# FINANCIAL ACCOUNTING

# Dedication

This book is dedicated to **Kathy, Kate, Andrew and Michael Trotman**, for their continued love and support

**Tom and June Trotman**, who gave up a lot to give me the education opportunities that resulted in the writing of this book

and

**Gordon Howitt**, for his outstanding contribution to accounting education over almost 50 years.

Second Edition

# FINANCIAL ACCOUNTING

## An Integrated Approach

Ken Trotman / Michael Gibbins

THOMSON

Australia · Canada · Mexico · Singapore · Spain · United Kingdom · United States

102 Dodds Street
Southbank Victoria 3006

Email highereducation@thomsonlearning.com.au
Website http://www.thomsonlearning.com.au

First published by ITP Nelson Canada as *Financial Accounting: An Integrated Approach*, second edition, by Michael Gibbins.
Authorised adaptation of the original edition by ITP Nelson Canada,
1120 Birchmount Rd, Scarborough, Ontario, Canada.

First edition published in 1998

First published in 2003
10 9 8 7 6 5 4 3 2
05 04 03



National Library of Australia
Cataloguing-in-Publication data

Trotman, K.T. (Kenneth Thomas).
Financial accounting: an integrated approach.

2nd ed.
Includes index.
ISBN 0 17 010772 8.

1. Accounting. I. Gibbins, Michael, 1942– . II. Title.
657.046

Editor: Bruce Gillespie
Project editor: David Parnham
Publishing editor: Glen Sheldon
Text designer: Jo Groud
Text illustrator: Shelly Communications
Cover designer: Fadi Abdel Massih
Cover art: Getty Images/FPG/Scott Morgan
Permissions researcher: Pamela Underwood
Typeset in 10pt Bembo, Officina Sans by Desktop Concepts P/L
Production controller: Carly McCormack
Printed in China by C&C Offset Printing Co. Ltd

This title is published under the imprint of Thomson.
Nelson Australia Pty Limited ACN 058 280 149 (incorporated in Victoria) trading as Thomson Learning Australia.

# Contents

## Chapter 15: Accounting policy choices

# Preface

One question I have been frequently asked since writing the first edition of this book is: given my busy schedule, why write an introductory accounting textbook?

First, I have been involved in teaching introductory financial accounting for over 25 years. I enjoy trying to get across the introductory concepts. Second, I have been surprised at the differences between how introductory accounting is taught in most undergraduate programs and how it is taught in MBA programs, such as those at Cornell, Michigan and AGSM. Ten to fifteen years ago there were good reasons for the differences, as most of our first-year undergraduate students were accounting majors. This is not the case today. Third, when I ask attendees at executive education programs what their accounting background is, many respond that they did first-year accounting ten-plus years ago but found it boring!

With all of the above in mind, we set about incorporating the following in the book. First, we have tried to make clear to students the importance of accounting information by frequent reference to current material, such as newspaper articles. Second, as companies are the most common business organisations in Australia today, we start by writing about companies, rather than spending many introductory chapters concentrating on sole traders. Third, to keep this book's material interesting and relevant, we have made frequent references to the content of annual reports. Students learn about real companies and can follow their performance in the newspapers or share market if they wish. Fourth, we believe that the depth of technical knowledge in this book will challenge both accounting and non-accounting majors.

The first edition of this textbook was adapted from the second edition of the best-selling Canadian introductory financial accounting textbook of the same name and written by Michael Gibbins. In the Australian edition, we have added five chapters as well as reorientating the material to the Australian context. Our second edition includes:

- new chapters 1 and 2, which provide a thorough understanding of the contents of financial statements and the uses of accounting information before introducing students to the double-entry process
- extensive re-writing of chapters 3, 4 and 5 to clarify the double-entry process
- extended material on liabilities
- an introduction to the implications of Australia's new GST system
- a great increase in the number of problems at the end of each chapter
- a new feature: a set of in-depth discussion questions at the end of each chapter
- a large number of new case studies, based on newspaper articles and annual reports.

The most attractive features of the first edition have been retained in the second edition:

- an easy-to-read writing style
- a wealth of extracts from company annual reports, newspapers and magazines
- a discussion in each chapter of how the material applies to the public sector

- 'How's your understanding?' activity questions throughout each chapter
- questions at the end of each chapter concentrating on the major case study for the book: the Woolworths annual report (appendix 2 at the end of the book)
- at the end of the book (in appendix 1), answers to some selected problems from each chapter.

Students should take advantage of the ancillary help that goes with this book, in particular the Web page, which includes practice questions and much interactive material. For instructors who wish to cover some management accounting in a course, we provide a management accounting supplement. Also, the publisher has made available all the usual materials for instructors.

We trust that you enjoy the book.

Ken Trotman

# Resources Guide

## For the student

As you read this text you will find a wealth of features in every chapter to help you explore the concepts and techniques that are used to prepare financial accounting information. Please take note of the following features:

**Learning objectives** let you know what you will learn in each chapter.

**Chapter overviews** give you a summary of the content of each chapter and relate this material to other chapters in the text.

**For your interest** sections give greater insights into the accounting profession and consolidate your understanding of the concepts covered in the chapter.

**How's your understanding** sections throughout each chapter allow you to check your comprehension of the key concepts you are learning as you work through each chapter.

**Homework and discussion to develop understanding** section at the end of each chapter enables you to revise the concepts that you have learnt and to apply accounting techniques. Problems are progressively more difficult to complete.

**Solution outlines** to some problems, which are marked with an asterisk, are provided in Appendix 1 on pages 698–727.

**Case studies** at the end of each chapter enable you to link the financial accounting concepts and practice you are learning to real-world examples.

**Woolworths Annual Report** can be found in Appendix 2 on pages 728–64.

To supplement your reading of *Financial Accounting: An Integrated Approach*, second edition, and further expand your study of financial accounting, you can utilise the following online resources:

**http://www.infotrac-college.com**

Included with this text is a passcode that gives you a four-month subscription to **InfoTrac College Edition**. This online library will provide you with access to full-text articles from hundreds of scholarly and popular periodicals, including *Australasian Business Intelligence*, *Australian Banking and Finance* and the *CPA Journal*.

**http://www.thomsonlearning.com.au/trotman**

For updates and news relating to *Financial Accounting: An Integrated Approach*, second edition please go to the companion website.

## For the instructor

Thomson Learning is pleased to provide you with an extensive selection of electronic and online supplements to help you lecture in financial accounting. These resources have all been specifically developed to supplement *Financial Accounting: An Integrated Approach*, second edition.

ExamView®

### ExamView Testbank®

ISBN: 0 17 010775 2

Helps you create, customise and deliver tests in minutes – both print and online. **The Quick Test Wizard** and **Online Test Wizard** guide you step by step through the test-creation process, while the unique WYSIWYG capability allows you to see the test you are creating on the screen exactly as it will print or display online. With **ExamView's** complete word-processing capabilities, you can add an unlimited number of new questions to the bank, edit existing questions, and build tests of up to 250 questions using up to 12 question types.

### Solutions Manual & PowerPoint® Presentation on CD-Rom

ISBN: 0 17 010774 4

The *Solutions Manual* provides you with fully worked solutions to all problems in the text. Also included on the CD-Rom are PowerPoint® presentation slides that include images and figures from *Financial Accounting: An Integrated Approach*, second edition. You can use this presentation as is or edit it to your own requirements.

THOMSON™

To request copies of these instructor resources please contact Thomson Learning:

PH: 1 800 654 831

FAX: 1 800 641 823

E-Mail: customerservice@thomsonlearning.com.au

# About the authors

**Ken Trotman** is Scientia Professor in the School of Accounting at the University of New South Wales. He has a MCom(Hons) from the University of New South Wales and a PhD from the Australian Graduate School of Management. He is a Fellow of both the Institute of Chartered Accountants in Australia and the Australian Society of CPAs. Ken's major research interests include examining the processing of information by users of accounting reports and auditors, and the factors that affect the quality of their decisions. He was awarded the 2001 Outstanding Educator Award by the Audit Section of the American Accounting Association and the 'Outstanding Contribution to the Accounting Research Literature' Award by the Accounting Association of Australia and New Zealand (AAANZ) in 1999. His research has resulted in him being made a Fellow of the Academy of Social Sciences in Australia. He is a former president of the AAANZ, a former Coopers & Lybrand visiting research professor and Director of Research for the audit section of the American Accounting Association. He has over 25 years of university teaching experience, much of which has covered introductory accounting. In addition to teaching in the Faculty of Commerce (UNSW), he has taught at Cornell University, the University of Michigan and the Australian Graduate School of Management. He has extensive consulting experience and has conducted many executive training programs in both the private and public sectors. He has published widely in Australian and international research journals and is on numerous editorial boards of leading international research journals.

**Michael Gibbins** is the Winspear Professor of Accounting in the Faculty of Business, University of Alberta. He has a BCom from the University of British Columbia, an MBA from York University and a PhD in accounting and psychology from Cornell University. He obtained his chartered accountancy designation in the Prince George office of what is now Deloitte & Touche. He has held appointments at Queens University School of Business, the Canadian Institute of Chartered Accountants and the University of British Columbia. His research and teaching interests lie in how people make decisions and judgements, and in the way accounting information is used in making important decisions in business and other economic spheres. A particular interest is in the professional judgement of public accountants, managers, and other professionals who cope with the pressures and risks of modern business life. He has published widely on judgement, accounting, financial disclosure and educational subjects; is a former editor of the Canadian accounting research journal Contemporary Accounting Research; has been on numerous editorial boards of academic journals; and is active in the Canadian Academic Accounting Association, the American Accounting Association and other professional bodies. He has received a number of education and teaching awards and in 1988 he received the honour of becoming a Fellow of both the Alberta and British Columbia Institutes of Chartered Accountants.

# Acknowledgements

The completion of this book only occurred with the help of many individuals. My greatest thanks go to my colleague Gordon Howitt, who 30 years ago inspired my interest in accounting. He taught me first year accounting and subsequently as a staff member provided me with guidance and support. Without his help I could not have written this book. During the first edition he encouraged me, regularly checked on progress, continually read drafts, provided many questions, authored the solutions manual and generally provided friendship and support. This support has continued with the reviewing of the second edition. For almost 50 years he has made an outstanding contribution to accounting education at the University of New South Wales. I certainly have never met a more dedicated accounting teacher. And it has been a privilege to work with him.

My co-author Mike Gibbins was kind enough to invite me to adapt his original Canadian textbook. Mike has an outstanding reputation as a researcher and I liked his version of the book so much that I decided to take on the task of co-author. While I have added five chapters, numerous problems, extensive Australian context and made many other changes, the book retains the structure and writing style that has made it so successful in Canada.

My life has been made much easier by the help of some very capable research assistants. On the first edition I was especially fortunate to have the help of Fernando Afonso, Elizabeth Carson, Kerry Humphries and Kate Trotman. For this second edition the assistance of Andrew Bowman, Christina Dimova, Mahreen Hasan, Amna Khalifa, Judith Quinn and Rebekah Solomon is greatly appreciated. Staff at the University of New South Wales and some other universities have been generous in providing me with material. Michael Pennisi provided material on GST in chapter 10, the rewrite of the appendix to chapter 5 and a consolidation illustrative example. Athol Carrington and Gordon Howitt provided me with some material in chapter 5, as well as numerous questions, and Malcolm Miller with some material in chapter 13. Rosina Mladenovic provided some material for chapter 6 and the appendix to chapter 5 as well as numerous comments on the book. Elizabeth Carson provided me with many questions and many helpful comments for improvements. Questions were also provided by Claudia Gormily, Cameron Hooper and Chris Poullaos. I was fortunate to have the expertise of Malcolm Miller in the next office and often sought advice from him on technical issues. Other useful comments were provided by Robert Czernkowski, Kar Ming Chong, Neil Fargher, Wendy Green, Roger Gibson, Noel Harding, Janice Loftus, Richard Petty, Baljit Sidhu and Roger Simnett. Russell Craig (Australian National University) has provided lots of detailed comments as well as some interesting reading that has been incorporated into cases. Advice from Peter Collett (University of Tasmania), Stephen Bali (University of Newcastle), Linda English (University of Sydney), Vic Fatseas (Charles Sturt University), Jack Flanagan (Australian Catholic University) and Greg Whittred (Australian Graduate School of Management) was appreciated. Thomson Learning also arranged for use of some material in chapter 6 from the US book by I. Solomon, L. Wither, P. Vargo and L. Plunkett.

In writing previous monographs and books I have thanked my family for adjusting through very busy times. Each year seems to get busier, so I again thank Kathy, Kate, Andrew and Michael for their love and support to allow me to take on these tasks.

Ken Trotman

**Copyright acknowledgements**

'Carol Altmann Scarfe's cooked books revealed', by Carol Altmann, *Weekend Australian*, 11–12 August 2001, reproduced courtesy of the Weekend Australian Newspaper, Nationwide News Pty Ltd; Amalgamated Holdings Limited for extract 'Deferred expenditure', *2001 Annual Report*, and material from 'Financial highlights 2001', used with the permission of Amalgamated Holdings Limited; American Accounting Association for 'Michelle's Cordial Stand: an introduction to accrual accounting', © American Accounting Association, 5717 Bessie Drive, Sarasota, Ph: 34233 2399; Australian Accounting Standards Board for extracts from SAC 4, courtesy Australian Accounting Standards Board; Australian Gas Light Company for extract taken from the 2001 financial statements of the Australian Gas Light Company; BHP for reproduction of various corporate materials © 2001 BHP Billiton, all rights reserved, used with permission; Billabong International Limited for extracts from 2001 financial statements, courtesy of Billabong International Limited; Blackwell Publishers for extract 'Australian accountants' attitudes on environmental reporting', by Craig Deegan, Sophie Geddes and John Stuanton, *Accounting Forum*, vol. 19m, no. 4, March 1996, this article was first published in *Charter Magazine*, April 1999, written by Craig Deegan; Cathy Bolt and *Australian Financial Review* for 'ERG's loss of gloss not so smart', 23 August 2001; J. Booker and R. Craig for *John Croaker: Convict Embezzler*, by J. Booker and R. Craig, Melbourne University Press; Boral Limited for extract, 'Boral accounting policy', 30 June 2001 and extracts from 2001 financial statements, reproduced with the kind permission of Boral Limited; *BRW* for 'Some companies are being taken to task over loose accounting in their financial reports', from *Lies, Damn Lies and Annual Reports*, by John Kavanagh; *BRW*, 15 October 1999, for extract 'Authorities aim for the objective on R&D', by Georgi Stickels, *BRW*, March 18 1996; *Canberra Times* for 'Accrual accounts worth the wait', courtesy of the *Canberra Times*, 17 May 1999; Emily Carr and *Australian Financial Review* for 'Rethink on directors taking stock', 19 October 1998; Coal & Allied for extract 'Exploration, evaluation and development expenditure'; Coles Myer Limited for extract from *Coles Myer Limited 2001 Annual Report*; New South Wales Department of Corrective Services, for statement of financial position 30 June 2000; CPA Australia for 'Show me the money', by Terry Chilvers, reproduced with permission of CPA Australia; CPA New York for extract from 'The development of international standards on auditing', by Robert Roussey, reprinted with permission of the *CPA Journal*, © 1999; CPI Group Limited for statement of financial position 30 June 2000, courtesy CPI Group Limited; Russell Craig for 'The missing $1b "cash reserves"', 'Account standards don't add up' and 'Jeremiah Murphy: Bank Account No. 1', *Australian CPA*, December 1998, Russell Craig is Professor of Accounting in the school of Business and Information Management at the Australian National University, reproduced with permission; CSR Limited, research and development, *2001 Annual Report*, © CSR Limited, reproduced with permission; Penelope Debelle for 'If Harris Scarfe boss wanted profit, he got it', by Penelope Debelle, *Sydney Morning Herald*, 7 August 2001; Craig Deegan for 'Triple bottom line reporting: a new reporting approach for the sustainable organisation', this article was first published in *Charter Magazine*, April 1999, and written by Craig Deegan; Department of Communications Information Technology and the Arts (DCITA) for 'Illustrative performance ratios for government departments', also extract from 'Guidelines of Steering Committee on National Performance Monitoring of Government Trading Enterprises'; John Fairfax Holdings Limited for extract from *2001 Annual Report* of John Fairfax Holdings Limited; Goodman Fielder for extract from 2001 financial statements, used with permission; Foster's Group for their consent to reproduce extracts from their inventory and financial reports; James Hardie for extract from *Annual Report 2001*, 'Intangible assets and deferred expenses'; Richard Hinds for Australian Cricket Board account numbers, *Sydney Morning Herald*, October 1997, Richard Hinds is a sportswriter with the *Sydney Morning Herald*; Anthony Hughes for 'Bad loans fail to halt Westpac's progress', by Anthony Hughes, *Sydney Morning Herald*, 5–6 May 2001; Institute of Chartered Accountants for extract from ICAA 2000 financial statements; ICAA for extract from ICAA 2000 financial statements, reprinted with the permission of the Institute of Chartered Accountants in Australia; Kaz Group Limited. The author and publisher gratefully acknowledge the contribution of Kaz Group Limited; Mark Lawson for 'Way clear for equity accounting', by Mark Lawson, *Australian Financial Review*; Lend Lease Corporation Limited for extract from 'Notes to the 2001 Accounts of Lend Lease Corporation Limited'; Matthew Kidman for 'Amcor's first fall in 18 years, lean times ahead', *Sydney Morning Herald*, 3 September 1996; Michael McDonald for 'A framework for ethical decision-making ethics shareware', by Michael McDonald, Centre for Applied Ethics, University of British Columbia, www.ethics.ubc.ca; New South Wales Department of Education and Training for extract from *NSW Department of Education and Training 2000 Annual Report*; New South Wales Waterways Authority for report extract, *1999–2000 Annual Report*, reprinted with courtesy of NSW Waterways Authority; News Corporation Limited for the reproduction of corporate material/reports, courtesy News Corporation; OPSM Protector Limited for 2001 inventory details, and extract 'Earnings per share' information, OPSM Group Limited, extract from 2001 financial statements reproduced with permission by OPSM Group Limited; Pasminco Limited for extract 'Sales revenue', from *Pasminco Limited 2000 Annual Report*; Rio Tinto Group for information reproduced from the Rio Tinto Group Accounts, which are publicly available; Roads & Traffic Authority, NSW for extract from *Annual Report 2001*; Seven Network Limited for report extracts, courtesy Seven Network Limited; Sigma Limited for 'Policy on inventory disclosures', extract from *Annual Report*, 30 June 2001, 'Intangibles', used with permission; State Library of New South Wales for Library Council of New South Wales notes, part of financial statements, 30 June 2000: 'Summary of significant accounting policies', reproduced with the permission of the State Library of New South Wales, Sydney; Sydney Airport Corporation for Statement of financial position 30 June 2000; Tabcorp Holdings Limited for the reproduction of corporate material/reports, courtesy Tabcorp Holding Limited; Telstra for extracts from *Telstra 2001 Annual Report*, Telstra Group statement of cash flows, 30 June 2001, courtesy of Telstra; Western Mining Corporation, for 'Capitalisation of borrowing costs, 2000' and extract from *2001 Annual Report*, courtesy Western Mining Corp; Professor Greg Whittred and AGSM for 'The road to insolvency', © Professor Greg Whittred Faculty of Commerce and Economics, University of New South Wales plus Figures 14.6 and 14.7; first published in *AGSM Magazine*, issue 3, 2001, pp. 12–15, Australian Graduate School of Management, Sydney.

# Chapter 1

# *Introduction to financial accounting*

## On completion of this chapter you should be able to:

- describe the basic purpose of financial accounting
- identify the users of accounting information and decisions they make that require accounting information
- identify who is involved in financial accounting
- describe how accrual accounting differs from cash accounting
- calculate accrual profit for an organisation
- explain the basic contents of the three key financial statements and describe the purpose of each statement
- describe the basic assumptions of accounting
- describe why accounting is important.

## 1.1 Use, preparation and concepts

### Use

Financial accounting has value because the information it produces is used in a variety of ways. Users include managers, investors, bankers, financial analysts and many others. Such people study accounting to learn how to use information effectively and do their jobs better. For accountants, this information is essential to the services they provide.

### Preparation

Accounting is a complex human activity. Accounting information doesn't just happen: it is produced by a large set of people, activities and computers. To be effective users of the information, people need to know something about how and why the information is prepared. Accountants' expertise is all about the how and the why.

### Concepts

Users, accountants and accounting form a connected system. The demand for useful information shapes how financial accounting information is prepared, for example, when producing annual or monthly performance reports. How it is prepared shapes its use, for example, in financial analysis and managerial decisions. Tying it all together are the whys: the reasons it is used and prepared, the principles that lie behind it. Many of these are quite interesting and controversial, but they are important in this book not so much for themselves as for the way they explain and connect the preparation and the uses.

The *hows* (preparation procedures and techniques), *whys* (concepts and principles) and *uses* (analysis and decisions) of financial accounting are throughout this book. Sometimes one of the three is emphasised for a while, but the others are never far away, because none can stand without the others. This diagram illustrates the relationships between and the importance of all three:

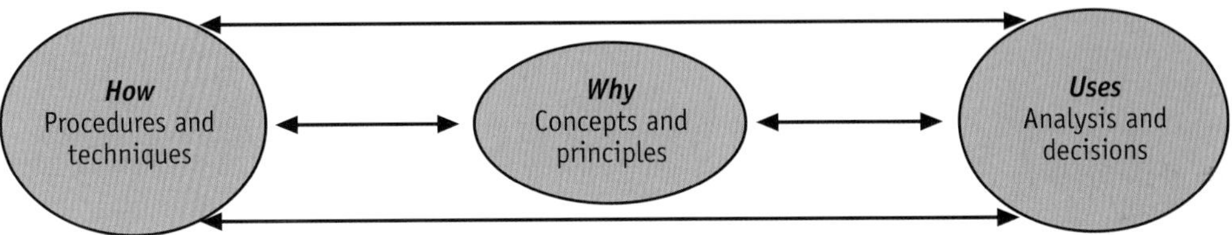


**Figure 1.1** The how, why and uses of accounting

### Chapter overview

This chapter introduces you to the subject of financial accounting and illustrates some useful concepts and techniques. It outlines a way of thinking about financial accounting that will be important to your career, whether you become an accountant or a user of accounting in business or in other walks of life. You will be introduced to the social setting of financial accounting and some of the people involved. Financial accounting is complex and requires much judgement, because it attempts to serve the needs of all these people, not all of whom necessarily see things the same way. You will then be introduced to one of the cornerstones of how financial accounting works: accrual accounting, the broad framework, within which financial accounting reports are prepared. You will also be introduced to the three key financial statements and the basic financial statement assumptions. Illustration from the financial press hopefully will convince you of the importance of accounting information.

## For your interest

Learning terminology is important. To help you with that, this book has a Glossary of Terms at the back. If you're not sure what a term means, look it up right away.

Accounting is a challenging discipline that involves many capabilities: assigning numbers to represent financial phenomena; providing explanations of those numbers; analysing and verifying the information prepared by others; understanding the needs of those who use accounting's reports to make decisions; engaging in oral and written communication with the many people involved in an organisation's financial activities; having familiarity with computers and other electronic media; and maintaining judgement that is sound, objective and ethical.

Much of the challenge of accounting is in figuring out which numbers to use, deciding what 'story' the numbers should tell. Adding and subtracting the numbers is often the easy part. This makes accounting both easier and harder to learn than you might have thought. Accounting is rooted in the financial setting, and has its own vocabulary and viewpoints, so don't expect it all to make perfect sense at the beginning. It will take a while for you to acquire the knowledge that creates an understanding of business and accounting as they really are in our world. This understanding will be based on your knowledge of both concepts and techniques, and of the viewpoints of both accountants and the users of accounting.

The going will not all be easy, but if you give it your best effort, you may be surprised at the high level of sophistication you will reach. Here is one important suggestion. The only way to learn accounting is to do problems. It is vital that you do more than just read the examples. After reading the chapter, come back and do the examples to check your understanding.

## For your interest

Accounting reports contain many examples of real art, humour and sophisticated design. Qantas uses pictures from its 'Spirit of Australia' adventures campaign, Cable and Wireless Optus and other large companies use pictures of leading sports stars, for example, Cathy Freeman, women's Olympic 400 metres athletic champion, for C+W Optus. Lion Nathan frequently reports its results using pictures of beer steins. You might enjoy looking at companies' web sites to see how they do their financial reporting. Try under Investor Relations, Investing, Financial and similar buttons.

# 1.2 Financial accounting

Financial accounting measures an enterprise's performance over time and its position (status) at a point in time, and does so in Australian dollars, US dollars, yen, euros or whatever currency is judged relevant to the enterprise. This measurement of financial performance and financial position is done for all sorts of enterprises: large and small businesses, governments from local to national level, universities, charities, churches, clubs, international associations and many others. The financial statements, which are financial accounting's reports, summarise the measurements of financial performance and position in standard ways thought to be useful in evaluating whether the enterprise has done well and is in good shape. These financial statements include notes, which contain many words (sometimes dozens of pages) of explanation and interpretation in addition to the numbers. The statements report on the economic and financial matters and are largely for the use of people outside the enterprise, such as investors, lenders, club members, regulatory agencies and taxation authorities.

In summary:

- *Financial performance* means generating new resources from day-to-day operations over a period of time.
- *Financial position* is the enterprise's set of financial resources and obligations at a point in time.
- *Financial statements* are the reports describing financial performance and position.
- *Notes* are part of the statements, adding explanations to the numbers.

As we will see throughout the book, financial performance and position are highly related. Good performance is likely to lead to a healthy financial position; if a company has been making profits, it will probably build up resources. On the other hand, a healthy financial position facilitates performance; if you have lots of resources compared to obligations, the company can undertake activities that lead to good performance.

Another branch of accounting, management accounting, is oriented toward helping managers and others inside the enterprise, in contrast to financial accounting's more external focus. While management accounting is not examined in this book, students interested in how financial accounting measures managerial performance will find frequent references to the relationship of managers with financial accounting. In the end, all forms of accounting exist to help people such as managers, investors, bankers, legislators and the public make financial decisions.

### How's your understanding?

Here is a question you should be able to answer, based on what you have just read. If you can't answer it, it would be best to reread the material.
What are the two main things that financial accounting measures?

## 1.3 The social setting of financial accounting

This book will show you the many ways in which financial accounting has been shaped by the development of business and society. Financial accounting:

- helps stock market investors decide whether to buy, sell or hold shares of companies
- helps banks and other lenders decide whether or not to lend
- helps managers run enterprises on behalf of owners, members or citizens (in addition to the help provided by management accounting and other sources of information)
- provides basic financial records for the purposes of day-to-day management, control, insurance and fraud prevention
- is used by governments in monitoring the actions of enterprises and in assessing taxes, such as income tax and the goods and services tax (GST).

Whole books can be, and have been, written about each of the many functions. Though this book emphasises externally oriented financial accounting for business firms, don't forget that there are many other organisations that use, and are affected by, accounting. When words like 'organisation', 'company', or 'enterprise' are used, the implications often go well beyond business firms.

The centre of our interest in this book, financial accounting for the enterprise, operates within and serves a complex social setting. It seeks to monitor and report on financial events initiated by or happening to the enterprise. Accounting is not a passive force within the social setting: it tells us what is going on, but in doing so it affects our decisions and actions and, therefore, also affects what is going on.

The social setting is composed of many people, including groups, companies, institutions and other parties interested in, or having an influence on, the company's financial accounting. As we will see many times in this book, these parties do not share the same interest in the company's accounting, and may even be in competition or conflict with each other. Most will be in the same country as the company and its management, but, increasingly, companies and other enterprises are operating internationally. The other groups interested in, and affecting, the company's financial accounting may be located anywhere on the planet.

## 1.4 The people involved in financial accounting

The main participants in the art of financial accounting are:

- the information users (the decision-makers)
- the information preparers, who put together the information to facilitate the users' decision-making
- the auditors, who assist the users by enhancing the credibility of the information, providing a professional opinion about the fairness and appropriateness of the information.

### Users (decision-makers)

In financial accounting, a user or decision-maker is someone who makes decisions on the basis of the financial statements, on his or her own behalf, or on behalf of a company, bank or other organisation. Financial accounting is utilitarian: ultimately, the nature and contents of financial statements are functions of the demand for decision information from users. If user demand is the fundamental reason for financial statements, understanding the demand is important.

A user's main demand is for *credible periodic reporting* of an enterprise's financial position and performance:

- *Credible* means that the information in the reports (the financial statements) appears to be sufficiently trustworthy and competently prepared for it to be used to make decisions. There is a cost–benefit issue here: huge amounts of money could be spent trying to make the reports absolutely perfect, but since that money would have to come out of the enterprise's funds, spending it would make its performance and position poorer. Users, such as owners and managers, may not want that to happen, so credibility is a relative condition, not an absolute one. Accounting information has to be worth its cost.
- *Periodic* means that users can expect reports on some regular basis (for example, yearly or quarterly). The longer the wait, the more solid the information. But waiting a long

time for information is not desirable: users are willing to accept some imprecision in the information in return for periodic reports with timely, decision-relevant information.

The main groups of users are as follows:

- *Owners* are individual business owners, such as proprietors, partners and other entrepreneurs; individual investors (shareholders) in shares on stock markets who can vote on company affairs; companies that invest in other companies; superannuation funds and other institutions that invest in companies; and people with quasi-ownership interests, such as members of clubs or voters in municipalities. In respect of companies, shareholders own portions of the corporation – shares that can be bought and sold – but the corporation is a legal entity existing separately from its shareholder owners.
- *Potential owners* are people of the same sort as the owners listed above, who do not at present have funds invested in the enterprise, but may be considering making such an investment. Because potential owners often buy shares from present owners – for example, by trading shares on the stock market – rather than investing directly, there is often a significant difference in outlook between present owners, who may wish to sell their shares for as much as possible, and potential owners, who would like to pay as little as possible.
- *Creditors and potential creditors* are suppliers, banks, bondholders, employees and others who have lent money to the enterprise, or who are owed funds in return for supplying something of value, or who are considering taking on such a role. Creditors do not have the legal control of the enterprise that owners have, but they often have a large say in enterprise decisions, especially if the enterprise gets into difficulty. In cases of extreme difficulty, creditors may have the right to take over control of the enterprise from the owners. Sometimes the difference between creditors and owners is hard to discern because it may depend on subtle legalities about who has what rights, and some people may play both roles for a given enterprise; for example, an owner invests money in a business, but in addition may lend the business further money, becoming a creditor as well as an owner.
- *Managers* are those who run the enterprise on behalf of the owners. They have a great interest in the way accounting reports on their activities and results. Often managers' salaries and bonuses, and the likelihood of staying in their jobs, are directly affected by the contents of the financial statements. In small businesses in particular, the owner may also be the main manager.
- *Employees* and their unions or other associations are interested in the enterprise's ability to pay wages, maintain employment levels, and keep such promises as paying superannuation contributions.
- *Regulators and other government bodies and agencies* are groups that may use the financial statements as a basis to evaluate whether the enterprise is following various rules and agreements.
- *Financial and market analysts* are people who study companies' performances and prepare reports for others by analysing those companies. Analysts often make recommendations about whether to invest, sell or do neither.
- *Competitors* may use the financial statements to try to understand the enterprise's operations for the purpose of making life more difficult for the enterprise. Sometimes, for example, managers are reluctant to disclose information to shareholders, because competitors can then also obtain it and act to reduce the enterprise's prospects.

- *Accounting researchers* are people, mostly university academics, but also some based in accounting firms and other organisations, who study accounting with the objective of understanding it and contributing to its improvement.
- *Miscellaneous third parties* are various other people who may get access to an enterprise's financial statements and use them in various ways. Once statements have been issued, many people may make use of them. For example, politicians may make judgements about industry efficiency or taxation levels, journalists may write stories about employment practices, and judges may evaluate the enterprise's ability to pay if it loses a lawsuit.

Think about all these users and decisions! It is a great challenge to develop one set of periodic financial statements for an enterprise so that they can be useful for all. Perhaps you will not be surprised to know that there is much controversy about whether financial statements do this well, and whether financial accounting methods serve some users or decisions better than others.

### For your interest

If you plan to be an accountant, the value of studying financial accounting is clear. It may not be so clear, however, if you have other plans, such as a career in management, marketing, finance, engineering, law, human resources or production. To provide some perspective if you are not planning an accounting career, and to help you understand the managers you will work with if you do become an accountant or auditor, comments will be made frequently about managers and financial accounting.

Financial accounting is directly relevant to managers because it reports on the managers' performances as decision-makers, caretakers of the enterprise, representatives of the owners, legal officers of the enterprise, and so on. Any manager cannot help but be interested in how her or his performance is being measured and in how that performance is analysed, projected and otherwise evaluated. Managers' bonuses, promotions, dismissals, transfers and other rewards and penalties are often directly based on the numbers and commentaries prepared by accountants. Every manager should have an intimate understanding of how accounting is measuring his or her performance and should be able to conduct a 'reasonableness check' of the information being provided. It is critical for managers to understand the impact of every decision they are making on accounting numbers as these numbers will measure their performance.

## Preparers (decision facilitators)

Three main groups are responsible for the information in the financial statements:

- *Managers* are responsible for running an enterprise, including issuing accounting and other information, and controlling its financial affairs. The fact that managers are also users, vitally interested in the results, has created a fundamental conflict of interest for them and has led to the development of the auditing function (see next pages). Managers are often referred to, as a group, as management.
- *Bookkeepers and clerks*, working under the direction of management, do the enterprise's basic record-keeping, creating the transactional data upon which accounting reports

are built. Many of the bookkeeping and clerical functions are now performed by computers.

- *Accountants* have the job of shaping the financial statements by applying the principles of accounting to the enterprise's records, under the direction of management. Many are members of professional societies, such as the Institute of Chartered Accountants in Australia, CPA Australia, the Institute of Chartered Accountants of New Zealand and the Hong Kong Society of Accountants. Accountants and their professional bodies also often have auditing experience and interests, and sometimes auditing roles, but the task of preparing the financial statements is quite different in principle from the task of verifying those statements once they are prepared.

## Auditors (credibility enhancers)

Auditors report on the credibility of the enterprise's financial statements, on behalf of owners and others. Auditors have the job of assisting the users, by verifying that the financial statements have been prepared fairly, competently and in a manner consistent with accepted principles. The auditing role is a very old one, arising because users demanded some assurance that managers' reports on their performance were not self-serving, biased or downright untruthful. This book refers frequently to external auditors, who report on the financial statements on behalf of external users, but there are also internal auditors, who work within the enterprise to support the credibility of information being used by management, and other auditors (such as tax auditors, who verify taxpayers' computation of tax). While external auditors may be asked for advice in preparing the statements, especially for small companies, they must avoid responsibility for the statements because their role is to scrutinise the preparation process. They cannot credibly audit statements they have prepared! (Professional accountants often do prepare financial statements, but in doing so they are not acting as external auditors, and they make this clear in covering letters and footnotes attached to the statements.)

The external auditors are formally appointed by the owners, for example, at the annual shareholders' meeting. But an enterprise's external auditor is not permitted to be an owner or manager of the enterprise too. This is to ensure that the auditor is financially and ethically independent and can therefore be objective about the enterprise's financial affairs. Independence and objectivity are fundamental ideas, to be encountered frequently in this book. The external auditing function is considered so important that the right to perform it is usually restricted to members of recognised professional accountants' societies, who therefore have auditing expertise and experience.

External auditors may work alone or in partnership with other auditors in accounting firms. Some of these firms are very large, having thousands of partners and tens of thousands of employees, and offices in many cities and countries. Accounting firms offer their clients not only external auditing, but also advice on income tax, accounting, computer systems and many other financial and business topics. In offering such other advice to enterprises that they also audit, accountants are not supposed to get so involved that they are in effect auditing their own work, or creating any conflict of interest problems. Managing this requires considerable professional skill and attention to ethics and rules of professional conduct, and whether this is being done successfully is a matter of much controversy at present. In early 2000, as just one example, a report accused one of the biggest American public accounting firms of not keeping its auditors sufficiently independent of the companies they audit.

## People and ethics

Ethics, mentioned on the previous page, will be raised throughout this book. Ethical issues can arise in just about any area of accounting. Here are some examples, all of them real:

- An enterprise has been sued by a recently fired employee, who claims that the firing was based on the employee's age and therefore broke employment laws. The enterprise's general manager denies any impropriety. The enterprise's chief accountant, who personally feels that the former employee's claim is justified, has suggested to the boss that the lawsuit should be mentioned in a note to the financial statements, so that users of the statements will know there is a potential for loss if the former employee wins. The general manager feels that the chief accountant should ignore the lawsuit in preparing the financial statements, to avoid embarrassment and to avoid the appearance of admitting guilt. The general manager fears that such an apparent admission could be used against the enterprise in court and so could cause the enterprise to lose the lawsuit. What should the chief accountant do?
- While doing the audit, the external auditor learns that the enterprise may have been cheating one of its customers. The customer, who is unaware of this and quite happy with things, is another client of the auditor. The auditor, who is bound by rules of conduct designed to protect the confidentiality of information gained during the audit, knows that saying anything to anyone could result in major lawsuits. Should the auditor just keep quiet about what was found?
- A third enterprise's general manager is paid a bonus each year, calculated as a percentage of profit. The general manager is considering a proposed change of depreciation method that will reduce depreciation expense and therefore raise accrual profit and increase the general manager's bonus. Should the general manager refuse to implement the accounting change, or request that the bonus calculation ignore the change, or just go ahead and enjoy the higher bonus?

These illustrative problems do not have easy answers, so none is offered here. They are dilemmas for the chief accountant, the auditor and the general manager. This book will address ethical issues from time to time, therefore helping you sharpen your ethical sense along with your accounting knowledge, for the two are inseparable.

## How's your understanding?

Here are two questions you should be able to answer, based on what you have just read:

1 Who uses financial reports, and what do they use them for?

2 What is the difference between a 'preparer' and an 'auditor', and why is the difference important?

# 1.5 Accrual accounting

Financial accounting's task of producing financial statements is a complex one. For even a small business, thousands of events (transactions) have to be recorded and their financial effects evaluated. For large corporations such as BHP Billiton, Lend Lease, Western Mining, Coles Myer, AMP, Qantas and Westpac, or organisations such as the University of New South Wales, Brisbane City Council or the Red Cross, the number of annual transactions runs into the millions or billions. Frequently, when the time comes to prepare the financial statements, transactions have not been completed, are in dispute or have an otherwise unclear status. Here are examples in which appropriate figures may be difficult to determine:

- The value of Westpac's overseas loans (that is, the money actually to be received back from those loans) depends on the health of the borrowing countries' economies, stability in international money transfer arrangements (often disrupted by wars, politics and natural disasters) and the relative values of various countries' currencies, which, like nickel prices, can change a lot from day to day.
- The value of donations promised to the Red Cross but not yet received depends on how committed donors are to actually producing the cash. This commitment can be affected by unemployment, rising prices for food and other goods the donors need and other factors beyond the Red Cross's control.
- The amount of profit that should be recognised during the year by Leighton Holdings for the construction of a major bridge that will take two years to complete will depend on future expenses.

To cope with these complexities, financial accounting for most businesses and organisations uses the accrual accounting approach. Under an accrual accounting system, the impact of transactions on the financial statements is recognised in the time periods during which revenues and expenses occur rather than when the cash is received or paid. Formal definitions of revenues and expenses can be quite complicated, and are left to chapter 2. At this stage we will provide examples of the main types of revenues and expenses.

The main form of revenue is usually the sale of goods or services. Other revenues include interest on investments held, dividends received on shares and rent from premises owned by the company.

Expenses include costs of services and resources consumed in the process of generating revenues. Examples of costs incurred would be labour, electricity, travel, commission and so on. An example of resources consumed is depreciation. Organisations depreciate the cost of an asset (such as a motor vehicle or a printing machine) over the useful life of the asset. These assets are helping in generating revenue, therefore a share of the cost should be treated as an expense in each accounting period during which the asset helps generate revenue.

Why do we depreciate the cost of an asset over its useful life rather than treat the cost of the asset as an expense in the first year? The reason is that the asset is used over many years and helps generate revenue over many periods. This depreciation expense is matched to the revenues earned during the period. Note that estimates need to be made. For example, a printing machine that cost \$480 000 would have annual depreciation of \$120 000, \$96 000 or \$80 000, depending on whether its estimated life is four, five or six years.

## Accrual accounting versus cash accounting

Before considering these complexities, let's consider the basic differences between cash accounting and accrual accounting.

- *Cash accounting* involves recording revenues and expenses at the time the cash is received or paid. This is reasonably precise because the accountant knows whether cash has been paid or received and the exact amount is easily determined (from accounting books or bank statements).
- However, often the timing of cash flow is in a different accounting period to the substance of the transaction. Examples include selling inventory on credit; a contractor fixes machinery but will not be paid until a later accounting period; or the use of

machinery, which reduces its future useful life. As noted above (but worth repeating) *accrual accounting incorporates these complexities by recording revenues and expenses at the time they occur, not when cash is received.*

To compare cash profit with accrual profit, consider the following:

- A company makes credit sales of $100 000 in June which will be collected in July. Under an accrual system $100 000 revenue would be included in June, whereas under a cash system the amount would be recognised in July.
- A contractor carries out repair work in June for $20 000, but the bill will not be paid until July. Under an accrual system the expense would be recognised in June but under a cash system would not be recognised until July.
- Under accrual accounting there will be an allocation of the cost of equipment to expenses over several accounting periods to recognise the consumption of the equipment's future economic value. This is called depreciation. If the equipment cost $80 000 and has a life of eight years, $10 000 depreciation would be included in expenses each year.

## Using accrual accounting to prepare financial statements

Using the accrual accounting approach in preparing the financial statements attempts are made to:

- include all the cash receipts and payments that have already happened, for example cash sale, cash payment for wages
- incorporate future cash receipts and payments that should be expected, based on existing transactions. For example, include the credit sale now, although the cash will not arrive until the next period
- measure the value of incomplete transactions, for example estimate the likely amount of accounts receivable that will not be collected, and treat the amount as an expense of this year
- estimate figures when exact amounts are unknown, for example estimate the amount of interest due from the bank at year-end, even though the bank does not add the interest to your account for another two months; the amount is interest revenue
- make an economically meaningful overall assessment of awkward problems. For example, a customer is suing you for $1 million because of a faulty product. You agree to pay $200 000 in settlement now, but the client takes the matter to court, with the case being held next year. You need to determine if there is an expense in this year.

## Estimates and assessments

Notice the use of the words 'estimate' and 'assessment' above, which illustrates the need for judgements when preparing financial statements. Further examples of estimates for the situations described earlier for Westpac, Red Cross and Leighton Holdings are:

- In order to judge the value of Westpac's uncollected loans, someone studies the loan repayment record of various countries for Westpac and estimates how much money the bank will be able to collect.
- To help the Red Cross make its spending plans, someone advises the Red Cross on how much of the promised donations are likely to be received.
- Someone calculates the costs involved in building the bridge to this point. Based on such estimates as the percentage of the job completed, he or she also estimates the

total likely profit of building the bridge and determines the percentage of profit to be included in this period.

## The importance of good judgement

Accrual accounting has been developed because financial statements cannot be based on merely the routine accounting records of what has happened. Measuring economic performance is more complex than that, and the appropriate measures can be elusive, or can depend on one's point of view. Many augmentations to the transactional record (estimates, adjustments, judgements and verbal explanations) must be made so that the statements will be meaningful. The resulting statements, therefore, depend to a great extent on the quality and fairness of such augmentations. Managers, accountants and auditors must use their judgement constantly.

Financial accounting, because it relies on many judgements, is far more imprecise than most people, even many regular users of financial statements, realise. To help students understand the reality of modern financial accounting, this book spends much space on the real-life imprecisions of preparing and using financial statements. Accrual accounting is therefore the presumed method in this book, though there will be some comparisons between it and simple cash-based accounting. Modern financial accounting starts with cash receipts and payments, then builds a very large accrual accounting process *in addition to* the cash records in order to provide the sophisticated measures of financial performance and position that today's world demands.

## Assembling information for accrual accounting

Figure 1.2 summarises the way accrual financial accounting information is assembled, and gives examples.

- The foundation is cash transactions, which even the simplest accounting records include.
- Most accounting systems also include credit transactions, because most enterprises extend credit to customers and/or use credit from their suppliers and employees.
- Short-term and long-term adjustments are needed in preparing financial statements, unless the company's accounting system is sophisticated enough to have already built them in (some are, though there are always new issues to be dealt with as the world keeps changing).
- Extensive narrative and supplementary disclosures (especially the 'notes' to the financial statements) are made, sometimes using many more pages than the statements themselves do.

The result is that accrual accounting is a very complex information system, and it will take the rest of this book to introduce you to it properly.

## How's your understanding?

Here are two questions you should be able to answer, based on what you have just read. If you can't answer them, it would be best to reread the material.

1 Does accrual accounting ignore cash transactions?

2 Why is accrual accounting thought necessary although a record of transactions already exists?

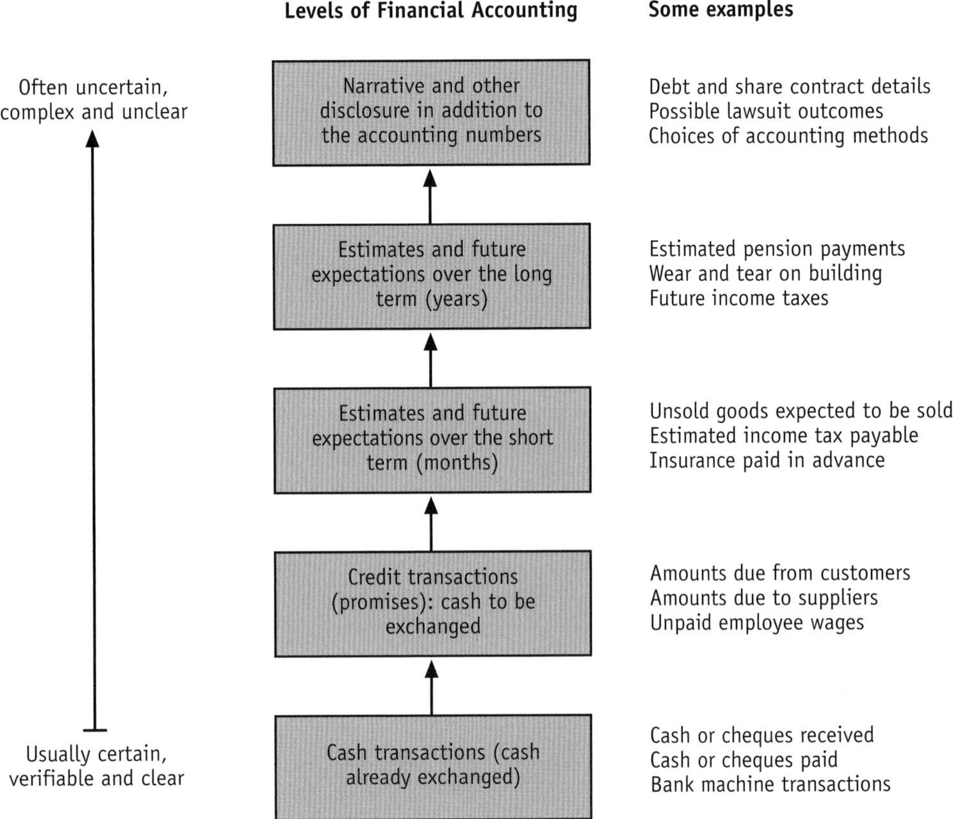


**Figure 1.2** Levels of of accrual accounting

## 1.6 Example: Simone's jewellery business

Here is an example of how accrual accounting works. The example is of a small business, one you should be able to imagine easily, but the accounting issues it raises are exactly the same as those faced by big businesses.

Simone works in an office during the day, but in the evenings and on weekends she makes silver jewellery in a studio she has set up in her basement. The jewellery is sold in local craft stores, and Simone keeps a separate bank account to deposit the cash from her sales and to pay the bills for supplies.

Accounting is a way of portraying an enterprise; another way, a visual image, may help you. Try to picture her working in her studio, driving around to craft stores to deliver her products and collect cash, and relaxing with her friends when things are going well. It is important that accounting's reports be consistent with the reality of her business, so keep the image in mind as this example develops.

### 2001 as first year in business

For 2001, her first year in business, Simone received $4350 in cash from the craft stores for sales of her jewellery and paid $1670 in cash for silver and for other supplies and expenses. How much money did she make from her business in 2001?

The simple answer is that she made a cash profit of $2680 ($4350 cash collected minus $1670 cash paid out). Her bank balance increased by that amount during the year. This is a simple, understandable calculation.

The notion behind accrual accounting is that maybe the simple calculation is too simple, that it really does not properly measure what Simone accomplished during the year. Accrual accounting tries to take into account a number of things.

- At the end of the year, Simone was still owed $310 for sales by one craft store because the owner had been out when she stopped by. The store paid her a few weeks later, but shouldn't that amount be counted as revenue for the year the sales were made? It was a credit transaction in that year, not a cash transaction yet. The amount was legally owed to Simone at the end of the year and she expected to collect the cash.
- At the end of the year, Simone had some unpaid bills for business expenses totalling $85. She paid those early in the next year, but aren't they really expenses for the year in which she incurred them, rather than for the year in which she paid them? She has bills for these, so they represent other credit transactions, but this time involving promises by Simone to pay rather than by her customers to pay her.
- In making the jewellery, she used some equipment she had bought earlier for $1200. If the equipment is expected to last about ten years, shouldn't the wear and tear on it during the year be counted as an expense? It is not easy to figure out how much wear and tear results from a particular period, but say that she feels the year was a normal one of the ten the equipment should last. The cost of the wear and tear, therefore, was about 10 per cent of the original cost of the equipment, or $120. (This $120 figure is what accountants call 'depreciation'. It can be calculated in several ways, as we will see later on.) This is an example of a long-term estimate or expectation. Because it involves prediction of an uncertain future, and for other reasons we'll look at, people have all sorts of disagreement about depreciation.

Just using these three additional pieces of information, accrual accounting would calculate Simone's accrual profit for the year 2001 (her first year in business) in the following way, taking into account the various estimates and incomplete transactions described:

**Simone's Jewellery Business**

Calculation of accrual profit for the year 2001

| | |
|---|---|
| **Revenue*** | |
| ($4350 collected plus $310 still to be received) | $4 660 |
| Expenses** | |
| ($1670 paid plus $85 unpaid plus $120 estimated depreciation) | 1 875 |
| **Accrual profit***** based on the information provided | $2 785 |

**Notes:**

* **Revenue** is the benefit received or expected from the sale of goods or services during the year, so it goes beyond cash received.

** **Expenses** are costs incurred or resources consumed during the year in order to earn the revenue, so they go beyond cash paid.

*** **Accrual profit** for the year is the difference between revenue and expenses.

Accrual accounting can and does handle many more complexities than the three included above. Even with this uncomplicated example, you can see that the $2785 accrual profit is a more complete measure of Simone's business performance than is the cash profit of $2680, which is the change in cash balance alone. (Accrual profit is not necessarily higher than cash profit – it just happens to be so in this example.)

There are some difficulties:

- The accrual profit requires extra calculation, therefore is more complex, as shown in figure 1.2. This might confuse some people, and it leaves more room for error than the simpler calculation.

- The accrual profit doesn't match the change in bank account balance any more, so Simone might be uncertain of how much she can take out of the bank for her next holiday. The accrual profit and cash profit can always be reconciled, however. We'll see how to do this in later chapters.
- Accrual accounting is a bit of a 'slippery slope'. Once you start trying to add and subtract things in calculating profit, where do you stop? For example, should there be some deduction for the cost of Simone's time in making all the jewellery? What about the costs of using the room in her basement for her house and her car for deliveries? Should some calculation of such costs be made, although it would be difficult to be exact about them? What about income tax? If she has to pay income tax on what she earns from her business, should that tax also be deducted as a business expense? What about unused supplies at the end of the period?

For now, let's not become mired in such complexities! Remember that accrual accounting tries to provide a more thorough measurement of financial performance and other aspects of an enterprise than simple cash-based accounting. In order to do so, it incorporates more complex ideas, as well as estimates and judgements. Much of your task is to understand the complexities, estimates and judgements so that you will be able to understand the resulting financial statements and what they say about the enterprise.

## Simone revisited

To finish the example of Simone's business, let's extend it to the case in which 2001 was *not* her first year in business, that is, just a normal business year. That means she may have had uncollected sales and unpaid bills at the end of 2000 (beginning of 2001). Would those make any difference to the cash profit calculation for 2001? No, they wouldn't – they don't involve any change in cash receipts or payments during the year. Would they make any difference to the accrual profit calculation for 2001? Yes, they would. Let's see how.

To keep the example uncluttered, let's use exactly the same numbers again, but add two new items as at the end of 2000: uncollected sales, $240; and unpaid bills, $50. Let's call this 'Simone revised'. What effect do these have on the accrual profit calculation?

Some of the $4350 cash received in 2001 was not for that year's activity, but rather was collecting $240 revenue that was part of the accrual profit calculation in the previous year, 2000. That amount has to be subtracted from $4350 in the 2001 accrual profit calculation because it was already in the 2000 accrual profit and shouldn't be counted twice.

The $50 of unpaid bills at the end of 2000 were included in the cash payments in 2001, therefore counted in the 2001 expenses above, although they had already been included in the 2000 expenses. So they are deducted from the 2001 expenses because they don't belong in 2001.

Now here's Simone's accrual profit *if 2001 was not her first year*:

**Simone's Jewellery Business**
Revised calculation of accrual profit for 2001

| | |
|---|---|
| **Revenue** | |
| ($4350 collected minus $240 from 2000 plus $310 still to be received) | $4 420 |
| **Expenses** | |
| ($1670 paid minus $50 from 2000, plus $85 unpaid at the end of 2000, plus $120 estimated depreciation for 2000) | 1 825 |
| Accrual profit based on the information provided | $2 595 |

Cash profit is still $2680, unaffected by the new information. But accrual profit is changed, *as it always is*, by non-cash items existing at *both* the beginning and the end of the year.

## How's your understanding?

Here are two questions you should be able to answer, based on what you have just read. If you can't answer them, it would be best to reread the material.

1 Your cousin, a medical student, says, 'In our course on managing a medical practice, we were told that our financial reports will use accrual accounting. What does that mean?'

2 Fred started his delivery business a few years ago. This year, he collected $47 000 from his customers and paid $21 000 in expenses. At the beginning of this year, his customers owed $3500 and he owed his suppliers $700. At the end of this year, his customers owe him $3200; he owes his suppliers $1450; and his truck depreciation for the year was $4600. Using just this information:

a What is this year's cash profit?

b What is this year's accrual profit?

(You should get: Cash profit $26 000 ($47 000 cash receipts minus $21 000 cash payments) and accrual profit $20 350 (revenue of $47 000 – $3500 + $3200 = $46 700; expenses of $21 000 – $700 + $1450 + $4600 = $26 350))

### For your interest

Many of you will end up working as accountants or managers for organisations that operate in many countries. This book should equip you to understand the financial statements prepared in most countries, including Australia, the United States, the United Kingdom, Canada, New Zealand, China, Singapore, Hong Kong, Indonesia, Malaysia and many others. The method of preparing financial statements in the above-mentioned countries is very similar. All use the accrual accounting system introduced in this chapter. While there are some differences in accounting principles and disclosures, these are gradually being reduced with the increased harmonisation of these principles and disclosures. When you come across these differences, you should have gained enough knowledge to interpret what is being stated.

## 1.7 The key financial statements

Organisations are required to provide the following types of information that are relevant to user needs: financial position, financial performance, financing activities and investing activities.

The key financial statements that provide this information are: a statement of financial position (formerly called a balance sheet), which shows the financial position at a point in time; a statement of financial performance (formerly called a profit and loss statement), which measures financial performance over a defined period (such as a month or a year) by deducting expenses from revenues during the period to obtain profit for the period; and a statement of cash flows, which shows the sources and uses of cash during the period. Both financing and investing activities are included in this statement.

The name changes (as well as other changes to be described in later chapters) from balance sheet and profit and loss statements occurred at 30 June 2001. However, you should still remain familiar with these names, as many overseas countries still use them (for example, Canada, USA, Singapore, Hong Kong and China), and it is likely that they will still be used in internal reports for Australian companies for many years. They are still included in Australian Corporations Law, and financial newspapers continue to use the terms profit and loss statement and balance sheet.

## Statement of financial position (balance sheet)

Exhibit 1.1 provides a simple statement of financial position. The statement of financial position shows an organisation's resources and claims on resources at a particular point in time. The heading provides the company name, the title of the report, and the date at which the financial position is shown. The three main elements of a statement of financial position are assets, liabilities and owners' equity. In this case, the organisation is a company, and owners' equity is described as shareholders' equity. If it were a sole trader or partnership, it would be called proprietor's equity or partners' equity respectively.

### Assets

Assets are future economic benefits controlled by an organisation as a result of past transactions or other past events. The value of every asset needs to be measurable in monetary terms. A brief discussion of the assets in exhibit 1.1 will make you familiar with the terminology.

- The cash at bank account records deposits and withdrawals from a bank.
- Accounts receivable (also called debtors) represents amounts owing from customers for goods or services provided to them. Accounts receivable is shown net, which indicates the amount that management expects to collect from customers after allowances have been made for likely uncollectable amounts.
- Inventory generally represents the cost of stock on hand – that is, unsold products.
- Property, plant and equipment includes items such as land, buildings, equipment, motor vehicles, computers and furniture.

### Liabilities

Liabilities are future sacrifices of economic benefits that an organisation is presently obliged to make to other organisations or individuals as a result of past transactions or events. For example, suppliers providing goods on credit and employees carrying out work are examples of past transactions that lead to liabilities. Liabilities can be legally owed debts, such as loans from the bank, mortgages, or amounts due to suppliers, but they also can be estimates of future payments based on past agreements, such as those arising from promises of future benefits to employees for long service leave, or of warranty repairs for customers when products break down. Liabilities involve the future use of assets, usually cash, or the performance of future services. An example of providing a future service would be carrying out warranty repairs on products previously sold.

Four examples of liabilities in Exhibit 1.1 are accounts payable, wages payable, provision for employee entitlements and long-term loans.

- Accounts payable (often called trade creditors) is the amount owed to various suppliers for goods or services they have provided to an organisation.

**EXHIBIT 1.1** XYZ Ltd

**Statement of financial position as at 30 June 2002**

| | $000 |
|---|---|
| **Assets** | |
| Cash at bank | 2 000 |
| Accounts receivable | 16 000 |
| Inventory | 12 000 |
| Property, plant and equipment | 90 000 |
| **Total assets** | **120 000** |
| | |
| **Liabilities and shareholders' equity** | |
| **Liabilities** | |
| Accounts payable | 17 000 |
| Wages payable | 2 000 |
| Provision for employee entitlements | 4 000 |
| Long-term loans | 30 000 |
| **Total liabilities** | **53 000** |
| | |
| **Shareholders' equity** | |
| Share capital | 40 000 |
| Retained profits | 27 000 |
| | |
| **Total shareholders' equity** | **67 000** |
| **Total liabilities and shareholders' equity** | **120 000** |

- Wages payable (also called accrued wages) is for work done by employees, but which has not been paid.
- Provision for employee entitlements refers to entitlements employees accumulate as a result of past work, such as holiday leave, sick leave, long service leave and superannuation.
- Long-term loans are loans that are not repayable within a year.

## Shareholders' equity

Shareholders' equity is the excess of assets over liabilities. It is a residual claim of the shareholders on the assets of the organisation. Shareholders' equity consists of two main elements, share capital and retained profits.

- Share capital is the amount owners have directly invested in the company.
- Retained profits represent the total cumulative amounts of profits that the company has retained in the business rather than distributed as dividends.

The relationship between assets, liabilities and owners' equity can be expressed in the following accounting equation:

**Assets = liabilities + owners' equity**

This equation shows that the resources of an enterprise are funded from two types of sources: debt or equity. The effects of transactions on this equation are discussed in chapter 2. At this point you should note that the equation balances at every point in time.

## Statement of financial performance (the profit and loss statement)

This statement provides information on an organisation's profitability for a period of time. It matches revenues during a period against expenses incurred in earning the revenues. The difference is the profit (revenue greater than expenses) or loss (expenses greater than revenue). Recall that under an accrual accounting system the cash related to the revenue or expense does not have to be received or paid in order for the revenue or expense to be included in the statement of financial performance. Discussion of when revenue and expenses are recognised is covered in chapter 2.

Exhibit 1.2 provides an example of a simplified statement of financial performance. Sales is the only revenue item listed. The next item in the statement of financial performance is cost of goods sold (COGS). For a retailer, this would be the purchase price of the goods that are sold. For example, if a retailer sells 100 items at \$20 each and the cost price of each of the items is \$8, sales revenue would be \$2000 (\$20 × 100) and cost of goods sold would be \$800 (\$8 × 100). The difference between sales revenue and cost of goods sold is called gross profit (also gross margin).

The statement of financial performance also lists various operating expenses, as shown in exhibit 1.2. These costs relate to the day-to-day running of the business.

Many other operating expenses, such as advertising, staff training, maintenance, telephone and motor vehicle expenses, could also be included. Deducting these operating expenses from gross profit gives operating profit before tax. Tax is then deducted to give operating profit after tax.

The profit figure of \$6 million can be paid out in dividends to shareholders or retained in the business. This is the connecting link between the statement of financial position and the statement of financial performance. The opening balance of retained profits plus the profit for the year minus dividends equals the closing balance of retained profits as shown in the statement of financial position.

**EXHIBIT 1.2** XYZ Ltd

**Statement of financial performance for the year ended 30 June 2002**

| | \$000 | \$000 |
|---|---|---|
| Sales revenue | | 21 000 |
| Less cost of goods sold | | 8 000 |
| **Gross profit** | | **13 000** |
| Less operating expenses | | |
| Salaries | 2 500 | |
| Depreciation | 500 | |
| Electricity | 300 | |
| Travel | 300 | |
| Postage | 400 | 4 000 |
| Operating profit before tax | | 9 000 |
| Less income tax expense | | 3 000 |
| **Operating profit after tax** | | **6 000** |

## Statement of cash flows

The statement of cash flows shows the changes during the period in one statement of financial position account, namely cash. It shows the receipt of cash and the payment of cash. Accounting standards require companies to present this statement in their published financial statements. Individual transactions are normally split into the following three categories:

- operating activities: related to the provision of goods and services
- investing activities: related to the acquisition and disposal of certain noncurrent assets, including property, plant and equipment
- financing activities: related to changing the size and composition of the financial structure of the entity, including equity and certain borrowings.

Exhibit 1.3 provides an example of a statement of cash flows. Under cash flows from operating activities, it shows that the company received $17 million from customers, and paid $7.7 million and $2.3 million to suppliers and employees respectively, as well as paying $4.5 million in other operating costs.

Note that these figures are not the same as those in the statement of financial performance. For example, the company could have made $21 million in credit sales but only collected $17 million from customers by the end of the year. There was only one investing item, being the cash paid for a new machine. Cash flows from financing activities show that the company received $4 million from an issue of shares but paid back a $3.6 million bank loan. The net effect on cash of all of the above transactions was an increase of $600 000. When added to the opening balance of $1.4 million it shows a closing balance

**EXHIBIT 1.3** XYZ Ltd

**Statement of cash flows for the year ended 30 June 2002**

| | $000 |
|---|---|
| **Cash flows from operating activities** | |
| Receipts from customers | 17 000 |
| Payments to suppliers | (7 700) |
| Payment to employees | (2 300) |
| Cash operating costs | (4 500) |
| | 2 500 |
| **Cash flows from investing activities** | |
| Purchase of machinery | (2 300) |
| **Cash flows from financing activities** | |
| Issue of shares | 4 000 |
| Bank loan | (3 600) |
| | 400 |
| Total net cash flows | 600 |
| Cash: 1 July 2001 (opening balance) | 1 400 |
| **Cash: 30 June 2002 (closing balance)** | **2 000** |

of $2 million, which is also the figure shown under cash in the statement of financial position. Statements of cash flows will be discussed in detail in chapter 12.

## 1.8 Financial statement assumptions

Now that you have seen the financial statements, it is important to understand the basic concepts underlying current accounting practice and the preparation of financial statements. The following concepts (or assumptions) are discussed below: accounting entity, accounting period, monetary, historical cost, going concern and materiality.

- *Accounting entity:* Under this concept the accounting entity is separate and distinguishable from its owners. For example, the accounting entity of a sole trader is differentiated from the financial affairs of the owner. Similarly, a company is a separate entity from its shareholders. If either the sole trader or a shareholder of a company goes out and buys a new set of golf clubs, it may affect his or her personal finances but does not affect the accounting entity. Accounting entities do not necessarily correspond to legal entities. For example, as noted above, the personal financial affairs of the sole trader can be separated from the finances of the business, although there is no legal distinction. This concept puts a boundary on the transactions that are to be recorded for any particular accounting entity. It also allows the owner to evaluate the performance of the business.
- *Accounting period:* The life of a business needs to be divided into discrete periods to evaluate performance for that period. Dividing the life of an organisation into equal periods to determine profit or loss for that period is known as the accounting period concept. The time periods are arbitrary, but most organisations report at least annually, with large companies preparing half-yearly and quarterly financial statements for outside purposes (in some countries) and at least monthly (sometimes more frequently) for management purposes.
- *Monetary:* Accounting transactions need to be measured in a common denominator, which in Australia is, not surprisingly, the Australian dollar. This allows comparisons across periods and across different companies. Transactions that cannot be reasonably assigned a dollar value are not included in the accounts. This concept also assumes that the value of the monetary unit is constant over time, which ignores inflation.
- *Historical cost:* Under the historical cost concept, assets are initially recorded at cost. As you will see in later chapters, many assets, such as inventory, will still be recorded at cost in the statement of financial position in subsequent periods although their value has increased. Some other assets, such as property, plant and equipment, can be revalued periodically. Thus, in reading a statement of financial position it is important to note at what valuation the assets are being recorded.
- *Going concern:* Financial statements are prepared on the premise that the organisation will continue operations as a going concern in the foreseeable future. If this is not the case, it is necessary to report the liquidation values of an organisation's assets.
- *Materiality:* Under the materiality concept, all transactions are recorded, but items that have a small dollar value are expensed rather than included as an asset on the statement of financial position. For example, a box of pens that costs $13 and has a useful life of two years would be treated as a stationery expense rather than as an asset.

Some of these basic concepts have already been briefly mentioned earlier in this chapter, and all will be referred to again throughout the book.

## 1.9 Is accounting really important?

In case you are not convinced that accounting numbers (profit and balance sheet figures) are important, we hope the following newspaper extracts may convince you. Quotes of this type appear in the financial section of most newspapers every day. The quotes are ones we thought you might find interesting. The quotes clearly show that a lot of emphasis is placed on accounting figures (especially profits) in decision-making by management, by users such as shareholders and creditors, corporate boards and consumer groups.

### Use by management in making business decisions

- Qantas responded to a sharp fall in earnings by eliminating 5 per cent of its workforce and culling several underperforming international routes. 'In the six months to December, net profit fell 22.2 per cent to $262.9 million ... Qantas will cut 25%, or 220, of its executive and middle management staff in Australia over the next two weeks, mostly through compulsory redundancies. It will reduce staff in other non-operational roles by 1250 positions within six months ... the job cuts would ... save the airline about $100 million a year' (*Sydney Morning Herald*, 23 February 2001).
- *Australian Financial Review*, 26 June 2001, noted that Qantas was considering the sale of its catering division as part of its cost cutting measures: 'if costs can be lowered by $25 million at the earnings before interest and tax line ... it will consider keeping the business'.
- 'Coles Myer is reviewing cost overheads for its underperforming Target division as it continues to review black spots on its balance sheet ... Target suffered a 39.5 per cent slide in earnings before interest and tax to $80.1 million in 1999–2000 ... Coles Myer last week sold off its loss-making Katies business to Miller's Retail ...' (*Australian Financial Review*, 7 November 2000).

### Decision-making by users such as shareholders

- 'Westfield Holdings is on track to deliver its 41st consecutive annual profit rise after a 13.5% gain in net profit to $76.6 million in the December half ... investor response was swift yesterday with the shares rising 28c to $13.50' (*Sydney Morning Herald*, 23 February 2001).
- 'Shares in F. H. Faulding dived 5.5% yesterday after the group turned in a lower than expected first half profit of $39.5 million' (*Sydney Morning Herald*, 7 March 2001).
- 'Investors wiped more than $4.7 billion from the market value of News Corporation Ltd after the company predicted its full year earnings would be lower than the market expected ... Analysts predicted that forecasts could be slashed by as much as 30 per cent' (*Australian*, 10 November 2000).

### Use by bankers and other creditor groups

- 'Austrim says it is confident it can negotiate a new financing facility with its bankers as the group looks to secure an additional $150 million to fund the New Zealand business plan' (*Australian Financial Review*, 31 July 2001).
- Re Harris Scarfe, *Australian Financial Review*, 3 April 2001: 'Creditors have become increasingly nervous about a 36 per cent blowout in accounts payable to $65 million in the first half of 2000–01 and heavy levels of debt, with gearing at 76 per cent'.

- 'Shares in Mayne Nickless closed at a nine year low yesterday after the healthcare and transport group received its second credit rating downgrade in a month. Standard and Poors cut Mayne's long term credit standing from A to BBB+ after placing it on credit watch with negative implications in September. S&P also said Mayne's outlook was still negative and "a further modest downgrade may result" if Mayne's performance did not improve' (*Australian Financial Review*, 3 December 1999).

## Use by corporate boards in rewarding and removing executives

- Executive remuneration plans are often specified in part according to accounting performance. For example, the chief executive of Brambles Industries, Mr C. K. Chow, receives performance bonuses contingent on company performance: 'if the company performs strongly, such as returning to its past 15% earnings per share growth, he will receive additional annual payments including up to $2 million in free shares, a cash bonus of up to $1.35 million and up to $2 million worth of market-priced options' (*Australian Financial Review*, 26 June 2001).
- Poor profits also often result in changes in chief executive officers: 'Orica's chief executive Mr Phillip Weickhardt yesterday paid the ultimate price for presiding over the destruction of $2 billion worth of shareholders' funds over the past four years, joining the growing list of chief executives to depart high-profile public companies in Australia in recent months. He joins Pacific Dunlop's Mr Rod Chadwick, Austrim's Mr Alan Jackson and Goodman Fielder's Mr David Hearn, who have all left their companies in recent months following a string of profit downgrades. The move also reflects a growing trend of institutional shareholder activism in Australia, led by Perpetual Funds Management. Perpetual is Orica's biggest shareholder and lobbied for executive changes at the Melbourne-based company ...' (*Australian Financial Review*, 6 July 2001)

## Use by consumer groups

- 'Fee income grew 14 per cent to $6.3 billion last year, outstripping growth in bank assets, with business paying around two-thirds of all fees ... households pay one-third of all bank fees totalling $2.1 billion ... the RBA found that fee income paid by households grew by 18 per cent last year, compared with 12 per cent for business customers ... the shadow assistant Treasurer, Mr Kelvin Thomson, said the banks had excessively profited from fees: "the banks still have their snouts in the trough ... banks continued their blatant profiteering at the expense of consumers and small business"' (*Australian Financial Review*, 20 July 2001).

## Use by unions and management in negotiating wage agreements

- 'Ansett will hold a crisis summit with union leaders, having warned that its balance sheet is too weak to support a pay rise for its 17 000 employees until at least March next year ... the airline has gone steadily downhill since the end of December, with operating losses spiralling from $14.3 million for the third quarter to an estimated $20 million to $30 million in the final three months ... the group would not be able to discuss a pay increase "until the company's balance sheet improves". "A 1 per cent increase on the current payroll will cost $10 million and the balance sheet is currently too weak to withstand such an increase in costs"' (*Australian Financial Review*, 1 July 1998).

### For your interest

Many people conduct research in an effort to understand and help with problems such as choosing appropriate accounting methods, maintaining auditor independence, share market responses to accounting information, disputes about accounting among contending parties, exercising professional judgement about accounting, ethics of professional accountants, history of accounting methods, social issues such as the role of women in accounting, practical solutions to computing management bonuses and other performance incentives, income tax calculation and even the use of graphs and pictures in accounting reports. There are many accounting research journals, with titles such as *ABACUS, Accounting and Finance, Accounting, Organisations and Society, The Accounting Review, Contemporary Accounting Research, Journal of Accounting and Economics* and *Journal of Accounting Research*. References to research results are made frequently in this book, wherever it helps in understanding an issue.

## 1.10 Public sector issues

There has been a recent trend in Australia to establish accounting standards for the three tiers of government: local government, the State Governments and the Commonwealth Government. In these tiers of government, there has been a move from cash to accrual accounting. There are many parties that require information about departments and councils for the purpose of making and evaluating decisions regarding the allocation of scarce resources. Users include departmental managers, responsible ministers, Members of Parliament, policy advisers, the Auditor-General, users of departmental services, ratepayers and those who perform oversight or review services on behalf of members of the community (for example, regulatory agencies).

These parties could use this information to determine, for example, whether a department is:

- achieving its objectives
- operating economically and efficiently in achieving its objectives
- using its resources for the purposes intended
- worthy of continued support for its activities and, if so, the amount of resources that should be committed to these activities
- able to continue to provide goods and services in the future.

Government departments and local government authorities are required to prepare financial reports that include an operating statement, a statement of financial position and a statement of cash flows. The differences in content and format between these and the private sector equivalents will be discussed in later chapters.

From 30 June 1999, each of the States and the Commonwealth have been required to prepare whole of government accounts. The financial reports of governments encompass the assets they control, the liabilities they have incurred and the related revenues and expenses. It is argued that these reports should be prepared because there are users who depend on the financial information contained in them for making and evaluating decisions about the allocation of resources. Users of these reports of governments include parliamentarians, the public, providers of finance, the media and other analysts. The financial reports will also assist governments in discharging their obligation of financial accountability.

An increasingly important area of the public sector is the performance of government trading enterprises (GTEs). These GTEs, which include Telstra, Australia Post and various electricity and water authorities, have become an increasing source of revenues for both the Commonwealth and the State Governments via dividends and taxation. Their financial performance therefore affects the performance of their owner governments. Accounting is the vehicle by which this financial performance is measured.

Many of these GTEs have recently experienced structural changes, including industry restructuring, improved accountability, commercialisation and corporatisation, privatisation and pricing reform. The focus of the reforms varies across industries. For example, in the water sector, where additional sources of supply are increasingly costly, pricing reform has been a high priority. In telecommunications, there has been increased emphasis on competition. Increased cost recovery has been an important issue for rail transport. In each of these cases, accounting reports and the development of accounting performance measures have been necessary to ensure focus on these reforms.

## 1.11 Homework and discussion to develop understanding

This section starts with simpler discussion questions that revise some of the basic concepts and are then followed by a set of problems.

*At the beginning of each homework section, some homework problems are marked with an asterisk (*).* For each of these, there is an informal solution outline at the end of the book. These outlines are intended to facilitate self-study and additional practice: *don't look at the solution for any of these without giving the problem a serious try first,* because once you have seen the solution it always looks easier than it is. Please note that *a problem can have several solutions* – it is possible for your answer to differ in some details from the solution outline provided and still be a good answer, especially if you have made valid, alternative assumptions or happen to know a lot about the particular situation in the problem.

### Discussion questions

**1** What is the basic purpose of financial accounting?
**2** Distinguish between financial performance and financial position.
**3** What is the difference between financial and managerial accounting?
**4** Who are the main parties that comprise the social setting of accounting?
**5** What is meant by credible periodic reporting? What prevents organisations making financial statements increasingly credible? (Consider cost-benefit implications.)
**6** List four important users of financial accounting and describe the use that each user would make of the information.
**7** Do all users of financial accounting have the same information needs? Why, or why not?
**8** List some similarities and differences between the need for financial information between shareholders and bankers.
**9** List five situations in which judgement is required by the preparers of financial information.
**10** What is the difference between a bookkeeper, an accountant and an auditor?
**11** What does an audit achieve?
**12** Describe what is meant by accrual accounting. How does it differ from cash accounting?
**13** Who uses accrual accounting?

**14** Which of the following terms would you see in financial statements prepared under (a) accrual accounting and (b) cash accounting: accounts payable, accounts receivable, cash and inventory.

**15** What are the three key financial statements, and what relevant information do they provide to users of accounting reports?

**16** Explain in simple terms each of the following account assumptions:

- **a** accounting entity
- **b** accounting period
- **c** monetary
- **d** historical cost
- **e** going concern
- **f** materiality.

**17** Do you think lecturers should have the right to use their own judgement in determining subject grades, or should those grades be based on objectively set exams administered by someone other than lecturers? Why? Do you think companies' management should have the right to choose the accounting policies and methods by which their performance is measured? Why? How do these two cases differ, if at all?

**18** An executive of an international economic consulting firm recently said: 'I find it interesting that as companies, or even countries, grow in sophistication, they tend to move from simple cash-based financial reports to accrual accounting reports.' If this observation is valid, why would you suppose this movement to accrual accounting is happening?

## Problem 1.1* Accrual profit

Pike Limited made cash sales of $640 000, credit sales of $490 000 ($270 000 of which had been collected by year-end). It paid $590 000 in expenses and owed $380 000 at year-end. What was the accrual profit?

## Problem 1.2* Cash balance and accrual accounting profit

Using the following information for Dawn's Diving Trips, calculate:

1. the cash in bank as at the end of 2002
2. the 2002 accrual accounting profit.

| | $ |
|---|---|
| Cash in bank as at the end of 2001 | 12 430 |
| Owing from customers as at the end of 2001 (collected in 2002) | 1 000 |
| Cash collected from customers during 2002 for 2002 trips | 68 990 |
| Owing from customers as at the end of 2002 (collected in 2003) | 850 |
| Payable to suppliers as at the end of 2001 (paid in 2002) | 1 480 |
| Cash paid to suppliers during 2002 for 2002 expenses | 36 910 |
| Payable to suppliers as at the end of 2002 (paid in 2003) | 2 650 |
| Depreciation on diving equipment during 2002 | 3 740 |

## Problem 1.3* Calculate accrual accounting profit

Joe Blow set up his own plumbing business on 1 January 2000. During the six months up to 30 June 2000 the following transactions occurred:

1. Joe put $20 000 of his own money into the business.

2 He borrowed $10 000 from the bank for one year at 5 per cent per annum, with interest to be repaid at the end of the loan.
3 He bought plumbing equipment for $4500, which has an expected useful life of three years.
4 He paid $11 600 in wages.
5 He paid other expenses of $15 200.
6 Joe sent bills for $40 000 to customers for work performed between 1 January and 30 June. By 30 June he had received $35 000 and expected the other $5 000 by August.

Using the concepts of accrual accounting, calculate Joe's profit for the six months ending 30 June 2000.

## Problem 1.4* Prepare a statement of financial position and calculate profit

1 Given the following balances prepare a statement of financial position as at 30 June 2002 for Broadway Limited.

| | $ |
|---|---|
| Bank loan | 50 000 |
| Share capital | 150 000 |
| Wages payable | 50 000 |
| Taxes payable | 40 000 |
| Inventory | 120 000 |
| Cash at bank | 60 000 |
| Equipment | 100 000 |
| Retained profits | 70 000 |
| Accounts receivable | 80 000 |

2 The company did not declare any dividends during the year. Its balance in retained profits at the start of the year was $50 000. What is the profit for the year?

## Problem 1.5 What are various people's interests in financial accounting?

Describe briefly what each of the following people would likely want to learn from the financial statements of BrandX Ltd, and how each might be affected if the statements showed good or bad financial performance or financial position:

1 the managing director of the company
2 the company's chief accountant
3 the chairperson of the company's board of directors (the board evaluates the president's performance on behalf of the shareholders)
4 the partner of auditing firm Dimbleby & Co., for whom BrandX is a client
5 the local manager of tax collections for the Australian Taxation Office
6 John Flatstone, who owns 100 shares of BrandX
7 Mildred Evans, who is thinking of buying some shares of the company
8 the local manager of Big Bank, which has made a large loan to BrandX.

## Problem 1.6 Users and their needs

Accounting information is demanded by a wide range of users, including shareholders, company management, suppliers, bankers, trade unions, the Australian Securities and Investments Commission and the Australian Taxation Office. Which one of the following types of information is likely to be sought by each user:

1 the likelihood of the company meeting its interest payments on time?

2 the profitability of each division in the company?
3 the financial position and performance of a company issuing shares to the public for the first time?
4 the prospects for future dividend payments?
5 the probability that the company will be able to pay for its purchases on time?
6 the profitability of the company based on the tax law?
7 the profitability of the company since the last contract with employees was signed?

## Problem 1.7 Accrual profit

During the accounting period, Green Limited received $750 000 from sales and paid out $580 000 in wages and other expenses. However, an extra $260 000 sales were made during the year but the cash has not been collected yet. The company also owes $240 000 for various expenses.

What is the accrual profit?

## Problem 1.8 Accrual profit

1 During the financial year, Gump Limited made cash sales of $300 000, credit sales of $800 000 ($700 000 of which had been collected by year-end). It paid out $600 000 for expenses and owed $200 000 at year-end. What was the accrual profit?
2 Gump Limited purchased 3000 items for $5 each on credit and sells 2000 of these items on credit for $8. What is the sales revenue and cost of goods sold for the period?

## Problem 1.9 Accrual profit

1 During the year ended 30 June 2002, French Horn Ltd made cash sales of $100 000, credit sales of $200 000 ($50 000 of which were still to be collected at year-end), and received $25 000 owing from credit sales, which occurred in May 2001. What is French Horn's sales revenue for the year ended 30 June 2002?
2 Also during the year ended 30 June 2002, French Horn paid $60 000 and owed $10 000 in employee wages. Of the $60 000 paid, $5000 related to wages payable as at 30 June 2001. What is the total of French Horn's accrual accounting expenses?
3 What is French Horn's accrual accounting profit for the year ended 30 June 2002?

## Problem 1.10 Calculate accrual accounting profit

Fred Jones started a consulting business on 1 March 2002. During the period up to 30 June 2002, the following transactions occurred:

1 Fred put $10 000 of his own money into the business.
2 He borrowed $30 000 from the bank at 10 per cent per annum for one year with interest to be repaid at the end of the loan.
3 He sent bills for $35 000 to customers for work performed. By 30 June he had received $30 000 and expected the other $5000 in July.
4 For $8100 he bought a computer that has an expected useful life of three years.
5 He paid $12 000 in wages.
6 He paid other expenses of $20 000.
7 He received a $500 bill for advertising (appeared in newspapers in May; will be paid in July).

Using the concepts of accrual accounting calculate Fred's profit for the four months ending 30 June 2002.

## Problem 1.11 Reconciliation of cash profit and accrual profit

Turku Services Company had a cash profit for its first year in business of $67 450 and accrual profit of $49 860. Show how the two amounts reconcile, using the following information:

1 Uncollected revenue at the end of the year was $18 730.
2 Unpaid bills for expenses at the end of the year totalled $24 880.
3 Expenses for the next year, paid already, totalled $2 300.
4 Depreciation on the company's equipment was $13 740 for the year.

## Problem 1.12 Calculate accrual profit and change in cash

'I just don't understand it!' Dwight Benat had received his accountant's calculation of Dwight's business profit, showing an accrual profit for his first year in business of $45 290. 'If I made so much money, why don't I have it in the bank? My bank account shows only $7540 on hand!'

Dwight operates Benat Supply, which provides stationery and office supplies to business customers. He has no store, just a small rented warehouse, and only one employee. Here are the data he and his accountant used. Explain clearly to Dwight:

1 how the accountant calculated the $45 290 profit
2 why there is only $7540 on hand.

| | $ |
|---|---|
| Collected from customers during the year | 143 710 |
| Still owing from customers at the end of the year (collected next year) | 15 220 |
| Paid for products to resell and for other expenses, including wages, during the year | 128 670 |
| Owing for products and other expenses at the end of the year (paid next year) | 9 040 |
| Cost of unsold products on hand at the end of the year (all sold next year) | 26 070 |
| Depreciation on equipment during the year | 2 000 |
| Personal withdrawals by Dwight during the year | 7 500 |

## Problem 1.13 Calculate accrual profit and change in cash

The accountant for Dale Rogers' new business, Greenbay, has calculated an accrual profit of $35 000. However, the bank balance for the business only shows a balance of $15 000.

Dale is confused by this, as the bank balance is much lower than the accountant's profit calculation.

1 Explain how the accountant calculated the accrual profit.
2 Explain why there is only $15 000 in the bank.

The data used by the accountant are as follows:

| | $ |
|---|---|
| Amounts collected from customers during the year | 122 000 |
| Amounts owing from customers at year-end | 21 000 |
| Amounts paid for stock and other expenses (e.g. wages) | 107 000 |
| Amounts owing for stock and other expenses at year-end | 13 000 |
| Cost of stock on hand (unsold) at year-end (all sold next year) | 16 000 |
| Depreciation of equipment during the year | 4 000 |

## Problem 1.14 Accrual profit and cash profit

Robyn began operating a part-time business, the Dressing Gown, repairing and making outfits. She does this from the spare room in her house and leases a sewing machine.

For the first year of operation, Robyn's business records show the following:

| | $ |
|---|---|
| Collections from customers | 4 000 |
| Payments to suppliers (materials etc.) | 1 600 |
| Rental payments for sewing machine | 1 200 |
| Amounts owing from customers at end of year | 450 |
| Amounts owing to suppliers at end of year | 220 |
| Cost of supplies on hand at end of year | 650 |

1 Calculate the business's cash profit for the year.
2 Calculate the business's accrual profit for the year.
3 Reconcile your answers to questions 1 and 2.

## Problem 1.15 Accounting equation

Mr Smiles opened his fruit shop at the beginning of last year. By the end of that year he had the following assets and liabilities:

| | $ (000) |
|---|---|
| **Assets** | |
| Cash | 350 |
| Fruit | 600 |
| Total assets | 950 |
| **Liabilities** | |
| Suppliers payable | 280 |
| Wages payable | 128 |
| Total liabilities | 408 |

1 What is Mr Smiles' owner's equity in his fruit shop at the end of the year?
2 If Mr Smiles' initial investment was $500 000, what was his profit for the year?

## Problem 1.16 Statement of financial performance

Given the following balances, prepare a statement of financial performance for the year ended 30 June 2002 for Bush Traders.

| | $ |
|---|---|
| Sales | 48 000 |
| Cost of goods sold | 21 000 |
| Wages | 8 000 |
| Electricity | 4 000 |
| Travel | 2 000 |
| Advertising | 1 000 |

## Problem 1.17 Statement of financial performance

Given the following information, prepare a statement of financial performance for Gerke Pty Ltd for the year ended 30 June 2002.

| | $ |
|---|---|
| Rent expense | 30 000 |
| Cost of goods sold | 100 000 |
| Sales | 250 000 |
| Wages | 75 000 |
| Marketing | 25 000 |
| Training expense | 8 000 |

## Problem 1.18 Prepare a statement of financial position and calculate profit

1 Given the following balances, prepare a statement of financial position as at 30 June 2002 for Bricks Ltd.

| | $ |
|---|---|
| Bank loan | 100 000 |
| Share capital | 400 000 |
| Accounts payable | 60 000 |
| Taxes payable | 40 000 |
| Inventory | 150 000 |
| Cash | 50 000 |
| Land and buildings | 500 000 |
| Retained profits | 200 000 |
| Accounts receivable | 100 000 |

2 The company did not declare any dividends during the year. Its balance in retained profits at the start of the year was $120 000. What is the profit figure for the year?

## Problem 1.19 Calculate shareholders' equity

Given the following information relating to Hybrid Ltd, what is the balance of shareholders' equity?

| | $ |
|---|---|
| Property, plant and equipment | 1 300 000 |
| Cash | 200 000 |
| Accounts receivable | 400 000 |
| Accounts payable | 300 000 |
| Loans to the company | 200 000 |

## Problem 1.20 Calculate shareholders' equity

Given the following information relating to Penguin Ltd, what is the balance of shareholders' equity?

| | $ |
|---|---|
| Property, plant and equipment | 1 500 000 |
| Accounts receivable | 400 000 |
| Cash | 100 000 |
| Inventory | 500 000 |
| Bank loan | 250 000 |
| Wages payable | 90 000 |

### Problem 1.21 Calculate shareholders' equity

Gomez Limited has the following assets and liabilities:

| | $ |
|---|---|
| Loan | 180 000 |
| Cash | 90 000 |
| Accounts payable | 110 000 |
| Accounts receivable | 170 000 |
| Equipment | 200 000 |

1 Classify each balance as an asset or liability.
2 Calculate shareholders' equity.

### Problem 1.22 Calculate shareholders' equity

Grey Limited has the following assets and liabilities:

| | $ |
|---|---|
| Accounts payable | 55 000 |
| Accounts receivable | 45 000 |
| Cash | 29 000 |
| Loan | 22 000 |
| Vehicle | 28 000 |
| Wages payable | 14 000 |

1 Classify each balance as an asset or liability.
2 Calculate shareholders' equity.

### Problem 1.23 The accounting equation

Cardigan Pty Ltd has total assets of $150 000 and liabilities that add to $70 000 as at 30 June 2002.

1 What is Cardigan's owners' equity as at 30 June 2002?
2 During the year to 30 June 2003, Cardigan's total assets increase by $63 000 while total liabilities increase by $25 000. What is the amount of Cardigan's owners' equity on 30 June 2003?
3 Now assume that in the year to 30 June 2003, Cardigan's total liabilities increase by $20 000 and its owners' equity decreases by $12 000. On 30 June 2003, what is the level of Cardigan's total assets?
4 Assume that in the year to 30 June 2003, Cardigan's total assets double while its owners' equity remains unchanged. What are its total liabilities as at 30 June 2003?

## Problem 1.24 The accounting equation

Use the accounting equation to answer the following.

1 Chocolat Pty Ltd doubled its liabilities during the year. At the beginning of the year, the amount of total assets was $40 000 and owners' equity was $30 000. What is the amount of Chocolat's total liabilities at the end of the year?

2 Walter & Co began the year with assets of $95 000 and liabilities of $40 000. Net profit for the year was $25 000. What is the amount of owners' equity at the end of the year?

3 During the last financial year, Goldsmart Industries tripled the amount of its assets. At the end of the year, total liabilities amount to $67 000 while owners' equity is $26 000. What was the amount of total assets at the beginning of the year?

## Problem 1.25 Correcting a statement of financial position

Cookiedough Limited began business on 1 July 2001, producing and selling cakes and pastries. One year later, the company's newly appointed accountant, Joe Biscuit, needs to produce a statement of financial position for a meeting of company executives. Unfortunately, Joe is more skilled at baking than he is in accounting and has requested your advice. He shows you the following statement of financial position he has prepared.

**Cookiedough Limited**
**Statement of financial position as at 30 June 2002**

| **Assets** | | **Liabilities and owners' equity** | |
|---|---|---|---|
| Cash | 2 170 | Accounts receivable | 5 230 |
| Net profit for the year | 12 360 | Share capital | 20 000 |
| Raw materials | 4 900 | Kitchen equipment | 25 400 |
| Accounts payable | 5 340 | | |

Assume that the account balances Joe has used are correct. Prepare (if necessary) a corrected statement of financial position. Provide an explanation of the main differences between your statement of financial position and the one Joe prepared.

## Problem 1.26 Primary assumptions made in preparing financial statements

Kelly Koedack opened a photography business in a small shop that she rented from a large retailer, Eastfield Limited. She paid the first month's rent of $400 by writing a cheque from her personal account. Kelly took some of her own photography equipment and materials (worth $5000) into the shop, and also bought some new cameras so that she could take pictures of her customers with the best available technology. The cameras had a recommended retail price of $2500 but she was able to buy them on sale for $2200, charging them to her personal credit card. Kelly's first customer paid her $900 for a set of portraits, so she opened a bank account for the company. Her other customers have not yet paid her, owing a total of $3100. At the end of the first month of business, Kelly prepared the following financial statements.

**Kelly's Professional Photography**
**Statement of financial position as at 31 May 2001**

| | | | |
|---|---|---|---|
| Cash | 900 | | |
| Equipment | 2 500 | Owner's equity | 3 400 |
| | 3 400 | | 3 400 |

**Kelly's Professional Photography**
**Statement of financial performance for the month ended 31 May 2001**

| | | |
|---|---|---|
| Sales | | 4 000 |
| Rent | 400 | |
| Equipment | 2 500 | 2 900 |
| | | 1 100 |

Identify the assumptions that Kelly has violated and explain how each event should have been handled. Prepare a corrected statement of financial position and statement of financial performance.

## Problem 1.27 (Challenging) Principles of performance evaluation

Suppose you have the job of designing a general system for measuring and evaluating the performance of managers on behalf of an enterprise's owners. List the principles (characteristics) that you think such a system would need in order to be acceptable to both the owners and the managers. Which principles would you expect the owners and managers to agree on fairly easily, and which would you expect to be more controversial?

## Problem 1.28 (Challenging) Calculate and reconcile cash and accrual profit

Leslie has a part-time business, Quick Crack-Fix, repairing small cracks and stars in car windshields, using a special polymer filler that makes the damage almost invisible and stops cracks from spreading. The repair takes only a few minutes, using equipment and supplies stored in the boot of Leslie's car. The main customers are used car lots, car rental companies, service stations and insurance companies, but some business is done with individual customers in the driveways of their homes.

For the current year, Leslie's business records showed the following:

| | $ |
|---|---|
| Collections from customers | 24 354 |
| Payments to suppliers | 5 431 |
| Royalty payments to owner of Crack-Fix trademark | 2 435 |
| Wages expense (all paid) | 14 000 |
| Depreciation on business equipment and car | 3 200 |
| Amounts owing by customers at end of previous year | 1 320 |
| Amounts owing by customers at end of current year | 890 |
| Amounts owing to suppliers at end of previous year | 436 |
| Amounts owing to suppliers at end of current year | 638 |
| Supplies on hand at the end of previous year | 0 |
| Cost of supplies on hand at the end of current year | 345 |

Leslie's business bank account showed a balance of $1332 at the end of the previous year.

1. Calculate the business's cash profit for the current year.
2. Calculate the bank account balance at the end of the current year.
3. Calculate the business's accrual profit for the current year.
4. Reconcile your answers to questions 1 and 3.

### Problem 1.29 (Challenging) Discuss ethical problems

Discuss the example on ethical problems given at the end of section 1.4. What ethical issues do you see? What do you think the chief accountant, the auditor and the general manager should do?

### Problem 1.30 (Challenging) Difficulties of determining appropriate figures under accrual accounting

For each of the following organisations suggest some difficulties in determining appropriate accounting numbers:

1. an oil exploration company
2. an airline company
3. a telecommunications company providing local, long-distance and overseas telephone calls
4. a wholesaler of jeans during a recession.

### Problem 1.31 (Challenging) Resentment of auditor by the person audited

The student tennis club is owned by the student association of the university. The student treasurer of the tennis club prepares an annual financial report to the executive committee of the student association, and that report is audited. A local accounting firm does the audit for a minimal fee, in order to help the students out. The club treasurer was heard complaining a little about the audit, because having one seemed to imply that the treasurer was not trusted and because the audit fee had to be paid by the club, which was always short of money.

The auditor thus has to deal with some resentment by the treasurer. Make a list of the difficulties the auditor might have because of this resentment, and any other difficulties you think might face such an auditor. (These problems are likely to be encountered by any auditor who is responsible for verifying financial statements prepared by management for use by owners and creditors.)

### Problem 1.32 (Challenging) Factors in comparing companies' performance

The general manager of Gobble Gobble Foods Pty Ltd, which makes everything from soup to nuts out of turkey meat, is comparing Gobble Gobble's performance to that of Curdled Products Pty Ltd, which does much the same using tofu and other bean curds. The general manager has the following data for Curdled Products, which she saw in the newspaper yesterday (note that figures inside brackets indicate a loss):

| | $ |
|---|---|
| Profit for 1996 | 1 565 000 |
| Profit for 1997 | 2 432 000 |
| Profit for 1998 | (985 000) |
| Profit for 1999 | 123 000 |
| Profit for 2000 | 1 249 000 |
| Profit for 2001 | 2 915 000 |
| Profit for first half of 2002 | 873 000 |

Without knowing much about accounting except the introductory ideas of this chapter, use your intelligence and experience in comparing things to make a list of the factors you think the general manager of Gobble Gobble should take into account in comparing her company's performance to that of Curdled.

## Problem 1.33 (Challenging) Accrual and cash profit in measuring performance

Wings Ltd is an airline services company with a plant near the Sydney Airport and service centres in several States. It provides meals, serviettes and other food-related items, cleaning, interior maintenance and several other services to various airlines. The company has been fairly successful, though recessions and deregulation of air services have put significant pressure on its operations. When the company began in the late 1970s, it had a relatively weak financial position (mainly because of borrowing to get set up) and its financial performance, while satisfactory, has not enabled it to reduce its debt load very much. It seems that every time the company gets a little ahead, new equipment must be purchased or new product lines developed, and the company finds itself borrowing again.

A recent year provides a good example. The company's accrual profit was $188 000 and its cash profit was $241 000. (The difference was because of depreciation expense of $96 000 and uncollected revenue being $43 000 higher at the end of the year than at the beginning. In the company's financial statements, the phrase 'net profit for the year' was used to describe the accrual profit and 'cash generated by operations' described the cash profit.) The general manager had looked forward to using some of the cash to pay debts, but late in the year the company had to buy new food-handling and wrapping equipment for $206 000 to meet revised standards announced by its airline customers. Therefore, the company ended up only a few thousand dollars ahead in cash, not enough to make much of a dent in its debts.

The general manager has a regular half-yearly meeting with the company's external auditor to discuss accounting and auditing issues. After the above results were known, the general manager phoned the auditor and made the following comments: 'I thought I'd ask you to think about a few things before our meeting next week. When it comes to our accounting, I think the company has too many masters and too many measures. What I mean is first that too many people are concerned with what our financial statements say. Why can't we just prepare financial statements that meet my needs as general manager? Why do we have to worry about all the other people outside the company? Sometimes I'm not even sure who all those other people are, since you accountants and auditors often just talk about "users" without being too clear what you mean. Also, I'm confused by the existence of both a "net profit" figure and a "cash generated by operations" figure in our financial statements. Why can't we just have one or the other to measure our performance?'

The general manager raised issues that will be addressed frequently as this book develops your understanding. But for now, what would you say to the general manager?

## Case 1A Woolworths Limited

Refer to the extracts of the annual report of Woolworths Limited in appendix 2. All questions relate to the consolidated accounts.

1 Provide indicators that Woolworths uses accrual accounting.
2 What were total assets at 24 June 2001?
3 What were total liabilities at 24 June 2001?
4 What was shareholders' equity at 24 June 2001?
5 State the accounting equation in dollar figures at 24 June 2001.
6 What was the operating profit before tax?
7 What was the operating profit after tax?
8 What was the largest cash inflow and outflow relating to operating activities?
9 Why is the cash flow from operations a different figure to operating profit after tax?

## CASE 1B Importance of profit to users

Listed below are six quotes from newspapers indicating the importance of profit to users of accounting information. For each quote, labelled (1) to (6), state what type of user is particularly concerned.

1 **Woolworths on attack after record half**

Woolworths Ltd is planning an acquisition spree to strengthen its retailing operations after yesterday reporting a record half-year profit of $237.7m (*Australian Financial Review*, 1 March 2001).

2 **Investors hit Coles on downgrade**

Coles Myer's shares plunged yesterday after it admitted annual profit could fall below $300m ... investors wiped $1.2b from the retailer's market value after it warned that net profit would be ... well below the $350m foreshadowed ... Its shares dived $1.04, or 14.5% ... Analysts immediately began winding back forecasts (*Australian Financial Review*, 26 June 2001).

3 Disenchanted investors have wiped more than $1.6 billion off market darling Brambles in the past two days, amid confirmation of an earnings downturn (*Australian*, 10 November 2000).

4 **AGL suspended after NZ losses**

The Australian Gas Light Co was in crisis last night, with its shares suspended on the stock exchange and its board thrashing out a plan to stem bleeding from its New Zealand operations.

AGL suspended its shares after media reports that it may be facing an asset writedown of up to $150 million on its 66 per cent NZ subsidiary, Natural Gas Corporation (*Australian Financial Review*, 22 July 2001).

5 **Pay cut for senior Goodman executives**

Goodman Fielder Ltd's two most senior executives have paid the price for the company's under-performance last financial year, missing out on their annual cash-based performance incentives ... A Goodman spokesman said the incentive payments were withheld after Goodman failed to achieve internal budget targets ... Last month the company reported a 4 per cent fall in net profits to $118 million and a bottom line loss of $78.3 million after writing off about $196 million in restructuring and other charges (*Australian Financial Review*, 3 October 2001).

6 **Fears grow for future of Ansett**

As the Air NZ board met for the second consecutive day to review its options, both governments said they were unable to agree to a capital restructuring plan until the company revealed its true financial position and equity requirements (*Australian Financial Review*, 7 September 2001).

## CASE 1C Michelle's Cordial Stand: An introduction to accrual accounting

During the first week of the summer holidays, Michelle and her family go to watch the cricket. They drive to the stadium, but it is a long walk from the car park to the cricket ground. It is a hot sunny day, and as she walks with her parents through the park leading to the stadium, Michelle (who is eight years old) notices a young girl selling cordial at one end of the park. She recognises the girl as one of her classmates, Jessica, and goes over for a chat. Jessica is doing a brisk business selling cordial for $1 per cup, and she shows Michelle a shoebox full of gold coins and five-dollar notes. She mentions that this is her last week selling cordial as Saturday morning tennis starts next week.

On the way home from the match, Michelle asks if she can set up a cordial stand next Saturday. Her Uncle Jeff, who likes to build things with wood, offers to build her a cordial stand if she can pay him for the materials – about $20, he thinks, plus $1 for his labour. Her little brother, Peter, offers to help and Michelle agrees to pay him $2 to be her assistant for the day.

On Friday, Michelle's mother estimates the amount of cordial and other supplies Michelle will need if she sells 60 cups of cordial. Michelle takes $25 from her money box and goes to the supermarket with her mother. They buy the items on her list for $10.

When they return home, they see that Uncle Jeff has delivered the cordial stand. It has a counter, a sign reading 'Cordial: $1' and a bench for Michelle to sit on. Michelle's father say that she can use this stand every Saturday for the rest of the holidays: a total of seven Saturdays. Uncle Jeff has already left, but he has left a message that he will be there at 9 a.m. tomorrow to fill his jug with cordial before going to play golf. He will collect the $21 for the cordial stand when he drops by again on Sunday afternoon.

While they are setting up the stand in the front yard, Michelle's cousin Tim pays a visit. After she tells him what she is planning to do, Tim gives her $5 and says that he will bring his family around the next day for five cups of cordial.

Michelle counts her money: she has already earned $20 from her business, and she hasn't even started working yet!

Saturday turns out to be a beautiful summer day. Michelle's house is well-positioned across from a school playground that is busy all day with netball, cricket and soccer matches. She serves her first four cups to Uncle Jeff at 9 a.m. for $4. During the rest of the day, business is brisk, and Michelle serves 72 more cups of lemonade, including five to cousin Tim and his family. At 2 p.m., her father takes $6 from her shoebox to the shops to buy more supplies.

At the end of the day, Michelle counts the money in her shoebox. It comes to $82. Peter asks for his $2, but she promises to pay him the next day. She has $3 worth of cordial supplies to use the following week. In addition, Mr Lee, one of the neighbours, owes her $4 for four cups she served to his family after he promised to pay her the next day.

Early on Sunday, Mr Lee stops by to pay Michelle the $4. Michelle then pays Peter his $2 in wages. After breakfast, she takes $20 from her shoebox to the shops to buy a toy. Uncle Jeff pays a visit later that afternoon and Michelle pays him the $21 for the cordial stand.

A summary of Michelle's Cordial Stand's transactions on Friday, Saturday and Sunday is shown in the table on the next page. The daily net cash flows are totalled at the bottom of the table. As can be seen, Michelle's business 'earned' $20 on Friday and another $62 on Saturday, but 'lost' $39 on Sunday.

(Adapted from Cushing, B. E. 1997, *Issues in Accounting Education*, vol. 12, no. 1, pp. 161–70.)

***Required:***

**1** Do you believe that Michelle's concept of 'profits' (the increase in the amount of cash that her business has) is a good way to measure how much she earned each day from her cordial business? Why or why not? What does it mean to 'earn' profit?

**2** Can you think of a better way to measure the profit from Michelle's Cordial Stand? If so, what was the daily profit of Michelle's Cordial Stand using this better method?

Hint: Analyse each of Michelle's transactions in terms of the accounting equation: Assets = Liabilities + Shareholders' Equity. Then analyse each of the transactions that affect the net worth of Michelle's Cordial Stand as either (a) investments and withdrawals or (b) revenues and expenses. The net profit of Michelle's Cordial Stand may then be measured in terms of another equation: Revenues – Expenses = Net Profit.

**Michelle's Cordial Stand**
Cash basis accounting
(for the first weekend of operations)

| | Frday $ | Saturday $ | Sunday $ |
|---|---|---|---|
| Friday | | | |
| 1 Michelle gets $25 from her money box to fund her business. | + 25 | | |
| 2 Michelle buys $10 of cordial supplies. | – 10 | | |
| 3 Uncle Jeff delivers stand and will collect money on Sunday. | — | | |
| 4 Tim pays $5 for 5 cups he will get on Saturday. | + 5 | | |
| Saturday | | | |
| 5 A total of 68 cups are sold for cash @ $1 each. | | + 68 | |
| 6 Mr Lee buys 4 cups but will pay tomorrow. | | — | |
| 7 Tim and his family pick up their five cups of lemonade. | | — | |
| 8 Michelle's father goes to the shops to buy $6 of supplies. | | –6 | |
| 9 Peter helps out and earns $2 in wages. | | — | |
| 10 Leftover ingredients and supplies amount to $3. | | — | |
| 11 The cordial stand is good for another 6 weeks. | | — | |
| Sunday | | | |
| 12 Mr Lee brings his $4 due for yesterday's purchase. | | | + 4 |
| 13 Michelle pays Peter his wages of $2. | | | –2 |
| 14 Michelle takes $20 to buy herself a toy. | | | –20 |
| 15 Uncle Jeff collects $21 for the cordial stand. | | | –21 |
| Net cash-basis 'earnings' | +20 | +62 | –39 |

## CASE 1D Australian Cricket Board

The following text describes how accounting numbers were used by the Australian Cricket Board and the players in negotiations over salaries. It provides further insights into the use of accounting numbers.

**1** How are accounting numbers being used in the pay dispute by the Australian Cricket Board (ACB) and the players?

**2** Why did the ACB order an independent audit?

**3** Given that the ACB ran at a $2.5 million loss in 1996–97, what effect would this have had on net assets (assets minus liabilities)?

**4** What is meant by the statement that 'the financial summary showed the ACB's "net asset position" as being $51.8 million in the black, although $30.3 million of this was tied up in assets such as the WACA Ground in Perth and the SACA's investments in the Adelaide Oval'?

5 Assume the reserves mentioned in the article refer to retained profits. (In fact it is not clear what they mean by reserves here!) How would that affect the arguments of the ACB and the cricket players?

6 If you were the cricket players' representative, what additional information would you want to see?

The Australian Cricket Board yesterday tabled a summary of cricket finances it believes justifies its tough stand on pay demands, then repeated its invitation to Australian Cricketers Association president Tim May to resume negotiations.

The independent audit for 1996–97 was shown first to May and the State captains, then the media, and painted the picture the ACB had predicted – one that portrays the game in robust financial health, despite its heavy reliance on revenue from the international arena, yet seemingly unable to grant pay rises of the magnitude demanded by the players.

It was immediately apparent the ACB will use the financial summary, collated by accounting firm Coopers and Lybrand using the books of the ACB and the six State associations, as its first and most formidable line of defence during future negotiations.

ACB chairman Denis Rogers was quick to quote the financial statement's major point – that Australian cricket had run at a $2.5 million loss last year, but had healthy revenue streams and assets – as evidence that the 10 per cent pay rise offered by the ACB was generous.

'We thought that was a sensible, responsible offer to the players given the financial situation we knew existed,' Rogers said. 'We are hoping now that they have a better understanding of the financial position; they've got a better understanding of the role of the board and the responsibility we exercise for the total Australian cricket community.'

One figure not released yesterday, but mentioned privately by the ACB, is that it would have needed to find an extra $12.5 million to meet the players' demand for 35 per cent of all revenue, based on figures from the past financial year.

In 1996–97, the players received about $9.5 million – or about 18 per cent – of the game's $51.8 million revenue.

May, who with the State captains was given a two-hour presentation of the figures, said he had been satisfied with the level of disclosure in the document, but gave little indication of how the ACA would react to its contents.

'The document is a large document,' May said. 'We spent a couple of hours up there and there is a lot to consider and we will do exactly that.'

**Cricket's finances**

What the Board revealed

Revenue by source

| | $ (m) | % |
|---|---|---|
| Sponsorship and media | 26.1 | 48.3 |
| Gate takings | 10.7 | 19.8 |
| Signage, catering and corporate boxes | 6.5 | 12.0 |
| Memberships | 2.9 | 5.4 |
| Interest income | 2.6 | 4.8 |
| Other | 2.3 | 4.3 |
| Tour guarantees | 2.2 | 4.1 |
| Merchandising | 0.7 | 1.3 |

Expenditure

| | $ (m) | % |
|---|---|---|
| Employee costs | 21.7 | 38.4 |
| Marketing | 6.9 | 12.2 |
| Ground operations | 5.6 | 9.9 |
| Administration | 5.2 | 9.2 |
| Development grants | 3.6 | 6.4 |
| Cricket resources | 3.0 | 5.3 |
| Travel and accommodation | 3.0 | 5.3 |
| Tour guarantees | 2.1 | 3.7 |
| Development resource | 1.9 | 3.4 |
| Interest expense | 1.8 | 3.2 |
| Depreciation | 1.7 | 3.0 |

Employee costs

| | $ (m) |
|---|---|
| Players | 10.0 |
| Team support | 0.6 |
| Administration | 3.6 |
| Marketing | 1.4 |
| Ground staff | 1.1 |
| Development staff | 4.0 |
| Coaches and umpires | 1.0 |
| | 21.6 |

May will convene a meeting of the ACA executive today to consider the figures and Rogers's invitation to resume negotiations, although a sticking point remains on the latter – the presence of ACA consultant James Erskine.

Rogers yesterday repeated that he had invited 'May and some of the leading players' to talks, but not Erskine.

However, regardless of when talks resume, the figures released yesterday indicated there was little chance the ACB would submit to the ACA's demands.

Among the figures which will be used by the ACB to justify its hard line:

- Cricket lost $2.5 million last year.
- Player payments have increased 106 per cent since 1992–93.
- State cricket earns just 8.8 per cent of cricket revenue, but is responsible for 16.6 per cent of expenditure.
- The majority of Sheffield Shield players earned between $30 000 and $50 000, although this figure was inflated by between $6000 and $7500 by payments for the Super Eights competition.

The one area of the finances on which the players were expected to – and may still – base some of their claims is the ACB's liquid reserves.

The financial summary showed the ACB's 'net asset position' as being $51.8 million in the black, although $30.3 million of this was tied up in assets such as the WACA Ground in Perth and the SACA's investments in the Adelaide Oval.

But while the ACB's ratio of assets to revenue was high in comparison with other sports bodies', such as the ARL's and the National Soccer League's, Peter Fekete of Coopers and Lybrand said this did not necessarily mean the ACB had large cash reserves that could be used to reward players.

'Either revenues have to be increased, or other overheads cut or development costs reduced, that's the framework in which [pay rises] can be accommodated,' he said. 'Otherwise you are eating into the reserves of cricket and you are operating with a deficit that isn't sustainable.'

ACB chief executive Malcolm Speed said he had told May he would contact him today or tomorrow in the hope of resuming negotiations on the pay dispute soon. However, he did not expect yesterday's financial disclosure to lead to a short-term resolution.

'I think it is a matter of wait and see,' Speed said. 'I don't think resolution is going to happen today or tomorrow; I think it's longer term than that. But this was a major step in satisfying the players. The players have asked to see what was the size of the pie and what were the constituent parts of the pie. I think that's been done today.'

(Source: Richard Hinds, *Sydney Morning Herald*, 30 October 1997, p. 48.)

Chapter 2

# Measuring and evaluating financial position and financial performance

## On completion of this chapter you should be able to:

- describe the contents of a statement of financial position
- carry out preliminary analysis based on the contents of a statement of financial position
- calculate key ratios such as the debt-to-equity ratio, the current ratio and the quick ratio
- draw up a statement of financial position
- draw up a statement of financial performance
- explain the nature of each of the items in the statement of financial position and statement of financial performance for a public company
- describe the contents of the note reconciling opening and closing retained profits
- explain the importance of both financial statements to managers
- interpret the contents of profit announcements in the financial press.

## 2.1 Chapter overview

Chapter 1 introduced accrual accounting, the key financial statements and the users and preparers of these statements. Now we turn to a set of three chapters that set out financial accounting's *results* and outline the *record-keeping system* that leads to those results. This chapter focuses on the content and use of the statements measuring financial position at a particular date and measuring financial performance (profit) over a period. Chapters 3 and 4 consider how the double-entry system produces accounts and how these accounts are assembled together to form financial statements.

In Australia, accounting standards changed the name from balance sheet to statement of financial position and profit and loss statement to statement of financial performance effective 30 June 2001. However, many executives still use the terms 'balance sheet' and 'profit and loss statement', as does the financial press (not surprisingly, given the term has been so common for hundreds of years). Most other countries continue to use the terms balance sheet and profit and loss statement (sometimes also called an income statement, particularly in the USA).

The statement of financial position (balance sheet) is financial accounting's oldest and most basic report. It measures the enterprise's financial position at a particular date and is the basis for much financial analysis. To outline what you will learn in the next three chapters, let's return to the diagram used at the beginning of chapter 1:

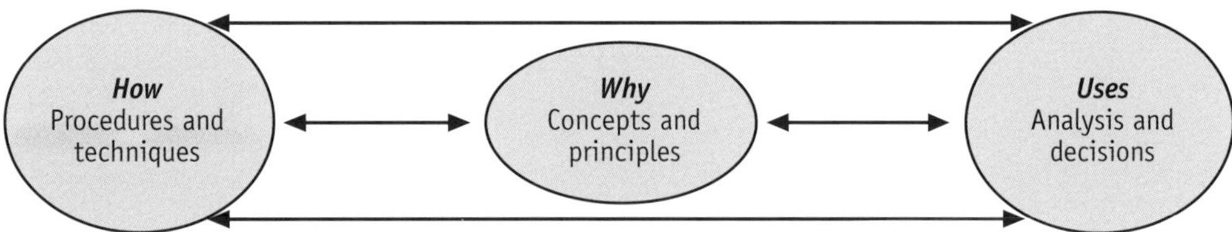


**Figure 2.1** The how, why and uses of accounting

In the next three chapters, you will learn:

- *procedures and techniques:* how the double-entry accounting system produces accounts, and how to assemble a statement of financial position and statement of financial performance from those accounts
- *concepts and principles:* why the statement of financial position and statement of financial performance are important, why they are arranged as they are, and some interesting history about where they came from
- *analysis and decisions:* using the financial statements to understand how an enterprise is put together financially, how it does its business and using it to do some analysis of the enterprise's financial health and performance.

The statement of financial position summarises, at a particular date, the enterprise's financial position as accounting measures it, in three categories of lists:

- resources (such as cash, products on hand, land and buildings) called assets
- obligations (such as loans owing and debts to suppliers) called liabilities
- owners' interests (what's left after subtracting the obligations from the resources) called equity.

The individual items in each of these lists are called accounts, so over the centuries the task of preparing them has been named account*ing*, and the people who do it are account*ants*. All these words are derived from *count*, which is where accounting began: just counting things and listing them.

The statement of financial position portrays the enterprise by arranging its lists of accounts so that the assets sum to the same total as the other two lists, and setting them beside (or below) each other, something like this:

| **Assets** | | **Liabilities and equity** | |
|---|---|---|---|
| Item a | $$ | Item x | $$ |
| Item b | $$ | Item y | $$ |
| Etc. | $$ | Etc. | $$ |
| Total | T$$ | Total | T$$ |

Because the left total equals the right total, accountants say that they balance. Hence the name balance sheet. The underlying accounting system maintains this balance by making sure that any changes in one side of the statement of financial position (balance sheet) are matched by changes in the other side. This requires that each change be recorded twice, so the accounting system is called double-entry. The statement of financial position turns out to be the accumulation of everything financial accounting has recorded about the enterprise since the day the enterprise began, so it is the fundamental cumulative accounting record, and is the anchor to which all the other financial statements are tied.

The statement of financial position provides important information about the enterprise's financial structure and strength, but its description of the enterprise's financial position is not the only story to be told. Its picture is static: it tells us what the position is. Most managers, owners and creditors also want to know how well the enterprise is performing and how it got to where it is. To provide that explanation we need to measure financial performance. This is provided by a statement of financial performance (often called a 'profit and loss statement' or 'income statement' in many countries).

Corporations, which are legally incorporated companies such as Qantas, Commonwealth Bank, Telstra, BHP Billiton, Coles Myer and thousands of local, national and international businesses, produce financial statements at least annually. So do many other kinds of organisations, such as the City of Brisbane, Salvation Army, the Government of Australia, and your university's student union. (We mainly focus on businesses, especially corporations, but other kinds of organisation are considered where appropriate. Each chapter finishes with a short section on public sector issues.)

For large corporations, especially public companies (such as the five examples above), whose shares are traded on stock markets, the financial statements are included in a larger document called an annual report. An annual report typically begins with narrative material on the corporation's performance and prospects, moves on to an extensive discussion and analysis by management, then turns to the financial statements: the statement of financial position, the statement of financial performance and the cash flow statement. The first two are discussed in this chapter, and the statement of cash flows is discussed in chapter 12.

## 2.2 Introduction to the statement of financial position (balance sheet)

The statement of financial position is only one of the set of financial statements, each of which is important for particular uses. But as the summary of the double-entry system, the statement of financial position is financial accounting's fulcrum. It balances, containing two lists that have the same dollar total and together describe the enterprise's financial position at a particular date.

The first list is the enterprise's financial *resources* at that date, as measured by the financial accounting methods you will learn. These resources, called assets, include the enterprise's cash, accounts receivable (money customers have promised to pay), inventory (goods for sale), land, buildings, equipment and many other resources that the enterprise has accumulated and can use in the future.

The second list is the sources, or financing, of those resources at that date, again as measured by financial accounting methods.

- These financing sources include existing obligations that will have to be paid in the future, such as loans from the bank, amounts due to be paid to employees and suppliers (wages payable and accounts payable respectively), mortgages and other long-term borrowings, and many other debts. Some estimates of future payments are included also, although they may not be legally owed just yet, such as promises to pay employee long service leave and estimated future income taxes based on profit already earned but not yet taxed. All these legal obligations and estimates together are called liabilities.
- The list of sources also includes amounts received from owners, which normally involve permanent financing and do not have to be repaid, plus any past accrual profits that have not been paid out to the owners. Owners can finance an enterprise by contributing money to the enterprise, or by not taking profit out of the enterprise, as we will see. The owners' investment is called owners' equity, or just equity. (For corporations, which are owned by shareholders, the term is usually shareholders' equity, while for unincorporated businesses the terms owners' capital or partners' capital are likely to be used, but all of these terms just mean owners' equity.)

Because the statement of financial position balances, the total amount of assets must equal the total of liabilities plus equity. Arithmetically, the accounting equation (often called the balance sheet equation) therefore is:

$$\text{Sum of assets} = \text{Sum of liabilities} + \text{sum of equity}$$
$$\text{Resources list} = \text{Sources (financing) list}$$

This equation is fundamental to financial accounting. Accounting procedures are designed to create and maintain this equality at all times. For example, if you obtain $100 by borrowing from the bank, your statement of financial position would list the $100 cash you received as a resource and the $100 obligation to repay as a liability. By maintaining this equality, financial accounting ensures that all the financing sources that go with the resources are identified, and vice versa. This balanced pair of lists is one of the main reasons for financial accounting's value as an information system.

The two lists are put side by side, or the first above the second, as in the standard style shown below.

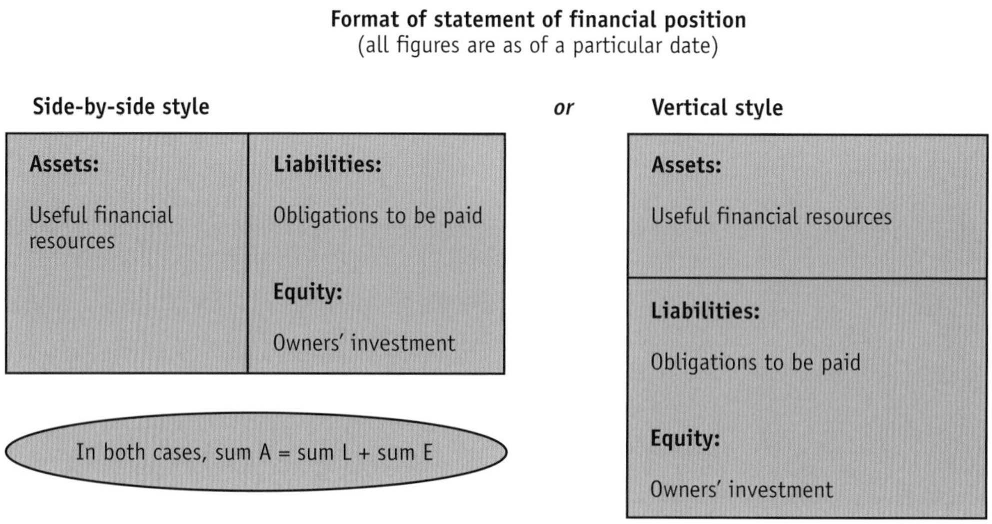

**Format of statement of financial position**
(all figures are as of a particular date)

**Side-by-side style**

| **Assets:** Useful financial resources | **Liabilities:** Obligations to be paid<br>**Equity:** Owners' investment |
|---|---|

In both cases, sum A = sum L + sum E

*or*

**Vertical style**

| **Assets:** Useful financial resources |
|---|
| **Liabilities:** Obligations to be paid<br>**Equity:** Owners' investment |

Figure 2.2 Statement of financial position

Below is a simple example statement of financial position using the side-by-side style to emphasise the equality of the two lists, with assets on the left and liabilities and equity on the right. Explanations of the terms used in the statement of financial position follow the example.

**EXHIBIT 2.1** **Sound and Light Pty Ltd**

**Statement of financial position as at 30 June 2002 (in thousands of dollars)**

| **Assets** | **$** | **$** | **Liabilities and equity** | **$** | **$** |
|---|---|---|---|---|---|
| **Current assets** | | | **Current liabilities** | | |
| Cash | 50 | | Bank overdraft | 30 | |
| Accounts receivable | 75 | | Accounts payable | 73 | 103 |
| Inventory | 120 | 245 | | | |
| **Noncurrent assets** | | | **Noncurrent liabilities** | | |
| Land | 100 | | Loan | | 87 |
| Equipment (net)* | 150 | 250 | Total liabilities | | 190 |
| | | | **Shareholders' equity** | | |
| | | | Share capital | 130 | |
| | | | Retained profits | 175 | 305 |
| **Total** | | 495 | **Total** | | 495 |

* A note to the statement shows that the equipment cost $272 000 less accumulated depreciation of $122 000 giving a net figure of $150 000.

Let's review some features of this statement of financial position:

- The title identifies the enterprise (Sound and Light Pty Ltd), the point in time at which it is drawn up (30 June 2002) and the currency in which amounts are measured (thousands of dollars).
- The statement of financial position (balance sheet) balances! As at 30 June 2002, total assets of $495 000 are exactly equalled by the total sources of these assets (that is, the liabilities and owners' equity). It is a summary, so we cannot tell exactly which source produced which assets; for example, the $50 000 of cash came partly from bank borrowing and partly from other sources, such as past profits. (More about sources shortly.)
- Assets are usually separated into shorter-term ones (current assets) and longer-term ones (noncurrent assets). (More about these categories below.)
- Like assets, liabilities are usually separated into shorter-term ones (current liabilities) and longer-term ones (noncurrent liabilities).
- The statement of financial position shows several individual accounts, telling us about the company's particular financial structure. For example, the company expects to receive $75 000 due from customers and owes $73 000 to its suppliers. The company owes $30 000 to the bank but has chosen not to pay it all back, keeping more than that ($50 000) on hand as cash. (These accounts are usually aggregates of many smaller accounts; for example, there is an account for each customer who owes money to Sound and Light.)
- The $495 000 of assets have been financed by $190 000 ($103 + $87) of liabilities and $305 000 of owners' investment.

## 2.3 Explanations of the three statements of financial position categories: assets, liabilities and equity

### Assets

These are a mixture of the resources that the company needs to do business, for instance, products to sell and a building to operate from, and the resources that it has accumulated as a result of doing business, including amounts due from customers for past sales. *Assets are future economic benefits controlled by the entity as a result of past transactions or other past events.* Sound and Light's assets include cash, accounts receivable, inventory, land and equipment.

Other 'assets' of Sound and Light might include happy employees, a safe working environment and the benefit of some market research on which products will be popular in the future, yet these do not directly appear on its statement of financial position. There is a distinction between the assets that accounting recognises and these other 'assets.' There are objective, standard measures for economic control of and demonstrating the probability of future benefits that will eventuate for the first group, but not for the second group. In the first group, an inventory of machine parts is owned by the enterprise and has a dollar cost that can be easily verified. The benefit will come from future use or selling the inventory. In the second group, a happy employee is, in theory, more productive than an unhappy employee, but it is difficult to measure reliably with any consistency how much more productive a very happy employee is compared with an only mildly happy employee.

Moreover, at least in our society, an enterprise does not own its employees! Accounting generally records assets only where there is economic control where the value of the asset can be reliably measured and it is probable the future benefits will eventuate. The expenditure from market research will not qualify as an asset because it is not possible at the date of expenditure to establish that it is probable that the future benefits will eventuate. This places limits on the scope of the financial statements.

Assets are usually separated into shorter-term ones (current assets) and longer-term ones (noncurrent assets). Current assets are those that are expected to be used, sold or collected within the next year, and noncurrent assets therefore are expected to have benefits for more than a year into the future. Sound and Light has $245 000 in current assets and $250 000 in noncurrent assets.

## Liabilities

These are amounts owed to creditors, such as to banks and suppliers, or amounts estimated to be due later, such as long service leave payments to employees, estimated future income taxes or interest building up on a bank loan. Liabilities are the future sacrifices of economic benefits that an entity is presently obliged to make to other entities as a result of past transactions or events. For example, if an electrician has done repair work on a company building, the electrician will be owed money (accounts payable). The electrician has done the work (past transaction) and the company has a present obligation. Not all liabilities are expected to be paid in cash; some are 'paid' by providing goods or services.

An example is a deposit received from a customer for goods to be shipped later. The enterprise has the money (an asset) and records a corresponding liability for the deposit, but expects to give the customer the agreed-upon goods to discharge the liability. In the meantime, the customer has a claim on the enterprise, expecting to get either the goods or the cash back if the goods are not supplied. Sound and Light's liabilities include amounts owing to the bank ('bank overdraft') and amounts owing to suppliers ('accounts payable') and a long-term loan.

Following the same rule as for assets, liabilities generally include only obligations that can be reliably measured. If you are in debt to a friend for $10, that would appear on your statement of financial position. But, if you are 'in debt' to a friend for saving your life, that would not appear on your statement of financial position. Requiring that the obligation has arisen from a past transaction means that a promise to pay is a liability if the enterprise has already received the benefit (for example, if it has received cash from the bank or goods from a supplier or hard work from an employee expecting a pension). An expectation to pay later is not a liability if the transaction bringing the benefit has not happened (for example, an agreement to borrow before the cash has been received is not a liability, nor is an order to purchase something before the goods have arrived). Because some of these expected or possible future events may result in future payments, even if they do not meet the definition of a liability and so do not appear in the statement of financial position, they are sometimes described in the notes to the financial statements so that the users of the financial statement are aware of them.

Like assets, liabilities are usually separated into shorter-term ones (current liabilities) and longer-term ones (noncurrent liabilities). Current liabilities are those that are due (expected to be paid or otherwise discharged) within the next year, and noncurrent liabilities therefore are due more than a year into the future. Some liabilities, such as many house mortgages, extend for years into the future, but are partly paid each year, so the statement of financial position would show both a current and a noncurrent portion for them. Sound and Light has $103 000 in current liabilities and $87 000 in noncurrent liabilities.

## Equity

This is the owners' interest in the enterprise.

- Interest can be derived from direct contributions the owners have made, or from the accumulation of profits that the owners have chosen not to withdraw.
- The details of the owners' equity section of the statement of financial position depend on the legal structure of the enterprise and its ownership arrangements, to be examined later in this chapter.
- The statement of financial position does not distinguish between assets whose sources are liabilities and assets provided by owners. Complex financial events make this impractical, so the assets represent a pool of resources provided by all sources.
- The owners' interest can also be considered as a 'residual' of the sum of the assets minus the obligations the enterprise has taken on. (If A = L + E, the equation can also be written A – L = E.)

Because the balance of shareholders' equity figure equals assets minus liabilities, this residual or net concept of equity is often referred to as the book value of the whole enterprise. Book value is an arithmetically valid idea, as the equation above shows. But it may not tell us very much. For example, if Sound and Light suddenly went out of business, the owners would be unlikely to receive exactly the equity of $305 000, because nobody knows what the assets would fetch if they had to be sold off all at once, and the liabilities perhaps would be settled for something other than the expected future payments used to record them.

Similarly, if the owners decided to sell the business, the price they'd get would depend on their and the buyers' views as to the future success of the business, not just on the accumulated assets and liabilities recorded in the statement of financial position. Thus the amount would be very unlikely to equal the statement of financial position equity figure.

Shareholders' equity is generally based on historical transactions, and does not except by coincidence equal the current market value of the whole business. You can see this with many high-technology and Internet companies in recent years: they may have small equity amounts in their statements of financial position but huge stock market values (market capitalisation, share price times number of shares outstanding). The stock market may be considering all sorts of 'assets' not included by accounting, such as competitive strength or smart employees, and/or expecting good future performance not part of accounting's historical measures.

Contributions from owners can come in many forms, which we will look at below. For a corporation like Sound and Light, the most usual is share capital: people give the corporation money in exchange for shares, which are portions of ownership interest. Sound and Light owners (shareholders) have contributed $130 000 to the corporation. For example, some owners probably contributed cash to get Sound and Light started, so they would be among the sources of the cash asset. Many corporations' shares, also called stocks in some countries (for example, the USA), are traded on stock markets (for example, the Australian Stock Exchange). In such markets, shares are traded between owners; the corporations issuing the shares receive money only when the shares were issued by them to the first owners. Therefore trades subsequent to the initial share issue are not reflected in the corporation's share capital; these trades are transactions for the owners, but not for the corporation.

Past profit retained, usually called retained profits (or retained earnings), represents past accrual profit not yet given to owners. (The terms 'earnings', 'income' and 'profit' are used pretty much interchangeably, but they all refer to accrual profit, as described in chapter 1.) As we'll see in later chapters, earning profit means that there will be more assets (such as cash) and/or fewer liabilities, so profit is a source of assets. Sound and Light has $175 000 in retained profits, which means it has $175 000 more in assets than it would have had if those profits had all been paid out. The owners could have withdrawn cash or other assets from the company (for instance, by declaring themselves a dividend, which is a payment of some of the retained profits to the owners), but they have chosen instead to leave the assets in the corporation. Thus those assets are resources of the corporation and retained profits are their source. The corporation can use the assets to earn more profit in the future.

Since E = A – L, it is arithmetically possible, and unfortunately seen sometimes in real enterprises, for equity to be negative. If the assets are less than the liabilities, which would indicate an enterprise has more obligations than resources (not a good position to be in!), the equity, and therefore the enterprise's book value, will be negative. Such a situation is a sign of serious financial problems and is likely to be followed by insolvency.

## 2.4 Some preliminary analysis of the Sound and Light statement of financial position

From the Sound and Light statement of financial position, we can answer some questions about the corporation's financial condition:

1 Is the enterprise soundly financed? Sound and Light has financed its $495 000 in assets by borrowing $103 000 short term and $87 000 long term, and by getting $130 000 in contributions from owners and not paying past earnings of $175 000 out to owners. Its $495 000 in assets are therefore financed by $190 000 (38.4 per cent) from creditors and $305 000 (61.6 per cent) from the owners. Its debt/equity ratio is $190/$305 = 62.3 per cent (often written 0.62:1). So, it is not much in debt, proportionately. What would you think if the creditors were owed $450 000 and the owners' equity was only $45 000? This would be a debt/equity ratio of $450/$45 = 1000 per cent (10:1), much more risky for the creditors because a lot more of their money than the owners' money would be at risk if the company ran into trouble.

2 Can the enterprise pay its bills on time? Sound and Light owes $103 000 in the short term and has only $50 000 in cash. Therefore, to pay its bills it will have to collect cash from its customers, either by getting them to pay what they already owe or by selling them some inventory for cash. There is likely no problem here: collections and sales, and payments to creditors, are probably going on continuously. The company has $245 000 of current assets that it should be able to turn into cash to pay the $103 000 of current liabilities. It is said to have $245 000 – $103 000 = $142 000 in working capital and a working capital ratio (also called the current ratio) of $245/$103, or 2.38. The working capital is positive, and the ratio indicates there is more than twice as much current assets as current liabilities, so Sound and Light appears to be fine.

3 You can see that if the company had a slow period of sales or collections, it could have difficulty paying its bills. But if you were concerned about the company's ability to sell inventory to pay its bills, you could calculate the quick ratio (also called the acid test ratio). It is like the working capital ratio but has only cash, very short-term investments that could be sold, and accounts receivable in its numerator. For Sound and Light, the

quick ratio would be ($50 000 + $75 000) ÷ $103 000 = 1.21. The company could pay its current liabilities without having to sell inventory. What would you think if the company had only $10 000 in cash and $160 000 in inventory? In that case, though its working capital and working capital ratio would be the same, it would likely be over-stocked and cash short, and might have trouble paying bills. Now the quick ratio would be ($10 000 + $75 000)/$103 000 = 0.83. The company would have to sell some inventory to meet its current liabilities. All ratios are only indicators. They require interpretation of the specific circumstances of each enterprise, so we don't know from our calculations if the company is in trouble, but a low quick ratio would give a signal to look further into the situation.

4 Should the owners declare themselves a dividend? If so, how large should it be? Legally, the board of directors (who manage the company on behalf of the shareholders) are able to declare a dividend to shareholders of $175 000, the full amount of the retained earnings. But there is not nearly enough cash for that. Those past earnings have been reinvested in inventory, land, equipment and so on, and are therefore not sitting around in cash waiting to be paid to owners. This is true of nearly all corporations: they invest past earnings in operating assets, so do not have a lot of cash on hand. Probably a dividend of more than about $25 000, only one-seventh of the retained earnings, would cause Sound and Light some cash strain. What would you think if the corporation had no land or equipment but $300 000 in cash instead? It would appear to be cash-rich in that case, and should either invest the cash productively or pay a dividend to the owners so they can do what they like with the money.

5 What is that negative 'accumulated depreciation' deducted from equipment cost to give equipment (net) in Sound and Light's statement of financial position? In the example of Simone's jewellery business in chapter 1, we deducted depreciation from Simone's revenue in calculating accrual profit, so that there would be an expense to represent the wear and tear on her equipment. Sound and Light has done the same: in calculating its profit, it has deducted depreciation expense on its equipment. The profit that is in the retained profits part of the equity is, therefore, smaller than it would have been without this deduction. The accumulated amount of that expense, built up over the years, is deducted from the assets in the statement of financial position to show how much of the economic value of the assets is estimated to have been used up so far. Accumulated depreciation is therefore a 'negative asset' used to reduce the amounts of other assets. In this case, the equipment cost $272 000, against which depreciation of $122 000 has accumulated, so the 'net' book value of the equipment is the remainder, $150 000. (It is normal for the statement of financial position to report only the net amount and give cost and accumulated depreciation amounts in the notes.) Comparing the cost and the accumulated depreciation tells us something about the age of the equipment. The $122 000 accumulated depreciation is less than half the equipment's cost, so the company estimates that less than half the economic value of the equipment has been used. What would you think if the accumulated depreciation was $250 000? The equipment would be nearing the end of its estimated life.

## For your interest

Probably you are getting tired of all the terms and definitions being introduced in this section! The vocabulary can be very important, as you can become very confused if it is not used clearly. The term 'book value' can refer both to the net value of depreciated assets (cost minus accumulated depreciation) and to the equity of the enterprise (assets minus liabilities).

## Common presentation styles for statements of financial position (balance sheets)

So you see that the statement of financial position provides interesting information if you know how to read it. Your skill in reading it will grow as you work with it. There are different styles of presentation of the statement of financial position; all show the same information, but it is arranged differently. Exhibit 2.1 showed you the side-by-side format for Sound and Light Pty Ltd. In exhibit 2.2, the vertical format is shown. It shows assets less liabilities equals shareholders equity.

**EXHIBIT 2.2** **Sound and Light Pty Ltd**

**Statement of financial position as at 30 June 2001 (in thousands of dollars)**

| | |
|---|---|
| **Current assets** | |
| Cash | 50 |
| Accounts receivable | 75 |
| Inventory | 120 |
| Total current assets | 245 |
| **Noncurrent assets** | |
| Land | 100 |
| Equipment (net) | 150 |
| Total noncurrent assets | 250 |
| **Total assets** | 495 |
| **Current liabilities** | |
| Bank overdraft | 30 |
| Accounts payable | 73 |
| Total current liabilities | 103 |
| **Noncurrent liabilities** | |
| Loan | 87 |
| Total noncurrent liabilities | 87 |
| **Total liabilities** | 190 |
| **Net assets** | 305 |
| **Equity** | |
| Share capital | 130 |
| Retained profits | 175 |
| **Total equity** | 305 |

## How's your understanding?

Here are two questions you should be able to answer, based on what you have just read:

1. The statement of financial position is a summary of certain things at a point in time. What things?
2. Assemble a statement of financial position for Northern Ltd from the following information and comment on the company's financial position at that point in time:

share capital, $1000; accounts receivable, $1100; accounts payable, $2100; inventory, $1700; retained profits, $2200; cash, $500; equipment, $2000. (Your result should be: current assets $3300, noncurrent assets $2000; total assets $5300; current liabilities $2100, noncurrent liabilities $0; contributed capital $1000, retained profits $2200; total liabilities and equity $5300. Working capital is $1200; the working capital ratio is 1.57, so it is not as strong currently as Sound and Light is. The quick ratio is 0.76, not strong either. Liabilities of $2100 are 39.6 per cent of total sources, with a debt/equity ratio of 65.6 per cent, so the company's financing is similar to Sound and Light's, though all of its liabilities are current, which is unusual. With $500 cash, it does not have enough cash to pay all of its $2200 retained profits to shareholders as dividends.)

## 2.5 A closer look at the statement of financial position

To gain further insights into the content of a statement of financial position, we will examine the content of Chez Pty Ltd's statement of financial position, shown in exhibit 2.3.

- It is *comparative*: it contains figures both for the most recent year and for the preceding year to help the users recognise changes. It is standard practice for the more recent figures to be to the left, closer to the words describing those figures.
- For clarity, the figures are shown in thousands of dollars, not exact amounts to the cent.
- References are made to various notes. It is not possible to explain every important item on the face of the statement of financial position, so extensive explanatory notes are referred to and appended to most statements of financial position. Chez's notes are not provided here because they raise issues we have not yet covered; remember to look for notes when you are using financial statements.
- The company has many different kinds of asset, liability and equity accounts. They are not necessarily easy to classify into the categories you saw in the Sound and Light Pty Ltd example. You probably won't understand all the accounts and how the company has categorised them; that understanding will develop as you work through the book.
- The balance date is 31 May, not 30 June. The end of the taxation year, 30 June, is the most popular accounting year-end (financial year-end), but many companies choose other dates, particularly subsidiaries of US companies, among whom 31 December is popular.

Some explanation of the detailed content of statements of financial position will be helpful now, before some examples of preparing statements of financial position are given.

Some of Chez's assets were described in chapter 1: cash, accounts receivable and inventory. Property, plant and equipment is split into land, buildings, equipment and furniture and fittings. Many Australian companies now show property, plant and equipment as one item on the face of the statement of financial position, with the split-up in one of the notes to the accounts.

Note that land is not depreciated, but buildings, equipment and furniture and fittings are shown net, meaning that accumulated depreciation has been deducted. The exact amount of the accumulated depreciation deducted will be shown in the notes. For example, if plant and equipment cost $1 000 000 and had an expected life of five years, the amount of depreciation each year would be $200 000. After three years, accumulated depreciation would be $600 000 ($200 000 + $200 000 + $200 000).

**EXHIBIT 2.3** Chez Pty Ltd

**Statement of financial position at 31 May (in thousands of dollars)**

| | 2002 | 2001 |
|---|---|---|
| **Assets** | | |
| **Current assets** | | |
| Cash and cash equivalents | 8 952 | 6 336 |
| Investments | 18 516 | 5 179 |
| Accounts receivable | 26 396 | 18 069 |
| Inventory | 22 831 | 20 427 |
| Prepayments | 3 586 | 2 015 |
| **Total current assets** | 80 281 | 52 026 |
| | | |
| **Noncurrent assets** | | |
| Land | 23 205 | 23 205 |
| Buildings (net) | 26 282 | 25 911 |
| Equipment (net) | 35 120 | 36 630 |
| Furniture and fittings (net) | 4 864 | 4 140 |
| Intangibles (net) | 2 398 | 3 586 |
| **Total noncurrent assets** | 91 869 | 93 472 |
| | | |
| **Total assets** | 172 150 | 145 498 |
| | | |
| **Liabilities and shareholders' equity** | | |
| **Current liabilities** | | |
| Accounts payable | 7 984 | 6 443 |
| Accrued expenses | 5 740 | 3 491 |
| Income taxes payable | 3 248 | 2 756 |
| Provision for employee entitlements | 4 898 | 1 598 |
| Provision for dividends | 5 925 | 2 883 |
| **Total current liabilities** | 27 795 | 17 171 |
| | | |
| **Noncurrent liabilities** | | |
| Long-term loans | 23 856 | 21 805 |
| Provision for employee entitlements | 14 006 | 13 647 |
| **Total noncurrent liabilities** | 37 862 | 35 452 |
| | | |
| **Total liabilities** | 65 657 | 52 623 |
| | | |
| **Net assets** | 106 493 | 92 875 |
| | | |
| **Shareholders' equity** | | |
| Share capital | 23 961 | 23 961 |
| Retained profits | 82 532 | 68 914 |
| **Total shareholders' equity** | 106 493 | 92 875 |

Chez Pty Ltd also has some other assets that were not introduced in chapter 1, including investments, prepayments and intangibles. These investments are short term – that is, included under current assets – and could be shares in other companies (such as Commonwealth Bank or Coles Myer), which Chez intends to convert to cash within a year.

Prepayments (or 'prepaid expenses') are amounts that have been paid in advance but for which the benefits have not yet been received. For example, if we pay a 12-month insurance premium on 1 April 2001, at 31 May 2001 we will have a prepayment equal to ten-twelfths of the amount paid. Prepayments are assets because they represent future economic benefits.

Chez Pty Ltd also has intangible assets. These are noncurrent assets that have no physical substance, such as copyrights, patents, trademarks, brand names and goodwill. They are discussed in chapter 8.

Chez Pty Ltd includes many liabilities that have not yet been discussed. Accounts payable and long-term loans were described in chapter 1.

Accrued expenses relate to expenses that have been incurred during the year but not yet paid. Consider two examples. Assume Chez Pty Ltd pays salaries and wages every two weeks for work done in the previous two weeks. If the last payday was 19 May, the company would owe employees salaries and wages from 20 May to 31 May. This is called accrued wages or wages payable. Another example of accrued expenses could be the amount owing to the electricity company. If it bills you quarterly and the last bill was for the period ending 30 April, you would owe the company for one month's electricity at the end of the accounting period. This would also form part of accrued expenses. Income taxes payable is the amount payable to the tax office in the next year.

Provision for employee entitlements relates to long service leave, holiday pay and some superannuation. It is an estimate based on years of service of the amounts owing to employees that will have to be paid in future periods. The provision for employee entitlements has both current and noncurrent proportions, depending on when the amounts are likely to be paid.

## Where do the figures come from?

A full understanding of what assets and liabilities are and how to measure them will take time and many examples. One thing you may be wondering about is where the figures used to measure these things come from. This is a deep and controversial question indeed. Only a superficial answer can be given now, but after a few more chapters, you will have a deeper understanding of it.

Accounting is generally a historical measurement system: it records what has happened, not what will happen or would have happened if conditions had been different. Therefore, asset and liability values are derived from the past. Assets are generally valued at *what they cost when they were acquired*, and liabilities are generally valued at *what was promised when the obligation arose*. In most countries, assets and liabilities are not valued at the current prices they might fetch if sold right now. This is something that confuses many users: looking at a statement of financial position, in the United States for example, a user might think that assets such as land and buildings are shown at what those assets would be worth right now if they were sold. They are, instead, valued at what they cost when acquired.

The differences in these values can be large. For example, a company may have bought land in the downtown area of a city twenty years ago for $50 000. The land may now be worth millions of dollars. But the statement of financial position normally will show the land asset at a figure of $50 000, its original cost. This is because the only thing that has happened is that the land was acquired 20 years ago, and the cost incurred then can be verified. Nothing further has happened: the land has not been sold, so its current value is hypothetical and difficult to verify. However, in Australia certain assets can be revalued in the statement of financial position to current market prices. They are shown at either independent valuation or directors' valuation. This important valuation issue is discussed in more detail in chapter 8.

The statements of financial position of most Australian companies actually show a little less detail than our Chez Pty Ltd example. For example, under liabilities it is quite normal to have a heading 'payables', which includes accounts payable and accrued expenses. The split-up of these amounts is then given in the notes to the accounts. The 2001 statement of financial position of Tabcorp Limited (taken from the 2001 annual report) is shown in exhibit 2.4 as an example.

Most of the items in exhibit 2.4 were discussed in earlier examples. Some differences include:

- the fact that under both current and noncurrent liabilities there is a payables liability (for example, accounts payable, which normally don't attract interest) and interest-bearing liabilities (for example, loans, which do incur interest)
- three items related to tax:
  - Current tax liabilities are an estimate of the amount of income tax to be paid in the next financial year.
  - Deferred tax assets and deferred tax liabilities result because of some different rules in calculating accounting profit and taxation profit (as per the company's tax return). When current reported accounting profit is greater than the profit reported on the tax return, a liability for income tax (called deferred tax liability) is implied for later, when the profit is reported in the tax return. Conversely, if the accounting profit is less than reported on the income tax return an asset is credited (called deferred tax liability). They are very difficult concepts, so at this stage just be aware they exist in the statement of financial position.

## How's your understanding?

Here are two questions you should be able to answer based on your reading of this chapter:

1 Comment on the short-term financial position of Chez Pty Ltd. (Working capital is $52 486 000; current ratio is 2.89:1. The interpretation of the working capital ratio depends very much on the nature of the enterprise and its way of doing business. However, you can see that Chez Pty Ltd is in quite a strong position; current assets are almost three times current liabilities.)

2 Prepare the statement of financial position of Mike's Tyre Repair (owner, Mike) from the following account balances: bank overdraft $250; accounts receivable $640; inventory of supplies $210; equipment cost $890; accumulated depreciation on equipment $470; accounts payable $360; owner's equity $660. (You should get total assets of $1270, total liabilities of $610, giving net assets of $660 and owner's equity also of $660.)

**EXHIBIT 2.4** Tabcorp Holdings Limited

## Statement of financial position as at 30 June 2001

| | Note | Consolidated 2001 $000s | Consolidated 2000 $000s | Tabcorp Holdings 2001 $000s | Tabcorp Holdings 2000 $000s |
|---|---|---|---|---|---|
| **Current assets** | | | | | |
| Cash assets | 8 | 123 534 | 91 019 | 3 989 | 403 |
| Receivables | 9 | 7 612 | 5 726 | 230 287 | 198 084 |
| Inventories | 10 | 4 968 | 4 925 | — | — |
| Other | 11 | 17 300 | 19 808 | 2 795 | 3 265 |
| Total current assets | | 153 414 | 121 478 | 237 071 | 201 752 |
| **Noncurrent assets** | | | | | |
| Receivables | 12 | — | — | 581 229 | 597 151 |
| Other financial assets | 13 | — | — | 3 241 | 3 192 |
| Property, plant and equipment | 14 | 850 258 | 898 251 | 5 077 | 5 212 |
| Intangible assets – licences | 15 | 836 515 | 839 133 | 597 450 | 597 476 |
| Intangible assets – other | 16 | 531 860 | 550 293 | — | — |
| Deferred tax assets | 17 | 38 784 | 60 408 | 3 576 | 2 782 |
| Other | 18 | 91 144 | 101 644 | 34 678 | 34 995 |
| Total noncurrent assets | | 2 348 561 | 2 449 729 | 1 225 251 | 1 240 808 |
| **Total assets** | | 2 501 975 | 2 571 207 | 1 462 322 | 1 442 560 |
| **Current liabilities** | | | | | |
| Payables | 19 | 105 025 | 98 724 | 119 640 | 112 878 |
| Interest-bearing liabilities | 20 | 229 052 | 196 871 | — | — |
| Current tax liabilities | 22 | 24 854 | 73 756 | — | 1 478 |
| Provisions | 23 | 121 798 | 114 201 | 98 846 | 91 336 |
| Other | 24 | 446 | 586 | — | — |
| Total current liabilities | | 481 175 | 484 138 | 218 486 | 205 692 |
| **Noncurrent liabilities** | | | | | |
| Payables | 25 | 5 745 | 9 928 | 23 767 | 23 950 |
| Interest bearing liabilities | 26 | 710 000 | 780 154 | — | — |
| Deferred tax liabilities | 27 | 52 408 | 48 086 | 510 | 662 |
| Provisions | 28 | 7 989 | 9 131 | 532 | 552 |
| Other | 29 | 1 448 | 1 706 | — | — |
| Total noncurrent liabilities | | 777 590 | 849 005 | 24 809 | 25 164 |
| **Total liabilities** | | 1 258 765 | 1 333 143 | 243 295 | 230 856 |
| **Net assets** | | 1 243 210 | 1 238 064 | 1 219 027 | 1 211 704 |
| **Equity** | | | | | |
| Contributed equity | 30 | 1 218 819 | 1 211 454 | 1 218 819 | 1 211 454 |
| Retained profits | 31 | 24 391 | 26 610 | 208 | 250 |
| **Total equity** | | 1 243 210 | 1 238 064 | 1 219 027 | 1 211 704 |

The accompanying notes form an integral part of this statement of financial position.

## 2.6 Managers and the statement of financial position (balance sheet)

Why do managers care about their companies' statements of financial position? The basic reason is that many outsiders do, including owners, creditors, tax authorities and unions. Read any issue of a business newspaper or magazine and you will see frequent references to the importance of the balance sheet and levels of debt.

> Thinn Ltd has a weak financial structure. Management must solve this problem before risk-shy investors can be expected to take an interest in the company.
>
> Huge Ltd has large cash reserves, so one can only guess that management is looking to buy another company to add to Huge's consolidated group.
>
> X Ltd's debt/equity ratio is high for the industry.
>
> The underlying strength of PBL's balance sheet is hard to ignore.

The statement of financial position reports what the organisation's position (assets, liabilities and owners' equity) is at a point in time (the financial year-end or any other date on which the statement of financial position is prepared). It shows the assets (resources) that management has chosen to acquire for the organisation, and how management has decided to finance those assets. Therefore, it provides a useful picture of the state of the company and is used by many outsiders to evaluate the quality of management's decisions on obtaining, deploying and financing assets. For better or worse, it is the summary of all the information recognised by accounting and is, to many people, the basic score card of management's stewardship of the company.

The statement of financial position does not directly state how management has performed in using assets to earn profit or in controlling cash flows to enable prompt payment of debts. Such information is contained in the statement of financial performance, but all of it correlates with the basic double-entry information contained in the statement of financial position. Good profit performance, for example, is reflected in increased assets and owners' equity (retained profits). The strengths and weaknesses of the statement of financial position, which will be explored throughout this book, are therefore fundamentally important to managers, who are responsible for managing companies' assets and liabilities.

Managers' own salaries, promotions, careers and reputations depend on other people's decisions (such as investors' decisions to buy and sell shares) that, in turn, rest to some extent on statement of financial position information.

## 2.7 Background: sole traders, partnerships, companies and financing

To help you further understand the statement of financial position, read the following background material. This section focuses on the right-hand side of the accounting equation, examining how the form of business organisation determines the way owners' equity is shown on the statement of financial position and outlining how both right-hand terms indicate how the assets are financed. This book's glossary will also help you to understand the terminology.

There are many important forms of organisation, such as businesses organised as partnerships, companies or cooperatives, and non-business organisations such as clubs, charities, governments and political parties. However, they cannot all be described here. Instead, we will focus on four main kinds of business organisations and their main methods of financing.

## Four kinds of business organisation

You have seen that each statement of financial position has an owners' equity section. The examples of Sound and Light Pty Ltd and Chez Pty Ltd indicated that the equity could be considered to be of two general kinds for a business enterprise:

- directly contributed equity, in which owners have provided money or other assets to the enterprise
- indirectly contributed equity (retained profits), in which owners have allowed profits earned by the enterprise to remain there, to help earn more profits in the future.

The legal meaning of being an owner depends on what kind of organisation exists. The equity section of the statement of financial position reflects that legal meaning, so that owners and other users will understand the status of their equity. Four main kinds of business organisations are the sole trader, the partnership, the company and the corporate group.

### Sole trader

A sole trader (sole proprietorship) is a business owned by one person (the proprietor), and does not legally exist separately from the owner. Because the business does not exist as a separate legal entity, it is said to be unincorporated. If Simone, the jeweller, just starts up a business one day on her own without further legal steps, the business is a sole trader. Legally, such a business is not distinguishable from Simone's non-business affairs. If she wishes, she can use the business cash to buy groceries (although separate records of business transactions must be kept for tax purposes), and if she does not pay her business bills, her creditors can claim against any non-business assets she has.

Because a sole trader has no legal existence, the equity section of the statement of financial position does not necessarily distinguish between the owner's direct contributions to the business and the indirect contributions by retained profits. Both kinds of equity are simply lumped together as owner's capital. The owner's equity section of the statement of financial position just says:

| **Owner's equity** | |
|---|---|
| Owner's capital | $XXXX |

### Partnership

A partnership is also unincorporated, but it has more than one owner. Partnerships are not separate legal entities, and all partners are personally responsible for the debts of the partnership. Again, the owners' personal assets can be claimed by business creditors, so there is the same somewhat arbitrary distinction between business affairs and personal affairs.

The fact that there is more than one owner introduces some formality into the business. For example, there is (or should be) an agreement about how the profits of the business are to be split among the partners and about how much each partner can withdraw from the business. Because stress can develop in partnerships, States and countries have partnership laws that provide some structure if the partners do not do so themselves. A partnership's owners' equity section of the statement of financial position, like that for a sole trader, does not necessarily distinguish between owners' direct contributions and retained profits. The only difference is that each owner's total capital is identified on the face of the statement of financial position (or, if there are many partners, as in firms of lawyers, accountants or engineers, in a separate schedule).

Therefore, the owners' equity section of the partnership's statement of financial position shows:

| **Owner's equity** | **$** |
|---|---|
| Partners' capital. | |
| Partner A | XXXX |
| Partner B | XXXX |
| Partner C | XXXX |
| Total capital | XXXX |

When an individual wishes to leave the partnership, it is necessary to obtain the permission of existing partners to transfer ownership to a new partner. As with sole traders, partnerships are not legal entities, but for accounting purposes are considered as a separate entity from the partners.

### Company

Companies are legal entities established under Corporations Law. The company's capital is divided into shares, and the owners are called shareholders. Companies are separate legal entities, therefore can buy, own and sell assets, enter into contracts in their own right and sue and be sued.

The major advantage of a company structure is that a company has limited liability in the event of its failure. This means that shareholders are not liable for debts incurred by a company once their shares have been paid for in full. That is, their liability is limited to the unpaid amount on any shares bought. All companies that have limited liability have the word 'Limited' or 'Ltd' after their name.

Other advantages of a company structure include the ease of transfer of ownership and increased borrowing powers. The shares of public companies can generally be sold freely and transfer of ownership does not affect the continuity of operations. Stock exchanges provide a convenient means for the disposal and acquisition of shares and for making known the prices that sellers are willing to accept and buyers prepared to offer.

In the case of the death of a shareholder in a company, ownership of the share normally passes to the beneficiary of the deceased shareholder, without interruption to the activities of the company.

A company has open to it a number of sources of funds that are denied to a sole proprietorship or a partnership. Debentures or unsecured notes may be issued by a company. A debenture is a document that evidences an undertaking by a company to repay a particular amount at or before an agreed date, and to pay interest at an agreed rate at specified intervals. The debt may be secured by a specific charge over certain assets, or by a 'floating charge' over all the assets of the company. Highly regarded companies may be able to obtain funds without pledging assets – that is, by the issue of unsecured notes or the acceptance of deposits.

Because of these advantages, particularly limited liability, most business enterprises are companies. Even your local newsagent, chemist and corner shop are likely to have adopted a company structure.

Companies can be either public or private companies. The main difference is that public companies can invite the public to subscribe to their share capital using a document called a prospectus. A private company (denoted by 'Pty' in the name) cannot invite the public to subscribe for shares. They also have limits on the number of shareholders (maximum 50) and other restrictions on transferability of the shares. Private companies have certain exemptions on requirements to provide full financial statements and appointment of auditors.

Listed public companies are those public companies that have chosen to be listed on the Australian Stock Exchange. This listing assists trading in the company's shares and helps in the raising of funds. However, it does involve additional disclosure to the stock exchange.

Companies can be very complex; just two complexities will be mentioned here.

#### *Forms of share capital*

People become owners of a company by buying shares that give them voting powers or other rights. When a share is first issued by a company, the money received for it is put in the company's bank account and the source of that asset is called share capital, which is an owners' equity item. If the person who paid the company for that share later sells it to someone else, the money for that sale goes to the person who owned the share, not to the company. Therefore, the company's share capital shows only the amount received by it the first time the share is sold. Most of the millions of share sales and purchases that take place on the world's stock exchanges every day have no effect on companies' statement of financial position accounts for share capital, because they are trades among owners, not issues by the companies.

There are several classes of shares, including:

- *ordinary shares*: owners of these vote; they are the company's basic (residual) owners, the ones who decide who will be on the board of directors that manages the company for the owners and declares dividends to owners
- *preference shares or otherwise special shares:* owners usually do not vote, but in return they have rights, such as receiving a fixed dividend each year and, in some cases, a preference in asset distributions if the company liquidates
- *Class A, Class B and other such categorisations:* whether these are more like ordinary shares or preference shares depends on the specific rights they carry. Many companies use these vague terms because the complexity of rights often prevents a simple categorisation as ordinary or preference.

The face of the statement of financial position or the notes to the accounts will list all the kinds of shares the company is authorised to issue, specify any special rights, and show the amount of share capital issued so far for each kind of share. The cash received for such share capital is the property of the company: except in specific circumstances, the owners (that is, shareholders, or stockholders as they are often also called, especially in the United States) have no right to get it back.

#### *Retained profits*

Profits of a company can be paid to the owners in the form of a dividend or retained within the company. The statement of financial position shows the amount of any retained profits (past profits minus past dividends) as a separate owners' equity item.

Thus, in addition to its lists of assets and liabilities, a company's statement of financial position has an owners' equity section showing various legal details to assist present and future owners:

| **Shareholders' equity** | **$** |
|---|---|
| Share capital: | |
| Class A shares (for example) | XXXX |
| Class B shares (for example) | XXXX |
| Total issued capital | XXXX |
| Retained profits | XXXX |
| Total shareholders' equity | XXXX |

Items other than issued capital and retained profits may appear in a company's owners' equity. Such items reflect legal and accounting complexities that are not important at this point. These items (including reserves) will be discussed in chapter 10.

*Corporate group*

Many companies you are familiar with, such as BHP Billiton, CSR, the Commonwealth Bank and Woolworths, are not single companies but are rather groups of many, often hundreds, of companies. The statement of financial position of such a corporate group attempts to represent what that group looks like as a 'consolidated' economic entity, although there is no such entity legally. Doing this requires complex accounting techniques that are mostly beyond the scope of this book. The statement of financial position of a corporate group looks like that of a single company, with the shareholders' equity section representing the equity of the primary, or parent, company in the group. In chapter 10, a brief examination will be made of the assumptions behind financial statements for corporate groups. For now, remember that such consolidated financial statements are aggregates of many legally separate companies. A summary of the different kinds of business organisations is given in exhibit 2.5.

**EXHIBIT 2.5** Kinds of business organisations

| Kind | Legality | Owner(s) | Equity accounts |
|---|---|---|---|
| Sole trader | Not separate from owner | One proprietor | Capital and retained profits are combined |
| Partnership | Not separate from owners | Several or many partners | Capital and retained profits are combined but each partner's total is calculated separately |
| Company | Separate from owners | Usually several or many shareholders | Legal share capital is disclosed separately from retained profits |
| Corporate group | Consists of legally separate companies | Usually several or many shareholders | Legal share capital of **parent** company is disclosed separately from retained profits |

## Business financing

The statement of financial position's right side lists the sources of the assets listed on its left side. As this book proceeds, many details about both sides of the statement of financial position will be explained. For now, here is a list of the main sources:

### Current liabilities (due within a year)

- Loans from banks due on demand or otherwise, at least potentially payable sooner rather than later

- Financing provided by suppliers and other trade creditors by allowing the enterprise to obtain credit for its purchases and pay for them later
- Wages earned by, but not yet paid to, employees and taxes withheld from them that are to be turned over to the taxation authorities
- Other amounts that will be paid in the next year related to such employee benefits as holiday pay and long service leave
- Estimates of amounts owing for things such as power, interest charges, legal costs and other debts building up, but not yet actually billed to the enterprise
- Income and other taxes owed by the enterprise
- Dividends owed by the enterprise (if it is a company), declared by the board of directors, but not yet paid to the shareholders
- Short-term portions of longer-term debts, such as the principal payments due over the next year on long-term mortgages

### Noncurrent liabilities (debts due more than a year in the future)

- Mortgages and other debts extending over several years
- Certain long-term liabilities, such as special loans from owners in addition to their share capital, long-term tax estimates, and estimated liabilities for amounts to be paid to employees in the future

### Owners' equity

- For a sole trader: owner's capital (contributed capital and profit not withdrawn by the owner)
- For a partnership: owners' capital (contributed capital and profits not withdrawn by the owners)
- For a company: share capital received for each kind of share plus retained profits (plus some other items if legal or accounting complexities require them).

## How's your understanding?

Here are three questions you should be able to answer, based on what you have read:

1 The owners of Blotz Consulting Partnership wonder if they should incorporate their business as Blotz Consulting Pty Ltd. What difference would this make to the owners' equity section of the business's statement of financial position?

2 What are some common examples of current and noncurrent liabilities, and how do the two types differ?

3 What are the main advantages of a company structure?

## 2.8 Statement of financial performance

In Australia, the name of the key statement providing information on a company's financial performance was changed from a profit and loss statement to a statement of financial performance (effective 30 June 2001). In addition to the name change, a basic difference is that the new statement has two basic components:

1 a profit and loss statement, which shows you how the company's accrued profit is calculated. (Think back to what you learnt about accrual profit in chapter 1. If this draws a blank, re-read section 1.5)

**2** a statement that shows total changes in equity other than those resulting from transactions with owners as owners. In this chapter we will only consider the profit and loss component, leaving **2** to chapter 10 – that is, we select examples in this chapter that do not have any items under **2**.

Also note that the terminology 'profit and loss statement' is still used in many countries, and is likely to be used on internal reports of Australian companies for many years. Consequently we will use the term 'profit and loss statement' to show the calculation of net profit.

A business exists over a period of time. If the owners and managers are successful, it may prosper for a long time. Suppose a measure of the company's financial performance were desired for comparison with other companies, for assessing income tax, for help in deciding how much to sell the company for, or for many other reasons we will come to. How could such performance be measured?

We might measure the company's financial performance by closing it down, selling off all its assets, paying off all its liabilities and discovering how much is left for the owners. Good performance would be indicated if the money left for the owners plus the amounts they withdrew over the years was greater than the amount they put in when they founded the company, perhaps adjusted for inflation over that time and for the owners' costs in raising the money they put in.

But killing the business to measure how well it has been doing is a little drastic! Waiting until it dies of natural causes seems hardly a better solution: many companies have outlasted many generations of owners and managers. It would be more useful to measure performance over selected shorter periods of time: annually, every three months (quarterly) or on a monthly basis. People could then make their decisions about investing in the company or getting out, and hiring managers or firing them, when they wanted to do so.

This is where the profit and loss statement becomes useful. This statement uses accrual accounting to measure financial performance over a period of time, usually a year, six months, three months or one month, indicating the bottom line net profit for the period, calculated as revenues minus expenses. Look back at the profit and loss statement for Simone's Jewellery Business in section 1.6 of chapter 1:

| | $ |
|---|---|
| **Revenue** | |
| ($4350 collected plus $310 still to be received) | 4 660 |
| **Expenses** | |
| ($1670 paid plus $85 unpaid bills plus $120 depreciation) | 1 875 |
| **Accrual profit** based on the information provided | 2 785 |

This simple profit and loss statement illustrates the form of most profit and loss statements as they are done in most countries of the world:

Net profit for the period = Revenue(s) – Expenses for the period

Simone's profit and loss statement shows no income tax on that profit. Her business is a sole trader, and any income tax is her personal responsibility. The profit and loss statements of companies, which are responsible for their own income taxes, do have income tax deducted as one of the expenses. The phrase 'net profit' is usually used to refer to the amount left after income tax. Net profit is based on accrual accounting, so it is a measure of economic performance, not cash profit (remember the different cash profit calculation we did for Simone's Jewellery Business in section 1.6).

## Revenues and expenses

Recall that in section 1.5 the concepts of revenues and expenses were introduced. As part of the conceptual framework of accounting, official pronouncements developed definitions of revenues and expenses. They were developed to be applicable to a range of measurement models and to include some transactions unique to the public sector. Consequently, the definitions are difficult to follow, especially for students in their second week of an accounting course. As a result we will defer discussion of these definitions until chapter 10. Below are some fundamental definitions that cover most revenues and expenses.

### Revenues

Revenues are described here as *increases in the company's wealth arising from the provision of services or sales of goods to customers*. Wealth increases because customers:

- pay cash for goods or services
- promise to pay cash (such promises are called accounts receivable for goods and services) or, more rarely,
- pay with other forms of wealth, such as by providing other assets to the company or forgiving debts owed by the company for goods and services.

If, *in return for services or goods*, a customer paid $1000 in cash, another customer promised to pay $1000 later, another gave the company $1000 in equipment, or another forgave a $1000 debt the company had owed the customer, each would be called a revenue of $1000.

Interest and dividends received are also examples of revenue because they are increases in wealth as a result of providing a service (lending or investing money in another organisation).

The key test for revenue recognition is *whether the goods or services have been rendered* (delivery to customers, for example, or provision of a service). Revenue recognition can become quite complicated for some companies. For example, if a company received a contract to build a new highway from Brisbane to Melbourne, when would revenue be recognised? This and other more complicated questions concerning revenue recognition will be addressed in chapter 11.

### Expenses

Expenses are the opposite of revenues. They are *decreases in the company's wealth that are incurred in order to earn revenue*. Wealth decreases because operating costs have to be paid; customers have to be given the goods they have paid for; long-term assets wear out as they are used to earn revenue and liabilities may be incurred as part of the process.

If, *as part of its attempt to earn revenues*, the company paid $600 in rent, or the goods bought by a customer cost the company $600 to provide, or the equipment depreciated by $600, or the company promised to pay an employee $600 in wages later on for work already completed, each of these would be called an expense of $600.

A major expense category that sometimes causes confusion is cost of goods sold (COGS) expense. In the examples above, if the goods bought by the customer cost the company $600 to provide, $600 is the cost of the goods sold that earned revenue of $1000.

The revenue is what the customer agrees to pay; the cost of goods sold is what it costs the enterprise to provide those goods. So a transaction with a customer who is buying goods has two aspects:

- The enterprise is better off because of the revenue gained.
- The enterprise is worse off because of the cost of the goods that the customer takes away.

When the enterprise buys the goods for sale, they begin on the statement of financial position in the asset account 'inventory of unsold goods'. When they are sold, their cost is transferred from the asset account to the expense account 'cost of goods sold'. This is done as a separate accounting activity from recording the revenue, because it is a separate economic event. Whether the enterprise makes money on the deal depends on whether the revenue gained is greater than the cost of goods sold (plus any other expenses incurred to make the sale, such as sales commissions and shipping costs).

### Profit

Both revenues and expenses are measured following the concepts of accrual accounting; therefore, they represent increases or decreases in wealth, whether or not cash receipts or payments occur at the same time. As net profit is the difference between revenues and expenses, it represents the *net inflow of wealth* to the company during the period. The reporting of net profit means that the company has become wealthier during the period. If net profit is negative—that is, if revenues are less than expenses—it is instead called net loss, and represents a net *outflow of wealth*. In this case, the company has become less wealthy.

Expenses include all the costs of earning the revenues, including income and other taxes, but they do not include payment of returns to owners (withdrawals by sole traders or partners, or dividends to shareholders of companies). Payments or promises of payment of returns to owners (such as when a company's board of directors *declares* (promises) a dividend) are considered to be *distributions* of net profit to owners. The undistributed remainder is kept in the company as retained profits.

## How's your understanding?

Here is a question you should be able to answer, based on what you have read. Calculate the total revenue and expenses for the month of June 2002, given the following:

1 Credit sales of $200 000 made in June; 50 per cent to be collected in June.

2 Cash sales of $300 000.

3 Received $20 000 as a deposit from a customer in June for a job to be carried out in July.

4 Paid salaries of $40 000; $10 000 related to work carried out in May and $30 000 related to June work.

5 Paid rent for the month of June of $6000 on 7 June.

6 Received a bill for $1500 from an electrician for work done on 20 June. This will be paid next month.

(Answers: Revenue 200 000 + 300 000; Expenses 30 000 + 6000 + 1500)

## The relationship of profit for the period to retained profits

Retained profits is the sum of past net profits, measured since the company began, minus dividends declared (even if not yet paid) to owners since the beginning. Retained profits from the end of the preceding period (year, quarter, month or whatever) are therefore increased by profits for the period and reduced by any dividends.

| | | |
|---|---|---|
| Retained profits at end of period | = | Retained profits at beginning of period |
| | = | + Net profit (or – Net loss) for the period |
| | | – Dividends declared during the period |

In some countries the above becomes a separate statement; in other countries it forms part of the 'profit and loss statement'. In Australia, a note is usually used to show the change in retained profits:

| | |
|---|---|
| Start with retained profits, beginning of period (end of previous period) | XXXX |
| Add net profit for the period | XXXX |
| Deduct dividends declared during the period | (XXXX) |
| Equals retained profits, end of period | XXXX |

In the above example, the company earned a profit. If the company performed badly, the profit could be negative (expenses greater than revenues, producing a net loss instead), and in that case, the net loss is deducted from the beginning retained profits. If things get really bad, retained profits can also be negative (losses having overwhelmed profits).

You might be interested to know that you can, *if you have the past records*, go back year by year, figuring out how much profit was added to retained profits each year and how much in dividends was deducted. You could go all the way back to the first day of the company, when there had not yet been any profit and therefore not yet any retained profits. Retained profits is therefore like an onion: you can keep peeling away each year's layer until you have peeled it all away and are back to zero. You can similarly peel away each year's transactions in every statement of financial position account; for example, you can trace all the changes in cash back to the very beginning. For this reason, the statement of financial position can be said to reflect everything that has ever been recorded in the accounts: it is the accumulation of everything that happened from when the company began until now. Accounting really is a historical information system!

In a company, the board of directors is the senior level of management, operating the company on behalf of the owners. When the board declares a dividend, the amount is deducted from retained profits at that time. At that point, the company has a liability to the owners, which it pays off later by sending the owners the promised cash. This involves two principles of financial accounting:

1. Transactions with owners, of which the main example is dividends, are taken out of retained profits. They are not an expense, and therefore not deducted in calculating profit for the period.
2. Owners can be creditors too, if they are owed dividends or have lent the company money in addition to the shares they bought.

## 2.9 Connecting statements of financial position and financial performance

The statement of financial position shows all assets, liabilities and shareholders' equity accounts at a point in time. Usually the statement of financial position is comparative, showing the accounts at both the beginning of the statement of financial performance's period (that is, the end of the previous period) and at the end of the statement of financial performance's period, and therefore showing both the beginning retained profits and the ending retained profits.

| | | |
|---|---|---|
| Assets at beginning | = | Liabilities + Equity (including retained profits) at beginning |
| Assets at end | = | Liabilities + Equity (including retained profits) at end |
| Change in assets | = | Change in liabilities + Change in equity (including retained profits) |

Suppose a corporation had assets of $1200 at the beginning of a year and $1450 at the end, and liabilities of $750 at the beginning and $900 at the end. We can deduce that its equity was $450 at the beginning and $550 at the end (that is, Assets – Liabilities = Equity). These data produce the following calculation of the changes in the statement of financial position categories:

| | | | |
|---|---|---|---|
| Beginning: | $1 200 Assets | = | $750 Liabilities + $450 Equity |
| Ending: | $1 450 Assets | = | $900 Liabilities + $550 Equity |
| Changes: | $250 Assets | = | $150 Liabilities + $100 Equity |

Where did the change in equity come from? Upon investigation, we find out that the company issued more share capital of $40, earned profit of $185 and declared a dividend of $125. Thus:

| | $ | $ |
|---|---|---|
| Share capital change: | | |
| Equity increase due to issued share capital | | 40 |
| Retained profits change: | | |
| Equity increase due to profit | 185 | |
| Equity decrease due to declaration of dividend | (125) | 60 |
| Change in equity between the two statements of financial position | | 100 |

We know what the profit was, but not what the company did to earn it. This is what the profit and loss component of the statement of financial performance is for: describing the revenues and expenses that produced the $185 profit. But once we have that, it is useful to know how that factors into the statement of financial position. The net profit is part of the change in retained profits, which in turn is part of the change in the statement of financial position over that period. The statement (or note) showing changes in retained profits therefore 'knits' the statements of financial position and financial performance together by showing that the net profit is part of the change in the statement of financial position over the period. (Accountants refer to this knitting together as the *articulation* of the two statements.) Profit is part of the change in retained profits for the period, therefore:

**Profit is part of the equity component of the accounting equation.**

Note that in chapter 10 you will see that the full statement of financial performance includes other equity changes that articulate through to the statement of financial position.

Make sure you understand how this works:

- A *revenue* increases wealth, so it either increases assets or decreases liabilities, and therefore increases equity.
- An *expense* decreases wealth, so it either decreases assets or increases liabilities, and therefore decreases equity.
- Positive *net profit* has the overall effect of increasing assets and/or decreasing liabilities, and therefore increases equity (increases due to revenues exceed decreases due to expenses).
- A *net loss*, which is negative net profit, does the opposite, decreasing equity (decreases due to expenses exceed increases due to revenues).

At this stage make sure you grasp the idea that profit is part of equity through retained profits.

### For your interest

People sometimes think that the whole balance of retained profits is available to pay dividends. Legally that may be true, but practically it is very unlikely to be true, because profit comes from changes in all the forms of wealth on the statement of financial position. A company that has made good profits and used the money earned to invest in new plant and equipment, for example, would have to sell the plant and equipment if it were to pay out all the retained profits as dividends. Also, since profit is based on accrual accounting, it is represented by changes in non-cash accounts such as accounts receivable (uncollected revenues) and accounts payable (unpaid expenses), so the profit in retained profits is not all cash, and the company might have to clear up all its receivables and payables to get the cash to pay a big dividend. The owners may not even want a dividend: many companies that pay small or no dividends have excellent share prices on the stock market, because shareholders believe that the companies will grow and prosper if the money that could have been paid as dividends is instead kept inside the company and used to make profitable business investments.

## A further example of articulation between the statements of financial position and financial performance

Bratwurst Pty Ltd had the following statement of financial position at the end of 2001 (beginning of 2002): assets \$5000; liabilities \$3000; equity \$2000.

- The beginning equity figure was made up of the shareholders' invested share capital of \$500 plus retained profit accumulated to the end of 2001 of \$1500. (That \$1500 was therefore the sum of all the net profits the company had ever had up to the end of 2001 minus all the dividends ever declared to owners up to that point.)
- During 2002, the company had revenues of \$11 000 and expenses of \$10 000, and declared dividends to owners of \$300.

**EXHIBIT 2.6** **Bratwurst Pty Ltd**

**Profit and loss statement (part of statement of financial performance) for 2002**

| | $ |
|---|---|
| Revenues | 11 000 |
| Expenses (including income tax) | 10 000 |
| Net profit for 2002 | 1 000 |

**Note showing change in retained profits for 2002**

| | $ |
|---|---|
| Retained profits beginning of 2002 (end of 2001) | 1 500 |
| Add net profit for 2002 (from profit and loss statement) | 1 000 |
| | 2 500 |
| Deduct dividends declared during 2002 | 300 |
| Retained profits end of 2002 | 2 200 |

**Statement of financial position at the beginning and end of 2002**

| Assets | | | Liabilities and equity | | |
|---|---|---|---|---|---|
| | End $ | Begin $ | | End $ | Begin $ |
| Assets | 5 900 | 5 000 | Liabilities | 3 200 | 3 000 |
| | | | Shareholders' equity | | |
| | | | Share capital | 500 | 500 |
| | | | Retained profits* | 2 200 | 1 500 |
| Total | 5 900 | 5 000 | Total | 5 900 | 5 000 |

- At the end of 2002, the company had assets of $5900, liabilities of $3200 and equity of $2700, made up of the shareholders' invested share capital of $500 plus retained profits of $2200.

Exhibit 2.6 shows the relationship.

You can see several things from this example:

- We have used the term 'retained profits' instead of 'retained earnings'. Both are used in Australia but the former is more common. In the USA and Canada, retained earnings is much more common.
- The profit and loss statement's bottom line is transferred to the statement of retained profits, which is generally shown as a note to the statement of financial position.
- The retained profits note's bottom line is transferred to the statement of financial position, showing that the statements tie together (articulate) through retained profits.

In addition, asset and/or liability accounts in the statement of financial position also have to change to reflect the wealth changes that revenues and expenses involve. These changes keep the statement of financial position in balance with the change in retained profits. This is true for all companies, not just simple ones like Bratwurst Pty Ltd.

The Bratwurst example also shows that the profit information and the retained profit note could be said to be detailed explanations of the change in the statement of financial position's retained profits figure. But the statement of financial position could instead have had the following format under the retained profits part of shareholders' equity:

| Retained profits | |
|---|---|
| Beginning balance | 1 500 |
| *Add* Revenues | 11 000 |
| | 12 500 |
| *Deduct* Expenses | 10 000 |
| | 2 500 |
| *Deduct* Dividends declared | 300 |
| Ending balance | 2 200 |

The information is there, but putting all this on the statement of financial position would make it rather cluttered, and there would hardly be room to provide any details about the various revenues, expenses and dividends. Also, the concept of profit as a measure of performance would be obscured.

## How's your understanding?

Here are two questions you should be able to answer, based on what you have just read:

1 In financial accounting, what is a revenue and what is an expense?

2 Suppose Bratwurst Pty Ltd's accounting records showed the following for the next year, 2002: revenues earned $14 200; cash collected from customers $13 800; expenses incurred $12 900; dividends declared $600; and dividends paid in cash $500. (Remember, retained profits equalled $2200 at the end of 2001.) What was Bratwurst's net profit for 2002 and its retained profits as at the end of 2002? (You should get $1300 and $2900.)

## 2.10 A closer look at the statement of financial performance

Social and economic forces have helped to produce a statement of financial performance that is more complex than the simple Bratwurst Pty Ltd example you saw earlier. More representative of the modern statement of financial performance and the associated note on retained profits are those of Tabcorp Holdings Limited, shown in exhibit 2.7.

Among the things you may notice as you review the two statements are:

- The statement covers a period of time (years ending 30 June in this case), not a point in time, as the statement of financial position does. It also is shown in thousands of dollars.
- As for statement of financial positions, extensive explanatory notes are referred to on the statement of financial performance and appended to them. The notes are not attached here; the content of such notes is important, however, so some comments are made about that below and further attention will be paid to it in later chapters.
- The right-hand columns refer to the parent company (Tabcorp Holdings Limited), and the left-hand columns are consolidated figures which refer to Tabcorp Holdings Limited and its controlled subsidiaries. A subsidiary is considered a controlled entity when

**EXHIBIT 2.7** Tabcorp Holdings Limited

**Statement of financial performance for the year ended 30 June 2001**

| | | Consolidated | | Tabcorp Holdings | |
|---|---|---|---|---|---|
| | Note | 2001 $000 | 2000 $000 | 2001 $000 | 2000 $000 |
| Total operating revenues | 2 | 1 811 599 | 1 595 831 | 21 702 | 20 980 |
| Other revenues from ordinary activities | 2 | 25 958 | 34 747 | 219 817 | 203 316 |
| **Revenues from ordinary activities** | 2 | 1 837 557 | 1 630 578 | 241 519 | 224 296 |
| Government taxes | | (556 526) | (500 423) | — | — |
| Commissions and fees | | (406 952) | (382 550) | (15 191) | (14 686) |
| Employee costs | | (238 997) | (187 188) | (16 949) | (18 287) |
| Depreciation and amortisation | | (113 398) | (95 094) | (1 709) | (1 623) |
| Borrowing costs | | (70 994) | (49 307) | (5 178) | (2 868) |
| Other expenses from ordinary activities | | (152 157) | (135 440) | (12 936) | (17 198) |
| **Profit from ordinary activities before income tax expense** | | 298 533 | 280 576 | 189 556 | 169 634 |
| Income tax (expense)/benefit relating to ordinary activities | 4 | (110 851) | (105 796) | 303 | (2 076) |
| **Net profit attributable to members of the parent entity** | | 187 682 | 174 780 | 189 859 | 167 558 |

| | Note | Consolidated 2001 $000 | Consolidated 2000 $000 |
|---|---|---|---|
| **Note 31** Retained profits | | | |
| Retained profits at the beginning of the financial year | | 26 610 | 26 469 |
| Net profit attributable to members of the parent entity | | 187 682 | 174 780 |
| Dividends provided for or paid | | (189 901) | (174 639) |
| Retained profits at the end of the financial year | | 24 391 | 26 610 |

the parent company has the capacity to dominate decision-making in relation to the financial and operating policies of that subsidiary (for instance, the capacity to dominate the composition of the board of directors). Consolidation basically involves aggregating revenues and expenses of the parent entity and all the subsidiaries after eliminating any transactions between these entities.

- At the top of the statement, the total revenue for the year is disclosed. In note 2 to the accounts, the various types of revenue are disclosed. These include waging and gaming revenue, casino revenue, other operating revenue and other revenue.
- Six expenses (including employee costs of $238 997 000) are then deducted to get operating profit before income tax. For Tabcorp Holdings Limited it amounts to $298 533 000.
- Income tax is levied on a company's profit because it is legally separate from its owners. Such tax is usually a percentage of profit before income tax (though there are many complications). Income tax expense of $110 851 000 is deducted to get 'operating profit after income tax' of $187 682 000. As there are no outside equity interests (this is discussed in chapter 10), Tabcorp Holdings Limited has labelled this figure 'net profit

attributable to members of the parent company'. Note 31 shows how the net profit after tax figure impacts retained profits.

- The net profit (or net loss) is carried to the statement of retained profits to be accumulated with past years' profits and losses. You can see that Tabcorp had a profit of \$187 682 000, which is added to the opening retained profits balance of \$26 610 000.
- Ending retained profits equals the beginning figure plus net profit minus dividends declared (provided for or paid). In this case, the dividends declared of \$189 901 000 were greater than the profit for the year (but less than opening retained profits plus profits for the year), giving a closing retained profits of \$24 391 000.
- Refer to exhibit 2.4 to see how the opening and closing balances of retained profits match the figures in note 31. That is, note 31 provides a description of how the balance of retained profits changed during the year ended 30 June 2001.

## How's your understanding?

Here is a question you should be able to answer, based on what you have just read:
If the opening balance of retained profits is \$850 000, net profit before tax \$150 000, net profit after tax \$120 000 and \$70 000 of dividends were declared, what is the closing balance of retained profits? (Answer: \$900 000.)

## 2.11 Managers and the statement of financial performance

The profit figure, as disclosed in the statement of financial position, has major impacts on managers' salaries, promotions, careers and reputations, especially where capital markets, such as stock markets, are concerned. Managers of large, publicly traded companies are under constant pressure because of the spotlight on profits and its components. Business and social observers often comment that this spotlight is too intense, that there is more to managerial performance than the profit figure.

An indication of the importance placed on the bottom line can be found in almost any issue of a financial newspaper, such as the *Australian* or the *Australian Financial Review*, in their regular announcements of companies' annual and/or half-yearly profits.

Exhibit 2.8 is a sample of yearly announcements from the *Australian Financial Review*.

These announcements presumably are meant to focus on the crucial bits of information. You can see quite a variation, from the brevity of Westfield and AGL to the longer information provided by Woolworths and BHP Billiton. The emphasis is on profit. There are almost never any data about non-financial performance, longer-term issues, or other aspects of managers' efforts. This is not to say that such other factors are not considered at some point, but when announcements tend to stress earnings; other things can be overlooked.

All of the announcements show sales, profits before tax (pre-tax), net profit after tax (net), earnings per share (Eps), interim and final dividends per share (includes the date of payment; *f* is fully franked, meaning that tax has already been paid on the profits by the company; *p* is partly franked), and the present share price includes the change from the previous day (shares yest.). Some figures are converted to per-share data (roughly, these are the profit figure divided by the number of ordinary shares issued by the company). Per-share amounts are thought to be helpful to the user who owns or is thinking of buying a particular number of shares and wonders what portion of the company's results can be

**EXHIBIT 2.8** AGL, BHP Billiton, Woolworths, Westfield Holdings

Announcements of company profits

**AGL**
(full year)

| | 2001 $m | 2000 $m |
|---|---|---|
| Sales | 3 498.0 | 2 292.2 |
| Pre-tax | 113.4 | 377.0 |
| Net | 115.0 | 450.0 |
| Eps | 32.8c | 133.8c |
| Interim div. | 25cp | 24cp |
| Final div.* | 27cp | 50cp |
| Shares (yest.) | 8.46 | +6 |

* Date payable 16 October

**BHP BILLITON**
(full year)

| | 2001 $USm | 2000 $USm |
|---|---|---|
| Sales | 19 079 | 18 402 |
| Interest | −476.0 | −489.0 |
| Depreciation | −1 672 | −1 748 |
| Pre-tax | 2 063.0 | 1 778.0 |
| Significant items | −1 094 | −760 |
| Net | 1 529.0 | 1 506.0 |
| Eps | 25.6c | 26.3c |
| Interim div. ($A) | 25cf | 25c |
| Final div.* ($A) | 26cf | 26c |
| Shares (yest.) | $9.13 | −11c |

* Date payable 2 July

**WOOLWORTHS**
(full year)

| | 2001 $m | 2000 $m |
|---|---|---|
| Sales | 21 648 | 20 557 |
| Interest | 1.2 | 3.1 |
| Depreciation | 300.6 | 280.7 |
| Significant items | Nil | −68.5 |
| Pre-tax | 693.5 | 499.9 |
| Net | 428.4 | 321.6 |
| Eps | 40.16c | 26.27c |
| Interim div. ($A) | 12.0cf | 10.0cf |
| Final div.* ($A) | 15.0cf | 13.0cf |
| Shares (yest.) | $10.92 | +1c |

* Date payable 5 October

**WESTFIELD HOLDINGS**
(full year)

| | 2001 $m | 2000 $m |
|---|---|---|
| Sales | 1 266.8 | 1 106.0 |
| Pre-tax | 221.7 | 192.4 |
| Net | 169.1 | 148.3 |
| Eps | 32.05c | 28.13c |
| Interim div. | 7.27cp | 6.44cp |
| Final div.* | 8.76cp | 7.71cp |
| Shares (yest.) | $14.66 | +7.7c |

* Date payable 31 August

(Source: *Australian Financial Review*)

related to that number of shares. If you own *n* shares of Woolworths, you can say that your shares earned $0.4016 *n* in the 2001 financial year, up from $0.2627 *n* in the previous financial year.

Share price information is given for the current period. For example, it shows that the share price of Woolworths at the last sale the previous day was $10.92, which was up one cent on the previous day's closing price.

Share market traders pay particular attention to the factors that produce good, or poor, profits. Share market prices and profits are positively correlated: when profits go up, share prices tend to be going up too, because investors want to buy the shares; and when profits go down, share prices tend also to be going down, because investors want to sell them. What seems to be happening is that investors learn about things like good (or poor) management decisions, and the attractiveness of the shares is increased (or decreased) accordingly. When the financial statements are produced and announcements like those above are made from them, the statements will also have reflected the same things, the same management decisions. Therefore, share prices on the share market will change when investors obtain news about the company that changes the shares' attractiveness. If this news comes out before the financial statements and the above announcements (which is usually the case, especially for well-known companies that are frequently in the news), the share prices will already have changed in the way you would expect from the announcements. If the announcement was not expected (surprisingly good or bad results), the share prices will change then, because the announcement is the news. In either case, share market prices and profit announcements tend to end up moving in the same direction, so are correlated.

Notice that all the key figures for AGL in exhibit 2.8 have gone down, but share price increased by \$0.06 per share on the announcement of these figures. How could this be the case? In December 2000, the AGL share price was \$11.90, and at 23 August was down to \$8.46. That is, lots of bad news had been impounded in the share price. The announcement of profit was a little better than the market expected, so the share price increased by \$0.06.

Some announcements include items such as interest, depreciation and significant items. This allows the reader to calculate other 'versions' of the profit figure. For example, some companies concentrate most of their profit discussion in EBIT (earnings before interest and tax). It is considered a good measure of operating performance, and is discussed in chapter 11. Items of expenses or revenues that are individually significant to users of the reports are required to be shown separately in the notes.

We can conclude that the performance factors measured by accrual accounting are similar to the factors share buyers and sellers are assessing when they decide to try to buy, or sell, a company's shares. Managers of companies with traded shares are therefore keenly aware of accounting's profit measurement, because accounting is tracking factors investors are concerned about, and if the investors do not learn about these factors from other sources, they will certainly learn about them from the accounting statements.

It is harder to tell if the statement of financial performance is as important for managers of smaller or private companies, the shares of which are not traded and about which there is less news in general, but there is no reason to think the importance is not comparable. Managers and owner–managers of smaller companies are at least as concerned as managers of larger companies are about management bonuses, income tax and other effects of profit figures. Managers of many companies – especially, but not only, larger corporations – go to great lengths to explain their performance to investors and to people on whom investors rely, such as share market analysts and business journalists.

In conclusion, every manager should be conversant with how her or his performance is measured in the statement of financial performance, because a lot of other people are.

Further evidence of regular profit warnings and their affect on share prices is provided by the following extract from an Ernst & Young study reported in the *Sydney Morning Herald* on 13 September 2001:

> The number of profit warnings from Australian listed companies doubled in the past financial year due to economic jitters and improved disclosure. Ernst & Young's profit warning study found there were 107 profit warnings in the year to August 31, 2001, and the share price of these companies fell an average 12pc 24 hours after the announcement.

## 2.12 Public sector issues

Public sector organisations are required to provide a statement of financial position that discloses assets, liabilities and equity of the government department (or other entity, such as municipality or State). They are also required to prepare a statement of financial performance, which, until 30 June 2001, has generally been called an 'operating statement'. Exhibit 2.9 shows a statement of financial position and exhibit 2.10 a statement of financial performance for the NSW Department of Corrective Services.

Note how similar the Department of Corrective Services statement of financial position is to the statements of Chez Pty Ltd and Tabcorp Holdings Ltd shown earlier in the chapter. The main difference is in the equity section of the statement. For public sector organ-

**EXHIBIT 2.9** **Department of Corrective Services**

**Statement of financial position as at 30 June 2000**

| | Notes | Actual 2000 $'000 | Budget 2000 $'000 | Actual 1999 $'000 |
|---|---|---|---|---|
| **Assets** | | | | |
| Current assets | | | | |
| Cash | 18 | 14 686 | 2 726 | 10 074 |
| Receivables | 8 | 6 949 | 5 198 | 5 912 |
| Inventories | 9 | 4 825 | 6 297 | 5 624 |
| **Total current assets** | | **26 460** | **14 221** | **21 610** |
| Noncurrent assets | | | | |
| Land and buildings | | 674 605 | 672 690 | 637 456 |
| Plant and equipment | | 44 186 | 53 978 | 46 187 |
| **Total noncurrent assets** | **10** | **718 791** | **726 668** | **683 643** |
| **Total assets** | | **745 251** | **740 889** | **705 253** |
| **Liabilities** | | | | |
| Current liabilities | | | | |
| Accounts payable | 11 | 17 048 | 9 680 | 12 603 |
| Employee entitlements | 12 | 24 748 | 21 488 | 18 964 |
| Other provisions | 12 | 1 446 | 2 055 | 1 238 |
| **Total current liabilities** | | **43 242** | **33 223** | **32 805** |
| Noncurrent liabilities | | | | |
| Employee entitlements | 12 | 23 477 | 14 912 | 19 993 |
| **Total noncurrent liabilities** | | **23 477** | **14 912** | **19 993** |
| **Total liabilities** | | 66 719 | 48 135 | 52 798 |
| **Net assets** | | **678 532** | **692 754** | **652 455** |
| **Equity** | | | | |
| Reserves | | 84 555 | 84 267 | 84 474 |
| Accumulated funds | | 593 977 | 608 487 | 567 981 |
| **Total equity** | 13 | **678 532** | **692 754** | **652 455** |

**EXHIBIT 2.10** **Department of Corrective Services**

**Operating statement for the year ended 30 June 2000 (will be called a statement of financial performance in future years)**

| | Notes | Actual 2000 $'000 | Budget 2000 $'000 | Actual 1999 $'000 |
|---|---|---|---|---|
| Expenses | | | | |
| Operating expenses | | | | |
| Employee related | 2(a) | 359 148 | 355 375 | 331 827 |
| Other operating expenses | 2(b) | 113 917 | 107 261 | 102 775 |
| Maintenance | 2(c) | 15 804 | 9 732 | 16 257 |
| Depreciation | 2(d) | 24 344 | 20 250 | 19 833 |
| Grants and subsidies | 2(e) | 3 009 | 2 298 | 2 461 |
| Other expenses | 2(f) | 133 | 926 | 144 |
| **Total expenses** | | **516 355** | **495 842** | **473 297** |
| Less: | | | | |
| Retained revenues | | | | |
| Sales of goods and services | 3(a) | 29 813 | 23 284 | 24 721 |
| Investment income | 3(b) | 368 | 306 | 403 |
| Grants and contributions | 3(c) | 2 458 | 1 694 | 2 045 |
| Other revenue | 3(d) | 1 007 | 275 | 4 601 |
| **Total retained revenues** | | **33 646** | **25 559** | **31 770** |
| Gain/(loss) on sale of noncurrent assets | 4 | 1 003 | 9 | (400) |
| **Net cost of services** | | **481 706** | **470 274** | **441 927** |
| Government contributions | | | | |
| Recurrent appropriation | 6 | 414 659 | 415 673 | 380 376 |
| Capital appropriation | 6 | 60 892 | 62 315 | 46 997 |
| Acceptance by the Crown Entity of employee entitlements and other liabilities | 5 | 32 232 | 31 641 | 33 127 |
| **Total government contributions** | | **507 783** | **509 629** | **460 500** |
| **Surplus (deficit) for the year** | | **26 077** | **39 355** | **18 573** |

isations, equity usually consists of the accumulated surplus (or deficit) and reserves (which are discussed in more detail in chapter 10). The accumulated surplus or deficit is the part of previous surpluses or deficits that have not been returned to consolidated revenues and is held by the government department. It is similar to retained profits for private sector companies. Most government entities do not have capital, and therefore do not include this item in their statement of financial position. The exception would be some government trading enterprises. The equity reported by local governments and governments represents the net assets of their constituent communities. Many government departments report this year's activities and budget together with the previous year's activities.

A statement of financial performance discloses revenues and expenses of a public sector entity. An example of a statement of financial performance (operating statement) for a government department is illustrated in exhibit 2.10 for the Department of Corrective Services. Note that this has some substantial differences to the statements of financial performance illustrated earlier in this chapter. First, the emphasis is on cost of services.

Operating revenue is shown separately and is deducted from operating expenses. Private sector operating statements generally deduct expenses from revenues. After the net cost of services is calculated, other revenues are included. For example, parliamentary appropriations are given to departments to assist them in providing services. There may be recurrent appropriations, capital appropriations (such as new equipment) or other appropriations.

Governments take over certain liabilities of departments, such as superannuation costs. These costs would have been included in employee entitlements in addition to salaries, leave and so on. They were included in expenses to get a more accurate assessment of the cost of services. When the government takes over that liability, it is effectively providing another appropriation, therefore this amount is recorded as a revenue. The net revenue from the disposal of noncurrent assets is discussed in chapter 8.

The statement of financial performance enables users to identify the cost of services provided by the department during the year, the extent to which these costs were covered by revenues, the sources of these revenues and the changes in resources controlled during the period as a result of operations. For the Department of Corrective Services, expenses are far greater than revenue, with the difference showing up as 'net cost of services'. These costs of services ($481 706 000) are covered by total contributions from government of $507 783 000. The difference is $26 077 000, which is the surplus for the year.

The format of the statement of financial performance can vary substantially, depending on the type of public sector entity involved. Many government departments no longer receive government grants. As a result, they need to sell their particular services. For example, the NSW Department of Public Works provides construction and repair services to other NSW government departments. It charges for these services, and must ensure these charges cover all of its costs. So how would you expect the statement of financial performance to look: (a) expenses deducted from revenue; or (b) revenue deducted from expenses? The answer is (a). From their operating surplus they even pay a tax equivalent (an amount equal to the income tax a private sector organisation would pay) to NSW Treasury and a $500 000 dividend to State Treasury.

As you can see from the financial statements of the Department of Corrective Services, most government departments include comparative budget figures for the latest financial year. In the notes to the accounts they provide information on how budget and actual differ.

## 2.13 Homework and discussion to develop understanding

### Discussion questions

1 Define the following terms in your own words:

- a revenue
- b expense
- c net profit
- d dividend
- e retained profits
- f shareholders' equity.

2 What is the difference between current and noncurrent assets?

3 What is the difference between current and noncurrent liabilities?
4 Do liabilities always involve future payments of cash?
5 Suggest two ways retained profits may decrease.
6 How can a statement of financial position answer the following questions:
   a Is a company financially sound?
   b Can a company pay its bills on time?
   c Should the board of directors declare a dividend?
   d How old is the equipment?
7 Explain the main differences between the alternative methods of setting out a statement of financial position: the side-by-side style and the vertical style.
8 List four liabilities that can be either current or noncurrent liabilities. What determines their categorisation?
9 The CEO of a large Australian company announced at a recent shareholders' meeting: 'Our people are our greatest assets'. If this is the case, why are they not included in the statement of financial position?
10 Explain the following in non-technical language that a business person who has not read this text would understand:
   a Why is net profit part of shareholders' equity?
   b If net profit is part of shareholders' equity, why is it necessary to have a separate statement of financial performance? Why not just report net profit on the statement of financial position?
   c Why are dividends to shareholders not considered to be an expense in calculating net profit? Employee wages are considered an expense, as is the cost of products delivered to customers, and shareholders must be kept happy, as must employees and customers.
11 Why are inventory and accounts receivable normally current rather than noncurrent assets? When would they be noncurrent assets?
12 Provide one example each of investments, intangibles, prepayments and accrued expenses.
13 Provide an indicator of whether a company is financially sound.
14 Provide an indicator of whether a company can pay its bills on time.
15 What accounts in the statement of financial position would you look at in deciding how much in dividends can be paid out?
16 Consider any company you are familiar with or interested in and make a list of all the people who might be interested in its statement of financial position. Make your list using the following headings:

| Person (decision-maker) | Use (decision to be made) |
|---|---|

   Try to think about the 'use' issue broadly: your list could easily be a long one. You might make it even more broad by including people you think might like to use the statement of financial position but whose needs are not served by it as you understand it, or who do not have timely access to it.
17 'Financial reports are no longer timely today.' Discuss.
18 Write a paragraph in which you identify a non-accounting career you or someone you know may pursue, and explain the interest in statement of financial position information that this career might imply. If you really cannot see any relationship between that career and anything reported in a statement of financial position, explain why not.

**19** Can a single statement of financial position ever satisfy all the users of a company's financial statements, or should there be different statements of financial position prepared to meet the differing needs of users? Write a paragraph giving your considered views.

**20** 'You can have a perfectly accurate statement of financial position 50 years after year-end.' Discuss.

## Problem 2.1* Prepare a simple statement of financial position, calculate working capital

Bluebird Bakery, a company that rents its bakery premises, had the following account balances at 30 June 2002.

| | $ | | $ |
|---|---|---|---|
| Bakery equipment cost | 129 153 | Shareholders' capital | 80 346 |
| Loan from bank | 14 500 | Accumulated depreciation | 43 996 |
| Supplies inventory cost | 13 220 | Cash on hand | 895 |
| Owing to suppliers | 11 240 | Owing by customers | 3 823 |
| Wages owing to employees | 2 246 | Cash in bank | 4 992 |
| | | Unsold baked goods cost | 245 |

**1** Prepare a statement of financial position for the company.

**2** Calculate the company's working capital and working capital ratio.

**3** Prepare another statement of financial position using account titles that you would see more commonly in financial reports.

## Problem 2.2* Examples of statement of financial position categories plus working capital

**1** Define each of the following and choose an example of each from the Chez Pty Ltd statement of financial position in this chapter (or from the statement of financial position of any company familiar or interesting to you):

- **a** a current asset
- **b** a noncurrent asset
- **c** a current liability
- **d** a noncurrent liability
- **e** an owners' equity item.

**2** Do you think the examples you selected will always be classified in the same way by all enterprises? Why or why not? Give examples if possible.

**3** Calculate the company's working capital and working capital ratio for the two years shown in the statement of financial position. Has the company's short-term position improved or deteriorated over the two years?

## Problem 2.3* Prepare a statement of financial position appropriately classified

From the following information prepare a statement of financial position, appropriately classified, as at 30 June 2002 for PSM Limited.

| | $000 |
|---|---|
| Share capital | 108 518 |
| Cash | 11 636 |

| | $000 |
|---|---|
| Accounts payable | 43 091 |
| Investments ($3 371 000 held for short-term investment) | 5 458 |
| Retained profits | 28 546 |
| Prepayments | 3 958 |
| Accounts receivable | 47 515 |
| Long-term borrowings | 30 866 |
| Inventory | 66 479 |
| Provisions for employee entitlements ($30 919 000 due within 1 year) | 34 888 |
| Property, plant and equipment | 67 760 |
| Other long-term assets | 42 742 |
| Other receivable (due more than 1 year) | 361 |

## Problem 2.4* Basic statement of financial position, net profit and retained profits ideas

Labott's Bottlery Pty Ltd had the following recent statement of financial position as at 30 September 2002:

| | | | |
|---|---|---|---|
| Cash | 1 642 | Mortgage | 1 000 |
| Inventory | 1 480 | Share capital | 3 000 |
| Land | 2 100 | Retained profits | 1 222 |
| | 5 222 | | 5 222 |

These questions start you out in chapter 2 and take you into Chapter 3, to help you think of accounting in an integrated way, not just as a set of disconnected chapter-by-chapter subjects.

1 Why is 'land' on the statement of financial position, and what does it represent?

2 On 5 October 2002, the company borrowed $2 410 from the bank and used the money immediately to buy more land. What was the total dollar figure of the company's assets after this point?

3 Why did the company not just use the $3000 share capital to buy more land instead of borrowing from the bank?

4 Explain how 'retained profits' comes to be on the statement of financial position and what it represents.

5 For the year ended 30 September 2002, the company's revenues were $10 116 and its expenses (including income tax) were $9881. What was its net profit for the year?

6 During the year ended 30 September 2002, the company declared dividends of $120. Considering this and point 5, what was the balance in retained profits at the beginning of that year (1 October 2001)?

7 If the 2002 expenses were $11 600 instead of the figure in point 5, and the company did not declare any dividends, what would the retained profits be at 30 September 2002?

8 The answer to point 7 is a negative number, which would be a debit. Would you think such a debit should be shown with the assets on the left side of the company's statement of financial position? Why, or why not?

## Problem 2.5 Explain statement of financial position ideas to a business executive

You are the executive assistant to Stephane Solden, a particularly hard-driving and successful owner of a chain of restaurants. Not long ago, Solden and you were flying to another city, and the inflight movie was so bad the two of you ended up talking about all sorts of things. One subject was Solden's impatience with accountants and accounting, which, probably because the annual audit of the company's accounts was then taking place, seemed particularly strong. How would you respond to the following questions from Solden?

1 The main thing that sticks in my mind about the statement of financial position is that the thing balances! Who cares? Why should it matter?
2 My auditor keeps wanting to talk to me about what the statement of financial position says about the company's finances and how I've managed them. But I always look to the future – why should I care about the statement of financial position when it's just a history?
3 Last year, I had a really good idea about the statement of financial position. You know, I consider our restaurant managers to be the most important asset the company has. I was going to have the managers added to the statement of financial position as assets, so it would show all our assets. But the accountants and auditors didn't seem interested in my idea. Why not?
4 Someone told me once that the statement of financial position is a photograph of the business at a particular instant in time, and that you have to be careful because some accountant might have touched up the photo, airbrushed away the warts. What did they mean? Isn't the statement of financial position an exact list of all the company's assets and liabilities?

## Problem 2.6 Preparing a statement of financial position

John Graham decided to set up a business as a downtown courier, calling his business QuickJohn Courier. Before he could operate his courier service, there were a few things he needed: a bicycle, a bike lock, a delivery bag, and a good pair of running shoes. He had $200 in savings, but quickly realised that he would need more funds to purchase all of the required items. John asked his Aunt Elizabeth for a loan of $200 and promised that he would pay her back as soon as he could. She said yes.

John purchased a bike for $500, placing $275 down and promising to pay the rest later. He then bought a bike lock for $15, a pair of shoes for $60, and a delivery bag for $25, paying cash for all these items. He began his business on 15 April 2001.

John asked a friend to prepare an initial statement of financial position for the new business. The friend had a couple of questions to ask first:

'John, when do you have to repay your Aunt Elizabeth?'

'She never said. But my intention is to pay her back by the end of 2002. I'm sure she would complain if I took longer than that. She wants the money for a big birthday party that year.'

'How about the amount you owe on the bicycle: when is that due?'

'The store wants the money right away. I told them I would have to raise the funds by sales in my business, so they said they wanted me to pay just as soon as I could. They made me sign a form saying they could take back the bike and the other stuff if I don't pay.'

With this information, prepare the initial statement of financial position for QuickJohn Courier as at 15 April 2001, including any notes you think might be useful, and comment on the business's financial condition.

## Problem 2.7 Answer questions about statement of financial position figures

Answer the question in each case below. No other statements besides the statement of financial position are involved or necessary to solve each case.

1 A. Ltd's property and plant are 40 per cent depreciated. The accumulated depreciation is $520 000. What is the cost of the property and plant?

2 B. Ltd's working capital ratio has fallen from 2.20 last year to 1.60 this year. Its current assets went up over that time, from $4 290 000 to $5 304 000. What was the dollar change in current liabilities?

3 C. Ltd has the following statement of financial position amounts: current assets $215 300; share capital $200 000; noncurrent liabilities $421 300; noncurrent assets $512 110; current liabilities $189 230. What is missing, and how much is it?

4 D. Ltd has decided to borrow some cash but does not want its debt/equity ratio to go above 2. According to the statement of financial position, the company has assets of $6 245 000 and liabilities of $4 116 000. How much can the company borrow?

5 E. Ltd's debt/equity ratio has been rising, although its working capital ratio has been rising too. There has been little change in current assets or in equity, so what has been happening to cause this change in ratios?

6 F. Ltd has decided to make a major change in its financial structure, by persuading some holders of its bonded debt to exchange their bonds for shares. The company's share capital is now $15 000 000 and its retained earnings (the only other item in equity) equal $32 000 000. The intention is to get the company's debt/equity ratio down from 2.1 to 1.4. How many dollars of bonds must be exchanged for shares to meet this goal?

## Problem 2.8 Personal statement of financial position and debt/equity ratio

1 List your own personal resources and obligations, and try to fit them into accounting's standard statement of financial position format, in which the resources are listed on one side and debts and claims against the resources are listed on the other, keeping in mind that total resources must balance total debts plus residual equity. In doing this, think about:

   a Which of your resources and obligations would or would not be reported in the statement of financial position?

   b What would likely be disclosed about each?

   c Which are short term and which are long term?

   d Which are easy or difficult to value numerically?

   (If you have completed a credit application or student loan application, the things you reported there might be a good starting point.)

2 What decision-making information might your list of resources and obligations provide?

3 Calculate your personal debt/equity ratio (total liabilities divided by total equity). Are you soundly financed?

## Problem 2.9 A real company's resources, sources and debt/equity ratio

Using the Chez Pty Ltd statement of financial position, or that of any other company as an example, answer the following questions:

1 What resources does the company have?

2 How are those resources financed?

3 What is the company's relative reliance on debt versus equity financing? Calculate the ratio of total liabilities to total equity (the debt/equity ratio) as a measure of this relative reliance.

## Problem 2.10 Recognise revenue

Calculate the total revenue for the month of February 2002, given the following:

1 Credit sales of $100 000 made in February; 50 per cent to be collected in February.
2 Cash sales of $150 000.
3 Received rental revenue of $5000 for the month for February rent on a property.
4 Interest of $8000 is credited to the company bank statement. It relates to interest earned for the six months from 1 August 2001 to 31 January 2002.
5 Received $10 000 as a deposit from a customer for a job to be carried out in March.

## Problem 2.11 Recognise expenses

Calculate the total expenses for the month of February 2002, given the following:

1 Paid salaries of $20 000; $5000 related to work carried out in January and $15 000 related to February work.
2 Paid commission expenses of $10 000 in February. The commission related to January sales.
3 Paid rent for the month of February of $3000 on 9 February.
4 Received a bill for $750 from a plumber for repair work done on 25 February. This will be paid next month.
5 Paid an $80 000 deposit on a block of land.

## Problem 2.12 Prepare simple statement of financial position, notes, 'what if' analysis

Prawns Galore Pty Ltd is a seafood eatery specialising in shellfish and soups. The premises are rented and all sales are for cash, so the company has only a few statement of financial position accounts. The accounts as at 30 June 2002 are as follows.

| Assets | $ | Liabilities and shareholders' funds | $ |
|---|---|---|---|
| Food supplies cost | 2 100 | Payable to suppliers | 5 300 |
| Equipment cost | 64 900 | Long-term loan | 25 000 |
| Other supplies cost | 4 500 | Wages payable | 900 |
| Cash at bank | 2 200 | Share capital | 10 000 |
| | | Accumulated depreciation | 27 400 |
| | | Retained profits | 5 100 |
| | 73 700 | | 73 700 |

*Required:*

1 Prepare a statement of financial position for Prawns Galore Pty Ltd as at 30 June 2002. Include any notes to the statement of financial position that you think might be useful.
2 Comment on the company's financial position as shown by your statement of financial position.
3 Suppose, when you were reviewing the company's accounts after preparing the statement of financial position, you found an error in the records. The company had paid a supplier

$2900, but that payment had inadvertently not been deducted from the company's bank account record or from its record of accounts payable to suppliers. You decided to record that payment. What changes resulted in the statement of financial position you prepared in question 1 and in your comments in question 2?

## Problem 2.13 Indicate the effects of transactions

With respect to the current accounting period, state whether each of the following independent transactions decrease (a) net profit; (b) the balance in the cash account; or (c) both.

1 recognition of depreciation
2 repayment of a loan
3 payment of a cash dividend
4 payment of an advertising invoice which had been recorded as an expense in the previous period
5 recording a bad debt
6 payment of wages for the period
7 purchase of a block of land for cash.

## Problem 2.14 Indicate the effect of failure to record transactions

Using the notation O/S (overstated), U/S (understated) and N/E (no effect), indicate the effect on assets, liabilities, shareholders' equity and net profit before tax of failing to record each of the following independent transactions or events:

- **a** a $200 000 piece of equipment purchased on credit
- **b** $30 000 inventory purchased on account
- **c** sale of inventory (costing $30 000) on credit for $50 000
- **d** a loan received from the bank for $80 000
- **e** payment of wages of $100 000 for the period.

Format your solution as follows:

| Transaction | Assets | Liabilities | Shareholders' equity | Net profit before tax |
|---|---|---|---|---|
| x | O/S | N/E | O/S | N/E |

## Problem 2.15 Statement of financial performance and statement of financial position

The following account balances are taken from the books of Century Cinemas on 31 December 2002. Revenues and expenses are for the year ended 31 December 2002. The Retained profits balance is as at 1 January 2002.

| | $ |
|---|---|
| Accounts receivable | $13 450 |
| Accounts payable | $13 910 |
| Advertising expense | $42 780 |
| Cash | $4 610 |
| Confectionery sales | $12 300 |
| Cost of confectionery sold | $10 500 |

| | |
|---|---|
| Electricity expense | $5 090 |
| Furniture and fittings | $34 000 |
| Inventory | $18 000 |
| Land and buildings | $60 000 |
| Loan payable | $35 000 |
| Projection equipment | $41 000 |
| Rent expense | $33 200 |
| Retained profits, 1 January 2002 | $59 720 |
| Share capital | $60 000 |
| Ticket revenue | $81 700 |

1 Prepare a statement of financial performance for Century Cinemas, for the year ended 31 December 2002.
2 Prepare a note for retained profits for the year ended 31 December 2002.
3 Prepare a statement of financial position as at 31 December 2002.

## Problem 2.16 Recording of assets

State whether or not an asset should be recorded in the statement of financial position of XYZ Ltd as at 30 June 2002 in each of the following situations. State the amount (if any) of the asset, and any assumptions made.

1 On 15 May 2002, XYZ Ltd paid Insurance Ltd $20 000 for an insurance premium. The premium covers losses incurred due to fire, theft or other causes up to 14 May 2003.
2 XYZ Ltd paid $15 000 for a patent in April 2002.
3 XYZ Ltd has just hired a new general manager who is an expert in the business carried on by XYZ Ltd. With the help of this person the company is expected to increase its annual profits by $500 000. The general manager's salary is $300 000 per annum.
4 XYZ Ltd purchased land in 1998 for $100 000. The market value of this land is $150 000 as at 30 June 2002.
5 A machine is purchased for $1 000 000 and costs an additional $400 000 to install.

## Problem 2.17 Recording of liabilities

State whether or not each of the following events would result in a liability being recognised in the accounts at 30 June.

1 Taxes for the year ended 30 June, which are not payable until October.
2 Wages to be paid on 2 July to cover the two-week period up to 30 June.
3 The company sells washing machines and gives a one year warranty to repair or replace any faulty machines.
4 A construction company receives a $10 million advance in June on a contract. The work will commence in July.
5 The company has signed a contract to pay its Managing Director $1 000 000 per annum (inflation adjusted) for the next four years.

## Problem 2.18 Effect of transactions on assets, liabilities and shareholders' equity

What is the effect on assets, liabilities and shareholders' equity of each of the following transactions:

1 contribute cash to the company in return for shares?
2 make a loan to the company?
3 receive payment from a debtor?
4 purchase inventory on credit?
5 purchase inventory for cash?
6 pay accounts payable?
7 receive interest that was due from the previous accounting period?
8 purchase furniture and fittings on credit?
9 an owner donates his motor vehicle to the company in return for additional shares?

## Problem 2.19 Effect of transactions on total assets

What is the effect of each of the following transactions on total assets:

1 purchased equipment for $200 000 cash?
2 purchased inventory for $30 000 cash?
3 received a loan of $50 000 from the bank?
4 received $20 000 from accounts receivable?
5 issued additional shares of $300 000?
6 returned to a supplier inventory that had been bought on credit for $2000?

## Problem 2.20 Prepare a classified statement of financial position

From the following information prepare a statement of financial position, appropriately classified, as at 30 June 2002 for Tin Ltd.

| | $ |
|---|---|
| Cash and cash equivalents | 43 000 |
| Notes payable | 30 000 |
| Prepayments | 10 000 |
| Long-term debt, excluding current portion | 200 000 |
| Accounts receivable | 68 000 |
| Long-term investments | 110 000 |
| Provision for employee entitlements (noncurrent) | 34 000 |
| Retained profits | 184 000 |
| Income taxes payable | 32 000 |
| Inventory | 81 000 |
| Property, plant and equipment, at cost | 550 000 |
| Accounts payable | 61 000 |
| Patents and trademarks | 55 000 |
| Current portion of long-term debt | 25 000 |
| Accumulated depreciation | 190 000 |
| Share capital | 161 000 |

## Problem 2.21 Prepare a classified statement of financial position

From the following information, prepare an appropriately classified statement of financial position as at 30 June 2001 for OPSM Protector Limited.

| | $000 |
|---|---|
| Share capital | 67 358 |
| Cash | 31 691 |
| Accounts payable | 52 672 |
| Retained profits | 39 346 |
| Receivables ($1 549 000 due in more than one year) | 49 132 |
| Interest-bearing liabilities ($8 732 000 due this year) | 96 185 |
| Intangibles | 49 053 |
| Deferred tax liabilities | 4 962 |
| Inventories | 55 117 |
| Provisions ($31 704 000 due within one year) | 35 438 |
| Property, plant and equipment | 90 574 |
| Reserves | 7 320 |
| Deferred tax assets | 16 974 |
| Other long-term assets (financial assets) | 2 416 |
| Other current assets (prepayments) | 8 324 |

## Problem 2.22 When is revenue earned?

Is revenue earned from the following transactions? Give reasons for your answer.

1 Goods costing $6000 are sold for $9500.
2 Goods costing $6000 are sold for $6000.
3 Goods costing $6000 are sold for $4500.
4 A surveyor sends an account for $15 000 to a builder for work in connection with a subdivision of a block of land.
5 An electrical store provides free service on a television set during the warranty period. The cost to the store was $250.
6 An investment company receives a dividend of $8000 on one of its investments.
7 Goods costing $100 are sold for $160. Instead of paying for the goods the customer cleans the store's windows. This cleaning is normally carried out by an outside contractor at a cost of $160.

## Problem 2.23 Identify items as revenues or expenses

State whether or not, and why, each of the following items is likely to be a revenue or expense for this year of the company indicated:

| Company | | Item |
|---|---|---|
| 1 | Email | Cost of advertising for new employees |
| 2 | Telstra | Collection of old accounts from customers who had skipped town and were tracked down by a collection agency |
| 3 | National Australia Bank | Cost of renovating its main Perth branch |
| 4 | Woolworths | Increased value of the land under certain department stores |
| 5 | Pizza Hut Restaurants | Food sold to customers who paid with their Visa cards |

| | | |
|---|---|---|
| 6 | Harvey Norman Discounts | Money paid by customers in advance on special furniture orders |
| 7 | Westpac | A lawsuit by a customer who fell down the escalator and was injured |
| 8 | Mount Isa Mines | Cost of issuing new shares to raise funds for exploration |
| 9 | Ford Motor Co | Income taxes paid in USA |
| 10 | BHP | Special good-performance bonuses promised this year but not to be paid until next year |
| 11 | BHP | Special dividend to owners, all of whom are also employees |
| 12 | Woolworths | Decreased value of the land under some of its inner-city locations |
| 13 | Email | Cost of scientific research aimed at developing new products |
| 14 | Western Mining | Estimated amount of money needed to provide long service leave to this year's employees to be paid in the future |
| 15 | Coles Myer | Goods lost to shoplifting |
| 16 | Coles Myer | Salary of floorwalker who tries to catch shoplifters |
| 17 | Leighton Construction | Contract payments to be received over the next five years for construction work on a large bridge project |

## Problem 2.24 Identify items as asset, liability or owners' equity

State whether or not, and why, each of the following items is likely to be an asset, liability or owners' equity account (perhaps both an asset and a liability in some cases) of the company indicated:

| **Company** | | **Item** |
|---|---|---|
| 1 | News Corporation | List of subscribers to a magazine |
| 2 | Qantas | Funds collected from employees, to be repaid to them after retirement as superannuation |
| 3 | Westpac | Westpac's satisfied customers |
| 4 | Any company | Lawsuit against the company by a builder who alleges the company failed to pay for work done on the company's premises |
| 5 | Consolidated Paper | Land that Consolidated Paper has agreed to sell to a real estate developer once it has been surveyed |
| 6 | Westpac | Westpac's dissatisfied customers |
| 7 | Fairfax Publications | *Australian Financial Review*'s skilled group of editors and reporters |
| 8 | Ampolex | Oil discovered on Ampolex's property, but still underground and likely to stay there for many years |
| 9 | Swans Football Club | Players under contract to the team |
| 10 | Harvey Norman | Deposits received from customers of Harvey Norman for furniture not yet delivered to them |

| | | |
|---|---|---|
| 11 | Sunbeam Victa | Profits earned by the Sunbeam Victa, but not yet paid out to the owners as dividends |
| 12 | TNT | A fleet of delivery trucks leased by TNT from several truck-leasing firms |
| 13 | Hertz | A car Hertz leases to real estate salesperson Don Wharton |
| 14 | Telstra | Funds owing to Telstra by a customer who recently declared bankruptcy |
| 15 | Keg Restaurants | The phrase 'The Keg' and the round logo, both registered trademarks |
| 16 | Westfield Holdings | The parking lot surrounding Roselands Shopping Mall, Sydney |
| 17 | Pacific Dunlop | A guarantee Pacific Dunlop has made on a bank loan owed by an associated company |
| 18 | Fosters | A newly developed beer with reduced calories that has yet to be approved by the government |

## Problem 2.25 Correcting a statement of financial position

Finewines Limited began business on 1 July 2001, producing and selling wine. One year later, the company's newly appointed accountant, Al Beer, needs to produce a statement of financial position for a meeting of company executives. Unfortunately, Al is more skilled at winemaking than he is in accounting and has requested your advice. He shows you the following statement of financial position he has prepared.

**Finewines Limited**
Statement of financial position
as at 30 June 2002

| **Assets** | | **Liabilities and owners' equity** | |
|---|---|---|---|
| Cash | 4 340 | Accounts receivable | 10 460 |
| Net profit for the year | 24 720 | Share capital | 40 000 |
| Raw materials | 9 800 | Kitchen equipment | 50 800 |
| Accounts payable | 10 680 | | |

Assume that the account balances Al has used are correct. Prepare (if necessary) a corrected statement of financial position. Provide an explanation of the main differences between your statement of financial position and the one Al prepared.

## Problem 2.26 (Challenging) Corrected financial statements

Deltamark Technologies is a marketer and distributor of computer games. The firm prides itself on its computerised accounting system: all transactions are entered into the system as they occur, and a 'state of the art' software package is used to produce financial statements at year-end.

Unfortunately, because of a temporary network failure, the file containing the company's 2001 financial statements was erased, and the backup copy cannot be located. All other records, however, remain intact. Deltamark's trainee accountant, Robin Sherwood, has been given the job of reproducing the company's financial statements. Below is the statement of financial performance and the statement of financial position Robin has prepared.

**Deltamark Technologies**
Statement of financial performance
for the year ended 31 December 2001

| | $ | $ |
|---|---|---|
| Revenues: | | |
| Software revenue – cash sales | 24 000 | |
| Accounts receivable | 13 200 | 37 900 |
| Expenses: | | |
| Salaries and wages | 17 800 | |
| Accounts payable | 12 700 | |
| Electricity expense | 4 200 | (34 700) |
| Net profit | | 3 200 |

**Deltamark Technologies**
Statement of financial position
as at 31 December 2001

| | $ | | $ |
|---|---|---|---|
| Cash | 5 700 | Software revenue – credit sales | 15 400 |
| Office equipment | 19 200 | Share capital | 25 000 |
| Land and building | 46 800 | Net profit | 3 200 |
| Less: Loan payable | (10 000) | Retained profits | 18 100 |
| | 61 700 | | 61 700 |

Robin is surprised by this year's level of profit, as Deltamark has achieved average net profits of $20 000 in the last few years. He wonders whether he has made a calculation error and seeks your advice.

1 Prepare a corrected statement of financial performance for the year ended 31 December 2001.
2 Prepare a statement of retained profits for the year ended 31 December 2001. The balance of retained profits on 1 January 2001 was $19 100. Note that the 31 December 2001 amount of retained profits shown on Robin's statement of financial position is incorrect (Robin used this as the 'plug' figure to make his statement of financial position balance).
3 Prepare a corrected statement of financial position as at 31 December 2001.
4 Robin is confused by the corrected financial statements. Explain to him the major differences between your statements and the ones he prepared.

### Problem 2.27 (Challenging) Accountants, ethics and statement of financial position

As has been indicated several times so far (in section 2.6, for example), managers of businesses and other organisations are very concerned about how the statement of financial position reflects their management of the enterprise. This is very natural, and generally appropriate too, because such concern is likely to lead managers to want to do a good job of managing. But it can also lead to a temptation to alter the information in a manager's favour. The possibility of such a temptation is part of the reason auditors are employed to examine financial statements, including the statement of financial position. This temptation can also produce ethical problems for professional accountants employed by the enterprise. On the one hand, such an accountant is bound by the ethical rules of the profession to see that proper accounting methods are followed in preparing the company's statement of financial position, which would imply that the information should not be altered in management's favour. On the other hand, such an accountant works for senior management and is likely to be bound by the contract of employment to put the enterprise's interests first. What does such an accountant (for example, the chief accountant responsible for preparing the enterprise's financial statements) do if senior management (for example, the general manager) wants to alter the statement of financial position to make things look better and makes a good case that such an action will help the enterprise get bank loans and other assistance it needs?

Discuss this situation, from the point of view of both the general manager and the chief accountant.

## CASE 2A Woolworths Limited case

Refer to the extracts of the annual report of Woolworths Limited in appendix 2. All questions relate to the consolidated accounts.

1. At what point in time is the statement of financial position drawn up?
2. What is the currency in which accounts in the statement of financial position are measured?
3. Illustrate how the 2001 statement of financial position of Woolworths Limited balances.
4. How were the assets financed?
5. How is the 'net assets' figure determined?
6. What are the balances of current assets, current liabilities, noncurrent assets and noncurrent liabilities at 24 June 2001?
7. What is the balance of working capital at 24 June 2001?
8. What dividends were paid or provided for during the year?
9. What is the amount of share capital issued?
10. What companies would be included in the consolidated figures?

## CASE 2B Interpreting statements about financial position

1. 'Telstra is banking on cost cutting, a strong balance sheet and a resumption of industry growth in the second half of the financial year to resurrect its earnings momentum ... Still boasting a strong balance sheet, unlike some much larger American and European telcos, it will also lie in wait for distressed telco businesses or assets, especially in Asia, the preferred growth area' (*Australian Financial Review*, 30 August 2001).
2. 'Credit Suisse Boston argues CSR has one of the strongest balance sheets within the Australian basic industrials universe and among its international peers' (*Australian Financial Review*, 28 May 2001).
3. 'Australian Gas Light Co has begun a wide-ranging review of its operations to counter a deteriorating balance sheet. The debt levels are not uncomfortable given the fact that AGL is still essentially a regulated business' (*Australian Financial Review*, 24 August 2001).
4. 'While Pasminco belatedly disclosed its restructuring plan the company also revealed a financial position far worse than the most pessimistic assessment by stockbroking and investment analysts, announcing a total debt position of almost 3 billion' (*Australian Financial Review*, 21 July 2001).

***Required:***

Discuss the implications of each of the quotes from the point of view of the comments made on their statements of financial position.

## CASE 2C Interpreting a statement of financial position

The principal activities of Sydney Airport Corporation are the provision and management of airport facilities at Sydney (Kingsford Smith), Bankstown, Camden and Hoxton Park Airports. The group is also involved in airport-related commercial operations and property management. The nature of the group's business has not changed during the financial year under review.

***Required:***

1 Describe the meaning of each of the items in the following statement marked with an asterisk.
2 Calculate the current ratio and debt to equity ratios for both years. Comment on the changes.
3 What is likely to be included in property, plant and equipment?

Statement of financial position
as at 30 june 2000

| | | Notes | Sydney Airports Corporation Limited Group | |
|---|---|---|---|---|
| | | | **2000 $000** | **1999 $000** |
| | Current assets | | | |
| | Cash assets | | 9 405 | 6 265 |
| * | Receivables | 5 | 28 629 | 33 957 |
| * | Prepayments | | 7 783 | 4 149 |
| | **Total current assets** | | **45 817** | **44 371** |
| | **Noncurrent assets** | | | |
| * | Receivables | | — | — |
| * | Investments | 6 | 196 | 196 |
| * | Property, plant and equipment | 7 | 3 198 171 | 2 868 773 |
| | Future income tax benefit | | 4 540 | 6 856 |
| | Prepayments | | 4 601 | 7 340 |
| | **Total noncurrent assets** | | **3 207 508** | **2 883 165** |
| | **Total assets** | | **3 253 325** | **2 927 536** |
| | **Current liabilities** | | | |
| * | Payables | 8 | 70 356 | 54 164 |
| * | Interest-bearing liabilities | 9 | 9 000 | 49 000 |
| | Tax liabilities | | 6 218 | 46 045 |
| * | Provisions | 10 | 18 562 | 21 290 |
| | **Total current liabilities** | | **104 136** | **170 499** |
| | **Noncurrent liabilities** | | | |
| * | Interest-bearing liabilities | 11 | 1 216 000 | 850 000 |
| | Deferred tax liabilities | | 13 959 | 4 712 |
| * | Provisions | 12 | 920 | 1 177 |

| | | Notes | Sydney Airports Corporation Limited Group | |
|---|---|---|---|---|
| | | | 2000 $000 | 1999 $000 |
| | **Total noncurrent liabilities** | | **1 230 879** | **855 889** |
| | **Total liabilities** | | **1 335 015** | **1 026 388** |
| | **Net assets** | | **1 918 310** | **1 901 148** |
| | **Equity** | | | |
| * | Contributed equity | 13 | 794 000 | 794 000 |
| | Reserves | 14 | 1 087 789 | 1 087 789 |
| * | Retained profits | 15 | 36 521 | 19 359 |
| | **Total equity** | | **1 918 310** | **1 901 148** |

## CASE 2D Interpreting newspaper announcements about profit

Losses on the implosion of One.Tel helped push Mr Kerry Packer's Publishing and Broadcasting Ltd to its first loss to date – the media and gaming company yesterday posted a full-year net deficit of $85 million.

The slump in earnings, from a $324 million profit a year earlier, followed one-off losses of $397 million, largely related to writedowns on PBL's stake in One.Tel, other investments, and losses on its Indian operations.

Excluding one-off items, PBL posted a profit of $312.6 million, above market expectations of a $300 million profit, with sales rising 3.4 per cent to $2.55 billion, buoyed by growth from its Crown casino unit.

Earnings before interest tax and depreciation fell 5 per cent to $625 million.

'You couldn't fault the operational result in a difficult environment,' said one analyst, adding that the performance from PBL's three units was broadly in line with expectations.

**PBL**

| Full year | 2001 $ | 2000 $m |
|---|---|---|
| Sales | 2 553 | 2 449 |
| Interest | 37.3 | 105.5 |
| Depreciation | 97.5 | 92.3 |
| Pre-tax | –47.2 | 414.1 |
| Significant items | –397.0 | 2.54 |
| Net | –84.6 | 323.96 |
| Eps | –12.76c | 49.18c |
| Interim div. | 10cf | 10cf |
| Final div.* | 10cf | 10cf |
| Shares (yest.) | $9.85 | +12c |

'The better than expected operating result helped push PBL's shares up 12c to close at $9.85, with Deutsche Bank doing the bulk of afternoon buying.'

(Source: *Australian Financial Review*, 23 August 2001, p. 15.)

***Required:***

Based on the above extract and what you learnt in the chapter, explain the contents of the PBL summary for the full year above.

# Chapter 3

# *The double-entry system*

## On completion of this chapter you should be able to:

- carry out transaction analysis and determine the impact of transactions on elements of the statements of financial position and financial performance
- describe how debits and credits work in the double-entry accounting system
- record transactions using debits and credits
- prepare journal entries
- determine the balance of an account after a series of transactions
- describe the normal balance for the following types of accounts: assets, liabilities, equity, revenues and expenses
- describe some developments in business and society that have had an impact on the development of financial accounting
- explain why financial accounting has become more sophisticated over the centuries.

## 3.1 Chapter overview

In chapter 2 we discussed the importance of the statements of financial position (balance sheet) and financial performance (profit and loss) to managers. It is therefore critical that every manager understand the impact of transactions on these financial reports. This chapter provides those skills by introducing transactional analysis, which considers the impact of specific transactions on the accounting equation. A good understanding of transactional analysis will make the rest of this book easier to follow. As well as being critical for managers and other users of accounting reports, transactional analysis is important to preparers of financial information, as it forms the basis of the double-entry system.

The double-entry system, involving debits and credits, which forms the basis of modern accounting, is then described. We then use this system to prepare journal entries and (via the use of spreadsheets) prepare financial statements. Preparing financial statements by the full accounting process is left to chapter 4. To put much of the above material in perspective, we then provide a brief history of accounting, including how accounting systems have developed in response to changes in society.

## 3.2 Maintaining the accounting equation

In section 2.2, the following equality (the accounting equation) was noted.

**Assets = Liabilities + Owners' equity**

Financial accounting is said to use the double-entry system, whereby the accounting equation is always kept in balance. If an asset goes up, a liability or equity must go up too (or another asset must go down). If a liability goes up, an asset must go up too, or an equity or another liability must go down. Here are some examples, using the statement of financial position descriptions in the Sound and Light example in section 2.2 and the equation $A_1 = L_1 + E_1$ to represent the statement of financial position before the events:

- cash of \$100 obtained from an owner for shares: 'cash' asset up, 'share capital issued' equity up, so $A_1 + \$100 = L_1 + E_1 + \$100$
- \$120 collected from a customer: 'cash' asset up, 'accounts receivable' asset down, so $A_1 + \$100 + \$120 - \$120 = L_1 + E_1 + \$100$
- goods for sale costing \$130 received from a suppler: 'inventory' asset up, 'accounts payable' liability up, so $A_1 + \$100 + \$120 - \$120 + \$130 = L_1 + \$130 + E_1 + \$100$.

After these three events, the new statement of financial position is \$230 higher on both sides and so still in balance:

$$\mathbf{A_1 + \$230\ (net) = L_1 + \$130 + E_1 + \$100}$$

The key point is that the equation will always be in balance. The equation would balance before recording these transactions and will balance after the transactions have been recorded.

## 3.3 Transaction analysis

The purpose of this section is to show you how various transactions affect the accounting equation. In this section we concentrate on transactions that affect the statement of financial position. In section 3.4, the accounting equation is expanded to show the effect on the statement of financial performance. Transaction analysis is a useful way of understanding how any transaction or event affects a company's financial statements.

Recall that the basic accounting equation is:

**Assets = Liabilities + Owners' equity**

After each transaction, the total assets must always equal the total liabilities and owners' equity. This equality remains regardless of the type of transaction.

To illustrate, consider the following transactions for LRM Pty Ltd for March 2002:

1 *Shareholders invest $200 000 cash in the business.* The effect of this transaction is to increase cash (an asset) and increase share capital (an owners' equity account).
2 *Land and building is purchased for $300 000, which is financed by a loan from the seller repayable in five years.* For this transaction, land and buildings (an asset) is increased. This is financed through a loan, so loan (a liability account) is also increased. Note that this transaction does not affect owners' equity. The shareholders do not have any more or less equity in the company, as assets and liabilities increased by the same amount. Note that after these first two transactions, the accounting equation is still in balance, as will be the case after every transaction.
3 *Inventory worth $50 000 is bought on account.* Inventory is purchased for $50 000, with an agreement to pay the suppliers at a later date (usually 30 days after the date of sale). Again, both an asset and a liability are increased. In this case they are inventory (asset) and accounts payable (liability).
4 *Equipment worth $90 000 is purchased, paying $20 000 cash and signing an agreement to pay the remainder in 90 days.* This involves the purchase of equipment (increase in an asset), which is financed by both paying out cash (an asset) and incurring a liability, which in this case is notes payable. Notes payable differ from accounts payable because the liability is evidenced by a promissory note or bill of exchange. Notes payable increased by $70 000.
5 *Damaged inventory which was purchased on credit at a cost of $5000 was returned to the supplier.* This reverses part of transaction 3. The damaged inventory is returned to the supplier, thus decreasing inventory (an asset). As less money is now owed to the suppliers, accounts payable (a liability) is also reduced.
6 *Paid $30 000 on accounts payable.* This results in the liability, namely accounts payable, being reduced by the payment which reduces an asset, namely cash.
7 *Purchased $10 000 inventory for cash.* All of the above six transactions have affected both sides of the equation. However, this transaction affects only the asset side. It results in one asset (inventory) increasing and another asset (cash) decreasing. Again, after all transactions have been recorded, the accounting equation balances.

A summary of the effect of each of these transactions is shown in exhibit 3.1. Based on the totals of the accounting equation in exhibit 3.1, a statement of financial position is produced in exhibit 3.2. As this is a new organisation and none of the transactions affected revenues or expenses, there is a zero balance for retained profits. Note that at this stage neither interest on the loan nor depreciation on the buildings and office equipment has been included.

## How's your understanding?

Here are two questions you should be able to answer, based on what you have just read:

1 If a company receives $10 000 cash from its accounts receivable, what effect will it have on the accounting equation? (You should get an asset (bank) increasing and another asset (accounts receivable) decreasing.)

2 Assume in the above example that you decrease accounts payable instead of accounts receivable. How would you know that you were incorrect? (The equation would not balance.)

**EXHIBIT 3.1** LRM Pty Ltd

**Accounting equation**

| | Assets | | | | = | Liabilities + Owners' equity | | | |
|---|---|---|---|---|---|---|---|---|---|
| | **Cash** | **Inventory** | **Land and buildings** | **Equipment** | | **Accounts payable** | **Notes payable** | **Long-term loan** | **Share capital** |
| 1 | +200 000 | | | | | | | | +200 00 |
| 2 | | | +300 000 | | | | | +300 000 | |
| 3 | | +50 000 | | | | +50 000 | | | |
| 4 | −20 000 | | | +90 000 | | | +70 000 | | |
| 5 | | −5 000 | | | | −5 000 | | | |
| 6 | −30 000 | | | | | −30 000 | | | |
| 7 | −10 000 | +10 000 | | | | | | | |
| | 140 000 | 55 000 | 300 000 | 90 000 | | 15 000 | 70 000 | 300 000 | 200 000 |
| | | | | **$585 000** | = | **$585 000** | | | |

**EXHIBIT 3.2** LRM Pty Ltd

**Statement of financial position as at 31 March 2002**

| **Assets** | **$** | **Liabilities** | **$** |
|---|---|---|---|
| **Current assets** | | **Current liabilities** | |
| Cash | 140 000 | Accounts payable | 15 000 |
| Inventory | 55 000 | Notes payable | 70 000 |
| | 195 000 | | 85 000 |
| **Noncurrent assets** | | **Noncurrent liabilities** | |
| Land and buildings at cost | 300 000 | Long term loans | 300 000 |
| Office equipment at cost | 90 000 | | |
| | 390 000 | **Total liabilities** | 385 000 |
| | | **Shareholders' equity** | |
| | | Share capital | 200 000 |
| | | Retained profits | 0 |
| | | **Total shareholders' equity** | 200 000 |
| **Total assets** | 585 000 | **Total liabilities and SE** | 585 000 |

## 3.4 Transaction analysis extended

We will now expand the LRM transaction analysis example in section 3.3 to include some revenue and expense transactions.

To do this we will expand the accounting equation as follows:

**Assets = Liabilities + Shareholders' equity**

**Assets = Liabilities + Issued capital + Opening retained profits + Net profit − Dividends**

**Assets = Liabilities + Issued capital + Opening retained profits + Revenue − Expenses − Dividends**

Recall from section 3.3 that, after the initial transactions were recorded, the closing balances were as follows as at 31 March 2002 for LRM Pty Ltd:

| | $ |
|---|---|
| Cash | 140 000 |
| Inventory | 55 000 |
| Land and buildings | 300 000 |
| Equipment | 90 000 |
| Accounts payable | 15 000 |
| Notes payable | 70 000 |
| Loans | 300 000 |
| Share capital | 200 000 |

Consider the following additional transactions for the month of April 2002:

**8** *Cash sales of $30 000 were made. The cost of the goods that were sold amounted to $12 000.* This transaction has two effects: one to recognise revenue and increase assets; and the other to recognise an expense and decrease assets. A cash sale of $30 000 was made. This increases a revenue account (sales revenue) and increases an asset (cash). We are also told that cost of goods sold, often abbreviated as COGS, amounted to $12 000. Cost of goods sold is what the company pays to acquire the goods that customers buy. It is not the same as sales revenue, but is rather an expense the company incurs to get sales revenue. In this case the expense (cost of goods sold) increases by $12 000 and inventory (an asset) decreases by $12 000. That is, the goods when purchased were added to inventory, and now that they are sold, inventory is decreased.

**9** *Credit sales of $40 000 were made. The cost of goods sold was $16 000.* This transaction has the same effect on the accounting equation as transaction 8, except that accounts receivable (an asset) is increased instead of cash (another asset). Because it was a credit sale, payment will be received in the future rather than now. Sales revenue and accounts receivable increase by $40 000, inventory decreases by $16 000 and cost of goods sold increases by $16 000.

**10** *Payments of $8000 were made to suppliers.* In this transaction, a payment was made and therefore cash, an asset, decreases. In addition, the payment to creditors reduces accounts payable, a liability account.

**11** *Paid wages for the first two weeks of April for $20 000.* Wages are an expense for the period. The payment of wages in this transaction increases this expense and reduces the cash account (an asset).

**12** *Received an advertising invoice for $2000 for a radio advertisement broadcast on 5 April. The bill will be paid next month.* The company receives an invoice for services that have already been provided to them. The expense should be recognised in the period when the service was received. Therefore an expense account (advertising) will be increased by $2000 and a liability account (accounts payable) will increase by $2000, as the amount has not yet been paid.

**EXHIBIT 3.3** LRM Pty Ltd

Transaction analysis

| | Assets | | | | | = | Liabilities | + | Shareholders' equity | | | | |
|---|---|---|---|---|---|---|---|---|---|---|---|---|---|
| Transaction | Cash | Accounts receivable | Inventory | Land and buildings | Equipment | Accounts payable | Notes payable | Wages payable | Loans | Share capital | Revenues | Expenses | Dividend |
| Balance | 140 000 | | 55 000 | 300 000 | 90 000 | 15 000 | 70 000 | | 300 000 | 200 000 | | | |
| 8 | 30 000 | | −12 000 | | | | | | | | 30 000 | −12 000 | |
| 9 | | 40 000 | −16 000 | | | | | | | | 40 000 | −16 000 | |
| 10 | −8 000 | | | | | −8 000 | | | | | | | |
| 11 | −20 000 | | | | | | | | | | | −20 000 | |
| 12 | | | | | | 2 000 | | | | | | −2 000 | |
| 13 | 25 000 | -25 000 | | | | | | | | | | | |
| 14 | | | | | | | | 18 000 | | | | −18 000 | |
| Total | 167 000 | 15 000 | 27 000 | 300 000 | 90 000 | 9 000 | 70 000 | 18 000 | 300 000 | 200 000 | 70 000 | −68 000 | |
| | | | | $599 000 | | = $599 000 | | | | | | | |

Note: All decreases to assets, liabilities or shareholders' equity are denoted by minus.

13 *Received $25 000 from accounts receivable.* This results in one asset (cash) increasing and another asset (accounts receivable) decreasing. No revenue is recognised as that occurred earlier when the sale was made (see transaction 9).

14 *At the end of the month $18 000 is owing in wages for the last two weeks of the month. It is due to be paid on 1 May.* The employees have carried out the work but have not yet been paid because the next pay day falls on the first day of the following month. As they have done the work an expense account (wages) increases by $18 000. Also, as the amount is owed to them a liability account (wages payable) increases by $18 000.

A summary of the effect of these transactions is provided in exhibit 3.3. Based on the totals of the columns in exhibit 3.3, a statement of financial performance and statement of financial position was prepared, as shown in exhibits 3.4 and 3.5. The statement of financial performance is based on the revenue and expense columns in exhibit 3.3. The retained profits figure

**EXHIBIT 3.4** LRM Pty Ltd

**Statement of financial performance for the month ended 30 April 2002**

| | $ | $ |
|---|---|---|
| Sales | | 70 000 |
| Cost of goods sold | | 28 000 |
| Gross profit | | 42 000 |
| Operating expenses | | |
| Wages | 38 000 | |
| Advertising | 2 000 | 40 000 |
| Net profit | | 2 000 |

**EXHIBIT 3.5** LRM Pty Ltd

**Statement of financial position as at 30 April 2002**

| **Assets** | | **Liabilities and shareholders' equity** | |
|---|---|---|---|
| | $ | | $ |
| **Current assets** | | **Current liabilities** | |
| Cash | 167 000 | Accounts payable | 9 000 |
| Accounts receivable | 15 000 | Notes payable | 70 000 |
| Inventory | 27 000 | Wages payable | 18 000 |
| | 209 000 | | 97 000 |
| **Noncurrent assets** | | **Noncurrent liabilities** | |
| Land and building at cost | 300 000 | Loans | 300 000 |
| Office equipment at cost | 90 000 | **Total liabilities** | 397 000 |
| | 390 000 | | |
| | | **Shareholders' equity** | |
| | | Share capital | 200 000 |
| | | Retained profit* | 2 000 |
| | | **Total shareholders' equity** | 202 000 |
| **Total assets** | 599 000 | **Total liabilities and shareholders' equity** | 599 000 |

* Retained profit = opening retained profits (0) + profit (2000) – dividends declared (0) = 2000

(same as profit for the period as there is no opening balance of retained profits and no dividends declared), together with the share capital account and the other assets and liabilities accounts, provides the information for the statement of financial position.

## How's your understanding?

What impact will each of the following have on profit for the period?

1 Purchase inventory on credit for $20 000.

2 Sell goods on credit for $30 000 (cost of goods sold was $14 000).

3 Pay accounts payable of $20 000.

4 Receive $30 000 from accounts receivable.

(Answer: 0; $16 000; 0; 0)

## 3.5 Recording transactions: double-entry bookkeeping

The above accounting equation is a useful technique for understanding how transactions can affect financial statements. However, it can be very unwieldy when there are many accounts and a large number of transactions. A system of accounting involving debits and credits has been invented centuries ago (see section 3.11 for the history).

One way to understand this double-entry system is to start with the statement of financial position. As noted in the previous section, the statement balances (this is why in many countries it is called a balance sheet); that is, the dollar value of all the resources on the left is equal to the dollar value of all the sources on the right. If the statement of financial position is to balance, every transaction and adjustment must also balance, that is, their effects on the two sides of the statement must be equal. To reinforce the earlier discussion on transaction analysis, consider the following:

- If a resource (asset) is increased, (a) a source (liability or equity) must be increased by the same amount; or (b) another resource decreased by the same amount; or (c) there must be some mixture of source increases and other resource decreases that equals the original resource's increase. For example, if the asset increased was inventory by $200, (a) there could be an increase in accounts payable of $200; (b) there could be a decrease in cash of $200; and (c) there could be an increase in accounts payable of $150 and a decrease in cash of $50.
- Conversely, if a resource is decreased, (a) a source must be decreased by the same amount; or (b) another resource increased by the same amount; or (c) some mixture of source increases/decreases and other resource increases that equals the original resource's decrease. For example, if cash is the resource that decreases by $500, (a) there could be a loan decreasing by $500; (b) there could be equipment increasing by $500; and (c) there could be equipment increasing by $4500 and loan increasing by $4000.

This is just arithmetic. Double entry is a form of algebraic notation, in which an equation (the accounting equation) must be maintained.

For reasons that are now largely lost in the mists of time, increases to resources (assets), on the left side, are called debits, and increases to sources (liabilities and equity), on the right side, are called credits. Perhaps confusingly, *decreases* on the left side are also called credits, and *decreases* on the right side are also called debits. Financial accounting uses only two names to cover the four kinds of effects, which will turn out to have some advantages as we learn more about the way accounting works. Thus the statement of financial position looks like this:

| Left side: Resources (Assets) | Right side: Sources (Liabilities, Equity) |
|---|---|
| Increases: debits | Increases: credits |
| Decreases: credits | Decreases: debits |
| Sum of resources | = Sum of sources |
| Assets | = Liabilities + Equity |
| Debits | = Credits |

Most students are confused by these terms, debits and credits. To avoid this confusion, simply think of a debit as a left-hand side entry and a credit as a right-hand side entry. An analogy may assist. When you drive, you stop at red lights and go on green. This is a convention. If it had been set up the opposite way, the system would still work. However, changing the system now or doing the opposite has some disastrous effects. Similarly with debits and credits. They could have been set up the opposite way around, but they weren't.

Consider the following summary:

| Type of account | Normal balance | Increases result in | Decreases result in |
|---|---|---|---|
| Assets | Debit | Debit | Credit |
| Liabilities | Credit | Credit | Debit |
| Shareholders' equity | Credit | Credit | Debit |

This can be expressed in terms of the accounting equation as follows:

| Assets | | = | Liabilities | | + | Shareholders' equity | |
|---|---|---|---|---|---|---|---|
| Debit to increase | Credit to decrease | | Debit to decrease | Credit to increase | | Debit to decrease | Credit to increase |

*Every* transaction, without exception, has two (or more) effects. One requires a debit entry and one requires a credit entry. The recording of increases to assets on the debit side and decreases on the credit side is opposite to that of liabilities and shareholders' equity. It thus provides the additional control on accuracy, in that the sum of the debit balances must equal the sum of the credit balances.

To understand this process, you need to be aware of some terms:

- Accounting records certain kinds of events measured in the country's currency (dollars in Australia). We will call those events transactions, a word used a few times already.
- Accounting's way of recording transactions is called the entry and, as you will see in section 3.11, the method follows the double-entry record-keeping system described by Pacioli 500 years ago. (Entries are summarised in records usually called journals, so are also called journal entries.)
- The entries are transferred to and summarised in accounts, which lie behind all the amounts and descriptions shown on the statement of financial position. Each account has a numerical balance that is either a debit or a credit. (All the accounts collected together are usually referred to as a ledger.)
- As you know, it is important that all the accounts together produce a balanced balance sheet. Before preparing the balance sheet from the accounts, accountants usually make a list of the account balances from the ledger and make sure that the sum of all the debit

balances equals the sum of all the credit balances. Because you never know for sure if it will work, this list is called the trial balance!

- The financial statements are prepared.

In this chapter we concentrate on you mastering journal entries and provide a simple spreadsheet method of maintaining account balances. The use of such tools as ledgers and trial balances is left to chapter 4, when we describe the full accounting process.

## Two simple examples of double entry

### Purchasing, on credit, goods for resale

- The resource (an asset) is an addition to the enterprise's inventory (unsold products).
- The source (a liability) is that an obligation is created to pay the supplier.

If the goods cost, say, $452, we have:

- a debit of $452: an addition to the account for the resource, in this case the inventory of unsold products; and
- a credit of $452: an addition to the account for the source, in this case the obligation to the supplier, usually called accounts payable.

The statement of financial position stays in balance because of this double entry, because both resources and sources are increased (are 'up') by $452:

| **Resources** | **Sources** |
|---|---|
| Up (debit) $452 | Up (credit) $452 |
| Assets up $452 | Liabilities up $452 (no change in equity) |

### Borrowing money from the bank on a long-term loan

- The resource (asset) is an addition to the amount of cash on hand
- The source (a liability again) is that an obligation is created to repay the bank.

If the borrowed cash is, say, $1000, we have:

- an addition to the asset 'cash', so total resources go up $1000; and
- an addition to the liability 'long-term bank loan', so the total sources also go up $1000.

Again, the statement of financial position stays in balance:

| **Resources** | **Sources** |
|---|---|
| Up (debit) $1000 | Up (credit) $1000 |
| Assets up $1000 | Liabilities up $1000 (no change in equity) |

These transactions would be recorded as follows:

| | | | |
|---|---|---|---|
| DR | Inventory | 452 | |
| CR | Accounts payable | | 452 |
| DR | Cash | 1 000 | |
| CR | Bank loan | | 1 000 |

Note that debits are abbreviated DR and credits as CR as is customary.

## Summary

These are simple examples, but they illustrate several features of the bookkeeping system. (For hundreds of years, accounting records were kept in bound books. In spite of the advent of computers, 'books' are still used by many enterprises, as we will see.) Some features illustrated by the examples include:

- Each double-entry record names one (or more) accounts that are *debited*, and one (or more) that are *credited*. Accounts contain all the transaction records and any adjustments, and therefore reflect everything recorded in the system. The cash account, for example, lists all transactions and adjustments that have affected cash. Accounts are used directly in preparing the statements of financial position and statement of financial performance.
- The double-entry records shown in the example are called journal entries. A journal entry can list as many accounts as are needed to record the transaction, but for *each* journal entry, *the sum of the debits must equal the sum of the credits*. If not, the accounting equation will not be maintained (the 'books' will not balance).

## For your interest

An interesting aspect of a transaction is that, because it is an exchange, both parties to the exchange would record it, each from that party's point of view. If Enterprise A gains cash for a loan from Enterprise B, Enterprise A would record an increase in cash (a debit) and in a loan liability (a credit), while Enterprise B would record a decrease in cash (a credit) and an increase in an asset for the loan receivable, to be collected (a debit).

Here are examples of some exchanges and of how both parties would record the two aspects of each. There is a tradition of recording the debits first in the double entry; that is sometimes disregarded here, so that you can see the parallels between Party A's and Party B's records.

| **Party A** | | | **Party B** | | |
|---|---|---|---|---|---|
| **1 Bob borrows $1000 cash from the bank** | | | **The bank lends Bob $1000 cash** | | |
| Bob's records: | | | The bank's records: | | |
| *Debit* Cash | 1 000 | | *Credit* Cash | | 1 000 |
| *Credit* Loan payable | | 1 000 | *Debit* Loan receivable | 1 000 | |
| To record bank loan | | | To record loan to Bob | | |
| **2 Jan pays a $500 phone bill recorded earlier** | | | **The phone company receives the $500 cash** | | |
| Jan's records: | | | The phone company's records: | | |
| *Credit* Cash | | 500 | *Debit* Cash | 500 | |
| *Debit* Accounts payable | 500 | | *Credit* Accounts receivable | | 500 |
| To record payment of phone bill | | | To record receipt of cash from Jan | | |

## How's your understanding?

Here are two questions you should be able to answer, based on what you have just read:

1 What are the effects on the statement of financial position of the following transaction? Whatzis Ltd. received $20 000 cash from a shareholder in return for $5000 in newly

issued shares and promised to pay the shareholder the other $15 000 back at the end of three years. (Cash up $20 000; Share capital up $5 000; Long-term loan up $15 000. Result is total increase to assets $20 000, total increase to sources of assets $20 000.)

2 What is the journal entry to record the following transaction, in which Whatzis used the cash from the shareholder? The company bought a large truck, which cost $89 000, by putting $20 000 down in cash and financing (borrowing) the rest from the truck dealer's finance company. (DR Truck 89 000, CR Cash 20 000, CR Truck loan 69 000. Result is net total increase to assets $69 000; total increase to sources of assets $69 000. Total debits 89 000, total credits 89 000.)

## 3.6 More about accounts

The statement of financial position and statement of financial performance are prepared from the underlying accounts, which have been recorded using the double-entry system so that the sum of the dollars in all the debit accounts equals the sum in all the credit accounts. But what is an account, exactly? A working definition is: an account is a record of the dollar amounts comprising a particular asset, liability, equity, revenue or expense. The net effect of these amounts is a debit or credit, and is called the account's balance.

### For your interest

Another term used more than one way! Accountants use the word 'balance' to refer to the equality of the assets, liabilities and equity, as in 'the statement of financial position balances'. They also use it to refer to the net sum of the debits and credits recorded in an account, as in 'the cash account's balance is $xxx'.

Below are some examples of how account balances are calculated. Modern computerised accounting systems can produce accounts in various formats thought to be useful, but they all use the arithmetic illustrated below.

- If the enterprise's cash began at $500 and there was a receipt of $400 and one of $750, and a payment of $300 and one of $525, the cash asset account would show a balance of $825 (a debit because there is a positive balance in this asset account).
  Cash = $500 DR + $400 DR + $750 DR − $300 CR − $525 CR = $825 DR
- If share capital began at $1000 and more shares were sold for $400 (which, let's say, caused the cash receipt above), the share capital equity account would show a balance of $1400 (a credit because there is a positive balance in this equity account).
  Share capital = $1000CR + $400CR = $1400CR
- If amounts owing to trade creditors began at $950 and a creditor was paid $300 (the first payment above), the accounts payable liability account would show a balance of $650 (a credit because there is a positive balance in this liability account).
  Accounts payable = $950CR − $300DR = $650CR
- If a cash collection from a customer was made for $750 (the second cash receipt above), the accounts receivable account, with a balance of, say, $2000 before the collection, would reduce by an amount of $750 (a credit because this reduces the accounts receivable asset, which has been transformed into cash through the collection transaction).
  Accounts receivable = $2000DR − $750CR = $1250DR

- If a $525 cash payment (the second cash payment above) was made on the company's bank loan, a liability account with a name like 'bank loan' would be debited with this payment. Suppose the loan had a balance of $15 000 before the payment. Then the account balance would be calculated to show the deduction of the payment.
  Bank loan (part of liabilities) = $15 000CR – $525DR = $14 475CR

## How's your understanding?

Here are two questions you should be able to answer, based on what you have just read:

1 Garf Pty Ltd had accounts receivable at the beginning of the year of $5290. During the year, it had revenue from sales on credit of $39 620 and collected $41 080 from its customers. What was the balance of accounts receivable at the end of the year? ($3830)

2 Garf Pty Ltd's net profit for this year was $2940, and it declared $900 in dividends to its shareholders during the year. Retained profits were $7410 at the beginning of the year. What are retained profits at the end of the year, after closing? ($9450)

## 3.7 How debits and credits work

Let's consider an example, CappuMania Pty Ltd, a small company that operates a coffee shop on the ground floor of an office building. At the end of March 2002, the company's statement of financial position was shown in exhibit 3.6.

- These accounts are assets, so have *debit* balances:
  cash, inventory of unsold food, inventory of supplies, and equipment.
- This account is deducted from an asset (it is often called a contra asset), so has a *credit* balance:
  Accumulated depreciation.
- These accounts are liabilities and equities, so have *credit* balances:
  accounts payable, taxes payable, loan, share capital, and retained profits.

Now let's see how the following four transactions, all happening on 1 April 2002, are recorded using accounting's double-entry method (ignoring the details of the particular computer or manual record-keeping system):

1 CappuMania pays $500 of its taxes owing.

2 CappuMania buys $450 more supplies, paying $100 cash and owing the rest.

3 A shareholder is given more shares in return for personally paying $1100 on the equipment loan.

4 CappuMania buys a new coffee machine for $200 cash.

Let's look at the entries.

1 *Resource effect:* Cash is reduced. Cash is an asset, so a decrease in an asset would be a credit.
*Source effect:* Tax liability is reduced. A liability is reduced, so the effect would be a debit.
*Entry*:

| | | $ | $ |
|---|---|---|---|
| DR | Taxes payable (liability) | 500 | |
| CR | Cash (asset) | | 500 |

**EXHIBIT 3.6** CappuMania Pty Ltd

**Statement of financial position as at 31 March 2002**

| **Assets** | | **Liabilities and shareholders' equity** | |
|---|---|---|---|
| | **$** | | **$** |
| **Current assets** | | **Current liabilities** | |
| Cash | 4 000 | Accounts payable | 1 200 |
| Inventory of unsold food | 800 | Taxes payable | 600 |
| Inventory of supplies | 1 900 | | 1 800 |
| | 6 700 | | |
| | | **Noncurrent liabilities** | |
| **Noncurrent assets** | | Loan | 5 000 |
| Equipment | 9 000 | | 6 800 |
| Accumulated depreciation | (1 500) | | |
| | 7 500 | **Shareholders' equity** | |
| | | Share capital | 3 000 |
| | | Retained profits | 4 400 |
| | | | 7 400 |
| | 14 200 | | 14 200 |

*Double-entry method:* There is both a DR and a CR and the two are the same. (The tradition is to list the DR(s) first in an entry.)

2 *Resource effects:* Inventory is increased $450. It is an asset, and an increase in asset is a debit. Cash is decreased $100 so this is a credit, as above.
*Source effect:* The liability to suppliers is increased $350. An increase in a liability results in a credit.
*Entry:*

| | | $ | $ |
|---|---|---|---|
| DR | Inventory of supplies (asset) | 450 | |
| CR | Cash (asset) | | 100 |
| CR | Accounts payable (liability) | | 350 |

*Double-entry method:* There are both DRs and CRs, and the sum of the DRs equals the sum of the CRs. (An entry can have any number of DRs and CRs as long as the sums of each are equal.) Note that this debit entry could have been achieved by two entries:

| | | $ | $ |
|---|---|---|---|
| DR | Inventory of supplies | 100 | |
| CR | Cash | | 100 |
| DR | Inventory of supplies | 350 | |
| CR | Accounts payable | | 350 |

3 *Resource effect:* None.
*Source effects:* The equipment loan, a liability, is decreased $1100, so this is a debit. The share capital, an equity, is increased $1100, so this is a credit.

*Entry*:

| | | $ | $ |
|---|---|---|---|
| DR | Loan (liability) | 1 100 | |
| CR | Share capital (equity) | | 1 100 |

*Double-entry method:* This transaction affects only the right side of the statement of financial position, but the statement stays in balance because one account on the right side goes up and another goes down.

4 *Resource effects:* Equipment, an asset, is increased $200, so this is a debit. Cash is decreased $200, which is a credit as in transactions 1 and 2.
*Source effect:* None.
*Entry*:

| | | $ | $ |
|---|---|---|---|
| DR | Equipment (asset) | 200 | |
| CR | Cash (asset) | | 200 |

*Double-entry method:* This transaction also affects only one side of the statement of financial position – this time, the assets side – but again the balanced entry keeps the statement of financial position in balance.

These journal entries form part of the accounting cycle, which records accounting transactions. The sequences of procedures by which these transactions enter the financial statements are discussed in chapter 4. For an illustration of how a journal entry affects the statement of financial position, these entries are recorded here by adding them to, or subtracting them from, the previous (31 March) balances in the accounts. This is done in exhibit 3.7, using a computer spreadsheet format (in this case, Microsoft Excel®, but the particular spreadsheet does not matter). Arbitrarily, the debits are recorded as positive and the credits as negative. This does not mean debits are good and credits are bad! It is simply an accounting convention.

You can see from the spreadsheet that at 31 March the total of adding all the debits and subtracting all the credits is zero. The transaction entries are in balance because the sum of the debits equals the sum of the credits. The 1 April debit balances also equal the credit balances.

It would be unlikely that another statement of financial position would be prepared, just one day after the 31 March one, but to complete the example, let's see how the debit balances would also equal the credit balances, after recording the four transactions (exhibit 3.8).

## How's your understanding?

Suppose that on 1 April 2002 a fifth transaction had occurred: CappuMania paid $800 on its loan. What would the following revised figures have been on the 1 April 2002 statement of financial position: cash, current assets, total assets, total liabilities and shareholders' equity? ($2400; $5550; $13 250; $4750; $8500)

**EXHIBIT 3.7** CappuMania Pty Ltd

**Example in spreadsheet form**

| | A | B | C | D | | E | | F |
|---|---|---|---|---|---|---|---|---|
| 1 | | | | | | | | |
| 2 | | | | | | | | |
| 3 | | | March 31/02 | | | | | April 1/02 |
| 4 | | | Balance | Transactions* | | | | Balance |
| 5 | | | Debit or credit | Debits | | Credits | | Debit or credit |
| 6 | | | | | | | | |
| 7 | Cash | | 4 000 | | | (1) | -500 | 3 200 |
| 8 | | | | | | (2) | -100 | |
| 9 | | | | | | (4) | -200 | |
| 10 | Inventory of unsold food | | 800 | | | | | 800 |
| 11 | Inventory of supplies | | 1 900 | (2) | 450 | | | 2 350 |
| 12 | Equipment | | 9 000 | (4) | 200 | | | 9 200 |
| 13 | Accumulated depreciation | | −1 500 | | | | | −1 500 |
| 14 | Accounts payable | | −1 200 | | | (2) | −350 | −1 550 |
| 15 | Taxes payable | | −600 | (1) | 500 | | | −100 |
| 16 | Loan | | −5 000 | (3) | 1 100 | | | −3 900 |
| 17 | Share capital | | −3 000 | | | (3) | −1 100 | −4 100 |
| 18 | Retained profits | | -4 400 | | | | | -4 400 |
| 19 | | | | | | | | |
| 20 | **Total** | | **0** | | **2 250** | | **−2 250** | **0** |

* The numbers in brackets have been added to the spreadsheet printout to refer to the events and transactions described in the text.

## 3.8 Debits and credits, revenues and expenses

In section 3.6, you saw how entries and accounts were used to record events as transactions in the double-entry accounting system. In the CappuMania Pty Ltd example, this was limited to statement of financial position accounts. Let's expand the example to bring in revenue and expense accounts.

To keep the example uncluttered, we group all the company's activities for the year ended 31 March 2003 into the following summary list.

First, the economic events to be recorded:

1 Revenue for 2003 was $89 740. The coffee bar does mostly cash business, so of this, $85 250 was in cash and the rest was on credit.
2 General expenses for 2003, not including depreciation or income tax, totalled $67 230. Most of the expenses were on credit, for coffee supplies and so on, so of this, only $2120 was in cash.
3 At the end of the year, it turned out that unsold food on hand cost $550 and supplies on hand (mainly paper cups and plastic spoons) cost $1740. Therefore, the food inventory account has to be reduced by $250 ($800 – $550) and the supplies inventory account has to be reduced by $610 ($2350 – $1740). Using up these inventories is part of the cost of earning revenue, so these reductions will be included in the company's

**EXHIBIT 3.8** CappuMania Pty Ltd

**Statement of financial position as at 1 April 2002**

| **Assets** | | **Liabilities and shareholders' equity** | |
|---|---|---|---|
| | **$** | | **$** |
| **Current assets** | | **Current liabilities** | |
| Cash | 3 200 | Accounts payable | 1 550 |
| Inventory of unsold food | 800 | Taxes payable | 100 |
| Inventory of supplies | 2 350 | | 1 650 |
| | **6 350** | | |
| | | **Noncurrent liabilities** | |
| **Noncurrent assets** | | Loan | 3 900 |
| Equipment | 9 200 | | **5 550** |
| Accumulated depreciation | (1 500) | | |
| | **7 700** | **Shareholders' equity** | |
| | | Share capital | 4 100 |
| | | Retained profits | 4 400 |
| | | | **8 500** |
| | **14 050** | | **14 050** |

general expenses. We could have described these expenses here as a cost of goods sold expense (abbreviated COGS) and put them as a separate expense category.

**4** Depreciation expense for the year was $2380.

**5** The company's income tax expense for 2003 was estimated as $4460. (This is an estimate because, until the income tax authorities issue a formal assessment of tax, the company does not know for sure what its tax will be for the year.)

**6** The company's board of directors declared a dividend of $1000.

Cash inflows and outflows by 31 March 2003 not already mentioned:

**7** Collections of the revenue on credit totalled $3330.

**8** Payments to suppliers totalled $59 420.

**9** The company paid $3000 toward its income tax.

**10** Only $800 of the dividend had been paid.

Before recording these transactions, we will extend the debit/credit rules to revenue and expense items. To help you understand the entries, remember that because profit is a part of retained profits, which is an equity account and therefore a credit account on the statement of financial position, anything that helps profit is a credit. A revenue is therefore a credit balance account. Conversely, anything that reduces profit reduces retained profits and equity, and is therefore a debit. An expense is therefore a debit balance account. When dividends are declared, they are deducted from retained profits, therefore such deductions are debits because they reduce equity. All this produces the following table of double-entry accounting's debits and credits:

| **Debits** | **Credits** |
|---|---|
| Increases in assets | Decreases in assets |
| Decreases in liabilities | Increases in liabilities |
| Decreases in equity: | Increases in equity: |
| Dividends declared | Contributed capital |
| Expenses | Revenues |

For completeness, the summary provided in section 3.5 is extended as shown below:

| Type of account | Normal balance | Increases result in | Decreases result in |
|---|---|---|---|
| Assets | Debit | Debit | Credit |
| Liabilities | Credit | Credit | Debit |
| Share capital | Credit | Credit | Debit |
| Retained profits | Credit | Credit | Debit |
| Revenues | Credit | Credit | Debit |
| Expenses | Debit | Debit | Credit |

Note that one way of decreasing retained profits is to declare a dividend, which results in a debit entry.

To further demonstrate this, the accounting equation can be rewritten in T-account format as follows:

| Assets | | = | Liabilities | | + | Shareholders' equity | |
|---|---|---|---|---|---|---|---|
| Debit to increase | Credit to decrease | | Debit to decrease | Credit to increase | | Debit to decrease | Credit to increase |

Increases in assets are debits; increases in liabilities or shareholders' equity are credits. As noted earlier, shareholders' equity accounts include share capital, retained profits, revenue and expenses. Remember, increases in expenses reduce shareholders' equity and are therefore debits, while an increase in revenue increases shareholders' equity and is therefore a credit. Therefore the revenue and expense accounts can be shown as:

| Revenue | | Expenses | |
|---|---|---|---|
| Debit to decrease | Credit to increase | Debit to increase | Credit to decrease |

Here are the journal entries for the ten items given earlier:

| | | DR<br>$ | CR<br>$ |
|---|---|---|---|
| 1 | **Revenue** | | |
| | Cash (assets increased) | 85 250 | |
| | Accounts receivable (assets increased) | 4 490 | |
| | Revenue (equity increased) | | 89 740 |
| 2 | **General expenses** | | |
| | General expenses (equity decreased) | 67 230 | |
| | Cash (assets decreased) | | 2 120 |
| | Accounts payable (liabilities increased) | | 65 110 |
| 3 | **Using up of inventories** | | |
| | General expenses (equity decreased) | 250 | |
| | Inventory of unsold food (assets decreased) | | 250 |
| | General expenses (equity decreased) | 610 | |
| | Inventory of supplies (assets decreased) | | 610 |
| 4 | **Depreciation of equipment** | | |
| | Depreciation expense (equity decreased) | 2 380 | |
| | Accumulated depreciation (assets decreased) | | 2 380 |

| | | | |
|---|---|---|---|
| 5 | **Estimated income tax expense** | | |
| | Income tax expense (equity decreased) | 4 460 | |
| | Taxes payable (liabilities increased) | | 4 460 |
| 6 | **Dividend declared** | | |
| | Retained profits (equity decreased) | 1 000 | |
| | Dividend payable (liabilities increased) | | 1 000 |
| 7 | **Collections of accounts receivable** | | |
| | Cash (assets increased) | 3 330 | |
| | Accounts receivable (assets decreased) | | 3 330 |
| 8 | **Payments of accounts payable** | | |
| | Accounts payable (liabilities decreased) | 59 420 | |
| | Cash (assets decreased) | | 59 420 |
| 9 | **Payments toward income tax** | | |
| | Taxes payable (liabilities decreased) | 3 000 | |
| | Cash (assets decreased) | | 3 000 |
| 10 | **Payment toward dividend** | | |
| | Dividend payable (liabilities decreased) | 800 | |
| | Cash (assets decreased) | | 800 |

We can enter these ten entries to the company's accounts, using the spreadsheet basis you saw in section 3.6. The resulting spreadsheet is shown in exhibit 3.9. Note that the 1 April 2002 figures, which are what we ended up with in exhibit 3.7, are now in the first column, as the starting figures. Some new accounts (such as accounts receivable and revenue) are needed to record the entries: the titles of these are shown in italics.

You can see that everything is still in balance. The sums of the debits and credits in the ten entries are $232 220, and the 31 March 2003 accounts add up to zero (remember that, arbitrarily, debits are shown as positive amounts and credits as negative ones).

To highlight the calculation of profit from the expanded set of accounts, a second version of the spreadsheet is shown in exhibit 3.10. It is the same as in exhibit 3.9, except that the statement of financial position accounts and the profit and loss accounts (part of the statement of financial performance) are now separately subtotalled. You will see that profit (the difference between the revenue and expense accounts) equals $14 810. It is a credit, which is what equity is. Also note that, without the revenue and expense accounts, the statement of financial position accounts are out of balance by the same $14 810. In chapter 4 you will see how these revenue and expense accounts are closed off. A separate note will show that the profit figure will be transferred to retained profits, that is, opening retained profits plus net profit for the year minus dividend declared equals closing retained profits (4400 + 14 810 – 1000 = 18 210). $18 210 will appear as the balance of the retained profits account in the statement of financial position.

The company's statement of financial performance showing profit for the year is shown in exhibit 3.11. The statement of financial position is given in exhibit 3.12.

This example has illustrated how accounting accumulates information about activities and how the financial statements are prepared from the accounts that are produced as the information is accumulated.

You can see how the two financial statements fit together (articulate) because they are all based on the double-entry accounting system:

**EXHIBIT 3.9** CappuMania Pty Ltd

**Example in spreadsheet form (continued)**

| | A | B | C | D | | E | | F |
|---|---|---|---|---|---|---|---|---|
| 1 | | | | | | | | |
| 2 | | | | | | | | |
| 3 | | | April 1/02 | | Events and | | Events and | March 31/03 |
| 4 | | | Balance | | Transactions* | | Transactions | Trial balance |
| 5 | | | Debit or credit | | Debit | | Credit | Debit or credit |
| 6 | | | | | | | | |
| 7 | Cash | | 3 200 | (1) | 85 250 | (2) | -2 120 | 26 440 |
| 8 | | | | (7) | 3 330 | (8) | -59 420 | |
| 9 | | | | | | (9) | -3 000 | |
| 10 | | | | | | (10) | -800 | |
| 11 | *Accounts receivable* | | 0 | (1) | 4 490 | (7) | -3 330 | 1 160 |
| 12 | Inventory of unsold food | | 800 | | | (3) | -250 | 550 |
| 13 | Inventory of supplies | | 2 350 | | | (3) | -610 | 1 740 |
| 14 | Equipment | | 9 200 | | | | | 9 200 |
| 15 | Accumulated depreciation | | -1 500 | | | (4) | -2 380 | -3 880 |
| 16 | Accounts payable | | -1 550 | (8) | 59 420 | (2) | -65 110 | -7 240 |
| 17 | Taxes payable | | -100 | (9) | 3 000 | (5) | -4 460 | -1 560 |
| 18 | *Dividend payable* | | 0 | (10) | 800 | (6) | -1 000 | -200 |
| 19 | Loan | | -3 900 | | | | | -3 900 |
| 20 | Share capital | | -4 100 | | | | | -4 100 |
| 21 | Retained profits | | -4 400 | (6) | 1 000 | | | -3 400 |
| 22 | *Revenue* | | 0 | | | (1) | -89 740 | -89 740 |
| 23 | *General expenses* | | 0 | (2) | 67 230 | | | 68 090 |
| 24 | | | | (3) | 250 | | | |
| 25 | | | | (3) | 610 | | | |
| 26 | *Depreciation expense* | | 0 | (4) | 2 380 | | | 2 380 |
| 27 | *Income tax expense* | | 0 | (5) | 4 460 | | | 4 460 |
| 28 | | | | | | | | |
| 29 | **Totals** | | **0** | | **232 220** | | **-232 220** | **0** |

* The numbers in brackets have been added to the spreadsheet printout to refer to the ten events and transactions described in the text.

- A set of accounts is created which is in balance (sum of all the debit account balances = sum of all the credit account balances).
- From these accounts are produced:
  - the statement of financial performance (profit and loss statement), the bottom line net profit after tax of which is transferred to
  - a note to the accounts showing a statement of retained profits, the bottom line ending retained profits of which is transferred to
  - the statement of financial position (balance sheet), which summarises all the accounts.

**EXHIBIT 3.10** CappuMania Pty Ltd

Example in spreadsheet form (continued) (with subtotals to show profit calculation)

| | A | B | C | D | E | F |
|---|---|---|---|---|---|---|
| 39 | | | | | | |
| 40 | | | | | | |
| 41 | | | April 1/02 | Events and | Events and | March 31/03 |
| 42 | | | Trial balance | transactions | transactions | balance |
| 43 | | | Debit or credit | Debit | Credit | Debit or credit |
| 44 | | | | | | |
| 45 | Cash | | 3 200 | 85 250 | -2 120 | 26 440 |
| 46 | | | | 3 330 | -59 420 | |
| 47 | | | | | -3 000 | |
| 48 | | | | | -800 | |
| 49 | *Accounts receivable* | | 0 | 4 490 | -3 330 | 1 160 |
| 50 | Inventory of unsold food | | 800 | | -250 | 550 |
| 51 | Inventory of supplies | | 2 350 | | -610 | 1 740 |
| 52 | Equipment | | 9 200 | | | 9 200 |
| 53 | Accumulated depreciation | | -1 500 | | -2 380 | -3 880 |
| 54 | Accounts payable | | -1 550 | 59 420 | -65 110 | -7 240 |
| 55 | Taxes payable | | -100 | 3 000 | -4 460 | -1 560 |
| 56 | *Dividend payable* | | 0 | 800 | -1 000 | -200 |
| 57 | Loan | | -3 900 | | | -3 900 |
| 58 | Share capital | | -4 100 | | | -4 100 |
| 59 | Retained profits | | -4 400 | 1 000 | | -3 400 |
| 60 | **Statement of Financial Position subtotals** | | **0** | **157 290** | **-142 480** | **14 810** |
| 61 | *Revenue* | | 0 | | -89 740 | -89 740 |
| 62 | *General expenses* | | 0 | 67 230 | | 68 090 |
| 63 | | | | 250 | | |
| 64 | | | | 610 | | |
| 65 | *Depreciation expense* | | 0 | 2 380 | | 2 380 |
| 66 | *Income tax expense* | | 0 | 4 460 | | 4 460 |
| 67 | **Profit and Loss subtotals** | | **0** | **74 930** | **-89 740** | **-14 810** |
| 68 | | | | | | |
| 69 | **Totals** | | **0** | **232 220** | **-232 220** | **0** |

Activities affecting profit therefore affect the statement of financial position through the double-entry system. Looking back at the entries above, for example:

- Entry 1 increased the statement of financial position's assets and increased revenue on the statement of financial performance (thereby also increasing profit, which is transferred to retained profits, therefore increasing equity, which keeps the statement of financial position in balance).
- Entry 2 decreased the statement of financial position's assets and increased its liabilities and increased expenses on the statement of financial performance (thereby also decreasing profit, therefore decreasing equity, which keeps the statement of financial position in balance).

You will see this sort of relationship among the financial statements many times. It is the basis of one of the most important uses of financial statements: analysing the financial statements in order to evaluate financial performance and financial position.

**EXHIBIT 3.11**

**CappuMania Pty Ltd**

**Statement of financial performance year ended 31 March 2003**

| | $ | $ |
|---|---|---|
| Revenue | | 89 740 |
| Expenses | | |
| General | 68 090 | |
| Depreciation | 2 380 | 70 470 |
| Net profit before income tax | | 19 270 |
| Income tax expense | | 4 460 |
| **Net profit after tax** | | **14 810** |

**EXHIBIT 3.12**

**CappuMania Pty Ltd**

**Statement of financial position as at 31 March 2003**

| **Assets** | | **Liabilities and shareholders' equity** | |
|---|---|---|---|
| | $ | | $ |
| **Current assets** | | **Current liabilities** | |
| Cash | 26 440 | Accounts payable | 7 240 |
| Accounts receivable | 1 160 | Taxes payable | 1 560 |
| Inventory of unsold food | 550 | Dividend payable | 200 |
| Inventory of supplies | 1 740 | | 9 000 |
| | **29 890** | | |
| | | **Noncurrent liabilities** | |
| **Noncurrent assets** | | Loan | 3 900 |
| Equipment | 9 200 | **Total liabilities** | **12 900** |
| Accumulated depreciation | (3 880) | | |
| | **5 320** | **Shareholders' equity** | |
| | | Share capital | 4 100 |
| | | Retained profits* | 18 210 |
| | | **Total shareholders' equity** | **22 310** |
| **Total assets** | **35 210** | **Total liabilities and SE** | **35 210** |

* Opening balance + Net profit – Dividends declared = Closing balance 4 400 + 14 810 – 1 000 = 18 210

## How's your understanding?

Here are two questions you should be able to answer, based on what you have just read:

1 At the end of 2001, Hinton Hats Pty Ltd had retained profits of $29 490. During 2002, it had revenue of $112 350, general expenses of $91 170, depreciation expense of $6210 and income tax expense of $3420. Dividends of $5000 were declared during 2002. What was the balance of retained profits at the end of 2002? (Your answer should be $36 040.)

2 The company's first event in 2003 was to pay $1200 cash for the rent on its store for the first month of 2003. What did this event do to: assets, liabilities, profit for 2003, retained profits, equity? (Your answers should be: down $1200; no effect; down $1200; down $1200; down $1200.)

## 3.9 Arranging accounts on the statement of financial position

In the Sound and Light example (chapter 2) and CappuMania example (chapter 3), you saw that accounts were organised into the statement's main categories: current assets, noncurrent assets, current liabilities, noncurrent liabilities and equity. This was done because the arrangement of accounts is meant to convey information beyond the account balances themselves. The placement of each account tells the reader of the statement of financial position what kind of account it is: a short-term asset, or a long-term one, a short-term liability or a long-term one, or an equity. This enables the calculation of meaningful ratios and other analyses. The statement of financial position is said to be classified, because accounts are classified into meaningful categories. This means that the accountant preparing the statement of financial position has to look into an account with a title like 'bank loan', for example, and determine whether it should be included in current liabilities or noncurrent liabilities. Moving items around within the statement of financial position (or within other financial statements) is called reclassification, and is done by accountants whenever it is thought to improve the informativeness of the financial statement.

### Three examples of account classification

#### Current and noncurrent portions of noncurrent liabilities

Many noncurrent liabilities, such as mortgages, bonds and debentures, require regular payments, so although most of the debt is noncurrent, not all of it is. Accountants therefore reclassify the amount to be paid on the principal of the debt within the next year into current liabilities, and show only the residual (due more than a year away) as noncurrent. (An interest owing but not yet paid would be treated as a separate liability. If it is due to be paid within the year it is a current liability.)

#### Bank overdrafts

Suppose a company has a bank overdraft of $500, which means that its cash-in-bank asset is negative (the bank has allowed the company to remove $500 more cash from the account than there was in it, in effect lending the company the $500). The company's other assets total $12 400. Its net assets are therefore $11 900, and this is also the total of its liabilities and owners' equity.

There are at least two ways of presenting this information:

| | | |
|---|---|---|
| Other assets of $12 400 minus bank overdraft of $500 | = | Liabilities and owners' equity of $11 900 |
| or | | |
| Other assets of $12 400 | = | Liabilities and owners' equity of $11 900 plus bank overdraft of $500 |

For bank overdrafts, it is customary to use the second method, to move the negative bank amount to the other side of the statement of financial position. Even if the company normally has cash in the bank so that the account is normally an asset, the account is a liability at this point because the bank has, in effect, lent the company $500 and will want the money back.

### Negative amounts left as deductions

Some negative amounts are left as deductions, not moved to the other side to make them positive, as was done with the overdraft. Accumulated depreciation is an important example of a negative-balance account. It is the amount of all the depreciation calculated to date on assets such as buildings and equipment. For accumulated depreciation, there are at least three ways of presenting the information, all of which maintain the balance sheet equation:

- It could be shown on the right side of the statement of financial position (in former times, it was, and in some countries, still is).
- Separate disclosure as a deduction on the left side of the statement of financial position as was used in the Sound and Light and CappuMania statements of financial position. This is very common, but if there are a lot of different kinds of assets and depreciation amounts, it can make the statement of financial position a little cluttered.
- It could be deducted from the assets' cost and just the net book value could be disclosed on the statement of financial position, so that accumulated depreciation is not mentioned on the face of the statement. This method, which is becoming quite popular, would be accompanied by a note to the financial statements, listing the cost and accumulated depreciation amounts separately, so keeping the statement of financial position uncluttered and allowing some additional explanations of the figures if that were thought useful.

## How's your understanding?

Here are two questions you should be able to answer, based on what you have just read:

1 Why are accounts classified, and sometimes reclassified, as they are on the statement of financial position?

2 Prepare a statement of financial position for Mike's Tyre Repair Pty Ltd from the following amounts: cash on hand, $90; bank overdraft, $120; accounts receivable, $640; inventory, $210; equipment cost, $890; accumulated depreciation on equipment, $470; accounts payable, $360; owner's equity, $880. (You should show the first, third, fourth and fifth amounts as positive assets and the sixth as a negative asset, with (net) total assets of $1360. The second and seventh amounts are liabilities, totalling $480, and equity equals $880, so that the total of liabilities and equity is also $1360.)

# 3.10 More journal entries

You will discover further in chapter 4 that the accounting process is reasonably mechanical once you have created your journal entries. Creating journal entries is very critical to your general understanding of accounting. The better you understand this and the earlier sections that gave you the knowledge to do this section, the easier you will find the rest of the course. A few extra hours on this material will save you many more hours later in this subject and subsequent subjects.

Let's go back to the LRM example from sections 3.3 and 3.4 and prepare the journal entries. The 14 transactions are repeated here for convenience.

1. Shareholders invest $200 000 cash in the business.
2. Land and building is purchased for $300 000, which is financed by a loan from the seller repayable in five years.
3. Inventory worth $50 000 is bought on account.
4. Equipment worth $90 000 is purchased, paying $20 000 cash and signing an agreement to pay the remainder in 90 days.
5. Damaged inventory, which was purchased on credit at a cost of $5000, was returned to the supplier.
6. Paid $30 000 on accounts payable.
7. Purchased $10 000 inventory for cash.
8. Cash sales of $30 000 were made. The cost of the goods that were sold amounted to $12 000.
9. Credit sales of $40 000 were made. The cost of goods sold was $16 000.
10. Payments of $8000 were made to suppliers.
11. Paid wages for the first two weeks of April for $20 000.
12. Received an advertising invoice for $2000 for a radio advertisement broadcast on 5 April. The bill will be paid next month.
13. Received $25 000 from accounts receivable.
14. At the end of the month, $18 000 is owing in wages for the last two weeks of the month. It is due to be paid on 1 May.

Below are the relevant journal entries and the reason for the debit and credit entries. Before looking at these journal entries, try to do them. If you are not getting them correct, go back to sections 3.3 and 3.4 for further detail on how the transactions affect the specific accounts.

## Journal entries for LRM Ltd

| | | $ | $ |
|---|---|---|---|
| 1 | DR Cash | 200 000 | |
| | CR Share capital | | 200 000 |
| Reason: | Cash (asset) increases; share capital (shareholders' equity) increases | | |
| 2 | DR Land and buildings | 300 000 | |
| | CR Long-term loan | | 300 000 |
| Reason: | Land and buildings (asset) increases; long-term loan (liability) increases | | |
| 3 | DR Inventory | 50 000 | |
| | CR Accounts payable | | 50 000 |
| Reason: | Inventory (asset) increases; accounts payable (liability) increases | | |

| | | | | |
|---|---|---|---|---|
| **4** | DR | Equipment | 90 000 | |
| | CR | Cash | | 20 000 |
| | CR | Notes payable | | 70 000 |
| Reason: | Equipment (asset) increases; cash (asset) decreases; notes payable (liability) increases | | | |
| **5** | DR | Accounts payable | 5 000 | |
| | CR | Inventory | | 5 000 |
| Reason: | Accounts payable (liability) decreases; inventory (asset) decreases | | | |
| **6** | DR | Accounts payable | 30 000 | |
| | CR | Cash | | 30 000 |
| Reason: | Accounts payable (liability) decreases; cash (asset) decreases | | | |
| **7** | DR | Inventory | 10 000 | |
| | CR | Cash | | 10 000 |
| Reason: | Inventory (asset) increases; cash (asset) decreases | | | |
| **8** | DR | Cash | 30 000 | |
| | CR | Sales revenue | | 30 000 |
| | DR | Cost of goods sold | 12 000 | |
| | CR | Inventory | | 12 000 |
| Reason: | Cash (asset) increases; sales revenue (revenue) increases; cost of goods sold (expense) increases; inventory (asset) decreases | | | |
| **9** | DR | Accounts receivable | 40 000 | |
| | CR | Sales revenue | | 40 000 |
| | DR | Cost of goods sold | 16 000 | |
| | CR | Inventory | | 16 000 |
| Reason: | Accounts receivable (asset) increases; sales revenue (revenue) increases; cost of goods sold (expense) increases; inventory (asset) decreases | | | |
| **10** | DR | Accounts payable | 8 000 | |
| | CR | Cash | | 8 000 |
| Reason: | Accounts payable (liability) decreases; cash (asset) decreases | | | |
| **11** | DR | Wages expense | 20 000 | |
| | CR | Cash | | 20 000 |
| Reason: | Wages expense (expense) increases; cash (asset) decreases | | | |

| | | | |
|---|---|---|---|
| **12** | DR Advertising expense | 2 000 | |
| | CR Accounts payable | | 2 000 |
| Reason: | Advertising expense (expense) increases; accounts payable (liability) increases | | |
| **13** | DR Cash | 25 000 | |
| | CR Accounts receivable | | 25 000 |
| Reason: | Cash (asset) increases; accounts receivable (asset) decreases | | |
| **14** | DR Wages expense | 18 000 | |
| | CR Wages payable | | 18 000 |
| Reason: | Wages expense (expense) increases; wages payable (liability) increases | | |

## 3.11 A brief history of early accounting

With the above overview of the double-entry accounting system we now provide a history review, because understanding how we got to where we are helps a lot in understanding why we do the things we do now and how to do them. Financial accounting is an ancient information system, with many of its ideas originating hundreds of years ago.

Like other complex human inventions, financial accounting did not just appear one day fully formed. It has developed over thousands of years and has been thoroughly intertwined with the development of civilisation. A science writer, quoting a brewery owner, had this to say on the topic of accounting and beer:

> Whatever the reason, [the early farmers in Mesopotamia] grew grain [and] 'if you have grain, you need storehouses; if you have storehouses, you need accountants; if you have accountants, bang – you're on the road to civilisation' (or the world's first audit).[1]

Our focus here is on accounting, not on history. Nevertheless, the past has a bearing on accounting, in that accounting evolves as business, government and other institutions in society evolve. As the needs for information change, accounting changes to meet those needs. Accounting's evolution is not always smooth, and not always efficient; at any given time there are aspects of accounting that may not seem to fit current needs well, but over time we can expect that accounting will, as it has in the past, meet those needs if they persist.

When commerce consisted mainly of trading among families or tribal units, information demands were not complicated. Money had not been invented, so even the simple financial reports you saw in chapter 1 could not have been prepared. People would want to know what they had on hand and would need some sort of documentation to accompany shipments, so that they and their customers would agree on what was being traded. To meet such needs, accounting began as simple list-making. Especially important would be lists of the family's or tribe's resources and, later, lists of debts to other tribes or families. Later still, as commercial activities became more complex, families began to employ others to run aspects of their businesses and began also to create large business units with several locations. Accounting had to become more complex too, providing records that could be used to monitor the activities of employees and businesses in farflung locations. People found that they needed to be able to verify what employees and traders said was happening. Because of these needs, the practice of having systematic records that could be audited later was begun.

To help you understand how present-day financial accounting concepts and techniques arose, we start with a brief history taking us from about 4500 BC in Mesopotamia to the early AD 1800s in England. We then cover the two succeeding centuries, bringing the history up to the present. Keep in mind that the purpose of the review is to help you understand accounting, not to explain general history.

Because modern accrual accounting, as practised in Australia and much of the rest of the world, has its roots in the development of Western civilisation, our review of accounting history is oriented to that development. The interesting stories of the development of accounting in other parts of the world, such as China, India and Africa, are therefore not included. The comments below are necessarily brief. If you would like to read further, some reading suggestions on accounting history are provided at the end of the chapter.[2]

## Mesopotamia to Rome: from 4500 BC to AD 400

For a society to demand accounting it must have active trade and commerce, a basic level of writing, methods of measuring and calculating and a medium of exchange or currency.[3] The earliest known civilisation with an active record-keeping system flourished in Mesopotamia (now Iraq and Syria). Generally, a common language (such as Babylonian) existed for business, and there was also a good system of numbers and currency and of record-keeping using clay tablets.

As far as we know, ordinary merchants and general traders did not keep official records. Officials of the government and religious leaders of the temples decided what records were to be maintained for official purposes, and scribes did the record-keeping. A scribe was apprenticed for many years to master the craft of recording taxes, customs duties, temple offerings and trade between governments and temples. Records consisted of counts and lists of grain, cattle and other resources, and of obligations arising from trade. We can still see that today: the statement of financial position (balance sheet) of any enterprise includes items such as unsold products and equipment, and trade obligations such as amounts due from customers and due to suppliers. All of these figures are summaries supported by detailed lists.

When a scribe determined that a particular record was complete and correct, the scribe's seal was pressed into a clay tablet to certify that this was so, and the tablet was baked to prevent alteration.[4] The scribe was a forerunner of today's accountants and auditors. (However, today's auditors do not use seals; instead, they sign an audit report to indicate that the financial statements are fairly presented.) This scribe-based form of record-keeping was used for many years, spreading across land and time to Egypt, Greece and Rome. Media other than clay tablets, such as papyrus, were used as time passed.[5] (Do you suppose people accustomed to clay tablets would have resisted the introduction of papyrus, just as some people accustomed to pencil and paper now resist the introduction of computers for accounting?)

Trade and commerce grew over thousands of years, from small family operations to very large activities involving kings, religious leaders and various levels of government. For example, as the Greek civilisation spread and then the Roman Empire grew very large, administrative regions were organised in conquered lands in order to simplify governing them. These regions were managed by local administrators or governors, who generally could neither read nor write. When an accounting of their management was required, an official of the central government would come out and listen to an oral report. This event was, therefore, a 'hearing', and the listening official was there to 'audit' (from the Latin word for 'hear'). Today, the person who comes to inspect and approve the financial statements of an enterprise is called an auditor, though a lot more goes on today than just listening.

## The Dark Ages to the Renaissance: from AD 400 to AD 1500

With the fall of the Roman Empire in about the fifth century AD, both trade and associated record-keeping became stagnant in Europe, though activities still continued in Constantinople, the Middle East, India, China and elsewhere. In Europe, great stimulus to trade began with the period of the Crusades, around the eleventh century, when kings and princes could not themselves provide the material to support their retinues of crusaders bound for the Holy Land. This was a prosperous time for the lesser nobles and private merchants, who supplied the crusaders from ports such as Venice. A shift of supply and economic power from governments to the private sector began, and large merchant banks developed, such as those of the Medici in Florence. These banks became heavily involved in the businesses and governments they helped to finance.

Because of all these activities, a more exact system of record-keeping was developed in order to keep track of materials supplied, cash received and spent, and especially who owed whom how much money.[6] For the traders, merchants and bankers, the stimulus provided by the Crusades set record-keeping off in a more organised and systematic direction. The new direction was made possible also by refinements in the use of numbers and arithmetic that had taken place in Arab countries during Europe's Dark Ages. The number system we use in accounting and in our daily lives originated from these refinements.

The exact way that accounting or, more precisely, the record-keeping basis of accounting we call bookkeeping, evolved during this busy time is a subject of debate among accounting historians. A major event, however, was the publication in 1494 of a treatise on 'double-entry' bookkeeping by Friar Pacioli of Venice. In the book, he referred to the method as an established procedure that had been in use in the Medici banks of Italy and in other businesses for some time. Pacioli's book was an important contribution to the knowledge of algebra and arithmetic, and of value specifically because of its detailed description and codification of the double-entry system. It was rapidly translated into all the major European languages and, using these translations, European scholars extended Pacioli's ideas.

## Double-entry bookkeeping

Pacioli's concepts were revolutionary but sound: they form the fundamental basis of modern financial accounting, providing a method of pulling together all the lists of resources and obligations in a way that helps to prevent errors. The idea is that each trade or other commercial transaction is recorded (entered) twice, hence double-entry:

- once to recognise the resource involved in the transaction
- once to recognise the source or effect of that resource change.

Instead of the disconnected lists that existed before double-entry bookkeeping was invented, the lists of resources and sources were now connected to each other. Now a statement of financial position (balance sheet) of the modern kind could be prepared. Double entry bookkeeping, which might be seen as a pretty humdrum sort of activity, turns out to have a solid conceptual basis and a long and important history.

If a dollar amount (or that in any other medium of exchange – pounds, francs, yen, marks and so on) can be assigned to each transaction, that amount can be used to record both the resources and sources sides of each. Then, by adding up all the resources amounts and all the sources amounts, the two sides act as a check on each other. If errors are made, they are likely to be found because the two sides will not add up to the same amount. If they do add up, we say they 'balance'. Hence, the 'balance sheet', which shows that the two sides do add up. The record-keeping system Pacioli described to the world is one of the most far-reaching of human inventions.

## Britain: from 1500 to the early 1800s

Before Pacioli, English record-keeping had much in common with Roman methods used hundreds of years earlier. 'Stewards' were employed to manage the properties of the English aristocracy, much as local governors had been in Roman-held areas. In 1300, Oxford University offered an accounting course: Roman record-keeping for stewards.[7] The concept of stewardship, of a person managing something on behalf of someone else, is still an important aspect of accounting. It is often said, for example, that an enterprise's financial statements demonstrate the quality of management's stewardship of the enterprise on behalf of its owners.

In the several hundred years after Pacioli's treatise, accounting developed to suit the social and business circumstances of each country. France, for example, had a strong, centralised government and developed a national accounting system written by a central board of administrators. On the other hand, England (which in combination with its neighbours became Great Britain) had less government involvement in commerce and trade, and a smaller civil service, and relied more heavily on the initiatives of the private sector and the courts.[8] The financial accounting system now used in Australia, New Zealand, the United Kingdom, Canada, the United States and many other countries relies heavily on the precedents set in England during this period. The English approach used Pacioli's double entry for the record-keeping and built the financial statements' reporting system on that. Other countries, including Australia, have developed that further. Financial accounting in continental Europe developed on a somewhat different path. Russia, China, Japan and many other countries took other financial accounting paths. However, the British–American–Australian approach is still gaining popularity worldwide; for example, China adopted it for much of its financial reporting in the early 1990s. Efforts are being made worldwide to 'harmonise' financial accounting to assist international trade, and the sort of financial accounting set out in this book seems likely to become the international standard. International issues will be outlined further in a later chapter.

### For your interest

John Croaker (1788–1824) was an English-born bank clerk who was convicted of embezzlement and sentenced to transportation for 14 years to the colony of New South Wales. He was granted an immediate ticket of leave by Governor Macquarie and was employed as a clerk in the justiciary. His arrival in New South Wales coincided with the Bank of New South Wales (now known as Westpac), and Croaker set up its bookkeeping procedures according to the system of double entry. Not only did he introduce double-entry bookkeeping to the bank but 'there are good reasons for believing that he introduced the system to the colony as a whole'.

Source: Booker, J. and Craig, R., *John Croaker: Convict Embezzler*, Melbourne University Press, p. 19.

Until the mid 1600s, accounting and record-keeping (bookkeeping) were largely synonymous. Records were a private matter for the attention of the lord, merchant or banker. But then a significant development occurred: the advent of companies that sold shares of ownership to private citizens. These citizens could not all crowd into the company's office to inspect the records, even if they could understand them. This produced a demand for some form of reporting to the shareholders, for financial statements that could be relied on as accurate summaries of the records. There was a demand that the balance sheet (now called a statement of financial position) be more detailed in its description of the owners' equity and the changes in it than had been necessary before there had been such dispersed ownership. There was even some demand for regulation of such reports: for example, in 1657 Oliver Cromwell, as Regent of England, required the East India Company to publish its balance sheet.[9] Accounting was on its way to developing the standards of calculation and disclosure that are very important in modern accounting and distinguish accounting from the underlying record-keeping. Progress in this direction was not rapid, but it gained momentum with the Industrial Revolution.

The developing Industrial Revolution of the late 1700s and early 1800s helped to fuel the emerging commercial sector of Britain, and accounting practices became an important part of the enterprise. In 1825, the British Parliament eased hundred-year-old prohibitions on trading shares in companies, and the modern era of share markets and publicly owned companies began in earnest. A few years later, Parliament required annual audits of the balance sheets of such companies. Accounting and auditing continued to develop in response to the changing needs of the society of which they were a part.

From then on, accounting's emphasis shifted from record-keeping to the choice of accounting method, professional ethics and the various standards and laws governing financial reporting and financial disclosure.

## 3.12 Financial accounting's recent history

### Developments in the nineteenth century[10]

Until the early nineteenth century, most business enterprises were formed for specific ventures, were financed by a few wealthy owners, and were disbanded when the ventures were completed. The sharing of profits among the owners of the enterprise or venture took place at the end, when all the assets were sold, the liabilities were paid off, and the net amount remaining was distributed among the owners. As industrialisation increased, large industrial plants began replacing short-term ventures as the major form of business enterprise and the traditional method of financing and profit-sharing was no longer acceptable. The large cost of constructing and maintaining these more capital-intensive enterprises was often more than a few owners could afford, and the long life of the assets made waiting for the winding up of the enterprise before sharing profits an unsatisfactory option.

Various pieces of companies' legislation were introduced in Britain in the 1830s, 1840s and 1850s. This legislation allowed companies to sell shares in stock markets (which, because the initial issuing of shares provides capital – that is, equity funds for the companies – are also called capital markets). The legislation also provided a major feature of companies: liability of the company's owners to the company's creditors was, and still is, limited to the amount of the owners' unpaid capital in the company. The justification for the limited liability feature was that individual investors could not always be aware of the actions of the directors they elected or the managers who were in turn engaged by the directors. Therefore, investors should not be liable for any more than the amount of money they invested in the enterprise. But no investors would want to lose even that, so as capital markets developed, the demand for information about the corporations involved grew.

Limited liability of its owners and an existence separate from its owners largely define the corporation. Modern laws and business practices complicate the operation of capital markets and can reduce the protection of limited liability, but the idea that a corporation is a 'legal person', able to act on its own and survive changes in owners, is still central to business and to much of the rest of our lives. In financial accounting, the focus is on the economic entity that is exchanging physical and financial goods and promises with other economic entities, but since laws began to define what corporations are (and sometimes what proprietorships, partnerships and corporate groups are, too), accounting also must reflect the legal nature of economic exchanges and the structure of the organisation.

An important legal issue is sharing profits. The problem of how to ensure fair calculation and sharing of ownership interests led legislators to require that a corporation present its balance sheet annually to its shareholders and that an auditor be present to report to the shareholders on the validity of that financial statement. Legislation also required that any annual payments to shareholders should not come out of the sale of, or by decreasing the value of, a corporation's long-term capital assets. Such payments should be made out of monies earned yearly from these assets after all yearly debts are paid. We can think of 'monies earned yearly' as revenues, and 'yearly debts' as expenses, so this meant, roughly, that payments to shareholders should come out of yearly profit. This is close to the dividend requirement placed on most corporations today (dividends can normally only be paid out of net profit). Corporations began to compute profit in statements or schedules separate from the balance sheet, so that they could demonstrate that they had performed well enough to permit the distribution of dividends or the issuing of more shares.

As businesses grew in size and complexity, the demand for information on financial performance increased. The static picture presented by the balance sheet was not good enough for the emerging stock markets, for the increasingly large group of non-owner professional managers, or for governments that wished to evaluate (and tax!) businesses' performance (to mention just a few of the groups interested in evaluating performance). The profit and loss statement (now called a statement of financial performance in Australia) came into its own as a central part of financial reporting in the last hundred years, and its measurement of financial performance is central to economic activity and performance evaluation in most of the world.

In responding to these demands for better performance information, accountants were limited by a lack of accounting theories or conventions to illustrate and define how to prepare balance sheets and income statements. There was no nationally organised association of accountants in Britain until the end of the nineteenth century (although the Accountants' Society of Edinburgh received a royal charter in 1854, an event that led to the term 'chartered accountant'). Financial accounting methods developed situation by situation, with no overall plan or concepts throughout this period. Some model financial statements and examples from legislation were being used, and income statements were becoming established, but it was becoming necessary to establish a rational basis, that is, principles, for preparing financial statements and for extending the principles to new settings, as business and commercial activity continued to increase. Toward the end of the nineteenth century, several British court cases had established that accountants and auditors had to decide what were proper and fair financial statements, and could not expect courts and legislatures to decide for them. A prominent accountant, Ernest Cooper, voiced his concern in 1894: 'the already sufficient responsibilities and anxieties of an Auditor will be extended beyond those known of any trade or profession'.[11] Accounting was on its way to formulating the professional rights, responsibilities and criteria for competence, as had the already established professions of law, engineering and medicine.

## How's your understanding?

Here are two questions you should be able to answer, based on what you have just read:

1 Why has financial accounting become more and more sophisticated over the centuries?

2 What sort of information demands prompted the development of the income statement?

### For your interest

Sergeant Jeremiah Murphy holds a unique place in Australian commercial history as being the first person in Australia in respect of whose affairs a ledger account prepared within a double-entry accounting system has been found. His bank deposit on 5 April 1817 was the first deposit taken by the Bank of New South Wales. The recording of this deposit appears to provide the earliest artefact that has survived of the operation of a double-entry accounting system in colonial Australia.

Source: Craig, R., 'Jeremiah Murphy: Bank Account No. 1', *Australian CPA*, December 1998, pp. 68–9.

## 3.13 Public sector issues

During the 1990s, local governments, State and Commonwealth Government departments, and whole of governments (for example, the Commonwealth of Australia and the NSW Government) have all moved from a cash-based accounting system to an accrual-based accounting system. They also use a double-entry accounting system involving debits and credits.

## 3.14 Homework and discussion to develop understanding

### Discussion questions

This section starts with simpler discussion questions that revise some of the basic concepts and are then followed by a set of problems.

1 If an asset increases, list what else may have happened to the accounting equation.

2 Which of the following is not possible?

   a One liability increases and another liability increases.

   b Shareholders' equity increases and liabilities decrease.

   c Assets increase and liabilities decrease.

3 Why does an increase in revenues result in an increase in shareholders' equity? What other part of the accounting equation is likely to be affected?

4 Why does an increase in expenses result in an decrease in shareholders' equity? What other part of the accounting equation is likely to be affected?

5 Which accounts normally have a debit balance and which normally have a credit balance?

6 Choose five transactions and show both the resource effect and the source effect.

7 Explain how the statement of financial position and statement of financial performance articulate.
8 Provide examples of how accounting has evolved as business, government and other institutions have evolved.
9 How did the practice of having systematic records that could be audited later begin?
10 Explain how the double-entry system developed by Pacioli works.
11 What development in Britain between 1500 and the early 1800s helped shape present-day accounting?
12 What development in the nineteenth century helped start present-day accounting?
13 What is meant by limited liability?
14 You have been working at a summer job as a clerk in a small store. The new owner of the store comes over to you, waving the statement of financial position for the store and saying, 'You're studying accounting, I hear. Can you explain to me what my statement of financial position is supposed to be telling me and why it is designed to have two sides? Where did such a way of measuring a business come from, anyway?' Give your reply.
15 Luca Pacioli's book on mathematics and double-entry bookkeeping was a huge best-seller across Europe 400–500 years ago. It was translated into many languages, including English. Merchants and other business people took to double entry with great enthusiasm and it quickly became the standard method wherever Europeans did business (such as in the Americas). Why do you think double-entry bookkeeping was (and is) so popular?

## Problem 3.1* Transaction analysis

Flashy Fashions Pty Ltd is a small company in a coastal town. It rents its premises and its sales are all on credit. It has only three expenses: cost of goods sold, rent, and income tax.

At the end of its previous financial year, 30 September 2001, Flashy's statement of financial position is as follows:

**Flashy Fashions Pty Ltd**
Statement of financial position
as at 30 September 2001

| Assets | $ | Equities | $ |
|---|---|---|---|
| **Current assets** | | **Current liabilities** | |
| Cash | 800 | Accounts payable | 600 |
| Accounts receivable | 400 | Rent payable | 300 |
| Inventory | 900 | | |
| | | **Shareholders' equity** | |
| | | Share capital | 500 |
| | | Retained profits | 700 |
| | 2 100 | | 2 100 |

During the year ended 30 September 2002, the following information was recorded in the company's accounts:

1 revenue from credit sales $10 000
2 collections from customers $9600
3 purchases on credit of inventory for sale $6100
4 payments to suppliers $6300
5 cost of goods sold $6400

6 rent charged by the landlord $2400
7 rent paid to the landlord $2900 (decreasing the liability)
8 income tax payable for the year $350
9 cash dividends declared and paid to shareholders $450.

*Required:*

1 Prepare transaction analysis for each of the above items.
2 Prepare a statement of financial performance and a statement of financial position.

## Problem 3.2* Complete the expanded accounting equation

Calculate the missing figure in each of the following situations:

| | Current assets | Noncurrent assets | Current liabilities | Noncurrent liabilities | Share capital | Opening retained profits | Revenue | Expense | Dividend |
|---|---|---|---|---|---|---|---|---|---|
| 1 | 50 000 | 200 000 | 25 000 | 50 000 | ? | 5 000 | 25 000 | 15 000 | 0 |
| 2 | 150 000 | 600 000 | 75 000 | 150 000 | 450 000 | 30 000 | 150 000 | ? | 0 |
| 3 | 150 000 | 600 000 | 75 000 | 150 000 | 450 000 | 120 000 | 135 000 | ? | 0 |
| 4 | ? | 250 000 | 25 000 | 50 000 | 250 000 | 50 000 | 45 000 | 30 000 | 0 |

## Problem 3.3* Prepare a simple set of financial statements from accounts

Following are account balances of Arctic Limo Services Pty Ltd. Prepare a 2003 statement of financial performance and comparative 2002 and 2003 statements of financial position. State any assumptions you feel are necessary.

| | 30 September 2003 | 30 September 2002 |
|---|---|---|
| | Debit (Credit) | Debit (Credit) |
| | $ | $ |
| Accumulated depreciation | (30 000) | (20 000) |
| Cash on hand | 2 000 | 4 000 |
| Dividends declared | 80 000 | |
| Due from Lucky Eddie | | 1 000 |
| Due to Amalgamated Loansharks | | (10 000) |
| Income tax expense | 35 000 | |
| Limousines depreciation expense | 10 000 | |
| Limousines cost | 90 000 | 60 000 |
| Long-term limousine financing | (50 000) | (30 000) |
| Other expenses | 70 000 | |
| Retained profits | (4 000) | (4 000) |
| Revenue | (300 000) | |
| Share capital | (1 000) | (1 000) |
| Wages expense | 100 000 | |
| Wages payable | (2 000) | |
| | 0 | 0 |

## Problem 3.4* Prepare a statement of financial position from simple transactions

South Shore Manufacturing Pty Ltd had this statement of financial position:

Statement of financial poisition
as at 30 June 2002

| | $ | | $ |
|---|---|---|---|
| **Assets** | | **Liabilities and shareholders equity** | |
| **Current assets** | | **Current liabilities** | |
| Cash | 24 388 | Bank overdraft | 53 000 |
| Accounts receivable | 89 267 | Accounts payable | 78 442 |
| Inventories, cost | 111 436 | Taxes payable | 12 665 |
| Prepayments | 7 321 | Current part of mortgage | 18 322 |
| | 232 412 | | 162 429 |
| **Noncurrent assets** | | **Noncurrent liabilities** | |
| Land, cost | 78 200 | Mortgage, less current | 213 734 |
| Factory and equipment cost | 584 211 | Employee entitlements | 67 674 |
| | 662 411 | Loan from shareholders | 100 000 |
| Accum. depreciation | (198 368) | | 381 408 |
| | 464 043 | **Shareholders' equity** | |
| | | Share capital | 55 000 |
| | | Retained profits | 97 618 |
| | | | 152 618 |
| | 696 455 | | 696 455 |

During July 2002, South Shore Manufacturing experienced the following transactions:

1 $10 000 of the shareholders' loan was repaid.
2 A customer paid one of the accounts receivable, $11 240.
3 Additional inventory costing $5320 was purchased on credit.
4 The company issued new shares for $22 000 cash.
5 The proceeds of the share issue were used to reduce the bank overdraft.
6 More land costing $52 000 was purchased for $12 000 cash plus a new long-term mortgage for the rest.
7 More factory equipment costing $31 900 was purchased on credit, with $13 900 due in six months and the rest due in 24 months.

*Required:*

1 Prepare journal entries for each transaction.
2 Prepare a new statement of financial position for the company as of 31 July 2002.

## Problem 3.5* Complete transaction analysis and prepare financial statements

The following transactions occurred for the month of November 2002 for Hoad Pty Ltd:

1 The company was incorporated, with shareholders investing $200 000 in cash.
2 Purchased inventory for cash, $20 000.
3 Paid $4000 for a month's rent on the premises.
4 Purchased inventory on credit, $30 000.
5 Received an advertising bill for newspaper advertisement to promote the new company. The $1000 will be paid in May.

6 Inventory with a cost of $40 000 was sold on credit for $90 000.
7 Paid $25 000 of accounts payable.
8 Received $30 000 from accounts receivable.
9 Paid wages of $15 000.
10 Paid sales commission at the rate of 1 per cent on sales made during the month.
11 Purchased a new computer for $6000, paid $3000 in cash and $3000 to be paid in 15 months' time.
12 Owed employees $2000 in wages at the end of the month.

*Required:*

1 Show the effect of each of the above transactions on the accounting equation.
2 Prepare a statement of financial performance and a statement of financial position at 30 November 2002.
3 Prepare journal entries for each transaction and determine the balances for each account.

## Problem 3.6 Examples of transactions

Provide an example of a transaction where:

1 one asset increases and one decreases
2 an asset increases and a liability increases
3 an asset increases and shareholders' equity increases
4 shareholders' equity increases and a liability decreases
5 an asset decreases and a liability decreases
6 one liability increases and another liability decreases.

## Problem 3.7 Transaction analysis and statement of financial position

Cynthia has just started a company she calls Beach Ready Pty Ltd. She will have a six-bed tanning salon and will sell various lotions, beachwear and other summery stuff. To get the business started, she contributed $15 000 from her savings plus a sound system for playing music in the tanning booths. She values the system at $1500.

She bought the needed tanning beds, a computer to keep track of customers' tanning minutes and other equipment for $21 200, paying $9200 down and agreeing to pay the rest in 24 monthly instalments of $500 plus interest at 10 per cent. After checking out several possible locations, she signed a two-year lease for space in a neighbourhood mall, costing $1100 rent per month. She painted the place and generally fixed it up, at a cost of $1600 cash. (This created an asset that you might call 'leasehold improvements' because she owns the improvements although not the property she improved.) The last thing she did before the grand opening was to stock up on lotions, beachwear and other things to sell. All that inventory cost $17 100. She paid the suppliers an initial $2300 and promised to pay the rest within 60 days.

1 Prepare a transaction analysis.
2 Prepare a classified statement of financial position for Beach Ready Pty Ltd.
3 Calculate the company's working capital and debt/equity ratios from your statement of financial position.

## Problem 3.8 Normal balances of accounts

What would be the normal balance (DR or CR) for each of the following account titles:

1 accounts receivable?
2 accounts payable?
3 inventory?
4 provision for employee entitlements?

5 taxes payable?
6 retained profits?
7 share capital?
8 investments?
9 plant and equipment?
10 accrued expenses?
11 prepayments?

## Problem 3.9 Complete the expanded accounting equation

Calculate the missing figure in each of the following situations:

| | Current assets | Noncurrent assets | Current liabilities | Noncurrent liabilities | Share capital | Opening retained profits | Revenue | Expense | Dividend |
|---|---|---|---|---|---|---|---|---|---|
| 1 | 100 000 | 400 000 | 50 000 | 100 000 | ? | 10 000 | 50 000 | 30 000 | 0 |
| 2 | 100 000 | 400 000 | 50 000 | 100 000 | 300 000 | 20 000 | 100 000 | ? | 0 |
| 3 | 100 000 | 400 000 | 50 000 | 100 000 | 300 000 | 80 000 | 90 000 | ? | 0 |
| 4 | ? | 500 000 | 50 000 | 100 000 | 500 000 | 100 000 | 90 000 | 60 000 | 0 |
| 5 | 100 000 | 400 000 | 50 000 | 100 000 | 300 000 | 20 000 | 100 000 | 50 000 | ? |
| 6 | 100 000 | 500 000 | 50 000 | 100 000 | 300 000 | ? | 100 000 | 50 000 | 20 000 |

## Problem 3.10 Ascertain the unknowns in the accounting equation

Find the unknowns for LAP Pty Ltd given the following information:

| | $m |
|---|---|
| Assets 1 July 2001 | 600 |
| Assets 30 June 2002 | ? |
| Liabilities 1 July 2001 | ? |
| Liabilities 30 June 2002 | 300 |
| Share capital 1 July 2001 | 180 |
| Share capital 30 June 2002 | 190 |
| Retained profits 1 July 2001 | 200 |
| Retained profits 30 June 2002 | ? |
| Revenues for the year | 800 |
| Expenses for the year | 650 |
| Dividends | 50 |

## Problem 3.11 Ascertain the unknowns in the accounting equation

| | $m |
|---|---|
| Assets 1 July 2001 | 600 |
| Assets 30 June 2002 | 800 |
| Liabilities 1 July 2001 | 200 |

| | |
|---|---|
| Liabilities 30 June 2002 | 300 |
| Share capital 1 July 2001 | 160 |
| Share capital 30 June 2002 | 180 |
| Retained profits 1 July 2001 | ? |
| Retained profits 30 June 2002 | ? |
| Revenues for the year | ? |
| Expenses for the year | 600 |
| Dividends | 100 |

## Problem 3.12 Prepare a statement of financial position from transactions

Fed up with her dead-end career with a big company, Tanya decided to start her own business, manufacturing and selling fresh pasta and a line of associated sauces, and selling cookware and other equipment to go with the food. It took her several weeks to get set up, before she made a single sale.

Based on the transactions given below:

1 Using transaction analysis, show the effect of the following transactions on the accounting equation for Tanya's new company, PastaPastaPasta Pty Ltd.
2 Prepare the company's statement of financial position at the end of Tanya's business set-up time.

*Transactions:*

1 Tanya put personal savings of $45 000 into a new bank account opened in the company's name. She decided that $35 000 of that would go for shares of the company and the rest would be a loan she hoped the company could pay back in a few years.
2 Tanya also provided her large set of recipes and her hatchback, to be owned by the new company. She thought the recipes would be worth about $500 and the hatchback about $7500. She was in no hurry to be paid for these items, but thought they should be included in the company's assets.
3 A group of friends and relatives gave her company $25 000 in cash, in return for shares.
4 The company rented space in a local shopping centre and paid $2000 as rent in advance.
5 Another friend, who had no cash but wanted to help, agreed to do some renovations and repainting in the new space, in return for some shares in the company. Tanya and the friend agreed that the work done would have cost $4500 if she had paid someone else to do it.
6 The company bought a large amount of food processing and storage equipment for $63 250, paying $28 000 in cash and agreeing to pay the rest in five equal annual instalments, beginning in six months.
7 Pasta-making supplies costing $4720 and cookware for resale costing $3910 were purchased for $1000 in cash, with the remainder to be paid in 60 days.
8 The company got a $20 000 line of credit from the bank and actually borrowed $2500 of that, repayable on demand. Tanya had to sign a personal guarantee for anything borrowed under the line of credit.
9 The company paid a lawyer $1800 for costs of incorporation.

## Problem 3.13 Complete transaction analysis and prepare financial statements

The abridged statement of financial position for Roche Pty Ltd at 31 August 2002 was as follows:

| Assets | $ | Liabilities and shareholders' equity | |
|---|---|---|---|
| Cash | 100 000 | Accounts payable | 200 000 |
| Accounts receivable | 400 000 | Long-term loan | 300 000 |
| Inventory | 600 000 | Share capital | 900 000 |
| Prepayments | 70 000 | Retained profits | 240 000 |
| Equipment | 600 000 | | |
| Accumulated depreciation | (130 000) | | |
| | 1 640 000 | | 1 640 000 |

The following transactions occurred during September:

1 Paid $100 000 of accounts payable.
2 Received $500 000 from accounts receivable.
3 Purchased inventory on credit $200 000.
4 Made credit sales of $700 000 (cost of goods sold was $450 000).
5 Administrative expenses of $30 000 paid in cash.
6 Depreciation of $10 000 was recognised.
7 $10 000 of prepayments expired during the month.
8 Dividends of $20 000 were paid.
9 Paid back $100 000 on the loan.
10 Issued additional shares $500 000.
11 Paid the wages bill of $50 000.

***Required:***

1 Show the effect of the above transactions on the accounting equation.
2 Prepare a statement of financial performance, a statement of retained profits and a statement of financial position at 30 September 2002.
3 Prepare journal entries for each transaction and determine the balances of the accounts.

## Problem 3.14 Identify debit and credit balances, and prepare a statement of financial position

BML Products Pty Ltd manufactures and sells children's toys. Here are the company's balance sheet accounts as at 30 June 2002, in alphabetical order.

| | $ | | $ |
|---|---|---|---|
| Accumulated depreciation | 63 700 | Owing from customers | 6 200 |
| Bank account balance | 14 300 | Owing to suppliers | 21 900 |
| Bank loan | 21 200 | Retained earnings | 47 500 |
| Building | 102 100 | Share capital issued | 25 000 |
| Cash on hand | 2 500 | Short-term part of mortgage | 8 000 |
| Employees' tax not yet remitted | 600 | Unpaid employee wages | 1 800 |
| Fixtures and equipment | 37 900 | Unsold finished products | 29 600 |
| Land | 48 000 | Unused office supplies | 1 400 |
| Long-term part of mortgage owing | 71 000 | Unused product raw materials | 18 700 |

*Required:*

1. Decide which accounts have debit balances and which have credit balances. According to the company's accounting system, total debits = total credits = $260 700.
2. Based on your answer to question 1, prepare the company's 30 June 2002 statement of financial position from the above accounts.
3. Rewrite the statement of financial position using account titles that you are more likely to see in actual financial statements.
4. Comment briefly on the company's financial condition as shown by the statement of financial position.

## Problem 3.15 Prepare financial statements from accounts

1. Look at the list of accounts of Geewhiz Productions, at 30 November 2001, which follow in no particular order, and decide which ones are statement of financial performance accounts.
2. Calculate net profit based on your answer to part 1.
3. Calculate ending retained profits based on your answer to part 2.
4. Prepare the following financial statements, demonstrating that your answers to parts 2 and 3 are correct:
   a. statement of financial performance for the year ended 30 November 2001
   b. a note calculating retained profits for the year ended on that date
   c. statement of financial position at 30 November 2001.
5. Comment briefly on what the financial statements show about the company's performance for the 2001 year and financial position at 30 November 2001.

| | $ | | $ |
|---|---|---|---|
| Salaries expense | 71 000 DR | Dividends declared | 11 000 DR |
| Income tax payable | 2 800 CR | Accumulated depreciation | 94 000 CR |
| Land | 63 000 DR | Cash at bank | 18 000 DR |
| Employee benefits expense | 13 100 DR | Income tax expense | 6 900 DR |
| Tax deductions payable | 5 400 CR | Credit sales revenue | 346 200 CR |
| Accounts receivable | 16 400 DR | Inventory on hand | 68 000 DR |
| Cash sales revenue | 21 600 CR | Prepaid insurance | 2 400 DR |
| Dividends payable | 5 500 CR | Beginning retained profits | 92 800 CR |
| Depreciation expense | 26 700 DR | Accounts payable | 41 000 CR |
| Cost of goods sold | 161 600 DR | Interest revenue | 1 700 CR |
| Insurance expense | 11 200 DR | Building | 243 000 DR |
| Share capital | 200 000 CR | Trucks and equipment | 182 500 DR |
| Office expenses | 31 100 DR | Salaries payable | 4 100 CR |
| Mortgage payable | 114 000 CR | Miscellaneous expenses | 8 200 DR |
| Bank loan owing | 21 800 CR | Interest expense | 16 800 DR |

## Problem 3.16 Prepare month-end financial statements from accounts

Matilda Jamison runs a successful second-hand clothing shop, Matilda's Boutique Pty Ltd. She buys quality new and used clothes from several sources and then sells them at reasonable prices.

To establish her business, Matilda invested $1500 of her savings and her mother contributed $500. Both received shares in the company in return for their investment, so the company's share capital is $2000. The company also took out a $3000 bank loan.

Matilda rents retail space in a shopping mall on a monthly basis at $200 per month. She pays rent in advance for a six-month period (in other words, $1200 twice a year) on 1 January and 1 July of every year. The company owns the display units, racks, shelving and hangers she uses in her business, which cost $2400 in total. She expects these items to last for five years and has, therefore, depreciated them by $480 per year ($2400 ÷ 5 years = $480 per year). The resulting accumulated depreciation is included on the statement of financial position. The insurance policy is an annual policy purchased on 1 January for $1200.

Matilda pays her employees for work done from the 1st to the 15th of each month, on or about the 20th of each month. As a result, half of the wages earned by employees during the month has been paid (that earned from the 1st to the 15th of the month) and the remaining half is still payable. The company's income tax rate is 20 per cent. Matilda closes her accounts monthly, so revenue and expense accounts contain only one month's data at a time.

**Account balances at 30 April 2002**

| | DR $ | CR $ |
|---|---|---|
| Cash | 780 | |
| Accounts receivable | 1 300 | |
| Inventory of unsold goods | 10 000 | |
| Office supplies on hand | 500 | |
| Prepaid insurance | 800 | |
| Prepaid rent | 400 | |
| Shelving/hangers/display units | 2 400 | |
| Accumulated depreciation | (1 120) | |
| Bank loan | | 3 000 |
| Accounts payable | | 2 800 |
| Wages payable | | 500 |
| Taxes payable | | 1 200 |
| Share capital | | 2 000 |
| Retained profits 31 March 2002 | | 4 360 |
| Revenue | | 7 000 |
| Cost of goods sold | | (3 500) |
| Wages | | (1 000) |
| Insurance | | (100) |
| Rent | | (200) |
| Cleaning and miscellaneous | | (580) |
| Office supplies used | | (50) |
| Interest | | (30) |
| Depreciation | | (40) |
| Income tax | | (300) |
| | 15 060 | 15 060 |

From the account balances at the end of April 2002, prepare a statement of financial performance for Matilda's Boutique Pty Ltd for the month of April 2002 and a statement of financial position as at 30 April 2002.

## Problem 3.17 Profit and loss and retained profits format

The accounts for Prentice Retail Pty Ltd for last year included the following (in alphabetical order):

| | | $ |
|---|---|---|
| Dividends declared | DR | 87 000 |
| Income tax expense | DR | 145 210 |
| Miscellaneous revenue from investments | CR | 23 570 |
| Operating expenses | DR | 1 703 470 |
| Retained profits, beginning of year | CR | 354 290 |
| Revenue from sales | CR | 2 111 480 |

Calculate net profit, and prepare a note to show the change in retained profits for the year.

## Problem 3.18 Transaction analysis

The following transactions pertain to Rosewall Pty Ltd for November 2001.

1. The company was incorporated with shareholders investing $250 000 in cash.
2. Purchased $43 000 worth of inventory on credit.
3. Rent of $8000 was paid.
4. Made credit sales of $110 000 (cost of goods sold was $45 000).
5. Received the $2000 bill for an advertising campaign to promote the new company. This amount will be paid in December.
6. Inventory was purchased for $27 000 cash.
7. Paid $30 000 of accounts payable.
8. Wages of $24 000 were paid (wages expense).
9. Received $45 000 from accounts receivable.
10. Sales commission was paid, at the rate of 1 per cent of total monthly sales.
11. Purchased new machinery at a cost of $9000. $4000 was paid in cash with the remainder to be paid in 15 months' time.
12. Owed employees $3500 in wages at the end of November.
13. Depreciation on the new equipment equals $1000.
14. Interest from the bank of $6000 is owed at the end of November. It will be received in January 2002.
15. Received $8000 from a client. Services to the client will be provided in December.

*Required:*

Show the effect of each of the above transactions on the accounting equation.

## Problem 3.19 Transaction analysis

Below is the abridged statement of financial position for Newcombe Pty Ltd as at 30 September 2001.

| Assets | | Liabilities and shareholders' equity | |
|---|---|---|---|
| | $ | | $ |
| Cash | 90 000 | Accounts payable | 110 000 |
| Accounts receivable | 106 000 | Long-term loan | 240 000 |
| Inventory | 118 000 | Share capital | 200 000 |
| Prepayments | 45 000 | Retained profits | 84 000 |
| Equipment | 400 000 | | |
| Accumulated depreciation | (125 000) | | |
| | 634 000 | | 634 000 |

The following transactions occur during October.

1 Received $23 000 from accounts receivable.
2 Additional shares worth $80 000 are issued.
3 Inventory (costing $32 000) is sold on credit for $76 000.
4 Recognition of $4000 of depreciation expense.
5 $60 000 of the loan is repaid.
6 Administrative expenses of $7000 are paid.
7 $9000 of prepayments are used up.
8 Payment of wages of $13 000.
9 Purchase of $28 000 worth of inventory for cash.
10 Dividends of $6000 are paid.
11 Payment of $36 000 of accounts payable.

*Required:*

1 Show the effect of each of the above transactions on the accounting equation.
2 Prepare a statement of financial performance, a statement of retained profits and a statement of financial position for Newcombe Pty Ltd at 31 October 2001.

## Problem 3.20 Explain and write entries for changes in account balances

Here are more account changes that occurred to Lotus Ltd. For each of the ten items, say in a few words what would have caused the changes and write a journal entry to account for them:

1 accounts payable down $3220, cash down $3220
2 income tax expense up $5900, cash down $5000, income tax payable up $900
3 travel advances receivable up $200, cash down $200
4 travel advances receivable down $200, cash up $11, travel expenses up $189
5 cash up $350, customer deposits liability up $350
6 auditing expense up $3000, accounts payable up $2400, cash down $600
7 equipment up $5200, share capital up $5200
8 share capital down $1000, cash down $1000
9 cash up $1200, accounts receivable up $3300, revenue up $4500, inventory down $2750, cost of goods sold expense up $2750
10 cost of goods sold expense down $147 670 (to zero), retained earnings down $147 670.

## Problem 3.21 Transactions

Provide illustrations of the following transactions relating to the business of I. Cameron, plumber:

1. one asset exchanged for another
2. an asset and a liability increased by the same amount
3. an asset and revenue increased by the same amount
4. one liability exchanged for another
5. an asset and a liability reduced by the same amount
6. a liability and an expense increased by the same amount
7. an asset and owner's equity increased by the same amount
8. an asset reduced and an expense increased by the same amount
9. a liability reduced and owner's equity increased by the same amount
10. an asset and owner's equity decreased by the same amount.

## Problem 3.22 Journal entries

**Knights Pty Ltd**
Statement of financial position
as at 30 June 2002

| | $ | | $ |
|---|---|---|---|
| **Assets** | | **Liabilities** | |
| **Current assets** | | **Current liabilities** | |
| Cash | 70 000 | Accounts payable | 60 000 |
| Accounts receivable | 180 000 | Wages payable | 30 000 |
| Inventory | 210 000 | | |
| | | **Shareholders' equity** | |
| | | Share capital | 200 000 |
| | | Retained profits | 170 000 |
| | 460 000 | | 460 000 |

During the year ended 30 June 2003, the following information was recorded in the company's accounts:

1. credit sales $1 000 000
2. cash sales $300 000
3. collections from customers $900 000
4. purchases of inventory $590 000 on credit
5. payments of accounts payable $400 000
6. cost of goods sold $600 000
7. wages expense $300 000, not yet paid
8. wages paid $320 000 (reduce wages payable)
9. income tax payable $100 000
10. cash dividends of $150 000 declared but not paid
11. other expenses paid $160 000
12. $200 000 was received for a service contract; services will be provided in the following year.

***Required:***

Prepare journal entries for the above transactions.

## Problem 3.23 Prepare journal entries

**Dragons Pty Ltd**
Statement of financial position
as at 30 June 2001

| | $ | | $ |
|---|---|---|---|
| **Assets** | | **Liabilities** | |
| **Current assets** | | **Current liabilities** | |
| Cash | 14 000 | Accounts payable | 12 000 |
| Accounts receivable | 36 000 | Tax payable | 6 000 |
| Inventory | 42 000 | | |
| | | **Shareholders' equity** | |
| | | Share capital | 40 000 |
| | | Retained profits | 34 000 |
| | 92 000 | | 92 000 |

During the year ended 30 June 2002 the following information was recorded in the company's accounts:

**1** credit sales $200 000
**2** cash sales $6000
**3** collections from customers $150 000
**4** purchases of inventory on credit $70 000
**5** payments of accounts payable $50 000
**6** cost of goods sold $80 000
**7** wages expense $90 000, not yet paid
**8** wages paid $22 000 (reduce wages payable)
**9** income tax payable $10 000
**10** cash dividends of $20 000 declared and paid.

***Required:***

Prepare journal entries, a statement of financial performance for the year ended 30 June 2002 and a statement of financial position as at 30 June 2002.

## Problem 3.24 Prepare a statement of retained profits

The accounts for Australian RST Limited for 30 June 2003 included the following (in alphabetical order):

| | | $000 |
|---|---|---|
| Dividends declared | DR | 49 444 |
| Income tax expense | DR | 571 |
| Operating profit before tax | CR | 58 884 |
| Retained profits, beginning of year | CR | 35 697 |

***Required:***

Prepare a statement showing closing retained profits.

## Problem 3.25 (Challenging) Statement of financial performance from partial information

A list of some events that occurred during the month of September at Tune Craft Instruments Pty Ltd follows. Review the list of events and decide whether each event is a revenue or an expense for Tune-Craft for September. Build a partial statement of financial performance for September from these revenues and expenses, putting in any important account titles you would expect to see on the statement of financial performance, even if the information you would need to come up with in dollar figures is lacking. The result will therefore be an outline of the September statement of financial performance, including whatever numbers you can determine so far.

| Date | Event |
|---|---|
| Sep 2 | Cash sales, $300. |
| 5 | Cheque received and recorded as revenue in August deposited in bank, $500. |
| 8 | Sale on account to M. Green, $650. |
| 8 | Showroom is painted. Tune-Craft will be billed $250. |
| 9 | Cash sales, $150. |
| 11 | Collection on outstanding account from customer R. Bowles, $75. |
| 14 | Instruments purchased for inventory, $1500. One-third is paid in cash, the rest is on account. |
| 17 | Collection from customer M. Green, $300. |
| 18 | An electricity bill is paid, $65. The amount had not previously been recorded as an expense. |
| 20 | Sales of $550 cash; $200 on account. |
| 23 | Office furniture is purchased, $710. Tune-Craft pays nothing down, no payments until six months from now. |
| 24 | Ordinary shares are issued for cash, $2000. |
| 25 | Cash sales, $275. |
| 30 | Two employees receive cheques for September totalling $1800. One of the employees also receives a cheque for overtime worked in August, $200. |

## Problem 3.26 (Challenging) General or user-specific statement of financial performances?

Do the accrual basis and the standard content and format of the statement of financial performance provide useful information to all people who are interested in companies' financial performance, or should there be different kinds of profit and loss statements prepared to suit the needs of different kinds of users?

Write a paragraph giving your considered views.

## Problem 3.27 (Challenging) Profit and loss smoothing and ethics

1 Income smoothing is a way of manipulating a company's net profit in order to create a desired impression of management's capability and performance. Other kinds of profit manipulation by management have also been alleged. Do you think it is ethical for management to manipulate the figures by which its performance is measured? Why or why not?

2 The usual answer to question 1 is that such behaviour is unethical. Can you think of any circumstances under which such manipulation of profit would be ethical? Putting it another way, are there any people, other than management, whose interests would be served by such behaviour?

## CASE 3A Woolworths Limited Case

Refer to the extracts of the annual report of Woolworths Limited in appendix 2. All questions relate to the consolidated accounts.

1 What period is covered by the profit and loss statement?
2 List the main types of revenues.
3 List some of the larger expenses incurred in earning revenue.
4 What are interest expense and interest revenue for the year?
5 What is cost of goods sold for the year?
6 What is total depreciation and amortisation for the year?
7 Explain the change in retained profits from 2000 to 2001.
8 What is income tax expense for the year?
9 What is the basic earnings per share for 2001?
10 What would be the normal balance Dr or Cr of each of the following accounts included in Woolworths Limited statement of financial position or the relevant notes: trade debtors, inventory, investments, land and buildings, advances to employees, trade creditors, provision for income tax, provision for dividends and retained profits?

## CASE 3B Financial reporting on the internet

This book mentions the Web pages for many companies. Increasingly, corporations and other organisations are putting out detailed information about themselves on the Internet. But how good is that information? Is it easy to find in the company's Web material, is it up to date, is it displayed usefully and can it be downloaded easily? This is a case you can construct for yourself, and discuss in class either by comparing various companies or by comparing various people's reactions to the same company.

Pick a company that interests you or that is assigned by your instructor, go to its Web site, and see what is there regarding the company's financial statements. If you don't know the company's Web address, type the company name into your search engine and you'll likely get to it easily. Once you get to the company's Web page, start your examination and consider questions such as those below, which could be addressed in a report or in a class discussion:

1 How attractive and user-friendly is the initial Web page? Does it concentrate on marketing the company's products, providing general information, telling you about recent news media attention to the company, or other purposes?
2 How easy is it to find the company's financial information, if it is there at all? (Many Web pages direct you to Investor Information or some such area for financial information, others specify the financial reports directly, while others make it quite hard to find.)
3 How much does the company tell you about itself to help you put the financial information in context? Can you easily relate the background to the financial stuff, or do you have to jump all over the Web pages to find it all?
4 How useful do you find the financial statements to be? Are they up to date, are they analysed or commented upon by the company, are they related to recent events affecting the company or just plunked on the Web as is? (You could look for a management discussion and analysis section if the statement of financial position is just included in the company's current annual report, posted as is on the Web.)

5 Are the statement of financial position, statement of financial performance and supporting material easy to download and/or print? Would they be readily available for insertion in an analysis of the company?

## CASE 3C Preparing journal entries

Shown below and on the next page is the statement of financial position from the 2001 annual report for George Weston Foods Limited. In addition, note that sales revenue for the year was $1 607 469 000 and operating profit was $54 980 000.

Additional information taken from the notes:

- Creditors and borrowings (current) includes trade creditors, other creditors and accruals, and bank overdrafts.
- Provisions (current) includes income tax, employee entitlements and declared final dividend.
- Creditors and borrowings (noncurrent) includes bank loan.
- Provisions (noncurrent) includes employee entitlements.
- Property, plant and equipment includes freehold land and buildings, plant and equipment, and motor vehicles.

There are three types of inventories: raw materials, work in progress and finished goods. These refer respectively to ingredients, partly completed products and products ready for sale.

Assume that during the year the following were some of the many transactions that occurred. Prepare journal entries for each transaction:

1 borrowed $977 000 from the bank, payable in 2006
2 purchased some flour (raw materials) from a supplier on credit for $80 000
3 received an advertising bill in July for a June advertisement of a new product called Golden Hotcakes. The bill was for $8000 and will be paid in August
4 in August paid wages outstanding from the previous year of $640 000
5 sent a cheque for $3000 to Expert Training to pay for a one-day course for six employees on marketing techniques
6 bought new icing sugar milling and handling equipment costing $400 000 (paid cash)
7 sold on credit 500 boxes of Wagon Wheels to a major supermarket for $25 000 (cost price $18 000)
8 paid last year's taxation bill of $6 231 000
9 paid May wages of $3 200 000
10 declared a final dividend of $7 567 000.

**George Weston Foods Limited**
Balance sheets as at 31 July 2001

| | Note | Consolidated | | The Company | |
|---|---|---|---|---|---|
| | | 2001<br>$000 | 2000<br>$000 | 2001<br>$000 | 2000<br>$000 |
| Current assets | | | | | |
| Cash assets | 6 | **30 448** | 41 379 | **29 386** | 36 884 |
| Receivables | 7 | **228 621** | 205 280 | **198 528** | 179 254 |

| | Note | Consolidated | | The Company | |
|---|---|---|---|---|---|
| | | 2001 $000 | 2000 $000 | 2001 $000 | 2000 $000 |
| Inventories | 8 | **168 304** | 154 730 | **146 385** | 133 782 |
| Other | 9 | **18 492** | 14 241 | **17 582** | 13 998 |
| **Total current assets** | | **445 865** | 415 630 | **391 881** | 363 918 |
| Noncurrent assets | | | | | |
| Receivables | 7 | **153** | 194 | **21 288** | 15 338 |
| Investments accounted | | | | | |
| For using the equity method | 10 | **11 156** | 8 327 | **—** | — |
| Other financial assets | 11 | **1 908** | 142 | **22 402** | 20 643 |
| Property, plant and equipment | 12 | **440 620** | 445 740 | **378 237** | 383 567 |
| Deferred tax assets | 3(d) | **5 912** | 3 135 | **5 620** | 2 808 |
| **Total noncurrent assets** | | **459 749** | 457 538 | **427 547** | 422 356 |
| **Total assets** | | **905 614** | 873 168 | **819 428** | 786 274 |
| Current liabilities | | | | | |
| Payables | 13 | **147 640** | 135 921 | **132 467** | 121 038 |
| Interest-bearing liabilities | 14 | **2 492** | — | **—** | — |
| Current tax liabilities | 3(b) | **6 231** | 10 619 | **9 090** | 11567 |
| Provisions | 16 | **52 291** | 51 378 | **49 102** | 48 178 |
| **Total current liabilities** | | **208 654** | 197 918 | **190 659** | 180 783 |
| Noncurrent liabilities | | | | | |
| Payables | 15 | **—** | — | **37 495** | 24 754 |
| Deferred tax liabilities | 3(c) | **1 390** | 524 | **—** | — |
| Provisions | 16 | **22 076** | 21 024 | **21 751** | 20 321 |
| **Total noncurrent liabilities** | | **23 466** | 21 548 | **59246** | 45075 |
| **Total liabilities** | | **232 120** | 219 466 | **249 905** | 225 858 |
| Net assets | | **673 494** | 653 702 | **569 523** | 560 416 |
| Shareholders' equity | | | | | |
| Contributed equity | 17 | **271 187** | 162 769 | **271 187** | 162 769 |
| Reserves | 18 | **130 974** | 128 133 | **116 527** | 116 527 |
| Retained profits | 19 | **271 333** | 362 800 | **181 809** | 281 120 |
| **Total shareholders' equity** | | **673 494** | 653 702 | **569 523** | 560 416 |

To be read in conjunction with the notes to and forming part of the accounts.

## Notes

1 Stone, J., 'Big Brewhaha of 1800 BC', *Discover*, January 1991, p. 14. (The words quoted in the excerpt are those of Fritz Maytag, owner of the Anchor Brewing Company of San Francisco.)

2 Information about the history of accounting and business is published in many places. A variety of professional and academic journals have shown an interest in such material, and there is a journal devoted specifically to it: the *Accounting Historians Journal.* See also the references below.

3 Coustourous, G. J., *Accounting in the Golden Age of Greece: A Response to Socioeconomic Changes*, Center for International Education and Research in Accounting, University of Illinois, Champaign, 1979.

4 Keister, O. R., 'The Mechanics of Mesopotamian Record-Keeping', in Chatfield, M. (ed.), *Contemporary Studies in the Evolution of Accounting Thought*, Dickenson Publishing Company Ltd, Belmont, 1968, pp. 12–20.
5 O ten Have, *The History of Accounting*, Bay Books, Palo Alto, 1976, pp. 27–30.
6 Ibid. pp. 30–46.
7 Chatfield, M., 'English Medieval Book-keeping: Exchequer and Manor', *Contemporary Studies in the Evolution of Accounting Thought*, p. 36.
8 Ibid., pp. 56–74.
9 O ten Have, *History*, p. 67.
10 Some of the ideas in this section were developed with reference to Ross Skinner's *Accounting Standards in Evolution*, Holt, Rinehart & Winston, Toronto, 1987. For a comprehensive treatment of the development of accounting standards, see part 1 of Skinner's book.
11 Ibid., p. 23.

# Chapter 4
# *Record-keeping*

## On completion of this chapter you should be able to:

- describe the importance of good record-keeping
- describe the criteria used to determine if an event involves an accounting transaction
- identify accounting transactions
- explain the various steps in the accounting cycle
- describe what source documents exist and how they provide data for the accounting system
- prepare journal entries
- post to ledger accounts and calculate the closing balances
- prepare a trial balance
- prepare closing entries and explain the need for these closing entries
- prepare financial statements from the trial balance.

## 4.1 The importance of good records

This chapter emphasises a very basic part of accounting: the record-keeping (bookkeeping) procedures that form the records on which accounting information is built.

Complete and accurate records are important: they provide the observations and the history of the enterprise. Without knowing what has happened, investors and managers cannot make plans for the future, evaluate alternatives properly or learn from past actions. In today's complex business environment, especially since enterprises have become very large, the number of events (or transactions, as we will call them) is much too great for anyone to keep track of without keeping accurate records (written or, these days, mostly on computer). Records provide the basis for extrapolations into the future, information for evaluating and rewarding performance, and a basis for internal control over the existence and quality of an enterprise's assets. Record-keeping, however, does cost money, and therefore records should be worth their cost. How complex and sophisticated to make one's records is a business decision, as are such decisions as how to price or market one's product.

## 4.2 Financial accounting's transactional filter

Accounting is an information system to filter and summarise data. Information systems select observations from the world, collect those results into data banks and organise and summarise the data to produce specific kinds of information. This is useful because decision-makers cannot cope with masses of raw, unorganised observations, and it is economically efficient to have one system organise data into information on behalf of various users.

An everyday example of the first reason is the daily newspaper: the editors group stories and features, so that you know where to look for what you want. There is a sports section, an entertainment section, a page for letters to the editor and so on. The daily paper is also an example of the second reason: while no newspaper contains exactly what you want, it gets close enough to what most people want, so that it can be published at a low cost compared with what it would cost you to hire reporters to get information just for you. In order to make this work, every information system has to be choosy: it must filter all the available data and pick what is relevant to its purpose. You don't expect the newspaper to contain glossy reproductions of Rembrandt paintings suitable for framing or to print the grades you received in your university courses: you go to other information sources for such things.

An information system such as financial accounting is inherently limited. It can report only what its sensors pick up as it seeks out data or filters data from the mass of ongoing events. No information system tells you 'the truth', and certainly not 'the whole truth', because it can only pass along information based on what it has been designed or permitted to gather as data. Figure 4.1 represents the situation. The gap in the wall is the system's filter or 'window on the world'. Once a piece of raw data is admitted, recording activity takes place and it is stored in a bank of data (in accounting: stored in manual or computerised accounts, ledgers, journals ('the books') and supporting records). The data in this bank are then organised to produce usable information (in accounting: financial statements and reports).

In accounting, we generally refer to the left part of the diagram, the data recording and some routine classifying and summarising, as 'bookkeeping'. We refer to the right part, the turning of data into information for users, as 'accounting' or 'reporting'. Financial

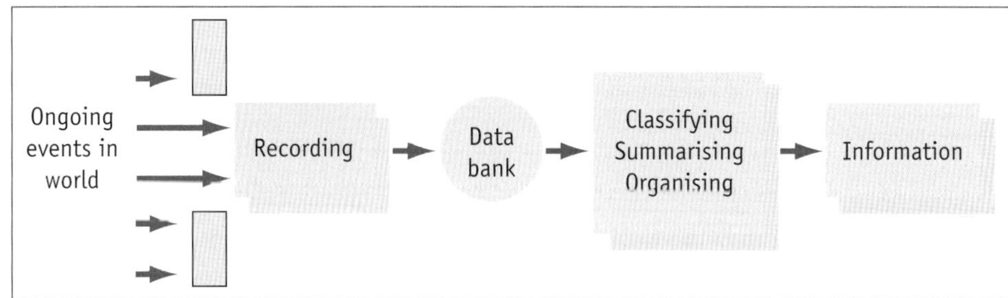


**Figure 4.1** Steps in the accounting information system

accounting information is contained in the system's final product, the financial statements and notes.

Accounting reports are based on, and are limited by, the data collected. Therefore, if you are to understand the reports, you have to understand how accounting filters, notices and chooses events to record into its data bank. Financial accounting's filter, its window on the world, is the transaction. Generally, if an event is a transaction, it is recorded in financial accounting's database; if it is not, the routine accounting system ignores the event. (You'll see in chapter 5 that one of the reasons for accrual accounting techniques is to provide for events or even non-event data that the transaction-based record-keeping system has ignored or treated improperly.)

The following are examples of external accounting transactions. They should be recorded routinely by the accounting system:

**1** The payroll department issues a cheque to pay an employee.
**2** A customer pays, in cash, an account owing since last month and gets a receipt.
**3** A sales clerk prepares an invoice for a customer, for the sale of goods the customer is taking with her and promises to pay for.
**4** The bank charges bank fees on an account.
**5** The storeroom receives a shipment of spare parts for the delivery trucks, along with an invoice from the parts supplier.

There is no limit to the number or kinds of transactions that human ingenuity can devise. Accounting has to deal with them, and must change as they change. Nowadays, many companies are scrambling to handle Internet transactions, those happening through Web pages and other areas of e-commerce, all of which are promising to change many accounting systems fundamentally.

Transactions are partly defined by the legal and economic system. In our society, promises to pay can be enforced in the courts, so they are considered transactions, as in example (3) above. Speaking very roughly, there are two general kinds of transactions important in accounting: cash transactions, which feature the concurrent exchange of cash, and credit transactions, which feature (partially or fully) promises to exchange cash in the future.

The following are examples of events that are *not* accounting transactions and that will therefore *not* be recorded routinely, if at all, by the accounting system:

**a** The chief executive officer (CEO) of the company breaks her leg while skiing.
**b** The credit department manager decides that a particular customer is probably never going to pay the account the customer owes.
**c** The main warehouse burns to the ground overnight.
**d** A customer orders a machine to be delivered next month.
**e** Real estate reports indicate the company's land has gone up in value by 14 per cent since last year.

Some such events may be brought into the system by special adjustments to the routine recording system that we will learn about later. Events (b) and (c) are examples. But many are never included in financial accounting's information system. Event (a) is an example.

Other events are recorded only after something more has happened. Event (d) is recorded by the accounting system only when the machine is delivered, and in Australian accounting, event (e) is recorded only when directors decide to revalue land (usually every three to five years).

Human ingenuity comes in here again: some large or innovative companies have accounting systems that routinely record events that are not transactions and that other or smaller companies ignore or leave to be done as special adjustments. Some examples are internal transfers of goods from department to department in the company, monthly changes in the market values of investments, estimated profit earned on partly completed construction contracts and revisions in estimates for future warranty payments. These may be included for various reasons, such as because other information systems in the company provide the necessary data so they can be used easily, or because management believes more finely tuned accounting information to be useful in decision-making.

What distinguishes accounting transactions, such as in the first list above, from the sorts of events in the second list? All of those in the second list may be important economically, but they are not routinely recorded by the accounting system. In order to qualify as a financial accounting transaction, an event must normally have all five of the following characteristics:

- Three fundamental economic and legal characteristics:
  - *exchange:* the event must involve an exchange of goods, money, financial instruments (such as cheques), legal promises or other items of economic value
  - *past:* the exchange must have happened, even if just seconds ago (financial accounting is essentially a *historical* information system)
  - *external:* the exchange must have been between the entity being accounted for and someone else, such as a customer, an owner, a supplier, an employee, a banker or a tax collector (the exchange must have been across the entity's boundary, so to speak).
- Two supplementary characteristics, needed for accounting's record-keeping:
  - *evidence:* there must be some documentation of what has happened (on paper or electronically recorded)
  - *dollars:* the event must be measurable in dollars or the currency unit relevant in the country where the transaction happens.

These transaction characteristics indicate the nature and value of financial accounting information.

- First, transactions are linked to the legal and economic concept of an exchange: completing a contract by giving or receiving consideration in return for the goods or services that change hands. The transactional basis of financial accounting thus has roots in the fundamental legal and economic processes by which society and business operate. It is no accident that accounting recognises as transactions events that have a broader legal and business importance too.
- Second, they constitute a large part of the underlying rationale for the historical cost basis of accounting, which is firmly founded on the transaction. If a transaction has *happened*, it should be in the accounting system and in the financial statements. It is history. If it has not yet happened, it is not yet the same sort of legal event and will not yet be in the historical accounting system. We can figure out how to get some events that have not happened into accounting anyway, but they often do not fit in well, and can be

controversial, because reasonable people often disagree about whether and how to bring them in.

- Third, the characteristics of the transaction provide the basis on which the records can be verified (audited) later as part of the process of ensuring that the accounting information is credible. Events that do not have these characteristics would be difficult to verify later, and therefore inevitably lack credibility as measures of financial performance or position.

Let's look at the five events from the first list above ((1) to (5)) and see that they fit the set of transaction characteristics:

| | Exchange | Past exchange | External party | Evidence | Dollars |
|---|---|---|---|---|---|
| 1 | Money | Yes | Employee | Cheque | Cheque |
| 2 | Money | Yes | Customer | Receipt | Cash |
| 3 | Goods, promise | Yes | Customer | Invoice | Price |
| 4 | Money | Yes | Bank | Bank statement | Cash |
| 5 | Goods, promise | Yes | Supplier | Invoice | Price |

The events in the second list lack several characteristics, especially that of being a past economic exchange. (Event **(4)**, for example, is not yet an exchange because the machine hasn't yet been delivered.)

What if an accountant is not satisfied with the set of data recorded by an accounting system and wishes to adjust those data to reflect some event he or she thinks is important in measuring financial performance or position? This can be done by recording special alterations to the data bank called adjustments or adjusting journal entries, which introduce new data or alter the recording of previous data. Deciding whether to make such adjustments and determining the dollar amounts to use in them require expertise and good judgement, since they involve events that are not exchanges, are not always accompanied by normal evidence, or are not readily measurable in dollars. You'll see much more about adjustments in the discussion of accrual accounting in chapter 5.

Most of this book involves the accounting (right-hand) side of the earlier information system diagram: deciding on adjustments, deciding on reporting format, making supplementary notes, and other such activities. Don't forget that the basic transactional recording system underlies the whole process, and the preceding definition of what is and isn't an external transaction gives the accounting system much of its valuable objectivity. However, also note that accrual accounting is designed to go beyond external transactions and add a further layer of information related to internal transactions such as depreciation, unpaid wages and prepayments. These are discussed in more detail in chapter 5.

## 4.3 Accounting's 'books' and records

### Accounting cycle

Figure 4.2 shows the sequence of accounting procedures from the original documentary evidence of a transaction (source documents) to the preparation of financial statements.

The source documents are the basis for journal entries, which in turn are posted to the general ledger accounts as a means of summarising the transactions. A trial balance is then taken out to ensure that the total of the debits equals the total of the credits. End of period

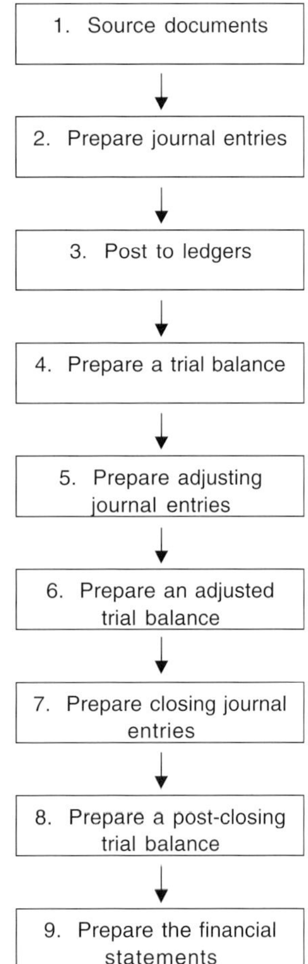


**Figure 4.2** Steps in the accounting cycle

accruals, corrections and other adjustments (covered in detail in chapter 5) are then incorporated via additional journal entries. A post-adjustment trial balance is taken out to ensure the total of the debits still equal the total of the credits. Further journal entries then close the revenue, expenses and dividend amounts to retained profits to make all of those accounts' balances zero in preparation for the next period's step 1. (The statement of financial position accounts continue into next period and so are not closed.) Financial statements are then prepared.

## The underlying accounting system

This section summarises some of the mechanics of the accounting system behind steps 1 and 9 above, to show you how transactions are summarised into the financial statements. Keep in mind, though, that this is a basic description: much has been left out in order to keep the portrayal clear. These days, for many companies, many of the 'books' referred to below are actually electronic records in computer systems.

## Source documents and the transactional cycle

Accounting record-keeping depends upon sets of documents to show that transactions have occurred. Such documents are kept so that the accounting records can be checked and verified to correct errors. They also permit auditing, and can be used in case of dispute

# LABELCRAFT

PTY. LTD. A.B.N. 61 002 533 244
40 GEORGE STREET, LEICHHARDT N.S.W. 2040
PHONE: 02-9550 0999 FAX: 02-9550 9734

TO No 19 GRAPHIC PRODUCTIONS

ORDER 32156 /620A
DATE 30 - 9 - 2001
WORK TICKET
DEL REQUIRED 18-10-2001

REFER: TERRY

NOTE: IF DELIVERY LATE, PLS. NOTIFY PURCHASING OFFICER.

| QTY. | DESCRIPTION OF GOODS | UNIT | COST | TOTAL |
|---|---|---|---|---|
| 200 | No 8 CARTON | | | 80-00 |
| 300 | No 9 CARTON | | | 120-00 |
| 100 | No 2 CARTON | | | 35-00 |
| 100 | No 10 CARTON | | | 35-00 |
| 100 | No 12 CARTON | | | 35-00 |
| | | SUB | | 305-00 |
| | | DELIVERY COST | | — |
| | | TRADING TERMS | 30 days net | |
| | | GST | | 30-50 |
| | | | TOTAL | 335-50 |

REQUISITIONED BY MATHEW
AUTHORISED BY GEORGE
DATE 30 - 9 - 2001

**DELIVERY ADDRESS:** 40 GEORGE STREET, LEICHHARDT NSW 2040.

**Figure 4.3** Example of a purchase order (reproduced courtesy of Labelcraft)

and to support income tax claims and other legal actions. The transactions themselves reflect various events in operating the business. Here are some examples from a real company, Labelcraft Pty Ltd.

1 Labelcraft, a manufacturer of self-adhesive labels and cartons, is located in Sydney. To manufacture these products it orders ink, paper and cardboard, among other things. Ordering the kinds of products it needs to produce products customers will want is an important early step. Ordering is not an accounting transaction, so orders are not recorded in the accounts, but documenting and keeping track of them is very important to Labelcraft, so it uses 'purchase order' forms for this. Figure 4.3 provides an example. You'll see that it is dated and prenumbered, so that it may be followed up in case of problems, and the items ordered are listed in detail so they can be checked against what actually arrives from the supplier. The amount of goods and services tax (GST) is added. The accounting entries for GST are covered in chapter 10.

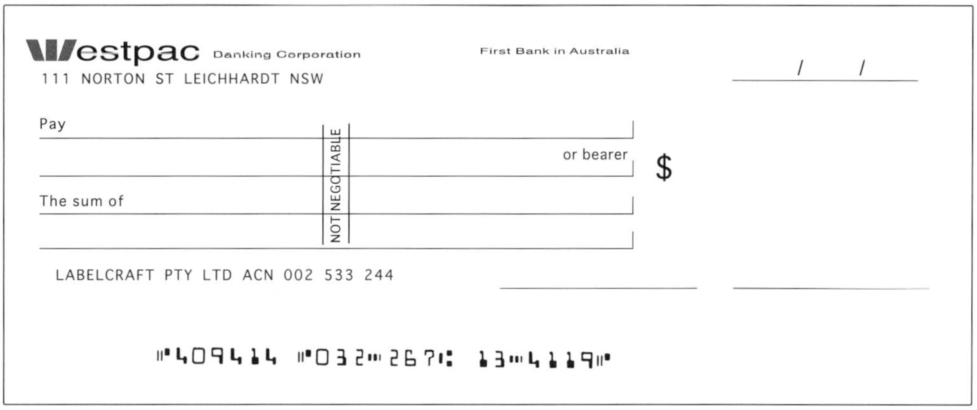

Westpac Banking Corporation
111 NORTON ST LEICHHARDT NSW
First Bank in Australia
/ /
Pay
NOT NEGOTIABLE
or bearer
$
The sum of
LABELCRAFT PTY LTD ACN 002 533 244
409414 032 2671 13 4119

**Figure 4.4** Example of a cheque (reproduced courtesy of Labelcraft)

2 When ordered items arrive, they are checked against purchase orders and the supplier's packing slips, to ensure all is proper. When Labelcraft accepts a delivery, this is an accounting transaction, and a purchases record is created to support the transaction *debit Inventory (asset) and credit Accounts payable (liability)*. Returns of goods to suppliers are recorded as well, in just the opposite way: *credit Inventory and debit Accounts payable*.

3 When Labelcraft pays the supplier, a cheque is written. A copy of that is the source document for recording the transaction *debit Accounts payable and credit Cash (bank)*. If Labelcraft receives a discount, the cheque will be for less than the amount owed; the difference *is debited to Accounts payable and credited to Cash discounts received*, an 'other revenue' account. Figure 4.4 shows Labelcraft's cheque. You'll see it is dated and pre-numbered. It also has other details on the cheque butt to allow reference later in case of problems.

4 Selling the products is what Labelcraft is in business to do. When a sale is made, a sales invoice is prepared, specifying various useful details. A copy of this invoice supports the transaction *debit Accounts receivable and credit Sales revenue*. (Through the company's computerised inventory system, the sales invoice also supports recording the cost of the goods taken by the customer, *debit Cost of goods sold expense and credit Inventory*.) You will cover the cost of goods sold calculation for a manufacturing firm in a later course on management accounting. It is determined based on the amount of material, labour and overhead incurred in the production process. Figure 4.5 provides an example of an invoice. Notice that the total amount charged is $707.30, which includes $64.30 GST. In effect, Labelcraft is collecting this amount on behalf of the government. While the entries will be shown in more detail in chapter 10, the journal entry will be: debit Accounts receivable $707.30 (that is, the amount owed by the debtor), credit Sales revenue by $643.00 (that is, revenue earned by the company) and credit GST liability account with $64.30 (that is, the amount being collected in GST on behalf of the government).

5 Collecting from customers is the last event we illustrate. When a customer pays Labelcraft, the payment is listed in the day's collections. That list is the source document to support the transaction *debit Cash (bank) and credit Accounts receivable*. It also supports the bank deposit made that day, so that if there are problems, someone can start with the monthly bank statement and trace the deposits shown on it back to the payments by individual customers. Figure 4.6 shows the list of collections for 15 October 2001.

6 These days, Labelcraft, like many businesses, relies on credit cards for customers' payments on some sales. When a customer pays by credit card, the credit card slip is

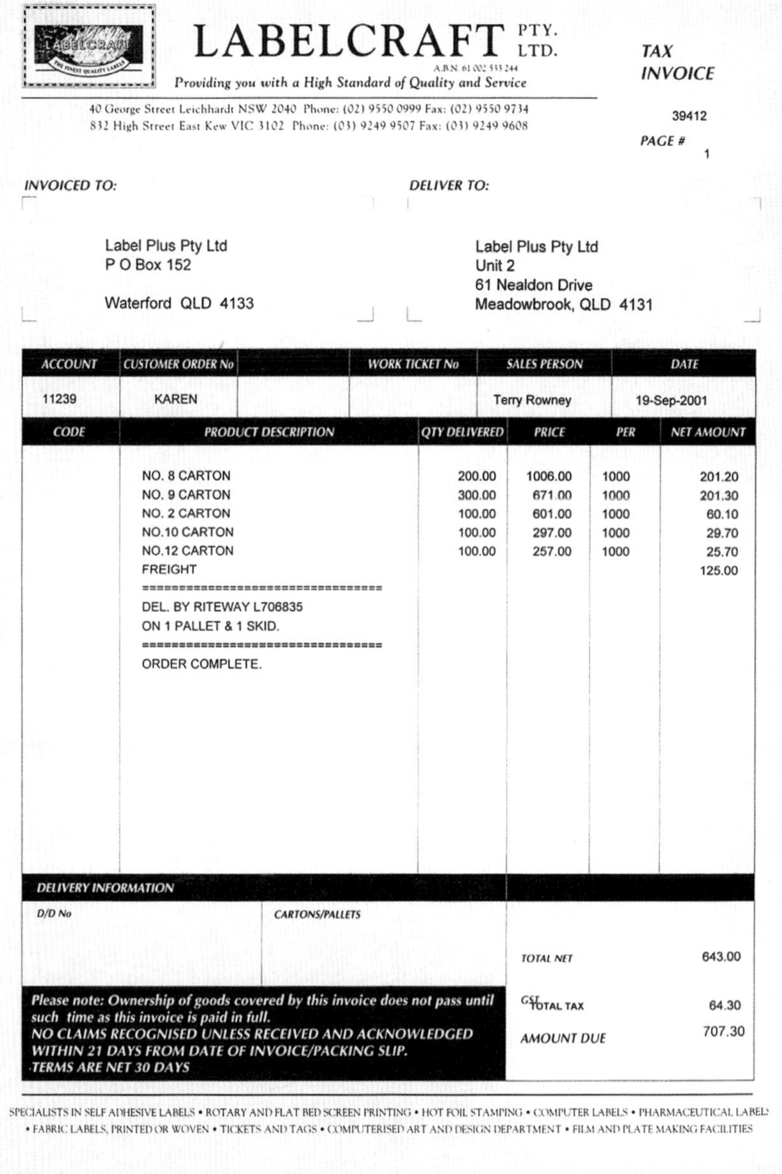
LABELCRAFT PTY. LTD.

A.B.N. 61 002 533 244

Providing you with a High Standard of Quality and Service

40 George Street Leichhardt NSW 2040 Phone: (02) 9550 0999 Fax: (02) 9550 9734
832 High Street East Kew VIC 3102 Phone: (03) 9249 9507 Fax: (03) 9249 9608

TAX INVOICE

39412

PAGE # 1

INVOICED TO:

Label Plus Pty Ltd
P O Box 152

Waterford QLD 4133

DELIVER TO:

Label Plus Pty Ltd
Unit 2
61 Nealdon Drive
Meadowbrook, QLD 4131

| ACCOUNT | CUSTOMER ORDER No | WORK TICKET No | SALES PERSON | DATE |
|---|---|---|---|---|
| 11239 | KAREN | | Terry Rowney | 19-Sep-2001 |

| CODE | PRODUCT DESCRIPTION | QTY DELIVERED | PRICE | PER | NET AMOUNT |
|---|---|---|---|---|---|
| | NO. 8 CARTON | 200.00 | 1006.00 | 1000 | 201.20 |
| | NO. 9 CARTON | 300.00 | 671.00 | 1000 | 201.30 |
| | NO. 2 CARTON | 100.00 | 601.00 | 1000 | 60.10 |
| | NO.10 CARTON | 100.00 | 297.00 | 1000 | 29.70 |
| | NO.12 CARTON | 100.00 | 257.00 | 1000 | 25.70 |
| | FREIGHT | | | | 125.00 |
| | ================================= | | | | |
| | DEL. BY RITEWAY L706835 | | | | |
| | ON 1 PALLET & 1 SKID. | | | | |
| | ================================= | | | | |
| | ORDER COMPLETE. | | | | |

DELIVERY INFORMATION

D/D No | CARTONS/PALLETS

| | |
|---|---|
| TOTAL NET | 643.00 |
| GST TOTAL TAX | 64.30 |
| AMOUNT DUE | 707.30 |

*Please note: Ownership of goods covered by this invoice does not pass until such time as this invoice is paid in full.*
*NO CLAIMS RECOGNISED UNLESS RECEIVED AND ACKNOWLEDGED WITHIN 21 DAYS FROM DATE OF INVOICE/PACKING SLIP.*
*TERMS ARE NET 30 DAYS*

SPECIALISTS IN SELF ADHESIVE LABELS • ROTARY AND FLAT BED SCREEN PRINTING • HOT FOIL STAMPING • COMPUTER LABELS • PHARMACEUTICAL LABELS • FABRIC LABELS, PRINTED OR WOVEN • TICKETS AND TAGS • COMPUTERISED ART AND DESIGN DEPARTMENT • FILM AND PLATE MAKING FACILITIES

**Figure 4.5** Example of an invoice (reproduced courtesy of Labelcraft)

deposited into the bank just like cash or a cheque (the credit card company bills Labelcraft for its fee monthly). Some customers pay Labelcraft by just notifying their and its banks to transfer the money to pay, without bothering with cheques or credit cards. This sort of electronic funds transfer (EFT) is becoming more common for many organisations, especially by large regular customers.

Without keeping track of EFTs and credit card payments, Labelcraft would have little idea of what its bank balances should be.

Labelcraft uses more kinds of documents. It has more electronic transfers, for example paying all employees by direct deposit into their bank accounts. There are many kinds of documents used by various companies. Each company adapts documents to its own needs, especially to provide legal evidence and support accounting transactions records. You can count on two things about any company, government, sports club or other organisation:

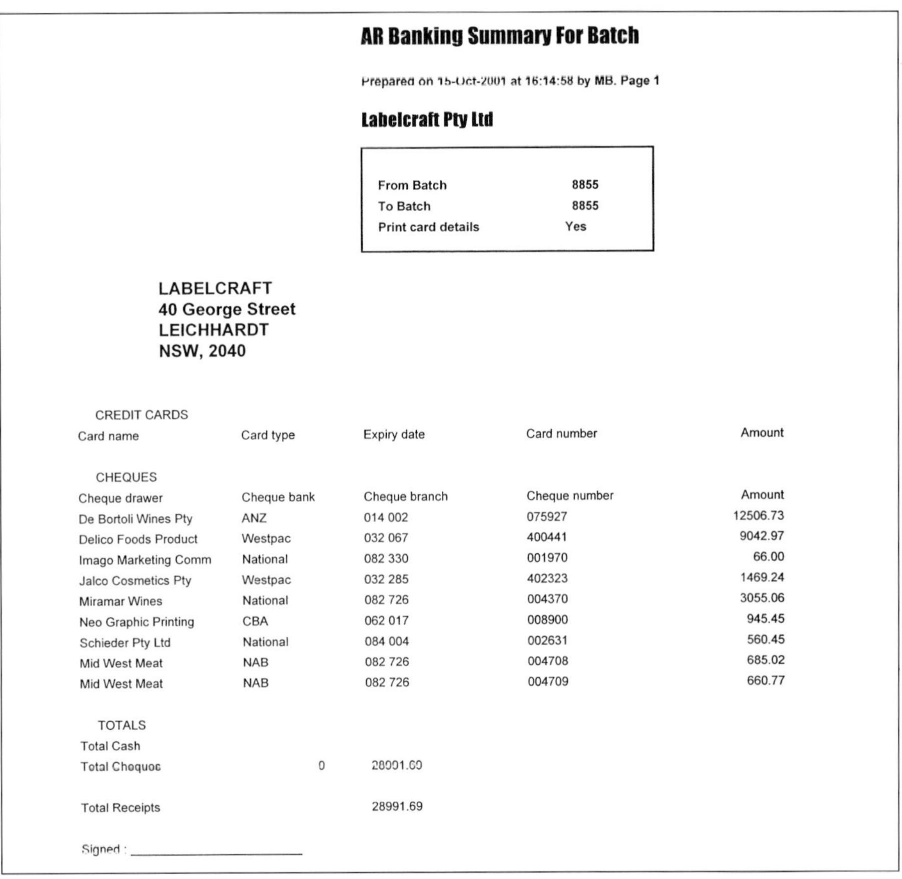

**AR Banking Summary For Batch**

Prepared on 15-Oct-2001 at 16:14:58 by MB. Page 1

**Labelcraft Pty Ltd**

| | |
|---|---|
| From Batch | 8855 |
| To Batch | 8855 |
| Print card details | Yes |

LABELCRAFT
40 George Street
LEICHHARDT
NSW, 2040

CREDIT CARDS

| Card name | Card type | Expiry date | Card number | Amount |
|---|---|---|---|---|

CHEQUES

| Cheque drawer | Cheque bank | Cheque branch | Cheque number | Amount |
|---|---|---|---|---|
| De Bortoli Wines Pty | ANZ | 014 002 | 075927 | 12506.73 |
| Delico Foods Product | Westpac | 032 067 | 400441 | 9042.97 |
| Imago Marketing Comm | National | 082 330 | 001970 | 66.00 |
| Jalco Cosmetics Pty | Westpac | 032 285 | 402323 | 1469.24 |
| Miramar Wines | National | 082 726 | 004370 | 3055.06 |
| Neo Graphic Printing | CBA | 062 017 | 008900 | 945.45 |
| Schieder Pty Ltd | National | 084 004 | 002631 | 560.45 |
| Mid West Meat | NAB | 082 726 | 004708 | 685.02 |
| Mid West Meat | NAB | 082 726 | 004709 | 660.77 |

TOTALS

| | | |
|---|---|---|
| Total Cash | | |
| Total Cheques | 0 | 28991.69 |
| Total Receipts | | 28991.69 |

Signed : ____________________

**Figure 4.6** Example of a bank deposit (reproduced courtesy of Labelcraft)

(1) it will have various documents to back up its accounting system; and (2) those documents will be suited to that organisation and so might not be quite like any other organisation's.

## Journal entries

Based on source documents, accounting transactions are recorded by preparing journal entries. Because this is when the business event is first recorded by the accounting system, these basic transactional records are often called books of original entry.

Journal entries were introduced in chapter 3 to illustrate the use of debits and credits. Journal entries provide in chronological order a record of all transactions recorded by an organisation.

Journal entries can take many different forms depending on such factors as the size of the organisation, the frequency of transactions and the frequency of providing reports. In this section we describe the simplest form known as a general journal entry. You had some practice in preparing journal entries in chapter 3 but it is worth reinforcing here. Consider the following transactions:

- A consulting company provides services to a client and sends it an invoice (source document) for \$10 000.
- The company buys a motor vehicle for \$30 000, paying \$12 000 cash and owing \$18 000 to be paid in two years.

These would be recorded as follows:

| Journal entry number | Date | Particulars | Posting reference | Debit | Credit |
|---|---|---|---|---|---|
| | 2002 | | | | |
| 1 | Feb 1 | Accounts receivable | 2 | 10 000 | |
| | | Consulting revenue | 316 | | 10 000 |
| Consulting services rendered on credit. | | | | | |
| 2 | Feb 3 | Motor vehicle | 27 | 30 000 | |
| | | Cash | 1 | | 12 000 |
| | | Long-term loan | 160 | | 18 000 |
| Purchased a motor vehicle paying $12 000 cash with remaining $18 000 to be paid in two years. | | | | | |

Note that an alternative format of the journal entries often puts the debit (DR) and credit (CR) before each account rather than as heading to the right hand column. For example:

| | | | |
|---|---|---|---|
| DR | Accounts receivable | 10 000 | |
| CR | Consulting revenue | | 10 000 |

From the above journal entries the following should be noted:

- All journal entries have one or more accounts debited and one or more accounts credited. A journal entry can list as many accounts as are needed to record the transaction, but each journal entry must be recorded so that the sum of the debits equals the sum of the credits for that entry. If not, the accounting equation will not be maintained (the books will not balance).
- It is traditional for the debits to be listed first in each journal entry and for the debits to be written to the left and the credits to the right. Neither of these is arithmetically necessary, but keeping a consistent style helps keep the records understandable.
- It is customary to omit the dollar signs in writing the entries. The transaction has to be measurable in dollars, so putting in dollar signs is thought redundant.
- It is also traditional to write a short explanation called a narration below each entry, as a memorandum of what the recorded transaction was about. Again, this is not necessary, but helps to make the record understandable.
- Every journal entry should also be dated, and is usually numbered, so there is no doubt about when the transaction was recorded. The date can have important legal and tax implications, and, of course, it is necessary to know to which financial period a transaction belongs when financial statements are being prepared.
- A posting reference is given to indicate the ledger account to which each journal entry is posted. This number can be obtained from the company's chart of accounts. In determining what accounts to use, accountants develop a chart of accounts and use it to determine the name of the account which is affected by a transaction. A chart of accounts is a listing of the titles of all accounts. For example, assets may be numbered 1 to 99, liabilities 100 to 199, shareholders' equity 200 to 299, revenues 300 to 399 and expenses 400 to 499. This allows room for expansion over time as new account titles are required for new types of transactions. An illustration is provided in section 4.5.

Enterprises with many transactions to record, which are most enterprises, do not create a separate journal entry for each transaction, but instead use special records for each frequent routine kind of transaction, such as a sales journal, a cash receipts journal, a cash payments journal and a purchases journal. These are illustrated in the appendix to chapter 5.

Many bookkeeping systems are computerised. These systems may or may not produce records that look like the preceding examples, but they have the same arithmetical objective of keeping all the debits equal to all the credits. You saw spreadsheet printout examples in chapter 3, but spreadsheets are a little cumbersome for handling large numbers of transactions, so most enterprises use special accounting software.

## Posting to ledgers

Consider the situation where during the month 500 journal entries were written, of which 80 included either a debit or credit to the cash account. If you were asked the balance of the cash account at the end of the month, how would you find out? One option is to get the opening balance, add on all debit entries affecting cash and deduct all credit entries affecting cash. But doing this is time-consuming, and it would be preferable to have a source that will give you the balance of the account at any point in time. Such a source is a ledger. Ledgers are books (or computer records) having a separate page or account code for each individual account referred to in the books of original entry. Each area or page contains a summary of all the transactions relating to that particular account and therefore 'posted' to it.

Here is an example of the 'Cash in Bank' account for a company:

**Cash in bank**

| Date | Description | Entry no. | Debits | Credits | Balance |
|---|---|---|---|---|---|
| Dec 1/02 | First deposit | 1 | 10 000 | | 10 000 DR |
| Dec 2 | Deposit | 3 | 1 146 | | 11 146 DR |
| Dec 2 | Cheque | 7 | | 678 | 10 468 DR |
| Dec 2 | Cheque | 8 | | 2 341 | 8 127 DR |

You see the idea. Each account is really just a convenient summary of the entries affecting it. In turn, the statement of financial position is a summary of all the account balances. The general ledger is the complete set of all the accounts (assets, liabilities, equity accounts, revenues and expenses) that lie behind the financial statements.

You might think of the ledger as a set of account pages (real pages, such as in the bound books the bookkeepers of old used, or representations in a computer system) such as the one above, in which the sum of all the debit balance accounts equals the sum of all the credit balance accounts. The picture in figure 4.7, using the accounting equation format and including the Cash in bank account above, might be useful.

For demonstration and analysis purposes, accountants and accounting instructors often use a simplified version of an account called a 'T-account', which includes only the debits and credits columns of the account, without calculating the balance after every entry. A T-account version of the above cash account example would look like this:

**Cash in bank**

| DR | CR |
|---|---|
| 10 000 | 678 |
| 1 146 | 2 341 |
| 8 127 | |

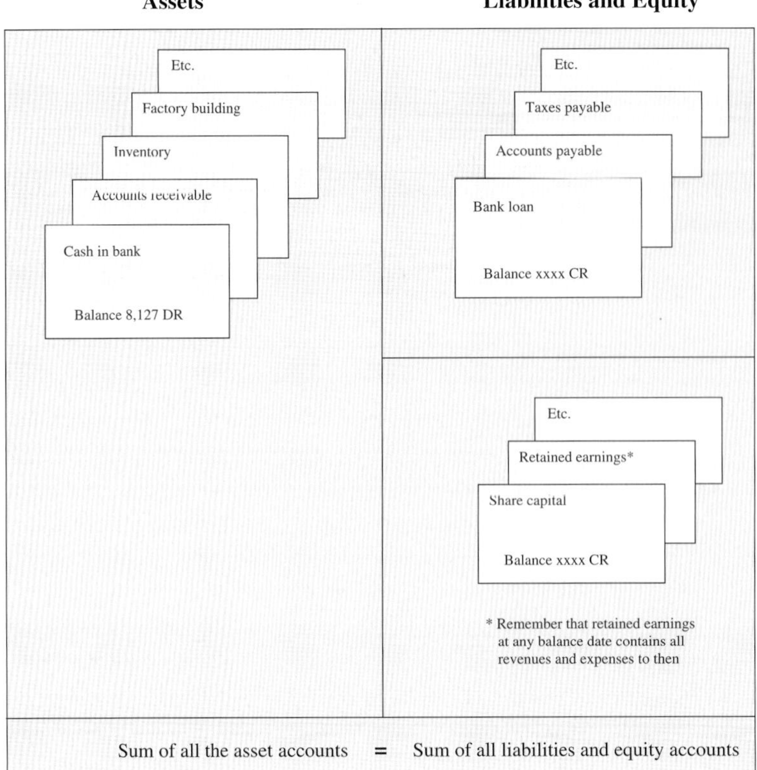


Figure 4.7

The balance of $8127 is simply the amount by which the debit entries exceed the credit entries.

Note that the normal balance of asset accounts is a debit and the normal balance of liabilities and equity accounts is a credit balance. (Also note that, as revenues increase equity, their normal balance is a credit and, as expenses reduce equity, their normal balance is debit).

By convention, left-hand entries to ledgers are called debits and right-hand entries are called credits. Here is an example of some ledger accounts:

Recall our earlier debit/credit conventions from chapter 3:

- For asset accounts, increases are recorded on the left-hand side (that is, debit) and decreases are recorded on the right-hand side (that is, credit).
- For liabilities and shareholders' equity accounts, the opposite occurs. Increases are recorded on the right-hand side (credit) and decreases are recorded on the left-hand side (debit).

Posting from the journal to the ledger is very mechanical. You simply do what the journal entry tells you to do. That is, if it says debit cash for $100, you place $100 on the debit side of the cash ledger account. To illustrate, we will post the two journal entries from the previous section.

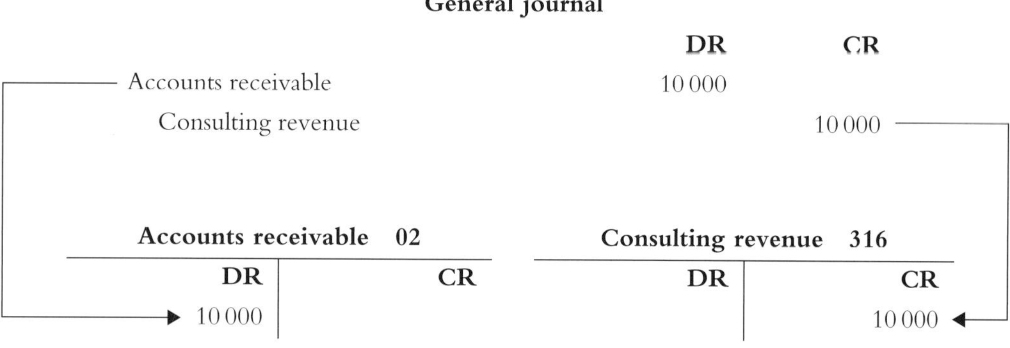


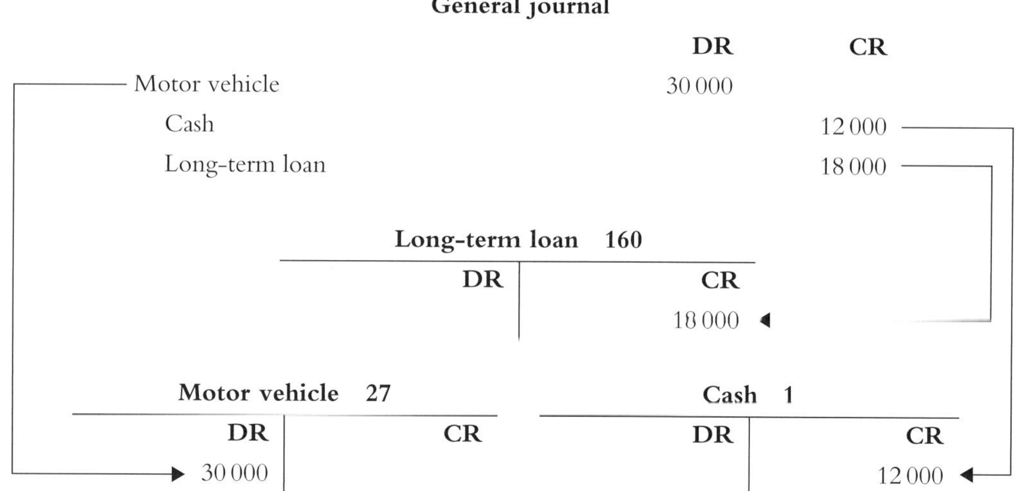


At this point you may be questioning why we need journal entries at all. That is, why not recognise a transaction, then put it straight to the ledger? The reason is that we want to have a complete record of all transactions, and the general journal does give us that. Each ledger account only records part of the transaction, so we would not have the whole transaction shown together.

The ledger accounts referred to above are called 'general ledgers' – the collection of all the asset, liability, equity, revenue and expense accounts, summarising the entire operations of the business. The general ledger is the central record of the financial accounting system, and is the basis on which the financial statements are prepared. The ledger may be a 'book' or it may be space on a computer disk.

In addition to the general ledger, most companies will maintain various subsidiary ledgers – accounts receivable and accounts payable ledgers are two examples of subsidiary ledgers. For instance, if a company extends credit to its customers, it may want to keep a separate ledger account for each customer. These ledgers are balanced by making sure that their accounts add up to the same amount as is shown in the relevant general ledger account (for example, the accounts receivable 'control' account in the general ledger, which is the account used to prepare the financial statements, should have the same balance as the list of customers' individual accounts). A subsidiary ledger does not 'balance' by having its debits equal its credits, but rather by having its sum equal the amount in the primary account in the general ledger. Making sure this is true is an important way of ensuring that individual customer accounts receivable, for example, are correct. Subsidiary ledgers, therefore, are part of the internal control system; their details are not in the financial statements, but they support the validity of the main 'control' account that does appear in the financial statements. Subsidiary ledgers are discussed further in the appendix to chapter 5 and 'Internal control' in chapter 6.

## Trial balance

Because the general ledger contains all the accounts, all of which came from balanced journal entries, it must balance (sum of debit-balance accounts equalling sum of credit-balance accounts) and it leads to a balanced statement of financial position. Because errors might have been made, a standard bookkeeping procedure is to check that the ledger does balance by adding up all the debit and all the credit account balances and making sure the two totals are equal. There is always a little uncertainty that this will work, so the calculation is called a trial balance.

An example of a trial balance is shown in exhibit 4.1.

**EXHIBIT 4.1** **Trial Balance**

**As at 30 June 2002**

| | DR | CR |
|---|---|---|
| | $ | $ |
| Cash | 15 000 | |
| Accounts receivable | 65 000 | |
| Inventory | 130 000 | |
| Accounts payable | | 40 000 |
| Sales | | 100 000 |
| Wages expense | 30 000 | |
| Other expenses | 20 000 | |
| Share capital | | 100 000 |
| Retained profits | | 20 000 |
| | 260 000 | 260 000 |

The above trial balance is for a company with only a very small number of accounts. In practice, the trial balance would include a balance of every account included in the company's chart of accounts.

What would you do if your trial balance doesn't balance? Here are some steps to follow:

- Re-add the trial balance.
- Check that you posted the correct amounts in the journal entries to the correct side of the ledger account.
- Check that you balanced each ledger account correctly.
- Check that each journal entry balances (that is, DR = CR).
- Determine how much the difference between the debits and credits is and look for an account with that balance. This would indicate you have left this ledger balance out. Also look for a journal entry with that amount, as this would indicate you have not posted one side of the entry.
- Divide the difference by 2 and look for a journal entry for that amount. It is likely that the amount is posted to the wrong side of the account.

- If the difference is divisible by 9, it is likely a transposition error has been made, for example, 21 instead of 12; 72 instead of 27.

Not all errors that are made will be picked up by the trial balance. Consider the journal entry:

| | | | |
|---|---|---|---|
| DR | Accounts receivable | 10 000 | |
| CR | Consulting revenue | | 10 000 |

If the following errors were made, would the trial balance still balance?

- The journal entry was not posted.
- The journal entry was posted by debiting consulting revenue and crediting accounts receivable.
- The accounts receivable amount was correctly posted, but the consulting revenue amount was posted to share capital by mistake.
- Posted $1000 instead of $10 000 for both accounts.

In all four cases, the trial balance will still balance!

## Adjusting entries

At the end of each accounting period it is necessary to adjust the revenue and expense accounts (and the related asset and liability accounts) to reflect expenses incurred but not yet paid, revenues earned but not yet received, cash received from customers before the work being done and the using up of assets, which creates an expense (for example, depreciation).

It is all about splitting an expense or revenue item across two different accounting periods. For example, an insurance payment could be made in March 2002 covering 1 April 2002 to 30 March 2003. At 30 June 2002, accounts have to be adjusted to reflect that 25 per cent of the payment is a 2002 expense and 75 per cent is a 2003 expense. Assuming that the payment for insurance (say, $200 000) was put to an asset account in March (that is, DR Prepayments $200 000; CR Cash $200 000), at 30 June it is necessary to reduce the asset (prepayments) to reflect that part of the asset is used up. Therefore:

| | | | | |
|---|---|---|---|---|
| 30 June 2002 | DR | Insurance expense | 50 000 | |
| | CR | Prepayments | | 50 000 |

This adjusting entry would be posted to the relevant ledger accounts, then another trial balance can be prepared. The various types of adjustments are discussed in chapter 5.

## Closing entries

To facilitate the preparation of the financial statements and to prepare the accounting records to begin the next period, a company may prepare closing entries. Closing entries formally transfer the balances of the revenue and expense accounts to a profit and loss summary, then to retained profits.

Closing entries also reset the revenue and expense account balances to zero to begin recording these items for the next accounting period.

Closing entries are simple to prepare. Revenue accounts have credit balances and are closed (reduced to zero) with debits to the revenue accounts and a credit to the profit and loss summary account. Expense accounts have debit balances and are closed (reduced to zero), with credits to the expense accounts and debits to the profit and loss summary account. The profit and loss summary account, which is simply a holding account, is then closed off to retained profits. If the profit and loss summary has a credit balance (that is, a profit has been made), the entry is debit profit and loss summary and credit retained profits. If the account has a debit balance (that is, a loss has been made), the entry is a credit to profit and loss summary and a debit to retained profits.

To illustrate closing entries, we will use exhibit 4.1 as an example. The only accounts that need to be closed off are the revenue and expense accounts (asset, liability and share capital accounts are carried forward as opening balance of the following period).

At 30 June 2002 the ledger accounts will appear as follows:

**Sales**

| DR | CR |
|---|---|
| | 100 000 |

**Wages expense**

| DR | CR |
|---|---|
| 30 000 | |

**Other expenses**

| DR | CR |
|---|---|
| 20 000 | |

To get the sales account back to zero, we would need to debit it with a corresponding credit to profit and loss summary. To get the expense accounts back to zero, we would have to credit both these accounts and correspondingly debit the profit and loss summary account. The profit and loss summary would then be closed by debiting it (it will have a credit balance because revenues are greater than expenses in this case) and crediting retained profits. This would result in the following journal entries:

| | | | |
|---|---|---|---|
| DR | Sales | 100 000 | |
| CR | P & L summary | | 100 000 |
| DR | P & L summary | 30 000 | |
| CR | Wages expense | | 30 000 |
| DR | P & L summary | 20 000 | |
| CR | Other expenses | | 20 000 |

At this point sales, wages expense and other expenses have zero balances, while profit and loss summary has a credit balance of $50 000. To clear it, the following entry is prepared:

| | | | |
|---|---|---|---|
| DR | P & L summary | 50 000 | |
| CR | Retained profits | | 50 000 |

**P & L summary**

| | |
|---|---|
| 30 000 | 100 000 |
| 20 000 | |
| 50 000 | |
| 100 000 | 100 000 |

**Retained profits**

| | |
|---|---|
| | 20 000 |
| | 50 000 |
| | 70 000 |

## Post-closing trial balance

A post-closing trial balance can now be prepared as follows:

| | DR | CR |
|---|---|---|
| Cash | 15 000 | |
| Accounts receivable | 65 000 | |
| Inventory | 130 000 | |
| Accounts payable | | 40 000 |
| Share capital | | 100 000 |
| Retained profits | | 70 000 |
| | 210 000 | 210 000 |

## Financial statements

The items in the P & L summary can be used as a basis for preparing the statement of financial performance (profit and loss statement), and the items in the post-closing trial balance can be used to prepare the statement of financial position (balance sheet). These statements are shown in exhibit 4.2.

**EXHIBIT 4.2**

**Statement of financial performance for the period ending 30 June 2002**

| | | |
|---|---|---|
| Sales | | 100 000 |
| less Operating expenses: | | |
| Wages | 30 000 | |
| Other | 20 000 | 50 000 |
| Net profit | | 50 000 |

**Statement of financial position as at 30 June 2002**

| | |
|---|---|
| **Assets** | |
| Cash | 15 000 |
| Accounts receivable | 65 000 |
| Inventory | 130 000 |
| | 210 000 |
| **Liabilities** | |
| Accounts payable | 40 000 |
| Net assets | 170 000 |
| **Shareholders' equity** | |
| Share capital | 100 000 |
| Retained profits | 70 000 |
| | 170 000 |

### For your interest

Above we noted that the asset accounts are not closed off. Their balances are carried forward as the opening balance of the next accounting period. This is not a new concept by any means.

Recall in chapter 3 where we mentioned that Sergeant Jeremiah Murphy is a significant person in Australian accounting history as he was the first person in Australia in respect of whose affairs a ledger account prepared within the double-entry accounting system was found. Professor Craig notes that 'Murphy's ledger account was balanced on 30 June 1817 and *that balance was carried down to form 1 July opening balance for the forthcoming account period* [emphasis added]. But some things have changed: when Murphy withdrew his deposit after five months it had not attracted a single bank fee!'

(Source: Craig, R., 'Jeremiah Murphy: Bank Account No. 1', *Australian CPA*, December 1998.)

## 4.4 An example: Northern Star Theatre Company

Record-keeping examples were used in prior chapters without exactly calling them that. Therefore, to help you tie down your knowledge, let's examine a specific example and follow the business events from transactions through to the financial statements.

A group of aspiring actors from Adelaide decided to form a theatre company to perform in Sydney and other festivals. Here are events that happened to Northern Star Theatre Company in its first production, presented at the Sydney Theatre Festival in 2002:

1 The theatre company was formed on 1 October 2001, and a bank account was arranged for in the company's name. Five actors each agreed to put $500 into the company, but not until the money was needed.
2 The company applied in December 2001 for a place in the August 2002 Sydney Festival, paying a fee of $400. Each actor paid $90 of the agreed capital amount to provide the money for the fee.
3 The Festival notified the company in January 2002 that it had been accepted and allocated seven performances.
4 The company would have to pay a royalty to the play's author after the performances. The details were agreed with the author in March 2002.
5 Rehearsals began in March, and costumes and other props costing $470 were purchased. To pay for those items, each of the actors paid $100 more of the agreed capital amount.
6 In early August, one of the actors, Elaine, drove to Sydney to see the venue and settle some staging details. The trip cost $290 in petrol and other expenses, all of which the company reimbursed after collecting another $100 from each member of the company.
7 In mid-August, the five actors drove to Sydney, a few days ahead of their performance date. They stayed with friends and spent the time constructing a set for the play and gathering other props. The set and props cost $610 in materials to construct, all of which was promised to be paid as soon as the play was over. The cost of the car petrol and motels along the way was $190, and the members who had paid for such expenses were also promised repayment after the play was over.
8 The play opened to an enthusiastic audience. The Festival collected $897. The money was deposited in the company's bank account using a Sydney branch of the bank.
9 Of the amounts owing for the props and set materials, $525 was paid in August.
10 The play was a moderate success. Total revenue for the remaining performances in August/September was $4840.

Now work through how these simple events are recorded (if at all) and accumulated in a very simple accounting system. Note that though this system is much simpler than large companies would have, it probably is all the company needs at this stage in its existence. It is important to match the accounting system to the needed level of sophistication.

## Step 1: Source documents

The five aspiring actors, who kept their other jobs, had a lot to plan and prepare, without worrying about accounting. But they knew they had to keep track of things, so one of them kept a box for all the company's documents. For the above events, the following items were in the box at the end of September:

**EXHIBIT 4.3** Northern Star Theatre Company

General journal

| No. | Date | Description | Debits | Credits |
|---|---|---|---|---|
| 1 | Nov 01 | No transaction so no entry | | |
| 2a | Dec 01 | Cash (bank) | 450 | |
| | | Share capital | | 450 |
| | | *Initial contributions by shareholders: 5 × $90, per bank records.* | | |
| 2b | Dec 01 | Performance fees expense | 400 | |
| | | Cash (bank) | | 400 |
| | | *Fee paid to the Sydney Festival to apply for a performance venue in 2002* | | |
| 3 | Jan 02 | No transaction so no entry | | |
| 4 | Mar 02 | No transaction so no entry | | |
| 5a | Mar 02 | Cash (bank) | 500 | |
| | | Share capital | | 500 |
| | | *Further contributions by five shareholders: 5 × $100* | | |
| 5b | Mar 02 | Costumes and props expense | 470 | |
| | | Cash (bank) | | 470 |
| | | *Costumes and props purchased per suppliers' bills* | | |
| 6a | Jul 02 | Cash (bank) | 500 | |
| | | Share capital | | 500 |
| | | *Further contributions by five shareholders: 5 × $100* | | |
| 6b | Jul 02 | Travel expense | 290 | |
| | | Cash (bank) | | 290 |
| | | *Reimbursement to Elaine for her trip to Sydney to check out the venue* | | |
| 7a | Aug 02 | Travel expense | 190 | |
| | | Accounts payable | | 190 |
| | | *Recording the liability to various people for travel expenses* | | |
| 7b | Aug 02 | Costumes and props expense | 610 | |
| | | Accounts payable | | 610 |
| | | *Recording the liability to various people for sets and props constructed in Sydney* | | |
| 8 | Aug 02 | Cash (bank) | 897 | |
| | | Performance revenue | | 897 |
| | | *Gate receipts for the first night* | | |
| 9 | Aug 02 | Accounts payable | 525 | |
| | | Cash (bank) | | 525 |
| | | *Paid some of what is owed for set and props* | | |
| 10 | Sept 02 | Cash (bank) | 4 840 | |
| | | Performance revenue | | 4 840 |
| | | *Gate receipts for remaining performances* | | |

**EXHIBIT 4.4** Northern Star Theatre Company

## General ledger

### Cash (bank)

| Date | Entry | Debit | Credit | Balance |
|---|---|---|---|---|
| Dec 01 | 2a | 450 | | 450 DR |
| Dec 01 | 2b | | 400 | 50 DR |
| Mar 02 | 5a | 500 | | 550 DR |
| Mar 02 | 5b | | 470 | 80 DR |
| Jul 02 | 6a | 500 | | 580 DR |
| Jul 02 | 6b | | 290 | 290 DR |
| Aug 02 | 8 | 897 | | 1 187 DR |
| Aug 02 | 9 | | 525 | 662 DR |
| Sept 02 | 10 | 4 840 | | 5 502 DR |

### Accounts payable

| Date | Entry | Debit | Credit | Balance |
|---|---|---|---|---|
| Aug 02 | 7a | | 190 | 190 CR |
| Aug 02 | 7b | | 610 | 800 CR |
| Aug 02 | 9 | 525 | | 275 CR |

### Share capital

| Date | Entry | Debit | Credit | Balance |
|---|---|---|---|---|
| Dec 01 | 2a | | 450 | 450 CR |
| Mar 02 | 5a | | 500 | 950 CR |
| Jul 02 | 6a | | 500 | 1 450 CR |

### Performance revenue

| Date | Entry | Debit | Credit | Balance |
|---|---|---|---|---|
| Aug 02 | 8 | | 897 | 897 CR |
| Sept 02 | 10 | | 4 840 | 5 737 CR |

### Performance fees expense

| Date | Entry | Debit | Credit | Balance |
|---|---|---|---|---|
| Dec 01 | 2b | 400 | | 400 DR |

### Costumes and props expense

| Date | Entry | Debit | Credit | Balance |
|---|---|---|---|---|
| Mar 02 | 5b | 470 | | 470 DR |
| Aug 02 | 7b | 610 | | 1 080 DR |

### Travel expense

| Date | Entry | Debit | Credit | Balance |
|---|---|---|---|---|
| Aug 02 | 6b | 290 | | 290 DR |
| Aug 02 | 7a | 190 | | 480 DR |

- a bank account agreement signed by the bank and two of the actors on behalf of the company, along with unused cheques and deposit slips for the account. There was also an agreement to issue 5000 shares and that each actor would put in $500 in return for one-fifth of the shares each
- a bank statement showing the $450 deposit and the $400 cheque, along with a receipt from the Festival for the $400 fee
- the Festival's notification of acceptance
- a note about the phone call making the royalty agreement with the author
- processed bills for the $470, along with a bank statement showing the deposit of the $500 and the $470 in cheques
- a bank statement showing the deposit of the $500 and the $290 cheque, along with various bills supporting the $290 travel cost
- bills for the $610 in props and the $190 in travel expenses
- a receipt for the deposit of the $897 and $4840 and a report from the Festival showing these amounts
- a cheque butt indicating the payment of $525.

## Step 2: Recording the transactions in a journal

A general journal to record the transactions is shown in exhibit 4.3. Exact dates would be necessary, but only the months were given above and they are used below.

## Step 3: Posting (summarising) journal entries in ledger

The recorded transactions, posted to general ledger accounts, are shown in exhibit 4.4. The accounts are listed in the order in which they arose in the entries, not necessarily in the order they would appear in the chart of accounts.

## Step 4: Trial balance to see if ledger balances

The general ledger trial balance is shown in exhibit 4.5.

It was agreed that a set of financial statements would be a good idea as soon as the production was over. It was decided to prepare the accounts at 30 September 2002 covering the full year. Before preparing them, a number of adjustments needed to be considered.

**EXHIBIT 4.5** **Northern Star Theatre Company**

**General ledger trial balance September 2002**

| | Debit $ | Credit $ |
|---|---|---|
| Cash (bank) | 5 502 | |
| Accounts payable | | 275 |
| Share capital | | 1 450 |
| Performance revenue | | 5 737 |
| Performance fees expense | 400 | |
| Costumes and props expense | 1 080 | |
| Travel expense | 480 | |
| Totals | 7 462 | 7 462 |

## Step 5: Accruals and adjustments

1 The play's writer was owed her royalty, which had been agreed at $450.
2 A group member had spent $215 on travel expenses during September but had not yet put her claim in for reimbursement.
3 The sum of $1080 had been spent on costumes and props. The group estimated that costumes and props costing about $420 were not reusable, but that the rest were reusable and would last on average about five engagements, including the just-finished Festival as one of the five. The actors agreed to keep going, and therefore agreed that the costumes and props could be accounted for on a going-concern basis – that is, assuming there would continue to be a theatre company and, therefore, that the usable costumes and props had some future value.
4 After talking to the bank, one of the actors estimated that, to 30 September, about $20 in interest would have been earned by the money in the bank account.

Exhibit 4.6 shows the journal entries to adjust the accounts to recognise the effects of the additional information.

**EXHIBIT 4.6** **Northern Star Theatre Company**

**General journal**

| No | Date | Description | Debits $ | Credits $ |
|---|---|---|---|---|
| 11 | Sept 02 | Royalties expense | 450 | |
| | | Accrued expenses | | 450 |
| | | *Royalty owed to author* | | |
| 12 | Sept 02 | Travel expense | 215 | |
| | | Accrued expenses | | 215 |
| | | *Travel costs owed to actors* | | |
| 13a | Sept 02 | Costumes and props asset | 660 | |
| | | Costumes and props expense | | 660 |
| | | *Capitalising the cost of the costumes and props having future value* | | |
| 13b | Sept 02 | Depreciation expense | 132 | |
| | | Accumulated depreciation | | 132 |
| | | *Depreciation of costumes and props assets: 1/5 of $660 for the Sydney engagement* | | |
| 14 | Sept 02 | Interest receivable | 20 | |
| | | Interest revenue | | 20 |
| | | *Estimated interest earned by the bank account to 30 September 2002* | | |

These entries have to be posted, just as the ones in step 3 were. The changes and additional ledger accounts are shown in exhibit 4.7.

## Step 6: Another trial balance

Exhibit 4.8 shows a trial balance at 30 September 2002 using the original accounts from step 4 and the additional accounts required by the entries in step 5.

**EXHIBIT 4.7** Northern Star Theatre Company

General ledger

**Cash (bank)**

| Date | Entry | Debit | Credit | Balance |
|---|---|---|---|---|
| Dec 01 | 2a | 450 | | 450 DR |
| Dec 01 | 2b | | 400 | 50 DR |
| Mar 02 | 5a | 500 | | 550 DR |
| Mar 02 | 5b | | 470 | 80 DR |
| Jul 02 | 6a | 500 | | 580 DR |
| Jul 02 | 6b | | 290 | 290 DR |
| Aug 02 | 8 | 897 | | 1 187 DR |
| Aug 02 | 9 | | 525 | 662 DR |
| Sept 02 | 10 | 4 840 | | 5 502 DR |

**Interest receivable**

| Date | Entry | Debit | Credit | Balance |
|---|---|---|---|---|
| Sept 02 | 14 | 20 | | 20 DR |

**Costumes and props**

| Date | Entry | Debit | Credit | Balance |
|---|---|---|---|---|
| Sept 02 | 13a | 660 | | 660 DR |

**Accumulated depreciation**

| Date | Entry | Debit | Credit | Balance |
|---|---|---|---|---|
| Sept 02 | 13b | | 132 | 132 CR |

**Accounts payable**

| Date | Entry | Debit | Credit | Balance |
|---|---|---|---|---|
| Aug 02 | 7a | | 190 | 190 CR |
| Aug 02 | 7b | | 610 | 800 CR |
| Aug 02 | 9 | 525 | | 275 CR |

**Accrued expenses**

| Date | Entry | Debit | Credit | Balance |
|---|---|---|---|---|
| Sept 02 | 11 | | 450 | 450 CR |
| Sept 02 | 12 | | 215 | 665 CR |

**Share capital**

| Date | Entry | Debit | Credit | Balance |
|---|---|---|---|---|
| Dec 01 | 2a | | 450 | 450 CR |
| Mar 02 | 5a | | 500 | 950 CR |
| Jul 02 | 6a | | 500 | 1 450 CR |

**Performance revenue**

| Date | Entry | Debit | Credit | Balance |
|---|---|---|---|---|
| Aug 02 | 8 | | 897 | 897 CR |
| Sept 02 | 10 | | 4 840 | 5 737 CR |

**Interest revenue**

| Date | Entry | Debit | Credit | Balance |
|---|---|---|---|---|
| Sept 02 | 14 | | 20 | 20 CR |

**EXHIBIT 4.7** Northern Star Theatre Company

## General ledger (continued)

**Depreciation expense**

| Date | Entry | Debit | Credit | Balance |
|---|---|---|---|---|
| Sept 02 | 13b | 132 | | 132 DR |

**Costumes and props expense**

| Date | Entry | Debit | Credit | Balance |
|---|---|---|---|---|
| Mar 02 | 5b | 470 | | 470 DR |
| Aug 02 | 7b | 610 | | 1 080 DR |
| Sept 02 | 13a | | 660 | 420 DR |

**Performance fees expense**

| Date | Entry | Debit | Credit | Balance |
|---|---|---|---|---|
| Dec 01 | 2b | 400 | | 400 DR |

**Royalties expense**

| Date | Entry | Debit | Credit | Balance |
|---|---|---|---|---|
| Sept 02 | 11 | 450 | | 450 DR |

**Travel expense**

| Date | Entry | Debit | Credit | Balance |
|---|---|---|---|---|
| Aug 02 | 6b | 290 | | 290 DR |
| Aug 02 | 7a | 190 | | 480 DR |
| Sept 02 | 12 | 215 | | 695 DR |

**EXHIBIT 4.8** Northern Star Theatre Company

## General ledger trial balance 30 September 2002

| | Debit<br>$ | Credit<br>$ |
|---|---|---|
| Cash (bank) | 5 502 | |
| Interest receivable | 20 | |
| Costumes and props | 660 | |
| Accumulated depreciation | | 132 |
| Accounts payable | | 275 |
| Accrued expenses | | 665 |
| Share capital | | 1 450 |
| Performance revenue | | 5 737 |
| Interest revenue | | 20 |
| Depreciation expense | 132 | |
| Costumes and props expense | 420 | |
| Performance fees expense | 400 | |
| Royalties expense | 450 | |
| Travel expense | 695 | |
| Totals | 8 279 | 8 279 |

## Step 7: Closing entries

As they are year end accounts, revenue and expense accounts are closed at this stage. The entries are as follows:

| | DR $ | CR $ |
|---|---|---|
| Performance revenue | 5 737 | |
| Interest revenue | 20 | |
| Profit and loss summary | | 5 757 |
| Profit and loss summary | 2 097 | |
| Depreciation expense | | 132 |
| Costumes and props expense | | 420 |
| Performance fees expense | | 400 |
| Royalties expense | | 450 |
| Travel expense | | 695 |
| Profit and loss summary | 3 660 | |
| Retained profits | | 3 660 |

The amount closed to retained profits from the profit and loss summary is the total profit shown in the statement of financial performance. So far, the company has a profit of $3660. As no dividends were paid, this amount remains in retained profits. The financial statements in exhibit 4.9 reflect this.

## Step 8: Financial statements

Note calculating closing retained profits:

| | |
|---|---|
| Beginning balance | 0 |
| Profit for the period | 3 660 |
| Dividends declared during the period | 0 |
| **Retained profits at end of the period** | **3 660** |

### How's your understanding?

Here are two questions your should be able to answer, based on what you have just read:

1 You are the owner of a business. Your bookkeeper has just given you the month-end trial balance of the company's accounts. What are the main records you would expect to have been used in coming up with that list of account balances?

2 Your bookkeeper rushes into your office to apologise for the fact that posting of cash sales to the general ledger has been accidentally forgotten for that month. The journal showed that cash received from cash sales during the month was $6782. Which ledger accounts would be incorrect because of the error, and by how much? (Cash would be too low by $6782, as would sales.)

**EXHIBIT 4.9** Northern Star Theatre Company

## Statement of financial performance year ending 30 September 2002

| | $ | $ |
|---|---|---|
| Performance revenue | | 5 737 |
| Interest revenue | | 20 |
| Expenses: | | |
| Depreciation of costumes and props | 132 | |
| Costumes and props not reusable | 420 | |
| Performance fees | 400 | |
| Royalties | 450 | |
| Travel | 695 | 2 097 |
| **Operating profit** | | **3 660** |

## Statement of financial position as at 30 September 2002

| | $ | $ |
|---|---|---|
| **Assets** | | |
| Current assets | | |
| Cash at bank | 5 502 | |
| Interest receivable | 20 | 5 522 |
| Noncurrent assets | | |
| Costumes and props, at cost | 660 | |
| less Accumulated depreciation | 132 | 528 |
| **Total assets** | | 6 050 |
| **Liabilities** | | |
| Current liabilities | | |
| Accounts payable | 275 | |
| Accrued expenses | 665 | 940 |
| **Total liabilities** | | **940** |
| **Net assets** | | **5 110** |
| **Shareholders' equity** | | |
| Share capital | 1450 | |
| Retained profits | 3 660 | **5 110** |

## For your interest

The changed role of accounting is illustrated here:

Accountants are no longer bean counters but business advisers: 'today's accountants are doing less number-crunching and more business advising and planning' (according to an analysis of 28 555 job ads done by Gottliebsen Research). The analysis showed 'big increases in employer demand for accountants with skills such as business consulting and advice, e-commerce, finance management and award knowledge'. As business becomes more competitive, there is a demand for constant information for decision making. 'Accountants have to provide information every day, every week and every month that the business can use to make decisions.'

(Source: Joycelyn Morton, national president of CPA Australia, quoted in 'Just for Kicks', *Sydney Morning Herald*, 3 March 2001.)

## 4.5 Another illustrative example

The purpose of this example is to reinforce the processes of preparing journal entries and posting to ledgers. In addition, the use of a chart of accounts and the use of folio numbers as a means of cross-referencing when posting journal entries are introduced.

Reval Pty Ltd is an importer and wholesaler of sporting goods to major department stores and specialist sporting goods retailers. The company commenced business last year.

The chart of accounts for Reval Pty Ltd is as follows:

| | |
|---|---|
| **Assets (1–99)** | |
| Cash | 1 |
| Accounts receivable | 2 |
| Inventory | 5 |
| Prepayments | 8 |
| Other assets | 10 |
| Land | 40 |
| Buildings | 42 |
| Accumulated depreciation – buildings | 43 |
| Plant and equipment | 50 |
| Accumulated depreciation – plant and equipment | 51 |
| **Liabilities (100–199)** | |
| Accounts payable | 100 |
| Salaries payable | 105 |
| Bills payable | 111 |
| Accrued expenses | 115 |
| Long-term loan | 140 |
| Mortgage loan | 145 |
| **Shareholders' equity (200–299)** | |
| Share capital | 200 |
| Retained profits | 210 |
| **Revenue (300–399)** | |
| Sales | 300 |
| Interest revenue | 305 |
| Consulting revenue | 310 |
| **Expenses (400–499)** | |
| Cost of goods sold | 400 |
| Wages | 404 |
| Staff training | 407 |
| Electricity | 408 |
| Rent | 415 |
| Interest | 419 |
| Depreciation | 430 |
| Municipal rates | 438 |
| Repairs and maintenance | 440 |
| Miscellaneous | 460 |

The trial balance at 30 April 2002 was as follows:

| | DR $ | CR $ |
|---|---|---|
| Cash | 25 000 | |
| Accounts receivable | 65 000 | |
| Inventory | 50 000 | |
| Accounts payable | | 21 000 |
| Share capital | | 100 000 |
| Retained profits | | 19 000 |
| | 140 000 | 140 000 |

During the month of May the following transactions occurred:

| Date | | Transaction no. | Transaction |
|---|---|---|---|
| May | 1 | 1 | Credit sales of $50 000. The cost of the goods sold was $28 000. |
| | 4 | 2 | Paid accounts payable of $15 000. |
| | 6 | 3 | Purchased additional inventory for $20 000 on credit. |
| | 8 | 4 | Five staff attended a seminar on understanding financial statements. The total bill received was for $3000. |
| | 11 | 5 | Received $30 000 for an account receivable. |
| | 18 | 6 | Of the goods purchased on 6 May, goods which cost $2000 were returned to the supplier as they were damaged. |
| | 20 | 7 | A local electrician carried out repairs. A cheque for $500 was paid to the electrician. |
| | 24 | 8 | Cash sales of $20 000 (cost of goods sold $11 200). |
| | 25 | 9 | Purchased land for $40 000 cash and obtained a bank loan of $35 000. The bank holds a first mortgage over the land. |
| | 26 | 10 | Paid the monthly wages bill of $12 000. |
| | 30 | 11 | Purchased equipment for $30 000 paying $20 000 cash and agreeing to pay the remainder in two years' time. |
| | 31 | 12 | Received the electricity bill of $2000, which covered the month of May. It will not be paid for another week. |

The general journal entries are shown in exhibit 4.10. Posting references have been included as a cross-reference to the account to which the amount will be posted. The folio numbers are obtained from the chart of accounts. A narration for each entry is not included.

While many of the above transactions should be familiar to you by now, some need additional emphasis and some are new. These are explained below. Note that in deciding which account names to use in the journal entries it is necessary to refer to the chart of accounts.

- Transaction 1 involves credit sales, which results in accounts receivable (an asset) increasing and sales, a revenue item, increasing. As the items sold had a cost, an expense (cost of goods sold) is increased and inventory (an asset) will decrease.
- Transaction 2 reduces an asset (cash) and reduces a liability (accounts payable).

**EXHIBIT 4.10** **Reval Pty Ltd**

**General journal**

| No. | Date | Description | Posting reference | Debits $ | Credits $ |
|---|---|---|---|---|---|
| 1 | May 1 | Accounts receivable | 2 | 50 000 | |
| | | Sales | 300 | | 50 000 |
| | | Cost of goods sold | 400 | 28 000 | |
| | | Inventory | 5 | | 28000 |
| 2 | May 4 | Accounts payable | 100 | 15 000 | |
| | | Cash | 1 | | 15 000 |
| 3 | May 6 | Inventory | 5 | 20 000 | |
| | | Accounts payable | 100 | | 20 000 |
| 4 | May 8 | Staff training | 407 | 3 000 | |
| | | Accounts payable | 100 | | 3000 |
| 5 | May 11 | Cash | 1 | 30 000 | |
| | | Accounts receivable | 2 | | 30 000 |
| 6 | May 18 | Accounts payable | 100 | 2 000 | |
| | | Inventory | 5 | | 2000 |
| 7 | May 20 | Repairs and maintenance | 440 | 500 | |
| | | Cash | 1 | | 500 |
| 8 | May 24 | Cash | 1 | 20 000 | |
| | | Sales | 300 | | 20 000 |
| | | Cost of goods sold | 400 | 11 200 | |
| | | Inventory | 5 | | 11 200 |
| 9 | May 25 | Land | 40 | 40 000 | |
| | | Cash | 1 | | 40 000 |
| | | Cash | 1 | 35 000 | |
| | | Mortgage loan | 145 | | 35 000 |
| 10 | May 26 | Wages | 404 | 12 000 | |
| | | Cash | 1 | | 12 000 |
| 11 | May 30 | Plant and equipment | 50 | 30 000 | |
| | | Cash | 1 | | 20 000 |
| | | Long-term loan | 140 | | 10 000 |
| 12 | May 31 | Electricity | 408 | 2 000 | |
| | | Accounts payable | 100 | | 2 000 |

- Transaction 3 increases an asset (inventory) and increases a liability (accounts payable).
- Transaction 4 involves an increase in an expense and an increase in a liability, as the bill has not yet paid. In deciding what expense account should be debited (that is, what to call the expense), it would be necessary to check the list of expenses in the chart of accounts. Staff training costs appears to be an appropriate account in which to put the cost of staff attending seminars.
- Note that for transaction 5 no revenue is recognised, as this occurred previously when the sale was made. The transaction simply converts one asset (accounts receivable) into another asset (cash).
- Transaction 6 involves the reversal of part of transaction 3. As part of the inventory is returned, the inventory balance reduces and the amount owing as accounts payable reduces.

**EXHIBIT 4.11** Reval Pty Ltd

## General ledger

**Cash — 1**

| | | | | | |
|---|---|---|---|---|---|
| 30/4 | | 25 000 | 1/5 | (2) | 15 000 |
| 11/5 | (5) | 30 000 | 20/5 | (7) | 500 |
| 24/5 | (8) | 20 000 | 25/5 | (9) | 40 000 |
| 25/5 | (9) | 35 000 | 26/5 | (10) | 12 000 |
| | | | 30/5 | (11) | 20 000 |
| | | | Bal c/d | | 22 500 |
| | | 110 000 | | | 110 000 |
| Bal b/d | | 22 500 | | | |

**Accounts receivable — 2**

| | | | | | |
|---|---|---|---|---|---|
| 30/4 | | 65 000 | 11/5 | (5) | 30 000 |
| 1/5 | (1) | 50 000 | Bal c/d | | 85 000 |
| | | 115 000 | | | 115 000 |
| Bal b/d | | 85 000 | | | |

**Inventory — 5**

| | | | | | |
|---|---|---|---|---|---|
| 30/4 | | 50 000 | 1/5 | (1) | 28 000 |
| 6/5 | (3) | 20 000 | 18/5 | (6) | 2 000 |
| | | | 24/5 | (8) | 11 200 |
| | | | Bal c/d | | 28 800 |
| | | 70 000 | | | 70 000 |
| Bal b/d | | 28 800 | | | |

**Land — 40**

| | | | | | |
|---|---|---|---|---|---|
| 25/5 | (9) | 40 000 | | | |

**Plant and equipment — 50**

| | | | | | |
|---|---|---|---|---|---|
| 30/5 | (11) | 30 000 | | | |

**Accounts payable — 100**

| | | | | | |
|---|---|---|---|---|---|
| 4/5 | (2) | 15 000 | 30/4 | | 21 000 |
| 18/5 | (6) | 2 000 | 6/5 | (3) | 20 000 |
| | | | 8/5 | (4) | 3 000 |
| Bal c/d | | 29 000 | 31/5 | (12) | 2 000 |
| | | 46 000 | | | 46 000 |
| | | | Bal b/d | | 29 000 |

**Long-term loan — 140**

| | | | | | |
|---|---|---|---|---|---|
| | | | 30/5 | (11) | 10 000 |

**Mortgage loan — 145**

| | | | | | |
|---|---|---|---|---|---|
| | | | 25/5 | (9) | 35 000 |

**Share capital — 200**

| | | | | | |
|---|---|---|---|---|---|
| | | | 30/4 | | 100 000 |

**Retained profits — 210**

| | | | | | |
|---|---|---|---|---|---|
| | | | 30/4 | | 19 000 |

**Sales — 300**

| | | | | | |
|---|---|---|---|---|---|
| | | | 1/5 | (1) | 50 000 |
| | | | 24/5 | (8) | 20 000 |
| | | | | | 70 000 |

**Cost of goods sold — 400**

| | | | | | |
|---|---|---|---|---|---|
| 1/5 | (1) | 28 000 | | | |
| 24/5 | (8) | 11 200 | | | |
| | | 39 200 | | | |

**Wages — 404**

| | | | | | |
|---|---|---|---|---|---|
| 26/5 | (10) | 12 000 | | | |

**Staff training — 407**

| | | | | | |
|---|---|---|---|---|---|
| 8/5 | (4) | 3 000 | | | |

**Electricity — 408**

| | | | | | |
|---|---|---|---|---|---|
| 31/5 | (12) | 2 000 | | | |

**Repairs and maintenance — 440**

| | | | | | |
|---|---|---|---|---|---|
| 20/5 | (7) | 500 | | | |

- Transaction 7 involves some electrical repairs, and the appropriate expense account is repairs and maintenance.
- Transaction 8 is the same as transaction 1, except that cash instead of accounts receivable is debited.

- Transaction 9 is divided into two parts: the purchase of the land and the obtaining of a loan. There are two account names in the chart of accounts that would be reasonable descriptions of the loan: long-term loan and mortgage loan. As the bank has taken out a mortgage over the land, the second description appears preferable.
- Transaction 10 involves the payment of an expense. There is no indication that an expense (and a liability) was previously recognised (for example, wages payable) in the opening trial balance.
- Transaction 11 involves the purchase of an asset (equipment) with the reduction of another asset and the creation of a liability (long-term loan).
- In transaction 12, the bill has been received and it relates to the month of May. The expense should therefore be recognised in May.

To post these journal entries to the ledger accounts, the T-account format of ledgers will be used (see exhibit 4.11). Only ledger accounts with an opening balance or ones affected by the transactions are shown on the previous page. They are recorded in the same order as they appear in the chart of accounts. The first step is to include the opening balances from the trial balance. Second, each journal entry is posted. Third, each account balance is calculated. Fourth, a new trial balance is prepared.

To illustrate how to balance accounts, the cash account will be used as an example. When the total debits exceed the total credits, the account will have a debit closing balance. Alternatively, if the total credits exceed the total debits, the account will have a closing credit balance. In this case, the total of the debits is $110 000 and the total of the credits is $87 500. Therefore the closing balance will be a debit of $22 500. This balance which is to be carried down (c/d) is put on the side with the lower balance (credit side in this example). The total of both sides (which is equal) is then inserted and the balance is brought down (b/d) under the total on the debit side.

**EXHIBIT 4.12**

**Reval Pty Ltd**

**Trial balance at 31 May 2002**

| | Debits $ | Credits $ |
|---|---|---|
| Cash | 22 500 | |
| Accounts receivable | 85 000 | |
| Inventory | 28 800 | |
| Land | 40 000 | |
| Plant and equipment | 30 000 | |
| Accounts payable | | 29 000 |
| Long-term loan | | 10 000 |
| Mortgage loan | | 35 000 |
| Share capital | | 100 000 |
| Retained profits | | 19 000 |
| Sales | | 70 000 |
| Cost of goods sold | 39 200 | |
| Wages | 12 000 | |
| Staff training | 3 000 | |
| Electricity | 2 000 | |
| Repairs and maintenance | 500 | |
| | **263 000** | **263 000** |

An alternative method of balancing accounts is to simply add both sides and insert the difference on the side with the highest value after ruling off the entries. In this case the cash account for Reval Pty Ltd would look as follows.

| | Cash | | 1 |
|---|---|---|---|
| 30/4 | 25 000 | 1/5 | 15 000 |
| 11/5 | 30 000 | 20/5 | 500 |
| 24/5 | 20 000 | 25/5 | 40 000 |
| 25/5 | 35 000 | 26/5 | 12 000 |
| | | 30/5 | 20 000 |
| Bal b/d | 22 500 | | |

The trial balance in exhibit 4.12 shows that the total of debits equals the total of the credits.

## 4.6 Electronic commerce

With the advent of sophisticated interconnected computer systems, especially via the Web, many business transactions are now being conducted entirely electronically. Electronic commerce ('e-commerce') is quite a challenge to financial accounting, and to internal control, because its essence is the absence of the painstaking 'paper trail' that has traditionally supported accounting records. Many people, not just accountants, think some sort of credible trail, even if not in paper, needs to be continued in some form, but how? Enterprises still need good records for all the reasons outlined at the beginning of this section, but clearly the form of those records is changing dramatically. These days, many companies see little cash and not as many cheques as they used to from customers, with most payments, even by other businesses, being made by credit card or electronically. They don't pay their own employees by cash or cheque, just depositing their pay directly into their personal bank accounts.

E-commerce has other interesting implications for accounting. One is that there needs to be some compatibility between computer systems, if the accounting systems on both sides of a transaction are to recognise it properly, and some trust in the electronic media to make the system work. The Web is developing interfaces that provide the compatibility, and credibility mechanisms with names like 'Encryption' and 'Web Trust' are beginning to appear.

A second implication is that there can be a lot of 'in transit' activities, because physical transfers (such as shipments and deliveries) are usually slower than the electronic system. If you order a book from an online retailer, you, the retailer and your credit card company will have all the electronic records completed much before the book shows up. The tendency of records to be speedier, and separated from the physical movements, means that in-transit items can be a challenge to control and reconcile.

A third implication for accounting is that the parties to e-commerce can be bound together quite closely, with the ability to make enquiries into each other's computer systems to find out order specifications, progress on production of goods, and other things to smooth the business relationship. This means that not only must the financial statements be right, but the underlying records must be good too, so that business partners' enquiries are answered reliably. Some external parties, such as banks, tax authorities or securities regulators, may want to go straight to the underlying records without waiting for financial statements. There's a bit of a paradox here: e-commerce both operates without paper and demands a good trail of evidence.

Financial reporting itself is going online and becoming continuous rather than waiting for ritual quarterly or annual reporting dates: numerous references to companies' Web pages have been made in this book, and many versions of online and even interactive financial reporting are being developed. E-commerce and electronic financial reporting are likely to change accounting and financial reporting dramatically in future years. Maybe in the future books like this will be available online, to match the online accounting they will then be describing!

## 4.7 Managers, bookkeeping and control

Not many managers think of record-keeping as a breathtaking topic. This chapter has demonstrated, however, that it is an important topic for managers, primarily for two reasons:

- Bookkeeping and associated record-keeping provide the underlying data on which accounting's information is built. To a large extent, management decision-making and evaluations of management performance depend on accounting information. Such decisions and evaluations may be constrained by the nature of the underlying data. For example, if certain events are not recognised as transactions by the bookkeeping system, they may not be reflected in the financial statements either.
- Bookkeeping and associated record-keeping provide the data and systems used in meeting management's important responsibility to safeguard assets and generally keep the business under control. Management's internal control responsibilities are discussed in chapter 6.

### For your interest

The importance of the integrity of accounting information is reflected in the severe penalties associated with incorrect records:

A South Korean court has sentenced former Daewoo Group officials to prison terms and levied fines of nearly $US20 billion ($39.5 billion) for falsifying financial accounts ... the fines were the largest ever levied by a South Korean court ... 19 former Daewoo Group executives [were found] guilty of distorting financial records and using falsified financial documents to procure funds for their companies ... [they] were fined a combined total of nearly $US20 billion, with five of them sentenced to prison ... terms of three to seven years.

(Source: *Australian Financial Review*, 26 July 2001.)

## 4.8 Public sector issues

The accounting process covered in this chapter applies equally to public sector organisations. The knowledge you have gained in this chapter concerning the use of debits, credits, journals, ledgers and so on is also useful in the preparation and understanding of public sector financial statements, with the move from cash to accrual accounting by the organisations.

The use of accrual accounting in the public sector can be illustrated in the journal entries required by a government department for the following nine transactions. Assume that a recent election in your State has resulted in a change of government. The new government has restructured the departments, creating a new department called Youth Affairs to provide greater opportunities for those in the 16–25 years age group. The department aims to provide better facilities (including sporting areas) as well as creating job opportunities particularly suited to this age group. Some of the transactions that occurred in the first month are as follows:

**1** On 1 April the Department of Youth Affairs was officially opened. Equipment ($200 000) and furniture and fittings ($300 000) were transferred to the department from another department. The transfer of assets between departments as a result of administrative restructuring is treated as a direct adjustment to the opening balance of accumulated funds (similar to 'retained profits' in the private sector). A result of this transaction is to increase assets and increase accumulated funds (an equity account). The journal entry would be:

| | | $ | $ |
|---|---|---|---|
| DR | Equipment | 200 000 | |
| DR | Furniture and fittings | 300 000 | |
| CR | Accumulated funds | | 500 000 |

**2** The department receives a recurrent appropriation of $1 000 000 from the State Government. This will result in an increase in cash and an increase in a revenue account called recurrent appropriation.

| | | $ | $ |
|---|---|---|---|
| DR | Cash | 1 000 000 | |
| CR | Recurrent appropriation | | 1 000 000 |

**3** The department purchases equipment on credit for $60 000. As a result, an asset (equipment) increases and a liability (accounts payable) increases.

| | | $ | $ |
|---|---|---|---|
| DR | Equipment | 60 000 | |
| CR | Account payable | | 60 000 |

**4** Wages of $80 000 are paid for the period.

| | | $ | $ |
|---|---|---|---|
| DR | Wages expense | 80 000 | |
| CR | Cash | | 80 000 |

**5** The department provided services on credit for a total of $200 000 during the period to other departments, local councils and youth groups. As a result both revenue (user charges) and an asset (accounts receivable) increase.

| | | $ | $ |
|---|---|---|---|
| DR | Accounts receivable | 200 000 | |
| CR | User charges | | 200 000 |

6 During the period, the department paid some of the creditors $40 000 related to the earlier purchase of equipment.

| | | $ | $ |
|---|---|---|---|
| DR | Accounts payable | 40 000 | |
| CR | Cash | | 40 000 |

7 The department made a grant of $40 000 to a suburban tennis club to support the construction of a junior tennis clubhouse. As a result, cash decreases and an expense called 'grants and subsidies' increases.

| | | $ | $ |
|---|---|---|---|
| DR | Grants and subsidies | 40 000 | |
| CR | Cash | | 40 000 |

8 The department receives and pays an invoice for advertising costs of $20 000 associated with advertising the new role of the department.

| | | $ | $ |
|---|---|---|---|
| DR | Advertising expense | 20 000 | |
| CR | Cash | | 20 000 |

9 The department collects $60 000 of the accounts receivable owing related to user charges.

| | | $ | $ |
|---|---|---|---|
| DR | Cash | 60 000 | |
| CR | Accounts receivable | | 60 000 |

# 4.9 Homework and discussion to develop understanding

## Discussion questions

1 What determines whether specific transactions are to be recorded in the accounting records?
2 What is the purpose of a journal entry?
3 What is a chart of accounts?
4 What determines the number of account names to be included in a chart of accounts?
5 Why is it beneficial for transactions to be entered into a journal rather than being entered directly to a ledger?
6 What is the purpose of the trial balance?
7 What is the purpose of closing entries?
8 Financial statements are highly summarised documents, representing thousands of transactions. Financial newspapers and commentators produce information about companies that is even more summarised. Why would users accept, or even prefer, summarised information to detailed data? How important is it for the user to understand the procedures and assumptions behind such summaries?

**9** At a recent Student Accounting Club wine and cheese party, local business people mixed with students. One small business entrepreneur was heard to say, 'All that financial accounting information you students learn about is not relevant to me. I just started up my business. I only have five employees: four people in the shop building the product and one person in shipping/receiving. I'm out on calls, drumming up business so I have my finger on the real pulse of the firm – that's sales. My brother pays the bills and does up the payroll every two weeks. Once in a while I write cheques too. It's all simple and smooth, so why add a lot of time-consuming, costly record-keeping to it all? All those books and financial statements are fine for the big public companies. I can do without the complications.' Prepare an appropriate response to his comments.

**10** Identify some differences you might expect to find between the transaction filters and accounting books and records of a large corporation and those of a corner store run by one person.

**11** In a flight of accounting passion, an accounting lecturer exclaimed, 'The double-entry transactional recording system is financial accounting's greatest strength and its greatest weakness!' He went on to explain this odd comment. Write down what the lecturer probably said in explanation.

**12** Make a list of the source documents you expect would be needed to back up the transactional records in an accounting system and briefly describe why each document would be useful.

**13** State whether or not you agree with each of the statements below and, in a few words, say why.

- **a** If an event satisfies all five of the transaction criteria, you can be sure it will be recorded by the entity's accounting system.
- **b** Purchases and sales by investors of existing issued shares of a company listed on the Australian Stock Exchange are not accounting transactions in the company's records.

**14** There have been frequent suggestions of the need to broaden the type of transactions that should be recognised by the accounting system. One such example has been the suggestion to include the value of an organisation's human capital. A consulting firm may have very few assets apart from its human capital, but this is not recorded on the statement of financial position. Why is this item not presently included? How would the item be measured if it was included?

**15** Why is it essential that an accurate source document be prepared for every transaction?

**16** Indicate the source documents that would be used for making entries for the following transactions:

- **a** a cash payment
- **b** a cash receipt
- **c** a credit sale
- **d** cost of goods sold
- **e** a purchase of inventory
- **f** receipt of inventory.

**17** Given the equality of debits and credits in a trial balance, what errors may still remain in a set of accounting records? How should these errors be guarded against?

**18** What types of errors may be detected from a perusal of the items in a trial balance? What procedure should be used to locate the source of the discrepancy?

**19** How does the accountant select the particular accounts to be included in the chart of accounts for a new enterprise?

## Problem 4.1* Identify transactions

Gould Ltd experienced the following events. For each, say whether or not it is an accounting transaction and why, or why not.

1 A painter repainted the reception lobby bright blue.
2 A customer, who had owed Gould money for several years, finally paid, to everyone's surprise.
3 The CEO decided that the company's main factory would be reorganised next month.
4 The company received shop supplies it had ordered earlier.
5 The company signed a new five-year lease on its Windsor warehouse.
6 The company sold some land, for which it would receive 10 annual payments, starting next year.
7 The company acquired a new truck for cash plus the trade-in of an old truck.
8 An employee was discovered to have stolen a large amount of cash.
9 The company received a bill from the supplier for the shop supplies in item (4).
10 The company was sued for a large amount by a customer who fell down in the parking lot.

## Problem 4.2* Journal entries for simple transactions

The events listed below all took place on 15 December 2001. Provide the journal entry necessary to record each event in the accounts of Company A for the year ended 31 December 2001. If no entry is required, indicate that and give reasons. In most cases an assumption is not necessary. If you feel an assumption is necessary, however, state it.

1 A new general manager is hired at an annual salary of $60 000.
2 Company A receives a bill for $200 from a newspaper for an advertisement to be run on 31 December 2001. Payment is not due for 60 days.
3 A bond is purchased by Company A for $2000 cash. The bond will have a maturity value of $2500 in three years because interest will accumulate.
4 A landscaper agrees to improve land owned by Company A. The agreed price for the work is $700.
5 An order for $900 of merchandise is received from a customer along with a cash deposit of $300.
6 A $600 insurance premium for coverage over the period from 1 December 2001 to 30 November 2002 is paid in cash.

## Problem 4.3* Make journal, ledger and trial balance entries

Take the transactions for Hoad Pty Ltd (problem 3.5 in chapter 3) and:

1 prepare journal entries
2 post to the ledger accounts
3 prepare a trial balance
4 prepare closing entries
5 prepare a statement of financial performance and a statement of financial position.

## Problem 4.4 Journal entries for a small new business

At the end of last year, Fergama Production Pty Ltd, a company in the movie industry, had the following closing accounts (in no particular order).

| | $ | | $ |
|---|---|---|---|
| Cash | 23 415 | Share capital | 20 000 |
| Accounts payable | 37 778 | Office equipment cost | 24 486 |
| Accum. depreciation | 11 134 | Accounts receivable | 89 455 |
| Retained profits | 51 434 | Inventory of supplies | 10 240 |
| Long-term loan payable | 15 000 | Taxes payable | 12 250 |

During this year, the company's activities resulted in the following:

**a** Revenue, all on credit, totalled $216 459.

**b** Production expenses totalled $156 320, $11 287 of which was paid in cash and the rest charged.

**c** Depreciation on the office equipment came to $2680 for the year.

**d** The company bought, on credit, new supplies costing $8657, and used up supplies costing $12 984 during the year.

**e** Income tax expense for the year was estimated to be $12 319.

**f** The board of directors declared a dividend of $25 000.

**g** Collections from customers totalled $235 260.

**h** Payments to suppliers totalled $172 276.

**i** Payments of taxes totalled $18 400.

**j** A $5000 payment was made on the long-term loan.

**k** The dividend was paid in cash to shareholders.

1. To get you started, prepare a statement of financial position for Fergama Productions Pty Ltd as at the end of the last year.
2. Record the activities for this year, using journal entries, and enter those entries to ledgers.
3. Prepare a trial balance of your accounts to show that it is in balance.
4. From those accounts, prepare the following financial statements:
   - **a** a statement of financial performance for this year
   - **b** a statement of financial position at the end of this year
   - **c** a note showing the change in balance of the retained profits account.
5. Comment on what the financial statements show about the company's performance for this year and financial position at the end of this year. Would you say the company is better off than it was last year?

## Problem 4.5 Identify accounting transactions

The following things happened to Bartlett Ltd last month. Decide if each is an accounting transaction and explain briefly why it is or isn't.

1. A customer ordered $6000 of products, to be shipped next month.
2. Another customer paid $528 for some marketing advice from the company.
3. Bartlett's share price went up by $0.50. As there are 100 000 shares outstanding, this was a value increase of $50 000.
4. Bartlett ran an advertisement on TV, and promised to pay the TV station the $2000 cost next month.
5. One of the company's employees worked overtime, earning $120 that would be paid next pay period.
6. The company paid a teenager $50 to compensate for a ripped shirt suffered when the teenager tried to run away after being accused of shoplifting.

7 Bartlett received a shipment of new goods for sale, paying $1000 cash and agreeing to pay the other $12 250 in a few days.
8 Bartlett paid the other $12 250.
9 The company made a donation to a political party of $500. (The donation turned out later to have been against the election law, to the company's embarrassment.)
10 Grand Bank made the company a $20 000 short-term loan.

## Problem 4.6 Identify whether or not events are accounting transactions

The following events happened at the Guzzle Beer Corporation. For each, indicate whether or not it is an accounting transaction for Guzzle Beer Corp. and state, in five or ten words, why.

1 A large tank containing beer mixture broke, and all of the mixture spilled.
2 A major shareholder sold 50 000 shares on the stock exchange.
3 The corporation paid $60 000 000 for a Mexican brewery.
4 An invoice for next week's TV advertising arrived.
5 A pub took delivery of its weekly shipment of Guzzle Beer.

## Problem 4.7 Chart of accounts

The Lightning Courier Service is engaged in the delivery of parcels in the city and suburbs. Three light vans are used and, in addition to the proprietor, one person is employed in the office.

1 Using the headings, owner's equity, liabilities, assets, revenue and expense, prepare a chart of accounts for the business.
2 What information will be available to the proprietor if your suggested chart of accounts is adopted?

## Problem 4.8 Chart of accounts and source documents

The Great Outdoors Ltd has been established to retail bushwalking and mountaineering equipment. It is proposed to open a shop in a suburban shopping centre which is at present under construction. To attract customers, a notice board will be provided for bushwalking clubs to post details of walks and other activities. The shop assistants will be experienced walkers, able to advise customers on equipment and routes for walking trips. An agency for the Youth Hostel Association will be established in the shop.

1 Indicate the information you would need to enable you to design a suitable accounting system.
2 Describe the source documents that would be employed in the system.
3 Prepare a suitable chart of accounts.

## Problem 4.9 Accounting cycle

The following transactions relate to the business of Romulus Pty Ltd, importer and dealer in exclusive continental cars. Cost of sales is recorded at the time of sale.

1 Enter the transactions in a journal.
2 Post to the ledger.
3 Prepare a trial balance.
4 Prepare closing entries.
5 Prepare a statement of financial performance for the month of December 2002 and a statement of financial position as at 31 December 2002.

| 2002 | | |
|---|---|---|
| Dec | 1 | Romulus commenced operations with $1 000 000 cash. |
| | 2 | Paid one month's rental of showroom, $29 000. |
| | 3 | Purchased ten Distincto vehicles for $200 000 each on 60-day credit terms. |
| | 4 | Retained one Distincto vehicle for demonstration purposes. |
| | 8 | Sold for cash three vehicles at $250 000 each. |
| | 9 | Paid account for advertising in motoring journals, $600. |
| | 21 | Purchased computer for $4000 cash. |
| | 24 | Sold one vehicle on the following terms: deposit $40 000, balance of $210 000 payable in 6 months. |
| | 29 | Sold one vehicle to old family friend for $249 600. |
| | 31 | Paid office salaries $900 and salesmen's commission $45 000. |

## Problem 4.10 Journal entry for a business acquisition

Big Ideas Pty Ltd decided to buy parts of the business of a competitor, which was cutting back operations. For a price of $4 200 000 (a $1 000 000 down payment and the rest in four equal annual instalments, plus interest at 12 per cent per annum), Big Ideas got inventory it valued at $280 000, land it valued at $1 500 000, a retail store building it valued at $1 800 000, furniture and equipment it valued at $470 000 and some dealership rights it valued at $40 000. Big Ideas also agreed to pay a bank loan of $130 000 secured by the inventory.

Write a journal entry to record Big Ideas Pty Ltd's purchase.

## Problem 4.11 Complete the accounting cycle from journal entries to financial statements

Cleaner Pools Pty Ltd was a small pool shop situated in Oatley in the southern suburbs of Sydney. The business sells and repairs pool filters as well as providing consulting services on pool layouts. At 30 June 2001 it had the following assets, liabilities and shareholders' equity account balances: cash $3000; accounts receivable $4000; inventory $4500; creditors $3500; retained profits $2000; share capital $6000. The company's chart of accounts is shown.

| | |
|---|---|
| 01 | Cash |
| 02 | Accounts receivable |
| 03 | Inventory |
| 04 | Prepayments |
| 11 | Furniture and fittings |
| 12 | Accumulated depreciation – furniture and fittings |
| 20 | Accounts payable |
| 22 | Accrued expenses |
| 30 | Share capital |
| 31 | Retained profits |
| 40 | Sales |
| 41 | Consulting revenue |
| 42 | Repairs revenue |
| 50 | Cost of goods sold |
| 51 | Salaries |
| 52 | Rent |
| 53 | Motor vehicle expenses |
| 54 | Stationery |
| 55 | Depreciation – furniture and fittings |
| 55 | Advertising |

The following transactions occurred during July 2001:

| Date | | Transaction |
|---|---|---|
| July | 1 | Paid $2400 for three months' rent on the premises, which covers from 1 July to 30 September 2001. |
| | 5 | Completed a consulting job providing advice to a local developer on the design of a pool. Invoiced the developer for $1400 to be paid in 15 days. |
| | 6 | Repaired a pool filter and received a cash payment of $100. |
| | 8 | Credit purchase of shelving for $2100 in the business office (payable in 30 days). Cash payment of $300 to a tradesman for installation of the shelves. |
| | 11 | Sold three filters for $900 cash each. (Cost of goods was $1600 in total.) |
| | 13 | Paid accounts payable $3500. |
| | 15 | Received $4000 from accounts receivable. |
| | 16 | Purchased for cash office furniture that had a list price of $4000 but was on sale for $3000. |
| | 18 | Received a bill for $400 for advertising payable in ten days. |
| | 19 | Paid the rental expense on the company photocopier of $400 which covers the month of July. |
| | 23 | Cash petrol expenses $50. |
| | 24 | Cash purchase of office stationery $100. |
| | 28 | Paid advertising bill. |
| | 29 | Paid salaries for the month of $2000. $200 in wages was still owing at the end of the period. |
| | 29 | Received $1400 for 5 July transaction. |
| | 31 | Charged depreciation on the furniture and fittings of $100. |

1 Show the relevant journal entries.
2 Post to the ledger.
3 Extract a trial balance at 31 July 2001.
4 Prepare a statement of financial performance for the month of July 2001 and a statement of financial position as at 31 July 2001.

## Problem 4.12 Make journal entries, post to the ledger and extract trial balance

Take the transactions for Roche Pty Ltd (problem 3.13 in chapter 3) and:

1 Prepare journal entries.
2 Post to the ledger accounts.
3 Prepare a trial balance.

## Problem 4.13 Accounting cycle and chart of accounts

Carlson Pty Ltd is a business selling freezers to the public. The chart of accounts for the business is as follows:

**Chart of accounts**

| | | | |
|---|---|---|---|
| **1–9** | **Owners' equity** | **30–39** | **Assets** |
| 1 | Share capital | 30 | Bank of NZ |
| 2 | Retained profits | 31 | Sundry debtors |
| 9 | Profit and loss summary | 32 | Inventories |
| | | 35 | Delivery truck |
| **10–19** | **Liabilities** | **40–49** | **Expenses** |
| 10 | Sundry creditors | 40 | Cost of goods sold |
| 15 | Loan from Finance Co. | 42 | Salary – shop assistants |
| | | 45 | Delivery truck expenses |
| | | 47 | Office expenses |
| | | 49 | Interest expense |
| **20–29** | **Revenue** | | |
| 20 | Sales | | |

Transactions for April 2002 were as follows:

| **2002** | | |
|---|---|---|
| Apr | 1 | Owners introduced $150 000 in share capital, deposited in Bank of New Zealand. |
| | 2 | Delivery truck bought from finance company for $80 000 to become long-term loan. |
| | 4 | Goods purchased on credit for resale for $200 000. |
| | 7 | Paid delivery truck expenses, $4800. |
| | 10 | Sales made for cash, totalling $50 000 invoice value – original cost $30 000. |
| | 15 | Sales made to credit customers $120 000 invoice value – original cost $70 000. |
| | 25 | Shop assistants' salary for month paid, totalling $8000. |
| | 27 | Paid office expenses, $26 000. |
| | 29 | Received $90 000 from credit customers. |
| | 29 | Paid sundry creditors, $100 000. |
| | 29 | Paid interest on loan, $800. |

1. Enter the transactions in a general journal.
2. Post to the ledger.
3. Extract a trial balance.
4. Prepare and post closing entries.
5. Prepare a statement of financial performance for April 2002.
6. Extract a post-closing trial balance and prepare a statement of financial position at 30 April 2002.

## Problem 4.14 Identify transactions and write journal entries for them

The following events happened today at Billowy Balloons Pty Ltd, a sightseeing and advertising company featuring large hot-air balloons. For each event listed below, state whether or not it is an accounting transaction for Billowy and why. If it is an accounting transaction, write a journal entry to record it.

1 The general manager, despondent over poor sales performance, jumped out of a balloon from 1000 feet up. His salary was $75 000 per year.

2 His widow immediately sued the company for $500 000, stating that job-related stress caused him to jump.

3 The company agreed with the barn owner that after the funeral it would pay $10 000 to repair the barn roof that the president had fallen through.

4 Learning about the general manager's action, shareholder Jumpy John sold his shares, which had cost him $20 000, to Happy Harry for $18 000.

5 Learning about the general manager's action and concerned about its possible effects on the company's share price, the board of directors declared a dividend of $25 000, to be paid in two weeks as a shareholder morale booster.

## Problem 4.15 Identify transactions and write journal entries for them

The following events took place on 1 February 2002. For each event, give the journal entry (if any) that should be made to record the transaction in the accounts of Smith Pty Ltd. Indicate clearly where in the financial statements you think the accounts involved belong. State any assumptions you feel are necessary.

1 The company purchased supplies to be used immediately. The purchase price of the supplies was $5000. Only $2000 was paid in cash, on delivery. The balance is due in 30 days.

2 The company decided to rent a service vehicle for $4800 per year. A rental contract was signed 1 February 2002, to take effect 1 March 2002. Smith Pty Ltd paid $400 cash to the rental company on 1 February 2002, which represented the rent for March 2002.

3 Some of Smith's repairers were not busy on 1 February. The manager had them paint the inside of a storage room to repair some water damage. Assume the repairers' salaries of $300 were paid in cash at the end of the day.

4 A shareholder sold her car to the company. The vehicle cost her $15 000 two years ago. An equivalent used vehicle would have been worth about $8000 on 1 February 2002. No cash changed hands, but the shareholder expects the company to pay her for the car eventually.

5 An invoice for $5000 was received, relating to repairs and maintenance work done in December 2001. The company's year-end is 31 December. This expense was not recorded in the 2001 financial statements.

## Problem 4.16 Identify transactions and write journal entries for them

Southward Stores Ltd is a general merchandise retailer operating in the suburbs. During a recent month, the events listed below happened. For each event, decide if it is an accounting transaction. If it is an accounting transaction, state briefly why and record it in journal entry form. Indicate where in the financial statements you wish each account to appear. If it is not an accounting transaction, state briefly why it is not.

1 Southward borrowed $500 000 from the Commonwealth Bank. Payment is due in three years, but the loan can be called on 10 days' notice if Southward fails to make any of the monthly interest payments, which begin next month.

2 The company ordered inventory for resale costing $300 000, to be delivered in 40 days, and sent a deposit of $10 000 with the order.

3 The company renewed its lease on the store premises, signing an agreement which provided that, beginning in three months, the monthly rent would rise from $21 000 to $23 000.

4 Southward was charged with unfair pricing of its main line of merchandise. News of this sent the company's shares (listed on the stock exchange) down in price from $10 to $8.50 each. The company has 1 000 000 shares issued, all publicly traded.

5 The company declared a dividend of $0.50 cents per share, to be paid in one week, on each of its 1 000 000 issued shares. This news sent the company's shares up by $0.40 each on the stock exchange.

## Problem 4.17 Accounting cycle, make journal entries, post to the ledger and extract trial balance

Morilla Ltd sells hair accessories. The statement of financial position for Morilla Ltd as at 31 January 2002 was as follows:

| **Assets** | | **Liabilities and shareholders' equity** | |
|---|---|---|---|
| Cash | 21 000 | Accounts payable | 13 000 |
| Accounts receivable | 25 000 | Long-term loan | 49 000 |
| Inventory | 36 000 | Share capital | 30 000 |
| Equipment | 24 000 | Retained profits | 11 000 |
| Accumulated depreciation | (3 000) | | |
| | 103 000 | | 103 000 |

The following transactions occurred during February 2002:

**a** Purchased 3000 bottles of GreyNoMore at $2.75 each (on credit).

**b** Made credit sales – 2200 bottles of Morilla Shinepoo at $5 each (cost $3.50) to Hair Today Supplies.

**c** Received $19 000 from accounts receivable.

**d** Paid $11 000 of accounts payable.

**e** Paid $1500 in electricity, petrol and phone bills.

**f** Paid $2600 in salaries.

**g** Expensed $200 in depreciation.

**h** $800 was paid off the loan.

1 Prepare journal entries.
2 Post to the ledger accounts.
3 Prepare a trial balance.
4 Prepare closing entries.
5 Prepare a statement of financial performance for the month of February 2002 and a statement of financial position as at 28 February 2002.

## Problem 4.18 Trial balances

Which of the following errors would be detected by the preparation of a trial balance?

1 Goods were sold to a customer for $540. The invoice showed $5.40, which was the amount duly paid by the customer.

2 To record the purchase of a computer on credit, both Computer Account and Accounts Payable Account were credited.

3 When an account from the service station was paid, Motor Vehicle Expenses Account was debited with $149 and Cash Account was credited with $194.

4 A photographic machine was repaired, but the invoice for the work was mislaid in the post.

5 Cash sales of $1470 were made. The bookkeeper correctly debited Cash Account, but the corresponding credit was never made.

6 A salesman left the keys in one of the firm's vehicles, which was stolen and never recovered. The accountant had omitted to renew the insurance policy on the vehicle.

7 In listing the balances of the accounts, the balance of Postages Account was shown as $541 instead of the correct figure of $514, and the balance of Donations Account was shown as $3 instead of the correct figure of $30.

## Problem 4.19 Incorrect trial balances

Fred Foster is the accountant at Flying Fox Ltd. During May, he records the following transactions in the general journal:

| | | | |
|---|---|---|---|
| 1 | Inventory worth $6000 was purchased for cash. | | |
| | Dr Inventory | $6 000 | |
| | Cr Cash | | $6 000 |
| 2 | $11 000 was paid to creditors. | | |
| | Dr Accounts payable | $11 000 | |
| | Cr Cash | | $11 000 |
| 3 | Wages of $7000 were paid | | |
| | Dr Wages expense | $7 000 | |
| | Cr Cash | | $7 000 |
| 4 | Payments totalling $14 000 were received from accounts receivable. | | |
| | Dr Cash | $14 000 | |
| | Cr Accounts receivable | | $14 000 |

Fred posts these entries to the general ledger accounts and prepares an updated trial balance as at 31 May. Shown below are a series of incorrect trial balances he has calculated.

***Required:***

Consider each trial balance and determine the most likely error Fred has made in each case.

1

**Flying Fox Ltd**
Trial balance at 31 May 2002

| | DR $ | CR $ |
|---|---|---|
| Cash | 37 000 | |
| Accounts receivable | 81 000 | |
| Inventory | 156 000 | |
| Accounts payable | | 29 000 |
| Share capital | | 200 000 |
| Retained profits | | 30 000 |
| Wages | 7 000 | |
| | 281 000 | 259 000 |

2

**Flying Fox Ltd**
Trial balance at 31 May 2002

| | DR<br>$ | CR<br>$ |
|---|---|---|
| Cash | 22 000 | |
| Accounts receivable | 81 000 | |
| Inventory | 156 000 | |
| Accounts payable | | 29 000 |
| Share capital | | 200 000 |
| Retained profits | | 30 000 |
| Wages | 7 000 | |
| | 266 000 | 259 000 |

3

**Flying Fox Ltd**
Trial balance at 31 May 2002

| | DR<br>$ | CR<br>$ |
|---|---|---|
| Cash | 15 000 | |
| Accounts receivable | 81 000 | |
| Inventory | 156 000 | |
| Accounts payable | | 29 000 |
| Share capital | | 200 000 |
| Retained profits | 30 000 | |
| Wages | 7 000 | |
| | 289 000 | 229 000 |

4

**Flying Fox Ltd**
Trial balance at 31 May 2002

| | DR<br>$ | CR<br>$ |
|---|---|---|
| Cash | 42 000 | |
| Accounts receivable | 81 000 | |
| Inventory | 156 000 | |
| Accounts payable | | 29 000 |
| Share capital | | 200 000 |
| Retained profits | | 30 000 |
| Wages | 7 000 | |
| | 286 000 | 259 000 |

5 Fred realises that the cash account in the general ledger is one in which errors have been detected in the past. The details of the cash account for May are extracted below.

| Cash | | | |
|---|---|---|---|
| o/b | 25 000 | Inventory | 6 000 |
| Accounts receivable | 14 000 | Accounts payable | 11 000 |
| | | Wages | 7 000 |
| c/b | 13 000 | | |

Given both the cash ledger account and the trial balance below, determine the error that Fred has made.

**Flying Fox Ltd**
Trial balance at 31 May 2002

| | DR<br>$ | CR<br>$ |
|---|---|---|
| Cash | 13 000 | |
| Accounts receivable | 81 000 | |
| Inventory | 156 000 | |
| Accounts payable | | 29 000 |
| Share capital | | 200 000 |
| Retained profits | | 30 000 |
| Wages | 7 000 | |
| | 257 000 | 259 000 |

## Problem 4.20 Closing entries

**Jones Ltd**
Pre-closing trial balance
at 30 June 2002

| | Debit<br>$ | Credit<br>$ |
|---|---|---|
| Cash | 120 000 | |
| Accounts receivable | 290 000 | |
| Inventory | 350 000 | |
| Prepaid insurance | 25 000 | |
| Equipment | 260 000 | |
| Accumulated depreciation | | 32 000 |
| Accounts payable | | 150 000 |
| Salaries payable | | 12 000 |
| Loan | | 186 000 |
| Share capital | | 300 000 |
| Retained profits | | 300 000 |
| Sales | | 320 000 |
| Cost of goods sold | 190 000 | |
| Depreciation expense | 2 000 | |
| Rent | 10 000 | |
| Salaries expense | 37 000 | |
| Insurance expense | 5 000 | |
| Telephone expense | 5 000 | |
| Electricity expense | 6 000 | |
| | 1 300 000 | 1 300 000 |

Prepare closing journal entries.

## Problem 4.21 Reconstruct journal entries from T-accounts

Sanderson Electronics is a new retail store that sells mainly small parts, such as switches, circuit boards and wire. Sanderson's ledger accounts are shown below in T-account form, with entries made for the first month of business.

| Cash | | | |
|---|---|---|---|
| (a) | 30 000 | (c) | 1 200 |
| (f) | 1 300 | (h) | 1 000 |
| (g) | 650 | (j) | 560 |

| Accounts receivable | | | |
|---|---|---|---|
| (e) | 900 | (g) | 650 |
| (f) | 1 400 | | |

| Supplies | | | |
|---|---|---|---|
| (i) | 300 | | |

| Equipment | | | |
|---|---|---|---|
| (c) | 3 600 | | |

| Inventory | | | |
|---|---|---|---|
| (b) | 5 000 | (e) | 540 |
| | | (f) | 1 620 |

| Accounts payable | | | |
|---|---|---|---|
| (h) | 1 000 | (b) | 5 000 |
| | | (d) | 700 |

| Notes payable | | | |
|---|---|---|---|
| (j) | 500 | (c) | 2 400 |

| Share capital | | | |
|---|---|---|---|
| | | (a) | 30 000 |

| Sales revenue | | | |
|---|---|---|---|
| | | (e) | 900 |
| | | (f) | 2 700 |

| Supplies expense | | | |
|---|---|---|---|
| (d) | 700 | (i) | 300 |

| Interest expense | | | |
|---|---|---|---|
| (j) | 60 | | |

| Cost of goods sold | | | |
|---|---|---|---|
| (e) | 540 | | |
| (f) | 1 620 | | |

For each of transactions (a) to (j), write the general journal entry that was used to post the accounts, including an explanation of the entry.

## CASE 4A Woolworths Limited case

Refer to the extracts of the annual report of Woolworths Limited in appendix 2. All questions relate to the consolidated accounts.

**1** What would be the most likely source document for Woolworths Limited to record:
- **a** a sale?
- **b** a purchase of goods for sale?
- **c** a payment to suppliers?
- **d** a payment of wages?
- **e** interest expense?

**2** Prepare an example of the assets component of the chart of accounts that could be used by Woolworths.

**3** What journal entry would Woolworths Limited write for each of the following:
- **a** a cash sale of $38?
- **b** the purchase of 1000 white folders for $3 each on credit for resale?
- **c** the payment of weekly wages of $1 800 000?
- **d** the purchase of shop fittings on credit for $800 000?
- **e** a bill to clients for management fees of $1 200 000?
- **f** the receipt of $1 200 000 in management fees from clients?

## CASE 4B Costs of accounting and record-keeping

An article from Business Week, 'A Day of Reckoning for Bean Counters', is below. Discuss the article's perspective on the cost of accounting and record-keeping. (The article mentions 'T&E': that's travel and entertainment expense claims. Also, the article considers accounting and record-keeping to be part of the 'finance function' in a business: not everyone would put it that way, but it's a reminder that accounting and financial statements are part of the business's overall financial management and control activity.) The article uses US companies, but seems equally applicable to most countries.

## A day of reckoning for bean counters

Now, finance departments are hearing the axeman's footsteps.

When Union Carbide Corp. spun off its industrial-gases business two years ago, that prompted a company-wide restructuring designed to pare some $400 million in costs. For Chief Financial Officer John K. Wulff, the exercise proved eye-opening. He decided to find out how the chemical company's costs of performing such simple finance functions as cutting (i.e. preparing) cheques, posting entries in accounting ledgers, and reviewing travel and expense reports compared with those of other large companies.

His conclusion? Carbide was a high-cost operation. It spent $9.45 to process a single invoice. Other companies spent an average of $8, with the best performers under $1. A journal entry cost Wulff's people $16.22 – about 10 times what other large industrial companies were spending. Carbide did do some things well, with T&E forms being processed at half the average $20 cost of comparative companies. But, overall, Carbide's performance left a lot of room for improvement. 'I knew our costs were high', says Wulff. 'But in certain areas, like general accounting, I was a little surprised.' Since then, Wulff has been aggressively reducing the costs of Carbide's finance operation. Some 200 positions have been eliminated, saving more than $20 million.

### *Shared services*

Carbide's experience, and that of some other big American companies taking similar measures, offers surprising lessons. Carbide has spent much of its recent history redesigning manufacturing operations, managing inventories more closely, and speeding up product-development cycles. But these very same companies – zealous in their ability to cut the cost of making products – had allowed their backroom bean counters to grow very flabby. Now, though, CFOs are giving finance the same makeover that manufacturing and marketing received in the late 1980s. Companies as diverse as Johnson & Johnson and General Electric Co. are finding they can cut overheads by a third or better with new ways to bill customers, pay employees and process cheques. 'This is going to be the agenda at every company within the next five years,' says consultant Robert W. Gunn, who has helped such companies as Hewlett Packard, Shell, and US West reengineer their finance shops.

In many ways, the changes afoot parallel what has happened on the shop floor. GE is using the very same techniques of mapping work processes that it uses to speed up production of appliances to increase the output of accounting clerks. But in other ways, the trend is counter to the latest dogma from management consultants. Leading-edge companies that are actively trying to push decision-making to the lowest point are just as quickly centralising their finance functions into one or two regional data centres under a system known as 'shared services'. Instead of each business unit having its own CFO and accounting operations, the businesses in effect become 'customers' of a centralised finance function. 'Once we got control of these functions, we could reengineer them,' says Walt Hazelton, manager of accounting service operations for Xerox Corp

### *Impact*

That's exactly what happened at GE. Its far-flung businesses once used 34 different payroll systems. But over the past five years, GE has transferred work from five different regional accounting centres to one megacentre in Fort Myers, Fla. Along the way, the number of finance department workers has fallen by 40 per cent, to 600. 'They do the work differently,' says Robert Frigo, manager of GE's Financial Services Operation. 'There's much more use of electronic media and local-area-network technology.' And with fewer workers, notes Frigo, come fewer supervisors.

Johnson & Johnson CFO Clark H. Johnson says he saw the light in the 1980s when the company participated in a benchmarking study. The survey found most large companies spent about 2.3 per cent of their annual sales on finance-department overhead. 'We were at 2.8 per cent, and that kind of woke us up,' says Johnson.

Armed with the data, J&J began a consolidation that combines regional data centres and undertook the use of uniform ledgers and accounts-payable systems. 'We had 100 manufacturing locations with 106 payroll people,' says Johnson. 'We're now doing our payroll of 40 000 people with 28 people.' All told, J&J slashed its finance-department head count by a third, or 600 positions, even as sales increased 30 per cent.

The cuts had a bottom-line impact. Johnson says that in the past four years, the company has reduced its worldwide finance budget by $84 million. To accommodate the downsizing, Johnson says the company used early retirement programs and tried to move affected workers to other jobs in the company. And Johnson cut back sharply on his use of temporary workers brought in to manage the paperwork overload.

The effort encouraged Johnson to push even harder for savings. Once, it took J&J 26 days to close its books. Now, it's down to 7 days. 'My target is 2 days,' says Johnson. 'It's really computerisation as well as different attitudes.' Johnson has also eliminated monthly closings, going to quarterly instead, and reduced much of the paperwork associated with a huge finance staff. 'We were producing too much paper that no one has time to use,' he says.

At Ford Motor Co., what began as an attempt in the mid 1980s to cut costs by 20 per cent in its accounts-payable department soon led to a wholesale reworking of the company's procurement system. In the old days, Ford would order a part, and when the supplier shipped it, accounts-payable clerks would attempt to match the purchasing order with a form produced at the receiving dock and reconcile that with the vendor's invoice. When all three agreed, payment was made to the vendor. Armies of clerical workers were spending hours chasing missing forms.

Nowadays, a clerk orders a part, enters the order into an electronic data base, and then awaits shipment. When the part comes in, a worker in receiving checks the database to make sure the part has been ordered and then approves it, at the same time prompting the computer to automatically issue payment to the vendor.

### *Entrenched*

The changes at Ford, J&J, GE and other companies have led to byproducts other than reduced costs and shrinking staffs. GE's Frigo says the goal is to get finance people integrally involved in overall business strategy. Instead of just checking T&E reports for errors, workers can now develop information about company spending practices that lead to better deals with vendors. 'It's more than just paying the bills,' says Frigo. 'We're trying to push the focus from processing transactions to adding value.'

But change is slow in coming in some companies, where the finance function is often a protected fiefdom. While outfits such as GE and Xerox are pacesetters, many companies are barely dealing with the growing costs of their finance units. 'I would say most people are groping,' says Patrick J. Keating, a business professor at San Jose State University who has studied the issue. 'Most finance people are so entrenched, they can't even visualise where they are trying to go.'

That's a shame. Consultant Gunn says finance staffs in large companies average nearly 5 per cent of the total employment and in some cases account for more than 10 per cent of the company's payroll – which creates major opportunities for big savings. Companies that seize those opportunities could get a big leg up on global competitors, especially since reengineering of back-office operations is something that American companies are far further along on than overseas companies. 'I think it's what is going to beat the Japanese,' says Gunn.

That may be carrying it too far. But it's still an incentive that any American company can appreciate.

(Source: *Business Week*, 14 March 1994, pp. 75–6, by special permission, copyright 1994 McGraw-Hill Ltd.)

Chapter 5

# Revenue and expense recognition in accrual accounting

## On completion of this chapter you should be able to:

- explain how the timing of revenue and expense recognition differs from cash inflows and outflows
- explain the purpose of accrual accounting adjustments
- describe prepayments, accrued revenue, accrued expenses, revenue received in advance, depreciation, doubtful debts and contra accounts
- calculate the impact on the financial statements of accrual accounting adjustments
- prepare journal entries for accrual accounting adjustments
- show the impact on the financial statements and prepare journal entries for inventory transactions using the perpetual inventory method
- show the impact on the financial statements and prepare journal entries for the depreciation of assets and the sale of assets
- show the impact on the financial statements and prepare journal entries for increasing the provision for doubtful debts and writing off bad debts.

## 5.1 Chapter overview

Accrual accounting exists because cash flow information is not complete enough to assess financial performance or financial position. Keeping track of cash flow is crucial for business success, but it is not enough. We have to go beyond cash flow to assess economic performance more broadly and to assess non-cash resources and obligations. We do this although it forces us to make estimates, judgements and other accounting choices that, in turn, make the results less precise than we would wish, and more subjective than transaction-based cash flow figures.

Imagine the following conversation between a student and a relative who is also a professional accountant:

> *Accountant*: Well, you spent the summer working at High-Class Boutique. How did you do?
>
> *Student:* I had a great time. Met some great people, learned a lot about retailing, and so decided to major in marketing.
>
> *Accountant:* No, I meant how did you do financially?
>
> *Student:* Let's see. I received $4260 over the three months. I have $2330 left in the bank, so I guess I must have spent $1930. Gee, $2330 doesn't seem much for a summer's work! But the boutique still owes me for my last week of work.
>
> *Accountant:* What did you spend the $1930 on?
>
> *Student:* I blew some of the money on beer and entertainment, and on that trip to the Gold Coast. But I also bought a good set of clothes for semester one, and I have the answering machine, and the fancy calculator I got so that I might be able to pass accounting.
>
> *Accountant:* Don't forget you have to pay your Uncle Al back the money he lent you in November. That's in your bank account too. You promised to pay him, plus interest, at the end of the summer. And then there's your university fees for next year. And didn't you say once that you owed a friend something for petrol for that trip to the Gold Coast?
>
> *Student:* I don't think we should count the fees because it doesn't really apply until I enrol. Although I guess that's why I was working. Now I'm not sure if I had a good summer or not!

This example illustrates many of the issues accrual accounting tries to deal with, including the following:

- The more you think about it, the more complex measuring performance and position seems to be, and the less satisfactory cash by itself seems to be as a measure.
- Some of what is earned may not yet have been received in cash (payment for the last week of work).
- Similarly, some costs incurred may not yet have been paid (the petrol for the trip).
- Some cash payments result in resources still having economic value at the end of the period (the answering machine, the calculator and maybe the clothes).
- Some cash receipts result in obligations still outstanding at the end of the period (Uncle Al's loan).
- The longer-term resources may have deteriorated during the period (not all the clothes purchased during the summer will still be valuable because fashions change, and the answering machine and calculator are now used items).
- Obligations may build up during the period (the interest on Uncle Al's loan).

- There is often doubt about whether some things should be included in measuring performance for a given period or position at a given point in time (the university fees).
- Generally, how do we relate the timing of cash flows to the period we're concerned with? Most of the above items involve cash flows sooner or later; the awkward cases are usually those for which the period when the cash moves and the period for which we're measuring performance don't match.

Think of accrual accounting as an attempt to measure economic performance and financial position in a more complex way than just using cash. There is always a trade-off here: the closer to cash, the more precise the measure, but also the more limited and less informative. The more accountants try to make the financial statements economically relevant, the more they must include estimates and other sources of imprecision or error.

## 5.2 Conceptual foundation of accrual accounting

Accrual accounting is the dominant form of financial accounting in the world today. This chapter builds on the foundation laid in earlier chapters and on the introduction in section 1.5; it explains why accrual accounting exists and distinguishes the accrual basis from cash basis accounting.

Accrual accounting is based on the idea that events, estimates and judgements important to the measurement of financial performance and position should be recognised by entries in the accounts (and therefore reflected in the financial statements), whether or not they have yet, or already, been realised by cash received or paid out. To slightly oversimplify, we might say that the objective is to recognise economic flows in addition to cash flows. To clarify this idea, we will focus on revenue and expense recognition.

Let's build the accrual accounting approach from some basics. These three cornerstones have come up already in this book, but we'll give them brief definitions again, then build from there. We will come back to these concepts in chapter 11 to provide the more inclusive concepts outlined in the *Australian Statements of Accounting Concepts* (specifically SAC 4).

- Revenues are *inflows* of economic resources from customers earned through providing goods or services. You might say that companies are in business to earn revenues.
- Expenses are *outflows* of economic resources to employees, suppliers, taxation authorities and others, resulting from business activities to generate revenue and serve customers. You might say that incurring expenses is the cost of earning revenues.
- Net profit is the *difference* between revenues and expenses over a period of time, such as a month, a quarter or a year. You might say that net profit is the measure of success in generating more revenues than it costs to do so.

Note some features of these cornerstones:

- Revenues and expenses refer to inflows and outflows of economic resources. These flows may be represented by the kinds of events recognised by the transactional record-keeping system described in chapter 4, but they may also involve other phenomena. In particular, they may involve phenomena that arise before or after cash changes hands, as well as at the point of the cash flow.
- Net profit is dependent on how revenues and expenses are measured. Accountants don't, or shouldn't, choose the profit number first, then force revenues and expenses to result in that number, but instead measure revenues and expenses as best they can,

then let net profit be whatever the difference is between properly measured revenues and expenses.

## For your interest

Above we noted that 'accountants don't, or shouldn't, choose the profit number first, then force revenues and expenses to result in that number'. However, there is plenty of anecdotal evidence that managers try to influence accountants' determination of the profit figure. Consider the following extract:

### If Harris Scarfe boss wanted profit, he got it

Harris Scarfe's figures were creatively altered to fit profit targets set by senior management, according to sworn evidence yesterday by the former chief financial officer of the collapsed retail group, Mr Alan Hodgson.

Mr Hodgson, who resigned in June and is unemployed, said he authorised the accounts to be changed if a profit result was requested or required by the company's managing director or chairman.

'If I was requested or ordered to produce a particular profit result and I didn't have the means of doing it in a conventional sense, I would take more out [of that accrual account] than I should have done,' he told the Supreme Court.

'Or the gross profit figures would be increased across the biggest stores to achieve a target result,' he said.

'I would simply sit down with [accountant] Michael Johnson and say this is the result I am required to achieve this year, for whatever reason, can you put an adjustment through? And he would put an adjustment through the department's stats,' he said.

Mr Hodgson distinguished between conventional profit, which was that achieved 'without making any creative adjustments', and unconventional profits, which were manipulated.

He said he was aware of the requirements of the corporations law but did not think about it, believing the issue was one of timing.

(Source: *Sydney Morning Herald*, 7 August 2001, p. 21.)

## A conceptual system for accrual profit measurement

Accrual accounting's purpose is to extend the measurement of financial performance and financial position by recognising phenomena *before* and *after* cash flows, as well as *at the point of* cash flows (which cash basis accounting already does). We need a system, therefore, that covers the following types of events:

1 recognition of revenue (resource inflow) or expense (resource outflow) at the same time as cash inflow or outflow
2 recognition of revenue (resource inflow) or expense (resource outflow) before cash inflow or outflow
3 recognition of revenue (resource inflow) or expense (resource outflow) after cash inflow or outflow.

Accrual accounting derives its value from recognising transactions in categories 2 and 3. These allow measurement of performance and position to be spread out in time. Category 2 extends the time horizon out prior to the cash flow, and category 3 extends the time horizon out subsequent to the cash flow. Category 1 already exists in the cash basis of accounting, so the accrual method includes the cash basis. As will be illustrated below, it also does much more.

## Implementing the accrual framework[1]

As you review the following examples, try to think about the general accrual accounting framework they represent. They are not the only examples that could be listed, but they help you understand the concept, so that you can choose or understand an accounting entry or financial statement item that you might not have seen before. Think about the patterns rather than trying to memorise the entries. Think about how accrual accounting recognises revenue when it is earned and recognises expenses when they are incurred, regardless of when the cash is collected.

In the following illustration, we show both the effect of the transactions on the accounting equation, then show the journal entry below. This should reinforce your understanding of journal entries.

In considering each of the entries below, remember the accounting equation must always balance: A = L + SE. An increase in revenue increases SE while an increase in an expense decreases SE.

### 1 Recognition of revenue or expense at the same time as cash inflow or outflow

These examples are simple cash basis revenue and expense transactions, which you have seen in earlier chapters. We present them again here to provide a complete picture of revenue and expense accounting under the accrual basis.

*Revenues:*

- A retail shop records a cash sale to a customer.

| | | |
|---|---|---|
| ↑ | Cash | $48 |
| ↑ | Sales revenue (↑ SE) | $48 |

| | $ | $ |
|---|---|---|
| DR Cash | 48 | |
| CR Sales | | 48 |

- An investor records a dividend cheque received from BHP Billiton.

| | | |
|---|---|---|
| ↑ | Cash | $150 |
| ↑ | Dividend revenue (↑ SE) | $150 |

| | $ | $ |
|---|---|---|
| DR Cash | 150 | |
| CR Dividend revenue | | 150 |

*Expenses:*

- A company pays Acme Rug Cleaners to shampoo the carpets in its customer waiting area.

| | | |
|---|---|---|
| ↑ | Office expenses (↓ SE) | $245 |
| ↓ | Cash | $245 |

Note that increasing an expense reduces equity.

| | $ | $ |
|---|---|---|
| DR Office expense | 245 | |
| CR Cash | | 245 |

- A company makes a donation to the accounting department of the local university to support teaching and research.

| | | |
|---|---|---|
| ↑ | Donation expense (↓ SE) | $10 000 |
| ↓ | Cash | $10 000 |

| | $ | $ |
|---|---|---|
| DR Donation expense | 10 000 | |
| CR Cash | | 10 000 |

## 2 Recognition of revenue or expense prior to cash flow

In the following situations, the revenue or expense is recognised before the cash inflow or outflow. Under accrual accounting, the revenue should be recognised (recorded in the accounting records) when it is earned, not when the cash is collected. Similarly, expenses should be recognised in the period in which the expense is incurred, not when the cash is paid. Assume the year-end is 30 June.

*Revenues:*

- A lawyer performs services for a client in June 2002 and bills the client $500 to be paid within 30 days.

| | | |
|---|---|---|
| ↑ | Accounts receivable | $500 |
| ↑ | Fee revenue(↑ SE) | $500 |

| | $ | $ |
|---|---|---|
| DR Accounts receivable | 500 | |
| CR Fee revenue | | 500 |

*Expenses:*

- A company receives a $2400 advertising bill on 10 June 2002 payable within 30 days.

| | | |
|---|---|---|
| ↑ | Advertising expense (↓ SE) | $2 400 |
| ↑ | Accounts payable | $2 400 |

| | $ | $ |
|---|---|---|
| DR Advertising expense | 2 400 | |
| CR Accounts payable | | 2 400 |

- A manufacturer estimates that it will incur future warranty costs of $3000 in the 2003 financial year on products sold in the 2002 financial year. (The warranty expense should be recognised in 2002, since that is the year in which the sales revenue was recognised and the warranty expense relates to that sale.)

| | | |
|---|---|---|
| ↑ | Warranty expense (↓ SE) | $3 000 |
| ↑ | Warranty liability | $3 000 |

(Warranty liability is sometimes called provision for warranty expense.)

| | $ | $ |
|---|---|---|
| DR Warranty expense | 3 000 | |
| CR Warranty liability | | 3 000 |

- On 30 June 2002, a company calculates that its 2002 income taxes are $1850. The company must pay its taxes by 10 October 2002.

| | | |
|---|---|---|
| ↑ | Income tax expense (↓ SE) | $1 850 |
| ↑ | Income tax payable | $1 850 |

| | $ | $ |
|---|---|---|
| DR Income tax expense | 1 850 | |
| CR Income tax payable | | 1 850 |

In the above examples, revenue and expenses are recognised before the cash flow transactions. When the cash flows occur, there is no longer a need to recognise revenue or expense. The cash flows will be recorded as offsets to the assets and liabilities created when the revenues and expenses were initially recorded. For example, the payment of the tax bill will decrease cash and decrease income tax payable. These entries are illustrated below.

## 3 Cash collections or payments related to previously recognised revenues and expenses

*Revenues:*

- The lawyer receives full payment from her client in July 2002.

| | | |
|---|---|---|
| ↑ | Cash | $500 |
| ↓ | Accounts receivable | $500 |

| | $ | $ |
|---|---|---|
| DR Cash | 500 | |
| CR Accounts receivable | | 500 |

*Expenses:*

- The advertising expense is paid on 10 July 2002.

| | | |
|---|---|---|
| ↓ | Accounts payable | $2 400 |
| ↓ | Cash | $2 400 |

| | $ | $ |
|---|---|---|
| DR Accounts payable | 2 400 | |
| CR Cash | | 2 400 |

- The manufacturer makes payments under the warranty in July 2002.

| | | |
|---|---|---|
| ↓ | Warranty liability | $3 000 |
| ↓ | Cash | $3 000 |

| | $ | $ |
|---|---|---|
| DR Warranty liability | 3 000 | |
| CR Cash | | 3 000 |

- The company pays a cheque to the Australian Taxation Office on 10 October 2002.

| | | |
|---|---|---|
| ↓ | Income tax payable | $1 850 |
| ↓ | Cash | $1 850 |

| | $ | $ |
|---|---|---|
| DR Income tax payable | 1 850 | |
| CR Cash | | 1 850 |

## 4 Cash inflow or outflow *before* revenue and expense recognition

In the following situations, the revenue or expense is recognised after the cash inflow, or outflow. Under accrual accounting, the revenue should be recognised when it is earned, not when the cash is collected. Similarly, expenses should be recognised in the period in which the expense is incurred, not when the cash is paid.

*Revenues:*

- A lawyer receives an advance of $2500 from a client for future services. The revenue will not be earned until a later date when services are performed. Recognition of revenue is deferred until the service has been performed.

| | | |
|---|---|---|
| ↑ | Cash | $2 500 |
| ↑ | Customer deposits (also called 'unearned revenue' or 'revenue received in advance') | $2 500 |

| | $ | $ |
|---|---|---|
| DR Cash | 2 500 | |
| CR Customer deposits | | 2 500 |

*Expenses:*

- In June 2002, Dogwood Limited pays $400 for a one-year fire insurance policy that becomes effective 1 July 2002. The insurance premium provides coverage during one year, and should be recognised as a 2003 expense. Expense recognition is deferred until 2003.

| | | |
|---|---|---|
| ↑ | Prepaid insurance | $400 |
| ↓ | Cash | $400 |

| | $ | $ |
|---|---|---|
| DR Prepaid insurance | 400 | |
| CR Cash | | 400 |

- In July 2002 Dogwood Limited purchases, for $400 000 in cash, a new building to be used as a retail location. Dogwood estimates that the building will be useful for ten years. The building will be used to produce revenues over ten future years. Recognition of an expense for the cost of using the building (depreciation expense) will be deferred.

| | | |
|---|---|---|
| ↑ | Building | $400 000 |
| ↓ | Cash | $400 000 |

| | $ | $ |
|---|---|---|
| DR Building | 400 000 | |
| CR Cash | | 400 000 |

- Dogwood Limited purchases $5000 worth of stereo components from a supplier for cash. Dogwood intends to resell these items to its customers. The purchases represent an asset (inventory) and recognising the cost as an expense is deferred until revenue is recognised through sale to customers.

| | | | | |
|---|---|---|---|---|
| ↑ | Inventory | $5 000 | | |
| ↓ | Cash | $5 000 | | |
| | | | $ | $ |
| DR | Inventory | | 5 000 | |
| CR | Cash | | | 5 000 |

## 5 Recognition of revenue or expense after cash inflow or outflow

*Revenues:*

- The lawyer completes the work promised for the client. The revenue has now been earned and should be recognised.

| | | | | |
|---|---|---|---|---|
| ↓ | Customer deposits | $2 500 | | |
| ↑ | Fee revenue (↑ SE) | $2 500 | | |
| | | | $ | $ |
| DR | Customer deposits | | 2 500 | |
| CR | Fee revenue | | | 2 500 |

*Expenses:*

- The fire insurance policy expires in June 2003. Coverage has been used during the year ending 30 June 2003; therefore, the cost of insurance should be recognised as an expense.

| | | | | |
|---|---|---|---|---|
| ↑ | Insurance expense (↓ SE) | $400 | | |
| ↓ | Prepaid insurance | $400 | | |
| | | | $ | $ |
| DR | Insurance expense | | 400 | |
| CR | Prepaid insurance | | | 400 |

- Dogwood recognises a portion of the cost of the building as an operating expense.

| | | | | |
|---|---|---|---|---|
| ↑ | Depreciation expense (↓ SE) | $4 000 | | |
| ↑ | Accumulated depreciation | $4 000 | | |
| | | | $ | $ |
| DR | Depreciation expense | | 4 000 | |
| CR | Accumulated depreciation | | | 4 000 |

- Dogwood sells all of the stereo components to customers. The cost of the inventory sold is an expense of earning revenue from the sale.

| | | | | |
|---|---|---|---|---|
| ↑ | Cost of goods sold (↓ SE) | $5 000 | | |
| ↓ | Inventory | $5 000 | | |
| | | | $ | $ |
| DR | Cost of goods sold | | 5 000 | |
| CR | Inventory | | | 5 000 |

## Summary

Based on the above:

- You can say that accrual accounting makes much of the statement of financial position into a sort of 'holding area' for incomplete revenue and expense events. For example, we record a credit sale as revenue and set up the related accounts receivable until cash is subsequently collected.
- You can see how accrual accounting spreads out these events over time. For example, a building is originally recorded as an asset, and the cost is periodically recognised as depreciation expense over the useful life of the asset.

There are complications, but the general pattern behind accrual accounting's revenue and expense recognition system is:

- Recognition of revenue before cash collection is done by creating an asset account (accounts receivable, usually), which stands in for the economic value gained until the cash has been collected.
- Recognition of expense before cash payment is done by creating a liability account (such as accounts payable, wages payable or tax payable), which stands in for the economic value lost until the cash is paid.
- Recognition of unearned revenue when cash is collected is provided for by creating a liability account (customer deposits or unearned revenue), which represents the commitment to the customer until the economic value is gained by providing the goods or services the customer has paid for. Revenue is later recognised when the goods or service are actually provided.
- An asset account (such as prepayments, inventory or machinery) is created when cash is paid. These assets represent the available resource until the economic value is lost by consuming the asset. Assets can be acquired by promises to pay, not just by cash; therefore, journal entries might credit accounts payable, mortgage payable or other liabilities rather than cash. But you can see that the 'asset' side of these entries still represents resources that are to be consumed later. Accrual accounting recognises the expense when the consumption happens, not when the asset is acquired, no matter how it is acquired.
- Not all cash flows involve revenues or expenses. Such flows have to be included in the accounts but, as they do not affect profit, are limited to statement of financial position accounts. There are other events even further removed from the profit calculation. Some examples of these are receipt of cash from an issue of share capital, disbursement of cash to make a mortgage payment, disbursement of cash to pay for an investment in another company and receipt of cash from a bank loan.

These examples were intended to help you think about what is going on, and see that there is a pattern behind the great variety of entries used in accrual accounting. For example, the following are all examples of asset consumption:

- reduction in economic value of a building (credit accumulated depreciation, debit depreciation expense)
- reduction in inventory as goods are sold (credit inventory, debit cost of goods sold)
- reduction in supplies asset as supplies are used (credit supplies inventory, debit supplies expense)
- reduction of prepaid insurance asset as the coverage is used (credit prepaid insurance, debit insurance expense)
- reduction in accounts receivable when customers fail to pay their accounts (credit accounts receivable, debit bad debts expense; more about this in section 5.8).

## How's your understanding?

Here are two questions you should be able to answer, based on what you have just read:

1 How do accrual accounting entries work to separate the earning of revenue from the receipt of cash? Is it always necessary to separate them, or can they happen at the same time?

2 In what way can it be said that depreciation expense and cost of goods sold expense are examples of the same thing?

# 5.3 Accrual accounting adjustments

The transactional records provide the foundation of the financial accounting system. In order to implement the accrual accounting system outlined above, such records usually require adjustments. Adjustments involve the implementation of routine accruals, such as those indicated in section 5.2: revenues earned but not yet collected, expenses incurred but not yet paid, cash received from customers before the related revenues having been earned and consumption of assets.

The degree to which accrual adjustments are needed in any accounting system depends on the sophistication of the system: sophisticated accounting systems may go beyond the transactional records and routinely include many adjustments that for simpler systems are made at year-end in a special set of journal entries. Many large companies have monthly accruals for interest expenses and other expenses as they build up, and monthly adjustments for depreciation and other consumptions of assets. Many small companies don't bother until annual financial statements are needed.

Accrual accounting adjustments follow the same double-entry format as do the transactional records:

- After each adjustment the accounting equation will still balance.
- Some account or accounts must be debited.
- Some account or accounts must be credited.
- The sum of the debits must equal the sum of the credits.

Accountants call such adjustments: adjusting journal entries. Their purpose is to *augment* the transaction-based (especially cash-based) figures (outlined in chapter 4), to add to the story told by the transactional records. They implement accrual accounting.

The objective of accrual accounting is to improve the measurement of financial performance and position. However, because different choices can be made about what accounts need to be adjusted and by how much, accrual accounting can be a mechanism for manipulating results and producing misleading reports. Therefore, the auditors give particular attention to the kinds of accrual adjustments a company makes, and most of the criticism of financial reporting is directed at subjective accrual adjustments, made using judgement, rather than at the more objective, verifiable transactional records. In spite of the subjectivity and criticism, most accountants believe the accrual accounting basis to be superior to the cash basis, because it provides a more complete record that is also more representative of economic performance than the cash basis.

There are four main types of routine adjustments that need to be accounted for:

- expiration of assets
- unearned revenues
- accrual of unrecorded expenses
- accrual of unrecorded revenues.

## Expiration of assets

Prepayments (prepaid expenses) are assets that arise because an expenditure has been made, but there is still value extending into the future. They are usually classified as current assets because the future value usually continues only into the next year. But sometimes the value extends beyond a year, and the company may then appropriately show a noncurrent prepaid expense. Prepaid expenses arise whenever the payment schedule for an expense does not match the company's financial period, such as for annual insurance premiums when the policy date is not the financial year-end, or council rates that are based on the council's rate assessment schedule rather than on the company's financial period.

Prepaid expenses are not assets in the same way as are receivables (to be collected in cash) or inventories (to be sold for cash). They arise from accrual accounting, in cases where the expense recognition follows the cash flow. This is conceptually the same reason inventories and fixed assets are on the statement of financial position: something of value exists, therefore its cost should not yet be deducted as an expense. Here, the value is in the fact that, having spent the money already, the company will not have to spend it in the next period. Alternatively, the value can be considered to be the fact that they are entitled to a service in the future for which they have already paid. So, prepaid expenses do not necessarily have any market value, but they have an economic value because future resources will not have to be expended. As the assets are consumed in the process of earning revenue, a portion of the cost is written off in each period as an expense.

The accounting for prepayments works as follows. When an amount is paid, for say, an insurance premium, prepayments (an asset) is increased and cash (an asset) decreases. At the end of the accounting period, some of the prepayment will have been used up. Therefore the amount of the asset is reduced and the expired portion of the asset is treated as an expense. Consider the following example.

On 1 June 2002, a company pays $24 000 for a one year insurance policy. The accounts would be affected as follows.

| | **Assets** | | **= Liabilities** | **+ Equity** |
|---|---|---|---|---|
| | | | | **Expense** |
| | **Cash** | **Prepayments** | | |
| 1 June | –24 000 | +24 000 | | |
| 30 June | | –2 000 | | –2 000 |
| Total | –24 000 | +22 000 | | –2 000 |

As one-twelfth of the asset was used up in June (that is, expense of $2000), the closing balance of the asset is $22 000.

The journal entry would be:

| | | | $ | $ |
|---|---|---|---|---|
| June 1 | DR | Prepayments | 24 000 | |
| | CR | Cash | | 24 000 |

| | | | $ | $ |
|---|---|---|---|---|
| June 30 | DR | Insurance expense | 2 000 | |
| | CR | Prepayments | | 2 000 |

These accounts now appear as follows:

| Prepayments | | | | | | Insurance expense | | |
|---|---|---|---|---|---|---|---|---|
| 1/6 | | 24 000 | 30/6 | 2 000 | 30/6 | 2 000 | | |
| 30/6 | Bal | 22 000 | | | | | | |

The prepayment balance of $22 000 represents 11 months of insurance that is prepaid and would be shown in the statement of financial position at 30 June 2002 as a current asset. The insurance expense account would appear on the June statement of financial performance (profit and loss statement). The transfer from the asset account (prepayments) to the expense account (insurance expense) will continue each month for the next 11 months, by which time the asset will have a zero balance.

You should note that there is an alternative way, which many companies also use, of treating prepayments. In this case they treat the initial cash payment as an expense, then at the end of the period reduce the expense by the amount that has not been used up, thus creating an asset (prepayments). The effect on the accounting equation would be:

| | Assets | | = Liabilities | + Equity Expense |
|---|---|---|---|---|
| | **Cash** | **Prepayments** | | |
| 1 June | –24 000 | | | –24 000 |
| 30 June | | +22 000 | | +22 000 |
| Total | –24 000 | +22 000 | | –2 000 |

The journal entries would appear as follows:

| | | $ | $ |
|---|---|---|---|
| June 1 | DR Insurance expense | 24 000 | |
| | CR Cash | | 24 000 |
| June 30 | DR Prepayments | 22 000 | |
| | CR Insurance expense | | 22 000 |

These accounts now appear as follows:

| Prepayments | | | | Insurance expense | | | | |
|---|---|---|---|---|---|---|---|---|
| 30/6 | Bal | 22 000 | | 1/6 | | $24 000 | 30/6 | $22 000 |
| | | | | 30/6 | Bal | $2 000 | | |

As you can see, the balances in the prepayments and insurance expense at 30 June are identical under both methods. In this book we will generally use the first method.

Prepayments are sometimes shown on the face of the statement of financial position (see exhibit 5.1, the Mayne Nickless example) or included in other assets and disclosed separately in the notes to the accounts (see the Seven Network example below).

Exhibit 5.1 shows that the Mayne Nickless group has $18 358 thousand of prepayments classified as current assets and shown on the face of their 2001 statement of financial position.

**EXHIBIT 5.1** **Mayne Nickless Limited**

**Extract of consolidated statement of financial position as at 30 June 2001**

| | Note | 2001<br>$000 | 2000<br>$000 |
|---|---|---|---|
| **Current assets** | | | |
| Cash and deposits | | **580 988** | 109 864 |
| Receivables | | **516 784** | 433 401 |
| Inventories | | **42 746** | 33 112 |
| Prepayments | | **18 358** | 27 684 |
| Assets held for resale | | **95 547** | — |
| Total current assets | | **1 254 423** | 604 061 |
| | | | |
| **Noncurrent assets** | | | |
| Deposits | | **3 777** | 698 |
| Receivables | | **14 868** | 15 720 |
| Investments accounted for using the equity method | | **8 798** | 9 169 |
| Other financial assets | | **18 068** | 14 854 |
| Property, plant and equipment | | **1 178 263** | 1 057 611 |
| Intangibles | | **506 793** | 555 182 |
| Deferred tax assets | | **131 237** | 64 992 |
| Other | | **97 568** | 55 884 |
| **Total noncurrent assets** | | **1 959 372** | 1 774 110 |
| **Total assets** | 12 | **3 213 795** | 2 378 171 |

In contrast the Seven Network in its 2001 annual report shows the following current assets:

| | | Consolidated | |
|---|---|---|---|
| | Note | 2001<br>$000 | 2001<br>$000 |
| **Current assets** | | | |
| Cash assets | | 25 555 | 49 230 |
| Receivables | 9 | 227 701 | 179 085 |
| Program rights and inventories | 10 | 66 317 | 143 042 |
| Other | 11 | 6 197 | 7 666 |
| **Total current assets** | | 325 770 | 379 023 |

'Other' current assets comprise prepayments as shown in Note 11 below.

| | | | |
|---|---|---|---|
| 11 Other assets | | | |
| Current | | | |
| Prepayments | | 6 197 | 7 666 |

Another example of expiration of assets is the using up of supplies. For example, on 3 June a company purchases supplies costing $10 000, which they pay cash for. At 30 June it is ascertained that $3000 of the supplies remains unused. Therefore the balance of the asset account (supplies) needs to be reduced by $7000 ($10 000 – $3000). The fact that $7000 of supplies has been used up results in an expense.

| | Assets | | = Liabilities | + Equity Expense |
|---|---|---|---|---|
| | **Cash** | **Supplies** | | |
| 3 June | –10 000 | +10 000 | | |
| 30 June | | –7 000 | | –7 000 |
| Total | –10 000 | +3 000 | | –7 000 |

The supplies expense balance of $7000 would appear in the June statement of financial performance. The supplies balance of $3000 would appear as a current asset in the statement of financial position as at 30 June.

The journal entries would appear as follows:

| | | $ | $ |
|---|---|---|---|
| June 3 | DR Supplies | 10 000 | |
| | CR Cash | | 10 000 |
| June 30 | DR Supplies expense | 7 000 | |
| | CR Supplies | | 7 000 |

Another example of reducing the balance of an asset and treating it as an expense upon consumption is depreciation. This concept has been introduced earlier, and will be discussed in more detail in section 5.7 of this chapter and in chapter 8.

## Unearned revenues

Unearned revenue is future revenue where the cash has been received in advance of earning revenue. Alternative names for the unearned revenue account include revenue received in advance, advances from customers and customer deposits. They relate to collections from customers for goods or services not yet provided, therefore the revenue cannot yet be recognised. Examples include deposits from customers for jobs, insurance premiums received, yearly magazine subscriptions received, golf club subscriptions and rental income received in advance. For example, a company that sells magazines by subscription would usually receive these amounts in advance, then send out magazines each month. Assume that at the start of the year the company receives subscriptions of $240 000 and has promised to send out magazines for twelve months. At the time of collection, the amount received would be a liability because goods or services are owing to the subscriber. As each magazine is delivered, the liability is reduced and revenue can be recognised.

| | Assets | = Liabilities | + Equity Revenue |
|---|---|---|---|
| | **Cash** | **Unearned revenue** | |
| January | +240 000 | +240 000 | |
| Monthly | | –20 000 | +20 000 |

The journal entries would be as follows:

| | | $ | $ |
|---|---|---|---|
| Jan | DR Cash | 240 000 | |
| | CR Unearned revenue | | 240 000 |

Each month, as the magazine is sent out, the following journal entry would be posted:

| | | $ | $ |
|---|---|---|---|
| (Date) | DR Unearned revenue | 20 000 | |
| | CR Sales revenue | | 20 000 |

Qantas Airways Limited, in its 'Statement of Significant Accounting Policies' in its 2001 annual report, provides the following details on unearned revenue: 'Passenger and freight sales are credited to revenue received in advance and subsequently transferred to revenue when tickets are utilised or freight uplifted.' This note indicates that when the cash is received, cash (an asset) will be debited and revenue received in advance (a liability) will be credited. When passengers take their flight or their ticket expires, the revenue received in advance account would be reduced (debited) and revenue increased (credited).

| | | **Qantas Group** | |
|---|---|---|---|
| | **Notes** | **2001 $m** | **2000 $m** |
| **Current liabilities** | | | |
| Accounts payable | 15 | 2 049.1 | 1 869.2 |
| Interest bearing liabilities | 16 | 974.7 | 582.4 |
| Net payables under hedge/swap contracts | | 257.9 | 233.5 |
| Provisions | 17 | 512.8 | 926.7 |
| Current tax liabilities | 18 | (8.8) | 119.9 |
| Revenue received in advance | | 1 187.8 | 1 181.0 |
| Deferred lease benefits/income | | 39.8 | 41.6 |
| Total current liabilities | | 5 013.3 | 4 954.3 |

Note that revenue received in advance is their second largest current liability.

Unearned revenue is also large in some service industries such as telecommunications. As an example, when you pay your phone rental in advance, the payment received by Telstra would increase cash and increase revenue received in advance. As it provides the service, the revenue would be increased and the liability decreased.

Telstra's 2001 annual report states:

> Revenue received in advance consists mainly of revenue from providing access to the fixed and mobile network and directories advertising revenue. This revenue is initially recorded as a liability and then transferred to earned revenue in line with the revenue policies described above.

The Institute of Chartered Accountants in Australia (ICAA), in its 2000 financial statements, includes receipts in advance of $11 116 000. In note 8, it describes them as follows:

| | Notes | 2000 $000 |
|---|---|---|
| **8 Receipts in advance** | | |
| Members' fees and subscriptions | | 6 113 |
| Professional year and continuing education course fees | | 4 140 |
| Applications for membership, advancement and Practising Certificates | | 280 |
| Other | | 583 |
| | | 11 116 |

Note that these items are included in the liability section because at year-end the ICAA has not yet provided the service. They are recognised as revenue in the following year, that is, the year the ICAA provides the service.

## Accrual of unrecorded expenses

This adjustment involves determining which expenses have been incurred by the organisation (but not paid in cash) during a particular period of time, generally a month. This usually involves checking which invoices have been received from suppliers and incorporating that information into the accounting system as accounts payable and making estimates for expenses for which invoices have not yet been received (for example, telephone, electricity and accounting fees). Generally speaking, accounts payable includes our trade suppliers, but accrued expenses include our other expenses incurred in running the business.

Accrued expenses are expenses that have been incurred during the current period but will not be paid until the following period. A common example is wages. Because the end of the pay period and the end of the financial period occur on different days, it is necessary to include an accrual for wages payable from the date of last payment to the day on which the accounting period finishes – that is, the employees have done the work but will not be paid for this work until after the end of the financial year. Therefore, at year-end, the organisation has a liability. It is usually called 'accrued wages' or 'wages payable'.

For example, assume wages are paid weekly on Thursday to cover the previous five working days before the Thursday. If 30 June falls on a Friday, two days' wages will be owing at 30 June. If the weekly wages bill is $500 000, then $200 000 (Thursday and Friday) will be owing.

| | Assets | = Liabilities | + Equity |
|---|---|---|---|
| | | **Accrued wages** | **Expense** |
| 30 June | | +200 000 | –200 000 |
| Total | | 200 000 | –200 000 |

Wages expense is increased because it is an expense of the period, and accrued wages (or wages payable) is increased because there is a liability at the end of the period. Other examples of accruals would be interest expense and electricity charges owing at the end of a period.

The journal entry will be:

| | | | $ | $ |
|---|---|---|---|---|
| June 30 | DR | Wages expense | 200 000 | |
| | CR | Accrued wages | | 200 000 |

The 2001 annual report of Coles Myer Ltd shows the following:

| | Notes | 2001 $m | 2000 $m |
|---|---|---|---|
| **Current liabilities** | | | |
| Payables | 16 | 2 186.8 | 2 245.0 |
| Interest-bearing liabilities | 17 | 12.5 | 44.1 |
| Loans | 18 | 115.3 | — |
| Tax liabilities | 19 | — | 108.8 |
| Provisions | 20 | 663.2 | 607.7 |
| **Total current liabilities** | | 2 977.8 | 3 005.6 |

| | 2001 $m | 2000 $m |
|---|---|---|
| 16 Payables (Current) | | |
| Trade creditors | 1 576.3 | 1 756.3 |
| Other creditors and accruals | 610.5 | 488.7 |
| | 2 186.8 | 2 245.0 |

The above shows that for 2001 the $2 186.8 million in payables includes other creditors and accruals of $610.5 million. Consider the effect on profit for the period and current liabilities if these items had not been included. Liabilities would show $610.5 million less, and expenses would also be $610.5 million less. You can see that these adjustments can have a major impact on the financial statements.

Consistent with the Coles Myer example above, accruals are normally included in the current liabilities section under the heading 'Creditors and borrowings', and the amount of the accrual is shown separately in the notes to the accounts. However, if they are large enough, they are shown on the face of the statement of financial position.

## Accrual of unrecorded revenues

The accrual of unrecorded revenues occurs when a service has been provided but cash will not be received until the following period. Common examples of accrued revenues include interest receivable on loans, commissions earned and unbilled revenues. For example, assume a company put $300 000 with a bank for one year at 10 per cent on 1 March 2002 (interest payable at the end of the period). At 30 June 2002, they would have earned $10 000 interest, although the total interest of $30 000 would not be received until 28 February 2003.

Accrued interest (also called 'interest receivable'), which is an asset, would be increased by $10 000, and interest revenue would be increased by $10 000.

| | Assets | = Liabilities | + Equity |
|---|---|---|---|
| | **Accrued revenue** | | **Interest revenue** |
| 30 June | +10 000 | | +10 000 |
| Total | +10 000 | | +10 000 |

Accrued revenue (or interest receivable) is a current asset that will appear in the statement of financial position, and interest revenue is a revenue account that will appear in the statement of financial performance for the year ending 30 June 2002.

The journal entry would be:

| | | $ | $ |
|---|---|---|---|
| June 30 | DR Accrued revenue | 10 000 | |
| | CR Interest revenue | | 10 000 |

An interesting example of accrued revenue is provided in the 2001 Telstra accounts. Telstra bills its customers either monthly or quarterly. When it bills customers, it increases accounts receivable and increases sales revenue. When the cash is received, cash is increased and accounts receivable is decreased. However, at 30 June there will be a lot of telephone calls that have been made but not yet billed. For example, if you receive a bill on 1 June (and you are billed quarterly), you will not receive another bill until 1 September. As telephone calls have been made in June, Telstra has provided the service, therefore is entitled to recognise the revenue. Telstra's statement of financial position shows accrued revenue of $1 055 million (2 000 – $1 010 million) under current assets. That is, at the end of the year, it increased accrued revenue and increased sales revenue.

## How's your understanding?

Here are two questions you should be able to answer, based on what you have just read:

1 What effect would failure to make adjustments for prepayments and accrued expenses have on the statement of financial position and the statement of financial performance?

2 A company has a $50 000 balance in the company's unearned service revenue account. Where would this account appear in the statement of financial position?

To further illustrate the above adjustments, consider the trial balance in exhibit 5.2 and the following information:

- The company prepares accounts annually.
- Ending office supplies on hand was $13 million.
- Prepayments related to insurance policies taken out on 1 October 2002 for one year.
- Unearned revenue relates to a six-month service agreement starting on 1 November.
- At the end of the year, wages of $3 million were still owing.
- An electricity bill was received on 10 January showing that electricity costs for December 2002 were $2 million.
- $27 million of the cash balance was on fixed deposit with the bank. The accrued interest at the end of the year was $1 million.

The following journal entries would be required:

| | | DR $m | CR $m |
|---|---|---|---|
| Dec 31 | Office supplies expense | 17 | |
| | Office supplies | | 17 |
| | *To record supplies used during the period.* | | |

**EXHIBIT 5.2** **Westbank Limited**

**Trial balance at 31 December 2002**

| | DR $m | CR $m |
|---|---|---|
| Cash | 30 | |
| Accounts receivable | 180 | |
| Inventory | 220 | |
| Office supplies | 30 | |
| Prepayments | 40 | |
| Accounts payable | | 150 |
| Unearned revenue | | 30 |
| Loan | | 100 |
| Share capital | | 80 |
| Retained profits | | 40 |
| Sales | | 950 |
| Interest revenue | | 50 |
| Cost of goods sold | 300 | |
| Insurance expense | 100 | |
| Wages expense | 400 | |
| Electricity expense | 20 | |
| Other expenses | 80 | |
| | **1 400** | **1 400** |

| | | | |
|---|---|---|---|
| Dec 31 | Insurance expense | 10 | |
| | Prepayments | | 10 |
| | *To record expiration of insurance coverage.* | | |
| Dec 31 | Unearned revenue | 10 | |
| | Fees revenue | | 10 |
| | *Recognising revenue for fulfilling part of service contract.* | | |
| Dec 31 | Wages expense | 3 | |
| | Accrued expenses | | 3 |
| | *To record accrued salaries at year-end.* | | |
| Dec 31 | Electricity expense | 2 | |
| | Accrued expenses | | 2 |
| | *To record accrued electricity at year-end.* | | |
| Dec 31 | Accrued revenue | 1 | |
| | Interest revenue | | 1 |
| | *To record accrued revenue at year-end.* | | |

The adjusted trial balance, after these entries have been posted to the ledger accounts, would appear as shown in exhibit 5.3 (see next page).

## 5.4 An example of cash basis vs accrual basis figures

To help you see how accrual accounting works by augmenting records of cash receipts and disbursements, here is an example that illustrates the difference between accrual profit and cash profit.

**EXHIBIT 5.3** **Westbank Limited**

**Trial balance at 31 December 2002**

| | DR $m | CR $m |
|---|---|---|
| Cash | 30 | |
| Accounts receivable | 180 | |
| Inventory | 220 | |
| Office supplies | 13 | |
| Prepayments | 30 | |
| Accrued revenue | 1 | |
| Accounts payable | | 150 |
| Unearned revenue | | 20 |
| Accrued expenses | | 5 |
| Loan | | 100 |
| Share capital | | 80 |
| Retained profits | | 40 |
| Sales | | 950 |
| Interest revenue | | 51 |
| Fees revenue | | 10 |
| Cost of goods sold | 300 | |
| Insurance expense | 110 | |
| Wages expense | 403 | |
| Electricity expense | 22 | |
| Other expenses | 80 | |
| Office supplies expense | 17 | |
| | **1 406** | **1 406** |

Information for Goblin Consulting Pty Ltd for this year is:

| | $ | $ |
|---|---|---|
| Cash in bank, end of last year | | 2 800 |
| Cash receipts: | | |
| Collections on last year's revenue | 1 600 | |
| Collections on this year's revenue | 75 200 | |
| Deposit received on next year's revenue | 1 000 | |
| Long-term debt issued | 6 000 | |
| Sale of old equipment (proceeds = book value) | 500 | 84 300 |
| Cash disbursements: | | 87 100 |
| Payment of last year's expenses | 900 | |
| Payment of this year's expenses | 61 300 | |
| Advance payment on next year's expenses | 2 200 | |
| Payments on long-term debt | 3 000 | |
| Purchase of new equipment | 14 000 | 81 400 |
| Cash in bank, end of this year | | 5 700 |
| Increase in cash during the year ($ 5700 – $2 800) | | 2 900 |

Additional information:

- Equipment depreciation for this year: $3100
- Uncollected revenue at the end of this year: $2500
- Unpaid expenses at the end of this year: $1700

If we did a cash-basis profit and loss statement for this year, we would get this:

| | $ |
|---|---|
| Operating receipts ($1600 + $75200 + $1000) | 77 800 |
| Operating expenditures ($900 + $61300 + $2200) | 64 400 |
| Cash profit for this year | 13 400 |

In contrast, the accrual-basis profit and loss statement for this year would look like this, recognising *this* year's earned revenues and incurred expenses:

| | $ | $ |
|---|---|---|
| Revenue ($75 200 + $2 500 uncollected) | | 77 700 |
| Expenses: | | |
| General ($61 300 paid + $1 700 unpaid) | 63 000 | |
| Depreciation | 3 100 | 66 100 |
| Operating profit | | 11 600 |

## How's your understanding?

Here are two questions you should be able to answer, based on what you have just read:

1 The owner of Frenzied Production Pty Ltd was looking at the company's profit and loss statement and said, 'I understand this statement was prepared using accrual accounting. What does accrual accounting try to do and why isn't it good enough just to report my company's cash receipts and disbursements?' Briefly answer the owner's questions.

2 In 2002, Frenzied collected $53 430 from customers for sales made in 2001 and $421 780 for sales made in 2002. In 2003, it collected $46 710 from customers for sales made in 2002. At that point, all 2001 and 2002 sales had been collected. What were the operating cash receipts for 2002 and the accrual accounting revenue for 2002? ($475 210; $468 490)

# 5.5 The financial period

Financial statements all have a time dimension. Statements of financial position (balance sheets) are prepared as at specific points in time, and statements of financial performance (profit and loss statements) cover specified periods of time. Business and other economic activities go on continuously, so if the financial statements are to be at, or begin and end at, particular dates, financial accounting must somehow find a way to separate all those activities into periods.

Here's an example of the problem. Quantum Ltd earns its revenue through a series of projects, done one at a time. Cash inflows (receipts) for revenues happen once or twice during each project, and cash outflows (disbursements) for expenses happen about a month after expenses are incurred. Projects affecting 2002 were:

| | Revenue | Expenses |
|---|---|---|
| **Project #39** | | |
| Work began on the project | | Nov 2001 |
| Some cash received from the customer | Dec 2001 | |
| Disbursements for expenses began | | Dec 2001 |
| Work completed on the project | | Feb 2002 |
| Disbursements for expenses ended | | Mar 2002 |
| Remaining cash received from the customer | Apr 2002 | |
| **Project #40** | | |
| Work began on the project | | Mar 2002 |
| Disbursements for expenses began | | Apr 2002 |
| All cash received from the customer | Sep 2002 | |
| Work completed on the project | | Oct 2002 |
| Disbursements for expenses ended | | Nov 2002 |
| **Project #41** | | |
| Some cash received from the customer | Nov 2002 | |
| Work began on the project | | Nov 2002 |
| Disbursements for expenses began | | Dec 2002 |
| Work completed on the project | | Mar 2003 |
| Disbursements for expenses ended | | Apr 2003 |
| Remaining cash received from the customer | Apr 2003 | |

Well, if we are to calculate net profit for 2002 using accrual accounting, we need to find a way to cut off the accounting records of what are continuous activities, so that 2002 can be separated from 2001 and 2003. The 2002 net profit is a measure of the economic value added by the project *during that year*, and following the matching concept that measure is produced by calculating the increase in resources (revenues) minus the decrease in resources (expenses), determined using comparable methods so that their difference is a meaningful profit figure.

Let's do this project by project.

- Project #40 seems easiest. All the revenue was earned and collected in 2002. All the expenses were earned and paid in 2002.
- Project #39 is more awkward. There were two cash inflows, December 2001 and April 2002. If the December 2001 inflow were less than the amount of revenue earned by the end of the year, there should be a 31 December 2001 account receivable created for the rest of the revenue earned but not collected. However, if the December 2001 inflow were greater than the amount of revenue earned by the end of the year, there should be a 31 December 2001 unearned revenue liability created for the unearned portion. For the expenses, it is the date the expense is incurred not the date it is paid. The expenses incurred in December would not be paid until January, so a 31 December 2001 account payable should be created for those.

- Project #41 has the same sort of awkwardness as #39, except that it has to be cut off properly at the end of 2002.
- So 2002 revenues, expenses and resulting net profit will be a combination of the part of Project #39's revenues and expenses not recognised in 2001, all of Project #40's revenues and expenses, and the part of Project #41's revenues and expenses recognised in 2002. You can see that both the cut off at the end of 2001 and the one at the end of 2002 have to be appropriate if the 2002 revenues, expenses and net profit are to be fair. Because of this, the 2002 results involve estimates on Projects #39 and #41 that also affect the fairness of the results for 2001 and 2003. The revenues and expenses for those projects have to be properly allocated among the years they involve, and the results for all those years will be affected by the quality of the allocations.

Making effective cut-offs for revenues and expenses is a major problem for accrual accounting. Much effort is put into determining whether revenues are placed in the appropriate years, whether there are bills outstanding for expenses that should be taken into account, whether inventories of goods and supplies are actually on hand, and so on. It is generally harder to do this, the larger and less frequent an enterprise's revenue and expense transactions are, and easier therefore for enterprises that have many short and simple transactions. But even there it can be difficult to keep track of just where the enterprise stands, if there are thousands of transactions in process across a year-end.

When should the financial (accounting) year begin and end? Companies have an initial choice, but once they make it, reasons of habit and legal and tax rules usually force them to stay with that choice indefinitely. They may select a financial year-end that is a relatively quiet time, so that there aren't many unfinished transactions in process and the revenue and expense cut-offs can be made more cleanly.

A large majority of Australian public companies have 30 June as their financial year-end. One reason is that it coincides with the end of the tax year, although this is certainly not the only reason, as it is possible in Australia to use a substituted accounting period for taxation purposes provided permission is received from the Australian Taxation Department. Financial year-ends vary substantially between countries. For example, in the United States, Canada, Singapore and Malaysia, 31 December is the most common date, while in the United Kingdom, New Zealand and Japan, 31 March is most common.

Examples of Australian companies with balance dates other than 30 June include those shown below.

| Date | Company |
|---|---|
| 31 March | James Hardie Industries |
| | Macquarie Bank |
| 30 April | Washington H Soul Pattinson |
| 31 August | Ten Network Holdings Limited |
| 30 September | Orica Australia |
| | Australia and New Zealand Banking Group |
| | Westpac |
| | National Australia Bank |
| | St George Bank |

| 31 December | Coal and Allied |
|---|---|
| | Coca-Cola Amatil |
| | Caltex |
| | George Weston Foods |

## 5.6 Introduction to accounting for inventory

As you will see in chapter 7, there are several different methods of controlling inventory. The most popular is called the perpetual inventory control method, and is briefly discussed below. In chapter 7 this method is explained in more detail, and is compared with the periodic inventory method.

Under the perpetual method, when inventory is purchased it is treated as an asset and the inventory account is increased. When the goods are sold, the cost price of the goods sold (cost of goods sold) is increased (that is, increase in an expense) and the inventory account is decreased (that is, a decrease in an asset).

For example, assume that Alpha Pty Ltd buys 2000 items of inventory at $5 each on credit on 1 March. On 10 March, it sells 1000 of these items on credit for $8 each. The impact on the accounting equation is shown below.

| | Assets | | = Liabilities | + Equity | |
|---|---|---|---|---|---|
| | **Inventory** | **Accounts receivable** | **Accounts payable** | **Sales** | **COGS** |
| 1 March | +10 000 | | +10 000 | | |
| 10 March | | +8 000 | | +8 000 | |
| | –5 000 | | | | –5 000 |
| Total | +5 000 | +8 000 | +10 000 | +8 000 | –5 000 |

The journal entries would be:

| | | $ | $ |
|---|---|---|---|
| Mar 1 | DR Inventory | 10 000 | |
| | CR Accounts payable | | 10 000 |
| Mar 10 | DR Accounts receivable | 8 000 | |
| | CR Sales | | 8 000 |
| | DR Cost of goods sold | 5 000 | |
| | CR Inventory | | 5 000 |

Thus, under this perpetual method, two journal entries are required when a sale is made. One records the sale and the other records the cost of the items sold. This second entry recognises the expense and reduces the asset inventory. The sales entry is recorded at the price the goods were sold for, and the cost of goods sold entry is based on the cost price of the goods as per the inventory record. Note that this is what you learnt in chapters 2 and 3, but we did not refer to it as the perpetual inventory method.

As will be discussed in the appendix to this chapter, a separate record is kept for each inventory item of the items purchased and sold. The total of the balances for each of these inventory items will equal the balance of the inventory account in the general ledger.

Another way the inventory account is affected is when a customer returns goods for credit. For example, in our Alpha example above, assume that the customer returns 100 of the items they purchased and asks for a credit. These returns also require two journal entries. The first entry records the sales returns by debiting sales returns and crediting accounts receivable because the customer now owes less.

Sales returns are deducted from the sales account in the profit and loss account. Assuming that the units returned are still suitable for sale, a second journal entry is needed to reduce the cost of goods sold and to increase inventory because of the items returned.

These entries for Alpha would be recorded as follows:

| | DR<br>$ | CR<br>$ |
|---|---|---|
| Sales returns | 800 | |
| Accounts receivable | | 800 |
| *100 items @ $8 each returned.* | | |
| Inventory | 500 | |
| Cost of goods sold | | 500 |
| *100 items with a cost price of $5 returned to inventory.* | | |

Based on the above transactions only, the profit for Alpha Pty Ltd would be:

| | $ |
|---|---|
| Sales | 8 000 |
| – Sales returns | 800 |
| Net sales | 7 200 |
| – Cost of goods sold | 4 500 |
| = Gross profit | 2 700 |

In the statement of financial position, the inventory figure would appear as $5500 (that is, $10 000 – $5000 + $500).

## 5.7 Contra accounts

Just about every statement of financial position account can be considered to be a control account. Cash is a record of the cash that should be there if counted. Accounts receivable is the sum of all the individual customers' accounts. Inventory is the amount that should be found if the company lists or counts all the unsold goods physically on hand. Accounts payable is the sum of all the individual suppliers' accounts. The number of shares outstanding should be traceable to the share capital account. (The particular owners may change, for example, because of trading on the stock market, but the company should always know how many shares it has issued and what it originally received for them.) Even the property, plant and equipment asset accounts are controls, as all the assets whose costs are included should be physically present.

The value of all these accounts as control accounts is that the amounts in them should be supported by, or reconcilable to, detailed lists or subsidiary ledgers, or some such background data. What do we do, then, when we want to make a change in a statement of financial position account without changing the underlying records and lists? Here are some examples of when we might want to change an asset account and why at the same time we might be reluctant to do it:

- There has been an overall decline in the market value of the inventory, so for conservatism we want to reduce the inventory asset account on the statement of financial position, but do not want to change the inventory control account because it should correspond to the sum of the costs of all the goods on hand.
- We have become worried that we might not collect all the accounts receivable, so for conservatism and proper profit measurement, we want to recognise that we have probably suffered some 'bad debts' expense, but do not want to change the accounts receivable control account because it should correspond to the list of all customers' accounts, and we are not yet giving up on collecting any, so the control feature is still useful.
- The property and plant assets are being used up economically, so we want to record depreciation expense as part of our profit measurement, but we do not want to change the asset cost account balances because their costs are not changing, but rather their economic values are being used.

In all these examples, the financial statement objectives of proper asset valuation and profit measurement seem to conflict with maintaining the accounts for control purposes.

What to do? Accrual accounting is very flexible. A perhaps peculiar kind of account called a contra account has been invented to allow us to recognise expenses and value changes without changing the control account. It is useful both for profit measurement and to preserve the internal control aspects of the accounts, therefore bridges between accounting's role in internal control (which is outlined in chapter 6) and in financial statement preparation.

Contra accounts have balances that are in the *opposite direction* to that of the control account with which they are associated: for example, contra asset accounts have credit balances that are 'contra' the assets' debit balances. They are mainly used for managing expense accruals separately from the asset accounts to which they relate, and therefore they keep the accruals from being mixed into those accounts. *Contra accounts only have meaning in conjunction with the control accounts to which they are matched.* We'll see below how this works.

Here we will focus only on the two most common uses of contra accounts: accumulated depreciation (amortisation) and allowing for doubtful accounts receivable. Virtually all enterprises have both. These accounts illustrate how the accounting system can meet one objective (expense recognition) and avoid compromising another objective (control) by creating accounts that recognise expenses but do not change the control accounts related to those expenses (asset costs and accounts receivable).

## Accumulated depreciation (amortisation)

Contra accounts are used to accumulate depreciation on fixed assets, such as buildings and equipment.

For example, the annual depreciation charge of $100 000 on a building would be recognised this way, as you've seen already several times:

| | $ | $ |
|---|---|---|
| DR Depreciation expense | 100 000 | |
| CR Accumulated depreciation | | 100 000 |

The debit is an expense account in the statement of financial performance. The credit is a contra asset account. The credit side of the journal entry could have been to the asset account 'Building'. Instead the contra account is used, so that by leaving the asset cost account alone, the statement of financial position presents the acquisition cost of the asset along with the accumulated amount of expense that has been recognised to date. Showing both these items allows users to make a rough guess as to how long the asset has been in service. Remember that accumulated depreciation on the statement of financial position is the amount of depreciation accumulated over the life of the asset to date, whereas the amount of depreciation charged this year (to match the revenues the asset consumption is presumed to have helped generate) can be determined from the depreciation expense account in the statement of financial performance (profit and loss statement).

Let's look at a simple example involving an electrician's purchase of a new truck. The truck cost $50 000 and an annual depreciation expense of $8000 was determined. Each year the expense account depreciation would be increased by $8000 and the contra asset account (called 'accumulated depreciation') would be increased by $8000.

The journal entry would be:

| | $ | $ |
|---|---|---|
| DR Depreciation expense | 8 000 | |
| CR Accumulated depreciation | | 8 000 |

On the statement of financial position, the asset account for the truck's cost would continue to show a balance of $50 000, but each year the accumulated depreciation contra asset account would increase by $8000. Deducting accumulated depreciation from the long-term asset account leaves a figure known as the net book value. So we would have:

| | **Cost** | **Accumulated depreciation contra** | **Net book value** |
|---|---|---|---|
| | $ | $ | $ |
| Date of purchase | 50 000 | 0 | 50 000 |
| End of first year | 50 000 | 8 000 | 42 000 |
| End of second year | 50 000 | 16 000 | 34 000 |

If the truck were sold at any time, the cost would be removed from the ledger, but so would the contra account. The contra is meaningful only in comparison to the cost – when the truck is gone, neither account is needed any more. Suppose the truck were sold for $37 000 at the end of the second year. At this point the accumulated depreciation is $16 000 ($8000 + $8000) and the book value is $34 000 ($50 000 – $16 000). If the company receives $37 000, it makes a profit of $3000. This profit (usually called 'gain on sale' or 'profit on sale') is a revenue item. These effects are shown below.

| | **Assets** | | | **= Liabilities** | **+ Equity** | |
|---|---|---|---|---|---|---|
| | **Cash** | **Truck** | **Accumulated depreciation** | | **Revenue** | **Expense** |
| Purchase | –50 000 | +50 000 | | | | |
| Year 1 | | | –8 000 | | | –8 000 |
| Year 2 | | | –8 000 | | | –8 000 |
| Subtotal | –50 000 | +50 000 | –16 000 | | | –16 000 |
| Sale of truck | +37 000 | –50 000 | +16 000 | | +3 000 | |

The journal entry is:

| | $ | $ |
|---|---|---|
| DR Cash (the proceeds) | 37 000 | |
| CR Truck asset (removing the cost) | | 50 000 |
| DR Truck accumulated depreciation (removing the contra) | 16 000 | |
| CR Gain on sale of truck | | 3 000 |

The gain on sale is just the difference between the proceeds and the net book value at the date of sale. If the proceeds had been $29 000 instead, the debit to cash would have been $29 000 and there would have been a debit to loss on sale (an 'other expense' account in the profit and loss statement) for $5000, the difference between the proceeds and the net book value.

When non-physical assets, such as goodwill, patents and franchise fees paid, are amortised, the accumulated amortisation account is used instead of accumulated depreciation. Gains, losses and write-offs on such assets are calculated just as for the physical assets illustrated above.

## 5.8 Accounts receivable and contra accounts

Before considering the other most common use of contra accounts, the provision for doubtful debts, we will provide a brief overview of the asset, accounts receivable. Most accounts receivable are *recognised but uncollected revenue*, created by the accrual accounting entry: DR accounts receivable, CR sales revenue. Such receivables arise from the company's day-to-day business activities, therefore are often called 'trade' receivables. They are included in current assets because they are usually expected to be collected within one year.

### Valuation of accounts receivable

Receivables are valued on the statement of financial position at the lower of cost or net realisable value. 'Cost' here is the original transaction value of the sale that gave rise to the receivable, plus any subsequent interest charges. Net realisable value is the amount expected to be collected (the cash value of the receivable, if you like). There is often col- [illegible] difficulties in collection, especially as time passes after the sale. So, if the collectable amount is now expected to be lower than originally anticipated, the receivable must be reduced to an estimated collectable amount. The method for doing this is by subtracting a provision for doubtful accounts from the accounts receivable balance.

The estimated collectable amount is gross accounts receivable minus the provision for doubtful debts, so the provision functions to adjust the net value down to the lower of cost (original value) and current estimated collectable amount. On the statement of financial position, accounts receivable are valued at this net amount. Australian companies show in the notes the amount of the provision for doubtful debts deducted from gross accounts receivable.

For example, Mayne Nickless Limited, in its 2001 statement of financial position, shows receivables of $516 784 000 in the current assets section. This amount is net accounts receivable and its breakup is shown in note 9 of the accounts as shown below.

| | Consolidated | |
|---|---|---|
| | **2001** | **2000** |
| | **$000** | **$000** |
| Receivables (current) | | |
| Trade debtors | 375 890 | 385 929 |
| Provision for doubtful debts | (12 815) | (12 003) |
| | 363 075 | 373 926 |
| Other debtors | 153 709 | 59 475 |
| | 516 784 | 433 401 |

Trade debtors are shown at their gross amount ($375 890 000), and the provision for doubtful debts ($12 815 000) is deducted. Other debtors are added in. It appears that none of the other debtors is doubtful for this company.

## Other receivables

There are two other main kinds of receivables. If large, these are shown separately, but if not, they are usually just lumped together under the heading 'Other debtors':

- The first kind is 'notes' receivable. These are supported by a signed contract between buyer and seller that specifies a payment schedule, an interest rate and often other legal details. Such notes are often used for large and/or long-term receivables, such as sales of motor vehicles, houses or appliances, and loans by banks and finance companies (long-term receivables would be properly classified as noncurrent rather than current assets). Notes are shown at 'present value' (only interest that has built up so far is included in the asset, not future interest).
- The second kind is loans to employees, officers and shareholders, loans to associated companies, tax refunds the company is waiting for and other receivables not arising from revenue transactions. They are accounted for and valued much as normal trade receivables and notes receivable are, but because some may arise from peculiar circumstances, companies often disclose the reasons for them and explain other circumstances about them. They are often included under the heading 'Other debtors'.

## Provision for doubtful debts

This section discusses further the provision for doubtful debts. When a company sells to a customer on account, there will always be some risk that the customer will fail to pay. Therefore, a portion of the sales on account will be doubtful, and that portion should be deducted from revenue in determining profit for the period.

The transaction analysis for the creation of a provision for doubtful debts based on some estimate of the likely level of doubtful debts is:

↑ Bad debts expense (↓ SE)

↑ Provision for doubtful debts (↓ total assets)

Note that the provision for doubtful debts is a contra asset account, which means that when we increase the provision we are actually reducing total assets. Let's assume that the company determines, by past experience or current evidence of customers' troubles, that about $500 of sales on account are not likely to be paid.

The journal entry to *recognise* the expense is:

| | $ | $ |
|---|---|---|
| DR Bad debts expense | 500 | |
| CR Provision for doubtful debts | | 500 |

The credit in this entry is again to a contra asset account, just as it was for depreciation. (That account was in the noncurrent assets section of the statement of financial position, while this one is generally in the current assets section.) The reason for not deducting the amount directly from the accounts receivable asset is that even after the usual collection time has passed, the company may still try to collect on the accounts and therefore doesn't want to alter the accounts receivable amount. The list of individual accounts should have the same total as that of the accounts receivable account for control reasons, so the account should not be changed just because collection is doubtful.

Eventually, after pursuing a non-paying customer for months, a company may decide to write the account off. Another journal entry is then needed. Suppose the account in question equals $100 (it was one of the risky ones contemplated when the provision was created above), then the transaction effect would be to reduce the provision for doubtful debts and reduce accounts receivable, both by $100.

The journal entry is:

| | $ | $ |
|---|---|---|
| DR Provision for doubtful debts | 100 | |
| CR Accounts receivable | | 100 |

This entry eliminates the account from the books of the company completely, but you'll notice that it does not affect expenses (and, therefore, profit); that effect was created when the provision and expense were recognised earlier.

Note that this write-off is handled differently from the noncurrent asset write-offs described earlier. The reason is that the provision for doubtful debts is considered to apply to the whole list of accounts receivable, in aggregate. We don't necessarily know which specific accounts receivable were provided for: for example, the $500 provision for doubtful debts was probably based on an average experience, such as that, say, 15 per cent of accounts over 60 days old will not be collected. We don't need to know which accounts in order to make such a provision for the aggregate risk being taken. There was a contra accumulated depreciation for each building or truck, but there is no particular contra for each account receivable, so both the account receivable asset and an equal amount of the provision for doubtful debts contra are just eliminated in the above bad debt write-off. It's like assuming that the written-off receivable had been 100 per cent allowed for.

Bad debt write-offs can throw the system off if they are large enough. For example, in the above case, what if a customer account for $800 had to be written off? That's more than there is in the provision! There are methods for adjusting the provision to take such problems into account, but this book will not include them beyond the next little example

It is possible to operate the accounting without a provision for doubtful accounts. Bad accounts can be written off directly to accounts receivable, by the so-called direct write-off method. This is used when a company has few accounts receivable or when a large account not contemplated in the provision suddenly goes bad. Suppose an account totalling $1500 is to be written off directly. Then the entry would be:

| | $ | $ |
|---|---|---|
| DR Bad debts expense | 1 500 | |
| CR Accounts receivable | | 1 500 |

This is equivalent to allowing for it first, then writing it off, using the entries shown earlier:

| | $ | $ |
|---|---|---|
| DR Bad debts expense | 1 500 | |
| CR Provision for doubtful debts | | 1 500 |
| DR Provision for doubtful debts | 1 500 | |
| CR Accounts receivable | | 1 500 |

As this example shows, the provision can be seen as a temporary holding account for amounts the company believes will not be collected, based on past experience and assessment of outstanding accounts. But during the holding period, an expense has been recognised and the asset value on the statement of financial position has been reduced. Using a provision is thought usually preferable to direct write-off, not only because of the internal control advantages the contra account provides, but also because the provision provides for a way to have an expense before the company gives up on collection, therefore is generally more conservative in its effects on the statement of financial position and the statement of financial performance.

Here is a final example of the use and effect of a provision for doubtful debts contra.

- Jellyroll Sweets Ltd sells chocolates to retail stores. At the end of 2001, it had accounts receivable of $53 000 and a provision for doubtful debts of $3100. *Therefore, the estimated collectable amount of the accounts receivable was $49 900 at the end of 2001.*
- During 2002, the company had credit sales of $432 800 and collected $417 400 from customers. Therefore, at the end of 2002, the accounts receivable stood at $68 400 ($53 000 + $432 800 – $417 400).
- At that point, the sales manager went through the list of accounts receivable and determined that accounts totalling $1200 were pretty much hopeless and should be written off, and furthermore, that an aggregate provision at the end of 2002 of $4200 was required. The amount of the provision was based on the percentage of the debtors that had not paid in the past. It also took into account the ageing of accounts receivable and the state of the economy.

The effect of the above is to write off bad debts by decreasing the provision for doubtful debts and decreasing the accounts receivable, both by $1200. The doubtful debts are allowed for by increasing the bad debts expense account and increasing the provision for doubtful debts by $2300.

The journal entries to accomplish what is needed are shown below:

| | | $ | $ |
|---|---|---|---|
| DR Provision for doubtful debts | | 1 200 | |
| CR Accounts receivable | | | 1 200 |

Allow for doubtful ones:

| | | $ | $ |
|---|---|---|---|
| DR Bad debts expense | | 2 300 | |
| CR Provision for doubtful debts | | | 2 300 |
| (Balance in allowance = $3100 – $1200 | = $1 900 | | |
| Provision needed at the end of 1999 | = $4 200 | | |
| Additional allowance = $4200 – $1900 | = $2 300 | | |

The accounts receivable balance is now $67 200 ($68 400 – $1200) and the contra balance is $4200. Therefore:

- The estimated collectable value of the accounts receivable (the net balance sheet value) is $63 000 at the end of 2002.
- Bad debts expense for 2002 is $2300.
- The write-off of the hopeless ones ($1200) cleared it out of the list of receivables, but did not affect either profit or the net balance sheet value.

The purposes of contra accounts are, like most other things in accounting, to provide useful information to the readers of financial statements and/or to assist in accounting's internal control functions. Internal control is discussed in chapter 6.

## How's your understanding?

Here are two questions you should be able to answer, based on what you have just read:

1 The term 'write-off' is used with reference to accounts receivable. What does this term mean?

2 [illegible]'s accounts receivable at the end of 2002 totalled $78 490. The provision for doubtful debts had been $2310, but it was decided that this would be increased by $1560, then that $1100 in hopeless accounts would be written off. What is the net collectable value of the receivables as shown on the balance sheet at the end of 2002 and the bad debts expense for 2002? ($74 620; $1560)

## 5.9 Illustrative example

Below we provide an example to reinforce the material covered in chapters 4 and 5. It will cover journal entries, posting to the ledger, trial balance, adjustments, closing entries and preparation of financial statements.

Scanlon Limited had the following trial balance at 1 January 2003:

| | Debit $ | Credit $ |
|---|---|---|
| Cash | 200 000 | |
| Accounts receivable | 600 000 | |
| Inventory | 700 000 | |
| Prepaid insurance | 60 000 | |
| Prepaid rent | 50 000 | |
| Equipment | 1 000 000 | |
| Provision for doubtful debts | | 20 000 |
| Accumulated depreciation | | 200 000 |
| Accounts payable | | 500 000 |
| Revenue received in advance | | 100 000 |
| Income tax payable | | 500 000 |
| Loan | | 570 000 |
| Share capital | | 400 000 |
| Retained profits | | 320 000 |
| | 2 610 000 | 2 610 000 |

During January 2003 the following transactions occurred:

**a** Cash sales $700 000.
**b** Credit sales $6 100 000.
**c** Cost of goods sold $3 000 000.
**d** Inventory purchased on credit $2 600 000.
**e** Cash collected from customers $5 800 000.
**f** Cash paid to suppliers $2 800 000.
**g** Paid income tax liability.
**h** Paid salaries $1 200 000, commission $600 000, other operating expenses $100 000.
**i** Paid $40 000 for insurance.
**j** Paid $30 000 in rent (the company debits prepaid rent).
**k** Bad debts of $8 000 were written off.
**l** It was decided that provision for doubtful debts should be 4 per cent of accounts receivable.
**m** Depreciation expense is calculated at 12 per cent per annum on cost.
**n** Closing balances in the prepaid insurance and prepaid rent at the end of January 2003 should be $70 000 and $60 000 respectively.
**o** The $100 000 revenue received in advance related to a service contract which has now been fulfilled in whole.
**p** The bank owes Scanlon Ltd $5000 for interest at the end of January.

The following steps will be carried out:

1. Prepare journal entries for the above transactions (exhibit 5.4).
2. Enter the opening balances in the ledger accounts and post the journal entries to the ledger (exhibit 5.5).
3. Prepare a trial balance at 31 January 2003 (exhibit 5.6).
4. Prepare closing entries (exhibit 5.7).

**EXHIBIT 5.4** **SCANLON LTD**

**Journal entries**

| | | | Debit $ | Credit $ |
|---|---|---|---|---|
| a | Jan 03 | Cash | 700 000 | |
| | | Sales | | 700 000 |
| | | *To record cash sales.* | | |
| b | Jan 03 | Accounts receivable | 6 100 000 | |
| | | Sales | | 6 100 000 |
| | | *To record credit sales.* | | |
| c | Jan 03 | Cost of goods sold | 3 000 000 | |
| | | Inventory | | 3 000 000 |
| | | *To record cost of goods sold.* | | |
| d | Jan 03 | Inventory | 2 600 000 | |
| | | Accounts payable | | 2 600 000 |
| | | *To record credit purchases.* | | |
| e | Jan 03 | Cash | 5 800 000 | |
| | | Accounts receivable | | 5 800 000 |
| | | *To record payments from debtors.* | | |
| f | Jan 03 | Accounts payable | 2 800 000 | |
| | | Cash | | 2 800 000 |
| | | *To record payment of accounts payable.* | | |
| g | Jan 03 | Income tax payable | 500 000 | |
| | | Cash | | 500 000 |
| | | *To record payment of tax.* | | |
| h | Jan 03 | Salaries expense | 1 200 000 | |
| | | Commission expense | 600 000 | |
| | | Other expenses | 100 000 | |
| | | Cash | | 1 900 000 |
| | | *To record payment of expenses.* | | |
| i | Jan 03 | Prepaid insurance | 40 000 | |
| | | Cash | | 40 000 |
| | | *To record payment of insurance premium.* | | |
| j | Jan 03 | Prepaid rent | 30 000 | |
| | | Cash | | 30 000 |
| | | *To record payment of rent.* | | |
| k | Jan 03 | Provision for doubtful debts | 8 000 | |
| | | Accounts receivable | | 8 000 |
| | | *To record write-off of certain debtors.* | | |
| l | 31 Jan 03 | Bad debts expense | 23 680 | |
| | | Provision for doubtful debts | | 23 680 |
| | | *To record the increase in the provision for doubtful debts (4% of accounts receivable = \$892 000 × 4% = \$35 680)*.* | | |
| | | *Provision increased by \$23 680 (\$35 680 – \$12 000).* | | |
| m | 31 Jan 03 | Depreciation expense | 10 000 | |
| | | Accumulated depreciation | | 10 000 |
| | | *To record one month's depreciation.* | | |

## EXHIBIT 5.4 SCANLON LTD

### Journal entries (continued)

| | | | Debit $ | Credit $ |
|---|---|---|---|---|
| n | 31 Jan 03 | Insurance expense | 30 000 | |
| | | Prepaid insurance | | 30 000 |
| | | *To record insurance expense for the month.* | | |
| n | 31 Jan 03 | Rent expense | 20 000 | |
| | | Prepaid rent | | 20 000 |
| | | *To record rent expense for the month.* | | |
| o | 31 Jan 03 | Revenue received in advance | 100 000 | |
| | | Service fee revenue | | 100 000 |
| | | *To record the earning of service fee revenue for the month.* | | |
| p | 31 Jan 03 | Accrued revenue | 5 000 | |
| | | Interest revenue | | 5 000 |
| | | *To record the earning of interest revenue for month.* | | |

* 600 000 + 6 100 000 – 5 800 000 – 8 000 = 892 000

## EXHIBIT 5.5 Scanlon Limited

### Ledger accounts

**Cash**

| | | | | | |
|---|---|---|---|---|---|
| 1/1/03 | | | | | |
| Bal b/d | | 200 000 | 1/03 | f | 2 800 000 |
| 1/03 | a | 700 000 | 1/03 | g | 500 000 |
| 1/03 | e | 5 800 000 | 1/03 | h | 1 900 000 |
| | | | 1/03 | i | 40 000 |
| | | | 1/03 | j | 30 000 |
| | | | Bal c/d | | 1 430 000 |
| | | 6 700 000 | | | 6 700 000 |
| 1/2/03 | | | | | |
| Bal b/d | | 1 430 000 | | | |

**Accounts receivable** 2

| | | | | | |
|---|---|---|---|---|---|
| 1/1/03 | | | | | |
| Bal b/d | | 600 000 | 1/03 | e | 5 800 000 |
| 1/03 | b | 6 100 000 | 1/03 | k | 8 000 |
| | | | Bal c/d | | 892 000 |
| | | 6 700 000 | | | 6 700 000 |
| 1/2/03 | | | | | |
| Bal b/d | | 892 000 | | | |

**Inventory**

| | | | | | |
|---|---|---|---|---|---|
| 1/1/03 | | | | | |
| Bal b/d | | 700 000 | 1/03 | c | 3 000 000 |
| 1/03 | d | 2 600 000 | Bal c/d | | 300 000 |
| | | 3 300 000 | | | 3 300 000 |
| 1/2/03 | | | | | |
| Bal b/d | | 300 000 | | | |

**Prepaid Insurance**

| | | | | | |
|---|---|---|---|---|---|
| 1/1/03 | | | | | |
| Bal b/d | | 60 000 | 31/1/03 | n | 30 000 |
| 1/03 | i | 40 000 | Bal c/d | | 70 000 |
| | | 100 000 | | | 100 000 |
| 1/2/03 | | | | | |
| Bal b/d | | 70 000 | | | |

**Prepaid rent**

| | | | | | |
|---|---|---|---|---|---|
| 1/1/03 | | | | | |
| Bal b/d | | 50 000 | 31/1/03 | n | 20 000 |
| 1/03 | j | 30 000 | Bal c/d | | 60 000 |
| | | 80 000 | | | 80 000 |
| 1/2/03 | | | | | |
| Bal b/d | | 60 000 | | | |

**Equipment**

| | | | | | |
|---|---|---|---|---|---|
| 1/1/03 | | | | | |
| Bal b/d | | 1 000 000 | | | |

## EXHIBIT 5.5 Scanlon Limited

### Ledger accounts (continued)

**Accrued revenue**

| Date | | Dr | Date | | Cr |
|---|---|---|---|---|---|
| 31/1/03 | p | 5 000 | | | |

**Accumulated depreciation**

| Date | | Dr | Date | | Cr |
|---|---|---|---|---|---|
| | | | 1/1/03 Bal b/d | | 200 000 |
| | | | 31/1/03 | m | 10 000 |
| | | | | | 210 000 |

**Provision for doubtful debts**

| Date | | Dr | Date | | Cr |
|---|---|---|---|---|---|
| 1/1/03 | k | 8 000 | 1/1/03 Bal b/d | | 20 000 |
| Bal c/d | | 35 680 | 31/1/03 | 1 | 23 680 |
| | | 43 680 | | | 43 680 |
| | | | 1/2/03 Bal b/d | | 35 680 |

**Revenue received in advance**

| Date | | Dr | Date | | Cr |
|---|---|---|---|---|---|
| 31/1/03 | o | 100 000 | 1/1/03 Bal b/d | | 100 000 |

**Accounts payable**

| Date | | Dr | Date | | Cr |
|---|---|---|---|---|---|
| 1/1/03 | f | 2 800 000 | 1/1/03 Bal b/d | | 500 000 |
| | | | 1/03 | d | 2 600 000 |
| Bal c/d | | 300 000 | | | |
| | | 3 100 000 | | | 3 100 000 |
| | | | 1/2/03 Bal b/d | | 300 000 |

**Income tax payable**

| Date | | Dr | Date | | Cr |
|---|---|---|---|---|---|
| 1/03 | g | 500 000 | 1/1/03 Bal b/d | | 500 000 |

**Loan**

| Date | | Dr | Date | | Cr |
|---|---|---|---|---|---|
| | | | 1/1/03 Bal b/d | | 570 000 |

**Share capital**

| Date | | Dr | Date | | Cr |
|---|---|---|---|---|---|
| | | | 1/1/03 Bal b/d | | 400 000 |

**Retained profits**

| Date | | Dr | Date | | Cr |
|---|---|---|---|---|---|
| | | | 1/1/03 Bal b/d | | 320 000 |

**Sales**

| Date | | Dr | Date | | Cr |
|---|---|---|---|---|---|
| | | | 1/03 | a | 700 000 |
| | | | 1/03 | b | 6 100 000 |
| | | | | | 6 800 000 |

**Service fee revenue**

| Date | | Dr | Date | | Cr |
|---|---|---|---|---|---|
| | | | 31/1/03 | o | 100 000 |

**Interest revenue**

| Date | | Dr | Date | | Cr |
|---|---|---|---|---|---|
| | | | 31/1/03 | p | 5 000 |

**Cost of goods sold**

| Date | | Dr | Date | | Cr |
|---|---|---|---|---|---|
| 1/03 | c | 3 000 000 | | | |

**Salaries expense**

| Date | | Dr | Date | | Cr |
|---|---|---|---|---|---|
| 1/03 | h | 1 200 000 | | | |

**Other expenses**

| Date | | Dr | Date | | Cr |
|---|---|---|---|---|---|
| 1/03 | h | 100 000 | | | |

**Bad debts expense**

| Date | | Dr | Date | | Cr |
|---|---|---|---|---|---|
| 31/1/03 | l | 23 680 | | | |

**Commission expense**

| Date | | Dr | Date | | Cr |
|---|---|---|---|---|---|
| 1/03 | h | 600 000 | | | |

**Insurance expense**

| Date | | Dr | Date | | Cr |
|---|---|---|---|---|---|
| 31/1/03 | n | 30 000 | | | |

**Depreciation expense**

| Date | | Dr | Date | | Cr |
|---|---|---|---|---|---|
| 31/1/03 | m | 10 000 | | | |

**Rent expense**

| Date | | Dr | Date | | Cr |
|---|---|---|---|---|---|
| 31/1/03 | n | 20 000 | | | |

5 Prepare a post-closing trial balance (exhibit 5.8).

6 Prepare a statement of financial performance for the month of January 2003 and a statement of financial position as at 31 January 2003 (exhibits 5.9 and 5.10).

Before preparing the financial statements, the revenue and expense accounts are closed via the closing journal entries (exhibit 5.7). They start with a zero balance in the next accounting period to enable profit for that period to be calculated.

**EXHIBIT 5.6** **Scanlon Ltd**

**Pre-closing trial balance at 31 January 2003**

| | Debit<br>$ | Credit<br>$ |
|---|---|---|
| Cash | 1 430 000 | |
| Accounts receivable | 892 000 | |
| Inventory | 300 000 | |
| Prepaid insurance | 70 000 | |
| Prepaid rent | 60 000 | |
| Accrued revenue | 5 000 | |
| Equipment | 1 000 000 | |
| Provision for doubtful debts | | 35 680 |
| Accumulated depreciation | | 210 000 |
| Accounts payable | | 300 000 |
| Revenue received in advance | | 0 |
| Income tax payable | | 0 |
| Loan | | 570 000 |
| Share capital | | 400 000 |
| Retained profits | | 320 000 |
| Sales | | 6 800 000 |
| Service fee revenue | | 100 000 |
| Interest revenue | | 5 000 |
| Cost of goods sold | 3 000 000 | |
| Salaries expense | 1 200 000 | |
| Bad debts expense | 23 680 | |
| Depreciation expense | 10 000 | |
| Insurance expense | 30 000 | |
| Rent expense | 20 000 | |
| Commission expense | 600 000 | |
| Other expenses | 100 000 | |
| | 8 740 680 | 8 740 680 |

After posting these journal entries a post closing trial balance is prepared (exhibit 5.8). The statement of financial performance and the statement of financial position are provided in exhibits 5.9 and 5.10.

## 5.10 Managers and accrual accounting assumptions

Accrual accounting's purpose is to move beyond cash flows toward a broader economic concept of profit and financial position. From a manager's point of view, this has several important implications:

- As a more inclusive way of measuring performance and position, accrual accounting should reflect more of what a manager is trying to do than cash flow can. This should make accrual accounting attractive to managers who want to be evaluated fairly and who are interested in comparing their companies with others.
- This attractiveness depends on how complete accrual accounting is in representing managers' performance. Here there is a limitation that often frustrates managers: accrual

**EXHIBIT 5.7** **Scanlon Ltd**

**Closing journal entries**

| | Debit $ | Credit $ |
|---|---|---|
| Sales | 6 800 000 | |
| Service fee revenue | 100 000 | |
| Interest revenue | 5 000 | |
| Profit and loss summary | | 6 905 000 |
| Profit and loss summary | 4 983 680 | |
| Cost of goods sold | | 3 000 000 |
| Salaries expense | | 1 200 000 |
| Bad debts expense | | 23 680 |
| Depreciation expense | | 10 000 |
| Insurance expense | | 30 000 |
| Rent expense | | 20 000 |
| Commission expense | | 600 000 |
| Other expenses | | 100 000 |
| Profit and loss summary | 1 921 320 | |
| Retained profits | | 1 921 320 |

**EXHIBIT 5.8** **Scanlon Ltd**

**Post-closing trial balance**

| | Debit $ | Credit $ |
|---|---|---|
| Cash | 1 430 000 | |
| Accounts receivable | 892 000 | |
| Inventory | 300 000 | |
| Prepaid insurance | 70 000 | |
| Prepaid rent | 60 000 | |
| Accrued revenue | 5 000 | |
| Equipment | 1 000 000 | |
| Provision for doubtful debts | | 35 680 |
| Accumulated depreciation | | 210 000 |
| Accounts payable | | 300 000 |
| Revenue received in advance | | 0 |
| Income tax payable | | 0 |
| Loan | | 570 000 |
| Share capital | | 400 000 |
| Retained profits | | 2 241 320 |
| | **3 757 000** | **3 757 000** |

**EXHIBIT 5.9** Scanlon Ltd

## Statement of financial performance for the month ending 31 January 2003

| | $ | $ |
|---|---|---|
| Sales: | | 6 800 000 |
| Cost of goods sold | | 3 000 000 |
| Gross profit | | 3 800 000 |
| Other revenue: | | |
| Service fee revenue | 100 000 | |
| Interest revenue | 5 000 | 105 000 |
| | | 3 905 000 |
| Operating expenses: | | |
| Salaries | 1 200 000 | |
| Bad debts | 23 680 | |
| Depreciation | 10 000 | |
| Insurance | 30 000 | |
| Rent | 20 000 | |
| Commission | 600 000 | |
| Other expenses | 100 000 | 1 983 680 |
| Net profit | | 1 921 320 |

**EXHIBIT 5.10** Scanlon Ltd

## Statement of financial position as at 31 January 2003

| | $ | $ |
|---|---|---|
| **Assets** | | |
| *Current assets* | | |
| Cash | | 1 430 000 |
| Accounts receivable (net) | | 856 320 |
| Inventory | | 300 000 |
| Prepaid insurance | | 70 000 |
| Prepaid rent | | 60 000 |
| Accrued revenue | | 5 000 |
| | | 2 721 320 |
| *Noncurrent assets* | | |
| Equipment | 1 000 000 | |
| Accumulated depreciation | 210 000 | 790 000 |
| **Total assets** | | **3 511 320** |
| **Liabilities** | | |
| *Current liabilities* | | |
| Accounts payable | | 300 000 |
| *Noncurrent liabilities* | | |
| Loan | | 570 000 |
| **Total liabilities** | | **870 000** |
| **Net assets** | | 2 641 320 |
| **Shareholders' equity** | | |
| Share capital | | 400 000 |
| Retained profits* | | 2 241 320 |
| | | 2 641 320 |

* Closing retained profits = 1 921 320 + 320 000 = 2 241 320

accounting, based on the historical transaction base of record-keeping, is better suited to measuring past performance than to looking into the future, as managers are inclined to do.

- Accounting runs into a fundamental problem here. While managers' expectations are a main reason for their actions, accounting cannot observe their expectations, but only their actions. (Expectations are not observable in general, so this is not just a problem for accounting.) So, accounting reports the results of actions, not the reasons for them (except by implication). Managers may therefore feel that the accounting statements are incomplete because they miss the 'why' behind the revenues, expenses, assets and liabilities.
- To many people, profits should be defined as changes in the value of the company. Economic earnings can be defined as increases in value. Value changes are a function of performance, but also of expectations and of the market prices for assets and whole companies. The evidence-based accounting procedures for revenue recognition, expense recognition, and matching them to measure profit may not relate very well to economic concepts of earnings, or to managers' struggles to increase the value of their companies.
- Accrual accounting's procedures require evidence to support entries and conservatism in estimating the effects of future events (provide for expected losses, but not for expected gains until they occur). To managers seeking an even-handed evaluation of their performance, accounting may seem overly sceptical about the future and downwardly biased in its measures. Accrual accounting goes beyond cash flows, and managers may wish that it went further, to recognise their optimism about the future more than it does.
- The criteria as to when and how to recognise revenues and expenses are inescapably judgemental and, therefore, to many managers' tastes, are both arbitrary and subjective. Earlier chapters have suggested that some managers may be motivated to manipulate the accounting results, and accrual accounting procedures can be a way of doing that, but it should also be said that many managers find accrual accounting too loose and flexible and would prefer less estimation and subjectivity. Prudence and conservatism are traits of many managers, not just of accountants and auditors!
- Modern finance theory, which is influential in the evaluations by financial markets, banks and takeover specialists, makes much of cash flows (especially discounted expected future cash flows, to be examined in chapter 13) but, as you have seen, cash flow does not necessarily connect well to accrual accounting's profit figure. This connection is worse the shorter the period (for example, cash flow and accrual profit are probably similar over a ten-year period, but unlikely to be similar over a month).

Another reason, therefore, for managers to take financial accounting seriously is so that they can know when the accounting measures seem appropriate and when not. Accrual accounting has many advantages and is very widely used, but managers should not accept it uncritically.

## 5.11 Accrual accounting in the public sector

Australia and New Zealand have made substantial progress in the introduction of accrual accounting in the public sector. While other public sectors, including those in the United States and the United Kingdom, have made some moves towards accrual accounting, Australia and New Zealand are ahead in producing accrual-based accounts. In Australia, local governments have been required since 1995 to produce financial statements using accrual accounting. All government departments were required to produce accrual-based financial statements for the first reporting period after 31 December 1996 (AAS29). In part, such accounts have been produced by all New South Wales government departments since 1994. Accrual accounting for whole of governments (for example, the State of South Australia, the Federal Government) has been required since 30 June 1999.

Accrual-based financial reports prepared by departments or governments will differ significantly from cash-based reports covering the same period. Some examples of the information provided in accrual based financial reports but not cash based financial reports include:

- non-cash assets such as land, buildings, motor vehicles and plant and equipment and their depreciation
- the value of receivables (such as the amount owing to departments or governments from others but not yet received) and the value of payables (such as amounts owed by departments or governments for goods or services that have been purchased but not yet paid for)
- liabilities, including those relating to employee entitlements that have not yet been paid and long-term contractual obligations
- the changing value of financial assets and liabilities, such as changes to amounts owed to overseas lenders resulting from exchange rate movements
- the full cost of department or government activities for the period, the revenues generated for the period and any differences therein
- the cost of consuming assets, which is included in expenses (such as depreciation)
- the value of goods or services received free of charge from other bodies, which is included in revenues.

In using accrual accounting for government departments, all of the adjustments considered in this chapter still apply. For example, the NSW Department of Education and Training 2000 annual report includes the following notes:

| | **Economic entity** | |
|---|---|---|
| | **2000** | **1999** |
| | **\$000** | **\$000** |
| **11 Current/noncurrent assets – receivables** | | |
| *Current:* | | |
| Trade debtors | 45 644 | 33 167 |
| Other debtors | 12 458 | 19 840 |
| Prepayments | 36 378 | 16 074 |
| Accrued income | 15 392 | 14 325 |
| | 109 872 | 83 406 |
| less Provision for doubtful debts | (1 028) | (911) |
| | 108 844 | 82 495 |
| *Noncurrent:* | | |
| Advances to schools | 124 | 167 |
| Other debtors | 2 310 | 8 360 |
| | 2 434 | 8 527 |

**16 Current/noncurrent liabilities – employee entitlements**

| *Current:* | | |
|---|---|---|
| Recreation leave | 38 780 | 35 451 |
| Accrued salaries and wages | 156 993 | 70 854 |
| Accrued payroll tax on recreation leave, and accrued salaries and wages | 19 033 | 11 615 |
| Other | 2 440 | 3 718 |
| | 217 246 | 121 638 |

In note 11 above, prepayments and accrued income (referred to as 'accrual of unrecorded revenues' in section 5.3) are included. In note 11, the provision for doubtful debts is deducted from debtors. Note 16 includes various accrued expenses.

## 5.12 Homework and discussion to develop understanding

### Discussion questions

1 Explain the difference between a revenue and a cash receipt.

2 Give examples of items that are revenue of a given period but not receipts of that period, items that are receipts but not revenue, and items that are both revenue and receipts.

3 Explain the difference between an expense and a cash disbursement.

4 Give examples of items that are expenses of a given period but not disbursements of that period, items that are disbursements but not expenses, and items that are both expenses and disbursements.

5 Outline some basic differences between cash and accrual accounting.

6 'The closer to cash, the more precise the measure.' Discuss in respect to cash and accrual accounting.

7 'The more accountants try to make financial statements economically relevant, the more they must include estimates and other sources of imprecision or error.' Discuss.

8 What is the purpose of accrual accounting adjustments?

9 For each of the accrual accounting adjustments, explain the impact on profit for the period and the statement of financial position.

10 Your old school friend has joined the maintenance group of a large airline. He asks you the following question: 'Our customers pay us large amounts of cash but we call this a liability. Surely it has to increase profits?' How would you answer?

11 The accountant at a large mining company tells you that they have some contractors who do the work but often don't get around to billing for about three months after the job is complete. She notes 'it's great for our cash flow but causes us lots of work at year-end'. Explain this statement.

12 What is the purpose of depreciating noncurrent assets?

13 What is the difference between depreciation and accumulated depreciation?

14 For a manager thinking about disposing of some assets, why is book value important?

15 What is the difference between a bad and a doubtful debt?

**16** Why do companies have a provision for doubtful debts?

**17** Discuss the following:

  **a** Speaking positively, it might be said that accrual accounting improves on the cash flow information. Speaking negatively, it might be said that accrual accounting messes up the picture by introducing non–cash flow factors. Whether or not you like the result they achieve, how do accrual accounting entries work to alter the cash flow story?

  **b** Why can it be said that timing is at the centre of accrual accounting?

**18** Respond, in point form, to the following complaint by a business person: 'I find modern financial accounting really annoying. The basis of financial strength is the availability and use of real resources, such as cash and machinery, yet accrual accounting produces a profit measure that is deliberately different from the cash return earned by the business. Why is this so? Why should accrual accounting diverge from the measurement of cash flow?'

**19** On 31 December, the end of the accounting period of Ultra Corp, the company accountant is about to make some adjustments. Describe a set of circumstances where, in making the typical year-end adjustments:

  **a** an expense is debited and a liability is credited

  **b** an expense is debited and an asset contra account is credited

  **c** an asset is debited and revenue is credited

  **d** a liability is debited and revenue is credited.

**20** A business executive remarked: 'Accountants use a dual standard for measuring assets. Some are on the balance sheet because they have real future economic value. Others are there only because they're left over from the profit measurement process . . . sort of expenses waiting to be deducted. Similarly with liabilities: some are really owed but some are just leftovers of the accrual accounting process for measuring profit.' Discuss the remark, citing examples of assets and liabilities that might fit the executive's four categories.

**21** Now that you are a famous business person, you are frequently asked to make after-dinner speeches on business topics. Without thinking about it too much, you agreed to make a speech on accrual accounting to a class of graduating business students. Now you have to think of something to say, and you have decided to title your talk, 'Why managers like me like accrual accounting and why we worry about it'. List the topics you plan to talk about under this heading.

**22** An economist might argue that revenue is created or earned continuously by a wide variety of the firm's activities (such as production, sales, delivery), yet the accountant in a typical case selects only one of these steps (the 'critical event') to signal the time at which all revenues are to be recognised.

  **a** Assuming that the economist's view is correct, under what circumstances would the accountant's method lead to an undistorted measure of periodic profit? In other words, under what conditions will the opinion that profit is continuously earned agree with profit as determined by accountants?

  **b** What are the obstacles to the practical implementation of the economist's view as the basis for accounting profit determination?

**23** A business person you know has just received the financial statements of a company in which that person owns shares. Answer the following questions asked by the person. Try to answer without jargon, and use examples that will make your answers clear.

  **a** I've been told that these accrual accounting numbers are 'mainly a matter of timing'. What does that mean?

  **b** I see that the company has a note in its financial statements describing its 'revenue recognition' method. Why would I want to know that?

- **c** I know from my business experience that sometimes you collect cash sooner or later than you expect. Customers may have cash, or not, for all sorts of reasons that have nothing to do with you. I understand that accrual accounting takes this into account so that it doesn't matter when cash is collected, you get the same revenue figure anyway. Is this true?
- **d** I understand that accountants try to be sure that revenues and expenses 'match', so the profit you get by subtracting expenses from revenues makes sense. It seems quite appropriate. But what effect, if any, does this matching procedure have on the balance sheet figures?

**24** A journalist said recently that accrual accounting was invented because managers wanted something they could manipulate to their own purposes more than was possible with transactions-based, cash-based data. Accrual accounting, the journalist continued, is a tool of management and has driven accounting away from the goal of producing information that is representative of any real phenomena and toward fanciful reports largely devoid of real meaning.

- **a** What do you think of the journalist's views? Are there any better reasons for accrual accounting?
- **b** The journalist said that academics and practitioners tend to differ in their responses to his views. What do you think the differences would be?
- **c** If the journalist is right, what does that say about the dictum that management bears the responsibility for providing financial information about an enterprise?

## Problem 5.1* Adjusting journal entries

It is the end of International Fabrics Ltd's financial year. You are working on the company's financial statements, and have discovered the items **a** to **h** listed below. For each item:

1. State whether or not the item requires that an adjustment be made in the company's accounts according to the principles of accrual accounting.
2. If the answer to part 1 is yes, write a journal entry to adjust the company's accounts.

*Items:*

- **a** $3200 of sales made on account just before the end of the financial year were not recorded until the beginning of the next year.
- **b** The cost of goods sold for those sales, totalling $1900, has not yet been recognised.
- **c** During the year, deposits of $5300 were made by customers on special orders and were credited to the deposit liability account. Deposits of $1400 are still being held, but all the other special orders have been completed and the customers have paid the rest of the price for those orders (those payments are included in sales revenue).
- **d** Maintenance expenses seemed rather high, and on investigation it turned out that an addition to the company's store, constructed over a period of several months at a cost of $62 320, had been included in the maintenance expenses.
- **e** Just before the year-end, the company was sued by a customer whose expensive curtains lost their colour as soon as they were exposed to sunlight. The lawsuit was for $4300 to replace the curtains and $50 000 in pain and suffering damages. Legal advice indicates that the curtains should be replaced (which would cost the company about what it is being sued for) but that the customer will not succeed with the pain and suffering damages.
- **f** The company's auditors sent a bill for $2350 for the year's audit work.
- **g** Effective just before the year-end, the company agreed to buy a motor vehicle from a major shareholder for $17 220.

**h** At the beginning of the year, the company had paid $2000 for the exclusive right to distribute in Australia fabrics made by Silk Dreams Ltd of Singapore. The exclusive distributorship is for a period of four years.

## Problem 5.2* Calculating accrual information

The following information has been extracted from the accounts of Star Ltd.

**Star Ltd**
Statement of financial position as at 30 June 2001

| **Assets** | **$** | **$** | **Liabilities and shareholders' equity** | **$** |
|---|---|---|---|---|
| Cash | | 19 000 | Accounts payable | 21 000 |
| Accounts receivable | | 22 000 | Accrued interest | 2 000 |
| Inventory | | 24 000 | | |
| Plant and equipment | 120 000 | | Loan | 30 000 |
| Accumulated depreciation | 25 000 | 95 000 | Share capital | 75 000 |
| | | | Retained profits | 32 000 |
| | | 160 000 | | 160 000 |

Cash receipts for the year ended 30 June 2002

| | $ |
|---|---|
| Cash sales | 78 000 |
| Receipts from accounts receivable | 262 000 |
| | 340 000 |

Cash payments for the year ended 30 June 2002

| | $ |
|---|---|
| Payments for accounts payable | 184 000 |
| Interest paid | 1 000 |
| Wages paid | 59 000 |
| Dividend payment | 45 000 |
| | 289 000 |

***Additional information:***

**a** Balances as at 30 June 2002:

| | |
|---|---|
| Accounts receivable | $18 000 |
| Accrued interest | $3 000 |

**b** Cost of goods sold during the year was $158 000.

**c** On 30 June 2002, Star owed $14 000 in salaries for services received during June.

**d** No additions or disposals of plant and equipment were made during the period. The depreciation rate is 10 per cent per annum. The straight-line method is used.

**1** Calculate total revenue for the year ended 30 June 2002.

**2** List all of the expenses for the year (including dollar amounts).

**3** Calculate the balance of cash as at 30 June 2002.

## Problem 5.3* Accounting transactions

The statement of financial position and statement of financial performance of Reconstruction Limited are reproduced below.

**Reconstruction Limited**
Statement of financial position

| | 31/12/2002 | 31/12/2001 |
|---|---|---|
| | $ | $ |
| **Assets** | | |
| Cash | — | 5 000 |
| Accounts receivable | 40 000 | 27 000 |
| Prepaid insurance | 3 000 | 2 000 |
| Equipment | 90 000 | 90 000 |
| less Accumulated depreciation | (31 000) | (22 000) |
| Motor vehicle | 25 000 | 25 000 |
| Less: Accumulated depreciation | (10 000) | (5 000) |
| Total assets | 117 000 | 122 000 |
| **Liabilities** | | |
| Accounts payable | 500 | 1 000 |
| Wages payable | 6 000 | 4 000 |
| Interest payable | 2 500 | 3 000 |
| Income tax payable | — | 2 000 |
| Long-term loan | 50 000 | 50 000 |
| Total liabilities | 59 000 | 60 000 |
| **Net assets** | **$58 000** | **$62 000** |
| **Shareholders' equity** | | |
| Share capital | 39 000 | 39 000 |
| Retained profits | 19 000 | 23 000 |
| **Total shareholders' equity** | $58 000 | **$62 000** |

**Reconstruction Limited**
Statement of financial performance for the year ended 31 December 2002

| | $ | $ |
|---|---|---|
| Fees revenue | | 105 000 |
| Depreciation expense | (14 000) | |
| Electricity expense | (8 000) | |
| Insurance expense | (17 000) | |
| Interest expense | (4 500) | |
| Rent expense | (24 000) | |
| Stationery expense | (3 500) | |
| Wages expense | (38 000) | |
| | | (109 000) |
| Profit/(loss) before tax | | (4 000) |
| Income tax expense | | 0 |
| Profit/(loss) after tax | | (4 000) |

1 How much cash was paid for insurance during the year?
2 How much cash was paid for electricity during the year?
3 How much cash was paid for interest during the year?
4 How much cash was paid for income tax during the year?
5 The last monthly rent payment was made on 15 December 2002. Monthly rent is $2 000 per month. How much rent is owing as at the end of the year?
6 Reconstruction Limited depreciates the motor vehicle (the company owns one vehicle) using straight-line depreciation with no residual value. On what date was the motor vehicle purchased?

## Problem 5.4* Cash versus accrual accounting

Greenfingers Pty Ltd opened a gardening consulting company on 1 August 2003 with each of the two owners contributing $10 000 cash. A one-year bank loan of $40 000 at 12 per cent per annum was obtained from the bank on 1 August, with principal and interest to be repaid at the end of the loan. An insurance policy for 12 months was taken out on 1 August 2003 for $600. Three months' office rental for $900 was paid in advance on 1 August 2003. Consulting revenue of $10 000 was earned during the month, but $6000 had not been received at the end of August. A truck that cost $36 000 was paid for in cash on 1 August. It had an expected life of three years and zero residual value. Cash expenses during the month were: wages $600; other expenses $400. Unpaid bills at month end were: electricity $100; wages $200.

Prepare a statement of financial performance for August 2003 under (a) an accrual basis and (b) a cash basis of accounting.

## Problem 5.5 Calculate accrual net profit from various accounts

Pottery Galore Pty Ltd has just finished its 2002 financial year. From the following data, calculate net profit before tax for 2002.

| | $ |
|---|---|
| Collections from credit customers during 2002 | 174 320 |
| Accounts receivable, end of 2001 | 11 380 |
| Accounts receivable, end of 2002 | 9 440 |
| Provision for doubtful debts, end of 2001 | 890 |
| Provision for doubtful debts, end of 2002 | 1 130 |
| Bad debts written off during 2002 | 520 |
| Payments to suppliers and employees during 2002 | 165 690 |
| Accounts and wages payable, end of 2001 | 12 770 |
| Accounts and wages payable, end of 2002 | 15 510 |
| Inventory of unsold goods, end of 2001 | 21 340 |
| Inventory of unsold goods, end of 2002 | 24 650 |
| Bank loan, end of 2002 | 12 000 |
| The loan was taken out a month before the end of 2002 at an interest rate of 8%. No interest has yet been paid. | |

## Problem 5.6 Simple accrual revenue calculation

A weekly newspaper began operations on 1 July, and collected payments for 1000 one-year subscriptions at $52.00 each in the first three days of that month. Editions were published on 7, 14, 21 and 28 July. How much revenue should the newspaper recognise in its accounts in July?

## Problem 5.7 Simple accrual expense questions

Before its opening, the Novelty Shop arranged for telephone service. The telephone company, the shop's owner was told, bills the customer for each month's service at the end of the month, and no deposit or installation fee is required.

1 Did the installation of the telephone increase the assets of the Novelty Shop? Did it result in an expense at the time of installation?
2 If the monthly service charge is $21, how will this affect the computation of profit for the first two weeks?
3 What would be the effect on assets and profit if the service charge for the first month were paid in advance at the beginning of the month?
4 What would be the effect on assets and profit if an installation charge of $10 were paid at the beginning of the month?

## Problem 5.8 Cash versus accrual accounting

Wizard Enterprises Ltd began business on 1 July 2001, with each of the three owners contributing $8000 cash. The company paid $2200 in advance for a two-year lease of its retail premises. Inventory worth $3500 was purchased in the first month of operation; by 30 June 2002, $1200 of inventory remained. Sales revenue of $9100 was earned during the year, although $1600 of this amount is yet to be collected. This amount also includes $400 for products that will not be delivered until December 2002.

During the year, wages totalling $1300 were paid to employees and $900 was paid for various administrative expenses. The company received an advertising invoice for $1100 as well as a utilities bill for $385; these are yet to be paid as at 30 June 2002.

1 Prepare a cash-basis statement of financial performance for Wizard Enterprises for the year ended 30 June 2002.
2 Prepare an accrual-basis statement of financial performance for Wizard Enterprises for the year ended 30 June 2002.

## Problem 5.9 Adjustments

The financial year-end for Flamingo Pty Ltd is 30 June.

a Prepaid insurance as at 1 July 2001 was $3200, representing the cost of a two-year insurance policy that expires on 30 June 2003.
b Flamingo [was entitled to a dividend revenue] of $5000 that will not be received until mid July
c Commissions to sales personnel for the five-day working week ending 2 July 2002, totalling $9600, will be paid on 2 July.
d Sales revenue for the year included $570 of customer deposits for products that have not yet been shipped to them.
e $900 of stationery was charged to office supplies expense during the year. On 30 June, about $490 worth of stationery is still considered useful for next year.
f The company has a bank loan and pays interest annually (in arrears) on 31 December. The estimated interest cost for the calendar year ending 31 December 2002 is $350.

1 Show the effect of each of the above on the accounting equation at 30 June 2002.
2 Give the adjusting journal entry for each of the above situations on 30 June 2002.

## Problem 5.10 Adjustments – accounting equation

Swan Ltd conducts three motels in large country centres. The accounts for the year ended 30 June 2002 have been finalised, with the exception of any adjustments that may result from the following:

**a** Bonuses due to the motel managers totalling $12 000 have not yet been recorded.

**b** On 1 October 2001, a comprehensive insurance policy covering building and contents was taken out for the year ended 30 September 2002, the annual premium of $2400 being paid on 1 November 2001.

**c** Interest on investments amounting to $450 is due but not yet received.

**d** A payment of $900 for embossed stationery has been charged in error to the advertising account.

**e** The accounts receivable balance is $171 500. Provision for doubtful debts is $7000. Bad debts of $350 are to be written off. Provision for doubtful debts is to be adjusted to stand at 5 per cent of accounts receivable.

**f** An amount of $4500 spent on a laptop computer had been charged to the office expenses account instead of the office equipment account.

**g** In May, commission of $360 had been received in advance for the six months ending 31 October 2002.

**h** Accrued electricity charges at 30 June 2002 were $92.

Show the impact of each transaction on the accounting equation.

## Problem 5.11 Effect of transactions

Consider the impact of each of the following transactions/events on net profit before tax, and cash flow for the year ending 31 March 2002 and total assets at 31 March 2002.

**a** Purchased new equipment on credit late in March 2002 (ignore any depreciation impact).

**b** Same as (a), but assume cash instead of credit.

**c** Carried out an installation project in March 2002. Invoiced the customer in March but will not receive payment until April.

**d** Signed a major contract in March with the work to be carried out between April and June 2002.

**e** Same as (d), but the customer pays $300 000 deposit.

**f** A piece of equipment purchased in 1998 was being depreciated over 8 years. In 2002 it was decided that its total useful life was really only six years. Show the changed effect on net profit and total assets.

**g** Some work was carried out by subcontractors in March 2002. The subcontractors are notoriously slow in billing, usually billing about two to three months after job completion.

**h** Insurance for the period 4 April 2002 to 3 April 2003 is paid on 27 March 2002.

## Problem 5.12 Prepare adjusting journal entries if necessary

The accountant for Super Office Supplies Ltd (SOS) is reviewing the year-end unadjusted trial balance and considering the following items of information. For each item, decide if an adjustment to the accounts is necessary. If it is, write a journal entry to make the adjustment.

**a** A shipment of inventory that arrived late on the last day of the year was not recorded. The shipment cost $11 240, and was paid for routinely about three weeks later.

**b** The accountant estimated that bank loan interest of $330 had built up between the last payment of interest to the bank and the end of the year.

**c** In the last few days of the year, the company's share price on the Australian Stock Exchange had fallen about $0.20 per share. The company has 500 000 shares outstanding.

**d** There had been an error in calculating amortisation expense during the year. To correct the error, additional expense of $14 500 would need to be recorded.

**e** A customer owing $2100 went bankrupt on the last day of the year, and SOS cannot expect to collect any of the money it expected.

**f** A review of the warranty liability indicated that the liability should be increased by $780.

**g** At a Board of Directors meeting on the last day of the year, the company's president and other senior executives were awarded raises totalling $11 100 annually, to begin the next day.

**h** The company had bought 12 months' building insurance two months before the end of the year, at a cost of $2400, and debited the cost to insurance expense.

**i** One of the cash receipts credited to sales revenue turned out to be a deposit of $400 made by a customer on an order that will be filled a week after the end of the year.

**j** The accountant determined that a major sales order had been filled on the last day of the year, although it was not recorded until three days later. The order was for $7200, and the goods supplied had cost SOS $3300. The customer paid two weeks later.

## Problem 5.13 Identify and describe common adjustments

The list below describes one side each of common accrual accounting adjustments. Describe the purpose of the adjustment, and state what the other side of the entry is. State any assumptions you feel are necessary.

**a** CR Accumulated depreciation

**b** CR Accrued interest liability

**c** DR Noncurrent assets

**d** DR Prepaid insurance asset

**e** CR Warranty liability

**f** CR Dividends payable

**g** CR Income tax payable

**h** CR Customer deposits liability

**i** DR Supplies inventory

**j** CR Bonuses payable.

## Problem 5.14 Record and post adjusting journal entries, close accounts

Here are the unadjusted accounts for Tucker Northern Ltd at the end of its first year in business:

| | | | |
|---|---|---|---|
| Cash | 25 600 | Employee deductions due | 2 500 |
| Accounts receivable | 88 200 | Sales taxes due | 3 220 |
| Inventory | 116 900 | Mortgage debt | 185 780 |
| Land | 100 000 | Share capital | 275 000 |
| Buildings and equipment | 236 100 | Revenue | 349 600 |
| Accounts payable | 74 900 | Cost of goods sold | 142 500 |
| | | Operating expenses | 181 700 |

The company has determined that the year-end adjustments listed below are required.

**a** An uncollectible account receivable of $2400 should be written off to expense.

**b** Depreciation of $13 000 should be recorded.

**c** Additional revenue of $11 200 has been earned and should be recorded.

**d** The COGS to go with the revenue in (c) is $4600.

**e** Accrued interest on the mortgage at the end of the year is $900.

**f** A bonus of $5000 was awarded to the CEO by the board of directors.

**g** Income tax for the year is estimated to be $2700. No tax has been paid yet.

1 Record these in journal entry form.
2 Post them to the accounts (creating new accounts if you need them).
3 Prepare a balanced adjusted trial balance.
4 Close the revenue and expense accounts to retained earnings.
5 Calculate the following: net profit; working capital; shareholders' equity.

## Problem 5.15 Simple prepaid and accrued expense question

1 In its 2000 annual report, Southcorp Limited shows the following:

| | 2000 $000 | 1999 $000 |
|---|---|---|
| Prepayments | 30 543 | 25 436 |

Assume this amount all related to insurance and that $20 million cash was paid during the year to the insurance company. What is the insurance expense for the 2000 financial year?

2 AXA Asia Pacific Holdings Limited, in note 14 of its 2000 accounts, shows an amount of $5 million ($9 million in 1999) for accrued management expenses. If the company paid $280 million in management fees during the year, what was the management expense?

3 Coca-Cola Amatil Limited, in its 2000 annual report, included an amount of $284.5 million in accrued charges ($285.9 million in 1999). Assume that all these accrued charges related to wages. If the wages paid during the year were $500 million, what was the wages expense for 2000?

## Problem 5.16 Adjusting entry for accrued expense

1 Employees of Donovan Ltd are paid every Friday for the five-day working week from Monday to Friday. The weekly wages expense is $115 000. The accounting year-end is 31 December. Assume this falls on a Thursday.

   a Prepare the adjusting entry for the year-end.

   b If no adjusting entry is made on 31 December, what will be the impact on net profit? What will be the errors in the statement of financial position?

   c What is the journal entry made on 1 January, when the staff are paid?

2 On 1 July 2002, Donovan obtained a bank loan of $100 000 at 12 per cent interest, payable yearly in arrears. The accounting year-end is 31 December.

   a What is the adjusting entry required on 31 December 2002?

   b The company's accountant forgets to prepare the above entry. What will be the effect of this omission on Donovan's financial statements?

   c Prepare the journal entry for 1 July 2003, when the first interest payment is made.

## Problem 5.17 Simple prepayment and accrual questions

1 In its 30 September 2000 annual report, Orica Australia Limited shows the following:

| | 2000 $ | 1999 $ |
|---|---|---|
| Prepayment | 21.7 million | 20.8 million |

Assume this amount is all related to insurance and that $30 million cash was paid during the year to the insurance company. What is the insurance expense for the year ended 30 September 2000?

2 In its 30 June 2001 annual report, Mayne Nickless Ltd shows the following:

| | 2001<br>$ | 2000<br>$ |
|---|---|---|
| Prepayment | 18 358 | 27 684 |

Assume this amount all related to insurance, and that $35 million cash was paid during the year to the insurance company. What is the insurance expense for the year ended 30 June 2001?

3 John Fairfax Holdings Limited, in note 13 of its 2001 accounts, shows an amount of $7 122 000 ($7 291 000 in 2000) for accrued interest on bank borrowings. If the company paid $20 000 000 in cash in interest payments during the year, what was the interest expense?

4 Burns Philp and Company Limited, in note 14 of its 2001 annual report, included an amount of $88.7 million in accrued expenses ($78.6 million in 2000). Assume that all these accrued expenses related to wages. If the wages paid during the year were $1200 million, what was the wages expense for the 2001 financial year?

5 The following is an extract from the statement of financial position of James Hardie Industries Limited. Assume all prepayments relate to insurance policies. If the cash paid for these policies during the year amounted to $50 million, what was the insurance expense for the year?

| | | James Hardie | |
|---|---|---|---|
| | **Note** | **31.3.01** | **31.3.00** |
| **Current assets** | | | |
| Cash | 7 | **153.2** | 254.2 |
| Receivables | 8 | **148.0** | 208.9 |
| Inventories | 9 | **178.9** | 117.7 |
| Prepayments | | **40.6** | 21.9 |
| **Total current assets** | | **520.7** | 602.7 |

## Problem 5.18 Journal entries of revenue received in advance

In the 2001 annual report of Telstra, the following appears as the financial policy on revenue received in advance:

*Revenue received in advance*

Revenue received in advance consists mainly of revenue from providing access to the fixed and mobile network and directories advertising revenue. This revenue is initially recorded as a liability and then transferred to earned revenue in line with the revenue policies described above.

1 What journal entries would be put through when the cash is received?

2 What journal entry would be put through when the revenue is recognised?

## Problem 5.19 Adjusting entry for accrued expense

ABC Pty Ltd pays its employees every Friday for a five-day working week from Monday to Friday. The weekly payroll amounts to $150 000. The accounting year-end is 30 June.

1 Assuming that 30 June falls on Wednesday, give the year-end adjusting entry.

2 If no adjusting entry was made on 30 June, by how much would net profit be overstated or understated? What would be the errors in the statement of financial position?
3 Give the entry to pay the staff on 2 July.

## Problem 5.20 Adjusting entry for revenue received in advance

XYZ Pty Ltd rents one office to a tenant who paid three months' rent in advance on 1 June. The firm credited unearned rental revenue to record the $6000 received. Year end is 30 June.

1 Prepare the adjusting entry for 30 June.
2 What are the effects on the firm's financial statements if the adjusting entry was omitted?
3 Prepare the entry in the next period to recognise the remaining portion of the rent revenue.

## Problem 5.21 Adjusting entry for prepaid expense

MNO Pty Ltd purchased a one-year insurance policy on 1 April. The entire premium of $6000 was recorded by debiting prepayments. Year-end is 30 June.

1 Give the 30 June adjusting entry.
2 What amount should be reported in the 30 June statement of financial position for prepayments?
3 If no adjusting entry was made on 30 June, by how much would net profit be overstated or understated? Would assets be overstated or understated?
4 What would your adjusting entry in **(1)** be if the premium of $6000 was recorded by debiting insurance expense?

## Problem 5.22 Adjusting journal entries

The annual accounting period for DEF Pty Ltd ends on 30 June. Prepare adjusting entries for each of the following:

1 DEF was entitled to a commission of $2000 during June, but it will not be received until July.
2 Wages of $3000 for the five-day work period ending 3 July will be paid on 3 July.
3 It has a $100 000 fixed deposit at 12 per cent, where interest is paid in arrears on 30 April and 30 November.
4 The office supplies account had an opening balance on 1 July 2001 of $1000. Supplies of $8000 were purchased during the year, and $900 of supplies are on hand on 30 June 2002.

## Problem 5.23 Classifying items in the statement of financial position

The adjusted trial balance for Jackson Pty Ltd at 30 June 2002 is shown below.

| | **Debit $000** | **Credit $000** |
|---|---|---|
| Accounts receivable | 1 600 | |
| Accounts payable | | 2 100 |
| Accrued revenue | 490 | |
| Accrued wages | | 3 500 |
| Accumulated depreciation | | 35 000 |
| Cash | 3 560 | |
| Income tax payable | | 210 |
| Inventory | 2 100 | |
| Long-term loan | | 8 000 |
| Prepaid rent | 3 000 | |
| Property, plant and equipment | 67 000 | |
| Provision for doubtful debts | | 20 |

| | Debit $000 | Credit $000 |
|---|---|---|
| Revenue received in advance | | 750 |
| Retained profits, 30 June 2001 | | 6 710 |
| Share capital | | 20 000 |
| Sales | | 15 800 |
| Cost of goods sold | 6 200 | |
| Depreciation expense | 5 400 | |
| Rent expense | 2 500 | |
| Income tax expense | 240 | |
| | 92 090 | 92 090 |

1 In the statement of financial position prepared as at 30 June 2002:
   a What will be the balance of total current assets?
   b What will be the balance of total current liabilities?
   c What will be the total amount of noncurrent assets?
   d What will be the closing balance of retained profits?
2 What was the balance of the accumulated depreciation account on 30 June 2001, assuming that no property, plant and equipment was disposed of during the year?

## Problem 5.24 Classifying statement of financial position items

An adjusted trial balance at 31 December 2002 for a toy manufacturer is given below:

| | Debit $ | Credit $ |
|---|---|---|
| Accounts receivable | 300 000 | |
| Accounts payable | | 120 000 |
| Property, plant and equipment | 1 000 000 | |
| Accumulated depreciation | | 400 000 |
| Income tax payable | | 40 000 |
| Revenue received in advance | | 10 000 |
| Prepaid expenses | 20 000 | |
| Provision for doubtful debts | | 5 000 |
| Accrued wages | | 25 000 |
| Inventory | 200 000 | |
| Cash | 60 000 | |
| Accrued revenue | 20 000 | |
| Long-term debt | | 100 000 |
| Share capital | | 700 000 |
| Retained profit at 1 Jan 2001 | | 150 000 |
| Sales | | 800 000 |
| Cost of goods sold | 500 000 | |
| Depreciation expense | 20 000 | |
| Other operating expenses | 150 000 | |
| Income tax expense | 80 000 | |
| | 2 350 000 | 2 350 000 |

1 In the statement of financial position prepared at 31 December 2002:
   a What would be the balance of total current assets?
   b What would be the balance of total current liabilities?
   c What would be the balance of total noncurrent assets?
   d What would be the closing balance of retained profit?

2 What was the balance of the accumulated depreciation account at 31 December 2001, assuming no property, plant and equipment was disposed of during the year?

## Problem 5.25 Adjusting entries and financial statements

The trial balance shown below has been extracted from the general ledger of R. James Electronics Pty Ltd at 30 June 2002. The following facts came to light after completion of the trial balance:

- **a** Investigation of a credit balance in a debtor's account in the subsidiary ledger showed that a credit sale of goods in May for $800 had not been recorded.
- **b** The last day of the period, 30 June 2002, was a Wednesday. The staff are paid on Friday for their five-day working week ending on Friday. Sales salaries are $2035 per week and office salaries are $475 per week.
- **c** Electricity expenses of $350 have been incurred, but not billed and not recognised. Telephone expenses of $200 have been incurred (in respect of calls) during June, but not recognised.
- **d** Rent expense includes an amount of $600 prepaid for the first two weeks of July 2002.
- **e** Depreciation of $2400 is to be charged on office equipment and $2805 on demonstration equipment.
- **f** Interest on the loan is at the rate of 12 per cent per annum payable quarterly in advance on the last day of each quarter. The loan was made on 1 October 2001.
- **g** Bad debts of $700 are to be written off, and provision for doubtful debts is to be 2 per cent of debtors.

| | Debit<br>$ | Credit<br>$ |
|---|---|---|
| Debtors | 407 700 | |
| Advertising | 81 800 | |
| Electricity | 5 400 | |
| Office equipment | 24 000 | |
| Postage and telephone | 9 300 | |
| Inventory | 145 000 | |
| Cost of goods sold | 689 900 | |
| Creditors | | 160 200 |
| Provision for doubtful debts | | 8 800 |
| Rent | 16 000 | |
| Sales salaries | 105 800 | |
| Office salaries | 24 800 | |
| Sales | | 1 105 800 |
| Accumulated depreciation: | | |
| Sales demonstration equipment | | 3 300 |
| Office equipment | | 4 800 |
| Sales demonstration equipment | 22 000 | |
| Share capital | | 50 000 |
| Retained profits | | 61 500 |
| Long-term loan | | 160 000 |
| Interest on loan | 19 200 | |
| General office expenses | 3 500 | |
| | 1 554 400 | 1 554 400 |

1 Prepare general journal entries for any period-end adjustments for the above items.
2 Prepare a statement of financial performance for the year ended 30 June 2002.
3 Prepare a statement of financial position as at 30 June 2002, suitably classified.

## Problem 5.26 Calculation of accrual profit from cash records

Mike Stammer is a private investigator. He keeps his accounting records on a cash basis and has produced the following statement of financial performance, as he calls it.

**Mike Stammer**
Statement of financial performance
year ended 30 June 2002

| | $ |
|---|---|
| Fees collected in cash | 85 000 |
| Less cash expenses | 34 600 |
| **Net profit** | **50 400** |

An examination of Mike's records shows these balances at the beginning and end of fiscal 2002:

| | 1 July 2001 $ | 30 June 2002 $ |
|---|---|---|
| Fees receivable | 10 350 | 3 900 |
| Client deposits on accounting investigations | — | 1 200 |
| Accrued expenses | 3 490 | 5 250 |
| Prepaid expenses | 1 700 | 2 500 |

1 a What amount of the fees Mike collected in 2002 was received for investigations he actually completed in 2001?
b What amount of the fees received in 2002 will he earn in 2003?
c How much in fees did he earn in 2002 but not collect?
2 a What amount of the expenses Mike paid in 2002 should be matched with his efforts in 2001 or 2003?
b What amount of expenses paid in previous years should be matched with revenues Mike earned in 2002?
3 Use your answers to questions 1 and 2 to calculate an accrual-basis profit for Mike Stammer for the year ended 30 June 2002.
4 Add or subtract whichever adjustments to the cash statement of financial performance are necessary to reconcile Mike's $50 400 'profit' to your figure.
5 Compare the two profit figures. Why might Mike Stammer (or others using his financial information) prefer to use the cash basis of accounting? Why might he (or others) prefer the accrual basis?

## Problem 5.27 Write adjusting journal entries

Write an adjusting journal entry, if required, for each of the following items, which have been encountered during preparation of Ajax Sales Pty Ltd's 31 January 2002 financial statements.
1 A pile of sales invoices totalling $3124 has yet to be recorded.
2 A customer had paid a deposit of $500 on a special order, which has not yet arrived. The deposit was included in the sales amount for the day it was paid.

3 The company has a $123 000 bank loan owing. Interest at 8 per cent per annum was last paid 23 days before the end of the year.

4 The credit manager decided to write off accounts receivable totalling $320, as the debtor had gone into liquidation.

5 A court case involving another company showed that one of the company's patents was worthless, so management decided to write the patent off. It was on the accounts at a cost of $74 500, and there was accumulated amortisation of $42 100 against it.

## Problem 5.28 Impact of transactions on financial statements

Management of Jane Limited are interested in the directional effect (that is, increase, decrease, no effect) on net profit before tax, total assets and the current ratio (presently 2:1) for the year ending 30 June 2002, if the following occurred in January to June 2002.

1 Paying back a loan of $200 000.
2 Purchasing inventory of $100 000 on credit.
3 Receiving $10 000 for a job to be done in July.
4 Making sales of $200 000 on credit for goods that cost $80 000.
5 Changing the depreciation policy by reducing the estimated lives of certain equipment.
6 Prepaying insurance on 30 June 2002 for $50 000. The policy covers the year commencing July 2002.
7 Increasing the provision for doubtful debts by $80 000.
8 Interest revenue is accrued at 30 June, and is $5000.
9 Accounts receivable totalling $10 000 are found to be uncollectable. The current balance of provision for doubtful debts is $100 000.

## Problem 5.29 Calculate bad debt expense and provision for doubtful debts

Windhook Technologies Pty Ltd has been having difficulty collecting its accounts receivable. For the year 2002, the company increased the provision for doubtful accounts by $43 000, bringing the balance to $71 000. At the end of 2002, accounts receivable equalled $415 000. When the year-end audit was being done, it was decided to write off a further $54 000 of accounts receivable which were doubtful, and $36 000 of accounts receivable previously deemed doubtful.

Calculate the following:

1 bad debts expense for 2002
2 provision for doubtful debts at the end of 2002
3 estimated collectable value of accounts receivable at the end of 2002.

## Problem 5.30 Adjusting entries and financial statements

On 31 December 2002, the accountant for NextGen Technologies prepared a trial balance, based on information from the company's general ledger.

| | Debit<br>$ | Credit<br>$ |
|---|---|---|
| Cash | 5 840 | |
| Salaries and wages | 24 500 | |
| Sales demonstration equipment | 159 200 | |
| Provision for doubtful debts | | 1 300 |

| | Debit<br>$ | Credit<br>$ |
|---|---|---|
| Accumulated depreciation: | | |
| Office equipment | | 11 000 |
| Sales demonstration equipment | | 35 600 |
| Creditors | | 43 760 |
| Electricity | 6 700 | |
| Sales | | 830 570 |
| Rent | 15 600 | |
| Inventory | 26 840 | |
| Share capital | | 60 000 |
| Commission | 76 500 | |
| Advertising | 43 100 | |
| Debtors | 56 890 | |
| Cost of goods sold | 550 620 | |
| Office equipment | 90 000 | |
| Interest on loan | 1 890 | |
| Retained profits | | 30 880 |
| Administrative expenses | 5 430 | |
| Long-term loan | | 50 000 |
| | 1 063 110 | 1 063 110 |

After the trial balance was completed, the following was discovered:

**a** Electricity expenses of $287 have been incurred during December, but not yet billed or recognised.

**b** 31 December falls on a Tuesday. Staff are paid on Friday for a five-day working week ending on Friday. The weekly payroll expense is $480.

**c** Interest on the loan is at 6 per cent per annum, payable quarterly in advance on the last day of each quarter. The loan was made on 1 September 2002.

**d** Investigation of a debtor's account in the subsidiary ledger showed that a credit sale of $560 made in April had not been recorded.

**e** Rent expense includes an amount of $800 prepaid for the first week of January 2003.

**f** Bad debts of $580 are to be written off. Provision for doubtful debts is to be [illegible] per cent of debtors.

**g** Depreciation of $10 200 is to be charged on demonstration equipment, and $1150 on office equipment.

**h** The sales team made record Christmas sales in December, earning commissions of $2450. The entire amount will be paid in the first week of January.

**1** Prepare general journal entries for any period-end adjustments required.

**2** Prepare a statement of financial performance for the year ended 31 December 2002.

**3** Prepare a (properly classified) statement of financial position as at 31 December 2002.

## Problem 5.31 Questions about accounts receivable and doubtful accounts

Dragon Designs Ltd had the following general ledger accounts for last year, using the T-account format. All the company's sales are on credit, to retail stores across the country. The first amount in each account is the balance at the beginning of the year; the last amount, under the solid line, is the balance at the end of the year. Other amounts are transactions and adjustments during the year.

**Accounts receivable**

| | |
|---|---|
| 244 620 | |
| 1 693 784 | |
| | 1 599 005 |
| | 8 293 |
| 331 106 | |

**Provision for doubtful debts**

| | |
|---|---|
| | 11 914 |
| | 9 117 |
| 8 293 | |
| | 12 738 |

**Bad debts expense**

| | |
|---|---|
| 0 | |
| 9 117 | |
| 9 117 | |

Answer these questions:

1 What was the company's revenue for the year?

2 How much was collected on account of revenue for the year?

3 How much of the uncollected revenue did the company give up on during the year?

4 What was the expense the company incurred from taking the risk of extending credit to customers during the year?

5 What was the estimated collectable value of the accounts receivable at the end of the year?

6 What was the estimated collectable value of the accounts receivable before the year-end write-off of uncollectable accounts?

## Problem 5.32 Journal entries, posting to the ledger, trial balance, adjustments, closing entries and preparation of financial statements

Status Cymbal is a chain of wholesaler/retailers that sells musical instruments all around Australia. Its trial balance at 1 June 2002 was as follows:

| | Debit $ | Credit $ |
|---|---|---|
| Cash | 95 000 | |
| Accounts receivable | 270 000 | |
| Inventory | 310 000 | |
| Prepaid insurance | 6 000 | |
| Prepaid rent | 24 000 | |
| Buildings and equipment | 540 000 | |
| Motor vehicles | 90 000 | |
| Accumulated depreciation | | 124 000 |
| Provision for doubtful debts | | 17 000 |
| Accounts payable | | 370 000 |
| Accrued wages | | 36 000 |
| Income tax payable | | 78 000 |
| Loan | | 200 000 |
| Share capital | | 390 000 |
| Retained profits | | 120 000 |
| | 1 335 000 | 1 335 000 |

During June 2002, the following transactions occurred:

- **a** Paid the annual insurance premium to begin 1 July 2002 (12 × \$6000 = \$72 000).
- **b** Paid wages outstanding at the end of May.
- **c** Made cash sales of \$132 000 (COGS \$88 000).
- **d** Made credit sales totalling \$250 000 (COGS \$165 000).
- **e** Paid \$290 000 to creditors.
- **f** Received \$300 000 from debtors.
- **g** Purchased \$150 000 inventory on credit.
- **h** Paid the first of two equal instalments on the tax liability.
- **i** Incurred wages expenses of \$42 000 for June.
- **j** Paid \$11 000 off the loan.
- **k** Paid rent for July of \$24 000 (rent is prepaid each month).
- **l** Paid other expenses, incurred during the month, of \$19 000.
- **m** Received news that Pianos Galore has gone bankrupt – this is a debtor whose balance is \$12 000.
- **n** After writing off Pianos Galore balance, management decided to increase the provision to \$19 000.
- **o** Depreciation expense is calculated as 12 per cent per annum for vehicles and 13 per cent for buildings and equipment based on cost.
- **p** Commissions are determined on the last day of the month at \$11 100. They will be paid next month.

1. Prepare journal entries.
2. Post to the ledger.
3. Prepare a trial balance.
4. Prepare any additional adjusting entries.
5. Prepare closing entries.
6. Prepare financial statements.

## Problem 5.33 Doubtful debts

OJ Pty Ltd has been having difficulty collecting its accounts receivable. For the year 2002, the company increased the provision for doubtful accounts by \$48 000, bringing the balance to \$70 000. At the end of 2002, accounts receivable equalled \$47[illegible] 000. When the year-end audit was being done, it was decided to provide for another \$50 000 of accounts receivable that were doubtful and write off \$32 000 of accounts receivable previously deemed doubtful.

Calculate the following:

1. bad debts expense for 2002
2. provision for doubtful debts at the end of 2002
3. estimated collectable value of accounts receivable at the end of 2002.

## Problem 5.34 Doubtful debts

On 1 July 2001, Morton Limited had accounts receivable of \$53 000 and a provision for doubtful debts of \$3100. During the year ended 30 June 2002, credit sales amounted to \$432 500 and cash collected from customers was \$417 400. At the end of the financial year, the credit manager decided that accounts totalling \$1200 should be written off as bad debts and the provision for doubtful debts increased to \$4200.

1. What was the estimated collectable value of accounts receivable as at 30 June 2002?
2. What was the amount of the bad debts expense for the year ended 30 June 2002?

**3** What are the main reasons for using the provision method of accounting for bad debts rather than the direct write-off method?

## Problem 5.35 (Challenging) Accrual versus cash accounting

The statement of financial position of ABC Ltd as at 31 December 2001 and the cash receipts and payments for the year ended 31 December 2002 are shown below.

***Additional information:***

a As at 31 December 2002, the balance of accounts receivable was $25 000 and the balance of accounts payable was $15 000.

b Salaries are now paid monthly on the second of the month for the preceding month. Wages and salaries total $7000 for the month of December, which was paid on 2 January 2003.

c Plant and equipment is shown net of accumulated depreciation of $50 000. Depreciation expense for the year is calculated using the straight-line method at 10 per cent per annum.

d The bank loan accrues interest at a rate of 10 per cent per annum payable on 30 March and 30 September. The loan was taken out on 1 January 2001.

e A physical stocktake, as at 31 December 2002, revealed that inventory costing $23 000 was on hand. Cost of goods sold for the year was calculated as $132 000.

f The insurance premium of $8000 provides cover for the year ending 30 September 2003.

**ABC Ltd**
Statement of financial position
as at 31 December 2001

| | $ | | $ |
|---|---|---|---|
| Assets | | Liabilities | |
| Cash | 5 000 | Accounts payable | 10 000 |
| Accounts receivable | 10 000 | Bank loan | 80 000 |
| Inventory | 20 000 | Shareholders' equity | |
| Plant and equipment | 200 000 | Share capital | 200 000 |
| Land | 100 000 | Retained profits | 45 000 |
| **Total** | 335 000 | **Total** | 335 000 |

Cash receipts and disbursements
for the year ended 31 December 2002

| | $ | | $ |
|---|---|---|---|
| Receipts | | Disbursements | |
| Cash sales | 150 000 | Salaries | 65 000 |
| Total collected from accounts receivable | 100 000 | Repairs | 2 000 |
| | | Rates and taxes | 3 000 |
| | | Interest | 6 000 |
| | | Total payments to accounts payable | 130 000 |
| | | Insurance | 8 000 |
| | 250 000 | | 214 000 |

**1** Calculate the following:

**a** total sales for the period

**b** gross profit

   **c** salaries expense and accrued salaries
   **d** interest expense and accrued interest
   **e** insurance expense and prepaid insurance.

**2** What was the profit/(loss) for the period?

**3** Prepare the statement of financial position as at 31 December 2002.

## Problem 5.36 (Challenging) Calculating accrual information from cash information

The following information has been extracted from the accounts of PQR Ltd.

**PQR Ltd**

Statement of financial position as at 30 June 2001

| **Assets** | **$** | **$** | **Liabilities and shareholders' equity** | **$** |
|---|---|---|---|---|
| Cash | | 25 000 | Accounts payable | 19 000 |
| Accounts receivable | | 14 000 | Revenue received in advance | 8 000 |
| Inventory | | 32 000 | Accrued interest | 1 000 |
| Plant and equipment | 150 000 | | Loan | 25 000 |
| Accumulated depreciation | 40 000 | 110 000 | Share capital | 80 000 |
| | | | Retained profits | 48 000 |
| | | 181 000 | | 181 000 |

Cash receipts for the year ended 30 June 2002

| | $ |
|---|---|
| Cash sales | 92 000 |
| Receipts from accounts receivable | 385 000 |
| | 477 000 |

Cash payments for the year ended 30 June 2002

| | $ |
|---|---|
| Payments for accounts payable | 172 000 |
| Repayments of loan ($25 000) and interest ($2000) | 27 000 |
| Administrative expenses | 46 000 |
| Dividend payment | 31 000 |
| | 276 000 |

***Additional information:***

**a** Balances as at 30 June 2002:

| | |
|---|---|
| Inventory | $20 000 |
| Accounts receivable | $24 000 |

**b** Credit purchases of inventory totalled $176 000 for the year.

**c** The services relating to the revenue received in advance at 30 June 2001 were provided during the year.

**d** No additions or disposals of plant and equipment were made during the period. The depreciation rate is 20 per cent per annum. The straight-line method is used.

**e** Administrative expenses included a prepayment of $4000 for July 2002.

**f** Accrued interest on 30 June 2001 related to the loan which was repaid during the year. There is no accrued interest as at 30 June 2002.

*Required:*

1 Calculate total revenue for the year ended 30 June 2002.
2 List all expenses for the year (including dollar amounts).
3 Calculate the balance of cash as at 30 June 2002.
4 Provide a statement of financial position as at 30 June 2002.

## Problem 5.37 (Challenging) Conversion from cash to accrual basis

Temporary Help Pty Ltd is a company offering specialised executive services (for example, secretarial assistance, delivery of advertising, errands and shopping for gifts). The company's accounts have been kept on a cash basis, but its banker has asked that the accounting be changed to the accrual basis. Profit for 2002 on the cash basis was $147 000. Using the following figures (note the order of the years), calculate the company's 2002 profit on the accrual basis:

| | Assets | | Liabilities | |
|---|---|---|---|---|
| | 2002 $ | 2001 $ | 2002 $ | 2001 $ |
| Cash basis: | | | | |
| Current | 98 000 | 56 000 | 35 000 | 35 000 |
| Noncurrent | — | — | — | — |
| Accrual basis: | | | | |
| Current | 182 000 | 112 000 | 70 000 | 49 000 |
| Noncurrent | 21 000 | 28 000 | 14 000 | — |

## CASE 5A Woolworths Limited case

Refer to the extracts of the annual report of Woolworths Limited in appendix 2. All questions relate to the consolidated accounts.

1 Is there any indication of the following in the accounts:
   a prepayments?
   b unearned revenue?
   c accrued expenses?
   d accrued revenues?
2 After all closing entries had been posted, what would the trial balance at 24 June 2001 probably have looked like? (Hint: Look at statement of financial position items including the details in the notes.)
3 Why would Woolworths Limited use 24 June 2001 (25 June 2000) rather than 30 June as the financial year-end?
4 Provide an example from note 1 of the accounts of a cut-off decision that would have needed to be made.
5 What is the net book value for:
   a land and buildings?
   b plant and equipment?

**6** How were trade debtors valued in the accounts?

**7** How much in bad debts was written off during the year? How did this compare with the previous year?

**8** What would have been the journal entry to record bad debts?

**9** Did the provision for doubtful debts increase/decrease? By how much?

## CASE 5B Examine published financial statements

### Waterways Authority of NSW 1999–2000 annual report

#### Waterways' profile
#### What are Waterways' responsibilities?

The Waterways Authority is a NSW statutory authority created on 1 July 1995 under the *Ports Corporatisation and Waterways Management Act 1995*. The Authority reports, through our Chief Executive, to the Hon Carl Scully MP, NSW Minister for Transport and Minister for Roads.

Our organisation manages the commercial and recreational waterways of the State, with a view to achieving the highest possible standards of safety for all waterway users, the protection of the marine and foreshore environment and the provision of essential marine infrastructure.

The role of the Authority was expanded on 28 July 1999 with the transfer from the NSW Department of Transport of the Maritime Assets Division. This Division is responsible for managing assets that were previously owned by the Marine Ministerial Holding Corporation, a separate statutory body with no staff. These assets include foreshore lands and the seabeds of the major ports of Sydney, Botany Bay, Newcastle and Port Kembla, which during the year were formally transferred to the Waterways Authority.

This broadened role of the authority includes responsibility for:

- issue of licences and registrations for recreational boaters
- periodic survey of commercial vessels
- management of private moorings and commercial mooring sites
- installation and maintenance of navigation aids across the State
- promotion of safety on the water through education and communication programs throughout NSW
- leasing of marinas, jetties and wharves in Sydney Harbour and Botany Bay
- enforcement of marine safety and environmental legislation and regulations
- provision of a Sydney Harbour cleaning service
- provision of waterways infrastructure through the Waterways Asset Development and Management Program
- development and construction consent for structures over the waters of Sydney Harbour and Botany Bay
- administration of the beds of Sydney Harbour, Botany Bay, Newcastle and Port Kembla and wetland leases
- management of the regional ports of Eden and Yamba.

Referring to notes 18 and 23 from the financial statements of the Waterways Authority of New South Wales, shown below:

**1** Provide examples of accrual accounting adjustments.

**2** Explain each of the adjustments.

| | | | 2000 $000 | 1999 $000 |
|---|---|---|---|---|
| 18 | **Receivables** | | | |
| | **Current** | | | |
| | Trade debtors | | 328 | 73 |
| | Rental debtors | | 939 | 180 |
| | Payments in advance | | 151 | 363 |
| | Accrued income | | 1 723 | 2 |
| | Land sale receivables | | 2 100 | — |
| | Other | | 1 623 | 149 |
| | less: Provision for doubtful debts | | (88) | (8) |
| | | | 6 776 | 759 |
| | **Noncurrent** | | | |
| | Prepaid superannuation | (a) | 13 397 | 5 901 |
| | Land sale receivables | | 18 525 | — |
| | Walsh Bay Commissions receivable | | 1 960 | — |
| | | | 33 882 | 5 901 |
| 23 | Other liabilities | | | |
| | **Current** | | | |
| | Boating fees in advance | | 15 126 | 14 575 |
| | Rent in advance | | 6 413 | 1 137 |
| | Maritime tower purchase | | 2 909 | — |
| | Provision for workers' compensation | | 860 | — |
| | Provision for dividend | | 3 000 | — |
| | | | 28 308 | 15 712 |
| | **Noncurrent** | | | |
| | Boating fees in advance | (a) | 5 175 | 5 089 |
| | Maritime centre lease | (b) | 24 920 | — |
| | Provision for workers' compensation | (c) | 4 290 | — |
| | | | 34 385 | 5 089 |

a Boating fees in advance comprises repayments by customers for licences, registrations and moorings for the service component which will be provided by the Authority in the future.

b Maritime tower purchase represents the amounts owing on the purchase of the Maritime Centre building, purchased in 1989 for a period of 96 years with payments made over the first 25 years. Tenure is secured by a lease.

c Workers' compensation provision includes \$2.7 m for dust diseases of which \$0.3 m is current.

## Case 5C Accrual accounting

The following editorial appeared in the *Canberra Times*, 17 May 1999. (Thanks to Russell Craig for bringing it to my attention.)

### Accrual accounts worth the wait

Accrual accounting has been a long time coming for the federal Budget, but all the signs are that it has been not only worth the wait, but will improve with the passage of time.

Compared with the traditional cash accounting methods used until now, which record only actual financial flows in the form of revenue, outlays, borrowings and repayments, accrual accounting gives depth and complexity to the Commonwealth's yearly financial ledger.

It incorporates all assets and liabilities in a single snapshot, so that governments can include such formerly ignored factors as asset depreciation, risks and contingencies (such as, in the 1999–2000 Budget, the cost of possible litigation against the Commonwealth, or the as-yet-unquantifiable cost of providing a safe haven for Kosovar refugees) and liabilities like superannuation for Commonwealth public servants. It can do the latter because it deliberately records the super liability as it arises as individual public servants 'earn' or accrue their super year by year rather than when it is handed over, in the form of an actual lump-sum payment or pension, at the end of those public servants' period of service.

Instead of recording money in and money out, accrual accounting records outcomes (aims) and outputs (the things a government does to achieve those aims). The individual portfolio Budget statements, used to scrutinise estimates, and issued for the first time this year to coincide with the Budget papers, list in minute detail the outcomes (for example, an efficiently functioning Parliament, for the Department of Finance and Administration's ministerial and parliamentary services group) and the outputs, which will help achieve them. For example, it lists the percentage of calls to be answered within three rings; the number of inquiries to be dealt with within a week, and so on.

Accrual accounting is the prevailing system in the private sector, but has been largely resisted by governments (the Federal Government is only the third national government to adopt the system; the ACT Government began accrual accounting a few years ago). Perhaps the reluctance has something to do with the fact that accrual accounting is so identifiable as a private-sector creation. It is a comparatively recent trend for governments to think of themselves as mega-corporations, or to use the language of capitalist profit and loss to describe government activity. A cultural change has been involved from the grass roots up.

Then, too, there is the not inconsiderable work which is required to make the change-over from cash to accrual accounting. The 1999–2000 Federal Budget is the handiwork of a single year, but the preparations began years ago, even before the election of the Coalition in 1996.

The full impact in terms of scrutiny of the Budget probably won't be known for some time. Early evidence suggests that while greater openness is one of the system's main claims to fame, detail can probably be concealed within the broader Budget lines as easily as – or more easily than – it ever could be under cash accounting. And a degree of subjectivity will probably always be inevitable in certain calculations, such as the valuing of Commonwealth assets or the anticipation of the cost of litigation and compensation involving the Commonwealth.

While the system promises greater transparency and greater honesty in the long term no one should be too surprised if it takes a year or so for government to perfect accrual budgeting, and for those whose job it is to scrutinise the Budget to perfect their methods of observation.

(Source: *Canberra Times*, 17 May 1999, p. 8.)

1 Based on your reading of this briefing, how do you believe accrual accounting helps public sector managers better perform their duties than they could have under a cash accounting system?

2 The article refers to the 'not inconsiderable work which is required to make the change over from cash to accrual accounting'. Provide examples of this work.

3 Does cash accounting limit the capacity for public sector managers to manipulate results as easily as they might under an accrual based system?

## CASE 5D Bad debts

Below is an extract of an article published in the *Sydney Morning Herald*, 5–6 May 2001, page 45. It deals with bad debts.

### Bad loans fail to halt Westpac's progress

*Anthony Hughes*

A sharp rise in bad loans has hit Westpac Banking Corp's profit for the March half but the bank has dismissed suggestions a bigger problem lies ahead.

Cost-cutting and surging volumes of mortgage and credit card lending more than compensated for the 200 per cent rise in its bad debt charge, helping the bank to report a 13 per cent rise in interim net profit to $924 million, slightly less than the market expected.

The 30 c fully franked interim dividend, up 4 c, is payable July 6. Westpac shares fell 21 c to $12.82, underperforming its rivals.

Chief executive Dr David Morgan said the increased bad debt charge was more a reflection of 'dynamic provisioning', where the bank estimates likely bad debts, than actual losses.

Dr Morgan said he did not expect a major recession in the next nine months, beyond which it was too difficult to forecast. Subject to the changes in the economy, Westpac would report double-digit earnings per share growth for the full year, he said.

The bad debt charge jumped from $59 million to $176 million. Total impaired assets still represent only 0.6 per cent of the total loan book.

The provisioning included the bank's estimate of losses on the $245 million secured exposure to HIH Insurance, which is in provisional liquidation.

Another dampener on the result was a $7.5 million write-down to the bank's $45 million in e-procurement technology company Metiom.

***Required:***

1. Explain by the accounting equation the statement in the first sentence of the above article.
2. What do you believe is meant by 'dynamic provisioning' (fourth paragraph)?
3. How will the increase in the bad debt charge from $59 million to $176 million affect (a) net profit; (b) total assets?
4. What would be the uncertainties in the bank's estimate of $245 million losses on its exposure to HIH?
5. How would the information in the final paragraph affect the financial statements? (Note: This is a transaction you would have not previously seen but allows you to think creatively.)

## Note

1 The assistance of Elizabeth Carson in writing parts of this section is gratefully acknowledged.

# Appendix to chapter 5

# *Special journals, subsidiary ledgers and control accounts*

This appendix is written for students who require a more detailed knowledge of recording systems.

Before going on, let's remind ourselves of the accounting cycle, as summarised in figure A5.1.

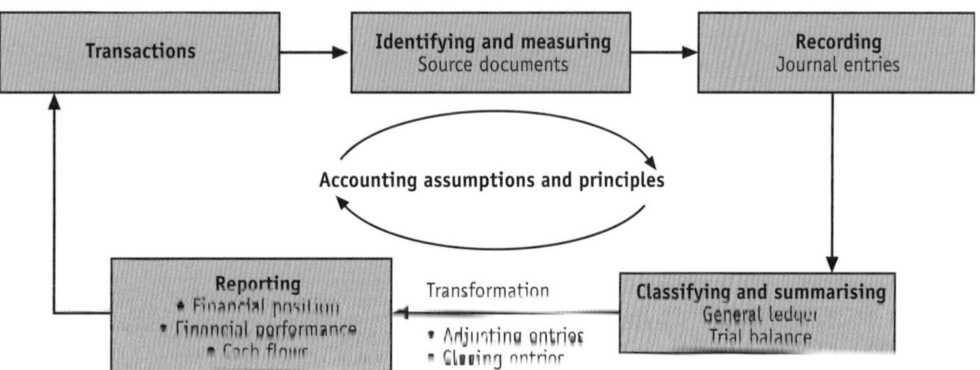


**Figure A5.1** The accounting cycle

To this point, we have assumed that the economic events captured in the accounting system are initially recorded in a general journal, then summarised through posting to the general ledger. Such a system is fine for a business with a small set of transactions. However, if you think back on the sorts of transactions you have already recorded and imagine a more complex business, you will have noticed that many of the transactions have common elements; for example, many transactions involve cash collections or payments. Given this feature, special systems can be put in place that allow a more efficient recording process for common transactions. These systems support and feed into the recording, classifying and summarising processes shown in figure A5.1.

Rather than all the accounting information being captured in one journal and posted to one ledger (or 'flat-file' database), a system of special journals and subsidiary ledgers can be used to streamline recording, storage and categorisation of data (similar to a relational database). Special journals are designed to allow easy recording of the most common transactions undertaken by a business, while subsidiary ledgers represent a detailed analysis of the information that is eventually transferred to a general ledger account.

In what follows, special journals and subsidiary ledgers are described in a manual framework to help you understand the relational nature of the databases used in a more sophisticated accounting system. Similar 'architecture' and processes are used in computerised systems. While many computerised accounting systems do not require the use of special journals, the journals can be produced by the system to provide summaries of transactions, if required.[1]

Let's briefly look at one example of how a common transaction for some businesses – credit sales – can be recorded in a system that uses special journals and subsidiary ledgers.

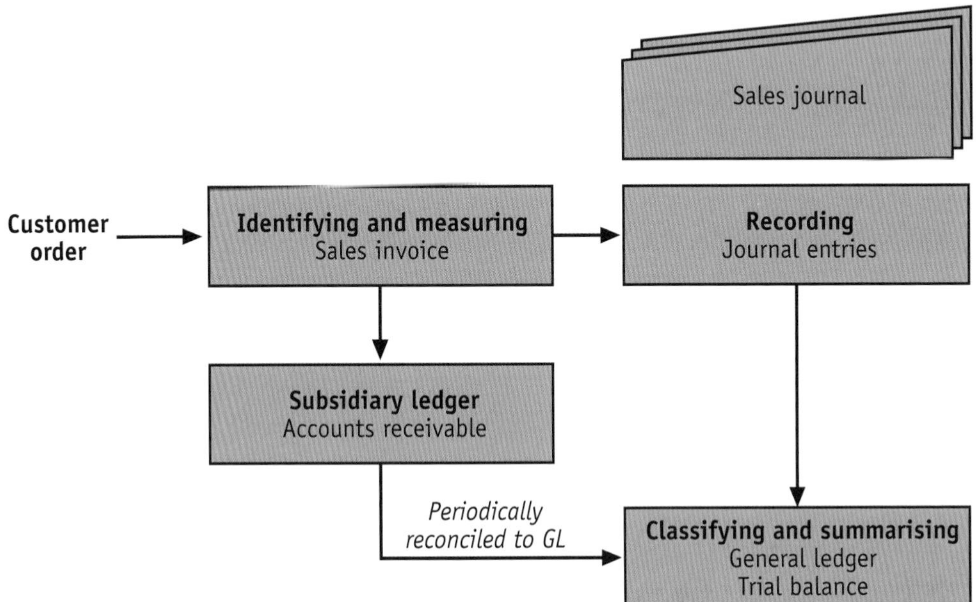


**Figure A5.2** Flow of information in accounting system using special journals and subsidiary ledgers

Figure A5.2 shows the receipt of an order from a customer who is allowed to buy from a business on credit. When the customer receives the product or service, a sales invoice is issued to the customer showing the product or service he or she bought, the amount owed and when it needs to be paid. The sales invoice becomes the source document that is used to record information in the accounting system. In this case, the business transaction is recorded in a special journal called a sales journal, because it is used to record all information about credit sales. At the same time, the customer's account is updated in the subsidiary ledger to show that he or she owes money to the business.

Periodically, information from the business's journals (including the sales journal) is transferred to the general ledger. This information is a summary of the more detailed records contained in the special journals and subsidiary ledgers.

Only a summary of all information needs to appear in the main accounting system if there are subsystems that contain more detailed records. In figure A5.2, a general ledger account called debtors (or accounts receivable) is supported by some form of detailed record showing how much each debtor owes the company and when he or she is expected to pay. This is the information contained in the subsidiary ledger. It is not much use knowing that you are owed $900 000 from debtors in total without knowing exactly who owes you what amounts and when you expect them to be received! For example, the $900 000 in the general ledger may be made up of the following three accounts in the subsidiary debtors ledger: M. Andrews $100 000; T. Blake $300 000; and A. Crawford $500 000. Whenever one of these customers buys from the business on credit, that transaction is recorded in the sales journal and the information is used to update the subsidiary ledger.

Refer back to the information flow diagrams at figures A5.1 and A5.2 as you learn more about special journals and subsidiary ledgers.

## A5.1 Prime entry records: special journals

The most common transactions undertaken by a business can be recorded in special journals. Typically, special journals are established to record the following transactions:

| **Special journal** | **Transactions recorded** |
|---|---|
| Sales | Credit sales of inventory |
| Purchases | Credit purchases of inventory |
| Cash receipts | All cash inflows (including cash sales) |
| Cash payments journal | All cash outflows (including cash purchases) |

In a special journal, each entry represents a transaction that belongs to the same class as others in the same journal. These special journals are used in addition to a general journal. Transactions that are not recorded in a special journal are recorded in a general journal (for example, depreciation, adjustments for prepayments and other accruals).

Apart from recording efficiency, other advantages of special journals are:

- Amounts can be posted from special journals to the general ledger as totals rather than as individual journal entries.
- More than one user can update the accounting system, because it consists of a number of related subsystems. For example, the general ledger, debtors subsidiary ledger and inventory subsidiary ledger could be updated by different individuals.
- The common nature of transactions eliminates the need for narrations.
- Information such as invoice or receipt number may be recorded in special columns provided for the purpose.
- Additional information can be recorded in a particular journal for convenience because it is available from the source document evidencing the transaction. For example, discount expense is generally recorded in the cash receipts journal because it is obtained from the duplicate receipt (which also shows the net amount of cash received).

## A5.2 Subsidiary ledgers and control accounts

The most common way of accommodating the need for detailed records in the accounting system, without grossly expanding the number of separate accounts in the general ledger, is to use subsidiary ledgers and control accounts. As already mentioned, a subsidiary ledger is a set of ledger accounts that collectively represents a detailed analysis of one general ledger account classification. The relevant ledger account in the general ledger is known as a control account. The accuracy of the detailed accounts in the subsidiary ledger can be periodically checked against the aggregate data and balance contained in the control account.

Subsidiary ledgers do not form part of the general ledger. They are separate ledgers that show more detail about a general ledger account (such as debtors).

Examples of general ledger accounts that have subsidiary ledgers are:

- debtors/accounts receivable: a separate account for each debtor
- creditors/accounts payable: a separate account for each creditor
- property, plant and equipment: separate records of each piece of property, plant and equipment; it is often called an asset register
- raw materials inventory: separate records of each type of raw material held
- finished goods inventory: separate records of each type of finished good held.

In each of these examples, the same principle applies. Every entry made to an account in the subsidiary ledger is contained within an aggregate amount in a general ledger control account. It follows that the total of all debit entries made to individual accounts in the subsidiary ledger must be equal to the debits made to the control account. Similarly, all credit entries made will be the same, in aggregate, between the subsidiary ledger and the control account. From this it follows that, at any time, when all required entries have been made in both records, the total of the balance appearing in the accounts in the subsidiary ledger should equal the balance appearing in the control account in the general ledger. If these amounts do not agree, it signals errors in one or both records.

Apart from providing a check on accuracy, subsidiary ledgers enable any desired amount of detail to be maintained to explain the composition of a selected general ledger account, without overloading that ledger. In some cases, subsidiary ledger accounts can include statistical data and written comments as well as dollar values. For example, the subsidiary ledger for equipment will include information beyond original cost and accumulated depreciation. It is likely to also include date of purchase, location in the organisation (a Burwood factory, for example), an identification number (which is also placed on the equipment for internal control purposes) and, possibly, details of maintenance, warranty and so on.

## A5.3 Trade discount and cash discount

Before illustrating the recording process using special journals and subsidiary ledgers, it is desirable to distinguish between two forms of discount, *trade discount* and *cash discount*. Each represents a reduction in the amount that a customer ultimately pays a vendor for goods or services supplied, but the two types differ in purpose and in the way they are customarily recorded in accounting systems.

### Trade discount

Trade discount, where compatible with trade practices legislation, is a means of adjusting the actual price charged to a customer from a standard 'list price'. Usually, the amount of reduction depends on the category of customer or their normal volume of business. For example, a manufacturer may sell at list price to the general public, allow a discount of 40 per cent off list price to retailers and a discount of 55 per cent to wholesalers. Although the amount of such discount is occasionally recorded in the books of account, most enterprises, whether receiving or giving the discount, record only the net amount of the transaction. This is because the effect of a trade discount is merely to set an actual price for the transaction.

### Cash discount

A cash discount, by contrast, is a conditional adjustment after determination of the actual selling price at which the transaction takes place. It is an incentive for prompt settlement of debts and is allowed only if there is compliance with payment terms. It is not, therefore, a change in the price of the original sales transaction, and is generally recorded as an additional transaction.

A common arrangement is to extend credit terms such as 2.5/10, n/30. This means that a discount of 2.5 per cent may be deducted from the amount due, if payment is made within 10 days; otherwise, the net amount (after adjusting for any trade discount) is payable within 30 days. Thus, if sales totalling $400 were made to a particular customer during April, on the above terms, $10 could be deducted from the payment, if settlement were made in the discount period. In the first instance, the gross selling price is recorded by both parties. If discount is allowed, it is commonly recorded in a discount allowed expense column in the cash receipts journal of the seller and in a discount received (revenue) column in the cash payments journal of the purchaser.

## A5.4 Operation of special journals and subsidiary ledgers

To illustrate the operation of accounting systems using special journals and subsidiary ledgers, we will examine their operation for the following transactions:

- credit sales
- credit purchases
- cash receipts
- cash payments.

### Sales

Exhibit A5.1 shows an extract from a sales journal in a business that uses the perpetual method to record inventory:

**EXHIBIT A5.1 Sales journal**

**Example**

**Sales journal** — **Page S1**

| Date 2002 | | Invoice No. | Customer | Post ref. | Cost of goods sold | Accounts receivable |
|---|---|---|---|---|---|---|
| Jul | 5 | 0001 | M. Andrews | ✓ | 50 000 | 100 000 |
| | 5 | 0002 | T. Blake | ✓ | 150 000 | 300 000 |
| | 20 | 0003 | A. Crawford | ✓ | 250 000 | 500 000 |
| | | | | | 450 000 | 900 000 |
| | | | | | (104/400) | (102/350) |

Had each of the credit sales been recorded in a general journal, each would have appeared as:

| | $ | & |
|---|---|---|
| DR Accounts receivable | XX | |
| CR Sales revenue | | XX |
| DR COGS | YY | |
| CR Inventory | | YY |

The purpose of special journals is to eliminate the need for such detailed recording in a general journal and the general ledger. Only the total for a suitable period (typically a month in a manual system) is posted to the general ledger. The general ledger account into which the total is posted is called a control account because aggregate amounts are posted to it. These totals are referenced in the general ledger account to the source of the information; in this case, the sales journal. If the sales journal in our example represents all the credit sales for the period, only the total $900 000 would be debited to accounts receivable (account 102) and credited to sales revenue (account 350) and $450 000 debited to COGS (account 104) and credited to inventory (account 400). The amounts are posted directly from the sales journal; there is no need to record the information again in a general journal.

A subsidiary ledger account might be established for each customer who buys on credit. The individual accounts in the debtors' ledger can be kept up to date by posting each line of the sales journal to the appropriate account in the subsidiary ledger. For example, the first entry in the sales journal shown earlier is recorded in the subsidiary ledger as a debit to the account of M. Andrews, the second to T. Blake and the third to A. Crawford. Part of this process is illustrated at exhibit A5.2: note that the accounts for T. Blake and A. Crawford are not shown, but would be updated in a similar manner. The use of the posting reference S1 in the ledger accounts indicates that the information in these accounts comes from page S1 of the sales journal. The tick in the posting reference column of the sales journal indicates that the amount has been posted to the subsidiary ledger.

At the end of the period, the total of the subsidiary ledgers can be checked against the balance of the accounts receivable control account. That is, if we add up the balance in the accounts for Andrews, Blake and Crawford, it should agree with the balance of the accounts receivable control account.

## Purchases

In its simplest form, the purchases journal is used only for recording the acquisition on credit of goods that are intended for resale. The relevant source document is the purchase invoice from the supplier, which is matched against the delivery docket and a copy of the official purchase order to ensure that the goods have been delivered in a satisfactory condition and that the agreed price has been charged.

Assume that the following credit purchases of furniture for resale were made during July 2002:

| **2002** | | | **$** |
|---|---|---|---|
| Jul | 2 | P. Renton | 1 400 |
| | 4 | J. Quincy | 320 |
| | 18 | R. Lemon | 3 500 |

The purchases journal is illustrated at exhibit A5.3.

## EXHIBIT A5.2 Credit sales

### Recording credit sales in a sales journal and posting to subsidiary and general ledgers

**Sales journal**

| Date 2002 | | Invoice no. | Customers | Post ref. | Cost of goods sold | Accounts receivable |
|---|---|---|---|---|---|---|
| Jul | 5 | 0001 | M. Andrews | ✓ | 50 000 | 100 000 |
| | 5 | 0002 | T. Blake | ✓ | 150 000 | 300 000 |
| | 20 | 0003 | A. Crawford | ✓ | 250 000 | 500 000 |
| | | | | | 450 000 | 900 000 |
| | | | | | (104/400) | (102/350) |

Post daily (Accounts receivable 100 000 → M. Andrews, Debit)

Post monthly (totals → General ledger accounts)

**Accounts receivable subsidiary ledger**

M. Andrews

| Date | Post ref. | Debit | Credit | Balance |
|---|---|---|---|---|
| Jul 5 | S1 | 100 000 | | 100 000 DR |

**General ledger**

Account receivable control 102

| Date | Post ref. | Debit | Credit | Balance |
|---|---|---|---|---|
| Jul 31 | S1 | 900 000 | | 900 000 DR |

Sales 350

| Date | Post ref. | Debit | Credit | Balance |
|---|---|---|---|---|
| Jul 31 | S1 | | 900 000 | 900 000 CR |

Cost of goods sold 104

| Date | Post ref. | Debit | Credit | Balance |
|---|---|---|---|---|
| Jul 31 | S1 | 450 000 | | 450 000 DR |

Inventory control 400

| Date | Post Ref. | Debit | Credit | Balance |
|---|---|---|---|---|
| | | 600 000 | | 600 000 DR |
| Jul 31 | S1 | | 450 000 | 50 000 DR |

In this case, note that P. Renton and J. Quincy expect payment within 30 days (their payment terms are n30) and no discount is available for early payment. R. Lemon allows a discount of 2 per cent if payment is received within 10 days; otherwise, the net amount is expected within 30 days of purchase. Because we're not certain that payment will be made within the discount period, the full amount owing is recorded in the journal, not 98 per cent of $3500. If we do qualify for the discount, our obligation of $3500 is satisfied and the discount received ($70) adjusts the amount of cash eventually paid to R. Lemon ($3430).

**EXHIBIT A5.3 Credit purchases**

**Recording credit purchases in a purchases journal and posting to subsidiary and general ledgers**

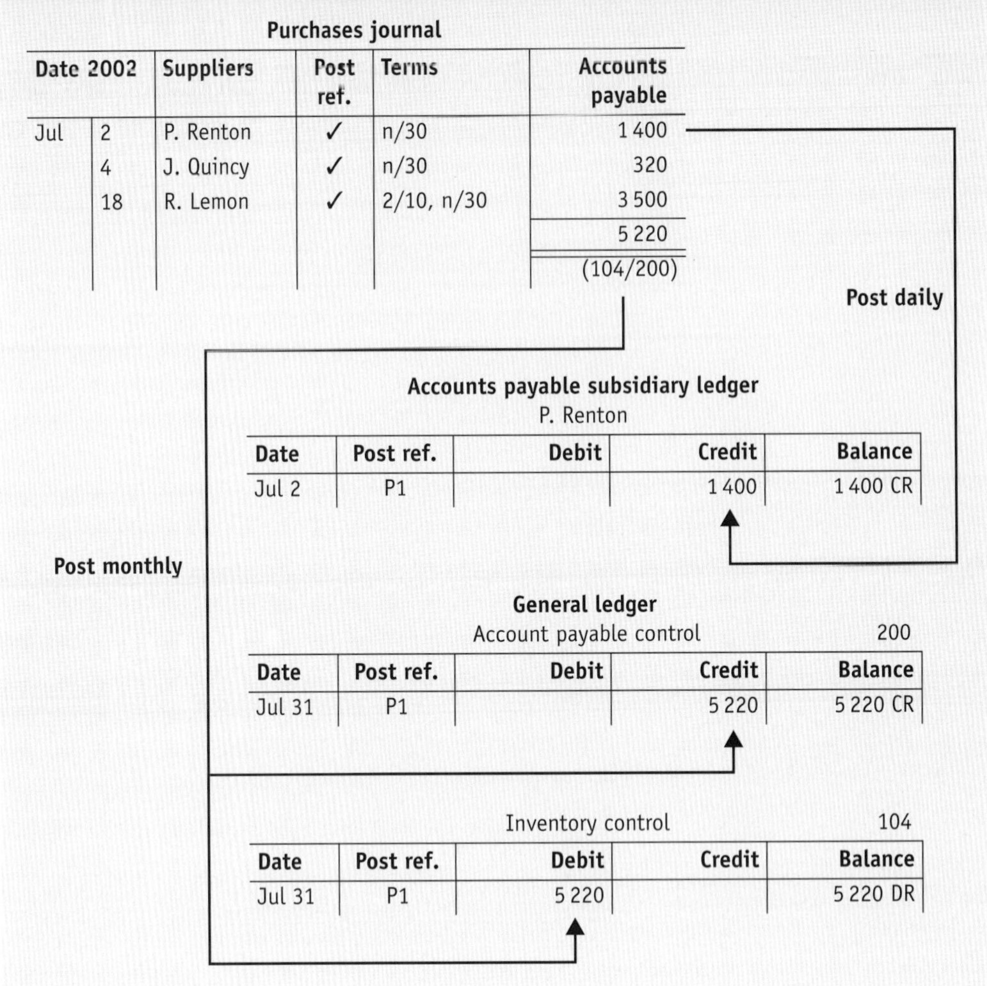

**Purchases journal**

| Date 2002 | | Suppliers | Post ref. | Terms | Accounts payable |
|---|---|---|---|---|---|
| Jul | 2 | P. Renton | ✓ | n/30 | 1 400 |
| | 4 | J. Quincy | ✓ | n/30 | 320 |
| | 18 | R. Lemon | ✓ | 2/10, n/30 | 3 500 |
| | | | | | 5 220 |
| | | | | | (104/200) |

**Accounts payable subsidiary ledger**

P. Renton

| Date | Post ref. | Debit | Credit | Balance |
|---|---|---|---|---|
| Jul 2 | P1 | | 1 400 | 1 400 CR |

**General ledger**

Account payable control 200

| Date | Post ref. | Debit | Credit | Balance |
|---|---|---|---|---|
| Jul 31 | P1 | | 5 220 | 5 220 CR |

Inventory control 104

| Date | Post ref. | Debit | Credit | Balance |
|---|---|---|---|---|
| Jul 31 | P1 | 5 220 | | 5 220 DR |



As in the case of the sales journal, subsidiary ledgers are updated each day for each creditor and for each item of inventory. In exhibit A5.3, only the account of P. Renton is shown; a similar process would be followed to update the accounts of J. Quincy and R. Lemon in the subsidiary ledger. The inventory subsidiary ledger is not shown.

At the end of the period, the inventory control account in the general ledger is debited with the total of $5220 and the creditors account is correspondingly credited. Alternative treatments for the recording of inventories are discussed in chapter 7.

Credit transactions involving the acquisition of fixed assets or items to be charged to expense accounts, such as repairs and maintenance and printing and stationery, are often recorded in a general journal. However, the above purchases journal can easily be expanded to include columns for other items, if they occur frequently.

## Cash receipts

The source document providing evidence of a cash receipt is usually a duplicate of the receipt given to a customer to acknowledge payment. Alternatively, a list of cheques

**EXHIBIT A5.4** Cash receipts

**Recording cash receipts in a cash receipts journal and posting to subsidiary and general ledgers**

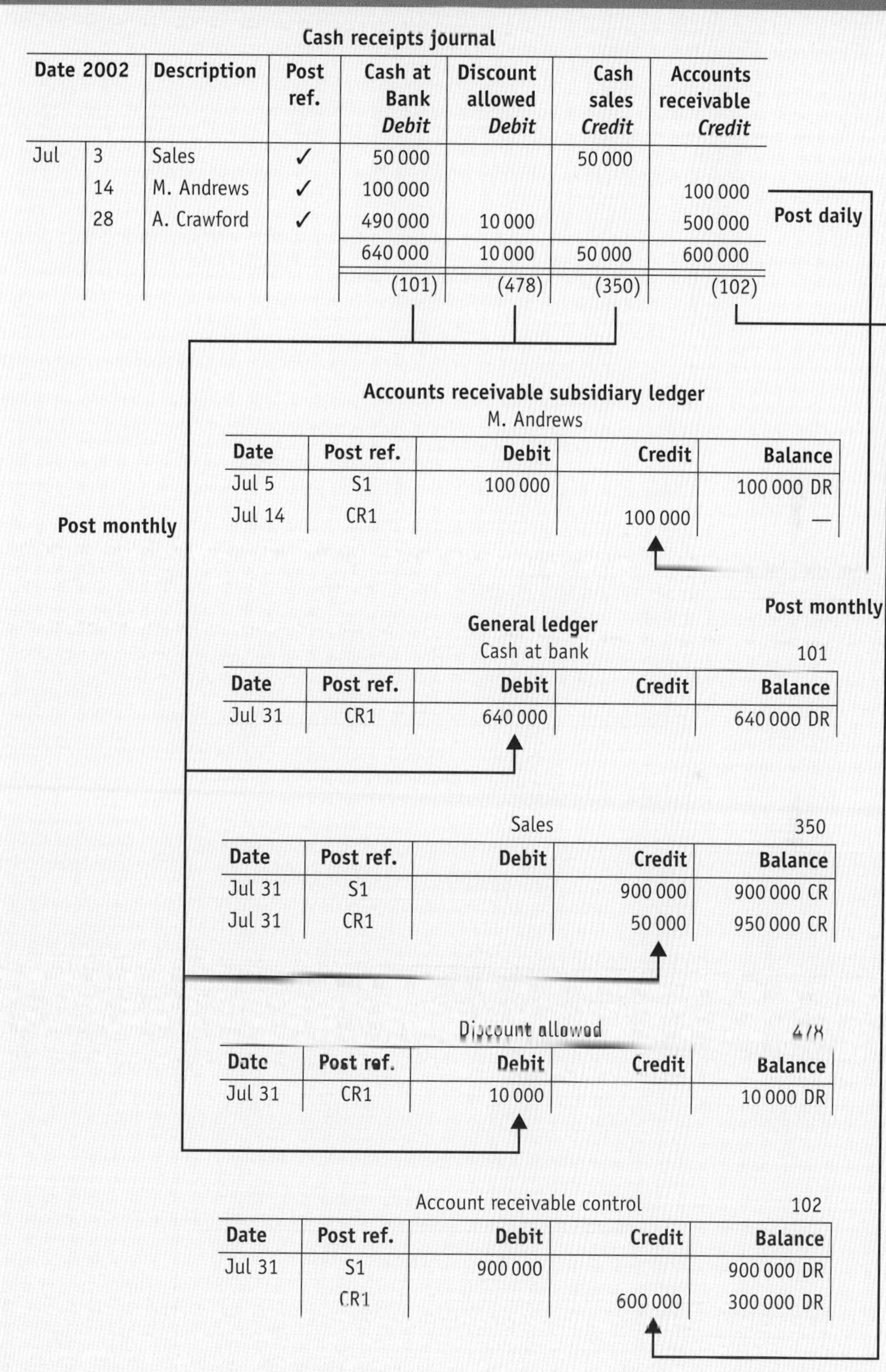

**Cash receipts journal**

| Date 2002 | | Description | Post ref. | Cash at Bank *Debit* | Discount allowed *Debit* | Cash sales *Credit* | Accounts receivable *Credit* |
|---|---|---|---|---|---|---|---|
| Jul | 3 | Sales | ✓ | 50 000 | | 50 000 | |
| | 14 | M. Andrews | ✓ | 100 000 | | | 100 000 |
| | 28 | A. Crawford | ✓ | 490 000 | 10 000 | | 500 000 |
| | | | | 640 000 | 10 000 | 50 000 | 600 000 |
| | | | | (101) | (478) | (350) | (102) |



**Accounts receivable subsidiary ledger**

M. Andrews

| Date | Post ref. | Debit | Credit | Balance |
|---|---|---|---|---|
| Jul 5 | S1 | 100 000 | | 100 000 DR |
| Jul 14 | CR1 | | 100 000 | — |

**General ledger**

Cash at bank 101

| Date | Post ref. | Debit | Credit | Balance |
|---|---|---|---|---|
| Jul 31 | CR1 | 640 000 | | 640 000 DR |

Sales 350

| Date | Post ref. | Debit | Credit | Balance |
|---|---|---|---|---|
| Jul 31 | S1 | | 900 000 | 900 000 CR |
| Jul 31 | CR1 | | 50 000 | 950 000 CR |

Discount allowed 478

| Date | Post ref. | Debit | Credit | Balance |
|---|---|---|---|---|
| Jul 31 | CR1 | 10 000 | | 10 000 DR |

Account receivable control 102

| Date | Post ref. | Debit | Credit | Balance |
|---|---|---|---|---|
| Jul 31 | S1 | 900 000 | | 900 000 DR |
| | CR1 | | 600 000 | 300 000 DR |

received or a direct deposit recorded on a bank account statement can serve as the source document.

A cash receipts journal is designed to meet the specific needs of an enterprise, so analysis columns are created for the types of cash inflow that occur most frequently. In most businesses, these are likely to include payments received from debtors and, possibly, cash sales. In addition to specific analysis columns, there is also a need for a sundry or miscellaneous column for cash receipts not otherwise identified by a specific column that represents a particular general ledger account. Examples of sundry cash receipts include proceeds from sale of fixed assets, refunds by creditors and new capital or mortgage funding. If a cash discount is allowed to debtors, a discount expense column is typically included in the cash receipts journal.

Exhibit A5.4 illustrates the process of recording and posting information about cash receipts. In contrast to the sales and purchases journals, separate columns are used to represent the debit and credit sides of transactions.

The July 3 entry represents a cash sale. In this case, the debit and credit amounts are equal. The next two entries represent the receipt of amounts owing from customers. These amounts were previously recorded in the sales journal. Assuming that we offer discount terms of 2/10, n30, A. Crawford qualifies for a discount and only pays $490 000 of the $500 000 owing; the balance is a financial expense of the business known as discount allowed.

No sundry accounts were affected by cash receipts during the period. If there had been, each item would be individually posted to the relevant general ledger account. The column total can't be posted because the amount represents the impact of transactions on a number of general ledger accounts.

In addition to the postings to the general ledger, each item appearing in the debtors column is posted as a credit to the account of the particular debtor in the debtors' subsidiary ledger. Note that the account for A. Crawford is not shown in the subsidiary ledger.

## Cash payments

The source document for cash payments is usually a duplicate of a cheque or a cheque butt. There is usually supporting evidence such as a statement and invoices from creditors, a receipt issued by the recipient or a payroll analysis certified as correct by a responsible staff member. The bank statement provides evidence of the amount of interest charged on any overdraft, together with information about other bank charges and fees.

In its simplest form, the cash payments journal comprises one column in which are listed the amounts of the cheques drawn by the business against its bank account. However, to minimise postings and to provide an analysis of payments, separate columns may be provided to record entries affecting those ledger accounts frequently involved. A sundry or miscellaneous column is necessary for those amounts which are to be posted to accounts for which there is no specific analysis column.

In the cash payments journal illustrated at exhibit A5.5, the amount of each payment is recorded in the cash at bank column and then entered, according to the nature of the payment, either in one of the analysis columns or divided over more than one column. For payments to creditors, the amount paid is entered into the bank column and any discount received is entered in the discount received column. The total of these two amounts is then entered in the creditors (accounts payable) column: this is the total amount by which accounts payable has decreased. The individual names of creditors are also included so the entry can be used to update the creditors' subsidiary ledger. Thus, when the journal is totalled at the end of each period, the aggregate of the bank and discount revenue columns should equal the sum of the totals of all the analysis columns, including the sundry column. This

**EXHIBIT A5.5** Cash payments

**Recording cash payments in a cash payments journal and posting to subsidiary and general ledgers**

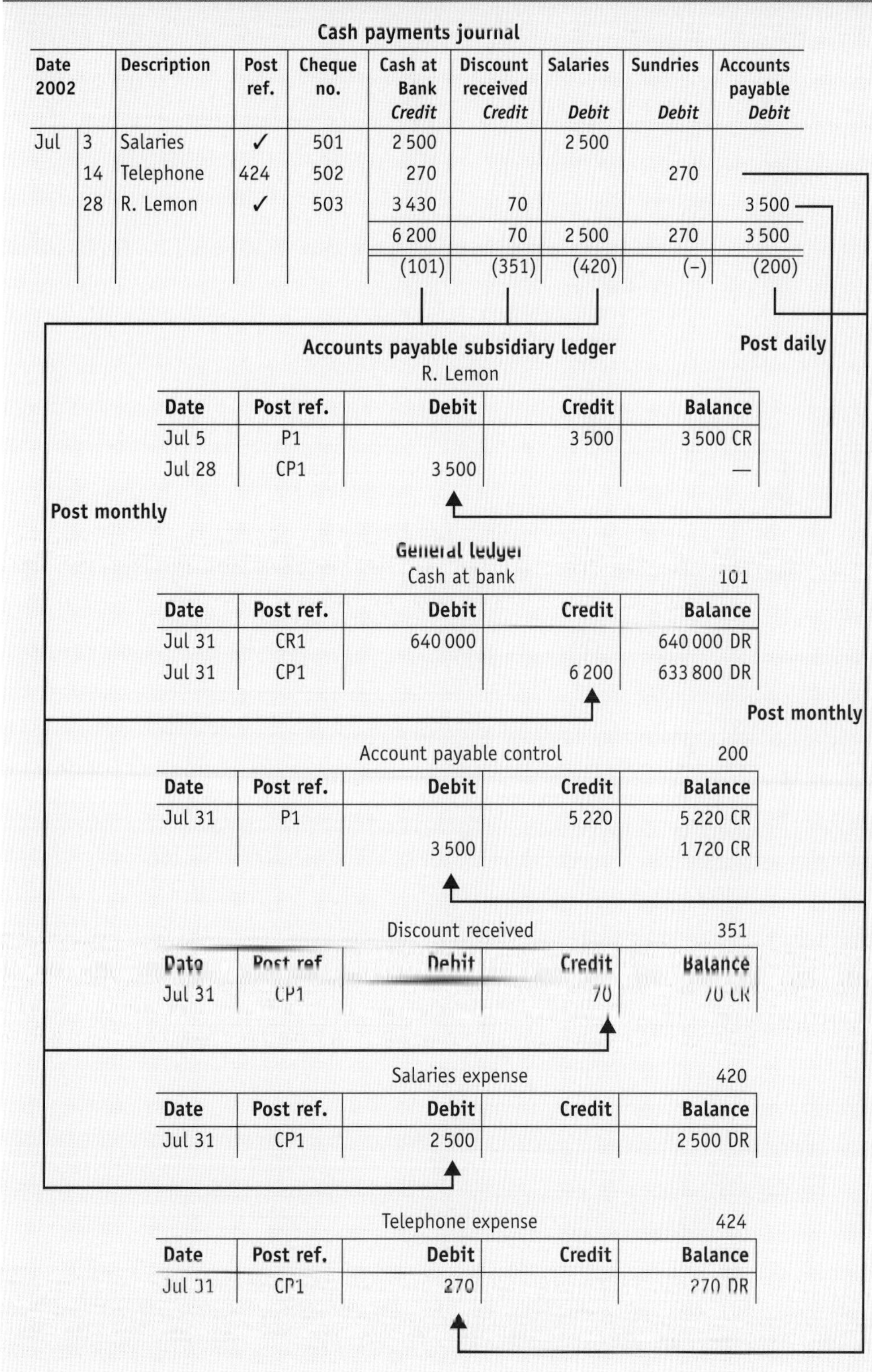

**Cash payments journal**

| Date 2002 | | Description | Post ref. | Cheque no. | Cash at Bank *Credit* | Discount received *Credit* | Salaries *Debit* | Sundries *Debit* | Accounts payable *Debit* |
|---|---|---|---|---|---|---|---|---|---|
| Jul | 3 | Salaries | ✓ | 501 | 2 500 | | 2 500 | | |
| | 14 | Telephone | 424 | 502 | 270 | | | 270 | |
| | 28 | R. Lemon | ✓ | 503 | 3 430 | 70 | | | 3 500 |
| | | | | | 6 200 | 70 | 2 500 | 270 | 3 500 |
| | | | | | (101) | (351) | (420) | (–) | (200) |



**Accounts payable subsidiary ledger**

R. Lemon

| Date | Post ref. | Debit | Credit | Balance |
|---|---|---|---|---|
| Jul 5 | P1 | | 3 500 | 3 500 CR |
| Jul 28 | CP1 | 3 500 | | — |

**General ledger**

Cash at bank 101

| Date | Post ref. | Debit | Credit | Balance |
|---|---|---|---|---|
| Jul 31 | CR1 | 640 000 | | 640 000 DR |
| Jul 31 | CP1 | | 6 200 | 633 800 DR |

Account payable control 200

| Date | Post ref. | Debit | Credit | Balance |
|---|---|---|---|---|
| Jul 31 | P1 | | 5 220 | 5 220 CR |
| | | 3 500 | | 1 720 CR |

Discount received 351

| Date | Post ref. | Debit | Credit | Balance |
|---|---|---|---|---|
| Jul 31 | CP1 | | 70 | 70 CR |

Salaries expense 420

| Date | Post ref. | Debit | Credit | Balance |
|---|---|---|---|---|
| Jul 31 | CP1 | 2 500 | | 2 500 DR |

Telephone expense 424

| Date | Post ref. | Debit | Credit | Balance |
|---|---|---|---|---|
| Jul 31 | CP1 | 270 | | 270 DR |

reflects the double-entry analysis of cash payments, which in all cases involves a credit to bank or discount revenue and a corresponding debit to some other account.

In this case, postings to the general ledger occur as follows:

1 Debit each account for which there is a specific analysis column with the total of that column.
2 Debit each account for which there is an individual entry in the sundry column with the amount of that entry. Do not post the total of the sundry column.
3 Credit bank with the total of the bank column.
4 Credit the discount received account for the amount of the discount received.

It should be noted that it makes no difference in the double-entry system whether bank is an asset or a liability (because it is in overdraft). In either case, a cash payment is a credit because it either reduces the bank asset or increases the bank overdraft liability.

In general, it is desirable in all books of prime entry (journals) to provide a reference to the source document for each entry. In the cash payments journal, this is usually done by recording the cheque number associated with each payment. This also facilitates preparation of bank reconciliation statements (covered in chapter 6).

In addition to the postings to the general ledger made at the end of the period, each individual item in the creditors column will be posted as a debit to the relevant individual creditor's account in the creditors' ledger.

## A5.5 Role of general journal and general ledger

Most of an organisation's transactions are recorded in special journals. There is, however, still a role for a general journal. A general journal is used to record a number of important transactions; for example:

- sales and purchase returns
- credit transactions other than those related to inventory, such as purchase of equipment
- adjusting entries
- closing entries.

As we have already seen, each entry in a general journal is individually posted to the appropriate account in the general ledger.

At the end of a period, all financial information will be posted in the general ledger, either as an individual entry sourced from a general journal (or from a sundry column in a special journal) or in aggregate form from the columns of the various special journals.

Once all financial information has been posted to the general ledger, the reporting process represented in figure A5.1 can begin and the accounting cycle can start again.

## A5.6 Homework and discussion to develop understanding

### Discussion questions

1 What are the purposes served by special purpose journals? What control information could more readily be made available to management as a result of their use?
2 What considerations determine whether a specialised journal should be brought into use rather than placing entries in the general journal? Is the need for a general journal ever eliminated?

3 On what basis should selection be made of the special analysis columns to be included in the cash payments journal?

4 Why should the sale of a fixed asset not be recorded in a simple sales journal?

5 What specialised journal handles the following types of transactions?

   a Cash sales

   b Credit sales

   c Receipts from debtors

   d Payments to creditors

   e Cash purchases

   f Credit purchases.

6 What is the purpose of a subsidiary ledger?

7 What are the advantages of a subsidiary ledger?

8 If a customer's account in the debtors ledger shows a credit balance, does this necessarily indicate that an error has been made?

9 Does the double-entry principle of an equal value of debits and credits in the system cease to apply when subsidiary ledgers are being employed?

10 'Subsidiary ledgers involve unnecessary duplication, increase the opportunity for error and involve a breach of the double-entry principle. Under no circumstances can their use be justified.' Comment critically.

## Problem A5.1 Preparation of control accounts

Smithers Pty Ltd, a manufacturer, maintains subsidiary ledgers for creditors and debtors. At 30 June 2002, the total amount owing to the business by trade debtors amounted to $4850 and the total amount owing by the business to its suppliers amounted to $3976.

The following is a summary of the transactions for the month of July 2002.

| | $ |
|---|---|
| Credit sales | 8 626 |
| Cash sales | 2 374 |
| Credit purchases | 6 945 |
| Cash received from debtors | 9 253 |
| Cash paid to creditors | 6 575 |
| Cash purchases | 1 600 |
| Promissory notes from customers | 420 |
| Discount received from creditors | 56 |
| Discount allowed to debtors | 78 |
| Creditors charged interest on overdue accounts | 25 |
| Freight paid and charged to debtors | 22 |

You are required to prepare the debtors and creditors control accounts as they would appear in the general ledger, and bring down the balances as at 31 July 2002. Disregard any transactions that do not relate to either of these accounts.

## Problem A5.2 Reconciliation of subsidiary ledgers with control accounts

M. King Pty Ltd, wholesaler, maintains subsidiary ledgers for debtors and creditors. The general ledger trial balance at 1 January 2003 is as set out below.

**M. King Pty Ltd**
Trial balance
as at 1 January 2003

| | $ | DR $ | CR $ |
|---|---|---|---|
| Share capital | | | 20 000 |
| Creditors: | | | |
| Adler | 1 000 | | |
| Barnes | 800 | | 1 800 |
| Mortgage loan | | | 10 000 |
| Bank | | 2 000 | |
| Debtors: | | | |
| Xavier | 400 | | |
| Young | 800 | | |
| Zoeller | 900 | 2 100 | |
| Inventory | | 4 000 | |
| Premises | | 18 000 | |
| Fixtures and fittings | | 5 700 | |
| | | **31 800** | **31 800** |

Transactions for the month of January

**Sales journal**

| | Sales $ | COGS $ |
|---|---|---|
| Young | 300 | 100 |
| Zoeller | 600 | 300 |
| Xavier | 700 | 350 |
| | 1 600 | 750 |

**Purchases journal**

| | $ |
|---|---|
| Barnes | 1 600 |
| Adler | 5 000 |
| | 6 600 |

**Cash receipts journal**

| | Debtors $ | Sundry $ | Bank $ |
|---|---|---|---|
| Rent | | 3 000 | 3 000 |
| Young | 800 | | 800 |
| Zoeller | 300 | | 300 |
| Dividends | | 4 000 | 4 000 |
| Xavier | 400 | | 400 |
| | 1 500 | 7 000 | 8 500 |

**Cash payments journal**

| | Debtors $ | Sundry $ | Bank $ |
|---|---|---|---|
| Salaries expense | | 700 | 700 |
| Barnes | 800 | | 800 |
| Rent expense | | 400 | 400 |
| Adler | 600 | | 600 |
| | 1 400 | 1 100 | 2 500 |

*Required:*

1 Post from the journals to the general ledger and to the debtors and creditors subsidiary ledgers.

2 Prepare supporting schedules of debtors and creditors at 31 January 2003 and agree with the balances in the control accounts.

## Problem A5.3 Specialised journals and subsidiary ledgers

Jupiter Pty Ltd uses multicolumn cash receipts and cash payments journals, and maintains control accounts for accounts receivable and accounts payable, supported by subsidiary ledgers. Balances in the subsidiary ledgers at 1 June 2002 were as follows:

| Accounts receivable | | Accounts payable | |
|---|---|---|---|
| | $ | | $ |
| Milky way | 3 000 | Venus | 6 000 |
| Mars | 14 000 | Mercury | 10 000 |
| Constellation | 10 000 | Sun | 6 000 |

During June 2002, the following amounts were received and paid:

| | | |
|---|---|---|
| Jun | 2 | Paid Venus [illegible] |
| | 3 | Milky Way paid an amount owing of $1100 less $30 discount. |
| | 8 | Cash sales, $500. |
| | 10 | Paid an amount owing to Sun of $4000 less $40 discount. |
| | 15 | Mars paid $7000 and was allowed $100 discount. |
| | 16 | Purchased goods for cash, $3000. |
| | 29 | Constellation paid $8000 less $200 discount. |
| | 30 | Paid Mercury $5000, discount of $200 was lost. |

*Required:*

Write up the cash receipts and cash payments journals. Use separate columns for bank, discount allowed, accounts receivable, cash sales, discount received, accounts payable and (cash) purchases. Post from those journals to both general and subsidiary ledgers, and prepare schedules of accounts receivable and accounts payable as at 30 June 2002.

## Problem A5.4 Preparation of control accounts

Prepare debtors and creditors control accounts for the year commencing 1 July 2002 from the following information:

| **Balances at 1 July 2002:** | |
|---|---|
| | $ |
| Debtors control | 15 425 |
| Creditors control | 9 870 |

| **Summary of transactions to 30 June 2003:** | |
|---|---|
| | $ |
| Credit sales | 101 700 |
| Cash sales | 3 540 |

| | |
|---|---:|
| Credit purchases | 71 620 |
| Cash purchases | 3 215 |
| Cash paid to creditors | 42 280 |
| Discount allowed by suppliers | 560 |
| Discount given to debtors | 725 |
| Cash received from debtors | 61 590 |

## Problem A5.5 Subsidiary ledgers and control accounts

James Stewart owns a general store in a country town. He keeps two subsidiary ledgers (an accounts receivable ledger and an accounts payable ledger) and a general ledger.

**Balances in the subsidiary ledgers as at 31 March 2002 were as follows:**

| Accounts receivable | $ | Accounts payable | $ |
|---|---:|---|---:|
| Brown | 900 | Blue | 580 |
| Green | 700 | Red | 1 500 |
| White | 460 | | 2 080 |
| | 2 060 | | |

**Transactions for the month of April 2002**

| Sales journal | | | | Purchases journal | | | |
|---|---|---|---:|---|---|---|---:|
| **Date** | | **Particulars** | **$** | **Date** | | **Particulars** | **$** |
| 2002 | | | | | | | |
| April | 2 | White | 1 240 | April | 7 | Red | 2 000 |
| | 13 | Brown | 2 400 | | 16 | Blue | 1 120 |
| | 16 | Sage | 1 160 | | 20 | Sage | 200 |
| | 20 | Ruby | 1 700 | | 22 | Grey | 750 |
| | | | 6 500 | | | | 4 070 |

**Cash receipts journal** **Page 35**

| Date | | Particulars | Cash sales | Accounts receivable | Bank | Sales discount |
|---|---|---|---:|---:|---:|---:|
| 2002 | | | $ | $ | $ | $ |
| Apr | 2 | Sales | 560 | | 560 | |
| | 4 | White | | 460 | 450 | 10 |
| | 7 | Sales | 350 | | 350 | |
| | 10 | Green | | 200 | 196 | 4 |
| | 15 | Brown | | 900 | 875 | 25 |
| | 25 | Ruby | | 700 | 682 | 18 |
| | | | 910 | 2 260 | 3 113 | 57 |

**Cash payments journal** — **Page 29**

| Date | | Particulars | Accounts payable | Sundries | Bank | Purchases discount |
|---|---|---|---|---|---|---|
| **2002** | | | **$** | **$** | **$** | **$** |
| Apr | 4 | Purchases | | 75 | 75 | |
| | 10 | Insurance | | 250 | 250 | |
| | 14 | Red | 1 500 | | 1 465 | 35 |
| | 20 | Advertising | | 150 | 150 | |
| | | Wages | | 140 | 140 | |
| | 24 | Blue | 1 700 | | 1 655 | 45 |
| | 27 | Rent | | 100 | 100 | |
| | | | 3 200 | 715 | 3 835 | 80 |

***Required:***

1. Post from the journals to the accounts receivable and accounts payable control accounts in the general ledger, and to the accounts receivable and accounts payable ledgers.
2. Prepare supporting schedules of accounts receivable and payable at 30 April 2002, and agree with the balances in the control accounts.

## Problem A5.6 Specialised journals and subsidiary ledgers

Harry Comfort is the proprietor of a business that maintains subsidiary ledgers for debtors and creditors. The general ledger trial balance on 1 July 2002 is set out below.

**Harry Comfort**
Trial balance
as at 1 July 2002

| | $ | DR<br>$ | CR<br>$ |
|---|---|---|---|
| Share capital | | | 12 000 |
| Creditors: | | | |
| James | 400 | | |
| King | 300 | | 700 |
| Bank overdraft | | | 2 300 |
| Debtors: | | | |
| King | 900 | | |
| Lane | 200 | | |
| Martin | 100 | 1 200 | |
| Inventory | | 7 000 | |
| Plant and equipment | | 4 000 | |
| Motor vehicle | | 2 800 | |
| | | 15 000 | 15 000 |

Transactions for the month of July were as follows:

| 2002 | | | $ |
|---|---|---|---|
| Jul | 2 | Cash sale to Prince, cost price $300, selling price | 450 |
| | 4 | King paid his account and was allowed $20 discount | |
| | 8 | Cash purchase of inventory from Hall | 1 200 |
| | 12 | Paid wages | 250 |
| | 14 | Paid James's account and was allowed $10 discount | |
| | 19 | Credit sale of inventory to King, cost price $450, selling price | 650 |
| | 20 | Lane paid his account and was allowed $5 discount | |
| | 22 | Credit purchase of inventory from James | 250 |
| | 26 | Paid wages | 270 |
| | 29 | Paid office expenses | 320 |
| | 30 | Cash dividends | 1 000 |
| | 31 | Credit sales of inventory to: | |
| | | King – cost price $200, selling price | 290 |
| | | Martin – cost price $320, selling price | 460 |

***Required:***

1. Record the transactions in the journals.
2. Post from the journals to the general ledger and to the subsidiary ledgers for debtors and creditors.
3. Extract supporting schedules of debtors and creditors at 31 July 2002.

## Note

1 Much of the material in this appendix was generously provided by Athol Carrington and Gordon Howitt. The material was rewritten by Michael Pennisi.

Chapter 6

# Internal control and cash

## On completion of this chapter you should be able to:

- outline the components of a good internal control system
- describe management responsibilities for maintaining control over an enterprise's assets
- provide information for evaluating an internal control system and for purposes such as fraud prevention
- develop internal control procedures to protect cash
- explain the role of bank reconciliations as part of an internal control system
- prepare a bank reconciliation statement
- explain the use of petty cash as an internal control for cash.

# 6.1 Chapter overview

This chapter looks at the importance of a good internal control system, and considers the internal control over one important asset, cash. The basic techniques for designing an internal control system are discussed. Some emphasis is given to a key internal control over cash, that is, the bank reconciliation.

# 6.2 Internal control

Record-keeping as outlined in chapters 4 and 5 has more value than just providing the data bank for the preparation of financial statements. An appropriate record-keeping system for any organisation is one that can be used to keep track of resources, thus discouraging misappropriation of the organisation's property or inefficient use of resources and helping management safeguard assets, yet is not overly cumbersome or bureaucratic. Records also help management meet its responsibility to run the enterprise effectively and generally to control what is going on. Such internal control is not only a matter of record-keeping; physical protection, insurance and proper supervision of employees are also important to internal control. The Labelcraft documents in section 4.3 were part of the company's internal control system: they were numbered and dated, and contained several details that could be used to follow up if problems arose.

This is a brief introduction to an interesting area of management responsibility that accountants and auditors consider part of their area of expertise, and it serves to demonstrate that record-keeping and accounting in general have more purposes than just preparing financial statements. Australian Auditing Standards (AUS 402) state that internal control structure refers to:

> management's philosophy and operating style, and all the policies and procedures adopted by management to assist in achieving the entity's objectives ... It is management's responsibility to maintain an adequate internal control structure. An effective internal control structure assists management in ensuring that, as far as practicable, the conduct of business is orderly and efficient, including:
> (a) irregularities being prevented, or detected and corrected should they occur;
> (b) assets being safeguarded from unauthorised use or disposition; and
> (c) financial records and other relevant data bases completely and accurately reflecting the entire operational activities of the entity and permitting the timely preparation of financial information.

## Main components of internal control

As the AUS excerpt above points out, internal control is a responsibility of management. Here are some ways in which management can establish proper control over the enterprise's affairs:

- *Run the enterprise competently.* Looking after the enterprise's assets and making sure various activities, including record-keeping, are done well is just part of being a good manager. A well-run enterprise has a climate of efficiency and records that cross-check each other, as well as competent managers who are likely to realise quickly when something is going wrong. Having a good internal control system contributes to the profitability and efficiency that good managers seek.

- *Establish clear lines of responsibility.* Once you have competent personnel it is important to clearly establish lines of responsibility, which need to be consistent with ability and authority. Each employee needs to know what their responsibilities are and who they report to. Rotation of duties has the likely benefit of reducing unauthorised activities as these are likely to be noticed by someone taking over the job at a later date. Similarly, ensuring that staff take annual leave has a similar benefit, as someone else takes over their responsibilities while on leave.
- *Maintain effective records.* Having a comprehensive, connected set of records, as was illustrated for Labelcraft in section 4.3, provides an early warning system and helps to motivate staff to perform well, because the records provide routine monitoring and act as the basis for hourly pay, performance appraisals, bonuses and other elements of the motivation system. Records also provide an audit trail of events that can be traced back to identify the causes of problems. An effective record-keeping system goes well beyond accounting transactions (we saw the example of the Labelcraft purchase order system), but accounting records are likely to be at the heart of it. Many modern organisations have integrated their accounting and other records into a decision-oriented management information system that can be used to support a wide range of management decisions and evaluations.
- *Separate record-keeping from handling assets.* An effective way of providing security over assets like cash, accounts receivable and inventories is to have records showing how much of each asset is supposed to be on hand at any time. But if the person who physically handles the asset (say, cash) also keeps the records of it, errors or fraud can be hidden by altering the records. Accountants call separation of record-keeping from handling assets 'segregation of duties'. One person collects the cash, and another person maintains the cash records. So if one or the other makes a mistake, a difference will arise between the count of cash on hand and what the record shows should be on hand. This difference can then be investigated and the cause corrected. Segregation of duties can also be used within the record-keeping system. For example, one person can maintain the general ledger, with the total accounts receivable account, and another can maintain the accounts receivable subsidiary ledger, with the detailed list of customer accounts. It is hard for smaller enterprises with few employees to spread the jobs around enough to segregate all the important tasks, but it should be done as much as is sensible. If segregation of duties doesn't exist, the boss needs to keep a close eye on important assets, such as cash and inventories.
- *Adequately pay and motivate employees.* A more positive side of internal control is to pay and reward people for their efforts on behalf of the enterprise, so that they try to do a good job and are not tempted to subvert record keeping and other control systems. Disgruntled employees may not care if things go wrong or may even take some pleasure when the enterprise suffers losses. As may already have occurred to you, the control provided by segregation of duties is destroyed if the people involved 'collude' (work together) to cover up errors or fraud, and while such actions can never be wholly prevented, their probability is reduced if people feel good about the enterprise.
- *Carry insurance on assets.* Like anything else, internal control has to be worth its cost. It is probably worth the cost to have an effective control system for the main part of the enterprise's activities, such as buying and selling goods, but there will be some unusual circumstances that are not anticipated or for which setting up elaborate controls doesn't seem worthwhile. Some events, such as earthquakes or fires, may be entirely or mostly beyond management's control. So it makes sense to protect the owners' investment by carrying insurance for some events against which internal control systems cannot provide adequate protection. There is a side benefit of insurance: insurance companies tend

to want to know a lot about how the enterprise is protecting and managing its assets, and satisfying the insurance company about this can result in improvements in controls.

- *Physically protect sensitive assets.* This control method is rather obvious, but is easy to overlook too. Sensitive assets, such as cash, inventories and tools, should be behind lock and key, kept in particular storage areas, or otherwise protected from unauthorised or casual access. Many enterprises are sloppy about access to their inventories in particular and sometimes protection is a good idea for assets you might not think of. For example, many manufacturers produce scrap as a byproduct, and the scrap can be very valuable. One manufacturer put its scrap in the backyard and found out later that thousands of dollars' worth had been lifted over the back fence and sold on the scrap market. Examples of physical controls include safes, locked storage areas, security guards and employee identification cards. More frequent use is being made of electronic devices. For example, most university libraries have electronically coded their books so that an alarm goes off if anyone tries to remove them without first taking them to the front desk to have them checked out.

There is much more to internal control. Designing effective control systems requires an understanding of management's objectives, a sensitivity to the cost–benefit balance needed between tight but costly controls and loose but cheap controls, knowledge of computer systems and other record-keeping methods, and considerable insight into the subtleties of human motivation and behaviour. It also requires some common sense: complete protection is not possible, and tying the enterprise up in red tape in order to try to get com plete protection is not what a good internal control system does.

Some specific examples of internal control procedures include:

- reporting, reviewing and approving reconciliations
- checking the arithmetical accuracy of records
- establishing controls over changes to computer programs and access to data files
- maintaining and reviewing control accounts (such as accounts receivable control) and trial balances
- comparing the results of cash and inventory counts to records
- limiting physical access to assets and records
- approving documents.

## How's your understanding?

Here are two questions you should be able to answer, based on what you have just read:

1 What should a good internal control system do?

2 What are some components of an internal control system?

## 6.3 Internal control of cash

Cash is the asset usually most susceptible to theft because of its liquid and generally anonymous nature.

**A real case:** Mike, a junior auditor, was assigned to do a surprise count of the cash on hand at a local clothing store. The cash counted was short compared with what was expected, based on the auditors' projections of cash from sales and bank deposit records. Mike was accused by the store's accounting clerk of stealing the cash himself while counting it, and he had to call the police and insist that they search him and so demonstrate that he had not stolen it. It turned out that the accounting clerk had been stealing cash and covering up the thefts by changing the sales records—a classic case of poor internal control through lack of segregation of duties, because the clerk had access to both the cash and the records of the cash. The theft was discovered only because Mike's surprise cash count referred to sales records that the clerk had not yet altered to cover up the shortage. The clerk was fired and promised to make restitution, though it was difficult to tell how much had been taken because sales records had been altered for several years. The owner of the store was quite critical of the auditors for 'not preventing the loss', but the auditors showed that they had indeed warned the owner, who had said that it would be too expensive to employ someone else to keep the sales records or control the cash.

For cash sales, a common control is to have locked-in sales registers or other carefully controlled records. Registers (such as you would see at any supermarket) usually print a consecutive number on the locked-in tape for each transaction. The access key is kept by a single person, perhaps a supervisor, who balances cash to sale records. The proceeds that should have been received will be recorded on the tape. The person who keeps the key should count the cash with the cashier, compare it with the sales proceeds, and check that the tape numbers are consecutive from one person's shift to that of the next person. If this sort of system is to work, there has to be no collusion between the people controlling the cash and checking the records—often collusion is difficult to prevent, so having yet another person provide overall monitoring of the process is a good idea. With the greater use of credit cards and the advent of electronic commerce, there are now many forms of 'cash' needing control attention, including currency, cheques, direct payments, credit cards and electronic funds transfers.

**A real case:** A large company established a 'petty cash' fund in its front office to be used to pay for small purchases such as office supplies and courier charges. The receptionist was given a fund of $1000, in cash, and when most of that was spent, submitted all the receipts in an envelope and was refunded the cash spent, to bring the petty cash fund back up to $1000. The internal control therefore was that, at any time, the receptionist should have cash on hand plus receipts for payments totalling $1000. What the company did not know was that the receptionist was involved with the delivery driver from the store from which the company got most of its office supplies, and nearly all invoices from that company paid through petty cash were inflated. The company paid far more than it should have for the supplies, but no one knew because the people who got the supplies did not see the invoices, which were kept by the receptionist as evidence of cash payouts. The people who reimbursed the receptionist had not seen the office supplies and so did not know the invoices were inflated. The thefts and the collusion between the receptionist and driver were discovered long after the two had moved to another city: someone noticed that office supplies costs were lower than they used to be! The company has no good idea of how much was stolen, but it probably exceeded $10 000 over the years.

Overall monitoring of petty cash summaries by a supervisor would probably have picked this up. Also, these are not the types of expenses that should be paid out of petty cash.

Another way to control cash from sales is to have multicopied, prenumbered sales invoices. The invoice copies are then removed by one person: for cash sales, the amounts are cross checked to cash records, and for credit sales, the amounts are cross-checked to accounts receivable records. Any gaps in the numerical continuity of the invoices are investigated. For this control to work, supervisors must ensure that an invoice is prepared for each sales transaction. An additional control is to regularly check inventory and compare it with the sales records. This should prevent, or at least detect, someone selling inventory and pocketing the cash.

Take, for example, the Mayfield Pro Shop, which accumulated $10 000 in sales at the end of a month according to the invoice copies in the locked box. If the inventory at the start of the month was worth $25 000 and at the end of the month was worth $14 000 (based on the retail price of the goods), the shop should have sold $11 000 worth of goods. The $1000 difference could be the result of one of the following:

- Someone could have kept $1000 worth of cash from sales and not written any invoices for those sales.
- Someone could have shoplifted $1000 worth of goods.
- The inventory could be inaccurate, or other errors could have occurred.

Thus, there could be other reasons for shortfalls besides theft by employees, but keeping track of cash and inventory together is one method of highlighting the possibilities and investigating them.

Cash collections received through the mail are normally in the form of cheques (but not always). You would be surprised at the variety of ways in which cheques received by a company are made out. These include cheques being made out to cash, the salesperson who made the sale or some other company official. Over the years there have been a number of examples of staff removing these cheques and banking some in their own accounts. So let's consider some basic controls to prevent this happening:

- The mail should be opened by more than one person.
- Cheques should be endorsed with a stamp to prevent the possibility of them being presented to a bank for cashing or deposited in some other account.
- A list of cheques received including amounts and customer name should be prepared.
- Copies should be distributed to the cashier with the cheques for banking, to the general ledger clerk for posting and to the accounts receivable section for updating of the subsidiary records.
- The mail openers should not also have duties related to the cashiers or record-keeping.

These procedures are based on the separation of record-keeping from handling assets.

There also needs to be good internal control over the payment of cash. Internal controls are needed to prevent payment for goods or services that have not been received or paying an invoice more than once. Some internal controls that are used by most larger companies include the following:

- Payments should only be made for properly authorised documentation. Before authorising the payment, a staff member should ensure that the relevant invoice is accompanied by some evidence of ordering and receiving the goods or service (such as a copy of the purchase order and goods received advice).
- The cheques should be signed by two staff members who are independent of invoice approval and accounting duties.
- The original invoice should be stamped 'paid' to ensure that it is not subsequently re-presented for payment.

The examples of cash control problems are presented here to illustrate the fact that accounting records have a variety of uses beyond preparing financial statements. The examples are not intended to suggest that employees or customers are crooks, but to show that management must be prudent in meeting its responsibility of good stewardship in taking care of the owners' assets. Part of that responsibility lies in not putting employees or others in such poorly controlled situations that they are tempted to steal, and paying people with responsibility for cash well enough that they do not start thinking of themselves as underpaid and therefore deserving of more money from the company!

**A real case:** An armoured truck company had developed a good business picking up cash from supermarkets and other stores and delivering it to banks. The company trusted its employees and had never had problems. Usually the trucks were staffed by two people, a driver and a second person who rode in the back. The two had to sign various forms and, in a sense, they kept an eye on each other so no one got tempted: there was often a million dollars or more in unmarked, untraceable cash in the truck. Sometimes, though, one of the two people was sick, or on vacation, or called away on some errand for the company, and there would be just one person to drive the truck and collect the money. On one day like that, there was a particularly large amount of money in the truck, and the driver, apparently on impulse, just took it and departed for foreign parts!

## 6.4 Bank reconciliations[1]

A company will have many cash receipts and disbursements during a given accounting period. Because of the high frequency of transactions and the potential for error, the accuracy of the cash balance in the general ledger (or your cheque book) should be examined periodically. This process, called a bank reconciliation, is based on the cash account and a document called a bank statement, which is received from the bank usually monthly.

### Bank statements versus cash accounts

Businesses and individuals receive monthly bank statements for every cheque account they maintain. An example of a bank statement appears in exhibit 6.1. Bank statements summarise the activity in a cheque account and report the ending monthly balance. It is important to understand that although the cash account of a depositor (such as Johnson Manufacturing) is an asset, the depositor's account is carried on the bank's records as a *liability*. Consequently, cheque and other debits by the bank *reduce* Johnson's account, while deposits and other credits *increase* the account.

At the end of a month, the bank statement cash balance and the company's cash records will normally not agree. A major reason for this discrepancy is the timing differences associated with the use of a cheque account. Timing differences result in an item being recorded on the depositor's books or the bank's books, but not both, in a given accounting period. Common examples of timing differences include the following:

- Items reflected on the company's records but not yet reported on the bank statement, such as:
  - *deposits in transit*—receipts entered in a firm's accounts but not yet processed by the bank. For example, a company could record certain cheques on the last day of the month, but not take the deposits to the bank until the next day.
  - *outstanding cheques*—cheques written by a business but not yet presented to the bank. Outstanding cheques are determined by comparing cheques reported on the bank statement against cheques written on the company's records.
- Items reported on the bank statement but not yet entered in the company's records, such as:
  - non-sufficient funds (NSF) cheques—customer cheques deposited but returned because of lack of funds. These cheques are reported on the bank statement via a debit memo notation, because the bank has reduced the depositor's account
  - bank service charges for account processing
  - notes receivable and interest collected by the bank. The collection of a note and interest is sometimes reported with a credit memo notation because of the increase in the depositor's account balance
  - interest earned on the account.

**EXHIBIT 6.1** **Sydney City Bank, George Street Branch**

**Bank statement**

Johnson Manufacturing Corporation
1 Anzac Parade
Peakhurst NSW 2210

Account no.
0008564201

Page no.
1

Statement period
31/7/02–31/8/02

| Date | Particulars | Debit | Credit | Current balance ($) |
|---|---|---|---|---|
| 31/7 | Balance | | | 19 507.50 CR |
| 01/8 | Deposit | | 10 031.87 | 29 539.37 CR |
| 04/8 | Cheque no. 630 | 6 791.45 | | 22 747.92 CR |
| 09/8 | Cheque no. 628 | 675.18 | | 22 072.74 CR |
| 09/8 | Cheque no. 629 | 375.00 | | 21 697.74 CR |
| 10/8 | Cheque no. 631 | 540.20 | | 21 157.54 CR |
| 12/8 | Deposit | | 4 925.75 | 26 083.29 CR |
| 12/8 | Deposit | | 5 242.70 | 31 325.99 CR |
| 15/8 | Cheque no. 633 | 728.40 | | 30 597.59 CR |
| 16/8 | Cheque no. 632 | 790.03 | | 29 807.56 CR |
| 18/8 | Note collection | | 4 600.80 | 34 408.36 CR |
| 19/8 | Cheque no. 634 | 3 574.24 | | 30 834.12 CR |
| 22/8 | Cheque no. 635 | 23 426.40 | | 7 407.72 CR |
| 25/8 | Deposit | | 9 312.28 | 16 720.00 CR |
| 26/8 | Cheque no. 637 | 2 470. 80 | | 14 249.20 CR |
| 26/8 | Cheque no. 639 | 740.15 | | 13 509.05 CR |
| 29/8 | Deposit | | 7 990.10 | 21 499.15 CR |
| 31/8 | Service charges | 20.00 | | 21 479.15 CR |
| 31/8 | FID | 80.80 | | 21 398.35 CR |
| 31/8 | Govt Debits Tax | 47.10 | | 21 351.25 CR |
| 31/8 | Interest | | 75.00 | 21 426.25 CR |
| | | **Total debits** | **Total credits** | |
| | | 40 259.75 | 42 178.50 | |

In addition to timing differences, errors may cause a discrepancy between the bank statement balance and company accounting records. Errors can be made by either the company or the bank and must be corrected as quickly as possible.

## The reconciliation process

Several different types of reconciliations can be prepared. One commonly encountered form results in determining the amount of cash a company has control over and reports on its end of period statement of financial position. An example appears in exhibit 6.2.

The exhibit reveals the thrust of a reconciliation. That is, we strive to isolate specific items that cause a difference between the depositor's records and the bank statement balance. The accountant considers these items and adjusts one cash balance or the other to bring both balances into agreement.

If the balances do not agree and the reconciling items are deemed correct there is an excellent chance that a record-keeping error has been made. Errors must be identified, then added or subtracted on the reconciliation to arrive at the corrected cash balance. For example, if a cheque written by a firm for $94.50 were incorrectly entered in the

**EXHIBIT 6.2** **Sydney City Bank**

**Bank reconciliation**

| | | $ |
|---|---|---|
| *Ending balance per bank statement* | | XXX |
| Add: Receipts/increases entered on company records but not reported on the bank statement | | XXX |
| Deduct: Disbursements/decreases entered on company records but not reported on the bank statement | | XXX |
| Adjusted cash balance: bank | → | XXX |
| *Ending balance per company records* | **These** | XXX |
| Add: Receipts/increases reported on the bank statement but not entered on company records | **amounts must** | XXX |
| Deduct: Disbursements/decreases reported on the bank statement but not entered on company records | **agree** | XXX |
| Adjusted cash balance: company records | → | XXX |

accounting records as $49.50, the accounting records would be overstated by $45.00 ($94.50 – $49.50). This amount ($45) should therefore be deducted from the ending cash balance per company records, since the company's books are in error. The bank, of course, will deduct the correct amount of the transaction ($94.50) when the cheque is received for payment. The reconciliation, then, not only highlights timing differences but also identifies errors made by either the bank or the depositor.

Most bank reconciliations contain adjustments to both the ending cash balance per bank statement and the ending balance per company records. After the reconciliation is completed, *general journal entries must be prepared for adjustments made to company records*. These adjustments are necessary to update the cash account (and others) for corrections of company errors and information already processed by the bank. It is important to note that no journal entries are needed for adjustments made to the ending bank statement balance. These adjustments reflect items that have already been recorded in a company's accounts; thus, no further updating is necessary.

Here is an example. Exhibit 6.3 contains summarised data and the bank reconciliation of Johnson Manufacturing Corporation for the month ended 31 August 2002. It will help if you refer back to Johnson's bank statement (in Exhibit 6.1), which serves as the source for much of the information presented.

The reconciliation reveals one increase to the bank statement cash balance: the deposit that was recorded prior to month end but awaiting deposit. Johnson had control over each of these items as of 31 August, and they should be included in the ending cash balance. The decrease to the bank statement cash balance was caused by cheques Johnson had written that had not yet cleared the bank. The bank will receive these cheques shortly, and the funds will then be deducted from the company's account.

The increase to company records arose from the note receivable and interest, both of which appear on the bank statement. These funds are now on deposit in Johnson's bank account and must therefore be entered in the company's records. The deductions for the government and service charges are also caused by items on the bank statement but not as yet in the company's ledger. The error in recording cheque no. 628 was discovered during the reconciliation. Because the bank deducted the correct amount of the cheque, an adjustment to Johnson's records is required to bring them into agreement with those of the bank.

**EXHIBIT 6.3** **Johnson Manufacturing Corporation**

**Data and bank reconciliation**

**Data**

a 31 August cash balance per bank statement, $21 426.25.

b 31 August cash balance per company records, $17 473.35.

c Government charges (FID) of $80.80 and government debits tax of $47.10.

d A customer's note receivable for $4600.80 was collected by the bank and reported on the August bank statement.

e A deposit for $1850.00 recorded by the company on 31 August did not appear on the bank statement.

f Monthly bank service charge, $20.00 and interest of $75.00 received.

g The following cheques written by Johnson were outstanding at the end of the month:

| | |
|---|---|
| No. 638 | $410.00 |
| No. 640 | 320.00 |
| No. 641 | 240.00 |
| No. 642 | 323.00 |

h Cheque no. 628, written for $675.18, was erroneously entered as $657.18 in the company's books. The cheque involved a payment to a supplier on account.

**Bank reconciliation**
**31 August 2002**

| | $ | $ | |
|---|---|---|---|
| *Ending balance per bank statement* | | 21 426.25 | CR |
| Add: Outstanding deposit | | 1 850.00 | |
| | | 23 276.25 | |
| Deduct: Outstanding cheques | | | |
| No. 638 | 410.00 | | |
| No. 640 | 320.00 | | |
| No. 641 | 240.00 | | |
| No. 642 | 323.00 | 1 293.00 | |
| **Adjusted cash balance: bank** | | **21 983.25** | CR |
| **Ending balance per company records** | | 17 473.35 | DR |
| Add: Note receivable collected by bank | 4 600.80 | | |
| Interest | 75.00 | 4 675.80 | |
| | | 22 149.15 | |
| Deduct: Government charges | 127.90 | | |
| Monthly service charge | 20.00 | | |
| Error in recording cheque no. 628 | 18.00 | 165.90 | |
| **Adjusted cash balance: company records** | | **21 983.25** | DR |

Note that, as the company is owed money, it has an asset, therefore it will show up as a debit balance in the bank reconciliation ($21 983.25 DR). However, as the bank owes money, it has a liability, therefore the amount will show up as a credit balance in the bank records ($21 983.25 CR).

On completion of the reconciliation, journal entries are needed for all items that affect company records. The following entries will be made on 31 August:

| | DR $ | CR $ |
|---|---|---|
| Cash | 4 675.80 | |
| Notes receivable | | 4 600.80 |
| Interest revenue | | 75.00 |
| Government charges | 127.90 | |
| Cash | | 127.90 |
| Bank charges | 20.00 | |
| Cash | | 20.00 |
| Accounts payable | 18.00 | |
| Cash | | 18.00 |

The first entry reflects the increase in cash caused by the collection of the note and interest. The second entry shows government charges for $127.90. The bank service charge is recorded in the third entry as expense. Finally, the error in recording cheque no. 628 was found to involve a payment on account; thus, Accounts Payable must be debited. These entries allow Johnson's records to reflect the true amount of cash held by the firm.

## 6.5 Performing a bank reconciliation from information in cash journals

In section 6.4, you were given lists of outstanding deposits, outstanding cheques and errors in bank charges, etc. In this section we will show you how to find this information by comparing the content of the bank statement and the organisation's cash records (cash receipts journal and cash payments journals). These two journals were discussed in the appendix to chapter 5. However, you can still follow this section even if you haven't read that appendix. Just note that a cash receipts journal (CRJ) lists all payments received and a cash payments journal (CPJ) records all cheques issued in cheque number order.

The following steps[2] should be undertaken to complete the bank reconciliation statement:

### Step 1

- Go through last month's bank reconciliation statement, ticking off any amounts that were outstanding last month (for example, unpresented cheques and outstanding deposits) and appear on this month's bank statement.
- Go through the bank statement and tick off items appearing both there and in the cash journals (tick them off in both places).
- Errors: if you see any cheques or deposits that are recorded incorrectly by the business or the bank (for example, a transposition error), deal with these as follows:
  - If the bank has made a mistake, inform the bank of its error and list it in the bank reconciliation.
  - If the business has made a mistake, correct the relevant cash journal (CPJ or CRJ).

### Step 2

- Go through the bank statements to see what amounts remain unticked. These unticked amounts may be dishonoured cheques, interest or cash transactions made directly through the bank and not yet recorded in the books. These should be entered into the appropriate CRJ or CPJ. After entering them, tick them off, both in the journals and in the bank statements.

- Go through the cash journals to see if there are any unticked amounts in the CRJ and CPJ. These will represent outstanding deposits and outstanding (unpresented) cheques respectively.

## Step 3

- If CRJ and CPJ have not yet been totalled and posted to the bank ledger account, this should be done.

## Step 4

- Prepare a bank reconciliation statement in a form similar to that shown in exhibit 6.3.

## Illustrative example

The bank reconciliation prepared by Onslow Ltd, as at 31 March 2002, showed a deposit in transit of $610 and the following outstanding cheques; # 204 for $615 and # 221 for $90. The balance, as per cash at bank account in the general ledger of Onslow Ltd at 31 March 2002, was $4667 DR.

**Bank Statement**

| **Date** | | **Particulars** | **Debit $** | **Credit $** | **Balance $** |
|---|---|---|---|---|---|
| 2002 | | Balance | | | 4 762 CR |
| April | 1 | Dep | | 610 | 5 372 CR |
| | 2 | Dep | | 115 | 5 487 CR |
| | 3 | 222 | 56 | | 5 431 CR |
| | 3 | DD car lease | 300 | | 5 131 CR |
| | 3 | Dep | | 630 | 5 761 CR |
| | 6 | 204 | 615 | | 5 146 CR |
| | 6 | Dep | | 220 | 5 366 CR |
| | 10 | Dep | | 105 | 5 471 CR |
| | 10 | 224 | 196 | | 5 275 CR |
| | 13 | Dep | | 832 | 6 107 CR |
| | 15 | DC | | 50 | 6 157 CR |
| | 17 | Dep | | 107 | 6 264 CR |
| | 17 | 226 | 852 | | 5 412 CR |
| | 17 | NSF | 312 | | 5 100 CR |
| | 20 | 225 | 846 | | 4 254 CR |
| | 22 | Dep | | 56 | 4 310 CR |
| | 24 | SC | 24 | | 4 286 CR |
| | 27 | 227 | 100 | | 4 186 CR |
| | 29 | 228 | 409 | | 3 777 CR |

NSF non-sufficient funds
DC Direct credit
SC service charge
DD Direct debit

**From the cash receipts journal**

| Date | Amount |
|---|---|
| April | $ |
| 2 | 115 |
| 3 | 630 |
| 6 | 220 |
| 10 | 105 |
| 13 | 832 |
| 17 | 107 |
| 21 | 56 |
| 30 | 403 |
| Subtotal | 2 468 |

**From the cash payments journal**

| Date | Cheque # | Amount |
|---|---|---|
| April | | $ |
| 3 | 222 | 56 |
| 3 | 223 | 124 |
| 10 | 224 | 169 |
| 14 | 225 | 846 |
| 17 | 226 | 852 |
| 23 | 227 | 100 |
| 28 | 228 | 409 |
| 29 | 229 | 900 |
| 29 | 230 | 556 |
| Subtotal | | 4 012 |

***Note:*** For any errors assume the bank's records are correct.

- Take the above information and tick off on the bank statement any outstanding cheques or outstanding deposits from the March bank reconciliation. Note that $610 outstanding deposit is included on the bank statement on 1 April, and the unpresented cheque #221 is still unpresented.
- Compare the amounts on the bank statement with those in the cash journal. The unticked amounts on the bank statements refer to a direct credit of $50, a dishonoured cheque for $312 (that is, the person who sent the cheque to Onslow did not have sufficient funds in the account), bank fees of $24 and direct debit for a car lease of $300. In addition there is an error of $27 for cheque #224 to Energy Australia.

  As a result of the above, the cash journals would be adjusted as follows:

**Cash receipts journals**

| | |
|---|---|
| Subtotal | 2 468 |
| Direct credit | 50 |
| NSF | –312 |
| | $2 206 |

**Cash payments journal**

| | |
|---|---|
| Subtotal | 4 012 |
| Error #224 | 27 |
| Fees | 24 |
| Car lease | 300 |
| | $4 363 |

- These amounts would then be posted to the cash at bank general ledger account.

**Cash at bank**

| | | | | |
|---|---|---|---|---|
| 1 April | Bal b/d | 4 667 | Payments | 4 363 |
| | Receipts | 2 206 | Bal c/d | 2 510 |
| | | 6 873 | | 6 873 |
| | Bal b/d | $2 510 | | |

- The unticked amounts in the cash receipts and cash payments journals represent outstanding deposits (deposit in transit) and outstanding cheques (unpresented cheques).
- These outstanding deposits would be added to the balance, as per bank statement, and the unpresented cheques would be deducted.

**Bank reconciliation statement for Onslow Ltd**
**at 30 April 2002**

| | | | |
|---|---|---|---|
| Balance per bank statement | | $3 777 | CR |
| add: Outstanding deposit | | 403 | |
| | | 4 180 | |
| less: Unpresented cheques | | | |
| #221 | 90 | | |
| #223 | 124 | | |
| #229 | 900 | | |
| #230 | 556 | 1 670 | |
| Balance per cash at bank ledger account | | $2 510 | DR |

- Note that the unpresented cheques include #221, which was outstanding in the previous bank reconciliation.

# 6.6 Petty cash[3]

Another element in the control of cash is a petty cash system. Under this system, a fund is established for use in making small payments, especially those that are impractical or uneconomical to make by cheque. Examples of such payments include those for minor items like taxi fares and other miscellaneous office needs.

A petty cash fund is created by cashing a cheque drawn on the company's regular cheque account. The proceeds from the cheque, sufficient to cover payments for a short period of time (several weeks, for example), are then placed in a petty cash box that is controlled by an individual known as the fund custodian. The custodian supervises the fund and is held accountable for any discrepancies. Assuming the petty cash fund is established at $200, the necessary journal entry follows. The petty cash account is an asset.

| | $ | $ |
|---|---|---|
| Petty cash | 200 | |
| Cash | | 200 |
| *To establish petty cash fund.* | | |

## Making disbursements from the fund

As payments are made from the fund, the custodian completes a form known as a petty cash voucher. Each voucher indicates the amount paid, the purpose of the expenditure, the date of the expenditure, and the individual receiving the money. Along with invoices and receipts, petty cash vouchers are used as evidence of disbursements.

The completed voucher is placed in the petty cash box by the custodian. Although a payment has been made, no journal entry is recorded at this time. Preparing a formal journal entry for each disbursement would give rise to considerable bookkeeping work and posting, all for relatively small amounts. At all times the following relationship should be true:

| | $ |
|---|---|
| Cash remaining in the fund | XXX |
| Plus: Petty cash vouchers | XXX |
| Original amount of the fund | 200 |

## Replenishing the fund

The petty cash fund is replenished when the amount of cash in the fund becomes low. For instance, assume that a count of the petty cash on hand totalled $32.40. Vouchers revealed that the following expenses had been incurred: postage $27.50; office supplies $50.80; transportation $73.40; coffee $15.90. The journal entry to record replenishment is as follows:

| | $ | $ |
|---|---|---|
| Postage expense | 27.50 | |
| Office supplies expense | 50.80 | |
| Transportation expense | 73.40 | |
| Miscellaneous expense | 15.90 | |
| Cash | | 167.60 |
| *To replenish petty cash fund* | | |

Notice that the credit is to the cash account and not petty cash. Although disbursements have been made from the petty cash box, the fund is restocked by writing a cheque for $167.60 on the company's regular cheque account. Thus, payment (and replenishment) is really from cash.

In addition to being restocked when the fund is low, petty cash is also replenished at the end of each accounting period. This procedure is necessary because no formal journal entries have been recorded for individual fund disbursements. Replenishment requires a journal entry, thereby ensuring that expenditures are charged to the period in which they arose.

## Errors in the petty cash fund

Occasionally, the sum of the petty cash vouchers and cash in the fund will not equal the original fund balance. This discrepancy usually occurs because of errors made by the fund custodian, some being in the company's favour and some against. In such cases, the cash short & over account is employed. Cash short & over is debited to record a shortage or credited to recognise an overage at the time the fund is replenished. The shortage is classified as a miscellaneous expense and the overage as a miscellaneous revenue item.

# 6.7 Disclosure of internal control in annual reports

Australian companies that are listed with the Australian Stock Exchange (ASX) are now required to include a section in their annual reports on corporate governance. A number of companies include in this section a description of their internal control systems. Examples from the 2001 annual reports of Coles Myer Limited, George Weston Foods Limited and Tabcorp Holdings Limited are given in exhibits 6.4 to 6.6.

Note some common aspects of these descriptions:

**EXHIBIT 6.4**

**Coles Myer Limited**

**Extract from 2001 annual report**

**Internal control**

*Group results*

The Board has overall responsibility for the appropriate reporting of the CML Group results. In order to effectively carry out this function, the Audit/Governance Committee monitors the effectiveness of the Group's systems and internal financial controls.

*Systems*

The systems of internal financial controls are designed to provide reasonable, but not absolute, assurance against material misstatement or loss. They are intended to enable the timely identification of problems that require the attention of the Board. The CML Group 's senior management has determined these controls.

*Monitoring*

The performance of the CML Group is monitored on a monthly basis through annual operating and capital budgets that have been established by the relevant business heads and approved by the Board.

*Internal audit* is used extensively to monitor the areas of greatest risk as identified by risk analysis. The external auditors review and test the system of internal control to the extent necessary for an opinion on the financial report.

**EXHIBIT 6.5**

**George Weston Foods Limited**

**Extract from 2001 annual report**

**Internal control framework**

The Company's internal control framework is based on policies, procedures and organisational structures that provide an appropriate division of responsibility and a program of internal auditing. The Board acknowledges its responsibility for the overall internal control framework. However, it recognises that no cost-effective internal control system will preclude all errors and irregularities. The internal control framework consists of:

*Financial reporting*

A comprehensive system is used, with an annual profit plan reviewed by the Board. Monthly and quarterly actual results are reported against plan and revised forecasts for the year are prepared regularly. The Company reports to shareholders half-yearly.

The Company's accounting and procedures manual states that employees must notify the Directors of any information that may affect share prices. This enables the Directors to report to the Australian Stock Exchange in accordance with continuous disclosure requirements.

*Operating unit controls*

Financial controls and procedures (including information systems controls) are in place in all units. Managers of each unit are required to sign certificates confirming compliance with procedures and disclosing any irregularities.

*Special functions reporting*

The Company has identified a number of key areas that must regularly report to the Audit Committee. These include departments involved with treasury, compliance, environmental, legal, insurance and superannuation matters.

*Investment appraisal*

The Company has clearly defined guidelines for capital expenditure. These include annual budgets, detailed appraisal and review procedures and levels of authority for approvals.

*Internal audit*

An internal auditor assists the Board in ensuring compliance with internal controls. The internal auditor reports directly to the Chief Executive.

**EXHIBIT 6.6** **Tabcorp Holdings Limited**

**Extract from 2001 annual report**

**Internal control framework**

The Board is responsible for the establishment and maintenance of the internal control structure of the company, but acknowledges that, within cost-effective parameters, errors and irregularities cannot be eliminated in their entirety.

Financial reporting is primarily in the form of the development of a detailed annual budget, which is subject to the approval of the directors. Actual monthly and year to date results for the company are reported to the Board to enable it to monitor performance against the pre-approved budget.

Forecasts for the company and each of the operating divisions are regularly updated and reported to the Board.

The company reports to shareholders both half-yearly and annually. Compliance with key regulatory requirements particular to the company's licences and the businesses conducted pursuant to those licences are the subject of specific reporting to the Board's Compliance Committee.

The company has detailed procedural guidelines for the approval of capital expenditure, including annual budgeting, review and approval of individual proposals and specific levels of authority between the Managing Director and the Board.

The company maintains a field audit program of its retail wagering outlets. This risk analysis-based program is carried out by staff from the Corporate Finance Group.

A detailed set of guidelines relating to the investment of surplus cash and management of debt has been established by the company's executives and approved by the Board.

- The board of directors has responsibility for the internal control system.
- The role of the audit committee in the evaluation of internal controls is noted.
- The internal control systems provide reasonable but not absolute assurance against errors and irregularities.
- Operating budgets are used to monitor performance.
- Internal audit is an important part of the internal control system.
- Controls are important in certain key areas including Treasury.
- There are clearly defined guidelines for capital investment.

## 6.8 Managers and internal control

As noted earlier, internal control is the responsibility of management. Internal controls are fundamental to the accurate recording of transactions and reliable financial reports.

A system of internal control should minimise and, where possible, eliminate errors and irregularities. Errors are unintentional mistakes, whereas irregularities are intentional. Even with a strong system of internal control errors can still occur but the system should detect these errors. Irregularities should also be detected except where there is collusion (two or more employees working together to cover up the irregularities) or management override (management using its power to instruct employees to ignore a particular control). Thus, no system of internal control can eliminate with certainty all errors and irregularities, but it can decrease substantially the possibility of them occurring and increase the chance of detecting them.

An important question for management is how much internal control is necessary. As each additional control is added, the risk of error and irregularity decreases, but there is a cost to implementing the controls. So a cost–benefit analysis is required, but this is difficult to do because the benefits of having the controls are often difficult to quantify. It becomes a matter of judgement by management as their estimate of the potential losses from errors and irregularities is compared with the cost of additional controls.

## 6.9 Public sector issues

Internal control is an integral part of the environment of all public sector entities. For example, the *NSW Public Finance and Audit Act 1983* provides the following obligation to establish a system of Internal Control as follows:

> The Head of an authority shall ensure that there is an effective system of Internal Control over the financial and related operations of the authority, including:
> (a) management policies and requirements made by the provisions of this Act and the prescribed requirements;
> (b) sound practices for the efficient, effective and economical management of functions by each organisational branch or section within the authority;
> (c) a system of authorisation and recording and procedures adequate to provide accounting control in relation to assets, liabilities, receipts and expenses;
> (d) proper segregation of functional responsibilities; and
> (e) procedures to review the adequacy of and compliance with the system of Internal Control.

Most State Treasurers have also established statements of best practice with respect to internal control. For example, in June 1995 NSW Treasury issued a 'Statement of Best Practice: Internal Control and Internal Audit', which provides guidance to government agencies on such topics as: responsibility for internal control; relationship between management processes and internal control; analysing risks and establishing controls; and effective collection of information, communication and monitoring. The document suggests the following four critical elements in an effective system of internal control for public sector entities:

- an appropriate 'tone at the top', which includes top management having appropriate skills and experience, timely and relevant information, a high level of integrity and ethics, a positive attitude to internal control and encouragement for the reporting of significant weaknesses and breakdowns in internal control
- a well-designed control system aimed at mitigating risks
- effective collection of information and effective communication throughout the Agency, recognising that different information is needed by different levels of management for performance measurement purposes
- effective monitoring of the system of internal control: periodically, the Board/CEO should undertake reviews of the internal control system, particularly where changes are frequent.

## 6.10 Homework and discussion to develop understanding

### Discussion questions

1 What is internal control?
2 List the main components of internal control.
3 Why is internal control over cash so critical?
4 What types of organisations need strong internal controls over inventory?
5 What is 'segregation of duties'? Provide three examples.
6 List four important internal controls over cash.

7 Provide three specific internal control procedures for:
   a cash
   b inventory
   c accounts receivable.
8 What is the purpose of the bank reconciliation statement?
9 If a company is owed $100 000 by the bank, why would it appear as a DR in the company's ledger accounts and a CR on the bank statement?
10 Why do outstanding (unpresented) cheques occur at month-end?
11 How does a petty cash system act as an internal control?
12 List some of the internal control disclosures made by companies and other organisations in their annual report.
13 'No system of internal control is perfect. There are always inherent limitations.' Discuss.
14 What does the concept of 'reasonable assurance' mean with respect to an internal control system?
15 Outline the importance of each of the following in an internal control system for cash:
   a that all cash should be banked daily intact
   b the bank reconciliation statement
   c the segregation of duties of the mail-opener, cashier, general ledger-keeper and receivable ledger clerk.
16 A school friend who has joined a new company tells you that the company has many controls over cash. He asks you to explain why the following controls exist.
   a Mail opening is carried out by two individuals. They won't allow the cashier or accounts receivable clerk to open the mail, although they have spare time during the morning.
   b Mail opening is time consuming, because the company requires all cheques to be crossed 'not negotiable' as well as making a listing of all cheques received.
   c As the cashier also has free time in the late afternoon, your friend suggested that the cashier receive the bank-validated deposit slips, but the company insisted that the slips be returned to someone else for checking.
   d The company has small expenses, so it would be useful to use some of the daily cash receipts to pay them. However, instead, they are forced to bank the receipts intact and set up a petty cash system to pay the small expenses.
   e The cashier takes flexitime every Wednesday afternoon, as he likes to attend the local race meeting. He asked management about not banking on Wednesday, keeping the Wednesday receipts in the safe, then combining them with Thursday's receipts, but the company would not give permission for this.
17 Over the next week, write down any internal controls you come across (consider the movies, for example, or football games, shopping, or visiting the library to do your accounting assignments).
18 The bank reconciliation of XYZ Ltd reveals a significant bank error in XYZ's favour that will probably go undetected. As accountant, you contact the general manager, who suggests that the bank has probably made errors in its favour in the past and that the bank should not be informed of its error. What should you do?
19 How much internal control is enough?
20 With respect to the internal control over cash, provide an example of each of the following:
   a independent checks, reviews
   b approval of transactions
   c matching documents

  - **d** prenumbering and sequence checking
  - **e** reconciliation to outside information
  - **f** access restrictions.

**21** Internal control is an important facet of sound business management and accounting. Explain at least four objectives served by internal controls.

**22** Discuss the following statements:
  - **a** Internal control is the responsibility of the accountants in an organisation.
  - **b** A properly designed system of internal control over cash should prevent employee theft of cash.

**23** Discuss the relationship between the corporate manager's responsibility for internal control and his or her responsibility to earn profit for the shareholders.

**24** You work for Sydney Industries Ltd. The CEO has been reading other companies' annual reports, and has become concerned that the company's internal controls may not be adequate. On the other hand, the CEO does not want to spend the company's money unnecessarily. List the factors that you would suggest the CEO consider in evaluating whether better internal controls would be worthwhile.

## Problem 6.1* Explain the nature and purpose of internal control to a manager

A friend, Janet, has accepted a job as general manager of a local company. During a meeting you attended, an accountant mentioned to Janet that she would be responsible for internal control of the company. When the accountant left the room, Janet turned to you and asked, 'What is internal control and why should I care about it?' Answer Janet's question, using clear language without technical jargon.

## Problem 6.2* Describe weaknesses in internal control

The following incidents took place in the Dag Company:

- Fred, the mail-opener, converted a cheque payable to the Dag Company for his personal use. The cheque was included in the list of mail receipts sent to the accountant. When he was doing the bank reconciliation, Fred treated the missing amount as a deposit in transit.
- Kylie, the cashier, pocketed cash received over the counter from customers paying their accounts. She then wrote off the receivables as uncollectable.

For each incident, describe the internal control weakness that made the above incidents possible and describe procedures that would remove each weakness.

## Problem 6.3* Prepare a bank reconciliation statement and explain the need for cash records

The bank reconciliation made by Johnson Ltd on 31 August of the current year showed a deposit in transit of $570 and two outstanding cheques, no. 597 for $260 and no. 603 for $180. The adjusted balance per books on 31 August was $7980 debit.

The bank statement shown on the next page is available for September. A list of deposits made and cheques written during September is shown here:

| Deposits made | | Cheques written | |
|---|---|---|---|
| | $ | | $ |
| Sep 1 | 350 | No. 607 | 450 |
| 4 | 420 | 608 | 325 |
| 8 | 296 | 609 | 192 |
| 12 | 580 | 610 | 285 |

| Deposits made | | Cheques written | |
|---|---|---|---|
| | $ | | $ |
| 16 | 404 | 611 | 410 |
| 24 | 535 | 612 | 242 |
| 29 | 256 | 613 | 214 |
| 30 | 430 | 614 | 453 |
| | 3 271 | 615 | 357 |
| | | 616 | 262 |
| | | | 3 190 |

The cash at bank account balance on 30 September was $8061. In reviewing cheques the bookkeeper discovered that cheque no. 610, written for $258 for repairs expense, was recorded in the cash payments journal as $285. The 'return' item for $335, which Johnson deposited on 24 September, was a payment on account from customer D. Lewis (dishonoured cheque).

**Bank statement**

**Johnson Ltd**
**Newtown, NSW**

**30 September 2002**

| | | | **Brought forward** | **$** |
|---|---|---|---|---|
| 31 Aug | | | | 7 850 CR |
| 1 Sep | Cash/cheques | | 570 | 8 420 CR |
| | 603 | 180 | | 8 240 CR |
| 2 Sep | Cash/cheques | | 350 | 8 590 CR |
| 5 Sep | Cash/cheques | | 420 | 9 010 CR |
| | 608 | 325 | | 8 685 CR |
| | 607 | 450 | | 8 235 CR |
| 8 Sep | 610 | 258 | | 7 977 CR |
| 9 Sep | 609 | 192 | | 7 785 CR |
| | Cash/cheques | | 296 | 8 081 CR |
| 15 Sep | Cash/cheques | | 580 | 8 661 CR |
| | 612 | 242 | | 8 419 CR |
| 17 Sep | Cash/cheques | | 404 | 8 823 CR |
| | 611 | 410 | | 8 413 CR |
| 25 Sep | 614 | 453 | | 7 960 CR |
| | Cash/cheques | | 535 | 8 495 CR |
| 30 Sep | Cash/cheques | | 256 | 8 751 CR |
| | Return | 335 | | 8 416 CR |
| | ACC fee | 15 | | 8 401 CR |

***Required:***

1. Prepare a bank reconciliation statement for Johnson Ltd at 30 September.
2. Prepare the necessary general journal entries to bring the cash at bank account up to date as at 30 September 2002.
3. Could a business dispense with its own cash records and rely entirely on bank statements?

## Problem 6.4 Identify violated components of internal control

In each of the following cases, what component of good internal control is being violated (if any)? (See section 6.2 if you can't remember the components.)

1 Tough Inc. pays all its employees minimum wages and does not have pleasant working conditions.

2 Fred is a very conscientious employee who does such a good job that he does pretty much all of Whisp Ltd's office tasks.

3 Garand Inc. has a sophisticated internal control system that prints out various reports on discrepancies, which company management asks the accounting clerks to investigate and resolve.

4 John runs a small warehousing business. He's proud of saving money on accounting. For example, the reason he gives for not keeping track of purchases and shipments of goods is that he can 'look at the shelves and see if everything is all right'.

5 Wildwood Restaurant is proud of its 'family approach' to its employees, taking great care to make them feel important and trusted. Everyone has a key to the restaurant and several employees can often be found there in off hours, helping to clean and prepare for the next day.

6 Hadlee Corp.'s founder, getting on in years, has turned the CEO's job over to his playboy son, who is quite interested in horse racing and turns up at the office only occasionally.

## Problem 6.5 Prepare journal entries relating to petty cash

A petty cash fund of $100 was established on 1 June 1997 by Green Pty Ltd. Disbursements were made during June as follows:

| Voucher no. | Voucher date | Amount $ | Details |
|---|---|---|---|
| 1 | 3 June | 20.00 | for postage |
| 2 | 6 June | 6.00 | for fares |
| 3 | 7 June | 15.50 | for staff tea supplies |
| 4 | 8 June | 20.00 | for postage |
| 5 | 10 June | 9.50 | for fares |
| 6 | 11 June | 4.80 | for stationery |
| 7 | 15 June | 20.00 | for postage |
| 8 | 17 June | 7.50 | for fares |
| 9 | 24 June | 10.00 | for taxis |
| 10 | 28 June | 17.00 | for staff tea supplies |

Reimbursement cheques were drawn on 16 June and 30 June.

Prepare journal entries to record the establishment and replenishment of the fund.

## Problem 6.6 Internal control of disbursements

You attend your local tennis club annual general meeting and get elected as secretary of the club. You are looking forward to your new role and realise you will be working with your old friend James King, who has been treasurer for the last twenty years. You know from previous experience that James is hardworking and honest. At a meeting with James to explain some of the accounting issues, he notes that the constitution requires two signatures on each cheque from among the following three individuals: president, secretary and treasurer. As the president is often overseas, James informs you that the treasurer and secretary usually sign the cheques. As you live about 10 km apart, James suggests you sign a few blank cheques as past secretaries have done so he can pay bills when needed. How would you react to this suggestion?

## Problem 6.7 Recommend improvements in internal control of cash in a church

You have been appointed to the finance committee of your local church. The collections for Sunday services are taken up by a team of ushers. At the end of each service the head usher counts the cash, then puts the total of the cash count and the cash in the safe. On Mondays the church treasurer, who has been doing the job for the last 15 years, re-counts the cash, deducts a float to pay for incidental church expenses during the week and deposits the balance and records it in the church records. The church treasurer takes frequent overseas trips, so when he is away the takings accumulate in the safe until he returns. Recommend improvements in control procedures.

## Problem 6.8 Explain cash control procedures and identify internal control weaknesses

**1** There are a number of procedures that a firm may employ to safeguard cash. These procedures are known as cash control procedures. List five examples of cash control procedures and explain their function. Follow the example given below:

| Cash control procedure | Function |
|---|---|
| Physical safeguards over cash, such as a safe. | To help protect the unbanked cash overnight until it can be banked the next day. |

**2** Identify the internal control weaknesses in the following two cases and suggest a way of improving each situation.

**a** A supplier was paid twice for the same shipment. One payment was made upon receipt of the invoice and the second payment upon receipt of the monthly statement. The first payment was not listed on the statement, as it arrived after statement date.

**b** The cashier pocketed cash received over the counter from a few customers who had paid their accounts. The cashier then wrote the accounts receivable off as uncollectable.

## Problem 6.9 Identify objectives of internal control and explain how theft may be prevented

Ekumhaha Pty Ltd is a small wholesaler of model aeroplanes. It has only a few employees. The owner of the business, who is also the manager, makes daily deposits of customers' cheques in the firm's bank account and writes all cheques issued by the firm. He also reconciles the monthly statement with the books when the bank statement is received in the mail.

The assistant to the owner renders secretarial services, which include taking dictation, typing letters and processing all mail, both incoming and outgoing. Each day the assistant gives the owner the cheques received from customers. The vouchers attached to the cheques are separated by the assistant and sent to the bookkeeper, along with any other remittance advices that have been enclosed with the cheques.

The bookkeeper makes prompt entries to credit customers' accounts for their remittance. From these accounts, the bookkeeper prepares monthly statements for mailing to customers. Other employees include marketing and warehouse personnel.

It is possible the owner's assistant takes customers' cheques (depositing them in his or her own account) and destroys the remittance advices and vouchers accompanying these cheques.

How would such a theft be concealed? What precautions could prevent the theft and/or its concealment?

## Problem 6.10 Top management responsibility for internal control

The proud owner of Beedle Ltd, a successful high-tech company, is very good at hiring and motivating excellent people to develop and sell products. Delegation is the key, says the owner: 'Hire good people and get out of their way!' As part of this philosophy, the owner hired the best accountants available and turned over to them all accounting, control and finance functions. The owner concentrates on strategy and business planning, and the company has grown steadily for several years.

Explain to the owner the top management responsibilities that are being neglected here. Given that the company is so successful, does such neglect really matter?

## Problem 6.11 Identify missing features of internal control

Read the following description of a sports club. Which features of good internal control seem to be missing? Are any of those offset by strengths in other features?

The club earns revenue from members' fees, and from selling tickets to its games and advertising in its programs. Advertising receipts are mainly by cheque; other receipts are primarily cash, with an increasing percentage by credit card. Most expenditures are in cash, except for equipment, facility rentals and the three employees' pay, all done by cheques. One employee does some coaching, schedules games and coordinates players and officials. The second employee (who is married to the first) looks after equipment, prepares rental facilities for games, makes travel arrangements and does various miscellaneous jobs. The third employee looks after cash, payroll and accounting. The club's board of directors meets monthly and always has monthly (or annual) financial reports to scrutinise. All three employees are members of the board, and other board members rely on them.

The club has a rented office/storeroom, where all employees work most of the time and where all the club's equipment and various supplies are stored. Cash, cheques and credit card slips are deposited into the bank every two weeks, and payment cheques are issued as needed. Cash expenses are paid out of cash collected from members' fees and ticket sales, so often there is not enough cash to bother depositing. Sometimes there is not enough cash to pay cash expenses, in which case the third employee, who is authorised to sign all cheques, just writes a cheque to 'cash' and cashes it at the nearby bank where the club's bank account is maintained. The board of directors discusses all major trips, equipment purchases and other large expenditures in advance, and gives general approvals (or denials) to the employees to then look after the details.

## Problem 6.12 Identify cash control problems

Many companies put a great amount of effort into controlling their cash, both that on hand and in banks, often more than for any other asset.

1. Why do you think such great effort is required to control cash?
2. List the control problems you'd expect in each of the following cases. To answer, try to visualise how the cash would probably flow into and out of the company and its bank accounts:
   - **a** cash collected at the sales counter of the local fast-food outlet
   - **b** wages being paid to construction employees working on a large highway project
   - **c** donations to the Heart Fund being collected by door-to-door volunteer canvassers
   - **d** money deposited into parking meters owned by your municipality
   - **e** cash provided to the receptionist at the main entrance of a large company, to be used to pay for deliveries, buy emergency supplies and other such minor things.

## Problem 6.13 Is internal control viewed too negatively in this chapter?

In this chapter's coverage of internal control, numerous parties were identified as playing a role in a company's internal control and/or in frauds and losses the company might experience. It could be argued that all this has represented an overly negative view of how enterprises operate and how people interact.

For the parties listed below, describe both positive and negative contributions the parties might be expected to make to an enterprise's internal control and the prevention or incurrence of losses. You might not be able to think of both pluses and minuses for every party, but if not, try to make a good description of whichever side you can think of.

- **a** top management
- **b** the board of directors and its audit committee
- **c** the external auditors
- **d** employees
- **e** customers
- **f** suppliers.

## Problem 6.14 Prepare a report on internal control

The NSW Golf Society operates a museum for the benefit and enjoyment of present and potential golfers. During hours when the museum is open to the public, two clerks who are positioned at the entrance collect a five dollar admission fee from each non-member patron. Members of golf clubs are permitted to enter free of charge upon presentation of their membership cards.

At the end of each day, one of the clerks delivers the proceeds to the accountant. The accountant counts the cash in the presence of the clerk and places it in a safe. Each Friday afternoon the accountant and one of the clerks deliver all the cash held in the safe to the bank, and receive an authenticated deposit slip, which provides the basis for the weekly entry in the cash receipts journal.

The board of directors of the Golf Society has identified a need to improve the system of internal control over cash admission fees. The board has determined that the cost of installing turnstiles for sales booths or otherwise altering the physical layout of the museum will greatly exceed any benefits that may be derived.

***Required:***

Identify weaknesses in the existing system of internal control over cash admission fees and recommend an improvement for each of the weaknesses identified.

## Problem 6.15 Simple bank reconciliation

Reconcile Henry's month-end bank account balance and, based on your analysis, indicate what corrections you would make to Henry's records:

- **a** month-end bank balance according to the bank's statement: $8791
- **b** month-end bank balance according to Henry's records: $7371
- **c** outstanding cheques (not processed by the bank yet): $1877
- **d** outstanding deposit (not processed by the bank yet): $250
- **e** bank charges Henry had not known about: $43
- **f** someone else's cheque put through Henry's account by the bank: $185
- **g** interest on the bank balance credited to Henry by the bank but not known to Henry: $21.

## Problem 6.16 Explain why bank reconciliation statements are prepared and then prepare one

1 Why are bank reconciliation statements prepared? Under what circumstances would it be unnecessary to prepare a bank reconciliation statement?

2 You have been supplied with the following information produced by comparing the records of the Swift Company with the most recent bank statement:

- a debit balance as per cash at bank account in ledger as at 30 June, $12 644.40
- b credit balance as per bank statement as at 30 June, $16 860.30
- c deposits not reflected on bank statement, $1880.00
- d unpresented cheques 30 June, $6185.90
- e service charge on bank statement not recorded in books, $30.00
- f error by bank – Switch Company cheque charged to Swift Company's account, $420.00
- g cheque for advertising expense, $480.00, incorrectly recorded in books as $840.00.

3 Prepare a bank reconciliation statement as at 30 June.

4 Prepare entries in general journal form to update the records of the Swift Company.

## Problem 6.17 Simple bank reconciliation

On 30 June 2002, the bank account for Holmes Traders showed a debit balance of $13 418 and the bank statement showed a credit balance of $20 208. A comparison of the two sets of records disclosed:

- a a bank service fee of $10
- b that the bank had collected $1000 on behalf of Holmes Traders on the redemption of debentures
- c that the date of a deposit of $2450 was shown by Holmes Traders as 30 June 2002, whereas the bank did not record the deposit until 1 July 2002
- d unpresented cheques totalling $8250.

Prepare a bank reconciliation statement at 30 June 2002.

## Problem 6.18 Prepare a bank reconciliation statement

The bookkeeper at Covington Ltd undertakes a bank reconciliation at the end of every month. On 31 August, the bank reconciliation showed a deposit in transit of $650 and two outstanding cheques (no. 463 for $170 and no. 471 for $350). The adjusted cash balance in the company records was $5906 debit.

The company's September bank statement is shown below.

**Bank statement**
State Bank

Covington Ltd
Kensington, NSW

Statement period
31/8/01–30/9/01

| | | | | $ |
|---|---|---|---|---|
| 31 Aug | Balance brought forward | | | 5 776 CR |
| 1 Sep | Deposit | | 650 | 6 426 CR |
| 2 Sep | Deposit | | 590 | 7 016 CR |
| | 482 | 260 | | 6 756 CR |
| 5 Sep | Deposit | | 340 | 7 096 CR |
| 7 Sep | 471 | 350 | | 6 746 CR |
| 8 Sep | Deposit | | 420 | 7 166 CR |

| | | | | |
|---|---|---|---|---|
| 11 Sep | Deposit | | 210 | 7 376 CR |
| | 484 | 350 | | 7 026 CR |
| 12 Sep | 483 | 850 | | 6 176 CR |
| 14 Sep | Deposit | | 810 | 6 986 CR |
| | 487 | 740 | | 6 246 CR |
| 19 Sep | Deposit | | 280 | 6 526 CR |
| 21 Sep | 485 | 680 | | 5 846 CR |
| 25 Sep | Deposit | | 760 | 6 606 CR |
| 28 Sep | 486 | 630 | | 5 976 CR |
| 30 Sep | 480 | 430 | | 5 546 CR |
| | Interest | | 18 | 5 564 CR |
| | Govt Debits Tax | 11 | | 5 553 CR |

Company records indicate the following deposits made and cheques written during September:

| **Deposits made** | | **Cheques written** | |
|---|---|---|---|
| | $ | No. | $ |
| Sep 2 | 590 | 479 | 240 |
| 5 | 340 | 480 | 430 |
| 8 | 420 | 481 | 345 |
| 11 | 210 | 482 | 260 |
| 14 | 810 | 483 | 850 |
| 19 | 280 | 484 | 350 |
| 25 | 760 | 485 | 680 |
| 29 | 630 | 486 | 360 |
| | 4040 | 487 | 740 |
| | | | 4255 |

The cash at bank account balance on 30 September was $5691. In reviewing cheques, a mistake was discovered: cheque no. 486, written for advertising expenses of $630, was recorded in the cash payments journal as $360.

***Required:***

1. Prepare a bank reconciliation statement for Covington Ltd at 30 September.
2. Prepare the necessary journal entries to bring the cash at bank account up to date as at 30 September.

## Problem 6.19 Prepare a bank reconciliation statement

The following information pertains to Bryant & Douglas Pty Ltd October 2002 cash transactions.

1. The following unpresented cheques appeared on the 30 September bank reconciliation:

| Cheque no. | Amount |
|---|---|
| | $ |
| 6539 | 603.80 |
| 6548 | 1 802.50 |
| 6549 | 158.70 |
| 6555 | 287.80 |
| 6558 | 495.00 |

2 All cheques except no. 6558 are included on the 31 October bank statement. On 30 September a deposit of $2581.50 was outstanding.

3 The adjusted debit book balance on 30 September was $19 829.78. All adjusting entries were properly made on 30 September.

4 Total cash payments of $49 782.80 were credited to cash at bank.

5 Total cash receipts for October were $52 145.70, but $1982.45 of 31 October receipts have not been received by the bank.

6 The bank statement shows an ending credit balance of $26 926.13; service charges of $32.40; a $95.40 cheque returned because of insufficient funds; and the 30 September deposit of $2581.50, which arrived at the bank on 1 October.

7 Cheque no. 6585, written for telephone expense and recorded in the cheque register as $989, was written for and paid by the bank as $998.

8 Paid cheques on the bank statement include a $582.50 cheque drawn by Bryant's Ltd.

9 The following cheques are included in the company's records but not in the company's bank statement:

| Cheque no. | Amount |
|---|---|
| | $ |
| 6598 | 287.40 |
| 6599 | 2 568.70 |
| 6614 | 2 090.60 |
| 6615 | 898.00 |
| 6616 | 1 095.50 |

*Required:*

Prepare a bank reconciliation at 31 October 2002. Prepare any necessary general journal adjusting entries.

## Problem 6.20 Prepare a bank reconciliation statement

The following information relates to the cash transactions of Mason and Coburn Ltd during November.

1 The 31 October bank reconciliation contained the unpresented cheques below:

| Cheque no. | Amount |
|---|---|
| | $ |
| 2812 | 513 |
| 2832 | 842 |
| 2845 | 657 |
| 2847 | 150 |

2 All cheques except no. 2847 are included in the 30 November bank statement. On 31 October, a deposit of $1345 was outstanding.

3 The adjusted cash balance in the general ledger on 31 October was $5292.

4 Total cash receipts for November were $5627, but $2382 of this amount was received on 30 November and has not been recorded by the bank.

5 Total cash payments of $5218 were credited to the cash at bank account.

6 The 30 November bank statement shows an ending credit balance of $3520. It includes service charges of $120, an $821 cheque returned because of insufficient funds, and the 31 October deposit of $1345, which arrived at the bank on 1 November.

7 Cheque no. 2932, written for maintenance expenses and recorded in the cheque register as $368, was written for and paid by the bank as $386.

8 Paid cheques on the bank statement include a $725 cheque drawn by Mason Bros Ltd.

9 The following cheques are included in the company's records but not in the company's bank statement:

| Cheque no. | Amount |
|---|---|
| | $ |
| 2903 | 317 |
| 2917 | 569 |
| 2944 | 411 |
| 2945 | 438 |

*Required:*

Prepare a bank reconciliation statement at 30 November. What entries must be made in the general journal to update the records of the company?

## Problem 6.21 Prepare a bank reconciliation statement

The following information comes from the records of Anthea's Homewares.

From the cash receipts records:

| | $ |
|---|---|
| April 1 | 687 |
| 8 | 805 |
| 15 | 412 |
| 22 | 903 |
| 29 | 246 |

From the cash payments records:

| Date | Cheque no. | $ |
|---|---|---|
| April 2 | 570 | 415 |
| 3 | 571 | [illegible] |
| 5 | 572 | 137 |
| 8 | 574 | 1 315 |
| 11 | 575 | 642 |
| 15 | 576 | 701 |
| 17 | 577 | 240 |
| 20 | 578 | 194 |
| 23 | 579 | 311 |
| 27 | 580 | 293 |
| 28 | 581 | 114 |

From the general ledger:

Cash at bank — Account no. 111

| Date | Item | Post ref. | Debit | Credit | Balance |
|---|---|---|---|---|---|
| March 31 | Balance | | | | 2 594 DR |

**Bank statement**

| | | | | | Statement Peiod 31/3/01–30/4/01 |
|---|---|---|---|---|---|
| | | | | | $ |
| March | 31 | Balance brought forward | | | 3 657 CR |
| April | 1 | Deposit | | 687 | 4 344 CR |
| | 3 | 568 | 372 | | 3 972 CR |
| | 4 | 570 | 415 | | 3 557 CR |
| | 8 | Deposit | | 805 | 4 362 CR |
| | | 572 | 137 | | 4 225 CR |
| | 9 | Direct credit | | 696 | 4 921 CR |
| | 10 | 574 | 1513 | | 3 408 CR |
| | 11 | 575 | 642 | | 2 766 CR |
| | 14 | 552 | 435 | | 2 331 CR |
| | 15 | Deposit | | 412 | 2 743 CR |
| | 16 | 571 | 82 | | 2 661 CR |
| | 19 | NSF | 421 | | 2 240 CR |
| | 20 | 576 | 701 | | 1 539 CR |
| | 22 | Deposit | | 903 | 2 442 CR |
| | | 578 | 194 | | 2 248 CR |
| | 25 | 560 | 97 | | 2 151 CR |
| | 27 | 577 | 240 | | 1 911 CR |
| | 30 | 581 | 114 | | 1 797 CR |
| | | Interest | | 58 | 1 855 CR |
| | | Govt Debits Tax | 24 | | 1 831 CR |

The NSF cheque was received from Bond Enterprises, a debtor. The direct credit represents a $650 bill collected by the bank, plus interest. Cheque no. 573 was prepared improperly and has been cancelled. Cheque no. 574 for a purchase of inventory was incorrectly recorded as a cash payment of $1315 instead of $1513. On 31 March, the only reconciling items were a series of unpresented cheques: no. 552 at $435, no. 560 at $97, no. 562 at $159 and no. 568 at $372.

***Required:***

Prepare a bank reconciliation statement for Anthea's Homewares at 30 April and any necessary adjusting journal entries.

## Problem 6.22 Prepare a bank reconciliation statement with overdraft

The following information comes from the records of Betty's Boutique.

**From the cash receipts records:**

| Date 2002 | | Cash (DR) amount $ |
|---|---|---|
| Nov | 1 | 1 828 |
| | 7 | 2 024 |
| | 14 | 6 480 |
| | 21 | 5 292 |

**From the cash payments records:**

| Date 2002 | | Cheque no. | Amount $ |
|---|---|---|---|
| Nov | 1 | 721 | 28 |
| | 2 | 722 | 566 |
| | 3 | 723 | 832 |
| | 4 | 724 | 54 |

| | | | | |
|---|---|---|---|---|
| 30 | 3 884 | 5 | 726 | 10 |
| | | 10 | 727 | 11 492 |
| | | 11 | 728 | 1 418 |
| | | 20 | 729 | 2 492 |
| | | 21 | 730 | 152 |
| | | 22 | 731 | 10 000 |

**From the general ledger:**

| **Cash at bank** | | | | | Account no. 111 |
|---|---|---|---|---|---|
| **Date 2002** | **Item** | **Post ref.** | **Debit** | **Credit** | **Balance** |
| Oct 31 | Balance | | | | 4 930 DR |

**Wolfpac National Bank** — **Statement of** Betty's Boutique

| **Date 2002** | | **Particulars** | **Debit $** | **Credit $** | **Balance $** |
|---|---|---|---|---|---|
| Nov | 1 | Balance | | | 7 570 CR |
| | 2 | 700 | 200 | | 7 370 CR |
| | 2 | 707 | 1 000 | | 6 370 CR |
| | 2 | Deposit | | 1 828 | 8 198 CR |
| | 4 | 720 | 920 | | 7 278 CR |
| | 4 | 721 | 28 | | 7 250 CR |
| | 6 | 723 | 832 | | 6 418 CR |
| | 8 | 724 | 54 | | 6 364 CR |
| | 8 | Deposit | | 2 024 | 8 388 CR |
| | 12 | 726 | 10 | | 8 378 CR |
| | 12 | NSF | 30 | | 8 348 CR |
| | 14 | 728 | 1 814 | | 6 534 CR |
| | 15 | Deposit | | 6 480 | 13 014 CR |
| | 22 | Deposit | | [illegible] | 10 306 CR |
| | 24 | 727 | 11 492 | | [illegible] |
| | 26 | 730 | 152 | | 6 662 CR |
| | 26 | 731 | 10 000 | | 3 338 DR |
| | 26 | DC | | 816 | 2 522 DR |
| | 30 | SC | 8 | | 2 530 DR |
| | 30 | IN | | 84 | 2 446 DR |

Code: DC—Direct credit; DD—Direct debit; IN—Interest; SC—Service charge; NSF—Non-sufficient funds

The NSF cheque was received from J. Pindar, a debtor. The direct credit represents an $800 bill collected by the bank plus interest. Cheque no. 725 was prepared improperly and has been cancelled. Cheque no. 728 for a purchase of inventory was incorrectly recorded as a cash payment of $1418 instead of $1814. On 1 November there were only the following unpresented cheques as reconciling items: no. 700 at $200; no. 707 at $1000; no. 719 at $520; no. 720 at $920.

*Required:*

Prepare a bank reconciliation statement as at 30 November 2002 and any necessary adjusting journal entries.

## Problem 6.23 Prepare a bank reconciliation statement where company has an overdraft

1 How can a bank reconciliation strengthen control over cash? Is it worth the time and effort, if internal control over cash records is already very strong? Why?

2 The bank reconciliation statement for Caramelle Pty Ltd at 31 March is shown below.

**Caramelle Pty Ltd**
Bank reconciliation
as at 31 March

| | $ | $ |
|---|---|---|
| Debit balance as per bank statement | | 3 521 |
| Plus unpresented cheques: | | |
| 6971 | 274 | |
| 6982 | 591 | |
| 6995 | 132 | 997 |
| | | 4 518 |
| Less outstanding deposit | | (894) |
| Credit balance as per company records | | 3 624 |

Cash receipts and cash payments for April are as follows:

| Cash receipts | | | Date | | Cash payments Cheque no. | $ |
|---|---|---|---|---|---|---|
| | | $ | | | | |
| April | 3 | 621 | April | 1 | 7002 | 98 |
| | 4 | 524 | | 4 | 7003 | 512 |
| | 7 | 895 | | 5 | 7004 | 467 |
| | 12 | 470 | | 7 | 7005 | 351 |
| | 15 | 152 | | 8 | 7006 | 661 |
| | 19 | 423 | | 11 | 7007 | 111 |
| | 22 | 609 | | 14 | 7008 | 474 |
| | 23 | 249 | | 18 | 7009 | 392 |
| | 26 | 311 | | 22 | 7010 | 187 |
| | 29 | 248 | | 24 | 7011 | 163 |
| | | 4 502 | | 28 | 7012 | 401 |
| | | | | 30 | 7013 | 32 |
| | | | | | | 3 849 |

The bank statement received at the end of April shows the following:

**Bank statement**

| | | Debit | Credit | Statement period 31/3/01–30/4/01 $ | |
|---|---|---|---|---|---|
| 31 March | Balance brought forward | | | 3 521 | DR |
| 1 April | Cash/cheque | | 894 | 2 627 | DR |
| 2 | 6971 | 274 | | 2 901 | DR |
| 4 | Cash/cheque | | 621 | 2 280 | DR |
| 5 | Cash/cheque | | 524 | 1 756 | DR |
| 7 | 7004 | 467 | | 2 223 | DR |
| 8 | 7003 | 512 | | 2 735 | DR |
| 11 | Return – NSF | 77 | | 2 812 | DR |
| 12 | 7007 | 111 | | 2 923 | DR |
| 13 | Cash/cheque | | 470 | 2 453 | DR |
| | 7002 | 98 | | 2 551 | DR |
| 15 | Dividend | | 190 | 2 361 | DR |
| 16 | Cash/cheque | | 152 | 2 209 | DR |
| 17 | 6995 | 132 | | 2 341 | DR |
| 19 | 7008 | 474 | | 2 815 | DR |
| 20 | Cash/cheque | | 423 | 2 392 | DR |
| 21 | 7006 | 661 | | 3 053 | DR |
| 23 | Cash/cheque | | 609 | 2 444 | DR |
| | 7009 | 392 | | 2 836 | DR |
| 24 | Cash/cheque | | 249 | 2 587 | DR |
| 25 | 7011 | 163 | | 2 750 | DR |
| 27 | Cash/cheque | | 311 | 2 439 | DR |
| 29 | 7010 | 187 | | 2 626 | DR |
| 30 | 7012 | 401 | | 3 027 | DR |
| | Interest on overdraft | 152 | | 3 179 | DR |

The 'Return' item on April 11 was a dishonoured cheque from a customer.

Complete a bank reconciliation statement as at 30 April and prepare journal entries for adjustments to be made to the records of the company.

3 What enquiries would be desirable following preparation of Caramello Pty Ltd's bank reconciliation statement at 30 April?

## Problem 6.24 Prepare journal entries relating to petty cash

A petty cash fund of $250 was set up by Snodgrass Ltd on 1 August by drawing cheque no. 232. Transactions relating to petty cash in August were as follows:

| Date | Voucher no. | Amount $ | Details |
|---|---|---|---|
| 1 Aug | | 250.00 | Establishment of fund (chq #232) |
| 3 | 53 | 25.00 | Staff tea supplies |
| 4 | 54 | 5.00 | Fares |
| 7 | 55 | 19.00 | Taxi |
| | 56 | 7.50 | Fares |
| 10 | 57 | 3.00 | Postage |

| | | | |
|---|---|---|---|
| 15 | 59 | 24.00 | Taxi |
| | | | Reimbursement of fund (chq #241) |
| 19 | 60 | 5.00 | Fares |
| | 61 | 28.00 | Taxi |
| 24 | 62 | 15.00 | Donation to charity |
| 25 | 63 | 22.50 | Stationery supplies |
| 26 | 64 | 110.00 | Entertaining clients |
| 31 | 65 | 7.00 | Fares |
| | | | Reimbursement of fund (chq #244) |

***Required:***

Prepare journal entries to record the transactions during August.

## Problem 6.25 Prepare journal entries relating to petty cash and explain safeguards inherent in a petty cash system

Sweet and Co established a petty cash fund on 1 December 2002, by drawing cheque no. 181 for $200. The newly appointed office boy was made responsible for the control of the fund and maintaining the records. Transactions relating to petty cash during December were as follows:

| Date 2002 | Voucher no. | Details | $ |
|---|---|---|---|
| Dec 1 | 1 | COD delivery of goods for sale | 70 |
| 3 | 2 | tea money | 20 |
| 4 | 3 | donation to charity | 50 |
| 5 | 4 | fares | 40 |
| | | Reimbursement cheque no. 192 drawn and petty cash fund increased to $500. | |
| 7 | 5 | tea money | 30 |
| 9 | 6 | cartage inwards | 40 |
| 10 | 7 | entertaining clients | 150 |
| 14 | 8 | fares | 50 |
| 16 | 9 | stationery | 120 |
| 18 | 10 | tea money | 20 |
| 19 | | reimbursement cheque no. 206 drawn | |
| 20 | | Petty cashier fails to attend for work and it is discovered that the petty cash tin is empty. | |
| | | The missing cash is immediately recovered but it is decided to reduce the fund to $250. | |
| 22 | 11 | entertaining clients | 150 |
| 24 | 12 | staff Christmas party | 30 |
| 29 | 13 | fares | 20 |
| 30 | 14 | payment to E. Lean, sundry creditor | 40 |
| 31 | | reimbursement cheque no. 231 drawn | |

*Required:*

1 Make the necessary entries in the journal.

2 What safeguards for the avoidance of error or defalcation should be inherent in a system of managing petty cash?

## Problem 6.26 Identify cash control problems

Many companies put a great amount of effort into controlling their cash, both that on hand and in banks, often more than for any other asset.

1 Why do you think such great effort is required to control cash?

2 List the control problems you'd expect in each of the following cases. To answer, try to visualise how the cash would probably flow into and out of the company and its bank accounts:

- **a** cash collected at the sales counter of the local fast-food outlet
- **b** wages being paid to construction employees working on a large highway project
- **c** donations to the Red Cross being collected by door-to-door volunteers
- **d** money deposited into parking meters owned by your local council
- **e** cash provided to the receptionist at the main entrance of a large company, to be used to pay for deliveries, buy emergency supplies, and other such minor things.

## Problem 6.27 Prepare report on internal control[3]

Maree Cruise operates a successful retail shop with a staff of three (apart from herself), these being a sales assistant, a cashier and a bookkeeper/general assistant. Maree helps the sales assistant serve customers in busy periods, makes occasional trips to the offices of suppliers to inspect new lines, decides on the lines to be purchased and organises the store display with the help of the sales assistant.

There is a cash register for the recording of cash sales. Credit sales are recorded in multi-copy carbon docket books. At the end of each day the cashier hands to the bookkeeper (a) the cash receipts for the day, (b) the cash register tape and (c) the copies of each sales docket. Delivery charges and incidental expenses are paid for using money from the register (derived from the day's takings). The bookkeeper fills out the deposit slip, uses (b) to write up the cash receipts records and (c) to write up the sales records. The bookkeeper maintains the journal and the general ledger, and sends out customer statements after they have been reviewed by Maree. Maree, the cashier, and the bookkeeper each take turns to do the daily banking depending on who is around and not too busy.

Maree and the bookkeeper open the mail, depending on who is available when it comes in. When Maree opens the mail she hands any cheques and remittance advices from customers to the bookkeeper. When Maree inspected the most recent bank statement she was surprised that there was so little 'money in the bank considering how well we've been doing'.

*Required:*

Identify the control strengths and weaknesses in the handling of cash receipts, and in the cash disbursements for delivery charges and incidental expenses. Make suggestions as to how control can be strengthened. In your discussion make reference to any potential strengths in present procedures which are not being fully utilised. You should also suggest new procedures if you feel any are necessary.

## Problem 6.28 Prepare a report on internal control following embezzlement

Following the embezzlement of $50 000 from Easy-Go Pinball Traders, you have been asked to appraise the information system of the business, with particular reference to the internal control procedures. An investigation soon discloses that there is, in fact, no system and internal control is neither understood nor practised.

Many payments are made from cash taken from the cash register and when it is necessary to draw a cheque it may be signed by any one member of the office staff. The bank statement has not been reconciled for several years. The weekly payroll normally amounts to approximately $5000 but last week it was prepared by an accounts clerk, Ian Pilfer. Pilfer wrote out a cheque for $50 000, recorded $5000 on the cheque butt, signed the cheque himself and drove the firm's car to the bank to collect the payroll. The police have been unable to locate Pilfer, the missing money or the vehicle.

***Required:***

Prepare a report for the management of Easy-Go Pinball Traders, making particular reference to:

**1** the purpose of the bank reconciliation statement

**2** deficiencies in the procedures followed by the business with respect to cash

**3** the changes you would recommend to safeguard the firm's liquid assets in the future.

## Problem 6.29 (Challenging) Prepare a report on internal control

Getwell Pty Ltd is a distributor of pharmaceutical products. Its customers include a wide range of hospitals, chemist shops, department stores and supermarkets.

The company's board of directors has identified a need to strengthen the internal control over Getwell's credit sales system. At present, customers' orders are received over the phone by the sales staff who prepare the sales order (three prenumbered copies). The sales order is approved by the sales manager, who is also the credit manager. The original is filed in numerical sequence in the sales department. One copy of the approved order is forwarded to the accounts department, where it is filed by the bookkeeper alphabetically under the customer name. The other copy is used as the stock request copy, which goes to the warehouse staff, who use it to fill the customer's order and update the perpetual inventory records.

When the order is sent to the customer, the dispatch personnel prepare a two-part delivery docket. One copy of the delivery docket is sent to the accounts department, where the bookkeeper uses it to initiate a two-part invoice, which is numbered manually as it is prepared. The invoices are posted to the sales register by the bookkeeper and mailed to the customer. The second copy is sent to the accounts receivable clerk for posting to the debtor's ledger. The invoices are filed in date order by the accounts receivable clerk.

***Required:***

Identify weaknesses in the present system of internal controls. In each case, state the potential problem and your recommendation to Getwell's board on how this should be overcome or improved upon.

## Problem 6.30 (Challenging) Prepare a report on internal control

The university recently opened a parking station on its lower campus area for the benefit of the students. A guard has been engaged to patrol the lot and issue parking stickers to university students who submit an application form and show evidence of enrolment. When the sticker is affixed to the car, the student may park in the lot for six hours by placing a dollar in the parking meter. The guard inspects the stickers on all parked cars to determine that only students are parking in the lot and also looks at the time gauges to ensure that the meter shows the necessary fees have been paid. The completed application forms are maintained in the guard's office.

Using a master key, the guard empties the meters weekly and delivers the cash to the university's central store department, where a clerk opens it, manually counts the coins, puts the cash in a safe and records the total on a weekly cash report. The report is sent to the university's accounting department. The day following the cash count, the university cashier picks up the cash and manually re-counts it, prepares the deposit slip and makes the deposit at the bank. The deposit slip, authenticated by the bank teller, is sent to the accounting department, where it is filed with the weekly cash report.

***Required:***

Describe any weaknesses in the existing system. Recommend for each weakness at least one improvement to strengthen the internal accounting control over the parking station cash receipts.

### Problem 6.31 (Challenging) Prepare a report on internal control

Cardshark Ltd supplies boxes of NBA basketball cards to various card swap shops around Australia. The company has more than 100 small clients purchasing boxes of cards on credit. Credit terms are net 30 days, with payments mostly being made by mail. Over the past few months, orders have been at a high level, reflecting an upswing in interest in basketball cards. This has meant a marked increase in both the volume of mail coming into the office and individuals paying over the counter. Mail is opened by the office junior, Sally Letter, and separated into payments on accounts and other mail. She also receives any monies that come directly over the counter. Sally sends the money to the cashier, Sam Moneybags, who puts it in the safe to await banking. The key to the safe is held by the accounts clerk, Sara Post. At the end of the week, Sara takes the money to the bank and uses the bank-stamped deposit slip to write up the cash receipts book. Monthly reconciliations of the bank account are prepared by Sara.

***Required:***

Based on this description of Cardshark Ltd's cash receipts system:

1 Identify the potential problems with Sara Post's duties.

2 Other than reassigning duties and responsibilities, give three recommendations in order to improve the current system of handling cash receipts.

## Case 6A Woolworths Limited case

Refer to the latest annual report of Woolworths Limited on the Web.

1 Are there any references to internal control by Woolworths Limited?

2 What details are provided about the internal audit function?

## Case 6B Internal control disclosures

You are provided below with two inserts from the 2001 annual reports of BHP Billiton and John Fairfax Holdings.

### BHP Billiton PLC

#### Internal control

The Directors are responsible for the system of internal controls and for regularly reviewing its effectiveness. The principal aim of the system of internal controls is the management of business risks that are significant to the fulfilment of the BHP Billiton Group's business objectives with a view of enhancing over time the value of the shareholders' investment and safeguarding the assets. Although no system of internal controls can provide absolute assurance that business risks will be fully mitigated, the internal control systems have been designed to meet the BHP Billiton Group's particular needs and the risks to which it is exposed.

### John Fairfax Holdings

#### Internal control framework

The Board is responsible for the Company's overall internal control framework. To assist in discharging this responsibility, the Board has approved an internal control framework summarised as follows:

- Financial reporting: there is a comprehensive budget process with the annual budget approved by the directors. Weekly and monthly results are reported against budget. The consolidated entity reports to shareholders half-yearly. Procedures are also in place to ensure that price-sensitive information is reported to the ASX in accordance with continuous disclosure requirements.
- Operating unit controls: financial controls and procedures including information systems controls are set out in procedures manuals. Management reports on material business issues to the Board at regular Board meetings.
- Investment appraisal: the consolidated entity has defined guidelines for capital expenditure and contract negotiations. These include annual budgets, appraisal and review procedures, levels of authority and due diligence requirements where assets are being acquired or divested.
- Treasury policy: the policy sets out procedures for the management of foreign currency and interest rate exposure, liquidity and credit risks. This policy restricts transactions to those for hedging purposes only and segregates implementation of transactions from account monitoring and settlement.
- Under the direction of the Finance and Audit Committee, management has established a Business Risk Group. Assisted by external experts, that Group undertakes regular reviews of business risk across the consolidated entity and is responsible for development and review of the Group's Business Risk Plan.

***Required:***

1. For both companies who is responsible for internal control?
2. For both companies what would be included in 'business risks'?
3. How does internal control enhance 'over time the value of the shareholders' investment'?
4. Why can't internal controls 'provide absolute assurance that business risks will be fully mitigated'?
5. How does budgeting form part of an internal control system?

## Case 6C Fraud in Colonial Australia

### The first Australian 'accountant': more colour than honesty

The Australian accounting profession has long maintained that its practitioners are imbued with an irreproachable honesty and an impressive commitment to ethical integrity. Current practitioners of accounting might be excused for finding it mildly amusing, if not slightly embarrassing, to discover that many of the first accountants to grace our shores were the very antithesis of the lofty ideals to which the profession lays claim.

There were many colourful individuals who were associated with the early commercial life of the New South Wales colony, 1788–1828 – a rich smorgasbord of convict rogues employed as clerks or accountants in the colony. One of the most remarkable was Thomas Ayliffe Gee (1784–1827), a convicted thief and embezzler.

Gee came to notice because his name is recorded under the only entry for 'Accountant' in the index of the colony's first paper, the *Sydney Gazette*, for the years 1803 to 1825. That entry relates to an advertisement that Gee placed in December 1814, seeking employment in 'keeping accounts'. His advertisement, complete with its deferential prose, is curious. It prompted further inquiry, which revealed Gee to be a rather special (or infamous?) accountant. He appears to be the first person transported to NSW who was described in the indent of details of arriving convicts, as an 'accountant' (in fact, as 'Clk & Acco't').

In 1813, Gee, with 'fair pale' complexion, light brown hair and hazel eyes, was a clerk in the accounting house of a London brewery. He was responsible for 'receiving money' for the brewery, entering the sums received in his own cash book, and then striking a reconciling balance weekly. Monies he received were handed over periodically to the brewery proprietors who would then make entries in their own cash books. But in March of 1813, Gee somehow 'failed' to make cash book entries for several cheques and bank notes totalling £96.5.0d that he had received from a customer. To conceal his fraud, he made false ledger entries.

In July 1813 Gee was discovered to be 'living in a most extravagant and profligate manner', and he was dismissed from the brewery's accompting house. The next day his embezzlement was discovered. An investigation revealed that the considerable sum of £1300 was missing. Warrants were issued for Gee's arrest and a reward was offered for his apprehension. Several days later a letter was received from Gee returning three bills of exchange and expressing his dread of the stigma that any punishment 'would bring upon his numerous and respectable relations'. He said that, if found, he would commit suicide, putting it quaintly thus: *If, by any untoward circumstance, my abode should be traced, I hope my Maker will excuse me if I should be my own executioner.*

His abode, in fact, was discovered two months later – but he reneged on his threat to kill himself. He was tried before the Old Bailey and sentenced to be transported to NSW for 14 years. He arrived in Sydney aboard the *Somersetshire* in October 1814 and appears to have been granted a Ticket of Leave from Governor Macquarie on arrival. Shortly afterwards, he placed his advertisement in the *Sydney Gazette*. Whether he was successful in obtaining employment is unknown. If he did so, it could not have been for long. Apparently, Gee found it difficult to resist the temptation to steal and he was soon in trouble with the authorities. In March 1815 he was found guilty of an unspecified crime and was transported for one year, as a secondary punishment, to the closed penal settlement at Newcastle.

What befell Gee in the next few years is unclear. There is evidence that he was employed as a clerk in the Principal Superintendent's Office sometime between 1816 and 1821. In September 1821 he was employed as a clerk in the Government Store, the Commissariat, in Sydney.

In December 1822 Gee obtained employment as a clerk with a Sydney merchant, Vickers Jacob, at No. 11 George Street. But in the following year, he was indicted before the Criminal Court in Sydney for feloniously stealing three cases of gin from Vickers Jacob. In May 1823, as Jacob's clerk, Gee had been responsible for 'entering cargo discharging' from a ship at King's Wharf and was required to forward it to his employer. But, Gee 'thought it proper to hire a carter and send home' to Mary McCarthy (with whom he co-habited), cases of gin 'for his own use'.

Gee was sentenced to a further term of secondary transportation – this time for seven years to Port Macquarie, where he died on 13 May 1827 'from a rupture of the bladder'. He was 43.

Gee appears to have been the first 'accountant' transported to NSW. He leaves the impression of being an excitable character, prone to imbibing excessively and enjoying the 'good life'. He was far from a paragon of virtue. Indeed, there was a sense of relief when he was sent to Port Macquarie. The *Sydney Gazette* opined that the Court had 'performed an act of great kindness on behalf of this part of the Colony in removing [Gee] to a distance'. He was not a good role model for contemporary accountants.

Russell Craig is Professor of Accounting at The Australian National University. He thanks Corn Num for her research assistance.

## References


- Archives Office of New South Wales, AO Reel 1028 4/3493, p. 477; Fiche no. 614-744.
- Colonial Secretary's Papers, 1788–1825, Reels 6004, pp. 476–477; 6016, p. 16; 6059, p. 126; 6023, p. 107.
- [illegible], C. and R. Howell, *The Windingsheet*, Port Macquarie Historical Society, [illegible].
- Index to the *Sydney Gazette*, 1803–1825, Mitchell Library, Sydney.
- International Genealogical Index, March 1993 version.
- NSW Pioneers' Index, Vol. 44b, No. 74.
- Old Bailey Proceedings, Part 2, 1794–1834, Reel 28.
- The *Sydney Gazette*, 17 December 1814; 29 May, 16 October 1823.
- The *Times*, 23 September, 1813, p. 3c.


(Source: Russell Craig, *Australian CPA*, October 1998, pp. 68–9.)

*Required:*

1 How has the role of the accountant changed since the time of Thomas Gee?

2 Outline any weaknesses in the internal control system of the London brewery.

3 How did Gee conceal the fraud from the London brewery? How was the fraud discovered? How else could it have been discovered?

## CASE 6D Records and internal control for Metcash

The 2001 annual report of Metcash Trading Limited includes in the operations summary some details of three of their major business units as shown below:

### IGA Distribution

#### Major activities

- 'Champion of the Independent Retailer'.
- Eight world-class Distribution Centres, benchmarked to international efficiency standards, carry around 14 000 items to meet the dry, chilled and frozen grocery requirements of approximately 4500 independent retail grocery stores in the eastern States and South Australia.
- A comprehensive range of services assists retailers, including 24-hour retail system support, in-store training, specialist advice on store refurbishment and building new sites and a non-trade procurement service.

#### Significant events

- An increase in the number of IGA stores to 1036.
- Sales growth of 16.9 per cent to $2.43 billion.
- 52 new stores (totalling 22 968 $m^2$), 10 store extensions (totalling 1 151 $m^2$) and 60 store refurbishments, with these 122 projects totalling an additional 24 119 $m^2$ of floor space.
- First combined National IGA Expo and Conference.

### Australian Liquor Marketers

#### Major activities

- ALM is the leading broad-range liquor wholesaler in Australia.
- Sixteen world-class, low-cost Distribution Centres across Australia and New Zealand, benchmarked against international players, carry more than 8000 products to meet the wine, spirits and beer requirements of over 13 000 licensed premises.
- ALM provides a viable alternative to direct supply by offering liquor suppliers a low cost route to market.

#### Significant events

- Sales growth of 22 per cent, attributable to successful strategies to attract customers away from direct supply and an increase of over 50 per cent in the sale of ready to drink (RTD) beverages.
- Rationalisation of warehouse locations and operations in Adelaide, Melbourne and Brisbane and relocation of warehouse operations in Auckland.
- Significant increase in supplier support, reflecting greater confidence in ALM's performance and ability to meet the standards required by suppliers in dealing with the independent market.
- Promotion of the 'ALM Advantage', a non-trade procurement offer to retailers offering them significant savings on petrol, communications services and EFTPOS services.

## Campbells Cash & Carry

### Major activities

- 40 wholesale cash and carry warehouses across New South Wales, Victoria, Queensland and South Australia carry 12 000 liquor, food service, grocery, dairy, frozen, confectionery and tobacco items to meet the requirements of more than 70 000 business customers.
- A broad product range has enabled Campbells to evolve into an effective wholesale distribution network catering for a combination of 'walk-in' trade and full delivery distribution facilities.

### Significant events

- Sales growth of 12.4 per cent.
- C Store Distribution has established itself as a specialist single-pick operation, well positioned to take advantage of the growing corporate, franchised and independent convenience store market.
- C Store Distribution assists customer groups in driving compliance with off-invoice promotional pricing, range control and electronic ordering facilities.
- Campbells' wide range and low warehouse costs have enabled it to provide an excellent source of supply for emerging e-commerce customers who choose to outsource their warehousing and logistics.

*Discuss:*

1 The kinds of transactions that would occur for such businesses, and the record-keeping that would be appropriate for them.

2 The kinds of internal control problems that seem likely, and some possible solutions for these problems.

## Notes

1 Section 6.4 is adapted with permission from L. Solomon, L. Wather, P. Vargo & L. Plunkett, South-Western College Publishing, Cincinnati, Ohio, 1996.

2 The material for the following steps and some questions were provided by Rosina Mladenovic. A number of the questions were provided by Gordon Howitt, Claudia Gormly, Chris Poullaos, Rosina Mladenovic and Peter Roebuck.

3 See note 1.

# Chapter 7
# *Inventory*

## On completion of this chapter you should be able to:

- explain the difference between perpetual and periodic inventory systems
- develop effective inventory controls
- analyse the effect of inventory transactions on the financial statements
- prepare journal entries for transactions under both the periodic and perpetual methods
- discuss the different types of cost flow assumptions
- calculate the impact of different cost flow assumptions on profit determination and inventory valuation
- apply the lower of cost and market rule to the write-down of inventory
- interpret the inventory disclosure policies of Australian companies
- explain why inventory valuation is important to managers.

# 7.1 Chapter overview

For many companies, inventory is one of the largest assets. In this chapter we will consider inventory control, and various aspects of inventory accounting. Inventory accounting affects both the statement of financial position (inventory valuation) and the expense recognised for the use of inventory (cost of goods sold expense).

# 7.2 Inventory control

Section 5.6 provided an introduction to inventory control. Chapter 6 emphasised the importance of keeping accurate records to provide information to both internal and external users. Many of the records kept have to do with the control of inventory. Inventory control is an important issue for management because a high percentage of working capital may be tied up in inventory. Inventory may be perishable or become obsolete if held too long, and, due to the physical attributes of some types of inventory, there may be a great potential for theft.

Several different inventory control systems may be used, depending on the nature of the inventory and the objectives of management. The methods explained below are the two most commonly used by business. Each provides a different amount of information at a different cost. It is important to note that the choice of inventory control system is a *record-keeping* choice as opposed to a *reporting* choice: management is simply deciding how to record the inventory. How inventory is reported on the financial statements will be dealt with in later sections of this chapter.

## The perpetual inventory control method

When an order of inventory items is received, the quantity received is added to the quantity recorded as being already on hand. When items are sold, they are deducted from the recorded quantity. Therefore, the perpetual inventory method shows how many items are supposed to be on hand at any time:

- Take the quantity on hand at the beginning of the period.
- Add the quantity purchased during the period.
- Deduct the quantity sold during the period.
- Equals the quantity that should be on hand at the end of the period.

The name perpetual inventory control comes from the idea that the accounting system has a continuously updated figure for the amount that should be on hand. If a physical count of the inventory fails to show that quantity, the company knows that some have been lost or stolen, or that there has been an error in the records. Just as for cash, bank accounts and accounts receivable, the records provide accounting control in addition to any physical protection. The accounting records tell the company what to expect to be on hand.

If the cost of items is included in the count along with the quantity, the perpetual record can be used to estimate the total cost of inventory at any time, without having to bother counting and pricing everything.

**Beginning inventory cost (support with physical count if desired)**
**+ Cost of purchases of inventory (records)**
**– Cost of inventory sold (records)**
**= Ending inventory cost (support with physical count if desired)**

The perpetual control method has been assumed in most of the examples so far in the text, because purchases have been recorded as debits to inventory asset, and cost of goods sold has been credited to the asset and debited to COGS expense.

The perpetual method provides additional management information. Suppose that after the above calculation, the expected ending inventory cost was $100 000, but a count to support that showed only $96 500 of inventory on hand. Management would know there had been a $3500 shortage or other error, and could intensify controls over inventory if that was thought to be cost effective. (If it cost $10 000 to improve the controls, management might well conclude that losing $3500 was the cheaper option.)

The inventory asset account would be adjusted to the count by an adjusting entry to reduce inventory and increase an expense. The accounts would then show the expense being incurred by the imperfect control.

If there were *more* inventory on hand than expected, there could instead be an inventory overage account, a credit balance so a sort of negative expense, though this would probably indicate an error somewhere as it is unlikely any thieves were breaking in and adding inventory.

The overage/shortage expense account would probably be included with COGS in the income statement, as management would usually consider this information to be an internal matter, and it would not likely, we hope, be large enough to be material in its effect on COGS.

## The periodic count method

When goods are bought, they are put on the shelf or in the storeroom, and when they are sold or used, they are taken off the shelf or out of the storeroom. With the perpetual control system, records are kept of these movements, to provide expected quantities or values on hand. But if complete records of such inventory changes are not kept, the enterprise does not have records to indicate what should be on hand. The only way to tell what is on hand is to go and count it. Because this sort of counting tends to be done only periodically, when an inventory figure is needed for financial statements or insurance purposes, this method is called the periodic inventory method. While there may be other features of internal control present, such as physical protection and insurance, it lacks the parallel record-keeping that gives the perpetual method its value. There is no way to reconcile counts to records in order to discover errors, but it is simple and cheap to operate because no continuing records are kept. Record-keeping does cost money!

**Beginning inventory (count)**
**+ Purchases (records)**
**– Ending inventory (count)**
**= Inventory sold (deduced), that is, cost of goods sold**

Because what has been sold is deduced rather than known from records, you can see that it might not all have been sold. Some could have been lost, stolen, evaporated and so on. So under the periodic method, cost of goods sold expense (cost of counted beginning inventory + cost of purchases – cost of counted ending inventory) includes all these other possibilities. If the periodic method is used, other forms of control need to exist to indicate theft and so on. For example, unexpected changes in the ratio of cost of goods sold to sales should be investigated.

## Inventory: cost and benefits of controls

The perpetual method can be costly in terms of record-keeping. Management must pay someone to record, sort and compile the information. What type of business uses a perpetual system? The local car dealership is a good example. Cars are expensive – therefore a large investment must be made if a good supply is to be on hand for customers to choose from. The high value of cars and the need to keep track for registration and insurance purposes mean that serial numbers and other identification information are easily available and usually recorded in various places. Automobiles have a high risk of becoming obsolete because consumer preferences change, and the cost of theft is high even if only one car is stolen. Because of the relatively small quantity of cars sold by most dealerships, record-keeping costs are not high. Similarly, companies selling more expensive items such as television sets, stereos, refrigerators, jewellery or furniture use the perpetual method.

In the past many organisations that have a large number of sales, particularly if each item has relatively low value, have used the periodic inventory method because of its lower costs. However, with the large increase in computer-based inventory systems, most organisations now use the perpetual system because of its advantages in controlling inventory. For example, many retail companies have cash registers that use optical scanners to read the barcodes attached to products. This reads the sales price and also updates the inventory records. Have you wondered recently why when you return an item of clothing to a department store to exchange for a larger size, they scan both the returned item and the replacement item? As the sales price is generally the same, the usual reason is to update inventory records. This not only assists with control but helps with planning for ordering additional inventory.

### How's your understanding?

Here is a question you should be able to answer, based on what you have read:
Does your university bookshop use a perpetual or periodic inventory system? Why? (Almost certainly you will find they use perpetual. If you ask them if they have a certain book they will check in their computer inventory records. The reasons are for better reordering and control of theft.)

## 7.3 Accounting entries for perpetual and periodic inventory

Brinkworth Pty Ltd uses a perpetual accounting control system for its inventory. It has the following data for a recent period:

| | $ | | $ |
|---|---|---|---|
| Beginning accounts receivable | 40 000 | Beginning inventory | 23 000 |
| Purchases during period (all cash) | 114 000 | Sales (all credit) | 150 000 |
| Cash collected in period | 115 000 | Ending inventory count | 28 000 |

The company's mark-up is 50 per cent on cost (that is, selling price is 150 per cent of cost). Just to make it easier, we'll assume that all sales, purchases and collections were in single transactions.

First we will consider the impact on the accounting equation:

| | | | $ |
|---|---|---|---|
| a | Purchases | Increase inventory | 114 000 |
| | | Decrease cash | 114 000 |
| b | Sales | Increase accounts receivable | 150 000 |
| | | Increase sales revenue | 150 000 |
| c | Cost of goods sold | Increase COGS | 100 000 |
| | | Decrease inventory | 100 000 |
| d | Adjustment | Increase inventory shortage expense (see below) | 9 000 |
| | | Decrease inventory | 9 000 |
| e | Collections | Increase cash | 115 000 |
| | | Decrease accounts receivable | 115 000 |

Here is a summary of the journal entries for the perpetual system:

| | | | DR<br>$ | CR<br>$ |
|---|---|---|---|---|
| a | Purchases | Inventory | 114 000 | |
| | | Cash | | 114 000 |
| | | *Purchases during the period.* | | |
| b | Sales | Accounts receivable | 150 000 | |
| | | Sales revenue | | 150 000 |
| | | *Sales on credit during the period.* | | |
| c | Cost of goods sold | Cost of goods sold expense | 100 000 | |
| | | Inventory | | 100 000 |
| | | *COGS expense: $150 000 revenue minus 50% mark-up on cost.* | | |
| d | Count adjustment | Inventory shortage expense | 9 000 | |
| | | Inventory | | 9 000 |
| | | *Shortage: record indicates inventory should be $23 000 + $114 000 – $100 000 = $37 000 but only $28 000 is on hand.* | | |
| e | Collections | Cash | 115 000 | |
| | | Accounts receivable | | 115 000 |
| | | *Customer collections during the period.* | | |

Let's review two accounts here, to ensure that you see how the accounting figures help with the control:

| | $ |
|---|---|
| **Inventory account:** | |
| Beginning cost balance | 23 000 |
| Purchases | 114 000 |
| Cost of goods sold | (100 000) |
| Expected balance on hand | 37 000 |

**The count showed less than expected on hand:**

| | |
|---|---|
| Adjustment for loss | (9 000) |
| Revised ending cost balance | 28 000 |

**Accounts receivable account:**

| | |
|---|---|
| Beginning | 40 000 |
| Sales | 150 000 |
| Collections | (115 000) |
| Ending balance | 75 000 |

We can check with the customers or otherwise verify that this amount really is a collectable asset.

Let's now consider the accounting entries under the periodic method.

| | | | $ |
|---|---|---|---|
| a | Purchases | Purchase expense increases | 114 000 |
| | | Cash decreases | 114 000 |
| b | Sales | Accounts receivable increases | 150 000 |
| | | Sales revenue increases | 150 000 |
| c | Collections | Cash increases | 115 000 |
| | | Accounts receivable decreases | 115 000 |

The journal entries for the periodic inventory system are as follows:

| | | | DR $ | CR $ |
|---|---|---|---|---|
| a | Purchases | Purchase expense | 114 000 | |
| | | Cash | | 114 000 |
| | | *Purchases during the period.* | | |
| b | Sales | Accounts receivable | 150 000 | |
| | | Sales revenue | | 150 000 |
| | | *Sales on credit during the period.* | | |
| c | Collections | Cash | 115 000 | |
| | | Accounts receivable | | 115 000 |
| | | *Customer collections during the period.* | | |

Note that under the periodic method there is no journal entry for cost of goods sold and inventory shortage (entries **c** and **d** under the perpetual method). Cost of goods sold is not affected at the time of sale. It is calculated at the end of the accounting period by adding purchases for the period to opening inventory and then deducting closing inventory. Inventory shortages are not known because there are no inventory records to compare the stock count total to. Under the periodic inventory method no adjustment has yet been made to the inventory account to show that it is different at the end of the period from what it was at the beginning of the period (because of purchases and sales). This adjustment to the inventory account will occur in the closing entries.

If the company did use the periodic count method, we would have the $23 000 from the beginning, plus the $114 000 purchased, less the $28 000 counted at the end, for an apparent cost of goods sold of $109 000. You can see that, had we had the perpetual records, we would know that this figure is actually the sum of $100 000 cost of goods really sold and $9 000 shortage. Both methods have the same revenue and the same total expense, $109 000; they differ in the information they provide to management about what is going on

The gross profit calculation under both methods is shown below.

## Perpetual inventory system

| | $ | $ |
|---|---|---|
| Sales | | 150 000 |
| Less: Cost of goods sold | 100 000 | |
| Less: Inventory shortage | 9 000 | 109 000 |
| Gross profit | | 41 000 |

## Periodic inventory system

| | $ | $ |
|---|---|---|
| Sales | | 150 000 |
| Cost of goods sold: | | |
| Opening inventory | 23 000 | |
| Purchases | 114 000 | |
| Cost of goods available for sale | 137 000 | |
| Less: Ending inventory | 28 000 | |
| Cost of goods sold | | 109 000 |
| Gross profit | | 41 000 |

In chapter 4 we discussed closing entries. The closing entries under the perpetual and periodic methods are shown below:

## Perpetual method

| | DR<br>$ | CR<br>$ |
|---|---|---|
| Profit and loss summary | 109 000 | |
| Cost of goods sold expense | | 100 000 |
| Inventory shortage expense | | 9 000 |
| Sales revenue | 150 000 | |
| Profit and loss summary | | 150 000 |

## Periodic method

| | DR<br>$ | CR<br>$ |
|---|---|---|
| Profit and loss summary | 137 000 | |
| Purchases | | 114 000 |
| Inventory (beginning) | | 23 000 |
| Inventory (ending) | 28 000 | |
| Sales revenue | 150 000 | |
| Profit and loss summary | | 178 000 |

Under both methods the profit and loss summary account and the inventory account will have the same balances. (Later in this chapter you will see situations where this is not the case because of certain inventory cost flow assumptions made.)

### Perpetual method

**Profit and loss summary**

| | | | |
|---|---|---|---|
| | 109 000 | | 150 000 |
| Bal. c/d | 41 000 | | |
| | 150 000 | | 150 000 |
| | | Bal. b/d | 41 000 |

**Inventory**

| | | | |
|---|---|---|---|
| Bal. b/d | 23 000 | | 100 000 |
| | 114 000 | | 9 000 |
| | | Bal. c/d | 28 000 |
| | 137 000 | | 137 000 |
| Bal. b/d | 28 000 | | |

### Periodic method

**Profit and loss summary**

| | | | |
|---|---|---|---|
| | 137 000 | | 178 000 |
| Bal. c/d | 41 000 | | |
| | 178 000 | | 178 000 |
| | | Bal. b/d | 41 000 |

**Inventory**

| | | | |
|---|---|---|---|
| | 23 000 | | 23 000 |
| | 28 000 | | |

Check the opening balance in the inventory accounts, then follow the posting from the journal entries to the ledgers to ensure that you can see what is happening. Using both methods $41 000 is the balance of profit and loss summary to be transferred to retained profits, and the inventory balance to be carried forward to next period is $28 000.

## How's your understanding?

Here are two questions you should be able to answer, based on what you have just read:

1 What is the role of record-keeping in internal control?

2 Granot Pty Ltd uses the perpetual inventory method. At the beginning of the month, inventory costing $145 020 was on hand. Purchases for the month totalled $267 540 and cost of goods recorded as sold totalled $258 310. At the end of the month, a count showed inventory costing $152 750 to be on hand. What, if anything, was the inventory shortage for the month? ($2390)

## 7.4 Inventory valuation and cost of goods sold

Inventory accounting, like accounting for other current assets, uses a modified version of the standard historical cost valuation basis: lower of cost or market. Because inventory is expected to be turned into cash (sold) or otherwise consumed within the next year, it is a current asset, and because it is normally a current asset, generally accepted accounting principles require that any impairment in the asset's value be recognised in the period in which the impairment occurred, not later when the asset is sold. Market is used only if it is lower than cost, so the historical cost basis is departed from only in one direction, down, if that is needed. This is an application of accounting conservatism: 'anticipate no gains but allow for all losses'.

In this section, we'll review briefly how to determine 'cost'. Inventory accounting affects both the statement of financial position (inventory valuation) and the expense recognised for the use of inventory (cost of goods sold expense).

## Inventory cost flow assumptions

Total cost is just the sum of quantity times unit cost for all items of inventory. This is a very simple calculation when the cost of an item in inventory remains constant. However, assume an item was purchased at various times throughout the year. There was an opening inventory of 200 items that cost $50 each. During the year the price has been increasing with subsequent purchases of 100 at $51, 200 at $53, 200 at $54 and 100 at $55. All the items are stored together and 400 were removed from inventory for sale during the year. What is the cost of goods sold and what is the value of closing inventory? It all depends on whether the items removed were those that cost $50, $51, $53, $54 or $55. Imagine the trouble of keeping track of the cost of each item removed from inventory.

In practice, the actual cost of inventory items is tracked only for high-value items (houses, motor vehicles, aircraft, expensive jewellery) that can be identified by serial numbers and other methods. This method is often called 'specific identification'. As the cost of keeping records decreases because of computerisation, more items can be tracked this way. Still, serial numbers or other ways to identify specific inventory items are needed.

For most inventories, because it is not worthwhile or even possible to keep track of the cost of individual items in inventory, most companies figure out their statement of financial position inventory cost and cost of goods sold expense by *assuming* some flow of costs through the business. We don't want to have to know exactly which ones are on hand, or which have been sold, so we make assumptions.

To illustrate the effects of different assumptions, we will first use a simple example based on the periodic inventory control method, in which no records are kept of changes in inventory levels during the accounting period. If the perpetual control method were used, the calculations would be more complex (you'll see those later). The example involves inventory purchased for resale (such as a retailer would purchase), but the ideas work just as well for inventory manufactured by a company: in that case, cost of *purchases* is replaced by cost of goods *manufactured*. Consider the following:

- Inventory at beginning of period: 120 units costing $2 each.
- Purchases during period (in the order in which they happened):
  100 units costing $3 each
  110 units costing $4 each.
- Sales during period: (based on an ending inventory of 150 units) 180 units.

The *cost of goods available for sale* equals the cost of the opening inventory plus the cost of those purchased (or manufactured). So we have 120 × $2 = $240, plus 100 × $3 = $300, plus 110 × $4 = $440, for a total cost of goods available of $980.

Our problem is how to *allocate* the $980 between the statement of financial performance for the period (cost of goods sold expense) and the statement of financial position at the end of the period (ending inventory asset). There are three common inventory cost flow assumptions that are used around the world:

- First in, first out (FIFO) assumes that the first items acquired are the first ones sold and, therefore, that any ending inventory on hand consists of the most recently acquired units (recent costs on statement of financial position, older costs in COGS expense).

**EXHIBIT 7.1** **Inventory cost flow assumptions**

**FIFO, AVGE and LIFO**

| Method | Ending inventory asset | Cost of goods sold expense |
|---|---|---|
| FIFO | (110 × \$4) + (40 × \$3) = \$560 | \$980 – \$560 = \$420<br>([120 × \$2] + [60 × \$3] = \$420) |
| AVGE | 150 × \$2.97 = 445<br>Average unit cost = \$980/330<br>= \$2.97 (rounded) | \$980 – \$445 = \$535<br>(180 × \$2.97 = \$535) |
| LIFO | (120 x \$2) + (30 x \$3) = \$330 | \$980 – \$330 = \$650<br>([110 x \$4] + [70 x \$3] = \$650) |

- Weighted average assumption (AVGE) assumes ending inventory and COGS are composed of a mixture of old and new units.
- Last in, first out (LIFO) assumes the opposite of FIFO, saying that any inventory on hand consists of the oldest units (older costs on statement of financial position, recent costs in COGS expense).

Exhibit 7.1 shows the three different assumptions of inventory cost flow. *In each case the sum of the ending balance sheet asset valuation and the cost of goods sold expense is \$980.* The different cost flow assumptions just allocate this available cost differently between the statement of financial position valuation and the expense in the statement of financial performance.

## 7.5 More about inventory cost flow assumptions

The above example introduced three cost flow assumptions, FIFO, AVGE and LIFO. This example applied to the periodic method. We know from section 7.2 that internal control over inventory may mean using the periodic or perpetual methods. If we put the three cost flow assumptions against the two control methods, we get the following:

| Assumption | Periodic control | Perpetual control |
|---|---|---|
| FIFO | FIFO | FIFO |
| AVGE | Weighted average | Moving weighted average |
| LIFO | Periodic LIFO | Perpetual LIFO |

First in, first out is not affected by the inventory control method, because it just assigns most recent cost to whatever is on hand. But the other two methods are affected by the control method, because they depend on what we know about what happened to inventory levels during the period. This gives us five potential methods: FIFO and two versions each of AVGE and LIFO. (There is a sixth, specific identification, as you have already seen and, at the end of this section, two more methods will be mentioned briefly. So there are at least eight different ways to account for inventory cost!) In Australia, the LIFO method is not allowed to be used for either financial reporting or tax purposes, but we will include it because the contrast with FIFO and moving average may help you understand the latter ones, and because LIFO is very common in the United States, so you will see it mentioned in many US financial statements.

Let's examine these assumptions and their interaction with internal control methods further. Remember that, because each assumption allocates the available inventory cost between the inventory asset and the cost of goods sold expense differently, the choice of assumption has an effect on both the statements of financial performance and financial position. The significance of the effect depends on how much purchase (or manufacturing) costs per unit rise or fall during the period: if there is little change in these costs, the various methods will show very similar results.

First in, first out assigns the more recent purchase costs to the inventory asset account and, therefore, older costs to the cost of goods sold expense account:

- It is used because it is convenient and produces inventory asset values that are close to current costs, which seems to many people to be appropriate for a current asset.
- It is convenient because all you really need to do is keep your purchase invoices and, when you know how many units are on hand, just go through recent invoices to find the costs.
- For example, suppose there are 620 boxes of chocolates on hand at 30 June, and recent purchase invoices showed the following costs: 29 June, 260 boxes at \$3.20; 14 June, 310 boxes at \$3.35; 1 June, 210 boxes at \$3; and so on. The FIFO ending inventory is found by starting with the most recent purchase and going back in time until all the ones on hand are accounted for (working on assumption, since we do not really know when any particular box was purchased). So the FIFO cost here would be:

  $$(260 \times \$3.20) + (310 \times \$3.35) + ([620 - 260 - 310 = 50] \times \$3) \text{ or } \$2020.50.$$

  You don't need complicated records, just a pile of invoices. Also, it doesn't matter what the internal control method is, because all you need to know is the quantity on hand, whether determined by count or by perpetual records.
- Australian Company Financial Reporting 1999[1] indicates that in 1998, 84 per cent of the 150 companies surveyed disclosed the cost flow assumption for inventories, and FIFO was the most popular, being used by 42 per cent of companies in the survey.
- First in, first out is considered appropriate for a current asset by many people because it is the most reasonable method of physically moving inventory, especially inventory that is perishable or subject to changes in style or features, such as groceries, clothing and other retail products. Picture a shelf in a grocery store: FIFO assumes that new stock is placed behind older stock on the shelf, so that the inventory keeps moving forward on the shelf. In Australia, accounting standards require that the cost flow reflects the underlying physical flow of the goods in question. This is not the case in the United States.

The AVGE method assigns the available cost equally to the inventory asset and to cost of goods sold expense. In the example in exhibit 7.1 above, both inventory asset and cost of goods sold used the same \$2.97 average cost per unit.

- When prices are rising, average cost shows a higher cost of goods sold (lower profit) and lower inventory balance sheet figures than the FIFO method.
- Australian Company Financial Reporting 1999 says that in 1998 the average cost method was used by 32 per cent of the companies reporting using the method employed. The two versions of the average cost method (the 'annual weighted average' method illustrated for the periodic inventory control example above and the 'moving weighted average' method, which can be used where the perpetual control method provides the required information) are illustrated below.

Last in, first out is, on the face of it, a strange valuation method. It assumes that the newer items are sold first and, therefore, that the oldest are the ones left on hand. In the extreme, this would imply that the grocery store's first loaves of bread are still at the back of the shelf, years later (possibly 100 years later). However, note that in the United States the cost flow assumption used for accounting purposes does not have to match the physical flow. So rest assured that while American bread may not be as tasty as Australian bread, it is not that old!

- Last in, first out is used in the United States for one very practical reason: it is an allowable method for income tax purposes. However, it can only be used for tax purposes if it is also used for accounting purposes. In a period of rising purchase costs (inflation), which is pretty much constantly the case, it produces a higher cost of goods sold expense and a lower inventory asset value than do FIFO or AVGE. Therefore, LIFO also produces lower profit and lower income tax, if it can be used for tax purposes.
- As noted earlier, it is not permissible in Australia to use LIFO for accounting or taxation purposes. In some countries, such as Canada, it is an allowable method for accounting but not for income tax purposes, so a Canadian company using it for the financial statements would have to compute inventory values all over again using one of the other methods when doing its income tax return.
- It can also be argued that LIFO matches revenues with expenses better than do the other two methods. For example, if a company changes its selling prices as its purchase costs change, its revenues reflect recent price changes and it then seems appropriate to deduct the more recent purchase costs as cost of goods sold expense against the revenues. The trouble is that LIFO produces inventory asset values that are based on older purchase costs and this can substantially underestimate the asset value.
- It would be nice to use current purchase prices for cost of goods sold expense and for the statement of financial position inventory value. But that can't be done if we stick to the historical cost accounting basis: the books wouldn't balance because some of the units would have been purchased at older costs and those costs would be in the accounts, too, in the inventory asset or expense accounts. (There have been proposals for using current costs, such as replacement costs, to be used in both statement figures, but these are not presently permitted to be used in practice.)
- Last in, first out is affected by whether its amounts are determined using the periodic or perpetual control methods, as the following example will show.

## 7.6 An example: Meeix Pty Ltd

Among the products Meeix Pty Ltd purchases and sells is Gloop. It began last year with 1000 units of Gloop on hand at a cost of $4 each and during the year its purchase and sales records showed:

| Date | Units purchased | Units sold | Units on hand | Purchase price |
|---|---|---|---|---|
| Jan 1 | | | 1 000 | $4 |
| Feb 15 | | 350 | 650 | |
| Mar 20 | 600 | | 1 250 | $5 |
| Apr 30 | | 750 | 500 | |
| Sep 12 | 800 | | 1 300 | $6 |
| Dec 11 | | 200 | 1 100 | |
| | 1 400 | 1 300 | | |

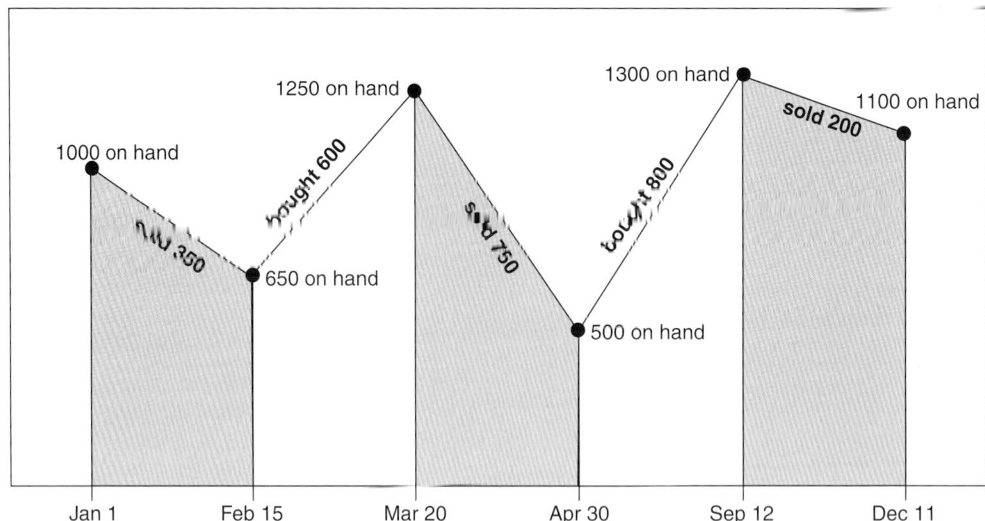


**Figure 7.1** Inventory balances and changes, Meeix's Gloop

The chart in figure 7.1 shows how the quantities of Gloop changed during the year. Note that the cost flow assumptions would identify the ending inventory's 1100 units as:

**FIFO**

- 1100 = 800 most recently bought + 300 of those bought 20 March

**AVGE**

- *Annual weighted:* 1100 = a proportionate mixture of those on hand at the beginning and those bought 20 March and 12 September
- *Moving:* the first average is the 1250 on hand at 20 March, a proportionate mixture of those on hand at beginning + those bought 20 March; second average, the 1300, is a proportionate mixture of the first average (on hand 30 April) and those bought 12 September

**LIFO**

- *Periodic:* the ups and downs during the year are not known (no records kept), so the 1100 = 1000 on hand at beginning + 100 bought 20 March
- *Perpetual:* during the year, the inventory hit a minimum of 500, so that's all of the beginning items that could still be on hand at the end, therefore 1100 = 500 from beginning + 600 bought 12 September

Now we can go on with the calculations. Regardless of the cost flow assumption used, we know that the beginning inventory cost is $4000 and that purchases costing $7800 (600 × $5 + 800 × $6) were made. Available cost, therefore, is the sum of beginning inventory and purchases, which is $11 800. Consequently, as long as the historical cost basis of accounting is used, any inventory cost allocation method must produce $11 800 as the sum of the ending inventory asset and cost of goods sold expense. You might think of it this way:

**Available for sale = Gone + Still here**
**Beginning inventory + Purchases = Cost of goods sold expense + Ending inventory**

The left side equals $11 800, so the right side must result in the same total. This gives us ways to check our calculations. If we calculate cost of goods sold expense and ending inventory asset cost separately, they must add up to $11 800. As a short cut, we can calculate *either* the expense or the asset value and deduce the other by deducting it from

$11 800. This is easier than doing it twice, but the calculations below will include both the expense and the asset so that you can see how it all works.

Based on the patterns shown in figure 7.1 and the summary of each method's assumption about the ending inventory quantity, here are the calculations for ending inventory cost and cost of goods sold.

## FIFO method

| | $ |
|---|---|
| Ending inventory cost: (800 × $6) + (remaining 300 × $5) | 6 300 |
| Cost of goods sold expense: | |
| (1000 × $4) + (remaining 300 × $5) | 5 500 |
| | 11 800 |

Alternatively, the calculations can be done as follows:

| Date | Purchases<br>$ | Cost of goods sold<br>$ | Ending inventory<br>$ |
|---|---|---|---|
| Jan 1 | | | 1 000 at $4 = 4 000 |
| Feb 15 | | 350 at $4 = 1 400 | 650 at $4 = 2 600 |
| Mar 20 | 600 at $5 = 3 000 | | 650 at $4 = 2 600 |
| | | | 600 at $5 = 3 000 |
| Apr 30 | | 650 at $4 = 2 600 | |
| | | 100 at $5 = 500 | 500 at $5 = 2 500 |
| Sep 12 | 800 at $6 = 4 800 | | 800 at $6 = 4 800 |
| Dec 11 | | 200 at $5 = 1 000 | 300 at $5 = 1 500 |
| | | | 800 at $6 = 4 800 |
| | | 5 500 | 6 300 |

## AVGE method

### *Annual weighted average*

| | $ |
|---|---|
| Average cost = $11 800 / (1000 + 600 + 800) = $4.917 (rounded) | |
| Ending inventory cost: 1100 × $4.917 | 5 408 |
| Cost of goods sold expense: 1300 × $4.917 | 6 392 |
| | 11 800 |

### *Moving weighted average*

The **moving average** works the same way as annual weighted average, but is recalculated after each purchase, weighted in accordance with the inventory on hand at that point.

| Date | Purchases<br>$ | Cost of goods sold<br>$ | Ending inventory<br>$ |
|---|---|---|---|
| Jan 1 | | | 1 000 at $4 = 4 000 |
| Feb 15 | | 350 at $4 = 1 400 | 650 at $4 = 2 600 |
| Mar 20 | 600 at $5 = 3 000 | | 1 250 at $4.48 = 5 600 |
| Apr 30 | | 750 at $4.48 = 3 360 | 500 at $4.48 = 2 240 |
| Sep 12 | 800 at $6 = 4 800 | | 1 300 at $5.415 = 7 040 |
| Dec 11 | | 200 at $5.415 = 1 083 | 1 100 at $5.415 = 5 957 |
| | | 5 843 | |

## LIFO method

### *Periodic basis*

| | $ |
|---|---|
| Ending inventory cost: (1000 × $4) + (remaining 100 × $5) | 4 500 |
| Cost of goods sold expense: (800 × $6) + (remaining 500 × $5) | 7 300 |
| | 11 800 |

### *Perpetual basis*

The perpetual records allow us to determine whether it is reasonable to assume that all the original 1000 units are still on hand. In this example it is not, because at one point the inventory was down to 500 units, so that 'layer' of cost has been partly used up. The calculation reflects the 'cost layer' information available from the records.

| Date | Purchases $ | Cost of goods sold $ | Ending inventory $ |
|---|---|---|---|
| Jan 1 | | | 1 000 at $4 = 4 000 |
| Feb 15 | | 350 at $4 = 1 400 | 650 at $4 = 2 600 |
| Mar 20 | 600 at $5 = 3 000 | | 600 at $5 = 3 000 |
| Apr 30 | | 600 at $5 = 3 000 | |
| | | 150 at $4 = 600 | 500 at $4 = 2 000 |
| Sep 12 | 800 at $6 = 4 800 | | 800 at $6 = 4 800 |
| Dec 11 | | 200 at $6 = 1 200 | 500 at $4 = 2 000 |
| | | | 600 at $6 = 3 600 |
| | | 6 200 | 5 600 |

The following summarises the Meeix example's results.

| Cost method | Ending inventory asset $ | Cost of goods sold expense $ | Total cost available $ |
|---|---|---|---|
| FIFO | 6 300 | 5 500 | 11 800 |
| AVGE | | | |
| Annual | 5 408 | 6 392 | 11 800 |
| Moving | 5 957 | 5 843 | 11 800 |
| LIFO | | | |
| Periodic | 4 500 | 7 300 | 11 800 |
| Perpetual | 5 600 | 6 200 | 11 800 |

This example illustrates a result that is common when using these methods. *In a period of rising purchase prices*, as here:

- FIFO tends to have the highest inventory asset value and lowest cost of goods sold expense (and therefore highest net profit).
- LIFO tends to have the lowest inventory asset value and highest COGS (and therefore lowest net profit).
- AVGE tends to be between the other two in asset values, COGS and net profit.

If *purchase prices are falling*, the positions of FIFO and LIFO reverse, with FIFO tending to have the lowest net profit and LIFO the highest. The AVGE method tends again to be between the other two. While falling prices are less common they can occur in some industries (such as computer software).

The differences among the methods are larger the more purchase cost prices rise (or fall) during the period. The differences tend to be smaller when inventory turnover is high, because price changes occurring during the time inventory is held are smaller and the size of the inventory asset relative to cost of goods sold expense is smaller. If a perpetual LIFO or moving average method is being used, the differences can also be in unexpected directions, depending on coincidental increases or decreases in inventory levels. The LIFO perpetual ending inventory for Meeix is higher than the annual average ending inventory because a large amount of the beginning inventory was sold, so the LIFO perpetual method used this information, but the annual average did not. The relationships among the methods also can stray from the typical pattern if purchase price changes and inventory quantities are moving in opposite directions (for example, if inventory levels are falling but prices are rising, or vice versa).

## How's your understanding?

Filo Ltd uses a perpetual inventory system. It has opening inventory of 200 items, which cost $10 each. It purchased another 500 items at $12 each, and 300 items at $13 each during the period. It has 100 items in closing inventory. What is the closing inventory valuation and the cost of goods for the period using FIFO and LIFO? (FIFO: closing inventory = $1 300; COGS = $10 600. LIFO: closing inventory = $1 000; COGS = $10 900.)

## 7.7 Lower of cost or market rule

The lower of cost or market rule states that the value of inventory should be written down from the cost price to market price in situations where market is below costs. In Australia, market is defined as net realisable value. Net realisable value is determined by taking selling prices and deducting any costs to complete (such as putting it in a box) or sell the item. Again, the focus is on items whose net realisable value is *below* cost, so we are concerned with items whose selling prices are falling or that have been damaged, or have become obsolete, or out of style so that we can't sell them for what we thought we could. The measurement of the lower of cost and net realisable value should be done on an item-by-item basis. When this is impossible because of the large number of homogenous items having an insignificant cost, the rule can be applied for a group of items.

Basically, to calculate the lower of cost or market value, we just take the cost of the items and match those costs against the net realisable value and use the lower as the balance sheet inventory value. In practice, companies usually focus mainly on items whose values are likely to be impaired (as might be identified during the physical count), rather than calculating net realisable value for everything.

For example, if inventory that costs $1000 had a net realisable value at year-end of $800, it would be necessary to write down an asset (inventory) and increase an expense (inventory write-down expense). The journal entry would be:

| | $ | $ |
|---|---|---|
| DR Inventory write-down expense | 200 | |
| CR Inventory | | $200 |

Note that the decision to write down the inventory has resulted in profit for the period reducing by $200. You can imagine that, if this figure were large, managers might not want to write down the value of inventory, and disputes between management and auditors arise over these issues.

Consider a company which has three products, X, Y and Z.

| **Item type** | **X** | **Y** | **Z** |
|---|---|---|---|
| Quantity | 100 | 300 | 200 |
| Cost | $5 | $9 | $10 |
| Net realisable value | $7 | $8 | $16 |

The inventory value under 'Lower of Cost and NRV' is $4900 ($100 \times \$5 + 300 \times \$8 + 200 \times \$10$). In this case, inventory of $300 would be written down because Y is presently included in the records at $2700 ($300 \times \$9$).

## 7.8 Retail inventory and standard costs

The retail inventory method, which, as you might expect, is most applicable for retailers' inventories, combines purchase costs and selling prices into a single calculation, or estimate.

This is like the perpetual method, except that records are based on selling prices of goods rather than just quantities or costs. In the retail inventory control method, a department or branch is charged with the total selling value (sales price times quantity) of all items for sale delivered to it. Revenue from sales is then deducted from this total value as the items are sold. This ties inventory control to cash control. At any point in time, the department or branch should have inventory, plus cash from sales made since the last revenue report, plus records of sales on credit or via credit cards, equal to the current total retail value:

- Start with the retail price of all goods received by the department (on hand at the beginning of the period plus received during the period).
- Deduct the department's sales (connected to cash, cheque, electronic funds transfer and credit card control procedures).
- Difference equals inventory that should be on hand, priced at retail.

If a physical count, with items priced at retail, fails to show the expected total retail value, the company knows that some items have been lost or stolen, or that there has been an error in the records. An adjustment for the shortage or overage can be made in the same way as for the perpetual method. Total cost of the inventory can be estimated at any time by deducting the average mark-up from the current total retail value. The retail method is, however, a little complicated in practice because of the need to keep track of markdowns, returned goods, special sale prices and other price adjustments if the method is to work accurately.

One other popular method for valuing inventory which is used in Australia is standard costs. You will learn about this method in detail if you take a course in management accounting or cost accounting. It is applicable to inventories manufactured by the company and uses estimated costs based on standard production costs and volumes. It is a predetermined cost that is applied to all movements in inventories including opening and closing balances, purchases and sales. For example, if the standard cost is $20 and the company sold 2000 units during the year and had 300 in stock at year-end, the cost of goods sold would be $40 000 ($20 × 2000) and the closing inventory $6000 ($20 × 300).

## How's your understanding?

Here are two questions you should be able to answer, based on what you have just read:

1 How does a company decide which method to use in determining the cost of inventory?

2 Meeix Pty Ltd also stocks a pet food called Dog's Breakfast, which it controls using the periodic inventory method. Last year, there were 200 crates of Dog's Breakfast on hand at the beginning of the year, and 1500 crates were purchased and 1450 crates were sold during the year. The crates on hand at the beginning cost $400 each. There were three purchases: early in the year, 500 crates costing $404 each were purchased; then 600 crates costing $390 each; and near the end of the year, 400 crates costing $384.50 each were purchased. What would be the cost of the inventory at the end of the year and the cost of goods sold expense under (a) FIFO (b) AVGE and (c) LIFO? ((a) $96 125; $573 675; (b) $98 500; $571 300; (c) $100 200; $569 600)

## 7.9 Disclosure of inventories policies

Accounting standards require the financial reports to disclose the value of inventory split between current and noncurrent assets and further split into the following classes: (a) raw materials and stores; (b) work-in-progress; (c) finished goods and (d) land held for resale. In addition, it requires disclosure of the general basis for inventory valuation (specific identification, average, FIFO or standard cost) and the methods used to assign costs to inventory quantities (for example, how overhead is allocated to inventories manufactured).

Examples from some 2001 annual reports are shown below. OPSM Protector Limited 2001 shows the details of inventory in note 9 as follows:

| | Consolidated | |
|---|---|---|
| | 2001 | 2000 |
| | $000 | $000 |
| **Note 9: Current assets inventories** | | |
| Raw materials and components | 14 826 | 22 335 |
| Work-in-progress | 963 | 1 089 |
| Finished goods | 39 328 | 65 429 |
| | 55 117 | 88 853 |

Examples of inventory policies as given in note 1 on statements of accounting policies are as follows.

**Coca-Cola Amatil Limited (2000)**

As a general principle inventories are valued at the lower of cost (including fixed and variable factory overheads where applicable) and net realisable value. Cost is determined on the basis of first in first out, average or standard, whichever is the most appropriate in each case.

> **News Corporation Limited (2001)**
> Inventories are valued at the lower of cost and net realisable value. Cost is determined by the first in first out or average-cost method for the greater part of inventories depending on the nature of the item, and by specific identification for the balance.
>
> **Coles Myer Limited (2001)**
> At balance date all stock of finished goods on hand or in transit is valued at the lower of cost and net realisable value, with cost being determined using the weighted average cost method.
>
> **Foster's Group Limited (2001)**
> Inventories of finished goods, raw materials and stores and work in progress are valued at the lower of cost (using average or FIFO basis) and estimated net realisable value.

The above disclosures show that FIFO, average, standard and specific identification methods are used to determine inventory in practice. Within the one organisation more than one method can be used and it may vary between the type of product or the class of inventories (raw material, work-in-progress or finished goods). The retail inventory method is used by Coles Myer and many other retailers. All of the disclosures refer to the fact that inventories are valued at the lower of cost and net realisable value.

For manufacturing firms, overheads costs are reported in the cost of goods manufactured. Manufacturing costs are beyond the scope of this book, and will be discussed in a management accounting subject.

## 7.10 Managers and the valuation of inventory

Managers have to make important decisions about the inventory control system. While the perpetual method has advantages over the periodic method for control purposes, it has a higher cost.

The valuation of inventory is important to managers, because it affects cost of goods sold (and therefore profit) as well as the statement of financial position via the value of inventory. Both profit figures and statement of financial position figures affect managers' performance reports. Managers therefore need to understand the effect of different cost flow assumptions on both financial statements across time.

Managers need also to make some important judgements related to inventory valuation. For example, which cost flow assumption most closely represents the actual physical flow? What inventory items have a net realisable value which is lower than cost?

## 7.11 Inventory in the public sector

Inventory is not normally a material item for most public sector organisations. However, there will be exceptions, such as health departments (for example, hospitals have bandages, medicines and so on), roads and traffic authorities (gravel, concrete and so on), government printing services (paper), and transport (spare parts, fuel). When inventory does exist, the same accounting standards apply as in the private sector. For example, the Statement of Accounting Policies in the 2001 annual report of the Roads and Traffic Authority, New South Wales states:

> Inventories are stated at the lower of cost and net realisable value. Cost is calculated using weighted average cost. Inventories consist mainly of raw materials and supplies used for the construction and maintenance of roads, bridges and traffic signals.

## 7.12 Homework and discussion to develop understanding

### Discussion questions

1 Explain the difference between periodic and perpetual inventory systems.

2 How is cost of goods sold determined under both the perpetual and periodic inventory systems?

3 Compare the periodic and perpetual systems as a control device.

4 What sorts of organisations are likely to use the periodic inventory system?

5 Under what circumstances will the perpetual and periodic inventory systems give the same cost of goods sold figure? How can this occur if one method treats purchases as an asset and the other method treats purchases as an expense?

6 How is inventory shortage detected under both perpetual and periodic inventory methods?

7 What does the term 'inventory cost flow assumption' mean?

8 Explain the impact on the financial statements of using FIFO, weighted average and LIFO. When will the three methods give similar profit figures? When would they give identical profit figures?

9 Which cost flow assumption do you believe gives the most appropriate asset figure in times of rising prices?

10 Explain the concept of lower of cost and net realisable value for inventory.

11 Why is the valuation of inventory important to managers?

12 In accounting for inventories and cost of goods sold, why are cost flow assumptions necessary? Why not just charge the actual cost of items sold to cost of goods sold and keep the actual cost of unsold items in the inventory asset account on the statement of financial position?

13 Under what circumstances would each of the following inventory cost flow assumptions be appropriate:

   a specific identification (actual cost of items on hand)?

   b LIFO cost flow assumption?

   c average cost flow assumption?

   d FIFO cost flow assumption?

   e cost estimate via deduction of mark-up from selling price (for example, retail method)?

14 Are inventories always current assets?

15 What is the connection (if any) between a company's revenue recognition policy and its inventory cost determination policy?

16 Suppose you were a shareholder in a company that switched its inventory costing method from FIFO to weighted average and, as a result, its reported net profit dropped $2 million. What would be your reaction? Explain.

17 If management overstated the valuation of inventory, would it affect profit for the year?

### Problem 7.1* Periodic and perpetual inventory control calculations

You are the senior accountant for a shoe wholesaler that uses the periodic inventory method. You have determined the following information from your company's records, which you assume is correct:

a Inventory of $246 720 was on hand at the start of the year.

b Purchases for the year totalled $1 690 000. Of this, $1 412 000 was purchased on account – that is, accounts payable was credited for this amount at the time of the purchase.

**c** The ending balance in accounts payable was $47 500 higher than the opening balance.

**d** A year-end inventory count revealed inventory of $324 800.

*Required:*

1. Calculate cost of goods sold according to the periodic inventory method.
2. Assume now that your company uses the perpetual method of inventory control, and that your records show that $1 548 325 of inventory (at cost) was sold during the year. What is the adjustment needed to correct the records, given the inventory count in item **d** above? What might the need for this adjustment indicate about company operations?
3. If the perpetual method generally provides more control over inventory for management, why don't all companies use it?

## Problem 7.2* LIFO, FIFO and AVGE inventory cost calculations

The following purchases of inventory were made by Anvil Pty Ltd in April:

| Date | Number of units purchased | Per unit amount | Total cost |
|---|---|---|---|
| | | $ | $ |
| Apr 2 | 100 | 5 | 500 |
| Apr 15 | 200 | 6 | 1 200 |
| Apr 23 | 50 | 7 | 350 |
| | 350 | | |

Sales of inventory during April were:

| Date | No. of units sold |
|---|---|
| Apr 6 | 70 |
| Apr 13 | 120 |
| Apr 18 | 200 |
| | 390 |

Anvil's inventory on 1 April consisted of 150 units valued at $4 each.

*Required:*

1. Calculate cost of goods sold for April, using **a** LIFO, **b** FIFO and **c** weighted annual average inventory cost flow assumptions, and assume that Anvil uses a periodic inventory control system.
2. Calculate ending inventory values under each of the three methods above as at 30 April.
3. Suppose the market price for these units was only $5 per unit at 30 April, and the lower of cost or market valuation is applied to each unit individually. Redo question 2.
4. Redo questions 1, 2 and 3, assuming that Anvil uses a perpetual inventory control system.

## Problem 7.3* Inventory cost and market calculations

Winedark Sea Pty Ltd sells prints of classic paintings. The prints are done on expensive paper and are quite costly. Pricing the prints to sell is hard because popularity of a print is difficult to predict. Sometimes prints don't sell well at all and are then disposed of in bulk for use in hotels and motels.

Here are data on two prints:

| | Print X | | Print Y | |
|---|---|---|---|---|
| | Units | Cost per unit $ | Units | Cost per unit $ |
| Inventory, 1 January 2002 | 4 | 340 | 11 | 500 |
| Purchases during 2002: | | | | |
| During summer | 10 | 350 | 25 | 480 |
| During autumn | 15 | 330 | 30 | 510 |
| Sales during 2002 | 23 | | 38 | |

*Required:*

1 Calculate the following:
   a Inventory cost, 31 December 2002, for Print X, FIFO basis.
   b Cost of goods sold, 2002, for Print Y, AVGE basis.

2 Print Y hasn't sold since September. No one seems to like it any more. An out-of-town hotel has offered $100 each for all that Winedark has left, if Winedark will pay the $10 per print shipping cost. What amount would you suggest be used for the inventory of Print Y on the 31 December 2002 balance sheet? Why?

## Problem 7.4 FIFO, LIFO, lower of cost and net realisable value

Dizzy Lizzy, an entrepreneurial fortune teller, also sells tarot cards. This is as a profitable sideline to her highly successful telephone clairvoyant service. The following information relates to transactions concerning inventory for the year 1 January 2002 to 31 December 2002.

| Date | Purchased | Sold | Balance |
|---|---|---|---|
| 1/1/02 | | | 110 @ $5 |
| 10/2/02 | 80 @ $6 | | |
| 14/4/02 | | 60 | |
| 9/5/02 | 110 @ $7 | | |
| 24/7/02 | | 120 | |
| 21/10/02 | 100 @ $8 | | |
| 12/11/02 | | 90 | |
| Total | 290 | 270 | |

*Required:*

1 Assuming a perpetual system of inventory flow calculate the cost of goods sold and closing inventory for:
   a FIFO
   b LIFO

2 You estimate that in the current market the net realisable value of tarot cards is $5 per unit. Do you need to make any adjustments to either of your calculations above to apply the lower of cost or net market rule? If so, calculate the adjustment.

## Problem 7.5 COGS/closing Inventory

XYZ commenced operations on 1 June 2000 selling one type of shirt. The company uses FIFO (first in first out) and perpetual inventory control. The June inventory and sales records for the shirts were:

| Date | Purchase price/unit | Units purchased | Units sold | Selling price/unit | Units on hand |
|---|---|---|---|---|---|
| June 1 | $11 | 1 500 | | | 1 500 |
| June 10 | $12 | 900 | | | 2 400 |
| June 12 | | | 300 | $15 | 2 100 |
| June 17 | $14 | 600 | | | 2 700 |
| June 23 | | | 1 800 | $15 | 900 |
| June 27 | $13 | 1 500 | | | 2 400 |
| June 29 | | | 700 | $17 | 1 700 |
| June 30 | $15 | 200 | | | 1 900 |

*Required:*

1 Calculate cost of goods sold for the month ended 30 June 2000.

2 Calculate the cost of ending inventory as at 30 June 2000.

3 Calculate gross profit for the month ended 30 June 2000.

4 Assume that on June 30, a total of 400 units (not 200 units) were purchased for $15 each. Calculate the gross profit for the month ended 30 June 2000 based on this assumption.

## Problem 7.6 Journal entries and profit and loss statements for perpetual and periodic inventory

The following information is taken from the accounting records of Bragg Ltd for year ended 30 June 2002:

| | $ |
|---|---|
| Inventory 1 July 2001 | 30 000 |
| Purchases (all credit) | 110 000 |
| Sales (all credit) | 180 000 |
| Inventory 30 June 2002 | 18 600 |
| Operating expenses (all cash) | 35 000 |
| The company's mark-up is 50% on cost | |

*Required:*

1 Assuming all purchases and sales were in single transactions prepare summary journal entries as well as closing entries using:

   **a** perpetual inventory

   **b** periodic inventory.

2 Prepare statements of financial performance for year ended 30 June 2002 using both inventory systems.

## Problem 7.7 Periodic and perpetual inventory control calculations

You are the senior accountant for a shoe wholesaler that uses the periodic inventory method. You have determined the following information from your company's records, which you assume are correct:

**a** Inventory of $246 720 was on hand at the start of the year.

**b** Purchases for the year totalled $1 690 000. Of this, $1 412 000 was purchased on account; that is, accounts payable were credited for this amount at the time of the purchase.

**c** The ending balance in accounts payable was $47 500 higher than the opening balance.

**d** A year-end inventory count revealed inventory of $324 800.

*Required:*

1 Calculate cost of goods sold according to the periodic inventory method.

2 Assume now that your company uses the perpetual method of inventory control, and that your records show that $1 548 325 of inventory (at cost) was sold during the year. What is the adjustment needed to correct the records, given the inventory count in item (d) above? What might the need for this adjustment indicate about company operations?

3 If the perpetual method generally provides more control over inventory for management, why don't all companies use it?

## Problem 7.8 Calculations for perpetual vs periodic inventory

Razzmatazz Ltd uses a perpetual inventory control system. The following data are available:

| | $ |
|---|---|
| Inventory on hand at beginning of year (100 000 units at $5 cost each) | 500 000 |
| Purchases for the year (850 000 units at $5 cost each) | 4 250 000 |
| Sales for the year (865 000 units at $11 price each) | 9 515 000 |
| Inventory on hand at end of the year (70 000 units at $5 cost each) | 350 000 |

*Required:*

1 Calculate the cost of goods sold expense for the year, based on the company's perpetual inventory system.

2 If the company had been using the periodic inventory method, what would the cost of goods sold expense for the year have been?

3 A perpetual system costs money to operate. Is it likely to be worthwhile for Razzmatazz?

## Problem 7.9 Journal entries for perpetual and periodic inventory

Barber Ltd has the following data for a recent period:

| | $ |
|---|---|
| Beginning inventory | 12 000 |
| Purchases (all credit) | 30 000 |
| Sales (all credit) | 46 200 |
| Ending inventory count | 7 000 |
| Operating expenses (all cash) | 5 500 |
| The company's mark-up is 40% on cost | |

*Required:*

Assuming all purchases and sales were in single transactions prepare summary journal entries as well as closing entries using:

1 perpetual inventory

2 periodic inventory.

## Problem 7.10 FIFO and LIFO inventory cost calculations

Hackack Pty Ltd sold various items just before the Great Depression. In the month of October 1929, Hackack began trading in widgets. The following transactions occurred in relation to the widget inventory of Hackack during that month.

| Date | | Transaction |
|---|---|---|
| Oct | 1 | Began widget operations by purchasing 300 widgets for $6.00 each |
| | 8 | Sold 50 widgets for $7.00 each |
| | 12 | Sold 150 widgets for $7.00 each |
| | 13 | Bought 500 widgets for $5.00 each |
| | 20 | Sold 400 widgets at $6.00 each |
| | 22 | Sold a further 100 widgets at $5.50 each |
| | 24 | Bought a further 200 widgets at $4.00 each |
| | 29 | Sold 150 widgets at $5.00 |

*Required:*

Prepare inventory cards and state the cost of goods sold and gross profit:

**1** assuming FIFO

**2** assuming LIFO.

## Problem 7.11 Inventory cost and effects calculations

You work for a large local company as inventory manager. The company uses FIFO in accounting for inventory. In June, the company began to stock a new product, Painto. The June inventory record for Painto was:

| Date | | Purchase price $ | Units purchased | Units sold | Units on hand |
|---|---|---|---|---|---|
| Jun | 1 | 10 | 1 250 | | 1 250 |
| | 10 | 11 | 1 000 | | 2 250 |
| | 12 | | | 250 | 2 000 |
| | 17 | 12 | 500 | | 2 500 |
| | 23 | | | 2 000 | 500 |
| | 27 | 13 | 1 500 | | 2 000 |
| | 30 | | | 800 | 1 200 |

*Required:*

**1** Calculate, using FIFO:

- **a** the cost of the 30 June inventory of Painto
- **b** the cost of goods sold for Painto for June.

**2** Calculate, using LIFO:

- **a** the cost of the 30 June inventory of Painto
- **b** the cost of goods sold for Painto for June:
  - **i** using periodic inventory
  - **ii** using perpetual inventory.

## Problem 7.12 AVGE, LIFO and FIFO inventory cost calculations

East Pty Ltd sells MP3 players for $200 each. At 1 November 2001 the inventory consisted of 15 units which had cost $105 each. During November the following transactions occurred:

| Date | | Transaction |
|---|---|---|
| Nov | 3 | Purchased 8 units @ $107 per unit |
| | 10 | Sold 9 units |
| | 16 | Purchased 10 units @ $115 per unit |
| | 21 | Sold 8 units |
| | 25 | Sold 8 units |

At 30 November 2001 there were eight units on hand. Total operating expenses for the month were $850.

*Required:*

1 Record the above information on perpetual inventory cards using each of the following cost flow assumptions:
   - a moving average cost
   - b LIFO
   - c FIFO.
2 Prepare profit and loss statements for East Pty Ltd for the month ended 30 November 2001 using the perpetual inventory system and each of the above cost flow assumptions.
3 Assuming the same facts as above, what would the net profit of East Pty Ltd have been for the month ended 30 November 2001 if it had used the periodic inventory system?

## Problem 7.13 Application of lower of cost or market rule

The following data relate to the Prosperomono Company which buys and sells only one product:

| Date | | Transaction |
|---|---|---|
| Jul | 1 | 1000 units on hand at $5 per unit |
| | 1 | 1000 units purchased at $5 per unit |
| | 12 | 900 units sold |
| | 23 | 800 units purchased at $8 per unit |
| | 30 | 500 units sold |
| | 30 | Net realisable value is $6 per unit.<br>A physical stocktake shows that 1400 units are on hand. |

*Required:*

1 Calculate the cost of ending inventory and the cost of goods sold, assuming:
   - a a perpetual system using the FIFO cost flow assumption
   - b a periodic system using the weighted average method.
2 Following on from **1** above, show the lower of cost or market valuation of ending inventory as at 30 July, assuming:
   - a a perpetual system using the FIFO cost flow assumption
   - b a periodic system using the weighted average method.

   In each case, state whether and why an adjusting entry would be necessary to apply the lower of cost or market rule. If an entry is necessary, indicate what it should be.
3 Using a T-account, show the inventory account as it would appear after all entries (including adjusting and closing entries) have been prepared and posted, assuming a periodic system using the weighted average method and the operation of the lower of cost or market rule.

## Problem 7.14 Effects of change from perpetual to periodic inventory

Frogmorton Fashions began the period with inventory costing $30 000. During the period, $125 000 more inventory was purchased. At the end of the period, a physical count showed that inventory costing $38 000 was on hand. The firm's perpetual inventory system showed that inventory costing $114 000 had been sold during the period.

The general manager says, 'It's a bother keeping track of our inventory the way we do – our perpetual system requires continuous attention to inventory costs. What if we just used the periodic method? What difference would it make?' Give your reply.

## Problem 7.15 FIFO and LIFO inventory cost calculations

The following transactions relate to a computer game sold by Wiley Louvres Pty Ltd for the period 1 January to 31 December 2001:

| Date | Transaction |
|---|---|
| Jan 1 | Beginning inventory – 4 units @ $150 |
| Mar 3 | Purchased 5 units @ $160 |
| Apr 9 | Sold 6 units |
| May 10 | Purchased 5 units @ $165 |
| Aug 22 | Sold 4 units |

***Required:***

**1** Determine the cost of ending inventory as at 31 December 2001 and the cost of goods sold for the year ended 31 December 2001, assuming:

- **a** a periodic system and the FIFO method
- **b** a periodic system and the LIFO method
- **c** a perpetual system and the LIFO method
- **d** a perpetual system and the FIFO method.

Show supporting calculations for each case.

**2** As the above data show, no units of the computer game were sold in the last four months of the year. The marketing manager is concerned that the cost of the remaining games will not be recovered. Explain what effect there would be on the financial statements, if any, if the following occurred:

- **a** The net realisable value of the game as at 31 December was estimated at $152 per unit *and* LIFO was used in conjunction with the perpetual system.
- **b** The net realisable value of the game as at 31 December was estimated at $155 per unit *and* FIFO was used in conjunction with the periodic system.
- **c** The net realisable value of the game as at 31 December was estimated at $152 per unit *and* LIFO was used in conjunction with the periodic system.

Show calculations to support your answer.

## Problem 7.16 Analyse various possible inventory costing policies

Yang Pty Ltd has been in business for three years and pays income tax at 30 per cent. The company manages its inventories well, so that there are no significant inventories for which cost is less than net realisable value. Here are the company's inventory asset and COGS expense for the past three years, computed under each of three methods:

| | 2002<br>$ | 2001<br>$ | 2000<br>$ |
|---|---|---|---|
| FIFO | | | |
| Ending inventory | 112 000 | 148 000 | 115 000 |
| COGS expense | 636 000 | 867 000 | 585 000 |
| AVGE | | | |
| Ending inventory | 108 000 | 126 000 | 106 000 |
| COGS expense | 618 000 | 880 000 | 594 000 |
| LIFO | | | |
| Ending inventory | 104 000 | 118 000 | 92 000 |
| COGS expense | 614 000 | 874 000 | 608 000 |
| Purchases in each year | 600 000 | 900 000 | 700 000 |

1. Determine the inventory cost policy that would produce the highest and lowest profit in each year and calculate the effect on net profit of choosing the former over the latter.
2. Given the variation of results you observed in part 1, how should a company choose its inventory cost policy?

## CASE 7A Woolworths Limited case

Refer to the extracts of the annual report of Woolworths Limited in appendix 2. All questions relate to the consolidated accounts.

1. Would you expect Woolworths Limited to use a perpetual or periodic method of inventory valuation?
2. Does the company use the lower of cost and net realisable value rule? Where is this noted?
3. What cost flow assumptions are used to value inventory?

## CASE 7B Creative accounting using inventory

Attached are two newspaper clippings on Harris Scarfe.

### Scarfe's cooked books revealed: skulduggery, double ledgers and deception have taken their toll

*by Carol Altmann*

Behind the candy-striped green and white of Harris Scarfe lies a once-mighty retailer which appears to have been eroded by deceit, manipulation and power plays.

Summonsed by the company's receivers, Harris Scarfe's former chief financial officer Alan Hodgson and former chief operating officer Daniel McLaughlin this week stood before the South Australian Supreme Court to give their version of how the 150-year-old retailer came to fall so heavily, so quickly.

They had a gripping story to tell.

The tiny courtroom in Adelaide was silent as Hodgson described under oath how then Harris Scarfe chairman Adam Trescowthick and former managing director Ron Baker ordered him to manipulate the books to create false profits.

Baker appeared in court Tuesday and has strenuously denied the claims. Trescowthick, scion of Melbourne's establishment family and son of Harris Scarfe founder Sir Donald, is yet to give evidence.

Hodgson had been with Harris Scarfe for six years and told the court of the pressure to create – by whatever means – the profit his superiors desired. 'Say five or six million' and he, in turn, would hammer his staff to find it.

'If the result that was required could not be achieved in the conventional sense, we would increase the gross profit and increase the gross stock artificially,' he said.

'I would simply sit down with (accountant) Michael Johnson and say Mike, this is the result I am required to produce this year for whatever reason – can you put an adjustment through?'

The method, as Hodgson described it, was relatively simple. The gross profits of each store could be gently manipulated and tweaked through their stock figures.

Stock that had not been invoiced by a supplier after six months, for example, would be reclassified as a profit rather than a debt, falsely inflating the stock value.

As the pressure to produce healthier profits mounted, Hodgson would dig deeper into the invoices, dragging across those which remained outstanding for only a few months.

'At the end of the day we brought up more than we should have done,' he said.

While bargain hunters rattled around below in Harris Scarfe's flagship store in Adelaide's Rundle Mall, those running the show from the fifth floor were creating two very different versions of the company's success. This behaviour, according to McLaughlin's evidence, continued until February this year.

With a few computer keystrokes, Johnson, acting on instructions from Hodgson, created a significantly better set of figures for presentation to the board compared with those contained in the company's general ledger.

'I don't know exactly how he (Johnson) did it, but he had a mechanism for going in and keying the adjustment to the cost of sales,' Hodgson said.

When asked by counsel for the receiver, Dick Whitington QC, if this had the effect of creating accounts which were 'no longer true and fair', Hodgson replied: 'Correct'.

While Hodgson maintained the company books were in 'first-class condition' at the end of the 1997–98 financial year, he admitted the figures had been fudged before, but always with the intent of 'washing it out' over time.

Earlier 'unbusinesslike adjustments' were apparently 'washed out' by a successful leasing arrangement struck with retailer David Jones for the former Adelaide department store John Martins and the purchase of John Martins' stock in the 1997–98 financial year.

'We had had a very good year and we were able to clear everything up that we wanted to,' Hodgson said.

According to spreadsheets tendered by the receiver, the adjustments dated back to at least 1995 where, month after month, the real gross profit margin fell below the 31 per cent to 33 per cent figure expected by the board.

The doctored figures presented to the board, however, failed to reflect the slide.

By the time the company fell over in April this year, the tweaking and fiddling to create a second set of books had left a gaping hole in its finances of at least \$46.3 million that no amount of 'washing' could repair.

A clue as to the possible motivation for the deception was provided by McLaughlin, a company veteran of 20 years. He referred in his evidence to Baker's preference to spend on capital works rather than floor stock and Trescowthick's penchant for dramatic, often costly changes.

On all the measures, 1995 was a sea change for the company. Ron Baker replaced Donald Trescowthick as managing director. Adam Trescowthick was deputy chairman and being groomed to take the reins from his father as company chairman, three years later, at the age of 33.

The company was on the move and thinking big. In just five years, the number of stores would almost double from 19 to 35, with plans for 50 by 2003.

It was around this period McLaughlin, as then head of buying, noticed 'suspicious' charges being added to the stockholding ledger that he could not account for.

'They were inflating my stock levels,' McLaughlin told the court. He didn't specify who 'they' were, but described in detail how he had approached Baker 'three, four or five' times with his concerns about the manipulations that in 1995–96 alone amounted to more than \$1.8 million.

Baker, he said, simply brushed him aside.

'(Baker said) McLaughlin, you really don't understand anything to do with accountancy. Again, will you please just go away and leave the accountants to do their job,' McLaughlin told the court.

In his evidence, Baker could not recall McLaughlin raising these concerns, or showing him any paperwork to support those concerns, only a frustration with the slowness of the new stocktake system.

'I cannot recollect that he came to me ... and raised those concerns,' Baker said.

In a dramatic flourish, Baker later swore on 10, then 20 bibles that he had never directed anybody to alter company figures under any circumstances.

(Source: Carol Altmann, *Weekend Australian*, 11–12 August 2001, p. 38.)

## If Harris Scarfe boss wanted profit, he got it

*by Penelope Debelle*

Harris Scarfe's figures were creatively altered to fit profit targets set by senior management, according to sworn evidence yesterday by the former chief financial officer of the collapsed retail group, Mr Alan Hodgson.

Mr Hodgson, who resigned in June and is unemployed, said he authorised the accounts to be changed if a profit result was requested or required by the company's managing director or chairman.

'If I was requested or ordered to produce a particular profit result and I didn't have the means of doing it in a conventional sense, I would take more out [of that accrual account] than I should have done,' he told the Supreme Court.

Or the gross profit figures would be increased across the biggest stores to achieve a target result, he said. 'I would simply sit down with [accountant] Michael Johnson and say this is the result I am required to achieve this year, for whatever reason, can you put an adjustment through? And he would put an adjustment through the department's stats,' he said.

Mr Hodgson distinguished between conventional profit, which was that achieved 'without making any creative adjustments', and unconventional profits, which were manipulated.

He said he was aware of the requirements of the corporations law but did not think about it, believing the issue was one of timing.

'I always believed it was a timing thing and that whatever took place would be resolved in the following period, one way or another', he said. He agreed with Mr Dick Whitington, QC, for the receivers Ferrier Hodgson, that if he 'robbed Peter this year he could pay Paul next year'.

Mr Hodgson's evidence was the first insight into the financial situation at Harris Scarfe's national chain of 35 stores in the lead-up to its unexpected collapse earlier this year. Despite a reported operating profit last year of $13.2 million, the company's finances were allegedly misrepresented for possibly as long as six years.

Ferrier Hodgson took the Supreme Court action in South Australia to win access to documents and information about the company and to locate assets.

Mr Hodgson told the court that in the past two years there were occasions when the cost of goods was decreased, or the value of stock increased, but that until July 1998 the books had been 'in first-class condition'.

This was challenged by Mr Whitington, who asked: 'Are you sure about that? You understand the receivers and managers have been picking over the accounts from top to bottom? And you understand you are under oath?'

Mr Hodgson then declined to say there had been no 'untoward or unbusinesslike adjustments' before 1 July 1998. 'No, I am not saying that,' he said.

Instead, he said, he meant that untoward entries prior to that time had been reversed as a result of opportunities opened up by the company's acquisition of the former John Martins and David Jones stores in SA, but after 31 July 1998 this had not been possible.

Before Master Peter Bowen Pain, Mr Hodgson agreed adjustments were made to the accrual accounts that, on reflection, should not have been made.

He said that by changing the way invoices were delivered by suppliers, accounts had built up to a substantial credit level which would then be written off by more than they should have been.

(Source: Penelope Debelle, *Sydney Morning Herald*, 7 August 2001, p. 21.)

***Required:***

1. What is meant by creative accounting?
2. What methods were used to adjust profits?
3. Provide an example of how 'untoward entries prior to that time had been reversed as a result of opportunities opened up by the company's acquisition of the former John Martins and David Jones stores in SA'.
4. How does increasing the value of inventory affect profit?
5. 'The gross profits of each store could be gently manipulated and tweaked through their stock figures'. Discuss how this manipulation could possibly occur.
6. Discuss some of the ethical issues raised by the chief financial officer.

## Note

1 J.B. Ryan and C. Heazlewood (eds), 'Australian Company Financial Reporting 1999', Accounting Research Study No. 14, Australian Accounting Research Foundation, 1999.

Chapter 8

# Noncurrent assets

## On completion of this chapter you should be able to:

- calculate the cost of an asset
- explain the concept of depreciation
- calculate the amount of depreciation using different depreciation methods
- explain how the different methods of depreciation have an impact on profit and the statement of financial position
- explain how the purchase and sale of a noncurrent asset impacts the financial statements and the performance of managers
- prepare journal entries for purchase, sale and depreciation of equipment
- identify the main types of intangible assets
- prepare the accounting entries for asset revaluations
- explain the disclosure requirements for noncurrent assets.

## 8.1 Chapter overview

In this chapter we will consider two major categories of noncurrent assets, namely property, plant and equipment, and intangible assets. Property, plant and equipment refers to long-term assets acquired by an organisation for the purpose of use in the organisation in two or more accounting periods for the production of goods and services. Examples include land, buildings, machinery, equipment, furniture, fittings and motor vehicles. Intangible assets are long-term assets that do not have a visible physical existence as do land, buildings, equipment and so on. Examples of intangible assets include patents, copyrights and goodwill. These and other intangible assets will be described later in the chapter.

## 8.2 The cost of an asset: basic components

The basic premise of historical cost valuation is to use the cost, at acquisition, of an asset to value it on the statement of financial position (balance sheet). On the surface, this looks simple. You buy a truck for $25 000 and value the truck at $25 000. However, there is often more to the cost of an asset than just the simple invoice cost or direct cost. For example, when you purchase a big computerised manufacturing machine, it may cost you $500 000 for the actual machine. But in order to use the machine, certain environmental conditions must exist, such as temperature control, a raised floor for wiring, and a fire protection system. Therefore, a section of the factory must be renovated to meet the specifications of the machine.

These costs, known as installation costs, are a good example of expenditures that are a component of the asset's cost. Overall, the cost of an asset includes all those costs required *to install it ready for use*. That can sometimes be difficult to determine. For example, suppose an enterprise constructs a specialised new manufacturing machine, using some of its regular employees and resources. The cost of such assets, which an enterprise constructs for itself rather than buying finished, will obviously include the cost of raw materials and labour needed to make them. But should the interest on monies borrowed to finance the project be included? This is a matter of judgement, and depends on the situation. Sometimes interest is included in the cost of such assets; most of the time it is not. Enterprises often have policies for how to determine whether expenditures, such as interest, are included in assets' costs. These policies are designed to ensure consistency in calculating cost and to fit the accounting to the enterprise's particular circumstances. Usually note 1 to the financial statements discloses the policy with respect to interest.

Deciding what to include in an asset's cost can make quite a difference to the enterprise's financial statements. Suppose Gondola Pty Ltd has spent $100 000 this year on supervisors' salaries in connection with setting up a new mountain gondola ride at Mount Kosciusko. If that cost is just deducted from revenue as an expense this year, that will reduce profit and income tax expense. But if the cost is added to the gondola ride asset instead, total assets will be higher, and this year's profit and income tax expense will be higher too. Over the next several years, profits and income tax expenses will be lower because of higher depreciation on the higher asset cost. So, aside from accounting appropriately and fairly for the asset, the decision about how to handle the supervisors' salaries will affect profit, assets and income tax expenses this year and in several future years. This decision is often called the capitalising versus expensing choice (including the expenditure with the assets versus deducting it as an expense in the current year), and you will see it several times in this book.

**EXHIBIT 8.1** **Common components of asset cost**

**Land, buildings, equipment**

a **Land**
- purchase price, including real estate agent commissions
- costs of obtaining clear title, such as legal fees and title searches
- costs of clearing, removing unwanted structures, draining, and landscaping

b **Building (purchased)**
- purchase price
- renovation and upgrading costs to make it suitable for the intended use
- initial painting and decoration

c **Building (self-constructed)**
- materials costs
- labour costs
- excavating, surveying, engineering and design costs
- insurance while constructing the building
- perhaps some overhead costs and even financing costs incurred during construction

d **Purchased equipment**
- purchase price including taxes
- transportation costs
- installation costs
- testing costs
- overhauls that extend the equipment's life or increase its value (betterments).

In summary, the components of the cost of an asset include all those costs that are required to make it suitable for the purpose intended, whether it be making a computer usable in the information-gathering process or bringing inventory into saleable condition. Some common components of the cost of an asset are listed in exhibit 8.1.

In the years following acquisition, the question of whether the asset cost should be changed will crop up again when repairs must be made. When a major repair or apparent improvement in the asset is done, the question to ask yourself is whether the asset's productivity or efficiency has been improved, or its useful life extended. If so, there has been a betterment of the asset and the cost of that should be capitalised (added to the cost of the asset). If not, the cost should just be charged to an expense, such as an account called repairs and maintenance expense.

## How's your understanding?

Here are two questions you should be able to answer, based on what you have just read:

1 Magnus Fabricators Pty Ltd has just constructed a new factory building, using company employees and equipment for most of the work. The company's accountant has said that 'various costs must be capitalised to produce an appropriate statement of financial position figure for the building's cost'. What does the accountant mean and what sorts of costs are likely meant?

2 How does a company determine when to stop adding expenditures to the cost of a new building and instead to add those expenditures to repairs and maintenance expense?

## 8.3 Depreciation of assets and depreciation expense

Assets such as property, plant and equipment have value because the company intends to receive economic benefits from using them in the future. However, with the exception of land, all these assets must eventually be retired from service. Thus, when purchasing an asset such as a building or equipment, the rational purchaser will at least have an approximate idea of how much benefit the asset will provide. For example, when buying a piece of equipment to slice bread, the baker must have a reasonable idea of how many years it will last or how many loaves it will slice, before it wears out. If we can estimate how many loaves it will slice we can then deduct the cost of the machine from revenue (in calculating profit) a part at a time, over the number of years it will take to bake that many loaves of bread. This process of allocating the cost over years of benefit is called depreciation, and the annual deduction from revenue is depreciation expense. All property, plant and equipment assets except land are depreciated under GAAP.

A short comment on terminology may be helpful here. This section and the book in general use the terms 'amortisation', 'depreciation' and 'depletion'. In Australia, depreciation is used when physical assets, such as buildings and equipment, are involved; depletion has been used when 'wasting assets', such as timber sales or ore bodies, are involved; and amortisation has been used when various intangible assets and leases are involved. The usage is changing in some countries (such as Canada) towards using the term 'amortisation' in all three cases.

Several questions need to be answered before we present examples of depreciation methods. These are outlined below.

### Why allocate the cost?

Assets are resources of the enterprise, used in order to generate revenue for the owners and, ultimately, a return on their investment. One of the objectives of accrual accounting is to attempt to match expenses with the revenue earned. In the case of long-lived assets, the cost will benefit many periods in which revenue is earned. Therefore, some method is needed to allocate the cost of long-lived assets over their useful lives. If the whole asset cost were deducted from profit in the period in which it was acquired, that would make that period's profit relatively low, and subsequent periods' profits relatively high. It would also mean that an asset which has further benefits is not recognised. So, depreciation spreads the cost out over all the periods that share in the using up of the asset's economic value.

- A bread slicer costs $5000 and will have no value after eight years, so depreciation of $5000 over eight years (for example, $625 of depreciation expense each year) shows that using up the slicer's value over those eight years costs us something. We have a $5000 asset now; in eight years we will have no asset.
- This cost allocation system is somewhat arbitrary, since it is based on expectations when the asset is acquired and not on tracking changes in market value, for example, over the time the asset is used. Over that time, the cost and resale value of slicers may keep changing due to inflation, market conditions or technological change. We may be able to resell the slicer for only $3000 after one year, so perhaps the economic value used up in that year is $2000, but if our depreciation method specifies $625 per year, that is what we use.

It is *essential* to understand that the accounting concept of depreciation involves an *allocation of cost* in order to measure *profit*: *it is not a system to track value changes in the assets or to measure the current value of those assets in the statement of financial position*. It recognises an expense (based on historical cost) that is presumed to *match* the revenue generated by using up the asset's economic value. The statement of financial position shows the net of the asset's original cost minus accumulated depreciation: it does not mean the asset's current value is that net amount.

In the above example, after one year the statement of financial position shows the slicer at $4375 ($5000 cost less $625), not at $3000 or any other measure of current value. The accounting meaning of depreciation (and amortisation and depletion) is very specific: *an allocation of cost as a deduction from profit over the useful life of the asset.*

## Why not depreciate land?

The basic answer is that land's economic value is not considered to decline through use. Land is not normally susceptible to physical or economic decline.

- As a machine is used in a production process it wears out, like the soles of your shoes as you walk. Other natural processes, such as wind, rain, rust, fatigue and corrosion, all keep assets from providing benefit indefinitely.
- There are also nonphysical causes of economic amortisation. A machine can become obsolete with the advent of newer and faster machines, economic conditions in an area can result in the closure of a plant that has many productive years left but cannot be profitable any more, and the whims of fashion can cause retail merchants to change display racks every two years when they were built to last for ten.

Land is considered immune from all this and so is not depreciated. If evidence of a loss of land value does appear, the land's cost can be reduced to a revised value, but that is a special case and is a 'write-down' rather than depreciation.

## When does cost allocation (depreciation expense) begin?

Depreciation is meant to provide an expense to match the economic benefit obtained from the use of the asset. Therefore, when the asset is put to use and the benefit begins to be realised, depreciation expense should begin. In chapter 5, journal entries for depreciating

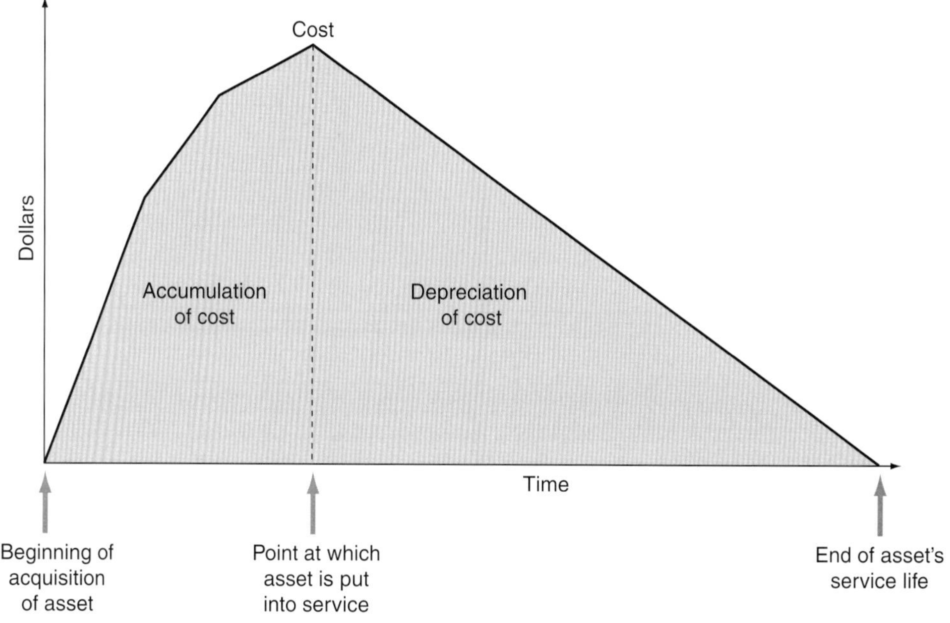


**Figure 8.1** When does depreciation begin?

assets as part of accrual accounting were explained. The general pattern is to capitalise costs incurred on the asset before putting it into service, and then, when the asset is put into service, to depreciate those costs.

This pattern is illustrated in the chart in figure 8.1. The line sloping downward from cost need not be a straight one, as you will see.

Once the asset has been put into service, further costs involved in painting, maintenance, repairs and so on are now considered to be expenses – they are part of the cost of keeping the asset on its planned path of decline over its useful life. If a cost that is incurred subsequent to the asset's going into service significantly changes its economic value in earning revenue or extends its useful life, such a 'betterment' may properly be capitalised as part of the asset's cost, then depreciated along with the rest of the asset's cost.

## Other questions

Does depreciation affect cash flow? Is it exact? What effect does it have on income tax?

Depreciation is recognised by the following journal entry:

DR Depreciation expense
CR     Accumulated depreciation

Accumulated depreciation (some companies refer to this as 'provision for depreciation') is a contra asset. The entry has no cash component, and so depreciation has no cash effect.

Depreciation, no matter how carefully calculated, is never exact. It involves a prediction of economic use and useful life, and such a prediction can easily be wrong. Any depreciation amount is fundamentally arbitrary; for that reason, most companies prefer fairly simple calculations rather than complex guesses!

In Australia, and most other countries, a company does not necessarily have the same depreciation figure for accounting and tax purposes. For example, the company may believe the asset has a life of 10 years and therefore depreciate it at 10 per cent per year for accounting purposes. Tax rules may stipulate (or provide advisory rates under self-assessment) that it is to be depreciated over 12 years, that is, 8.33 per cent per year. Thus, the choice for accounting purposes does not affect the tax paid.

Depreciation does not match actual market value changes in assets, it has no cash effect, it is an estimate only and it has no income tax effect! What good is it? That's a question often asked, and the answer goes back to the matching criterion and historical cost basis of accrual accounting. We know that some economic value is being used up as a depreciable asset is used in earning revenue. We end up with a way of spreading the cost out over the useful life to match the presumed consumption of that cost to the benefits (revenue) gained from the use.

# 8.4 Depreciation bases and methods

Several depreciation methods are commonly used today. Different methods attempt to approximate different economic use patterns of the assets over their lives. In each case, the purpose is to *match* the depreciation expense for each period to the presumed economic benefit obtained during that period, often in a simple way, since depreciation is an estimate rather than an exact measure of value changes.

As noted in section 5.7, which discusses contra accounts, the accumulated depreciation account is a statement of financial position offset account to the asset cost account. Over time, it accumulates the total of the depreciation expense recorded over the years.

There are three basic assumptions about how an asset brings economic benefit, and one general kind of depreciation for each:

| Assumption | Kind of cost allocation |
|---|---|
| 1 *Evenly over the asset's life*<br>The consumption of economic benefits is equal throughout its useful life. | *Straight-line*<br>Expense is the same each year of the useful life. |
| 2 *Falling over the asset's life*<br>The consumption of economic benefits is higher in the earlier years than in the later years. | *Reducing balance method*<br>Expense is larger in the earlier years than in the later years. |
| 3 *Variable over the asset's life*<br>The consumption of economic benefits varies according to how much production is achieved each year. | *Units of production*<br>Expense depends on each year's volume of production. |

These three general kinds are compared graphically in figure 8.2. Each has a different depreciation expense per period and a different pattern of book value. (Book value equals cost minus accumulated depreciation, so, because cost is constant, the book value pattern comes from the accumulation of the depreciation.)

Let's see how to calculate depreciation using the three different bases.

## 1 Straight-line depreciation

Straight-line depreciation, depicted in the top panel of figure 8.2, is the simplest and most widely used of all the depreciation methods. Three pieces of information are necessary in order to calculate straight-line depreciation.

- *cost of the asset* – the total cost to be depreciated over time (the amount capitalised to the date the asset is put into service)
- *estimated useful life of the asset* – the number of periods for which the asset is expected to benefit the enterprise
- *estimated 'salvage value'* – the amount expected to be recovered via the sale of the asset at the end of its useful life. (This amount is likely to be only an educated guess and is often assumed to be zero for purposes of calculating depreciation over long periods of time.)

The formula for straight-line depreciation is:

$$\textbf{Depreciation for one period} = \frac{\textbf{Cost minus estimated salvage value}}{\textbf{Estimated useful life (no. of periods)}}$$

Using the above formula, annual depreciation on a delivery truck used by a local business would be calculated this way:

- Cost of the truck = \$5000
- Estimated useful life = 6 years
- Estimated salvage value after 6 years = \$800

$$\text{Depreciation for one year} = \frac{5000 - 800}{6}$$

$$= \$700$$

At the end of the first year, the net book value of the truck will be:

$$\text{Cost} - \text{Total depreciation to date} = \$5000 - \$700 = \$4300$$

Each year the following journal entry would be made:

| | $ | $ |
|---|---|---|
| DR Depreciation expense | 700 | |
| CR Accumulated depreciation | | 700 |

Depreciation expense for each of the six years will be $700, reducing the book value by $700 per year. As shown in figure 8.2, the constant expense produces a linear increase in accumulated depreciation and so a linear decline in book value.

A common practice for many firms is to assume the salvage value of the asset to be zero, which then enables depreciation to be expressed in terms of percentages instead of years. For example, a company might use straight-line depreciation expressed as $16\frac{2}{3}$ per cent of historical cost, rather than as a term of six years.

## 2 Reducing balance method

Some assets contribute more of their benefit to the enterprise in the early parts of their lives. For example, a new computer may benefit the company greatly when it is first purchased, but because of quickly changing technology and changing needs as the company grows, this same computer may be relegated to less important tasks within a few years of its purchase, as better computers are acquired. Therefore, even though the computer will continue to benefit the company, most of its economic value has been consumed near the beginning of its life.

In Australia, the reducing balance method is the next most common depreciation method after straight-line.

Information needed for this procedure is:

- *cost of the asset*
- *accumulated depreciation*—total depreciation recorded since the acquisition of the asset
- *depreciation rate*—the percentage of the book value (cost minus depreciation to date) of the asset that is to be depreciated in the period

The formula for the reducing balance method is:

$$\textbf{Depreciation for one period} = (\textbf{Cost} - \textbf{Accumulated depreciation}) \times \textbf{Rate} = \textbf{Remaining book value of the asset} \times \textbf{Rate}$$

Let's use the reducing balance method to calculate depreciation for the six-year life of the same truck you saw above. With this method, the depreciation rate is established such that over the asset's life, the cost will be fully depreciated. Doing this exactly requires complex algebra, so approximate rates are usually used. For example, Australian companies that use this method normally use 150 per cent of the straight-line percentage assuming no salvage value. This is what many of them use for taxation purposes.

The truck has a life of six years (straight-line depreciation is $16\frac{2}{3}$ per cent per year). As 150 per cent of the straight-line rate would be 25 per cent, we will use 25 per cent to approximate the economic consumption pattern.

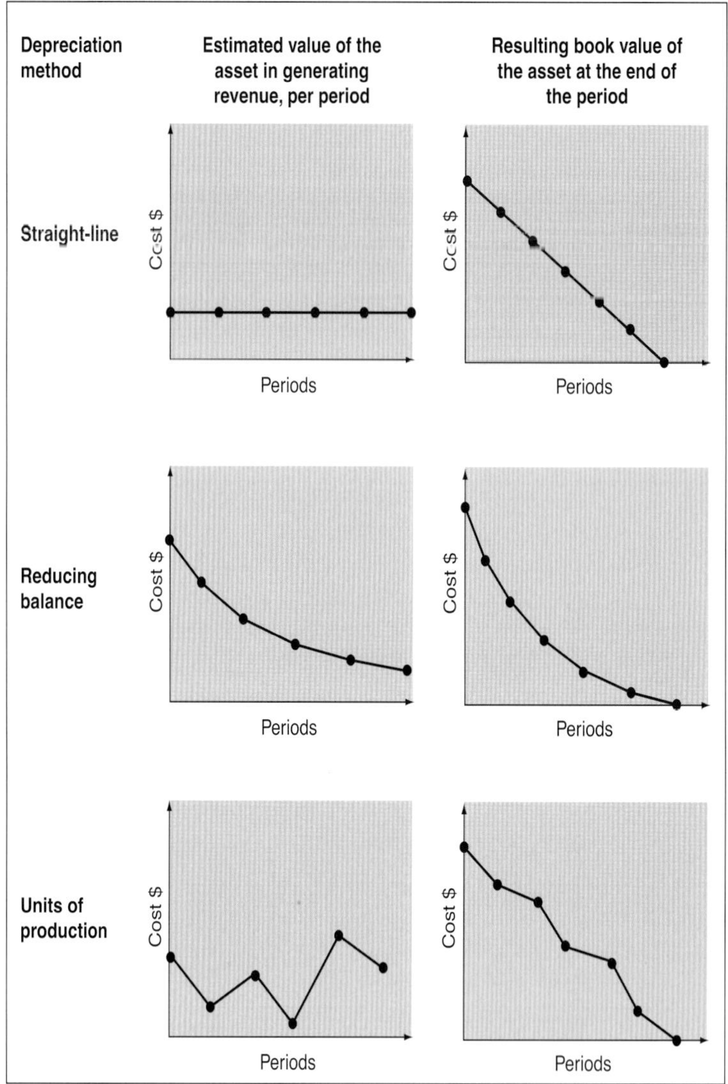


Figure 8.2 Three depreciation methods

- cost = \$5000
- depreciation to date = \$0 (at beginning)
- depreciation rate = 25%

*Year 1*

| | |
|---|---|
| Depreciation for the year | = (\$5000 – \$0) × 25% |
| | = \$1250 |
| Total depreciation to date | = \$1250 |
| Remaining book value | = \$3750 |

*Year 2*

| | |
|---|---|
| Depreciation for the year | = (\$5000 – \$1250) × 25% |
| | = \$937.50 |
| Total depreciation to date | = \$2187.50 |

Remaining book value = $2812.50

Depreciation expense gets smaller with each year.

*Year 3*

Depreciation for the year = ($5000 – $2187.50) × 25%

= $703.13

Total depreciation to date = $2890.63

Remaining book value = $2109.37

*Year 4*

Depreciation for the year = ($5000 – $2890.63) × 25%

= $527.34

Total depreciation to date = $3417.97

Remaining book value = $1582.03

*Year 5*

Depreciation for the year = ($5000 – $3417.97) × 25%

= $395.51

Total depreciation to date = $3813.48

Remaining book value = $1186.52

*Year 6*

Depreciation for the year = ($5000 – $3813.48) × 25%

= $296.63

Total depreciation to date = $4110.11

Remaining book value = $889.89

Although in this example the remaining book value of the truck at the end of five years is fairly close to the expected salvage value of the truck, reducing balance depreciation does not normally take salvage value into account. Consequently, the book value at the end of six years would be the same whether or not the company expected to recover any of the cost of the truck.

The second panel of the chart in figure 8.2 shows the kind of patterns of depreciation expense and book value we calculated for the truck. The expense and book value lines are curves instead of straight lines.

The reducing balance percentage is sometimes calculated using the following formula, which is applied to the original cost.

$$r = 1 - \sqrt[n]{\frac{s}{c}}$$

where $r$ = required depreciation rate

$n$ = estimated life in years

$s$ = estimated residual value

$c$ = original cost

This formula operates satisfactorily only if the estimated residual value is substantially greater than zero, as the result is very sensitive to small movements near zero.

If an asset has an original cost of $30 000, a life of five years and an estimated salvage value of $5000 the rate would be

$$1 - \sqrt[5]{\frac{5000}{30\,000}} = 30\% \text{ (approximately)}.$$

In the United States a method called 'sum-of-the year's digits' is sometimes used. The effect of this method on profit and balance sheets figures is similar to that of the reducing balance method. Both methods provide larger amounts of depreciation in the first years of an asset's life, with the depreciation expense gradually decreasing each year. These methods are both referred to as accelerated depreciation methods.

The sum-of-the-year's digits method calculates the depreciation charge by multiplying the original cost minus estimated residual value by a fraction. The numerator is the number of years of life remaining for an asset. The denominator is the sum of the years of the asset's life. For example, the sum of the years for an asset with a life of five years is $5 + 4 + 3 + 2 + 1 = 15$. In years one to five the following fractions would be used:

$$\frac{5}{15}, \frac{4}{15}, \frac{3}{15}, \frac{2}{15}, \frac{1}{15}$$

For the asset that cost $30 000 and had an estimated disposal value of $5000 at the end of five years, depreciation for year 1 would be $8333 ([$30 000 – $5000] × $\frac{5}{15}$).

## 3 Units-of-production depreciation and depletion

The economic consumption of many assets is not necessarily a function of time, but rather of use. For example, it may make more sense to say that the delivery truck is expected to last so many kilometres rather than so many years. The consumption of natural resources ('wasting assets') is also often accounted for using units of production, because the value to the enterprise of a stand of timber, or an oil well, is tied to the number of trees remaining to be felled or the amount of oil left to be recovered. Therefore, the units-of-production method of depreciation is also used to compute depletion of natural resources.

To compute depreciation or depletion per unit of usage, the following information is needed:

- *cost of the asset*
- *estimated salvage value*
- *estimated number of units to be produced during life of asset*—the estimated number of tonnes of ore extracted from a mine, or the estimated number of kilometres that the delivery truck will travel, or other production measures.

The formula for computing units-of-production depreciation is:

$$\textbf{Depreciation or depletion for one unit of use or production (e.g. a kilometre)} = \frac{\textbf{Cost} - \textbf{Estimated salvage value}}{\textbf{Estimated no. of units of use or production during life}}$$

To determine depreciation for the year, the charge per unit is multiplied by the number of actual units produced or used. Using the delivery truck as an example again, depreciation of the truck over its expected useful life might be:

- cost = $5000
- estimated salvage value = $800
- estimated number of km to be driven = 210 000

$$\text{Depreciation per km} = \frac{\$5000 - \$800}{210\,000}$$
$$= \$0.02 \text{ depreciation/km}$$

*Year 1*

If the truck is driven 20 000 km during the year, the depreciation charge for the year will be:

$\$0.02 \times 20\,000 = \$400$

*Year 2*

If the truck is driven 80 000 km during the second year, the depreciation charge for the year will be:

$\$0.02 \times 80\,000 = \$1600$

*Year 3*

Say the truck is driven 65 000 km during the year. The depreciation charge for the year will be:

$\$0.02 \times 65\,000 = \$1300$

*Year 4*

Suppose the truck is driven 50 000 km during the year; however, after 45 000 km, the truck will be fully depreciated (it has been driven the estimated 210 000 km). Therefore, the depreciation charge for the year will be just the remaining \$900, which is less than $\$0.02 \times 50\,000$ km.

The bottom panel in figure 8.2 illustrates units-of-production depreciation. It is the only method that can result in the annual depreciation expense going up and down from period to period.

Depletion of a wasting asset and units-of-production depreciation of a fixed asset are computed in the same manner, but depletion refers to the physical consumption of an asset, rather than just the economic consumption. For the timber stand, salvage value may be the value of the land after all the timber has been cut. In Australia, this method is often used in the mining industry.

## 8.5 Depreciation example

Here is an example. Greco Limited has purchased a factory at a cost of \$23 000 000 (not including land). The general manager wants to know what difference it would make if the company used straight-line, reducing balance or units-of-production depreciation.

- Estimated useful life is 20 years, during which time the company plans to make about 100 million boxes of its standard product.
- Estimated salvage value after the end of the useful life is \$5 000 000.
- If reducing balance depreciation were used, the probable rate chosen would be 10 per cent per year on the reducing balance.
- Production plans call for production over the next six years of 4, 9, 9, 8, 9 and 5 million boxes per year, and likely stable production of about 4 million boxes per year for the remaining 14 years.

  The resulting depreciation bases would be:

  - straight-line
    \$23 000 000 – \$5 000 000 = \$18 000 000 over 20 years (5% of base per year)

- reducing balance
  $23 000 000 – accumulated depreciation × 10% per year
- units-of-production
  $18 000 000/100 000 000 boxes = $0.18 per box produced

If everything turns out as expected, annual depreciation expense for the next 20 years will be as follows:

| | Straight-line expense | Reducing balance | | Units-of-production expense |
|---|---|---|---|---|
| | | Begin book value | Expense | |
| | | $ | $ | $ |
| 1 | 900 000 | 23 000 000 | 2 300 000 | 720 000 |
| 2 | 900 000 | 20 700 000 | 2 070 000 | 1 620 000 |
| 3 | 900 000 | 18 630 000 | 1 863 000 | 1 620 000 |
| 4 | 900 000 | 16 767 000 | 1 676 700 | 1 440 000 |
| 5 | 900 000 | 15 090 300 | 1 509 030 | 1 620 000 |
| 6 | 900 000 | 13 581 270 | 1 358 127 | 900 000 |
| 7 | 900 000 | 12 223 143 | 1 222 314 | 720 000 |
| 8 | 900 000 | 11 000 829 | 1 100 083 | 720 000 |
| 9 | 900 000 | 9 900 746 | 990 075 | 720 000 |
| 10 | 900 000 | 8 910 671 | 891 067 | 720 000 |
| 11 | 900 000 | 8 019 604 | 801 960 | 720 000 |
| 12 | 900 000 | 7 217 644 | 721 764 | 720 000 |
| 13 | 900 000 | 6 495 880 | 649 588 | 720 000 |
| 14 | 900 000 | 5 846 292 | 584 629 | 720 000 |
| 15 | 900 000 | 5 261 663 | 526 166 | 720 000 |
| 16 | 900 000 | 4 735 497 | 473 550 | 720 000 |
| 17 | 900 000 | 4 261 947 | 426 195 | 720 000 |
| 18 | 900 000 | 3 835 752 | 383 575 | 720 000 |
| 19 | 900 000 | 3 452 177 | 345 218 | 720 000 |
| 20 | 900 000 | 3 106 959 | 310 696 | 720 000 |
| Total | 18 000 000 | | 20 203 737 | 18 000 000 |

At the end of 20 years, if everything works out as expected, the book value of the factory will be, for each method:

- straight-line: $23 000 000 – $18 000 000 = $5 000 000
- reducing balance: $23 000 000 – $20 203 737 = $2 796 263
- units-of-production: $23 000 000 – $18 000 000 = $5 000 000

If at the end of 20 years the factory is sold, there will be a gain or loss on sale equalling the sale proceeds minus the book value. The proceeds may not be the expected $5 000 000. If they are not, there will be a gain or loss on sale for even the simplest method (that is, straight-line).

The reducing balance method, however, will be a little off target at the end of 20 years, with a book value of less than $3 million. In fact, it will reach a $5 million book value in the fifteenth year. If the expected $5 000 000 salvage value is actually obtained at the end of 20 years, the reducing balance method will result in a gain on sale at the date of sale of the factory equalling $2 203 737 ($5 000 000 proceeds minus $2 796 263 book value), which is really a correction of the over-depreciation that the reducing balance method produced. The method will have been off target by this $2 203 737 amount.

The units-of-production method will almost certainly result in a book value not exactly equal to $5 000 000, even though it is planned to equal that. This is so because the actual production will be very unlikely to equal exactly 100 million boxes over 20 years.

Whichever method is adopted, the company can always adjust its calculations later, if the expectations about length of useful life or salvage value begin to look seriously incorrect. For now, note that it is usual to allocate the remaining book value over the remaining useful life. For example, an asset was expected to have a useful remaining of life of 10 years, but after the fifth year it had a book value of $60 000; it was decided that it would only be used for another three years. The depreciation for each of the last three years would be $20 000.

## How's your understanding?

Here is a question you should be able to answer, based on what you have just read: Explain to the general manager of Cold Lake Manufacturing Pty Ltd, which opened for business at the beg0inning of this year, what depreciation expense is supposed to accomplish and the criteria you would recommend the company use in choosing the most appropriate method.

## 8.6 Gains and losses on noncurrent asset disposals and write-offs

Gains, losses and write-offs have been mentioned and illustrated in various ways since chapter 4. This section is intended to pull the ideas together for you and show you how they are partly the consequences of accounting policy choices.

In the above Greco example, there was a possibility of a gain or loss on the sale of the factory in the twentieth year. When a noncurrent asset is sold, it could be handled as ordinary revenues are: the proceeds could be added to revenue and the book value of the asset added to the cost of goods sold. But this would mix day-to-day revenues from the activities for which the enterprise exists with the occasional (and presumably less important economically) revenues from reducing long-term fixed assets or other investments.

Therefore, such events are kept separate from ordinary revenues via the following kind of journal entry, which we have seen before:

| | | | |
|---|---|---|---|
| DR Cash or non-trade receivables (proceeds) | XXXX | | |
| CR Noncurrent asset (for original cost) | | | XXXX |
| DR Accumulated depreciation on that asset (all that has accumulated) | XXXX | | |
| DR (loss) or CR (gain on sale) | XXXX | or | XXXX |

The gain or loss is just the difference between the proceeds and the book value (cost minus accumulated depreciation, if any). Here is an example: Company X has a truck that cost $84 000. The accumulated depreciation at the date of sale is $46 000. Therefore, book value is $38 000 at the date of sale. If the company:

- sells it for $52 000, there is a gain on sale of $14 000 ($52 000 – $38 000). The journal entry would be:

| | $ | $ |
|---|---|---|
| DR Cash | 52 000 | |
| DR Accumulated depreciation | 46 000 | |
| CR Truck | | 84 000 |
| CR Gain on sale | | 14 000 |

- sells it for $30 000, there is a loss on sale of $8000 ($38 000 – $30 000). The journal entry would be:

| | $ | $ |
|---|---|---|
| DR Cash | 30 000 | |
| DR Accumulated depreciation | 46 000 | |
| DR Loss on sale | 8 000 | |
| CR Truck | | 84 000 |

Think of gains and losses as depreciation corrections:

- If the company knew in advance what the proceeds would be and when the sale would happen, it could have depreciated the asset down exactly to the proceeds amount by that date. So if the proceeds equal book value, there is no gain or loss.
- If the proceeds are less than book value, there is a loss: in effect, more depreciation is needed and that's what the loss really is.
- If the proceeds are *more* than book value, there is a gain: in effect, too much depreciation was taken and the gain is really just that excess (which caused the lower book value) being recognised.

Also note that in Australia AASB 1004 requires gross proceeds from the sale of non-current assets to be separately disclosed under 'Other revenue'.

## 8.7 Assets revaluations

Australian companies are allowed to partly depart from historical cost by revaluing non-current assets. While this is also allowable in New Zealand and the United Kingdom, it is not permitted in the United States or Canada.

Accounting standards state that each class of noncurrent assets must be measured on either (a) the cost basis or (b) the fair value basis. *Fair value* is defined as the amount for which an asset could be exchanged between knowledgeable willing parties in an arm's length transaction. The measurement of fair value assumes the highest and best use of the asset for which market participants would be prepared to pay.

Assets can either be revalued upwards (revaluation increment) or downwards (revaluation decrement) from their carrying amounts (often called 'book value'). The accounting standards on revaluations have the purpose of ensuring that users of the financial statements have relevant and reliable information for evaluating the performance, financial position, financing and investing of the organisation. Surveys of users of financial statements have also indicated that the revalued assets' values are desired.

When there is an increment, the amount of the increment goes to an asset revaluation reserve, which appears in the shareholders' equity section of statement of financial position. (The concept of a reserve is discussed in more detail in chapter 10.) So if you see a balance in an asset revaluation reserve, it simply tells you the amount by which assets have been revalued over time. For example, if land is revalued from $11 million to $12 million, both the land account and the asset revaluation account would increase by $1 million. However, because of conservatism, if there were a revaluation decrement to $10 million, the decrement would be recognised as an expense in the profit and loss account. That is, an expense (loss on devaluation of land) would increase, and land would decrease. In summary, increments in asset valuations do not generally affect the profit and loss statement directly, but decrements do reduce the profit for the year (see exceptions below). Also note that changes in asset valuation (except for land) result in different depreciation expenses in subsequent years.

When a class of noncurrent assets is measured on the fair value basis, revaluations need to be made with sufficient regularity to ensure carrying amount does not materially differ from fair value. Revaluing every three years is quite common.

The standards state that when an asset is revalued, all assets within the same class of assets should be valued at the same time on a consistent basis. For example, if one block of land is revalued, all other blocks of land should be revalued on a consistent basis; similarly for buildings, plant and equipment. There is an exception, in that, for downward revaluations of a particular noncurrent asset, the revaluation of all other assets of that class is not required. Note that a downwards revaluation of a noncurrent asset must be undertaken when its carrying amount is greater than its recoverable amount. Recoverable amount refers to the net amount that is expected to be recovered through the cash inflows and outflows arising from the asset's continued use and subsequent disposal. When the fair value basis is used, the method used in determining fair value must be disclosed as well as whether an independent valuation has been obtained.

Now let's consider the debits and credits. Where there is an asset revaluation increment, the amount of the increment is credited to an asset revaluation reserve. For example, if land is revalued from $11 million to $12 million, the entry would be:

| | $ | $ |
|---|---|---|
| DR Land | 1 million | |
| CR Asset revaluation reserve | | 1 million |

However, if there had been a revaluation decrement to $10 million the decrement would be recognised in a profit and loss account. The entry would be:

| | $ | $ |
|---|---|---|
| DR Loss on devaluation of land | 1 million | |
| CR Land | | 1 million |

Again there are exceptions. If an increment reverses a revaluation decrement previously recognised as an expense in the profit and loss account in respect of that same class of assets, the increment would be recognised as revenue. Similarly, if the revaluation decrement reverses a previous revaluation increment previously credited to asset revaluation reserves for the same class of assets, it will be debited directly to the asset revaluation reserve.

Further complications arise when we consider assets that are depreciated, such as equipment. At the time of revaluation the accumulated depreciation on those assets is credited to the asset account. The asset account is then increased or decreased by the amount of the revaluation increments or decrements. For example, if equipment cost $2 000 000 (with accumulated depreciation of $500 000) and was revalued to $2 500 000, the entries would be:

| | $ | $ |
|---|---|---|
| DR Accumulated depreciation | 500 000 | |
| CR Equipment | | 500 000 |

This entry transferred the relevant accumulated depreciation as an offset to the equipment account. The equipment is now carried at a net balance of $1 500 000. To revalue it to $2 500 000, the following entry would occur:

| | $ | $ |
|---|---|---|
| DR Equipment | 1 000 000 | |
| CR Asset revaluation reserve | | 1 000 000 |

When the asset that has previously been revalued is sold, the gain or loss on disposal is measured as the difference between the carrying value at the time of disposal and the net proceeds. You will cover these and other more advanced issues in subsequent courses.

We realise that the above sections are difficult for an introductory book. However, at least by seeing the journal entries, even if you don't fully understand them at this stage, you will be in a better position to understand the meaning and value of the noncurrent assets section and the asset revaluation reserve in the statement of financial position.

## 8.8 Intangible assets

Intangible assets are long-term assets that do not have a visible physical existence, as do land, buildings or equipment. Examples of intangible assets include:

- *Patents, copyrights, trademarks* and other such legal property.
  For example, the 2001 statement of financial position of Telstra states, under the heading of 'Identifiable intangible assets':

  > Identifiable intangible assets include patents, trademarks, brand names, customer bases and licences (including network and business software and spectrum licences). When the costs spent on such assets have a benefit or relationship to more than one accounting period, these costs are deferred and amortised on a straight-line basis over the period of expected benefit, which averages 12 years for fiscal 2001 (2000: 13 years). The recoverable amounts of identifiable intangible assets are reviewed annually and the carrying amount is adjusted down where considered necessary.

  Thus an asset is created for these items. The asset is then amortised over the period during which the company believes they will provide benefit.
- *Brand names*, which can be registered to maintain exclusive use.
  For example, consider some of the brand names of the Foster's Brewery Group Limited that you may be familiar with: Fosters, Victoria Bitter, Carlton Cold, Crown Lager, Light Ice and Rothbury Estate Wines. Note 16 to the 2001 financial statements shows the following:

**Note 16. Intangibles**

| | | |
|---|---|---|
| Brand names, mailing lists, patents and licences | | |
| At cost | 1 947.5 | 1 043.9 |
| Accumulated amortisation | (12.6) | (9.5) |
| | 1 934.9 | 1 034.4 |
| Goodwill at cost | 825.5 | 354.6 |
| Accumulated amortisation | (91.0) | (56.4) |
| | 734.5 | 298.2 |
| | 2 669.4 | 1 332.6 |

Goodwill is discussed below. At this stage, note that the brand names (together with patent and licences) are valued at either directors' valuation or cost. Unlike the reporting of intangibles in the Telstra accounts, these intangibles are not amortised. The Foster's Brewery Group annual report 2001 states:

> Brand names, patents and licences are included in the financial statements at the lower of cost and recoverable amount. The cost of acquired brand names is determined by reference to independent valuations performed on the acquisition of businesses.
>
> The carrying value of these brands is reviewed each year to ensure that it is not in excess of recoverable amount . . .
>
> The Directors believe that any depreciable amounts of the Group's brand names is negligible based on expected residual values compared with carrying values. Further, the Directors believe that the useful lives of the brands are of such duration that any amortisation charge on the brands will be immaterial

Sigma Ltd, on the other hand, does amortise brand names, but the period of amortisation depends on the brand name.

> Effective 1 February 1999, a review was conducted of the consolidated entity's trademarks and product brands to reassess their useful lives. This review resulted in the trademarks and product brands, with the exception of the Amcal and Guardian brand names, being amortised on a straight-line basis over 20 years.
>
> Effective 1 August 1999, the useful lives of the Amcal and Guardian brand names were reassessed, and are being amortised on a straight-line basis over 60 years.

- *Franchises, distributorships* and other such rights to sell someone else's products in a certain geographical area (McDonald's Restaurants, Midas Mufflers, LJ Hooker, Shell Australia Service Stations, Bob Jane T-mart and Pizza Hut are examples in which the local operator has paid for the right to use the name and sell the products).
- *Deferred charges* such as incorporation costs, financing costs, and other items that are really long-term prepaid expenses.

Examples from 2001 annual reports of deferred charges include:

> **Amalgamated Holdings Limited**
>
> ***Deferred expenditure***
>
> Material items of expenditure are deferred to the extent that they are recoverable out of future revenue; do not relate solely to revenue which has already been brought to account; can be measured reliably; and will contribute to the future earning capacity of the consolidated entity.
>
> Deferred expenditure is amortised over the period in which the related benefits are expected to be realised. Expenditure deferred in previous periods is reviewed annually. Any amounts no longer considered recoverable out of future revenue are written off.

**Tabcorp Holdings Limited**

***Casino licence***

The casino licence is amortised over the life of the casino licence, being ninety-nine years, from the date of issue, 14 December 1994.

**Western Mining Corporation (2000)**

***Capitalisation of borrowing costs***

For qualifying assets under construction, which are normally major projects and where development or construction extends over more than one year, borrowing costs directly attributable to the funds invested in the project are included as a capital cost during the period up to the commencement of production. To the extent that additional funds have been borrowed for the purpose of, and are associated with the project, the interest rate used is that applicable to those funds. The interest rate for any funds utilised in excess of specific borrowings is the weighted average rate for all other borrowings. Capitalised borrowing costs are amortised (from the commencement of commercial production) over a period not exceeding the economic life of the projects, which are subject to a maximum of twenty years.

- *Research and development costs* (including product development costs and mineral exploration costs) that are capitalised and later expensed at the time they earn revenue in the future. The Australian Accounting Standards require organisations to charge research and development costs to an expense account when incurred except where future benefits related to the costs are expected to be greater than the costs 'beyond any reasonable doubt'. Because of different interpretations of the term 'beyond any reasonable doubt', there is variation between companies on when they capitalise research and development costs.

  Two examples from the 2001 annual report of CSR Limited, and the 2000 annual report of Western Mining Corporation:

  **CSR Limited**

  ***Research and development***

  All expenditure on research and development is written off in the year in which the expenditure is incurred except where future benefits can be assured beyond reasonable doubt. Projects are continually under review.

  **Western Mining Corporation**

  ***Research and development***

  Research and development expenditure is charged against profit and loss as incurred, except that when a regular evaluation of projects concludes that an individual project is expected beyond any reasonable doubt to recover its costs from subsequent use or disposal, the costs of the project for that and subsequent reporting periods are capitalised. Such deferred capital is amortised over the reporting periods that are expected to benefit from the project. In establishing this economic life, due regard is given to the economic life of the related area of interest or, if this is not relevant, a maximum life of five years is applied.

- *Purchased goodwill* arises when more is paid for a group of assets, such as a whole business, than the assets seem to be worth individually. The rationale for paying the additional amount may be based on such factors as how the business is organised or the number of customers. As a result, there is an intangible asset called goodwill that keeps the accounts in balance. Here is an example: Great buys all the business assets of Small for \$800 000 cash. The best estimate of the fair market values of those assets are: receivables

$60 000; inventories $110 000; land $100 000; building $260 000; equipment $130 000; total $660 000; no liabilities are assumed by Great.

Great would record the purchase as follows:

| | $ | $ |
|---|---|---|
| DR Accounts receivable | 60 000 | |
| DR Inventories | 110 000 | |
| DR Land | 100 000 | |
| DR Buildings | 260 000 | |
| DR Equipment | 130 000 | |
| CR Cash | | 800 000 |

No problem. Except that the entry doesn't balance! So a new account called Goodwill is created and debited with $140 000, which is the $800 000, cost of the whole, minus $660 000, the sum of the fair values of the parts. This keeps the books in balance but creates an account of which the value and meaning are unclear. If goodwill represents unrecorded assets, what are they? If it represents a good location, good managers or 'synergy' with the operations of Great, what are these things really worth? How much future value do they have? How long will this value last?

For accounting purposes, it is important that you understand the difference between externally and internally generated goodwill. The situation discussed in the previous paragraph refers to externally generated goodwill, which is recognised by the accounting system. This is a transaction, supported by documentation, that shows how much was paid, then some judgements need to be made about the fair value of the assets, with the remainder being goodwill. However, if an organisation builds up the business by such methods as better management and improving the friendliness of staff, this would be called internally generated goodwill, which would not be included in the financial statements. While someone else may now be willing to pay more for the business, this extra value is not represented in the accounts. While there are a number of reasons for this, at this stage note that problems in measuring this amount is one reason why it is not included.

## What are intangible assets worth?

Because such assets are intangible, their existence and value may be doubtful. Generally, the more clearly identifiable and documented the assets are (especially via external evidence such as contracts and legal documents), the less difficulty they pose. However, even for clearly owned assets such as patents and franchises, there may be considerable doubt about their future economic value. For example, what is a McDonald's franchise worth? It depends on ever-changing consumer tastes, on whether a competitor does or doesn't open across the street and on many other business and economic factors. Difficulties in valuing brand names and trademarks also abound.

For assets such as product development expenditures included as part of research and development, there is often a real question as to whether they belong on the statement of financial position at all. Capitalising expenditures on such items may appear to create better matching, and is usually seen to be proper by those making such expenditures, but this depends on whether they will ever return future value. Will the great new product sell? Will it produce revenues greater than costs? This is a difficult judgement to make, and many people have concluded that such assets should not appear, because these people favour conservatism in accounting, are afraid of manipulation or just feel that recognising such assets is not fair or appropriate. As noted above, Australian Accounting Standards require expenditures on such things to be expensed immediately and not capitalised, unless the costs will be recovered in the future beyond any reasonable doubt.

### Cost of intangibles

Goodwill's cost is determined as illustrated above. For other intangibles, cost is determined in the same way as that of any other asset: purchase cost and other expenditures made prior to putting the asset into service (getting economic benefits from it). There may be substantial ambiguity about the cost of internally developed assets, such as research and development expenditures, because it may be difficult to determine exactly what was spent to develop the asset, separately from normal expenses incurred, and for this reason many companies decline to recognise (capitalise) such assets. Internally developed goodwill is never capitalised (for example, expenditures on office parties that create happy employees are expensed, not capitalised).

### Amortisation of intangibles

Intangible assets are generally amortised over their useful lives, just like fixed assets. Determining legal useful life may be fairly straightforward for assets supported by contracts or other documents (for example, leases have a specified term, as do most franchises, and patents are good for a specific number of years), but whether this is also the economic useful life is harder to say. For other assets, such as incorporation costs or goodwill, useful life is anyone's guess. Australian standards specify a *maximum useful life* of 20 years for goodwill. This is a less optimistic estimate than the 40 years used in the United States and Canada. Other intangibles, such as brand names, are often not amortised, as illustrated in the Foster's Brewing example earlier.

Because of all this ambiguity, intangibles are generally amortised simply, using the straight-line basis.

## 8.9 Finance leases

Leases are rental agreements in which one individual (a lessee) pays to the owner of a property (lessor) a certain amount in return for the right to use that property over a predetermined period. The property could be a building, a motor vehicle, equipment, aircraft, computers or furniture and fittings. Before the issuing of accounting standards on leases, there was some concern that companies were using leases to avoid putting assets and liabilities on the statement of financial position. For example, instead of borrowing $100 000 from a bank to buy a new piece of equipment (resulting in assets and liabilities both increasing by $100 000), some companies were using an alternative form of financing, namely leases, and avoiding the need to include the asset and related liability on the statement of financial position. As a result, the Australian Accounting Standards defined two types of leases: finance leases (called 'capital leases' in the United States) and operating leases. Leases are classified as finance leases when all the risks and benefits incidental to ownership are substantially transferred to the lessee.

Such finance leases are included on the statement of financial position as follows:

- The 'cost' is the present value of the future lease payments, using an appropriate interest rate usually deduced from the lease agreement (discussed in appendix to chapter 13).

- At the same time, the present value of those payments is recorded as a liability.
- So the journal entry to put the leases on the statement of financial position is:

| | | |
|---|---|---|
| DR Finance lease asset | XXXX | |
| CR Finance lease obligations liability | | XXXX |

- After that:
  1. The leased asset is amortised, just as the owned assets are depreciated, following a policy that is consistent with that used for owned assets but also taking into account the terms of the lease.
  2. The liability is reduced as payments are made on the lease. Each payment is divided into deduced principal and interest portions, so that only the principal portion is deducted from the liability and the rest is considered interest expense. This maintains the liability at the present value of the remaining lease payments.
  3. The expenses for using the leased asset, therefore, are amortisation and interest. Such amounts are usually combined with other amortisation and interest expenses because the intent is to represent the economic situation fairly.
  4. Various particulars of significant capital leases are usually disclosed in the notes to the financial statements, so that the readers of the statements may judge the effects of such capitalisation. Such separate disclosure is usual for the lease obligations liability, the terms of the lease, and related amortisation and interest expenses.

The result of these procedures is that the leased asset is treated essentially as if it were owned. Accrual accounting recognises the economic value of the asset and disregards the legalities of who owns it.

If the lease does not result in an economic equivalence of ownership (for example, if it is really a rental situation where the owner continues to do the repairs and maintenance, generally controls the asset and regains use of the asset after a certain period), the lease is termed an 'operating lease'. For such leases, there is no asset or lease obligation liability recognised, and the lease payments are just expensed as rent expense. If the operating lease is significant to the company, some of its particulars may be disclosed in the notes to the financial statements.

## 8.10 Reporting of noncurrent assets and associated depreciation/amortisation

Corporations Law and the Australian Accounting Standards require certain disclosures concerning noncurrent assets and the related depreciation/amortisation. These include:

- depreciation and amortisation expenses
- cost and accumulated depreciation by major classes of assets (where revalued the revalued amount is shown in place of cost)
- a description of the enterprise's accounting policies with respect to depreciation/amortisation
- details concerning revaluations including the year, the basis of valuation, whether this was an independent valuation
- a statement that assets have not been valued above their recoverable amount.

Concerning this last point, accounting standards require that the carrying value of noncurrent assets be written down to their recoverable amount when their carrying amount is greater than their recoverable amount. Recoverable amount means the net amount that is expected to be recovered through the cash inflows and outflows arising from the continued use of the asset and its disposal. It is necessary to disclose whether these expected cash flows, used in determining recoverable amounts of noncurrent assets, have been discounted to their present value. Not-for-profit entities are excluded from the requirement to write down to their recoverable amount assets that are not held for the primary purpose of generating net cash inflows.

## 8.11 Managers and noncurrent assets

Managers need to make many judgements related to noncurrent assets. Examples include:

- What should be included in the cost of an asset, and over what period should it be depreciated?
- When should assets be revalued, and who should do the revaluation?
- Should research and development costs be capitalised or expensed?
- Should costs such as incorporation and pre-opening costs be capitalised or expensed?
- Over what period should goodwill be amortised?
- What value should be put on brand names, trademarks and so on?

All of the above judgements will affect the valuation of assets, which in turn affects certain performance measures such as return on assets, which managers are responsible for. All of the above judgements (except the upward revaluation of assets) will affect the enterprises' profit figure, which is again a key indicator of manager performance.

## 8.12 Public sector issues

Australian Accounting Standard 29 (AAS 29) outlines some guidelines for handling the recognition, measurement, revaluation and depreciation of noncurrent assets of government departments. Some interesting and unique (to the public sector) issues arise.

AAS 29 adopts the view that all assets, including infrastructure assets (for example, roads, bridges and tunnels), heritage assets (for example, historical buildings and historical monuments), community assets (for example, parks and sporting fields) and other assets that provide services or economic benefits over long periods of time should be recognised as assets provided that: it is probable that the service potential or future economic benefits embodied in the asset will eventuate; and the asset possesses a cost or other value that can be measured reliably.

Infrastructure system assets include items such as roads, bridges, sewerage systems, water supply and reservoirs, power generation plants and transmission lines. These items are generally valued by government departments at cost or written-down replacement value (that is, estimated replacement value minus accumulated depreciation). Consider the difficulty of obtaining these figures. For example, as accrual accounting was not used at the time of construction of many assets, costs are difficult to know; determining the replacement value of the major bridges in each capital city is costly.

Heritage assets refer to those noncurrent assets that a government intends to preserve indefinitely because of their unique historical, cultural or environmental attributes. One common feature of heritage assets is that they cannot be replaced. Because of the difficulty of valuation, certain heritage assets are not valued and are included in a department's assets at a nominal value of $1. The valuation of $1 highlights to readers that an asset exists but at this point in time it is not clear how to value it. An example is the library collection held by the State Library of New South Wales, which is included in the assets at $1. The notes to the financial statements state that 'this is justifiable due to the unique or cultural attributes of the vast majority of acquisitions, which will be retained in perpetuity'

In general, a number of factors affect the difficulty of reliably measuring the assets of public sector entities. These include completeness of asset registers and other accounting records not required prior to the adoption of accrual accounting, the type of asset, the extent of the asset's similarity to other assets used in other government departments and the time period that has elapsed since the asset was acquired. Examples of assets for which such difficulties may exist include land under roads, transport infrastructure, monuments, historic buildings, parks and gardens. For example, what value would you put on the train lines in your State or the botanical gardens in the nearest capital city?

## 8.13 Homework and discussion to develop understanding

### Discussion questions

1 What is included in the cost of an asset?
2 What is the purpose of depreciation?
3 'Without depreciation, the asset values in the statement of financial position would not be appropriate.' Discuss.
4 What judgements need to be made by managers and accountants in calculating depreciation?
5 What different methods of depreciation are available? How do the methods affect profit for the year?
6 How do gains and losses on disposal affect the financial statements?
7 What is the purpose of an asset revaluation?
8 What is the impact of a land being revalued upwards on the profit for the year?
9 What is recoverable amount?
10 List five different types of intangibles.
11 What is goodwill? How is it valued in the statement of financial position?
12 Provide three examples of deferred expenditure. Where would they appear in the financial statements?
13 What determines whether research and development costs are capitalised or expensed?
14 Why record depreciation expense by debiting the expense and crediting accumulated depreciation? Why not just credit the asset cost so that the balance sheet shows just the remaining undepreciated cost? (After all, the latter method is used for prepaid expenses.)
15 What are the circumstances under which these depreciation policies would be appropriate:
   a straight-line (even periodic expenses over asset's life)?
   b reducing balance (declining periodic expenses over asset's life)?
   c units of production (variable periodic expenses depending on the use of the asset)?
16 Briefly explain what is meant by the statement: 'under historic cost accounting, depreciation is a process of allocation'. Include in your answer some reference to the key assumptions that support the view of depreciation as an allocation process, and a brief explanation as to why the residual value of depreciable noncurrent assets is not 'depreciated'.
17 Why is capitalising costs such as intangible assets a reasonable idea? Why is it not such a good idea?

18 Explain clearly why and how capitalising the costs of a development project as a 'deferred costs' asset affects the profit and loss statement and the balance sheet.

19 If an asset is leased, it is not owned. How can accounting standards that require creating a balance sheet account for some such leased assets be justified?

20 If a lease is treated as a finance lease rather than an operating lease, what effects does that have on the balance sheet and the profit and loss statement?

21 A State Government department asks you how it should value the botanical gardens in a capital city for inclusion in the department's statement of financial position. Draft a suitable reply.

22 'This depreciation business appears to involve a lot of guesswork. To calculate the annual charge you guess the life of the asset, its scrap value and expected pattern of reduction in value. You tell us that there is a choice of methods available and that no method can be claimed to be correct in particular circumstances. You admit that the rate of depreciation charged for taxation purposes differs from the rate used in the accounting records. It seems to me that the company will run into difficulties with the taxation department.' Discuss.

## Problem 8.1* Depreciation, calculations, entries and effects

At the beginning of 2001, Garrison Pty Ltd acquired machinery costing $100 000 and having a useful life of 10 years and zero scrap value. The company depreciated this machinery during 2001 and 2002, using the straight-line method. During 2003, it decided to change to the reducing balance method of depreciation of the machinery at a rate of 20 per cent. Garrison is taxed at an income tax rate of 40 per cent.

1 Calculate the depreciation expense Garrison has recognised for 2001 and 2002 and write a journal entry to record either year's amount.

2 Calculate the depreciation expense Garrison would have recorded, had it been using the reducing balance method for 2001 and 2002.

3 Calculate the effects of changing from straight-line to reducing balance on the following:
   - a the statement of financial position at the end of 2001
   - b the statement of financial performance for 2002
   - c the statement of financial position at the end of 2002.

## Problem 8.2* Depreciation questions and calculations

1 Your friend Z has just completed the first year of operating a one-truck delivery company. Z explains to you that, because of careful care of the truck, the price the truck would fetch on the used truck market is not much different from the price paid for the truck a year ago. As a result, says Z, no depreciation expense on the truck is needed for accounting purposes this year. Next year, Z believes, the truck's value will drop a noticeable amount, but this is not a problem because the cash obtained from deducting tax depreciation will compensate for the decline in market value over the year.

   Explain to Z what the accounting concept of depreciation is and how Z's thinking is in error with respect to that concept.

2 Another friend is just starting a lawnmowing service and has purchased a group of new lawnmowers for $20 000. The friend expects the mowers to last five years and to have negligible resale value at that point. The friend's business plan projects cutting 5000 lawns over the five years, with per year projections of 500, 1000, 1200, 1800 and 500 lawns over the five years.
   - a Calculate the accumulated depreciation balance at the end of the second year using each of the following depreciation bases:

i straight-line

ii reducing balance (25 per cent rate)

iii units-of-production.

b Based on your calculations, which depreciation basis would produce the highest retained profits at the end of the second year?

c Your friend has never heard of the units-of-production basis. Explain why companies use it and comment on whether it would make sense for your friend's business.

d If the 25 per cent reducing balance method is used, accumulated depreciation will be $15 254 at the end of the fifth year. Suppose that on the first day of the sixth year, all the lawnmowers are sold as junk for $100 cash in total. Ignoring income taxes:

i Calculate the loss on sale that would be recorded that day.

ii Suppose your friend objects to recording the loss on sale, pointing out that $100 more was received for the lawnmowers than had been expected five years earlier, and claims that, in any case, profit for the sixth year should not be reduced by the loss when it happened on the first day of the year. Reply to your friend.

## Problem 8.3* Determining cost of noncurrent assets

On 1 January 2002, Combo Pty Ltd purchased a factory (and the land on which it stood) together with the machinery in it for $700 000 in total. The independently determined appraisal values were:

| | $ |
|---|---|
| Land | 320 000 |
| Building | 180 000 |
| Machinery | 200 000 |

In January a portion of the building was demolished, at a cost of $1200, before the extension of the building to house new machinery. Two hundred dollars was received for materials salvaged from the demolition. However, in the course of demolition, existing machinery was damaged, requiring expenditure of $400 on repairs. This amount was not recoverable from the demolition company. In February and March the extensions were built. Construction costs were $40 000, architect's fees were $4000, legal fees were $500. In April new machinery was purchased for $50 000 (list price). Sales tax of 4 per cent was paid, as were freight and installation costs of $750. In addition, $500 was spent on making changes to an existing machine to extend its useful life.

*Required:*

1 If a statement of financial position were to be prepared at the end of April 2002, what amounts would be shown for the cost of land, buildings and machinery? Prepare separate schedules, listing individual components of the cost of land, buildings and machinery, in support of your answer.

2 What is the effect on shareholders' equity of the above transactions (if any), assuming all payments were made in cash? Briefly explain your answer.

## Problem 8.4 Cost of an asset, expenses

The following events took place at Liz's Mobile Coffee Shop during 2002:

a On 1 January, Liz bought a van for $20 000. She had a coffee machine and storage units installed for a total cost of $4800. She paid an additional $500 to a signwriter to paint her name along the side of the van for advertising purposes. The van is expected to last for four years, then be sold for $800. Liz uses diminishing value method to depreciate this vehicle at a rate of 40 per cent per annum.

**b** On 1 April, Liz purchased 10 cartons of disposable cups at auction for $500. She believes that the market value of the cups would be at least $650. Liz will use all the disposable cups this year.

**c** On 1 February, Liz paid Sydney Council $4500 for a three-year licence to operate her business at Circular Quay.

**d** Liz also has an older truck, which cost $16 000 when purchased on 1 September 1996. It was expected to last eight years and have a salvage value of $800. Liz used straight-line method to depreciate the truck. The truck was sold on 31 December 2002 for $1000.

**1** What cost (at date of purchase) would be assigned to:
   **a** the new van?
   **b** the disposable coffee cups?
   For each situation, give reasons for your calculation.

**2** Name the type of expense and the amount of the expense to be recorded for the year ending 31 December 2002 for each of the following:
   **a** the new van
   **b** the disposable coffee cups
   **c** the licence
   **d** the older truck.

## Problem 8.5 Depreciation methods and selection of method

Dombey & Son acquired a new machine on 1 January 1999 at a cost of $135 000. Freight and installation charges amounted to $25 000. The machine was expected to have a useful life of four years and a residual value at the end of that period of $10 000. During its useful life it was expected to be operated for 25 000 hours.

***Required:***

**1** Prepare a table showing the annual depreciation expense in respect of the machine for each of the years ending 31 December 1999, 2000, 2001 and 2002 using:
   **a** the straight-line method
   **b** the reducing balance method
   **c** the sum-of-the-year's digits method.

**2** Assuming that Dombey & Son had used the units of production method and that the machine had been operated for 7000 hours during the year ending 31 December 2002, show the journal entry to record the depreciation expense for that year.

**3** How should Dombey & Son decide which depreciation method to use? Will the choice of depreciation method have any effect on the reported profit and financial position of Dombey & Son over the life of the asset?

## Problem 8.6 Correcting errors relating to noncurrent assets

The following errors were discovered in the books of the Deep Appreciation Company during the current year, before the books were closed as at 31 December.

**1** Depreciation of $2140 relating to machinery was incorrectly credited to the 'Accumulated depreciation – buildings' account.

**2** A machine with a cost of $22 500 and accumulated depreciation to the date of sale of $16 000 was sold for $8000. The sale was recorded by debiting the cash at bank account and crediting the machinery account for $8000.

3 The cost of delivery equipment purchased on 1 July for $7900 was debited to the purchases account. The equipment has a useful life of four years and estimated residual value of $900. Straight-line depreciation is used for delivery equipment.

4 The cost of installing lighting in the company car park ($12 000) was charged to the maintenance expense account on 4 January, the date of purchase. The lights have a useful life of eight years and no residual value. Assume straight-line depreciation.

5 A machine with a cost of $26 000 and accumulated depreciation to date of $19 000 was exchanged on 23 December for a new machine with a cash price of $35 000. A trade-in allowance of $9000 was allowed on the old machine and a cheque was drawn to cover the difference between the trade-in and the cash price. The bookkeeper made the following entry at the time of sale:

| | | $ | $ |
|---|---|---|---|
| DR | Machinery | 33 000 | |
| DR | Accumulated depreciation – machinery | 19 000 | |
| CR | Machinery | | 26 000 |
| CR | Cash at bank | | 26 000 |
| | (Old machine traded in for new machine) | | |

***Required:***

Prepare general journal entries to correct the errors (if any).

## Problem 8.7 Cost of an asset, depreciation

The following events took place at Leonardo's Sketching Studio during 2002:

**a** On 1 January, Leonardo bought a van for $20 000. He had a tool chest and side racks for ladders installed for a total cost of $4800. He paid an additional $500 to a signwriter to paint his name along the side of the van for advertising purposes. The truck is expected to last for four years and then be sold for $800. Leonardo uses diminishing value method to depreciate this vehicle.

**b** On 1 April, Leonardo purchased 10 cases of paint trays and roller covers at auction for $500 (market value, $650). Leonardo will use all the paint trays and roller covers this year and next year. The paint trays and roller covers have no salvage value at the end of this time.

**c** On 1 February, Leonardo paid Sydney Council $4500 for a three year licence to operate his sketching business at Circular Quay

**d** Leonardo also had a truck, used in the business for large deliveries, which cost $16 000 when purchased on 1 September 1997. It was expected to last eight years and have a salvage value of $800. Leonardo used straight-line method to depreciate the truck.

1 What cost would be assigned to:

   a the van?

   b the paint trays and the roller covers?

   For each situation, give reasons for your calculation.

2 Determine the amount of depreciation or other expense to be recorded for each asset for the year ending 31 December 2002.

3 How would these assets appear on Leonardo's statement of financial position as at 31 December 2002?

## Problem 8.8 Classify expenditure as assets or expenses

Anne and Tony own a guesthouse and spent the following:

1. $200 000 on construction of an extension to the guesthouse
2. $10 000 painting the extension
3. $1500 demolishing a cow shed which was on the site of the extension
4. $15 000 painting the old section of the guesthouse
5. $45 000 replacing carpets with floorboards in the original section of the guesthouse
6. $20 000 replacing existing carpets in the original section of the guesthouse
7. $300 on new curtains (the old ones were destroyed by a guest).

For each item, state whether it is an asset or an expense.

## Problem 8.9 Classify expenditure as assets or expenses

Classify the following expenditure as an asset or as an expense and state your reasons why:

1. Rosco Pty Ltd bought three new cars for its sales team, for a cost of $96 000. Two cars were air-conditioned at a cost of $4000 and a mobile phone was installed in one car for $750.
2. Boney Pty Ltd bought a new point-of-sale inventory system for $150 000 and at a cost of $15 000 trained two employees to use it. Two months later both employees left and an additional $10 000 was spent training a replacement.
3. Davo Pty Ltd has spent $15 000 developing a new product called Davo Plus. Development is not yet complete. At a recent board meeting, directors voted to continue development.
4. An equipment overhaul is estimated to have increased the productive capacity of the equipment by 15 per cent but has not increased its useful life.

## Problem 8.10 Correction of errors and revaluation of noncurrent assets

During the audit of the accounts of Hogarth Pty Ltd for the year ended 31 December 2002, it was discovered that the following errors had been made during the year:

1. Store fixtures which had cost $12 000 were sold for $1200 cash. The accumulated depreciation at the date of sale was $8500. The sale was recorded by a debit to Cash at Bank and a credit to Store Fixtures for $1200.
2. On 1 July 2002 a fence was erected around the company's office building at a cost of $9000, which was charged to maintenance expense. The fence is expected to have a useful life of 10 years and no residual value. Assume straight-line depreciation.
3. A truck was purchased on 1 January 2002 at a cost of $10 000, which was debited to purchases account. The truck is expected to have a useful life of four years and a residual value of $1296. It is to be depreciated by the reducing balance method.
4. Another block of land, which had been purchased for $20 000 in 1998 and had been revalued at $25 000 during 2000, was found to have a fair value of only $15 000 at 31 December 2002. No entry had yet been made to record the fall in the value of this land.

***Required:***

Prepare general journal entries to correct the above errors together with any necessary adjusting entries as at 31 December 2002.

## Problem 8.11 Depreciation calculations, entries, effects and choice

At the beginning of 2001, SD Corporation acquired machinery having a cost of $100 000 and an anticipated useful life of 10 years. It depreciated this machinery for 2001 and 2002, using the straight-line method. During 2003, it decided to change to the reducing balance method of depreciation. SD is taxed at an income tax rate of 40 per cent.

1 Prepare the journal entry to record depreciation expense for 2002, using the straight-line method.
2 Prepare the journal entry to record depreciation expense for 2002 using the reducing balance method, at a rate of 20 per cent.
3 Show the effects of changing from straight-line to the 20 per cent reducing balance method on:
   a the net profit for 2002
   b the total assets for 2002.
4 In what circumstances is the use of reducing balance depreciation more appropriate than use of the straight-line method?

## Problem 8.12 Depreciation and gain/loss calculations and effects

Fred's Freighthauling Pty Ltd has a small fleet of delivery trucks. Each one is depreciated on the reducing balance method (rate 20 percent; half that in the year of acquisition and in the year of disposal) with no salvage value. Truck 4 was purchased on 1 July 1999, for $46 000 and sold three years later, on 30 June 2002, for $15 000. The company's financial year-end is 31 December.

1 What was the total depreciation on Truck 4 to the date of its disposal?
2 Based on your answer to question 1, write a journal entry to record the disposal of Truck 4.
3 Redo questions 1 and 2, assuming the company uses straight-line depreciation at 15 per cent per year and an estimated salvage value of $6000.
4 Calculate the difference in effects between the two depreciation methods on the company's 2002 profit. Ignore income tax effects.
5 What implications (if any) would the use of different depreciation methods by the company have for potential creditors or investors?
6 The use of different depreciation methods could affect financial performance comparability between financial years of a particular company, and between different companies for the same financial year. How are these differences mitigated?

## Problem 8.13 Depreciation calculations and selection of method

An item of equipment was purchased on 1 July 1998 at a cost of $625 000. It was estimated to have a useful life of four years and a salvage value at the end of that period of $81 000.

*Required:*

1 Calculate the depreciation expense which would be charged in respect of this equipment in each of the years ending 30 June 1999, 2000, 2001 and 2002 using:
   a the straight-line method
   b the sum-of-the-year's digits method
   c the reducing balance method.
2 Outline the main factors to be considered in selecting an appropriate depreciation method.

## Problem 8.14 Various depreciation methods

On 1 January 2002, Yip Pty Ltd acquired additional equipment at a cost of $120 000 less a trade discount of 25 per cent. The terms of payment were 2/10, *n*/30. Payment was made on 20 January 2002. Freight charges were $7500 and installation and testing cost $2500.

The equipment was expected to have a useful life of five years and a salvage value of $3125. During its life the equipment was expected to produce 775 000 units of output. During the year ended 30 June 2002, the equipment was used to produce 70 000 units.

*Required:*

Calculate the depreciation expense to be charged in the accounts of Yip Pty Ltd in respect of this new equipment for the financial year ended 30 June 2002 using:

1 the reducing balance method (assuming a rate of 50 per cent)
2 the straight-line method
3 the units-of-production method.

## Problem 8.15 Comparison of methods of depreciation

Alley Limited recently purchased certain manufacturing equipment for $810 000. The equipment is expected to have a useful life of four years and a salvage value of $10 000. The manager of Alley Limited wishes to know the effect that various depreciation methods will have on the reported profit of the company and asks you to prepare a schedule comparing the straight-line and the reducing balance methods of depreciation.

*Required:*

1 Prepare a schedule, as set out below, and calculate the annual depreciation expense and end-of-year carrying amount of the equipment for each year of its estimated useful life. Show your workings.

| Year | Straight-line | | Reducing balance | |
|---|---|---|---|---|
| | Depreciation expense | Carrying amount $ | Depreciation expense | Carrying amount $ |
| Acquisition | | 810 000 | | 810 000 |
| 1 | | | | |
| 2 | | | | |
| 3 | | | | |
| 4 | | | | |

2 What are the main factors likely to influence the useful life of a depreciable asset? What factors are likely to influence the manager in selecting a depreciation method?

## Problem 8.16 Calculate any goodwill on a business purchase

Foofaraw Pty Ltd paid $200 000 for land, buildings, inventories and accounts payable of another business that will become a branch. The assets (after deducting the accounts payable of $50 000) had an aggregate fair market value of $187 000.

1 What (if anything) is the resulting asset on Foofaraw's statement of financial position?
2 If Foofaraw had paid $185 000, what would be your answer to question **1**?

## Problem 8.17 Intangibles

Shown below are the accounting policy disclosure for John Fairfax Ltd on intangibles.

### Intangibles

#### Mastheads and tradenames

Mastheads and tradenames are carried at cost and are not amortised. In accordance with AASB 1021, no amortisation is provided against the carrying value of these assets because the directors believe that the life of these assets is of such duration and the residual value would be such that the amortisation charge is not material.

**Goodwill**

Goodwill is amortised by the straight-line method over the period during which benefits are expected to be received. This is taken to be 20 years. The carrying amount of intangibles is reviewed annually by directors to ensure it is not in excess of the recoverable amount. The recoverable amount is assessed based upon the present value of expected future cash flows.

*Required:*

1 Explain what each of the following would represent for John Fairfax Limited:
   a mastheads
   b tradenames
   c goodwill.
2 Compare the treatment of amortisation for mastheads and amortisation for tradenames.
3 Why would these treatments be different?
4 If the goodwill amortisation policy were adopted for mastheads and trademarks, what would be the impact on the financial statements?

## Problem 8.18 Comparison of depreciation methods

*Part A*

Waking Hours Pty Ltd owns a nightclub in the centre of Sydney. In a major refurbishment, it purchased a new sound system and a new lighting system on 1 April 2002.

The sound system cost $27 000 to purchase and $3500 to install. The lighting system cost $44 000.

The sound system has a useful life of five years, and the lighting system, four years. Both are depreciated on a straight-line basis, assuming no residual value.

*Required:*

1 What is the cost and the written-down value for the assets discussed above as at 31 December 2002?
2 Would Waking Hours' profit be higher or lower for the year ending 31 December 2002 if it had adopted the diminishing value method of depreciation? Use the same data in the question above to calculate your answer.

*Part B*

This question continues the scenario outlined above.

On 1 May 2002 it was found that the lighting system was no longer flashing ultraviolet rays in time with the music (as it should). It cost $700 to have this fixed.

On 1 October 2002, $5000 was spent to give the sound system a heavier bass beat.

*Required:*

What is the appropriate accounting treatment of the events that occurred on 1 May 2002 and 1 October 2002?

## Problem 8.19 Asset revaluations

The following is an extract from the statement of financial position of ABC Limited as at 30 June 2000.

| | 2000 | 1999 |
|---|---|---|
| Land (at cost) | — | 200 000 |
| Land (at directors' valuation) | 3 500 000 | — |
| The company's land was revalued upwards during the year. | | |

*Required:*

1 What impact would the revaluation have on net profit for the year ended 30 June 2000?

2 Do you have any concerns with regard to the revaluation?

## Problem 8.20 Revaluation of noncurrent assets

Eaglehawk Pty Ltd had the following noncurrent asset on its statement of financial position on 30 June 2001. The company adopts a policy of depreciating all relevant items on a straight-line basis at an annual rate of 10 per cent.

| | $ |
|---|---|
| Building | 200 000 |
| Accumulated depreciation | 50 000 |
| | 150 000 |

1 What is the carrying amount of the building on 1 January 2002?

2 On 1 January 2002, the directors of Eaglehawk decide to revalue the building to $400 000 to reflect its market value. Prepare the necessary journal entries.

## Problem 8.21 Revaluation of noncurrent assets

At 30 June 2000, the statement of financial position of Lyrebird Ltd disclosed the following non current assets:

| | $ | $ |
|---|---|---|
| Land | | 500 000 |
| Plant and equipment | 250 000 | |
| Accumulated depreciation | 50 000 | 200 000 |
| Patents | 60 000 | |
| Accumulated amortisation | 12 000 | 48 000 |
| | | 748 000 |

On 1 July 2000, the plant and equipment was revalued to $220 000. On 1 July 2001, the land was revalued to its recoverable amount of $400 000, and the plant and equipment was revalued to $150 000. Depreciation for all relevant items is straight-line, charged at 10 per cent per annum.

1 Prepare journal entries to record the revaluations of the plant and equipment and land on 1 July 2000 and 1 July 2001.

2 Construct the 'Noncurrent assets' section of Lyrebird's statement of financial position as at 30 June 2002.

## Problem 8.22 Revaluation of noncurrent assets

At 30 June 2000, the balance sheet of Fragrant Flowers Pty Ltd disclosed the following noncurrent assets:

| | $ | $ |
|---|---|---|
| Land | | 60 000 |
| Building | 130 000 | |
| Accumulated depreciation | 50 000 | 80 000 |
| | | 140 000 |

On 1 July 2000, the land was revalued upwards by $20 000 and the building was revalued at $90 000. Depreciation expense in respect of the building was $4500 for each of the years ended 30 June 2001 and 2002. On 1 July 2002 the land was revalued at its recoverable amount of $70 000 and the building at $55 000.

***Required:***

Prepare journal entries to record the revaluations of the land and buildings on 1 July 2000 and 1 July 2002.

## Problem 8.23 Revaluation of noncurrent assets

Kingfisher Ltd had the following noncurrent assets on its statement of financial position at 30 June 2000:

| | $ | $ |
|---|---|---|
| Land | | 320 000 |
| Plant and equipment | 150 000 | |
| Accumulated depreciation | 30 000 | 120 000 |
| | | 440 000 |

On 1 July 2000, the land was revalued to $300 000, and the plant and equipment was revalued to $140 000. One year later, on 1 July 2001, the recoverable amount of the plant and equipment was determined to be $100 000, and it was revalued accordingly. Depreciation for all relevant items is straight-line, at an annual rate of 10 per cent.

***Required:***

1. Prepare journal entries to record the revaluation of the land on 1 July 2000.
2. Prepare journal entries to record the revaluation of the plant and equipment on 1 July 2000.
3. Prepare journal entries to record the revaluation of the plant and equipment on 1 July 2001.
4. Assuming that there are no acquisitions or disposals of noncurrent assets, construct the 'Noncurrent assets' section of Kingfisher's statement of financial position as at 30 June 2002.

## Problem 8.24 (Challenging) Identify possible asset valuation methods

Sports Forever Pty Ltd has recently agreed to purchase a local sports ground at a price of $100 000. The realtor had listed the property at $115 000, but Mark Johnson, SFL's general manager, managed to talk the present owner, Shattered Dreams Pty Ltd, down to the lower price by promising full payment in cash. Mark has seen the local council's valuation of the arena, which revealed the following information:

- total assessed value: $80 000
- land value equal to: 70 per cent
- building value equal to: 30 per cent.

Mark is also aware that the sports ground has firm contracts (regardless of change in ownership of the arena) for the next 20 years with both a popular football team and a highly successful local cricket team. Net total cash flows from the two contracts are expected to be approximately $25 000 per year over the full term of the contracts. This is rather convenient, since the remaining expected life of the sports ground is projected by a professional estimator to be 20 years.

Upon consultation with a contractor, Mark learned that the cost to replace the sports ground in its original condition is currently $150 000. The managing director of Shattered Dreams Pty

Ltd felt that the price offered by Mark was more than appropriate, since the net book value of the building on his company's books is only $30 000. Sports Forever Pty Ltd can borrow or invest at an interest rate of 10 per cent.

*Required:*

1 Identify all possible valuations of the arena for which sufficient information has been supplied. Where calculations are required, show your work.
2 List the potential users of each valuation and describe how they would use the information.

## Problem 8.25 (Challenging) Reconstruction of ledger accounts

The (double-entry) accounting records of The Enemy Within Pty Ltd are computerised. Unfortunately, a treacherous employee has introduced a computer virus into the system and disappeared with the backup disks. The following information has been salvaged in relation to the year ended 31 December 2002:

1 As at 1 January 2002, the balance of the Machinery account was $40 000. During the year, machinery costing $20 000 was purchased for cash. In addition, a machine costing $5000 was traded in on a new machine costing $8000 (on 31 March 2002). As at 30 June 2002, a machine was revalued, there having been no previous revaluation increment or decrement in respect of that machine. Accumulated depreciation up to that date on that machine was $7000. The balance of the machinery account as at 31 December 2002 was $55 000.
2 As at 1 January 2002, the balance of the 'Accumulated depreciation – machinery' account was $30 000. Depreciation expense of $100 was recognised as at 31 March 2002 with respect to the machine traded in on that date. Similarly, depreciation expense of $300 was recognised as at 30 June 2002 in respect of the machine revalued as at that date. In addition, the regular year-end adjusting entry for depreciation (as at 31 December 2002) was $7000. The balance of the 'Accumulated depreciation – machinery' account as at 31 December 2002 was $26 600.
3 During the year a block of land costing $91 000 was purchased for cash; while, in a separate transaction, another block of land costing $50 000 was sold for $95 000 (cash). In addition, a third block of land was revalued downwards by $11 000, having previously been revalued upwards by $15 000 during the year ended 31 December 2001 (resulting in an asset revaluation reserve in that year). The balance of the land account as at 31 December 2002 was $180 000.

*Required:*

Using the above information, reconstruct appropriate ledger accounts and provide answers to the following questions:

1 With respect to the machine revalued as at 30 June 2002, what was the amount of the revaluation, and was it upwards or downwards?
2 What was the total amount of accumulated depreciation relating to the machinery traded in on 31 March 2002?
3 What was the balance of the land account as at 1 January 2002?

## Case 8A Woolworths Limited case

Refer to the extracts of the annual report of Woolworths Limited in appendix 2. All questions relate to the consolidated accounts.

1 Is land depreciated?
2 Are buildings depreciated?
3 What is the total depreciation and amortisation for the year?
4 How much did the accumulated depreciation and accumulated amortisation accounts increase by?
5 Why aren't the answers to 3 and 4 the same?

6 What method of cost allocation is used by the company to determine depreciation?

7 Which assets are recorded at directors' valuation and which at cost (less accumulated depreciation or amortisation)?

8 How did the company arrive at directors' valuation figures?

9 Did Woolworths sell any property, plant and equipment during the year? If so what were the proceeds? Did they make a profit or loss on these sales? How would this profit or loss be calculated?

10 Does the company revalue any assets? If so, how frequently?

11 How is the balance of accumulated depreciation handled at the time of revaluation?

12 What intangibles does the company have? How are they valued? Over what period are they amortised? Where are they located in the financial statements?

13 What are pre-opening expenses? How are they handled?

14 The company has both operating and finance leases. Which are more common for Woolworths Limited? How are both types of leases accounted for?

15 What does Woolworths say about recoverable amount?

## Case 8B Research and development capitalisation

Shown below is an extract from *Business Review Weekly*, 18 March 1996, on the capitalising of research and development expenses.

### Expenditure on innovation should be capitalised if it is recoverable beyond a reasonable doubt – but the definition is of doubtful value

*By Georgi Stickels*

The impending review of AASB 1011 by the Australian Accounting Research Foundation, covering research and development expenditure, seems poised to remove the scope for subjective judgement that has drawn the ire of the Australian Securities Commission.

The standard in its present form states that all expenditure on research and development must be written off through the profit and loss statement unless some, or all, of it is recoverable 'beyond reasonable doubt'. Where it is recoverable, such as through sales of a newly developed product or a licensing arrangement, it is capitalised as an asset and amortised once it starts generating revenue.

However, precisely what constitutes reasonable doubt has never been defined, resulting in almost as many interpretations of the standard as there are companies conducting R&D.

The pharmaceutical company Biota Holdings, which has developed a drug that may ward off influenza, writes off all its R&D costs immediately. Chief financial officer Richard Wadley says: 'We always have. You can spend an awful lot of money looking and not getting much success. We have no problems in writing it off because we know exactly what we've got.' Wadley describes Biota's balance sheet as 'very clean', with $24 million in shareholder equity, no intangibles and few liabilities. He says shareholders appreciate a company that is upfront about its expenditure, particularly in a risky industry such as pharmaceutical development.

The drug, GG167, is in clinical trials, and Biota has signed an agreement for royalties with the international company Glaxo Wellcome. Wadley says that even at this stage the company cannot say beyond reasonable doubt that all, or a portion, of the cost of developing the drug will be recovered.

Wadley expects Biota to continue to write off costs even if the drug goes into production. 'It might generate X amount of income in one year and quite a different level in another year,' he says. 'If we valued our expenditure at one level one year and something else the next, our shareholders would never know where they were at.'

Biota's stance is conservative. A more typical policy is that of Peptide Technology (Peptech), which has only recently changed its guidelines on how to assess recoverability. Peptech's old guidelines were based on discounted cashflow calculations. This meant that in practice the company capitalised virtually everything it spent developing various peptides (chemical compounds that are the building blocks for many proteins) for application in the cosmetics, veterinary and pharmaceutical industries.

The new guidelines, introduced at the end of the company's reporting year last September, stipulate that R&D expenditure can only be capitalised if it meets the old requirements and arises from a project that has reached the second stage of clinical trials (on humans) or for which a commercial agreement has been negotiated. Group vice-president Darryl Mellish says that little will now be capitalised. 'It means we are more in line with what happens overseas, but it's a Catch-22. For companies involved in R&D their key assets are their research and their know-how. To a certain extent the investor would like to see the assets in the balance sheet. On the other hand, another investor would say we've got all that to write off later and our income is going to be lower.'

Concerned by such variations in the interpretation of the standard, the ASC last September announced a crackdown on companies that capitalised, promising close scrutiny of those that delayed the arrival of the expenditure at the bottom line. The commission's main concern is that companies are holding over costs incurred early in a project, when it is impossible to tell whether the venture will succeed. This can result in substantially higher short-term profit.

The ASC announcement is in line with international accounting standards, which take a hard line against capitalising costs, and it seems to have been heeded by industry. The Australian Society of CPAs says most companies now write off their R&D costs straight away. Several companies have changed their R&D accounting policy, either immediately before the statement, or following it, to avoid being caught unprepared.

One such company is Orbital Engine Corporation, which announced its decision to change policies in its half-yearly report released last month. The decision to change from capitalisation to writing off expenditure in the year incurred resulted in a $16-million contribution to its total loss of $20.6 million. The change has been implemented just as production gets under way of engines using what the company calls the Orbital Combustion Process. Directors say that the change will mean considerably lower short-term earnings, but higher profits in the longer term because of reduced future amortisation charges, which means dividends can be paid earlier. This now seems to be a greater influence on investor confidence than the bottom line.

(Source: *Business Review Weekly*, 18 March 1996.)

***Required:***

1. Outline the basic arguments for and against capitalising research and expenditure costs.
2. What is the relative effect on the balance sheet and profit and loss statements of capitalising versus non-capitalising?
3. What is meant by a 'very clean' balance sheet?
4. What were the main concerns of the Australian Securities Commission (ASC) with respect to the capitalisation of research and development as outlined in the article?
5. Evaluate the arguments made in the last paragraph of the extract.

## CASE 8C Accounting policy for noncurrent assets

Shown below is the accounting policy for Boral at 30 June 2001 for property, plant and equipment.

**Boral, 30 June 2001**

*Property, plant and equipment*

**Acquisition:** Items of property, plant and equipment are initially recorded at cost and depreciated as outlined below. The cost of property, plant and equipment constructed by the consolidated entity includes the cost of materials and direct labour. The proportion of overheads and other incidental costs directly attributable to its construction are also capitalised to the cost of property, plant and equipment. Borrowing costs are also capitalised to the cost of constructed property, plant and equipment using a weighted average capitalisation rate.

**Disposal of assets:** The gain or loss on disposal of assets is calculated as the difference between the carrying amount of the asset at the time of disposal and the proceeds of disposal, and is brought to account as profit or loss in the period in which the disposal occurs.

Any realised revaluation increment relating to the disposed asset standing in the asset revaluation reserve at the time of disposal is transferred to retained earnings.

**Leased plant and equipment:** Leases of plant and equipment which are classified as finance leases are capitalised and amortised over the period during which benefits are anticipated. Other leases are classified as operating leases and the lease costs are expensed as incurred.

**Depreciation and amortisation:** Depreciation and amortisation are charged on property, plant and equipment at rates which provide for the write-down from cost or valuation over the anticipated period of their useful life to the consolidated entity. Predominantly the straight line method of calculation has been used for items of property, plant and equipment.

***Required:***

1 Show the effect on the accounting equation of acquisition, disposal, leasing and depreciation.

2 Provide journal entries for each item in part 1.

3 What judgements do accountants need to make for the above four items and how do they impact profit?

4 Provide four actions by management that could move profit from one accounting period to another.

## CASE 8D Intangibles

### Sigma Annual Report, 30 June 2001
### Intangibles

The unamortised balance of intangibles is reviewed semiannually and any material diminution in value is immediately charged to the profit and loss statement.

#### Goodwill

Goodwill represents the excess of the purchase consideration over the fair value of the net assets of the business or entity acquired, including any liability for restructuring costs. A liability for restructuring costs is recognised as at the date of acquisition of an entity or part thereof, when there is a demonstrable commitment to a restructuring of the acquired entity and a reliable estimate of the amount of the liability can be made.

Goodwill is amortised on a straight line basis over the period during which benefits are expected to be received, being no greater than twenty years.

#### Brand names and trademarks

Effective 1 February 1999, a review was conducted of the consolidated entity's trademarks and product brands to reassess their useful lives. This review resulted in the trademarks and product brands, with the exception of the Amcal and Guardian brand names, being amortised on a straight-line basis over twenty years.

Effective 1 August 1999, the useful lives of the Amcal and Guardian brand names were reassessed and are being amortised on a straight-line basis over sixty years.

#### Deferred expenditure

Deferred expenditure is amortised on a straight-line basis over no more than five years.

## Tabcorp, 30 June 2001
## Goodwill

Goodwill, representing the excess of the purchase consideration plus incidental costs over the fair value of the identifiable net assets acquired on the acquisition of a controlled entity, is amortised over the period of time during which benefits are expected to arise.

Goodwill is amortised on a straight-line basis over 20 years.

The unamortised balance of goodwill is reviewed at least at each reporting date. Where the balance exceeds the value of expected future benefits, the difference is charged to the statement of financial performance.

In establishing the fair value of the identifiable net assets acquired, a liability for restructuring costs is only recognised at the date of acquisition where there is a demonstrable commitment and a detailed plan.

The liability is only recognised where there is little or no discretion to avoid payment to other parties in settlement of costs of the restructuring and a reliable estimate of the amount of the liability as at the date of acquisition can be made.

## James Hardie, 30 June 2001
## Intangible assets and deferred expenses

### Goodwill

On acquisition of some, or all, of the assets of another entity or, in the case of an investment in a subsidiary, on acquisition of some, or all, of the equity of that subsidiary, the identifiable net assets acquired are measured at fair value. The excess of the fair value of the cost of acquisition over the fair value of the identifiable net assets acquired, including any liability for restructuring costs, is brought to account as goodwill and amortised on a straight-line basis over 20 years, being the period during which the benefits are expected to arise.

### Patents and trademarks

Significant costs associated with patents and trademarks are deferred and amortised on a straight-line basis over the periods of their expected benefit. Patents and trademarks held at the reporting date are being amortised over 20 years.

***Required:***

Questions 1–5 relate to Sigma. Question 6 relates to Sigma, Tabcorp and James Hardie.

1 Explain what is meant by the first paragraph above.
2 Why is the liability for restructuring costs included in the calculation of goodwill? How is the amount determined?
3 Why is goodwill amortised over 20 years?
4 Why do different brand names have different lives? How does this impact profit?
5 Provide an example of deferred expenditure.
6 Compare Sigma's policy on goodwill to that of Tabcorp Holdings and James Hardie Industry Limited. What are the main differences? Who provides the most detail and is the additional detail beneficial?

# CASE 8E Revaluations

## Coca-Cola Amatil, 31 December 2000
## Valuation of noncurrent assets

Freehold and leasehold land and buildings have been revalued at three-yearly intervals including 2000. The value of the land and buildings is assessed on their worth to the Group on an existing use basis and does not exceed the net amount expected to be recovered from their continued use and subsequent disposal.

Investments in bottlers' agreements were revalued in 1999 using discounted cash flow techniques. This revaluation was not part of a regular program for revaluation of this class of noncurrent assets. No valuation was carried out in 2000. Investments in controlled entities in the parent entity accounts were revalued in 1999 consistent with the revaluation of investments in bottlers' agreements.

All noncurrent assets are carried at amounts that do not exceed their recoverable amount. The expected net cash flows included in determining the recoverable amounts of noncurrent assets are discounted to their present value.

### James Hardie, 30 June 2001
### Land and buildings

Land and buildings are revalued at three-yearly intervals. Revaluations reflect independent assessments of the fair market value of land and buildings based on existing use. Revaluation increments are credited directly to the asset revaluation reserve, unless they are reversing a previous decrement charged to the profit and loss statement, in which case the increment is credited to the profit and loss statement. Valuations adopted by the Directors are not in excess of those given by the independent valuers. Revaluations do not result in the carrying value of land or buildings exceeding their recoverable amounts. The expected net cash flows included in determining recoverable amounts of land and buildings have not been discounted to their present values.

### News Corporation, 30 June 2001
### Property, plant and equipment

The directors have elected under section 334(5) of the Corporations Act 2001 to apply Accounting Standard AASB 1041 'Revaluation of Noncurrent Assets' [Revised 2001] for the financial year ended 30 June 2001

In accordance with the requirements of AASB 1041 'Revaluation of Noncurrent Assets', land and buildings previously carried at valuation were reverted to a cost basis of measurement. For the purpose of transitioning to a cost basis, the existing revalued carrying amounts at 1 July 2000 were deemed to be their cost. This change in accounting policy had no impact on the financial position or financial performance of the Company as presented in this financial report.

Depreciation is provided on property, plant and equipment at rates appropriate to write off the net book value over the expected useful life of each class of asset. Leasehold land and buildings are amortised over the shorter of the period of the lease or the useful life of the asset.

### Qantas, 30 June 2001
### Revaluation of noncurrent assets

The Qantas Group has applied AASB 1041 'Revaluation of Noncurrent Assets' (reissued July 2001) for the first time from 1 July 2000. The standard requires each class of noncurrent asset to be measured on either the cost or fair value basis. AASB 1041 does not apply to inventories, foreign currency monetary assets, goodwill, deferred tax assets and other assets measured at net market value where the market value movements are recognised in the statement of financial performance.

Under AASB 1041, the Qantas Group has adopted the cost basis for all noncurrent assets, and has deemed the cost to be equal to the carrying value of those assets as at 1 July 2000. As a consequence of making this election, the balance of the asset revaluation reserve at 1 July 2000 amounting to $52.6 million is no longer available for asset write-downs. The change in accounting policy has no financial effect in the current or prior financial years.

***Required:***

Compare and contrast the asset revaluation policies of the four companies. How does the revaluation policy impact future profits and asset figures?

Chapter 9

# Financial reporting, principles, accounting standards and auditing

## On completion of this chapter you should be able to:

- list and explain the contents of annual reports in Australia
- describe what users are likely to expect from a set of financial statements
- define GAAP and its components
- describe the set of principles and concepts that guide the preparation of financial reports
- list and define the principles of financial accounting and explain how each directly affects the process of financial accounting
- provide examples of trade-offs among accounting principles
- explain the nature and purpose of an audit
- describe the types of audit reports issued
- make judgements on the appropriate responses to certain ethical dilemmas
- define assets, liabilities and equity, and determine whether certain items meet these definitions
- determine when an asset or liability is to be recognised.

## 9.1 Chapter overview

You have now seen an overview of the key financial statements, including the preparation of the statement of financial position and statement of financial performance. You have then had a detailed look at the accounting for cash, receivables, inventory and noncurrent assets. Before completing your more in-depth examination of the remainder of the statement of financial position and further issues relating to the statement of financial performance, this chapter introduces you to generally accepted accounting principles (GAAP).

GAAP is the system of principles and rules that governs the way the financial statement figures are calculated and presented. This chapter also covers three topics associated with GAAP: the annual report, issued by larger companies, containing the set of financial statements and much more; the presence of an auditor's report to add credibility to the financial statements; and examples of specific accounting principles for assets and liabilities values. The concepts and techniques you learn in this chapter will provide a foundation for the rest of the book.

## 9.2 The annual report and financial statements

Financial reporting is important for many organisations. All incorporated companies, and most other legally constituted organisations, are required to prepare a set of financial statements at least annually, explaining their financial performance and position. Listed companies, which are those whose shares are traded on a stock exchange, usually also issue some interim financial information, especially on the subject of profits (earnings). Most sole traders and partnerships also prepare annual financial statements, at their bankers' request or for inclusion with the proprietor's or partners' income tax returns, even if there are no other reasons for doing so.

The standard set of financial statements has four components:

- statement of financial position
- statement of financial performance
- statement of cash flows
- notes to the financial statements.

A fifth item accompanies the financial statements and notes: the auditor's report on the truth and fairness of the set. The contents of the statements and its notes are the responsibility of management, and the auditor's report consists of the auditor's opinion about those statements and notes. You should be sceptical of financial statements that have not been audited or those whose audit report is not attached.

Public companies and other organisations include their set of financial statements in a much larger annual report. This report usually contains:

1. summary data on the company's performance for the year, usually in a graphical or other easy-to-read form, and comparisons going back five or more years
2. a letter to the shareholders from the company's chairperson of the board of directors or the managing director. It often includes highlights of the performance for the year and plans for the future.
3. an often extensive 'managing director's report', including a description of the economic, financial and other factors behind the company's business, usually broken down by its main products or departments

4 for listed companies, a corporate governance statement, which is required under stock exchange regulations. This would include such items as the composition and membership of the board of directors; remuneration policy for directors; the availability of independent professional advice to directors; the composition of the audit committee; procedures for identifying and managing business risks and statement of ethical standards.
5 the set of financial statements containing the statement of financial performance, statement of financial position, cash flow statement and notes to the accounts
6 a directors' statement and an independent audit report. The directors' statement, which is required by the Corporations Law, includes a statement by the directors of whether, in their opinion, the financial statements give a true and fair view of the financial performance and position of the company as at year-end. The directors also provide an opinion on whether the company can pay its debts as and when they fall due, and whether the financial statements comply with the requirements of the Corporations Law. The audit report is discussed in section 9.5.
7 a directors' report, which includes such items as the names of directors, principal activities of the company, operating results, significant changes in the state of affairs of the company, and certain information on directors
8 for listed companies, information on substantial shareholders, distribution of ownership of shares, twenty largest shareholders and voting rights of shareholders.

If you have not seen an annual report, you might find it interesting to browse through one. Most public companies have their most recent annual reports (as well as some more current financial information) on their Web site, or they will normally make their annual report available on request. In appendix 2 of this book are the 2001 financial statements and notes of Woolworths Limited, plus the auditor's report and the directors' declaration. These items are taken from the '2001 Financial Report to Stockholders'.

## Full versus concise financial reports

Traditionally in Australia all of the above information has been contained in one set of financial statements. The *Corporations Act 2001* now requires the publication of both full general purpose reports (GPFR) and concise financial reports.

The full financial statements contain a statement of financial position, a statement of financial performance and a statement of cash flows. In addition, it contains all of the notes to the financial statements, the auditor's report and the directors' declaration. It may also contain various other information the company decides to include.

The concise financial statements are sent to all shareholders, with a statement that the report is a concise report and that the GPFR will be sent to the shareholder if requested. The content of the concise report is drawn up in accordance with the relevant Accounting Standards, and all disclosures must be derived from the GPFR. While there are minimum content requirements, there is scope for additional content, which will vary with regard to the particular circumstances of the organisation and the presentation of relevant, reliable, understandable and comparable information.

The concise financial statements include a statement of financial position, a statement of financial performance and a statement of cash flows as these must be presented as in GPFR. In addition, there must be a discussion and analysis of these financial statements to assist the user's understanding.

Examples of the discussion and analysis would include:

| **Statement** | **Examples of discussion and analysis** |
|---|---|
| Statement of financial performance | Trends in revenue<br>The effects of significant economic or other events on the operations of the entity<br>The main influences on cost of operations<br>Measures of financial performance |
| Statement of financial position | Changes in the composition of assets<br>Significant movements in account balances<br>The relationship between debt and equity |
| Statement of cash flows | Changes in cash flows from operations<br>Financing of capital expenditure programs<br>Servicing and repayment of borrowings |

In addition, there will be a variety of other disclosures, including segment information (separate disclosures of revenues, profits and assets for the main segment of the business) and details of revenues and dividends.

## 9.3 Accounting principles and the use of accounting information

Financial accounting has a surprisingly large set of concepts and principles to guide accountants in preparing financial statements, auditors in verifying them, and users in interpreting them. A very large amount has been written about the conceptual and theoretical side of accounting, and as you saw earlier, several groups are involved in setting financial accounting standards and otherwise regulating accounting information.

All this material occupies many metres of library shelves and much space in computer databases. This section will give you a glimpse of the conceptual structure behind financial accounting, by focusing on some concepts of particular value to the users of accounting information. These concepts have been deduced by accountants, researchers and standard-setters from logic and observation of good practices, and they are used to guide everyone who prepares, audits, uses and studies financial accounting.

A phrase often used in respect to accounting's conceptual structure is generally accepted accounting principles (GAAP). These are the rules, standards and usual practices that companies are expected to follow in preparing their financial statements. They are a combination of the authoritative standards and concept statements issued by accounting standard-setters (such as the Australian Accounting Standards Board (AASB) in Australia and the Financial Accounting Standards Board in the United States) and the accepted ways of doing accounting that are not included in such standards. Year by year, the set of authoritative standards gets larger, but the world continues to increase in complexity, so the standards are never extensive enough to include everything. Probably they should not try to cover everything, because if they did, financial accounting would be bound by a boring, inflexible set of rules.

The development of GAAP can be traced back to the evolution of financial accounting, as well as to the efforts of standard-setting bodies that attempted to improve accounting principles and practices by increasing the authoritative, documented part of GAAP. Until this century was well along, authoritative accounting standards did not exist. As noted in chapter 3, the catalyst that produced increased financial disclosure and brought more rules governing it was the stock market crash of 1929. Poor financial reporting and disclosure were seen as contributing to the crash. It was argued that had investors been better informed, they could have made sounder financial decisions, thus preventing the stock market collapse and its harmful economic and social consequences.

In Australia, GAAP consist of accounting standards, statements of accounting concepts, accounting guidance releases and Urgent Issues Group statements. It all sounds a bit complex, but if we describe them one by one it should become clearer. Think of them as a package that together forms GAAP.

There are two forms of accounting standards, Australian Accounting Standards Board (AASB) standards, which apply basically to companies, and Australian Accounting Standards (AAS), which apply to certain non-corporate reporting entities, including public sector organisations and not-for-profit organisations. At present, the AASs are gradually being eliminated, with the AASBs applying to both private and public sector organisations.

Statements of Accounting Concepts (SAC) have been developed by the accounting profession in Australia to establish general concepts and principles to be used in preparing and presenting financial statements. They form part of a conceptual framework to help in the developing of new standards and in developing consistency of treatments across standards. At this point there are four SACs:

- SAC 1 Definition of a Reporting Entity
- SAC 2 Objective of General Purpose Financial Reporting
- SAC 3 Qualitative Characteristics of Financial Information
- SAC 4 Definition and Recognition of the Elements of Financial Statements.

The purpose of the accounting guidance releases (AAG series) is to give guidance on the application of concept statements and accounting standards. In addition there is an Urgent Issues Group (UIG), set up by the Australian Accounting Research Foundation, whose role is to provide guidance on urgent financial reporting issues. In providing such guidance, the UIG attempts to avoid the development of divergent or unsatisfactory financial reporting practices in new areas that are not presently dealt with by accounting standards.

Well, let's bring all this down to earth. The 'Financial Highlights' section of the 2001 annual report of Amalgamated Holdings Limited is shown in exhibit 9.1. Amalgamated Holdings Limited is a leisure and entertainment business, with activities which include Greater Union cinemas, film processing interests and ownership or management of hotels in Australia and New Zealand. The company owns and operates the Thredbo Alpine Ski Resort and has other ventures in the leisure and entertainment area.

## Information use scenarios

Let's consider some possible users of the financial statements summarised in these highlights:

- The company's board of directors manages the company on behalf of the shareholders. One function of the board that involves the financial statements is hiring the company's top operating management, especially the chief executive officer (CEO). Suppose you are a member of the board and are preparing for a discussion at the next board meeting. The board evaluates the CEO's performance continuously, which is its responsibility. The June 2001 financial statements have been provided to the board prior to the meeting, and will be a major input to this evaluation.

**EXHIBIT 9.1**

## Amalgamated Holdings Limited

### Financial highlights

| 30 June | 2001 | 2000 | 1999 | 1998 | 1997 |
|---|---|---|---|---|---|
| | | ($ million unless indicated) | | | |
| Sales | 440.0 | 455.5 | 440.4 | 394.7 | 381.1 |
| Earnings before interest and tax | 51.5 | 59.1 | 69.9 | 66.5 | 74.7 |
| Operating profit before tax | 34.0 | 45.0 | 54.3 | 54.5 | 62.2 |
| Operating profit before extraordinary items | 23.4 | 28.0 | 40.2 | 47.4 | 44.7 |
| Loss on extraordinary items after tax | (0.5) | (1.4) | (1.7) | (5.7) | (5.6) |
| Return on average shareholders' funds (%) (see note 2) | 5.9 | 7.2 | 11.5 | 15.7 | 16.2 |
| Basic earnings per share (cents) | 19.0 | 22.0 | 32.0 | 38.0 | 37.6 |
| Dividend per ordinary share (cents) | 10.0 | 14.0 | 13.0 | 12.0 | 11.0 |
| Total assets | 778.4 | 733.2 | 741.6 | 669.0 | 580.1 |
| Shareholders' equity | 402.9 | 388.2 | 386.8 | 314.8 | 287.9 |
| Borrowings net of cash | 261.1 | 250.3 | 241.2 | 210.4 | 167.5 |
| Gearing (%) (see note 3) | 39.3 | 39.2 | 38.4 | 40.1 | 36.8 |

**Notes**

1 The consolidated entity applied the equity method of accounting for investments in associates for the first time in 1999. Years 1997–1998 have not been adjusted to reflect this change.

2 Calculated before extraordinary items.

3 Gearing is defined as borrowings net of cash, as a percentage of borrowings plus shareholders' equity.

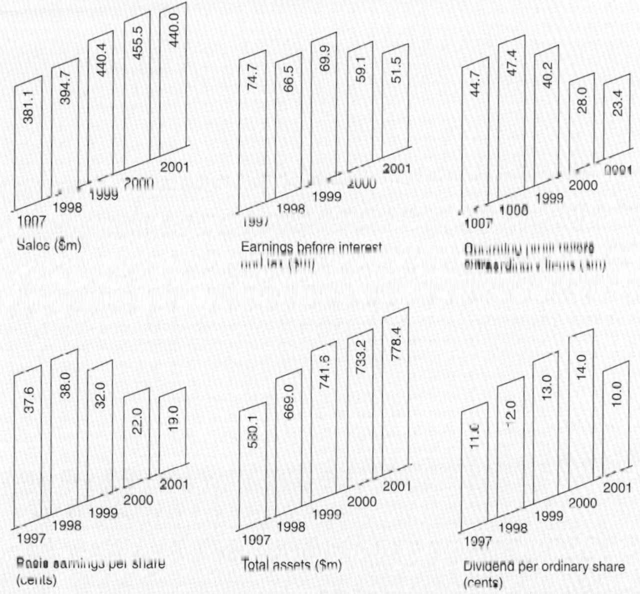


**Figure 9.1** Illustration of financial highlights, Amalgamated Holdings Limited

- The company's shares are listed (that is, can be bought and sold) on the Australian Stock Exchange. Suppose you are a financial analyst for an investment dealer and are preparing a report projecting future earnings and making recommendations about whether the company's shares are worthwhile to buy, or to keep if already held, or instead should be sold. You have the June 2001 financial statements and will use them to support your report.
- The company has several hundred millions of dollars in bank borrowing and has lines of credit (preauthorised borrowing capability) for millions of dollars more. Suppose you are a commercial lending officer for a bank, conducting a regular review of the company's borrowing status. You must consider the quality of the company's financial performance and assets (many of which have been assigned as security on bank loans and, therefore, could be seized if the company didn't pay its loans back on schedule). Financial performance is important because net profit generates cash to pay loans, and a good past record suggests that the company is likely to be able to earn profit in the future. You have requested the 2001 financial statements to use in your review.
- The company depends on a large number of suppliers to obtain the food and beverages for its hotels. Suppose you are the sales manager of a food and liquor supplier and are considering signing a long-term contract to supply the company. You want to sign the contract because your company needs the business, but you have to be satisfied that your shipments will be paid for. More positively, you hope that if you do a good job, you will have an opportunity to grow with the company. Most of the information you need has been received already, but you have obtained the 2001 financial statements and are reviewing them as you make your final decisions about the contract.

In summary, these scenarios involve the following reasons for using the 2001 financial statements of Amalgamated Holdings Limited:

- evaluation of the CEO's performance by a member of the board of directors
- preparation of 'buy', 'sell' or 'hold' recommendations by a financial analyst
- review of the company's borrowing status by a bank lending officer
- development of a supply contract with the company by a food and liquor supplier's sales manager.

These scenarios have been chosen to add to your insight into the use of financial accounting information. They are not complete. In all cases, the financial statements would be only part of the set of information used in the decision making. Also, there are many other uses of financial statements, some of which might make different demands on the quality of the information than are discussed here.

## Demands on the quality of financial accounting information

Let's think about what the users in these scenarios might reasonably expect of the financial statements. The important accounting concepts and principles involved are described in italics.

1. The financial statements need to contain information that is useful to those who are making the decisions. The information must have value in helping the financial analyst or bank lending officer make their recommendation. In addition, the information to be provided needs to be made in a timely manner. For example, some of the decisions by the board, the analyst, the banker and supplier noted above need to be made at a certain point in time. While the outcome of a particular contract may be relevant information, the decisions often can't wait until that contract is finalised.

*This is the concept of relevance. If information is to assist users in making decisions about the allocation of scarce resources, it should help them make, confirm or correct predictions about the outcomes of past, present or future events. Timeliness refers to the need to provide the relevant information in time for the decision to be made.*

**2** The financial statements should not be deliberately misleading. They should be free from bias. They should not be designed to lead users toward conclusions desired by the preparers. If accounting information is to tell people about the economic forces affecting the company and the business arrangements the company has made to deal with those forces, it should connect to such important underlying phenomena. The bank loans officer would want to feel confident that the statements were not prepared in such a way as to make the company appear to be a better lending risk than it is. Similarly, the board of directors would want the statements to provide an objective portrayal of the CEO's performance in running the company.

*This is the criterion of reliability. The financial statements should report the economic substance of events happening to the company, and the numbers should measure the events neutrally, neither overstating nor understating their impact. Reliable information will, without bias or undue error, faithfully represent those transactions and events that have occurred.*

**3** Preparing financial statements, like any other activity, costs money and takes time. Most people would be satisfied if the statements were fair about the important things and would not mind a few minor errors in them, especially if preventing small errors would have cost the company money (reducing the company's profit and cash flow) or delayed the release of the statements. The food and liquor sales manager would not want to wait for the statements while Amalgamated accountants changed the cost of the company's inventory of unsold souvenirs (part of the multi-million-dollar inventory account) to $1199 from $1189.

*This is the criterion of materiality (significance). The materiality concept is concerned with assessing whether omission, misstatement or non-disclosure of a piece of information would affect the decisions of users of the accounting reports. Just what is or is not material is a matter of judgement and has been the subject of considerable research and study by accountants and auditors. Usually, people judge materiality by considering the size of a possible error compared to the net profit or the total assets. For example, an accountant or auditor might judge that an error over 5 per cent of net profit or 1 per cent of total assets is material and a smaller one is not. But, as you might expect, the materiality judgement depends on any particular uses of the information that are expected, and on whether the error moves the profit to a loss or violates some loan condition.*

**4** There needs to be some standard against which an accounting method or number can be judged. The financial analyst would like to know that Amalgamated Holdings' financial statements were presented fairly, in all material respects, given accepted current methods. In the statement of financial performance, for example, sales revenue should mean what a knowledgeable analyst or other user would expect for such a company. The company is actually a group of companies, so its financial statements are consolidated, and it would be reasonable to expect that the company's method of calculating consolidated figures was proper.

*This is where GAAP come in. To assure the users that accepted methods have been followed, the auditor's report also says that the auditor's opinion is that the statements have been prepared in accordance with generally accepted accounting principles. This does not mean that one particular method has been followed: GAAP often include several acceptable methods, depending on the circumstances. Therefore, the auditors are saying that the company's accounting methods and the resulting figures are appropriate to its circumstances.*

**5** In many countries GAAP suggest that it is prudent to be cautious when estimating uncertain amounts, such as future collections and the value of unsold inventory.

*This leads to another criterion, conservatism. This often controversial criterion states that under uncertainty, assets, revenues and profit should not be overstated and liabilities, expenses and losses should not be understated. Conservatism should involve being careful, not deliberately biasing important numbers, although just where prudence ends and bias begins is a matter of judgement.*

**6** The previous criteria indicate that the financial statements necessarily reflect judgement on the part of the preparers. Also, the figures in the statements are summaries of many accounts: for example, 'accounts receivable' and 'long-term debt' may include dozens or thousands of different customers or debts. The bank loan officer may want to know what sort of long-term debts the company has, so that those may be evaluated against the bank borrowing by the company. The bank would not want other creditors to interfere with the company's ability to pay the bank back. The financial analyst may want to know if the company has made commitments to issue more shares (such as in a plan to motivate senior management by issuing shares to them cheaply if they perform well), because those might reduce the equity of anyone buying the shares now.

*This raises the principle of disclosure. The financial statements include a large number of notes and account descriptions intended to make it clear to the reader which important accounting methods have been followed (especially if those methods are not what might be expected) and to provide supplementary information on debts, share capital, commitments, law suits and other things thought to be helpful, or necessary, in understanding the statements. Disclosure beyond the accounting figures is increasingly extensive: many pages of notes often accompany the set of statements, and companies disclose additional information to taxation authorities, to securities regulators (such as the Australian Securities and Investments Commission and the US Securities and Exchange Commission) and to important other parties who have a reason to get the information (such as the bank loan officer and the financial analyst).*

**7** The board, the banker, the analyst and the supplier would like information they can understand. No doubt their ability to understand will depend on their knowledge of accounting.

*This principle is called understandability. Reports should be prepared having regard to the interests of users who are willing to exercise diligence in examining the reports and who possess the skills and ability to comprehend contemporary accounting practices.*

**8** The banker and the financial analyst are also involved with other companies. They would like to be able to compare Amalgamated Holdings' financial statements to those of similar companies. It may be difficult to be sure that a company is performing well or badly in an absolute sense, but it can always be compared to others, as long as the financial statements have been prepared in a comparable way.

*You will not be surprised that this principle is called comparability. It will be important when we review techniques for financial statement analysis in chapter 14.*

**9** The banker, the analyst and the board of directors' member will also want to study the trend in financial performance and position over time. Is the net profit improving over time, or deteriorating? How about liquidity? Or the ratio of debt to equity financing? It is important to know if significant events have happened to make comparisons over time difficult or even impossible. It is also important to know if the company has changed its accounting methods over time, because such changes may affect the comparability of the accounting figures from year to year.

*Keeping the same accounting methods over time is called consistency. Recently, the auditor's report said specifically whether the financial statements were prepared consistently, but now it is presumed that if the company is following GAAP, that includes using consistent methods or else telling the reader of the statements that a change has been made and what the effects of changes in accounting methods are (if they are material). Note that consistency does not mean that a company has to use the same accounting method in all parts of the company. For example, different depreciation methods can be used for different assets. Some parts of the organisation may use FIFO, while others use weighted average for inventory valuation.*

## Trade-offs among accounting principles

If you think about the criteria and principles mentioned above (relevance, reliability, timeliness, materiality, conformance with GAAP, conservatism, disclosure, comparability and consistency), you may see that they do not always fit together well. Here are some examples:

- It is often argued that conservatism is a bias that interferes with reliability.
- If some other companies with which a company is likely to be compared (such as others in its industry) change their accounting methods, the company has to decide whether to change its methods too for the sake of comparability, even though that will mean inconsistency in its own figures over time.
- Similarly, when a new or revised accounting standard is issued by the AASB, following the new standard (that is, conforming with GAAP as they now exist) will mean inconsistency over time for all companies that did not previously use the approved new method.
- It would seem sensible that the more reliable the accounting information is, the better. You get more reliable information by being very careful about how you prepare it, checking it carefully and having the auditors come in and verify it, maybe even waiting until some major uncertainties are resolved, so you do not have to estimate them. It also seems sensible that decision makers need information relevant to their decisions when they are making the decisions. This means that information should be timely: people should not have to wait for the information they need.

So, let's take the example of a company trying to report on its liability for long service leave to employees. It has thousands of employees, who will take this leave over the next forty years, if they do not leave (voluntarily or involuntarily!). The dollar amount of long service leave paid will depend on how much the employees earn when they take the leave, and that is not known yet for most of them. The amount of leave depends on how long the employees have been with the firm. Under most awards it starts to accumulate after 10 or 15 years' service. For each extra year of service it increases at different rates. If the employee leaves before 10 years' service, no amount normally needs to be paid unless the employee's leaving was involuntary.

How is that for a mass of uncertainty? Any number you come up with for the long service leave liability will be based on all sorts of estimates of unknown future events. So to get a liability figure that is at all reliable, you really have to wait 20 or 30 years until most of the employees have retired or taken their leave. You can always expect to get reliability by just waiting a while, even years, to see how things turn out. But waiting 20 or 30 years will hardly provide timely information, relevant to decisions such as those being made by the board of directors, investment analyst, banker and supplier mentioned above. Such decisions require the best information we can come up with now, even if it is necessarily based on estimates and assumptions. Therefore, there is almost never a solution that produces both the most reliable and the most timely, relevant accounting information. As time passes, reliability rises and timely relevance falls, so we have to try to find some midpoint where there is enough of both, but not as much as we would like of either.

## SAC 3

As part of an overall conceptual framework for financial reporting, the Accounting Standards Review Board and the Public Sector Accounting Standards Board developed Statement of Accounting Concepts 3 (SAC 3) entitled 'Qualitative Characteristics of Financial Information'. Some key points of this statement that relate to our above discussion are listed here:

- The qualitative characteristics are useful in providing assistance when choices need to be made between reporting policies by preparers, auditors, standard-setters and others.
- Relevance and reliability are the primary qualitative characteristics that financial information should possess.
- The concept of conservatism, as described earlier, is at odds with many of the desirable qualitative characteristics, including reliability.
- Once it is determined that financial information can be classified as relevant and reliable, there is a need to consider whether the information is material given the individual circumstances of the entity. The materiality test involves an assessment of whether omission, misstatement or non-disclosure of an item of relevant and reliable information could affect the decisions made by users.
- An important implication of the concept of comparability is that users need to be informed of the policies employed in the preparation of the general-purpose financial reports, changes in those policies and the effect of those changes particularly on profitability. As a result all companies provide a note to the accounts (usually note 1), which sets out the accounting policies used by the firm.
- Consistency should not be an end in itself. A company should not remain rigid in its accounting policies for the sake of consistency when more reliable and relevant alternatives exist.
- Preparers should present information in the most understandable manner without sacrificing relevance or reliability. However, it is not always possible to report complex transactions and events in simple or simplified terms. It is also noted that users can obtain professional advice where necessary.
- Disclosure is an important means of understanding new financial information. Financial information that does not meet the recognition criteria to be included in the balance sheet because of material uncertainties can still be disclosed in notes or supplementary schedules. The manner of presenting such information can ensure that users do not place undue reliance on it.
- Financial information which is relevant and reliable may lose its relevance if there is undue delay in reporting it. This has implications for the frequency of financial reports and the length of time that should elapse between the year-end and the reporting date to users.
- Preparers, auditors, standard setters and others must consider whether the cost of providing certain information exceeds the benefits of providing that information.

## Summary

This section has illustrated decision settings using accounting information and identified some accounting principles that respond to those settings. There are many more principles, some of which will be mentioned as this book proceeds, but be sure you understand the ones described above at this stage.

### How's your understanding?

Here are two questions you should be able to answer, based on what you have just read:

1 You have just opened the annual report of a company and found that the auditor's report says that it is the auditor's opinion that the financial statements have been prepared in accordance with applicable accounting standards. What concepts of information value would the auditors have assumed as part of GAAP?

2 Can accounting numbers in financial statements and highlights be relevant, reliable and conservative all at once?

## 9.4 Accounting regulation in Australia[1]

Earlier chapters have emphasised the importance of financial accounting information to various user groups. Credible financial reporting is hard to achieve without an accounting regulatory system. Effective regulation depends on the existence of accounting rules based on the right concepts to guide information processing and disclosure. Also necessary is an enforcement mechanism that ensures sufficient compliance with the rules. The *Corporate Law Economic Reform Program Act 1999* (CLERP Act 1999), which came into effect on 1 January 2000, modified the institutional arrangements for the setting of accounting standards in Australia, recognising that financial reporting requirements can play an important role in Australian companies' ability to compete effectively and efficiently in a global environment.

The purpose of this section is to provide an overview of the Australian regulatory system in respect of corporate financial reporting. A system of co-regulation has evolved. It is based on collaboration between the Federal Government and its agencies and the accounting profession. Figure 9.2 depicts the main elements in the system.

The government's role is highlighted in the top section of figure 9.2. After an agreement with the States and the Northern Territory in 1990 to overcome the constitutional obstacles, the Federal Government took over the responsibility for companies and securities law. The broad legal framework for corporate financial reporting is set out in the *Corporations Act 2001*, with subordinate detail contained in the *Corporations Regulations 2001*.

Also shown in figure 9.2 are two statutory bodies established by the *Australian Securities and Investments Commission Act 2001*; the Australian Securities and Investments Commission (ASIC) and the Financial Reporting Council (FRC). Both play an important role in the operation and oversight of financial reporting in Australia. ASIC is the agency charged with the administration and enforcement of the *Corporations Act*, while the FRC is responsible for providing broad oversight of the accounting standard-setting process in the private and public sectors.

The role of ASIC is to regulate and enforce laws that promote honesty and fairness in financial markets, products and services and in Australian companies. In doing so, it underpins the strength, growth and international reputation of Australia's financial markets. As part of this role, it monitors compliance with accounting standards and takes appropriate enforcement action where necessary. ASIC is directed by three full-time Commissioners appointed by the Governor-General on the nomination of the Treasurer. It reports to the Commonwealth Parliament directly and through the Treasurer.

The FRC is an advisory body, setting the general strategic direction for the development of accounting standards. It reports to the Treasurer, who also appoints the members of the FRC. Members' appointments are based on nominations put forward by key stakeholder

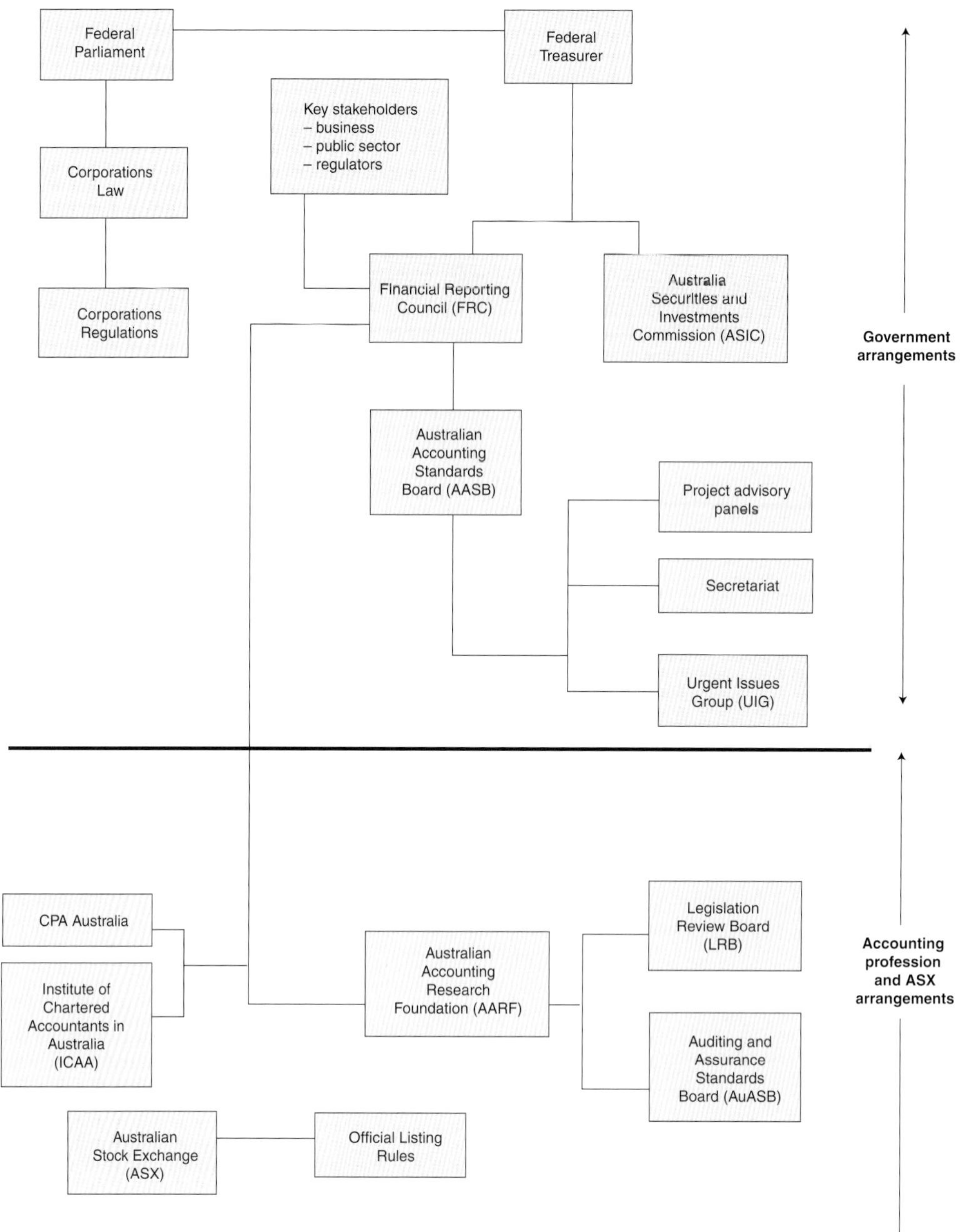


Figure 9.2 The regulatory framework

groups: representatives from the business community, the public sector, regulatory agencies and the professional accounting bodies. These groups all have an interest in the standard-setting process, and representation on the FRC allows them an opportunity to provide input to the process, resulting in greater ownership of the resulting standards. The FRC is a new body, introduced as part of the government's Corporate Law Economic Reform Program (CLERP), and its membership, broadly based upon a variety of stakeholder groups, enables the accounting standard-setting process to be more responsive to the needs of users and preparers of financial statements.

One of the key functions of the FRC is to oversee the operation of the Australian Accounting Standards Board (AASB). The AASB prepares, approves and issues accounting standards for the purposes of the *Corporations Act*, and for the public and not-for-profit sectors. It is comprised of a full-time Chairman, appointed by the Treasurer, and nine part-time members. Members are appointed by the FRC, selected on the basis of their knowledge and experience in business, accounting, law or government. The Board is required to follow the directions, advice and feedback of the FRC on matters of general policy. The FRC is also responsible for approving the priorities, business plan, budget and staffing arrangements of the AASB. However, it cannot influence the AASB's technical deliberations, and hence the content of particular accounting standards.

The Urgent Issues Group (UIG) is a committee of the AASB, whose purpose is to review on a timely basis accounting issues that are likely to receive divergent or unacceptable treatment in the absence of authoritative guidance. In doing so, it seeks to reach a consensus as to the appropriate accounting treatment, dealing with all issues within the framework of existing accounting standards. The AASB has a reserve power of veto over UIG consensus views. A UIG consensus view is published in an Abstract, which is expected to be followed in the preparation of general-purpose financial reports, and is mandatory for CPAs and members of the ICAA.

The lower section of figure 9.2 shows the role of the accounting profession, represented by CPA Australia and the Institute of Chartered Accountants in Australia (ICAA). The profession plays a part in the financial reporting process through its representation as a key stakeholder group on the FRC. In addition, the ICAA and CPA Australia jointly established the Australian Accounting Research Foundation (AARF) in 1966. Within this body are a number of specialised boards. The Auditing and Assurance Standards Board (AuASB) is responsible for the development of auditing and assurance standards. The Legislation Review Board (LRB) aims to lobby and comment on proposed government legislation that affects the accounting profession.

To complete the picture of the regulatory framework for corporate financial reporting, figure 9.2 shows the Australian Stock Exchange Limited (ASX). This body increases the reporting obligations of entities that are listed on the Stock Exchange by issuing official listing rules. Companies must comply with these if they wish to be listed, and remain listed, on the Stock Exchange. The listing rules may be enforced by the ASX's power of suspension or delisting. Further, the rules have statutory backing in the Corporations Law, as a court order may be obtained to enforce them.

In recent years, the ASX has been emphasising its continuous disclosure rule 3A(1) and the need for information on corporate governance. On the latter issue, the rules require a company to state whether it has an audit committee and, if it does not, to explain why not. In addition, companies are required to state in their annual reports the main corporate governance practices they had in place during the reporting period. To assist companies, an indicative list of corporate governance matters is provided in the listing rules.

## 9.5 The external auditor's report

Several references to the auditors were made above. The auditor's report is normally a routine statement by the auditors that provides an opinion on whether the financial statements are fairly presented. But if it is not routine, the auditors are trying to tell the users something they think is important. The auditor's report may be qualified in some way, indicating that the auditors have some concern about the statements; in extreme cases, the report may even 'deny' the fairness of the statements, saying that the auditors have some very serious objection.

Before we turn to some examples of applying GAAP to financial statement preparation and use, it will be useful to point out a few things about the auditor's role in financial reporting. (In the discussion below, the auditor will be referred to in the singular for simplicity. Most of the time, auditors are members of accounting firms of auditors and related professionals, and so are often referred to in the plural.)

*External auditing* refers to the evaluation of an organisation's financial statements by an auditor who should be unconnected with, and therefore independent of, the management of the organisation. The role of the external auditor has two fundamental parts:

- to have an independent, unbiased and professional perspective
- to render a competent opinion on the fairness of the financial statements (given GAAP, as discussed in section 9.3).

Many companies, governments and other organisations also have *internal auditors*. Such auditors work within the organisation and help management operate the organisation. Their work is not dealt with in this book.

Let's begin with independence and professionalism. Auditors are members of professional associations, such as CPA Australia and/or the Institute of Chartered Accountants in Australia. Overseas equivalents include the American Institute of Certified Public Accountants, the Canadian Institute of Chartered Accountants, the Institute of Chartered Accountants of England and Wales, the Institute of Chartered Accountants of New Zealand, the Hong Kong Society of Accountants, the Institute of Certified Public Accountants of Singapore, and the Malaysian Institute of Accountants.

A fundamental objective of these professional associations is to protect society by ensuring the professionalism and independence of the external auditors who belong to them. Protecting society should be consistent with protecting the association's members' professional reputations. To this end, there are complex rules of professional ethics that prohibit the external auditor from having a financial interest, directly and in most indirect ways as well, in the client companies or other organisations being audited. These rules and similar ones related to other relationships between the auditor and the client are intended to ensure that the auditor has no personal interest in whether the financial statements report one kind of performance or another. In other words, the auditor should be an unbiased, professionally sceptical reviewer of the financial statements and not someone who wants the result to turn out one way or another.

Maintaining this independence is not easy because the auditors are business entrepreneurs themselves and their clients pay them for doing the audit. The idea is that independence is maintained because the auditor is appointed by, and reports to, the shareholders, not management. Since the financial statements are reports on management's stewardship performance, the auditor is presumed to be working for the shareholders in verifying management's reports. In practice, however, external auditors must have a close working relationship with client management.

Also, managers are in a strong position to recommend a change of auditor if the relationship is not to their liking. Maintaining independence under these circumstances is difficult and is complicated further by the fact that auditing (accounting) firms offer non-auditing services, the revenue for which may exceed the fee for doing the audit. It is also complicated by the fact that if users of financial statements suffer losses, they can, and often do, sue the auditor, so the auditor must be very careful not to be compromised by the relationship with management.

The second part of the auditor's role is to render a competent opinion on the financial statements. If you refer to an audit report such as that for Woolworths Limited at the back of this book, you will see that it says the auditors have reached an opinion as to whether the financial statements have been properly drawn up to give a true and fair view in accordance with the provision of the Corporations Law and applicable accounting standards. It is an opinion, not a guarantee, nor does it say that the company has performed well or badly. It simply says that the performance and the position have been measured and presented in a generally accepted and unbiased way.

Given the complexity of accounting, auditing and business in general, the auditor's opinion is fundamentally a professional judgement. The auditor must be competent but, in addition, must weigh all sorts of factors in arriving at his/her opinion. Concerned about the quality of their judgement, auditing firms in North America have sponsored a great deal of research into the professional judgement of auditors. The results of much of this research have been incorporated into international practices including those in Australia.

The form and content of the auditor's report change every few years, as auditors rethink how best to communicate with the users of financial statements. Because the auditors are formally reporting to the owners of the company, not to management, the report is usually specifically addressed to the owners (the shareholders). The usual title of the report is 'Independent Audit Report'. The latest standard version of the auditor's report has three paragraphs:

1. The first identifies the company and the set of statements and their date, and states that they are the responsibility of management and that the auditor's responsibility having conducted an independent audit of the financial report is to express an opinion on them.
2. The second contains the following statements:
   - that the audit has been conducted in accordance with Australian Auditing Standards to provide reasonable assurance on whether the financial report is free of material misstatement
   - that the auditor's procedures included the examination, on a test basis, of evidence supporting the amounts and other disclosures in the financial report, and the evaluation of accounting policies and significant accounting estimates
   - a statement indicating that these procedures have been undertaken to form an opinion on whether, in all material respects, the financial report is presented fairly in accordance with the relevant accounting standards as to present a view which is consistent with the auditor's understanding of the entity's financial position, the results of its operations and its cash flows
   - a statement that the audit opinion expressed in the report has been formed on the above basis.
3. Normally the third paragraph provides the auditor's opinion that the financial statements give a true and fair view, that they are in accordance with the provisions of the *Corporations Act 2001*, applicable accounting standards and other professional mandatory reporting requirements.

You should expect to find most auditors' reports to be worded pretty well the same. This sounds boring, but there is a purpose: any nonstandard wording is likely to be a warning to anyone planning to use the financial statements in decision-making.

There are three main exceptions to this *unqualified opinion*: an *except for opinion*, when the auditors are generally satisfied except for a specified problem in doing their work or a specified departure from GAAP in the statements; an *adverse opinion*, when the auditors say that their opinion is that the financial statements are not presented fairly in accordance with GAAP; and *inability to form an opinion*, when the auditors are unable to express an opinion either way because of a limitation in the work the auditors were able to do. This last form of opinion is very unusual.

In certain limited circumstances, the auditor will issue an unqualified opinion, but will draw attention to or emphasise a matter that is relevant to the users of the audit report, but is not of such a nature that it affects the audit opinion. For example, there may be a major uncertainty that could affect the company's ability to remain a going concern, but this uncertainty is adequately disclosed by the company.

### How's your understanding?

Here are two questions you should be able to answer, based on what you have just read:

1 The external auditor's report states that 'Our audit has been conducted in accordance with Australian Auditing Standards'. Why is the auditor referring to these auditing standards?

2 The general manager of a small company recently said, 'We need to have an external auditor for our financial statements so we can guarantee their accuracy to our bank.' Will that be the result if an auditor is appointed?

## 9.6 The nature of a profession and professional ethics

Many of the people involved in financial accounting consider themselves to be professionals. Evolving systems of standards such as GAAP work reasonably well partly because professionals, who are both expert and ethical, are involved. Ethical behaviour comes from personal standards plus various written codes of ethical conduct.

For many people today, there is strong concern with being professional. There are, however, certain occupations that have established status as the professions. In today's world some groups that have this status are physicians, lawyers, engineers, architects and professional accountants.

Part of the reason these groups stand out is that entry into each of them requires a post-secondary education, including training and examination by practitioners, and members are bound by a code of conduct or professional ethics. Members of each professional group usually enjoy a monopoly in their particular area of expertise. Associations of architects, physicians, engineers, lawyers and other members of legally recognised professions can all prevent people from calling themselves members of their particular professions and practising in that capacity. Such groups have to convince the public (as represented by governments, for example) that they have expertise and appropriate codes of ethical conduct, but also that entrance to their area of expertise should be regulated for the public good.

The Institute of Chartered Accountants in Australia (ICAA) and CPA Australia are the professional accounting bodies in Australia. There are no legal requirements governing the employment of accountants in Australia although some specialist accounting functions (auditing, taxation, liquidation) are subject to statutory requirements. You, your friends or anyone can call yourselves 'accountants' and advertise in the paper or Yellow Pages to attract clients. However, professional designations, such as ACA and CPA, are protected by law and can only be attained if you meet the various requirements specified by the relevant accounting body. For these accountants there are both powers and restrictions (for example, advertising must meet certain standards of content and decorum).

The rights that a particular profession enjoys come in return for promises made about the quality and ethics of its members' work. If a professional accountant has not lived up to the standards of conduct held by the profession, he or she can be reprimanded or expelled by the profession and/or sued in court. (Anyone can be sued, of course, but professionals are usually held to a higher standard of performance than are non-professionals.)

All told, being in a profession has many advantages (including service to society, monopoly over an area of work, collegial support, social prestige and good pay), but one must remember that in return there is the social responsibility of discharging one's duties competently and in accordance with the profession's code of ethics. Professional codes of ethics involve not only behaving in a professional manner (for example, with integrity and objectivity), but also maintaining the level of expertise required in order to perform skilfully. This involves following procedures that will, or should, ensure that high standards of work and performance are met, and exercising informed judgement.

Here are examples of ethical problems that may be faced by professional accountants. What would you, as a member of a professional body or as someone who may rely on accounting information or auditors' reports, think would be appropriate ethical behaviour in each case?

- Mary works for a Big 5 accounting firm and is part of the team doing the external audit of Westward Industries Ltd. Staff at Westward are all very friendly, and Mary is offered the chance to buy one of the company's high-quality sound systems for only about half the usual price. Should she accept the deal?
- Andrew is also on the Westward external audit team. He is a member of a local football team. During drinks after a game, he hears a member of another team boast of cheating Westward systematically by over-billing on printing invoices. Should he tell Westward?
- Lisa and Sean fall in love and decide to marry. Both are professional accountants: Lisa is the chief accountant of Westward, responsible for preparing all the company's financial statements, and Sean is a partner of a Big 5 firm and is in charge of the external audit of the company. Should Sean turn the audit over to another partner, or perhaps even ask the accounting firm to resign as auditor (because as a partner, he shares in the firm's profits from all audits)?
- Michel is another member of the Westward external audit team. During some audit tests, she discovers that Westward engaged in some business activities that appear to be illegal. Breaking that particular law can bring large fines and even jail terms. Should Michel go to the police?
- Erin works for the same Big 5 firm. During the audit of Basic Electronics Ltd, she discovers that an employee of Basic is overcharging Westward by applying too high a mark up to services contracted with Westward. Documents indicate that Basic's management is aware of this and is happy to be getting away with it, because it has a material effect on Basic's profit. Should she tell the management of Basic that she knows what they are doing? Should she tell Sean, the partner responsible for the Westward audit? Should she tell Westward?
- George is a partner of the same Big 5 firm. For years, his father has owned a few shares of Westward, among a whole portfolio of shares of many companies. His father has just died and willed all the shares to George. Should he sell the Westward shares?

One of the more interesting and challenging aspects of being a professional is dealing with such ethical issues. Some of these examples do not have clear answers, but here are some ideas:

- The external auditors are supposed to be independent scrutineers of their clients' financial affairs. Mary should probably not accept the deal, unless it is available to anyone who turns up at a retail store, because accepting it would undermine her independence. Being friendly with clients is fine, but auditors also have to maintain some distance from clients to protect their independence and integrity.

- Andrew should tell Westward what he heard and suggest they look into their printing costs. When doing their work, auditors acquire much confidential information about their clients and must be very careful about how they use it. In this case, the information was not acquired under circumstances of confidentiality. He may find himself in court over the issue, however, so he may need to seek legal advice before speaking to Westward.
- Sean needs to take some action to remove himself from the job of auditing his wife's work, to protect both her and his integrity. The firm probably has rules about such relationships, which likely involve transferring the job to another partner and keeping Sean entirely ignorant of the work on the Westward audit. The firm might have to resign the audit.
- Michel's situation is very complex. There is a mixture of confidentially acquired information and a duty to society. Much more has to be known before any advice could be offered to Michel. At the very least, Michel and the firm would have to get legal advice immediately. The board of directors of most large companies has an audit committee to give the auditors a way to bring criticisms of management to the board's attention. Michel's firm would likely raise this with Westward's audit committee.
- Erin's is another very complex situation. Erin is responsible for protecting the confidentiality of her client, Basic, and would be in trouble if she told another company what she learned on the audit. But her firm is responsible to both clients. Again, she and the firm would need immediate legal advice.
- Most firms have rules prohibiting members of the firm from having an interest in any clients audited by the firm. George would have to sell his shares in Westward.

## How's your understanding?

Here are two questions you should be able to answer, based on what you have just read:

1 Why do professional accountants have to abide by codes of ethics, and what difference might that make to the users of their services?

2 What ethical issues do you see in the following situation? During the audit of Westward Industries Ltd, Sonya discovered that an accounting clerk, needing money for a child's operation, had temporarily taken some cash collected from customers. The clerk had returned the money a short time later, before anyone had known it was missing and was otherwise a very competent and valued employee. The company's controls over cash have since been tightened, and it is unlikely that the clerk would be able to repeat the theft. Sonya is the only person, other than the clerk, who knows about the theft.

## 9.7 Applying generally accepted accounting principles

You have seen that financial accounting has developed over hundreds of years and that in the twentieth century there has been an increase in the regulation and standardisation of financial statements and other financial disclosures. But financial accounting is by no means completely rule-bound and regulated. There are many accounting methods that are not covered by specific rules but are so well accepted that they are taken for granted as proper, and there are many problems that no rules seem likely to settle and that must be solved using the professional judgement of managers, accountants and auditors. Generally accepted accounting principles are mostly stable, so people can know what to expect, yet they are not fixed. They change as demands for information change and as new solutions are developed. They are 'generally accepted', but not always easy to tie down, because they are flexible enough to be tailored to the circumstances of particular companies and other organisations. They are often controversial because people feel they are too flexible, or not flexible enough, or too detailed, or not specific enough. Their combination of technicality and judgement makes them both interesting and frustrating to learn about.

It is all very well to know that GAAP exist, but how do you know when and how to apply them? The answer is that this requires significant expertise in today's world of complicated businesses, complicated governments and complicated accounting. Basically, you have to get to know what GAAP are for the kind of company or financial statement item you are concerned about. This can require both a lot of reading of published standards, texts and other material, consultation with others, and a lot of experience in making it all work. You have already learned many parts of GAAP, as you learned about the set of financial statements. The rest of this book will show you many more aspects of GAAP in order to get your interpretative expertise started.

The following sections of this chapter offer examples of the application of GAAP to particular financial accounting issues.

- Section 9.8 considers the definition and recognition of the elements of financial statements (SAC 4).
- Section 9.9 examines the general question of how to determine the values (figures) of items included on the statement of financial position.
- Section 9.10 reviews the usual contents of the notes to the financial statements. The notes often take many more pages than the financial statements do.

## 9.8 Definition and recognition of assets and liabilities

Statement of Accounting Concepts 4: Definition and Recognition of the Elements of Financial Statements considers the following elements: assets, liabilities, equity, revenue and expenses. Each of these elements has been introduced earlier in this book. In this section we expand the earlier discussion to examine recognition issues related to assets, liabilities and equity. Revenue and expense issues are left to chapter 11.

### Assets

Accounting concept SAC 4 defines assets as 'future economic benefits controlled by the entity as a result of past transactions or other past events'. Based on this definition, assets need to have three essential characteristics:

- *Future economic benefits (or service potential)* is described as being the essence of assets. In profit-seeking organisations, the future economic benefits are used to provide goods and services for exchange with the objective of generating net cash flows (for example, through the sale of the asset or sale of the output produced through the use of the asset). In not-for-profit organisations, the provision of goods or services may not result in the generation of net cash inflows. For example, monuments, cathedrals and museums may not generate cash, but do benefit the organisation by enabling it to meet its objective of providing needed services to beneficiaries.

  Consider the following examples of assets and how they provide future economic benefits. Cash balances benefit an organisation because of their command over the future economic benefits it provides. Assets such as debtors and investments are direct claims to cash inflows (receipt of payment from debtors or interest on investments); prepayments provide rights to receive services; inventories can be exchanged for cash or claims to cash; property, plant and equipment and patents can provide goods or services.

- *Control by the entity* relates to the capacity of an entity to benefit from the asset in pursuing its objectives and to deny or regulate the access of others. The entity controlling the asset is the one that can exchange it, use it to provide goods and services, charge others for its use and use it to settle liabilities.

  Although the ability to control the future economic benefits may be a result of legally enforceable rights, this is not an essential characteristic of an asset. For example, under a lease agreement, the owner (lessor) may transfer to the lessee control over the leased property for a certain period of time.

  Some future economic benefits will not be controlled by an entity because the entity cannot deny others access to the benefits of the asset. For example, consider a property developer who builds a series of townhouses and is required by the local council to put in road improvements or a public park as part of project. If access to the road or the park is open to the general public without charge then the developer does not have control over the asset.
- *Occurrence of past transactions or other past events* means that the transaction or other event giving the entity control over the future economic benefits must have occurred. Most assets are obtained by an entity from cash, credit or barter transactions. For example, this may involve the purchase of an asset for cash, by credit, exchange for other assets, issue of shares or release from a liability. Alternatively, the transactions may be non-reciprocal transfers such as donations or grants.

## Asset recognition

A further question addressed by SAC 4 is the criteria that should be used to recognise assets. Recognition refers to the reporting of an item on the face of the financial statements. For assets, the relevant financial statement is the statement of financial position.

Accounting concept SAC 4 states an asset should be recognised when and only when:

- it is probable that the future economic benefits embodied in the asset will eventuate
- the asset possesses a cost or other value that can be measured reliably.

The term 'probable' means that the chance of the future economic benefits arising is more likely rather than less likely. For example, a credit sale to a reputable customer still involves some probability that the amount will not be collected. However, if the likelihood of non-receipt is remote at reporting date, the debt would satisfy the criteria for recognition as an asset. However, for some expenditures, such as those on exploration and research and development, the degree of certainty for the item to satisfy the criteria for recognition of an asset often does not exist.

An expenditure that fails the recognition criteria at one point in time may qualify for recognition as an asset at a later date. Confirmation of the existence of a valuable mineral deposit would be an example.

For an asset to satisfy the recognition criteria, it is also necessary that it possesses a cost or other value that can be measured reliably. In most cases, assets have a cost that can be reliably measured. An example where this is not the case is a mining company that may have discovered, at an immaterial cost, some evidence of minerals on its exploration site, but at the date of reporting does not know the extent of the minerals or their value.

### For your interest

You may have heard CEOs say that their staff are their biggest asset. Yet you will have noted that staff are not listed on any statement of financial position (balance sheet). One of the reasons is the difficulty of putting a value on staff. In the 1970s and 1980s, there was a lot of accounting research called 'human resource accounting' that examined this question. Some suggestions for valuing staff included:

- all costs spent on the staff member (such as the cost of training)
- the present value of the future cash the staff member will generate
- the cost of training a replacement.

## Liabilities

Accounting concept SAC 4 defines liabilities as 'future sacrifices of economic benefits that the entity is presently obliged to make to other entities as a result of past transactions or other past events'.

There are two essential characteristics of liabilities:

- a present obligation exists
- the obligation involves settlement in the future via the sacrifice of service potential or future economic benefits.

Most obligations are legally enforceable; for example, they arise out of contractual arrangements including money borrowed, amounts owing on assets purchased or for services provided, or obligations to provide services to parties who have paid in advance. Obligations can also be imposed on the entity, including damages awarded by courts, workers' compensation claims and income tax payable.

While most obligations are legally enforceable, obligations can also be equitable and constructive. Accounting concept SAC 4 states that an equitable obligation is governed by social or moral sanctions or custom rather than legal sanctions; that is, to do what one ought to do in the pursuit of one's objectives rather than only what one is legally required to do. An example of an equitable obligation is where a profit-seeking entity, based on moral considerations, undertakes to rectify faults in one of its products even where these become apparent after the warranty period has expired. As a result, the amounts expected to be sacrificed in accordance with this policy in relation to goods already sold would constitute an obligation. A constructive obligation is created, inferred or construed from the facts in a particular situation rather than contracted by agreement with another entity or imposed by government. An example of a constructive obligation is where an entity has a policy of paying periodic bonuses to employees even though it is not contractually bound to do so, and bonuses for the current reporting period have not yet been paid.

Accounting concept SAC 4 also outlines the importance of distinguishing between present obligations and future commitments. The mere intention to sacrifice economic benefits in the future is not sufficient to give rise to a liability. For example, the management of an entity may decide to acquire assets in the future. Such a decision does not, of itself, create a present obligation. A liability would normally only arise when the entity had acquired the assets and was obliged to pay for them. That is, future work remains to be carried out by the seller of the asset and non-delivery of the asset would break the contract. No obligation on the part of the buyer to pay the seller exists until the work is performed (for example, delivery and installation of the asset) and therefore no liability exists before that.

The other essential characteristic of a liability is that it has adverse financial consequences for the entity in that the entity is obliged to sacrifice economic benefits to one or more entities. Thus, the existence of a liability depends on the present obligation being such that the legal, social, political or economic consequences of failing to honour the obligation leave the entity little, if any, discretion to avoid the future sacrifice of economic benefits to another entity. Accounting concept SAC 4 provides the example where an entity places an order for the purchase of goods. This action would not normally give rise to a liability, since the entity would normally have the discretion to avoid the future sacrifice of economic benefits by being able to cancel the order. The receipt of the goods would normally be the event that would create the liability. However, if the goods were to be made to the specifications of the purchaser, it might not be possible to cancel the order after, say, the supplier commenced manufacture of the goods without significant penalties. In these circumstances a liability would exist when the supplier commenced manufacture of the goods.

There are two essential criteria for the recognition of a liability:

- it is probable that the future sacrifice of economic benefits will be required
- the amount of the liability can be measured reliably.

The term 'probable' means that the chance of the future sacrifice of economic benefits being required is more likely rather than less likely. This probability can range from virtual certainty to highly unlikely. An example of virtual certainty would be that wages during the month of June are due to be paid on 1 July. An example of highly unlikely would be that the company has guaranteed a loan from the bank to a highly profitable subsidiary; the future sacrifice of economic benefits would only occur if the subsidiary defaulted on the loan. While the first example would meet the criteria for recognition of a liability, the second example would not.

The second essential criterion is that the amount of the liability can be reliably estimated. Verifiable evidence of the amounts to be paid and the dates of payment are available for the majority of liabilities (such as payments to creditors and repayments of loans). However, some probable future sacrifices of economic benefits, such as law suits, cannot be reliably estimated, and therefore are not included as a liability at this point in time. In between the above examples are future sacrifices related to future warranty expenses on products already sold. These can normally be estimated reliably based on previous experience with the products.

## Equity

Equity is defined in SAC 4 as the residual interest in the assets of the entity after deduction of its liabilities. A statement of financial position comprises amounts assigned to the assets of the entity, amounts assigned to its liabilities, and a net amount, being the difference between the amounts assigned to its assets and liabilities. This net amount represents an element of the statement of financial position which is referred to as equity. Other names by which equity is sometimes called include 'owners' equity', 'shareholders' equity' and 'shareholders' funds'.

The approach taken in SAC 4 of defining equity as a residual is based on the view that equity cannot be defined independently of the other elements comprising the statement of financial position. Accordingly, the concepts of assets and liabilities must be defined before a definition of equity can be made operational.

Equity ranks after liabilities as a claim to the assets of an entity. In the event of the entity being wound up, all liabilities must be met before a distribution can be made to owners.

This characteristic implies that equity is a residual interest; it is the claim to the net assets of the entity – that is, to the assets after liabilities have been deducted.

**For your interest**

In the better-known recent corporate failures, such as One Tel and HIH the likelihood of shareholders getting a distribution appears to be very low. Keep an eye on the financial press for the outcomes of the investigations into these corporate failures.

## 9.9 Assets and liabilities: valuation and measurement

When we look at financial information, what do the numbers, the numeric values assigned to assets and liabilities, mean? The asset valuation question is both complex and controversial. You may intuitively think that the assets should be valued at what they are worth, but what does that mean? There are five basic methods often suggested for measuring (valuing) assets and liabilities:

- historical cost
- price-level-adjusted historical cost
- current or market value
- value in use
- liquidation value.

As you read the description below of each measurement and valuation method, think about which one you believe is appropriate, and in which circumstances. There is much variety and judgement within generally accepted accounting principles, so no one method, even the main one (historical cost), is considered best in all circumstances.

Asset and liability valuation is often controversial, partly because of a concern that the values should be useful in people's decision-making and a suspicion that historical cost values are not as useful as those that look more to the future. Would you drive your car looking only in the rear-view mirror to see where you have been and not look out the front window to see where you are going? One worry is that historical cost valuation, the most common method, leaves financial statements too much a history, when there are equally important needs to recognise changes in market conditions and to predict the future when making decisions.

Two controversies will serve as examples. For asset valuation, one issue is whether market values may actually be better than historical cost, at least in some cases, such as for the financial and monetary assets of banks and similar financial institutions. For liability valuation, an issue is whether obligations due well into the future, such as warranty obligations, should be valued at the 'present value' of the likely future payments (future cash flows minus interest lost by waiting for the money), rather than just at the estimated future cash outflow itself, as is done now.

Now let's turn to the five valuation methods.

### Historical cost

Historical cost, otherwise known as acquisition cost, values assets at the amount of the payments made or promised to acquire the assets, and values liabilities at the amounts of any associated promises. These amounts can generally be found by referring to transactional evidence, such as invoices, receipts or contracts. The ability to document the cost is a major reason historical cost is the usual valuation method for most assets and liabilities.

Another principal reason is that an enterprise will rarely purchase assets or make promises for more than the enterprise believes them to be worth. If you believe that an asset will provide you with $10 000 worth of productive capacity, you will not rationally pay or promise more than $10 000 for it. Under this method an asset valued at historical cost is valued at its expected lowest or most conservative value of future benefits at the date of acquisition. In most cases, GAAP imply the use of historical costs, unless some other valuation basis is more appropriate and is specifically disclosed in the financial statements.

For example, note 1 of BHP Billiton Limited's 2001 financial statements states: 'Subject to the exceptions noted in the paragraphs below dealing with valuation of investments and property, plant and equipment, the accounts are drawn up on the basis of historical cost principles.'

Some additional points in connection with this method are worth noting:

- At the point of acquisition, historical cost = market value = value in use, in most cases. (We assume that rational people would pay only what the asset is worth to them in the future in their business, and that in general such use valuation would therefore tend to determine the market value of the asset.)
- Much of the criticism of historical cost has to do with time issues. That a piece of land was purchased ten years ago for $50 000 has little meaning today. Is the land worth $200 000 or $100? That is something you do not know with historical cost.
- If an asset's market value later falls below its original cost, the asset may be written down to the market value. This violation of strict historical cost accounting is very much part of generally accepted accounting principles, largely because of conservatism. It is behind two important accounting phenomena: 'writing down' of unproductive assets, and the 'lower of cost or market' rule used in valuing inventories and some other current assets. You will see more about these later in this book.
- It has been said that many of the assets on the statement of financial position (especially the less liquid ones) are, because historical cost is used, valued not so much as assets but as 'costs waiting to be deducted from revenue in the future' or 'unexpired costs'. While this residual view of such assets is quite consistent with the profit measurement and consistency provisions of GAAP, it is opposed by some accountants, who feel that asset values should represent something more meaningful than just unexpired costs, that they should, for example, represent more current value using current prices.

Concerns over how assets are valued using historical cost have led people to suggest alternative methods for valuing assets and liabilities on the statement of financial position. Some of the more popular alternatives are shown below.

## Price-level-adjusted historical cost

This approach adjusts for changes in the value or purchasing power of the dollar (the measuring unit), rather than for changes in the values of particular assets. The historical cost values of the assets and liabilities are adjusted for changes in the value of the dollar (using economy-wide indices such as the Consumer Price Index) since the assets were acquired or liabilities were incurred. Though this is a venerable idea, first proposed early in this century, and has been used by some companies (for example, the Philips electronics company in the Netherlands) and by some countries that had high inflation (Brazil for one), it has not found much favour in Australia or North America. One reason for its lack of popularity is that, if historical cost is unsatisfactory compared to current values, adjusting the cost for inflation still leaves it unsatisfactory, only now less understandable.

## Current or market value (value in exchange)

This approach records the individual assets and liabilities at their current particular market value. It focuses on the individual values of the assets and liabilities items, not on changes in the dollar itself, as price-level-adjusted accounting does. It assumes that value is market determined and that profit should be measured using changes over time in market values. The argument is that if, for example, your house's market worth is greater today than yesterday, you have made money on it today, even if you have not sold it. If its market worth is less, you have lost money on it, even if you have not sold it. This method has been the subject of much writing and experimentation and has some theoretical attraction, but it does not seem likely to replace historical cost as the most popular method because of difficulties and costs in estimating current values.

Current value accounting can use either, or a mixture of, input or output values:

- *Input market value*, or entry value, refers to the amount it would cost to bring the asset into the company if it were not now in, usually measured by estimating 'replacement cost' to purchase it again or 'reproduction cost' to make it again. The same idea holds for the hypothetical reborrowing of liabilities.
- *Output market value*, or exit value, is the amount an asset is worth if sold now (in other words, its 'net realisable value') or the amount that a liability could be paid off at now, usually measured by quoted prices, appraisals and similar estimates.

## Value in use

This approach considers that value flows from the way the company will use the asset to generate future cash flows (cash generated from revenues net of expenses).

- Value in use is usually estimated by calculating the 'net present value' of future cash inflows (the cash flows minus lost interest implied by waiting for the cash) expected to be generated by the asset, or cash outflows it will make unnecessary.
- Present value is the future cash flows minus lost future interest implied by waiting for the cash. For example, suppose you are getting $1.00 in a year. If you had money now, you would be able to earn 10 per cent on it, but by waiting a year, you give up that interest. The present value of the $1.00 is the amount before the lost interest, the amount that would build up to $1.00 in a year at 10 per cent. That would be 91 cents. In a year, 91 cents at 10 per cent would earn 9 cents interest, bringing the total to the $1.00 you will get in a year. The present value (91 cents) is thus always smaller than the future cash payment ($1.00), which is said to be 'discounted' to a lower amount to remove the effects of future interest. More on this is in the appendix to chapter 1[illegible].

For example, a machine might be valued according to the products that it will make and that will be sold. Modern theories of finance and management accounting presume that value in use, measured by net present value value, is an appropriate method for managerial decisions about asset acquisition and financing, and many people presume it underlies market values, but the approach has been little used in producing financial accounting numbers.

## Liquidation value

Liquidation value is like output market value, but used on a 'going out of business, sell it for what you can' basis. It is the value that the company's assets would bring upon being sold and that liabilities would be paid off for, if the whole company went out of business.

It is used when the company is not felt to be a going concern; that is, if its continued viability cannot be assumed. Therefore, the reader of financial statements prepared on the historical cost basis should be entitled to presume that the company in question is a going concern. This presumption is an important part of financial accounting, but every year it turns out to be wrong for some companies that unexpectedly fail. Such bad outcomes remind us that good judgement is required in selecting the valuation basis, as with other aspects of financial accounting. A judgement that a company is a going concern and so should use historical cost accounting will turn out to have been wrong if the company fails. On the other hand, a judgement that it is not a going concern might be self-fulfilling: it might panic creditors and investors, and spark a failure no one wants.

## An example: Current market value as an alternative to historical cost

Let's look at a realistic and relevant example. In most countries there are many companies that specialise in acquiring and developing real estate for office buildings, shopping centres, industrial plants, housing developments and many other uses. As you probably know, real estate values are highly variable, with frequent booms and busts. Consider two real estate development companies operating in the Sydney market. Let's call them Oxbridge and Bramview:

- Oxbridge has undeveloped land, bought during a downturn in the Sydney real estate market, that cost \$5 000 000 and has an estimated current market (output) value of \$8 000 000. The company's net profit has been about \$700 000 per year in the last few years.
- Bramview also has undeveloped land, comparable to Oxbridge's, except bought during an overheated period of the Sydney market at a cost of \$11 000 000. Its estimated current market value is also \$8 000 000, and the company's net profit has also been about \$700 000 per year.

The two pieces of land are about the same, but the companies' historical-cost-based statements of financial position (balance sheets) certainly do not look the same:

- Oxbridge: undeveloped land, at cost \$5 000 000
- Bramview: undeveloped land, at cost \$11 000 000.

Also, Oxbridge will show a higher ratio of net profit to total assets, indicating apparently stronger performance than Bramview, because its total assets will be lower than Bramview's. Now, we could argue that this is as it should be, that Bramview has not really done as well because, in hindsight, too much was paid for the land. But another argument is that, since the two pieces of land are comparable economic assets, net profit should be related to the economic value (for example, market value) of the assets, not to costs that depend on historical events rather than currently relevant economic conditions.

Let's consider the idea of changing both companies' asset valuations for the land to current market value. Using the concepts from earlier in this book, what might be some pros and cons of this idea?

### Pros

- More relevant valuation for users in assessing company's value
- More useful in comparing companies with similar economic assets

- Fairer way of relating performance (income) to the economic value that managers are managing on behalf of owners
- More timely data than the 'obsolete' cost figures
- Not costly to implement (unless real estate appraisers have to be paid)
- Understandable to users who know something about real estate

## Cons

- Less reliable numbers, because based on estimated selling value of land that has not been sold
- Less consistent statement of financial position values, because real estate values tend to vary a great deal over time
- Not transaction based, and therefore not verifiable
- Not conservative in the long run, because land values have tended to rise over time, especially as measured in dollars subject to inflation
- Can be costly if valuations need to be paid for
- Not a generally accepted procedure, so users accustomed to GAAP would have to adjust their performance evaluation methods and rewrite contracts, such as for lending agreements and management compensation, that depend on financial statement information
- No effect on cash flow directly or through income tax because the land has not been sold, so there might be doubt that moving the financial statement numbers around in the absence of real economic effects would be very helpful to anyone

You can probably add more pros and cons. We don't know the significance (materiality) of the land valuation issue to the companies' financial statements or the income tax and other consequences of changing the accounting numbers. But you should see that the accounting concepts are useful in figuring out what would be the appropriate accounting procedure to use.

How might changing to market values be implemented in the accounts? Here are some possibilities (all ignoring income tax considerations):

1 Any difference between current market value and the value on the companies' statement of financial position (cost, so far) could be just included in the current year's net profit:
   - Oxbridge's land asset would be debited \$3 000 000 to bring it up to the \$8 000 000 market value, and the credit would go to a profit and loss account such as 'Other revenue', raising the current year's profit by more than 400 per cent to \$3 700 000
   - Bramview's land asset would be credited \$3 000 000 to bring it down to the \$8 000 000 market value, and the debit would go to a profit and loss account such as 'Other expense', changing the current year's profit to a loss of \$2 300 000 (more than three times the current profit).

2 The difference could be put directly into retained earnings. Oxbridge's retained earnings would rise \$3 000 000, and Bramview's would fall \$3 000 000. Oxbridge would appear more able to pay a dividend; Bramview would appear less able. As would also happen with method (**1**), this could paradoxically hurt Oxbridge more than Bramview, because the accounting change could produce pressure from shareholders for increased dividends, although there is no additional cash to pay such dividends.

3 The difference could be put into owners' equity but not into retained earnings, by creating a new equity account called something like 'Unrealised changes in asset valuations'. This would increase Oxbridge's equity by \$3 000 000 with a new credit

balance account, but would decrease Bramview's equity by $3 000 000 with a new debit balance account. Since it would not be part of retained earnings, the new account might not affect the owners' demand for dividends, thus avoiding the implication that the valuation change is similar to the kinds of events behind the revenues and expenses that form net profit and retained earnings. (Some methods of implementing current value and price-level-adjusted accounting that have been developed, and adopted by a few countries, have used such an 'Unrealised gains and/or losses' account.)

4 Perhaps the principle of conservatism should be invoked, whereby one of the above methods (most likely the first) would be followed only when the market value is less than the present balance sheet value. In this case, only Bramview would adjust its figures, because its cost is higher than current market value. The other side of the adjustment would probably go to profit as in the first possibility, but could also go to retained earnings or a special equity account. Though the companies' accounting would still show different figures for the same sort of land, using 'lower of cost or market' would be conservative, so users could rely on the asset values not being overstated relative to current conditions. This might be done particularly if a decline in market value indicated a serious impairment in the land's value. GAAP in most countries already require such a write-down if there is a permanent or long-term impairment in an asset's value.

5 Perhaps the historical cost numbers should not be changed, but each company could disclose the current market value of the land on its statement of financial position or in a note:
- Oxbridge: undeveloped land (current market value estimated at $8 000 000), at cost $5 000 000
- Bramview: undeveloped land (current market value estimated at $8 000 000), at cost $11 000 000.

This method provides users with information about the market values, but does not presume what they mean, as the other methods do. Users probably can make intelligent use of information as long as they know about it (that is, if it is disclosed). With full information and 'what if' analytical skill, they can adjust the financial statements to reflect the information in whatever way they consider relevant to their needs, using any of the above adjustment methods they thought appropriate.

Because any change from historical cost in the absence of actually selling the land would not affect cash flow (no proceeds) and, we will assume, would not affect income tax either, there is no net effect on the cash flow statement. Cash from operations would not be affected, nor would any of the other cash flow categories discussed in chapter 12.

## Australian position

Australia is one of the few countries in the world that allows upward revaluation of noncurrent assets. In Australia, companies basically adopt the historical cost basis, with the exception that they can revalue classes of noncurrent assets (such as land and buildings) upwards or downwards. That is, as described in chapter 8, they can value these assets at either cost or fair value. When a revaluation is made to fair value, companies must disclose the basis of the valuation, and whether there was an independent valuation or whether it is a directors' valuation. Unlike the market value system discussed above, the change in valuation does not generally affect profit for the year. This was discussed in more detail in chapter 8, where it was shown that upward revaluations are normally credited to an asset revaluation reserve.

## How's your understanding?

Here are two questions you should be able to answer, based on what you have just read:

1 The owner of Staely Industries Ltd is grumbling about the limitations of historical cost accounting for valuing the company's assets and liabilities. Tell the owner what other valuation or measurement methods can be used and what each does that the historical cost basis does not do.

2 What are some reasons that valuation methods other than historical cost have not replaced it in general use?

# 9.10 Notes and other supplementary information

The four standard financial statements are not enough to transmit all the information felt to be needed by users of the statements. Therefore, GAAP require that a variety of supplementary narrative and tabular data be appended to the statements. Companies may add more if they wish, but GAAP provide that at a minimum, certain added pieces are sufficiently important that they are considered an integral part of the statements.

Here are outlines of the kinds of information typically covered by the notes and supplementary disclosures. See the financial statements of Woolworths Limited in appendix 2 for examples, or again go to the annual reports on the Web pages of major Australian or overseas companies.

1 *Normally required by authoritative standards:*
  - **a** a description of the company's significant accounting policies, understanding of which is necessary in interpreting the statements' figures (usually the first note following the statements)
  - **b** backup details on any statement figures needing further explanation, typically including the depreciation figures, tax expense, long-term debts, share capital, employee entitlements and any accounts unusually calculated or very significant for the particular company
  - **c** information on some things not included in the figures, such as 'contingent' (potentially possible) liabilities, purchase commitments, lawsuits, relationships with associated companies or persons, significant 'subsequent' events since the official balance date (for example, a major fire)
  - **d** analysis of revenues and contributions to profit of any significant product line or geographical 'segments' of the company's business (for example, contribution of hardware lines versus food lines, or operations in Australia versus the United States). This is usually referred to as segment information.

2 *Also pretty much part of GAAP, especially for larger companies:*
  - **a** comparative profit and financial position figures going back at least five years, often ten. If a company changes any important accounting policy, it has to go back and change such trend analyses to keep past figures comparable
  - **b** an explanation of corporate governance for the company (required for listed companies by the stock exchange)
  - **c** a 'management discussion and analysis' of the decisions and results for the year.

3 *Still largely voluntary:*
  - **a** graphs and other pictorial supplements
  - **b** details about products, business policies, business objectives and other such details

**c** lists of senior managers and various policies, including training and safety, and human resource management

**d** reports on pollution control, environmental policies, donations and contributions to the community. This is often referred to as social responsibility information.

## 9.11 Managers and financial accounting standards

Managers may be interested in accounting standards for several reasons. On the positive side, standards should:

- make reporting managers' performance clearer
- make for easier comparisons with other companies
- reduce the costs of accounting (each company would not have to work through and invent accounting methods on its own)
- increase the company's credibility to important users of financial statements in general
- help to evaluate the conceptual and numerical effects of accounting choices and business decisions managers may have to make.

On the negative side:

- Standards may specify general methods that do not work well for or even mismeasure some specific companies or situations.
- Not all managers may wish to be measured clearly or to have their company's performance easily comparable to that of other companies.
- Some complex standards may be quite costly to follow for some companies.
- New standards may cause difficulty for loan agreements, bonus plans or other arrangements that depend on accounting information and that were agreed to before the implementation of the new standards.

With reasons like these, it should be no surprise that the top management of many companies (and of the firms of auditors who have the companies as clients) take accounting standards very seriously. Many companies seek to influence accounting standards through lobbying standard setters, lobbying securities commissions and other government agencies, doing their own studies of the effects of proposed standards, looking for audit firms that will help them avoid the negative effects they fear and even launching law suits.

## 9.12 Accounting standards in the public sector

Three accounting standards have been prepared specifically for the public sector: AAS 27 (Financial Reporting by Local Governments), AAS 29 (Financial Reporting by Government Departments) and AAS 31 (Financial Reporting by Whole of Governments).

The following extract from note 1 of the Roads and Traffic Authority 2001 annual report illustrates the impact of accounting standards on government departments:

> **(b) Basis of Accounting**
>
> The RTA's financial statements are a general purpose financial report which has been prepared on an accruals basis and in accordance with:
>
> - applicable Australian Accounting Standards;
> - other authoritative pronouncements of the Australian Accounting Standards Board (AASB);
> - urgent Issues Group (UIG) Consensus Views;
> - the requirements of the *Public Finance and Audit Act 1983* and Regulations; and

- the Financial Reporting Directions published in the Financial Reporting Code (FRC) for Budget Government Sector Agencies or issued by the Treasurer under Section 9(2)(n) in the *Public Finance and Audit Act*.

One major issue discussed in this chapter is asset measurement. Both AAS 29 and AAS 31 encourage but do not prescribe the use of current costs in the valuation of non-current assets. For example, AAS 29 encourages certain assets to be initially recognised at their written-down current cost and departments to regularly revalue certain assets to their written-down current cost.

The above standards do not specify what measure of written-down current value should be used. One method that is used by many government trading enterprises and the one recommended by the Steering Committee on National Performance Monitoring of Government Trading Enterprises is deprival value.

The following quote provides you with a background to this choice:

> The Guidelines adopt the concept of deprival value as the appropriate current value basis for GTE asset valuation.
>
> Deprival value of an asset is the value to the entity of the future economic benefits that the entity would forego if deprived of the asset. Under this approach, assets are valued at an amount that represents the loss that might be expected to be incurred by an entity if that entity was deprived of the service potential or future economic benefits of these assets at the reporting date. Thus the value to the entity in most cases will be measured by the replacement cost of the services or benefits currently embodied in the asset, given that deprival value will normally represent the cost avoided as a result of controlling the asset and that the replacement cost represents the amount of cash necessary to obtain an equivalent or identical asset.
>
> In applying deprival value concepts, the basic principles are:
>
> - Where an entity would replace the services potential embodied in an asset if deprived of it, the asset should be measured at its *current cost* (i.e. the lowest cost at which the *gross* service potential of the asset could currently be obtained in the normal course of business). This is the amount which an entity would need to receive in compensation to restore the asset to its former capacity.
> - Where an entity would not replace an asset if deprived of it, the asset would be measured at the greater of its *market value* and the *present value* of future net cash inflows expected from continued use of the asset. This is the amount by which an entity would be worse-off if deprived of the asset.
> - Where an asset is surplus to requirements, the asset should be measured at its market value.[2]

Deprival value accounting has been used extensively by Public Trading Enterprises (PTEs) over the last decade. Some examples include Sydney Water Corporation, Prospect County Council (an electricity utility) and Pacific Power (New South Wales' major utility generator).[3]

## 9.13 Homework and discussion to develop understanding

### Discussion questions

1 What are the three key financial statements in an annual report?

2 What is the purpose of the notes to the financial statements?

3 What purpose does the auditors' report serve?

**4** Go to the Web page for a listed company, find its annual report and describe the contents of the managing director's (or CEO's) report.

**5** What is the difference between a directors' report and a directors' statement?

**6** Define each of the following:
- **a** relevance
- **b** reliability
- **c** materiality
- **d** conservatism
- **e** disclosure
- **f** understandability
- **g** comparability
- **h** consistency.

**7** Provide three examples of trade-offs among accounting principles.

**8** What is the purpose of an external financial statement audit?

**9** What are the types of audit reports, and what does each indicate to the users of financial statements?

**10** Why is ethics so important to a profession? Is there really a necessity for ethical guidance for members of a profession?

**11** Ideally accounting information should be both relevant and reliable (SAC 3), but it is difficult to achieve both simultaneously. Why is this so?

**12** Define an asset. What are the essential characteristics of an asset?

**13** Define a liability. What are the essential characteristics of a liability?

**14** Describe each of the following methods for measuring assets and liabilities:
- **a** historical cost
- **b** price-level adjusted historical cost
- **c** value in use
- **d** liquidation value.

**15** Compare the concepts of value in use with value in exchange.

**16** In addition to the financial statements, what else is included in an annual report?

**17** Auditors play an important role in the financial reporting system, and their independence from their clients is an essential feature of this system. Why is such independence considered necessary? Why is it difficult to maintain?

**18** You happen to be walking past your boss's office and you hear her exclaim, 'These generally accepted accounting principles give me a headache! How can I figure out which ones apply to my business and decide how to apply them?' Wanting to impress your boss, you rush into her office and blurt out some answers to the question. What do you say?

**19** Argue both for, and against, the following proposition: 'Historical cost accounting is irrelevant to users' decision-making.'

**20** Write a paragraph or two discussing the following topic: 'The only thing worse than the large and complex set of practices, standards and theories that make up GAAP would be if there were no such thing as GAAP.'

**21** Your friend John operates a successful small business. He recently came to you, saying, 'I went to the bank to borrow some money for my business, but the banker said before the bank would consider a loan, I had to submit a "proper" set of financial statements. I'm not sure what that includes!' After wondering to yourself how your friend ever got this far in business, you explained the components that normally comprise a set of financial statements and described what each of them does. Outline what you said to John.

**22**
- **a** What purpose is served by the external auditor of a company?
- **b** Review the auditor's report included with the financial statements of any company you like. What is the report telling you?

- c To an investor, what value has been added to the financial statements by the auditor's report? Why?
- d Suggest some limitations of the value of the auditor's report that an investor should be aware of.

**23** Do you think governments should follow the same GAAP that business enterprises follow in their financial accounting? Why, or why not?

**24** Do you think not-for-profit organisations should follow the same GAAP that business enterprises do? Why, or why not?

**25** Discuss the major factors in today's society that have made the need for independent audits much greater than it was 25 years ago.

**26** Give examples of cases where there is conflict of interest between preparers of financial statements and users of them.

**27** Why are independence and an objective state of mind essential in an auditor? Are they necessary in all professions?

**28** Should a senior financial manager who works for a company, and who is a professional accountant, have to meet the same standards of professional ethics as does a colleague who is an external auditor in public practice? Why, or why not?

## Problem 9.1* Identify some accounting concepts and principles

Identify the accounting concepts or principles that relate to each of the following sentences and explain what effect the concepts or principles have on financial statements:

1. Users of financial statements should be able to believe that the numbers represent real events.
2. Financial statements should avoid undue optimism about the future.
3. It is hard to say absolutely that a company is performing well or badly, but you can evaluate its relative performance.
4. Financial accounting should be helpful both in understanding the past and looking ahead to the future.
5. The content of financial statements should not depend on who prepares them.

## Problem 9.2* Recognition of liability

BRK Limited is being sued for $3.5 million by a client for defamation resulting from statements made in newspapers by one of its executives. In each of the situations below, state whether a liability should be recognised in the statement of financial position.

1. BRK receives legal advice that it is unlikely that the claim will be successful.
2. BRK receives legal advice that the claim has about a 50 per cent chance of being successful.
3. BRK receives legal advice that the claim is likely to be successful, with damages somewhere between $500 000 and $3 million.
4. BRK offers the client $1 000 000 in full settlement, but the client refuses.
5. At year-end, BRK is informed that legal costs to date are $400 000, and will increase substantially in the new year, depending on whether the matter goes to court or not.

## Problem 9.3* Accounting assumptions

Consider the following statements relating to how we might account for certain transactions or events. What accounting assumption or principle underlies each?

1. 'Inventory is recorded at cost unless the net realisable value of inventory is below cost. In that case, inventory is written down to the net realisable value.'

2 'Accounting financial statements are primarily based on historical costs. They should, however, be primarily about the contemporary cash value of a company's net assets.'

3 'At the end of each period, a company has to calculate any salaries that have accrued and recognise an expense and a liability for that amount.'

4 'If a company changes its depreciation policy, it needs to disclose (in the notes to the financial statements) the nature of the change, and its financial effects.'

5 'Many businesses do not record "freight in" as part of the acquisition cost of inventory, but any freight charges of the period, which are normally small amounts, are expensed in the gross profit section of the profit and loss statement.'

## Problem 9.4 Accounting concepts

Listed below, in journal entry form, are certain unrelated accounting situations and (where applicable) the accounting treatment, that has been followed by the firms concerned.

1 YZ Ltd has purchased for $2 million a computer that it expects to use for three years. At the end of this period it plans to acquire a faster computer with greatly increased storage capacity for $4.5 million. The directors decided to 'provide for one-third of the estimated cost of a new computer during the current year'.

**Accounting treatment:**

| | | |
|---|---|---|
| DR | Depreciation expense | $1 500 000 |
| CR | Accumulated depreciation | $1 500 000 |

2 During the current year, geologists and engineers hired by the Duchess Oil Company revised upward the estimated value of natural gas and oil on property leased by the company. The directors instructed the accountant to record goodwill of $5 million, the estimated value of gas and oil deposits in excess of previous estimates.

**Accounting treatment:**

| | | |
|---|---|---|
| DR | Goodwill | $5 000 000 |
| CR | Gain on revaluation of gas and oil deposits | $5 000 000 |

3 The board of directors of Ryan Corporation disposes of a major segment of the enterprise, but omits any mention of this in the annual report 'to protect the interests of shareholders'. Profit is correctly stated and total figures in the statement of financial position are correct in total.

4 Zig-Zag Ltd changes its method of depreciation every three years, but clearly discloses the change in its published financial statements.

5 The financial year of Saturated Ltd ends on 31 December. It is now 21 January, and financial statements for the year just ended are being prepared. On 10 January, a cyclone destroyed a warehouse servicing the northern part of the country, and most of the inventories stored in the warehouse were rendered worthless. Because there is some doubt concerning the payment of the insurance premium by the due date, it remains unsettled whether the loss is in fact covered by insurance. This possible loss was reflected in the financial statements for the year just ended.

**Accounting treatment:**

| | | |
|---|---|---|
| DR | Cyclone loss | $450 000 |
| CR | Inventory | $450 000 |

6 It has been customary for HPB Ltd, one of the country's largest corporations, to capitalise and depreciate all newly acquired assets costing more than $200. This year, the board of directors has instructed that in future all acquisitions of less than $500 are to be immediately written off as expenses.

7 BNM Insurance, by action of the board of directors, wrote down the value of its head office building to a nominal amount of $1. The objective was to bolster its policyholders' confidence in the financial strength of the enterprise by obviously understanding assets.

**Accounting treatment:**

| | | |
|---|---|---|
| DR | Retained profits | $19 999 999 |
| CR | Buildings | $19 999 999 |

*Required:*

In each of the given situations, indicate which basic accounting concepts are involved, and whether they have been used appropriately. In those situations where you consider that the accounting concepts have not been used appropriately, discuss the effect of the departure on the financial statements.

## Problem 9.5 Accounting assumptions

Accounting practice is influenced by a series of assumptions. Consider the following journal entries:

| | | | $ | $ |
|---|---|---|---|---|
| A | Dr | Prepaid rent | 500 | |
| | Cr | Cash | | 500 |
| B | Dr | Accounts receivable | 9 000 | |
| | Cr | Sales | | 9 000 |
| C | Dr | Inventory write-down expense | 300 | |
| | Cr | Inventory | | 300 |
| D | Dr | Cash at bank | 2 000 | |
| | Cr | Share capital | | 2 000 |
| E | Dr | Bad debts expense | 240 | |
| | Cr | Provision for doubtful debts | | 240 |
| F | Dr | Cost of goods sold | 310 | |
| | Cr | Inventory | | 310 |
| G | Dr | Wages expense | 620 | |
| | Cr | Cash | | 620 |
| H | Dr | Income tax payable | 1 000 | |
| | Cr | Cash | | 1 000 |

For each of the following assumptions or principles of accounting practice, identify one journal entry from the list above that demonstrates the adoption of that assumption or principle. You may only use a particular journal entry once. Briefly explain how it demonstrates that assumption or principle:

**a** conservatism principle

**b** accounting entity assumption

**c** matching principle.

## Problem 9.6 Usefulness of accounting concepts and principles

Jason is a hard-driving, impatient business executive. You work for him and can feel the grey hair sprouting on your head from all the pressure. One day, he returns from a lunch meeting with his accountant and says, 'That accountant told me that there are accounting concepts and principles that tell me important things about why my financial statements are useful, why they are worth all the money they cost to produce and audit. I'm not convinced.'

Choose any five of the concepts and principles listed at the end of section 9.3 and explain to Jason why those five are useful. Make your explanations brief and to the point: Jason hates longwinded answers!

## Problem 9.7 Recognition of asset

The general manager of Ericnokoroloa Limited is considering spending $10 000 000 on the development of a new mobile phone that can also be used as a television.

What conditions would need to be met before the $10 000 000 can be recognised as an asset on the statement of financial position?

## Problem 9.8 Qualitative characteristics

SAC 3's 'Qualitative Characteristics of Financial Information' examines the characteristics of accounting information that make it useful for decision-making. It also points out that various limitations inherent in the measurement and reporting process may necessitate trade-offs among the characteristics of useful information.

***Required:***

**1** Describe briefly the following characteristics of useful accounting information:
- **a** relevance
- **b** reliability
- **c** understandability
- **d** comparability
- **e** consistency.

**2** For each of the following pairs of information characteristics, give an example of a situation in which one of the characteristics may be sacrificed in return for a gain in the other:
- **a** relevance and reliability
- **b** relevance and consistency
- **c** comparability and consistency
- **d** relevance and understandability.

**3** What criterion should be used to evaluate trade-offs between information characteristics?

## Problem 9.9 Conceptual components of asset cost

The new accountant for Mactaggart Industries is wondering how to calculate the cost of a new machine the company just installed. Explain briefly whether or not you think each of the following items should be part of the machine's cost, and why:

1. the invoice price of the machine
2. sales tax paid on the machine
3. shipping charges to get the machine to the company's factory
4. the cost of the factory manager's trip to the machine manufacturer's plant to choose the machine
5. the cost of painting the machine light green, as other machines in the factory are painted

6 estimated revenue lost because the machine arrived late
7 the cost of substandard products made while the factory personnel were learning how to operate the machine (all thrown away so as not to damage the company's reputation for quality products)
8 interest cost on the bank loan used to finance the machine's purchase
9 the cost of moving three other machines in the factory to make room for the new one.

## Problem 9.10 Determine asset costs from various possible components

Determine the costs of land and building that would appear on the statement of financial position of Smith Co Pty Ltd, based on the following information:

| | |
|---|---|
| Purchase price of plant site | 175 000 |
| Building materials (includes $10 000 in materials wasted due to worker inexperience) | 700 000 |
| Machinery installation charges | 40 000 |
| Grading and draining plant site | 20 000 |
| Labour costs of construction (Smith Co. used its own workers to build the plant rather than laying them off because business was slack. However, the labour to build the plant cost $40 000 more than outside contractors would have charged, due to inside workers' inexperience and inefficiency.) | 500 000 |
| Machinery purchase cost | 1 000 000 |
| Machinery delivery charges | 10 000 |
| Parking lot grading and paving | 60 000 |
| Replacement of building windows shot out by vandals before production start-up | 7 000 |
| Architect's fees | 40 000 |

## Problem 9.11 Asset recognition

State whether or not an asset should be recorded in the statement of financial position of LMR Ltd as at 30 June 2002 in each of the following situations. State the amount (if any) of the asset and any assumptions made.

1 On 15 May 2002, LMR Ltd paid $10 000 for an insurance premium. The premium covers losses incurred in the period up to 14 May 2003.
2 LMR Ltd paid $100 000 for a patent in April 2002.
3 LMR Ltd has just hired a new general manager who is an expert in the business carried on by LMR Ltd. With the help of this person the company is expected to increase its annual profits by $850 000. The general manager's salary is $450 000 per annum.
4 LMR Ltd purchased land in 1994 for $500 000. The market value of this land is $750 000 as at 30 June 2002.
5 On 29 June 2002, LMR Ltd paid $900 000 for a printing service business consisting of machines worth $500 000 and a list of 75 established clients.
6 Over the years LMR Ltd has created goodwill among its clients, whereby it now enjoys good relations with over 2000 customers. It is estimated that if the business was sold as at 30 June 2002, LMR Ltd could demand an additional $400 000 above the sale price of its physical assets.
7 A machine is purchased for $500 000 and costs an additional $200 000 to install.

## Problem 9.12 Recognition of assets

For each situation below, state whether an asset would be recognised in the statement of financial position. If the answer is no, state which of the essential characteristics of an asset has not been met.

1 Equipment is purchased on credit.
2 Cash is received from a cash sale.
3 A yearly insurance policy is paid in advance.
4 A department store receives goods from a manufacturer on consignment. A consignment is a selling arrangement whereby a company (consignor) ships goods to an agent (the department store) who agrees to sell the goods on behalf of the company for a commission. Under the agreement, title to the goods remains with the consignor until the goods are sold to a third party.
5 Land is donated to a sporting association.
6 A sporting association receives a grant from the local council to build a new tennis court.
7 A patent is purchased for cash.
8 Money is spent on research and development that is unlikely to lead to any new product in the near future but has the potential to lead to developments in the long term.
9 A company hires a new general manager who has the reputation of increasing profits in the first year with her new employer.
10 BHP shares are purchased for cash.
11 A council swimming pool offers free admission to ratepayers who provide identification.
12 A luxury resort paves a gravel road from the highway to the resort. The road can also be used by others to get to a number of sporting facilities in the area, including a golf course that is not owned by the resort.
13 A new printing press is acquired.
14 A piece of equipment has a written-down value of $100 000 and is no longer used by the company. It has no scrap value.

## Problem 9.13 Recognition of liabilities in the statement of financial position

State whether or not each of the following events would result in a liability being recognised in the accounts at 30 June. If so, what will the liability be called? If not, explain the reasons.

1 Taxes for the year ended 30 June, which are not payable until October.
2 Wages to be paid on 2 July to cover the two-week period up to 30 June.
3 The company sells washing machines and gives a one-year warranty to repair or replace any faulty machines.
4 A construction company receives a $5 million advance in June on a contract. The work will commence in July.
5 The company has signed a contract to pay its managing director $500 000 per annum (inflation adjusted) for the next four years.
6 On 1 June the company is informed that it is being sued for damages of $1 000 000 caused by a faulty product. The company denies liability.
7 The company will go to arbitration in July to determine the amount of payment to repair environmental damage caused by one of their factories.

## Problem 9.14 Recognition of various items in the financial statements

Samantha is the accountant for Prior Pty Ltd. How would you advise her to account for the following items in the financial statements as at 30 June 1998?

1 A production manager was appointed on 1 May 1998 under a two-year contract that specifies an annual salary of $50 000 for each of the two years. The contract can be terminated with six months' notice from either party.

2 The company pays into a bonus pool 5% of the profits reported at the end of June for distribution to participating employees.

3 A subsidiary of Prior Pty Ltd has just been placed in receivership. In April 1998, Prior Pty Ltd signed as guarantor for a $800 000 two-year loan to the subsidiary from a finance company.

4 Based on his experience in previous years, the customer service manager expects warranty claims against sales made during 1998 to amount to $70 000.

5 Gower and Co is suing Prior Pty Ltd for breach of contract. Samantha thinks Gower and Co will probably lose the case.

## Problem 9.15 Asset recognition

Indicate whether each of the events described below gives rise to an asset under SAC 4. If so, show the amount of the asset. What would the asset be called?

1 A temporary excess of cash is used to purchase shares in BHP Billiton for $8500.

2 $5000 is paid as a deposit on custom-designed equipment, to be completed and delivered next year. The total purchase price of this equipment will be $20 000.

3 A supplier sends notice that $900 worth of raw materials have been shipped by freight, with payment due in 30 days. The buyer obtains title to the goods as soon as they are shipped by the seller.

4 A customer places an order for $600 worth of goods.

5 A production manager has been hired to oversee the company's operations, with employment commencing next month. One-twelfth of the annual salary of $96 000 is to be paid at the end of each month worked.

6 Inventory is acquired at a list price of $1200, with payment made in time to secure a 2 per cent discount for prompt settlement. Cash discounts are treated as a reduction in the acquisition cost of the inventory.

## Problem 9.16 Liability recognition

Indicate whether each of the events described below results in a liability under SAC 4. If so, show the amount of the liability. What would the liability be called?

1 A bank loan of $10 000 is obtained, with the company signing an agreement to repay the amount in six months, together with interest of 8 per cent per annum.

2 Electricity used in the past month, worth $230, has not been paid for.

3 A $3000 cheque is received from a tenant for three months' rent in advance.

4 A company signs a two-year employment contract with a marketing manager. Employment begins next month, at a contract price of $150 000 per year.

## Problem 9.17 Effects of asset accounting change to market from cost

Beauport Ltd owns several parcels of land in the Sydney area. The area has been subject to wide swings in real estate values, and the general manager is doubtful that the historical cost basis is appropriate for accounting for the company's land and buildings. Give short but careful answers to the following questions asked by the general manager.

1 If we changed to market values for the real estate instead of cost, would that make our statement of financial position look better or worse?

2 Similarly for profit, would using market value instead of cost make us look more profitable or less?

3 Does it matter what we do, as long as we disclose both cost and market value somewhere in our financial statements?
4 In what way do the general managers' questions reflect a choice between the concepts of value in use and value in exchange?
5 What other bases for valuing the parcels of land and buildings would be available to the company?

### Problem 9.18 Asset valuation

**Pioneer tops off Hymix for $300 m**

Building materials group Pioneer International Ltd said yesterday that it had completed the acquisition of Hymix Australia Pty Ltd at a net cost of about $300 million.

'We estimate the benefit of gaining access to substantial aggregate reserves in the Sydney region adds about $60 million in net present value terms,' Dr Schubert said.

'That synergy and business efficiency improvement will, at a minimum, contribute a further $30 million in net present value.'

(Source: *Australian Financial Review*, 17 February 1999.)

***Required:***

1 How should this asset be valued in the balance sheet?
2 What type of asset measurement is Pioneer interested in and why?
3 Why do accountants record the value of an asset at historical cost and not net present value?

### Problem 9.19 Asset recognition

**Southcorp tastes harsh drop of red**

Southcorp Ltd is relying on its wine business to drive double-digit operating profit growth this financial year after more than $130 million in write-downs and restructuring costs in other divisions pushed the group into the red.

The group booked a net loss of $53.5 million for the December half compared with a $67.7 million profit last year.

Before abnormals, Southcorp's operating profit rose 14 per cent to $80 million. This result was partly boosted by accounting changes, which involves the company capitalising $4.8 million in interest costs.

(Source: *Australian Financial Review*, 3 March 1999.)

***Required:***

1 Explain what is meant by 'capitalisation of interest'. Why is it an asset?
2 Provide journal entries to show the process of interest capitalisation.
3 What impact will the capitalisation have on 1999 profits and later year profits?

### Problem 9.20 (Challenging) Judgements involved in accounting policy choice

Here is an extract from Seven Network Ltd's 2001 annual report:

#### Program rights

Television program rights are carried at the lower of cost less amortisation and net realisable value. Cost comprises acquisition of copyright and, for programs produced using the company's facilities, direct labour and materials and an appropriate proportion of fixed and variable overheads.

**Recognition**

Television program assets and program liabilities are recognised from the commencement of the rights period of the contract. Contract payments made prior to commencement of the rights period are disclosed as a prepayment and included under television program rights and inventories.

**Amortisation policy**

The consolidated entity's amortisation policy requires the amortisation of features and cartoons straight line over three years from commencement of the rights period or over the rights period of the contract (whichever is the lesser). All other purchased program product is amortised straight line over the lesser of 12 months or the rights period. Locally produced programs are expensed on telecast or in full on the twelfth month after completion.

In addition an annual review is carried out to identify any programs which are not expected to be aired. These programs are written off when identified.

***Review:***

1 Why are program rights an asset?
2 What judgements are involved in the valuation of the asset program rights?
3 Why do you think the amortisation policies differ between program types (for example, cartoons versus locally produced programs)?

## Problem 9.21 (Challenging) Materiality, reliability and conservatism

Some of the criteria involved in justifying the accounting method and the disclosure choices are troublesome to many people. Using the following opinions as starters, discuss the theoretical, social and ethical merits of each of the criteria commented on:

1 *Materiality*

'Using materiality as a criterion implies that some accountant has the arrogance to suppose that he or she can judge on behalf of all sorts of other people what information those people should or shouldn't have.'

2 *Reliability*

'Reliability seems to be an empty assurance. It refers to the financial statements being not misleading, but wouldn't it be more useful to go back to earlier times and ask the auditors to state whether the statements are correct?'

3 *Conservatism*

'Conservatism benefits the potential investor or lender to the disadvantage of the present owners and managers. How can accountants who think seriously about the value of objective, independent information consider conservatism as an even remotely legitimate factor in choosing the numbers to report?'

## Problem 9.22 (Challenging) Threats to an auditor's independence

Pat is the partner on the audit of Hardwood Emporium Pty Ltd. Comment on whether or not, and why, each of the following may be a threat to Pat's independence.

1 Pat and the chief financial officer of Hardwood Emporium play golf together every few weeks.
2 During the audit, Pat notices that the company has a serious problem with its computer system. Pat's accounting firm is then hired by Hardwood Emporium to do a major redesign of the system, for a large fee.
3 As part of the completion of the audit, Pat works with the company to determine its likely income tax liability for the year, including helping to prepare the company's income tax returns. Pat bills the company for the tax advice separately from the audit fee.

4 Pat's former assistant on the Hardwood Emporium audit is hired by the company as the chief financial accountant, responsible for preparing all the company's financial statements.

5 Pat is asked to submit a bid on the next year's Hardwood Emporium audit fee, in competition with several other accounting firms. Pat decides to submit a very low bid because the revenue from tax and consulting services would make up for the lower audit revenue.

## CASE 9A Woolworths Limited case

Refer to the full financial statements of Woolworths Limited on the Web. All questions relate to the consolidated accounts.

1 Find each of the following and indicate the page:
   - a summary data on the company's performance
   - b a letter to shareholders from the company's chairperson of the board of directors or managing director
   - c management discussion and analysis
   - d a corporate governance statement
   - e directors' statement
   - f auditor's report
   - g directors' declaration
   - h five-year summary.

2 Who is the auditor?

3 What are the main items covered in the auditor's report?

4 What are the main items covered in the directors' statement?

5 What are the main items addressed in the corporate governance statement?

6 What risk management policies are discussed?

7 What does the company say about corporate ethical standards?

8 Provide examples from the accounts of the accounting principles of materiality, comparability, conservatism and consistency from note 1 of the accounts.

9 Identify two different groups of users of financial statements of Woolworths Ltd.
   - a What decisions do they make based on corporate financial statements?
   - b What specific components of the Woolworths Ltd financial statements would they be most interested in?

## CASE 9B Should GAAP be extended to cover environmental reports?

Attached are some extracts from two articles on environmental and social reporting:

### Triple bottom line reporting: A new reporting approach for the sustainable organisation

*by Craig Deegan*

Triple bottom line reporting, a term coined by management consultant and author John Elkington, is reporting which provides information about the economic, environmental and social performance of an entity. It represents a departure from traditional approaches that focus solely on an entity's financial or economic performance. The notion of also reporting on an entity's environmental and social performance is directly tied to the concept of sustainable development.

For an organisation or community to be sustainable (a long run perspective) it must be financially secure (as evidenced through such measures as profitability); it must minimise (or ideally eliminate) its negative environmental impacts; and it must act in conformity with society's expectations. Obviously these three elements of the triple bottom line are closely connected.

Since the late 1980s, sustainability has become a central part of the language of government and business worldwide. The 1987 report by the World Commission of Environment and Development, *Our Common Future* (better known as the Brundtland Report, after Commission chairman Gro Harlem Brundtland, the then Norwegian Prime Minister), defines sustainable development as 'development that meets the needs of the present world without compromising the ability of future generations to meet their own needs.'

The Brundtland Report clearly identified that equity issues are central to the sustainability agenda. This includes both intragenerational equity issues as well as those associated with intergenerational equity (the latter meaning that globally, we must ensure that present consumption patterns do not negatively impact future generations' quality of life).

Many organisations are now explicitly stating that their focus is on longer-run sustainability considerations, which, although having implications for near-term profitability, are essential for long-term survival (at both the corporate and global level). For example, the recently released report of the Royal Dutch Shell Group of Companies, *Profit or Principles: Does There Have to be a Choice?* (available at www.shell.com), states:

'Shell companies have responsibilities to a wide range of interested parties, such as shareholders, employees, customers and others in society. And the responsibilities relate to our financial, environmental and social impacts on each of these groups. Living up to their expectations demands a long-term perspective, embraces many non-financial considerations and calls for balance when requirements conflict.'

Within Australia, numerous companies (such as WMC Ltd, RGC Ltd, Rio Tinto Ltd, North Ltd, BHP Ltd and Body Shop Australia) are also explicitly committing to sustainable development. For example, Placer Pacific Ltd's 1998 document *Taking on the Challenge towards Sustainability* states: 'We need to adopt sustainability, not as an added extra, but as a core aspect of our business strategy.'

(Source: Craig Deegan, *Charter*, April 1999, p. 38.)

## A survey of Australian accountants' attitudes on environmental reporting

*by Craig Deegan, Sophie Geddes and John Staunton*

### Abstract

*This paper reports the results of a study of Australian accountants' attitudes on various issues related to environmental reporting. Using a questionnaire, the study shows that there is a distinct lack of consensus on numerous issues relating to the environment. It would appear that, on average, Australian accountants only mildly support the view that environmental issues should be incorporated within business entities' financial statements. The minimal support for the recognition of environmental issues is proposed as a reason to explain the current lack of environmental reporting requirements pertaining to the environment. The paper further indicates that if the issue of environmental reporting remains voluntary, then left to accountants, future disclosures may be minimal.*

### Introduction

Within Australia there is a general absence of professional and legislative requirements for organisations to provide information within their annual accounts about their environmental performance, or about any environmental initiatives they may have undertaken. The only specific requirement is provided in 'Abstract 4: Disclosure of Accounting Policies for Restoration Obligations in the Extractive Industries' issued by the Urgent Issues Group (UIG). The UIG release requires reporting entities in the extractive industries to disclose information about the amount of restoration obligations that have been recognised and the accounting methods adopted in recognising them. Against this lack of regulation, it is nevertheless commonplace for Australian firms to provide some form of information pertaining to their relationship with the environment.

This paper explores potential explanations for the general absence of Australian guidance and rules being provided by the accounting profession in relation to accounting for the environment. Specifically, the paper considers Australian accountants' views on whether general purpose financial reports should provide information pertaining to environmental issues. This paper documents the results of a survey of Australian accountants.

### Evidence of Australian environmental disclosures

Even with the lack of environmental disclosure requirements, a recent review of Australian company annual report disclosures (Deegan and Gordon, 1996) indicates that numerous Australian firms do provide environmental information within their annual reports. Out of a random sample of 197 listed firms, 71 were identified by Deegan and Gordon as producing environmental information. Such disclosures were largely qualitative in nature. The disclosures were typically found within the companies' Chairman's Report, Managing Director's Report or equivalent. The disclosures tended to be very self-laudatory, emphasising the positive environmental aspects of the organisations without tending to disclose any negative environmental attributes. Assuming rationality on behalf of the management of the firms surveyed, those which provided environmental information must have considered that such information was of relevance to annual report users.

It is also interesting to note that even though the Australian accounting profession does not publicly seem to consider environmental issues are an important element of financial reporting, the adjudicators of the Australian Annual Report Award have placed environmental disclosures on their list of preferred disclosures. Specifically for those entities applying within the divisions of Business Enterprise, Public Administration and Professional Community and Health classifications, the adjudicators require the disclosure of 'the impact of the organisation's activities on the environment, giving factual data wherever possible' (*1991 Award Handbook*, page 34).

Hence, in summary to this point, there does seem to be a view that the environmental performance of reporting entities is relevant to a large cross-section of annual report users. Yet this apparent concern has not led to moves to place the environment on the agenda of the Australian accounting standard setters.

(Source: Craig Deegan, Sophie Geddes and John Staunton, 'A Survey of Australian Accountants' Attitudes on Environmental Reporting', in *Accounting Forum*, vol. 19, no. 4, March 1996.)

***Required:***

Do you think the kinds of accounting concepts and standards this chapter has illustrated as being part of GAAP can or should apply to companies' environmental and social reports? Discuss the pros and cons of such an expansion and interpretation of GAAP, given the reasons you think companies would want to produce environmental and social reports and people would want to get them.

## Case 9C Ethics of an accounting manager's behaviour

Discuss the ethical issues involved in the situation described below.

Leslie was chief accountant for a municipal council. The job included responsibility for the council's computer systems, which are mostly used for financial records such as rate billings and collections, budgets, operating expenditures, payrolls and services such as parks and swimming pools, but also are used by the police, fire department, welfare office and other municipal operations. Recent budget pressures and technological developments have created some information system challenges, so the council set up a task force to respond to the challenges and put Leslie in charge. The task force was specifically directed to find ways to save money that the municipality desperately needed elsewhere, in particular for services to several kinds of disadvantaged citizens.

Leslie was recently fired by the council for 'insubordination and incompetence' resulting from the task force's work. Two problems were especially irritating to the council:

1 The task force developed an integrated computer system for recording and responding to emergency calls. The system would connect the emergency response system to rate records and other information about citizens, to discourage abuse and ensure that the council billed people for all services provided. Considerable financial benefit to the municipality would result, but at the cost of delays in responding to emergency calls and substantially reduced

privacy for callers. Leslie was concerned about these costs, because delays could cost lives and loss of privacy might discourage needy people from calling. However, a meeting of the task force with the Finance Committee of Council, chaired by the mayor, resulted in instructions to Leslie to disregard those concerns because the efficiencies gained would allow other needy people to be helped with the funds saved. Leslie was not satisfied with this, feeling that the impact on emergency response was too high a price to pay, and as the person responsible for computer systems and head of the task force, wrote a confidential memo to the mayor stating that the Finance Committee's instructions were inappropriate and giving careful reasons. Someone leaked the memo to the local media, with sensational results that were quite embarrassing to the council.

2 As the council investigated the first problem, a second one came to light. Earlier in the task force's work, a list of abuses of municipal resources and services had been developed, so that the new system could be designed to reduce or eliminate them. The list included such things as people avoiding rate increases on home improvements, cleaning streets of important citizens first, municipal employees taking unauthorised holiday leave, sending several vehicles to one emergency call because of duplications in recording calls, senior citizens receiving more than authorised discounts on recreation fees and gifts by some contractors to council employees who send business their way. In the interests of task force efficiency, because not everything could be solved at once, Leslie had shortened the list and asked the task force to focus only on the remaining abuses. Leslie had thought a lot about which abuses to keep on the list and had eliminated several that potentially involved large dollars but seemed to Leslie to be socially acceptable, such as the seniors' discounts. Council members questioned Leslie's judgement on these issues and criticised Leslie for presuming to make the eliminations in the first place.

## Case 9D Audit reports

Read the article below:

### Meeting bowls up questions to the auditor

*by Damon Kitney*

A senior partner with Arthur Andersen yesterday became one of the first auditors in Australian corporate history to address an annual general meeting when he took the floor to defend BHP's valuation of various assets on its 1997 and 1998 balance sheet.

The auditor, Mr Fergus Ryan, was answering questions put to him by the Australian Shareholders' Association over the board's decision to buy Magma Copper in 1996 for $A3.2 billion, the valuation of BHP's copper assets and the value of the Beenup mineral sands mine in Western Australia.

Under changes to the Corporations Law passed by Federal Parliament earlier this year, auditors can now be asked direct questions by shareholders on the floor of an annual general meeting, following a practice that has become commonplace in Britain.

The only previous occasion on which auditors have been questioned at an AGM in Australia was in 1993, when Burns Philp's external auditor, KPMG Peat Marwick partner Mr Doug Jukes, appeared at its Sydney meeting.

Mr Ryan said yesterday the audit of BHP was undertaken at all the main operating sites of the company across the globe, and that the process was carried out through testing of the management's processes and procedures and inspection of supporting evidence.

He assured shareholders that the audit was conducted according to the auditing standard issued by the Australian Auditing Standards Board and that the report to shareholders set out in the 1998 annual report was 'unqualified'.

He said he could find nothing in BHP's financial statements to indicate that they did not give a true and fair value of assets and cash flows.

Mr Ryan indicated that the auditors were satisfied that the residual value of the Beenup mine was $134 million at May 31, 1998, and that there was no difference between the procedures employed to evaluate the reasonableness of the valuation of BHP's copper assets at May 31, 1998, compared with May 31, 1997.

However, he conceded that the process had been a difficult one because in conducting their assessment the auditors had been required to form a judgement on fluctuating commodity prices, which had varied from 118 cents a pound in June 1996 down to 90¢ in August, up to 121¢ the following May and down to 76¢ by August 1998.

There were also difficulties forming judgements on the appropriateness of estimated future production and sales for BHP's commodities and products which include copper, coal, iron ore, steel, petroleum, titanium, manganese and platinum.

(Source: Damon Kitney, *Australian Financial Review*, 23 September 1998.)

***Required:***

**1** In your opinion, is it appropriate for auditors to be answering questions at annual general meetings?

**2** What is meant by an 'unqualified audit report'?

**3** How did the auditors come to this opinion?

**4** What uncertainties did the auditors face and what judgements did they make?

## CASE 9E International harmonisation and new services of the accountancy profession

Read the following extracts:

### The development of international standards on auditing

*by Robert Roussey*

The explosive growth of investing and raising capital in the global markets has put new emphasis on the development of international accounting, auditing, and ethical standards. The worldwide accountancy profession, together with preparers, users, regulators, and other bodies, have been exerting great effort in the development of high-quality standards that can be implemented in the global as well as the domestic capital markets. The harmonisation of these standards is receiving greater and greater attention by the participants in these markets.

International standards on auditing are promulgated by the International Auditing Practices Committee (IAPC) of the International Federation of Accountants. A codified core set of international standards on auditing were completed and released in 1994. The release of the core set has led to a growing acceptance of the standards by national standards setters and auditors involved in global reporting and cross-border financing transactions. In addition, the growth of assurance services has led to the development of a new framework and a new direction for the work of the IAPC . . .

#### *The growing information needs of users*

While there are many changes in this area, three are most important. They are the information needs arising from:

- the global information technology and communications revolution
- the global expansion of business
- the global information and knowledge flow.

These three changes are not just increasing the need for information but also the need for its reliability. Most importantly, this information is not just financial in nature, but also relates to a broad range of other areas. (It is clear to the IAPC that the current financial statement audit model – the current basis of the ISAs – does not fit the new information needs of users. The solution was the development of a new framework described in a proposed international standard on 'Assurance Engagements'.

Part of the solution was to broaden the definition of information to include:

- nonfinancial information
- process and performance information
- qualitative information
- database information

### New services of the accountancy profession to meet those needs

The accountancy profession does not stand still when it sees new market opportunities. What are the opportunities for new services for the accountancy profession, and what does the IAPC have to do in developing new standards to cover them? Some examples that relate to the new assurance services framework are as follows:

- expanded reporting on financial information by directors and management, such as management's discussion and analysis (for example, the US SEC requirement for public companies)
- reporting on nonfinancial information by directors, such as directors' reports to shareholders on corporate governance (for example, the reports required by the London Stock Exchange)
- reporting on the results of processes by directors and management, such as directors' reports on the adequacy of internal controls (for example, the reporting required by the banking industry in a number of countries)
- reporting on compliance with laws and regulations (for example, the oxygen content in gasoline required in the US)
- reporting on qualitative information by directors, such as ethical guidelines (for example, the government contract industry guidelines on ethical conduct)
- reporting on database information, such as the reliability of data warehouse information (for example, a company's customer information database).

(Source: Robert Roussey, *CPA Journal*, October 1999, pp. 12–14.)

***Required:***

1 Discuss how the needs of users of accounting reports are changing.

2 Why is the international harmonisation of accounting and auditing standards important?

3 From your knowledge of the work accountants do, what role can accountants play in providing each of the assurance services mentioned?

4 Outline some differences in the type of report that might be provided for these new assurance services compared to a typical financial statement audit.

## Notes

1 This section is heavily based on material provided by Malcolm Miller, including Malcolm C. Miller, 'The Credibility of Australian Financial Reporting: Are the Co-Regulation Arrangements Working?', *Australian Accounting Review*, vol. 5, no. 2, 1995 and Accounting Regulations and the Roles Assumed by the Government and the Accounting Profession: The Case of Australia, working paper, University of NSW, 1996. Additional material was provided by Mahreen Hasan.

2 Steering Committee on National Performance Monitoring of Government Trading Enterprises, 'Overview: Guidelines on Accounting Policy for Valuation of Assets of Government Trading Enterprises Using Current Valuation Methods', October 1994.

3 A detailed description of their cases can be found in R. G. Walker, F. L. Clarke and G. W. Dean, 'Use of CCA in the Public Sector: Lessons from Australian Experience with Public Utilities', *Financial Accounting and Management*, February 2000.

Chapter 10

# Completing the statement of financial position

## On completion of this chapter you should be able to:

- provide the accounting entries for both short-term and long-term investments
- interpret a set of financial statements that include both equity and consolidated accounting information
- describe the types of liabilities that appear on a statement of financial position
- interpret the liabilities section of a statement of financial position
- prepare the accounting entries for liabilities and shareholders' equity
- explain the components of the shareholders' equity section of a statement of financial position
- prepare the accounting entries for dividends, bonus issues and other items affecting shareholders' equity
- describe the disclosure requirements for liabilities and shareholders' equity.

## 10.1 Chapter overview

Chapters 6 to 8 were about the 'left-hand side' of the statement of financial position (assets). To complete your understanding of the statement of financial position, we start with an elementary understanding of accounting for a company's investments. The remainder of the chapter is about the 'right hand side' (liabilities and equity). Most sections are not detailed, for two reasons: we have encountered many of the issues already when considering asset and profit accounting, and the accounting practices for many liabilities and equity items are very complex, beyond what this introductory book can sensibly cover. Therefore, the objectives of this chapter are to set out some important principles about liability and equity accounting and provide a general understanding of some topics that are covered more fully in advanced accounting courses. The goal is to equip you to understand what you see on a typical corporate statement of financial position and its accompanying notes, so that you will know the principles of how accounting is done for the right-hand side of the statement of financial position.

The right-hand side of the statement of financial position is where much of the complexity of modern financial arrangements has to be worked out. One complex arrangement is corporate groups created by growth of a single company into a group or by business combinations: acquisition of one company by another, and mergers of companies. Accounting for corporate groups also has a significant impact on profit measurement and on the asset side of the statement of financial position, and thus could have been covered earlier. The topic is in this chapter because it raises important issues that are specific to the right-hand side. It is an example of an accounting method that is very complex in practice, but has principles that are understandable without the practical complexities. It is also part of the goal of understanding a corporate set of financial statements, because, as we saw in chapter 2, most are consolidated, portraying corporate groups.

## 10.2 Intercorporate investments and corporate groups

Modern business organisations, especially large ones, are often groups of separately incorporated companies. You will have heard terms like 'takeover', 'parent' and 'subsidiary': these all come from the phenomenon of grouping corporations together. Lend Lease Corporation, National Australia Bank, Coles Myer, Amcor and Western Mining are examples of organisations that are actually made up of several, even hundreds, of companies. Such groups are linked in many ways, including:

- by formal ownership of all or parts of each member by one or more of the group. For example, Coles Myer owns Grace Bros, Coles Supermarkets, Liquorland, Target and K-Mart
- by internal patterns of performance reporting, motivation and promotion that encourage managers and other employees to feel part of the larger group (the general manager of Target may have been promoted from another company in the group and may be promoted to yet another, if he or she does well in the Target operations)

Most of the financial statements included in published annual reports are consolidated; that is, they are really those of groups of companies. Accounting for corporate groups is a complicated part of financial accounting, and is covered in detail in advanced courses. This book only introduces you to the main principles behind it and shows you how to apply the principles to do some basic calculations. In this section we cover short-term investments and long-term investments in shares.

## Short-term investments

Short-term investments are securities that management intends to hold for less than one year. These investments are held primarily to put extra cash to work. They include shares, commercial paper (such as notes issued by finance companies), government bonds and treasury bills, short-term money market investments and term deposits in banks. Not all of these are really intercorporate investments, in that there may not be any ownership or business relationship connecting the holder of the security to the issuer.

Because there is no intention to hold such investments for long or to try to influence the operations or policies of the organisations that issued the securities, such investments are included in current assets usually under the heading of marketable securities. The investments are valued at the lower of cost or market (net realisable value). Dividends and interest from such investments are usually also included in other revenue.

Wildrose Ltd has short-term investments costing $520 000. Suppose the investments' market value slipped to $484 000 on balance date. What would happen to profit, given the lower of cost or net realisable value rule? The difference, $36 000, would be included as an expense. Profit before tax would go down by $36 000. Working capital would be reduced by the write-down. The journal entry would be:

| | $ | $ |
|---|---|---|
| DR Loss on marketable securities | 36 000 | |
| CR Marketable securities | | 36 000 |

If the value of the investments then increased to $540 000, the value of the investments can be written up to $520 000 but not above this original cost.

Suppose instead that the investments' market value went up to $585 000. In this case, the market value of the security is greater than cost, but the unrealised gain is not recorded and the marketable securities are recorded at cost.

## Long-term investments

These are investments that management does not intend to convert to cash within one year. These include both debt and equity securities. Only the latter are discussed here. Long-term investment in shares can be accounted for using the cost method, the equity method or the consolidation method. The specific circumstances where each are used are discussed below.

### Cost method

Under the cost method the investment is recorded at the cost of acquisition. For example, if a company purchases shares for $500 000, the entry would be:

| | $ | $ |
|---|---|---|
| DR Investment | 500 000 | |
| CR Cash | | 500 000 |

When dividends of $20 000 are received on those shares, the entry is:

| | $ | $ |
|---|---|---|
| DR Cash | 20 000 | |
| CR Dividend revenue | | 20 000 |

Consistent with the treatment of other noncurrent assets (see chapter 8), the investment account can be revalued periodically.

## Equity method

When an investing company has significant influence but not control of an investee company, the investee company is an associated company of the investor. In this case, AASB 1016 requires the investor, in the financial statements of the investor, to account for the associate by using the equity method of accounting. Under this basis, the investing company includes in its statement of financial performance and statement of financial position its share of earnings by the investee company, because it is in a position to influence significantly that company's performance.

Under the equity basis:

- The investment asset is still valued initially at cost, as it was for the cost basis.
- As the investee company earns profit (or incurs losses), the asset is increased for the investing company's share of that profit (or decreased for its share of losses), and that share is included in the investing company's revenue. This is an accrual of revenue the investing company is entitled to, so it is taking credit for its share of the investee's profit (increase in retained profits). Other revenue is credited with this share and the investment asset account is debited, so the asset account is treated like an account receivable for the accrued revenue.
- When the investee company pays a dividend, the investing company receives some of the accrued revenue as its share of the dividend, so the dividend received is deducted from the investment asset account, just as collection of an account receivable would be deducted from the account receivable asset. The dividend is not called revenue by the investing company, because the revenue has already been accrued, instead, the dividend is deducted from the investment asset because it is considered a return of some of the money invested.
- There are some other more complicated features of equity accounting we will not get into here.

Before considering an example, it should be noted that the use of the equity method requires that the investor have significant influence over the investee company. Accounting standards define significant influence as 'the capacity of an investor to affect substantially, either or both of the financial and operating policies of an investee'. Generally, the higher the percentage shareholding an investor has, the greater the likely influence it will have. As a general rule, where an investor holds 20 per cent or more of the shares of a company, it can be presumed that it has significant influence over the company, unless there is evidence to the contrary.

Assume XYZ buys 30 per cent of the shares of ABC Ltd for $1 000 000 on 1 July 2001. On 30 June 2002 ABC records an after-tax profit of $240 000, from which it pays a dividend of $90 000. The journal entries would be as follows:

| **2001** | | $ | $ |
|---|---|---|---|
| Jul 1 | DR Investments | 1 000 000 | |
| | CR Cash | | 1 000 000 |
| | *To record acquisition of the investment.* | | |
| **2002** | | | |
| Jun 30 | DR Investments | 72 000 | |
| | CR Share of associated company's profits | | 72 000 |
| | *To equity account 30% of associated company's profits.* | | |
| Jun 30 | DR Cash | 27 000 | |
| | CR Investments | | 27 000 |
| | *To record receipt of dividends.* | | |

To further clarify the differences between the cost basis and equity basis, consider the following summary of how the two methods work (ignoring complexities including any asset revaluations).

| | Cost basis | Equity basis |
|---|---|---|
| Initial carrying value of the investor's intercorporate investment asset | Original cost | Original cost |
| Investor's share of profit earned by investee | Nothing done | Add to investment asset and to other revenue |
| Investor's share of dividend paid by investee | Add to cash and to other revenue | Add to cash and deduct from investment asset |
| Resulting balance sheet value of the investor's intercorporate investment asset | Original cost | Original cost plus accrued profit share minus share of dividends received by investor. |

Here is an example. Grand Ltd acquired investments in other companies on 1 January 2002.

**a** 145 000 shares (29% of the voting interest) in B Ltd were purchased for $4 640 000 cash.
**b** On 30 June 2002 B Ltd announced its earnings per share for the first six months of 2002 at $2.10 per share.
**c** On 10 December B Ltd paid dividends to shareholders at $1.60 per share.
**d** On 31 December B Ltd announced its earnings per share for 2002 at $3.90 per share (that is, $1.80 additional since 30 June).

The effects of items **a** to **d** on the financial statements of Grand Ltd at the end of 2002 are:

- *Investment in B Ltd (cost basis)*
  **a** Long-term investment asset starts out at the purchase price of $4 640 000 (cash reduced by same amount).
  **b** Earnings announcement is ignored for accounting purposes.
  **c** Cash received and dividend revenue are recorded for $232 000 (145 000 shares × $1.60).
  **d** Earnings announcement is ignored for accounting purposes.
  Using the cost basis, Grand Ltd's financial statements as of 31 December 2002 will therefore include for B Ltd:

| | $ |
|---|---|
| Investment in B Ltd (noncurrent asset) | 4 640 000 |
| Dividend revenue (in other revenue) | 232 000 |

- *Investment in B Ltd (equity basis)*
  **a** Long-term investment asset starts out at the purchase price of $4 640 000, the same as if the cost basis were used.
  **b** Upon earnings announcement, both investment revenue and investment asset are increased by $304 500 (145 000 shares × $2.10).
  **c** Cash is increased by, and investment asset is reduced by, $232 000 (145 000 shares × $1.60): the dividend is therefore deemed to be a return to Grand Ltd of some of its investment.

**d** Upon earnings announcement, both investment revenue and investment asset are increased by $261 000 (145 000 shares × $1.80).

Using the equity basis, Grand Ltd's financial statements as at 31 December 2002 will therefore include for B Ltd:

| | $ |
|---|---|
| Investment in B Ltd (noncurrent asset) | 4 973 500 |
| ($4 640 000 + $304 500 – $232 000 + $261 000) | |
| Investment revenue (in other revenue) | 565 500 |

## How's your understanding?

Here are two questions you should be able to answer, based on what you have just read:

1 If Gretel Ltd buys a non-controlling number of shares of Hansel Ltd for $460 000, what are the criteria by which management of Gretel should decide if the investment is to be accounted for on the equity basis in the financial statements?

2 During the year, Gretel receives a $45 000 dividend from Hansel. At the end of the year, Hansel reports a net profit. If Gretel's proportion of the Hansel voting shares is applied to Hansel's net profit the resulting figure is $78 500. What revenue from its investment in Hansel will Gretel report if it is using the cost basis? The equity basis? What is the 'Investment in Hansel' asset on Gretel's books at the end of the year on the cost basis? The equity basis? ($45 000; $78 500; $460 000; $493 500)

### Consolidation

Where the investor (X) has control over another entity (Y), X is referred to as a parent entity, Y is the subsidiary entity, and the combination of X and Y is called the economic entity. Control is defined in AASB 1024 as the 'capacity of an entity to dominate decision-making, directly or indirectly, in relation to the financial and operating policies of another entity so as to enable that other entity to operate with it in pursuing the objectives of the controlling entity'.

Whether an entity has control over another entity is always a matter of judgement, and accordingly involves the preparer (and auditor) of financial reports in exercising professional skill and judgement. While owning over 50 per cent of the shares normally results in the investor having control, control can also exist where, for example, the investor has the capacity to dominate the composition of the board or the capacity to control the majority of votes cast at a meeting of the board of directors or at a general meeting. This may occur, for example, when an investor has less than 50 per cent of the shares of another entity, but the ownership of the remainder of the shares is widely dispersed. Where control exists, accounting uses a technique called consolidation to present the parent company and all of its subsidiaries as one economic entity. While there is a consolidated entity for accounting purposes, there is no consolidated entity for most legal purposes. Rather, it is legally a group of separate companies with connected ownership. The idea is to present the group of companies as if it were a single entity. This method is thought to represent the economic and business circumstances more faithfully than would reporting separate statements for all the legally separate companies and leaving the user to try to add them together.

Consolidation uses a simple idea: to prepare the financial statements of a group of companies, put the statements of financial position and the statements of financial performance and other statements for all the companies side by side and, mostly, add them up. The consolidated cash figure would be the sum of all of the companies' cash figures, the consolidated sales figure would be the sum of their sales figures, and so on. To apply this simple idea to the complexities of modern businesses, a quite complicated set of GAAP for consolidation has arisen. In this book, the complexities will be left out in favour of a focus on four main issues in consolidation accounting:

- what to do if the parent company owns less than 100 per cent of the subsidiary's voting shares
- determining the asset and liability values that are to be added together
- determining any 'goodwill' arising from the acquisition price paid by the parent
- determining consolidated profit.

## Outside equity interests

Outside equity interests (also called 'minority interests') refer to the interests of the shareholders who have shares not owned by the parent company. For example, if a company buys 80 per cent of a subsidiary's shares, the remaining 20 per cent belongs to outside equity interests (minority shareholders). On consolidation, all of the assets and liabilities of the subsidiary are included in the consolidated statement of financial position. This provides the reader with the total assets and liabilities under the control of the parent company. The outside equity interest in the net assets (assets less liabilities) is shown separately in the shareholders' equity section of the balance sheet. Exhibit 10.1 shows an example of the disclosure of outside interests in the consolidated financial statements of CSR Limited. It can be seen that for 2001, \$97.9 million of the net assets of \$4081.0 million is owned by outside interests and the remainder is owned by the shareholders of CSR Limited (\$3983.1 million).

## Asset and liability values

The idea of consolidation is just to add the accounts together: the parent's accounts receivable are added to the subsidiary's accounts receivable, the land is added to the land, the accounts payable are added to the accounts payable, and so on. But some changes to the parent's and subsidiary's statement of financial position are made before that is done. One such change is that any intercompany balances are offset against each other. If S Ltd owes P Ltd \$40 000, for example, that would be on S Ltd's statement of financial position as an account payable and on P Ltd's statement of financial position as an account receivable. If the consolidated statement of financial position is to represent the two companies as if they were one entity, this \$40 000 amount is an internal matter to that entity: it is not owed to or receivable from anyone outside the entity, so it is not like the other accounts payable and accounts receivable. Therefore, it is just left out of the consolidated figures by eliminating the intercompany receivable against the intercompany payable. (Intercompany sales and expenses, such as management fees, are also left out of the profit and loss account, and any profit made by one company in dealing with the other is left out as well. Eliminating these can be complex.) Another example is the account for the parent company's investment in the subsidiary, which is also an intercompany account, so it too is eliminated in the consolidation.

## Goodwill arising on consolidation

What if P Ltd paid more for the shares of S Ltd than the sum of the fair values of S Ltd's assets minus its liabilities? This indicates that P Ltd is buying something else *not on* S Ltd's statement of financial position, something in addition to all the individual parts of S Ltd. This something is called consolidated goodwill, or goodwill arising on consolidation. It might represent good managers, a good location, faithful customers, economies

**EXHIBIT 10.1** CSR Ltd

**Extract of the statement of financial position as at 31 March**

| CSR Ltd and its controlled entities | Note | Consolidated 2001 A$ m | Consolidated 2000 A$ m | CSR Limited 2001 A$ m | CSR Limited 2000 A$ m |
|---|---|---|---|---|---|
| **Net assets** | | **4 081.0** | 3 819.4 | **2 822.5** | 3 140.5 |
| Shareholders' equity | | | | | |
| Capital | 22 | **2 322.4** | 2 647.0 | **2 322.4** | 2 647.0 |
| Reserves | 23 | **386.8** | 151.5 | **101.6** | 106.3 |
| Retained profits | | **1 273.9** | 860.8 | **398.5** | 387.2 |
| Shareholders' equity attributable to members of CSR Limited | | **3 983.1** | 3 659.3 | **2 822.5** | 3 140.5 |
| Outside equity interests in controlled entities | 24 | **97.9** | 160.1 | | |
| Total shareholders' equity | | **4 081.0** | 3 819.4 | **2 822.5** | 3 140.5 |

of scale with the parent, reduced competition or other factors the parent company took into account in agreeing to a price for the subsidiary's shares.

**Goodwill asset = Cost of parent's investment**
**minus**
**Parent's portion of (fair values of subsidiary's assets**
**– fair values of its liabilities)**

For example, if Very Big Ltd paid \$1 200 000 for 80 per cent of the voting shares of Not So Big Ltd, and at that date Very Big evaluated Not So Big's assets to be worth \$4 300 000 and its liabilities to be \$3 000 000, then consolidated goodwill at date of acquisition would be \$160 000 (\$1 200 000 – .80 (\$4 300 000 – \$3 000 000)).

Goodwill is shown among the noncurrent assets on the consolidated statement of financial position, and it is amortised over time by charges against consolidated profit (goodwill amortisation expense).

## Consolidated statements of financial performance

Consolidated statements of financial performance are prepared by combining the revenues and expenses of the parent company and all subsidiaries. This is done after eliminating any transactions between these entities. For example, intercompany sales and expenses, such as management fees, are left out of the consolidated statements of financial performance and any profit made by one company in dealing with the other is also left out. Amortisation of goodwill is also deducted. Any share of profits of the subsidiaries that belongs to outside interests is also deducted.

## How's your understanding?

Here are two questions you should be able to answer, based on what you have just read:

1 Where does outside equity interest appear in the statement of financial position? What does it represent?

2 X Ltd is the parent company with sales of \$1 million. Y Ltd, a subsidiary, had sales of \$500 000 which included \$100 000 of sales to X Ltd. What was the consolidated sales figure? (\$1 400 000)

## Example: consolidation examples[1]

To illustrate the above principles, here is an example. While the example is normally beyond an introductory accounting course, it is hoped that it will be of interest to the student who wants more information.

Assume that the current statements of financial position of two companies are as follows:

| | Massive Ltd | Piddling Ltd |
|---|---|---|
| **Assets** | | |
| General assets | 115 800 000 | 14 600 000 |
| Total | 115 800 000 | 14 600 000 |
| **Liabilities and owners' equity** | | |
| General liabilities | 83 700 000 | 8 200 000 |
| Equity | 32 100 000 | 6 400 000 |
| Total | 115 800 000 | 14 600 000 |

Further assume that the assets and liabilities of Piddling Ltd are expressed at fair value.

If Massive Ltd buys 100 per cent of Piddling Ltd's shares using cash, then Massive Ltd shows an investment in Piddling Ltd among its assets:

| | Massive Ltd | Piddling Ltd |
|---|---|---|
| **Assets** | | |
| General assets | 109 400 000* | 14 600 000 |
| Investment in Piddling Ltd | 6 400 000** | |
| Total | 115 800 000 | 14 600 000 |
| **Liabilities and owners' equity** | | |
| General liabilities | 83 700 000 | 8 200 000 |
| Equity | 32 100 000 | 6 400 000 |
| Total | 115 800 000 | 14 600 000 |

* Reduced by $6 400 000 as a result of Massive Ltd buying 100 per cent of Piddling Ltd's shares using cash.

** The investment in Piddling Ltd is equivalent to Massive Ltd buying the net assets of Piddling Ltd of $6 400 000.

To prepare the consolidated balance sheet for Massive plus Piddling Ltds as one economic entity, the assets and liabilities of the two companies are combined, and any intercompany transactions are eliminated:

| | | | Eliminations | | |
|---|---|---|---|---|---|
| | Massive Ltd | Piddling Ltd | Dr | Cr | Consolidated |
| **Assets** | | | | | |
| General assets | 109 400 000 | 14 600 000 | | | 124 000 000 |
| Investment in Piddling Ltd | 6 400 000 | | | 6 400 000 | 0 |
| Total | 115 800 000 | 14 600 000 | | | 124 000 000 |
| **Liabilities and owners' equity** | | | | | |
| General liabilities | 83 700 000 | 8 200 000 | | | 91 900 000 |
| Equity | 32 100 000 | 6 400 000 | 6 400 000 | | 32 100 000 |
| Total | 115 800 000 | 14 600 000 | 6 400 000 | 6 400 000 | 124 000 000 |

If investment in Piddling Ltd were not eliminated, the net assets of Piddling Ltd would be counted twice in the consolidated statement of finacial position. From the perspective of the shareholders in Massive Ltd, Piddling Ltd appears as the net assets that are included in the consolidated balance sheet, and there is no separate equity representing Piddling Ltd.

## Outside equity interest

If, instead of buying 100 per cent of Piddling Ltd, Massive Ltd bought only 80 per cent, the balance sheets of the individual companies would appear as follows:

| | Massive Ltd | Piddling Ltd |
|---|---|---|
| **Assets** | | |
| General assets | 110 680 000 | 14 600 000 |
| Investment in Piddling Ltd | 5 120 000 | |
| Total | 115 800 000 | 14 600 000 |
| **Liabilities and owners' equity** | | |
| General liabilities | 83 700 000 | 8 200 000 |
| Equity | 32 100 000 | 6 400 000 |
| Total | 115 800 000 | 14 600 000 |

Consolidation requires that the assets and liabilities of Piddling Ltd be combined with those of Massive Ltd. However, there remains an ownership interest in the net assets of Piddling Ltd, that is, 20 per cent of $6 400 000 – $1 280 000. This ownership interest is additional to that of the shareholders in Massive Ltd, and is known as the outside equity interest in the economic (consolidated) entity. Therefore, the consolidated statement of financial position is determined by including this outside interest separately from the equity of Massive Ltd.

| | Massive Ltd | Piddling Ltd | Eliminations Dr | Cr | Consolidated |
|---|---|---|---|---|---|
| **Assets** | | | | | |
| General assets | 110 680 000 | 14 600 000 | | | 125 280 000 |
| Investment in Piddling Ltd | 5 120 000 | | | 5 120 000 | 0 |
| Total | 115 800 000 | 14 600 000 | | | 125 280 000 |
| **Liabilities and owners' equity** | | | | | |
| General liabilities | 83 700 000 | 8 200 000 | | | 91 900 000 |
| Outside equity interest | | | | 1 280 000 | 1 280 000 |
| Equity | 32 100 000 | 6 400 000 | 6 400 000 | | 32 100 000 |
| Total | 115 800 000 | 14 600 000 | 6 400 000 | 6 400 000 | 125 280 000 |

The consolidated statement of financial position indicates that the ownership of the economic entity is divided between the shareholders of Massive Ltd and the minority shareholders of Piddling Ltd.

## Goodwill on consolidation

Finally, imagine that Massive Ltd paid $6 000 000 for its 80 per cent share of Piddling Ltd. In this case, the investment in Piddling Ltd is greater than the fair value of the 80 per cent of the net assets of Piddling Ltd that has been acquired. The excess of the purchase price over the fair value of net assets acquired is goodwill.

Following the investment, the balance sheets of the individual companies appear as follows:

| | Massive Ltd | Piddling Ltd |
|---|---|---|
| **Assets** | | |
| General assets | 109 800 000 | 14 600 000 |
| Investment in Piddling Ltd | 6 000 000 | |
| Total | 115 800 000 | 14 600 000 |
| **Liabilities and owners' equity** | | |
| General liabilities | 83 700 000 | 8 200 000 |
| Equity | 32 100 000 | 6 400 000 |
| Total | 115 800 000 | 14 600 000 |

Given that the value of investment in Piddling Ltd is greater than the fair value of the net assets of Piddling Ltd that are combined with those of Massive Ltd in the consolidated statement of financial position, an additional asset is created: goodwill on consolidation:

| | Massive Ltd | Piddling Ltd | Eliminations Dr | Cr | Consolidated |
|---|---|---|---|---|---|
| **Assets** | | | | | |
| General assets | 109 800 000 | 14 600 000 | | | 124 400 000 |
| Investment in Piddling Ltd | 6 000 000 | | | 6 000 000 | 0 |
| Goodwill on consolidation | | | 880 000* | | 880 000 |
| Total | 115 800 000 | 14 600 000 | | | 125 280 000 |
| **Liabilities and owners' equity** | | | | | |
| General liabilities | 83 700 000 | 8 200 000 | | | 91 900 000 |
| Outside equity interest | | | | 1 280 000 | 1 280 000 |
| Equity | 32 100 000 | 6 400 000 | 6 400 000 | | 32 100 000 |
| Total | 115 800 000 | 14 600 000 | 7 280 000 | 7 280 000 | 125 280 000 |

* 880 000 = 6 million – 0.8 × 6.4 million

## 10.3 Current liabilities

In much of liability accounting, the principal difference between current and noncurrent liabilities is just their timing. A bank loan due in five months is shown as a current liability, and one due in five years is a noncurrent liability. Their due dates may be the primary feature that distinguishes them. Similarly, an accrual for an expense that is expected to be paid in five months is a current liability, and one that is expected to be paid in five years is a noncurrent liability. Both are accruals used for profit measurement; they may also differ primarily in timing. Because noncurrent liabilities tend to be harder to estimate as the future is farther away, there may be more practical complexities for noncurrent liabilities than for current ones.

Getting the current liabilities right is important for several reasons. The total current liabilities are part of the calculation of working capital, and the working capital ratio is very important in assessing an enterprise's financial strength. Many of the current liability accounts are accruals of expenses, so measuring profit properly requires getting the accruals right.

### For your interest

When auditors are examining the accounts, they pay particular attention to ensuring that no current liabilities have been left out of the statement of financial position, because an understatement of liabilities results in an overstatement of profit (think back to the accounting equation). Banks are asked to provide written confirmation of loans, payments in the next period are reviewed to see if any are for liabilities and corresponding expenses that should have been recorded in this period, and accruals for unpaid wages, income taxes, interest and other expenses are checked.

As is true of assets, liabilities are significant both for their effect on statement of financial position valuation and for their connection to profit measurement. Their principal effect on profit measurement is through their association with expenses. Expenses arise from consuming the economic value of assets, such as inventory or fixed assets, and also from incurring liabilities. Such liability incurrence arises from expense recognition prior to the cash flow, such as accounts payable, income tax payable, employee entitlement liability and warranty liability, topics mentioned in earlier chapters and examined in this chapter. Liabilities are also sometimes associated with revenues, such as via the unearned revenue liability for revenue collected before it is earned, but their main importance to profit measurement is through expenses.

This section summarises some important things you should know about accounting policies for liabilities – their valuation on the statement of financial position and their connection to profit measurement. Only some parts will be new to you, but you should find the summary useful.

## Legal debts

Bank loans, trade accounts payable, wages payable, employees' income tax deducted from their pay and due to governments, other employee deductions and fringe benefits due, GST collected and due to governments, bonded debt, mortgages and other legal debts are recorded when incurred, and are reported at the amounts incurred (minus anything paid so far).

- Historical cost accounting applies here too. The amounts shown are those that arose when the debt was incurred. This is normally the same amount as will actually be paid, but sometimes it is not. (An example of where it is not, bonds issued at a discount or premium, is included in section 10.5.)
- There is no recognition of nonhistorical interpretations of the debt, even if the economic meaning of the debt would increase because of such recognition. Three things therefore not recognised are:
  - interest that will have to be paid but has not yet accrued (for example, if a debt is due in two years, only the interest to date is added, not the interest for the next two years)
  - inflation (although being in debt during a period of inflation is a good idea, because you pay back with dollars worth less than those you borrowed)
  - market value changes in public debt (for example, if interest rates have risen so much that a bond issued for $1000 but paying a now unattractive interest rate is now selling on the bond market for only $780, the debt liability is not revalued on the statement of financial position to reflect the lower market value).

- Unless there is evidence to the contrary, the company is assumed to be a 'going concern' and, therefore, debts are shown at the amounts that would normally be paid, and are expected to be paid, not at some other liquidation value that might be negotiated with creditors if the company got into serious financial trouble.
- For important debts, some of the legal details are disclosed (usually by footnote). The main details here are the interest rate on the debt (especially for noncurrent debt), any assets or other securities given, repayment terms and any special conditions, such as being convertible to equity.

## Current portion of noncurrent debts

In one way, current and noncurrent debts are just two parts of the same debt. In order to determine current liabilities properly, and conservatively, GAAP require that, if there is a noncurrent debt on which some payment is to be made within the next year, payment be included in current liabilities. So a single debt is split into two parts: current and noncurrent. This does not affect the legal debt in the slightest: it is just done for accounting purposes.

## Short-term accruals and other current liabilities

Accrued interest, estimated after-sale service costs, estimated income tax payable and other such estimated but not yet legally payable short-term liabilities are accounted for by debiting an expense account and crediting a current liability. Although they are not yet actual debts, they are reported in the same way as the legal debts. Such accruals are a product of the matching process behind profit measurement, and they are usually done very carefully, because if they are not, an imprecise 'cut-off' of the expenses involved would make both the current year's and next year's profit wrong.

An example of collecting *money the enterprise owes on behalf of others* is deducting income tax, superannuation contributions, union dues, medical insurance fees and many other possible deductions from employees' pay. You've probably experienced these employee deductions: you think you have earned, say $250, but your pay cheque is, say, only $180 because of all the deductions. Here again, the employer is acting as a channel to get your income tax and other contributions to the government, the union, the medical insurer or wherever they go.

Employee deductions have some complications that the accounting system has to handle. One is that each deduction normally has to be sent to a different place; for example, income tax deducted goes to the government, union dues deducted go to the union and medical benefits deducted go to the medical fund. A second complication is that the employer often has to pay 'on costs' in addition to the amount deducted from the employee. Superannuation and many kinds of medical and other insurance are examples. Therefore the wages the employee earns are not the only expense the employer incurs.

Suppose an employee earns $1100 a week and the following deductions are made: income tax $300, superannuation $50, union dues $40, medical coverage $65. Therefore the employee will receive only a net 'take-home pay' of $645. In addition, the employer has to pay some 'on costs': superannuation $45, workers' compensation insurance $15, payroll tax due $67. So, to the employer, the total cost of having the employee for the period is $1100 plus benefits, or $1227. Let's see how the accounting records would show all this (in the two entries below or one combined entry):

| | $ | $ |
|---|---|---|
| DR Wages expense | 1 100 | |
| CR Income tax deductions due | | 300 |
| CR Superannuation due | | 50 |
| CR Union dues due | | 40 |
| CR Medical premiums due | | 65 |
| CR Wages payable | | 645 |
| | | |
| DR On costs expenses (or include in wages expense) | 127 | |
| CR Superannuation due | | 45 |
| CR Workers' compensation insurance due | | 15 |
| CR Payroll tax due | | 67 |

In the above example, superannuation contributions are made by both the employee and the employer, which is common practice.

Current liabilities also include other credit-balance accounts.

- One, already mentioned above, is unearned revenue or customer deposits (also called revenue received in advance), which represent revenue collected before it has been earned. This was discussed in chapter 5. This is not necessarily a legal debt, but it is viewed as an economic one, in that the enterprise has not yet earned the money. In a business sense, it is also a debt, because it would be a poor business practice to collect money in advance from customers and refuse to either do the agreed revenue-earning work or return the money.
- Another kind of credit balance account is an asset that has gone negative because of an event that is not typical of the asset. Two common examples are a bank overdraft (overspent bank balance) and a credit balance in accounts receivable resulting from a customer overpaying the account. This last is like a customer deposit, but usually results from inadvertent overpayment or a billing error. (The enterprise may overpay an account payable for the same reasons; if so, the debit balance in accounts payable should be transferred to accounts receivable.) Reclassification of accounts between current liabilities and current assets is important only if the amounts involved are material to the total of either category.

## How's your understanding?

Here are two questions you should be able to answer, based on what you have just read:

1 Current liabilities arise for several reasons. What are they?

2 Why is it important to measure the current liabilities properly?

## Off balance sheet financing

Sometimes companies will arrange for sources of financing that do not meet the accounting definition of a liability or an equity and that therefore do not appear on the right-hand side of the statement of financial position (balance sheet). There may be a concern among users of financial statements that such sources of financing are sought by management because they do not appear on the statement of financial position and therefore do not affect the debt/equity ratio, the working capital ratio or other measures. Perhaps such sources of financing might not be disclosed at all, so that the user would not be aware of the financial commitment they imply. This concern led accounting standards to deem one such source, long-term leasing of important fixed assets, to be equivalent to a liability and require its recognition and disclosure, as described in chapter 8. This source of financing has therefore been brought onto the statement of financial position as a capital lease liability.

New financial arrangements are being invented all the time, and the impact they have on the statement of financial position, or might have depending on the company's accounting policies, is likely to be a factor in their acceptability and popularity.

### Contingent liabilities

Contingent liabilities are not included on the statement of financial position, but are shown by way of a note to the accounts. They include:

- liabilities of the company that have not been recognised because (a) there is significant uncertainty as to whether a sacrifice of future benefits will be required. For example, a company provides a guarantee to a lender for a loan taken out by a supplier and the capacity of the supplier to repay the loan is uncertain at the end of the financial year, or (b) the amount of the obligation cannot be measured reliably. An example is a law suit against a company where the likely amount to be paid on the claim cannot be reliably determined
- where there is significant uncertainty as to whether an obligation presently exists and therefore the item has not been recognised as a liability. An example is a dispute with the taxation department, where legal advice suggests that the company will win the dispute.

However, it should be noted that in chapter 9 a liability would not be recognised as a contingent liability merely because estimation procedures were necessary to determine its amount. In most situations, the use of estimation techniques will provide measurements that are sufficiently reliable to enable a liability to be recognised.

## 10.4 Goods and Services Tax (GST)

We have already seen that companies pay tax levied on their profit to the Australian government. Like other expenses, income tax expense is subtracted from revenue to determine the financial performance of a company over a period, that is, the company's net profit or loss.

While company taxes have a direct impact on financial performance, companies and other organisations can also be affected by the other two types of tax that form part of the taxation system – direct (personal) and indirect taxes. While a company is not itself liable for these types of tax, it acts as an *agent* for the Australian Taxation Office in their collection and remittance. For example, as was discussed in section 10.3, while employees are individually liable for personal income tax on their salaries or wages, companies are required to withhold this tax when they pay their employees and remit it to the Australian Taxation Office under the Pay As You Go (PAYG) withholding system. From the company's perspective, salaries and wages paid to employees is an operating expense. That portion of the salary or wage that is withheld does not change the operating expense of the company, but does create a liability to a third party, the Australian Taxation Office (ATO).

Companies are also affected by indirect taxes. The most common examples of indirect taxes are sales tax (usually levied on the final retail sale of finished goods) and what are called value added taxes. Many countries, including New Zealand, the UK and Canada, operate a system of value added tax. In Australia, a 10 per cent value added tax, known as a goods and services tax (GST), was introduced on 1 July 2000.

Formally, a GST is a broad-based consumption tax – 'broad-based' because it applies to most transactions in the economy and 'consumption' because it applies to the amounts spent for goods, services and activities.

Exhibit 10.2 highlights the key features of the Australian GST system. The choices available to a business under the GST system depend on turnover, a concept roughly equivalent to total annual revenue. If a business is registered for the GST, it collects 10 per cent tax on its sales on behalf of the government. Smaller businesses have the choice of accounting for GST on either a cash or accrual basis; this choice is independent of whether the business uses cash or accrual accounting to prepare its financial statements. Smaller businesses are also able to remit amounts to the ATO quarterly or monthly. As of February 2001, some businesses with an annual turnover of $2 million or less can choose to pay GST instalments quarterly and lodge a GST return annually. Large businesses account for the GST on an accrual basis and remit amounts monthly.

GST is recorded in the accounting system as part of the process of preparing the statement of financial position and to support the preparation of a business activity statement (BAS), which includes a GST return and is submitted to the ATO.

## How the GST system works

The following examples illustrate how the GST system operates.

The simplest case is that of a supply chain with two parties. Let's assume that R. Chan provides $1000 of consulting services to M. Baker. Under the GST system, the consulting services represent a taxable supply (services are supplied by R. Chan to M. Baker) and 10 per cent GST is added to the price paid for the service:

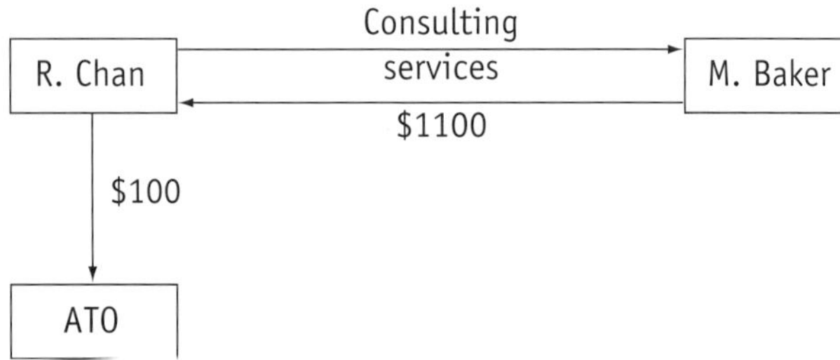


**Figure 10.1 Simple model of GST system as it affects two parties**

We see that M. Baker acquires consulting services in exchange for $1100. From the perspective of R. Chan, $1100 is to be collected; $1000 of this amount represents revenue for the services supplied and $100 represents the GST collected on behalf of the ATO, which is to be remitted at the end of the tax period. The following journal entry records the transaction:

| | | $ | $ |
|---|---|---|---|
| DR | Cash or accounts receivable | 1 100 | |
| CR | Consulting revenue | | 1 000 |
| CR | GST payable | | 100 |

The GST payable account is a current liability account that accumulates the GST collected on all applicable sales. When the GST due is paid to the ATO, the liability account is reduced. At any date, the GST payable account shows what has been collected, but not

## EXHIBIT 10.2 Goods and Services Tax (GST)

**Simplified flow chart showing the main elements of the GST system for Australian business**

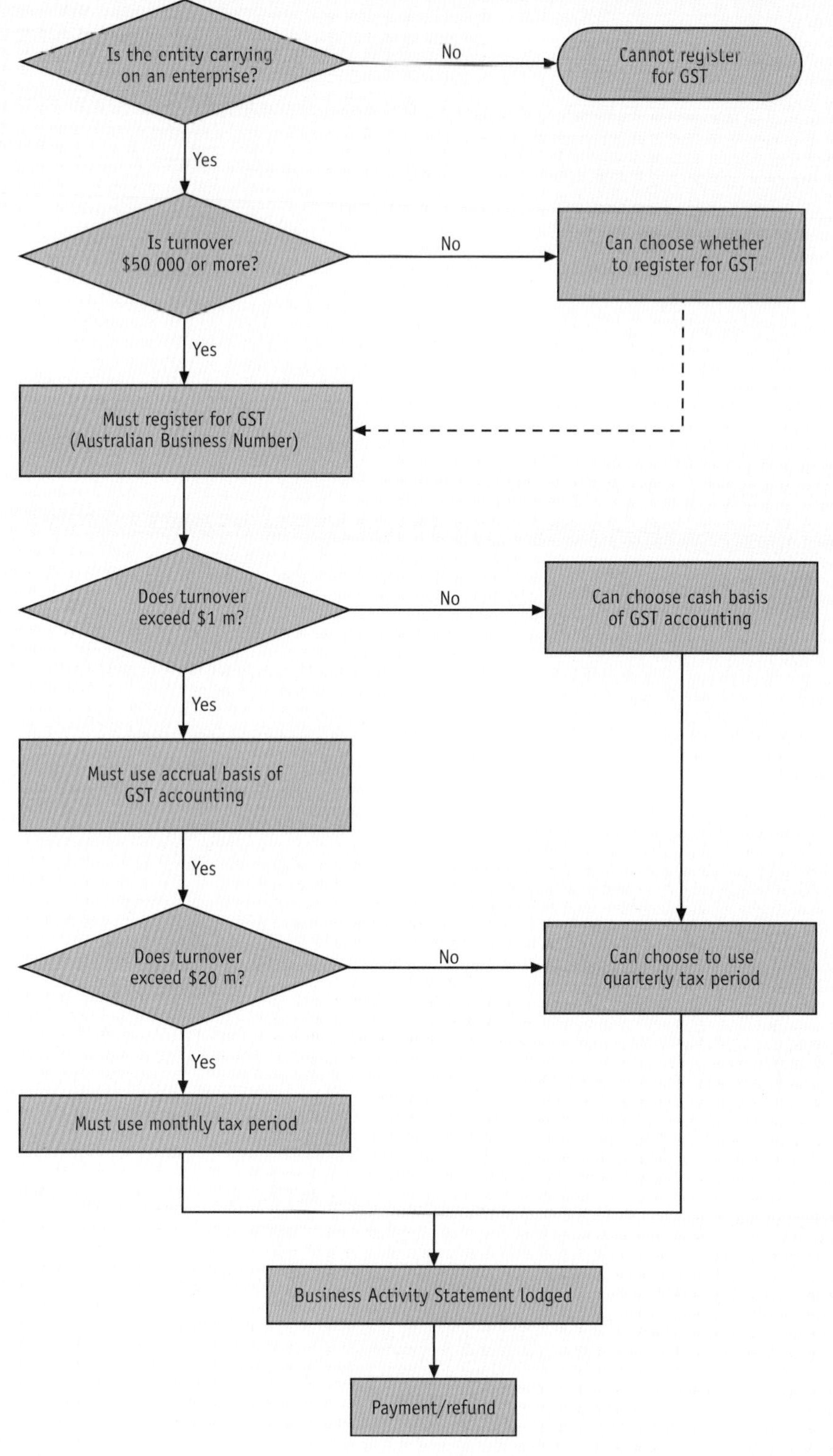

yet remitted. It is, therefore, a control account for the seller's obligation to the government. It shows the way the seller has been a channel for the government's money, because it goes up when sales subject to GST are made and down when the money is sent to the ATO.

Because M. Baker is the final consumer, this example is similar to the operation of a sales tax system, except that the tax is being levied on the provision of a service. However, things are usually a bit more complicated than this, because R. Chan is likely to have to pay GST on purchases made from suppliers.

Let's assume that R. Chan pays $44 for paper supplies from P. Lee. A value added tax system such as the GST operates through the collection of GST each time a taxable supply is made in the supply chain. In this case, the paper represents a taxable supply, so GST is included in the price paid by R. Chan. To work out the amount of GST, we can divide the price by 11: $44/11 = $4. However, because R. Chan is registered for GST and intends to use the paper for business purposes, it becomes a creditable acquisition for R. Chan. This means that R. Chan is able to deduct any GST on its own purchases and expenses from the amount to be sent to the ATO. Therefore, the GST due to the government is the difference between GST collected and GST paid. In this way, the effective responsibility for the payment of GST is shifted along the supply chain.

If we extend our simple example, we can see how this works:

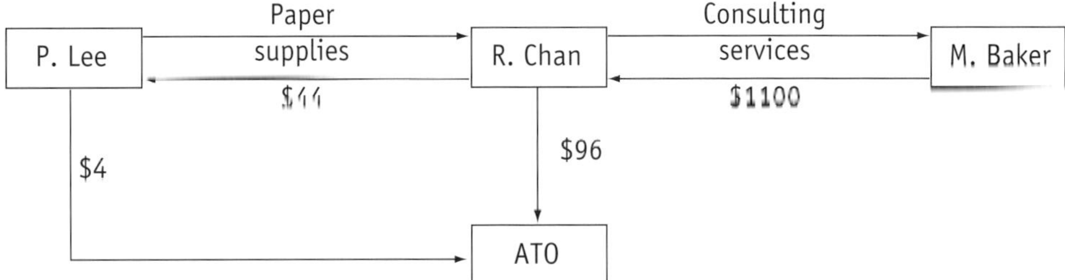


**Figure 10.2** Simple example of how the GST system works along the supply chain.

There are a number of things to notice in this example:

- P. Lee has no business inputs, because it is the first link in the supply chain, and therefore has no creditable acquisitions. On making a taxable supply to R. Chan, P. Lee collects $4 GST and remits the amount to the ATO.
- R. Chan pays GST on its acquisitions and collects GST when it supplies consulting services. The amount remitted to the ATO is the difference between the GST paid and collected in any tax period. In the above example, R. Chan pays $4 GST to P. Lee and collects $100 from M. Baker. The difference of $96 is remitted to the ATO.
- M. Baker pays $100 GST on the consulting services bought from R. Chan. Because M. Baker is the final consumer, there is no GST collection to offset the GST payment.
- The ATO continues to receive a total of $100.

So how does R. Chan record its purchase of paper supplies? The first thing to note is that part of the $44 paid to P. Lee is for GST, and that this provides an input tax credit of $4 for R. Chan. The paper itself is valued at $40. The following journal entry records the transaction:

| | | $ | $ |
|---|---|---|---|
| DR | Supplies expense/asset | 40 | |
| DR | GST recoverable | 4 | |
| CR | Cash/payable | | 44 |

Assuming that the GST collected in a business is usually greater than the GST paid, the GST recoverable account could be treated as a contra account to the GST payable account. It is possible for the GST payable account to be a debit (an asset), if the company makes particularly large purchases and has small sales in a given period. For example, this might occur if a business acquires noncurrent assets where the GST paid is claimed immediately as an input tax credit in the current tax period. Alternatively, the GST recoverable account could be classified as a current asset, and only the net amount of the GST recoverable and GST payable accounts appears in the statement of financial position.

If a business does not maintain extensive subsidiary records for GST, it might be easier for that business to clear the GST recoverable and GST payable accounts to another account at the end of a tax period. This allows a record to be kept of the net amount owing or refundable for a period in such a clearing account, and resets the other accounts to accumulate information for the new period.

Our discussion suggests a number of generalisations:

- GST is not a business tax. The main impact for business might be on cash flow planning because of differences in timing between GST paid and collected (assuming no significant elasticity effects or uncompensated administrative costs).
- The final consumer bears the cost, because he or she is not able to claim input tax credits on his or her acquisitions.
- If input tax credits are available, any GST paid does not become part of an expense or the cost of acquisition of an asset.
- Any GST collected does not form part of a business's revenue.
- GST is collected at each point in the supply chain, bringing forward the collection of tax.

This same pattern is repeated in every enterprise operating in the Australian economy!

## GST: three special cases

Let's consider three special cases:

1. *Private use.* The GST system allows input tax credits to be claimed only to the extent that the acquisition relates to a business purpose or the operations of an enterprise.
2. *GST-free supplies.* In this case, GST is not charged when goods or services are supplied to customers, but input tax credits can be claimed for any GST paid on business inputs. Examples of GST-free supplies are fresh food items, health and medical care, education services and child care.
3. *Input taxed supplies.* Here GST is not charged when goods or services are supplied to customers but there is no entitlement to input tax credits. Effectively, the business is deemed to be the 'final consumer'. Examples include financial services and residential rents.

To illustrate the effect of the last two cases, let's redo the journal entries we recorded in our last example. In the case of GST-free supplies, the journal entries become:

| | $ | $ |
|---|---|---|
| DR Cash or accounts receivable | 1 000 | |
| CR Revenue | | 1 000 |
| | | |
| DR Supplies expense/asset | 40 | |
| DR GST recoverable | 4 | |
| CR Cash/payable | | 44 |

Note that there is no GST collected on supply, but GST can be recovered for business inputs.

In contrast, the journal entries for input taxed supplies are:

| | $ | $ |
|---|---|---|
| DR Cash or accounts receivable | 1 000 | |
| CR Revenue | | 1 000 |
| | | |
| DR Supplies expense/asset | 44 | |
| CR Cash/payable | | 44 |

Note that there is no GST collected on supply, and the full amount paid or payable for inputs is the expense recognised or cost of acquisition for an asset.

There is much more to the operation of the tax system than can be covered in this brief introduction. For those who are interested, current information can be obtained at: http://www.taxreform.ato.gov.au. As you will find, tax is a very challenging and dynamic area!

# 10.5 Noncurrent liabilities

## Long-term debts

Debts that are due more than a year into the future are included in noncurrent liabilities, minus any part due within the next year, which is included in current liabilities. Most non-current liabilities are supported by specific agreements about repayment terms between the enterprise and its lenders. These usually involve some security to protect the lender. There are several common kinds of security, which can exist in various combinations with each other:

- a mortgage held by the lender on the enterprise's property or equipment so that the lender can claim title to those assets if the enterprise does not make the agreed payments on time
- a debenture, which is a more general kind of right by the lender to take some degree of control over the enterprise if necessary
- a loan agreement (or a clause in the debenture trust deed), which has a set of specifications that the enterprise must meet, otherwise the lender can demand payment or take other action. Such specifications may be that the enterprise maintains a particular level of working capital, a particular working capital ratio or a particular debt/equity ratio, or meet other conditions defined on the financial statements. (Such agreements may tempt management to choose accounting policies designed to help the financial statements meet the agreed specifications.)
- a fourth kind of security, often used by banks with smaller company borrowers, whereby the owners of the company are asked to provide personal guarantees in case the enterprise's assets are not sufficient to repay the debt if trouble comes. GAAP require some disclosure of important security on long-term debts, plus repayment terms and some other details, so the financial statement notes about long-term debts can be extensive.

Some long-term debts, such as loans from shareholders, may be unsecured and have an unspecified due date, which will also be disclosed if informative.

A common kind of noncurrent debt is an agreement to pay for an asset over a period of time. For land or buildings, such an agreement is usually a mortgage. But equipment and vehicles may also be acquired with such agreements. These are usually not large in comparison to other noncurrent liabilities, so there may not be much disclosure about them. Another way of acquiring economic assets, explained in section 8.9, is via capital leases. The liability for such leases, once recorded by the process described in section 8.9, is included in noncurrent (and current) liabilities just as if it was a regular debt, because the accounting principle is that they are economic debts.

## Discounts or premiums on noncurrent debts

Sometimes noncurrent debt is issued at a discount or a premium. This is easiest to explain with bonded debt. A bond is an instrument, similar to a share, that usually can be traded among investors, but instead of carrying ownership rights, carries a portion of a mortgage, indenture agreement or other security, has a limited term before it must be repaid and has the right to interest in the meantime. Suppose the enterprise decides to borrow using a bond issue composed of $1000 bonds carrying 7 per cent interest. When the bond issue is all ready, interest rates in the market for such bonds may have risen a bit, say to 8 per cent. Lenders would not want a 7 per cent bond. So the enterprise sells the bonds at a discount, a lower price such that the amount the lender pays will earn 8 per cent. The lender gives the company less than $1000 for each bond, and that lower amount is such that the $70 interest (7 per cent of $1000) represents the 8 per cent the lender wants. If the interest rates have fallen, say to 6 per cent, the lender will be willing to pay more than $1000 for each bond, such that the $70 interest represents the 6 per cent return the lender wants. So the enterprise gets a premium for the bonds, more than $1000 each. (This explanation is a little simplified; the present value calculations behind bond prices are included in the appendix of chapter 13.)

Here is an illustration: an issue of 10 000 $1000 bonds, thus having a total legal debt of $10 000 000, which sold for a total of either $8 760 000 (a discount) or $11 180 000 (a premium). (The selling prices can be said to be the appropriate price for that bond at prevailing market interest rates, so in the first case, the bond pays interest at a rate below market rates, and in the second case, pays at a rate above market rates.) At the date of issue of the bonds, the proceeds and discount or premium are recorded this way:

| | $ | $ | | $ | $ |
|---|---|---|---|---|---|
| **Discount** | | | **Premium** | | |
| DR Cash (proceeds) | 8 760 000 | | DR Cash (proceeds) | 11 180 000 | |
| CR Bonded debt | | 10 000 000 | CR Bonded debt | | 10 000 000 |
| DR Bond discount | 1 240 000 | | CR Bond premium | | 1 180 000 |

The bonded debt account is a liability. The premium or discount account works as a contra account, to change the valuation of the liability without changing the legal debt account. (The premium is a credit balance account, so it is not opposite in sign, as are contra accounts, such as the allowance for doubtful accounts and accumulated depreciation.) The legal debt is what has to be repaid; the discount or premium is just an adjustment to get the proceeds to what will bring the bond market the return it requires. So on the day of issue, the enterprise's statement of financial position would show a liability called bonded debt, at the amount of $8 760 000 (in the case of the discount: $10 000 000 –

$1 240 000), or $11 180 000 (in the case of the premium: $10 000 000 + $1 180 000). Thus the reported liability meets the historical cost criterion: it is what was received for the bonds.

But the amount of the proceeds is not what will eventually be repaid to the lenders. That is $10 000 000 in both cases. So the discount or premium is amortised over the period until the bonds are due. It therefore shrinks away until, on the due date, it is zero, and the $10 000 000 is correctly shown as the debt on that date. The period's amortisation amount is included with interest expense reported in the calculation of net profit. The discount is a debit, so amortising it adds to the interest expense, making the reported expense higher than the $70 cash interest paid per bond. This makes sense, as the reason for the discount is that the bond market demanded a rate higher than 7 per cent, and by selling the bonds at a discount, the enterprise provided that. The real interest cost is higher than $70. In the case of a premium, the amortisation reduces the reported interest expense, which again makes sense, because the bond market was happy with a rate lower than 7 per cent, and, by selling the bonds at a premium, the enterprise provided that. Thus the reported interest expense approximates the market rate demanded when the bonds were sold. Methods for calculating amortisation of a discount or premium are in more advanced accounting books.

## Long-term accruals

These are in principle just longer-term versions of the short-term accruals. Like the current liability accruals, they are created by debiting an expense account. But, since there will not be a payment for a long time, the credit is to a noncurrent liability. Many of these are approximate estimates, depending on many assumptions: they are recorded in order to account for the future consequences of arrangements made to help earn profit today, so their main purpose is profit measurement rather than statement of financial position valuation.

Three examples of long-term accruals, often called provisions, are:

- *warranty liability:* the estimated future cost of providing warranty service for products already sold (revenue already recognised). In the period in which a product is sold, an expense is recognised to match to the revenue by the expense recognition entry debit warranty expense, credit warranty liability (or provision for warranty). When a warranty cost is incurred, the liability is reduced by the payment entry debit warranty liability, credit cash, or if a replacement product is provided, debit warranty liability, credit inventory. If, as is likely, some of the warranty cost will be paid within the next year, that amount is included in current liabilities.

### For your interest

In the 1960s, General Motors in the USA produced a little rear engined car called the Corvair. It was popular and seemed trouble free. There were Corvair clubs of devotees. It was all very sweet. GM did not have to have a very large warranty provision for the Corvair. In his famous book *Unsafe at Any Speed*, Ralph Nader criticised the Corvair, as well as other cars. People returned to their car dealers in droves, complaining about their Corvairs. It was no longer so sweet. Suddenly, GM had to increase its warranty provision, current and noncurrent, because of the cost of fixing real or imagined problems. Its warranty expense estimates had been fine under previous conditions, but were suddenly made wrong by the unanticipated event of Nader's book. It's an example of the unavoidable fact that accrual accounting estimates of the future, no matter how carefully made, can easily turn out later to have been wrong.

- *superannuation liability:* the estimated future cost of providing superannuation for work already done by employees, minus cash paid to a superannuation trustee to be invested to fund the eventual pensions. The accounting for superannuation (called pension plans in North America) varies around the world, and can be very complicated. In its simplest form, companies' obligations are restricted to paying *x* per cent of the salary of the employee to a superannuation fund each month. For example, if the salary bill for the month is $1 million and there is an agreement for 10 per cent extra to be paid to the superannuation fund, the following entries would occur: at the end of the month, debit superannuation expense $100 000, credit superannuation liability $100 000; when paid, we would debit superannuation liability $100 000, credit cash $100 000. However, if the employer keeps the legal liability for the superannuation payment but uses a fund to accumulate amounts towards the liability, the situation starts to get more complicated. For example, if an employee has worked five years and is already entitled to some part of a superannuation 30 years from now based on that work, the estimated present value of that superannuation entitlement is recorded as a liability. Cash paid to the trustee is deducted from the liability. You can see the problems in trying to estimate such a liability when you think of all the things that can change in those 30 years: the employee might die first, be fired or quit; interest rates (used in the present value calculation) will doubtless vary; laws governing such plans may change; and so on. When the employee earns a superannuation entitlement, that is presumed to be an expense of the period in which it is earned, and is recorded by the expense recognition entry: debit superannuation expense, credit superannuation liability. When a payment is made to a trustee or directly to a retired employee, the payment is recorded by: debit superannuation liability, credit cash. Superannuation liabilities continually need adjustment as conditions and assumptions change, and those adjustments are just included in wages or other expense of the period of the adjustment, because they are a routine consequence of accrual accounting, just as adjustments to asset depreciation, provision for doubtful accounts and other estimates are routinely made.
- *provision for employee entitlements:* part of the conditions of employment of most staff is that they receive annual holidays (they may take them in the current year or they may accrue them to subsequent years), and if they stay a certain number of years with the same company they receive a long service leave payment. For example, after 10 years of service they may receive six weeks' pay. The amount of pay increases as they remain with the company for more years. So each year the company will debit annual leave expense and long service leave (LSL) expense and credit an appropriate liability account (for example, provision for annual leave and/or provision for LSL). There are lots of assumptions that need to be made in determining the dollar amount of the liability. We will leave these complications to later courses.

  As an example, assume a company starts accruing LSL after five years for staff. It decides not to accrue earlier, because it finds on average that it has a high staff turnover in the early years, therefore these staff don't eventually get LSL. Assume the company (based on past history of length of employment and estimated future salaries) determines that the long service leave expense for a particular employee for years 6 to 10 is $10 000 per year. Also assume that in year 11 the staff member takes long service leave. In this simplified example the accounting equation would look like this:

| | A | = L | + SE |
|---|---|---|---|
| Year | Cash | Provision for LSL | LSL expense |
| 6 | | +10 000 | +10 000 |
| 7 | | +10 000 | +10 000 |
| 8 | | +10 000 | +10 000 |
| 9 | | +10 000 | +10 000 |
| 10 | | +10 000 | +10 000 |
| 11 | –50 000 | –50 000 | |

- That is, the provision will be building up each year to $50 000 in year 10. In year 11 when the person takes the leave, the liability is reduced to zero (debit provision for LSL, credit cash).

**For your interest**

Staff often wonder why management want them to take long service leave. One reason is that pay generally increases, so they want them to take the leave at the lower rate. More important can be the impact on the financial statements. When the person takes the LSL, cash decreases and a liability decreases (provision for LSL). Therefore it does not reduce profit (that is, expenses were taken up in earlier years). However, if the employee had not taken leave, the entry would be debit wages expense and credit cash, both for $10 000. In this case, there is a wages expense in this period, therefore profit will decrease. In both cases, cash remains the same. Thus, staff taking LSL has no effect on cash, but has the dual benefits of increasing profits and reducing liabilities.

## 10.6 Shareholders' equity

The shareholders' equity section of the statement of financial position has three main components:

- issued capital
- reserves
- retained profits/accumulated losses.

Accounting standards require that each of these is required to be disclosed separately. The purpose of keeping them separate is related to the concept of capital maintenance. Under this concept profit is only earned after the capital of the company has been maintained. Dividends can only be paid when there are retained profits and revenue reserves to cover them. That is, they cannot be paid out of issued capital. This is to ensure that the original capital is maintained within the company, which benefits the creditors because the amount of capital (in the form of net assets) is available for repayment of the creditors.

So what does the balance of shareholders' equity represent? First recall the basic accounting equation introduced in chapter 1:

**Assets = Liabilities + Shareholders' equity**

**or**

**Assets – Liabilities = Shareholders' equity**

Shareholders' equity thus represents the difference between asset and liabilities – that is, net assets. It shows how these net assets have been financed. For example, consider the following sample statement of financial position:

| **Assets** | **$** |
|---|---|
| Cash | 1 000 |
| Accounts receivable | 10 000 |
| Property, plant and equipment | 89 000 |
| **Total assets** | 100 000 |
| **Liabilities** | |
| Accounts payable | 5 000 |
| **Total liabilities** | 5 000 |
| **Net assets** | 95 000 |
| **Shareholders' equity** | |
| Share capital | 70 000 |
| Retained profits | 19 000 |
| General reserves | 6 000 |
| **Total shareholders' equity** | 95 000 |

General reserves will be discussed in section 10.8. For now, assume that they were created by debiting retained profits and crediting general reserves. Total shareholders' equity of $95 000 indicates that net assets of $95 000 have been financed by original contributions from owners (share capital) of $70 000, and $25 000 ($19 000 + $6000) from past accumulated profits that have not been distributed in dividends. The transfer of $6000 from retained profits to general reserves provides a signal to users that this $6000 is unlikely to be paid out in dividends in the future although it is still legally possible to do so. Note that neither retained profits ($19 000) nor general reserves ($6000) indicate there is cash or some 'pot of gold' for this amount. In fact, in the above example you can see that cash only totals $1000.

Share capital, reserves and retained profits are now discussed in sections 10.7, 10.8 and 10.9 respectively.

## 10.7 Share capital

The majority of shares issued by companies are *ordinary shares*, which confer no special rights or privileges on their holders. The ordinary shareholders are the main risk-takers of companies, receiving no dividend unless adequate profits are earned. There is, however, no upper limit to the rate of dividend that may be recommended by the directors if profits permit. Normally the holders of ordinary shares have full voting rights.

Preference shares confer special rights on their holders. Generally, these involve priority with respect to dividends at a prescribed rate and, in addition, the holders may enjoy preferential treatment with respect to return of capital if the company terminates in a liquidation or winding up. Profits must be available before any dividends may be declared and, to protect the interests of preference shareholders, provision is generally made for the priority of unpaid preference dividends to accumulate from year to year until profits are adequate. Shares with this entitlement are termed cumulative preference shares. A company may also issue participating preference shares, which means that after the fixed amount of preferred dividend is paid, preference shareholders may participate in other dividends with the ordinary shareholders if profits exceed a specified level.

Except for some defined exceptions under the *Corporations Act 2001*, a company invites the public to subscribe for shares by the issue of a *prospectus*, which contains the relevant application form. The content of the prospectus must conform with the requirements of the *Corporations Act* and must contain an audit report. The prospectus is designed to inform potential shareholders or their advisers about the financial position of the company, its prospects and the rights attached to the securities being issued.

In its simplest form, the journal entry for the issue of 100 000 fully paid $2.50 ordinary shares would be:

| | $ | $ |
|---|---|---|
| DR Cash | 250 000 | |
| CR Share capital | | 250 000 |

This form is appropriate where the shares are issued to an institutional investor or where the share issue is administered by an underwriter.

Public companies can also issue shares direct to the public based on a prospectus. Assume the above issue of 100 000 shares at $2.50 were all payable at the time of application. In this case the payment of $250 000 must be held in a special cash trust account, since the board of directors has not yet formally resolved to issue the shares to the applicants. The journal entry would be:

| | $ | $ |
|---|---|---|
| DR Cash trust | 250 000 | |
| CR Application | | 250 000 |

*To record receipt of cash of $2.50 per share on 100 000 shares.*

Once the minimum subscription is received and the directors allot the shares to the applicants, the amount of money paid by successful applicants would be transferred from the cash trust account to the cash at bank account.

| | $ | $ |
|---|---|---|
| DR Cash at bank | 250 000 | |
| CR Cash trust | | 250 000 |

*To record the transfer of application payments into the cash at bank account.*

If there had been excess application funds, the application money of the unsuccessful applicants would be refunded with the following entry:

DR Application

CR Cash trust

The last step is to transfer the balance from the application account to the share capital account, as the shareholders have now been issued with shares:

| | $ | $ |
|---|---|---|
| DR Application | 250 000 | |
| CR Share capital | | 250 000 |

The statement of financial position under shareholders' equity would show an amount of $250 000 under share capital.

For most Australian companies the full payment for shares is required at the time of issue. As a result, for the majority of companies the entries discussed above will be all you need to know. However, it is possible for a company to require shareholders to pay the amounts in instalments. In this case the entries become a little more complex and are discussed below.

Assume the conditions of the earlier share issue of 100 000 shares at $2.50 required $1.70 per share down payment with the application. On allotment another $0.50 is due and a further $0.30 when determined by the board of directors. The application money was received on 10 April. On 28 April the shares were issued (or allotted) with the amount payable on allotment received on 10 May. On 12 July the directors called for the remaining amount owing on the shares, which was received on 28 July. The journal entries would be as follows:

| | | DR<br>$ | CR<br>$ |
|---|---|---|---|
| Apr 10 | Cash trust | 170 000 | |
| | Application | | 170 000 |
| | *Cash received on application.* | | |
| Apr 28 | Cash at bank | 170 000 | |
| | Cash trust | | 170 000 |
| | *Transfer to cash at bank on allotment.* | | |
| Apr 28 | Application | 170 000 | |
| | Share capital | | 170 000 |
| | *To record the amounts due on application.* | | |
| Apr 28 | Allotment | 50 000 | |
| | Share capital | | 50 000 |
| | *Allotment amount of 50 cents per share.* | | |
| May 10 | Cash at bank | 50 000 | |
| | Allotment | | 50 000 |
| | *Allotment money received.* | | |
| Jul 12 | Call | 30 000 | |
| | Share capital | | 30 000 |
| | *Call of 30 cents per share.* | | |
| Jul 28 | Cash at bank | 30 000 | |
| | Call | | 30 000 |
| | *Receipt of call money.* | | |

The general ledger accounts would appear as follows:

**Cash trust**

| | | | |
|---|---|---|---|
| Application | 170 000 | Cash at bank | 170 000 |

**Cash at bank**

| | | | |
|---|---|---|---|
| Cash trust | 170 000 | | |
| Allotment | 50 000 | | |
| Call | 30 000 | | |
| Balance | 250 000 | | |

**Share capital**

| | | | |
|---|---|---|---|
| | | Application | 170 000 |
| | | Allotment | 50 000 |
| | | Call | 30 000 |
| | | Balance | 250 000 |

**Application**

| | | | |
|---|---|---|---|
| Share capital | 170 000 | Cash trust | 170 000 |

**Allotment**

| | | | |
|---|---|---|---|
| Share capital | 50 000 | Cash at bank | 50 000 |

**Call**

| | | | |
|---|---|---|---|
| Share capital | 30 000 | Cash at bank | 30 000 |

If these were the only transactions for the company, the statement of financial position would appear as follows:

| **Assets** | **$** |
|---|---|
| Cash | 250 000 |
| | |
| **Shareholders' equity** | |
| Share capital | 250 000 |

The issue of share capital can get much more complex, and topics such as oversubscription, undersubscription, forfeiture of shares, reissue of forfeited shares and the issue of preference shares are left to later courses.

So far, we have been dealing with the issue of shares. A common practice at present is for companies to buy back their own shares. Share buybacks occur when companies have surplus cash and they use this to buy back their own shares, thus reducing the number of shares issued and the dollar amount of shareholders' equity. If they can maintain profits at approximately the same level, this action will result in increases in such ratios as return on equity and earnings per share.

The overall input on the accounting equation of a share buyback is to decrease an asset (cash) and decrease shareholders' equity. In terms of debits and credits, the credit entry will be to cash. Companies are allowed some flexibility in which shareholders' equity account to debit. Three possibilities are share capital, retained profits and reserves. In the unusual situation where shares were bought back at the same price as they were issued, the debit entry would be to share capital. If they were bought back at a price above the issue price, a possibility would be to debit the share capital account for the amount of the issue price and debit retained profits or a reserve account for the additional amount.

## 10.8 Reserves

Reserves are not defined in the Corporations Law, Australian Accounting Standards or the Statements of Accounting Concepts. However, every annual report you pick up will have reserves included in the statement of financial position category of shareholders' equity. Reserves can take many different forms, and the terminology between companies varies greatly, which is not surprising given the lack of professional guidance.

Accounting standard AASB 1034 requires the disclosure of reserves in the statement of financial position and requires further disclosure in the notes for each 'class of reserves', a description of the nature and purpose of the reserve, the amount of the reserve at the beginning of the financial year, the nature and amount of changes during the year and the amount at the end of the financial year.

It is important to understand the nature of each type of reserve account in a company's financial statements, because under the *Corporations Act* dividends can only be paid out of profits. It is therefore important to know whether each reserve account is a form of accumulated profits or not. One type of reserve is based on *Corporations Act* requirements, namely capital redemption reserves created when preference shares are redeemed out of profits. These reserves cannot be used to pay a cash dividend. Other reserves may be created by the appropriation of profits and the revaluation of noncurrent assets. These would include general reserves and asset revaluation reserves. Cash dividends can be paid out of general reserves. Case law indicates that cash dividends can be paid out of across-the-board revaluation of assets, but it is uncertain whether cash dividends can be paid out of a selective or partial revaluation.

Three of the more common reserves you are likely to come across are the general reserve, asset revaluation reserve and foreign currency translation reserve. The general reserve account is an amount transferred from retained profits by the entry debit retained profits (that is, decrease in a shareholders' equity account) and credit general reserve (that is, an increase in a shareholders' equity account). The purpose of this transfer is often to indicate to shareholders that the amount of the transfer is unlikely to be paid out in dividends and will be retained in the business. However, the directors can later decide to transfer the amount back to retained profits. As a result, the entry does not achieve a great deal, as there is no change in where funds are invested, nor are the amounts earmarked for specific future use.

Another reserve account that was discussed in chapter 8 was the asset revaluation reserve. Recall that the entry to revalue, say, land and buildings upwards was:

DR Land and buildings

CR Asset revaluation reserve

A third common example of a reserve account is the foreign currency translation reserve that relates to exchange differences, which arise in translating the accounts of a self-sustaining foreign operation into domestic currency. Again, these issues are left to a more advanced accounting course.

## 10.9 Retained profits and dividends

A note showing the changes in retained profits was introduced in chapter 2. The contents of this note can now be expanded to include a transfer to reserves.

The appendix to AASB 1018 shows the following example of the contents of a note on changes to retained profits.

| **Note 11: Retained profits** | **2002**<br>**$** | **2001**<br>**$** |
|---|---|---|
| Retained profits at the beginning of the financial year | X | X |
| Net profit (loss) attributable to members of the parent entity | X | (X) |
| Net effect of adoption of a new Standard | (X) | X |
| Dividends recognised as a liability or paid if not previously recognised as a liability | (X) | (X) |
| Transfers to and from reserves: | | |
| Foreign currency translation reserve | X | — |
| .... | X | X |
| Retained profits at the reporting date | X | X |

In the above example you can see that there are four main ways in which the balance of retained profits changes:

- a profit or loss for the year
- adoption of a new standard, which requires the making of an initial accounting entry to give retroactive effect to the changes, with any resulting revenue or expense directly adjusted to retained profits
- dividends provided for paid
- a transfer to or from a reserve, such as a general reserve or the foreign currency translation reserve.

## 10.10 Cash dividends

Dividends may be provided for on the basis of share capital, or paid according to the number of shares held. With respect to the former, a dividend of 5 per cent could be declared, which means that 5 per cent of the share capital is paid. If shares are only partly paid up, only a proportion of the dividend for those shares would be received. With respect to the latter method, the dividend is declared on the per share basis, such as 20 cents per share, which would mean that a shareholder with 5000 shares would receive $1000.

Generally companies have the right to make a payment of interim and final dividends. Interim dividends are usually authorised by the board of directors during the year, based on an expectation of adequate profits. When an interim dividend is declared, there is a debit to interim dividends declared and a credit to dividends payable. When paid, dividends payable is debited and cash is credited. At the end of the financial year, the interim dividend declared would be closed off to retained profits. For example, assume XYZ Ltd declared an interim dividend on 15 January 2002 of 3 cents per share (1 000 000 issued shares), and paid it on 4 February 2002. The journal entries for the 2002 financial year would be:

| | | DR<br>$ | CR<br>$ |
|---|---|---|---|
| Jan 15 | Interim dividends declared | 30 000 | |
| | Interim dividends payable | | 30 000 |
| | *To record declaration of interim dividend.* | | |
| Feb 4 | Interim dividends payable | 30 000 | |
| | Cash | | 30 000 |
| | *To record payment of interim dividend.* | | |
| Jun 30 | Retained profits | 30 000 | |
| | Interim dividends declared | | 30 000 |
| | *To record transfer of interim dividends declared to retained profits.* | | |

The main reason for the original debit to interim dividends declared rather than straight to retained profits is to create a ledger account that identifies the interim dividends paid before the year-end transfer of balances.

Directors recommend a final dividend to be authorised by the shareholders at the annual general meeting of the company, which is held after the end of the company's financial year. Shareholders may not increase the amount beyond that recommended by directors, but may reject or reduce the recommended amount. However, they almost invariably ratify the directors' resolution. Following the directors' meeting, the amount of the dividend recommended is debited to the final dividends declared account and credited to the final dividends payable account. In view of the high degree of probability that the dividend as recommended will be paid, final dividends payable is classified as a current liability. At the end of the financial year, the final dividends declared account is closed to retained profits (that is, debit retained profits and credit final dividends declared). When the dividend has been authorised at the general meeting, dividend cheques are drawn and a debit is made to final dividends payable with a corresponding credit to cash.

For example, assume XYZ Ltd at a meeting on 30 June 2002 declared a final dividend of 10 cents per share on its 1 000 000 shares. The dividend is ratified by shareholders at an annual general meeting on 28 September 2002 and dividend cheques are prepared and sent on 5 October 2002. The journal entries would be as follows:

| | | DR<br>$ | CR<br>$ |
|---|---|---|---|
| Jun 30 | Final dividends declared | 100 000 | |
| | Final dividends payable | | 100 000 |
| | *To record recommendation of final dividend.* | | |
| Jun 30 | Retained profits | 100 000 | |
| | Final dividends declared | | 100 000 |
| | *To record transfer of final dividends declared to retained profits.* | | |

Final dividends declared, together with interim dividends declared, will appear as an appropriation in the retained profits note for the year ended 30 June 2002. Final dividends payable will be included in the statement of financial position as a current liability. When the final dividend is paid on 5 October, the journal entry is:

| | | DR<br>$ | CR<br>$ |
|---|---|---|---|
| Oct 5 | Final dividends payable | 100 000 | |
| | Cash | | 100 000 |

As noted in section 10.8, dividends can only be paid out of profits, including both this year's profit and previous years' profits. Therefore, directors must ensure that profits are legally available before they recommend a certain level of dividends. They also need to ensure that there will be adequate cash available to pay the dividend. Changes in dividends are important signals to shareholders, therefore directors need to exercise care in determining the level of dividends each year.

## 10.11 Bonus issues and share splits

Dividends do not have to be cash dividends. Companies can also issue **share dividends**, which are normally called bonus issues in Australia.

Consider the case of a company that has 5 million fully paid ordinary shares. Assume it has the following shareholders' equity section at 1 August 2002.

| **Shareholders' equity** | **$** |
|---|---|
| Share capital | 5 000 000 |
| Asset revaluation reserve | 1 800 000 |
| Retained profits | 1 400 000 |
| **Total shareholders' equity** | 8 200 000 |

Assume that on 10 August the company declares a 1:4 bonus issue out of the asset revaluation reserve. This means that for every four shares in existence, one additional share will be issued to shareholders free of charge. The shares were issued on 3 September. The journal entries would be as follows.

| | | | |
|---|---|---|---|
| Aug 10 | Bonus issue declared | 1 250 000 | |
| | Bonus issue payable | | 1 250 000 |
| | *To record declaration of bonus issue.* | | |
| Aug 10 | Asset revaluation reserve | 1 250 000 | |
| | Bonus issue declared | | 1 250 000 |
| | *To record reduction of asset revaluation reserve* | | |
| Sep 3 | Bonus issue payable | 1 250 000 | |
| | Share capital | | 1 250 000 |

The shareholders' equity section of the statement of financial position before and after the bonus issue would appear as follows:

| | Before bonus issue<br>$ | After bonus issue<br>$ |
|---|---:|---:|
| **Shareholders' equity** | | |
| Share capital | 5 000 000 | 6 250 000 |
| Asset revaluation reserve | 1 800 000 | 550 000 |
| Retained profits | 1 400 000 | 1 400 000 |
| **Total shareholders' equity** | 8 200 000 | 8 200 000 |

Note that total shareholders' equity has remained constant and that there has been only internal movement within the shareholders' equity section of the statement of financial position. Have shareholders gained from this issue? Shareholders will only gain if the market value of the combined shares is greater than it was before the bonus issue. Total shareholders' funds have remained constant, so it is unlikely that the value of the firm has increased. If a shareholder owned 5 per cent of the company shares before the bonus issue, he or she would still own 5 per cent after the bonus issue. Thus, the share market will normally adjust the price of the shares accordingly so the total value of each shareholder's shares remains the same. However, if it is believed that the bonus issue will be accompanied by increased total dividends (for example, the dividend per share remains the same), the share market will incorporate this information in determining the new share price.

So why do companies make bonus issues? There are a number of potential reasons. First, they provide a return to shareholders without affecting cash. While the value of that return has been questioned above, many shareholders may perceive it to be a benefit. Second, it reduces the market price of each share, which may make the shares available to a wider range of investors. Third, it can be used to capitalise reserves – that is, turn them into permanent share capital. Fourth, they can be a useful takeover defence by forcing the offerer to withdraw and resubmit the offer or extend the original offer price to the newly created shares.

Share splits simply increase the number of shares available. For example, a company has 100 000 fully paid-up shares. If there was a 2:1 share split, there would be 200 000 shares. The share split does not change the balance of any of the shareholders' equity accounts. For example, share capital is $200 000 before and after the share split. Therefore no journal entry is required to record the share split. The purpose of the share split is generally to reduce the unit market price of each share so that the shares are appealing to a wider range of investors.

## 10.12 Managers, investments, liabilities and shareholders' equity

In earlier chapters we emphasised the importance of the financial position of a company. Items such as total assets, total liabilities and total shareholders' equity, form the basis of performance measures that can be used to evaluate the company and its managers. Many of these indicators, such as return on total assets and the ratio of debt to equity, have been mentioned earlier and will be covered in detail in chapter 14. Therefore, it is important that managers understand how decisions they make affect some statement of financial position items such as investments, liabilities and shareholders' equity.

When purchasing shares, investment managers need to be aware that the percentage of shares they buy will affect the influence or control they have over the investment, which in turn affects how these investments are accounted for in the financial statements. Decisions on dividends, bonus issues and so on will affect the closing statement of financial position. An understanding of the nature of retained profits and the various reserve accounts is important in determining the level of dividends that can be paid or the amount of a bonus issue.

## 10.13 Public sector issues

A full discussion of public sector issues related to this chapter is beyond the scope of this book. In fact, it would require a number of other chapters. However, a number of differences and similarities between private and public sector statements of financial position are discussed below. The emphasis in this section will be on government departments. The three issues to be discussed are consolidations, liabilities assumed by the government and the components of equities.

The financial statements of government departments must encompass all entities controlled by the government department. Government departments conduct activities through a variety of administrative and organisational structures. For example, they may manage commercial activities separately from noncommercial activities, operate certain trusts and a number of programs. Combining all of the above in consolidated financial statements is intended to provide users with an overview of the government department's performance, financial position and investing activities.

Liabilities of a government department may include amounts payable to:

- suppliers of goods and services
- employees in respect of wages, salaries and other employee entitlements
- lenders where, in respect of any of the activities conducted by the government department, the department has the obligation to repay loan funds
- other entities that the government department is presently obliged to pay as a result of past transactions or other past events.

Some interesting accounting issues arise for the treatment of liabilities of a government department that are assumed by the government. For example, the obligation to make payments to employees of Federal Government departments in respect of long service leave and some other employee entitlements eventually rests with the Federal Government (that is, they are assumed by the Federal Government). However, as the costs of long service leave and other employee entitlements are part of the cost of goods and services provided by the government department for which those employees work, it is important that these employee costs be included in determining the total cost of services. Therefore, the typical accounting treatment is that on initial incurrence of the liability by the government department, the department recognises the liability and the expense (for example, debit long service leave expense and credit provision for long service leave). On the assumption of the liability by the government, the government department extinguishes the liability and recognises revenue equivalent to the liability assumed (for example, debit provision for long service leave and credit acceptance by the consolidated fund entity of employee entitlement).

Equities of a public sector entity can comprise capital, reserves and accumulated funds. It is rare for government departments to have a capital account as contributions by owners or distributions to owners do not normally occur. Reserve accounts were discussed in section 10.8. There has been a move towards restricted use of reserves by government departments. For example, the NSW Financial Reporting Code for Budget Dependent Agencies suggests that reserve accounts are to be created and shown in the financial statements only if such accounts are required by specific legislation or Australian Accounting Standards. Examples include asset revaluation reserves and foreign currency translation reserves. The accumulated funds account is the sum of all net surpluses (surpluses minus deficits) made by the department that have not been returned to the government.

## 10.14 Homework and discussion to develop understanding

### Discussion questions

1 What is the difference between a short-term and a long-term investment?

2 Explain the difference between the equity method and the cost method for the valuation of investments.

3 What is consolidation?

4 What is meant by 'outside equity interests' in the statement of financial position?

5 Why are each of the following items classified as liabilities: provision for warranty, provision for LSL, unearned revenue, GST payable, income tax deductions due?

6 Explain why contingent liabilities do not appear on the statement of financial position. Give two examples of a contingent liability.

7 List three examples of reserves.

8 A company decides to split its existing shares in half (that is, replace existing shares with two shares). What impact will it have on the statement of financial position?

9 What is the difference between liabilities and equity?

10 What is the difference, if any, between liabilities and legally enforceable debts?

11 Suggest two examples each of short-term and long-term accruals that require difficult estimates, and indicate what the difficulty is in each case.

12 Explain the conditions that must be met before a final cash dividend may be paid to ordinary shareholders of a company.

13 Explain how the following benefit from the issue of share dividends (bonus shares):

   a existing shareholders

   b future shareholders

   c the company.

14 Why does a subsidiary have to be consolidated with the parent's accounts?

15 Why doesn't consolidating a newly acquired subsidiary affect consolidated retained profits? (After all, the subsidiary has retained profits too.)

16 Since it is the sum of more than one company, won't a consolidated statement of financial position present a stronger financial picture than the parent's unconsolidated statement of financial position does?

17 What does 'goodwill on consolidation' on the consolidated statement of financial position mean?

18 Why can't the terms 'reserves' and 'provisions' be used synonymously?

19 What purpose is served by transferring amounts from retained profits to reserves, when the amounts may be transferred back if the directors so decide?

20 Explain the accounting differences between a bonus issue (share dividend) and a share split.

## Problem 10.1* Cost versus equity basis for non-consolidated investment

China Sports Ltd purchased 40 per cent of the voting shares of Brassy Ltd at the beginning of this year for $4 100 000. During the year, Brassy earned net profit of $600 000 and paid dividends of $250 000. China Sports, which has been accounting for its investment in Brassy on the cost basis, has profit of $800 000 for this year. If the equity basis were used instead, what would China Sports Ltd's profit be?

## Problem 10.2* Issue of shares

The following transactions relate to the issue of shares by Tindale Ltd.

| Date 2002 | Transaction |
|---|---|
| Feb 1 | The public was invited to make application for 100 000 shares at $1.00 each, 20c per share being payable on application. |
| Feb 28 | Applications were received for 70 000 shares. |

| Date 2002 | Transaction |
|---|---|
| Mar 15 | The directors allotted 60 000 shares and the successful applicants were advised that 30c per share was due on allotment. |
| Mar 31 | The balance due on allotment was received. |
| May 1 | A first call of 25c per share was made. |
| May 31 | $14 000 was received in respect of the first call. |

*Required:*

Record the above transactions in the appropriate journals, and prepare a note to the accounts showing the capital structure at 31 May 2002.

## Problem 10.3* Long-term accruals

1 Balmer Ltd. has a warranty plan. Estimated warranty liability was $50 000 at the beginning of the year, and based on the company's sales for the year, warranty service costing $78 500 in wages and other costs, plus $62 000 in replacement products, was expected to have to be provided eventually. Actual expenditures for the year were $84 000 in wages and other costs and $78 000 in replacement products. Calculate warranty expense for the year and estimated warranty liability at the end of the year.

2 Write one or more journal entries to record Balmer Ltd's warranty experience for the year.

## Problem 10.4 Valuation of investments

The following shares were held by Roxby Pty Ltd at 30 June 2002.

| Share | Market | Cost |
|---|---|---|
| Riley Ltd | 115 000 | 110 000 |
| Blytheswood Ltd | 80 000 | 90 000 |
| Roland Ltd | 15 000 | 45 000 |
| Total | 210 000 | 245 000 |

***Required:***

1 Prepare the journal entry for 30 June 2002 to reduce the shares to the lower of cost or net realisable value.

2 What is the reasoning behind this entry? How would it be reflected in the financial statements?

## Problem 10.5 Intercorporate investments and the equity method

On 1 July 2001, Big Limited purchased 10 per cent of Small Limited as a long-term investment for $5.00 a share (a total of $250 000). Big Limited paid 1 per cent brokerage and 0.15 per cent stamp duty on the transaction. On 1 January 2002, Small Limited paid an interim dividend of 35c per share relating to the period 1 July 2001 to 31 December 2001. Small Limited's operating profit for this half-year was $180 000.

1 Prepare journal entries to record:
   a purchase of shares in Small Limited by Big Limited
   b receipt of dividend by Big Limited.

2 Small Limited's share price was $3.75 at 31 December 2001. What would you do with this information when preparing financial statements for 31 December 2001?

3 Assume that for $250 000 plus brokerage and stamp duty, Big Limited purchased 25 per cent of Small Limited's shares on 1 July 2001 (instead of 10 per cent). Prepare Big Limited's journal entries using the equity method to account for the investment in Small Limited.

## Problem 10.6 Equity and cost bases of accounting for an investment

Baxter Investments Ltd owns 23 per cent of the voting shares of Bluebird Hotel Ltd. It bought them last year for $1 500 000 and, since then, Bluebird has reported net profit of $400 000 and declared dividends totalling $160 000. Baxter accounts for its investment in Bluebird on the cost basis.

1 Give the figures for:
   a the revenue Baxter will have recognised from its investment since acquisition
   b the present balance in the company's statement of financial position account for investment in Bluebird Hotel Ltd.

2 Give the same figures requested in question 1 if Baxter accounted for its investment on the equity basis.

## Problem 10.7 Equity basis of accounting versus consolidation

International Printers Ltd owns 45 per cent of the voting shares of Nomad Printers Ltd. It acquired the shares several years ago for $10 000 000. Nomad lost money for some years after acquisition, but has recently begun to be profitable: since International acquired its shares, Nomad has had losses totalling $790 000 and profits totalling $940 000, for a total net profit since acquisition of $150 000. Last year, Nomad paid its first dividend, $100 000.

1 International accounts for its investment in Nomad on the cost basis. What is the present figure for investment in Nomad on the statement of financial position of International?

2 International presents supplementary statements using the equity method. What does this mean? What would be the present figure for investment in Nomad on the statement of financial position of International using the equity method?

3 What difference would it make to the statement of financial position of International if the Nomad investment were consolidated instead of using the equity method?

4 Suppose that International had bought 65 per cent of the Nomad voting shares for its $10 000 000 and that at that date the following values existed for Nomad: book value of

assets $18 000 000; sum of fair values of assets $19 000 000; book value of liabilities $7 000 000; sum of fair values of liabilities $10 000 000. Calculate the goodwill that would have been shown on the consolidated statement of financial position of International if the Nomad investment had been consolidated at that date.

## Problem 10.8 Cost and equity methods

On 1 July 2000, Kokos Ltd acquired a 25 per cent interest in Pier Ltd for $220 000 in cash. Kokos Ltd has no other investments. Extracts from Pier Ltd's financial statements for the years ended 30 June 2001 and 30 June 2002 are as follows:

| | 30/06/2002 | 30/06/2001 |
|---|---|---|
| | $ | $ |
| Net profit | 250 000 | 180 000 |
| Dividends paid (30 March) | (15 000) | (15 000) |

*Required:*

1 For the year ended 30 June 2001, prepare the journal entries for Kokos Ltd to account for its investment in Pier Ltd under the:
   a cost method
   b equity method.

2 Calculate the present value in the Kokos Ltd's statement of financial position for investment in Pier Ltd as at 30 June 2002 under the:
   a cost method
   b equity method.

## Problem 10.9 Basic consolidated figures

Fat Furniture has decided to purchase 65 per cent of Banana Appliances Ltd for $43 000 000 in cash. The two companies' statements of financial position as at acquisition date are (in millions of dollars):

| | Fat | Banana | | Fat | Banana |
|---|---|---|---|---|---|
| | $m | $m | | $m | $m |
| **Assets** | | | **Liabilities and equity** | | |
| Cash equivalent assets | 112 | 10 | Cash equivalent liabilities | 128 | 0 |
| Other current assets | 304 | 45 | Other current liabilities | 160 | 10 |
| Noncurrent assets (net) | 432 | 25 | Noncurrent liabilities | 272 | 15 |
| | | | Share capital | 160 | 15 |
| | | | Retained profits | 128 | 40 |
| | 848 | 80 | | 848 | 80 |

Fat Furniture has evaluated all of Banana's assets and liabilities as having fair value equal to book value, except for its noncurrent assets, which Fat Furniture believes have a fair value of $33 million.

*Required:*

Calculate the consolidated goodwill that would appear on the consolidated statement of financial position at acquisition date.

## Problem 10.10 Goodwill amount and reasons; later consolidated profit

White Knight Acquisitions Ltd recently purchased a 70 per cent interest in Premier Publications, a small magazine wholesaler. Premier's balance sheet on the date of acquisition appears below.

| | $ | | $ |
|---|---|---|---|
| **Assets** | | **Liabilities and equity** | |
| Cash | 10 000 | Liabilities | 102 000 |
| Accounts receivable | 55 000 | Shareholders' equity | 108 000 |
| Inventory | 70 000 | | |
| Fixed assets (net) | 75 000 | | |
| | 210 000 | | 210 000 |

Premier's receivables have an adequate provision for doubtful accounts. Inventories are carried at cost and current replacement value is about $70 000. Land with a book value of $20 000 has a market value of $29 000. In the purchase agreement, White Knight assumed all of Premier's liabilities. Before the sale was final, the then owners of Premier were allowed to withdraw all cash from the company as a dividend.

*Required:*

1 If White Knight paid $104 000 (in addition to the $102 000 to pay the liabilities) for its interest in Premier Publications, what was the amount of purchased goodwill? (Hint: all White Knight got for its money were receivables, inventories and fixed assets.)
2 Why would White Knight have been willing to pay this amount for goodwill?
3 Assume that in the year following the acquisition, Premier made a net profit of $14 000. Therefore, decide whether the following statement is true or false and explain why: To record Premier's earnings, the consolidated retained profits of White Knight Acquisitions will be increased by $14 000.

## Problem 10.11 Accounting for GST

Vincent Barbarino Ltd undertakes consulting services for large food-processing enterprises. The company is registered for GST and accounts for GST on the cash basis.

At the end of March 2002, the GST payable account had a balance of $400 and the GST recoverable account a balance of $144.

During April 2002, Vincent Barbarino Ltd recorded these transactions:

| | |
|---|---|
| 6 April | Received from DeadChickenFarmers (for analysis of rotating knife machine) the sum of $4000 + $400 for GST. |
| 8 April | Received from Vegetable Killers Inc the sum of $4950 (including GST) for compliance testing at its vegetable abattoir. |
| 15 April | Sent cheque to the ATO for the net amount of GST payable for the March quarter. |
| 23 April | Performed crucial system maintenance for The French Snail Mangling Co. The client was immediately billed $1320 (including GST) and given 10 days to pay. |

*Required:*

Prepare general journal entries to account for the month of April.

## Problem 10.12 GST reporting on a Business Activity Statement

Tony Cheng recently opened a restaurant in Hobart serving Asian Creole food, as well as exporting its own brand of spice mixture. The business is registered for GST, and accounts for GST on the accrual basis using a monthly tax period.

Summarised below are the events that need to be considered in preparing the Business Activity Statement for June 2002:

- On 2 June, a grinding machine was acquired for $1100 (including GST). It is estimated that 85 per cent of the grinder's usage will be for the restaurant business and the rest to make spice mixture for export.
- Fresh food was purchased for $65 000 (GST free).
- Invoices for other purchases totalled $9900. At the end of the month, inventory to the value of $230 was still in store and Cheng still owed $2475.
- Cash sales in the restaurant were $264 000, including GST.
- Credit sales of spice mixture totalled $13 500, of which only $12 000 was collected during the month.
- The restaurant owner estimates that 5 per cent of all acquisitions are for private use.

***Required:***

Determine the following items for Tony Cheng's Business Activity Statement for the month of June:

| | |
|---|---|
| GST on sales | $ |
| less input tax credit | |
| GST to pay | $ |

## Problem 10.13 Bond discount or premium calculations

In each case below:

1. Calculate the amount of any discount or premium on issue of the bonds.
2. Record the issue of the bonds.
3. State whether interest expense over the life of the bonds will be higher, lower or the same as the cash interest paid on the bond each year.

   a A Ltd. issued 10 000 $100 bonds and received $97.50 cash for each.

   b B Ltd. planned to issue 10 000 $100 bonds, but found that the planned interest rate of 7 per cent was lower than market rates, and so received $915 000 for them.

   c C Ltd issued 10 000 $100 bonds for a premium of 5 per cent on legal value.

## Problem 10.14 Accounting for warranty expenses and liabilities

The accounting records of Gizmo Pty Ltd showed the following: at 1 January 2002 provision for warranty claims was $7400; for the year ending 31 December 2002, sales were $260 000. In the past, Gizmo's warranty expense has been 9 per cent of sales. During the current period, Gizmo paid $14 032 to satisfy warranty claims.

1. Record Gizmo's warranty expense for the year to 31 December 2002 and cash payments for warranty claims made during the year ending 31 December 2002.
2. What is the closing balance of provision for warranty claims recorded on the balance sheet as at 31 December 2002?

## Problem 10.15 Events giving rise to current liabilities

The following events occurred during the year ended 30 June 2002.

1 On 1 May 2002, Regal Rubber signed a three-month 12 per cent per annum bill payable to purchase a new stretching machine costing $48 000. Interest and principal are paid at maturity.

2 On 15 May 2002, Regal Rubber received rent in advance of $6000 from Sophie's Soaps for a three-month lease of premises.

3 June sales totalled $212 000. Regal Rubber collected GST of 10 per cent on this amount. This is due to be paid to the tax office by the seventh day of the month following collection.

4 Electricity charges of $40 000 from 24 April to 23 June are payable on 10 July.

5 On 30 June 2002, Regal Rubber took out a loan for $110 000 from Oscar Bank. Repayments of principal are scheduled evenly over a five-year period. Interest on the loan is paid in the year it is incurred.

6 Regal Rubber's main product is backed by warranty. Sales of this product for the year totalled $445 000. The opening balance of provision for warranty claims was $10 600. During the year Regal Rubber's warranty expense was $31 700 and claims paid to customers totalled $25 200.

***Required:***

For each item, indicate the account and the amount to be included as a current liability on Regal Rubber's statement of financial position.

## Problem 10.16 Record GST and employee deductions

Montane Tours Pty Ltd provides tours to ski areas and operates Mountain Crest souvenir shops in some resort towns. Two groups of transactions the company recently had are described below. The payments indicated were for the amounts due before these transactions, because such remittances follow the transactions creating the amounts due.

1 The company earned sales revenue of $72 000, on which it charged GST of $5040 (some services were for overseas trips). Customers paid $69 030 of the total during the month, and the company expected to collect the rest within 60 days. The company paid the tax office $3100 in GST. GST paid was lower, because the company incurred $1940 GST on its own $26 286 purchases.

2 Employees earned $39 250 in wages, from which the company deducted income tax of $11 180 and other deductions of $4990. The company incurred fringe benefits costs of $6315 on those wages. During the month, the company remitted $12 668 to the tax office on account of income taxes and remitted $11 894 to various government bodies, superannuation trustees and other organisations on account of other deductions and fringe benefits.

Record the transactions described above.

## Problem 10.17 Prepare statement of financial performance and statement of shareholders' equity

The trial balance of Laser Ltd as at 30 June 2002 is as follows:

| | DR<br>$ | CR<br>$ |
|---|---|---|
| Sales | | 800 |
| Cost of goods sold | 330 | |
| Interest received | | 100 |
| Marketing expenses | 100 | |

| | | |
|---|---|---|
| Interest expense | 50 | |
| Rent expense | 80 | |
| Depreciation | 130 | |
| Bad debts expense | 20 | |
| Legal expenses | 100 | |
| Tax expense on operating profit | 90 | |
| Share capital | | 5 000 |
| Retained profit 1 July 2001 | | 1 000 |
| General reserve | | 300 |
| Accounts receivable | 480 | |
| Provision for doubtful debts | | 40 |
| Plant and equipment | 2 000 | |
| Accumulated depreciation | | 500 |
| Inventory | 450 | |
| Cash | 670 | |
| Accounts payable | | 120 |
| Interim dividend declared | 600 | |
| Final dividend declared | 100 | |
| Provision for tax | | 80 |
| Final dividend payable | | 100 |
| Deferred tax liability | | 10 |
| Land | 3 850 | |
| Loan from bank | | 1 000 |
| | 9 050 | 9 050 |

***Additional information:***

- Legal expenses were unusually large for the year ended 30 June 2002. Legal expenses were not tax deductible.

***Required:***

1 Prepare a statement of financial performance displaying any extraordinary items in the statement. Notes are not required.

2 Which operating expense items would be disclosed in the notes to the accounts?

3 On 1 September 2002, the directors declared and paid an additional 10 per cent interim share dividend paid out of the general reserve. Prepare all journal entries.

4 Prepare a statement of shareholders' equity after the share dividend referred to in question 3.

## Problem 10.18 Shareholders' equity

The shareholders' equity section of Journal Limited is reproduced below.

| | 2002<br>$ | 2001<br>$ |
|---|---|---|
| Share capital | 1 400 000 | 1 300 000 |
| Reserves | 150 000 | 200 000 |
| Retained profits | 250 000 | 350 000 |
| Total shareholders' equity | 1 800 000 | 1 850 000 |

*Required:*

1 Provide two plausible reasons for the above reduction in retained profits.

2 What could be included in reserves?

3 Give possible reasons for the change in share capital.

4 The manager of Journal Limited is contemplating a bonus issue. What impact would a bonus issue ($100 000) have on total shareholders' equity?

## Problem 10.19 Shareholders' equity

Reproduced below is the shareholders' equity section of the statement of financial position of Locomotion Limited.

| | Note | Consolidated | | Parent | |
|---|---|---|---|---|---|
| | | 2002 $000 | 2001 $000 | 2002 $000 | 2001 $000 |
| Share capital | 23 | 314 | 298 | 314 | 298 |
| Reserves | 24 | 206 | 194 | 175 | 182 |
| Retained profits | | 391 | 342 | 103 | 95 |
| Outside equity interests in controlled entitites | 25 | 13 | 12 | — | — |
| | | 924 | 846 | 592 | 575 |

*Required:*

1 Briefly describe what information would be contained in note 23.

2 What is the difference between the parent and consolidated columns?

3 Apart from the general reserve, list two other common reserves that might be shown in note 24.

4 What might have caused the movement in retained profits from 2001 to 2002?

5 What is outside equity interest? Why might it have increased?

## Problem 10.20 Oversubscriptions

1 Prepare journal entries for each of the following transactions:

  a XYZ Ltd issues 200 000 shares to an institutional investor on 10 October 2001 for $2.70 a share.

  b On September 2001, ABC Ltd issued a prospectus offering 500 000 shares at $3.00 per share, all payable at the time of application. On 15 October, $1 800 000 had been received, and the directors allotted the 500 000 shares to subscribers in proportion to their applications and refunded the balance of the application monies.

  c Assume that in **b** $2.00 was payable on application, $0.50 on allotment and $0.50 on call and there was no oversubscription.

2 Prepare the shareholders' equity section of the statement of financial position, assuming that retained profits were $100 000 and that there were no other reserves.

## Problem 10.21 Explain the nature of certain reserves

The note on reserves is provided on the next page. Explain the nature of each of the reserves.

**Note 17. Reserves**

| | Consolidated | | Company | |
|---|---|---|---|---|
| | **2002 $'000** | **2001 $'000** | **2002 $'000** | **2001 $'000** |
| **Capital** | | | | |
| Balance at start of year | 26 874 | 26 494 | 23 896 | 23 896 |
| Transfer from retained profits | — | 380 | — | — |
| Balance at end of year | 26 874 | 26 874 | 23 896 | 23 896 |
| **General** | | | | |
| Balance at start and end of year | 13 337 | 13 337 | 13 010 | 13 010 |
| **Asset revaluation** | | | | |
| Balance at start of year | 31 188 | 31 704 | 157 923 | 15 590 |
| Increase (Decrease) arising from revaluation of freehold land and buildings and investments | — | (516) | (16 700) | 142 333 |
| Balance at end of year | 31 188 | 31 188 | 141 223 | 157 923 |
| **Foreign currency translation** | | | | |
| Balance at start of year | 6 575 | 2 825 | 47 | 47 |
| Translation adjustment on controlled foreign entities financial statements | (1 197) | 3 750 | — | — |
| Balance at end of year | 5 378 | 6 575 | 47 | 47 |

## Problem 10.22 Examine note on reserves in annual report

Shown below is the note on reserves from CSL Limited's 2001 annual report.

**Note 22 Reserves**

| | Economic entity | | Chief entity | |
|---|---|---|---|---|
| | **2001 $000** | **2000 $000** | **2001 $000** | **2000 $000** |
| Composition | | | | |
| Asset revaluation reserve[a] | **22 308** | 22 308 | **22 824** | 22 824 |
| Foreign currency translation reserve | **45 203** | 5 667 | **—** | — |
| General reserve | **5 618** | 5 618 | **5 618** | 5 618 |
| Options reserve | **1 274** | 2 785 | **1 274** | 2 785 |
| | **74 403** | 36 378 | **29 716** | 31 227 |
| Movements | | | | |
| Foreign currency translation reserve | | | | |
| Opening balance | **5 667** | 2 367 | **—** | — |
| Net exchange differences on translation of foreign controlled entities | **39 536** | 3 300 | **—** | — |
| Closing balance | **45 203** | 5 667 | **—** | — |
| Options reserve | | | | |
| Opening balance | **2 785** | 6 574 | **2 785** | 6 574 |
| Net options issued during the year | **1** | — | **1** | — |
| Options exercised during the year | **(1 512)** | (3 789) | **(1 512)** | (3 789) |
| Closing balance | **1 274** | 2 785 | **1 274** | 2 785 |

a All land and buildings previously revalued are now carried at deemed cost.

***Required:***

1 How much of the $74 403 would be shown on the face of the statement of financial position?

2 Could a bonus issue be made out of:

a the asset revaluation reserve?

b the general reserve?

3 If the company wanted to increase general reserves to $10 000 000, what journal entry would be made?

4 In problem 10.21, the company used the headings 'consolidated' and 'company', whereas in this problem, CSL Limited uses 'economic entity' and 'chief entity'. What are the differences, if any?

## Problem 10.23 Issue of shares, bonus issues and revaluations

The abridged statement of financial position of Brace Ltd at 30 June 2002 was as follows:

**Brace Ltd**
Statement of financial position as at 30 June 2002

| | $ | | $ |
|---|---|---|---|
| Inventories | 10 000 | Trade creditors | 60 000 |
| Trade debtors | 20 000 | Bank overdraft | 40 000 |
| Plant | 100 000 | Share capital (shares of $1) | 200 000 |
| Freehold premises | 270 000 | Retained profits | 100 000 |
| | 400 000 | | 400 000 |

Fifty thousand shares were issued to the public at $1.50 per share, the full amount of $1.50 per share being payable on application. Applications were received for 80 000 shares, and a refund was made to the unsuccessful applicants.

The freehold premises were revalued at $350 000. The directors resolved to make a bonus issue of one fully paid share for every five shares held (including the 50 000 recently issued). It was decided to use for this purpose the full credit balances in the asset revaluation reserve accounts and a portion of the retained profits account.

***Required:***

Assuming that no other transactions took place, record the above transactions in the journal, post to the ledger and prepare the balance sheet.

## Problem 10.24 Liabilities and dividends

Notes 13, 14 and 16 for the financial statements of Emm Limited are shown below.

**Note 13. Creditors and borrowings**

| | Consolidated | | Company | |
|---|---|---|---|---|
| | 2002 $'000 | 2001 $'000 | 2002 $'000 | 2001 $'000 |
| **Current** | | | | |
| Trade creditors and accruals | 231 473 | 217 868 | 75 394 | 65 567 |
| Loans—unsecured | 547 | — | — | — |
| Bank loans—unsecured | 72 804 | 64 262 | 64 000 | 60 000 |
| Amounts owing to controlled entities | — | — | 217 126 | 214 624 |
| | 304 824 | 282 130 | 356 520 | 340 191 |

| | Consolidated | | Company | |
|---|---|---|---|---|
| | 2002 $'000 | 2001 $'000 | 2002 $'000 | 2001 $'000 |
| **Noncurrent** | | | | |
| Promissory notes | 150 000 | 115 000 | 150 000 | 115 000 |
| Loans—unsecured | 1 160 | 20 970 | 970 | 20 970 |
| Bank loans—unsecured | 305 437 | 150 000 | 300 000 | 150 000 |
| Amounts owing to controlled entities | — | — | 114 400 | 129 635 |
| | 456 597 | 285 970 | 565 370 | 415 605 |
| **Note 14. Provisions** | | | | |
| **Current** | | | | |
| Self insurance | 6 048 | 5 041 | — | — |
| Employee leave entitlements | 31 006 | 30 779 | 11 241 | 10 990 |
| Warranty and service on goods sold | 8 404 | 6 962 | 2 212 | 2 436 |
| Dividends (Note 16) | 28 691 | 37 559 | 28 691 | 37 559 |
| Income tax (Note 4B) | 5 566 | 24 606 | 9 267 | 1 794 |
| | 79 715 | 104 947 | 51 411 | 52 779 |
| **Noncurrent** | | | | |
| Self insurance | 250 | 250 | 250 | 250 |
| Employer leave entitlements | 41 613 | 36 110 | 18 668 | 15 548 |
| Warranty and service of goods sold | 961 | 708 | 542 | 548 |
| | 42 824 | 37 068 | 19 460 | 16 346 |
| **Note 16. Dividends paid and proposed** | | | | |
| Ordinary | | | | |
| —Interim paid 23% (2001—23%) | 32 585 | 30 946 | 32 585 | 30 946 |
| —Final proposed 20% (2001—27%) | 28 691 | 37 559 | 28 691 | 37 559 |
| | 61 276 | 68 505 | 61 276 | 68 505 |
| Preference—paid 6% for year | 12 | 12 | 12 | 12 |
| | 61 288 | 68 517 | 61 288 | 68 517 |

***Required:***

1 Provide examples of trade creditors and accruals.

2 Assume that there are no new loans unsecured during the year. What journal entries would have been made during the year?

3 The bank loan of $150 000 000 in 2001 is repayable in 2005. What journal entry would be made with respect to long-term unsecured bank loans during the year?

4 Assume that a total of $6 000 000 was paid in warranty costs during 2002. What was the warranty expense for 2002?

5 What would be included in the provision for employee leave entitlements? Why is it both a current and a noncurrent liability? What journal entry is made to increase this amount?

6 Provide journal entries that would have been made in 2002 with respect to dividends.

7 Profit after tax was $55 136 000. How could total dividends of $61 288 000 be paid and declared during the year? Why would the company pay out more in dividends than it earned in profits?

## Problem 10.25 Prepare a statement of financial performance and details of shareholders' equity

Provided below are certain balances of Weldon Ltd at 30 June 2002.

| | DR $ | CR $ |
|---|---|---|
| Share capital | | 125 000 |
| General reserve | | 18 000 |
| Retained profits | | 25 000 |
| Asset revaluation reserve | | 20 000 |
| Profit before tax | | 22 000 |
| Interim dividend (paid 31 January 2002) | 5 600 | |

***Additional information:***

- Provide for taxation on 2002 profits, $9000
- Provide for final dividend, $2800
- Transfer $10 000 to general reserve

***Required:***

Complete the statement of financial performance and note of retained profits for the year ended 30 June 2002, and show how the shareholders' equity section would appear in the statement of financial position as at 30 June 2002.

## Problem 10.26 Prepare financial statements

On 31 May 2002 the following figures were extracted from the general ledger of Leonora Ltd.

| | DR $ | CR $ |
|---|---|---|
| Share capital | | 156 000 |
| Retained profits | | 20 000 |
| Mortgage | | 27 000 |
| Plant | 200 000 | |
| Cash | 6 100 | |
| Goodwill | 15 000 | |
| Accounts receivable | 7 400 | |
| Accounts payable | | 5 200 |
| Prepayments | 620 | |
| Accrued expenses | | 470 |
| Accumulated depreciation | | 55 000 |
| Inventory | 84 450 | |
| Government bonds | 10 000 | |
| General reserve | | 17 900 |
| Land | 100 000 | |
| Profit before tax | | 142 000 |
| | 423 570 | 423 570 |

***Additional information:***

On 31 May 2002, the directors of Leonora Ltd resolved to:

- provide for estimated tax liability, $65 000
- transfer $2100 to general reserve
- propose a dividend at the rate of 5 per cent on share capital.

*Required:*

1 Prepare a statement of financial performance and a note of retained profits for year ended 31 May 2002.

2 Prepare a statement of financial position as at 31 May 2002.

## Problem 10.27 Analysis of leave provisions

An extract from a public sector organisations's annual report is provided here.

**Note 2. Schedule of leave entitlements**

| | Recreation leave | | Extended leave | | Total provisions | |
|---|---|---|---|---|---|---|
| | 2002 | 2001 | 2002 | 2001 | 2002 | 2001 |
| | $ | $ | $ | $ | $ | $ |
| Balance 1 July | **98 515** | 105 771 | **274 855** | 244 172 | **373 370** | 349 943 |
| Paid during year | **51 315** | 86 751 | **830** | 21 350 | **52 145** | 108 101 |
| | **47 200** | 19 020 | **274 025** | 222 822 | **321 225** | 241 842 |
| Provided during year | **67 875** | 79 495 | **51 884** | 52 033 | **119 759** | 131 528 |
| Liability 30 June | **115 075** | 98 515 | **325 909** | 274 855 | **440 984** | 373 370 |
| Current | **115 075** | 98 515 | **310 847** | 267 120 | **425 922** | 365 635 |
| Noncurrent | **—** | — | **15 062** | 7 735 | **15 062** | 7 735 |
| Total liability | **115 075** | 98 515 | **325 909** | 274 855 | **440 984** | 373 370 |

*Required:*

1 What do you think recreation leave and extended leave are likely to include?

2 What was the opening balance of recreation leave as at 1 July 2001?

3 By dollar value, did the staff take more recreation leave or extended leave in 2002?

4 By dollar value, did the staff accrue (become entitled to) more recreation leave or extended leave in 2002?

5 Why has the extended leave provision increased by $51 054 from 2001 to 2002?

## Problem 10.28 (Challenging) Equity accounting, consolidation

One of Vast Ltd's investments in partly owned businesses is the Red Robin Baseball Club, of which Vast owns 45 per cent and for which Vast accounts on the equity basis. The Robins have been losing money for years. Vast originally invested $20 000 000 in the club. The club lost $8 000 000 in the year ended 30 April 2002 (Vast's share of the loss would be $3 600 000), bringing its total accumulated losses by 30 April 2002 to $18 000 000 (Vast's share of which would be $8 100 000). Needless to say, the Robins have paid no dividends to their owners, having had losses all along.

1 The investment in the Robins is accounted for on the equity basis. What does this mean?

2 What is the book value of Vast's investment in the Robins as at 30 April 2002 on the equity basis?

## CASE 10A Woolworths Limited case

Refer to the extracts of the annual report of Woolworths Limited in appendix 2. All questions relate to the consolidated accounts.

1 What information does Woolworths provide about its consolidation policies in its notes on significant accounting policies?

2 What is included in contingent liabilities?

3 How are investments valued?
4 What is the total value of investments in the consolidated accounts?
5 What does goodwill in the statement of financial position represent? How much goodwill was amortised during the year?
6 Does the company provide equity accounting information? Explain.
7 Did Woolworths borrow more money from the bank during the year?
8 What items could be included in accrued expenses?
9 What do employee entitlements include?
10 What was the journal entry to propose the final dividend? Why is the final dividend included as a current liability?
11 How many shares were issued during the year?
12 Were there any transfers between general reserves and retained profits during the year?

## CASE 10B Shareholders' equity and liabilities

The shareholders' equity section of CSR Limited's 2001 statement of financial position is shown below.

| | Note | Consolidated | | CSR Limited | |
|---|---|---|---|---|---|
| | | **2001 $A m** | **2000 $A m** | **2001 $A m** | **2000 $A m** |
| **Shareholders' equity** | | | | | |
| Capital | 22 | **2 322.4** | 2 647.0 | **2 322.4** | 2 647.0 |
| Reserves | 23 | **386.8** | 151.5 | **101.6** | 106.3 |
| Retained profits | | **1 273.9** | 860.8 | **398.5** | 387.2 |
| **Shareholders' equity attributable to members of CSR Limited** | | **3 983.1** | 3 659.3 | **2 822.5** | 3 140.5 |
| Outside equity interests in controlled entities | 24 | **97.9** | 160.1 | **—** | — |
| **Total shareholders' equity** | | **4 081.0** | 3 819.4 | **2 822.5** | 3 140.5 |

Another extract from the statement of financial position of CSR Limited for 2001 shows the following:

| | Note | Consolidated | | CSR Limited | |
|---|---|---|---|---|---|
| | | **2001 $A m** | **2000 $A m** | **2001 $A m** | **2000 $A m** |
| **Current liabilities** | | | | | |
| Accounts payable | 19 | **824.2** | 688.2 | **971.0** | 1 367.9 |
| Borrowings | 19 | **70.1** | 65.2 | **1.0** | 1.7 |
| Provisions | 21 | **426.3** | 444.5 | **255.4** | 302.0 |
| **Current liabilities** | | **1 320.6** | 1 197.9 | **1 227.4** | 1 671.6 |
| **Noncurrent liabilities** | | | | | |
| Accounts payable | 19 | **33.1** | 16.5 | **0.6** | 0.9 |
| Borrowings | 19 | **2 230.0** | 1 149.4 | **1 047.0** | 1 158.8 |

| | Note | Consolidated 2001 $A m | Consolidated 2000 $A m | CSR Limited 2001 $A m | CSR Limited 2000 $A m |
|---|---|---|---|---|---|
| Provisions | 21 | 796.9 | 699.9 | 336.1 | 307.8 |
| Noncurrent liabilities | | 3 060.0 | 1 865.8 | 1 383.7 | 1 467.5 |
| Total liabilities | | 4 380.6 | 3 063.7 | 2 611.1 | 3 139.1 |
| Net assets | | 4 081.0 | 3 819.4 | 2 822.5 | 3 140.5 |

*Required:*

1 What would you expect to be included in notes 22, 23 and 24?

2 Explain what is meant by outside equity interests in controlled entities.

3 Retained profits have increased from $860.8 million to $1273.9 million. What items would be used to reconcile these two figures?

4 Given the balances in question 3 and the following information, prepare the retained profits note for year ended 31 March 2001:

   a transfers of $1.5 million from reserves to retained profits

   b interim dividends paid in 2001 of $108.1 million and final dividend proposed of $114.4 million.

5 What would you expect to see in notes 19 and 21?

6 What would CSR be likely to include in contingent liabilities? Why would these items not be included in the statement of financial position?

## CASE 10C Reserves

### The missing $1b 'cash reserves'

THE FINGER of blame for the Ansett debacle has been pointed across the Tasman at incompetent management by Air New Zealand and at a dithering New Zealand Government. But perhaps part of the problem was closer to home, in particular an element of gullibility in Canberra.

Would any household that found itself struggling to meet mortgage and credit-card payments, with action by repossession agents likely, keep a large sum of money stashed away unused? And then tell the world about it?

That sort of behaviour appears to be what we are invited to believe in the Ansett debacle.

Part of the reason for the Commonwealth Government's seemingly blase attitude in the prelude to the demise of Ansett seems to have been the 'curious' financial assurances the Government received from Gary Toomey, chief executive of Ansett's parent company, Air New Zealand.

These assurances were conveyed at a critical meeting in Canberra on June 27. Toomey and a delegation from Air New Zealand met Prime Minister John Howard and his deputy, and Minister for Transport, John Anderson.

The Air New Zealand delegation provided no 'paper' or a 'set of financials', so aural accuracy in recollecting what was said would have been critical.

Anderson has said Toomey told the meeting that Ansett could call upon 'a billion dollars in cash reserves' held by the Air New Zealand group of companies (including Ansett). Toomey's alleged use of the term 'cash reserves' is remarkable.

For Ansett staff, it is especially significant. They do not need reminding that their entitlements are to be paid in cash, not aircraft parts or anything else.

The Government's demeanour after the meeting, when ministers seemed to reflect a cavalier attitude to Ansett's plight in media interviews, was consistent with its having been comforted by the prospect that money was available to Air New Zealand to meet any extraordinary cash needs.

Whether the Government and its advisers were captured by such a prospect merits pondering. Or would it be uncharitable to attribute the apparent lassitude of the Government to its fervour for 'free-market' principles? Was the Government prepared, as early as June and July, to risk sacrificing Ansett and the jobs of 16 000 Ansett employees because of its love affair with competition and market efficiency?

Anyone exercising ordinary financial common sense ought to know that it would be unusual for a business in financial distress to have a large sum safely put aside unused.

A 'nest egg' philosophy might have resonated agreeably with sections of the Government, but it ought not to have.

Anderson told Parliament he had been assured by Air New Zealand that there was no danger of its running into cash problems. If this were the case, presumably Toomey and Air New Zealand management had access to a crystal ball or a cash-flow forecast. Why wasn't Toomey asked to submit a projected cash-flow statement to support his assurances?

With the benefit of hindsight in September, Anderson asked in Parliament, 'Would anyone believe it remotely reasonable' that the Air New Zealand group 'had $1 billion in cash reserves'?

If $1 billion in cash was held in a reserve on June 27, where did it go? Why wasn't it available to meet the entitlements of retrenched Ansett workers? The simple answer is that there was no $1 billion.

If a genuine reserve existed, the consolidated balance sheet of Air New Zealand, drawn up as at June 30, could reasonably be expected to show it. That balance sheet was prepared in compliance with accepted accounting practices. As is customary, it was provided to the New Zealand Stock Exchange, unaudited, as part of the company's routine 'Preliminary Full Year Report Announcement'. What does it reveal about cash and reserves?

It shows cash of $NZD812 million. There were also a 'bank overdraft and short-term borrowings' of $NZ47 million, presumably repayable on demand. There were two 'reserve accounts': a 'foreign-currency translation reserve' of $NZ348 million and a 'revaluation reserve' of $NZ9 million.

The 'cash' of the Air New Zealand group might be calculated at $NZ765 million, after deducting the overdraft. Could this have been the alleged cash reserve (or part thereof) of $1 billion that had been regarded as available to pay retrenched Ansett staff?

Consider the merits of such an argument. First, most Ansett employees are to be paid in Australian dollars. At the June 30 exchange rate, $NZ765 million converts to only $A609 million.

Second, in no sense could this sum be regarded as being in reserve. It was needed on a day-to-day basis to service the working capital needs of the company – to pay suppliers, to meet weekly wages, to meet debt repayments, and to help the company sustain ongoing operating losses estimated at $18 million a week. It was not a 'special sum' set aside for extraordinary purposes.

Could the Government's statement that Toomey had said there was a $1 billion cash reserve be inaccurate? Under questioning in Parliament on September 18 and I9, ministers seemed slightly confused as to exactly what Toomey had said.

Hansard reports both Anderson and Senator MacDonald describing the $1 billion as 'cash reserves' on several occasions each. Howard did not use the term 'cash reserves', but he referred to 'financial reserves', 'group reserves' and 'reserves'.

Now all of this may seem like an exercise in hairsplitting, but the subtleties of terminology are critical. The misunderstandings fostered may have unwittingly helped seal Ansett's fate.

There is a crucial difference between the terms 'cash reserves' and 'reserves' used by accountants in balance sheets.

Contrary to common parlance, 'reserves' do not represent stacks of cash kept in a vault. Strange as it may seem, the peculiarities of accepted accounting practices are such that 'reserves' usually have no immediate monetary equivalence. That is, the balances shown for 'reserves' cannot be exchanged immediately for cash.

Thus, the two 'reserve' accounts on the Air New Zealand consolidated balance sheet at June 30 do not represent cash set aside and retained to pay bills or wages.

But it would be a different matter if a balance sheet item was described as 'cash reserves'. It would probably represent quick access to a set-aside amount of cold hard cash. However, use of the term 'cash reserves' in modern balance sheets is rare.

Although 'reserves' cannot usually be called on directly to pay bills or to meet wages, 'cash reserves', if they exist, most likely can.

Under vigorous questioning about the meeting on June 27, Anderson begged the forgiveness of the House for 'having genuinely misheard' a question posed by Opposition Leader Kim Beazley. Could it be that he also misheard Toomey? Could Toomey have said Air New Zealand had 'reserves', not 'cash reserves', of $1 billion? If so, it would make more financial sense and accord with the Prime Minister's recollection.

More importantly, was Government policy on Ansett influenced by such a critical mishearing? Was there a failure by Government and its advisers to appreciate the technical subtleties of the accounting terminology used by Toomey and respond in a way that might have saved Ansett?

(Source: Russell Craig, *Canberra Times*, 1 October 2001, p. 9.)

***Required:***

**1** Based on your reading of this article, explain the relationship between reserves (in the balance sheet) and cash.

**2** How are reserves created in the accounts?

## CASE 10D Assets

The following article relates to both chapters 9 and 10.

### Accounting standards don't add up

THE ROYAL Commission into the collapse of HIH will begin in Sydney today, headed by Western Australian Supreme Court Justice Neville Owen.

The terms of reference are broad. But are they broad enough?

Owen is to determine the extent to which actions of HIH's directors, officers, auditors, actuaries and advisers contributed to the company's failure. He will seek evidence of undesirable corporate governance practices and assess the adequacy of prudential supervision arrangements for insurance companies.

But missing is any explicit direction to inquire into the adequacy of the 40 or so accounting standards and the generally accepted accounting principles on which HIH prepared its annual accounts.

Australian accounting standards are proposed by the Australian Accounting Standards Board. They have legal backing after approval by the Commonwealth Parliament. Accountants are obliged to implement approved accounting standards when preparing company financial statements.

HIH's accountants are no exception. On October 16 last year, external auditors attested that HIH's accounts for the year ended June 30 last year were prepared in accordance with accounting standards and gave a 'true and fair view' of financial position.

HIH policyholders and creditors can be forgiven if they are still scratching their heads in puzzlement. How would a company that received a clean bill of health in its audited annual accounts collapse nine months later with a deficiency of funds formally estimated at between $3.6 billion and $5.3 billion?

A major confounding factor is that accounting standards routinely yield balance sheets and profit and loss statements at odds with ordinary financial common sense. They lead to financial statements that are prone to be misleading and deceptive.

Indeed, it is surprising that an aggrieved creditor has not relied on consumer protection legislation to argue that contemporary accounting leads to financial statements of unmerchantable quality.

All of this lends weight to a call for a greater public scrutiny of the accounting standards underpinning financial reporting in Australia. Perhaps, Owen's terms of reference should be extended.

What arguments support such a call?

Company accounts, such as those of HIH, define key terms and report on much financial activity in ways that are at odds with everyday practice and common sense. Financial reports are unfathomable to other than those who are familiar with accountant-speak and who have received full tribal rites as an accountant.

There seems no sustainable reason for ordinary people to be disadvantaged. Why should they routinely need to take financial statements with a grain of salt? Why should published accounts need to be 'adjusted' to make them more realistic and useful?

Let's examine the HIH accounts more closely.

The HIH balance sheet at June 30 last year reported total assets of $8.32 billion and total liabilities of $7.38 billion. The excess of assets over liabilities was $939 million. HIH also reported an annual operating profit after income tax of $19 million.

Seemingly, there was little need for concern about the company's solvency. But awareness of the perversities of the accounting involved should have set alarm bells ringing loudly.

HIH's 'total assets' figure is comprised of several items most people would not regard to be an asset, even in a wild flight of fancy.

Most people consider an asset to be something they can cash in to buy a hamburger. They think that balance sheet numbers preceded by dollar signs represent the cash amount for which assets can be exchanged, either now or in the near future.

Such a view is as it should be. But that is not the way accountants define, measure and report assets.

The 'accountants' assets' reported in the HIH balance sheet at June 30 last year comprised (in $ million): cash – $162; trade accounts receivable – $1604; investments – $2378; reinsurance recovery receivables – $1820; plant and equipment – $165, deferred acquisition costs – $304; goodwill – $475; management rights – $19, prepayments and deferred expenses – $41; future tax benefit – $228; NSW workers' compensation statutory fund – $831, total assets – $8327.

A non-accountant would be entitled to believe that HIH had assets of $8.32 billion to meet its reported debts of $7.38 billion. But the dollar amounts of HIH's 'assets' did not necessarily represent any equivalence to what HIH would have to use to discharge its debts – access to money or a near equivalent of money.

Many 'accountants' assets' arise from money expended in the past. Some are not exchangeable into cash, now or ever. But accountants regard them as assets now, because they embody some notional 'future benefit'.

As with most balance sheets, HIH's assets are a mixture of 'money in possession now' (for example, cash – $462 million), 'claims to receive money in the future' (for example, receivables – $3424 million), and 'money amounts expended in the past' (for example, plant and equipment, shown at written down cost of $165 million).

A closer look at the following three HIH 'assets' is revealing. All should be excluded when calculating HIH's ability to pay debts and remain in business.

'Deferred acquisition costs' relates to sums expended in the past to acquire another business. It is defined as an 'asset' and is gradually 'written off' over time as its 'benefits' are deemed to have been used up. But the $304 million shown for this asset cannot be received in cash, now, or at any future time.

The same can be said about 'goodwill' ($475 million). It represents the excess of past sums paid out to acquire 'assets' over the value of assets so acquired. 'Goodwill' cannot be sold separately. Nor can it be used to buy a hamburger, pay an insurance claim or meet the wages of employees.

And so it is, too, with 'future tax benefit' ($228 million). This 'asset' does not have any real world manifestation. You cannot satisfy the claims of creditors with 'future tax benefit'. It does not represent anything that can be exchanged for cash now, or in the near future.

'Future tax benefit' is a peculiar artefact arising from the Accounting Standard on 'tax effect accounting'. That accounting standard has been described, by informed commentators, as 'hocus pocus' and as leading to 'accounting fictions'.

If we adjust the HIH balance sheet for these three dubious 'assets', 'total assets' are reduced by $1 billion to $7.32 billion. That is, to $68 million less than reported total debts.

But these three adjustments are only a start. Several other assets on the balance sheet, calculated in accordance with accounting standards, are also highly dubious. For example, the auditors' report directs attention to the 'inherent uncertainty' of realising all of the 'reinsurance recoveries receivable'.

In their book, *Corporate Collapse*, F. Clarke, G. Dean and K. Oliver review the way accounting has been implicated in the procession of corporate failures in Australia over several decades.

They conclude with a damning lament: 'Corporate accounting does not do violence to the truth occasionally, and trivially, but comprehensively, systematically, and universally, annually and perennially.'

They express surprise that, to date, no litigation has been taken alleging that company accounts were misleading because they complied with accounting standards. They also speculate that sooner or later a financial victim of a corporate collapse will instigate legal action against those responsible for devising accounting standards.

If this occurs, the defence of accounting standards will not be easy. According to Clarke, Dean and Oliver, 'the financial nonsense promoted in Accounting Standards will be nigh impossible to defend'.

The accounting establishment will be miffed by all of this. They will say, with some good reason, that the measurement and reporting of financial phenomena is a complex task, best left to practising accountants. They will offer well-rehearsed arguments and a stout defence of the current habits and rituals of accountants.

The Treasury will point to some commendable initiatives of the Commonwealth Law and Economic Reform Program. But, generally, the political establishment will duck for cover.

Perhaps the mystique of accounting has politicians totally intimidated. If so, this seems all the more reason to remind them that the Commonwealth Parliament has endorsed the Accounting Standards used to prepare HIH's accounts.

A strong case can be made that the Australian community deserves better company accounting and financial reporting. That it is time for the quality of accounting standards, and the way they are implicated in financial calamities, to be put under strong, independent scrutiny. The HIH Royal commission seems a suitable venue to do that.

Or perhaps, as with tobacco products, we should take a softer option. Simply insist that financial statements have a 'financial health warning' attached?

• Recommended reading: F. L. Clarke, G. W. Dean and K. G. Oliver, *Corporate Collapse: Regulatory, Accounting and Ethical Failure*, Cambridge University Press, 1997.

(Source: Russell Craig, *Canberra Times*, 1 September 2001, p. C4.)

***Required:***

Evaluate Professor Craig's arguments. In your answer, outline the pros and cons of including or excluding in the statement of financial position (balance sheet) the assets referred to in the article.

## Note

1 Example developed by Michael Pennisi.

Chapter 11

# Revenue and expense recognition: additional concepts

## On completion of this chapter you should be able to:

- explain the criteria used to decide whether revenue and expenses should be recognised
- calculate the amount of revenue and expense that should be recognised in a particular period
- calculate the impact on profit of different revenue recognition methods
- apply the concepts in SAC 4 to revenue and expense recognition
- understand the contents of a statement of financial performance.

# 11.1 Chapter overview

This chapter discusses revenue and expense recognition concepts in greater detail. Businesses and other entities must choose an appropriate point at which to recognise revenue and related expenses. Several alternatives are available, and this important decision is the core of this chapter. The contents of the statement of financial performance (introduced in earlier chapters) are then discussed in detail.

# 11.2 Revenue recognition

## Reliability versus decision relevance

It can be said that profit over the life of an enterprise is easy to determine. At the end of the enterprise's life, all expenses have resulted in cash outflows and all the revenue earned has resulted in cash inflows. There is no need for estimates; the results are known with certainty. Profit for the life of the firm is simply the difference between the total cash contributed to the business by the owners and the total cash withdrawn by the owners plus any cash remaining at the end.

The difficulty in reporting profit periodically, which is how economic decision-makers require information about the operations of a firm, is that of finding a way to put the essentially continuous operations of a firm into discrete time periods. The result is that profit determined earlier, so that it is relevant for evaluating the enterprise's performance over shorter decision periods, is unavoidably subject to estimates and judgements because the whole story is never known until the end, but no one wants to wait for the end.

We are back to the ever-present trade-off between reliability and relevance in profit measurement. If revenues and expenses are recognised earlier, so that they are more relevant for decision-making, they will not be as reliable as they would be if recognition were delayed until later, when outcomes of the various economic activities are better known. Figure 11.1 illustrates the trade-off.

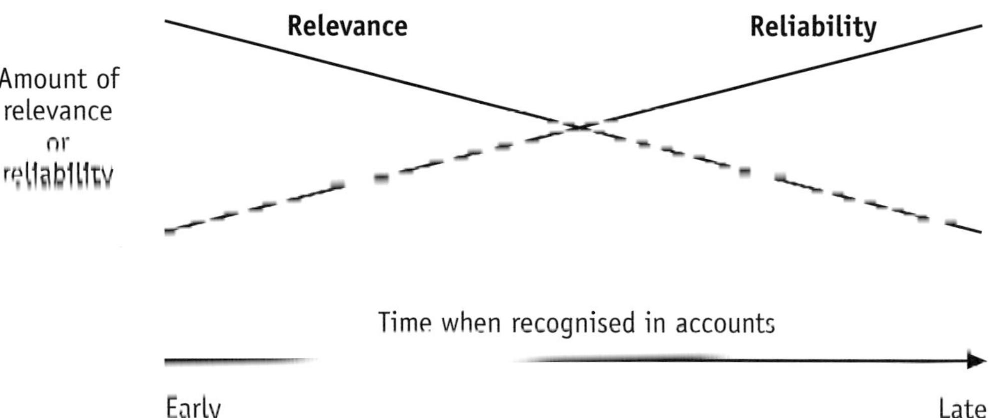


Figure 11.1 Trade-off between relevance and reliability

## Critical event simplification

If we are to describe the firm's operations for a given period by calculating the profit for that period, we must define a means by which to measure the amount of profit that can be attributed to that period. We accomplish this by:

- defining how much revenue can be recognised in that period; then
- determining the expenses that were incurred to generate the revenue.

Profit, the value added by the activities of the firm, is just the difference between the recognised revenue and the recognised expenses.

But what are the revenues, or the expenses, for a period? From an economic and business point of view, profit is earned by a wide variety of actions taken by the firm. There is a whole sequence of activities intended to help generate profit, which therefore generate revenue and incur expenses, including, for example:

- organising the firm in the first place
- building the factory
- buying or making inventory
- advertising
- selling
- delivering to the customer
- billing
- collecting cash
- providing warranty service.

How should we recognise revenue when there is such a series of activities as those listed above? Should we recognise it a bit at a time as each activity is carried out? This would approximate the economic process underlying the business. This would be relevant, all right, but by the same token it would be very subjective and imprecise, because it is difficult to say what each activity actually adds. How do you tell, when the company is just being organised, what revenue that form of organisation will help to generate, for example? It would also be expensive to implement, with armies of accountants scurrying about measuring minute value changes generated by the various activities and writing masses of journal entries to recognise each value change.

Instead, for greater objectivity and verifiability and lower accounting cost, accountants usually choose one activity in the sort of sequence above as the critical event in the revenue-generation sequence that can be readily documented, and recognise all of the revenue at that point. This is a simplification, because clearly some revenue could have been recognised when earlier activities were carried out, and probably some should be recognised when later activities take place. For some companies, such as those building big projects such as power stations, pipelines, highways and bridges, it is worthwhile estimating revenue at several points along the way, but for most the simplification of the critical event is followed. *The most common critical event used is the point of delivery of the goods or services to the customer.*

## Criteria for revenue recognition

Revenue recognition, then, becomes the first step in determining profit for the period. The revenue recognition criteria discussed below have been formulated for the purpose of making sure that revenue will be recognised only when there is objective evidence that revenue has indeed been earned. The following four criteria must normally all be met in order for revenue to be recognised. For most firms, the activity nearest to fitting these criteria is chosen as the critical event. However, as you'll see, there are exceptions (as usual!).

- all or substantially all of the goods or services to be provided to customers have been provided or performed
- most of the costs to generate the revenue have been incurred, and those remaining can be measured with reasonable accuracy

- the amount of the revenue can be reasonably measured in dollar terms
- cash, a promise of cash (a receivable), or other asset that can be measured with reasonable precision has been received.

Although the above criteria seem fairly clear, there are still many judgements to be made about when the criteria are met. For instance, how should 'substantially all of the services have been performed' be defined? Is it when 100 per cent of the services have been performed, or 90 per cent or 80 per cent? To deal with such problems, there are several points in the revenue-earning process at which revenue is commonly recognised, though as noted above, point of sale or delivery is the most common. You'll see those points below.

To recognise the earning of revenue when the critical event has taken place, we make the following recognition entry:

| | | | |
|---|---|---|---|
| DR | Cash or accounts receivable or unearned revenue liability | XXXX | |
| CR | Revenue | | XXXX |

Let's take a closer look at the four most commonly used methods of revenue recognition and a fifth very conservative method.

## 1 At point of sale or delivery

For most retail, service and manufacturing businesses, revenue is recognised when the product or service is sold. 'Sold' is usually defined as being when the goods or services have been shipped to the purchaser, when legal title passes to the purchaser.

- At that point substantially all of the service has been performed, terms and price have been set, and cash has been received or there is an agreement to pay it in the future (for example, accounts receivable).
- Even though there is some risk involved in extending credit, this can usually be adequately estimated and deducted from the gross revenue by way of the bad debts expense account.
- Another risk at the point of sale is the possibility of returns and the likely service obligation under the warranties for the product or service sold. Again, this can usually be adequately estimated and recognised as an expense of the business and matched against the revenue of that period.

Point of sale or delivery is so common a revenue recognition method that most companies do not mention in their financial statements that they are using it. You are expected to assume it is the one being used if you are not told otherwise, as you probably would be if any of the other four methods below were used.

## 2 During production

Sometimes the earnings process extends well beyond one financial period, as is the case in building construction, road building, ship building and other lengthy processes. In such situations, if a firm waited until the point of delivery to recognise revenue, it might report no revenue for one or more years, then, when the project was complete, would report all the revenue. This would distort the performance picture of the company for the duration of the project: some years with no revenue, then one year with huge revenue, even though the company was working faithfully on the contract all along. There are not likely to be many projects going on at once (few, anyway, in comparison to the number of sales made by a grocery retailer), and projects include enough documentation that the value added can usually be estimated and verified. Therefore, in an attempt to provide users with useful information and reflect the economics of what is happening, revenue may be recognised during production. (This also means recognising expenses and therefore profit during production.)

Percentage of completion is the most common method of recognising revenue during production. This method entails determining what proportion of the project has been completed during the year and recognising that proportion of total expected revenue, expenses (costs) and, therefore, profit. Often this is done by measuring the proportion of expected total costs incurred during the period. In order to recognise revenue in this manner, total costs must be reasonably determinable, the contract price (total revenue) must be reasonably certain and there must be reasonable assurance of payment. The frequent use of the word 'reasonable' here shows that a lot of judgement is required in using this method!

Let's assume Greenway Construction had a large, three-year project with total revenue of $4 000 000 and total costs of $3 400 000. (Before expense recognition, project costs are charged to an inventory account for costs of construction in process. Like other inventories, this account holds costs until they are expensed.) Total profit for the project over the three years was therefore $600 000. The project was 20 per cent completed at the end of the first year, 65 per cent completed at the end of the second year, and 100 per cent completed at the end of the third year. Ignoring complications that arise when revenues and costs do not work out as expected, here are journal entries to implement percentage of completion revenue (and matched expense) recognition during production. (For presentation purposes, all amounts are in thousands of dollars.)

| | **Year 1** | | **Year 2** | | **Year 3** | |
|---|---|---|---|---|---|---|
| Percentage of contract done in the year | 20% | | 45% | | 35% | |
| | **$000** | | **$000** | | **$000** | |
| Revenue recognition: | | | | | | |
| DR Accounts receivable | 800 | | 1 800 | | 1 400 | |
| CR Revenue | | 800 | | 1 800 | | 1 400 |
| *Percentage earned each year* | | | | | | |
| Expense recognition: | | | | | | |
| DR Cost of goods sold expense | 680 | | 1 530 | | 1 190 | |
| CR Construction in process inventory | | 680 | | 1 530 | | 1 190 |
| *Percentage of expenses each year* | | | | | | |
| *Resulting profit each year* | 120 | | 270 | | 210 | |

You can see the *timing* effect of accrual accounting here. The annual entries have the effect of spreading the $600 000 project profit out over the three years: 20 per cent to the first year, 45 per cent to the second, 35 per cent to the third.

### 3 On completion of production

In the percentage of completion method, revenue is recognised as the work proceeds. It is also possible to wait until the work is all done and recognise the revenue then. This is like the point-of-sale method, except that if the work took a long time, perhaps several accounting periods, then it is very conservative because no revenue would be recognised for a long time, then all of it at once. In the Greenway Construction example above, if revenue and the associated expenses were recognised on the completion of production, the project profit would be:

- $0 in Year 1
- $0 in Year 2
- $600 000 in Year 3.

Compared to the percentage of completion method, profit would be:

- $120 000 *lower* in Year 1
- $270 000 *lower* in Year 2
- $390 000 *higher* in Year 3 ($600 000 – $120 000).

So if the company wanted to know 'what if' it changed to the completion of production (or 'completed contract') method, there's the answer, ignoring income tax.

Note that if a company has a reasonably large number of construction contracts (say 25 construction sites going at once) and an approximately equal number of projects are completed each year, it is possible that the percentage of completion and completed contract methods give similar profits.

### 4 When cash is received

If there is serious doubt as to the collectability of cash from a revenue-generating transaction, revenue recognition is delayed until the collection has taken place. This does not mean that any time a business extends credit to a customer, revenue recognition is delayed; this is only the case when the risk is great and the amount collectable cannot be reasonably determined, or is not sufficiently predictable.

For example, certain real estate transactions that are speculative in nature and/or for which the collection of cash is contingent upon some future condition (such as the purchasers of a shopping centre successfully leasing a certain percentage of the space) will not be recognised as revenue until the cash is received.

Another example of revenue recognition at time of collection is the 'instalment sales' method. When the majority of the revenue will come in over a long series of instalments, and there is substantial uncertainty that a given customer will actually make all the payments, the revenue is recognised in stages as the cash comes in. The instalment sales method has some complexities, but in principle it is just a way of recognising revenue on a cash-received basis.

### 5 At some point after cash has been received

Revenue recognition methods 1, 2 and 3 use accrual accounting, while 4 uses the cash basis for recognising revenue. It is also possible to defer recognition for some time after the cash has been collected. Even though cash has been received, all revenue may not be recognised immediately because of some circumstance, such as a guaranteed deposit refund policy or a policy of 'satisfaction guaranteed or money back'. A current liability account (unearned revenue) is credited when the cash is collected:

DR Cash
CR Unearned revenue or deposits received liability

Revenue will be recognised at a point in the future, normally after the refund time has expired or the required after-delivery service has been performed:

DR Unearned revenue or deposits received liability
CR Revenue

## Examples of revenue recognition

Lend Lease Corporation Limited, and Leighton Holdings Limited are two large Australian companies that are involved in long-term contracts. The relevant notes from their 2001 accounts are as follows:

**Lend Lease**

Profits are brought to account:

- for property construction, progressively at an amount equivalent to general overheads or an amount equivalent to the value of work performed when the outcome of a contract can be reliably determined (Lend Lease does not consider that the outcome of a construction contract can be reliably determined until it is at least 50% complete)
- for property held for resale whilst under development where an unconditional sales contract is in place or when all conditions under the sales contract have been met or are reasonably likely to be met, progressively at an amount equivalent to the value of work performed when both revenues and costs to complete can be reliably determined (Lend Lease does not consider that revenues and costs can be reliably determined until a development is at least 50% complete)
- for completed properties held for resale, upon exchange of an unconditional sales contract
- for goods and services, when such goods or services have been supplied or rendered
- for rental income, when earned
- for profits on sale of investments, where an unconditional contract is in place.

Stage of completion is measured by reference to actual costs to date as a percentage of total forecast costs for each contract.

**Leighton Holdings**

**(e) Revenue and profit recognition**

(i) Construction revenues includes revenues from building, civil, mining and telecommunications contracting services. Revenue and profit is recognised on the basis of the value of work completed. Stage of completion is measured by reference to costs incurred to date as a percentage of estimated total costs for each contract. The whole of any expected loss is recognised in the financial statements as soon as a loss has become apparent.

The Lend Lease note provides an interesting example of the variety of revenue recognition methods that are used in practice. For goods and services, consistent with most companies, they recognise revenue when such goods and services have been supplied or rendered. They also use both the percentage of completion and the completed contract method, depending on the difficulties in determining total revenues and costs for the project. A more conservative approach is adopted for property held for resale, with revenue recognition awaiting settlement.

Leighton Holdings uses the percentage of completion on construction contracts. It also notes that the whole of any expected loss on a contract is recognised in the period as soon as the loss has become apparent. This is an example of conservatism; profits are recognised gradually as they are earned, whereas losses are recognised immediately.

## 11.3 Extending the revenue concept: SAC 4

The above discussion of revenues has concentrated on the main type of revenue generated by the majority of companies – that is, the recognition of revenue for providing goods and/or services. However, this discussion has not been broad enough to encompass every type of revenue, such as an appropriation to a government department from the Commonwealth Government.

A more encompassing definition of revenue that is applicable to a range of measurement models and different types of organisations including public sector entities is provided in SAC 4, which states that:

> revenues are inflows or other enhancements, or savings in outflows, of future economic benefits in the form of increases in assets or reductions in liabilities of the entity, other than those relating to contributions by owners, that result in an increase in equity during the reporting period.

This definition relates back to the definitions of assets and liabilities in chapter 9. With respect to revenue, SAC 4 states that:

> the above inflows, other enhancements of future economic benefits or savings in outflows of future economic benefits that constitute revenues may be of various kinds. For example, revenues in the form of inflows or other enhancements of future economic benefits can arise from the entity providing goods and services, investing in or lending to another entity, holding and disposing of assets, or by receiving contributions such as grants, donations and bequests. Revenues in the form of savings in outflows of future economic benefits can arise where inflows of assets are foregone in return for extinguishment of liabilities, where liabilities are forgiven and where exchange gains arise on translation of loans denominated in a foreign currency.

In the case of the forgiveness of liabilities, the revenues arise simultaneously with that forgiveness. For example, when the Commonwealth Government takes over the superannuation liabilities of a department, this would result in revenue for the department of the amount by which the liability was reduced.

Revenues only arise where the entity controls the future economic benefits arising from the transaction or other event. Consequently, as discussed in section 11.2, revenues will not normally arise before the provision of goods or services by an entity. For example, where a company rents out a property, revenues will not arise until the company has a claim against the tenant for rent in respect of the property. This claim arises progressively as the tenant uses the rental property.

According to SAC 4, a revenue should be recognised when and only when:

**a** it is probable that the inflow or other enhancement or saving in outflows of future economic benefits has occurred; and

**b** the inflow or other enhancement or saving in outflows of future economic benefits can be measured reliably.

For **a** above, 'probable' means more likely rather than less likely. For many entities, the majority of revenues will result from the provision of goods and services, and these will involve little or no uncertainty that an inflow or other enhancement or saving in outflows of future economic benefits has occurred, since the entity will either have received cash or have an explicit claim against an external party. However, an absence of an exchange transaction will often raise doubts about whether the requisite degree of certainty has been attained.

For **b** above, in most cases the revenue will be able to be reliably measured. However, in some cases there is a need for estimates. For example, in using the percentage of completion method in accounting for construction contracts, the stage of contract completion and/or the amount of revenues that will ultimately be recognised can be uncertain and would need to be estimated. In such cases, revenues would qualify for recognition only if the inflow or other enhancement or saving in outflows of future economic benefits can be measured reliably.

While the above two criteria may appear different to those set out in section 11.2, it should be noted that they are consistent with the criteria in section 11.2 and just cover a broader array of possible transactions. For example, SAC 4 suggests that if all the criteria set out in section 11.2 were met, the definition and recognition criteria for revenues will be satisfied, because it will be probable that an inflow of future economic benefits has occurred in respect of the entity's acts of performance and because the future economic benefits that have been, or will be, received can be measured reliably. However, SAC 4 also notes that there will be situations where the criteria for recognition of revenues will be considered to have been met even though one or more of the tests in section 11.2 were not satisfied.

## 11.4 Expense recognition and matching

According to the 'matching' concept, expense recognition should be timed to match the revenue recognition method. The basic idea is that expense accounts should be debited in the same accounting period as the revenue, to which the expenses relate, was recognised. In practice, this is done quite routinely for most expenses. When expenses such as wages, interest, electricity, municipal rates or advertising are incurred, they are recognised as expenses on the assumption that they were incurred to help earn revenues in the same period. Sometimes this assumption is a bit strained; for example, advertising may stimulate revenue over more than the current period, but the subjectivity of estimating multi-period effects and the simplicity of just expensing such costs when incurred lead most companies to just expense them, matching them to current revenues.

In some cases it is clear that an expense will benefit more than one year and therefore it is capitalised. This may occur for items such as research and development and interest on a construction project. Examples of capitalising of these expenses by Australian companies were given in chapter 8.

You saw above an example of expense recognition matching to the revenue recognised during production. Just to help you see the potential accrual accounting offers for fine tuning revenue and expense recognition, here's another example, from the growing field of franchising.

WonderBurgers Ltd is a franchiser, which means it sells the right to sell its products in particular geographic areas. For example, a franchisee might pay $25 000 for the right to set up a WonderBurgers fast-food restaurant in Alice Springs, and no one else would be able to use the WonderBurgers name in Alice Springs.

Let's suppose that the management of WonderBurgers estimates that it takes three years for a franchise to become viable and knows that during that time it will have to provide a lot of help. Suppose the sort of schedule of cash flows and economic activity that WonderBurgers has experienced for a typical $25 000 franchise fee is much like the one shown below. The 'percentage-of-fee-earned' amounts could have been determined by how much revenue was collected or how much support cost was spent, but because of the kinds of effort the company and its franchisees go through in getting a franchise going, management has worked out a general policy of recognising 40 per cent of the revenue in the first year of a franchise and 30 per cent in each of the next two years. (It's a lot like the percentage of completion method you saw above, which is no accident. Franchise accounting is a form of the percentage of completion method.)

| Year | Cash paid by franchisee $ | Cash cost to help franchisee $ | Percentage of fee earned % |
|---|---|---|---|
| 1 | 15 000 | 4 000 | 40 |
| 2 | 5 000 | 3 000 | 30 |
| 3 | 5 000 | 1 000 | 30 |
| | 25 000 | 8 000 | 100 |

Using management's estimates of percentage of fee earned as the basis of revenue recognition, the revenue recognised from the franchise sale would be:

- Year 1, $10 000 (40 per cent of $25 000)
- Years 2 and 3, $7500 each (30 per cent of $25 000 each).

According to the matching criterion, the expense of helping the franchisee should be recognised on the same schedule, so the expense recognised would be:

- Year 1, $3200 (40 per cent of $8000)
- Years 2 and 3, $2400 each (30 per cent of $8000 each).

This matching process means that the profit from the contract follows the same pattern. The total expected profit is $17 000 ($25 000 minus $8000), and the matching process produces a profit pattern of:

- Year 1, $6800 (40 per cent of $17 000), which is $10 000 revenue recognised minus $3200 expense recognised
- Years 2 and 3, $5100 (30 per cent of $17 000 each) which is $7500 revenue minus $2400 expense.

The resulting profit schedule and differences between accrual basis and cash basis are below.

| | Accrual basis profit | | |
|---|---|---|---|
| **Year** | **Revenue (a) $** | **Expense (b) $** | **Profit (c) $** |
| 1 | 10 000 | 3 200 | 6 800 |
| 2 | 7 500 | 2 400 | 5 100 |
| 3 | 7 500 | 2 400 | 5 100 |
| | 25 000 | 8 000 | 17 000 |

| | Cash basis profit | | |
|---|---|---|---|
| **Year** | **Received (d) $** | **Spent (e) $** | **Profit (f) $** |
| 1 | 15 000 | 4 000 | 11 000 |
| 2 | 5 000 | 3 000 | 2 000 |
| 3 | 5 000 | 1 000 | 4 000 |
| | 25 000 | 8 000 | 17 000 |

| | Difference | | |
|---|---|---|---|
| **Year** | **(a) – (d) $** | **(b) – (e) $** | **(c) – (f) $** |
| 1 | (5 000) | (800) | (4 200) |
| 2 | 2 500 | (600) | 3 100 |
| 3 | 2 500 | 1 400 | 1 100 |
| | 0 | 0 | 0 |

You can see the point again about accrual accounting being a matter of timing. Both the accrual and the cash basis get to the same point, $17 000 profit over the three years, but they take different routes to get there. In Year 1, the accrual profit is $4200 less than the net cash inflow of $11 000, but in Years 2 and 3, the accrual profit is greater than the net cash inflows.

## How's your understanding?

Here are two questions you should be able to answer, based on what you have just read:

1 Why is revenue recognition not always so simple as just debiting accounts receivable and crediting revenue at the point of sale?

2 In 2002, Flimsy Construction Ltd has recognised 38 per cent of the total expected revenue from a contract to build a house extension. The total contract price is $43 000, and Flimsy expects its costs for the contract to be $29 500. Costs so far have been in line with expectations. How much contract expense should Flimsy recognise for 2002 and what would be the resulting contract profit for 2002? ($11 210: $5130)

# 11.5 Extending the expenses concept: SAC 4

In SAC 4 it is stated that: 'Expenses are consumptions or losses of future economic benefits in the form of reductions in assets or increases in liabilities of the entity, other than those relating to distributions to owners, that result in a decrease in equity during the reporting period.'

For example, future economic benefits will be consumed during the current accounting period as stationery supplies are used. In addition, there will be an outflow of future economic benefits in a future accounting period as a result of incurring a liability for property taxes in the current accounting period. Some other expense names mentioned in SAC 4 are wages and salaries, depreciation, amortisation, cost of goods sold, rent and interest.

According to SAC 4, an expense should be recognised when and only when:

**a** it is probable that the consumption or loss of future economic benefits resulting in a reduction in assets and/or an increase in liabilities has occurred; and

**b** the consumption or loss of future economic benefits can be measured reliably.

Most expenses result from the production or delivery of goods and services during the accounting period and the large majority of these involve little or no uncertainty that future economic benefits have been consumed; for example, cost of goods sold, cost of employee services and supplies used and equipment used. However, in some cases there will be uncertainty; for example, it may be difficult to determine whether the future economic benefits embodied in noncurrent assets have suffered commercial impairment (in addition to physical wear and tear) during the reporting period.

In addition, generally the consumption or loss of future economic benefits will be capable of being measured with a high degree of reliability. However, in some cases this measurement will be subject to estimates (future warranty claims, for example). In such cases, it depends on whether the estimates can be made reliably in determining whether an item would qualify as an expense. In general, estimates such as warranties, long service leave, doubtful debts and so on can be made reliably based on past experience and are therefore recognised as expenses.

In section 11.4 the importance of the matching concept was noted. In SAC 4 it is stated that for profit-seeking entities determining profitability, matching of revenues and expenses is typical. However, while application of the concepts in SAC 4 typically result in matching of expenses and revenues, matching is not the criterion used in determining whether an expense should be recognised in a particular accounting period.

The following extract from SAC 4 provides further insight:

> The reporting of relevant and reliable information about the profitability of a profit-seeking entity will typically involve the matching of revenues and expenses in an appropriate manner. This could include the following types of matching of revenues and expenses:
>
> (a) matching of expenses with revenues where those items result directly and jointly from the same transactions or other events; for example, simultaneous recognition of sales and cost of goods sold, and recognition of project revenues arising from performance under construction contracts simultaneously with recognition of project expenses;
>
> (b) matching of revenues with progressive performance by an entity over a period; for example, recognition of interest revenues by lenders over the period of credit, and recognition of insurance premiums by insurers over the period of risk; and
>
> (c) matching of expenses with the entity's productive operations; for example, the systematic recognition of depreciation over the periods during which the entity consumes the future economic benefits embodied in its long-lived assets. Where expenses are not related directly to particular revenues, their recognition will largely be independent of the recognition of revenues. However, a matching of those expenses will occur in the sense that they will be recognised concurrently with revenues generated by the entity's operations in the reporting period …
>
> While application of this Statement would generally give rise to matching of revenues and expenses, there would be instances where matching will not be achievable if relevant and reliable information is to be reported. For example, there could be instances where costs, such as research and development costs, are incurred in the expectation of future benefits but it is not possible, at the reporting date, to establish that it is probable that future economic benefits will eventuate. In those circumstances, the costs would be recognised as expense prior to recognition of any revenues which eventually are generated by a successful outcome from the activity concerned.

## 11.6 Statement of financial performance

In Australia, as noted in chapter 1, the name of the key statement providing information on a company's financial performance was changed from a profit and loss statement to a statement of financial performance (effective 30 June 2001). In addition to the name change, an important difference is that the new statement has two basic components:

- a profit and loss statement, which shows you how the company's accrued profit is calculated
- a statement that shows total changes in equity other than those resulting from transactions with owners as owners.

The following line items and *recognised revenues* and *expenses* must be disclosed separately on the face of the statement of financial performance.

**a** revenues from ordinary activities, excluding any shares of net profits of associates and joint ventures accounted for using the equity method
**b** expenses from ordinary activities, excluding borrowing costs expense and any shares of net losses of associates and joint ventures accounted for using the equity method
**c** borrowing costs expense
**d** shares of net profits or losses of associates and joint ventures accounted for using the equity method
**e** profit or loss from ordinary activities before income tax expense (income tax revenue)

**f** income tax expense relating to ordinary activities
**g** profit or loss from ordinary activities after related income tax expense
**h** profit or loss from extraordinary items after related income tax expense
**i** net profit or loss
**j** net profit or loss attributable to outside equity interest
**k** net profit or loss attributable to members of the parent entity.

Some further explanations of the terms above are now given:

- The definition of ordinary activities is very broad, and virtually all items of revenue and expense included in the determination of net profit or loss for the reporting period arise in the course of the ordinary activities of the entity. It is extremely rare for a transaction or other event to give rise to an extraordinary item.
- Examples of transactions or other events that may give rise to extraordinary items are:
  - *the expropriation of assets:* the expropriation of an asset in a political environment where expropriations are rare may qualify as an extraordinary item. By contrast, the expropriation of assets in a region where the risk of expropriation is high would not qualify as an extraordinary item
  - *an earthquake or other natural disaster:* losses sustained as a result of an earthquake or other natural disaster may qualify as an extraordinary expense for entities that do not operate in a region subject to such events.
- The equity method refers to the situation in which an investing company has significant influence but not control of an investee company (investee company is called an associate company of the investor). Using the equity method, the investing company includes in its profit and loss statement its share of earnings of the investee company, because it is in a position to significantly influence that company's performance (refer back to chapter 10).
- Operating profit or loss after income tax means the profit or loss for the period before extraordinary items and after applicable income taxes.
- Outside equity interests in net profit is a deduction from profit. It is an amount reflecting the share of profit, earned by consolidated companies, that is attributed to owners other than the parent company. For example, if CSR owns 80 per cent of a company, 100 per cent of the revenues and expenses are included in the consolidated figures, but 20 per cent of that company's net profit is deducted as an outside equity interest, so that consolidated net profit only includes CSR's 80 per cent share.

When a revenue or an expense from ordinary activities is of such size, nature or incidence that its disclosure is relevant in explaining the financial performance of a company, its nature and amount must be disclosed separately in the notes in the financial report. These are normally referred to as 'individually significant items'. They are not extraordinary items as described above. Their disclosure is likely to be relevant to users in understanding financial performance and in making decisions.

Some of the circumstances that may give rise to the separate disclosure of the nature and amount of revenues and expenses include:

- the write-down of inventories or noncurrent assets
- litigation settlements
- restructuring of operations
- some changes in accounting policies.

The statement of financial performance for Tabcorp is shown below. We have shown it because of its relative simplicity. It has no non-owner changes in equity.

**EXHIBIT 11.1** **Tabcorp Holdings Limited**

**Statement of financial performance for the financial year ended 30 June 2001**

| | Note | Consolidated | | Tabcorp Holdings | |
|---|---|---|---|---|---|
| | | 2001 $000 | 2000 $000 | 2001 $000 | 2000 $000 |
| Total operating revenues | 2 | 1 811 599 | 1 595 831 | 21 702 | 20 980 |
| Other revenues from ordinary activities | 2 | 25 958 | 34 747 | 219 817 | 203 316 |
| **Revenues from ordinary activities** | 2 | 1 837 557 | 1 630 578 | 241 519 | 224 296 |
| Government taxes | | (556 526) | (500 423) | — | — |
| Commissions and fees | | (406 952) | (382 550) | (15 191) | (14 686) |
| Employee costs | | (238 997) | (187 188) | (16 949) | (18 287) |
| Depreciation and amortisation | | (113 398) | (95 094) | (1 709) | (1 623) |
| Borrowing costs | | (70 994) | (49 307) | (5 178) | (2 868) |
| Other expenses from ordinary activities | | (152 157) | (135 440) | (12 936) | (17 198) |
| **Profit from ordinary activities before income tax expense** | | 298 533 | 280 576 | 189 556 | 169 634 |
| Income tax (expense)/benefit relating to ordinary activities | 4 | (110 851) | (105 796) | 303 | (2 076) |
| **Net profit attributable to members of the parent entity** | | 187 682 | 174 780 | 189 859 | 167 558 |

Among the things you may notice as you review the statement are:

- The statement covers a period of time (years ending 30 June in this case), not a point in time, as the statement of financial position does. It also is shown in thousands of dollars.
- Extensive explanatory notes are referred to on the statement of financial performance and appended to them. The notes are not attached here; the content of such notes is important, however, so some further attention will be paid to it later in this chapter.
- The right-hand columns refer to the parent company (Tabcorp Holdings Limited), and the left-hand columns are consolidated figures that refer to Tabcorp Holdings Limited and its controlled subsidiaries. As noted in chapter 10, a subsidiary is considered a controlled entity when the parent company has the capacity to dominate decision-making in relation to the financial and operating policies of that subsidiary (for instance, the capacity to dominate the composition of the board of directors). Consolidation basically involves aggregating revenues and expenses of the parent entity and all the subsidiaries after eliminating any transactions between these entities.
- At the top of the statement, the total revenue for the year is disclosed. In note 2 to the accounts, the various types of revenue are disclosed. These include waging and gaming revenue, casino revenue, other operating revenue and other revenue.
- Six expenses (including employee costs of $238 997 000) are then deducted to get operating profit before income tax. For Tabcorp Holdings Limited, it amounts to $298 533 000.
- Income tax is levied on a company's profit because the company is legally separate from its owners. Such tax is usually a percentage of profit before income tax (though there are many complications). Income tax expense of $110 851 000 is deducted to get operating profit after income tax of $187 682 000. As there are no outside equity interests,

Tabcorp Holdings Limited has labelled this figure 'net profit attributable to members of the parent entity'. Note 31 shows how the net profit after tax figure impacts retained profits.

| | Note | Consolidated 2001 $000 | 2000 $000 |
|---|---|---|---|
| **Note 31 Retained profits** | | | |
| Retained profits at the beginning of the financial year | | 26 610 | 26 469 |
| Net profit attributable to members of the parent entity | | 187 682 | 174 780 |
| Dividends provided for or paid | | (189 901) | (174 639) |
| Retained profits at the end of the financial year | | 24 391 | 26 610 |

- The net profit (or net loss) is carried to the statement of retained profits to be accumulated with past years' profits and losses. You can see that Tabcorp had a profit of $187 682 000, which is added to the opening retained profits balance of $26 610 000.
- Ending retained profits equals the beginning figure plus net profit minus dividends declared (provided for or paid). In this case, the dividends declared of $189 910 000 were greater than the profit for the year (but less than opening retained profits plus profits for the year), giving a closing retained profits of $24 391 000.

Accounting standards also require disclosure, in a separate component of the statement of financial performance, of non-owner changes in equity not recognised in net profit and loss.

In considering these non-owner changes, think back to chapter 10, and recall how shareholders' equity could be changed. Some possibilities include issue of shares, buyback of shares, paying dividends, earning profit and valuation adjustments (for example, changes in reserves). Some of the above changes in equity are the result of transactions with owners in their capacity as owners (contribution by owners who buy shares; payments to owners for share buybacks; payment of dividends). These amounts are not included in the statement of financial performance. However, changes in total equity can arise from revenues, expenses and valuation adjustments (for example, asset revaluation reserve), and these are called non-owner changes in equity. Some of these items will be included in the profit and loss calculation (for example, increased sales) and some will not (for example, an increase in an asset revaluation reserve).

The new accounting standards require disclosure in a separate component of the statement of financial performance of these non-owner changes in equity not recognised in net profit or loss. Examples of such items are:

- some revaluation increments or decrements
- gains and losses on the translation of the financial statements of self-sustaining foreign operations
- transitional provisions, on the introduction of accounting standards, that require an initial adjustment against opening retained profits.

The appendix to AASB 1018 provides an illustrative statement of financial performance, as shown in exhibit 11.2:

**EXHIBIT 11.2** XYZ Limited

**Statement of financial performance for the financial year ended 30 June 2002**

| | Note | Consolidated 2002 $000 | 2001 $000 |
|---|---|---|---|
| Revenues from ordinary activities | | X | X |
| Expenses from ordinary activities, excluding borrowing costs expense | | (X) | (X) |
| Borrowing costs expense | | (X) | (X) |
| Share of net profits (losses) of associates and joint ventures accounted for using the equity method | | X | (X) |
| **Profit (loss) from ordinary activities before income tax expense (income tax revenue)** | | X | (X) |
| Income tax revenue (income tax expense) relating to ordinary activities | | (X) | X |
| **Profit (loss) from ordinary activities after related income tax expense (income tax revenue)** | 9 | X | (X) |
| Profit (loss) from extraordinary items after related income tax expense (income tax revenue) | 10 | (X) | — |
| **Net profit (loss)** | | X | (X) |
| Net profit (loss) attributable to outside equity interests | | X | (X) |
| **Net profit (loss) attributable to members of the parent entity** | 11 | X | (X) |
| Increase (decrease) in asset revaluation reserve | 12 | X | (X) |
| Net exchange difference on translation of financial report of self-sustaining foreign operations | 13 | (X) | X |
| Increase (decrease) in retained profits on adoption of a new Standard | 11 | (X) | X |
| **Total revenues, expenses and valuation adjustments attributable to members of the parent entity and recognised directly in equity** | | X | X |
| **Total changes in equity other than those resulting from transactions with owners as owners** | 14 | X | X |
| Basic earnings per share | | X | (X) |
| Diluted earnings per share | | X | (X) |
| Dividends per share | | X | X |

As illustrative examples we have shown in exhibits 11.3 and 11.4 the statements of financial performance for both John Fairfax Holdings Limited and Qantas. Note the following similarities and differences. (Numbers refer to the numbers at the left side of each financial statement.)

1 Both statements are labelled 'Statement of financial performance for the year ended 30 June 2001'.
2 Both show columns for the consolidated group and the company.
3 Qantas figures are in millions, while Fairfax figures are in thousands.
4 Both show revenue from ordinary activities excluding interest revenue (Fairfax $1320.5 million, Qantas $10 188.2 million). Qantas divides up the revenue on the face of the statement while Fairfax does it in the notes.

**EXHIBIT 11.3** **John Fairfax Holdings Limited and controlled entities**

**Statement of financial performance for the year ended 30 June 2001**

| | | | Consolidated | | Company | |
|---|---|---|---|---|---|---|
| 2 | | Note | 2001 $000 | 2000 $000 | 2001 $000 | 2000 $000 |
| 3 | | | | | | |
| 4 | **Revenue from ordinary activities, excluding interest income** | 2 | **1 320 545** | 1 346 788 | **130 504** | 109 211 |
| 5 | Share of net profits/(losses) of associates | 2 | **5 277** | 59 382 | — | — |
| | **Expenses from ordinary activities, excluding depreciation and borrowing costs** | 3 | **(1 025 997)** | (1 015 883) | **(58 836)** | (88 448) |
| | **Profit from ordinary activities before depreciation, interest income, borrowing costs and income tax** | | **299 825** | 390 287 | **71 668** | 20 763 |
| | Depreciation and amortisation | 3 | **(65 172)** | (64 681) | **(1 736)** | (1 371) |
| 6 | **Profit from ordinary activities before interest income, borrowing costs and income tax** | | **234 653** | 325 606 | **69 932** | 19 392 |
| | Interest income | 2 | **1 882** | 2 419 | **127 271** | 127 203 |
| | Borrowing costs | 3 | **(45 733)** | (50 002) | **(108 635)** | (78 803) |
| 7 | **Profit from ordinary activities before income tax** | | **190 802** | 278 023 | **88 568** | 67 792 |
| | Income tax (expense)/revenue relating to ordinary activities | 4 | **(62 733)** | (92 552) | **(5 519)** | 3 752 |
| 8 | **Net profit** | | **128 069** | 185 471 | **83 049** | 71 544 |
| 9 | Net profit attributable to outside equity interest | | **—** | 280 | **—** | — |
| | **Net profit attributable to members of the Company*** | 19 | **128 069** | 185 751 | **83 049** | 71 544 |
| | Net increase/(decrease) in asset revaluation reserve | 18 | **(125)** | (1 352) | **—** | — |
| | Net exchange difference on translation of financial report of foreign-controlled entities | 18 | **(214)** | 134 | **—** | — |
| 10 | **Total revenues, expenses and valuation adjustments attributable to members of the Company and recognised directly into equity** | | **(339)** | (1 218) | **—** | — |
| 11 | **Total changes in equity other than those resulting from transactions with owners** | | **127 730** | 184 533 | **83 049** | 71 544 |
| | *** Net profit attributable to members of the Company comprises:** | | | | | |
| | Ongoing operations | | **126 199** | 168 708 | **83 049** | 85 433 |
| 12 | Significant items referred to in Note 3(d), net | | **1 870** | 17 043 | **—** | (13 889) |
| | | | **128 069** | 185 751 | **83 049** | 71 544 |
| 13 | Basic earnings per share (cents) | 21 | **17.5** | 25.5 | **—** | — |

5 Fairfax shows 'share of net profits of associates' as a separate line on the face of the statement. For Qantas, this figure is part of the sales and operating revenue figure, but the associated components are shown in the notes separately.

6 Both show earnings before interest and tax (EBIT) (Fairfax \$234.7 million; Qantas \$695.8 million). However, they do it in different ways. Fairfax deducts expenses from ordinary activities, excluding depreciation, amortisation and borrowing costs (often called EBITDA by companies; that is, earnings before interest, tax, depreciation and amortisation). Depreciation and amortisation are then deducted to show EBIT. For Fairfax, more details of the expenses are shown in the notes. Qantas provides details of its expenses on the face of the report. It does not show EBITDA separately, but we could easily calculate it (EBIT plus depreciation and amortisation).

7 Both companies add on interest revenue and deduct borrowing costs (mainly interest expense) to obtain profit from ordinary activities before income tax (Fairfax \$190.8 million; Qantas \$597.1 million).

**EXHIBIT 11.4** Qantas

**Statement of financial performance for the year ended 30 June 2001**

| | | Notes | Qantas Group 2001 $m | Qantas Group 2000 $m | Qantas 2001 $m | Qantas 2000 $m |
|---|---|---|---|---|---|---|
| 2 | | | Qantas Group | | Qantas | |
| 3 | | Notes | 2001 $m | 2000 $m | 2001 $m | 2000 $m |
| | **Sales and operating revenue** | | | | | |
| | Net passenger revenue | | 7 941.8 | 6 975.6 | 7 385.5 | 6 452.8 |
| | Net freight revenue | | 596.3 | 543.0 | 588.9 | 535.7 |
| | Tours and travel revenue | | 604.3 | 551.8 | — | — |
| | Other sources* | | 1 045.8 | 1 036.4 | 1 550.3 | 979.6 |
| 4 5 | **Sales and operating revenue** | 2 | 10 188.2 | 9 106.8 | 9 524.7 | 7 968.1 |
| | **Expenditure** | | | | | |
| | Manpower and staff related | | 2 549.9 | 2 295.8 | 2 142.6 | 1 983.4 |
| | Selling and marketing | | 1 141.6 | 1 051.0 | 1 146.8 | 1 058.5 |
| | Aircraft operating – variable | | 2 023.0 | 1 732.7 | 2 019.1 | 1 700.3 |
| | Fuel and oil | | 1 329.8 | 863.2 | 1 247.8 | 799.1 |
| | Property | | 246.9 | 215.2 | 228.9 | 206.3 |
| | Computer and communication | | 365.0 | 352.4 | 409.1 | 403.2 |
| | Depreciation and amortisation | | 706.7 | 634.0 | 563.7 | 479.1 |
| | Non-cancellable operating lease rentals | | 181.8 | 127.9 | 132.5 | 120.8 |
| | Tours and travel cost of sales | | 525.7 | 482.8 | — | — |
| | Capacity hire, insurance and other | | 422.0 | 477.8 | 489.5 | 587.7 |
| | **Expenditure** | 3 | 9 492.4 | 8 232.8 | 8 380.0 | 7 338.4 |
| 6 | Earnings before interest and tax (EBIT) | | 695.8 | 874.0 | 1 144.7 | 629.7 |
| | Borrowing costs | 3 | (167.7) | (199.7) | (181.9) | (200.6) |
| | Interest revenue | 2 | 69.0 | 88.5 | 56.5 | 79.9 |
| | **Net interest expense** | | (98.7) | (111.2) | (125.4) | (120.7) |
| 7 | Profit from ordinary activities before income tax expense | | 597.1 | 762.8 | 1 019.3 | 509.0 |
| | Income tax expense relating to ordinary activities | 4 | (177.4) | (244.9) | (190.3) | (170.1) |
| 8 | Net profit | | 419.7 | 517.9 | 829.0 | 338.9 |
| 9 | Outside equity interests in net profit | | (4.3) | (0.6) | — | — |
| | Net profit attributable to members of the company | | 415.4 | 517.3 | 829.0 | 338.9 |
| | Non owner transaction changes in equity | | | | | |
| 10 | Net exchange differences on translation of financial statements of self-sustaining foreign operations | 21 | 0.3 | 1.2 | — | — |
| 11 | Total changes in equity from non-owner related transactions attributable to members of the company | 23 | 415.7 | 518.5 | 829.0 | 338.9 |
| 13 | Basic earnings per share | 38 | 33.0 cents | 42.8 cents | | |
| | Diluted earnings per share | 38 | 32.8 cents | 42.7 cents | — | — |

* Excludes proceeds on sale (and on sale and leaseback) of noncurrent assets Group $163.9 million, Qantas $159.0 million (2000: Group $889.7 million, Qantas $879.6 million), and interest revenue Group $69.0 million, Qantas $56.5 million (2000: Group $88.5 million, Qantas $79.9 million) which is included in net interest expense.

8 Both companies deduct income tax to arrive at the net profit figure (Fairfax $128.1 million; Qantas $419.7 million). The net profit figure is sometimes described as the 'bottom line'.

9 Both companies deduct outside equity interests in net profit (in some countries this is referred to as 'minority interest') to obtain net profit attributable to members of the

parent company. For example, assume one of the subsidiaries in which the parent owns 90 per cent of the shares makes a profit of $100 000. The whole $100 000 would be included in consolidated net profit. However, $10 000 (10 per cent of $100 000) is really owned by outsiders, therefore this is deducted from net profit to obtain net profit attributable to members of the parent company.

**10** Both companies include non-owner transaction changes in equity (excluding this years' profit and loss). For Fairfax these amount to $(339 000), and consist of a decrease in the asset revaluation reserve and an exchange difference on translation of the financial statements of foreign-controlled entities. For Qantas, the amount is $300 000, and relates to an exchange difference on the translation of financial statements of a foreign controlled entity.

**11** While they use different headings, both companies come up with a total for 'total changes in equity other than those resulting from transactions with owners'. This is the sum of **10** above, as well as this year's net profit attributable to members of the parent company. For Fairfax, this figure is $127.7 million, and for Qantas, it is $415.7 million.

**12** Fairfax shows significant items separate from ongoing operations on the face of the statement. Qantas adopts the more normal procedures of disclosing these significant items in the notes to the accounts. The list of individually significant items for Qantas were:

| | **2001** **$m** |
|---|---|
| Change in accounting policy for software development costs | 46.0 |
| Profit on sale of Mascot Head Office land and buildings | 41.2 |
| Revenue relating to assets sold by an associated company | 43.3 |
| Provision for redundancy costs | (35.0) |

**13** Both companies provide earnings per share figures. This divides the net profit figure by the average number of issued shares. These will be discussed in chapter 14 in more detail.

## 11.7 Managers and the recognition of revenues and expenses

Profit determination is of vital interest to both shareholders and managers, as it is a key component in their performance evaluation. As profit depends on revenue recognition and expense recognition, an understanding of these concepts is important when various decision alternatives are being considered by management.

Revenue and expense recognition also require many different judgements by managers. For example, assume a company is involved in long-term contracts and uses the percentage of completion method to recognise revenues. Two examples of judgements that need to be made by management are **a** how to calculate the percentage of completion and **b** at what point can the outcome of the contract be reliably estimated. With respect to the first point, managers must decide whether to use such methods as physical estimates, or the proportion of costs incurred to date compared to the estimated total costs. While the outcome of a contract is never certain until it is complete, the percentage of completion method allows managers to recognise profit earlier, provided the outcome is 'reliably estimated'. Determining this level of reliability is the second judgement outlined above.

## 11.8 Public sector issues

As was noted in chapter 5, government departments use accrual accounting in measuring revenues and expenses. Examples of revenues of government departments include the proceeds of user charges, fines and fees the department gains control of during the reporting period. Control will usually occur when the goods or services are provided or when the fines are levied. However, some departments do not gain control of the assets arising from charges, fees and fines. For example, the Office of State Revenue would collect payroll and land tax on behalf of the Crown. In this case, no revenue is recognised in their financial statements.

Another example of revenue is parliamentary appropriations (such as recurrent appropriations, capital or works and services appropriations). However, complications, which are beyond the scope of this book, arise in determining the date at which the government department gains control and therefore when the revenue should be recognised. For example, AAS 29 argues that accounts appropriated to a department for such things as unemployment benefits, pensions, family allowances and so on should not be recognised as revenues in the department's financial statements.

## 11.9 Homework and discussion to develop understanding

### Discussion questions

1 Provide an example of a trade-off between relevance and reliability for revenue recognition.

2 What criteria are used to recognise revenue?

3 Compare revenue recognition under the percentage of completion, and completed contract methods.

4 What conditions need to be met before revenue can be recognised?

5 What conditions need to be met before expenses can be recognised?

6 A statement of financial performance shows profit and loss for the period, and total changes in equity other than those resulting from transactions with owners as owners. Provide three examples of these changes in equity.

7 What is an extraordinary item? Provide three examples.

8 What is a significant item? Provide three examples.

9 You are told by a friend who builds upstairs extensions to houses that he estimates the profit on a job at the time of quoting, and recognises 10 per cent of profit each week based on the fact that most jobs take 10 weeks. Do you agree?

10 Explain why revenue is sometimes recognised at the point of sale. When would it be appropriate to recognise revenue at the time of production?

11 Describe the matching principle. How is it dealt with in SAC 4?

12 Discuss when each of the following types of businesses is likely to recognise revenues:

   a a shipbuilding company

   b a magazine company for which yearly subscriptions are received yearly in advance and the magazines are posted each month

- **c** a coal-mining company that has a long-term contract to supply a local company at a set price
- **d** a printer
- **e** an installer of hotwater systems.

**13** Discuss when each of the following types of business are likely to recognise revenues:

- **a** a telecommunications company that provides local and interstate calls
- **b** an airline
- **c** a real estate developer who constructs 'speculative' houses and later sells them
- **d** an engineering business that receives orders for special-purpose machinery accompanied by deposits
- **e** a meat pie stand at the football ground.

**14** Which of the following items are likely to be treated as extraordinary items in the profit and loss account:

- **a** Differences in movements of foreign exchange rates?
- **b** A large profit on the sale of an investment portfolio?
- **c** A large profit on the sale of all assets of a significant business?
- **d** A bad debt write-off equal to 50 per cent of operating profit before tax?
- **e** The destruction of one of the company's largest factories by earthquake (the factory was not insured)?

**15** Would a large write-down of inventory that has become obsolete be included as an extraordinary item? Why, or why not?

**16** What is the main benefit of providing separate disclosure of significant items?

## Problem 11.1* Likely revenue recognition policies for various cases

When is a sale a sale? When does the accounting system recognise revenue as having been earned? Indicate what you think would be the revenue recognition policy in each of the following cases. Remember to think of whether the general criteria for revenue recognition have been met, the concept of a 'critical event' for revenues recognised all at once, and the proportionate recognition that is available for revenue earned over several accounting periods:

1. coffee shop
2. sales of housing subdivisions
3. sales of natural gas to businesses and residences
4. magazine subscription sales
5. ticket sales for concerts
6. instalment sales of appliances and furniture
7. revenue from drilling oil wells on others' properties
8. revenue from oil production on its own land
9. revenue from sales of pottery on consignment through local craft shops
10. a TV station's revenue from advertising on sports programs
11. revenues from sales of manufactured plumbing products
12. computer stores sales of microcomputer software
13. department store revenue from clothing sales (some people pay cash; some use their store credit cards; some use other credit cards; and some return their purchases after deciding they don't like them)
14. your university's or college's revenue from student tuition fees
15. a charity's revenues from donations
16. a gardener's revenues from contract landscaping work for home owners.

## Problem 11.2* Revenue and expense recognition for a franchiser

The Pie Place Ltd (TPP) was started in 2001 to franchise a chain of fast-food outlets that would sell only pies: meat, chicken, seafood, apple and the like. A speciality was to be 'pi-pie', a recipe made from various roots (ginger, ginseng and so on) and invented by Janet Randolph, the founder and owner of TPP.

Janet has divided each major city into population sectors of about 200 000 each and plans to sell one franchise per sector. For smaller cities, franchises will cover rural areas as well. The franchises will be good for ten years, renewable for at least two more ten-year periods, and will sell for $20 000 each. Each franchisee must pay TPP $5000 down in cash, pay the remainder in three equal annual instalments (with no interest charges), and agree to buy various ingredients from TPP. In return, TPP will provide expert advice (Janet's), recipes, help with locating and constructing the food outlet, management training and some national advertising. (Most advertising costs will be charged back to the franchises on a pro rata basis.)

Here are data for TPP's first year, ended 31 August 2002:

| | |
|---|---:|
| Franchise agreements signed | 28 |
| Down payments received | 26 |
| Fast-food outlets opened | 18 |
| Franchise-related costs | $230 000 |
| Other general expenses | $55 000 |

One of the franchises has already gone out of business (having paid only the initial $5000), two others of those that have opened do not look as if they are going to make it, and one of the unopened franchises looks as if it will never get going.

***Required:***

1 List as many methods as you can think of for recognising revenue from franchise sales.

2 Rank those methods from least conservative to most conservative.

3 List as many methods as you can think of for recognising expenses from franchise-related costs.

4 Match each expense recognition method to the revenue recognition method that seems most appropriate.

5 Compare the profit before tax for 2002 that would be produced by two or three of the more reasonably matched methods of recognising revenue and expense.

6 Choose a matched method that you think would be most appropriate for TPP.

7 Draft an 'accounting policy' footnote describing your chosen revenue/expense recognition method for TPP's 31 August 2002 financial statements.

## Problem 11.3 Revenue and expense recognition

Indicate whether each of the events described below gives rise to a revenue or an expense under SAC 4. If yes, what would be the other side of the transaction?

1 A temporary excess of cash is used to purchase $8500 of shares in BHP Billiton.

2 $5000 is paid as a deposit on custom-designed equipment, to be completed and delivered next year. The total purchase price of this equipment will be $20 000.

3 A supplier sends notice that $900 of raw materials have been shipped by freight, with payment due in 30 days. The buyer obtains title to the goods as soon as they are shipped by the seller.

4 A customer places an order for $600 worth of goods.

5 A production manager has been hired to oversee the company's operations, with employment commencing next month. One-twelfth of the annual salary of $96 000 is to be paid at the end of each month worked.

6 Inventory is acquired at a list price of $1200, with payment made in time to secure a 2 per cent discount for prompt settlement. Cash discounts are treated as a reduction in the acquisition cost of the inventory.

## Problem 11.4 Revenue and expense recognition

Indicate whether each of the events described below gives rise to a revenue or an expense under SAC 4. If yes, what would be the other side of the transaction?

1 A bank loan of $10 000 is obtained, with the company signing an agreement to repay the amount in 6 months, together with interest of 8 per cent.

2 Electricity used in the past month, worth $230, has not been paid for.

3 A $3000 cheque is received from a tenant for 3 months' rent in advance.

4 A company signs a two-year employment contract with a marketing manager. Employment begins next month, at a contract price of $150 000 per year.

## Problem 11.5 Choose suitable revenue recognition policies

In each of the following independent cases, indicate when you think the company in question should recognise revenue. Support your decision with reference to the generally accepted criteria for revenue recognition.

1 Outback Gold mines and refines gold. To sell the gold, the company waits until it feels the market price is favourable. The company can, if it wishes, sell its entire inventory of gold at any time at the prevailing market price.

2 Crazy Freddie sells cheap, ugly furniture on the instalment plan. His customers take delivery of the furniture after making a down payment. In the course of the past year, Crazy Freddie has had to repossess over 50 per cent of the furniture that he sold, because of customers defaulting on payments.

3 Tom and Mark's Construction undertakes long-term construction contracts. The company only accepts contracts that will pay a fixed fee. Costs can be estimated with reasonable accuracy, and there has never been a problem collecting from customers.

4 Cecily Cedric is a toy manufacturer producing toys that are shipped to various retail customers upon receipt of their purchase order. Sales are billed after shipment. The company estimates that approximately 2 per cent of credit sales prove to be uncollectable.

## Problem 11.6 Interpret expense recognition footnotes

Read the following excerpts from past annual reports, and explain what is going on and why the companies have the policies described.

**Mayne Nickless, 2001**
**(a) Capitalisation of interest**
Building projects:
To establish the costs of capital projects, interest is capitalised on capital projects during development. The interest is amortised over the estimated useful life of the relevant fixed asset.

**Coal and Allied, 2000**
**(b) Exploration, evaluation and development expenditure**
Exploration and evaluation expenditure incurred by or on behalf of the entity is accumulated separately for each area of interest. Such expenditure comprises net direct costs.

Exploration expenditure for each area of interest is carried forward as an asset provided that one of the following conditions is met:

i such costs are expected to be recouped through successful development and production of the area of interest, or alternatively, by its sale; or

ii exploration activities in the area of interest have not yet reached a stage which permits a reasonable assessment of the existence or otherwise of economically recoverable reserves, and active and significant operations in relation to the area are continuing.

Exploration expenditure that fails to meet at least one of the conditions outlined above is written off to the extent that it is considered not recoverable. In the event that an area of interest is abandoned, or the Directors consider the expenditure to be of no value, accumulated costs carried forward are written off in the period in which that assessment is made.

## Problem 11.7 Recommend revenue and expense recognition policy

Gary Slapstick Promotions Ltd (GSP) acquired the rights to use the names of a number of football players on life-sized stuffed dolls it purchases from a toy manufacturer. The dolls are marketed through mail-order advertisements in the TV-listings inserts of large newspapers. When an order is received (with a money order, cheque or credit card number), GSP contacts the toy manufacturer. The toy manufacturer is responsible for manufacturing and shipping the doll to the lucky boy or girl. GSP is notified at the time of shipment. The customer has the option of returning the doll within two weeks of the day it is received. GSP pays the toy manufacturer within 30 days after delivery. Response to the dolls this Christmas has been overwhelming. In fact, the toy manufacturer is working extra shifts to try and keep up with the demand.

1 Identify three points in time at which GSP could recognise revenue on the dolls. Which would you recommend? Why?

2 Identify two different points in time at which the toy manufacturer could recognise revenue on the dolls.

3 Discuss how GSP should account for its payments to football players for the right to use their names. (Assume that each player is paid a lump sum initially and a royalty on each doll sold that uses his name.)

## Problem 11.8 Builder's revenues, expenses and assets

A builder formed a construction company in September. After several months' effort, the company completed a residence at a total cost of $70 000 and advertised it for sale. By 31 December, the company had received three offers: one of $78 000 cash; another of $83 000 to be paid in monthly instalments over 20 years at 10 per cent annual interest; and another of $50 000 cash plus a residential lot worth $31 000. The builder decided to wait for a higher offer, which he seemed certain to get.

1 What was the amount of the construction company's revenue for the year?

2 How much were its expenses?

3 In what form, if any, were its assets on 31 December?

4 Taking each offer separately, assume the offers were accepted and calculate the amount of revenue and expense for the four-month period ended 31 December in each case. Assume that for each situation the sale was settled on 26 December.

## Problem 11.9 Recognition in accordance with standards and SAC 4

For each of items 1 to 5 listed below, state whether, in accordance with existing accounting standards and SAC 4, it would be recognised as:

a an asset

b a liability

c a contingent liability

**d** revenue

**e** an expense

**f** none of the above.

*Items:*

1. A provision for annual leave
2. A million dollars payable under a guarantee in the event of a third party being unable to pay
3. Purchased goodwill
4. A patent
5. The excess of research and development costs over the expected future economic benefits of the project

## Problem 11.10 Expense recognition

The Ten Group Pty Ltd included the following note in their statement of significant accounting policies.

> **Program development**
> The consolidated entity's long term commitment to program planning and development requires significant expenditure on an infrequent basis. Accordingly, where appropriate, amounts are set aside as a charge against revenue to reflect more properly the ongoing nature of these expenses in the periods in which they accrue.

Discuss whether you agree with this expense recognition policy.

## Problem 11.11 Franchise revenue amounts and policies

Pickin Chicken Ltd and Country Delight Ltd both sell franchises for their chicken restaurants. The purchaser of the franchise (the franchisee) receives the right to use Pickin Chicken's and Country Delight's products and benefit from national training and advertising programs for 10 years. The buyers agree to pay $50 000 for a franchise. Of this amount, $20 000 is paid upon signing the agreement and the remainder is payable in five equal annual instalments of $6000 each.

Pickin Chicken recognises all franchise revenue when franchise agreements are signed. Country Delight recognises franchise revenue as cash is received. In 1999 the companies each sold eight franchises. In 2000 they each sold five. In 2001 and 2002, neither company sold a franchise.

1. Determine the amount of franchise revenue recognised by each company in 1999, 2000, 2001 and 2002.
2. Do you think that revenue should be recognised when the franchise agreement is signed, when cash is received, or over the life of the franchise agreement? Why? Fully support your answer.

## Problem 11.12 Preparing a statement of financial performance

The Ten Group Pty Ltd included the following amounts in their financial statements for the year ended 31 August 2001.

| | $000 |
|---|---:|
| Revenue from ordinary activities | 664 157 |
| Television costs | (401 061) |
| Other costs | (96 782) |
| Borrowing costs | (93 263) |

| | $000 |
|---|---|
| Share of net profit of associates and joint ventures accounted for using the equity method | 588 |
| Income tax expense relating to ordinary activities | (23 822) |
| Net (profit)/loss attributable to outside equity interests | 5 451 |
| Net exchange difference on translation of financial report of foreign controlled entities | 18 |

***Required:***

Prepare a statement of financial performance for the year ended 31 August 2001.

## Problem 11.13 Disclosure of a change in expense recognition policy

News Corporation included the following note in their June 2001 statement of significant accounting policies.

> At the beginning of the current financial year, the Company changed its accounting policy with regards to, amongst other things, the treatment of marketing and development costs incurred in the production and distribution of films whereby marketing and certain development costs, previously capitalised and expensed over time, are now expensed as incurred. This change in accounting policy provides better comparability of the Company's results against its competitors and has also ensured continued consistency with United States' generally accepted accounting principles for producers and distributors of films. The net impact of this change in accounting policy net of outside equity interest was a one-off pre-tax charge to profit of $1107 million, with an associated tax benefit of $421 million.

***Required:***

How should the above information be disclosed in the financial statements? Possibilities include:

**a** on the face of the statement of financial performance

**b** in a note on significant items

**c** no further disclosure is required.

## Problem 11.14 Interpret revenue recognition notes

Pasminco was formed in 1988 by the merger of the zinc lead silver mining, smelting and international marketing activities of two of Australia's leading resource-based companies, CRA Limited and North Broken Hill Peko Limited. The new company became Australia's only primary producer of refined zinc and lead metals, and is now the world's largest zinc producer.

Read the following excerpt from the 2000 annual report of Pasminco Limited, and explain what it means.

> **p Sales revenue**
> Sales revenue is stated on a gross basis, with freight and realisation expenses included in the cost of sales. Sales revenue is stated net of the impact of gains and losses arising on foreign exchange hedging contracts relating to sales commitments and designated borrowings effectively hedging future revenues. Sales of metals, concentrates, ores and byproducts are recognised when the product passes out of the physical control of the selling company to external customers pursuant to enforceable sales contracts. As the final value of concentrate sales can only be determined from weights, assays, prices and exchange rates applying after a shipment has arrived at its destination, sales of concentrates are recorded at estimated values pursuant to contract terms, with adjustments being subsequently recognised in the period when final values are determined.

## Problem 11.15 Significant Items

OPSM Limited reported a net profit before tax of $1 554 000 and a net profit after tax of $1 431 000 for the year ended 30 June 2001. It also reported the following earnings per share information:

| | Consolidated | |
|---|---|---|
| | **2001 cents** | **2000 cents** |
| Basic earnings per share before individually significant items | 15.87 | 17.30 |
| Basic earnings per share after individually significant items | 1.08 | 12.72 |

Note 4 is shown below.

| **Note 4: Individually significant items** | **2001 $000** | **2000 $000** |
|---|---|---|
| **Gains** | | |
| Profit on sale of Protector Supply business | 7 814 | — |
| **Expenses/losses** | | |
| Write-down of the carrying value of Protector Technologies business | 28 349 | — |
| Strategic restructuring including redundancies | 1 114 | 9 513 |
| **Total individually significant expenses/losses before income tax** | 29 463 | 9 513 |
| **Net individually significant expenses/losses before income tax** | 21 649 | 9 513 |
| Less: Income tax benefit on individually significant items | (2 022) | (3 343) |
| **Net individually significant expenses after income tax** | 19 627 | 6 170 |
| **Profit from ordinary activities before income tax expense** | 1 554 | 25 830 |
| Total individually significant net expenses/losses before income tax | 21 649 | 9 513 |
| Profit from ordinary activities before income tax and individually significant items | 23 203 | 35 343 |

***Required:***

Explain how the note on significant items would assist shareholders in their decision-making.

## Problem 11.16 Preparing a statement of financial performance

Leighton Holdings Limited provides the following information for the year ending 30 June 2001.

| | | Consolidated | |
|---|---|---|---|
| | **Note** | **2001 $000** | **2000 $000** |
| Revenues from ordinary activities | | **4 393 254** | 3 577 364 |
| Expenses from ordinary activities | | **(4 183 361)** | (3 371 494) |
| Borrowing costs | | **(10 872)** | (5 453) |
| Share of net profits of associates and joint venture entities | | **3 219** | 957 |

| | Note | Consolidated 2001 $000 | 2000 $000 |
|---|---|---|---|
| Income tax expense relating to ordinary activities | | **(42 312)** | (43 371) |
| Net profit attributable to outside equity interests | | **(3 772)** | (23 923) |
| Net exchange difference on translation of financial statements of self-sustaining foreign operations | 20 | **12 229** | (1 180) |
| Increase in asset revaluation reserve | 20 | **—** | 19 |

*Required:*

Prepare a statement of financial performance for the years ending 30 June 2000 and 2001.

## Problem 11.17 Interpreting a statement of financial performance

**Billabong International Limited**
Consolidated statement of financial performance
for the year ended 30 June 2001

| | 2001 $000 |
|---|---|
| Revenue from ordinary activities | 387 074 |
| Less: Operating expenses prior to depreciation, amortisation, interest and borrowing costs | (311 791) |
| Earnings before interest, tax, depreciation and amortisation | 75 283 |
| Depreciation expense | (2 520) |
| Amortisation expense | (3 018) |
| Interest received | 661 |
| Borrowing costs expense | (6 591) |
| Profit from ordinary activities before income tax expense | 63 815 |
| Income tax expense | (21 756) |
| Net profit attributable to members of Billabong International Limited | 42 059 |
| Net exchange differences on translation of financial reports of foreign controlled entities | 3 009 |
| Total revenues, expenses and valuation adjustments attributable to members of Billabong International Limited recognised directly in equity | 3 009 |
| Total changes in equity other than those resulting from transactions with owners as owners | 45 068 |

*Required:*

1 Provide examples of what would be included in revenue from ordinary activities.
2 Where would cost of goods sold be disclosed?
3 Calculate EBIT.
4 What is the 'bottom line'?
5 Does the company have any outside equity interests?
6 Which figure would be included in the note that reconciles opening and closing retained profits?

## Problem 11.18 Company transactions including extraordinary items

The following transactions occurred for Andrew Ltd for the year ended 30 June 2002:

- **a** There was a major change in the Australian dollar resulting in a large exchange rate loss.
- **b** Income tax expense for the current period was determined at year-end.
- **c** Rent was prepaid for July 2002.
- **d** Ordinary dividends were declared.
- **e** One shareholder sold its shares in Andrew Ltd to another company. The shares were sold at a loss.
- **f** A fire destroyed most of Andrew's inventory. The inventory was uninsured.
- **g** Management believes it will probably be able to win a major contract to service the government's computers, although no expenditure has been incurred to date.
- **h** The price of shares of Andrew Ltd fell.
- **i** A major segment of the business, which comprised only land and investments, was sold for cash. The sale proceeds were below the carrying amount of the assets.
- **j** Accounts payable were paid.
- **k** Andrew Ltd provided for future warranty claims.
- **l** Depreciation was charged on a building.
- **m** A provision was created for obsolete stock.
- **n** At a meeting of the board of directors it was decided that the company would obtain foreign currency through forward exchange contracts in future.
- **o** Interest was paid for the year ended 30 June 2002 on that date.
- **p** Internally generated goodwill declined throughout the year.
- **q** Inventory was sold below cost on credit.
- **r** Andrew Ltd may be liable for damages incurred by a consumer of one of its products. It is likely that some payment will be required. The amount is dependent upon the outcome of a court case.
- **s** A bad debt was written off. No amount had been provided in previous years. The debt represented 8 per cent of year-end debtors. Bad debts over the last two years have represented 1 per cent of year-end debtors.

***Required:***

1. Which of the above transactions would not require a journal entry?
2. Which transactions would involve an extraordinary item?
3. Which of the expenses would affect the operating profit?

## Problem 11.19 (Challenging) Interpret expense notes

Shown below are three notes from the 2001 financial statements of Amalgamated Holdings Limited for deferred expenditure, research and development costs and construction rights.

**(m) Deferred expenditure**

Material items of expenditure are deferred to the extent that they are recoverable out of future revenue; do not relate solely to revenue which has already been brought to account; can be measured reliably; and will contribute to the future capacity of the consolidated entity.

Deferred expenditure is amortised over the period in which the related benefits are expected to be realised. Expenditure deferred in previous periods is reviewed annually. Any amounts no longer considered recoverable out of future revenue are written off.

**(n) Research and development costs**

Research and development costs are deferred where future benefits from those costs are expected beyond any reasonable doubt to be recoverable out of future revenue.

Research and development costs are amortised over the period in which the related benefits are expected to be realised. Costs deferred in previous periods are reviewed annually. Any amounts no longer considered recoverable are written off.

**(o) Construction rights**

Construction rights relate to a controlled entity's ability to develop accommodation in the Thredbo Alpine Resort. The costs are being amortised as the rights are either sold or developed. The carrying value of construction rights is reviewed annually. Any amounts no longer considered recoverable are written off.

## Problem 11.20 (Challenging) Profit on various revenue recognition bases

The Latanae Company produces a single product at a cost of $6 each, all of which is paid in cash when the unit is produced. Selling expenses of $3 a unit are paid at the time of shipment. The sale price is $10 a unit; all sales are on account. No customer defaults are expected, and no costs are incurred at the time of collection.

During 2001, the company produced 100 000 units, shipped 76 000 units, and collected $600 000 from customers. During 2002, it produced 80 000 units, shipped 90 000 units, and collected $950 000 from customers.

1 Ignoring income tax for now, determine the amount of profit that would be reported for each of these two years:
   a if revenue and expense are recognised at the time of production
   b if revenue and expense are recognised at the time of shipment
   c if revenue and expense are recognised at the time of collection.
2 Would the asset total shown on the 31 December 2002 statement of financial position be affected by the choice among the three recognition bases used in question 1? What would be the amount of any such difference?
3 Redo question 1, assuming that the company's income tax rate is 30 per cent.

## Problem 11.21 (Challenging) Cost capitalisation, rental income issues

A company stops accumulating costs (capitalising) in a long-term asset account (for example, a building asset) and begins charging expenditures to expense and calculating depreciation expense on the asset when the asset is put into service and begins to earn revenue. This is usually fairly straightforward, but consider the following.

A company owns an office building that is scheduled to be completely finished on 1 September 2002. As of 1 July 2002, construction costs totalled $3 000 000, including interest on construction financing of $150 000 ($10 000 from 1 April 2002 to 1 July 2002). The first tenant moved in on 1 April 2002, and was followed by several others. At 1 July 2002, approximately 40 per cent of the space had been rented. Projections indicate that 70 per cent of the office space needs to be rented before the building will be profitable. Unfortunately, the vacancy rate is extremely high for office space in this area of the city because of a recent economic downturn. Average occupancy is 60 per cent in other office buildings nearby, with no expectation of improvement for at least three years. To date, rent of $50 000 has been paid by the tenants, in addition to expenses amounting to $10 000 to reimburse the company for some of the utilities, cleaning and other common-area costs of the building that total $25 000 from 1 April to 1 July 2002. The rental revenue, common-area costs and common-area cost reimbursements have been netted and capitalised, reducing construction costs to date by $35 000 in total ($50 000 + $10 000 – $25 000).

As well, the construction costs to date include $100 000 paid to these tenants by the company to cover some of their leasehold improvements (alterations the tenants had to make to their office space to make it suitable for their use – interior walls, painting, carpeting). These payments to the tenants were inducements to lure them away from their old premises in other nearby buildings and into signing long-term rental agreements (five years) with the company.

1 Is the company 'correct' in capitalising some or all of the above items? Why or why not?
2 When might be an appropriate time to record cash receipts and disbursements related strictly to rental activity as statement of financial performance items, rather than statement of financial position items (that is, to recognise revenues and expenses)?

## Problem 11.22 (Challenging) Real company's revenue, expense recognition

Using the financial statements of any company you are interested in, write a comprehensive review of the company's revenue and expense recognition policies. Cover such points as:

1 what the nature of the company's business is and how it earns its revenue and incurs its expenses
2 what the company's financial statements and notes disclose about its important revenue and expense recognition policies
3 based on **1** and **2** and on your own thinking about the company, the appropriateness of the company's revenue and expense policies and the questions or concerns that you have about them.

## Case 11A Woolworths Limited

See appendix 2.

1 Which of the notes under 'significant accounting policies' (note 1) deal with revenue and expense recognition?
2 Select three notes related to expense recognition and prepare an alternative policy for the recognition of the expense. Does your alternative increase or decrease profit for the year?
3 Find the dollar values for each of the following for 2001:
   a total sales revenue
   b cost of goods sold
   c depreciation
   d interest expense
   e bad and doubtful debts
   f income tax expense
   g net profit attributable to outside equity interests.
4 What is meant by net profit attributable to outside equity interests?
5 What expenses and valuation adjustment were recognised directly to equity in 2000 and 2001?

## Case 11B Revenue recognition policies

Shown below are a range of revenue recognition disclosures for Australian companies from their 2001 financial statements.

### Qantas
### Passenger and freight sales revenue

Passenger and freight sales revenue is included in the statement of financial performance at the fair value of the consideration received net of sales discounts and net of goods and services tax (GST). Passenger and freight sales commissions are treated as a cost of sale. Passenger and freight sales are credited to revenue received in advance and subsequently transferred to revenue when tickets are utilised or freight uplifted.

### News Corp

Revenue from the theatrical distribution of motion pictures is recognised when motion pictures are exhibited. Revenue from video sales, net of a reserve for returns, is recognised on the date that video units are made widely available for sale by retailers. Revenue from the licensing of feature films and television programming is recorded when the material is available for telecasting by the licensee and when certain other conditions are met.

Television advertising revenue is recognised as the commercials are aired. Subscriber fees received from cable system operators and direct broadcast satellite services are recognised as revenue when services are provided.

Advertising revenue from newspapers, magazines and inserts is recognised when the advertisements are published. Revenue from magazine subscriptions is deferred and recognised proportionately as the magazines are delivered to subscribers. Revenue from books and magazines sold on newsstands is recognised upon shipment, net of a reserve for returns.

## OPSM

Revenue is recognised in the Optical business at the time of commitment to purchase by the customer. In the Protector business, revenue is recognised either when the goods have been dispatched to a customer or used by the customer under a consignment arrangement.

## Tabcorp

Wagering and Gaming revenue is recognised as the residual value after deducting the statutory return to customers from the Wagering and Gaming turnover.

Casino revenue is the net gaming win plus the retail sales of food, beverages, accommodation and other services.

## Goodman Fielder Ltd

Sales revenue represents revenue earned from the sale of the economic entity's products, net of returns, trade allowances and duties and taxes paid. Sales revenue is recognised when control of the goods passes to the purchaser. Other revenue in the case of the parent entity includes dividends received from controlled entities.

## Mayne Nickless

Sales revenue is recognised when the service has been performed. Prepaid revenue for freight satchels and stickers is deferred and recognised when the service has been completed using systems which monitor sales and service patterns.

## Fosters

### Beer and spirits

Sales are recorded when the goods leave the warehouse. Credit terms for the beer business are generally 14 days from the date of invoice and 35 days from the date of invoice for the spirits business.

### Leisure and hospitality

Sales are recorded when the customer receives the goods or service.

## Telstra

### Installation and connection fees

Installation and connection fee revenues are deferred and recognised over the average estimated customer contract life. For basic access installation and connections this is an average of five years. For mobile phone connections, this is an average of two years. Incremental costs directly related to these revenues are also deferred and amortised over the customer contract life. Any costs in excess of the revenue deferred are recognised immediately.

### Sale of goods

Our revenue from the sale of goods includes revenue from the sale of customer equipment and similar goods. This revenue is recorded on delivery of the goods sold.

### Rent of network facilities

We earn rent mainly from the rent of dedicated lines, customer equipment, property, plant and equipment and other facilities provided. The revenue is recorded on an accrual basis over the rental period.

### BHP

Revenue from the sale of goods and disposal of other assets is recognised when the economic entity has passed control of the goods or other assets to the buyer.

***Required:***

1 What would be the journal entries for Qantas to recognise revenue?
2 Discuss the different points at which News Corporation recognises revenue. How do these meet the criteria of SAC 4?
3 Discuss whether the OPSM recognition policies meet the criteria of SAC 4.
4 What alternatives could Tabcorp use to recognise revenue?
5 Goodman Fielder and BHP use the term 'when control of the goods passes' to the purchaser. What does this mean?
6 What judgements need to be made in Mayne Nickless' recognition of freight satchels?
7 Outline alternative ways in which Telstra could have recognised revenue.

## CASE 11C Revenue recognition

The following extract refers to the refusal of the auditors to recognise a revenue transaction:

### ERG's loss of gloss not so smart

Shares in smart card group ERG Ltd plummeted more than 20 per cent yesterday, to 66c, after it reported an unexpected 83 per cent slump in net profit to $6.1 million for the year to June 30, damaging already fragile confidence in the stock.

The result was forced on the Perth-based company by its auditors, who refused to sign off on a $31 million contribution to earnings from the sale of software licence fees to German smart card joint venture, card.etc AG, for which it received shares.

ERG's chief executive, Mr Peter Fogarty, criticised the auditor's approach and said the result would have been in line with analysts' forecasts if the transaction, completed on June 28, had, in line with previous practice, been recognised as revenue rather than deferred.

Mr Fogarty said licence fee revenue was a recurring part of ERG's business and should be recognised in the year of transaction, as it had been when it received shares for licensing its software to its UK joint venture, Prepayment Cards Ltd.

However, Pricewaterhouse–Coopers was not willing to accept the shares in card.etc AG were sufficiently measurable or there was sufficient probability that economic benefit would flow. 'We do not want to just get paid in cash,' Mr Fogarty said. 'We want the upside of equity in the operation.'

The last-minute dispute with the auditor – the accounts were signed off just after midnight yesterday – is ill timed for ERG, given the thrashing its share price has taken over the past six months and the market's heightened sensitivity to earnings quality.

Analysts said ERG's results reflected the newfound caution being exercised by auditors, given the recent focus on their role.

(Source: Cathy Bolt and Mandy Bryan, *Australian Financial Review*, 23 August 2001, p. 46.)

**ERG Limited**

| **Full year** | **2001 ($ m)** | **2000 ($ m)** |
|---|---|---|
| Sales | 299 | 416 |
| Pre-tax | 6.4 | 35.49 |
| Net | 6.1 | 35.2 |
| EPS | 1.0c | 16.7c |
| Interim div* | 0.0c | 0.0c |
| Final div* | 1.0c | 2.0c |
| Shares (yest) | 66c | –20c |

*Date payable: 30 November

***Required:***

1 Consider the requirements for recognising revenue outlined in the chapter. Which requirement would the auditors have been concerned about when they refused to recognise revenue in this situation?
2 What have been some of the impacts of this transaction not being recognised?
3 Explain the contents box headed 'Erg Limited: Full year'.
4 What events may have caused 'the new-found caution being exercised by auditors'?

## Case 11D Deferred expenditure

Outlined below are accounting policies for Optus, Boral, Mayne Nickless, Billabong and AGL with respect to deferred expenditure.

### Boral 2001

#### Deferred expenses

Expenditure is deferred to the extent that management considers that it is probable that future economic benefits embodied in the expenditure will eventuate and can be measured. Deferred expenses are amortised over the period in which the related benefits are expected to be realised. The carrying value of deferred expenditure is reviewed in accordance with the policy set out under recoverable amount of noncurrent assets.

### Mayne Nickless 2001

#### Deferred expenditure

Material items of expenditure are deferred to the extent that future economic benefits can be measured reliably, are recoverable out of future revenue, do not relate solely to revenue which has already been brought to account and will contribute to the future earning capacity of the economic entity.

### Billabong 2001

#### Deferred expenditure

Deferred expenditure is expensed as incurred except where future benefits are expected, beyond reasonable doubt, to exceed those costs. The costs arising from development of products are carried forward. Deferred expenditure is amortised over future financial years to match such costs with related benefits. Any amortisation required is charged to the profit and loss account for the financial year. The recoverable amount of unamortised costs in respect of each development project are reviewed regularly and at each balance date.

### AGL

#### Deferred expenditure

Borrowing expenses relating to long-term facilities are deferred and amortised over periods not exceeding the term of each borrowing.

Other expenditures which provide benefits beyond the current accounting period are deferred and amortised over the periods during which the benefits are expected to arise, ranging from two to fifty years. These expenditures principally relate to computer software and gas and electricity industry operations (the connection of new customers to the gas system, the conversion of existing customers' appliances to the use of natural gas and other gas and electricity industry expenditures).

***Required:***

For each company, provide a rationale for the company treating the expenditure as an asset 'deferred expenditure' rather than treating it as an expense.

## CASE 11E Cricket, revenue recognition and expense recognition

I recently received the following offer from the Sydney Cricket Ground Trust:

### Premium collectables
### Steve Waugh fine art limited edition print

Now you can own this magnificent piece of official ACB memorabilia – a limited edition fine art print of Australian cricket captain, Steve Waugh.

Renowned Australian sports artist Mark Sofilas has produced this fine art print of Steve Waugh to honour a great cricketing legend.

There are only 1500 of these limited edition prints, each one individually signed and numbered by Steve Waugh and Mark Sofilas, with a certificate of authenticity accompanying each print.

Retail Price (unframed): $275 each (plus $10 postage)

Trust members' price: $250 (plus $10 postage)

To order, complete the order form and return to the Trust.

Allow 30 days for delivery.

***Required:***

1. Assume the Trust is the promoter of the limited edition prints (that is, it receives all revenues and pays all costs). Describe the alternatives the Trust has as to when it recognises revenue. Which would you suggest?
2. How would your answer differ if the Trust included an offer that the prints could be returned within two months if the purchaser is not completely satisfied? The purchaser would receive a refund of $200.
3. Assume the Trust is not the promoter but is a selling agent; that is, it sends out the brochures, collects the order forms, retains 20 per cent ($55) per print and passes the order on to the promoter, who fills the order. Assume a 'no refund' policy. When should the Trust recognise revenue?
4. Does the accounting profession have the skills to provide the certificate of authenticity? Do you believe the Trust or any other seller of 'collectibles' is likely to see advantages in members of professional accounting bodies providing this certificate of authenticity?
5. A Trust member was sitting behind two accounting students at a recent match and heard them discussing 'cost of goods sold'. He shows you the above brochure, buys you a beer each and asks you what would be the COGS for the limited edition print.
6. Assume Steve receives a flat fee for signing the prints. When would the Trust recognise this expense?
7. Assume Steve gets paid a commission based on sales. When would the Trust recognise this expense?

## CASE 11F Recognition of expenses

Shown below is an article that discusses employee options as a form of remuneration.

### One.Tel's $110m write-off satisfies ASIC

*by Christine Lacy*

Emerging telecommunications company One.Tel will write off $110 million in expenditure following discussions with Australia's corporate regulator over its accounting policies and stave off possible legal action under the Corporations Law.

The write-off at June 30 means One.Tel, whose major shareholders include Mr Kerry Packer's Publishing and Broadcasting Ltd and News Corp, will almost certainly record a substantial bottom-line loss at the full year, and follows a tense meeting with the regulator on Tuesday.

It is understood months of negotiations between the Australian Securities and Investments Commission and company officials failed to resolve the conflict over interpretation of the Corporations Law, which One.Tel maintains it has complied with, and its amortisation of marketing expenses.

ASIC's other option, had it chosen to pursue the matter further, would have been an application in the Federal Court. However, One.Tel's decision to write off the sum has satisfied the regulator, and the matter is now settled.

ASIC chief accountant Ms Jan McCahey welcomed One.Tel's decision, and said the regulator's action reflected its belief that Australian companies operating in the new economy must also operate within the traditional legal framework.

'It has been ASIC's view that One.Tel's policy of recording this expenditure as an asset did not comply with accounting standards and the Corporations Law,' the regulator said.

One.Tel, which recorded a net loss of $19.6 million in the December half, outlined its change in accounting policy in a statement to the exchange that also reiterated its intention to seek a dual listing of its shares on the London Stock Exchange.

One.Tel says that as a reseller it now commands one million customers in the United Kingdom, and is eager to afford them the opportunity to invest in its stock.

However, a spokeswoman for the group said One.Tel had a six-month time frame for the potential compliance listing, which would not raise any fresh equity, with no broker yet mandated to handle the process. One.Tel has an established relationship with Morgan Stanley in the UK.

She said the decision to change its accounting policy of capitalising deferred costs, which the company believes did not breach the Corporations Law, was in part driven by the need to comply with standard accounting practice in the UK.

The spokeswoman said One.Tel's decision to amortise its marketing expenses was in line with other industry players. However, she acknowledged that its practice was more aggressive than its counterparts on the strength that it was acquiring new customers faster.

One.Tel's shares ended 15c down at $1.49.

(Source: Christine Lacy, *Australian Financial Review*, 6 April 2000.)

***Required:***

1 What is an option? How does the receipt of options by employees act as incentive? Why is it part of a performance-based pay?
2 Evaluate the alternatives outlined in the article for accounting for options.
3 Why do the proposed accounting treatments put 'the explosion in the use of employee options and executive performance-based pay under threat'?
4 Do you believe the issue of the options and/or the exercise of the options fit the definition of an expense?

***Required:***

1 Outline the main arguments in favour of One.Tel capitalising the expenditure.
2 What differences will there be in the financial statements if the marketing costs are capitalised, as opposed to expensed?
3 What arguments does ASIC raise against capitalising this expenditure?

Chapter 12

# The cash flow statement

## On completion of this chapter you should be able to:

- explain the contents of a statement of cash flows
- distinguish between cash flow from operations, cash flow from investing and cash flow from financing
- interpret a statement of cash flows
- calculate cash flow from operations, using both the direct and indirect methods
- prepare a statement of cash flows.

## 12.1 Chapter overview

General purpose financial reports should provide information useful to users for making and evaluating decisions about the allocation of scarce resources. A statement of cash flows provides relevant information to users about the cash inflows and cash outflows of an enterprise during a financial year. Evaluating the enterprise's cash management is so important that the result of this analysis, called the cash flow statement, is included as part of the set of financial statements. Since 1992, accounting standards have required an enterprise to present a statement of cash flows with their published financial statements.

Understanding the cash flow statement is important for all users of accounting reports in gaining a better insight into the health of a company. Making the detailed analysis required for preparing a cash flow statement is a good way to cement your understanding of what the financial statements contain and the interrelationship between different accounts.

## 12.2 The purpose of cash flow analysis

Performance in generating additional wealth for the enterprise, as measured by accrual profit, is very important to managers, investors, tax authorities and many others. But the world is a complex place, and there is more to performance than generating accrual profit. An additional important aspect of performance is managing the inflow and outflow of cash so that the enterprise has enough cash to pay its bills, finance its growth and keep its borrowing under control. This will not be a surprise to you – everyone has to worry about cash flow, about how much cash is available, and where needed additional cash will come from.

No business enterprise can survive without cash. (Nor can other organisations, such as governments, as we have seen in recent years with governments struggling to raise enough cash from taxes and other charges to meet their financial and social obligations.) Employees, suppliers and tax authorities must be paid, loans must be repaid and assets must be kept up to date. Many new and established firms have had positive net profit figures, yet have still run out of cash and gone bankrupt. Thus it is important for present and potential investors and creditors to have information about a firm's cash inflows and outflows and its resulting cash position. Can the firm meet all its debts and obligations as they fall due, an ability commonly referred to as solvency, and does it have enough cash and short-term assets now to cover its immediate debts and obligations, a condition commonly called liquidity? Enterprises can get into difficulty by not managing their cash properly. On the other hand, some enterprises seem to have rather a lot of cash, raising questions about what is being done with the cash. Keeping a large supply of cash lying around idle is no way to earn a return for owners: the cash should be put to work by making investments, improving the buildings and equipment, attracting new customers or paying off interest-bearing debt.

The cash situation can be obscured somewhat by accrual accounting. Let's take an extreme example. Suppose a company has revenue of $1000 but it is all on credit, and none of the customers has paid yet. In order to generate the revenue, the company has expenses of $700, and they all have to be paid soon. The accrual profit will be the revenue minus the expenses, or $300. Looks good: a 30 per cent return on revenue. But the company is in trouble: it has no cash to pay its expenses; instead, it has $1000 of accounts receivable, which cannot be used to pay expenses unless the customers pay or some other way is found to get cash for the receivables. The company is likely to want to borrow money from a bank or other lender to provide it with the needed cash: how much should it borrow? Should it hound the customers for payment? Should it ask its creditors for more time to pay the $700 in expenses? How will it be able to afford a planned new machine to keep its product quality competitive? All these questions are about the management of cash, and they are not easy to answer based on the accrual accounting profit.

To assist with such questions, the cash flow statement provides information about a firm's generation and use of cash and highly liquid short-term assets, and, therefore, assists in evaluating the firm's financial viability. The analysis of cash flows provides different information from the summary of accrual-based performance in the statement of financial performance.

In the example of Simone's jewellery business in chapter 1, it was shown that accrual profit is not the same as cash profit. Some revenues and expenses do not involve an inflow or outflow of cash in the present period. The example of uncollected revenue has already been mentioned. Depreciation is another example here: the cash flow happened when the asset was acquired, so the depreciation expense does not involve any current cash flow.

Even cash profit is not a complete measure of what has happened to cash. Certain inflows of cash (such as those resulting from getting a bank loan or issuing shares) or outflows of cash (such as dividends or a purchase of land) are not part of the day-to-day process of generating revenue and incurring expenses, so they would not be covered even by a cash profit measure. They reflect management decisions beyond generation of profit in the current period, though they may well tell us something about what ability to generate profit the firm might have in the future.

The purpose of the analysis of cash flow is therefore twofold.

- To produce a measure of performance that is based on day-to-day cash flow, cash generated by ordinary business activities, instead of accrual accounting. This measure, which we have called cash profit and which the cash flow statement calls cash flow from operations, does not imply that accrual profit is invalid; rather, it provides a different perspective on performance, so enhances the information for users.
- To incorporate other non-operating cash inflows and outflows, such as from investing in new assets, selling old ones, borrowing or repaying debts, obtaining new capital from shareholders or paying dividends to shareholders. By including these non-operating cash flows, the cash flow statement can provide a complete description of how the firm's cash was managed during the period. It can tell the full story of why the firm has more, or less, cash at the end of the period than it had at the beginning.

With all this information, the user can evaluate management's strategy for managing cash and make a better judgement of the company's liquidity, solvency, risk and opportunities than could be made just from the statement of financial position and statement of financial performance.

## 12.3 Overview of cash flow statements

### Classification of cash flow transactions

Accounting standards suggest that for profit-seeking organisations it would be normal to divide cash flow transactions into operating activities, investing activities and financing activities.

- Operating activities means those activities that relate to the provision of goods and services.
- Investing activities means those activities that relate to the acquisition and disposal of noncurrent assets, including property, plant and equipment and other productive assets, and investments such as securities, not falling within the definition of cash.

- Financing activities means those activities that relate to changing the size and composition of the financial structure of the entity, including equity, and borrowings not falling within the definition of cash.

Exhibit 12.1 provides the classification of typical cash inflows and outflows.

**EXHIBIT 12.1** **Classification of cash flow transactions**

**Operating, investing and financing**

| **Operating** | **Investing** | **Financing** |
|---|---|---|
| *Receipts from:*<br>Sale of goods and services<br>Interest or dividends received | *Receipts from:*<br>Sales of property, plant and equipment<br>Repayment of loans by other entities<br>Sale of shares held as investments | *Receipts from:*<br>Issue of shares<br>Borrowings |
| *Payments for:*<br>Purchase of inventory<br>Wages of employees<br>Taxes to governments<br>Interest to lenders | *Payments for:*<br>Acquisition of property, plant and equipment<br>Acquisition of shares and debentures for investment purposes | *Payments for:*<br>Dividend distributions<br>Share buybacks<br>Repayment of borrowings |

## Format of the statement of cash flows

The cash flow statement, like the other statements, has a standard format (see exhibit 12.2). It is useful to know, because variations from that format may be a signal of special circumstances or problems.

Some important features of this format are:

1. The cash flow statement covers the same period as the statement of financial performance.
2. Cash includes some equivalents: very liquid near-cash assets that can be turned into cash without any risk of loss, such as demand bank deposits and certificates with a maturity of three months or less.
3. In some cases, cash may include temporary negative bank balances (overdrafts) if they are just a result of cash management activity and the bank balances regularly vary from positive to negative.
4. If there is anything unusual about the enterprise's definition of cash (and equivalents), or any other category of the statement, that should be explained in the notes to the financial statements. You may even see a little reconciliation at the bottom of the cash flow statement.
5. The cash flow statement follows some rules to ensure that its focus stays on cash. For example, if a dividend has been declared but not all paid, only the paid part is included in the cash flow statement's financing activities section. Another example: if there is an account payable for a noncurrent asset, the investing activities figure shows only the amount paid so far.
6. Following from point 5, any asset acquisitions, borrowing or share issues that are done without cash, such as acquiring land in return for shares, are excluded from the cash flow statement. (They would be disclosed in a note to the cash flow statement.)
7. Any of the numbers in the cash flow statement can be positive or negative, according to what happened during the period. For example, a really bad year can result in cash from operations being negative, in which case it might be described as cash used in operations! As another example, a company undergoing significant restructuring

**EXHIBIT 12.2** Cash flow statement

**Standard format**

**Operating activities:**
Cash generated by operations, from day-to-day cash receipts and payments related to the activities that generate profit.

**Investing activities:**
Cash used to invest in additional noncurrent assets, including investments in other companies, minus any cash proceeds obtained by disposing of such assets.

**Financing activities:**
Cash obtained from borrowing and from issuing share capital, minus borrowing repaid or shares redeemed.
Any cash transactions in retained earnings (that is, not included in calculating net profit) are also included here, especially dividends and share issue costs.

**Change in cash (and equivalents) for the period:**
Net sum of the above three categories.

**Cash (and equivalents) at the beginning of the period:**
Brought forward from last period's cash flow statement and statement of financial position.

**Cash (and equivalents) at the end of the period:**
Equals what is shown on the statement of financial position at the end of the period.

could have more cash coming in from selling off assets than going out to buy more, so its investing section could be a positive cash inflow instead of the usual cash outflow.

8 Deriving the cash flow from day-to-day operations is one of the main reasons for having the cash flow analysis. The cash from operations figure takes away accrual accounting's many adjustments, which are very important in measuring profit but obscure the cash effects. To emphasise this, cash flow statements in many countries begin with the net profit figure, then explicitly remove the effects of changes in accounts receivable, accounts payable, depreciation and other accruals. This is called the indirect method of deriving cash from operations, as distinct from the direct method of just listing operating cash receipts and deducting operating cash payments (also called disbursements). In Australia the direct method is used with a note showing the indirect method.

The following diagram compares the two methods, both of which end up with the same figure for cash from operations.

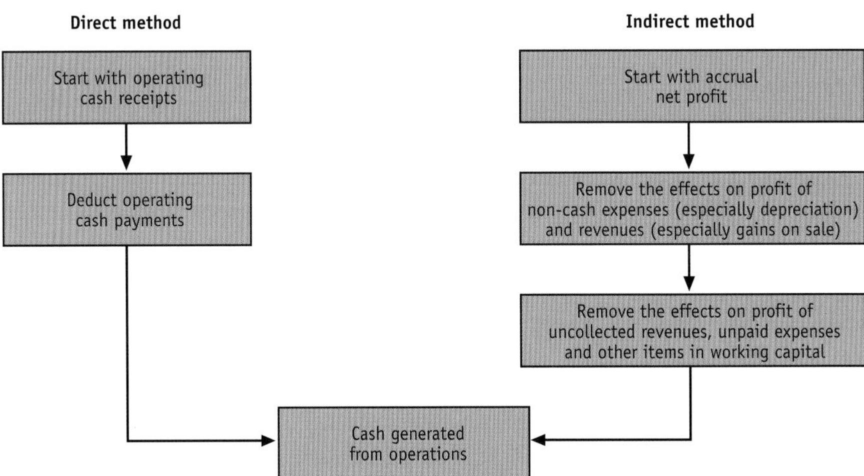


**Figure 12.1** Comparing the direct and indirect methods of deriving cash from operations.

## How's your understanding?

Here are two questions you should be able to answer, based on what you have just read:

1 What are the summary categories of cash flow used in the cash flow statement?

2 Dubroy Ltd defines its cash and equivalents to include the following (this year's and last year's figures shown in that order for each): cash ($13 000; $4000), demand deposit in MegaBank ($25 000; $50 000), and occasional bank overdraft ($7000; $3000). What is the net total change in cash that the cash flow statement for this year will explain? (Cash and equivalents at the beginning = $4000 + $50 000 – $3000 = $51 000. At the end they equal $13 000 + $25 000 – $7000 = $31 000. So the change in cash is negative $20 000.)

## Direct vs indirect method of reporting cash flow from operations

Cash flow from operations can be reported using either the direct or the indirect method. The direct method reports gross cash inflows and gross cash outflows. An example of using the direct method is shown for XYZ Limited in exhibit 12.3. The information for the direct method can be obtained by:

**a** using the accounting system, which directly records and analyses the cash flows in relation to cash transaction

**b** adjusting sales, cost of sales and other profit and loss items for non-cash items.

Method **b** will be illustrated in section 12.4 below. To illustrate method **a** refer back to the Reval Limited example in exhibits 4.10 and 4.11. The cash flow statement (including cash flow from operations) could be obtained from dissecting the general ledger account 'cash' in exhibit 4.11. You may need to refer back to exhibit 4.10 to obtain further details of some of these transactions. Summarising the entries in the cash ledger account we can see the following.

| | $ |
|---|---|
| 1 Opening balance | 25 000 |
| 2 Cash from accounts receivable | 30 000 |
| 3 Cash sales | 20 000 |
| 4 Cash from mortgage loan | 35 000 |
| 5 Payments to accounts payable | 15 000 |
| 6 Payments for repairs and maintenance | 500 |
| 7 Purchase of land | 40 000 |
| 8 Payments of cash for wages | 12 000 |
| 9 Purchase of plant and equipment for cash | 20 000 |
| 10 Closing balance | 22 500 |

Items 2, 3, 5, 6 and 8 all affect cash flow from operations. Item 4 would be classified under financing activities. Items 7 and 9 would be classified as investing activities. The cash flow from operations would be calculated as follows:

| | $ |
|---|---|
| Receipts from customers (30 000 + 20 000) | 50 000 |
| Payments to suppliers and employees (15 000 + 500 + 12 000) | (27 500) |
| Cash flow from operations | 22 500 |

**EXHIBIT 12.3** XYZ Limited

**Statement of cash flows for the financial year ended 30 June 2002**

| | Inflows (Outflows) | | | |
|---|---|---|---|---|
| | 2002 | | 2001 | |
| | $000 | $000 | $000 | $000 |
| **Cash flows from operating activities** | | | | |
| Receipts from customers | 30 150 | | 27 130 | |
| Payments to suppliers and employees | (27 600) | | (25 040) | |
| Dividends received | 100 | | 250 | |
| Interest received | 300 | | 270 | |
| Interest paid | (270) | | (240) | |
| Income taxes paid | (900) | | (810) | |
| Royalty received | 180 | | — | |
| **Net cash provided by operating activities** | | **1 960** | | **1 560** |
| **Cash flows from investing activities** | | | | |
| Purchase of shares in other companies | (550) | | — | |
| Payment for property, plant and equipment | (350) | | (1 200) | |
| Proceeds from sale of equipment | 20 | | 10 | |
| **Net cash used in investing activities** | | **(880)** | | **(1 190)** |
| **Cash flows from financing activities** | | | | |
| Proceeds from issue of shares | 300 | | 200 | |
| Proceeds from borrowings | 200 | | 240 | |
| Repayments of borrowings | (90) | | (80) | |
| Dividends paid | (1 200) | | (1 080) | |
| **Net cash used in financing activities** | | **(790)** | | **(720)** |
| Net increase/(decrease) in cash held | | 290 | | (350) |
| Cash at the beginning of the financial year | | 120 | | 470 |
| **Cash at the end of the financial year** | | **410** | | **120** |

A full cash flow statement from Reval Limited is shown in exhibit 12.4 below.

Australian Accounting Standards require the direct method of presentation for cash flow from operations because it provides information that is not otherwise available in the balance sheet and the profit and loss statement. Accounting standards suggests that it provides a more useful basis for estimating future cash flows than the indirect method, which shows only the net amount of cash flows from operating activities and does not report the individual components of cash flows from operations.

Under the indirect method, the accrual-based profit figure is adjusted to get the cash flow from operations by adding or subtracting:

- adjustments to remove accruals for non-cash expenses (or revenues) arising from non-current asset changes, such as depreciation expense, and profit or loss on the sale of non-current assets
- adjustments to remove accruals for uncollected revenues, revenues received in advance, prepaid expenses, and unpaid expenses, represented by changes in non-cash working capital accounts (current assets and current liabilities).

The indirect method will be discussed further in section 12.6.

**EXHIBIT 12.4** Reval Limited

**Statement of cash flows for the month ended 31 May 2002**

| | $ | $ |
|---|---|---|
| **Cash flows from operating activities** | | |
| Receipts from customers | 50 000 | |
| Payments to suppliers and employees | (27 500) | |
| | | 22 500 |
| **Cash flows from investing activities** | | |
| Purchase of land | (40 000) | |
| Purchase of plant and equipment | (20 000) | |
| | | (60 000) |
| **Cash flows from financing activities** | | |
| Proceeds from mortgage | | 35 000 |
| Net increase/(decrease) in cash held | | (2 500) |
| Cash at the beginning of the month | | 25 000 |
| **Cash at the end of the month** | | **22 500** |

# 12.4 Preparation using the direct method[1]

Under the direct method of presenting cash flows from operations, it is necessary to calculate cash receipts from customers, payments to suppliers and employees as well as other expense and revenue items affecting cash flows. The cash flows from investing and financing are then calculated.

## Cash flows from operating activities

To determine the cash flows from operations using the direct method it is necessary to convert the accrual-based figures to a cash basis for each of the items outlined below.

### Cash receipts from customers

Cash receipts from customers will not be the same as sales, because not all trade debtors will have paid by year-end. Cash received from customers will be less than sales if the balance of trade debtors increases and will be greater than sales if the trade debtors balance decreases. Therefore, to determine the cash received from customers, we need the sales figure from the profit and loss account and the opening and closing balances of trade debtors from the statement of financial position.

To understand the relationship between trade debtors, sales and cash received from customers, you may need to think through the debits and credits affecting the trade debtors account. To keep things simple at this stage, we assume all sales are on credit and that there are no bad debts.

Trade debtors increases when credit sales are made:

DR Trade debtors
CR Sales

Trade debtors decreases when cash is received:

DR Cash
CR Trade debtors

As a result, the trade debtors account would normally appear as follows:

**Trade debtors**

| | | | |
|---|---|---|---|
| Opening balance | | Cash recived from customers | |
| Credit sales | | | |
| Closing balance | | | |

Alternatively, it can be expressed as follows:

Opening balance + credit sales – cash received from customers = closing balance

or

Cash received from customers = credit sales + opening balance – closing balance

For Michael Limited, whose financial statements are shown in exhibits 12.5 and 12.6, the cash receipts for customers can be determined given that we know that the opening and closing balances of accounts receivable were $70 000 and $90 000 respectively, and from the profit and loss that credit sales were $421 000.

**Trade debtors**

| | | | |
|---|---|---|---|
| Opening balance | 70 000 | | |
| Credit sales | 421 000 | Cash received | **401 000** |
| Closing balance | 90 000 | | |

Alternatively, using the formula above:

Cash received from customers = 421 000 + 70 000 – 90 000
= 401 000

Additional information:

- All purchases are on credit.
- Loans payable of $150 000 were paid back during the year.
- The land was revalued upwards by $50 000.
- Equipment that cost $30 000 was sold during the year.

### Cash paid to suppliers

To calculate the cash paid to suppliers requires a two-stage process. First it is necessary to calculate the amount of purchases. This can be found from the inventory account, given that you know the opening and closing balances of inventory from the statement of financial position and the cost of goods sold used in calculating net profit.

Recall that the main journal entries that affect trade creditors are as follows:

- purchase of inventory on credit (assuming perpetual inventory method)

  DR Inventory
  CR    Trade creditors

- payment to suppliers.

  DR Trade creditors
  CR    Cash

**EXHIBIT 12.5** Michael Limited

**Profit and loss statement* for the year ended 30 June 2002**

| | $ | $ |
|---|---|---|
| Sales | | 421 000 |
| Cost of goods sold | | 151 000 |
| Gross profit | | 270 000 |
| Less operating expenses | | |
| Wages | 100 000 | |
| Insurance | 13 000 | |
| Interest | 20 000 | |
| Depreciation | 20 000 | |
| Loss on sale of equipment | 4 000 | |
| Other | 37 000 | 194 000 |
| Net operating profit before tax | | 76 000 |
| Income tax expense | | 27 000 |
| **Net operating profit** | | **49 000** |

* As this is an internal document, it is more likely to be called a profit and loss statement than a statement of financial performance. Therefore the label 'profit and loss statement' will be used throughout this chapter.

Assuming all inventory is purchased on credit, we can determine the cash paid to suppliers for inventory by Michael Limited as follows. Note that the missing figures calculated in each T-account are in bold to make the example easier to follow.

**Inventory**

| | | | |
|---|---|---|---|
| Opening bal | 45 000 | COGS | 151 000 |
| Purchases | **168 000** | | |
| Closing bal | 62 000 | | |

**Trade creditors**

| | | | |
|---|---|---|---|
| | | Opening bal | 40 000 |
| Cash | **148 000** | Purchases | 168 000 |
| | | Closing bal | 60 000 |

By solving for the missing purchases figure in the inventory account and transferring it to trade creditors via the double-entry system (that is, DR inventory, CR trade creditors) we can solve for the missing cash paid to suppliers.

If you prefer, solve the above algebraically. From the above you can determine that:

Purchases = COGS + Closing inventory – Opening inventory

and

Payment to suppliers = COGS + Closing inventory – Opening inventory + Opening trade creditors – Closing trade creditors

= 151 000 + 62 000 – 45 000 + 40 000 – 60 000

= 148 000

EXHIBIT 12.6

Michael Limited

Comparative statements of financial position as at 30 June 2001 and 2002

| | 2002<br>$ | 2001<br>$ |
|---|---|---|
| **Current assets** | | |
| Cash | 25 000 | 40 000 |
| Accounts receivable | 90 000 | 70 000 |
| Inventory | 62 000 | 45 000 |
| Prepaid insurance | 8 000 | 5 000 |
| **Total current assets** | **185 000** | **160 000** |
| **Noncurrent assets** | | |
| Land | 400 000 | 200 000 |
| Equipment (at cost) | 280 000 | 150 000 |
| Less: accumulated depreciation | (58 000) | (45 000) |
| **Total noncurrent assets** | **622 000** | **305 000** |
| **Total assets** | **807 000** | **465 000** |
| **Current liabilities** | | |
| Trade creditors | 60 000 | 40 000 |
| Wages payable | 4 000 | 7 000 |
| Provision for income tax | 6 000 | 5 000 |
| Interest payable | 11 000 | 10 000 |
| **Total current liabilities** | **81 000** | **62 000** |
| **Noncurrent liabilities** | | |
| Loans payable | 250 000 | 200 000 |
| **Total liabilities** | **331 000** | **262 000** |
| **Net assets** | **476 000** | **203 000** |
| **Shareholders' equity** | | |
| Issued capital | 367 000 | 163 000 |
| Asset revaluation reserve | 50 000 | 0 |
| Retained profits | 59 000 | 40 000 |
| **Total shareholders' equity** | **476 000** | **203 000** |

## Payments to other suppliers for services, and to employees

Under an accrual system, payment for expenses such as wages, interest, insurance, tax, electricity, rent and so on may be the same, more or less than the actual expense figure in the profit and loss statement. The differences result because of increases/decreases in prepayments/accruals. For example, in Michael Limited, prepaid insurance increases from $5000 to $8000; therefore, the payment for insurance is $3000 greater than the expense for the period. Wages payable reduces from $7000 to $4000, which means that the payment for wages was $3000 greater than the expense of the period. Taxes payable and interest payable both increased by $1000 during the year, meaning that both expense amounts were $1000 greater than the cash paid.

There are no other statement of financial position accounts indicating further accrual of expenses or prepayments. Therefore, the 'other expenses' category in the profit and loss account of $37 000 was all paid in cash. The depreciation amount of $20 000 does not affect cash and therefore is not included in the cash flow statement (recall that the entry for depreciation is DR depreciation expense CR accumulated depreciation, thus cash is not affected). Similarly, the loss on sale of equipment does not affect cash.

We will now determine the cash paid for insurance, wages, interest and taxes. First we consider insurance. When an insurance premium is paid, the entry is:

DR Prepaid insurance
CR Cash

At the end of the accounting period, the insurance expense is determined by the amount of insurance used up:

DR Insurance expense
CR Prepaid insurance

For Michael Limited, the cash payment for insurance can be determined as follows, given that we know the opening and closing balance for insurance from the comparative statements of financial position and the insurance expense from the profit and loss account.

**Prepaid insurance**

| | | | |
|---|---|---|---|
| Opening balance | 5 000 | Insurance expense | 13 000 |
| Cash | **16 000** | | |
| Closing balance | 8 000 | | |

Alternatively, using a formula:

$$\text{Closing prepaid insurance} = \text{Opening prepaid insurance} + \text{Payments} - \text{Insurance expense}$$

Therefore:

$$\begin{aligned}\text{Payment for insurance} &= \text{Insurance expense} + \text{Closing prepaid insurance} - \text{Opening prepaid insurance}\\ &= 13\,000 + 8\,000 - 5\,000\\ &= 16\,000\end{aligned}$$

The cash payments for wages can be determined, given that we know the opening and closing balances of wages payable from the comparative statements of financial position and the wages expense from the profit and loss account.

**Wages payable**

| | | | |
|---|---|---|---|
| | | Opening balance | 7 000 |
| Cash | **103 000** | Wages expense | 100 000 |
| | | Closing balance | 4 000 |

The cash paid for wages is $103 000. Alternatively, by formula we have:

Closing wages payable = Opening wages payable + Wages expense
– Cash paid for wages

Cash paid for wages = Wages expense + Opening wages payable
– Closing wages payable
= 100 000 + 7 000 – 4 000
= $103 000

The cash payments for interest can be determined in a similar manner.

**Interest payable**

| | | | |
|---|---|---|---|
| | | Opening balance | 10 000 |
| Cash | **19 000** | Interest expense | 20 000 |
| | | Closing balance | 11 000 |

Alternatively, by formula we have:

Closing interest payable = Opening interest payable + Interest expense
– Cash paid for interest

Therefore:

Cash paid for interest = Interest expense + Opening interest payable
– Closing interest payable
= 20 000 + 10 000 – 11 000
= 19 000

Finally, we will calculate the taxes paid during the year. Recall that when tax is calculated at the end of the year the journal entry is:

DR Income tax expense
CR Provision for income tax

When the amount is paid:

DR Provision for income tax
CR Cash

**Provision for income tax**

| | | | |
|---|---|---|---|
| | | Opening balance | 5 000 |
| Cash | **26 000** | Income tax expense | 27 000 |
| | | Closing balance | 6 000 |

The cash paid for income taxes during the year, determined from the provision for income tax ledger account, is shown to be $26 000. Alternatively, by formula it could be calculated as follows:

Closing provision for income tax = Opening provision for income tax + Income tax expense – Income tax paid

Therefore:

$$
\begin{aligned}
\text{Income tax paid} &= \text{Income tax expense} + \text{Opening provision for} \\
&\quad \text{income tax} - \text{Closing provision for income tax} \\
&= 27\,000 + 5000 - 6000 \\
&= 26\,000
\end{aligned}
$$

Calculation of income tax paid becomes a little more complicated when deferred tax is introduced, thus the cash flow implications are left to later courses.

All the calculations necessary to show the cash flows from operating activities have been completed and are shown below:

| **Cash flows from operating activities** | **$** |
|---|---|
| Receipts from customers | 401 000 |
| Payments to suppliers and employees | (304 000) |
| Interest paid | (19 000) |
| Income tax paid | (26 000) |
| Net cash provided by operating activities | 52 000 |

Interest and income tax paid are shown separately as required by Australian Accounting Standards.

## Cash flows from investing activities

Our next step is to calculate cash inflows and outflows from investing activities. To do this we need to examine any changes in the noncurrent assets in the statements of financial position together with any additional information we have on sale or purchase of non-current assets. This additional information may give details of any sale of any assets during the year and any asset revaluations (up or down). When there are changes in noncurrent assets, the potential explanations are an acquisition, disposal, asset revaluation or a combination of the above.

For Michael Limited, there are changes in two noncurrent assets, namely land and equipment. Changes in these accounts result from net acquisitions. It is necessary to check whether the changes are only the result of acquisitions or if some disposals are involved. This can be ascertained by seeing if there is any profit or loss on disposal in the profit and loss statement or some mention of disposals or revaluations in the notes. For Michael Limited a loss on sale of equipment of $4000 was reported. Additional information provides more details about the sale of equipment and notes the revaluation of land.

Land has increased from $200 000 to $400 000. There is no indication of any disposals of land, and the land was revalued upwards by $50 000 (see asset revaluation reserve). The entry for this revaluation would have been:

DR Land

CR Asset revaluation reserve

Based on the above, land which cost $150 000 was purchased during the year ($200 000 – $50 000).

The general ledger account would appear as follows:

**Land**

| | | | |
|---|---|---|---|
| Opening balance | 200 000 | | |
| Cash | **150 000** | | |
| Asset revaluation | 50 000 | | |
| | 400 000 | | |

We know that equipment that cost $30 000 was sold during the year and that there was a loss on sale of $4000. To determine the purchases of equipment, first consider the journal entry when equipment is sold with a loss on sale:

| | | |
|---|---|---|
| DR Cash | ? | |
| DR Loss on sale | 4000 | |
| DR Accumulated depreciation | ? | |
| CR Equipment | | 30 000 |

We can first determine the accumulated depreciation on the equipment sold from the accumulated depreciation account, as we know opening and closing balances from the comparative statements of financial position and depreciation expense from the profit and loss statement.

**Accumulated depreciation**

| | | | |
|---|---|---|---|
| | | Opening balance | 45 000 |
| Disposal | **7 000** | Depreciation | 20 000 |
| | | Closing balance | 58 000 |

As shown in the above account, the accumulated depreciation for the equipment sold was $7000.

We now have additional information for the journal entry.

| | | |
|---|---|---|
| DR Cash | ? | |
| DR Loss on sale | 4000 | |
| DR Accumulated depreciation | 7 000 | |
| CR Equipment | | 30 000 |

Therefore $19 000 was received from the equipment sold. Next we can calculate the amount of cash paid for the equipment purchased by calculating the debit to the equipment account as follows:

**Equipment**

| | | | |
|---|---|---|---|
| Opening balance | 150 000 | Disposal | 30 000 |
| Cash | **160 000** | | |
| Closing balance | 280 000 | | |

Note that the disposal of the equipment is entered in the equipment account at cost. New equipment at a cost of $160 000 was purchased.

The cash flows from the investing activities section of the cash flow statement would appear as follows:

| **Cash flows from investing activities** | **$** |
|---|---|
| Purchase of land | (150 000) |
| Purchase of equipment | (160 000) |
| Proceeds from sale of equipment | 19 000 |
| Net cash used in investing activities | (291 000) |

## Cash flows from financing activities

The next step is to determine the cash flows from financing activities. Finance comes from internal and external sources. The former is generated through operations, and is disclosed as cash flow from operations. External finance is generated from lenders or shareholders. To determine the cash flow from financing, it is necessary to examine the noncurrent liability accounts and the shareholders' equity account.

For Michael Limited, loans payable has increased from $200 000 to $250 000. The difference could be the result of a combination of both debt repayments and debt raising. The journal entries would be as follows:

Debt repayment

DR Loans payable

CR Cash

Debt raising

DR Cash

CR Loans payable

We can determine the amount of debt raising from the general ledger account for loans payable, as we know the opening and closing balances as well as debt repayment of $150 000.

**Loans payable**

| | | | |
|---|---|---|---|
| | | Opening balance | 200 000 |
| Cash (repayment) | 150 000 | Cash (raising) | **200 000** |
| | | Closing balance | 250 000 |

As shown, new debt of $200 000 was raised during the year.

Turning now to the shareholders' equity accounts, you can see that issued capital increased by $204 000 from $163 000 to $367 000. As there was no mention of share buy-backs, the difference of $204 000 must have resulted from the issue of shares. The change in the asset revaluation reserve has already been explained as a revaluation of the land and there is no effect on cash. Retained profits changes can result from: profit or loss from the period, or dividends or transfers to or from general reserves. As there are no other reserve accounts besides asset revaluation reserve in this case, the transfer to or from reserves is not a possibility. By reconstructing the retained profits accounts, we can see the amount of dividends paid or declared during the year, given that we know the profit for the year.

**Retained profits**

| | | | |
|---|---|---|---|
| Dividends | **30 000** | Opening balance | 40 000 |
| | | Profit | 49 000 |
| | | Closing balance | 59 000 |

From the above it can be seen that dividends total $30 000. These could be paid in cash (DR retained profits, CR cash) or could be provided for at balance date pending ratification at the annual general meeting, which will be held in the next financial year.

In the latter case the entry would be:

DR Retained profits

CR Provision for dividends (or dividends payable)

For Michael Limited, there is no provision for dividends account, therefore all of the dividends of $30 000 must have been paid in cash.

Based on the above, the cash flows from financing activities are as follows:

| **Cash flows from financing activities** | **$** |
|---|---|
| Issue of debt | 200 000 |
| Debt repayment | (150 000) |
| Issue of shares | 204 000 |
| Dividends paid | (30 000) |
| Net cash provided from financing activities | 224 000 |

Combining all of the above, the full cash flow statement is shown in exhibit 12.7.

**EXHIBIT 12.7** **Michael Limited**

**Statement of cash flows for the year ended 30 June 2002**

| | **$** |
|---|---|
| **Cash flows from operating activities** | |
| Receipts from customers | 401 000 |
| Payments to suppliers and employees | (304 000) |
| Interest paid | (19 000) |
| Income tax paid | (26 000) |
| **Net cash provided by operating activities** | **52 000** |
| **Cash flows from investing activities** | |
| Purchase of land | (150 000) |
| Purchase of equipment | (160 000) |
| Proceeds from sale of equipment | 19 000 |
| **Net cash used in investing activities** | **(291 000)** |
| **Cash flows from financing activities** | |
| Issue of debt | 200 000 |
| Debt repayment | (150 000) |
| Issue of shares | 204 000 |
| Dividends paid | (30 000) |
| **Net cash provided from financing activities** | **224 000** |
| Net increase (decrease) in cash held | (15 000) |
| Cash at 1 July 2001 | 40 000 |
| **Cash at 30 June 2002** | **25 000** |

## 12.5 Interpreting a cash flow statement (direct method)

To illustrate some of the information you can gain from examining statements of cash flow, we will consider the statement of cash flows for Coca-Cola Amatil Limited, which is shown in exhibit 12.8. We have included the comparative figures for the 1995, 1994 and the 1999 financial statements. This allows you to make some comparisons of how cash flows can change over time.

The following should be noted about the statement of cash flows in 1995 in exhibit 12.8:

**EXHIBIT 12.8** Coca-Cola Amatil Ltd and its subsidiaries

**Statements of cash flows for the financial years ended 31 December 1995, 1994, 2000 and 1999**

| Inflows/(outflows) | 1995 $m | 1994 $m | 2000 $m | 1999 $m |
|---|---|---|---|---|
| **Cash flows from operating activities** | | | | |
| Receipts from customers | 2 917.9 | 2 204.9 | 4 191.0 | 3 867.0 |
| Payments to suppliers and employees | (2 657.3) | (1 926.1) | (3 494.2) | (3 370.3) |
| Dividends received | — | — | 0.3 | — |
| Interest and bill discounts received | 33.5 | 23.6 | 43.8 | 37.4 |
| Interest and other costs of finance paid | (127.5) | (77.0) | (214.6) | (191.0) |
| Income tax paid | (49.7) | (52.4) | (58.0) | (80.1) |
| | **116.9** | **173.0** | **468.3** | **263.0** |
| **Cash flows from investing activities** | | | | |
| Proceeds from sale of property, plant and equipment | 33.0 | 17.1 | 42.6 | 19.8 |
| Payment for: | | | | |
| Property, plant and equipment | (480.8) | (323.7) | (228.9) | (349.8) |
| Investments in securities | (32.9) | (0.4) | (0.9) | (4.0) |
| Acquisitions of entities, net of cash acquired | (770.9) | (12.7) | — | — |
| Other | — | (2.1) | (8.6) | (0.6) |
| | **(1 251.6)** | **(321.8)** | **(195.8)** | **(334.6)** |
| **Cash flows from financing activities** | | | | |
| Proceeds from issue of shares | 737.6 | 50.2 | 58.0 | 90.5 |
| Proceeds from borrowings | 695.7 | 164.3 | 1 535.8 | 698.3 |
| Borrowings repaid | (233.5) | (95.2) | (1 631.9) | (339.1) |
| Dividends paid | (75.9) | (64.5) | (124.5) | (122.6) |
| | **1 123.9** | **54.8** | **(162.6)** | **327.1** |
| Net increase/(decrease) in cash held | (10.8) | (94.0) | 109.9 | 255.5 |
| Cash held at the beginning of the year | 326.2 | 433.5 | 377.1 | 129.9 |
| Exchange rate adjustments to cash held at the beginning of the year | 3.7 | (13.3) | (7.3) | (8.3) |
| Cash at the end of the year | **319.1** | **326.2** | **479.7** | **377.1** |

1 Cash held remained fairly constant, reducing from $326.2 million to $319.1 million.
2 There were large cash flows for investing activities, in particular acquisition of property, plant and equipment ($480.8 million) and acquisitions of other entities ($770.9 million).
3 Other points to note about investing activity are the sale of certain property, plant and equipment and the purchase of some securities.
4 Only a small proportion of the investing activities was funded by cash flow from operations ($116.9 million). While the cash flow from customers was very large ($2917.9 million), most of it was used on payments to suppliers and employees ($2657.3 million). Some of the difference paid interest and tax bills.
5 There was a substantial increase in financing inflows as a result of the issue of shares and new borrowings. This additional finance was required to cover the cash outflows for investments.

6 Under financing activities, note that some borrowings were repaid during the year ($233.5 million) and dividends of $75.9 million were paid during the year. However, there were significant additional borrowings of $695.7 million and cash received from the issue of shares.

From the 2000 statement of cash flow, observe the following:

1 There is a large cash flow from operations of $468.3 million, which has increased substantially from 1999 and earlier years. Over the period from 1994, there have been large increases in both cash receipts from customers and payments to suppliers and employees. This is consistent with a growing organisation.
2 While the company is still investing in new property, plant and equipment ($228.9 million), this is down on previous years. There can be a range of explanations for this, including: (a) large investments in earlier years have reduced the need for investments this year; and (b) a priority could have been to reduce debt this year (as shown in the cash flow from financing).
3 From the cash flow from financing section it can be seen that, while there have been very large new borrowings ($1535.8 million), the repayments of debt have been even larger ($1631.9 million).

## 12.6 Indirect method: preparation

The indirect method of presenting cash flow from operations is used in many overseas countries, including Canada and the United States (where companies can use either direct or indirect but generally choose the indirect method). As noted above, it is also necessary to show this information in Australia in a note to provide the reconciliation between operating profit and cash flow from operations. Consider for a minute why these two items should reconcile. The two will reconcile when you eliminate all the accruals in operating profit, which will get you back to a cash profit – that is, cash flow from operations.

It is important to note that the direct and indirect methods give the same results. The only difference is in how they report cash flow from operations. The reporting of cash flows from investing and financing are identical under both methods. The indirect method of reporting cash flow from operations starts with operating profit, then makes adjustments to this figure from non-cash items to arrive at cash flow from operating activities. There are two main types of non-cash adjustments: (a) depreciation, losses and gains; and (b) credit and accrual transactions that form part of the calculation of profit.

To adjust for depreciation, losses and items that are expenses but do not affect cash, these items are added back to operating profit. These include depreciation, amortisation and loss on sale of noncurrent assets. In addition, non-cash revenues such as profit on sale of noncurrent assets are deducted from operating profit.

Let's take a simple example with only one adjustment, namely depreciation, to illustrate the above. Assume a company has only cash sales amounting to $100 000, cash expenses of $60 000 and depreciation of $10 000. Therefore net profit is $30 000. Cash flow from operations can be determined by deducting $60 000 from $100 000, giving $40 000 (the direct method), or by adding back the $10 000 depreciation to operating profit of $30 000, again giving cash flow from operations of $40 000 (indirect method).

The second type of adjustment removes the accruals relating to current assets and current liabilities. For example, if accounts receivable increases during a period by $10 000, credit sales will be greater than cash received from customers by $10 000. Under accrual accounting, sales are recognised when earned, whereas the cash receipts from customers can be before, after or at the same time as revenue recognition. Therefore, to adjust from operating profit to cash flow from operations, it would be necessary to deduct $10 000 from operating profit to get cash flow from operations. This has eliminated the non-cash portion of sales from profit. Similarly, other working capital items, including inventories, prepayments, accounts payable and accrued expenses, need to be adjusted.

Therefore the following rules apply in adjusting for working capital changes:

- deduct from operating profit increases in working capital assets (debtors, inventory and prepayments)
- deduct from operating profit decreases in working capital liabilities (accounts payable, accruals)
- add to operating profit decreases in working capital assets
- add to operating profit increases in working capital liabilities.

We can summarise the indirect method of calculating cash from operations as follows:

| | |
|---|---|
| | Operating profit after tax |
| + | Non-cash expenses (e.g. depreciation) |
| – | Non-cash revenues (e.g. profit on sale of plant) |
| + | Decrease in accounts receivable, inventory and prepayments |
| + | Increase in accounts payable and accrued expenses |
| – | Decrease in accounts payable and accrued expenses |
| – | Increase in accounts receivable, inventory and prepayments |
| = | Cash flows from operating activities |

To illustrate the preparation of a cash flow statement using the indirect method, we'll redo the Michael Limited example from section 12.4 (see exhibit 12.9).

You should note that the cash flow from operations using the indirect method gives the same total cash flows from operations as did the direct method. To complete the statement of cash flows, it would be necessary to add on the cash flows from investing and financing, which would be exactly as outlined in exhibit 12.7.

**EXHIBIT 12.9** **Michael Limited**

**Cash flows from operating activities – indirect method**

| | $ |
|---|---|
| Operating profit after tax | 49 000 |
| Depreciation | 20 000 |
| Loss on sale of equipment | 4 000 |
| Changes in current assets and liabilities: | |
| Increase in accounts receivable | (20 000) |
| Increase in inventory | (17 000) |
| Increase in prepaid insurance | (3 000) |
| Increase in trade creditors | 20 000 |
| Increase in provision for income tax | 1 000 |
| Increase in interest payable | 1 000 |
| Decrease in wages payable | (3 000) |
| **Cash flows from operating activities** | **52 000** |

**EXHIBIT 12.10** Tamarack Systems Ltd

**Balance sheets for 2002 and 2001 (with changes calculated)**

| | 2002<br>$ | 2001<br>$ | Change<br>$ | |
|---|---|---|---|---|
| **Assets** | | | | |
| *Current assets* | | | | |
| Cash | 16 064 | 12 440 | 3 624 | CCE |
| Temporary investments | 0 | 65 000 | (65 000) | CCE |
| Accounts receivable | 220 668 | 143 962 | 76 706 | OP |
| Inventories | 176 962 | 187 777 | (10 815) | OP |
| Prepaid expenses | 9 004 | 14 321 | (5 317) | OP |
| **Total current assets** | **422 698** | **423 500** | **(802)** | |
| *Noncurrent assets* | | | | |
| Land cost | 82 500 | 75 000 | 7 500 | INV |
| Building cost | 600 898 | 420 984 | 179 914 | INV |
| Accumulated depreciation | (243 224) | (173 320) | (69 904) | OP |
| **Net total noncurrent assets** | **440 174** | **322 664** | **117 510** | |
| **Total assets** | **862 872** | **746 164** | **116 708** | |
| **Liabilities** | | | | |
| *Current liabilities* | | | | |
| Bank overdraft | 64 900 | 43 200 | 21 700 | CCE |
| Accounts payable | 199 853 | 163 866 | 35 987 | OP |
| Income taxes payable | 17 228 | 16 090 | 1 138 | OP |
| Dividends payable | 0 | 6 000 | (6 000) | FNC |
| Current portion of bonds payable | 22 000 | 20 000 | 2 000 | FNC |
| **Total current liabilities** | **303 981** | **249 156** | **54 825** | |
| *Noncurrent liabilities* | | | | |
| Bonds payable | 213 000 | 235 000 | (22 000) | FNC |
| Provision for employee entitlements | 52 364 | 50 773 | 1 591 | OP |
| **Total noncurrent liabilities** | **265 364** | **285 773** | **(20 409)** | |
| **Net assets** | **293 527** | **211 235** | **82 292** | |
| **Equity** | | | | |
| Share capital issued | 150 000 | 100 000 | 50 000 | FNC |
| Retained profits | 143 527 | 111 235 | 32 292 | OP, FNC |
| **Total equity** | **293 527** | **211 235** | **82 292** | |

Exhibit 12.10 illustrates how the cash flow from operations using the indirect method can be prepared from the changes in the statement of financial position from the beginning to the end of the period. The cash flow category to which the account change is assigned is shown to the right of the 'Change' column.

Additional information:

- The change in retained profits is composed of net profits $56 292 minus dividends declared of $24 000.
- Cash and equivalents are defined as cash plus temporary investments minus bank overdraft.
- Current and noncurrent portions of the bonds payable will be included together in the financing section of the statement of cash flows.

EXHIBIT 12.11

**Tamarack Systems Ltd**

**Statement of cash flows for the year ended 30 June 2002**

| | $ | $ |
|---|---|---|
| **Cash flow from operating activities** | | |
| Net profit for the year | | 56 292 |
| Adjustments for non-cash expenses: | | |
| Depreciation of building | 69 904 | |
| Employee entitlements | 1 591 | 71 495 |
| Adjustments for changes in non-cash working capital: | | |
| Accounts receivable | (76 706) | |
| Inventories | 10 815 | |
| Prepaid expenses | 5 317 | |
| Accounts payable | 35 987 | |
| Income taxes payable | 1 138 | (23 449) |
| **Cash from operations** | | **104 338** |
| **Investing activities** | | |
| Additions to land | (7 500) | |
| Additions to building | (179 914) | (187 414) |
| **Financing activities** | | |
| Dividend payments | (30 000) | |
| Repayment of bonds ($22 000 – $2 000) | (20 000) | |
| Share capital issued | 50 000 | 0 |
| **Net total change in cash and equivalents** | | (83 076) |
| Cash and equivalents – beginning of year ($12 440 + $65 000 – $43 200) | | 34 240 |
| Cash and equivalents – end of year ($16 064 + $0 – $64 900) | | (48 836) |

Using the categorisations indicated above for the changes, we get the statement of cash flows shown in exhibit 12.11. Every account change is shown below, so you can trace each back to the balance sheet changes. Most companies would group changes together to make a less detailed cash flow statement.

From this cash-focused summary of balance sheet changes, we can make several observations:

- The company's total cash flow was strongly negative for the year.
- Cash from operations was almost twice accrual net profit.
- Cash from operations has been severely reduced by a large rise in accounts receivable (uncollected revenue).
- Operations were the major source of cash during the year – there was no new borrowing and the issue of shares brought in only half the cash that operations did.
- The major use of cash was additions to noncurrent assets.
- The company's cash balance reversed from $34 240 to a cash deficit of $48 836.

We do not know the reasons for the effects shown in the statement of cash flows, but we certainly do know several things we might like to ask management about. In particular, we might like to know how management proposes to get cash back onto the positive side.

## How's your understanding?

Here are two questions you should be able to answer, based on what you have just read:

1 How does a statement of cash flows explain what happened to cash and cash equivalents during the year?

2 The following changes occurred in Bradee Ltd's accounts during the past year: non-cash current assets increased by $270; cost of noncurrent assets increased by $600; accumulated depreciation increased by $250; non-cash current liabilities increased by $340; warranty provision in noncurrent liabilities increased by $80; noncurrent debts decreased by $120; share capital increased by $200; net profit was $475; and $215 in dividends was paid. Calculate the change in cash and cash equivalents for the year. ($475 + $250 + $80 + $340 – $270 – $215 – $600 – $120 + $200 = $140 increase)

## 12.7 Interpreting a cash flow statement (indirect method)

The indirect method is used extensively in North America. As noted earlier, in Australia the indirect method is shown as a note to the statement of cash flows. In exhibit 12.12 we have provided an example that we call Tyson Limited. The example is a simplified version of some real figures for a US company. Note that it is comparative for three years, and that the three years vary a great deal in the details of their cash flows. A great deal of information is provided about various financing and investing activities.

Let's see some of the things Tyson's cash flow statement tells us.

- The company's cash from operations is very large in relation to its other cash flows. This allows the company to finance most of its activities from such internally generated cash, rather than having to borrow or issue more share capital.
- The company does not keep much cash on hand relative to its annual flow. Cash from operations has been about, or more than, ten times cash on hand in each of the three years.
- Interesting changes are suggested in the company's relationship with its customers and suppliers. Accounts receivable had been increasing each year in 20X1 and 20X2, but were significantly decreased in 20X3. (It turns out that new arrangements were made to sell accounts receivable continuously to a bank, speeding up the company's receipt of cash.) Inventories rose quite a lot in 20X3 and accounts payable were paid off faster: these two items reduced cash from operations by more than $100 million.
- The company acquired more noncurrent assets during 20X3. Those acquisitions cost more than $250 million in 20X3, more than twice what was spent in 20X2, and more than was spent in 20X1. Such acquisitions have been Tyson's major use of the cash it generates from operations.
- These acquisitions help the company keep its assets renewed as they lose their value through use. The sum of the company's amortisation and depreciation for the year gives an indication of that lost value, which is only about $90 million less than the spending on noncurrent assets.
- Tyson did a major refinancing of its long-term debt during 20X3, trying to take advantage of financial market changes such as interest rate reductions. The company has a large amount of 'revolving' prearranged credit lines and other flexible arrangements, so it was able to rearrange its debts. You can see that though nearly a billion dollars was rearranged, the net amount of additional borrowing was small.

**EXHIBIT 12.12** Tyson Foods Ltd

**Consolidated statements of cash flows for three years ended 30 June 20X3**

| | 20X3 $000 | 20X2 $000 | 20X1 $000 |
|---|---|---|---|
| **Cash flows from operating activities** | | | |
| Net profit | 185 712 | 178 417 | 149 282 |
| Adjustments to reconcile net profit to cash provided by operating activities: | | | |
| Depreciation | 145 756 | 119 363 | 106 630 |
| Amortisation | 30 753 | 29 502 | 29 201 |
| Loss on dispositions of property and equipment | 695 | 218 | 816 |
| (Increase) decrease in accounts receivable | 35 344 | (25 259) | (3 810) |
| (Increase) decrease in inventories | (66 909) | 10 606 | (14 238) |
| Increase (decrease) in trade accounts payable | (41 001) | 7 414 | (6 396) |
| Net change in other current assets and liabilities | 18 052 | (54 381) | 35 589 |
| *Cash provided by operating activities* | *308 402* | *265 880* | *297 074* |
| **Cash flows from investing activities** | | | |
| Additions to property, plant and equipment | (268 682) | (107 990) | (213 576) |
| Proceeds from sale of property, plant and equipment | 7 387 | 6 615 | 15 294 |
| Net change in other assets and liabilities | (41 393) | (3 309) | (7 424) |
| *Cash used for investing activities* | (302 688) | (104 684) | (205 706) |
| **Cash flows from financing activities** | | | |
| Net increase (decrease) in notes payable | (29 200) | (10 000) | 10 000 |
| Proceeds from long-term debt | 977 421 | 131 941 | 155 500 |
| Repayments of long-term debt | (954 497) | (278 694) | (246 642) |
| Dividends paid | (4 951) | (2 836) | (1 716) |
| *Cash used for financing activities* | (11 227) | (159 589) | (82 858) |
| Increase/(decrease) in cash | (5 513) | 1 607 | 8 510 |
| Cash and cash equivalents at beginning of year | 27 060 | 25 453 | 16 943 |
| **Cash and cash equivalents at end of year** | 21 547 | 27 060 | 25 453 |

- The company does not pay much in dividends. This is presumably part of the company's internal financing strategy: retained profits is the largest single account on the right side of the company's 20X3 statement of financial position.
- Net total cash flow ('increase (decrease) in cash') is small compared to the size of the operating, investing and financing flows. The company appears to be doing a careful job of balancing incoming and outgoing cash flows.

## How's your understanding?

Here are two questions you should be able to answer, based on what you have just read:

1 It was stated above that Tyson Foods relies on internal financing of its investing activities. How can you tell?

2 Comparison of which figures on the statement of cash flows gives an indication of whether a company appears to be renewing its assets as they lose their value through use?

## 12.8 Cash flow and the manager

Managers are responsible not only for earning profit for the company, but also for managing cash so that bills can be paid on time, excess borrowing and interest costs can be avoided, and the company's liquidity and solvency can be generally protected. Effectively employing available cash so that it does not remain idle, earning nothing, is also important. Cash flow and profit are generally positively correlated (good performance tends to move them both up, and poor performance tends to move them both down), and over a long enough time (years), they are almost the same. But in the short run their relationship can be complex. For example, a problem new businesses can have is to grow too fast. Often the product demand and the entrepreneurial enthusiasm are high: the business was founded in the hope that people would want the product or service, and it is exciting to everyone when they do! The income statements of such businesses often show high profits, but the cash flow and the balance sheet may tell a different story. In the enthusiasm of making sales and satisfying customers, inventory levels often get too high (making sure there is something for everyone on hand) and collections from customers often lag (receivables get too high as the entrepreneur concentrates on the pleasures of selling rather than the nuisance of collecting). The cash flow deducts the increases in inventories and receivables from accrual-basis net income, and may show that operating cash flows are small or even negative. When this happens, you do not need cash flow to know you are in trouble: your bank balance tells you that! But the statement of cash flow reports the whole story to others, so that they can see what you have accomplished in obtaining and using cash in your operating, financing and investing activities. You then have to be prepared to explain such activities to users of the financial statements.

The statement of cash flows provides a measure of managerial performance in managing cash, so smart managers must be aware of how their efforts are reflected in it, just as they are aware of the measures of performance and position offered by the statements of financial position and financial performance.

## 12.9 Cash flow statements in the public sector

Public sector entities are also required by AAS 28 to provide a statement of cash flows. The statement identifies the sources of the cash flows during the period, the purposes for which the cash was used during the period and where the government entity can retain cash balances, the cash balance at the reporting date. For a government department the information in the cash flow statement will be relevant to assessment of future cash flow needs of the department and to discharge accountability obligations (AAS 29).

In addition to cash flows from operating activities, investing activities and financing activities, government departments usually include cash flows from government, which would include such items as recurrent appropriation, capital appropriation and asset sale proceeds that are transferred to consolidated funds. The sum of these items provides 'net cash from government'.

An example of a statement of cash flows for a government department is provided in exhibit 12.13. It can be seen that, as the New South Wales Roads and Traffic Authority has limited capacity to collect users' charges, total receipts from operations in 2001 are considerably less than total payments for operations. When the cash flows from government (recurrent appropriations and capital appropriations) are added, the cash flows from operations are highly positive. This amount approximately covers the cash inflow from investing. There was also a net increase in borrowings of $39 732 000.

**EXHIBIT 12.13**

## Roads and Traffic Authority, New South Wales

## Statement of cash flows for the year ended 30 June 2001

| | Notes | Actual 2001 $000 | Budget 2001 $000 | Actual 2000 $000 |
|---|---|---|---|---|
| **Cash flows from operating activities** | | | | |
| **Payments** | | | | |
| Employee related | | (167 755) | (173 091) | (187 957) |
| Grants and subsidies | | (19 386) | (23 220) | (33 662) |
| Finance costs | | (76 400) | (89 800) | (96 372) |
| Other | | (997 233) | (921 562) | (979 585) |
| **Total payments** | | **(1 260 774)** | **(1 207 673)** | **(1 297 576)** |
| **Receipts** | | | | |
| Sale of goods and services | | 143 548 | 126 168 | 139 067 |
| Retained taxes, fees and fines | | 5 347 | 3 498 | 3 203 |
| Investment income received | | 18 423 | 3 566 | 18 247 |
| Other | | 155 087 | 24 935 | 37 069 |
| **Total receipts** | | **322 405** | **158 167** | **197 586** |
| **Cash flow from Government** | | | | |
| Recurrent appropriation | | 1 069 099 | 1 035 756 | 1 042 464 |
| Capital appropriation | | 882 682 | 884 925 | 853 151 |
| **Net cash flows from Government** | | **1 951 781** | **1 920 681** | **1 895 615** |
| **Net cash flows from operating activities** | 25 | **1 013 412** | **871 175** | **795 625** |
| **Cash flows from investing activities** | | | | |
| Proceeds from sale of land and buildings, plant and equipment and infrastructure systems | | 33 482 | 29 102 | 41 115 |
| Purchases of land and buildings, plant and equipment and infrastructure systems | | (1 091 176) | (908 077) | (911 656) |
| **Net cash flows from investing activities** | | **(1 057 694)** | **(878 975)** | **(870 541)** |
| **Cash flows from financing activities** | | | | |
| Proceeds from borrowings and advances | | 40 000 | 40 000 | 110 000 |
| Repayment of borrowings and advances | | (268) | (32 200) | (16 351) |
| **Net cash flows from financing activities** | | **39 732** | **7 800** | **93 649** |
| **Net increase/(decrease) in cash** | | **(4 550)** | | **10 733** |
| **Opening cash and cash equivalents** | | 45 770 | 23 037 | 27 037 |
| Closing cash and cash equivalents | 9 | **41 220** | **23 037** | **45 770** |

# 12.10 Homework and discussion to develop understanding

## Discussion questions

1 Why is managing cash flow important?

2 Can a company have a good net profit and little cash generated from operations in the same year? If it can, how does this happen?

3 Why is cash generated from operations usually larger than net profit?

4 What are cash and cash equivalents?

5 Explain the difference between the direct and indirect method of calculating cash flow from operations.

6 Provide three examples of transactions that will affect:

a cash flow from operations

b cash flows from financing activities

c cash flows from investing activities.

7 How can cash flow from operations be negative when net profit is positive?

8 Companies are required to classify cash flows as either 'operating', 'investing' or 'financing'. Which of these three categories is most likely to have a net cash outflow over a number of years? Briefly explain your answer.

9 At the Annual General Meeting of Scotlay Ltd, the Managing Director made the following statement:

> Although the year was one characterised by poor sales performance, Scotlay Ltd maintained strong operating cash flows. Operating profit for the year was $1 000 000, and net operating cash flows were $4 000 000. The difference between operating profit and operating cash flows is primarily explained by depreciation charges of $3 000 000. Scotlay's continuing investment program will ensure that operating cash flows are even higher next year, as depreciation charges are expected to increase to $5 000 000.

a Explain how depreciation charges can create a difference between 'operating profit after tax' and 'net cash flow from operating activities'.

b Briefly comment on the validity of the managing director's prediction of an increase in operating cash flows next year.

10 Briefly explain why managing cash flow is important for the success of a business.

11 A senior financial executive for a large public company remarked to a stockmarket analyst: 'I don't know why you people worry so much about what is in our cash flow statement. Managing cash flow is our responsibility as managers; it involves paying close attention to cash on a daily basis. Why don't you pay attention to our profit and just forget about cash flow? We'll look after that!'

Respond to the executive's comments. You do not have to agree or disagree entirely.

### Problem 12.1* Prepare a cash flow statement[2]

Shown below are the statements of financial position for Mato for the six months ending 31 August 2002, as well as the company's opening statement of financial position (1 March 2002). A profit and loss statement for the six months ended 31 August is also provided.

**Mato Pty Ltd**
**Statement of financial position**
as at 31 August and 1 March 2002

| **Assets** | | | **Liabilities and shareholders' equity** | | |
|---|---|---|---|---|---|
| | **August $** | **March $** | | **August $** | **March $** |
| **Current assets** | | | **Current liabilities** | | |
| Cash | 4 507 | 130 000 | Bank loan | 75 000 | 0 |
| Receivables | 18 723 | 0 | Payables | 45 616 | 1 100 |
| Inventory | 73 614 | 0 | Loan payable | 15 000 | 15 000 |
| | **96 844** | **130 000** | | **135 616** | **16 100** |
| **Noncurrent assets** | | | **Shareholders' equity** | | |
| Equipment cost | 54 640 | 10 000 | Share capital | 125 000 | 125 000 |
| Accumulated depreciation | (3 234) | 0 | Retained profits (deficit) | (49 378) | 0 |
| Leasehold (net) | 57 568 | 0 | | | |
| Software (net) | 4 320 | 0 | | | |
| Incorporation costs | 1 100 | 1 100 | | | |
| | **114 394** | **11 100** | | **75 622** | **125 000** |
| **Total** | **211 238** | **141 100** | **Total** | **211 238** | **141 100** |

**Profit and loss statement**
for the six months ended 31 August 2002

| | $ | $ |
|---|---|---|
| Revenues | | 42 674 |
| Cost of goods sold | | 28 202 |
| Gross profit | | 14 472 |
| Operating expenses: | | |
| Salaries | 25 480 | |
| Travel | 8 726 | |
| Telephone | 2 461 | |
| Rent | 12 000 | |
| Utilities | 1 629 | |
| Office and general | 3 444 | |
| Amortisation and depreciation | 10 110 | 63 850 |
| **Net loss for the six months (no tax)** | | **49 378** |

An analysis of the noncurrent assets shows that the following investments were made: equipment $44 640 (computer $14 900; other equipment and furniture $29 740); leasehold cost $63 964; software costs $4 800.

***Required:***

1 Prepare a cash flow statement for the six months ended 31 August 2002.

2 Comment on what we learn from the cash flow statement.

3 Prepare a reconciliation between the net loss and the cash flow from operations. What do we learn from this reconciliation?

## Problem 12.2* Cash flow basics plus some 'what if' questions

1 Beta Company's statement of cash flows showed the following figures: cash generated from operations $127 976; cash used in investing activities $238 040; and cash obtained in financing activities $107 000. What was the net change in the company's cash and cash equivalents for the year?

2 Indicate the effect on Beta Company's statement of cash flows (direct method) of each of the following events, *if they had occurred during the year*:

 a A new truck was purchased at a cost of $38 950, and of this, $10 000 was paid in cash and the remainder was borrowed long term.

 b The company sold a machine that had a book value of $3220 for $4100 cash.

 c Collections of accounts receivable were $6000 less than actually happened.

 d The company declared an additional dividend of $15 000, but had not paid any of it by the end of the year.

 e The company borrowed $25 000 from the bank as a demand loan.

3 Answer question **2c** using the indirect method.

## Problem 12.3* Prepare a statement of cash flows

The following information relates to Tut Ltd.

**Tut Ltd**
**Comparative statements of financial position**
**as at 30 June 2002**

| | 2002 $000 | 2001 $000 |
|---|---|---|
| **Current assets** | | |
| Cash | — | 20 |
| Accounts receivable | 143 | 105 |
| Inventory | 200 | 220 |
| Prepaid insurance | 10 | 10 |
| **Noncurrent assets** | | |
| Equipment | 640 | 450 |
| Accumulated depreciation – equipment | (200) | (150) |
| Land | 680 | 600 |
| Motor vehicles | 485 | 520 |
| Accumulated depreciation – motor vehicles | (183) | (210) |
| **Total assets** | 1 775 | 1 565 |
| **Current liabilities** | | |
| Bank overdraft | 10 | — |
| Accounts payable | 205 | 265 |
| Income tax payable | 44 | 70 |
| Final dividend payable | 85 | 60 |
| **Noncurrent liabilities** | | |
| Borrowings | 470 | 430 |
| **Total liabilities** | 814 | 825 |
| **Net assets** | 961 | 740 |
| **Shareholders' equity** | | |
| Paid up capital | 620 | 450 |
| Asset revaluation reserve | 210 | 130 |
| Retained profits | 131 | 160 |
| **Total shareholders' equity** | 961 | 740 |

**Profit and loss statement**
**for year ended 30 June 2002**

| | $000 | $000 |
|---|---|---|
| Sales | | 560 |
| Less: Cost of goods sold | 170 | |
| Insurance expense | 45 | |
| Other expenses | 220 | |
| Loss on sale of motor vehicles | 25 | 460 |
| Profit before tax | | 100 |
| Less: Income tax expense | | 44 |
| Profit after tax | | 56 |

Additional information (dollar amounts expressed in full units):

- Land was revalued upwards during the year by $80 000.
- Motor vehicles with an original cost of $145 000 and accumulated depreciation of $65 000 were sold for $55 000.
- Equipment to the value of $60 000 was acquired with the issue of a long-term note. The amount payable has been included in borrowings on the balance sheet.

***Required:***

Prepare a statement of cash flows for Tut Ltd for the year ended 30 June 2002. Also prepare a reconciliation of cash from operating activities to net profit.

## Problem 12.4 Interpreting cash flow statements

You are evaluating two companies, Adelaide Airways Ltd and Perth Express Ltd, as possible investments. The two companies, similar in size, are in the commuter airline business. They fly passengers from Adelaide and Perth to smaller cities in their States. Assume that all other available information has been analysed and that the decision on which company's shares to purchase depends on the information given in their statements of cash flows, which appear below.

**Adelaide Airways Ltd**
**Statement of cash flows**
for the years ending 30 September 2002 and 2001

| | 2002 | 2001 |
|---|---|---|
| **Cash flows from operating activities** | | |
| Receipts from customers | 580 000 | 561 000 |
| Payments to suppliers and employees | (563 000) | (430 000) |
| Net cash provided by operating activities | 17 000 | 131 000 |
| **Cash flows from investing activities** | | |
| Purchase of equipment | (120 000) | (91 000) |
| Proceeds from sale of equipment | 118 000 | 39 000 |
| Proceeds from sale of investments | 52 000 | 4 000 |
| Net cash provided by (used in) investing activities | 50 000 | (48 000) |
| **Cash flows from financing activities** | | |
| Proceeds from short-term loans | 122 000 | 143 000 |
| Repayment of short-term loans | (179 000) | (134 000) |
| Payment of dividends | (45 000) | (64 000) |
| Net cash used in financing activities | (102 000) | (55 000) |
| Net increase (decrease) in cash | (35 000) | 28 000 |
| Cash balance at the beginning of the year | 131 000 | 103 000 |
| Cash balance at the end of the year | 96 000 | 131 000 |

**Perth Express Ltd**
**Statement of cash flows**
for the years ending 30 September 2002 and 2001

| | **2002** | **2001** |
|---|---|---|
| **Cash flows from operating activities** | | |
| Receipts from customers | 776 000 | 632 000 |
| Payments to suppliers and employees | (528 000) | (439 000) |
| Net cash provided by operating activities | 248 000 | 193 000 |
| **Cash flows from investing activities** | | |
| Purchase of equipment | (303 000) | (453 000) |
| Proceeds from sale of equipment | 46 000 | 39 000 |
| Proceeds from sale of investments | 0 | 33 000 |
| Net cash used in investing activities | (257 000) | (381 000) |
| **Cash flows from financing activities** | | |
| Proceeds from short-term loans | 43 000 | 35 000 |
| Proceeds from long-term loans | 131 000 | 83 000 |
| Repayment of short-term loans | (66 000) | (18 000) |
| Net cash provided by financing activities | 108 000 | 100 000 |
| Net increase (decrease) in cash | 99 000 | (88 000) |
| Cash balance at the beginning of the year | 116 000 | 204 000 |
| Cash balance at the end of the year | 215 000 | 116 000 |

***Required:***

1 What information is contained in the statements of financial performance and financial position? Why is the additional information contained in the statement of cash flows important when evaluating a company's performance?

2 Based on an examination of their statements of cash flows, discuss the relative strengths and weaknesses of Adelaide Airways and Perth Express. Which company would you recommend as an investment? Why?

## Problem 12.5 Interpret a statement of cash flows and answer two 'what if' questions

A high school friend of yours, Natasha Wheeler, is currently in second-year fine arts and, in addition to many other talents, also happens to have an entrepreneurial flair. For the last two summers, she has operated a bicycle rental business near a local park. In 2000, even though the business was just getting started, she made enough money to pay for tuition and get herself through the school year. Encouraged by this initial success, she bought several more bikes in 2001 and constructed a moveable shed, out of which she operated her business and serviced the bikes.

Business was even better this summer, but Natasha is confused. Although her business profit was great, there is no cash for her to withdraw. She does not know how she will pay for tuition this year, not to mention living expenses. Knowing that you are taking an accounting course, she comes to you for help. She realises that you cannot lend her any money, but maybe you can explain what is going on with her business.

1 Using the statement of cash flows, explain to Natasha how it is possible that the profit and loss statement can show a profit, while there is no cash for her to withdraw from the business. Explain to her where all the cash went.

2 In order to pay her tuition and keep a roof over her head, Natasha decides that she will have to borrow another $4000 from her parents, who will not expect her to repay the money in

the near future, and another $2000 from the bank, which is looking very carefully at Natasha's cash position (and at her very saleable bicycles) and expecting to be repaid as soon as possible. What effect will these two events have on the statement of cash flows?

**Wheeler's Bicycle Rental Pty Ltd**
**Statement of cash flows**
**for the year ended 28 February 2002**

| | 2002<br>$ | 2001<br>$ |
|---|---|---|
| **Cash flows from operating activities** | | |
| Receipts from customers | 20 000 | 11 000 |
| Payments to suppliers and employees | (8 000) | (4 500) |
| Net cash provided by operating activities | 12 000 | 6 500 |
| **Cash flows from investing activities** | | |
| Payment for property, plant and equipment | (20 000) | (5 000) |
| Net cash used in investing activities | (20 000) | (5 000) |
| **Cash flows from financing activities** | | |
| Proceeds from borrowings | 7 000 | 3 000 |
| Proceeds from issue of shares | — | 2 000 |
| Dividends paid | — | (5 500) |
| Net cash provided/(used) in financing activities | 7 000 | (500) |
| Net increase/(decrease) in cash held | (1 000) | 1 000 |
| Cash at beginning of financial year | 1 000 | — |
| Cash at end of financial year | — | 1 000 |

## Problem 12.6 Effect of transactions on cash flows

For each of the following transactions, indicate the directional effect (increase, decrease, no change) on cash from operating activities, cash from investing activities, and cash from financing activities. Ignore taxes.

***Transactions:***

1 The company borrows $100 000 as a long-term loan from the local bank.
2 The company increases its depreciation expense for the year.
3 The company declares and pays a dividend to shareholders.
4 The company collects $1000 from a customer who had previously purchased merchandise on credit.
5 The company sells a motor vehicle for $5000 cash. The carrying amount of the motor vehicle at the time of sale is $9000.

## Problem 12.7 Interpreting cash flows

Narooma Limited reported the following information on cash flow for the year 2001.

| | $ |
|---|---|
| Cash flows from operations | 180 000 |
| Cash flows from investing activities | 400 000 |
| Cash flows from financing activities | (600 000) |
| Net cash flows | (20 000) |
| Opening cash balance | 78 000 |
| Closing cash balance | 58 000 |

*Required:*

1 Does Narooma Limited appear to be expanding or contracting its operations?
2 Describe three activities that could explain the use of cash by financing activities.
3 Using only the cash flow information presented, make an assessment of the condition of Narooma Limited. Is it growing, mature/stable or declining? State reasons for your answer (including any assumptions you make).

## Problem 12.8 Effect of transactions on cash flows

The financial year for Alpha Limited ends on 30 June 2002. Management has asked you what effect each of the following June transactions will have on net profit before tax, cash flow from operations, cash flow from financing and cash flow from investing for the year ended 30 June 2002:

1 sent invoices for $20 000 to customers during June for work carried out in June; $8000 of this had been collected by year-end
2 borrowed $300 000 from the bank on 10 June, with principal and interest repayable in six months. Accrued interest at 30 June is $1300
3 paid salaries for the month of $70 000, with $5000 in wages owing at year-end
4 received $20 000 deposit on a job that will be carried out in July 2002
5 paid accounts payable $30 000, which was outstanding at 31 May 2002
6 sold old equipment for $20 000. The equipment originally cost $300 000 with accumulated depreciation at the time of sale of $250 000
7 purchased new equipment on 20 June 2002 for $320 000 cash. Depreciation on this equipment for June 2002 amounted to $1100
8 declared dividends of $200 000 in June 2002, to be paid after year-end.

## Problem 12.9 Interpreting a cash flow statement

Outline the *five* most important things you learn about Tabcorp Holdings Limited from the consolidated cash flow statement for the year ended 30 June 2000.

| | 2000<br>$000 | 1999<br>$000 |
|---|---|---|
| **Cash flows from operating activities** | | |
| Net cash receipts in the course of operations | 1 639 929 | 1 067 952 |
| Payments to suppliers, service providers and employees | (710 884) | (421 675) |
| Payment of State Government betting taxes | (501 901) | (372 604) |
| Dividends received | — | — |
| Interest received | 3 730 | 5 469 |
| Interest and other costs of finance paid | (51 751) | (684) |
| Income tax paid | (92 170) | (73 331) |
| Net operating cash flows | 286 953 | 205 127 |
| | | |
| **Cash flows from investing activities** | | |
| Loans pursuant to employee share plan | 4 102 | 4 141 |
| Payment for controlled entities (net of cash acquired) | (473 347) | — |
| Payment for unlisted securities | (258) | — |
| Redemption of unlisted securities | — | — |

| | 2000<br>$000 | 1999<br>$000 |
|---|---|---|
| Payment for property, plant and equipment | (75 916) | (86 116) |
| Proceeds from sale of property, plant and equipment | 13 975 | 2 275 |
| Payment for the acquisition of licences | (30) | — |
| Payment of acquisition costs | — | (390) |
| Other | (135) | 2 163 |
| Loans advanced to controlled entities | — | — |
| **Net investing cash flows** | (531 609) | (77 927) |
| | | |
| **Cash flows from financing activities** | | |
| Loans from controlled entities | — | — |
| Proceeds from issue of securities | 92 270 | — |
| Proceeds from borrowings | 629 898 | 47 000 |
| Repayment of borrowings | (310 133) | (9 000) |
| Proceeds from loans repaid | 703 | — |
| Return of capital and associated costs paid | — | (100 475) |
| Dividends paid | (170 683) | (121 569) |
| Other | (29) | — |
| **Net financing cash flows** | 242 026 | (184 044) |
| **Net increase/(decrease) in cash held** | (2 630) | (56 844) |
| **Cash at the beginning of the financial year** | 84 816 | 141 660 |
| **Cash at the end of the financial year** | 82 186 | 84 816 |

## Problem 12.10 Comment on a company's cash management (indirect method)

Axiomatic Ltd's cash flow statement for last year is shown below. Make as many observations as you can about how the company managed its cash during the year.

**Axiomatic Ltd**
Cash flow statement for last year

| | $ | $ |
|---|---|---|
| Operations: | | |
| Net profit for the year | | 94 900 |
| Add back non-cash expenses: | | |
| Depreciation expense | 216 800 | |
| Deferred income tax expense | 14 200 | |
| Superannuation expense | 38 900 | 269 900 |
| Non-cash working capital changes: | | |
| Increase in accounts receivable | (143 900) | |
| Increase in inventories | (71 600) | |
| Increase in accounts payable | 87 000 | (128 500) |
| Cash generated by operations | | 236 300 |
| Investing activities: | | |
| Additions to noncurrent assets | (429 100) | |
| Proceeds on disposal of noncurrent assets | 27 700 | (401 400) |

**Axiomatic Ltd**
Cash flow statement for last year

| | $ | $ |
|---|---|---|
| Financing activities: | | |
| Short-term bank loan | 30 000 | |
| Additions to noncurrent debt | 343 200 | |
| Repayments of noncurrent debt | (316 000) | |
| Share capital issued | 200 000 | |
| Dividends paid during the year | (40 000) | 217 200 |
| Increase in cash for the year | 52 100 | |
| Cash, beginning of year | (93 500) | |
| Cash, end of year | (41 400) | |

## Problem 12.11 Cash flow analysis from account information

Prepare a cash flow statement from the following cash account information.

| | $ | | $ |
|---|---|---|---|
| Bank loan obtained | 60 000 | Dividends paid ($20 000 declared) | 15 000 |
| Cash expenses | 8 920 | Employee wages and salaries paid | 223 610 |
| Cash sales | 31 610 | Income tax paid | 14 920 |
| Cash, beginning of year | 68 920 | Land purchased for cash | 81 000 |
| Cash, end of year | 93 620 | Payments to suppliers | 513 600 |
| Collections on accounts receivable | 797 640 | Proceeds from sale of old truck | 7 000 |
| Ordinary shares issued | 140 000 | Repayments on mortgage | 80 500 |
| Cost of redeeming preference shares | 25 000 | Truck purchased ($5000 still owing) | 49 000 |

## Problem 12.12 Prepare and interpret a basic cash flow analysis from financial statements

1 Prepare a cash flow statement from the following financial statements of Fuzzy Wuzzy Wines Ltd. Include a reconciliation of cash and cash equivalents, and a reconciliation of operating profit after tax to cash flows from operating activities.

2 Comment on what your statement tells you about the company's cash management during the year ended 31 August 2002. If you were a shareholder in Fuzzy Wuzzy, would you be happy with management's performance?

**Fuzzy Wuzzy Wines Ltd**
Statements of financial position as at August 31, 2002 and 2001

| **Assets** | **2002** | **2001** | **Liabilities and equity** | **2002** | **2001** |
|---|---|---|---|---|---|
| | **$** | **$** | | **$** | **$** |
| **Current assets** | | | **Current liabilities** | | |
| Cash | 80 | 175 | Bank loan | 140 | 100 |
| Term deposits | 0 | 150 | Payables | 425 | 200 |
| Receivables | 520 | 350 | | 565 | 300 |
| Inventories | 340 | 250 | Noncurrent liabilities | | |
| | 940 | 925 | Long-term loans | 225 | 400 |
| | | | | 790 | 700 |
| **Noncurrent assets** | | | **Shareholders' equity** | | |
| Factory | 1 450 | 925 | Share capital | 700 | 500 |
| Accumulated depreciation | (475) | (350) | Retained earnings | 425 | 300 |
| | 975 | 575 | | 1 125 | 800 |
| | 1 915 | 1 500 | | 1 915 | 1 500 |

**Fuzzy Wuzzy Wines Ltd**
**Profit and loss statement**
for year ended 31 August 2002

| | **$000** | **$000** |
|---|---|---|
| Revenue | | 3 000 |
| Expenses: | | |
| Depreciation | 210 | |
| Building write-off* | 45 | |
| General | 2 320 | 2 575 |
| Profit before income tax | | 425 |
| Income tax expense | | 190 |
| Net profit for the year | | 235 |

* Building written off had a historical cost of $130 and accumulated depreciation of $85.

**Fuzzy Wuzzy Wines Ltd**
Note showing changes in retained earnings

| | |
|---|---|
| Retained earnings as at 1 September 2001 | 300 |
| add: Net profit for the year ended 31 August 2002 | 235 |
| less: Dividends declared and paid | (110) |
| Retained earnings as at 31 August 2002 | 425 |

## Problem 12.13 Prepare a statement of cash flows

The information below relates to Nata Ltd.

**Nata Ltd**
**Comparative statements of financial position**

| | 2002 $000 | 2001 $000 |
|---|---|---|
| **Current assets** | | |
| Cash | 72 | 20 |
| Accounts receivable | 205 | 120 |
| Inventory | 140 | 120 |
| **Noncurrent assets** | | |
| Marketable securities | 160 | 160 |
| Equipment | 180 | 185 |
| Accumulated depreciation – equipment | (88) | (85) |
| Buildings | 265 | 265 |
| Accumulated depreciation – buildings | (100) | (80) |
| Land | 400 | 400 |
| **Total assets** | 1 234 | 1 105 |
| **Current liabilities** | | |
| Accounts payable | 140 | 135 |
| Provision for income tax | 50 | 35 |
| Final dividend payable | 50 | 50 |
| **Noncurrent liabilities** | | |
| Borrowings | 340 | 330 |
| **Total liabilities** | 580 | 550 |
| **Net assets** | 654 | 555 |
| **Shareholders' equity** | | |
| Share capital | 375 | 375 |
| Asset revaluation reserve | 70 | 70 |
| General reserve | 30 | 30 |
| Retained profits | 179 | 80 |
| **Total shareholders' equity** | 654 | 555 |

**Profit and loss statement**
**for the year ended 30 June 2002**

| | $000 | $000 |
|---|---|---|
| Sales | | 640 |
| Profit on sale of equipment | | 2 |
| | | 642 |
| Less: | | |
| Cost of goods sold | 190 | |
| Other expenses | 253 | 443 |
| Profit before tax | | 199 |
| Less: Income tax expense | | 50 |
| Profit after tax | | 149 |

***Additional information (dollar amounts expressed in full units):***

- Equipment with an original cost of $30 000 and accumulated depreciation of $25 000 was sold for $7000.
- Equipment to the value of $10 000 was acquired with the issue of a long-term bank loan. The amount payable has been included in borrowings on the balance sheet.

***Required:***

1. Prepare a statement of cash flows for Nata Ltd for the year ended 30 June 2002.
2. Prepare a reconciliation of operating profit after tax and cash provided by operating activities.

## Problem 12.14 Prepare a statement of cash flows

The following information relates to Nile Ltd.

**Nile Ltd**
**Comparative statements of financial position**

| | 2002 $000 | 2001 $000 |
|---|---|---|
| **Current assets** | | |
| Cash | 405 | 360 |
| Accounts receivable | 570 | 225 |
| Inventory | 400 | 320 |
| **Noncurrent assets** | | |
| Land | 430 | 400 |
| Equipment | 620 | 590 |
| Accumulated depreciation – equipment | (320) | (280) |
| Vehicles | 270 | 260 |
| Accumulated depreciation – vehicles | (90) | (90) |
| Buildings | 470 | 470 |
| Accumulated depreciation – 'buildings | (300) | (250) |
| **Total assets** | 2 455 | 2 005 |
| **Current liabilities** | | |
| Accounts payable | 850 | 800 |
| Income tax payable | 220 | 230 |
| Final dividend payable | 100 | 100 |
| **Noncurrent liabilities** | | |
| Borrowings | 910 | 520 |
| **Total liabilities** | 2 080 | 1 650 |
| **Net assets** | 375 | 355 |
| **Shareholders' equity** | | |
| Paid-up capital | 310 | 240 |
| Asset revaluation reserve | 20 | 0 |
| Retained profits | 45 | 115 |
| **Total shareholders' equity** | 375 | 355 |

**Profit and loss statement**
**for the year ended 30 June 2002**

| | $000 | $000 |
|---|---|---|
| Sales | | 1 200 |
| Profit on sale of equipment | | 130 |
| | | 1 330 |
| Less expenses: | | |
| Cost of goods sold | 620 | |
| Other expenses | 435 | 1 055 |
| Profit before tax | | 275 |
| Less: Income tax expense | | 220 |
| Profit after tax | | 55 |

***Additional information (dollar amounts expressed in full units):***

- Vehicles with an original cost of $90 000 and accumulated depreciation of $40 000 were sold for a price of $180 000.
- Land was revalued upwards by $20 000.
- Equipment to the value of $30 000 was acquired with the issue of a long-term note. The amount payable has been included in Borrowings on the statement of financial position.
- Interim dividends were paid during the year. (Hint: reconstruct retained earnings.)

***Required:***

1 Prepare a statement of cash flows for Nile Ltd for the year ended 30 June 2002. Prepare a reconciliation of cash from operations to net profit.

2 Comment on what the statement of cash flows reveals about the financial stability of Nile Ltd.

## Problem 12.15 Prepare a statement of cash flows

The following information relates to Willow Ltd.

**Willow Ltd**
**Comparative statements of financial position**

| | 2002 $000 | 2001 $000 |
|---|---|---|
| **Current assets** | | |
| Cash | 335 | 110 |
| Accounts receivable | 110 | 150 |
| Inventory | 260 | 250 |
| **Noncurrent assets** | | |
| Land | 540 | 460 |
| Equipment | 120 | 170 |
| Accumulated depreciation – equipment | (80) | (90) |
| Vehicles | 205 | 165 |
| Accumulated depreciation – vehicles | (72) | (45) |
| Buildings | 260 | 260 |
| Accumulated depreciation – buildings | (180) | (110) |
| **Total assets** | 1 498 | 1 320 |

| | 2002<br>$000 | 2001<br>$000 |
|---|---|---|
| **Current liabilities** | | |
| Accounts payable | 390 | 360 |
| Income tax payable | 210 | 145 |
| Final dividend payable | 50 | 60 |
| **Noncurrent liabilities** | | |
| Borrowings | 400 | 320 |
| **Total liabilities** | 1 050 | 885 |
| **Net assets** | 448 | 435 |
| **Shareholders' equity** | | |
| Share capital | 300 | 250 |
| Asset revaluation reserve | 92 | 52 |
| Retained profits | 56 | 133 |
| **Total shareholders' equity** | 448 | 435 |

**Profit and loss statement**
**for the year ended 30 June 2002**

| | $000 | $000 |
|---|---|---|
| Sales | | 710 |
| Gain on sale of equipment | | 30 |
| | | 740 |
| Less: | | |
| Cost of goods sold | 320 | |
| Other expenses | 219 | 539 |
| Profit before income tax | | 201 |
| Less: Income tax expense | | 210 |
| Profit/(loss) after tax | | (9) |

***Additional information (dollar amounts expressed in full units):***

- Equipment with an original cost of $120 000 and accumulated depreciation of $50 000 was sold for a profit of $30 000.
- Land was revalued upwards by $40 000.
- Vehicles to the value of $40 000 were acquired with the issue of a long-term note. The amount payable has been included in borrowings on the balance sheet.
- Interim dividends were paid during the year. (Hint: reconstruct retained earnings.)

***Required:***

1. Prepare a statement of cash flows for Willow Ltd for the year ended 30 June 2002. Prepare a reconciliation of cash from operations to net profit.
2. Explain briefly how it is possible to generate a net inflow of cash in the same year as a loss was recorded in the profit and loss statement.

## Problem 12.16 Preparation of a statement of cash flows

The following information relates to Kim Ltd.

**Comparative statements of financial position**

| | 30 June 2001 $000 | 30 June 2002 $000 |
|---|---|---|
| Current assets | | |
| Cash | 240 | 193 |
| Accounts receivable | 470 | 400 |
| Provision for doubtful debts | (47) | (50) |
| Inventory | 380 | 420 |
| Prepaid insurance | 40 | 30 |
| Noncurrent assets | | |
| Land | 620 | 605 |
| Buildings | 840 | 1 205 |
| Accumulated depreciation – buildings | (310) | (390) |
| Trucks | 215 | 215 |
| Accumulated depreciation – trucks | (40) | (80) |
| Office equipment | 400 | 610 |
| Accumulated depreciation – office equipment | (210) | (220) |
| Goodwill | 190 | 170 |
| **Total assets** | 2 788 | 3 108 |
| Current liabilities | | |
| Accounts payable | 290 | 210 |
| Accrued Expenses | 140 | 120 |
| Interest payable | 40 | 40 |
| Income tax payable | 480 | 510 |
| Final dividend payable | 200 | 270 |
| Noncurrent liabilities | | |
| Borrowings | 1 100 | 770 |
| **Total liabilities** | 2 250 | 1 920 |
| Shareholders' equity | | |
| Paid-up capital | 300 | 400 |
| Asset revaluation reserve | 10 | 60 |
| General reserve | 50 | 110 |
| Retained earnings | 178 | 618 |
| **Total shareholders' equity** | 538 | 1 188 |
| | 2 788 | 3 108 |

**Profit and loss statement**
year ended 30 June 2002

| | $000 | $000 |
|---|---|---|
| Sales revenue | | 4 800 |
| Proceeds from sale of land | | 380 |
| Proceeds from sale of office equipment | | 280 |
| | | 5 460 |
| Less Expenses: | | |
| Cost of goods sold | 2 200 | |
| Bad debts expense | 30 | |
| Insurance expense | 20 | |
| Interest expense | 40 | |
| Other expenses | 1 400 | |
| Carrying amount of land sold | 200 | |
| Carrying amount of office equipment sold | 160 | 4 050 |
| Profit before income tax | | 1 410 |
| Income tax expense | | |
| Current year | 510 | |
| Over provision from previous year | (20) | 490 |
| Profit after tax | | 920 |

***Additional information (dollar amounts expressed in full units):***

- **a** The office equipment sold had been originally purchased by Kim Ltd three years ago at a cost of $300 000.
- **b** Land with an original value of $240 000 was revalued to $290 000.
- **c** An interim dividend was paid during the year. (Hint: balance retained earnings.)

***Required:***

1. Prepare a statement of cash flows for Kim Ltd for the year ended 30 June 2002.
2. Prepare the reconciliation of cash from operations to net profit after income tax. No other notes are required.

## Problem 12.17 Prepare a cash flow statement from statement of financial position changes

Lambic Beverages Ltd. makes special high-powered beers, some fermented in the bottle, and nonalcoholic sparkling drinks. Below are the company's statements of financial position for the end of this year and last year, and some information about profit and dividends during this year. From this information, prepare a cash flow statement for this year and comment on what it tells you. Also, calculate the company's working capital ratio and debt/equity ratio for both years and comment on those, in relation to the cash flow analysis.

**Lambic Beverages Ltd.**
Comparative statements of financial position for this year and last year

| **Assets** | **This year** $ | **Last year** $ | **Liabilities and equity** | **This year** $ | **Last year** $ |
|---|---|---|---|---|---|
| Current assets | | | Current liabilities | | |
| Cash | 560 | 1 120 | Bank loan | 400 | 1 500 |
| Accounts receivable | 3 210 | 2 060 | Accounts payable | 7 240 | 6 220 |
| Inventory | 4 440 | 4 910 | Income tax payable | 0 | 330 |
| | 8 210 | 4 910 | | 7 640 | 8 050 |
| Noncurrent assets | | | Noncurrent liabilities | | |
| Property and plant | 26 670 | 24 820 | Long-term debt | 14 060 | 14 350 |
| Accumulated depreciation | (7 760) | (5 130) | | | |
| | 18 910 | 19 690 | Shareholders' equity | | |
| | | | Share capital | 1 500 | 1 200 |
| | | | Retained earnings | 3 920 | 4 180 |
| | | | | 5 420 | 5 380 |
| | 27 120 | 27 780 | | 27 120 | 27 780 |

***Other information:***

**a** The company had a net loss of $210 this year. Not expecting the loss, the company paid a $50 dividend early in the year.

**b** Depreciation expense for the year was $2630.

## Problem 12.18 Effects on cash flow statement of unpaid dividends and building disposal

**a** You have just prepared a cash flow statement for Frogmorton Ltd, and it works out to the correct change in cash and cash equivalents. You then discover that included in the current liabilities is an account for dividends payable that you had not realised was there. Explain why the cash from operations and financing figures on your cash flow statement are incorrect and why the total change in cash is correct in spite of your error.

**b** You are struggling with the cash flow statement for Magdalen Ltd. You know that the net total change in noncurrent assets over the year is an increase of $459 200, and that the depreciation expense for the year was $236 100. You then learn that during the year the company sold a building for $200 000. The building had cost $840 000, and there was accumulated depreciation on it of $650 000 at the date of sale.

***Required:***

**1** Calculate the apparent amount spent on acquisitions of noncurrent assets during the year.

**2** Calculate the gain or loss on the sale of the building.

**3** Specify the adjustments to profit in the operations section of the cash flow statement arising from noncurrent assets.

**4** Specify the figures in the investing activities section of the cash flow statement.

## Problem 12.19 Interpreting a cash flow statement

**Foster's Group Limited**
**Statements of cash flows**
for the financial year ended 30 June 2001

| | Note | FGL 2001 $m Inflows/ (Outflows) | FGL 2000 $m Inflows/ (Outflows) | Consolidated 2001 $m Inflows/ (Outflows) | Consolidated 2000 $m Inflows/ (Outflows) |
|---|---|---|---|---|---|
| **Cash flows from operating activities** | | | | | |
| Receipts from customers | | | | **6 156.8** | 4 684.4 |
| Payments to suppliers, governments and employees | | **(43.6)** | (40.2) | **(5 388.3)** | (3 976.0) |
| Dividends received | | **257.0** | 200.0 | **0.2** | — |
| Interest received | | | | **90.1** | 118.9 |
| Borrowing costs | | | | **(269.6)** | (183.0) |
| Income taxes paid | | **(16.5)** | (24.6) | **(306.0)** | (167.5) |
| Net cash flows on behalf of controlled entities | | **(257.0)** | (200.0) | | |
| **Net cash flows from operating activities** | 29 | **(60.1)** | (64.8) | **283.2** | 476.8 |
| **Cash flows from investing activities** | | | | | |
| Payments to acquire controlled entities (net of cash balances acquired) | 29 | | | **(2 315.9)** | (205.1) |
| Payments to acquire outside equity interest in controlled entities | 29 | | | **(4.9)** | (24.1) |
| Payments for property, plant, equipment and agricultural assets | | **(5.0)** | (1.3) | **(322.9)** | (209.8) |
| Payments for acquisition of investments | | | | **(2.3)** | (34.9) |
| Proceeds from repayment of loans | | **7.6** | 3.7 | **10.4** | 36.9 |
| Proceeds from sale of controlled entities | | | | **—** | 2.6 |
| Proceeds from sale of property, plant and equipment | | | | **33.4** | 19.2 |
| Proceeds from sale of investments | | | | **3.1** | 31.4 |
| **Net cash flows from investing activities** | | **2.6** | 2.4 | **(2 599.1)** | (383.8) |
| **Cash flows from financing activities** | | | | | |
| Payments for shares bought back | 21 | **(12.6)** | (112.3) | **(12.6)** | (112.3) |
| Proceeds from issue of shares | 21 | **1 031.7** | — | **1 031.7** | — |
| Proceeds from borrowings | 19 | | | **3 726.8** | 2 689.4 |
| Repayment of borrowings | 19 | | | **(2 294.5)** | (2 074.0) |
| Proceeds from exercise of options and capital called up | 21 | **15.1** | 7.7 | **15.1** | 7.7 |
| Distributions to outside equity interest | | | | **(0.4)** | — |
| Dividends paid | | **(131.7)** | (240.3) | **(131.7)** | (240.3) |
| Net cash flows on behalf of controlled entities | | **(840.2)** | 407.0 | | |
| **Net cash flows from financing activities** | | **62.3** | 62.1 | **2 334.4** | 270.5 |
| **Total cash flows from activities** | 19 | **4.8** | (0.3) | **18.5** | 363.5 |
| **Cash at the beginning of the year** | | **0.1** | 0.4 | **504.8** | 139.4 |
| Effects of exchange rate changes on foreign currency cash flows and cash balances | | | | **11.2** | 1.9 |
| **Cash at the end of the year** | 29 | **4.9** | 0.1 | **534.5** | 504.8 |

***Required:***

What are the main points you learn about Foster's from the above cash flow statements?

## Problem 12.20 Interpreting a cash flow statement

**Jupiters Limited**
Statements of cash flows
for the year ended 30 June 2001

| | Note | Consolidated | | Chief entity | |
|---|---|---|---|---|---|
| | | 2001 $000 | 2000 $000 | 2001 $000 | 2000 $000 |
| **Cash flows provided by operating activities:** | | | | | |
| Cash receipts in the course of operations | | **753 647** | 666 154 | **564 147** | 568 465 |
| Cash payments in the course of operations | | **(565 244)** | (475 441) | **(417 051)** | (413 508) |
| Distributions received | | **—** | 1 019 | **1 777** | 1 019 |
| Interest received | | **6 316** | 4 312 | **4 099** | 3 655 |
| Borrowing costs | | **(27 007)** | (22 015) | **(26 674)** | (22 015) |
| Income taxes paid | | **(49 732)** | (19 372) | **(41 495)** | (14 283) |
| Net cash provided by operating activities | 15(b) | **117 980** | 154 657 | **84 803** | 123 333 |
| **Cash flows used in investing activities:** | | | | | |
| Purchase of property, plant and equipment | | **(44 458)** | (32 070) | **(33 136)** | (20 507) |
| Purchase of/proceeds from sale of businesses | | **(2 803)** | 956 | **—** | — |
| Proceeds from sale of property, plant and equipment | 2 | **326** | 417 | **141** | 336 |
| Increase in equity investment and acquisition of management contract | | **—** | (10 693) | **—** | (17 352) |
| Purchase of controlled entity | | **—** | (132 566) | **—** | (145 879) |
| Net cash used in investing activities | | **(46 935)** | (173 956) | **(32 995)** | (183 402) |
| **Cash flows provided by/(used in) financing activities:** | | | | | |
| Repayment of borrowings | 12 | **(126 500)** | — | **(126 500)** | — |
| Repayment of finance lease | 16(c) | **(1 919)** | (1 919) | **(1 919)** | (1 919) |
| Loan repayments from controlled entities | | **—** | — | **25 906** | 784 |
| Dividends paid | | **(45 330)** | (36 204) | **(43 444)** | (36 204) |
| Proceeds from borrowings | 12 | **96 500** | 96 500 | **96 500** | 96 500 |
| Net cash provided by/(used in) financing activities | | **(77 249)** | 58 377 | **(49 457)** | 59 161 |
| Net increase/(decrease) in cash | | **6 204** | 39 078 | **2 351** | (908) |
| Cash at the beginning of the financial year | | **122 946** | 83 868 | **79 198** | 80 106 |
| Cash at the end of the financial year | 15(a) | **116 742** | 122 946 | **81 549** | 79 198 |

***Required:***

Explain the main differences in cash flows between 2000 and 2001.

## Problem 12.21 (Challenging) Why not just have cash basis accounting?

A business commentator made the following remark during a discussion of the financial performance of a large, but struggling, company. 'These accountants are something to behold! They spend lots of money to create complicated financial statements, especially profit and loss statements, that use what they call "accrual" accounting, and come up with a profit number they expect us to take seriously. Then they spend a whole lot more money creating cash flow statements, which are just as complicated as the other statements, and they take away all the accruals and supposedly return us to the cash profit number we would have had anyway, if they hadn't bothered with accrual accounting in the first place! Nice work! You get paid to create a dubious profit measure and then more money to uncreate it. What kind of idiots do they take the business community for? Why don't they just give us the cash profit and leave it at that? We can understand that, and it would make a simple profit and loss statement and no need for a cash flow statement to just cancel out the profit number, as we have now.'

If you were an accountant involved in the discussion and everyone turned to you to hear what you would say in response to the commentator, what would you say?

## Problem 12.22 (Challenging) Interpret trends in cash management

Apex Accessories Limited makes, imports and sells various goods for the fashion trade, including costume jewellery, belts and other leather goods, hats and many kinds of apparel. The business is both seasonal and very unstable, with products coming and going as fashions and availability from foreign suppliers change. During a very interesting 'business issues' TV program about the fashion industry, some of Apex's financial results were displayed in an onscreen table, while a narrator gushed about the marvellous management the company had. Here is that table:

| Year | Year-end total assets<br>$ | Year-end total bank borrowing<br>$ | Net profit for the year<br>$ | Year's cash flow from operations<br>$ |
|---|---|---|---|---|
| 1993 | 24 400 000 | 8 300 000 | 2 100 000 | 3 200 000 |
| 1994 | 29 100 000 | 9 600 000 | 2 400 000 | 3 900 000 |
| 1995 | 28 500 000 | 8 900 000 | 2 300 000 | 3 200 000 |
| 1996 | 34 700 000 | 10 300 000 | 2 600 000 | 2 500 000 |
| 1997 | 37 800 000 | 12 000 000 | 2 800 000 | 2 200 000 |
| 1998 | 35 400 000 | 14 100 000 | 3 000 000 | 1 800 000 |
| 1999 | 37 000 000 | 14 200 000 | 3 100 000 | 3 800 000 |
| 2000 | 39 600 000 | 15 200 000 | 3 300 000 | 3 400 000 |
| 2001 | 43 000 000 | 16 400 000 | 3 200 000 | 2 800 000 |
| 2002 | 45 700 000 | 18 500 000 | 3 400 000 | 1 900 000 |

***Required:***

1 Which column of figures do you suppose the narrator was referring to when gushing about the 'marvellous management'?

2 Provide as many comments as you can about the company's results. Do you think the management is marvellous?

3 For this particular company (which is listed on a stock exchange), would you expect market traders to respond much to the cash flow information once they know the net profit figures?

Put another way, do you think the cash flow information has any added value to the net profit information?

### Problem 12.23 (Challenging) Ethics of cash flow manipulation

There is an interesting ethical issue behind the very reason the cash flow statement is thought by some people to have advantages over the profit and loss statement. The reason is that people are often mistrustful of the profit and loss statement, because they feel its accrual accounting methods can be used to manipulate net profit as a measure of performance, and think that the cash flow figures are more 'real'. For example, a company might claim large revenues, not yet collected, that make its revenue higher (via the entry DR Accounts receivable, CR Revenue), but if the cash has not been collected, the increase in accounts receivable will be deducted from net profit on the statement of cash flows, and the lack of 'real' cash inflow will be apparent because cash from operations will be lower than would be expected from the profit number. Thus, it is thought, the statement of cash flows cash from operations figure is more believable than net profit and will even, if it is too different from net profit, unmask manipulations of the net profit.

The ethical issue is that it is possible to manipulate the cash flow figures too. For example, a company might accelerate or delay receivables collections in order to change the cash flow figures, whether or not the net profit is also being manipulated. There may be a difference from manipulating net profit, because changing cash flow figures requires real actions, affecting customers or suppliers or employees, so there are real consequences, such as irritating customers or having to offer inducements for early payment. Nevertheless, it can be done.

It seems that most people would feel that altering the accruals just to make net profit better (or worse, or smoother) is ethically questionable, even if it is understandable because of the way management is evaluated and rewarded. But is altering the cash flow ethically questionable? Is there an ethical problem if management decides to put pressure on customers to accelerate collections and improve the company's cash position? Sounds like good management, not like manipulation.

Suggest two or three ways, not included above, by which operating, investing or financing cash flows could be altered from their normal levels. For each, discuss whether, or under what conditions, you would think there is an ethical problem in such alteration.

### Problem 12.24 (Challenging) Prepare a full set of statements, including statement of cash flows

Grandin Ltd manufactures a single product and has revenue from related service activities. The company had been growing slowly but steadily until this year (2002), when revenue, especially from services, increased substantially.

The company's bookkeeper was part way through preparing the 2002 and 2001 financial statements, and asked you for help in completing them. When you went to the company's offices you got the information below. Assume these figures are correct.

1. Prepare a set of statements, including a comparative statement of financial position, profit and loss statement, and statement of retained profits for 2002 and 2001.
2. Define 'cash and cash equivalents' for Grandin.
3. Prepare a 2002 statement of cash flows in the usual format. Note that the 2001 statement of financial position is relevant to this task, but that the 2001 profit and loss and retained profits statements are not, because they are for a period before the beginning of 2002.

| | 2002 | | 2001 | |
|---|---|---|---|---|
| | Debit<br>$ | Credit<br>$ | Debit<br>$ | Credit<br>$ |
| Accounts payable | | 12 300 | | 8 900 |
| Accounts receivable | 44 200 | | 21 300 | |
| Accumulated depreciation | | 36 000 | | 32 000 |
| Administrative expenses | 14 600 | | 11 900 | |
| Bank loan – current | | 29 000 | | 19 000 |
| Cash | 4 700 | | 5 400 | |
| Cost of goods sold | 103 190 | | 71 650 | |
| Depreciation expense | 4 000 | | 5 800 | |
| Dividends paid | 4 000 | | 6 000 | |
| Electricity expense | 9 200 | | 6 200 | |
| Equipment | 87 000 | | 87 000 | |
| Equipment financing | | 20 000 | | 24 000 |
| Income tax expense | 5 450 | | 3 500 | |
| Income tax payable | | 6 550 | | 5 100 |
| Interest expense | 4 800 | | 3 900 | |
| Inventory | 42 500 | | 37 000 | |
| Prepaid expenses | 2 100 | | 800 | |
| Retained profits – opening | | 37 500 | | 33 300 |
| Revenue – product sales | | 163 290 | | 116 250 |
| Revenue – service | | 73 700 | | 32 600 |
| Share capital | | 25 000 | | 25 000 |
| Shipping expense | 8 100 | | 7 500 | |
| Wage expense | 69 500 | | 28 200 | |
| | 403 340 | 403 340 | 296 150 | 296 150 |

## CASE 12A Woolworths Limited case

Refer to the extracts of the annual report of Woolworths Limited in appendix 2. All questions relate to the consolidated accounts.

1 What are the main components of cash flows from operating activities?
2 What are the main components of cash flows from investing activities?
3 What are the main components of cash flows from financing activities?
4 Reconcile the dividends paid and provided figure in the retained profits note with dividends paid in the cash flow statement.
5 What does the company define as cash and cash equivalents?
6 How does the cash flow statement relate back to the statement of financial position?
7 Why does cash flows from operations differ from operating profit after tax for Woolworths?
8 Did the company have any accrued interest (or interest payable) at year-end?
9 Reconcile sales in note 2 to receipts from customers in the statement of cash flows.

10 Write a paragraph summarising the major causes of the change in cash experienced by the company during the year. What major activities occurred?

## CASE 12B Statement of cash flows for Qantas Ltd

**Qantas Group**
**Statement of cash flows**
for the year ended 30 June 2001

| | Notes | 2001 $m | 2000 $m |
|---|---|---|---|
| **Cash flows from operating activities** | | | |
| Receipts from customers | | 10 527.8 | 9 066.6 |
| Payments to suppliers and employees | | (9 145.5) | (7 135.8) |
| Interest received | | 69.9 | 90.5 |
| Interest paid | | (151.8) | (175.5) |
| Dividends received | | 43.8 | 26.9 |
| Income taxes paid | | (243.5) | (272.9) |
| **Net cash provided by operating activities** | 40 | 1 100.7 | 1 599.8 |
| **Cash flows from investing activities** | | | |
| Payments for property, plant and equipment | | (995.5) | (1 141.8) |
| Receipts/(payments) for aircraft security deposits | | 44.4 | (10.6) |
| Total payments for purchases of property, plant, equipment and aircraft security deposits | | (951.1) | (1 152.4) |
| Proceeds from sale of property, plant and equipment | | 16.4 | 10.3 |
| Proceeds from sale and leaseback of property, plant and equipment | | 147.5 | 819.0 |
| Proceeds from sale of investments | | — | 60.4 |
| Payments for investments, net of cash acquired | | (17.1) | — |
| Loans to associates | | (67.0) | — |
| Net funding to related parties | | — | — |
| **Net cash used in investing activities** | | (871.3) | (262.7) |
| **Cash flows from financing activities** | | | |
| Repayment of borrowings/swaps | | (1 028.0) | (798.9) |
| Debt prepayments on sale and leaseback of property, plant and equipment | | — | (819.0) |
| Total debt repayments | | (1 028.0) | (1 617.9) |
| Proceeds from borrowings | | 804.8 | 505.9 |
| Proceeds from the issue of shares | | 19.0 | — |
| Dividends paid | | (454.8) | (430.0) |
| **Net cash used in financing activities** | | (659.0) | (1 542.0) |
| **Reconciliation of cash provided by/(used in):** | | | |
| Operating activities | | 1 100.7 | 1 599.8 |
| Investing activities | | (871.3) | (262.7) |
| Financing activities | | (659.0) | (1 542.0) |
| Net decrease in cash held | | (429.6) | (204.9) |
| Cash at the beginning of the financial year | | 688.8 | 893.7 |
| **Cash at the end of the financial year** | 40 | 259.2 | 688.8 |

1 Write a paragraph summarising the major causes of change in cash and cash equivalents experienced by the company during the year. What major activities seem to have been going on? (Hint: the following extract may give you some ideas.)

> Profit for the year to June 30 was $246 million (just matching prospectus estimates), compared with $246 million a year earlier and a loss in 1993–94.
>
> Earnings rose 2.1% in the latest half year, to December 31. More significantly, in the same period revenue rose 2.5% but people costs jumped 6.3%. Reductions in other costs contained the overall cost rise to 2.7%. If other factors had stayed the same, the remarkable changes made at the airline over three years would have given current profit a big boost.
>
> The number of passengers carried by Qantas has risen 32% over the past three years. In that time, the airline has added capacity equal to Boeing 767 aircraft yet it has only bought enough aircraft to provide the capacity of six 767s. There has been better utilisation. Strong says Qantas has become a world leader in aircraft utilisation. It has also reduced its finance costs as a result of lower interest rates and by using its cash flow to reduce net debt by more than $2 billion in the past three years. Gearing has fallen from 73% to 56%.
>
> (Source: *Business Review Weekly*, 7 April 1997.)

2 What do you learn about Qantas from the statement of cash flows for the year ended 30 June 2001?

## CASE 12C Interpreting the One.Tel Limited statement of cash flows

| | Consolidated | |
|---|---|---|
| | **2000 $m** | **1999 $m** |
| **Cash flow from operating activities** | | |
| Receipts from customers | **510.9** | 300.1 |
| Payments to suppliers and employees | **(684.8)** | (328.1) |
| Interest received | **16.9** | 1.9 |
| Interest and other borrowing costs paid | **(11.9)** | (3.5) |
| Income tax refunded | **—** | 0.7 |
| Net cash used by operating activities | **(168.9)** | (28.9) |
| **Cash flow from investing activities** | | |
| Proceeds from sale of investments | **—** | 1.6 |
| Proceeds from sale of plant and equipment | **—** | 19.2 |
| Payment for plant and equipment | **(87.5)** | (34.0) |
| Purchase of licences | **(525.6)** | (9.5) |
| Purchase of Controlled Entities | **—** | (6.9) |
| Payment of deferred consideration | **(1.8)** | |
| Loans provided to wholly owned entities | **—** | — |
| Loans provided to other parties | **—** | (2.6) |
| Net cash used by investing activities | **(614.9)** | (32.2) |

| | Consolidated | |
|---|---|---|
| | 2000 $m | 1999 $M |
| **Cash flow from financing activities** | | |
| Proceeds from issue of shares | **818.5** | 280.3 |
| Proceeds from borrowings | **139.8** | 59.0 |
| Finance lease principal repayments | **(11.2)** | (4.2) |
| Dividends paid | **(1.8)** | (2.5) |
| Share buyback | **—** | (106.4) |
| Net cash provided by financing activities | **945.3** | 226.2 |
| Net increase in cash held | **161.5** | 165.1 |
| Cash and cash equivalents at beginning of year | **172.6** | 8.4 |
| Exchange rate adjustment | **1.6** | (0.9) |
| Cash and cash equivalents at end of year | **335.7** | 172.6 |

*Required:*

1 Outline what you learn about One.Tel from the above statement of cash flows.

2 Which factors in the cash flow statement indicate the company would fail within one year, and which factors indicate they would not?

## CASE 12D Variations in the pattern of cash flows

Shown below are the 2001 statements of cash flow for Leighton Holdings, Stockland Corporation Limited and Toll Holdings Limited. For all companies, the pattern of cash flows has varied substantially between 2000 and 2001. Explain these changes for each of the four companies.

**Leighton Holdings**
**Statement of cash flows**
for the year ended 30 June 2001

| | Consolidated | |
|---|---|---|
| | 2001 $000 | 2000 $000 |
| **Cash flows from operating activities** | | |
| Cash receipts in the course of operations | **4 101 727** | 3 637 367 |
| Cash payments in the course of operations | **(3 484 360)** | (3 205 455) |
| Dividends received | **1 424** | — |
| Interest received | **17 119** | 12 256 |
| Borrowing costs paid | **(11 560)** | (10 741) |
| Income taxes paid | **(50 573)** | (59 073) |
| **Net cash provided by operating activities** | **573 777** | 374 354 |
| **Cash flows from investing activities** | | |
| (Increase) in investment in controlled entities and businesses | **(34 873)** | (86 314) |
| Payments for property, plant and equipment | **(346 998)** | (299 803) |
| Proceeds from sale of assets | **99 816** | 117 313 |
| (Increase) in investment in other entities | **(49 430)** | (18 197) |
| (Loans to)/repayments by executives | **(970)** | 78 |
| **Net cash used in investing activities** | **(332 455)** | (286 923) |
| **Cash flows from financing activities** | | |
| Proceeds from share issues | **14 707** | 2 007 |

| | | |
|---|---|---|
| Proceeds from borrowings | **166 170** | 183 667 |
| Repayment of borrowings | **(182 282)** | (207 440) |
| Distributions to outside equity interests | **(24 192)** | — |
| Dividends paid | **(89 705)** | (81 296) |
| **Net cash provided by/(used in) financing activities** | **(115 306)** | (100 006) |
| **Net increase/(decrease) in cash held** | **126 020** | (15 631) |
| **Net cash at the beginning of the financial year** | **348 029** | 363 704 |
| Effects of exchange rate changes on the balances of cash held in foreign currencies at the beginning of the year | **26 084** | (44) |
| **Net cash at reporting date** | **500 133** | 348 029 |

**Stockland Corporation Limited**
**Statements of cash flows**
for the year ended 30 June 2001

| | Note | Consolidated 2001 $000 | 2000 $000 |
|---|---|---|---|
| **Cash flows from operating activities** | | | |
| Cash receipts in the course of operations | | **389 863** | 188 739 |
| Cash payments in the course of operations | | **(375 926)** | (304 600) |
| Interest received | | **1 572** | 1 368 |
| Interest paid | | **(21 514)** | (13 245) |
| Income taxes paid | | **(14 281)** | (6 514) |
| **Net cash used in operating activities** | 30(b) | **(20 286)** | (134 252) |
| **Cash flows from investing activities** | | | |
| Proceeds from sale of plant and equipment | | **375** | 719 |
| Dividends received | | **—** | 10 |
| Repayment of loans by directors and executives | | **1 983** | 1 654 |
| Payments for investment | | **(925)** | (6 092) |
| Payments for plant and equipment | | **(3 423)** | (3 639) |
| Payments by/(to) partnership | | **1 220** | (1 020) |
| Hotel pre-opening expenses | | **(646)** | (1 741) |
| Purchase of controlled entity | | **(942)** | (4 609) |
| Advances to directors and executives under the executive share scheme | | **(10 493)** | (3 717) |
| Advances to controlled entities | | **—** | — |
| **Net cash used in investing activities** | | **(12 851)** | (18 435) |
| **Cash flows from financing activities** | | | |
| Proceeds from issue of shares | | **46 945** | 5 275 |
| Loans from a related entity | | **12 500** | 161 387 |
| Proceeds from borrowings | | **100 000** | |
| Repayment of borrowings | | **(100 000)** | — |
| Dividends paid | | **(21 656)** | (18 971) |
| **Net cash provided by financing activities** | | **37 789** | 147 691 |
| **Net increase/(decrease) in cash held** | | **4 652** | (4 996) |
| Cash at the beginning of the financial year | | **1 943** | 6 939 |
| Cash at the end of the financial year | 30(a) | **6 595** | 1 943 |

**Toll Holdings Ltd**
**Cash flows**
from annual report 2001

| | Notes | Consolidated 2001 $000 | Consolidated 2000 $000 | The Company 2001 $000 | The Company 2000 $000 |
|---|---|---|---|---|---|
| **Cash flows from operating activities** | | | | | |
| Cash receipts in the course of operations | | **1 659 799** | 1 350 718 | **57 310** | 40 923 |
| Cash payments in the course of operations | | **(1 544 343)** | (1 276 084) | **(34 631)** | (30 899) |
| Restructure costs paid | | **(6 118)** | (10 957) | **—** | — |
| Interest received | | **1 113** | 472 | **86** | 2 |
| Dividend received | | **551** | 329 | **—** | — |
| Interest and other costs of finance paid | | **(5 729)** | (3 239) | **(4 645)** | (2 037) |
| Income taxes paid | 5(b) | **(8 009)** | (165) | **(553)** | (29) |
| **Net cash inflow/(outflow) from operating activities** | | **97 264** | 61 074 | **17 567** | 7 960 |
| **Cash flows from investing activities** | | | | | |
| Proceeds on disposal of controlled entities | | **1 213** | — | **—** | — |
| Payment for entities and businesses, net of cash acquired | 33(d) | **(132 536)** | (9 917) | **(122 579)** | — |
| Payment for property, plant and equipment | | **(58 101)** | (50 958) | **(4 999)** | (22 915) |
| Proceeds from sale of property, plant and equipment | 2 | **30 244** | 20 261 | **—** | 29 970 |
| Payment for investments | | **(1 615)** | (350) | **—** | — |
| **Net cash inflow/(outflow) from investing activities** | | **(160 795)** | (40 964) | **(127 578)** | 7 055 |
| **Cash flows from financing activities** | | | | | |
| Proceeds from borrowings | | **125 298** | 34 605 | **124 927** | 44 772 |
| Repayment of borrowings | | **(32 332)** | (40 688) | **(6 500)** | (49 525) |
| Dividends paid | 6 | **(12 538)** | (10 438) | **(12 538)** | (10 438) |
| Proceeds from share issue | | **4 291** | 183 | **4 291** | 183 |
| Finance lease payments | | **(983)** | — | **—** | — |
| **Net cash inflow/(outflow) from financing activities** | | **83 736** | (16 338) | **110 180** | (15 008) |
| Net increase/(decrease) in cash held | | **20 205** | 3 772 | **169** | 7 |
| Cash at the beginning of the financial year | | **26 691** | 22 919 | **10** | 3 |
| **Cash at the end of the financial year** | 33(a) | **46 896** | 26 691 | **179** | 10 |
| Financing arrangements | 16 | | | | |
| Non-cash financing and investing activities | 33(e) | | | | |

## Notes

1 Useful information for this section was provided by Professors Jack Flanagan and Greg Whittred.
2 A number of problems in this chapter were developed by Cameron Hooper and Elizabeth Carson.

Chapter 13

# Prelude to financial statement analysis

## On completion of this chapter you should be able to:

- describe the social setting of financial accounting
- describe the way in which capital markets operate
- describe the role of financial accounting information in capital markets
- explain the relationship between risk and return
- explain what is meant by an efficient capital market
- explain the implications for financial accounting of agency relationship
- develop possible solutions to agency problems
- carry out 'what if' analysis.

## 13.1 Chapter overview

Previous chapters have developed your understanding of the financial statements and how they are prepared using transaction records and accrual accounting. Chapters 14 and 15 will describe techniques for the analysis of financial statements and the effects of accounting policy choices made by management in preparing those statements. This chapter is a bridge to those analytical chapters. It expands the description of the roles of financial accounting so that analysis and policy choice may be understood in context. As has been emphasised already, financial accounting does not exist in a vacuum: it plays a role in the world – in fact, it plays many roles. To help make your learning about analysis and policy choice meaningful, this chapter adds some perspective and depth to understanding those roles.

## 13.2 The social setting of financial accounting

We already know that financial accounting has been shaped by the development of business and society and that it has many functions, including the following:

- it helps share market investors decide whether to buy, sell or hold shares of companies
- it helps managers run companies on behalf of owners
- it provides basic financial records for the purposes of internal control, insurance and fraud prevention
- it is used by governments in monitoring the actions of enterprises and in assessing taxes, such as income tax and sales tax.

We could go on for some time listing major and minor functions of financial accounting. Whole books can be, and have been, written about each of the many functions! And, though we will focus on companies because the ideas in this chapter are most fully worked out for them, don't forget that there are many other organisations that use, and are affected by, accounting.

The centre of our interest in this book, financial accounting for the enterprise, operates within and serves a complex social setting. It seeks to monitor and report on financial events initiated by or happening to the enterprise. These events come from and in turn affect the social setting, so the accounting is not passive: it tells us what is going on, but in doing so it affects our decisions and actions and, therefore, also affects what is going on.

The social setting is composed of many people. There are at least three parties directly concerned with what financial accounting says about the enterprise:

- the owners (shareholders of a company, for example)
- the managers, who are running the company on behalf of the owners
- the auditors, who are employed by the owners to evaluate the accounting reports presented by the managers.

These parties have relationships with each other, as well as with financial accounting.

- Managers, for example, may work for a company throughout their careers and, therefore, may have as much a feeling of ownership as do shareholders who may, through buying and selling shares on the share market, be part-owners of the company for only a few months before moving on to another investment.
- In smaller companies, managers and owners may be the same people.
- The auditors are formally appointed by the owners, at the annual shareholders' meeting, for example, but they work with the managers on a day-to-day basis and may also offer advice on tax, accounting and other topics of practical interest to managers, which are separate from the knowledge they use in their role as auditors.

In addition to these three central parties, and often hard to distinguish from them, is a host of other groups, companies, institutions and parties interested in, or having an influence on, the company's financial accounting. Some of these others are:

- share markets (where shareholders may buy and sell their shares)
- other capital markets, such as bond markets
- share market regulators, such as stock exchanges and securities commissions
- governments
- employees
- creditors
- competitors
- potential owners, creditors, employees or competitors
- the accounting profession
- society in general.

As you have already seen, these parties do not share the same interest in the company's accounting, and may even be in competition or conflict with each other. Most will be in the same country as the company and its management, but, increasingly, companies and other enterprises are operating internationally. So, the other groups interested in, and affecting, the company's financial accounting may be all around the world.

## 13.3 Capital markets

### Share markets and other markets for financial capital

As business corporations developed, ownership rights in them were sold more and more broadly. The owners (shareholders) began to invest in several businesses at once and to buy and sell their shares from and to each other. To facilitate such buying and selling ('trading') of shares among investors, share markets organised as stock exchanges developed. Today there are many such exchanges, including the major international ones in New York, London, Tokyo, Paris and Toronto. The Australian Stock Exchange (ASX) provides the tenth-largest national equities market in the world, and the largest in the southern hemisphere. There are also 'over-the-counter' markets and other alternatives to the major exchanges. Brokers, investment banks, market analysts and others conduct, assist in and advise on trading.

Trading goes on in more than just shares of companies. There is also trading of rights (using terms such as 'warrant' or 'options') to buy or sell shares in the future, to convert from one kind of share to another, to receive dividends and to perform a wide variety of other future actions. New rights and financial instruments to convey such rights are being invented and traded all the time. Special markets have been developed for some of these, such as an options exchange in Chicago, but many are traded on regular stock exchanges, including the Australian Stock Exchange. Corporate and government bonds are also traded, and there is such a variety of financial instruments that the distinction between ownership shares, creditorship bonds and other rights and instruments is often blurred. For example, some bonds carry the right to be converted into shares at the option of the holder.

Many exchanges and over-the-counter markets use computerised trading systems for the listed companies whose shares and other securities (the usual general name for all these shares, bonds and other financial instruments) trade on the exchanges and other markets, and, increasingly, investors can buy or sell securities somewhere in the world pretty well 24 hours a day. Taken together, all these exchanges, markets and buying and selling activities are usually called capital markets. They include both share trading and trading of all the other securities that corporations and governments use to finance their assets.

It is important to emphasise that these markets operate quite separately from the organisations that initially issue the securities.

- For example, when a company decides to issue some shares, these securities are offered to the market(s), and the company receives the proceeds of the initial sale of them (less commissions to brokers and others involved). After that, however, the company ceases to be a direct participant. Investors buy the securities from each other and sell them to each other with no participation from the company.
- Investors may even act in the face of opposition from the company. For example, an investor may try to get enough shares together to get voting control of the company (a 'takeover'). There is always a risk for so-called public companies (companies whose shares members of the public are able to buy or sell from each other without permission of the companies) that the markets will behave in ways companies do not like.
- There are other examples of investors acting in ways not desired by the company. One is that the company may announce a new management team that it expects will improve the company's performance, only to see the price of its shares fall because the people buying and selling the shares do not like the new team, and more people want to sell their shares than want to buy them, producing a fall in the share price.
- The markets often create new securities out of the ones the company initially issued, then trade those. For example, a share may carry the right to buy another share in the future. That right may be bought and sold separately on the market, so that you could own the share without any such right, or the right without any such share. You might even be able to buy an 'option', consisting of a bet as to whether the share price will rise or fall in the next month or year, or buy a bet as to the overall price of the market's shares in the future. (Overall price measures, such as the Dow Jones Average (United States) and the Australian All Ordinaries Index, are closely watched by many.)

To prepare you for financial accounting analysis, five particular aspects of capital markets are outlined in this section. These are:

- the way securities are traded and security prices are established
- the role of information (such as accounting reports) in such a market
- the idea of a 'risky return'
- the fact that markets are 'aggregates'
- the concept of 'market informational efficiency'.

These aspects, among many others, are dealt with in capital market theory. This theory is very down-to-earth, and incorporates much practical knowledge of how markets work. It has been a powerful impetus to economics, finance and accounting research, and to changes in the way capital markets are operated.

## Security trading and security prices

Capital markets work in the same way as any market. People trade (buy and sell) what they own for something else, usually money or a promise of it.

- There are people who own securities, such as shares in BHP Billiton. Some of these will be willing to sell their shares, if the price is right. If no one was willing to sell at any price, there would be no trading!
- There are people who don't own the securities, but who are willing to buy them from the above people, if the price is right. If no one was willing to buy at any price, there

would be no trading! Let's call the first group the sellers and the second group the buyers. Suppose we had the following list of possible prices of BHP shares:

| Price | Sellers' willingness to sell | Buyers' willingness to buy |
|---|---|---|
| $31 | Everyone would sell | No one would buy |
| $30 | Most would sell | A few would buy |
| $29 | Half would sell | Half would buy |
| $28 | Some would sell | Most would buy |
| $27 | None would sell | All would buy |

You'll recognise from this hypothetical list of prices that we have a supply curve and a demand curve. Capital market prices are set by the interaction between those wanting to sell and those wanting to buy. At a price of $31, there would be lots of shares for sale but no buyers; at a price of $27, there would be lots of buyers but no sellers. Each day's market price for the shares is set by the balance between people willing to buy and people willing to sell:

- If there are more sellers than buyers, the price will fall, roughly down to the level at which there is an equal number of buyers and sellers (or at least, shares demanded and shares for sale).
- If there are more buyers than sellers, the price will rise, roughly up to the level at which there is an equal number of sellers and buyers (or shares for sale and shares demanded).

In the above example, we would expect the buyers and sellers to agree to trade (buy and sell) at a price around $29. So if we looked up BHP Billiton's shares in the newspaper's listing of Australian Stock Exchange prices, we would expect to see today's price to be about $29. But the daily price is set by the pressures of supply and demand, so it will vary depending on how many buyers and sellers make offers to buy or sell, and, therefore, it will vary around $29 as those pressures vary.

## Role of information in a capital market

Why would the pressures of supply and demand vary? Broadly speaking, there are three kinds of reasons that are of interest in accounting analysis:

1 *No information-based trading*. The circumstances of some buyers and sellers may require them to sell, or even buy, almost regardless of anything to do with the particular company whose shares are being traded. An owner of some shares may die and the estate may have to sell the shares in order to distribute the money to the beneficiaries of the owner's will. Or an 'institutional' investor, such as a superannuation fund, may need some cash to pay superannuation or other payments. Or a person may win a lottery and buy shares in a managed fund (an investment consisting of a sample of shares of many companies), so that the mutual fund in turn has to buy some shares. Therefore, some trading is likely to be occurring continuously for reasons of raising or spending available cash. Such trading is referred to as 'liquidity trading'.

2 *General information-based trading*. Companies whose shares are traded are part of a general economic system, and some general events may change people's views on the wisdom of investing in anything, and so cause changes in all or most shares traded on an exchange. The share price of companies such as the BHP Billiton may therefore change along with the rest. Examples of such general events are changes in national

interest rates, announcements of trends such as inflation or consumer confidence, wars, illness or death of important people and elections that change the party in power. If the Australian Federal Government announced a new special tax on company profits, we might expect pretty well every company's share price to fall, including BHP Billiton's, because investors would see this as hurting every company's future profits and, therefore, the returns investors would get from owning shares in any company. Market-wide price changes coming from the economic system are often called 'systemic' effects. Some of the trades may happen because investors think some companies will be hurt or helped more than others, and some investors may be getting out of that market altogether, such as by selling their shares and buying gold or real estate.

3 *Specific information-based trading.* Information specifically about BHP Billiton's future prospects may also cause changes in the willingness of people to buy or sell its shares. For example, if BHP Billiton announces that it is going to buy a mining company, some people may like that idea (and, wanting to buy, increase the demand for shares) and other people may dislike the idea (and, wanting to sell, increase the supply of shares). If most people think BHP Billiton's buying the other company is a good idea, the share price will rise; if most people think it is a bad idea, the share price will fall. This phenomenon, in which share prices reflect people's evaluation of the impact or meaning of an event on the wisdom of holding a company's shares, is very important to understanding share prices and accounting's information role. We can say that the share market 'prices' the information, in that the change in the trading price of the shares (up, down, or not at all) is a measure of the value of the information to the market. Harking back to the accounting concepts of chapter 9, we might say that in a share market sense, *decision-relevant information is material* to the market if knowing about it changes, or would change, a security's market price or, perhaps, would prompt trading (buying and selling) even if the net effect on price were zero.

A great amount of analysis and research in accounting, finance and economics uses this idea to measure the apparent value of all sorts of company-specific information, such as a company's annual announcement of its net profit ('earnings announcement'), announcements of changes in management and news about other events initiated by or affecting the company. (Presuming that change in share market prices is a measure of information value requires some faith in the market system as a social good and confidence in the market's ability to respond appropriately ('efficiently') to information.)

## Return and risk

The return you earn by owning a security (a share or bond) is the sum of:

- the cash you get (from dividends or interest payments) plus
- the change (hopefully an increase) in the market price of the security.

So, you get a cash return plus a holding gain or 'capital gain' (or loss). Capital market theory develops much of its power from analysing the nature of these two kinds of returns, particularly the second kind. If the security you own varies in market price, that variation is, according to the theory, a measure of the risk from owning the security, since price could go up or down. Risk is calculated as the variance or standard deviation of the prices around the average price, or trend in average price, of that security. A risky security, therefore, is one whose price varies all over the place. As described above, a security's price may vary because the whole share market or bond market is going up or down, or because of information specific to that security or to the company issuing the security. So, analytically, the risk is separated into:

- *systematic risk* – the portion of the security's variation that relates to or correlates with variation in the overall market
- *unsystematic risk* – the security's own residual variation not related to the market. 'Beta' (a term coming from the mathematical model used to relate a firm's returns to those of the market overall) is a measure of the security's relationship to overall market variations. Securities can be classified according to this relationship: a low beta security's prices vary less than overall market prices do, while a high beta security's prices vary more than the market.

Risk can be controlled to some extent by holding a variety of securities with different betas. More will be said about this in the section on aggregates below.

A natural question at this point might be, 'Does accounting information (especially profit or cash flow) help to predict security prices and, therefore, risks and returns?' Market prices are pretty hard to predict, full stop. Therefore, accounting information isn't much help, but neither is anything else. However, accounting information can be helpful indirectly. When important events that do affect security prices are also represented in the accounting information (perhaps later on, since accounting reports come out only quarterly or annually), the accounting information will indirectly be predictive too. It depends on how well accounting does represent the original event: it seems that if phenomena reported in the accounting information have a clear economic meaning (such as when they represent an impact on cash or risk), they do have some incremental predictive value.

After the fact, however, it is clear that accounting information (especially profit) does correlate highly with market prices. The longer the accounting–price relationship is measured, ordinarily the better it is: accounting profit, for example, usually correlate better with share prices over several years than over a few months. Accounting does relate to whatever affects markets, though calling the shots in advance is hard!

## Aggregates

Security markets involve aggregate behaviour. Capital market theory proposes that a sensible investor will invest in a group of securities termed a *portfolio*. By choosing a group with various individual betas (risk measured by variation in returns), the investor can assemble a portfolio with whatever overall risk the investor wishes. Generally, a portfolio is less risky than any individual security because, by adding together a group of securities with different unsystematic risks, the unique variations in each partially cancel each other out. When the price of one goes up, another price may go down. Thus, a portfolio is a way of diversifying away the unsystematic risk.

Portfolio thinking has become pervasive in the investment community. Most research on the impact of accounting information presumes that investors have portfolios of securities, and companies accounting for their own investments (marketable securities and superannuation funds, for example) increasingly make the same presumption.

## Market informational efficiency

Efficiency of information use means that markets respond so quickly and smoothly to information that, once the information becomes public, its effects are immediately reflected in prices through the trading of securities. People who think the information implies that they should buy do so, from people who think they should sell. This fast response means that if the market is efficient, you can't use publicly available information (such as public financial statements everyone can read) to 'beat' the market; by the time you have the information and can act, the market will already have reacted to the information and produced a new trading price that reflects that information. You, as an individual trader, don't have the power to do much about the price that the overall sum of buys and sells has produced, so, unless you can trade on your information before anyone else knows it, you will find that the price already reflects the value of the information. If everyone gets an accounting report at the same time, probably only those traders nimble enough to act immediately will be able to take advantage of any news in the report. (More comments on whether accounting reports are likely to be news are below.)

Capital markets operate on information, but they do so in light of expectations already formed, in accordance with what was already known. Therefore, the markets tend to respond to new information only if it is unexpected. The argument can be made that for an efficient capital market, only the *unexpected* portion of earnings (or of any other such item or announcement) is information to the market. The market will not respond much to financial results that are exactly as everyone expected. There always is some response, though, because various market traders have different expectations and beliefs – these differences make the markets work!

Research indicates that some markets (such as the New York Stock Exchange) are quite efficient with respect to publicly available information, but many people don't believe these findings. The research is by no means conclusive, and the behaviour of many markets is not well understood (the Australian Stock Exchange, for example, has been studied much less than the New York Stock Exchange). Because informational efficiency is a difficult phenomenon to demonstrate conclusively, it is often called a hypothesis about how markets work: the efficient market hypothesis.

Securities commissions, such as the US Securities and Exchange Commission and Australian Securities and Investments Commission, are responsible for ensuring that securities trading is as fair as possible. One problem securities commissions worry about is so-called 'asymmetric information': some market traders know more than others do about a security and, therefore, potentially take advantage of the more ignorant traders. If you know that bad things are ahead, you sell to people who don't know that the price will fall when everyone learns about the bad things, or if you know that good things are ahead, you buy from people who don't know their shares are worth more than they think. A major role of financial accounting is to reduce information asymmetries by producing information that informs everyone.

An example of the effects of asymmetric information is that people on the 'inside' of the company might use their private knowledge to take advantage of other investors. Such insiders can buy or sell before other investors learn about something and, therefore, before the market can reach a new price based on the information. If you were a senior executive of a company, and you knew that tomorrow the company will release an unexpectedly good earnings report that will cause the share price to rise, you could buy today from share sellers who are ignorant of what you know. Securities commissions require that any significant information be released quickly and to everyone at once, and they keep an eye on insider trading, which is illegal.

## 13.4 Corporate disclosure

Financial statements are one of the ways in which companies disclose information about themselves to outsiders. Securities markets certainly pay attention to financial accounting information, but in a world in which many people buy and sell bonds, shares and options several times a day, half-yearly or annual financial statements only provide part of the picture. Much of the information in the financial statements leaks out over the year, in press releases, announcements and official information filings with securities commissions or stock exchanges. For example, the audit of a company's 30 June financial statements may be completed in August and the financial statements printed and issued in November, but throughout the prior year there will have been announcements about important events. Not surprisingly, accounting research shows that share price changes generally happen before the official earnings reports are released, and this is more likely to happen for larger firms, about which there tends to be more information available between accounting reports.

There is, therefore, a continual flow of financial statement-related and other significant information from public companies to securities markets. The general idea is that information should be released as soon as it is known, so that general market traders are not disadvantaged compared to insiders. This helps to keep the system fair for all, but also it should assist the market's pricing system to reflect informed evaluations of companies' prospects, so that the market prices are consistent with society's overall interest in appropriate allocation of economic resources.

A cornerstone policy for stock exchanges is that all persons investing in securities listed on the exchange have equal access to information that may affect investment decisions. Confidence of investors in the integrity of an exchange requires timely disclosure of material information concerning the company listed on the exchange, with the result that all participants in the market have equal opportunities.

Trading on an exchange can be affected by both material information and the existence of rumours and speculation. In this case, an exchange may require an announcement from a company as to whether such rumours and speculation are factual or not.

Insider trading laws prohibit insider trading, which can result in very large fines as well as jail sentences.

## How's your understanding?

Here are two questions you should be able to answer, based on what you have just read:

1 If a particular capital market is described as being 'efficient', what does that imply about the role and usefulness of financial accounting information in that market?

2 Why is timely disclosure of financial accounting and other information important to capital markets?

# 13.5 Contracts and financial accounting information

The previous sections may have left you with the impression that reporting to capital markets is about all that financial accounting is good for, or that managers worry about. It is not. There are many other roles financial accounting plays that are important to managers and other parties. Financial accounting information is used by banks and suppliers in making lending and credit decisions, in resource-allocation decisions made by governments, in assessing income taxes, in negotiations with and by labour unions, and perhaps also in enhancing or attacking the political power of certain groups (such as the corporate sector) in society.

To illustrate the different perspective on accounting you can get from examining another role, this section sets out some of the ideas behind agency (contract) theory, an important area of economic and accounting thought that focuses on contractual relationships among people. The area goes by several other names, with differences that aren't important to this discussion, including 'principal–agent theory' and 'positive accounting theory'. Some of the work is quite theoretical and mathematical, and some uses data to predict how people, such as managers or investors, behave in an economic environment that includes accounting information. The research is based in economics, so focuses on economic forces rather than social or psychological ones.

Agency theory is concerned with contractual relationships among people in which one or more people (the *agents*, who might be managers, auditors, lawyers or physicians) are entrusted with acting on behalf of one or more other people (the *principals*, who might be owners, creditors, defendants or patients). Contracts may be formally written ones (such as legally binding debenture trust deeds providing protection to debenture holders), less formal employment contracts or supplier agreements, or informal arrangements such as a handshake between partners.

Agency theory examines a fundamental characteristic of contracts among self-interested participants: they are unlikely to have the same interests. Conflicts of interest are not viewed as being bad, but rather as being the natural state of affairs. For example, if the agent is to provide effort on behalf of the principal, it would be natural for the agent to want to work less hard than the principal wishes. For the agent, effort is costly and, therefore, is to be minimised, whereas for the principal, the agent's effort should improve results and is, therefore, to be maximised. The theory develops ideas about how the agents can be induced to act 'properly' on behalf of the principals – for example, to do things that are in the principals' best interests and not shirk their responsibilities or lie about what they've done when the principals cannot observe their actions.

Agency theory tends to focus on the stewardship role of accounting information (in monitoring the stewardship of the agent on behalf of the principal) rather than on the future-oriented, decision-making role of such information that capital market theory emphasises. It doesn't deny that both roles exist – it just emphasises the former. The theory views information that is produced by financial accounting, management accounting or auditing as resulting from the wish by the various parties to provide incentives and controls over each other's behaviour. This wish exists because agents are assumed to want to act in their own interests and, in the absence of appropriate incentives and controls, their interests are assumed not necessarily to coincide with those of their principals.

The theory has very practical implications, proposing that if conditions change between various parties, accounting and auditing will change to meet the new conditions. Accounting information is viewed as an economic good that changes to meet changes in demand, not as something that is in any sense 'right' or 'wrong'. Principals and agents will demand whatever information they require to manage the contractual relationship between them, and information, therefore, can be judged only in terms of that specific relationship. Is it what they need, or isn't it?

Information is 'good' to the extent that it helps the contracting parties agree on what each party should do and on how to allocate the positive or negative results that occur. In a typical example, suppose the shareholders of Lakewood Ltd wanted management to work hard to maximise the price of Lakewood's shares, which are traded on a stock exchange. The higher the price, the better the return to the owners from owning the shares and the higher their wealth. The owners might, through their representatives on Lakewood's board of directors, propose a management contract that specifies that the top managers get no salary, but instead get 20 per cent of the change in the company's share price over each year. The top managers might well reply that this is too risky for them, because all sorts of things might affect share price, including things they have no control over, such as wars, recessions or other unexpected problems. The share price could go up, but it might as likely go down. The managers may then propose that they should be paid a flat salary of $200 000 each, regardless of changes in share price, believing that the owners should take the risks. This isn't what the owners want, because they are concerned that the managers will not be sufficiently conscientious if they are guaranteed a salary regardless of performance. Therefore, the two parties negotiate. Finally, a contract is agreed upon, according to which the managers will get $150 000 each plus performance bonuses of 5 per cent of the annual net profit and 3 per cent of the increase in share price, with no penalty for negative profit or negative change in share price, but with no bonuses then either. (The owners, interested in maximising the share price, and the managers, feeling that they have more control over net profit than share price, would in this case have agreed to include both factors in the bonus calculation. Management compensation contracts are often very complex, and a subcommittee of the board of directors may be created specifically to design and monitor such contracts. Regulatory agencies increasingly require public companies to disclose the nature of such contracts and the compensation that results from them, especially for the chief executive officer and other senior managers.)

The result is that the managers, as agents for the owners (the principals), have agreed to work for the owners, and the owners have agreed to employ the managers. Both parties entered into the contract for their own reasons, and both have agreed with it. Now the financial accounting information can be used by the owners to monitor the managers' performance and to calculate their bonuses based on net profit. Both parties, because of their contract, are interested in the accounting information; neither would be satisfied without accounting. They may specify in their contract that GAAP be used to calculate net profit, for the sake of convenience or because they prefer it that way. They also may specify other ways of calculating net profit that they think are to their mutual advantage.

You can see the role for auditors that we saw earlier: if the managers are responsible for the accounting information and are being paid on the basis of it, the owners (who are perhaps some distance from the company's offices and in any case would not want to have to show up to ask questions about accounting) may not be inclined to trust the managers' figures, and would prefer having an outside auditor evaluate them.

## How's your understanding?

Here are two questions you should be able to answer, based on what you have just read:

1 What is the 'agency' or 'contractual' view of the value of financial accounting information?

2 Green Ltd has a set of management bonus contracts for its senior executives, specifying that their pay will be based partly on how well the company performs. Brown Ltd, however, just pays its managers a flat salary. What differences would you expect in the attitudes of the two groups of managers to their company's financial statements?

## 13.6 'What if' (effects) analysis

Suppose you are a financial analyst trying to determine what a recently released set of financial statements tells you about the company's performance. You can do various standard analyses (as will be described in chapter 14), but before you do that you find that the company's accounting isn't quite comparable to that of another company you want to compare it to, or that the company has used an accounting method you don't agree with. You therefore want to alter the numbers to show 'what if' the company used the other company's accounting method, or a method you do agree with.

Or perhaps you are the managing director of a company, and are assessing some alternative accounting methods to determine which would be the most appropriate for the company. You know that there are restrictions on the company's debt/equity ratio imposed by a major lender, and that there are expectations of the year's net profit resulting from a forecast you made during a speech earlier in the year. You also know that various financial analysts examine your company's performance quite closely and that, if that performance declines, your bonus and even your job could be in jeopardy. You therefore want to know what the effects on the company's financial statements would be if the company adopted each alternative accounting method.

Such questions are very common in business. Answering them requires analysis of the accounting information: we'll call this 'what if' (effects) analysis. The ability to analyse accounting information to tell managers, bankers and others what difference various accounting choices, or business events in general, would make to the financial statements is very important to accountants. If you are going to be an accountant, you have to develop this skill. If you are not going to be an accountant, you should have some idea of what the accountants are doing in such analyses, so that you can evaluate the results they give you. You may even want to do some basic analysis yourself. Computer spreadsheets are particularly good for this sort of analysis, but you have to know what to tell the spreadsheet to do.

## Examples of 'what if' effects analysis

A good way to think about what would result if one method were used instead of another, or one event happened instead of another, is to figure out the accounting numbers both ways and compare them. There are shortcuts to this, and if you see one, go ahead and use it! But for now, let's take the longer, and hopefully clearer, way.

### Example a Cash versus accrual

Back in section 5.4, you saw an example comparing cash and accrual figures for Goblin Consulting Pty Ltd. Suppose Goblin's managing director said, 'I know we use accrual accounting, but what difference would it make to this year's profit if we used the cash basis instead?'

This year's accrual profit is $11 600 (profit and loss statement), and this year's cash from operations is $13 400. Therefore, the answer to the general manager's question is that profit would be $1800 higher this year on a cash basis.

### Example b Revenue recognition: during or after production

In section 11.2, you saw the example of Greenway Construction, which uses percentage of completion to recognise its construction revenues and expenses. Suppose the company's banker, more used to revenue recognition at completion of production (completion of the contract), wanted to know what difference there would be to profit if the completion of production method were used instead.

The percentage of completion project profit (totalling $600 000 over three years) was:

- $120 000 for Year 1
- $270 000 for Year 2
- $210 000 for Year 3.

If revenue and expenses were recognised only at completion of the project, the project profit would be:

- $0 in Year 1
- $0 in Year 2
- $600 000 in Year 3.

So the answer to the banker's question would be that profit would be:

- $120 000 *lower* in Year 1
- $270 000 *lower* in Year 2
- $390 000 *higher* in Year 3.

There has been no change in the three-year total, but the yearly figures are rearranged if the completion of production method is used.

### Example c Franchise revenue recognition

In section 11.4, the accrual and cash basis ways of recognising profit from WonderBurgers Ltd's franchising operations were compared. It should be easy for you to see now that, if you used the cash basis instead of the accrual basis, you would have the following effects on profit over the three years of the example:

- Year 1 profit would be $4200 *higher*.
- Year 2 profit would be $3100 *lower*.
- Year 3 profit would be $1100 *lower*.

## Examples of income tax effects in this analysis

### Example d Income tax effects on examples b and c

Suppose Greenway Construction pays income tax at a rate of 35 per cent and WonderBurgers pays at a rate of 30 per cent. What effect would that have on our figures above? The answer is that the income tax reduces all the effects by the tax rate, because that proportion goes to the government. As you'll see below, a useful rule is to just multiply the before-tax effect by (1 – tax rate), in this case (1 – .35) = .65 for Greenway and (1 – .30) = .70 for WonderBurgers.

Here is a table of the effects, before and after income tax (for presentation purposes, Greenway's figures are in thousands of dollars):

| | Greenway | | | WonderBurgers | | |
|---|---|---|---|---|---|---|
| Year | Gross effect 100% $ | Tax effect 35% $ | After-tax effect 65% $ | Gross effect 100% $ | Tax effect 35% $ | After-tax effect 65% $ |
| 1 | (120 000) | (42 000) | (78 000) | 4 200 | 1 260 | 2 940 |
| 2 | (270 000) | (94 500) | (175 500) | (3 100) | (930) | (2 170) |
| 3 | 390 000 | 136 500 | 253 500 | (1 100) | (330) | (770) |
| Total | 0 | 0 | 0 | 0 | 0 | 0 |

Income tax reduces both positive and negative differences. The assumption here is that an increased profit is taxed, and a decreased profit produces tax savings (by reducing tax payable on other profit or creating tax credits that can be used to get refunds on past years' taxes or reduce future taxes).

Without knowing the details of the income tax law (which are beyond the scope of this book), we cannot say for sure how much of the income tax effect is current and how much is deferred.

### Example e 'Net of tax' analysis

Revenues and expenses can be considered to increase or decrease income taxes on their own, and, therefore, the effects on net profit of changes in revenues and expenses can be estimated directly, net of tax, once the income tax rate is known (or approximated). Here's how it works. Suppose Alcatraz Fencing Ltd has one revenue, one expense and an income tax rate of 35 per cent. Its profit and loss statement might look like this:

| | $ |
|---|---|
| Revenue | 1 000 |
| Expense | 700 |
| Profit before income tax | 300 |
| Income tax expense (35%) | 105 |
| Net profit | 195 |

Note that the net profit is 65 per cent of the profit before tax. We can state this in a formula, as suggested in part d above:

**Net profit = (1 – tax rate) × Profit before income tax**

You can look at net profit as the residual after the income tax has been deducted. But this works just as well for the revenues and expenses. Suppose we recast the profit and loss statement as if the revenues and expenses were taxed directly, so that they are shown net of tax, and the income tax effect is, therefore, included in them rather than being a separate expense:

| | Original<br>$ | Net of tax<br>$ |
|---|---|---|
| Revenue (net = $1000 × (1 – .35)) | 1 000 | 650 |
| Expense (net = $700 × (1 – .35)) | 700 | 455 |
| Profit before income tax | 300 | |
| Income tax expense (35%) | 105 | |
| Net profit | 195 | 195 |

The net-of-tax way of looking at things can be very useful analytically. Suppose the general manager of Alcatraz has a plan to increase revenue by $200 without any increase in the $700 expense. What would that do to net profit? The new net profit would be higher by $200 × (1 – .35) = $130, and so would be $325 ($195 + $130). There is no need to recalculate the whole profit and loss component of the statement of financial performance.

If you are doubtful, you can always do the analysis the longer way, by recalculating the profit and loss statement:

| | $ |
|---|---|
| New revenue | 1 200 |
| Expense still | 700 |
| New profit before tax | 500 |
| New tax expense (35%) | 175 |
| New net profit | 325 |

Net-of-tax analysis got us to this answer more quickly by focusing just on what *changes*.

## How's your understanding?

Here are three questions you should be able to answer, based on what you have just read:

1 The general manager of a company is thinking about changing the company's method of accounting for insurance expense, and wants to know what the effect of the policy will be on net profit. Explain why all you need to know to estimate the effect is the amount of the expense under the present and proposed methods and the company's income tax rate.

2 A company had revenues of $10 499.7 million in a recent year. Its income tax rate was 30 per cent. If its revenues increased by 2 per cent, with no effect on expenses other than income tax, what would be the effect on net profit for that year?
(Revenue effect = 2% x $10 499.7 = $210.0 million more revenue. Net profit effect = $210 (1 – .30) = $147.0 million higher.)

3 Hinton Ltd has found an error in its revenue account: an invoice for $1400 was recorded as revenue in 2001 when it should have been recorded in 2002. The company's income tax rate is 35 per cent and there was no corresponding error in cost of goods sold. What is the effect of the error on: 2001 net profit; 2001 cash from operations; 2002 net profit; retained profits at the end of 2001; retained profits at the end of 2002?
($1400 [1 – .35] = $910 too high; no cash effect; $910 too low; $910 too high; no effect as the sum of 2001's and 2002's profits is unaffected)

## 13.7 Managers and performance information

One of the main reasons top managers of public companies pay close attention to their companies' financial statements, earnings announcements and other disclosures is that share markets and other securities markets respond quickly to information, and do so in accordance with the value of that information to the market traders. Markets impose a sort of 'discipline' on such corporations and their management. Whatever the managers may hope, the market evaluates the information and quickly applies rewards, by bidding companies' share prices up, or penalties, by bidding them down, regardless of whether management thinks the reward or penalty is justified.

The less a company is in the public eye and/or the less it is involved in various securities markets, the less it is disciplined by such markets. However, even private companies are not immune to such discipline, because they often compete or cooperate with, or are suppliers to or customers of, more directly affected companies, and also because even private owners often wish to sell their companies, borrow heavily, or take other action that brings their performance information under scrutiny. (For example, common ways of calculating the value of a private business make extensive use of financial statements and of the performance and trends they reveal.)

Managers also pay close attention to their companies' financial statement figures, because important contracts are based on those, explicitly or indirectly. Many top managers are compensated based on the profit shown in the financial statements, many own shares in their companies and, if the company is public, the top managers may lose their jobs if stock market prices decline or fail to rise as the board of directors wishes.

Managers' stewardship performance in running the company for the owners is scrutinised by the external auditors, so managers are also faced with justifying what the financial statements show. The statements are really the representations of senior management so, in the end, they should be what those managers think is an appropriate reflection of their performance, within the constraints of GAAP and the auditors' scrutiny.

## 13.8 Public sector issues

Obviously the social setting of financial accounting is quite different in the public sector compared with the private sector. However, much of the material discussed in this chapter does apply in the public sector. For example, while most government entities are not listed on the Australian Stock Exchange, some entities, such as Telstra, have partly privatised, with the result that they are listed on the stock exchange. Governments also borrow money by issuing bonds. Given that many public sector managers have moved toward performance-based contracts, our discussion of agency theory is relevant.

For both public sector managers and users of public sector reports, the application of 'what if' analysis can be useful. However, as most public sector entities (such as departments) do not pay tax, there is often no need to make the tax adjustment we discussed.

## 13.9 Homework and discussion to develop understanding

### Discussion questions

1 Describe the main parties who form the social setting of financial accounting.

2 What is the role of information in a capital market?

3 What is meant by the efficient market hypothesis?

4 What is the major purpose of a stock exchange?

5 Explain the terms 'agency theory' and 'stewardship'.

6 How does 'what if' analysis assist analysts?

7 Briefly describe two important implications capital market theory has for the use of accounting information.

8 Briefly describe two important implications agency (contract) theory has for the use of accounting information.

9 Many external parties rely on statements such as the statement of financial position and the statement of financial performance by a company. Identify two different types of major users of financial information and briefly explain how each of the preceding two financial statements will help them. (This is a similar question to some asked in earlier chapters, but now you should be able to give a more sophisticated answer.)

10 a It appears that some top managers attempt to manage their companies' financial disclosure, including their financial accounting, to alter the story each disclosure tells. Why might managers be motivated to do this?

b Do you think managers should be prohibited from practising such disclosure management?

11 How useful is financial statement information in a modern business setting? In your answer you may consider, among other things, the historical development of accounting practice and the implications of capital market theory and agency theory.

12 Why should the shareholders of a large, publicly traded company want to have the company's financial statements audited?

13 The auditors' report is normally written in a standard wording. The idea is that, if things are not all right, variations from the standard wording will alert users of the financial statements. Is that consistent, or inconsistent, with capital market theory?

14 Why do changes in accounting methods usually have no effect on cash or cash flow?

15 Can you suggest a situation in which an accounting method change would affect cash flow as reported on the statement of cash flows?

16 Why is it important to take income tax into account when doing 'what if' effects analysis?

## Problem 13.1* Basic multi-year effects analysis, with income tax

Mistaya Ltd has decided to change its revenue recognition policy to increase revenue $10 000 in the current year and by a total of $8000 in prior years (accounts receivable are increased correspondingly). Matched expenses increase $4000 in the current year and $3000 in prior years (so accounts payable go up as well). The company's income tax rate is 35 per cent.

Determine all effects of the change on the company's profit for the current year and statement of financial position as at the end of the current year. Show your calculations and demonstrate that all the effects balance.

## Problem 13.2* Settle an argument about financial accounting's purpose

Two students are arguing. One says that financial accounting exists in order to provide information to outsiders (for example, capital markets) for assessing company performance. The other says that it exists in order to provide a monitoring and control system over managers who are running the company as the agents of the owners. Settle the argument.

## Problem 13.3* Accounting concepts and economic agents

1 Explain why each of the following concepts is important in financial reporting to markets and other economic agents who rely on such reporting:
   - a economic entity assumption
   - b historical cost basis of accounting
   - c reliability
   - d generally accepted accounting principles
   - e professional ethics of the accountants and/or auditors involved in producing financial statements.

2 How have each of these concepts been incorporated into the financial statements of a large public company you know about? Give specific examples.

3 Now apply these ideas to a small private company, such as your local Thai takeaway, newsagent or pharmacy. Are these concepts still relevant? Why or why not?

## Problem 13.4 Disclosure regulation and management strategy

1 The general manager of a smallish company, Brandex Pty Ltd, is thinking about listing the company's shares on the Australian Stock Exchange, because doing so might facilitate issuing a large block of new shares, bringing the company needed capital. Describe for the general manager a few ways in which life might be more difficult if Brandex becomes a publicly listed company.

2 The general manager feels that if the company becomes listed, a strategy for handling financial disclosure will have to be adopted so that disclosure is managed as other company activities are. What would be some likely components of a managed financial disclosure strategy?

## Problem 13.5 Authoritative standards, capital markets and contracts

Many of the accounting methods you are studying in this book are based on authoritative standards (AASB and AAS Statements, and so on) that attempt to specify how companies' financial accounting should be done. Such standards don't cover everything: companies must still make many choices when they are preparing their financial statements.

Why are there authoritative standards for companies to follow? Why don't they cover everything? Should we have more or less of them? Put your answer in the context of this chapter's theories about information use.

## Problem 13.6 Capital markets and contracts for a corporation

Choose any large, well-known corporation you are interested in and answer the following, based on your choice.

1 What kinds of capital markets are likely to be important to the company?

2 Suppose those capital markets are 'efficient' and an unexpected and important piece of information about the company is released. What is likely to happen? Would it make a difference if the markets expected the information?

3 List some of the explicit, implicit or even casual contractual relationships between the company and other internal or external parties that are likely to be important to the company's success.

## Problem 13.7 Multi-year effects analysis with income tax

Amalgamated Ltd has a large amount of excess cash invested temporarily because it is winding down and selling off several of its divisions. Data with respect to its cash and temporary investments are:

| | 31 December 2002 | 31 December 2001 |
|---|---|---|
| Cash on hand | $2 134 600 | $1 814 910 |
| Temporary investments (cost) | $16 493 220 | $8 649 270 |
| Temporary investments (market) | $15 829 300 | $10 100 500 |
| Investment revenue for the year | $1 492 814 | $948 653 |
| Income tax rate for the year | 37% | 36% |

The company has been valuing its temporary investments at cost, but this year the company's auditor resigned, and the new auditor insists the company value the investments at the lower of cost or market.

*Required:*

1 What effect will the new accounting policy have on net profit for 2002?

## Problem 13.8 Effects of changing the provision for doubtful debts, with tax

Karl and Tanya are having the following conversation:

> 'Karl, we have a problem in our accounts receivable. We've made a provision for doubtful debts of 2 per cent of the gross receivables, but during this recession more customers are running into trouble. The provision should be raised to 5 per cent.'
>
> 'Tanya, we can't do that. It would wipe out our profitability and ruin our cash flow.'

Given the data on the next page, prepare an analysis for Karl and Tanya.

| | |
|---|---|
| Gross accounts receivable at year-end | $8 649 000 |
| Net profit for the year at present | $223 650 |
| Income tax rate | 30% |

## Problem 13.9 Effects of recognising supplies inventory, with tax

Magnic Manufacturing Pty Ltd has large amounts of manufacturing supplies that have been recorded as an expense when purchased. Now the company is considering recognising the supplies on hand as an asset. If this were done, a new supplies inventory account would appear in the current assets. Its balance would be $148 650 at the end of last year and $123 860 at the end of this year. The company's income tax rate is 30 per cent.

Calculate the effect on each of the following that would result if the company changed its accounting to recognise the supplies inventory:

1 retained profits at the end of last year
2 income tax liability at the end of last year
3 supplies expense for this year
4 net profit for this year
5 current assets at the end of this year
6 income tax liability at the end of this year
7 retained profits at the end of this year
8 cash flow for this year
9 cash flow for next year.

## Problem 13.10 (Challenging) Auditors and forecast information

Recently, there has been pressure to expand the role of auditors because investors and other groups are demanding more forward-looking information. If these demands are met, auditors may be expected to review the plans and forecasts of a company that will be reporting to the public, and to determine the fairness of such forward-looking financial statements.

Discuss the implications of this expanded role for auditors, using such concepts as independence, information value, comparability, agency theory, capital market theory, relevance, reliability, objectivity and any other concepts that you feel are important.

## Problem 13.11 (Challenging) Capital markets, auditors and contracts

1 On 31 October 2001, analysts predicted that the earnings per share of Oakes Ltd would equal $4.80 for the year ended 31 December 2001. Actual results were announced on 27 February 2002. Earnings per share for 2001 came to $3.95. Consider the three dates noted above (31 October 2001, 31 December 2001 and 27 February 2002). At which of these dates would you expect to see share prices react to earnings information? Why? Can you predict the direction in which share prices would react on any of these dates? Explain why or why not.

2 Explain the importance of the audit function in the context of a large company where the ownership (composed of a large number of private investors) and the management are separated. To whom are the auditors primarily responsible? By whom are they hired? What would the investors expect of the auditors? Do your answers indicate anything inconsistent in the auditor's role as an independent party?

3 Agency theory describes the problems inherent in a situation in which one party (the principal) hires a second party (the agent) to do work on the former's behalf. Choose one contractual relationship existing between parties connected with a corporation, and describe this relationship in an agency theory context.

## Problem 13.12 (Challenging) Can financial statements meet various needs?

The chairperson of the board of directors of a large public company said in frustration, 'The company's written and unwritten contracts with its shareholders are so different from those with its managers that it's impossible to design financial statements that will meet the needs of both shareholders and managers.' What do you think?

## Problem 13.13 (Challenging) Multiple-issue effects analysis, with tax

Cranberry Costumes Pty Ltd has been operating for several years now. So far the profit for the current year is $75 000, before income tax at 30 per cent. (The preceding year's profit before tax was $62 000 and the tax rate then was also 30 per cent.) Owner Jan Berry is considering a few changes and has asked your advice. The possible changes are:

- Change the revenue recognition policy to recognise revenue earlier in the process. This would increase accounts receivable by $26 000 immediately and $28 000 at the end of the previous year.
- Make a monthly accrual of the bonuses paid to employees at the end of each fiscal year. This would increase accounts payable by $11 000 immediately and $7000 at the end of the preceding year.
- Postpone for five years repayment of a $19 000 loan (by Jan to the company), which has until now been classified as a current liability.
- Capitalise as a trademark asset $14 000 of advertising, supplies and wages expense recorded in the preceding year.

***Required:***

1 Calculate the net profit after income tax for the current year that will result if all the changes are adopted, and discuss the economic reasons for considering each change.

2 Calculate the effect on the amount of cash in the bank account of Cranberry Costumes Pty Ltd that these changes will have.

3 Explain any difference between results calculated for questions **1** and **2**.

## CASE 13A Woolworths Limited case

Refer to the extracts of the annual report of Woolworths Limited in appendix 2.

1 List some of the parties who will be directly concerned with what financial accounting says about the company.

2 What stock exchange is Woolworths Limited listed on? How many shares are issued? Look up a newspaper to discover its share price.

3 List three accounting-related events that are likely to increase the company's share price.

4 Are there any form of incentive contracts for executives in place (see Web page)?

5 What does the company say about its regulatory environment for financial reporting?

## CASE 13B Executive compensation plans

Shown below are two articles about executive compensation. With capital market and agency (contract) theory as a background, discuss the compensation used by each company.

1 What features of each plan relate to the performance of the company's shares on the stock market?

2 What features of each plan relate to management's stewardship of the company on behalf of the shareholders?

3 What role does accounting information play in compensation for each company?

## Rethink on directors taking stock

*by Emily Carr*

Australian companies are coming under increased pressure to pay their non executive directors with shares, and follow a trend in the US, where almost 80 per cent of American directors are now paid in some form of company stock.

The practice has long been anathema to Australian boards and proponents of corporate governance, but the present round of annual general meetings will see at least three Australian corporates seek approval partly to pay outside directors with shares and options.

Goodman Fielder is seeking approval to pay 25 per cent of annual fees for non-executive directors in ordinary shares, a move aimed at aligning director fees with company performance and shareholder interests.

Perpetual Trustees is also seeking to introduce a plan under which non-executive directors can choose to take up to half their normal fees as fully paid shares.

Cinema Plus Ltd, operator of the giant-screen Imax theatres, will ask shareholders to approve the issue of 150 000 remuneration options to each of its three non-executive directors.

Korn/Ferry International's 25th Annual Board of Directors' Study of more than 1000 directors of major US corporations revealed that 78 per cent of all outside directors received some part of their directors' fees in the form of company stock or a combination of stock options and grants in 1998, up from 62 per cent in 1995.

A whopping 98 per cent of directors in the biggest US companies ($20 billion-plus) said directors should be paid with some stock.

A recent comparable study of Australian directors, also by Korn/Ferry, showed that only one-third of Australian directors believed the practice was worthwhile, though only a handful of listed Australian companies actually pay their outside directors in scrip.

Rural merchandising company IAMA received approval for a plan to pay its directors with options in February this year, but not before pressure from at least one institutional shareholder forced the board to raise the hurdles for the exercise of the options.

Cinema Plus Ltd was forced to withdraw a resolution to issue its three outside directors with options, but will resubmit the proposal at its AGM on November 25.

The Korn/Perry report said the practice of rewarding outside directors with shares would continue to grow in the US, with more directors to be paid all or partly in stock.

'Directors and CEOs will, over the next five years, be required to own a specific number of shares,' the report says.

A senior associate with Korn/Ferry's Sydney office, Ms Jan Buck, says the US study should be cause for renewed debate on the issue in Australia.

'Why do we reject it out of hand?' she said. 'We have always followed the UK thinking along the lines of directors losing independence, but they don't seem to be experiencing that problem in the US. Shouldn't we at least be playing around with the idea?'

(Source: Emily Carr, *Australian Financial Review*, 19 October 1998.)

## New deal for senior execs

*by Brett Clegg*

The Telstra board has attempted to modernise its executive remuneration policies in line with the wider market, unveiling a new compensation plan for senior managers that intends to better align their interests with that of shareholders.

Telstra senior managers are now expected to have 'significant shareholdings' in the company. Over a five-year period, CEO Mr Ziggy Switkowski and senior executives are required to build a stake at least equivalent to their annual salary or, in the case of the CEO, one and a half times annual salary.

The new Senior Manager Equity Participation Plan (SMEPP), which is revealed in the T2 offer document, replaces the existing plan in which executives were paid cash incentives based on internally agreed return-on-investment targets.

Under the SMEPP, they will be allocated shares and options that vest over five years. Because the company is not able to issue new shares under the Telstra Act, shares will be bought on-market and this cost will be expenses in the Telstra accounts.

Before executives receive their allocation, they must clear a performance hurdle. the Telstra Accumulation Index must exceed the average of the All Industrials Accumulation Index for 30 consecutive days in the final two years of the vesting period.

However, as the SMEPP requires no new shares to be issued, under stock exchange listing rules the Telstra Board did not need to submit the plan for shareholder approval. The allocation itself is determined by 'individual performance and other criteria judged relevant by the Board'.

Mr Switkowski was paid $1.17 million in the year to June. Thus, he must build up at least $1.755 million in Telstra shares, though the most recent notification to the ASX disclosed his current interest as 57 120 shares, or $460 000.

The CEO has been allocated 50 000 shares ($402 500) and 300 000 options under the new plan. Less than 50 of his senior managers will participate in 1999, with a total of less than 50 000 shares ($4.025 million) and 3 500 000 options to be allocated.

(Source: Brett Clegg, *Australian Financial Review*, 7 September 1999.)

## CASE 13C Corporate governance

This case incorporates some earlier discussion in the book on disclosure. It specifically addresses a corporate governance issue related to audit committees, and allows you to consider it in the light of the material in this chapter.

Shown below is an article discussing the collapse of Harris Scarfe Holdings Limited and corporate governance issues.

### The unravelling of the house of Scarfe

*by Jim Pasaros and Michael Seamer*

In a press release dated 16 March 2001, the executive chairman of Harris Scarfe, Adam Trescowthick, attempted to explain a 45 per cent reduction in net profit for the six-month period ended 31 January 2001. He indicated that trading conditions were 'some of the toughest . . . for a very long time'. He further rationalised that Australian consumer patterns had been hit by the introduction of the GST, the Sydney 2000 Olympics, petrol prices, a falling Australian dollar, a slowing economy and interest rate rises.

All of these factors may have played some role in the poor performance of Harris Scarfe, but it wasn't because of these factors that Harris Scarfe appointed voluntary administrators on 3 April 2001. Rather, the company announced the appointment of voluntary administrators because, according to Reuters' news agency, 'the directors were shocked to discover critical financial management accounting irregularities, which had given the board a deliberately false and misleading view of the company's true financial position over a period of up to six years'.

Adam Trescowthick said the board had acted in good faith on financial information provided by senior management, and that the accounts had been cleared by the auditors at least three times in the last 15 months. Trescowthick went on to explain that 'in light of the serious nature of the irregularities, the company has notified all relevant authorities with a request to examine the actions of senior management and the role of the auditors'.

In due course, there is no doubt that the role of the auditors will be scrutinised. This article makes no comment about their performance. Instead, its purpose is to examine the corporate governance practices of Harris Scarfe.

#### *Corporate governance*

The Australian Stock Exchange defines corporate governance as involving 'those monitoring and control mechanisms that are put in place by companies with the objective of enhancing shareholder value'. Within the context of this definition, corporate governance takes on a very wide meaning.

However, two important mechanisms inherent in having effective corporate governance are an independent and well-performing board of directors, and similarly an independent and well-performing audit committee.

#### *The board of directors*

The board of directors is the ultimate decision-making body of an organisation and thus plays a crucial role in many areas, including corporate governance. An effective board will contain ethical, skilled and critically thinking individuals who contribute special expertise to the company. The highly authoritative US *Blue Ribbon Report* states explicitly, 'Most importantly, the board overall should consist of a majority of independent directors' (p. 21).

*The Blue Ribbon Report* also states that 'the rationale supporting the call for a majority of independent directors on a board of directors... [is] that independence is crucial to ensuring that the board fulfils its objective oversight role and holds management accountable to shareholders.'

The Australian Investment and Financial Services Association is also of the view that the majority of the board should consist of independent directors. It explains that the composition of the board is one of the most crucial issues of corporate governance. 'International best practice requires that the majority of the individuals on the board should be genuinely independent . . . the independent board majority is a key mechanism to assure shareholders that their company will run competently in its own interests and consequently in the best interests of all shareholders.'

The Association defines an independent director as a director who:

- is not a substantial shareholder of the company
- has not within the last three years been employed in an executive capacity by the company
- is not a principal or professional adviser to the company
- is not a significant supplier or customer of the company
- has no significant contractual relationship with the company
- is free from any interest or relationship which could interfere with the director's ability to act in the best interests of the company.

In view of the above comments, let's look at the composition of Harris Scarfe's board of directors as at 31 July 2000:

**Table 1 Composition of Harris Scarfe Board of Directors, 31 July 2000**

| Director | Association with company | Independence status |
|---|---|---|
| A. J. Trescowthick | Executive Chairman | Non-independent |
| J. M. Patten | | Independent |
| R. A. Curtis | Company solicitor | Non-independent |
| R. D. Mattingly | | Independent |
| R. G. Oakley | | Independent |
| A. J. Trescowthick | Supplier to company | Non-independent |

As is apparent from table 1, Harris Scarfe's board of directors contained three independent and three non-independent directors. This falls short of the best practice guidline of the AIFSA, which recommends a *majority* of independent directors. It is also important to note that the board for the 2000 year was no more independent than at any time during the four previous years. In fact, 2000 appears to be the relative high point for independence.

Consider the composition of the board for the five years from 1996 to 2000.

**Table 2 Composition of the Harris Scarfe Board of Directors, 1996–2000**

| Independence status | 2000 | 1999 | 1998 | 1997 | 1996 |
|---|---|---|---|---|---|
| Number of independent directors | 3 | 3 | 3 | 3 | 2 |
| Number of non-independent directors | 3 | 3 | 4 | 5 | 5 |
| Total | 6 | 6 | 7 | 8 | 7 |

Table 2 indicates that, for the years 1996 to 1998, the board of Harris Scarfe consisted of a majority of non-independent directors. The board may have contained many (possibly all) of the skills necessary to succeed. However, it did not pass the test of independence.

But what are the implications of having a board that is not truly independent? Stated simply, if the board does not contain a majority of independent directors, then the board will not have the power to implement policy that may be contrary to the wishes of management or a major shareholder. Conversely, where there is a majority independent board, there is a greater expectation on independent directors to act with due diligence, plus a greater perception of independence, thus creating a better board culture.

## *The audit committee*

An audit committee is also a crucial component of effective corporate governance. It can perform a range of functions, but, in summary, it serves to strengthen the auditor's independence by providing an independent forum to which issues relating to the audit can be referred on a timely basis.

In Australia, audit committees are not required by law. However, all companies listed on the Australian Stock Exchange are required to disclose in their annual reports whether they have an audit committee and its composition. Recent studies suggest that more than 90 per cent of Australian listed companies now have an audit committee.

### *Audit committee composition best practice*

In terms of the composition of the audit committee, most authoritative reports recommend that either the audit committee be comprised solely of independent directors (e.g. Treadway (1987), MacDonald Commission (1988), Cadbury (1992), Toronto Stock Exchange, New York Stock Exchange), or be comprised of a majority of independent directors (e.g.

Bosch (1990, 1993, 1995), Ernst & Young (1992), KPMG (1995), AARF (1997), Investment and Financial Services Association (1999), National Association of Security Dealers and the Blue Ribbon Committee (2000)).

Harris Scarfe had an audit committee for the three years ended 31 July 1998, 1999 and 2000 comprised as follows:

**Table 3 Composition of the Harris Scarfe Audit Committee, 1998–2000**

| Position in organisation | Independence status |
|---|---|
| Independent director | Independent |
| Executive Chairman | Non-independent |
| Chief Financial Officer | Non-independent |

As noted in table 3, Harris Scarfe's audit committee was comprised of a majority of non-independent directors.

Clearly, on the basis of non-independence, the Harris Scarfe audit committee did not meet best practice guidelines. This raises the important question of why independence, both in fact and appearance, is crucial to the effective operation of an audit committee.

The fundamental issue is that an audit committee should be in a position to discuss matters with the external and internal auditor *in the absence of management and non-independent directors*. This is essential so that the external and internal auditors are not constrained or intimated by the presence of senior management or non-independent directors on the audit committee.

Accordingly, as the majority of the Harris Scarfe audit committee comprised senior management, it was arguably not possible for it to operate to its full potential.

### Audit committee: regularity of meetings

With respect to best practice on the regularity with which audit committees should meet, there is less guidance. However, the authoritative *Blue Ribbon Report* (1999) states that 'The [audit] Committee shall meet at least four times annually, or more frequently as circumstances dictate' (p. 68).

In contrast, for not one of the previous five financial years had the audit committee of Harris Scarfe met on four occasions. Specifically, in 1998 it met three times, in 1997, 1998 and 2000 it met twice, and in 1996 it had met only once. While it is difficult to speculate about how effective these meetings were, their infrequency is not a good sign.

### Concluding comments

The Corporate Governance Statement contained in Harris Scarfe's 2000 financial accounts proudly proclaims that the 'Directors are committed to the principles underpinning best practice in corporate governance'.

However, the evidence suggests that the corporate governance practices of Harris Scarfe were less than ideal. Neither the board of directors nor the audit committee possessed the recommended degree of independence to enable them to act at an optimal level.

Whether improved levels of independence could have prevented, or detected more quickly, the alleged accounting irregularities is a moot point. However, there is no doubt that accounting irregularities are less likely to occur in an organisation with effective corporate governance practices.

In the context of the current problems encountered by Harris Scarfe, *The Blue Ribbon Report* makes a particularly pertinent comment. 'Several recent studies have produced a correlation between audit committee *independence* and two desirable outcomes: a higher degree of active oversight and a lower incidence of financial statement fraud [emphasis added]' (p. 22).

While many more facts are still likely to emerge from the Harris Scarfe case, there are some important lessons that should be apparent for the respective legislators.

First, it seems impossible to justify the Australian regulatory situation where listed public companies are not compelled to have an audit committee. Clearly, all Australian publicly listed companies should be compelled to have an audit committee – and that committee should contain a majority (ideally 100 per cent) of independent members. Second, legislation should also be enacted to ensure that the composition of the board of directors comprises a majority of independent directors.

(Source: Jim Psaros and Michael Seamer, *Charter*, June 2001, pp. 44–7.)

***Required:***

1 What is meant by corporate governance, and how is it related to audit committees?

2 What criticisms do the authors make of the corporate governance of Harris Scarfe?

3 What lessons about corporate governance should legislators draw from the Harris Scarfe case?

4 Describe the relationship between this article and description of agency theory provided in this chapter.

# Appendix to chapter 13
# Future cash flows: present value analysis

## A13.1 Future cash flows

Earlier in this book, you saw that cash flow is important to a company. In chapter 14 you will see that assessing cash flow is a significant part of the analysis of a company's financial performance and position. You will also see that sorting out the impact of interest rates on the company's returns is important to understanding how it has performed. This chapter has reviewed ideas about capital markets, which are concerned with the company's expected ability to generate returns in the future, especially cash returns that can be used to pay dividends or reinvest in the company. Many financial contracts, such as for management compensation and supply or service arrangements, focus on future financial performance. Generally, management should be looking to the future and trying to combine its asset acquisition, borrowing and profit-generation strategies to produce a good future return for the owners.

An important way of thinking about future performance, especially future cash flows, is present value (PV) or discounted cash flow (DCF) analysis. Future cash flows are not the same as present ones, because you have to wait for them. Because you have to wait, you lose interest or other returns you could have earned if you had had the cash sooner.

Detailed PV or DCF techniques are examined in management accounting and finance courses, and you may well have seen them already in economics or business statistics courses. In this section, basic ideas will be outlined to prepare you for the financial analysis to follow in chapter 14 and to help you think about how traders in capital markets may use expectations of future cash flows and future interest rates when deciding on prices of securities. (Note that such traders don't necessarily do explicit PV or DCF calculations, but research shows that capital market prices behave as if they are doing something like that.)

### Interest and the time value of money

In Western society, it is permissible — even expected — that the owner of capital should charge a person who wants to use that capital a fee for that use. That fee is called interest, and is computed by applying a specified percentage rate to the amount lent, which can be referred to as either the investment or the principal. For example, an 8 per cent interest rate on a \$200 loan would produce annual interest of \$16 (\$200 × .08). The existence of interest, which builds up as time passes, gives money a **time value**.

Some simple formulas you probably already know ($P$ = principal or investment, $i$ = interest rate):

Annual interest = $P \times i$
Amount due at the end of one year = $P(1 + i)$
Amount due after $n$ years, with annual compounding, if no payments at all are made = $P(1 + i)^n$

Suppose a loan provides for repayment of the principal plus interest after several years, with no payments in the meantime. If the interest is compounded, which is normally the case, that means interest builds up on the unpaid interest as well as on the unpaid principal. In order to know how this works, you need to know how frequently interest compounds. Do you get interest on the interest:

- as soon as any interest arises ('continuous compounding')?
- after a day's interest has been added ('daily compounding')?
- after a month's interest has been added ('monthly compounding')?
- only after a year's interest has been added ('annual compounding')?

Here's an example of annual compounding. We have the same \$200, 8 per cent loan as above, which is to be repaid in five years with annual compounding. We can then calculate the amount that the loan has built up to at the end of each year (its 'future value', FV below) as follows:

| Year | FV at beginning of year | Annual interest at 8% | FV at end of year |
|---|---|---|---|
| | \$ | \$ | \$ |
| 1 | 200.00 | 16.00 | 216.00 |
| 2 | 216.00 | 17.28 | 233.28 |
| 3 | 233.28 | 18.66 | 251.94 |
| 4 | 251.94 | 20.16 | 272.10 |
| 5 | 272.10 | 21.77 | 293.87 |

You can see that the FV increases every year. Using the third formula above, we can calculate the FV at the end of any year:

- End of year 3: FV = $P(1 + i)^n$
  = \$200 $(1 + .08)^3$
  = \$251.94
- End of year 5: FV = \$200 $(1 + .08)^5$
  = \$293.87

## A13.2 Interest and present value

The concept of interest can be 'turned on its head' by considering what you lose by waiting some period of time for your money, or, putting it another way, what a future payment is worth in present terms if you assume your money should earn interest between now and when you get it back.

Suppose someone promises to give you \$100 a year from now. If you were given the money now instead, you'd be earning 9 per cent interest on it. Therefore, if you'd had some amount of $P$ now and earned 9 per cent on it, you'd be in the same position as you will be after waiting the year. Using the second formula above, $\$100 = P(1 + .09)$, where $P$ is the amount you could have earned interest on.

Solving for $P$ we get $P = \$100/(1.09) = \$91.74$. If you had \$91.74, you could have invested it at 9 per cent and ended up with \$100 (\$91.74 + [.09 × \$91.74] = \$100) at the end of the year.

We say that \$91.74 is the present value of \$100 received after waiting one year, 'discounted at 9 per cent'. This present value concept is another way of thinking of the time value of money: it reminds us that as long as we wait for cash that could have earned interest, we lose that interest we could have earned. This idea is referred to as an 'opportunity cost', which you may recall from introductory economics. As long as the interest rate is greater than zero, present value is less than the actual future amount of cash that will be received.

Analogous to the above interest formulas are the following present value formulas (where $C$ = future cash flow, and $i$ = interest rate):

Present value waiting one year $= \dfrac{C}{1 + i}$

Present value waiting $n$ years with no payments in the meantime, interest compounded annually $= \dfrac{C}{(1 + i)^n}$

Combining these two, present value of a constant cash payment over $n$ years, interest compounded annually $= \dfrac{C}{i}\left(1 - \dfrac{1}{(1 + i)^n}\right)$

Therefore the present value of \$1000 received three years from now, discounted at an opportunity cost interest rate of 12 per cent, would be \$711.78 (this is \$1000 divided by $(1.12)^3$). The phrase 'opportunity cost' is often used, because by waiting three years for the \$1000, you lose the *opportunity* to invest your money at 12 per cent in the meantime.

Here's an example of present value calculations. A company is considering an investment that will cost \$10 000 and will return \$2400 at the end of each year for five years. This looks good: 24 per cent of the investment cost received each year, a total of \$12 000 back on the \$10 000 invested. To make the investment, the company will have to borrow at an interest rate of 7 per cent. Should it go ahead?

Before we do the calculations, note three things about problems like this:

1. What we are trying to determine is if the money coming in is equivalent to a cost of capital of 7 per cent. If the company has to raise its money at 7 per cent, it will want the investments it makes to return at least that. A greater rate of return would be desirable, otherwise there would be little point in investing, but 7 per cent is the minimum acceptable return.
2. The idea of present value analysis is to take the future returns and subtract the 7 per cent that the company has to pay on its borrowing, to determine if, after considering the borrowing cost, the returns equal the \$10 000 that has to be invested. *Is the present value of the future cash flows equal to the present cost outlay that has to be made to get those flows?*
3. The 24 per cent quoted above is irrelevant to the analysis. It compares the annual return to the investment cost, but it does not consider the interest cost of waiting several years for some of that return. The whole idea of present value analysis is to build that interest cost, the time value of money, into the analysis.

Here's the present value analysis:

- Using the second present value formula above:

| | $ |
|---|---|
| PV of first year's return is $\$2400 / (1.07)^1$ | 2 242.99 |
| PV of second year's return is $\$2400 / (1.07)^2$ | 2 096.25 |
| PV of third year's return is $\$2400 / (1.07)^3$ | 1 959.11 |
| PV of fourth year's return is $\$2400 / (1.07)^4$ | 1 830.95 |
| PV of fifth year's return is $\$2400 / (1.07)^5$ | 1 711.17 |
| Total PV | 9 840.47 |

- Since the annual flows are constant, the third present value formula above could have been used instead:

  $PV = (\$2400 / .07)(1 - [1 / 1.07]^5) = \$9840.48$

  This is the same answer as using the second present value formula. We can draw the needed conclusion from this and also see the effects of waiting for returns:

- The conclusion is that the investment is not a good idea. It will cost $10 000, but after calculating the interest cost of waiting for the money to be returned, the present value of the $12 000 returned is only $9840. Therefore, the investment is returning less than the 7 per cent rate the company has to pay to finance it. It's close, but still not attractive.
- From the annual calculations above, you can see that the present value of the $2400 is smaller the longer we wait for it. The $2400 received after one year has a PV of $2243, but the $2400 received after four years has a PV of $1831. This is a necessary result: the longer the wait, the lower the PV, because the greater is the amount of interest assumed included in the cash flow and, therefore, the lower is the residual PV.

## Some present value examples

As you saw in the example above, the concept of present value is very useful in evaluating investment possibilities ahead of time. Here are some more examples.

1 Suppose you are offered the chance to invest $2000 in a project that will pay you back $4500 after six years. Is it a good deal? Suppose, alternatively, you could invest your $2000 at 11 per cent. The present value of the $4500 in 6 years is $\$4500/(1 + .11)^6$, or $2406. Therefore, the present value of what you'll get ($2406) exceeds your cost ($2000), and it does seem a good deal.

2 Usually, in modern financial arrangements, 'blended' payments are made to cover the specified interest plus some payment on the principal. House mortgages and car loans are two common examples. In such cases, to understand what is going on, we have to separate the return on investment (the interest) from the return of investment (repayment of the principal). Here is an example: a loan of $7998 carrying an interest rate of 10 per cent is being repaid by a blended annual payment of $2110, made at the end of each year, which will cover all interest and pay off the principal as well in five years. In such a case, the interest amount gets smaller every year because the principal balance is falling, but the rate of return on investment is a constant 10 per cent.

| Date | Total blended payment $ | Return on investment (interes) $ | Residual paid on principal $ | Principal balance $ |
|---|---|---|---|---|
| Loan date | | | | 7 998 |
| 1 year later | 2 110 | 800* | 1 310 | 6 688 |
| 2 years later | 2 110 | 669 | 1 441 | 5 247 |
| 3 years later | 2 110 | 525 | 1 585 | 3 662 |
| 4 years later | 2 110 | 366 | 1 744 | 1 918 |
| 5 years later | 2 110 | 192 | 1 918 | 0 |
| | 10 550 | 2 552 | 7 998 | |

* $800 = $7998 × .10; $669 = $6688 × .10; and so on.

Using this example, the present value of $2110 paid every year for five years, discounted at 10 per cent, compounded annually, is $7998. This is ($2110/.10) (1 – 1/[1.10]$^5$): check it and see.

## How's your understanding?

Here is a question you should be able to answer, based on what you have just read: What is the present value of $300 you will receive after two years if your opportunity cost of waiting is 11 per cent? ($243.49, which is $300/[1 + .11]$^2$)

# A13.3 Homework and discussion to develop understanding

### Problem A13.1 Basic present value analysis

You have an opportunity to invest $200 000. You will be paid a single-interest payment of $100 000 (and get your investment back) at the end of five years.

1 If 8 per cent is the return you require, should you invest? Show all calculations

2 Describe one other factor you should consider before you invest

### Problem A13.2 Basic ideas of present value analysis

1 Explain what the 'time value of money' or 'present value' concept is all about. Why would business people be sensitive to it?

2 Calculate the present value of each of the following:

   a $1000 to be received a year from now. If it were on hand now, it would be invested at 10 per cent interest

   b $1000 to be received at the end of each of the next three years. The opportunity cost of interest or cost of capital in this case is 12 per cent.

3 Answer question **2b** again but assume a rate of 10 per cent. Why is the present value higher when the rate is lower?

## Problem A13.3 Present value analysis – which AFL team?

Elbows Murphy has come to you for financial advice. The Canberra Stars, in a bid to strengthen their team, have made him a contract offer that would pay a signing bonus now of $90 000, plus a salary of $85 000 for each of the next three years. Elbows is considering turning down the offer, because he knows he can earn $120 000 per year for the next three years at his present club. Assuming no tax is deducted from his earnings or investment earnings:

1. If Elbows could invest his earnings (including signing bonus) at 11 per cent, which team should he play for?
2. If Elbows could invest at only 7 per cent, what should he do?
3. At what interest rate would it make no difference to Elbows which team he should play for?

## Problem A13.4 Present value analysis – proposed investment in shares

Surprising Sleepwear Ltd is considering making an investment in shares of a company that makes fibreglass boats. The investment will cost $110 000 and will return $8000 cash per year for four years. At the end of four years, Surprising expects to be able to sell the shares for $125 000. Surprising pays 11 per cent to raise financing for such ventures. Based just on this data, should Surprising buy the shares?

## Problem A13.5 Present value analysis – buy or lease a truck?

Speedy Trucking is trying to decide whether it should buy a new truck for its business or lease the truck from another company. If Speedy decides to buy the truck, it must pay $140 000 cash immediately, and the truck is expected to last for five years. At the end of the five years, the truck will have no remaining value and will be disposed of. If Speedy decides to lease the truck, it must pay $30 000 at the end of each year for five years, at which point the truck must be returned to the leasing company. Assume zero taxes.

1. If the current market interest rate (which Speedy has to pay to borrow) is 10 per cent, should Speedy lease or buy the truck?
2. Suppose Speedy discovers that if the truck were bought, it could be sold at the end of the five years for $35 000. Would your answer to question **1** change?
3. Identify one or two important assumptions made in your analyses and explain why those assumptions are important.

# Chapter 14

# Financial statement analysis

## On completion of this chapter you should be able to:

- describe the objectives of financial statement analysis
- recognise the limitations of financial statement analysis
- prepare common size statements
- calculate the ratios in common use to analyse a firm's performance, activity, liquidity and financing
- use ratios to analyse a firm's financial performance and financial position
- explain the Du Pont system of integrative ratio analysis.

## 14.1 Chapter overview

With the background you now have on the content of financial statements and how financial markets work, you are now ready to carry out financial statement analysis. This chapter provides tools for analysis and evaluation of financial position and performance. The main focus is on ratio analysis, but analysis of cash flow, which you first encountered in chapter 12, is revisited, and there are more examples of 'what if' effects analysis.

When you evaluate a company's performance, you need to evaluate it relative to the company's circumstances (for example, comparisons with previous years, similar companies and budgets).

Ratio analysis is the main technique described in this chapter. Ratios need to be grouped under specific categories: profitability, activity, liquidity and financial structure. The combination of ratios in each of these categories provides lots of insight into the company performance.

## 14.2 Investment and relative return

An investment is made to earn a return. The return is usually thought of in relation to the amount of the investment required to earn it. For example, you might be pleased with a \$1000 annual return if you had invested \$2000, but horrified if you had invested \$2 000 000. One way to relate the two components is via return on investment, in which the return is the numerator and the initial investment is the denominator:

$$\textbf{Relative return (return on investment)} = \frac{\textbf{Return}}{\textbf{Investment}}$$

Later, we will examine relative returns, such as return on investment (ROI), in more depth. For now, note that we have to have some way of measuring both return and investment if we are to be able to calculate (and evaluate) relative return.

Much of financial statement analysis is based on ratios such as ROI. Some points you should remember about ratios:

- The purpose of a ratio is to produce a scale-free, relative measure of a company that can be used to compare with other companies, or other years for the company. Such a measure is scale free because both numerator and denominator are measured in the same units (dollars) and are both dependent on the size of the company. A large company will have a larger investment than a small one, and should be expected to have a larger return as well, but a ratio like ROI cancels out some of the effects of size, and so allows the large and small companies to be compared.
- The ratio will be unreliable as a comparison, or even misleading or useless, unless its numerator is appropriate. This means that the numerator must be properly calculated, as well as suitable for the comparison being made. The word 'return' in ROI could be represented by several possible quantities, including net profit, cash generated by operations or interest. The appropriate quantity for the numerator depends on the context of the analysis, as you will see. Also, the role of GAAP and other rules in making figures such as net profit meaningful is very important to the conclusions that may be drawn from ratio analysis.
- These same points apply equally to the denominator of the ratio. Possible denominators include total assets, gross assets and shareholders' equity. Additionally, sometimes a doubtful or ambiguous accounting method can create a problem in both the numerator and the denominator, bringing the whole ratio into question. An example here is that

if a company chooses a revenue recognition method that makes net profit doubtfully valid, that will also make the retained profits figure doubtful, throwing into question one of the most widely used ROI-type ratios, called return on equity (ROE), which is calculated as net profit divided by equity (including retained profits).

## 14.3 Introduction to financial statement analysis

The purpose of financial statement analysis is to use the financial statements to evaluate an enterprise's financial performance and financial position. Therefore, the value of the analysis depends on the value of the financial statements.

### Financial evaluation is not just calculation

When you have completed this chapter, you will be able to take a set of financial statements of pretty well any company and make an evaluation of its performance and prospects. But remember that such an evaluation is not just a calculation, it is a judgement based on the calculations that make sense for that company and based on substantial knowledge of the company. The more you know about a company, its business, its management and its accounting, the more useful and credible will be your analysis.

Financial accounting information is not used in a vacuum, but is part of a vast array of information available to investors, creditors, managers and others. Its use is affected by its own quality, such as whether a company's financial statements have been carefully prepared and are comparable with other companies' statements. Use is also affected by the availability of other sources of information that may contain all or part of what is in the financial statements. Remember the idea from the discussion of capital market research in section 13.3: it is difficult to 'beat the market' using financial statement information, because the statements reflect business events people already know something about and because there are many other people, all with their own sources of information, also trying to analyse what is going on and taking action on the basis of their analyses. You should always view financial accounting information as part of a network of information, not as standing alone. To explain and illustrate various techniques, however, this chapter deals with them separately.

### Preparation for intelligent analysis

Unless you know why you're doing the analysis – that is, what decision or evaluation is dependent on it – you can't get very far with it. Also, unless you have substantial knowledge of the enterprise, you can't interpret the figures your analysis produces (for example, what is good performance for a new company in a troubled industry may be unsatisfactory for an established company in a prosperous industry).

Much of financial analysis involves ratios. They have little meaning on their own: they are merely indicators, which can be interpreted and used meaningfully only with a good understanding of the company and the accounting policies used in preparing the financial statements. The scale-free nature of a ratio means that it allows comparisons over certain periods of time, among companies of different sizes, and with other indicators such as interest rates or share prices. But it also can be tempting to think that when you have calculated a ratio, you have something meaningful in itself. While there is some fundamental meaning in each ratio, as you will see, what the comparisons mean to the analyst's decision must be added by the analyst, using knowledge and information beyond ratios.

Therefore, in order to do an intelligent and useful financial statement analysis, you should do the following:

1 Learn about the enterprise, its circumstances, and its plans. This is essential in any real analysis: don't be misled by the limited information given for the examples in this book. The annual report's descriptive sections and the footnotes to the financial statements will help you learn about the enterprise.
2 Get a clear understanding of the decision or evaluation to which the analysis will contribute, who the decision-maker is (investor, lender, creditor, management) and what assistance he or she requires.
3 Calculate the ratios, trends and other figures that apply to your specific problem. Don't calculate indiscriminately.
4 Find whatever comparative information you can to provide a frame of reference for your analysis. Industry data, reports by other analysts, results for similar companies or the same company in other years and other such information is often plentiful.
5 Focus on the analytical results that are most significant to the decision-maker's circumstances, and integrate and organise the analysis so that it will be of most help to the decision-maker.

There are many sources of information about companies to help you become knowledgeable about them and able to place your analysis in context. As you might expect, there is more information about large companies than small ones and more about public listed companies (those whose shares and other securities are listed on stock exchanges) than about private ones (those that are closely held by a few owners). Companies will often send you their annual reports and other information about them, and company Web sites provide you access to the company's annual report and lots of other data.

The preparer of financial statements has a choice from among a number of accounting policies on which to base the financial information. (You've seen this already in chapters 7, 8 and 11 and in some 'what if' effects analysis examples in chapter 13, and you'll see more about it in chapter 15.) As the analyst of these statements, you may wish to recast them using other policies that you prefer before computing any of the ratios. For example, some analysts deduct intangible assets, such as goodwill, from assets and owners' equity before computing ratios. They reason that, because these assets are not physical in nature, some people may doubt their value; deleting them, therefore, may improve comparability with companies that don't have such assets.

The validity of financial analysis based on accounting ratios has been challenged. Among the criticisms are that future plans and expected results, not historical numbers, should be used in computing ratios, especially liquidity ratios; current market values, not historical numbers, should be used for assets, debts and shareholders' equity in computing performance ratios; and cash flow, not accounting profit, should be used in computing performance ratios. Another objection is that because, at least for public companies, stock markets and other capital markets adjust prices of companies' securities as information comes out, ratios based on publicly available information cannot tell you anything the markets have not already incorporated into security prices. While these criticisms are controversial, they are reminders to use ratios with care and intelligence.

## Common size statements

While the emphasis in this chapter will be on ratio analysis, it should be noted that another, complementary, method of explaining financial results are common size statements. By calculating all statement of financial position figures as percentages of total assets and all profit and loss figures as a percentage of total revenue, the size of the company can be approximately factored out. This procedure assists in comparing companies of different sizes and in spotting trends over time for a single company.

For example, consider the following profit and loss statement for the years ended 30 June 2002 and 2003.

| | | **2003** | | **2002** |
|---|---|---|---|---|
| | | **$000** | | **$000** |
| Sales | | 1 549 | | 1 289 |
| Cost of goods sold | | 387 | | 258 |
| Gross margin | | 1 162 | | 1 031 |
| Operating expenses | | | | |
| Administration | 101 | | 82 | |
| Selling | 125 | | 104 | |
| Distribution | 77 | | 66 | |
| Depreciation | 124 | | 97 | |
| Other | 39 | 466 | 32 | 381 |
| Operating profit before tax | | 696 | | 650 |

If we expressed these numbers as a common size statement, the following would result:

| | | **2003** | | **2002** |
|---|---|---|---|---|
| | | % | | % |
| Sales | | 100.0 | | 100.0 |
| Cost of goods sold | | 25.0 | | 20.0 |
| Gross margin | | 75.0 | | 80.0 |
| Operating expenses | | | | |
| Administration | 6.5 | | 6.4 | |
| Selling | 8.1 | | 8.1 | |
| Distribution | 5.0 | | 5.1 | |
| Depreciation | 8.0 | | 7.5 | |
| Other | 2.5 | 30.1 | 2.5 | 29.6 |
| Operating profit before tax | | 44.9 | | 50.4 |

You can see that operating profit before tax as a percentage of sales has dropped from 50.4 per cent to 44.9 per cent. This change is brought about almost exclusively because of cost of goods sold expense becoming a higher percentage of sales.

## 14.4 Woolworths Limited: an example company

To help you see how the analyses in this chapter work, they will be illustrated using the financial statements of Woolworths Limited, a company that all Australians will be familiar with. This company is used in this book because it provides the necessary scope for illustrating a wide variety of analyses. The main reason it is included, though, is to give you a sense of *accomplishment* as you work through this chapter. You will find that, with the accounting knowledge you already have and the techniques outlined in this chapter, you can understand a lot about such a company as Woolworths. While there will be some head scratching as you go, you will be pleased at how knowledgeable you become.

As you are aware, Woolworths Limited is a large retail organisation with virtually all of its operations carried out in Australia. It has three main operating groups:

- supermarkets group (including Woolworths Supermarkets, Safeway and Mac's Liquor)
- general merchandise group (including Big W and Woolworths Variety)
- the specialty retail group (including Dick Smith Electronics, Tandy Electronics and Rockmans).

The company closes its books on the penultimate or last Sunday in June of each year, not at the end of the month. The financial period is therefore measured in weeks.

The financial statements from Woolworths' 2001 annual report are at the back of the book. *Before you go further*, go to the company's Web site and read its latest Chairman's Report, This Year's Highlights, Group Managing Director's Report and Company Overview, and the financial statements. From the 2001 financial statements in appendix 2 find:

- the 2001 net profit number (called 'net profit after ordinary activities after income tax', $476.1 million)
- the 24 June 2001 retained profits ($279.9 million)
- the decrease in cash held for 2001 ($94.0 million)
- the 24 June 2001 total assets ($5083.2 million), total liabilities ($3557.6 million) and shareholders' equity ($1525.6 million).

As you familiarise yourself with the general content and format of the financial statements, here are a few things to keep in mind:

- The financial statements are consolidated because Woolworths is really a group of companies.
- Woolworths provides figures for the prior year, 2000. In addition, on the page before the financial statements is a five-year summary. We'll make extensive use of the prior-year figures to help you understand the 2001 figures.
- In the auditors' report, the auditors state their opinion that the financial statements present a true and fair view of the state of affairs as at 24 June 2001 and the profit and cash flows for the financial year.

## 14.5 Financial statement ratio analysis

If you're familiar enough with Woolworths' financial statements to have a good idea of where to look for information, let's turn now to consider the use of ratio analysis of the financial statements.

Various kinds of ratios that could be used to analyse a company's financial performance and position are outlined in the following pages. (More than this set have been proposed and used. You may wish to invent more yourself if you have particular analytical uses in mind.) Each ratio is illustrated by showing how it is calculated from Woolworths' financial statements at the back of this book. Some interpretive and comparative comments are made as illustrations, but the main purpose of this section is to show you how to figure out the ratios.

Most figures below are given in millions of dollars, as they are in Woolworths' statements. Ratios are calculated here to two decimal places. They could be done to more decimals, but that would be false accuracy, because the ratios depend on all sorts of judgements and estimates made in assembling the financial statements and, therefore, should not be thought of as precise quantities, but rather as indicators.

## Performance ratios

### Return on equity

Sometimes called return on shareholders' funds or return on net worth, return on equity is calculated as operating profit after tax divided by shareholders' equity. Operating profit after tax is calculated before deducting outside equity interests, and generally excludes any extraordinary items. Return on equity (ROE) indicates how much return the company is generating on the historically accumulated shareholders' investment (contributed share capital, reserves, retained profits). Shareholders' equity can be taken straight from the statement of financial position or can be computed from the accounting equation as total assets minus total liabilities. The denominator can be year-end equity or average equity over the year; for a growing company, you'd expect a slightly larger ROE figure for the latter.

For Woolworths, ROE (based on year-end equity) for the last two years has been:

$476.1 ÷ $1525.6 = 31.21% for 2001
$321.7 ÷ $1630.9 = 19.73% for 2000

The profit return relative to equity is up from 2000. Woolworths issued a small number of shares during the year, under the employee share plan and the dividend reinvestment plan, but they bought back more shares, with the result that shareholders' equity decreased (see note 18, which provides details of the movements in share capital). However, operating profit during 2001 increased substantially, which resulted in an increase in the ratio. The effect of changes in shareholders' equity on profit for the year may depend on when the change occurred. For example, if a large increase occurred in July 2000, you would expect profits to increase more than if it increased in May 2001, because the additional shareholders' funds were available for use for a longer period. For internal purposes, a company would be able to calculate a more accurate return on equity figure by calculating the average equity over the year, which will vary, depending on such things as when new shares are issued or when dividends are declared (recall that declaring dividends reduces retained profits). For the 2001 year for Woolworths, factors affecting profitability are noted in the Group Managing Director's Report to Shareholders and in the Discussion and Analysis of the Statement of Financial Performance. The main explanations were strong sales growth and a reduction in costs.

Note that differences between versions of ratios are common. They are usually not large and, as long as you calculate your ratio in the same way from year to year, you should be able to spot major changes and trends regardless of how you calculated the ratio.

### Return on assets

This ratio is usually calculated as earnings before interest and tax divided by total assets. Earnings before interest and tax (EBIT) is a measure of profit based on the operating profit before interest and taxes are deducted. As EBIT is not always shown in the financial statements, it can be calculated by adding interest back to net profit before tax (that is, EBIT equals net profit before tax plus interest. For Woolworths, it is shown in the statement of financial performance ($706.6 million).

As with equity in ROE, the total assets figure can be the year-end figure or the average over the year. Return on assets (ROA) indicates the company's ability to generate a return on its assets before considering the cost of financing those assets (interest). It helps in judging whether borrowing is worthwhile: presumably if it costs *x* per cent to borrow money, the company should expect to earn at least *x* per cent on the assets acquired with the money. (This relationship between ROA and borrowing cost is explored further in section 14.6.)

Different companies use different versions of the numerator. These include operating profit after tax, operating profit after tax but before interest expense, and operating profit before tax and interest expense. For the denominator, the total assets figure can be the year-end figure or the average over the year. Other versions of the denominator include gross assets (that is, total assets before accumulated depreciation is deducted) and net assets employed (usually total assets minus current liabilities). In this book, our examples will use EBIT divided by total assets (year-end). We have given you the other alternatives so that you can exercise some care when comparing ratios calculated and presented by different companies. Again, provided a consistent method is used by a company each year, the major trends should show up.

You can see the value of being able to calculate ratios that you understand yourself, because the versions produced by companies may not be fully clear, since each company fits the ratios to its own circumstances.

For Woolworths the return on assets figures are:

| | **2001** | **2000** |
|---|---|---|
| EBIT ÷ Total assets | 706.6 | 527.7 |
| | 5 083.2 | 4 816.8 |
| | 13.90% | 10.96% |

## Profit margin

Profit margin is often calculated as operating profit after tax divided by sales. Profit margin indicates the percentage of sales revenue that ends up as profit, so it is the average profit on each dollar of sales. For example, a 10 per cent profit margin would mean that 10 cents in net profit, after income tax and all other expenses, is generated from each dollar of sales, on average. It is a useful measure of performance, and gives some indication of pricing strategy or competition intensity. You might expect a discount retailer in a competitive market to have a low profit margin, and an upscale jeweller to have a high margin, for example.

For Woolworths, the profit margins for 2001 and 2000 can be calculated as shown below. Sales figures are provided in the statement of financial performance. Note that for 2000, there are two possible sales figures to use: one including wholesale sales tax ($20 019.9 million) and one adjusted to exclude this tax ($18 988.8 million). Because sales revenue for the 2001 period is reported exclusive of the wholesale sales tax, the $18 988.8 million figure for 2000 is used, in order to be consistent.

| | **2001** | **2000** |
|---|---|---|
| Operating profit after tax ÷ Sales | 476.1 | 321.7 |
| | 20 915.1 | 18 988.8 |
| | 2.28% | 1.69% |

An alternative version of profit margin can be calculated by dividing earnings before interest and tax (EBIT) by sales revenue. For Woolworths Limited, this would result in the following ratios:

| | **2001** | **2000** |
|---|---|---|
| EBIT ÷ Sales | 706.1 | 527.7 |
| | 20 915.1 | 18 988.8 |
| | 3.38% | 2.78% |

These ratios are labelled as 'trading profit to sales' in the Five Year Summary. The EBIT/sales ratio for the supermarkets, general merchandise and specialty retail groups are provided on pages 8 and 9 of the annual report in the Overview of Operating Groups. In the subsection of this chapter headed 'Activity (turnover) ratios', we will use this alternative version of the profit margin ratio to show the relationship between profit margins and ROA.

### Gross margin

Also known as the gross profit ratio, this is calculated as gross profit divided by sales. Woolworths' gross profit is shown on its statement of financial performance. If this were not disclosed, an alternative would be to use sales minus cost of goods sold.

The gross margin provides a further indication of the company's product pricing and product mix. For example, a gross margin of 33 per cent indicates that the company's average mark-up on cost is 50 per cent (revenue equals 150 per cent of cost, so cost is 67 per cent of revenue and gross margin is 33 per cent). This is a rough indicator only, especially for companies with a variety of products or unstable markets.

For Woolworths, the gross margin is calculated as follows:

| | **2001** | **2000** |
|---|---|---|
| Gross profit ÷ Sales | 5 354.1 | 5 038.6 |
| | 20 915.1 | 18 988.8 |
| | 25.60% | 26.53% |

### Cash flow to total assets

This is calculated as (cash generated by operations plus interest paid plus tax paid) divided by total assets. Cash generated by operations, tax paid and interest paid are found in the cash flow statement, and total assets may be the year-end statement of financial position figure or an average of the beginning and ending figures. This ratio relates the company's ability to generate cash resources to its size, which approximately factors out size. It provides an alternative return measure to ROA, focusing on cash return rather than on accrual profit return as used in ROA. To be comparable to the ROA, the ratio should be calculated before tax and interest payments are deducted.

For Woolworths Limited, using year-end assets, the ratio was 21.06 per cent in 2001 (1070.4 divided by 5083.2) and 25.99 per cent in 2000 (1252.1 divided by 4816.8), a small decline. Note that 1070.4 is the sum of 809.0 plus 35.7 plus 225.7.

### Earnings per share

This ratio is calculated as (net operating profit minus dividends on preference shares) divided by weighted average number of ordinary shares outstanding. Earnings per share (EPS) relates earnings attributable to ordinary shares to the number of ordinary shares issued.

Accounting standards require basic earnings per share to be disclosed in every set of accounts. The numerator is operating profit after tax (profit after tax not including extraordinary items) minus any preference dividends. For consolidated financial statements, the profit figure is after deducting outside equity in the operating profit. The weighted average number of ordinary shares issued is provided in the annual report, as it could not be calculated by outsiders. It can become quite a complicated calculation, and will be discussed further in later courses.

If a company has potential commitments to issue further shares, such as in stock-option plans to motivate senior management or preference shares or debt convertible to ordinary shares at the option of the holder of the preference shares, the potential effect of the exercise of such commitments is calculated by showing both basic EPS and 'fully diluted' EPS. ('Dilution' refers to the potential lowering of return to present shareholders resulting from other people's exercising rights arising from commitments already made by the company.)

For Woolworths Limited, the earnings per share is shown on the statement of financial performance for 2001 and 2000 as $0.4016 (428.0 divided by 1065.8) and $0.2627 (295.5 divided by 1125.0) respectively. It is also noted that diluted earnings per share is not materially different from basic earnings per share.

### Price to earnings ratio

This is calculated as current market price per share divided by EPS. The price to earnings (PE) ratio relates the accounting earnings and market price of the shares but, since the relationship between such earnings and changes in share market prices is not straightforward (as noted in chapter 13 and in other earlier material), the interpretation of PE is controversial. Nevertheless, it is a widely used ratio, appearing in many publications and analyses of companies. Many newspapers around the world include PE in their daily summaries of each company's share market trades and prices.

The idea is that, because market price should reflect the market's expectation of future performance, PE compares the present performance with those expectations. A company with a high PE is expected to show greater future performance than its present level, while one with a low PE is not expected to do much better in the future. High-PE companies are those that are popular and have good share prices, while low-PE companies are not so popular, having low share prices relative to their present earnings. PE is highly subject to general increases and decreases in market prices, so it is difficult to interpret over time, and is more useful when comparing similar companies listed in the same stock market at the same time.

For Woolworths, the ordinary shares had an average price on the Australian Stock Exchange of about $10.85 in the year ended 24 June 2001, and about $6.18 in the year ended 25 June 2000 (corresponding to our 2001 and 2000 periods). The average PE ratio was, therefore, about 27.0 for 2001 ($10.85 divided by $0.4016) and 23.5 for 2000 ($6.18 divided by $0.2627). Because PE changes as share prices change, with each announcement of an EPS number, it can be monitored regularly to track changes in the market's expectations, particularly changes relative to other companies' PEs.

### Dividend payout ratio

This ratio is calculated as annual dividends declared per share divided by EPS. This is a measure of the portion of earnings paid to shareholders. For example, if the dividend payout ratio is 0.40, 40 per cent of profit was distributed to shareholders and the remaining 60 per cent was kept in the company (retained profits) to finance assets or reduce debts. A stable ratio would suggest that the company has a policy of paying dividends based on profits, and a variable ratio would suggest that factors other than profits are important in the board of directors' decisions to declare dividends.

For Woolworths, the Five Year Summary (and note 6 to the financial statements) indicates that dividends were $0.27 per share (15 cents plus 12 cents) in 2001 and $0.23 (13 cents plus 10 cents) in 2000, EPS were $0.4016 and $0.2627, so the dividend payout ratios for 2001 and 2000 would be 67.23 per cent (0.27 divided by 0.4016) and 87.55 per cent (0.23 divided by 0.2627) respectively. This can be seen also from the total figures indicated in note 6, which show that dividends of $517.0 million were declared in 2001 and $490.5

million in 2000. These are 108.59 per cent of net profit in 2001 ($517.0 divided by $476.1) and 152.47 per cent in 2000 ($490.5 divided by $321.7).

## Return on funds employed (ROFE)

A ratio that is relatively new to Australian financial reports is return on funds employed. It is calculated as earnings before interest and tax (EBIT) divided by average funds employed. Funds employed is normally working capital (current assets minus current liabilities) plus fixed assets (property, plant and equipment). However, there are variations on the above.

For Woolworths, funds employed includes inventory, receivables, trade and other payables, and fixed assets. It excludes cash, tax balances and dividend provisions.

| | 2001<br>$m | 2000<br>$m |
|---|---|---|
| **Funds employed** | | |
| Inventory | 1 731.8 | 1 648.3 |
| Trade payables | (1 666.4) | (1 571.8) |
| Net investment in inventory | 65.4 | 76.5 |
| Receivables | 320.0 | 298.5 |
| Other creditors | (855.5) | (798.8) |
| **Working capital** | (470.1) | (423.8) |
| Fixed assets | 2 587.7 | 2 339.1 |
| **Total funds employed** | 2 117.6 | 1 915.3 |

To calculate the return on funds employed for 2001 from the above figures, we get:

$$\text{ROFE} = \frac{\text{EBIT}}{\text{Av. funds employed}} = \frac{706.6}{.5(1915.3 + 2117.6)} = 35.04\%$$

This was up from 29.08 per cent the previous year, as reported in the company's financial highlights. The importance of this ratio relates to the need to finance the funds employed. For example, inventory that is not financed by accounts payable needs to be funded. The purchase of property, plant and equipment needs to be funded. It is important that the return on funds employed is higher than the cost of those funds employed.

## Activity (turnover) ratios

### Total asset turnover

Calculated as a ratio of sales to total assets, this and similar turnover ratios relate the company's dollar sales volume to its size, thereby answering the question: how much sales volume is associated with a dollar of assets? Turnover and profit/margin ratios are often useful together, because they tend to move in opposite directions. Companies with high turnover tend to have low margins, and those with low turnover tend to have high margins. Those extremes represent contrary marketing strategies or competitive pressures; pricing low and trying for high volume versus pricing high and making more on each unit sold. (Find more about using profit margin and turnover together in section 14.6.)

Woolworths' total asset turnover ratio was 4.11 in 2001 ($20 915.1 million divided by $5083.2 million) and 3.94 in 2000 ($18 988.8 million divided by $4816.8 million). Turnover rose in 2001 because revenue grew faster than assets did. The company is getting more business out of each dollar of assets.

### Inventory turnover

This is calculated as cost of goods sold expense divided by average inventory assets. This ratio relates the level of inventories to the volume of activity: a company with low turnover may be risking obsolescence or deterioration in its inventory and/or may be incurring excessive storage and insurance costs. In recent years, many companies have attempted to reduce inventories to the minimum, keeping just enough on hand to meet customer demand or even ordering inventory as it is demanded by customers (as in the 'just in time' method of minimising inventories without running out of stock and irritating customers).

Average inventories were $1690.1 million ([$1731.8 million plus $1648.3 million] divided by 2) for 2001, and $1650.5 million ([$1648.3 million plus $1652.7 million from the 1999 balance sheet, not included in this book] divided by 2). These result in turnovers relative to COGS of 9.49 for 2001 ($16 034.6 million divided by $1690.1 million) and 9.30 for 2000 ($15 353.7 divided by $1650.5). The company appears to have managed its inventories in about the same way in both years.

Inventory turnover can be converted to measure how long, in days, inventory is held on average. This can be achieved by dividing 365 by the inventory turnover rate. This is usually referred to as 'days' inventory on hand' and 'number of days' stock'. For Woolworths Limited, converting the above inventory turnover ratios (based on sales) we get 38.46 days (365 divided by 9.49) and 39.25 (365 divided by 9.30) for 2001 and 2000.

### Debtors turnover

Also called 'accounts receivable turnover', this ratio is calculated by dividing credit sales by trade debtors. As credit and cash sales are not disclosed separately in an annual report, it is necessary to make some assumptions about the percentage of sales that are on credit. For companies where most sales are on credit (such as BHP, CSR or Telstra), it is normal to use the sales figure given in the annual report. As cash sales are collected immediately, using this figure for retailers such as Woolworths or Coles Myer is meaningless, as most of their sales are for cash. The trade debtors' figure in the ratio refers to gross trade debtors (that is, before deducting the provision for doubtful debts). Again, either year-end or average trade debtors can be used, with the latter common particularly where there are substantial fluctuations in debtors.

This ratio can be converted into a time period often called 'days in debtors' or 'days sales in receivables'. This ratio indicates how many days it takes, on average, to collect a day's sales revenue. It becomes large when accounts receivable become larger relative to sales, so a large collection ratio is a negative signal, raising questions about the company's policies of granting credit and the vigour of its collection attempts. The ratio is subject to significant seasonal changes for many companies, usually rising during heavy selling periods (such as just before Christmas for a retailer) and falling during slow times.

As we do not know the percentage of Woolworths' sales that are on credit, calculation of the accounts receivable turnover ratio will be rather uninformative. However, for illustrative purposes we will show you how to calculate it using the information in the annual report, plus an assumption that 3 per cent of Woolworths' sales in 2001 were on credit.

| | 2001 |
|---|---|
| 3% of sales (3% of $20 915.1m) | $627.453 m |
| Average trade receivables (0.5[$91.8 m + $85.9 m]) | $88.85 m |
| Accounts receivable turnover (627.453 ÷ 88.85) | 7.06 |
| Days in accounts receivable (365 ÷ 7.06) | 51.70 |

Before we move on to liquidity, let's consider three ratios discussed above that are interrelated: return on assets, profit margin and asset turnover. For Woolworths 2001 and 2000:

**Return on assets = Profit margin × Asset turnover**

$$\frac{EBIT}{Total\ assets} = \frac{EBIT}{Sales} \times \frac{Sales}{Total\ assets}$$

**2001**

$$\frac{706.6}{5\,083.2} = \frac{706.6}{20\,915.1} \times \frac{20\,915.1}{5\,083.2}$$

$$13.90\% = 3.38\% \times 4.11$$

**2000**

$$\frac{527.7}{4\,816.8} = \frac{527.7}{18\,988.8} \times \frac{18\,988.8}{4\,816.2}$$

$$10.96\% = 2.78\% \times 3.94$$

Thus a change in either profit margin or asset turnover increases or decreases the return on assets. We can also tell whether a change in return on assets is caused by a change in profit margin, asset turnover or both. For 2001, return on assets increased from 10.96 per cent to 13.90 per cent. This was caused by a substantial improvement in profit margin (2.78 per cent to 3.38 per cent) and a smaller increase in asset turnover (3.94 to 4.11).

You can see above how profit margin and asset turnover interact to produce the return on assets. In one company, a low margin and a high turnover may generate the return. In another, a high margin and a low turnover may generate the return. Profit margin and turnover are likely to offset each other in generating the return on assets, because competitive pressures are likely to force down selling prices, and therefore profit margins, if a high turnover is desired. Conversely, if you want to cater to the high-priced end of the market, you are not likely to have much sales volume. Think of what great results you'd get if you could get both high margin and high volume (hence our worry about monopolies), or of how disastrous things are for companies stuck with both low margin and low volume.

## Liquidity ratios

### Current ratio

Current ratio is calculated as current assets divided by current liabilities. This ratio has already been used several times in this book. It indicates whether the company has enough short-term assets to cover its short-term debts. A ratio above 1 indicates that working capital is positive (current assets exceed current liabilities), and a ratio below 1 indicates that working capital is negative. Generally, the higher the ratio, the greater the financial stability and the lower the risk for both creditors and owners. However, the ratio should not be too high, because that may indicate that the company is not reinvesting in long-term assets to maintain future productivity. Also, a high current ratio can actually indicate problems if inventories are getting larger than they should or collections of receivables are slowing down.

The current ratio is a very commonly used indicator. Many writers use a rough rule that says the current ratio should be around 2 (twice as much in current assets as current liabilities), but this is simplistic. Many large companies regularly operate with a current ratio closer to 1 than 2. The ratio's interpretation depends on the specific circumstances of each company. Interpretation of it is also complex, because it is a static ratio, measuring financial position at a point in time and not considering any future cash flows the company may be able to generate to pay its debts. This ratio is most useful for companies having cash flows that are relatively smooth during the year and hardest to interpret for those that have unusual assets or liabilities or that depend on future cash flows to pay current debts. An example of the latter would be a company that owns a rented building: there may be few current assets and large current liabilities for mortgage payments, but, as long as the building is mostly rented and rental revenue is steady, the company is not in difficulty, even though its current ratio is low. However, it is more at risk than a similar company with a higher current ratio, because that company could more easily weather a loss of tenants because of recession or the opening of a competing building.

Woolworths' current ratio was 0.81 at the end of 2001 ($2388.5 million divided by $2959.4 million), and 0.90 at the end of 2000 ($2345.1 million divided by $2594.9 million). The Five Year Summary shows that this is the highest the ratio has been in the last five years. This level of the ratio is reasonably common for large Australian companies, particularly those with a relatively quick cash flow cycle.

### Quick ratio

The quick ratio is also called the acid test. It is calculated as (current assets minus inventory) divided by current liabilities. This is a more demanding version of the current ratio, and indicates whether current liabilities could be paid without having to sell the inventory. The ratio is particularly useful for companies that cannot convert inventory into cash quickly if necessary. This is not normally the case for retailer companies. As a result, the quick ratio normally has little significance for retailers such as Woolworths Limited. If calculated, it would be ($2388.5 million minus $1731.8 million) divided by $2959.4 million = 0.22.

## Financial structure ratios

### Debt to equity ratio

This is generally calculated as total liabilities divided by total shareholders' equity. This ratio measures the proportion of borrowing to owners' investment (including retained profits), and thus indicates the company's policy of financing its assets. A ratio greater than 1 indicates that the assets are financed mostly with debt, while a ratio less than 1 indicates that the assets are financed mostly with equity. A high ratio is a warning about risk: the company is heavily in debt relative to its equity and may be vulnerable to interest rate increases, general tightening of credit or creditor nervousness. (A high ratio also indicates that the company is highly geared or leveraged, which means it has borrowed to increase its assets over the amount that could be acquired with owners' funds only, and hopes thereby to increase returns and benefit the owners.)

Woolworths' statement of financial position makes this calculation straightforward, by totalling both liabilities and shareholders' equity. Thus the ratio for 2001 is 2.33 ($3557.6 million divided by $1525.6 million), and for 2000 is 1.95 ($3185.9 million divided by $1630.9 million). These ratios show that the company relies on debt more than on equity, and that its relative reliance on debt increased during 2001.

## Debt to assets ratio

This ratio is calculated by dividing total liabilities by total liabilities plus shareholders' equity. This is equivalent to dividing total liabilities by total assets (given that total assets equal total liabilities and shareholders' equity). This ratio will be highly correlated with the debt/equity ratio, and indicates the proportion of assets financed by liabilities.

For Woolworths Limited, this ratio equals 69.99 per cent ($3557.6 million divided by $5083.2 million) for 2001, and 66.14 per cent ($3185.9 million divided by $4816.8 million) for 2000. Consistent with the debt/equity ratio, this ratio shows an increase in reliance on liabilities to finance assets.

The debt/assets ratio can also be calculated by just comparing long-term debt or external debt to assets. For example, Woolworths, in its Five Year Summary, includes the gearing ratio as 20.26 per cent in 2001. It defines gearing as net repayable debt divided by (net repayable debt plus total equity).

## Leverage ratio

This is defined as (total liabilities plus shareholders' equity) divided by shareholders' equity. Given the accounting equation, it can also be defined as total assets divided by shareholders' equity. The ratio considers how much of assets is financed by equity. The higher the ratio, the smaller the proportion of total assets funded by shareholders' equity, and therefore the more that is funded by debt.

For Woolworths, the leverage ratio was 3.33 (5083.2 divided by 1525.6) in 2001, and 2.95 (4816.8 divided by 1630.9) in 2000.

## Interest coverage ratio

Usually calculated as EBIT divided by net interest expense, this and similar coverage ratios based on cash flow figures indicate the degree to which financial commitments (in this case, those to pay interest on debts) are covered by the company's ability to generate profit or cash flow. (Net interest refers to the difference between interest expense and interest revenue.) A low coverage ratio (especially below 1) indicates that the company is not operating at a sufficiently profitable level to cover the interest obligation comfortably, and may also be a warning of solvency problems (difficulty in meeting obligations over the long term).

For Woolworths, net interest expense in shown in note 3. The interest coverage ratio, calculated using the above formula, is 53.94 in 2001 (706.6 divided by 13.1) and 18.98 in 2000 (527.7 divided by 27.8). The Five Year Analysis also shows the interest coverage ratio; for 2001 it was 11.62, and for 2000 it was 11.53. To obtain these figures, you need to add the net interest ($13.1 million) to a WINS distribution ($47.7 million), which is shown in the Five Year Summary under the interest figure. That is 706.6 divided by (13.1 plus 47.7) equals 11.62. The WINS distribution relates to Woolworths income notes included in the equity section of the statement of financial position. In note 21, it is stated that the holders of WINS are entitled to a distribution each quarter. This just goes to show there are many different ways of calculating ratios. The reader may sometimes have difficulty in determining exactly how certain ratios were calculated by companies in their annual reports.

## Summary

Ratios are a quick method of breaking the information in the financial statements down into a form that allows for comparability with similar companies and with the financial performance of the company over a number of years. Ratios also offer the advantage that different ratios consider different parts of a company's performance. Thus, if you do not want to investigate anything more about a company than its liquidity, you might only calculate liquidity ratios, such as the quick and current ratios.

Users rely on more than ratios and other calculations from the financial statements when analysing a company's performance. They also rely on the parts of the annual report that precede the financial statements, the auditor's report, notes to the financial statements, reports by various analysts, personal knowledge of management, news media reports and much more.

Some possible pieces of information that users could find in the first part of an annual report would include management's interpretation of past and prospective performance, new ventures or growth strategies for the company, and indications of the areas of operations that were undergoing stress or change.

Notes to financial statements provide further explanations of some key areas in the statements, as you saw in the calculation of ratios for Woolworths. These can include information about a company's accounting policy for particular accounts, detailed calculations of how some account values were determined and notifications of any accounting policy changes, significant litigation and other possibly significant items. All this information, along with the statements themselves, and any ratios or other analyses, helps users get a well-rounded picture of the company.

Exhibit 14.1 summarises our ratio calculations.

## Cash flow ratios

Use of cash flow information, particularly cash flow from operations, allows the analyst to determine both the cash sufficiency and cash efficiency of an entity. Cash sufficiency ratios examine when the entity is generating enough cash flows for payment of such items as dividends, asset purchases and repayment of debt. Cash flow efficiency ratios consider the relationship between cash from operations and certain statement of financial performance and statement of financial position items. They examine how efficient the entity is in generating cash from operations in relation to sales, profit and total assets. Exhibit 14.2 provides you with a sample of potential cash flow ratios you can use.

## How's your understanding?

Here are two questions you should be able to answer, based on what you've just read:

1 How well did Woolworths perform in 2001 compared with 2000?

2 With which companies would Woolworths compare its financial performance?

# 14.6 Integrative ratio analysis

With knowledge of the company and the purpose of the analysis, the long list of ratios in section 14.5 can be used to reveal many things about a company. You learned much about Woolworths in section 14.5, but it may not be obvious how to pull all the information together into an overall picture of the company's performance. It's clear that the company

**EXHIBIT 14.1** Ratio calculations

| Ratio | Numerator | Denominator |
|---|---|---|
| **Performance ratios** | | |
| Return on equity | Operating profit after tax | Shareholders' equity |
| Return on assets | Earnings before interest and tax | Total assets |
| Profit margin | Operating profit before tax | Sales |
| Gross margin | Sales – cost of goods sold | Sales |
| Cash flow to total assets | Cash provided by operations | Total assets |
| Earnings per share | Operating profit after tax – preference share dividends | Weighted average number of ordinary shares outstanding |
| Price/earnings ratio | Current market price per share | Earnings per share |
| Dividend payout ratio | Annual dividends declared per share | Earnings per share |
| Return on funds employed | Earnings before interest and tax | Funds employed |
| **Activity (turnover) ratios** | | |
| Total asset turnover | Sales | Total assets |
| Inventory turnover | Cost of goods sold | Average inventory assets |
| Days in inventory | 365 | Inventory turnover ratio |
| Debtors turnover | Credit sales | Average trade debtors |
| Days in debtors | 365 | Debtors turnover ratio |
| **Liquidity and solvency ratios** | | |
| Current (working capital) ratio | Current assets | Current liabilities |
| Quick ratio | Current assets – inventory | Current liabilities |
| **Financing ratios** | | |
| Debt/equity ratio | Total liabilities | Total shareholders' equity |
| Debt/assets ratio | Total liabilities | Total assets |
| Leverage ratio | Total assets | Total shareholders' equity |
| Interest coverage ratio | Earnings before interest and tax | Interest expense |

is performing well, that its performance generally improved across 2001 and 2000. Can we fit the ratios together more systematically? Can we use the fact that the ratios are all calculated on the same financial statement figures and thus tend to connect to each other?

The system we will use to link ratios together is known as the Du Pont system of ratio analysis. This name is used because Du Pont was the first company to formally integrate it into its organisational and control system back in the 1920s.

The Du Pont formula uses the idea of leverage, which is an important objective and consequence of borrowing money, then using it to generate returns. Leverage, also called 'trading on the equity', 'financial leverage' and 'gearing', works like this:

1 Michael Grunion wants to invest $15 000 in a real estate project.
2 Grunion has $5000 available in personal funds.
3 So Grunion borrows $10 000 from the bank at 11 per cent interest.
4 Grunion invests the total $15 000 in the project and receives an annual return of $2100.
5 The project's return is 14 per cent before tax ($2100 / $15 000).

**EXHIBIT 14.2** Cash flow ratios

| Ratio | Sufficiency and efficiency ratios formula | Indication |
|---|---|---|
| **Sufficiency ratios** | | |
| Cash flow adequacy | Cash from operations / (Dividends paid + Asset purchases + Long-term debt paid) | Ability to generate cash to cover primary cash requirements. A value greater than 1 deemed satisfactory cover. |
| Long-term debt payment | Long-term debt payments / Cash from operations | Adequacy measure for contractual payments. |
| Dividend payout | Dividends / Cash from operations | Payout ratio measure for discretionary distributions. |
| Reinvestment | Asset purchases / Cash from operations | Outlay ratio measure for discretionary investments. |
| Debt coverage | Total debt / Cash from operations | Coverage – used as payback – how many years, at current flows, it will take to retire debt. |
| Depreciation-amortisation impact* | (Depreciation + amortisation) / Cash from operations | Ratio of non-cash items to cash from operations. |
| **Efficiency ratios** | | |
| Cash flow to sales | Cash from operations / Cash | Ratio of sales dollar realised as cash from operations. |
| Operations index | Cash from operations / Income from continuing operations | Measures cash-generating productivity of continuing operations. |
| Cash flow return on assets | Cash from operations / Total assets | Measures return on assets (on cash generation basis). |

* Comparison of this ratio with the reinvestment ratio can indicate the adequacy of a firm's reinvestment and the maintenance of its asset base. Over time the reinvestment ratio should exceed this ratio to ensure sufficient replacement of assets at higher current costs.

(Source: R. Juchau and P. Ross, 'Putting Cash into Ratios', *Australian Accountant*, November 1994, pp. 29–36.)

6 Out of that, Grunion pays the bank interest (11 per cent of $10 000 = $1100).
7 Grunion keeps the rest ($2100 – $1100 = $1000).
8 Grunion's before-tax return on the equity invested is 20 per cent ($1000 / $5000).

Not bad! The project returns 14 per cent, but Grunion gets 20 per cent on the equity invested. The reason is that Grunion has borrowed at 11 per cent but has used the borrowed funds to earn 14 per cent. The extra 3 per cent return on the borrowed funds is Grunion's to keep in return for taking the risk of investing in the project:

- overall return = 14 per cent on $15 000 = $2100
- paid to the bank = 11 per cent on $10 000 = $1100
- kept by Grunion: 14 per cent on $5000 own funds + 3 per cent on $10 000 borrowed funds

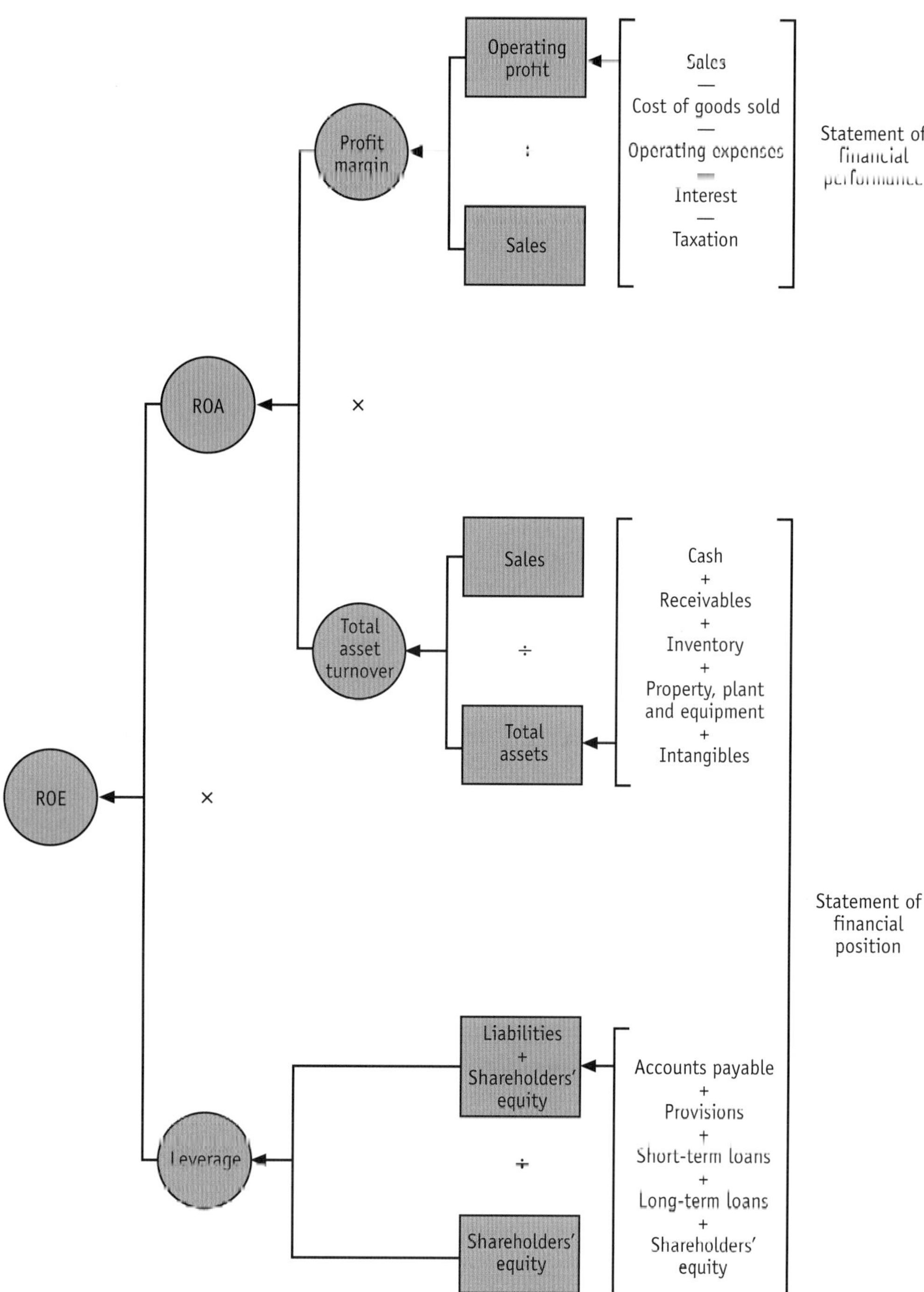


**Figure 14.1** Du Pont system of ratio analysis

- Grunion's return = the 14 per cent ($700) + the 3 per cent ($300) = $1000, which is 20 per cent of the $5000.

Grunion has benefited from leverage: borrowing money to earn money.

Leverage is a good way to increase your return, as long as you can ensure that the project's total rate of return is greater than your borrowing cost. It's a double-edged sword, though, because leverage can hit you hard if returns are low or negative. Suppose Grunion's real estate project returns only 7 per cent. Then look what happens:

- overall return = 7 per cent on $15 000 = $1050
- paid to the bank = 11 per cent on $10 000 = $1100
- kept by Grunion: 7 per cent on own funds *minus* 4 per cent on $10 000 borrowed funds
- Grunion's return = 7 per cent ($350) – 4 per cent ($400) = –$50, which is –1% of $5000.

Grunion has been hurt by leverage.

So, Grunion in this case loses on every dollar borrowed, because the project returns less than the cost of borrowing. It's not such a great deal anymore! Grunion is losing 1 per cent on the equity invested, but if just that equity had been invested, with no borrowing, Grunion would have made 7 per cent, the project's return. Leverage is now hurting, not helping.

Now that you have this basic understanding of leverage we will return to the Du Pont system. The relationships among the various ratios and how they connect to the financial statements are shown in figure 14.1.

The relationship between the return in equity ratio and its two components can be seen below.

$$\text{ROE} = \text{ROA} \times \text{Leverage}$$

$$\frac{\text{Operating profit after tax}}{\text{Shareholders' equity}} = \frac{\text{Operating profit after tax}}{\text{Total assets}} \times \frac{\text{Total assets}}{\text{Shareholders' equity}}$$

Notice that, for the above relationship, the measure of profit used in the return on assets (ROA) formula is 'operating profit after tax'. This is used because it is consistent with the profit measure used for ROE. The above equation shows that ROE can be explained by

**EXHIBIT 14.3** **Du Pont analysis for Woolworths**

Du Pont analysis is internationally recognised as an instructive way to analyse ROE (return on equity) and financial performance. It subdivides ROE into:

| | | | $m | |
|---|---|---|---|---|
| 1 | Sales return | EBIT/sales | 707/20 915 | 3.38% |
| 2 | Debt burden | NPbT/EBIT | 646/707 | × 0.91 |
| 3 | Tax burden | NPaT/NPbT | 428/646 | × 0.66 |
| 4 | Asset turnover | Sales/Average gross assets | 20 915/4 963 | × 4.21 |
| 5 | Financial leverage | Average gross assets/average shareholders' funds | 4 963/992 | × 5.00 |
| = | Return on equity | NPaT/Average shareholders' funds | 428/992 | = 43% |

NPbT = net profit before tax
NPaT = net profit after tax
Gross assets = assets before deducting accumulated depreciation

Note that if you multiply the first five ratios together, everything will cancel out except NPaT/Average shareholders' funds. However, by looking at the five ratios individually, we can see what component is changing and how it affects ROE.

The aim of Woolworths is to:

- increase the EBIT to sales ratio over time as a result of sharing 'Project Refresh' cost savings between customers and shareholders
- reduce the debt burden as EBIT increases
- reduce the tax burden as Australian tax rates fall
- improve the asset turnover as gross assets grow more slowly than sales
- improve the financial leverage as shareholders' funds grow more slowly than gross assets.

Therefore, improve ROE over time.

two factors, namely ROA and leverage. Both these factors can in turn be explained by factors to the right of them, in figure 14.1.

The above analysis can be made more sophisticated if so desired. For example, Woolworths' Web site (www.woolworths.com.au, accessed October 2001) provides the information shown in exhibit 14.3, which is a more detailed use of the Du Pont formula.

The above example shows the choices companies have in calculating these ratios. Here, Woolworths uses gross assets (that is, without deducting accumulated depreciation), whereas above we used total assets as per the statement of financial position (that is, after accumulated depreciation has been deducted). Different forms of the ratios are used, depending on which better reflect what management is trying to measure.

## 14.7 'What if' effects, ratios and cash flow

This section continues the 'what if' effects analysis examples, to include an analysis of effects on ratios and cash flow. As before, this analysis will be done on an after-tax basis. Therefore, remember the following general points:

- Changes in specific accruals or general accounting policies do not directly affect cash because they do not involve cash. For example, correcting a depreciation expense involves an entry to depreciation expense (for the current year), and accumulated depreciation. Cash isn't part of the entry. Even when an accrual or accounting policy change is implemented in the accounts, there is no direct cash effect because, by the nature of accrual accounting, such choices are implemented by journal entries involving balance sheet accounts other than cash (such as receivables, payables, inventories and accumulated depreciation).
- Such changes *do* generally affect income tax expense and liability, as you have already seen, because tax is assessed on an accrual accounting basis, by and large. The income tax effect on any current or prior year change, $X$, is approximately $tX$, where $t$ is the tax rate estimated from the financial statements. The after-tax effect is therefore $(1 - t)X$. Without detailed tax knowledge, it may not be possible to tell whether it is the current or the deferred part of the tax that is affected, but that is unlikely to matter for the purpose of most 'what if' analysis.
- The effect on income tax expense and liability is also a likely effect on accruals, and so involves no *immediate* cash effect either. However, there will be a cash effect fairly soon, when the extra tax is paid or the tax refund is collected.

### For your interest

Accounting research has shown that share prices tend to reflect the above analysis. If there is no effect on cash at all, now or ever, the share market is likely to largely ignore the change. If there is a tax effect, the market may react in accordance with it because of its cash implications. For example, if a public company takes a write-down or makes a change in accounting that reduces profit, but saves income tax in doing so, the price of its shares might rise a bit to recognise the cash saving.

Below we will examine three 'what if' effects analysis examples. For each, we will ask seven standard questions, just to help you see the extent of the analysis that is possible. We will ask what the effect is on each of the factors listed on the next page.

| | | Abbreviation |
|---|---|---|
| 1 | Net profit for the current year | Net profit |
| 2 | Income tax liability at the end of the current year | Tax liability |
| 3 | Cash from operations for the current year | Op cash flow |
| 4 | Current ratio at the end of the current year | Current ratio |
| 5 | Return on equity for the current year | ROE |
| 6 | Return on assets (using EBIT) for the current year | ROA |
| 7 | Debt/equity ratio at the end of the current year | D/E ratio |

Here are the three examples (assume a 40 per cent income tax rate for all):

**1** Handee Hardware Ltd is considering borrowing a short-term loan of $1 000 000 from the bank.

**2** Eastern Mining Ltd proposes to write an unproductive mine down by $25 000 000.

**3** Gibson Ltd decides to write off goodwill over 10 years instead of over 20 years.

## Solution notes: example 1

*Net profit:* no effect on current profit (until after the borrowing, when interest begins to accumulate).

*Tax liability:* no effect on income tax (until after the borrowing, when interest incurred becomes a tax-deductible expense).

*Operating cash flow:* no effect on operating cash flows.

*Current ratio:* cash is a current asset and the bank loan is a current liability, and both are increased, so there is no effect on working capital. But to think about effects on the current ratio, consider the following possible situations:

| | Current assets | | Current liabilities | | Current ratio | |
|---|---|---|---|---|---|---|
| | **Before** | **After** | **Before** | **After** | **Before** | **After** |
| a | 6 000 000 | 7 000 000 | 3 000 000 | 4 000 000 | 2.00 | 1.75 |
| b | 6 000 000 | 7 000 000 | 5 000 000 | 6 000 000 | 1.20 | 1.17 |
| c | 6 000 000 | 7 000 000 | 7 000 000 | 8 000 000 | .86 | .88 |
| d | 6 000 000 | 7 000 000 | 9 000 000 | 10 000 000 | .67 | .70 |

You can see from these situations that such an event drives the current ratio toward 1: down toward 1 if it was higher, up toward it if lower. So, there is no effect on working capital because it is the *difference* between current assets and current liabilities, and the effects on each cancel one another out. But there is an effect on the current ratio, because it is current assets *divided* by current liabilities, and the effects on each depend on the level of the ratio before the change.

*ROE:* no effect until interest starts to accumulate and any revenues or decreased costs for which the money is used begin. Whether ROE ultimately goes up or down depends on whether the company has borrowed wisely. For example, the money may be used to pay suppliers sooner and get early-payment discounts that are greater than the interest paid to the bank for the money, in which case ROE will go up eventually.

*ROA:* in this case, total assets increases and there is no effect on profit until interest starts to accumulate. At this point ROA will decrease.

*D/E ratio:* this will go up because the company has more debt and there has been no immediate effect on equity (no effect on profit).

## Solution notes: example 2

*Net profit before tax:* the mine asset cost will be credited, accumulated depreciation will be debited, and an expense, loss on mine closure, will be debited. The full effect would be: a $25 000 000 reduction on current profit.

*Tax liability:* probably some reduction in income tax liability. The exact effect depends on resolving the tax deduction uncertainty.

*Operating cash flow:* no effect on cash or cash from operations.

*Current ratio:* no effect on working capital or on the current ratio, unless there was a reduction of current income tax liability. In such a case, working capital and the ratio would increase.

*ROE:* profit would fall, therefore so would ROE. The write-off would equally reduce profit and equity (retained profits after including the lower profit), so the ratio's fall would be reduced a little by the decline in the denominator as well as the numerator.

*ROA:* like ROE, this would fall because of the effect on profit.

*D/E ratio:* this will go up because the company has less equity.

## Solution notes: example 3

*Net profit:* profit would decrease because of the increased amount of goodwill amortisation expense.

*Tax liability:* no impact on tax as goodwill amortisation is not an allowable tax deduction in Australia.

*Operating cash flow:* no impact on cash flow from operations.

*Current ratio:* as neither current assets nor current liabilities are affected, the current ratio would not be affected.

*ROE:* both profit and equity (via retained profits) would fall by the same amount. Assuming the ratio is less than 100 per cent, the ratio would fall.

*ROA:* both profit and total assets (via accumulated amortisation) would decrease by the same amount. Assuming the ratio is less than 100 per cent, the ratio would fall.

*D/E ratio:* would increase because equity falls because of the drop in retained profits.

## How's your understanding?

Here are two questions you should be able to answer, based on what you have just read:

1 Strapped Ltd, which has $190 000 in current assets and $170 000 in current liabilities, borrows $40 000 from the bank as a long-term loan, repayable in four years. What is the effect of this loan on working capital? On the current ratio? On current net profit? (Up $40 000; up from 1.12 to 1.35; none immediately, but it should be helped, as the money is put to work and hurt as interest is paid)

2 Slipshod Ltd has discovered that it has not estimated enough warranty expenses because more customers are returning products for repair than had been expected. The company decides to recognise an additional $130 000 in noncurrent warranty liability, and therefore in corresponding expenses. The company's income tax rate is 35 per cent. What will this do to the current year's net profit? To cash from operations? To the current ratio? (Down by $130 000 × (1 – .35), or $84 500; no effect; no effect because no current assets or liabilities are involved)

## 14.8 Measuring a manager's performance

Financial statements don't measure a manager's performance without sensitive and informed interpretation, and even then, often not fully satisfactorily! For example, if a company follows standard financial accounting methods uncritically, making no attempt to adjust them to fit its own circumstances, the resulting financial statements will provide clear, but sometimes very arbitrary, measures of the performance of the company's management. On the other hand, if the company ignores standard methods entirely, designing its own accounting methods for everything, the resulting financial statements will provide a relevant but hard-to-compare measure of management performance. Most companies are in between these extremes, which means that there are some arbitrary aspects of financial statements and some difficulties in comparing them.

It is hard to determine how much a company's performance is really due to management and how much depends on other factors, such as economic trends, product price changes, union pressure and even pure luck (good or bad). Also, in most companies management is a group, so it is difficult to set one manager's performance apart from the group's. The result is that evaluating a manager's performance with financial statements requires great care and knowledge of the company and its industry.

The ratios and other computations used in financial analysis can easily compound the problem. Let's take the example of return on assets. Consider the case of two companies, A and B. Company A has assets of $100 000 and EBIT of $20 000, for a 20 per cent ROA. Looks great. But the manager is not looking into the future much, so is not keeping the company's assets or maintenance up to date.

Company B is exactly the same, except that the manager is very aware of the need to stay competitive and look after the assets, and so has spent $10 000 on new assets and $2000 (after tax) on an improved maintenance program. B's assets are, therefore, $110 000 and its EBIT is $18 000, for a 16 per cent ROA. Consequently, A looks better than B: ROA is reduced both by a smaller numerator and a larger denominator in the case of B.

You can see that, unless the person doing the financial analysis really understands the situation, the prudent and responsible manager of B will look worse than the neglectful manager of A!

Consider another example of two managers of printing companies. Both of the companies have an EBIT of $100 000. Both companies' only material asset is a printing machine which cost $1 000 000, and has a life of 10 years. Company C bought the machine two years ago (accumulated depreciation $200 000; book value $800 000) and company D bought its machine four years ago (accumulated depreciation $400 000; book value $600 000). In this simplified situation, company C would have an ROA of 12.5 per cent ($100 000 ÷ $800 000), while company D would have an ROA of 16.67 per cent ($100 000 ÷ $600 000). Again, care needs to be taken in interpreting the figures and evaluating managers' performances based on ratios.

## 14.9 Ratio analysis in the public sector

Traditional measures of assessing financial performance and financial position in the private sector are often not relevant for assessing the performance of public sector entities. In the private sector, operating performance is concerned with profitability and financial position is concerned with liquidity, solvency and asset management.

**EXHIBIT 14.4** Illustrative performance ratios

| Government departments | |
|---|---|
| **Self-sufficiency** | |
| $\frac{\text{Revenue from independent sources x 100}}{\text{Total operating expenses}}$ | Shows the reduction in budget dependency resulting from user charges and asset sales |
| **Government funding** | |
| $\frac{\text{Revenues from government x 100}}{\text{Net cost of services}}$ | Shows the extent to which the net cost of producing goods and services is funded by government |
| **Tax administration costs** | |
| $\frac{\text{Net cost of services}}{\text{Number of tax returns}}$ | Shows the net annual administration cost for each tax return |
| **Benefits administration costs** | |
| $\frac{\text{Net costs of services}}{\text{Number of benefit payments}}$ | Shows the net annual administration cost for each benefit payment (e.g. pension payments, unemployment) |
| **Average employee costs** | |
| $\frac{\text{Employee expenses}}{\text{Average number of employees}}$ | Shows the average annual employee cost (including accrued entitlements) |
| **Employee support costs** | |
| $\frac{\text{Administration expenses}}{\text{Average number of employees}}$ | Shows the annual administration cost for each employee (e.g. rent, power, depreciation of plant and equipment) |
| **Rate of change** | |
| $\frac{\text{Change in item or total x 100}}{\text{Previous year item or total}}$ | Highlights material changes in the amounts of items that may warrant further inquiry (e.g. above a particular threshold) |
| **Change in composition** | |
| Change in % item to total | Highlights material changes in the composition of revenues and expenses that may warrant further inquiry |

(Source: Department of Finance, 'The New Financial Reports of Agencies', 1994, p. 49.)

In the public sector, some of these issues are not always relevant:

- Profit is not an objective of many budget-dependent departments, whose aim is to deliver goods or services consistent with government policy. As a result, performance needs to be measured by a wider range of criteria.
- Information about financial structure is less relevant because the ongoing viability of budget-dependent bodies is determined by the government (via the will of Parliament).
- Liquidity issues become less important, because creditors know they have a claim against the government as a whole.

- Liquidity and solvency become less important from a lending perspective, because the agencies generally do not have the ability to borrow in their own right.

Given the above differences, it has become necessary for public sector entities to develop new or modified ratios. For example, evaluations of financial performance of government departments can focus on the relationship between costs, physical output and changes in efficiency. Efficiency is defined in AAS 29 as the extent to which an entity maximises the outputs produced from a given set of inputs or minimises the input cost of producing a given level and quality of outputs. Therefore it is useful to measure the input costs of program delivery (cost of services) and relate that cost to input about physical outputs (for example, number of tax returns processed, benefit payments made).

Exhibit 14.4 shows performance ratios for government departments.

For government trading enterprises, such indicators as profitability and gearing become important. As these are government businesses that sell products or services, they are evaluated on their profitability performance. For example, all NSW government businesses report return on total assets as measured by EBIT as a percentage of total revalued assets. For these organisations, return on assets is a fundamental indicator of performance and enables comparisons between industries and sectors. Other ratios calculated include: rate of return on shareholders' funds (operating profit before tax but after interest divided by total shareholders' funds). This ratio indicates: the return on public capital invested in the agency; debt/equity ratio (gross external debt as a percentage of shareholders' funds), where a lower ratio indicates a higher rate of internal funding and less vulnerability to adverse interest rate movements; and times interest earned (EBIT divided by the total interest expense), which measures the ability of the enterprise to meet its interest expenses from profits.

## For your interest

A large number of people make it their business to analyse financial statements, and many forecasts of earnings and other financial statement numbers are made by such analysts. The importance of this activity is demonstrated not only by the resources put into it, but also by the existence of professional associations of financial analysts and by the considerable prominence given to many of the analyses and forecasts by business newspapers and other media.

Here is some of the evidence about financial statement analysis produced by accounting research:

- If the financial statements have new or unexpected information (as would those of most private and/or small companies), analysis of them is valuable in order to interpret the results.
- Ratios computed from financial statements have some value in predicting company failure or other financial problems. Research indicates that, for some companies, financial problems can be predicted several years in advance using accounting ratios.
- Financial analysis is an important activity in the monitoring of lending agreements, management bonus plans and other contractual arrangements. Many such agreements involve analysis because they specify that deterioration of some ratios (such as debt/equity) will trigger penalties or even the termination of the agreement, or because ratios are used in computing bonuses or other payments.

- Even though annual reports come out rather a long time after the fiscal year-end, there is enough reaction by stock markets to them to indicate that analysis of the reports still has something to say to market traders.
- People cannot cope with masses of disaggregated data. It takes too long and requires too much special expertise. So summarising techniques such as financial analysis play a major role in users' decision making.
- Analysts' forecasts of earnings, based partly on financial statement data, do help to predict companies' future earnings performance. The analysts often can anticipate significant changes in earnings because they are following companies closely, so market prices regularly change before the new financial statements are released.
- Risk and return are generally related. Investments with a higher potential return often are riskier, and those with a low risk usually have a low potential return. Different investors have different risk preferences: some prefer to hold risky shares that may generate high returns (or large losses!); others prefer more secure investments. Financial statement analysis helps to assess risk, and thus helps investors choose the shares that seem appropriate for their risk preferences.
- Financial statement analysis is useful to corroborate what people already believe about a company's performance, position or risk. Even if such analysis turns up little that is 'new', it acts as a check on the other flows of information about companies, because the validity of that information can be verified later when the financial statements come out. Also, sometimes financial statement analysis does turn up new information, allowing people to fine tune their expectations about future performance.

## 14.10 Homework and discussion to develop understanding

### Discussion questions

1 What is the purpose of financial statement analysis?

2 What is a common size statement? When is its use most appropriate?

3 What information should you gather about a company before you start calculating ratios?

4 What ratios would you calculate to evaluate a company's profitability?

5 What ratios would you calculate to evaluate a company's turnover?

6 What ratios would you calculate to evaluate a company's liquidity?

7 What ratios would you calculate to evaluate a company's financial situation?

8 Explain the Du Pont system of ratio analysis.

9 Outline some of the main limitations of ratio analysis.

10 List the advantages and disadvantages you see in using ratio analysis of financial statements as a way of evaluating management's performance. For the disadvantages, try to think of a way around each problem you identify.

11 Use non-technical language to answer the following:

   a What is financial leverage?

   b Why is such leverage risky?

   c How does the Du Pont formula incorporate leverage?

**12** In this chapter you have seen several types of ratios used to analyse financial statements and information.

- **a** Select two types of ratios and describe what information is conveyed by each.
- **b** Calculate ratios of these types for any company you are interested in.

**13** Write the rough notes for a speech you have been asked to give to a local investment club. The members of the club are all experienced share investors and want a better understanding of companies' accounting information. The topic of your speech is 'Analysis and use of financial accounting information'.

**14** A senior member of a large public company's management complained: 'Accountants' financial analyses don't seem very useful to me. The analyses don't reveal the business management factors that are important to my company's success. They are biased toward the past rather than the future. And, anyway, the share market is way ahead of the accountants in judging the company's performance'. Comment on the manager's complaint.

**15** Why is it true that changing financial accounting accruals does not affect cash flow (ignoring any tax effect)?

**16** Why does changing depreciation method (that is, changing the depreciation numbers in the financial statements) change the debt/equity ratio?

**17** A company is considering creating a new account, a liability for warranty repairs, by estimating the costs of warranty repairs not yet done for customers but likely to be necessary. Would such an accounting method affect the return on assets? Why?

**18** Briefly explain the differences in profit margin, asset turnover, accounts receivable turnover, inventory turnover and any other important differences between a retailer of fast moving consumer goods (for example, a food retailer); a manufacturer of consumer durables (for example, whitegoods or electrical goods) and a manufacturer or distributor of tobacco products.

**19** Prepare a speech for a meeting of local business people, all of whom are active managers and investors, on the following topic: 'Methods and value of financial statement analysis in the age of computer spreadsheets and efficient capital markets'. There will be a question period after you talk, so include a few notes on any awkward issues you may decide not to deal with directly in your talk.

**20** Explain how the following are possible:

- **a** Kylie Limited has a high current ratio, but has difficulty paying its bills.
- **b** Jason Limited has a high quick ratio, but has difficulty paying its bills.
- **c** Craig Limited has a low quick ratio, but no difficulty paying its bills.

## Problem 14.1* Integrating ratios

TMC Ltd, a large producer of telecommunications equipment, retails its products through suburban outlets. Shown below are the calculations of some of its key ratios for 2002 and 2001.

| | **2002** | **2001** |
|---|---|---|
| Return on shareholders' equity | 13% | 12% |
| Return on total assets (ROA) | 8% | 9% |
| Profit margin | 20% | 18% |

| | 2002 | 2001 |
|---|---|---|
| Asset turnover | .40 | .50 |
| Days in inventory | 72 days | 55 days |
| Days in debtors | 42 days | 42 days |
| Current ratio | 1.6:1 | 1.5:1 |
| Quick ratio | 0.7:1 | 1.1:1 |
| Debt to equity ratio | 1.4:1 | 1.0:1 |

Let's consider how the ratios are linked.

*Required:*

1 Comment on TMC's profitability, asset management, liquidity and financial structure.
2 Why could ROE and ROA move in different directions?
3 What caused the fall in ROA?
4 What caused the fall in asset turnover?
5 What caused the increase in the current ratio?

## Problem 14.2* Ratios to measure different kinds of performance

1 Many financial performance measures are ratios of some return over some investment base. Why is such a concept of performance important in business?
2 With your answer to question **1** in mind, how might you measure the performance of each of the following investments owned by Ann Mandel:
   a her $1200 in a savings account at Solid Bank?
   b her investment of $15 000 in a little consulting business she runs?
   c her Slapdash 210 sports car?

## Problem 14.3* Change effects analysis, with ratios

Suppose that on 31 December, the last day of its fiscal year, a large company borrowed $150 000 000 cash, to be paid back in six years. The money was used on the same day to reduce the company's short-term bank loans by $50 000 000 and buy additional equipment for $100 000 000.

1 Calculate the changes to the following that would result from the above:
   a total current assets
   b total assets
   c total current liabilities
   d current ratio
   e total shareholders' equity
   f net profit for the year ended on the day of the borrowing
   g cash and cash equivalents
   h cash used for investments
   i cash provided from financing
   j leverage ratio.
2 How could you predict the effect on return on equity for the period after the loan?

## Problem 14.4* Answer questions using ratio analysis

Company A is 100 per cent owned by Mr A. A summary of Company A's financial statement information is as follows:

| **Statement of financial position as at 30 September 2002** | **$** |
|---|---|
| Total assets | 80 000 |
| Total liabilities | 35 000 |
| Total shareholder's equity | 45 000 |
| Total liabilities and shareholder's equity | 80 000 |

| **Statement of financial performance for the year ended 30 September 2002** | **$** | **$** |
|---|---|---|
| Revenue | | 30 000 |
| Expenses | | |
| Interest | 2 000 | |
| General and operating expenses | 19 000 | |
| Income tax ($33\frac{1}{3}$%) | 3 000 | 24 000 |
| Net profit for the year | | 6 000 |

| **Note showing changes in retained profits for the year ended 30 September 2002** | **$** |
|---|---|
| Balance at beginning of the year | 17 000 |
| Net profit for the year | 6 000 |
| Balance at end of year | 23 000 |

***Required:***

1 Calculate Company A's return on equity for 2002.

2 Company A is considering borrowing $50 000 for additional assets that would earn the company the same return on assets it has historically earned, according to the financial statement information above. The cost of borrowing this money is 8 per cent. Should the company borrow the money? (Assume there are no alternative sources of funding.) Show all calculations.

3 Place yourself in the role of the local bank manager. Mr A has approached you to lend the company the required $50 000 mentioned above. Detailed financial statement information has already been presented to you.

What additional information would you require, if any? What financial statement ratios, in addition to those calculated in previous parts of this problem, would be useful in aiding your decision? Do not calculate the ratios, just mention or describe them.

## Problem 14.5 Calculation and interpretation of ratios

**White Star Limited**
**Statements of financial position**
as at 30 June

| | **2002 $m** | **2001 $m** |
|---|---|---|
| **Current assets** | | |
| Cash | 50 | 330 |
| Receivables | 540 | 310 |
| Inventories | 450 | 260 |
| Total current assets | 1 040 | 900 |

| | 2002 $m | 2001 $m |
|---|---|---|
| **Noncurrent assets** | | |
| Property, plant and equipment | 160 | 140 |
| Total noncurrent assets | 160 | 140 |
| Total assets | 1 200 | 1 040 |
| **Current liabilities** | | |
| Creditors and borrowings | 630 | 510 |
| Provisions | 15 | 10 |
| Total current liabilities | 645 | 520 |
| **Noncurrent liabilities** | | |
| Creditors and borrowings | 245 | 195 |
| Provisions | 10 | 15 |
| Total noncurrent liabilities | 255 | 210 |
| Total liabilities | 900 | 730 |
| **Net assets** | 300 | 310 |
| **Shareholders' equity** | | |
| Share capital ($1 ordinary shares) | 80 | 80 |
| Reserves | 35 | 35 |
| Retained profits | 185 | 195 |
| Total shareholders' equity | 300 | 310 |

***Additional information:***

Net operating profit after tax is $25 million (2000: $38 million).

***Required:***

1 Use the information above to calculate for 2002 and 2001:
   - a working capital
   - b current ratio
   - c quick ratio
   - d debt/equity ratio
   - e return on equity ratio
   - f earnings per share ratio.

2 Identify two warning signals that could have negative implications with respect to the company's ability to generate cash flows to meet its future needs. In each case, explain why the signal you have identified could reflect a cash flow problem.

3 At the Annual General Meeting of White Star, the Managing Director Ms Rose Dawson made the following statement: 'Recently a number of articles in the financial press have questioned the financial position of our company. This criticism is totally unjustified. Net profit was $25 million and total assets have increased by $160 million. These results show that 2002 was a very successful year for White Star.'

## Problem 14.6 Calculation and interpretation of ratios

Comparative financial statements for Celebration Limited are given below.

**Celebration Limited**
**Statements of financial position**
as at 30 June

| | 2002 $000s | 2001 $000s |
|---|---|---|
| **Current assets** | | |
| Cash | 41 | 43 |
| Receivables | 79 | 74 |
| Inventories | 210 | 203 |
| Other | 4 | 5 |
| Total current assets | 334 | 325 |
| **Noncurrent assets** | | |
| Property, plant and equipment | 160 | 141 |
| Total assets | 494 | 466 |
| **Current liabilities** | | |
| Creditors and borrowings | 77 | 64 |
| Provisions | 40 | 30 |
| Total current liabilities | 117 | 94 |
| **Noncurrent liabilities** | | |
| Loan | 140 | 140 |
| Total liabilities | 257 | 234 |
| **Net assets** | 237 | 232 |
| **Shareholders' equity** | | |
| Share capital ($1 shares) | 90 | 90 |
| Reserves | 115 | 115 |
| Retained profits | 32 | 27 |
| Total shareholders' equity | 237 | 232 |

**Celebration Limited**
**Profit and loss statements**
for the year ending 30 June

| | 2002 $000s | 2001 $000s |
|---|---|---|
| Sales | 790 | 773 |
| Less: Cost of goods sold | 494 | 456 |
| Gross profit | 296 | 317 |
| Less: Administrative and selling expenses | 220 | 241 |
| Less: Interest expense | 15 | 14 |
| Operating profit before income tax | 61 | 62 |
| Income tax expense | 30 | 32 |
| Operating profit after income tax | 31 | 30 |

During the year ended 30 June 2002, Celebration Limited declared and paid dividends of $26 000. On 30 June 2002, the market price per ordinary share was $2.70.

*Required:*

1. Assume you are a banker evaluating a request for a short-term loan from Celebration Limited. The company would like to borrow on 1 July 2002 and repay on 31 December 2002. Name and calculate three 2002 ratios that you would use to determine the likelihood that the company will be able to make the loan repayment when it falls due.
2. Assume you are a potential investor evaluating a share purchase in Celebration Limited. You are looking for an investment that will provide a steady stream of dividend income over the years. Name and calculate three 2002 ratios that you would use to make your decision about whether to buy shares in Celebration Limited.
3. List and briefly explain three disadvantages of basing your decisions solely on ratio analysis.
4. List other tools that analysts and other users of financial statements might use to overcome the limitations associated with the use of ratios alone.

## Problem 14.7 Calculation and interpretation of ratios

Maggie Wong is considering an investment in one of two fast-food chains, Quik Burger and Big Steak, whose financial statements follow:

**Statements of financial position**

| | Quik Burger $000 | Big Steak $000 |
|---|---|---|
| **Assets** | | |
| Cash | 2 000 | 4 500 |
| Accounts receivable (net) | 2 000 | 6 500 |
| Inventory | 2 000 | 5 000 |
| Property, plant and equipment | 20 000 | 35 000 |
| Other assets | 4 000 | 5 000 |
| Total assets | 30 000 | 56 000 |
| **Liabilities** | | |
| Accounts payable | 4 000 | 7 000 |
| Loan payable | 10 000 | 30 000 |
| Total liabilities | 14 000 | 37 000 |
| **Net assets** | 16 000 | 19 000 |
| **Shareholders' equity** | | |
| Share capital | 1 000 | 3 000 |
| Reserves | 9 000 | 9 000 |
| Retained profits | 6 000 | 7 000 |
| Total shareholders' equity | 16 000 | 19 000 |

**Profit and loss statements**
(in $ thousands, except per share amounts)

| | Quik Burger | Big Steak |
|---|---|---|
| Sales | 53 000 | 86 000 |
| Less: Cost of goods sold | (37 000) | (61 000) |
| Gross profit | 16 000 | 25 000 |
| Less: Operating expenses | (11 000) | (15 000) |
| Less: Interest expense | (1 400) | (3 200) |
| Less: Income tax expense | (1 800) | (3 400) |
| Net profit | 1 800 | 3 400 |
| Earnings per share | 1.80 | 1.13 |

From the Statement of cash flows, cash from operations was $2 200 000 for Quik Burger and $3 000 000 for Big Steak. Dividends of $500 000 were paid for Quik Burger and $600 000 for Big Steak. The market price of shares for Quik Burger and Big Steak were $30 and $20 respectively. Financial information relating to prior years is not readily available to Maggie Wong.

1 Conduct a comprehensive financial analysis of Quik Burger and Big Steak and compare the results. You should include the following in your analysis:
   a performance
   b activity
   c liquidity
   d financial structure.
2 What other information should Maggie consider before making an investment decision?

## Problem 14.8 Impact of transactions on ratios

Analyse the effect of each of the following transactions on the current ratio, quick ratio, debt/equity ratio and earnings per share. Assume that the current ratio, quick ratio and debt/equity ratio are each greater than 1, and that earnings per share is positive. Determine if the ratio increases, decreases or is unchanged. Consider each transaction independently of all the other transactions.

1 Purchased inventory of $48 000 on credit.
2 Made repayments of $78 000 on the long-term loan.
3 Declared, but did not pay, a $31 000 cash dividend on shares.
4 Borrowed an additional $56 000 on the long-term loan.
5 Sold the short-term investments for $34 000.
6 Issued 140 000 shares at the beginning of the financial period for cash of $168 000.
7 Received $6000 owing in cash from a customer.
8 Repaid short-term loans payable of $51 000.

## Problem 14.9 Impact of transactions on ratios

Winslet Limited is consistently profitable. Winslet's normal financial statement relationships are as follows:

| | |
|---|---|
| Current ratio | 3:1 |
| Inventory turnover | 4 times |
| Debt/assets ratio | 0.5:1 |

*Additional information:*

- **a** Winslet declared, but did not pay, a cash dividend.
- **b** Customers returned invoiced goods for which they had not paid.
- **c** Accounts payable were paid on the last day of the financial year.
- **d** Winslet decided to revalue land it had purchased many years previously.
- **e** Early in the financial year, Winslet increased the selling price of one of its products that had a demand in excess of capacity. The number of units sold last year and this year was identical.

For each of the above transactions or events, determine the effect on each of the ratios in the table above (increase, decrease, no effect).

## Problem 14.10 Effect of transactions on ROA and ROE

State whether the following transactions would affect ROA (using EBIT), ROE, both or neither:

- **a** asset revaluation upwards
- **b** increase in interest expense
- **c** increase in depreciation expenses
- **d** purchase new equipment for cash (ignore depreciation effects)
- **e** issue bonus shares
- **f** issue ordinary shares to pay off a loan
- **g** increase the provision for long service leave
- **h** purchase equipment on credit (ignore depreciation).

## Problem 14.11 Effects analysis of disposal of investments

The following extract appeared in the *Sydney Morning Herald* on 20 March 1997.

Qantas Airways has quit its shareholding in rival Air New Zealand for about $363 million, removing the last hurdle to the looming all-out battle between the two carriers.

The Australian airline's directors yesterday voted to sell the 19.4 per cent stake at a board meeting in Canberra.

Qantas chief executive Mr James Strong said the board accepted an 'unsolicited offer' from stockbroking firm ANZ Securities to buy its 112 million Air New Zealand B class shares for $NZ3.80 ($3.36) a share. The broker sold to a number of institutions worldwide.

Qantas' capital gain from the eight-year investment was about $99 million before tax, Mr Strong said.

'We regard it as a very satisfactory outcome,' he said.

'The proceeds of the sale will decrease net debt, reducing gearing.'

Stockbroking analysts reacted positively to the news, saying the sale would reduce Qantas's gearing ratio of net debt/equity to just over 100 per cent by the end of the year. It was about 200 per cent in 1995.

Qantas may even receive an upgraded credit rating because of its improved gearing.

This will further impress the market after Qantas reduced costs by $468 million in the 1996 financial year and cut an additional $237 million in the first half of 1997.

By Michael Sharp

*Required:*

1. Explain the effect on the sale of the shareholding on gearing.
2. Why was it considered good news by share analysts?
3. Would every sale of investments be considered good news?
4. Why might the credit rating improve?
5. How would a better credit rating assist Qantas?

## Problem 14.12 Effects analysis of truck fleet purchase and financing

Suppose that on 1 May 2002 Large Corporation decides to purchase a new fleet of delivery trucks at a total cost of $5 800 000. The trucks will be paid for in cash, which Large Corporation will raise by using $2 200 000 cash on hand, issuing shares for $2 000 000 and borrowing $1 600 000 over 20 years from the bank.

1 Using the preceding information, fill in the blanks below, indicating the magnitude and direction of the change in each category the truck purchase will cause.

**Large Corporation**
**Changes in statement of financial position**
**at 1 May 2002**

| | $ | | $ |
|---|---|---|---|
| Cash equivalent assets | ______ | Cash equivalent liabilities | ______ |
| Other current assets | ______ | Other current liabilities | ______ |
| Noncurrent assets | ______ | Noncurrent liabilities | ______ |
| | ______ | Share capital | ______ |
| | ______ | Retained profits | ______ |
| **Total assets** | ______ | **Total liabilities & shareholders' equity** | ______ |

2 What effect (if any) will this event have on the financing activities section of the cash flow statement for the year?

3 What effect (if any) will this event have on the statement of financial performance for the year?

4 Which important financial statement ratios would you expect this event to affect?

5 Record the above event as a journal entry.

## Problem 14.13 Calculate and explain return on equity and effect of debt

A neighbour of yours finds out that you are taking business courses and engages you in a conversation to get some cheap investment advice. As it turns out, she was raised during the Depression and is very averse to debt. She believes that solid companies should be debt free and raise all their capital by issuing shares or by retaining profits. You have handy a set of financial statements for a company she knows, which you use to discuss the matter with her.

Use the financial information below, extracted from the financial statements, to calculate the company's return on equity. Explain to your neighbour the effect debt has on the company's return on equity, and, specifically, whether this return is helped or hindered by the debt.

| | |
|---|---|
| Total assets | $251 600 |
| Total liabilities | 98 980 |
| Interest-bearing long-term debt | 42 580 |
| Share capital | 87 150 |
| Income tax rate | 43% |
| Retained profits | $ 65 470 |
| Total revenues | 313 450 |
| Interest expense | 5 070 |
| Profit before tax and extraordinary item | 36 100 |
| Net profit | 28 060 |

## Problem 14.14 Examine components of return on assets ratio

Information taken from the recent annual reports of two retail companies appears below (amounts in millions). One of these companies is a discount chain store and the other is a specialty retailer of fashion clothes. Which company is likely to be the discount chain store? Briefly explain.

| | Company X $m | Company Y $m |
|---|---|---|
| Sales | 4 069 | 4 130 |
| Interest expense | 42 | 18 |
| Net profit before tax | 245 | 168 |
| Total assets | 2 061 | 1 149 |

## Problem 14.15 Calculate ratios and comment on performance

JRP Pty Ltd is a mail-order business selling a variety of consumer products. At the end of 2001, its major shareholder instigated changes in management in order to improve performance. The financial statements for the years ending 30 June 2001 and 2002 are shown below.

***Required:***

1. Calculate the following ratios:
   a. return on assets (using EBIT)
   b. asset turnover
   c. profit margin
   d. return on shareholders' equity
   e. current
   f. quick asset
   g. inventory turnover
   h. days in inventory
   i. debtor's turnover
   j. days in debtors
   k. debt/equity
   l. interest coverage.
2. Comment on the company's performance, indicating any changes you would suggest.

**Statement of financial position as at 30 June**

| | 2002 $000 | 2001 $000 |
|---|---|---|
| **Current assets** | | |
| Inventory | 2 400 | 750 |
| Accounts receivable | 1 650 | 1 500 |
| **Total current assets** | 4 050 | 2 250 |
| **Noncurrent assets (at net book value)** | | |
| Land and buildings | 3 750 | 3 015 |
| Machinery | 1 200 | 1 010 |
| **Total assets** | 9 000 | 6 275 |

| | 2002<br>$000 | 2001<br>$000 |
|---|---|---|
| **Current liabilities** | | |
| Bank overdraft | 800 | 275 |
| Accounts payable | 1 700 | 600 |
| Provision for employee entitlements | 200 | 250 |
| **Total current liabilities** | 2 700 | 1 125 |
| **Noncurrent liabilities** | | |
| Bonds | 3 950 | 2 000 |
| **Shareholders' equity** | | |
| Share capital | 1 000 | 1 000 |
| Retained profits | 1 350 | 2 150 |
| **Total shareholders' equity** | 2 350 | 3 150 |
| **Total shareholders' equity and liabilities** | 9 000 | 6 275 |

**Statement of financial performance**
**for the year ending 30 June**

| | 2002<br>$000 | 2001<br>$000 |
|---|---|---|
| **Sales** | 9 000 | 8 125 |
| *Less* Cost of goods sold | 6 300 | 5 687 |
| **Gross profit** | 2 700 | 2 438 |
| *Less* Expenses: | | |
| Selling and administration | 1 260 | 1 382 |
| Interest charges | 400 | 256 |
| Profits before tax | 1 040 | 800 |
| *Less* Tax | 140 | 150 |
| **Net profit after tax** | 900 | 650 |

## Problem 14.16 Explain reasons for changes in ratios

The following is a summary of the information in the financial statements of ABC Ltd for the years 2001 and 2002.

| | 2002<br>$000s | 2001<br>$000s |
|---|---|---|
| Current assets | 50 | 100 |
| Noncurrent assets | 350 | 200 |
| Total assets | 400 | 300 |
| Current liabilities | 50 | 50 |
| Noncurrent liabilities | 210 | 150 |
| Shareholders' equity | 140 | 100 |
| | 400 | 300 |
| Sales | 800 | 750 |
| Expenses | 752 | 720 |
| Net profit (before interest and tax) | 48 | 30 |

| | 2002 $000s | 2001 $000s |
|---|---|---|
| Interest | 13 | 10 |
| | 35 | 20 |
| Tax payable | 14 | 8 |
| Net profit after tax | 21 | 12 |

The manager of ABC Ltd has given the following information relating to the firm:

| | 2002 % | 2001 % |
|---|---|---|
| Return on assets (using EBIT) | 12 | 10 |
| Current ratio | 100 | 200 |
| Quick asset ratio | 100 | 100 |
| Debt/assets ratio | 65 | 66.7 |
| During 2002 land which cost $50 000 was revalued to $90 000 | | |

***Required:***

1 Suggest possible reasons for the change in ROA.
2 Comment upon the changes in liquidity during the period.
3 What changes have taken place in the firm's long-term financial position during the period?
4 Why does a great deal of care need to be taken in the use and interpretation of financial ratios?

## Problem 14.17 Effect of transactions on ratios

Fad Foods Pty Ltd completed a series of transactions listed below. Before the transactions, both the current and quick asset ratios are greater than one. The cash account has a debit balance.

Indicate the effect of each of the transactions listed below on the ratio listed opposite it. For each transaction, state whether the ratio would increase, decrease or have no effect. Treat each transaction independently.

| Transaction | Ratio |
|---|---|
| 1 Redeemed debentures by issuing ordinary shares | Rate of return on ordinary shareholders' equity |
| 2 Purchased inventory on credit | Quick ratio |
| 3 Sold inventory for cash with a 40% mark-up on cost | Current ratio |
| 4 Issued additional ordinary shares for cash | Debt/equity ratio |
| 5 Collected an account receivable balance | Debtors turnover |
| 6 Paid accounts payable | Rate of return on total assets |
| 7 Paid accounts payable | Profit margin |

## Problem 14.18 Effect of transactions on ratios

Indicate the effects (increase, decrease, no effect) of each of the following independent transactions on **(1)** the rate of return on shareholders' equity, **(2)** the current ratio, and **(3)** the debt/equity ratio. State any necessary assumptions.

**a** Inventory costing $410 000 is purchased on account.
**b** Inventory costing $240 000 is sold on account for $300 000.
**c** Collections from customers on accounts receivable total $100 000.

- **d** Payments to suppliers on accounts payable total $160 000.
- **e** A machine costing $80 000, on which $60 000 of depreciation had been charged, is sold for $20 000.
- **f** Dividends of $80 000 are declared. The dividends will be paid during the next accounting period.
- **g** Ordinary shares are issued for $175 000.
- **h** A machine costing $60 000 is acquired. Cash of $10 000 is given, and a note for $50 000 payable five years from now is signed for the balance of purchase price.

## Problem 14.19 Use statement analysis to evaluate general manager's claims

The general manager of a medium-sized manufacturing company wants to renew the company's operating loan. In discussions with the bank's lending officer, the general manager says, 'As the accompanying financial statements show, our working capital position has improved during the past year, and we have managed to reduce operating expenses significantly.'

The partial financial statements are shown below.

***Required:***

1. Evaluate the general manager's comments. Incorporate appropriate ratio analysis in your discussion.
2. What additional financial information (if any) would you request of the general manager? Why?

**Titan Manufacturing Pty Ltd**
**Partial statement of financial position**
**as at 31 December 2002 and 2001**

| | 2002<br>$ | 2001<br>$ |
|---|---|---|
| **Current assets** | | |
| Cash | 50 000 | 200 000 |
| Accounts receivable | 250 000 | 100 000 |
| Inventories | 500 000 | 400 000 |
| **Total current assets** | 800 000 | 700 000 |
| **Current liabilities** | | |
| Accounts payable | 250 000 | 200 000 |
| Operating loan | 100 000 | 100 000 |
| **Total current liabilities** | 350 000 | 300 000 |

**Titan Manufacturing Pty Ltd**
**Statement of financial performance**
**for the years ended 31 December 2002 and 2001**

| | 2002<br>$ | 2001<br>$ |
|---|---|---|
| Sales | 1 200 000 | 1 500 000 |
| Less cost of goods sold | 780 000 | 900 000 |
| **Gross profit** | 420 000 | 600 000 |
| Operating expenses | 350 000 | 400 000 |
| Profit before taxes | 70 000 | 200 000 |
| Income taxes | 14 000 | 40 000 |
| **Net profit** | 56 000 | 160 000 |

## Problem 14.20 Interpretation of ratios

The following ratios describe the performance of Ratio Ltd for 2001 and 2002:

**Ratio Ltd**

| | 2001 | 2002 |
|---|---|---|
| Debt to equity ratio | 1.36 | 1.86 |
| Inventory turnover | 6.7 | 8.00 |
| Quick ratio | 0.91 | 0.70 |
| Gross margin | 63.2% | 65.0% |
| Interest coverage | 2.8 | 2.00 |
| Current ratio | 1.89 | 1.29 |
| Receivables turnover | 7.3 | 7.5 |
| Days inventory on hand | 54.5 | 45.6 |
| Return on assets | 13.24 | 14.40 |
| Return on equity | 38.43 | 34.97 |

***Required:***

1 Based on the ratio values supplied, comment on the company's performance in 2002.

2 Explain:

   a Why do the return on assets and return on equity ratios differ?

   b Why calculate the return on assets ratio if you had already calculated the return on equity ratio?

3 Consider the inventory turnover ratio and the days inventory on hand ratio.

   a What information do these ratios provide?

   b From the viewpoint of management, what are the limitations relating to these ratios?

4 During 2002, the chief financial officer (CFO) of Ratio Ltd employed an independent valuer to assess the current value of the land and buildings owned by the company. The valuer had advised the CFO that the value of the land and buildings had increased by $50 000 (10 per cent). Assume that this increased value is reflected in the ratios provided earlier. What impact would this revaluation have had on each of the ratios?

## Problem 14.21 (Challenging) Use ratios to evaluate relative performance

A friend has asked you to evaluate information about two companies in the same industry. Your friend wants to invest in one or the other, but not both. Both companies are publicly traded, started with $10 000 of cash, have been in operation exactly one year, have paid the interest owing on their long-term debts to date, and have declared dividends of $1 per share.

The beginning statements of financial position for the two companies at 1 January 2002 were as follows:

| **Alpha Company** | **$** | **Omega Company** | **$** |
|---|---|---|---|
| Total assets | 10 000 | Total assets | 10 000 |
| Long-term debt | 1 000 | Long-term debt | 9 000 |
| Shareholders' equity | | Shareholders' equity | |
| (900 ordinary shares issued) | 9 000 | (100 ordinary shares issued) | 1 000 |
| Total assets | 10 000 | Total assets | 10 000 |
| Net profit for 2002 | 2 400 | Net profit for 2002 | 1 600 |

Your friend says, 'Alpha Company seems the better investment. Its return on assets is 24 per cent, and Omega's is only 16 per cent.'

Comment on your friend's observation and on the relative performance of the companies, and give your friend some investment advice.

## Problem 14.22 (Challenging) Performance evaluation using ratios

International Business Computers (IBC) has enjoyed modest success in penetrating the personal computer market since it began operations a few years ago. A new computer line introduced recently has been received well by the general public. However, the general manager, who is well versed in electronics but not in accounting, is worried about the future of the company.

The company's operating loan is at its limit and more cash is needed to continue operations. The bank wants more information before it extends the company's credit limit. The general manager has asked you, as financial controller, to do a preliminary evaluation of the company's performance, using appropriate financial statement analysis, and to recommend possible courses of action for the company. The general manager particularly wants to know how the company can obtain additional cash. Use the summary financial information shown below to do your evaluation and make your recommendations.

**International Business Computers**
**Statements of financial position**
**as at 31 December**

| | 2002 $000 | 2001 $000 | 2000 $000 |
|---|---|---|---|
| **Current assets** | | | |
| Cash | 19 | 24 | 50 |
| Marketable securities | 37 | 37 | 37 |
| Accounts receivable (trade) | 544 | 420 | 257 |
| Inventory | 833 | 503 | 361 |
| **Total current assets** | **1 433** | **984** | **705** |
| **Noncurrent assets** | | | |
| Land | 200 | 200 | 100 |
| Buildings | 350 | 350 | 200 |
| Equipment | 950 | 950 | 700 |
| | 1 500 | 1 500 | 1 000 |
| Less: Accumulated depreciation buildings and equipment | (447) | (372) | (288) |
| **Net noncurrent assets** | **1 053** | **1 128** | **712** |
| **Total assets** | **2 486** | **2 112** | **1 417** |
| **Current liabilities:** | | | |
| Bank loan | 825 | 570 | — |
| Accounts payable (trade) | 300 | 215 | 144 |
| Other liabilities | 82 | 80 | 75 |
| Income tax payable | 48 | 52 | 50 |
| **Total current liabilities** | **1 255** | **917** | **269** |
| **Shareholders' equity:** | | | |
| Share capital | 1 000 | 1 000 | 1 000 |
| Retained profits | 231 | 195 | 148 |
| **Total shareholders' equity** | **1 231** | **1 195** | **1 148** |
| **Total liabilities and shareholders' equity** | **2 486** | **2 112** | **1 417** |

**International Business Computers**
**Statement of financial performance**
**for the years ended 31 December**

| | 2002<br>$000 | 2001<br>$000 | 2000<br>$000 |
|---|---|---|---|
| Sales | 3 200 | 2 800 | 2 340 |
| Cost of goods sold | 2 500 | 2 150 | 1 800 |
| Gross profit | 700 | 650 | 540 |
| Expenses | 584 | 533 | 428 |
| Net profit | 116 | 117 | 112 |

Other related information included in total expenses:

| | 2002<br>$000 | 2001<br>$000 | 2000<br>$000 |
|---|---|---|---|
| Interest expense | 89 | 61 | — |
| Income tax expense | 95 | 102 | 97 |

International Business Computers
Note showing changes in retained profits
for the years ended 31 December

| | 2002<br>$000 | 2001<br>$000 | 2000<br>$000 |
|---|---|---|---|
| Opening retained profits | 195 | 148 | 96 |
| Add: Net profit | 116 | 117 | 112 |
| Less: Dividends | 80 | 70 | 60 |
| Closing retained profits | 231 | 195 | 148 |

## Problem 14.23 (Challenging) Inventory valuation, depreciation and ratios

Jeans F' All and Jeans 'R' Us are very similar companies in size and operation. Jeans F' All uses FIFO and the straight-line depreciation method and Jeans 'R' Us uses LIFO and diminishing value depreciation. Identify which company will report the higher number for each of the following ratios:

1 Current ratio
2 Inventory turnover
3 Profit margin
4 Return on assets

State any assumptions you need to make in answering this question.

## CASE 14A Woolworths annual report

Go to the Woolworths Limited financial statement in appendix 2.

1 What ratios are calculated for you?
2 What do we learn about Woolworths from all of the above ratios?

## CASE 14B Hooker Corporation

This case is based on Hooker Corporation. Shown below is an extract from an article by Jack Flanagan and Greg Whittred from the *Australian Accounting Review,* vol. 1, no. 3, May 1992.

### Hooker Corporation: A case for cashflow reporting?

Hooker, arguably one of Australia's premier real-estate developers, collapsed in July 1989. At November 1989 its principal banker, Westpac Banking Corporation, was owed an estimated $A200 million; the Commonwealth Bank $A90 million; PNG International $A66 million; and the State Bank of NSW, Mitsubishi Bank, Citibank, Bank of Nova Scotia, First Fidelity and First Chicago $A50 million.

It is easy to see, with hindsight, that the confidence of Hooker's bankers had been sorely misplaced. But were there any forewarnings of the impending problems?

Certainly, none would have been apparent from a traditional ratio analysis. But a careful examination of the company's cashflows would probably have

**Figure 14.2 Profitability ratios**

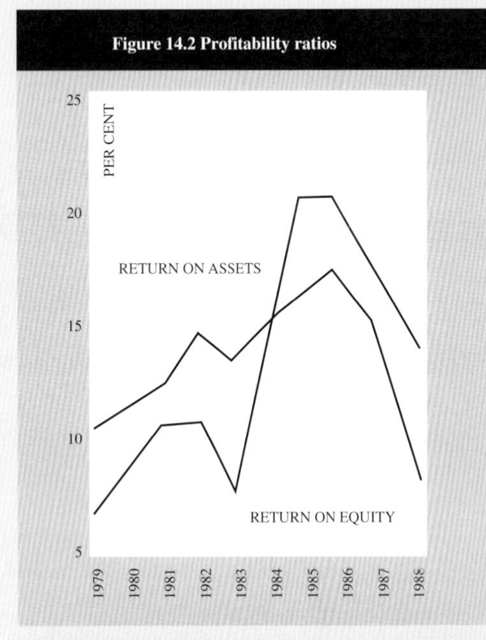


**Figure 14.3 Liquidity ratios**

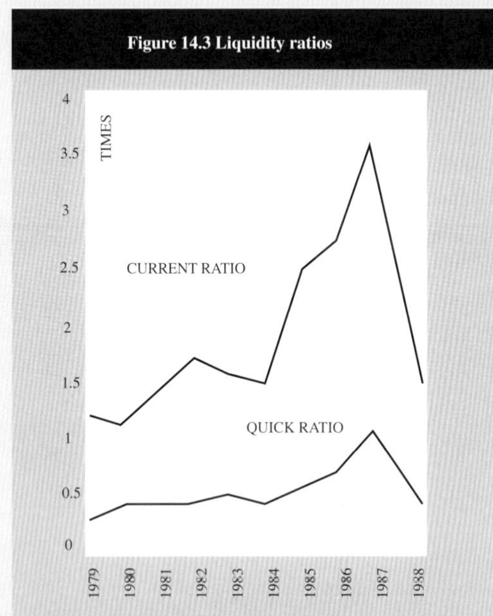


**Figure 14.4 Solvency ratios**

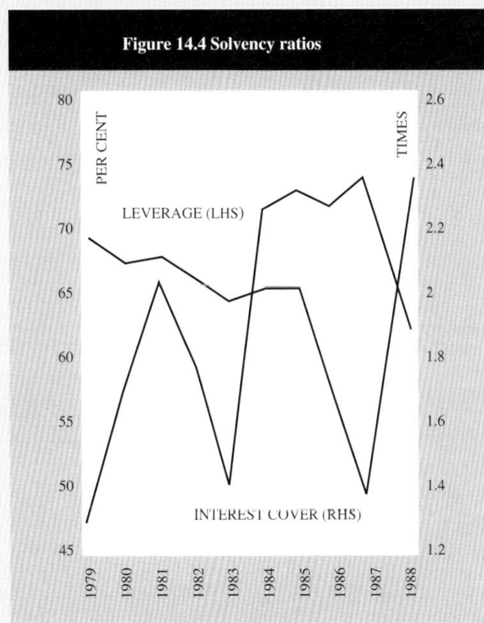


**Figure 14.5 Net profit and cash flow**

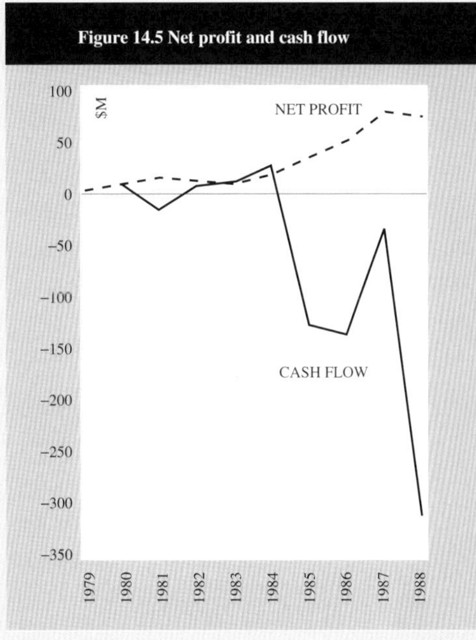

suggested that considerable caution was warranted. Indeed, the most striking characteristic of Hooker Corporation during the years before its collapse was its inability to generate cash internally—that is, from operations.

### *Conventional analysis*

Figures 14.2, 14.3 and 14.4 show Hooker's profitability, liquidity and solvency for the decade before its collapse. The figures are based on the financials, as presented, in each of the respective years.

Return on equity trends upwards for most of the decade, but falls off moderately after 1986. Return on assets shows a similar, if less volatile, pattern. The liquidity ratios are relatively stable during the early years and actually show significant improvements up to 1988, the year preceding failure. Leverage improves (i.e. decreases) slowly until the year preceding failure. The pronounced drop in 1987 is caused mainly by Hooker's controversial treatment of $141.4 million deferred profits arising on a liability assumption agreement. If these are treated as a non-current liability (as Hooker was obliged by the National Companies and Securities Commission to do in its 1988 accounts), then leverage in fact increases in both 1987 and 1988. Interest cover, while variable, always exceeds 1x.

This study was prepared from public information as a basis for classroom discussion, rather than to illustrate effective handling or otherwise of an administrative situation. It was suggested by an earlier case analysis of the WT Grant bankruptcy in the US by James A. Largay III and Clyde P. Stickney, which appeared in the *Financial Analysts Journal* (July/August 1980).

In the 1988 annual report of Hooker Corporation, the chief financial officer's review of performance contained the following: 'The confidence of major banks with regard to Hooker's strategy is reflected in the large increase in banking lines negotiated during the year, with a number of United States and Canadian banks joining the group as lenders.'

Note 1 The debt/assets ratios were 63.1 per cent (up from 49.3 per cent) and 73.6 per cent respectively. Note that the increase in 1988 occurs even after asset revaluations of approximately $100 million.

***Required:***

1. Discuss the levels and trends in return on assets, return on equity, current ratio, quick ratio, leverage (measured by debt/assets), interest cover and cash flow from operations. What is the best indicator of potential problems in this case?
2. Provide an explanation of why ROE may be more volatile than ROA.
3. What is the problem of having a quick ratio at the level indicated in figure 14.3?
4. Why would the current ratio be so high in 1986–87?
5. In a note to the article referring to leverage the authors state: 'Note that the increase in 1988 occurs even after asset revaluations of approximately $100 million.' Would this revaluation affect ROA and ROE?

## CASE 14C Harris Scarfe Holdings

The article below provides an interesting analysis of the Harris Scarfe collapse.

### The road to insolvency

*by Greg Whittred*

At the time of its collapse, Harris Scarfe Holdings was one of Australia's largest department store chains, boasting more than 150 years of continuous operation. It had 35 stores in a national network, sales of $406 million, more than 2500 employees and 10 500 individual shareholders.

When the end came it was swift. What happened to HSH – and why – are questions that, with the passage of time, will no doubt be answered. However, why the symptoms of the company's prolonged illness were not diagnosed and treated earlier is difficult to understand.

#### *Reading the entrails*

Since its reorganisation in late 1995, HSH had reported bottom-line profit growth. Figures 14.6 and

| | Financial year ending July | | | | | |
|---|---|---|---|---|---|---|
| Year | 1995 | 1996 | 1997 | 1998 | 1999 | 2000 |
| Retail sales ($000) | 255 000 | 246 000 | 236 527 | 348 110 | 373 452 | 406 586 |
| Operating profit, reported ($000) | 401 | 4 622 | 7 558 | 12 428 | 12 502 | 13 245 |
| Dept store profit, estimate 1 ($000) | –7 841 | –3 958 | 3 338 | –1 063 | –1 006 | –2 056 |
| Dept store profit, estimate 2 ($000) | –4 906 | –1 473 | 5 881 | 1 866 | 2 421 | 1 653 |
| Dept stores, year-end (no.) | 18 | 20 | 24 | 32 | 32 | 35 |
| Square metres (e) = estimate | 94 000 | 105 000 | 138 000 | (e) 178 352 | (e) 178 352 | (e) 195 506 |
| Sales per square metre ($000) | 2.71 | 2.34 | 1.71 | 1.95 | 2.09 | 2.08 |
| **Inventory** | | | | | | |
| Finished goods inventory ($000) | 39 300 | 38 640 | 54 414 | 76 128 | 91 717 | 95 395 |
| HSH inventory turnover (times) | 4.9 | 4.7 | 3.8 | 4.0 | 3.3 | 3.3 |
| Inventory (days) | 74.2 | 77.1 | 95.7 | 91.3 | 109.4 | 112.0 |
| David Jones' inventory turnover (times) | | 3.8 | 3.6 | 3.8 | 3.8 | 3.7 |
| **Receivables** | | | | | | |
| Trade debtors, as reported ($000) | 11 289 | 7 528 | 7 150 | 11 091 | 11 957 | 10 657 |
| Trade debtors, ex-securitisation ($000) | 32 289 | 29 828 | 33 750 | 39 469 | 46 204 | 46 518 |
| **Estimated securitisation costs** | | | | | | |
| Financing, average receivable 6% ($000) | 1 931 | 1 864 | 1 907 | 2 197 | 2 570 | 2 782 |
| Management fee, average receivable 2% ($000) | 644 | 621 | 636 | 732 | 857 | 927 |
| Total | 2 575 | 2 485 | 2 543 | 2 929 | 3 427 | 3 709 |
| Receivables turnover (times) | 15.4 | 21.7 | 31.3 | 38.2 | 32.4 | 36 |
| Receivables (days) | 23.6 | 16.8 | 11.6 | 9.6 | 11.3 | 10.2 |
| Receivables turn, ex sec. (times) | 7.9 | 7.9 | 7.4 | 9.5 | 8.7 | 8.8 |
| Receivables, ex sec. (days) | 46.1 | 46.1 | 49.1 | 38.4 | 41.9 | 41.6 |
| Operating lease rentals ($000) | 11 876 | 13 024 | 15 334 | 20 708 | 22 531 | 25 119 |
| Retail/sales (%) | 4.7% | 5.3% | 6.5% | 5.9% | 6.0% | 6.2% |

**Figure 14.6** Harris Scarfe Holdings financial statements

14.7 show that reported profit grew from $4.6 million to $13.2 million. However, a closer look at the accounts reveals that the growth is attributable to a profitable receivables securitisation operation rather than its department store operations *per se*. Included in total revenues are miscellaneous non-retail revenues, including the results of the 'securitisation' operation.

Unfortunately, existing accounting requirements do not require the disclosure of operating costs by line of business. This makes it difficult, but not impossible, to estimate the relative contribution of each to overall profitability. When you remove non-retail revenues (interest, dividends, trust distributions and sundry), net of the estimated costs of generating these revenues[1] , along with any gain/loss on asset disposals, it is possible to draw the inference that in only one of the last six years has the department store operation been other than marginally profitable. And this was despite continuing sales growth, both in total and on a like-for-like basis, up until 2000.

There are many things that must be done well to run a successful discount department store – but among the most critical are efficient management of

### 3 October 2000, chairman 's address

'I believe we can look back with pride on the service and dedication of our employees, and the loyalty of our customers. Your board believes we can face the future with confidence, building upon the strong foundations for growth which have been created.'
– Adam Trescowthick, HSH executive chairman.

### 16 March 2001, HSH half yearly report

The company posted an interim profit of $5.03 million, down from $9.2 million a year earlier, on sales of $204.2 million. These sales were down from $219.9 million for the corresponding period a year earlier. The interim dividend was axed.

### 27 March 2001

HSH chief operating officer, Dan McLaughlin, resigns.

### 30 March 2001

Directors request the suspension of trading in HSH's shares.

### 3 April 2001

HSH appoints KPMG as voluntary administrator and calls for an investigation into accounting irregularities. Within a day shareholders are reported to be considering a class action, and by the end of a tumultuous week the company's principal creditor, ANZ banking group (with a total exposure of around $67 million), appoints Ferrier Hodgson as receiver and manager.

**Figure 14.7** Fast-track demise

space, inventories, receivables and margins. In the case of discounters, the last translates into tight control of costs.

### Use of space

HSH's growth on a store-for-store basis was impressive in a tough retail market. Though much less impressive was the declining yield per square metre (psm) devoted to retail. In his 1999 report, the chairman observed that HSH had acquired or opened 15 new stores in an 18-month period. Figure 14.6 shows that as the network expanded from 18 to 35 stores, sales declined from $2710 to $2110 psm, (or 23 per cent). In contrast, Wal-Mart, which is arguably the world's leading discount department store, achieved sales of around $US3333 psm.

Even in the upmarket retail sector, the David Jones department store business averages around $4200 psm. Coles Myer, which sits in between the discount and upmarket sectors, averages between $3000 psm (Apparel and Home) and $4000 psm (Myer Grace Bros). The comparisons are noteworthy, since players at the discount end of the market require higher (not lower) turnover to compensate for the lower margins.

HSH's aggressive growth strategy also should have raised concerns. Not only did HSH expand into two States where it had never before operated, it did so with stores significantly larger than its existing ones. At the end of financial 1997, the average net retail space in HSH's 24 stores was 5750 square metres. Yet, three of the five stores it acquired from David Jones in 1998 were two to three times larger than this.[2]

### Inventories

Any analysis of this aspect of HSH performance is complicated by the suggestion of significant accounting irregularities, related in part to the company's inventories.[3] The irregularities are reported to have resulted in a cumulative overstatement of profits of $125 million – an amount far in excess of the cumulative reported profits for the last six years. But this is after the fact. What inferences might have been drawn before the fact?

Getting a feel for HSH's retail efficiency (or inventory turnover) is problematic in the absence of disclosure of its cost of goods sold (COGS) – although given the recently proposed changes in accounting standards, this situation will soon be remedied. At a macro-level, it is evident that while HSH sales grew by 65 per cent between 1996 and 2000, its inventories grew by 146 per cent in the same period. For each dollar of sales in 1996, HSH held $0.16 of stocks at year-end. In 2000 the value of stock held had risen to $0.23 (Wal-Mart held $0.17 of stock for each dollar of sales at this time, and David Jones held $0.19).

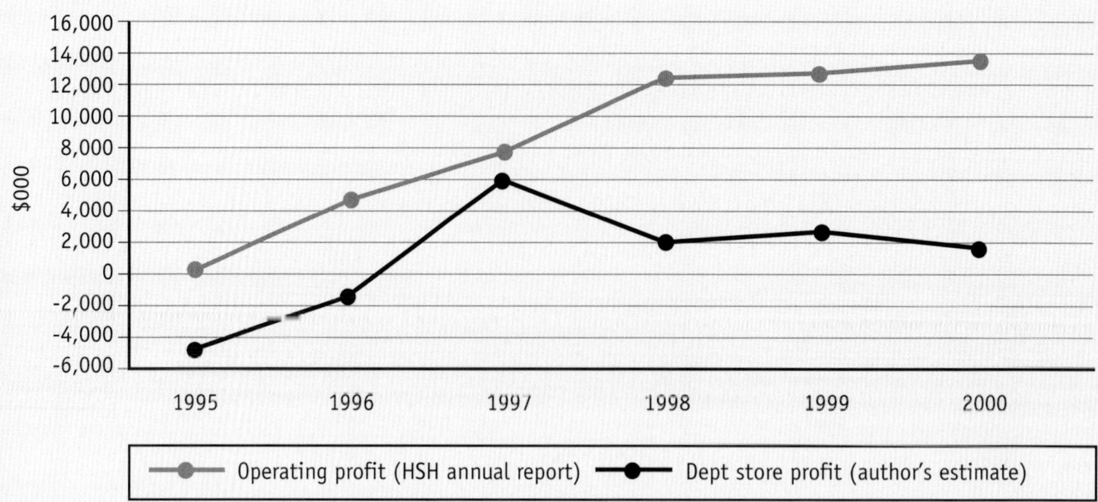


**Figure 14.8** HSH profits

Another approach is to assume HSH's ratio of COGS:Sales is equal to world best practice. For at least the last decade Wal-Mart has operated at a gross margin of around 25 per cent – with COGS sitting consistently at around 75 per cent of retail sales. On this basis, HSH's inventory turnover (COGS:Average Inventory) is as reported in figure 14.6. Turnover declined by about one-third – from 4.9 times in 1996 to 3.3 times in 2000, with the number of days in inventory increasing from 74 to 112. Different (higher) estimates of the ratio of COGS:Sales do not change the underlying downward spiral. By 2000 HSH's inventory turnover was less than half that of Wal-Mart (3.3 versus 7.3). In recent years it has been even lower than the inventory turnover of David Jones, which sits at the top end of the department store market (see figure 14.9).[4]

In short, while the 'true' inventory position of HSH may not have been clear, even the reported numbers ought to have raised questions regarding the company's operating performance.

### *Receivables*

On the basis of the reported figures, HSH's receivables turnover increased from around 15 to 36 times, with a reduction in the number of days in receivables from 23 to 10. This performance is due entirely to the fact that from 1993 HSH had securitised increasing proportions of its credit card receivables portfolio – a practice that both frees up capital and typically generates a revenue stream for the department store operation (as discussed above).

The notes to the accounts explain that these receivables were sold into a securitisation trust (in which the company retained a 10 per cent interest). The department store subsidiaries had the right of first refusal to repurchase any doubtful debts offered for sale by the trust and, as a matter of practice, had always exercised that right.

This practice means that the receivables have been effectively, though not technically, sold on a 'with recourse' basis. Over the period of interest, the year-end balance of receivables in the trust grew from $26 to $43 million.

An alternate picture of how well the receivables were being managed is to re-calculate the figures as if their sale had not taken place. On this basis, receivables turnover runs at between 7.4 and 9.5 times; with days in receivables sitting between 38 and 49 (see figures 14.6 and 14.10).

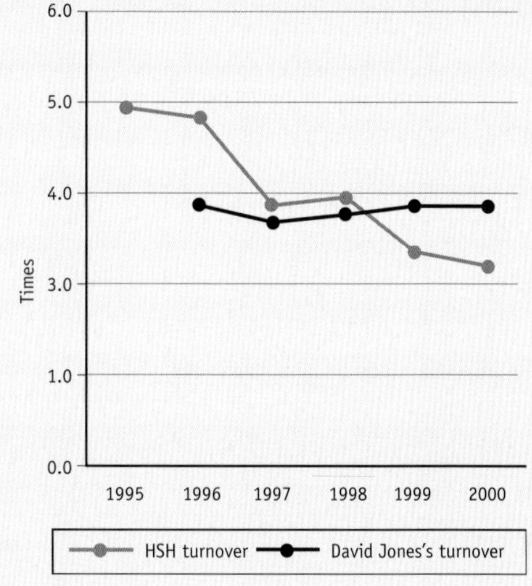


**Figure 14.9** Inventory turnover

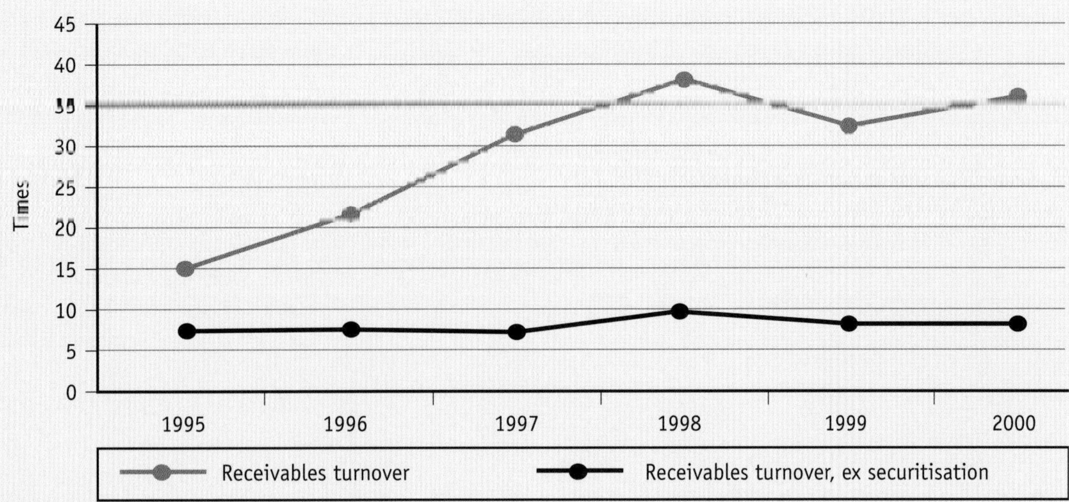


**Figure 14.10** Receivables turnover ratios

The receivables operation does appear to have been the end of the business at which earnings were being generated. What can be said about the quality of these earnings? Two observations are possible – neither of which is fatal, but both of which would warrant further investigation. These observations relate to: (1) the adequacy of the provisioning for receivables; and (2) the revenue recognition principles adopted for the sale of receivables.

With respect to the former, note that the provisions for doubtful debts relate to the estimated buybacks from the trust. In recent years there have been no disclosures regarding this matter. But between 1993 and 1997 the company's footnote disclosures are instructive. Repurchases from the trusts exceeded the provisions for doubtful debts in four of the five years – by amounts ranging from 10 to 214 per cent! Repurchases ran at 1.7 per cent of year end receivables in 1997. The provisions set aside in the three most recent years are somewhat lower, and sit at around 1.3 per cent of year-end receivables.

It has already been observed that HSH was effectively selling its receivables with recourse. Under generally accepted accounting principles in the US, receivables sold with recourse can only be accounted for as a sale if: (a) the seller gives up control of the economic benefits associated with the receivables; (b) the seller can make a reliable estimate of any obligations due to the default and prepayment risks; and (c) the buyer cannot require the seller to repurchase the receivables. Otherwise the transaction should be treated as a loan (collateralised by the receivables).

## *Margins*

While HSH provides the required statutory disclosures in its operating statement, these are of limited assistance in assessing this aspect of the company's performance. It is clear from references in the chairman's address from 1999 forward that the company was concerned about declining margins. While gross margins were presumably positive, it is also clear that operating costs (selling, general and administrative costs) quickly eroded these.

One of the company's largest single expenses was store rental (non-cancellable operating leases). These had more than doubled in size between 1995 and 2000 – from $11.9 million to $25.1 million, or from 4.7 per cent to 6.2 per cent of retail sales – a number that ought to have raised a red flag. Discount operators, by definition, operate out of stores that are low-cost to fit out and cheap to run. Wal-Mart, for example, has rental expenses of 3 per cent of retail sales. The average for the US discount department store industry is 3.3 per cent. Closer to home, David Jones, whose stores should cost more than HSH's to fit out and operate, has rental expenses estimated at around 4 per cent of sales – lower than those of its discount competitor.[5]

## *Missed signals*

With the advantage of hindsight, detective work is comparatively easy. However, it does seem that, with some effort, the signs were there to be seen and had been for some time. It is, therefore, difficult to understand why the problems were not diagnosed and treated earlier.

There are many contributors in a corporate collapse. Those that my analysis suggests are present in this case include: the adequacy of the disclosures being made – particularly the lack of data on margins (by line of business);[6] the adequacy of the corporate governance mechanisms in place; and management's strategy development and implementation. What is clear is that HSH is a textbook example of how to 'grow broke' and a cogent reminder that we seem doomed to repeat the lessons of history.

## Footnotes

1 Assuming the securitisation trust operates along similar lines to others in this sector, it is likely that the receivables were sold into the trust at face value, the financiers being paid their cost of capital (around 6.5 per cent), plus a management fee – say 2 per cent on the average balance in the portfolio. The coupon on the credit card receivables is around 21.5 per cent – with an effective interest rate around 15 per cent. The spread, net of the costs of generating it, is returned to HSH.

2 For example, Campbelltown (NSW) was 12 243 square metres and Elizabethtown (SA) was 18 062 square metres. As a rule of thumb, around 75 per cent of the gross area is available for selling space.

3 Concerns were first raised by the HSH board in its 3 April advice to the Australian Stock Exchange regarding the suspension of trading in the company's shares. That the accounting irregularities may have been more pervasive has become evident in recent court proceedings brought by the receivers (see Katherine Towers, 'Auditor Questioned Retailer's Expansion' and 'Harris Scarfe Inflated 1997 Profit by $7m, Court Told ', in the *Australian Financial Review*, 3 and 5 October, respectively).

4 David Jones has operated on a gross margin of around 35 per cent (COGS:Sales of 65 per cent) since its reorganisation in 1995. On this basis its inventory turn fluctuates around four times. The differences in retail strategy imply HSH should have a lower margin and higher turnover than David Jones.

5 Note that in 2000, DJs still owned its major stores in Sydney and Melbourne, though in October 2000 it entered into sale and leaseback arrangements for these properties. The implied rental on these properties was backed out of analysts' forecasts of property contributions to EBIT for the period 2001–2002.

6 While it is not possible to know exactly what information on margins went to the board, the various stakeholders in the company would, arguably, have been better served by this sort of disclosure.

(Source: Greg Whittred, *AGSM*, Issue 3, 2001, pp. 12–15.)

***Required:***

**1** Outline both the financial and non-financial ratios discussed in the article.

**2** Discuss what you learn from the article about each of the following:

- **a** space
- **b** inventories
- **c** receivables
- **d** margins.

**3** Are there any lessons for corporate disclosure and corporate governance?

## CASE 14D Use of cash flow ratios

The following extract provides some interesting insight into the use of cash flow ratios.

### Right on the bottle

*by Roger Juchau*

While warnings of investing in dotcom companies continue to flourish amid claims of strong cash outflows and negligible cash inflows, there are ways for stakeholders to assess a company's viability.

The increased availability of cash flow data and the reforms in financial disclosure standards, such as cost of sales figures, offers an improved database to derive cash measures for use in making assessments and predictions.

There are three well-known approaches – cash gap analysis, liquidity assessment and going concern analysis – that can be employed to assist understanding of the financial soundness of companies. To illustrate, the 1999 financial data of three Australian wine companies has been analysed. The companies encounter the classical range of business challenges and conditions of climate: markets, fashion, production and distribution.

#### *Cash gap analysis*

The cash gap is defined as being equal to inventory days on hand plus receivables collection period minus accounts payable period. Where a gap exists, then this has to be financed. Benchmark gaps vary with industry sector and also according to impacts of seasonal, trading and location factors. Widening gaps must be of concern to stakeholders since the cost of financing the gap quickly eats into the bottom line and threatens survival.

Consider a typical wine producer company where the cash gap may often be 200 days. If that company's annual sales per day is $96 000, and its cost of sales was 60 per cent, then it would have to finance $57 600 for each day of its cash gap. If the company's finance costs were 10 per cent, it would be paying $5760 for each day in its cash gap, i.e. $1.152 million for 200 days.

To manage the cash gap, companies may opt to extend payment to payables, reduce the collection period and/or increase turnover of inventory (see figure 14.11).

Such options may not be commercially available, nor is there the possibility of moving their inventory or receivables off the balance sheets. The danger for companies is that growth will not necessarily improve the situation where the cash gap remains 'commercially fixed'.

There is a point of sales growth where cash outflows will outpace cash inflows – the faster the sales growth rate, the faster the loss of cash. In this situation a company must reduce the gap, increase its margin or slow sales growth. In short, it must select a commercially sustainable option.

Where trading and production conditions vary, causing inventories to fluctuate and margins to shift about, cash gap management will benefit from computer models to predict the gap.

#### *Liquidity assessment*

Conventional ratios, current (CR) and quick ratios (QR) have been used to secure a view of liquidity status of companies. These ratios do not consider cash flows and, importantly, the capacity of cash flow to cover contractual obligations. In recent times three cash ratios have been used to further assess the liquidity conditions: the operating cash flow ratio (OCF) = cash flow from operations divided by current liabilities; cash interest coverage ratio (CIC) = cash flow from operations plus interest paid plus

Generally the shorter the cash gap, the better. Some businesses – such as Amazon.com – have a negative cash gap. We can compare our three wine companies with some other industry data. Service industries generally have average gaps of about 20 to 30 days, retailers 35 to 70 days and manufacturers 45 to 80 days

| Number of days in: | Receivables + | Inventory | Payables – | Cash gap | Sales revenue $m | Total assets $m |
|---|---|---|---|---|---|---|
| Petaluma | 91 + | 317 – | 99 = | 309 | 35.7 | 97.8 |
| McGuigan | 153 + | 368 | 152 = | 369 | 36.0 | 63.2 |
| Peter Lehmann | 99 + | 314 – | 136 = | 277 | 35.2 | 51.1 |

Assumes cost of sales of 55 per cent is a reasonable median (based on US data). Based on year-end data in 1999 annual reports.

**Figure 14.11** Cash gap: three wine companies

| Company | Ratio | | | | |
|---|---|---|---|---|---|
| | CR | QR | OCF | CIC | CCD |
| Petaluma | 2.8 | 1.4 | 0.02 | 2.01 | (0.13) |
| McGuigan | 1.8 | 0.85 | 0.13 | 12.7 | (0.01) |
| Peter Lehmann | 1.4 | 0.56 | 0.05 | 5.53 | (0.06) |

These ratios may not be totally representative, given that data is drawn from 1999 annual reports, and does not accommodate seasonal and trading variations or trends.

**Figure 14.12** Ratios revealing liquidity: three wine companies

taxes paid divided by interest paid; cash current debt coverage ratio (CCD) = operating cash flow minus cash dividends divided by current debt (as in figure 14.12). The cash ratios reveal a different picture of financial strength. Some analysts would argue that the low and negative ratios would indicate the companies have to find other sources for financing normal activity. Conclusions drawn about the strength of the companies from conventional ratios would need to be reframed, given the additional information supplied by these cash ratios.

## *Going concern analysis*

Conventional financial statement ratios, debt to equity (DE) and time interest earned (TIE) are used to inspect a company's longer-term prospects. They provide a view of the ability to carry long-term debt and to maintain solvency. The advent of more cash flow information has provided an opportunity to produce cash ratios that permit a sharper grasp of how well a company will meet its ongoing commitments and obligations. Such cash ratios include: capital expenditure ratio (CE), which equals cash flow from operations divided by capital expenditure; total debt ratio (TD), which equals cash flow from operations divided by total debt; total free cash ratio (TFC), which equals net profit plus accrued and capitalised interest plus depreciation and amortisation plus operating lease and rental expense minus dividends declared minus capital expenditure divided by accrued and capitalised interest plus operating lease and rental expense plus current portion of long-term debt plus current portion of capitalised lease obligations; cash flow adequacy ratio (CFA), which equals earnings before interest, taxes, depreciation and amortisation minus taxes paid minus interest paid minus capital expenditures divided by average annual debt maturities scheduled over the next five years. These ratios are shown in table 14.13.

Of course, cash ratios have been used by finance houses, credit raters and analysts for a long period to scrutinise the financial capacity of firms.

For example, the CE ratio evaluates whether funds are available to meet capital expenditures as well as spare capacity to meet debt obligations. The TD ratio indicates the time taken to repay debt, assuming all operational cash flow is used to discharge debt.

The free cash flow ratios can highlight the viability of a firm as a going concern. TFC and CFA ratios rated against forthcoming debt obligation give indications of the credit risk of the firm.

In examining the ongoing viability of the three wine companies, these ratios in figure 14.13 need to be interpreted in the contexts of each firm and the segment of the industry in which they operate.

Unfavourable indications in these ratios need to be checked against variables that may irregularly affect cash flow performance (e.g. wine gluts) and may explain adverse indicators.

Importantly, these ratios will also indicate whether wine firms will be able to withstand the adverse trading and production conditions that the wine industry confronts.

(Source: Professor Roger Juchau, *Australian CPA*, February 2001, pp. 60–2.)

| Company | Ratio | | | | | |
|---|---|---|---|---|---|---|
| | DE | TIE | CE | TD | TFC* | CFA* |
| Petaluma | 1.08 | 4.9 | 0.04 | 0.005 | 0.71 | 1.21 |
| McGuigan | 0.73 | 22.1 | 0.83 | 0.10 | 0.45 | 1.48 |
| Peter Lehmann | 0.85 | 13.8 | 0.27 | 0.04 | 0.11 | 2.60 |

* In the TFC and CFA ratios, some variables have been based on mandatory data in the annual report which may not reflect total amounts required to be attributed to each of the ratio variables.

**Figure 14.13** Ratios revealing ongoing viability

***Required:***

1. What is meant by cash gap analysis? What are the implications for a company if this gap increases? How can they reduce this gap?
2. Compare profit and cash ratios available to assess liquidity.
3. Compare profit and cash ratios available to assess going concern.

## Case 14E Bank evaluation

The following article discusses the performance of the big four banks.

### How the banks rate

*by Anthony Hughes*

Commonwealth Bank of Australia has retained its spot as investors' highest-rated bank, although Westpac has begun to stake its claim in another strong year of profitability for the sector.

All of the banks showed robust profit growth in the latest reporting season, but both CBA and Westpac's shares now trade at a 15 to 20 per cent premium to National Australia Bank, the country's biggest, and ANZ, based on arguably the fairest measure, the relative price to earnings ratio.

CBA also shows the highest return on equity and earnings per share growth of the big four, albeit helped by accounting changes associated with its $10 billion acquisition of Colonial earlier in 2000.

Some cracks have appeared in CBA's armoury, with official figures showing signs of a leakage of home lending customers as a result of the merger – as expected and as is often the case with major bank acquisitions. But CBA received a boost this week when broker Ord Minnett upgraded its earnings per share forecast by 8 per cent for this financial year after reassessing the cost savings from integrating Colonial.

On the cost front, ANZ is leading the charge with the most efficient operation, but some dispute the calculation of its 51.7 per cent cost to income ratio, or the ratio of its expenses to income.

ANZ has been particularly aggressive in setting a target into the 40s, but as Westpac managing director Dr David Morgan pointed out yesterday, a number of the banks are taking restructuring expenses below the line.

ANZ has booked a $361 million one-off restructuring charge for a reconfiguration of its branch network and NAB took a $136 million one-off charge, in part to cover the planned closure of another 100 branches. This is the last year that companies will be able to book abnormal charges and both banks look to have taken advantage of that to improve their ratios.

UBS Warburg's analyst, Mr James Ellis, said Westpac was his preferred choice because it was a simple 'organic growth story', even though it lacked an easily identifiable catalyst such as a large corporate transaction.

Stockbroking analysts say NAB's market rating has suffered due to uncertainty about its next strategic move, with the expectation NAB will sell its US bank Michigan National (whose interest margins fell by 100 basis points in the last two quarters) and buy a big UK bank. But managing director Mr Frank Cicutto appeared to play this prospect down at Thursday's results announcement.

NAB's UK strategy was further muddied yesterday after London's *Financial Times* reported that

| Measure | CBA* | ANZ | NAB | WBC |
|---|---|---|---|---|
| Historic price earnings ratio (times) | 16 | 13.1 | 13.2 | 15 |
| Cost to income ratio (%) | 54.7 | 51.7 | 54.5 | 54.5 |
| Return on equity (%) | 22.1 | 18.8 | 18.1 | 18.4 |
| Interest margin (%) | 2.88 | 2.87 | 2.88 | 3.13 |
| EPS growth (%) | 21 | 15 | 13.2 | 15.3 |
| EOS (c) | 185 | 106.5 | 211.3 | 88.8 |

* CBA results are for the year to June, the rest to September.

**Figure 4.15** How the banks rate

Abbey National and Bank of Scotland were in merger talks. Both banks had been considered possible merger candidates for NAB.

But NAB did receive a boost this week when broking house Merrill Lynch added the bank to its preferred list of favoured stocks outside North America, joining only News Corp among the Australian stocks in the list.

'We believe NAB is poised to dominate the wealth creation market in Australia by building a powerful retail financial services and asset management operation,' the broker said.

But in a note after NAB's result, Macquarie Entities said the bank was strategically stymied and maintained its 'underperform' recommendation.

The Australian operations were in good shape, but 'outside Australia NAB is a collection of local, low brand-value businesses that are sub-scale.

'In both the US and UK, competitors are investing and cutting costs around NAB's subsidiaries at a rate NAB is apparently unable or unwilling to match,' the broker said. 'We continue to feel the best solution is a scale-enhancing acquisition in the UK, coupled with a divestment of Michigan.'

Deutsche Bank has a 'marketperform' recommendation, raising concern about weak underlying growth from the overseas operations. A restructure separating the UK banks from the Irish banks could suggest NAB was looking to divest them and could 'be part of a broader plan to boost the overall English profile'.

Some fund managers remain positive that the banks can continue to rise, despite the bank index already jumping 18 per cent this year.

(Source: Anthony Hughes, *Sydney Morning Herald*, 4 November 2000.)

***Required:***

1. The cost to income ratios and interest margin ratio are two bank-specific ratios. They are not defined in this book. What do you think they may measure? What impact would a change in these ratios have on return on equity?
2. How are the ratios in figure 14.15 used to evaluate the banks?
3. The article mentions various accounting changes and accounting treatments. How do these affect the ratios listed?

# Chapter 15

# *Accounting policy choices*

## On completion of this chapter you should be able to:

- explain the impact of accounting policy choices on financial statements
- describe typical accounting policy choices
- discuss opportunities for manipulation by accounting policy choices and discuss the constraints on management
- calculate the before and after tax effects of changes in accounting policies.

## 15.1 Introduction

The many differences among organisations, the complexity of users' demands for information and the reluctance of regulatory authorities to specify a single solution in the face of all this variation and complexity encourage a diversity of financial accounting methods, which form part of GAAP. Thus organisations have some choices as to how to prepare financial statements to suit their circumstances. Analysing financial performance and position, and understanding the effects of such accounting policy, require knowledge of accounting methods, the principles of accrual accounting and GAAP that guide and constrain choices, and methods of analysis. It is important to extend some of the techniques you learned in earlier chapters, including ratio analysis and 'what if' effects analysis, to explore the consequences of accounting policy choices and develop an understanding of how to make sense of financial statements that reflect such choices.

## 15.2 Background to accounting policy choices

This section explains what is meant by 'accounting policy choices' and outlines some aspects that are worth thinking about when working through the rest of the chapter.

### What is an accounting policy?

Imagine the following scenario: the bookkeeper for MegaMega Stores Ltd has to decide whether or not each sales invoice should be recorded as revenue (credit revenue, debit cash or accounts receivable) and so, each time, phones the general manager and asks whether that invoice should be recorded. Pretty silly, eh? What the company needs to do is decide, *in advance and in general*, what sort of transaction constitutes a sale that is to be recorded as revenue. Then this decision can be communicated to the bookkeeper, who can apply the criteria to each invoice, and so decide what to record without phoning the general manager. The general manager can run the company instead of talking to the bookkeeper every few minutes.

An accounting policy is a decision made in advance about how, when and whether to record or recognise something. Typically, companies make policy choices in areas such as:

- when and how to recognise revenue (chapter 11)
- how to compute depreciation on plant and equipment assets (chapter 8)
- how to value inventories (chapter 7)
- how to value receivables, including how to estimate the provision for doubtful debts (chapter 5)
- which expenditures on fixed assets should be capitalised (added to the asset accounts) and which should be included with expenses such as repairs and maintenance (chapters 8 and 9)
- which product development expenditures should be expensed and which (if any) should be capitalised (this chapter)
- how to compute amortisation on intangible assets (chapter 8)
- which assets and liabilities should be included in cash and cash equivalents for the purpose of preparing a cash flow statement (chapter 12)
- how accounts of subsidiary and partly owned companies are to be reflected in the parent company's financial statements (chapter 10).

When you choose the location of an account in the financial statements (such as putting it in current liabilities rather than noncurrent liabilities), you are making an accounting policy choice!

Accounting policy choices are very important to the interpretation and analysis of the financial statements. Without knowing how the statements were assembled, it is difficult to use them intelligently. For this reason, the first of the notes following the financial statements is usually a summary of the company's significant accounting policies. The other notes provide further details on important policies.

## Why is there a choice?

Accounting, in spite of being numerical, is not mathematically cut and dried. Preparers of financial statements are forced to make choices, whether they like it or not, for the following main reasons:

1 There is information value in the location of an account in the statements (for example, current versus noncurrent or revenue versus other income). Choice of location ('classification') of accounts is therefore potentially important.

2 Even the basic transactional records of accounting, the bookkeeping records, require decisions about what is a transaction, which accounts should be used, and how and when transactions are to be recorded.

3 The basis of accrual accounting, as you have seen, is to augment the transactional records to produce a more complete (in the economic sense) picture of the enterprise's performance and position. How to do this is a matter of judgement and of criteria such as matching, fairness and economic substance. Accrual accounting therefore *necessitates* choices about accounting figures, notes and methods.

4 In Australia, the United States, Britain, Canada, New Zealand and many other countries, governments and professional accounting standard-setters have been reluctant to specify all solutions and require all enterprises to follow them. Such authorities appear to believe that choices in accounting are appropriate to fit the accounting to each enterprise's circumstances, and perhaps inevitable in our free enterprise economic system. Stock market participants, financial analysts and others who rely on financial statements are expected to attain sufficient knowledge of accounting and the enterprise to make informed decisions, just as they would when buying the enterprise's products or having other interactions with the enterprise.

   It should be noted that authorities in many countries (such as China, France, Germany and Japan) specify accounting methods much more strictly than is done in Australia. In such countries, the material covered in this chapter would put more emphasis on how to implement the approved accounting methods and less on how to choose among a variety of acceptable methods.

5 Because the complete financial statements include the figures and the footnotes and other narrative disclosures, there is frequently a decision to be made as to whether to adjust the figures for something or to disclose it in the narrative material instead, or even both. For example, if the company has been sued by a disgruntled customer, should that be recorded as a liability? Should it instead be disclosed only in the notes, or recorded as a liability with an explanatory note? Or are none of these appropriate?

## General criteria for accounting policy choices

When deciding how to account for revenues, inventories, depreciation and other matters (including what to say in footnote disclosures), companies have to consider the following kinds of criteria and how they apply to the specific policy choice situation:

- reliability (objectivity, lack of bias, correspondence with economic substance of the situation)
- relevance (have value in assisting users in making decisions)

- consistency over time
- comparability with other companies (especially in the same industry)
- conformance with authoritative standards and less formal aspects of generally accepted accounting principles
- materiality to (significance to decisions of) known or presumed users of the information
- cost of implementing the policy.

## How much freedom of choice is there?

As the earlier historical material indicated, companies used to have much more freedom to decide what and how to report than they do now. Some laws specify the use of particular reporting methods: for example, information about a company's transactions with its shareholders. But, more importantly, there is now a vast array of accounting standards that operate to constrain enterprises' choices about their accounting. Some of these standards (such as which partly owned companies should be consolidated) are specified in authoritative sources, such as the AASB standards. Others (such as that business enterprises should deduct depreciation expense in computing profit) are part of a more informal set of traditional, accepted procedures. The authoritative standards and the traditions *together* form generally accepted accounting principles (GAAP).

In some areas, the choices have already been largely made by a standard-setting body, legislators or accepted practice. In others, there is no such guidance, and the enterprise is free to make its own decisions.

- Examples of the first kind, which are already set, are consolidation method, accounting for income taxes and accounting for leases. These are still subject to revision when needed.
- Examples of the second kind, where choice is allowed, are which of several depreciation methods to use, which of several inventory cost methods to use and how to determine provision for doubtful debts.

## Professional judgement and professional standards

Even when there is an authoritative standard or a clear tradition, the necessity of fitting the accounting policy to the particular circumstances of the enterprise necessitates, in turn, the exercise of professional judgement by the preparers and auditors of the information.

For example, a document entitled 'Understanding Financial Statement Audits: A Guide for Financial Statement Users' (issued by the International Federation of Accountants and endorsed by the Australian Auditing Standards Board)[1] lists four specific ways in which the judgements management make on accounting matters affect financial statements:

- Financial measurement involves measuring the monetary amounts of the effects of events and transactions. Such measurement is not always as easy as determining the amount of a payment, as many financial statement amounts involve significant accounting estimates. Examples include: What portion of credit sales will be uncollectable? How long will depreciable assets remain in use? What product warranty claims will have to be paid?
- There are many different accounting policies in use even in relation to the same subject. Consequently, judgement is required in determining and applying those that are best suited, in the circumstances, to present fairly an entity's financial position and results of operations. For example, there are many acceptable methods for valuing inventory (chapter 7) or depreciating noncurrent assets (chapter 8).

- Management must make judgements about the amount and types of disclosures. For example, disclosures may be made in the body of the financial statement or in the notes to the accounts.
- In the preparation of financial statements, an entity's ability to continue as a going concern is assumed. However, if there is a doubt about an entity's ability to continue as a going concern in the next year, then management should disclose, in the notes to the financial statements, the pertinent conditions that raise doubt about the entity's ability to continue as a going concern and the possible effects of such conditions.

## For your interest

A research study on professional judgement in financial reporting listed several reasons for professional standards and commented on their relationship to professional judgement.[2] Some of the main points under the two categories of findings are summarised below.

Why have professional standards?

- To carry out the profession's responsibility to society for reducing the risk of error and impropriety.
- To bring collective wisdom to bear on difficult or complex issues.
- To remove the inefficiency that would result if everyone had to solve every reporting issue anew on their own.
- To state the official wisdom of the profession, and so provide some protection to accountants and auditors.
- To develop and communicate a consensus on issues that may lack objectively arrived-at 'right' answers.

There is a relationship between professional judgement and professional standards:

- Standards reduce the need for (and risk entailed by) unfettered individual judgement.
- Standards provide a framework within which judgement on unresolved issues may be exercised.
- Judgement is needed to determine whether a given standard applies to a particular circumstance.
- Judgement is needed to apply standards, especially where estimates and allocations are involved or materiality (significance of something) is in doubt.
- Judgement is needed to match relatively static standards to ever-changing circumstances.

## Manipulation

Does accounting policy choice provide a way for company management to alter the picture presented in the financial statements — to present the story they want to tell rather than the truth? The short answer is yes. However, there is a fine line between choosing the accounting policies that suit the company's circumstances and so produce fair reporting, and choosing policies that tell a desired story that may not be fair. *The vast majority of companies and their managers are scrupulous about their accounting* and consider producing fair financial statements to be both ethical and good business practice. But we do learn of companies that have stepped over the line and 'doctored' their accounts to make themselves look better or to hide some embarrassing result.

Here are some examples that the user of financial statements may want to consider:

- A company may choose accounting methods, for receivables, inventories, amortisation or any other accounts, that tend to make profits higher than would have been produced by other methods. This could involve optimistic estimates of earned revenue, of the useful life of assets or of the value of patents or exploration expenditures.
- Another company, concerned about its income tax burden, might make choices that would reduce profit and, in this way, put off paying taxes.
- Having promised the bank that a current ratio would be maintained at a certain level, a company may choose accounting methods that help the ratio look as high as possible, such as classifying longer-term receivables as current assets or likely short-term obligations as noncurrent liabilities.

There may be reasons for manipulating the financial statement figures in any direction, but good knowledge of the enterprise may be necessary to predict what that direction is likely to be.

A dramatic example of profit manipulation is the 'big bath'. The method works in this way: the management of a company that has a bad year may write off extra costs (for example, writing inventories, receivables or intangibles way down) on the assumption that the company is already going to be criticised, so the criticism won't be much stronger if the results appear even worse. By transferring such costs to expenses now, instead of in later years, future expenses are reduced and therefore future profits will look better. The company will appear to have bounced back quickly. Management hopes for praise for this recovery, even though it is not all real, because of the manipulation. Large write-offs become more critical when executive compensation packages are tied to changes in accounting profits.

Manipulation dangers can be overrated. First, managers cannot simply change accounting policies wherever they wish. There is a need for consistency, and if there is a change it must be disclosed in the notes to the accounts, together with the effect of the change on profit. Second, most managers are honest and anxious that their accounting be fair and truthful. Most consider that good financial reporting is important to the company's reputation and ability to borrow, raise share capital and generally do business. Most consider good financial reporting to be part of good business and professional ethics. However, the danger of manipulation is always there, so accountants, auditors and users who rely on profit and other measures for their decisions must be vigilant. It is especially dangerous to rely on financial statements that have not been audited by independent public accountants.

## A few technical points

- *Cash flow.* Generally, accounting policy choice does not affect cash flow. You saw the reasons for this in chapters 12 and 13: policy choices are made by accrual accounting entries, which do not affect cash directly. There may be indirect or eventual effects, especially through income tax. But at the instant an accounting policy choice is implemented, there is no cash or cash flow effect.
- *General form of policy change journal entry.* You can see the lack of a cash effect from the following general form of an entry to implement a change in an accounting policy (cash is not part of the entry):

| | |
|---|---|
| DR or CR | Some statement of financial position account (receivables, payables, inventories, accumulated depreciation and so on) |
| CR or DR | Some profit and loss account for the current year's effect of the change (revenue, expenses, depreciation and so on) |
| DR or CR | Current year's income tax expense (current or deferred portion) for the income tax consequences of the current year's profit and loss effect |

- *Dual effects of changes.* As noted in prior chapters, and as the above entry shows, most accounting policy changes affect both the statement of financial position and the statement of financial performance. They *must* affect both if they are to affect net profit. Here are some examples:

| **Statement of financial position accounts** | **Main statement of financial performance accounts** |
|---|---|
| Accounts receivable | Revenue, bad debts expense |
| Inventories | Cost of goods sold expense |
| Prepaid and accrued expenses | Various expense accounts |
| Property and plant assets | Depreciation expense |
| Intangible and leased assets | Amortisation expense |
| Liabilities | Various expense accounts |
| Equity | None* |

*Transactions with owners, such as share capital issues and redemptions and dividends, are ordinarily not considered part of the measurement of profit. However, there are some technicalities that may allow this to be violated – this book will not cover such technicalities.

- *Classification and disclosure.* There are accounting policy choices in two areas that do not affect profit:
  - *Classification* policies (decisions about where within the statement of financial position or where within the statement of financial performance to show accounts) do not affect profit because they do not involve *both* statements, as do recognition policies, but instead affect only one or the other.
  - *Disclosure* policies relate to what is said about the figures in the words used in the statements and in the notes to the statements.

## How's your understanding?

Here are two questions you should be able to answer, based on what you have just read:

1 Sue Wong, an experienced investor, reacted in frustration on having difficulty comparing the financial statements of two companies she was considering investing in. 'There is too much judgement being exercised in financial accounting! Why are companies allowed to choose their accounting policies, not just told how to do it?' What are some pros and cons of allowing enterprises to make accounting policy choices?

2 Indicate the probable direction of the effect of each of the following possible accounting policy changes on the item given:

| Policy change | Effect on |
|---|---|
| Accrue greater employee benefits expense | Liabilities |
| Recognise accounts receivable sooner | Revenue |
| Capitalise some repairs expenses | Net profit |
| Disclose board's intention to declare dividend | Net profit |
| Separate bank loan into current and long-term | Net profit |
| Recognise doubtful accounts sooner | Net profit |
| Write off spoiled inventories | Net profit |

(Increase, increase, increase, no effect, no effect, decrease, decrease)

## 15.3 Inventory valuation and cost of goods sold: effects

Refer back to the Meeix example in section 7.6. The following is a summary of the results for the Meeix example:

| Cost method | Ending inventory asset<br>$ | Cost of goods sold expense<br>$ | Total cost available<br>$ |
|---|---|---|---|
| FIFO | 6 300 | 5 500 | 11 800 |
| AVGE | | | |
| Annual | 5 408 | 6 392 | 11 800 |
| Moving | 5 957 | 5 843 | 11 800 |
| LIFO | | | |
| Periodic | 4 500 | 7 300 | 11 800 |
| Perpetual | 5 600 | 6 200 | 11 800 |

Let's assume Meeix is using FIFO for its inventory of Gloop. What would be the effects on Meeix's financial statements if it changed to one of the other four methods beginning this year (that is, without changing past years and so without changing the $4 cost of the 1 January inventory)? Meeix's income tax rate is 30 per cent.

If it *changed to moving weighted average*:

- Cost of goods sold expense would go up by $343 ($5843 – $5500), so net profit would decline by 70 per cent of that, or $240.
- Income tax expense and liability would go down by the other 30 per cent, or $103.
- Working capital would go down by $343 (inventory asset declines) and up by $103 (income tax liability decline) for a net decrease of $240, the same as the net profit decline.
- There would be no immediate effect on cash or cash flow.

You should be able to fill in the analysis for changes to any of the other methods. For your reference, the results for changes to the other three are shown in the notes at the end of this chapter.[3]

## 15.4 Depreciation effects analysis

This accounting policy choice has its main effect on profit. Use of an accelerated method, such as reducing balance, increases depreciation in the early years of assets' lives, relative to the depreciation resulting from the use of the straight-line method. Therefore, profit will be lower in the early years if reducing balance is used, and higher in the later years, when the reducing balance depreciation falls below straight-line.

Refer back to the Greco Ltd example in section 8.5. The results of using various depreciation methods were as follows:

| Year | Straight-line expense | Reducing balance | | Units-of-production expense |
|---|---|---|---|---|
| | | Begin book value | Expense | |
| | $ | $ | $ | $ |
| 1 | 900 000 | 23 000 000 | 2 300 000 | 720 000 |
| 2 | 900 000 | 20 700 000 | 2 070 000 | 1 620 000 |
| 3 | 900 000 | 18 630 000 | 1 863 000 | 1 620 000 |
| 4 | 900 000 | 16 767 000 | 1 676 700 | 1 440 000 |
| 5 | 900 000 | 15 090 300 | 1 509 030 | 1 620 000 |
| 6 | 900 000 | 13 581 270 | 1 358 127 | 900 000 |
| 7 | 900 000 | 12 223 143 | 1 222 314 | 720 000 |
| 8 | 900 000 | 11 000 829 | 1 100 083 | 720 000 |
| 9 | 900 000 | 9 900 746 | 990 075 | 720 000 |
| 10 | 900 000 | 8 910 671 | 891 067 | 720 000 |
| 11 | 900 000 | 8 019 604 | 801 960 | 720 000 |
| 12 | 900 000 | 7 217 644 | 721 764 | 720 000 |
| 13 | 900 000 | 6 495 880 | 649 588 | 720 000 |
| 14 | 900 000 | 5 846 292 | 584 629 | 720 000 |
| 15 | 900 000 | 5 261 663 | 526 166 | 720 000 |
| 16 | 900 000 | 4 735 497 | 473 550 | 720 000 |
| 17 | 900 000 | 4 261 947 | 426 195 | 720 000 |
| 18 | 900 000 | 3 835 752 | 383 575 | 720 000 |
| 19 | 900 000 | 3 452 177 | 345 218 | 720 000 |
| 20 | 900 000 | 3 106 959 | 310 696 | 720 000 |
| Total | 18 000 000 | | 20 203 737 | 18 000 000 |

The general manager wants to know what effects the depreciation choice has. Some things you could tell the general manager are:

**1** The straight-line method shows the same depreciation every year.
- The reducing balance method starts out with much higher depreciation than that of the straight-line method and ends up with much lower depreciation.
- The units-of-production method starts out lower, rises, then falls back in accordance with production plans.

2 Accordingly:
- The declining balance method will show lower net profits than straight-line in the earlier years and higher in the later years.
- The units-of-production method result is greatly different from that produced by the straight-line method in years two to five, but in other years they are not much different.

3 After subtracting the 30 per cent income tax effect on profit, the differential effect on net profits of moving from straight-line to either of the other two methods in a sample of years would be, if everything works out as expected, as shown below.

| | **Reducing balance compared with straight-line** | | **Units-of-production compared with straight-line** | |
|---|---|---|---|---|
| **Year** | **Depreciation expense effect** | **Net profit effect (70%)** | **Depreciation expense effect** | **Net profit effect (70%)** |
| | **$** | **$** | **$** | **$** |
| 1 | 1 400 000 | (980 000) | (180 000) | 126 000 |
| 5 | 609 030 | (426 321) | 720 000 | (504 000) |
| 10 | (8 933) | 6 253 | (180 000) | 126 000 |
| 15 | (373 834) | 261 684) | (180 000) | 126 000 |
| 20 | (589 304) | 412 513 | (180 000) | 126 000 |
| Cumulative 20 years | 2 203 737 | (1 542 616) | 0 | 0 |

4 If reducing balance or units-of-production is chosen, the company will look less profitable in the early years and more profitable in the later years.

5 The statement of financial position effects are in the book value of the factory, and therefore also in the book value of the total assets of the business, which decline least rapidly with the straight-line method, and in the deferred income tax liability and retained profit. The liability will have 30 per cent of the difference in book value, and retained profits will have the other 70 per cent.

6 The effects on return on equity and return on assets are reduced somewhat because both the numerators and denominators are affected by the depreciation choice. (If the ROA was 10 per cent, reducing both the numerator and the denominator by the same amount will reduce the ratio. If you don't follow, make up some numbers and try it.) For example, reducing balance shows lower net profit in year five than does straight-line but, by then, book value and retained profits are both also lower and, therefore, ROE and ROA are pushed a little closer to the values they would have under the straight-line method.

7 Greco Ltd should choose the depreciation method that would best match its depreciation expense to the apparent economic value provided by using the factory. But, since depreciation does not affect cash flow or current assets, and because in this case the straight-line method provides higher net profits in the early years, it might be that the general manager will want to use that method. The general manager is likely to be concerned about the reaction to the company's performance over the next few years, and it may take a good deal of explanation to demonstrate that the non-straight-line methods do result in a fairer way of determining profit and asset figures. As you saw earlier, most large Australian companies use straight-line, so that method probably also has comparability with other companies in Greco's industry in its favour.

## How's your understanding?

Here is a question you should be able to answer, based on what you have just read:

1 Cold Lake management is trying to decide whether to use straight-line or reducing balance depreciation for its assets. If it used straight-line, the depreciation expense for this first year would be $1 120 000; but if it used reducing balance with the rate management believes would be appropriate, the expense would be $1 860 000. The company's income tax rate is 35 per cent. Calculate how much higher or lower each of the following would be if the reducing balance method were used rather than the straight-line method: depreciation expense, net profit, cash from operations, net book value of assets, retained profits, current ratio. ($740 000 higher; $481 000 lower; no effect; $740 000 lower; $481 000 lower; no effect)

## 15.5 Intangibles effects analysis

Let's look at an example. Checkup Auto Services Ltd, which has been in business for one year, has a chain of heavily advertised automobile service centres. The company's income tax rate is 30 per cent. The company makes it a practice to capitalise a portion of its advertising costs as a 'deferred asset'. An accountant suggested to the company's financial controller that the policy of capitalising advertising should be ended because the future economic benefit from the expenditures is not clearly determinable. The controller wants to know what effect such policy changes would have.

*Data:*
- The amount of advertising capitalised was $75 000 this year.
- The capitalised amount is being amortised at 20 per cent per year.

*Present method:*
- Amortisation expense is $15 000 this year (20 per cent of $75 000).
- Asset is $75 000 – $15 000 = $60 000 at end of this year.

*Proposed method:*
Expenses this year would be $75 000.

*Effects:*
If advertising were not capitalised:
- This year's net profit would be lower by 70 per cent of ($75 000 – $15 000) = $42 000.
- Income tax liability would go down by $18 000 (the other 30 per cent).
- Retained profits this year would be lower by $42 000.
- Assets would be lower by the removal of $60 000 net capitalised advertising asset.
- Accounts equation proof. ($60 000) = ($18 000) + ($42 000).
- No effect on cash flow, cash balance or working capital.

## 15.6 Accounting policy disclosure

You have seen that a company may have a variety of accounting policies chosen to fit its circumstances. Generally accepted accounting principles require that companies disclose what their significant policies are and any changes in them since the previous period. The idea is to help the users of the financial statements understand and interpret the figures and notes in the statement, as this chapter has tried to prepare you to do.

Accounting standard AASB 1001 covers accounting policies and includes the following key statements:

- *Accounting policies* must be selected and applied in a manner which ensures that the resultant financial information satisfies the concepts of *relevance* and *reliability*, thereby ensuring that the substance of the underlying transactions and other events is reported.
- *Accounting policies* must be disclosed in a manner which ensures that the resultant financial information is *comparable* and *understandable*.
- A summary of *accounting policies* must be presented in the initial section of the notes to the *financial report*. The summary must:
  (a) state that the financial report is a *general purpose financial report* which has been prepared in accordance with *Accounting Standards*;
  (b) identify the accounting policies adopted in preparing and presenting the financial report where alternative accounting policies are permitted in an Accounting Standard, or an accounting policy has been adopted in the absence of a requirement specified in an Accounting Standard; and
  (c) identify the fact and reasons for not applying the *going concern* or *accrual accounting bases*, where the financial report has been prepared otherwise than in accordance with the going concern or accrual accounting bases.
- Where there is a change in the accounting policies from those applied in the *preceding financial year* which has a *material* effect in the *current financial year* or is expected to have a material effect in a subsequent *financial year*, the summary of accounting policies must disclose, or refer to a note disclosing:
  (a) the nature of the change;
  (b) the reasons for the change; and
  (c) the effect of the change.

A summary of the significant policies usually appears as the first of the notes to the financial statements. The user should be able to tell from this note the company's policies for inventory, depreciation, accounting for intercorporate investments and any other policies the company and its auditors feel are necessary for an understanding of how the financial statements have been prepared. For an example of this accounting policy disclosure, see note 1, Significant Accounting Policies, to the Woolworths Limited financial statements in appendix 2 of this book. Policy specifics are often not disclosed if the methods used are what you'd expect; for example, if revenue is recognised at the point of sale or delivery, or if normal accruals are made for expenses.

Changes in accounting policies are also disclosed, including a description of the change and a calculation of the effect the change has had on the financial statements. Many changes have to be given retroactive effect. For example, if the revenue recognition method is changed, past years' financial statements have to be recalculated to show them on the new basis. Therefore, if a company has changed its accounting policy in some area, the prior year's figures in this year's annual report may not be the same as the ones you would have seen in last year's annual report.

## 15.7 Accounting policy choices: management's objectives

Each chapter of this book has included a few words about managers and accounting to bring a managerial perspective to the topics and help to answer the question, 'Why should a manager care about financial accounting?'

In the case of accounting policy choice, the answer should not be hard to see. Management is responsible for the financial statements, as it is for other aspects of the business, and must see that it chooses the best accounting policies for its company for several reasons:

- As this book has emphasised, such choices are an inevitable consequence of accrual accounting. They are part of the judgemental fabric that is at the heart of accrual accounting, and, properly made, they add to the value of the financial statements. Improperly made, they detract from the value. In either case, they make a difference!
- Management is in the best position to make valid accounting policy choices, because management knows the company best. Professional advisers can provide great assistance to management here, but management should have the data that would drive rational accounting policy choices.
- Management's performance on behalf of the owners is evaluated partly via the financial statements. While this provides a motivation for self-serving managers to abuse accrual accounting in order to make themselves look good, it also provides an opportunity for those more professional managers to create financial measures that show the company's performance in the clearest, most valid light. Such a portrayal should, in the long run, benefit everyone.
- In the company overview section that is in most annual reports, management reviews the year's performance and takes responsibility for it. This naturally leads management to be interested in the policy choices behind the financial statements, for not only do they help determine how management's performance is measured, but they too are the responsibility of management.
- Agency (contract) theory, based on the idea that self-interested behaviour is to be expected of everyone, provides a straightforward objective for management's accounting policy choices: to increase managers' share of corporate returns (and therefore decrease the returns of owners, creditors and employees). Agency theory puts no negative cast on this, simply treating it as a natural function of economically rational behaviour. But many people see this as manipulation, and are very critical of managers who appear to put their own interests first. Such behaviour may be prompted by managers' concerns about their performance bonuses, about avoiding complications due to investor or creditor nervousness regarding poor performance or about avoiding standing out as being too profitable. Managers' objectives are likely to be complex, including in many cases a simple wish to 'tell it like it is' in a fair and unbiased manner.

Readers of this book should now have considerable sensitivity to the position of the manager in the financial accounting situation and be able to interpret or prepare financial statements more intelligently, given that sensitivity. If you are a present or future manager, many of the use techniques should be helpful. For example, the ability to do, arrange for or at least use 'what if' effects analysis forms an important part of the manager's analytical toolkit. Graduates of accounting courses should be in a particularly good position to answer others' 'what if?' questions. Financial statements are thus closer to the centre of effective management than you might have imagined. This closeness should motivate managers to pay close attention to their financial statements and should motivate others (users, accountants and auditors) to understand management's role in preparing any financial statements with which they are involved.

## For your interest

In this chapter it has been noted that accounting policy choices usually don't have direct cash flow implications. But they may have various indirect future cash effects:

- If a manager's bonus depends on the company's net profit, and a policy choice will affect net profit, there will be an effect on the cash paid to the manager.

- If a policy choice changes the debt/equity ratio, the company's risk might appear different enough to affect interest rates on its debts, therefore changing future interest payments.

## 15.8 Public sector issues

Managers in the public sector also have to make accounting policy choices, which in turn affect figures in the operating statement and the statement of financial position. Go to the Web site of a government department and look at note 1 of its financial statements for some of its accounting policy decisions.

## 15.9 Homework and discussion to develop understanding

### Discussion questions

1 What is an accounting policy choice?

2 In what areas do organisations often make policy choices?

3 Select five accounting policy choices. Describe the impact on profit and total assets of each of the choices.

4 Why is the location of an item in the financial statements an accounting policy choice?

5 Why do organisations have a choice on what accounting policies to choose?

6 Are there any limits on the choices companies have?

7 As you have seen, there is a general conflict between two financial reporting objectives. The first objective is to fit the accounting to each company's circumstances so that the resulting reports are relevant to understanding or evaluating that company. The second is to make accounting consistent from company to company so that intercompany comparisons may be facilitated and the overall credibility of the information maintained. Write a paragraph giving your views on how important this conflict is and how (if at all) it should be dealt with.

8 Should management have the responsibility and authority to choose companies' accounting policies, or should that role be someone else's (for example, the government's, the auditor's or an independent board's)? If you think it should be management's role, explain why. If you think it should be someone else's role, explain whose, and why.

9 A commentator on the accounting scene remarked, 'Management makes its accounting choices to serve its own interests, and there's no way the poor lonely auditor can hold the fort of fairness when you consider how vague and judgemental accrual accounting's criteria for accounting policy choices are.' What are your views on the commentator's remarks?

10 a Outline the kinds of information you would expect to see in a company's significant accounting policies note to the financial statements.

b How should a company decide what to include in that note?

c A business commentator suggested that, when a company uses an accounting policy that is unusual, its significant accounting policies note should include a calculation of the effect on profit of using that policy as compared to the more usual practice. What do you think of that idea?

11 Comment briefly on the following remarks by a business person:

a No one cares what our accounting policy choices are, because they have no effect on the price of the company's shares.

b Last year we sold some equipment that had a book value of $70 000 for $54 000. I was really angry at our general manager for losing $16 000 and nearly fired him.

c I don't allow our company to include any intangible assets on its balance sheet, because I prefer a conservative balance sheet that doesn't contain questionable assets.

d Once we have established proper accounting policies, all those notes at the end of the financial statements are really an irrelevant nuisance.

**12** Write a paragraph on each of the following topics, using the perspective on accounting policy choice and methods provided in this chapter:

a Why the auditor's report refers to whether the company's financial statements have been prepared in accordance with GAAP.

b Why professional judgement is needed in preparing financial statements.

c Whether it is justifiable to use an aggressive (in other words, early in the production sale collection cycle process) revenue recognition policy.

**13** A shareholder in a large public company threatens to sue management, the auditors and the AASB for 'approving conservative accounting policies that have resulted in poor apparent performance and low stock prices that have reduced my investment value'. What do you think of the shareholder's complaint?

**14** During lunch with a senior executive of a large public company, you are asked to respond to several comments, including the following:

a Accounting standards and principles evolve too slowly to keep up with the rapidly changing needs of businesses such as ours. Why don't we just ignore standards and GAAP, and do our accounting the best way for our needs?

b I would be glad to see our goodwill asset written off. I can't see the sense in including such a thing with the statement of financial position assets anyway. To me, it's not like the other assets.

c You just referred to judgement in applying accounting principles. That's foolish: judgement is just a word people use when they'd prefer not to follow the rules.

d I've heard that the auditors may not agree with our planned accounting changes. Who cares? We can always change auditors.

**15** A new CEO is appointed to an organisation. Why may he or she have incentives to write off particular capitalised assets, write down some investments and write off a lot of bad debts?

**16** Given that accounting choices provide management with the opportunity to act in its own self-interest, what are the benefits for financial statement users of allowing managers to choose accounting policies?

**17** Refer to the following statement and answer questions that follow.

> In an accrual accounting setting, altering policies by, for example, choosing to capitalise rather than expense an interest cost or using straight-line depreciation versus reducing balance, achieves nothing more than to shift the recognition of expenses from one period to another. Consequently, across time, such choices ought to count for little, if anything at all.

a On what basis might this have been argued?

b What reasons are there to suspect that the conclusion reached may be oversimplistic?

## Problem 15.1* Accounting policy choice – software development costs

Kaz Computer Services provides the following information in its 2001 financial statements:

> **Software development costs**
>
> Software development costs are charged to operating profit from ordinary operations before income tax as incurred or deferred where it is expected beyond any reasonable doubt that sufficient future benefits will be derived so as to recover those deferred costs.

Software development costs are amortised on a straight-line basis over the period during which the related benefits are expected to be realised once commercial production is commenced, but not exceeding three years.

*Required:*

Discuss the judgements to be made by the accountant. How does each judgement affect profit in 2001 and 2002?

## Problem 15.2* Effects analysis: expensing versus capitalising, plus tax

The controller of Squiffle Ltd is having some disagreements with senior management about some company accounting policies.

**1** Squiffle, in business for only a year, has capitalised $67 000 in development costs. The controller argues that such costs should be expensed instead. Assume that this accounting policy affects current income tax liability and that the company's income tax rate is 30 per cent. What would the controller's proposal do to:

- **a** the current year's net profit?
- **b** the current year's cash flow?
- **c** working capital at the end of the current year?

**2** Top management is likely to go grudgingly along with the controller regarding question **1** because of the income tax saving. If that is done, the first year's statement of financial performance will show income before income tax of $100 000. The income tax law allows an extra deduction of $25 000, to postpone payment of the tax on that $25 000 for several years – the company has received this as an inducement to locate in a depressed region. Top management wants to take advantage of the income tax inducement by showing income tax expense for the year of only $22 500 (which is 30 per cent of $100 000 – $25 000), because that is all the income tax the company will have to pay. The controller believes that the company should create a deferred income tax liability for the inducement, because the tax will have to be paid after several years. What would the controller's proposal do to:

- **a** the current year's net profit?
- **b** the current year's cash flow?
- **c** working capital at the end of the current year?

## Problem 15.3 Inventory policies

Shown below are the disclosures with respect to inventory for Kaz Computer Services Limited and Sigma Limited.

**Kaz Computer Services Limited**

Inventories are valued at the lower of cost or net realisable value. Cost comprises direct materials and inwards freight charges and is assigned to individual items of stock on the basis of weighted average cost.

**Sigma Limited**

Inventories are valued at the lower of cost and net realisable value. Cost is determined on the first-in-first-out basis and includes all direct costs and an appropriate proportion of overheads directly related to production, where appropriate.

*Required:*

**1** What are the main differences in accounting policies for inventory?

**2** If all other things were equal (for example, same sales, same expenses), which company would have the higher profit for 2001 and the higher inventory figure?

## Problem 15.4 Interest capitalisation policies

### Boral Limited, 30 June 2001

**Borrowing costs:** Borrowing costs include interest, amortisation of discounts or premiums relating to borrowings, amortisation of ancillary costs incurred in connection with arrangement of borrowings and lease finance charges. Borrowing costs are expensed as incurred unless they relate to qualifying assets. Qualifying assets are assets which take more than 12 months to get ready for their intended use or sale. Where funds are borrowed specifically for the acquisition, construction or production of a qualifying asset, the amount of borrowing costs capitalised is that which is incurred in relation to that borrowing, net of any interest earned on those borrowings. Where funds are borrowed generally, borrowing costs are capitalised using a weighted average capitalisation rate.

### Coca-Cola Amatil, 31 December 2000

Capitalisation of interest: Interest relating to the financing of qualifying assets is capitalised in non-current assets up to the date of commissioning and subsequently amortised over the useful life of the asset. Interest capitalised has been calculated at varying rates dependent on the location and timing of the expenditure on qualifying assets incurred throughout the Group.

*Required:*

Compare the content of the accounting policy disclosure on capitalisation of interest for these two companies. How does the policy on interest capitalisation have an impact on profit in different accounting periods?

## Problem 15.5 Revaluation of noncurrent asset policies

### Amcor, 30 June 2001

**Changes in accounting policy revaluation of noncurrent assets**

The consolidated entity has applied revised AASB 1041 (Revaluation of Non-current Assets) for the first time from 1 July 2000 and, in accordance with the standard, has elected to apply the cost basis for noncurrent assets. In respect of land, land improvements and buildings, the consolidated entity has deemed the cost of these assets to be equal to their carrying value as at 1 July 2000. The change in accounting policy has no financial effect in the current or prior periods. As a consequence of making this election on the adoption of AASB 1041 the balance of the asset revaluation reserve at 1 July 2000 relating to land, land improvements and buildings is no longer available for asset write-downs.

*Required:*

1 How was the deemed cost at 1 July 2000 calculated?
2 Why did the change in accounting policy have no financial effect in the current or previous period?
3 Will the change affect profit in future years?

## Problem 15.6 Inventory policies

Under Australian accounting standards, directors have a choice in determining the cost of closing inventory. They may use specific identification, weighted average, or FIFO.

During the year ended 30 June 2002, the unit costs of merchandise purchased for resale by Wattle Limited rose steadily, ending 50 per cent higher at 30 June 2002 than at 30 June 2001. The inventory turnover was 4.

***Required:***

Assuming the choice is between FIFO and weighted average, which will result in the highest profit for the year ended 30 June 2002? Explain your answer.

## Problem 15.7 Inventory cost and effects calculations

You work for a large local company as inventory manager. The company uses FIFO in accounting for inventory. In June, the company began to stock a new product, Painto. The June inventory record for Painto was:

| Date | Purchase price | Units purchased | Units sold | Units on hand |
|---|---|---|---|---|
| Jun 1 | $10 | 1 250 | | 1 250 |
| 10 | $11 | 1 000 | | 2 250 |
| 12 | | | 250 | 2 000 |
| 17 | $12 | 500 | | 2 500 |
| 23 | | | 2 000 | 500 |
| 27 | $13 | 1 500 | | 2 000 |
| 30 | | | 800 | 1 200 |

***Required:***

1 Calculate, using FIFO:
  - a the cost of the 30 June inventory of Painto
  - b the cost of goods sold for Painto for June.

2 Calculate, using LIFO (either perpetual or periodic):
  - a the cost of the 30 June inventory of Painto
  - b the cost of goods sold for Painto for June.

3 The company's income tax rate is 35 per cent. Based on your calculations in questions **1** and **2**, what would be the effect of changing from FIFO to LIFO on the company's:
  - a net profit for June?
  - b balance sheet at the end of June?

## Problem 15.8 Research and development policies

You are preparing the financial statements for Ironore Ltd and the Chief Financial Officer (CFO) asked you to capitalise $2 000 000 worth of research and development expenses, previously recorded during the current financial year.

***Required:***

1 What journal entries would you use to record this transaction?

2 How will this transaction affect the following statements:
  - a profit and loss summary?
  - b statement of financial position?
  - c cash flow statement?

3 What does capitalising an expense mean?

4 Suggest reasons for the CFO's decision.

## Problem 15.9 Impact on profit of goodwill accounting policy change

An extract from the Amalgamated Holdings 2001 annual report is presented here:

**r Goodwill**

Goodwill representing excess of the purchase consideration plus incidental costs over the fair value of the identifiable net assets acquired on the acquisition of a controlled entity or the acquisition of assets of another entity, is amortised on a straight-line basis over a period not exceeding 15 years, being the period during which benefits are expected to arise.

The unamortised balance of goodwill is reviewed at least each reporting date. Where the balance exceeds the value of expected future benefits, the difference is charged to the statement of financial performance.

**Note 17 Intangibles**

| | Consolidated | | The Company | |
|---|---|---|---|---|
| | 2001 $000 | 2000 $000 | 2001 $000 | 2000 $000 |
| Goodwill | 20 170 | 20 028 | — | — |
| Less: Accumulated amortisation | (8 815) | (7 274) | — | — |
| | 11 355 | 12 754 | — | — |
| Liquor licence | 82 | 82 | — | — |
| | 11 437 | 12 836 | — | — |

If Amalgamated Holdings changed its goodwill amortisation policy to 10 years or to 20 years, would profit increase or decrease? Briefly explain why.

## Problem 15.10 (Challenging) Impact of goodwill accounting policy change

An extract from the Amcor Limited 2001 annual report is presented here.

**18 Goodwill**

The consolidated entity recognises goodwill on acquisitions of controlled entities and businesses as required by Accounting Standard AASB 1013 (Accounting for Goodwill).

All goodwill is amortised in equal instalments over the period of time during which the benefits are expected to arise, but for a period not exceeding 20 years. The unamortised balance of goodwill is reviewed at reporting date and adjusted where it is considered that the carrying amount exceeds the expected future benefits.

However, prior to 30 June 1995 the Economic Entity systematically amortised goodwill using the inverted-sum-of-the-digits method over the period of time during which the benefits were expected to arise, but for a period not exceeding 20 years.

The inverted-sum-of-the-digits method of amortisation of goodwill is similar to the sum-of-the-digits method in section 8.4, but instead of the largest amounts of amortisation being recognised in earlier years, the smallest amounts are (1/210, 2/210, 3/210 rather than 20/210, 19/210, 18/210 for assuming a 20-year amortisation period). This method was disallowed for use in Australia for the year ending 30 June 1995.

1 Why do you think this method of amortising goodwill was disallowed?

2 What would be the effect on net profit and total assets of Amcor's change to straight-line amortisation of goodwill back in 1995?

## Problem 15.11 (Challenging) Brand name policy choices

**Pacific Dunlop, 30 June 2001**

**Brand names:** Brand names acquired since 1 July 1987 are recorded in the financial statements at cost. No amortisation is provided against the carrying value of these brand names on the basis that the lives of these assets are considered unlimited at this point in time.

Brand names have an unlimited legal life, and the brand names recorded in the financial statements are not currently associated with products which are likely to become commercially or technically obsolete.

***Required:***

1. Suggest two alternative accounting policies for accounting for brand names.
2. What would be the impact on profit and total assets for 2001 of adoption of the above alternative policies?

## Problem 15.12 (Challenging) Accounting policy change calculations

Humungus Ltd is a retailer of consumer products. The general manager of the company had two concerns: the company's worsening cash position ($3000 cash and no bank loan at the end of 2001, no cash and a $7000 bank loan at the end of 2002) and what the general manager believed was an inadequate level of net profit.

1. The general manager was confused because the company had a $9000 profit, yet seemed, as noted above, $10 000 worse off in its cash position. Explain briefly how, in general, this difference between profit and cash change can happen.
2. The general manager proposed changes in the company's accounting policies in a few areas in an attempt to show a higher profit. He met the company's auditors to discuss these ideas. What do you think the auditors should have said?
3. For each of the proposed changes below, considered separately and independently, calculate the effect on 2002 net profit and total assets as at 31 December 2002. Assume a 30 per cent income tax rate.
   - **a** The general manager suggested recognising revenue at an earlier point. If this were done, net accounts receivable would be increased by $12 000 at 31 December 2001, and by $23 000 at 31 December 2002.
   - **b** The general manager suggested changing the inventory cost policy to FIFO (which would still produce costs less than net realisable value). Doing so would increase 31 December 2001 inventories by $4000 and 31 December 2002 inventories by $1000.
   - **c** The general manager suggested the company not account for deferred income taxes, but rather treat income taxes payable in each year as the income tax expense. The deferred income tax liability was $2800 at 31 December 2001, and without this change was $2600 at 31 December 2002.
   - **d** The general manager suggested capitalising more of the company's product development costs and amortising additional capitalised amounts over five years, using the straight-line method. If this were done, $4000 of 2001 expenses would be capitalised at 31 December 2001, and $6000 of 2002 expenses would be capitalised at 31 December 2002.

## Problem 15.13 (Challenging) Accounting policies, effects and entries

Refer to the Grandin Ltd trial balances for 2002 and 2001 in problem 12.24 and the financial statements you originally prepared. Assume that upon further inquiry you have discovered the following information:

- At the very end of 2002, some equipment that had cost $4500 eleven years earlier was sold for $1800. The bookkeeper had debited the sale proceeds to cash and credited service revenue.
- The company's depreciation policy for its equipment is straight-line, with an estimated useful life of 15 years and no salvage value. No depreciation is recorded in the year of sale. Depreciation on the remaining assets has been recorded in the accounts.
- No other equipment was bought or sold during 2002.

- The company uses the average inventory costing policy. There were 2000 units on hand at the end of 2001 (costing $18.50 each), and during 2002 there were the following purchases, in this order: 800 at $19; 1200 at $16.20; 2000 at $17.50; 1500 at $19.20; and 500 at $20.50. Sales for 2002 were recorded at 5666 units. On the average cost basis, 2002 cost of goods sold for 5666 units was $103 190 and inventory at the end of 2002 was $42 500. (Weighted average cost was $18.21; the two figures above are rounded.)
- The company has decided to change its inventory costing policy to FIFO (which will be less than net realisable value, as is cost on the average basis). The change will be implemented for 2002, but the inventory cost per unit at the end of 2001 ($18.50) will not be changed. The bookkeeper has no idea how to implement the accounting policy change.
- The company has failed to correctly accrue bonuses owing to the company general manager for the last three years. The bonuses, related to the 2000, 2001 and 2002 year-ends, were paid and recorded as expenses on the 2002 statement of financial performance in service wage expense. The bonuses were as follows:

  2000 $2 000 2001 $3 000 2002 $4 000
- Grandin's applicable tax rate is 25 per cent. All income tax adjustments will be paid or refunded currently.

***Required:***

1. Prepare adjusting journal entries to correct the company's records.
2. Calculate the effect of the above entries on:
   - **a** net profit for 2002
   - **b** 2002 beginning retained profits
   - **c** 2002 ending retained profits.
3. Prepare corrected statements of financial position and financial performance for 2002.
4. Comment on the company's performance for 2002 and its position at year-end.

## Problem 15.14 (Challenging) Intangibles

Shown below are extracts from note 1 of the financial statements of Ten Network Holdings Limited and Seven Network Limited.

### Ten Network

#### Television licenses

Television licences are stated at cost and are supported by independent advice recieved from Grant Samuel & Associates Pty Limited in October 2000. The television licences continue to be subject to Government legislation and regulation by the Australian Broadcasting Authority (ABA). The Directors have no reason to believe that the licences will not be renewed in due course.

The Directors regularly assess the carrying value of licences so as to ensure that they are not carried at a value greater than their recoverable amount. No amortisation is provided against these assets as the Directors believe that the television licences do not have a limited useful life.

[The following paragraph appeared only in the 2000 Annual Report, but was excluded from the 2001 Annual Report.] Television licences have been included as a separate category under noncurrent assets. These assets are the principal assets of the consolidated entity and it is considered separate disclosure in the balance sheet is necessary for the consolidated financial report to show a true and fair view of the state of affairs of the consolidated entity at balance date ...

#### Television program rights

[This paragraph is taken from the 2001 Annual Report.] Television programs which are available for broadcast are recognised as an asset and stated at residual cost. Series programs are written off in full upon initial airing. Features are amortised over their estimated useful lives. Furthermore, the carrying values of television program rights are reviewed on a periodic basis and, where required, written down to their recoverable amount. Television programs at balance date for which the telecast licence period has commenced or will commence in the succeeding year has been classified as a current asset.

## Seven Network

### Television licences

The television licences are renewable every five years under the provisions of the *Broadcasting Services Act 1992*. The directors have no reason to believe that they will not be renewed.

Television licences are carried at deemed cost. In prior years the television licences were carried at independent valuation, carried out by Grant Samuel & Associates Pty Limited on the basis of market value of the television licences as at 31 December 1998. This valuation was adopted as the deemed cost effective 25 June 2000.

No amortisation is provided against the carrying amount as the directors believe that the lives of these assets are of such duration, and the residual value would be such, that the amortisation charge, if any, would not be material. The directors review the carrying amounts of these assets at balance date to ensure that they do not exceed their recoverable amounts.

The potential impact of capital gains tax has not been taken into account on the grounds that the licences are an integral part of the consolidated entity's operations, and that there is no current intention to sell the licences.

### Program rights

Television program rights are carried at the lower of cost less amortisation and net realisable value. Cost comprises acquisition of copyright and, for programs produced using the company's facilities, direct labour and materials and an appropriate proportion of fixed and variable overheads.

### Recognition

Television program assets and program liabilities are recognised from the commencement of the rights period of the contract. Contract payments made prior to commencement of the rights period are disclosed as a prepayment and included under television program rights and inventories.

### Amortisation policy

The consolidated entity's amortisation policy requires the amortisation of features and cartoons straight-line over three years from commencement of the rights period or over the rights period of the contract (whichever is the lesser). All other purchased program product is amortised straight-line over the lesser of 12 months or the rights period. Locally produced programs are expenses on telecast or in full on the twelfth month after completion.

In addition, an annual review is carried out to identify any programs which are not expected to be aired. These programs are written off when identified.

***Required:***

**1** What are the differences between the accounting policies of the two companies for television program rights and television licences?

**2** Which company do you believe has the more conservative accounting policies? Why?

## CASE 15A Woolworths Limited case

Refer to the extracts of the annual report of Woolworths Limited in appendix 2.

**1** Provide examples of some accounting policy choices disclosed in note 1 of the accounts.

**2** Do any of the other notes provide further details on important policy choices?

**3** Referring to note 1 'Significant Accounting Policies', discuss a possible alternative treatment of the pre-opening expenses, purchase and promotional inventories and borrowing costs. In each case state the effect on net profit for 2001 and on total assets at 24 June 2001 if the alternative had been used.

**4** Assume there was a change of accounting policy to write off intangibles over 10 years. What effect would this have on net profit and total assets?

**5** If operating leases had been treated as finance leases, what effect would this have on total assets and total liabilities?

**6** Would a downward revaluation of liquor licences have any effect on profit?

**7** Will the figures in the 2000 column of the 2001 annual report be the same as they would have appeared in the 2000 annual report?

## CASE 15B Intangibles

Read the following article:

### Some companies are being taken to task over loose accounting in their financial reports

*by John Kavanagh*

When shareholders of Australia's biggest gold miner, Normandy Mining, opened their 1999 annual reports last month, they would have been drawn to the proud claim by the company's executive chairman, Robert de Crespigny, 49, that the profit after tax and abnormals of $103.8 million was the third highest in the company's history. A close reading of the accounts would have shown this to be a meaningless claim, which told more about the company's attitude to its shareholders than about the state of its earnings.

Such are the vagaries of company reporting that de Crespigny's statement can be supported, but a summary of the company's performance since 1992 shows that its 'consolidated profit after tax' for the 1998–99 financial year was the lowest in six years. The company's cost of gold production had gone up and the margin over the spot gold price it realised on its hedging positions (an important contributor to earnings) had gone down. Shareholders' equity fell from $1.49 billion to $1.37 billion. None of this, which tends to contradict the bullish tone of the executive chairman's remarks, is explained.

Accounting standards are being exploited by companies wanting to present their results in the best light, making it increasingly difficult for investors to gain a clear understanding of how the companies in which they invest are performing. The Australian Securities and Investments Commission (ASIC) has started a campaign to get companies to observe the spirit of the accounting standards and to communicate meaningful and timely information to shareholders.

Last year, for the first time, ASIC ran a surveillance program on more than 180 company financial reports. ASIC chief accountant Jan McCahey, 40, says the overall standard of reporting was good but there were problems. She says a number of companies are failing to amortise their intangible assets, others wrongly classify amounts (usually losses) as abnormal items to improve the presentation of profit-and-loss statements, and others are over-provisioning to create 'hollow logs' that will smooth future earnings.

ASIC went public on requests it made to three companies to amend their financial reports or make additional disclosure. They were Novogen, a biotechnology company, Seven Network and Media Entertainment Group (MEG), a cinema and television advertising production company.

Novogen was asked to make additional disclosure about an asset writedown to clarify whether the carrying value of the asset was recoverable. In its 1998 financial statements, it had described the write-off as resulting from a change in accounting policy. But ASIC's view was that the assets were not recoverable beyond reasonable doubt. Novogen's treatment did not comply with the accounting standard.

MEG was challenged over an accounting policy that booked sales when contracts to screen advertising were signed, rather than after the screenings had occurred. ASIC started court action, which was settled in April when MEG agreed to lodge revised financial statements for 1998.

Seven was forced to revise its accounts for 1997 and 1998 after ASIC objected to the treatment of its investment in the Hollywood studio Metro–Goldwyn–Mayer (MGM). Seven did not include unrealised foreign-exchange losses and gains on the investment in its profit-and-loss statement, which had the effect of dramatically altering reported earnings in 1997 and 1998. According to ASIC, if Seven had prepared its accounts in accordance with the standard, it would not have been permitted to pay dividends for the 1997–98 financial year.

In addition, Seven capitalised the interest on the borrowings relating to the investment in MGM. ASIC took the view that this was not an appropriate accounting treatment, and that the consolidated profit after tax for the 1996–97 financial year was overstated by $8.7 million.

ASIC is running a surveillance program again this year, and it has already identified two companies whose financial reporting needs clarification. It has queried the resources company North Limited over a change to its accounting policy that has affected the valuation of forest reserves. And it has challenged Brisbane Airport Corporation over the amortisation of its airport lease premium (the licence to operate the airport).

McCahey says: 'If a company doesn't amortise its intangible assets it is, in effect, overstating its earnings. It may be paying dividends when there is no buffer to cover those payments. In the worst case, the situation runs on until the bubble bursts, as it did at Burns Philp, and then shareholders suffer.

'Provisioning is the problem in reverse. Companies acquiring other companies often create provisions for undefined future expenses. What this gives them is a "hollow log" – expenses can be written off against these provisions in a bad year so that the profit-and-loss statement is protected. The heart of the problem is that shareholders are getting a distorted picture of how the company is performing.'

Wayne Lonergan, 53, a partner at PricewaterhouseCoopers, agrees: 'What is worrying about the trend is that managers and directors have vested interests in this misreporting. If their remuneration is tied to reported profits or movements in the share price, there is a strong incentive for them to use techniques that smooth earnings. What the accounting profession would like to see is representational neutrality, which means giving investors a real insight into the progress of the company, year on year.'

Lonergan says it is up to shareholders to look more deeply into companies' financial statements and call directors to account over issues of poor reporting.

This may well happen at Normandy's annual general meeting, which is scheduled for 27 October in Adelaide. Last year Normandy produced more than 1.5 million ounces of gold; it reached its leading position in the Australian gold industry through a series of acquisitions throughout the 1990s. Normandy spent $1.8 billion over about eight years, yet the value of shareholders' funds grew only about $340 million – from $1.03 billion in 1992 to $1.37 billion at 30 June.

A byproduct of Normandy's takeover activity has been a dramatic increase in the number of shares on issue – from 437 million in 1992 to 1.67 billion at 30 June. As a result, earnings per share have plunged. In 1992, consolidated profit after tax of $90.6 million brought earnings per share of 20 cents. In 1999, profit of $119.4 million translated into earnings per share of just 7 cents.

To compensate for the big fall in earnings per share, Normandy has boosted its dividend payout. At the start of this decade, the dividend payout ratio was 25–30 per cent of net profit, but this year the dividend payout of $102.6 million represented 85 per cent of net profit. Directors offer no explanation in the 1999 accounts for the change to dividend policy, or its effect on the company's capacity to carry out exploration or mining development.

Normandy earned $386 million from its gold production last year. Its cash cost of production was $329 million and its total cost of production (including depreciation, amortisation and mine closure costs) was $413 million. Normandy depends on its hedging operations to make a profit out of gold production. Last year, the margin it earned on hedging contracted as a result of currency and metal-price movements, and the margin will shrink further this year.

Seven and its executive chairman, Kerry Stokes, may be in ASIC's sights again this year after Seven's decision to double the value of its television licences. The move was made without the benefit of any independent analysis and was based largely on the view that the valuation of Seven's licences should be brought into line with those of the other networks. This is despite the fact that Seven's 13.3 per cent profit margin (earnings before interest and tax as a percentage of sales) is well below that of rivals Nine (29.3 per cent) and Ten (32 per cent).

Media companies are at the centre of a dispute with ASIC and accounting bodies over the treatment of intangible assets, such as mastheads and broadcasting licences. ASIC supports the introduction of an international accounting standard that would make companies write down the value of intangibles over a set period, usually 20 years. Further, the international standard under consideration by local accounting bodies does not allow for any value to be attached to internally generated intangibles.

McCahey says although the general rule is that intangible assets should be amortised, there are cases in which it is legitimate to attach a higher valuation to them. What ASIC expects to see in such cases is full disclosure of the treatment of those assets, with reasons for the revaluation.

Lonergan says companies complain too much about having to amortise intangibles. 'It is cash flow that drives a company's value, and amortisation does not affect cash flow. Directors who complain about it are either displaying their ignorance or indicating their belief in the basic ignorance of the average investor.'

Pacific Dunlop directors will be preparing for some pointed questions from shareholders at the annual general meeting at the Melbourne Convention Centre on 3 November 1999. In July 1998, the company announced that it had signed a contract for the sale of its GNB battery-making business to Quexco of Texas for $US550 million. Pacific Dunlop accounted for the transaction in its 1997–98 accounts, even though the sale was completed after the end of the financial year. It argued that the sale process was largely completed in 1997–98.

Pacific Dunlop chief executive Rod Chadwick, 53, said the sale would give the company a huge boost, allowing it to retire a substantial amount of debt and make investments in its more profitable businesses, such as the rubber-goods manufacturer Ansell. But if ever there was a case of counting chickens before they hatched, this was it. By October, the sale price had come back to $US500 million and Pacific Dunlop announced that it had agreed to help Quexco finance the purchase with up to $US100 million of vendor finance.

In June, Pacific Dunlop announced that the sale had fallen through. In its 1999 annual report, the company restated its 1998 figures to reallocate the sale proceeds. A loss of $94 million reported in the December half (a result of the sale negotiation) has been retained because it was a 'clear indication of the impairment of value' in GNB.

Several analysts rerated Pacific Dunlop after the report of the sale last year. They had been worried that the company's debt level, at 70 per cent, was too high and that it was operating in too many low-margin businesses. By getting out of GNB the company seemed to be tackling both issues. Pacific Dunlop's share price rose from about $2.50 in June to a 12-month high of more than $3 in August. The prospect of a fundamental recovery at Australia's biggest manufacturer encouraged investors to back the stock. Today the share price is again languishing, at about $2.30.

Lonergan says companies can avoid such problems if they stop trying to finesse their accounts and accept the principle that assets should marked to market. If the balance date is 30 June, then sales entered in the profit-and-loss statement should end on that date, and assets in the balance sheet should be stated at their market valuation on the day.

'Again, it is a question of companies saying that their shareholders will not understand the process, that they will be frightened by the volatility introduced by that valuation method. There are shortcomings; there is potential for confusion and in some cases it is hard to get an accurate market price for an asset. But what we have now, which is a mix of historical cost and current valuation, is useless. What you paid for something five years ago is not useful information for an investor. Already we are seeing life insurance companies and general insurers using the mark-to-market method, and we have just moved to ... that method for valuing rural and agricultural assets.

'Directors must recognise that investors allow quite a bit of margin in their share-price valuations because of all this fudging. The effect is a higher cost of capital. It is time for Australian companies to get in step with what is going on around the world.'

(Source: John Kavanagh, *Business Review Weekly*, 15 October 1999, pp. 91–7.)

***Required:***

1 Explain the effect on profit, total assets and total liabilities of not amortising goodwill and over-provisioning 'to create hollow logs'.
2 Explain the issue with Novogen and how it would have an impact on profit.
3 Explain the issue with Seven Network and how it would have an impact on profit.
4 Explain the issue with Media Entertainment Group and how it would have an impact on profit.
5 How can not amortising goodwill affect the payment of dividends?
6 What is the problem with over-provisioning?
7 'There is a strong incentive for them to use techniques that smooth earnings.' Why might management do this? How would it be achieved?
8 How does Normandy's dividend policy affect the company's capacity to carry on exploration or mine development?
9 Discuss how an auditor may test the reasonableness of Seven's revaluation of television rights.
10 Discuss the impact of the international accounting standard on intangibles.
11 Lonergan comments: 'It is cash flow that drives a company's value, and amortisation does not affect cash flow. Directors who complain about it are . . . displaying their ignorance . . .' Discuss.
12 Do you agree with Pacific Dunlop's revenue recognition policy concerning the GNB battery?

## CASE 15C Accounting policy choices

Shown below is an extract from an article in the *Australian Financial Review* on 15 August 1996. There are a few items in the article we have not covered in this book, but you should be able to comprehend the key elements. Note 1 from the 1996 accounts of Sydney Harbour Casino Holdings Limited notes that 'Pre-opening expenses consist primarily of set-up costs, establishment costs and the costs associated with the organisation of the Casino licence, share issue and finance costs. Pre-opening expenses have been written off as incurred'.

### Sydney: We're as good as Crown

Sydney Harbour Casino Holdings Ltd recorded a mere $1 million net profit for its first full six months of operations, falling well short of both prospectus forecasts and its booming Melbourne counterpart.

But chairman Mr Dick Warburton yesterday rejected suggestions that Melbourne's Crown Ltd was outperforming the Sydney gaming house, saying the better bottom line down south was largely a function of accounting methods, and had little to do with real operations.

Sydney Casino has chosen to account for large chunks of its expenses as they occur – rather than follow Crown's lead and capitalise those costs – leaving the company with large abnormal losses.

'When you get such a significant difference in accounting practices, it skews the results,' Mr Warburton told reporters. 'What we're just trying to point out is that when you put it on a like-to-like basis, you'll see the result is exceptionally good.'

Mr Warburton produced a string of numbers to show that when indicators other than bottom-line profit were used, Sydney Casino's position was equal to or better than its competitor.

He said Crown was a bigger casino — with 2820 'gaming spaces' available against Sydney Casino's 1700 – and as such was always expected to show bigger overall numbers.

However, on a win-per-table or win-per-visitor basis, Sydney Casino was trading more strongly than Crown, he said.

Mr Warburton said Sydney Casino's pre-abnormal $24.8 million result was wiped out by $22 million in pre-opening costs and amortisation of pre-paid rentals.

Before accounting for interest, tax, abnormals, depreciation and amortisation, earnings were $47 million – a result that Mr Warburton said confirmed the company was performing exceptionally well in a competitive market.

However, the result was well short of prospectus forecasts.

**Table 1 Sydney Harbour Casino**

| Half-year | 1996 ($m) | 1995 ($m) |
|---|---|---|
| Sales | 178.3 | nil |
| Other revenue | 4.4 | 1.6 |
| Depreciation | –10.6 | –2.2 |
| EBIT | 36.5 | –0.5 |
| Net Interest | –11.6 | –0.3 |
| Pre-tax Profit | 24.8 | –0.8 |
| Abnormals | –22.4 | –25.0 |
| Less Tax | –1.4 | 8.9 |
| Minorities | nil | nil |
| Net Profit | 1.0 | –17.0 |
| Interim div c | nil | nil |
| Div (nil) | nil | nil |
| EPS c | –0.9 | –18.9 |
| Shares (yest) | +1c | $1.76 |

Revenue for the 1996 financial year came in 22 per cent weaker than prospectus forecasts: the casino pulled in $303 million against a promised $387 million.

Also, it predicted a net profit of $37 million, based on an operating profit of $67 million. Instead, its year to June result was a $4.7 million net loss, and an operating profit of just $48.5 million.

Problems with restaurants and bars continued to plague the temporary operation, with revenue from the food operations well below expectations.

Acting managing director Mr Don Tatzin said the catering side of the business had been repositioned, away from being a profit centre in its own right to more of a promotional tool.

The casino also renewed its call for a new, lower tax rate for high-roller gamblers, saying it would bring in millions more in revenue to government coffers.

(Source: *Australian Financial Review*, 15 August 1996).

***Required:***

1 Explain, as simply as possible, what is included in pre-opening costs.
2 How does the accounting treatment of pre-opening costs differ between the two casinos? What effect do the differences have on the profit and loss and balance sheets of the two companies?
3 Why may Sydney Casino have chosen to account for pre-opening costs in this way?
4 Is the choice of accounting method an excuse for not reaching profit forecasts?

## CASE 15D International accounting policies

Read the following article:

### US view lowers Telstra's profit

*by Christine Lucy*

Telstra Corp's $4.1 billion net profit in 2001 was 12 per cent lower when calculated under American accounting rules, amplifying the premium at which the telco's stock is trading, compared to those of its regional sector peers.

According to accounts lodged in the US over the weekend, Telstra's operating revenue fell by 15 per cent to $19.4 billion for 2001 when calculated under US generally accepted accounting principles (US GAAP), while net income dropped from $4.1 billion to $3.6 billion. This meant earnings per share for the year fell 12.5 per cent from 32 cents to 28 cents which, based on Telstra's closing price on Friday of $5.20 a share, representing a price–earnings ratio of 18.6 times 2001 earnings, based on US GAAP profits, compared to the 16.5 times based on Australian reported earnings.

Reporting of the Telstra accounts under US GAAP included increased amortisation of software assets, redundancy and restructuring costs and differing accounting principles relating to Telstra's Asian joint ventures.

Under Australian accounting principles, Telstra's profit was 10.4 per cent higher than last year's but was boosted by several one-off gains, including a $725 million superannuation writeback.

A new report by Deutsche Bank said Telstra would need to show an earnings growth rate of more than 6 per cent to justify its trading premium when compared with its sector peers. Instead, Telstra is forecasting a flat outlook in the interim, with the full-year increasingly uncertain.

(Source: Christine Lucy, *Australian Financial Review*, 8 October 2001, p. 14.)

*Required:*

1 What caused Telstra to show a different profit in Australia compared to the USA?
2 Why would accounting policies vary between countries? Is variation more or less important than it was 10 years ago?
3 Why don't different countries align their accounting policies?

## CASE 15E Differences in international GAAP

Rio Tinto reports in the UK, and its financial statements at 31 December 2000 show the following reconciliations between Australian GAAP and US GAAP:

**Reconciliation with Australian GAAP**
31 December

| 2000 A$m | 1999 A$m | 2000 £m | 1999 £m | | 2000 US$m | 1999 US$m |
|---|---|---|---|---|---|---|
| **2 600** | 1 986 | **995** | 792 | **Net earnings under UK GAAP** | **1 507** | 1 282 |
| | | | | Increase/(decrease) net of tax in respect of: | | |
| **—** | (454) | **—** | (181) | Abnormal increase in provisions | **—** | (293) |
| **(250)** | (235) | **(96)** | (94) | Goodwill amortisation | **(145)** | (152) |
| **3** | (5) | **1** | (2) | Taxation | **2** | (3) |
| **(43)** | — | **(17)** | — | Higher costs of sales resulting from acquisition accounting | **(25)** | — |
| **17** | 17 | **7** | 7 | Other | **9** | 11 |
| **2 327** | 1 309 | **890** | 522 | **Net earnings under Australian GAAP** | **1 348** | 845 |

**Reconciliation with US GAAP**
31 December

| 2000 A$m | 1999 A$m | 2000 £m | 1999 £m | | 2000 US$m | 1999 US$m |
|---|---|---|---|---|---|---|
| **2 600** | 1 986 | **995** | 792 | **Net earnings under UK GAAP** | **1 507** | 1 282 |
| | | | | Increase/(decrease) net of tax in respect of: | | |
| **(180)** | (173) | **(69)** | (69) | Goodwill amortisation | **(104)** | (112) |
| **(5)** | (90) | **(2)** | (36) | Asset writedowns | **(3)** | (58) |
| **—** | (76) | **—** | (30) | Provision against receivable | **—** | (49) |
| **(212)** | — | **(81)** | — | Exchange differences taken to earnings under US GAAP | **(123)** | — |
| **3** | (5) | **1** | (2) | Taxation | **2** | (3) |
| **(159)** | (69) | **(61)** | (28) | Other | **(92)** | (45) |
| **2 047** | 1 573 | **783** | 627 | Income before cumulative effect of change in accounting principle | **1 187** | 1 015 |
| **—** | (88) | **—** | (35) | Cumulative effect of change in accounting principle for start-up costs | **—** | (57) |
| **2 047** | 1 485 | **783** | 592 | **Net income under US GAAP** | **1 187** | 958 |

***Required:***

1. Why would Rio Tinto provide this information?
2. In Australian dollars, compare net profit using Australian GAAP, UK GAAP and USA GAAP.
3. In US dollars, compare net profit using Australian GAAP, UK GAAP and USA GAAP.
4. What caused the differences above?

## Notes

1. Australian Society of CPAs and the Institute of Chartered Accountants in Australia, 'Understanding Financial Statement Audits: A Guide for Financial Statement Users', in *Auditing Handbook 1997*, pp. 3–26.
2. See M. Gibbins and A.K. Mason, *Professional Judgement in Financial Reporting*, chapter 5, Canadian Institute of Chartered Accountants, Toronto 1988. Reprinted by permission of the Canadian Institute of Chartered Accountants, Toronto, Canada.
3. *Effects of changing to the annual weighted average method:* cost of goods sold expense would go up $892, so net profit would decline by 70 per cent of that, $624. Income tax expense and liability would go down by the other 30 per cent, $268. Working capital would go down by $892 (inventory asset decline) and up by $268 (income tax liability decline) for a net decrease of $624, the same as the net profit decline. There is no immediate effect on cash or cash flow.

   *Effects of changing to the periodic LIFO method:* the figures, in the same order as above, are up $1800, decline $1260, decline $540, down by $1800, and up by $540 for net decrease of $1260. No cash effect.

   *Effects of changing to the perpetual LIFO method:* the figures, in the same order again, are up $700, decline $490, decline $210, down by $700, and up $210 for a net decrease of $490. No cash effect.

# Appendix 1

# Solution outlines to asterisked homework and discussion problems

Several homework and discussion problems in each chapter are marked with asterisks. For your use in self-study, outlines of solutions to these problems have been prepared. The outlines are informal and often chatty, and you should take them as suggestions of valid approaches, not as the only valid approaches. Students and instructors have various views of the world, and such views colour the way answers to accounting problems, as with other important problems, are developed. Coming up with a coherent personal view of accounting is the responsibility of each student, and the solutions provided here should be fitted to that view, not override it. The solution outlines are intended to help you, so they are written to be clear, not vague or evasive. But they can never be complete, nor can they anticipate the intelligence and creativity that you will bring to the problems.

Sometimes, the solution to a problem will require some assumptions or data not explicitly given in the problem. That is the way real-world problems tend to be formed: not necessarily completely laid out or unambiguously phrased. Become comfortable with stating your assumptions and knowing where they make a difference, because in dealing with the real problems you will face in your career, such assumptions can be replaced by evidence to produce high-quality solutions, but only if you know what the assumptions are and when they matter.

*Always* try each problem on your own, or with friends, and make rough notes of your solution, before you look at the solution outline. If you look at the solution outline before you think about the problem, you will rob the solution of its main value to you, which is feedback on your own learning. Problems always look easier if you look at the solutions prematurely, so if you do that, you can fool yourself about what your ability is.

## Solution outline for problem 1.1

| | |
|---|---:|
| **Sales** | |
| Cash sales | 640 000 |
| Credit sales | 490 000 |
| Total sales | 1 130 000 |
| **Expenses** | |
| Paid | 590 000 |
| Outstanding | 380 000 |
| Total expenses | 970 000 |
| Accrual profit | 160 000 |

Accrual profit = Total sales – Total expenses
= 1 130 000 – 970 000
= 160 000

## Solution outline for problem 1.2

**1** Cash in the bank as at the end of 2002:
$12 430 + $1000 + $68 990 – $1480 – $36 910 = $44 030.

**2** Accrual accounting profit for 2002:
$68 990 + $850 – $36 910 – $2650 – $3740 = $26 540.

## Solution outline for problem 1.3

| | |
|---|---:|
| Revenue | 40 000 |
| Expenses | |
| Interest (10,000 × 0.05 × 0.5) | (250) |
| Wages | (11 600) |
| Depreciation ([4500 ÷ 3] × 0.5 | (750) |
| Other | (15 200) |
| Joe's profit | $12 200 |

## Solution outline for problem 1.4

**1**

**Broadway Limited**
**Statement of financial position**
**as at 30 June 2002**

| | |
|---|---:|
| **Assets** | |
| Cash at bank | 60 000 |
| Accounts receivable | 80 000 |
| Inventory | 120 000 |
| Equipment | 100 000 |
| **Total assets** | **360 000** |
| **Liabilities and shareholders' equity** | |
| *Liabilities* | |
| Bank loan | 50 000 |
| Wages payable | 50 000 |
| Taxes payable | 40 000 |
| **Total liabilities** | 140 000 |

| | |
|---|---|
| *Shareholders' equity* | |
| Share capital | 150 000 |
| Retained profits | 70 000 |
| **Total shareholders' equity** | **220 000** |
| **Total liabilities and shareholders' equity** | **360 000** |

2 Profit for year ended 30 June 2002
= Retained profits at end of year – Retained profits at start of year
= 70 000 – 50 000 = $20 000

## Solution outline for problem 2.1

1

**Bluebird Bakery**
**Statement of financial position**
**as at 30 June 2002**

| **Assets** | **$** | **Liabilities** | **$** |
|---|---|---|---|
| *Current assets* | | *Current liabilities* | |
| Cash on hand | 895 | Owing to suppliers | 11 240 |
| Cash in bank | 4 992 | Wages owing to employees | 2 246 |
| Owing by customers | 3 823 | | **13 486** |
| Supplies inventory cost | 13 220 | Noncurrent liabilities | |
| Unsold baked goods cost | 245 | Loan from bank | 14 500 |
| | **23 175** | | **14 500** |
| *Noncurrent assets* | | **Total liabilities** | **27 986** |
| Bakery equipment cost | 129 153 | **Equity** | |
| Accumulated depreciation | (43 996) | Shareholders' capital | 80 346 |
| | **85 157** | **Total equity** | **80 346** |
| **Total assets** | **108 332** | **Total liabilities and equity** | **108 332** |

2 Working capital = $23 175 – $13 486 = $9689
Working capital ratio = $23 175 ÷ $13 486 = 1.72.

3

**Bluebird Bakery**
**Statement of financial position**
**as at 30 June 2002**

| **Assets** | **$** | **Liabilities** | **$** |
|---|---|---|---|
| *Current assets* | | *Current liabilities* | |
| Cash | 5 887 | Accounts payable | 11 240 |
| Accounts receivable | 3 823 | Wages payable | 2 246 |
| Inventory – baked goods | 245 | | **13 486** |
| Inventory – supplies | 13 220 | *Noncurrent liabilities* | |
| | **23 175** | Bank loan | 14 500 |
| *Noncurrent assets* | | | **14 500** |
| Bakery equipment | 129 153 | **Total liabilities** | **27 986** |
| Accumulated depreciation | (43 996) | **Equity** | |
| | **85 157** | Share capital | 80 346 |
| | | **Total equity** | **80 346** |
| **Total assets** | **108 332** | **Total liabilities and equity** | **108 332** |

## Solution outline for problem 2.2

1 Here are the definitions, in enough detail for you to see if you've chosen the appropriate items from the Chez statement of financial position.

  a A current asset is an item carrying future benefit that will be realised in cash or consumed within a year. This includes 'cash equivalent' assets, which are assets that are cash or can be converted at any moment, and other current assets, which can be converted within the year, but not immediately. Examples: cash and cash equivalents, short term investments, receivables, prepaid expenses and inventories.

  b A noncurrent asset is an asset that will be converted to cash or consumed in more than one year. Examples: land, buildings, equipment, long-term investments, and other assets, such as development costs.

  c A current liability is any obligation that must be paid in cash within one year, or an estimated payment incorporated as part of accrual accounting. Examples: accounts payable, dividends payable, income taxes payable, portion of long-term debt due within a year, and deferred revenue (revenue or deposits collected from customers before it has been earned, so still an obligation to the customers).

  d A noncurrent liability is an obligation or accrual that is due to be paid more than one year in the future (minus any part included in current liabilities). Examples: mortgages, long-term bank loans, debentures, pension liabilities and deferred income taxes.

  e Equity represents the residual ownership interest in a company. It is one of the ways in which assets such as cash and long-term investments are financed (liabilities are the other way). It is composed of direct investments by owners (such as share capital) and the indirect investment represented by retained profits, which is accumulated profit the owners have chosen to leave in the company rather than withdrawing as dividends. Chez has share capital and retained profits.

2 Assets, liabilities and equity have general definitions such as those above, but each company's particular circumstances may produce variations in how some items are classified. For a manufacturing company, the land that its factory is on is a noncurrent asset, but for a real estate company that buys and sells land, land may be a current asset (inventory for sale). For you and Chez, a bank loan is a liability, but for a bank, which is a lender rather than a borrower, a bank loan is an asset (an amount receivable from the borrower). Some kinds of debt are so much like shares that they may be classified as equity, while some shares are so much like debt that they may be classified as liabilities. Every company's statement of financial position must fit its circumstances so that it will be a valid measure of the company's financial position.

3

| | **2002** | **2001** |
|---|---|---|
| Working capital | 80 281 − 27 795 = 52 486 | 52 026 − 17 171 = 34 855 |
| Working capital ratio | 80 281 ÷ 27 795 = 2.89 | 52 026 ÷ 17 171 = 3.03 |

The working capital ratio is positive in both years, showing that there is about three times as much current assets as current liabilities. The company has a strong short-term financial position, although this has deteriorated slightly in 2002, with the working capital ratio falling to 2.89.

## Solution outline for problem 2.3

**PSM Limited**
**Statement of financial position**
**as at 30 June 2002**

| | $ |
|---|---|
| **Current assets** | |
| Cash | 11 636 |
| Accounts receivable | 47 515 |
| Inventory | 66 479 |
| Prepayments | 3 958 |
| Investments | 3 371 |
| | 132 959 |

| | $ |
|---|---|
| **Noncurrent assets** | |
| Other receivables | 361 |
| Investments | 2 087 |
| Property, plant and equipment | 67 760 |
| Other long-term assets | 42 742 |
| | 112 950 |
| **Total assets** | **245 909** |
| **Current liabilities** | |
| Accounts payable | 43 091 |
| Provisions for employee entitlements | 30 919 |
| | 74 010 |
| **Noncurrent liabilities** | |
| Long-term borrowings | 30 866 |
| Provisions for employee entitlements | 3 969 |
| | 34 835 |
| **Total liabilities** | **108 845** |
| **Net assets** | **137 064** |
| **Shareholders' equity** | |
| Share capital | 108 518 |
| Retained profits | 28 546 |
| **Total shareholders' equity** | **137 064** |

## Solution outline for problem 2.4

1 Land is on the statement of financial position because it is an asset – that is, a resource owned or controlled and having economic value. Land carries the potential to produce revenues for the company in the future, as do other assets.

2 Assets = $5222 + $2410 = $7632.

3 Share capital is one of the sources of funds used to acquire the assets on the left side of the statement of financial position. Therefore, it is not an asset that can be used to purchase more land, but a co-creator of the assets that now exist. Assets can only be used to buy other assets. Therefore, you must use $3000 cash or another asset to buy a new asset. The company did not have enough cash, since some had already been used to buy inventory and land, so more cash had to be borrowed.

4 Retained profits is the accumulation of net profit minus dividends for each year of the company's history. It is the accumulated residual undistributed earnings of the company, and is on the statement of financial position because it is a source of present assets (because assets created in the process of earning profit were not all distributed to owners).

5 Net profit = $10 116 – $9881 = $235.

6 Ending retained profits were $1222. Subtracting profit that had been added ($235) and adding back dividends that had been deducted ($120) gives beginning retained profits of $1107. To check this, going the other way gives $1107 + $235 – $120 = $1222.

7 Ending retained profits would be $1107 + $10 116 – $11 600 = –$377. There would have been a net loss for the year of $1484, and that would have turned the retained profit at the beginning into a deficit at the end of $377.

8 If the debit for the deficit were shown among the assets, that would indicate that the company had something of value for the future, a resource that could be used to generate profit in the future. This is not at all the case: instead, the company has incurred more expenses than revenue and has, therefore, diminished some of the equity (share capital) put into it by the owners. Its resources were decreased by this, not increased as would be indicated by showing it as an asset. That's why a deficit is deducted from other equity (such as share capital) and shown as a negative item on the right-hand side of the statement of financial position.

## Solution outline for problem 3.1

**1**

| | Assets | | | = Liabilities | | | + Owners' equity | | |
|---|---|---|---|---|---|---|---|---|---|
| | **Cash** | **Accounts receivable** | **Inventory** | **Accounts payable** | **Rent payable** | **Tax payable** | **Retained profits** | **Revenue** | **Expenses** |
| 1 | | +10 000 | | | | | | +10 000 | |
| 2 | +9 600 | –9 600 | | | | | | | |
| 3 | | | +6 100 | +6 100 | | | | | |
| 4 | –6 300 | | | –6 300 | | | | | |
| 5 | | | –6 400 | | | | | | –6 400 |
| 6 | | | | | 2 400 | | | | –2 400 |
| 7 | –2 900 | | | | –2 900 | | | | |
| 8 | | | | | | 350 | | | –350 |
| 9 | –450 | | | | | | –450 | | |
| Total | –50 | 400 | –300 | –200 | –500 | 350 | –450 | 10 000 | –9 150 |
| | | 50 | = 50 | | | | | | |

NB: Increases in expenses have been entered as minus figures.

**2**

**Flashy Fashions Pty Ltd**
**Statement of financial performance**
**for the year ended 30 September 2002**

| | $ |
|---|---|
| Sales | 10 000 |
| Less: Cost of goods sold | 6 400 |
| Gross profit | 3 600 |
| Less: Operating expenses | |
| Rent | 2 400 |
| Profit before tax | 1 200 |
| Less: Tax expense | 350 |
| Net profit | 850 |

**Flashy Fashions Pty Ltd**
**Statement of financial position**
**as at 30 September 2002**

| **Current assets** | **$** | **Current liabilities** | **$** |
|---|---|---|---|
| Cash | 750 | Accounts payable | 400 |
| Accounts receivable | 800 | Tax payable | 350 |
| Inventory | 600 | | |
| Prepaid rent | 200 | **Shareholders' equity** | |
| | | Share Capital | 500 |
| | | Retained profits | 1 100 |
| | **2 350** | | **2 350** |

## Solution outline for problem 3.2

1 $160 000
2 $105 000
3 $180 000
4 $140 000

## Solution outline for problem 3.3

**Arctic Limo Services Pty Ltd**
**Statement of financial performance**
**for the year ended 30 September 2003**

| | $ | $ |
|---|---|---|
| Revenue | | 300 000 |
| Less: Expenses: | | |
| Wages | 100 000 | |
| Other expenses | 70 000 | |
| Depreciation | 10 000 | 180 00 |
| Profit before income tax | | 120 000 |
| Less: Income tax expense | | 35 000 |
| **Net profit** | | 85 000 |

**Arctic Limo Services Pty Ltd**
**Statement of retained profits**
**for the year ended 30 September 2003**

| | $ |
|---|---|
| Beginning balance (30 September 2002) | 4 000 |
| Net profit for the year | 85 000 |
| Dividends declared | (80 000) |
| Ending balance (30 September 2003) | 9 000 |

**Arctic Limo Services Pty Ltd**
**Statement of financial position**
**as at 30 September 2003**

| | 2003<br>$ | 2002<br>$ |
|---|---|---|
| **Assets** | | |
| *Current assets* | | |
| Cash | 2 000 | 4 000 |
| Accounts receivable | 0 | 1 000 |
| | 2 000 | 5 000 |
| *Noncurrent assets* | | |
| Equipment (limos) | 90 000 | 60 000 |
| Less: Accumulated depreciation | (30 000) | (20 000) |
| | 60 000 | 40 000 |
| **Total assets** | 62 000 | 45 000 |
| **Liabilities and equity** | | |
| *Current liabilities* | | |
| Loan | 0 | 10 000 |
| Wages payable | 2 000 | 0 |
| | 2 000 | 10 000 |
| *Noncurrent liabilities* | | |
| Long-term limo financing | 50 000 | 30 000 |
| *Shareholders' equity* | | |
| Share capital | 1 000 | 1 000 |
| Retained profits | 9 000 | 4 000 |
| | 10 000 | 5 000 |
| Total liabilities and equity | 62 000 | 45 000 |

*Assumptions:*

- Receivable amount due from Lucky Eddie appears to have been current because he paid it within a year.
- Loan also appears to have been current.
- Wages are payable over a short term; a reasonable assumption is that employees would not allow their wages to remain unpaid for long.
- Noncurrent liabilities have no current portion payable within the next year.

## Solution outline for problem 3.4

**1** The journal entries are shown below:

| | | | $ | $ |
|---|---|---|---|---|
| 1 | DR | Loan from shareholders | 10 000 | |
| | CR | Cash | | 10 000 |
| 2 | DR | Cash | 11 240 | |
| | CR | Accounts receivable | | 11 240 |
| 3 | DR | Inventory | 5 320 | |
| | CR | Accounts payable | | 5 320 |
| 4 | DR | Cash | 22 000 | |
| | CR | Share capital | | 22 000 |
| 5 | DR | Bank overdraft | 22 000 | |
| | CR | Cash | | 22 000 |
| 6 | DR | Land | 52 000 | |
| | CR | Cash | | 12 000 |
| | CR | Mortgage | | 40 000 |
| 7 | DR | Equipment | 31 900 | |
| | CR | Accounts payable | | 31 900 |

**2**

**South Shore Manufacturing Pty Ltd**
**Statement of financial position**
**as at 31 July 2002**

| | $ | | $ |
|---|---|---|---|
| **Assets** | | **Liabilities and shareholders' equity** | |
| **Current assets** | | **Current liabilities** | |
| Cash | 13 628 | Bank overdraft | 31 000 |
| Accounts receivable | 78 027 | Accounts payable | 97 662 |
| Inventories, cost | 116 756 | Taxes payble | 12 665 |
| Prepayments | 7 321 | Current part of mortgage | 18 322 |
| | 215 732 | | 159 649 |
| **Noncurrent assets** | | **Noncurrent liabilities** | |
| Land, cost | 130 200 | Accounts payable | 18 000 |
| Factory and equipment cost | 616 111 | Mortgage, less current | 253 734 |
| | 746 311 | Employee entitlements | 67 674 |

| | $ | | $ |
|---|---|---|---|
| Accumulated depreciation | (198 368) | Loan from shareholders | 90 000 |
| | 547 943 | | 429 408 |
| | | **Shareholders' equity** | |
| | | Share capital | 77 000 |
| | | Retained profits | 97 618 |
| | | | 174 618 |
| | 763 675 | | 763 675 |

## Solution outline for problem 3.5

**1**

| | **Assets** | | | | **= Liabilities** | | | **+ Owners' equity** | | |
|---|---|---|---|---|---|---|---|---|---|---|
| | **Cash** | **Accounts receivable** | **Inventory** | **Office equipment** | **Accounts payable (current)** | **Expenses payable** | **Accounts payable (noncurrent)** | **Share capital** | **Revenue** | **Expenses** |
| | $ | $ | $ | $ | $ | $ | $ | $ | $ | $ |
| 1 | +200 000 | | | | | | | +200 000 | | |
| 2 | −20 000 | | +20 000 | | | | | | | |
| 3 | −4 000 | | | | | | | | | −4 000 |
| 4 | | | +30 000 | | +30 000 | | | | | |
| 5 | | | | | | +100 000 | | | | −1 000 |
| 6 | | +90 000 | −40 000 | | | | | | +90 000 | −40 000 |
| 7 | −25 000 | | | | −25 000 | | | | | |
| 8 | +30 000 | −30 000 | | | | | | | | |
| 9 | −15 000 | | | | | | | | | −15 000 |
| 10 | −900 | | | | | | | | | −900 |
| 11 | −3 000 | | | +6 000 | | | +3 000 | | | |
| 12 | | | | | | +200 000 | | | | −2 000 |
| Total | 162 100 | 60 000 | 10 000 | 6 000 | 5 000 | 3 000 | 3 000 | 200 000 | 90 000 | −62 900 |
| | | 238 100 | | | = | | | 238 100 | | |

NB: Increases in expenses have been entered as minus figures.

## Solution outline for problem 4.1

These are definitely transactions: **1**, **2**, **6**, **7**. Item **4** is also, assuming there is documentation with the shipment to show the cost (otherwise recording the transaction may have to await an invoice). Therefore item **9** would be a transaction unless already recorded in item **4**. Item **8** is a transaction, even if not a nice one, assuming that the amount stolen can be determined. Probably it would be recorded as a reduction in cash as best could be determined, and whether recorded as an expense or loss, or instead as an amount due from the employee or Gould Inc.'s insurance company, would depend on whether a recovery was expected. Items **3**, **5** and **10** are not transactions; not yet anyway.

## Solution outline for problem 4.2

**1** No transaction so no entry.

**2**

| | | $ | $ |
|---|---|---|---|
| DR | Advertising expense | 200 | |
| CR | Accounts payable | | 200 |

(Entry may not be recorded until 31 December, as there is no economic exchange until the ad is run.)

**3**

| | $ | $ |
|---|---|---|
| DR Bond asset | 2 000 | |
| CR Cash | | 2 000 |

The interest will be recorded periodically during the three years. In addition to cash interest, entries debiting bond asset and crediting interest revenue will eventually raise the asset value to the $2500 to be received in three years. (Such entries are beyond the scope of this book.)

**4** No transaction yet, so no entry.

**5**

| | $ | $ |
|---|---|---|
| DR Cash | 300 | |
| CR Deferred revenue liability (or Customer deposits liability) | | 300 |

**6**

| | $ | $ |
|---|---|---|
| DR Insurance expense (1/12 × 600) | 50 | |
| DR Prepaid insurance | 550 | |
| CR Cash | | 600 |

*Assumption: that the insurance is consumed equally over the twelve months.*

## Solution outline for problem 4.3 (parts 1 and 5 only)

**1** Journal entries:

**Hoad Pty Ltd**
**General journal**

| No. | Description | Post ref. | Debits | Credits |
|---|---|---|---|---|
| | | | $ | $ |
| 1 | DR Cash | 1 | 200 000 | |
| | CR Share capital | 21 | | 200 000 |
| 2 | DR Inventory | 3 | 20 000 | |
| | CR Cash | 1 | | 20 000 |
| 3 | DR Rent expense | 31 | 4 000 | |
| | CR Cash | 1 | | 4 000 |

**5**

**Hoad Ltd**
**Statement of financial performance**
**for the month of November 2002**

| | $ | $ |
|---|---|---|
| Sales | | 90 000 |
| Less: Cost of goods sold | | 40 000 |
| Gross profit | | 50 000 |
| Less: Operating expenses | | |
| Rent | 4 000 | |
| Advertising | 1 000 | |
| Wages | 17 000 | |
| Sales Commission | 900 | 22 900 |
| Net profit | | 27 100 |

**Hoad Ltd**
**Statement of financial position**
**as at 30 November 2002**

| **Current assets** | **$** | **Current liabilities** | **$** |
|---|---|---|---|
| Cash | 162 100 | Accounts payable | 5 000 |
| Accounts receivable | 60 000 | Expenses payable | 3 000 |
| Inventory | 10 000 | | 8 000 |
| | 232 100 | **Noncurrent liabilities** | |
| **Noncurrent assets** | | Accounts payable | 3 000 |
| Office equipment | 6 000 | **Total liabilities** | 11 000 |
| | | **Shareholders' equity** | |
| | | Share capital | 200 000 |
| | | Retained profits | 27 100 |
| | | | 227 100 |
| **Total assets** | 238 100 | **Total liabilities and equity** | 238 100 |

## Solution outline for problem 5.1

| **Adjust?** | | **Journal entry** | $ | $ |
|---|---|---|---|---|
| a | Y | DR Accounts receivable | 3 200 | |
| | | CR Revenue | | 3 200 |
| b | Y | DR Cost of goods sold expense | 1 900 | |
| | | CR Inventory | | 1 900 |
| c | Y | DR Customer deposits liability | 3 900 | |
| | | CR Revenue | | 3 900 |
| d | Y | DR Store building (asset) | 62 320 | |
| | | CR Maintenance expense | | 62 320 |
| e | Y | DR Warranty expense | 4 300 | |
| | | CR Warranty liability | | 4 300 |
| *No adjustment seems required for the pain and suffering claim.* | | | | |
| f | Y | DR Audit expense | 2 350 | |
| | | CR Accounts payable | | 2 350 |
| g | Y | DR Automobile (asset) | 17 220 | |
| | | CR Accounts payable | | 17 220 |
| h | Y | DR Distribution rights amortisation expense | 500 | |
| | | CR Distribution rights (asset) | | 500 |

## Solution outline for problem 5.2

**1**

| | $ |
|---|---|
| Cash sales | 78 000 |
| Credit sales (18 000 + 262 000 – 22 000) | 258 000 |
| **Total revenue** | 336 000 |

2

| | $ |
|---|---|
| Cost of goods sold | 158 000 |
| Interest (3 000 + 1 000 – 2 000) | 2 000 |
| Wages expense (59 000 + 14 000) | 73 000 |
| Depreciation expense (10% × 120 000) | 12 000 |
| Total expenses | 245 000 |

3

| | $ |
|---|---|
| Opening cash balance | 19 000 |
| Cash receipts | 340 000 |
| Cash payments | (289 000) |
| Closing cash balance | 70 000 |

## Solution outline for problem 5.3

1 18 000 (17 000 + 3000 – 2000).
2 8000.
3 5000 (4500 + 3000 – 2500).
4 2000.
5 1000.
6 31 December 2000.

## Solution outline for problem 5.4

**Greenfingers Pty Ltd**
**Statement of financial performance**
**for August 1997**

| | **Accrual basis** | | **Cash basis** | |
|---|---|---|---|---|
| | **$** | **$** | **$** | **$** |
| Revenue | | 10 000 | | 4 000 |
| Less expenses: | | | | |
| Interest | 400 | | — | |
| Rent | 300 | | 900 | |
| Depreciation | 1 000 | | — | |
| Wages | 800 | | 600 | |
| Electricity | 100 | | — | |
| Insurance | 50 | | 600 | |
| Other expenses | 400 | 3 050 | 400 | 2 500 |
| Net profit | | 6 950 | | 1 500 |

## Solution outline for problem 6.1

The answer to this problem could be quite wide-ranging. One approach is to say that internal control involves managing and safeguarding assets, and that managers such as Janet should care about it because they are responsible for such managing and safeguarding on behalf of the owners. Some details that might be included would be to list particular components of internal control and note management's responsibility for each. Such components include:

- Keeping control over the company is part of management's general objective, so internal control is consistent with and helpful to managers' general purposes.
- Some specific aspects of internal control Janet may want to think about include:
  - physical protection of assets (fences, dry storage, safes, locks and so on)
  - economic protection of assets (avoiding obsolescence, keeping assets maintained and so on)
  - insurance against loss (probably cheaper the better the control is)
  - generally staying aware of the location, condition, economic value and other important features of assets.
- Some techniques that are helpful to managers like Janet include:
  - segregation of duties
  - good, reliable records
  - timely reports on assets' use and condition
  - periodic verification of records
  - cost-effective physical protection
  - proper motivation and monitoring of employees, customers and others with access to assets.

## Solution outline for problem 6.2

1 The company has not properly segregated the duties of accounting for cash and handling cash. The person who prepares the bank reconciliation should not have access to cash. Someone other than the mail-opener should prepare the bank reconciliation.

2 Again, there has been poor segregation of duties; in particular, record-keeping has not been kept separate from cash handling. Some sort of device with a locked-in record (such as a cash register to which the cashier does not have access) should be used to record over-the-counter transactions, while customers could be encouraged to insist on a receipt or some other evidence of payment. The cashier should not be responsible for record-keeping, particularly making entries in customers' accounts. All write-offs should be approved by someone other than a cashier or bookkeeper.

## Solution outline for problem 6.3

1 Bank reconciliation statement:

**Johnson Ltd**
**Bank reconciliation statement**
**30 September 2002**

| | | $ | $ | |
|---|---|---|---|---|
| Ending | Balance as per bank statement | | 8 401 | CR |
| | Add: Deposit not credited by bank | | 430 | |
| | | | 8 831 | |
| | Less: Outstanding cheques: | | | |
| | No. 597 | 260 | | |
| | No. 613 | 214 | | |
| | No. 615 | 357 | | |
| | No. 616 | 262 | 1 093 | |
| Adjusted | Balance as per cash at bank account | | 7 738 | DR |
| Ending | Balance per company records | | 8 061 | DR |
| | Add: Increase reported bank statement but not entered in company records: | | | |
| | Error in recording Cheque 610 | | 27 | |
| | | | 8 088 | |
| | Deduct: Decreases reported on bank statement but not entered in company records: | | | |
| | Accounts receivable – dishonoured cheque | 335 | | |
| | Add: Bank charges | 15 | 350 | |
| Adjusted | Balance as per cash in bank account | | 7 738 | DR |

**2** General journal entries:

| Date | | Description | Debit $ | Credit $ |
|---|---|---|---|---|
| 2002 | | | | |
| Sep | 30 | DR Cash at bank | 27 | |
| | | CR Repairs expense | | 27 |
| | | *To correct error in recording $258 cheque as $285.* | | |
| | 30 | DR Accounts receivable – D. Lewis | 335 | |
| | | CR Cash at bank | | 335 |
| | | *To record dishonoured cheque.* | | |
| | 30 | DR Bank charges | 15 | |
| | | CR Cash at bank | | 15 |
| | | *To record bank service charge.* | | |

**3** Points to note:

- A business could dispense with its own cash records and rely entirely on bank statements, but in most cases such an arrangement would fail to provide information adequate for internal control purposes.
- Bank errors are rare, because of the rigid internal checks in force so that the bank statements provided would generally be accurate records. Problems would arise in respect of lack of detail and absence of an up-to-date record.
- The bank statement furnishes adequate details of charges levied by the bank. However, it provides little information concerning cheques that have been cleared and deposits that have been made. Businesses require details of other parties involved in transactions, and about the accounts affected by these transactions, and these are not forthcoming from the bank.
- The information shown on the bank statement may not be sufficiently up to date for internal control purposes. Such statements are normally obtained from the bank on a weekly or monthly basis, but if they constituted a firm's sole cash record it would be necessary to arrange for them to be furnished more frequently.
- Sums deposited are normally recorded by the bank very promptly. However, cheques that are written by the customer can only be debited to his or her account when presented for payment. Delay in presentation will inevitably lead to an overstatement of cash at bank and could mislead management. Decisions could be made, on the assumption that ample funds were available, that could lead to financial embarrassment when all cheques had been cleared.
- In general, most businesses will prefer to maintain their own cash records. This is so that they will be:
  - in a form that is useful to the enterprise
  - in sufficient detail
  - kept up to date.

## Solution outline for problem 7.1

**1** Cost of goods sold:

| | $ |
|---|---|
| = Beginning inventory | 246 720 |
| + Purchases | 1 690 000 |
| Ending inventory | (321 000) |
| | 1 611 920 |

**2** If the correct COGS is $1 548 325, this means that some of what appeared to have been sold was not. It was lost or stolen, or it strayed! The amount lost is $63 595, which could be left in the COGS expense or could be shown separately, so that the COGS expense would be the accurate, smaller amount. Total expense would not be different; the perpetual method just allows it to be split into $1 548 325 COGS and $63 595 loss, which were lumped together under the periodic method. The need for the $63 595 adjustment indicates that the company has what seems a serious problem somewhere: there are errors in the records, inventories are being lost somehow or there are more sinister things going on, such as employee theft.

3 Companies may not use the perpetual method because of its greater cost to operate. It may be felt that the improved record-keeping is not worth its cost. Here, the losses are large enough that a reasonable perpetual control system would probably be affordable.

## Solution outline for problem 7.2

**1 a** Flows of physical units:

| **Date** | | **Purchases** $ | **Sales** $ | **Balance** $ |
|---|---|---|---|---|
| Apr | 1 | | | 150 |
| | 2 | 100 | | 250 |
| | 6 | | 70 | 180 |
| | 13 | | 120 | 60 |
| | 15 | 200 | | 260 |
| | 18 | | 200 | 60 |
| | 23 | 50 | | 110 |
| | | 350 | 390 | |

Available cost: (150 × $4) + (100 × $5) + (200 × $6) + (50 × $7) = $2650
Cost of goods sold (periodic basis):

LIFO = most recently purchased 390 units
= (50 × $7) = (200 × $6) + (100 × $5) + (40 × $4)
= $2 210
(or = $2 650 – ending inventory
= $2 650 – (110 × $4)
= $2 210)

**b**

FIFO = earliest purchased 390 units
= (150 × $4) + (100 × $5) + (140 × $6)
= $1 940
(or = $2 650 – ending inventory
= $2 650 – [(50 × $7) + (60 × $66]
= $1 940

**c**

Weighted average = average of available cost
= 390 × ($2 650 ÷ 500 units)
= $390 × $5.30
= $2 067
(or = $2 650 – ending inventory
= $2 650 – (110 × $5.30)
= $2 067)

**2 a** Ending inventories (calculated in part **1**):
LIFO = 110 × 4 = $440
**b** FIFO = (50 × $7) + (60 × $6) = $710
**c** Average = (110 × $5.30 = $583

3 **a** Using lower of cost or market: LIFO would not be affected, because its unit cost of $4 is already below market.

**b** FIFO cost is above market, so the inventory value would be reduced to $5 per unit, or $550. The $160 difference would be transferred to an expense account.

**c** Average cost is also above market, so the inventory value would also be reduced to $550. The $33 difference would be transferred to an expense account (This would leave profit under FIFO and average cost the same, since both begin with the same inventory value (150 × $4) and end with the same value ($550).)

4

| | Ending inventory | COGS |
|---|---|---|
| **a** LIFO: | | |
| Ending = (60 × $4) + (50 × $7) | $590 | |
| COGS = $2650 – ending | | $2 060 |
| **b** FIFO: | | |
| Same as **1** and **2** | $710 | $1 940 |
| **c** Moving average: | | |
| First average: $4 | | |
| Second average: $\dfrac{(150 \times \$4) + (100 \times \$5)}{150 + 100} = \$4.40$ | | |
| Third average: $\dfrac{(60 \times \$4.40) + (200 \times \$6)}{60 + 200} = \$5.63$ | | |
| Fourth average: $\dfrac{(60 \times \$5.63) + (50 \times \$7)}{60 + 50} = \$6.25$ | | |
| Ending: 110 × $6.25 | $688 | |
| COGS = $2 650 – ending | | $1 962 |

Regarding lower of cost or market, there would now be no difference in profit for any of the methods, because all have ending inventory costs higher than market ($550) and all ending inventories would therefore be reduced to that $550.

## Solution outline for problem 7.3

1 **a** Inventory cost, 31 December 2002 for Print X, FIFO basis.

| | $ |
|---|---|
| First calculate units in ending inventory: | |
| Beginning inventory | 4 |
| Purchases (10 + 15) | 25 |
| Sales | (23) |
| Ending inventory | 6 |

Ending inventory value: 6 × $330 = $1 980

**b** Cost of goods sold 2002, for Print Y, Average basis

| | Units | Cost $ | Total cost $ |
|---|---|---|---|
| Beginning inventory | 11 | 500 | 5 500 |
| Summer purchases | 25 | 480 | 12 000 |
| Autumn purchases | 30 | 510 | 15 300 |
| Goods available for sale | 66 | | 32 800 |

Cost of goods sold: 38 ($32 800 ÷ 66) = $18 885.

2 Ending inventory value Print Y:

| | $ |
|---|---|
| Market value (100 – 10) | 90 |
| Units remaining (11 + 25 + 30 – 38) | × 28 |
| Inventory value | 2 520 |

GAAP require that inventory be valued at the lower of cost or market. In this case, the market value would be net realisable value, i.e. selling price less any costs required to complete the sale. Since this amount is lower than cost, the inventory must be written down.

## Solution outline for problem 8.1

1 Depreciation would be 10 per cent of cost per year: $10 000 in 2001 and 2002. The entry would debit depreciation expense and credit accumulated depreciation with the $10 000.

2 Depreciation for 2001 would be 20 per cent of $100 000 = $20 000.
Depreciation for 2002 would be 20 per cent of ($100 000 – $20 000) = $16 000.

3 Effects analysis:

| **Statement of financial position end last year** | $ | **+ Profit and loss statement this year** | $ | **= Statement of financial position end this year** | $ |
|---|---|---|---|---|---|
| **Assets** | | **Revenue** | | **Assets** | |
| Acc. depreciation up | (10 000) | No effect | | Acc. depreciation up | (16 000) |
| **Liabilities** | | **Expenses** | | **Liabilities** | |
| *Other than tax:* | | *Other than tax:* | | *Other than tax:* | |
| No effect | | Depreciation expense up | 6 000 | No effect | |
| *Income tax:* | | *Income tax:* | | *Income tax:* | |
| Down | (4 000) | Down | (2 400) | Down | (6 400) |
| **Equity** | | | | **Equity** | |
| *Retained profits:* | | *Net profit:* | | *Retained profits:* | |
| Down | (6 000) | Down | (3 600) | Down | (9 600) |

## Solution outline for problem 8.2

1 The purpose of depreciation of the cost of an asset is to attempt to match the cost of the asset to the benefit generated through the use of the asset. In Z's case, the benefit of the use of the truck is the delivery revenue earned by using the truck. Therefore, the purpose of depreciating assets is not to provide a market valuation of the asset on the statement of financial position. The truck could be used more in the first year than in subsequent years. If no depreciation expense is recorded because the value of the truck has not declined, there will be an improper matching of revenues and expenses in that first year.

2 **a** Accumulated depreciation at the end of the second year:

**i** Straight line:

| | | |
|---|---|---|
| 20 000 ÷ 5 | = $4 000 per year | |
| 4 000 × 2 | = $8 000 | |

**ii** Reducing balance (25% rate):

| | | |
|---|---|---|
| 20 000 × 0.25 | = $5 000 | Year 1 depreciation |
| (20 000 – 5 000) × 0.25 | = $3 750 | Year 2 depreciation |
| | = $8 750 | |

**iii** Units of production:

| | | |
|---|---|---|
| 20 000 ÷ 5 000 | = $4 per lawn | |
| 500 × 4 | = $2 000 | Year 1 depreciation |
| 1 000 × 4 | = $4 000 | Year 2 depreciation |
| | = $6 000 | |

**b** The units of production method would result in the highest retained profits at the end of the second year because the expense for the first two years taken together is lower, resulting in net profit for the two years taken together being higher.

**c** Revenue is generated when a unit is sold. If the total units that an asset is capable of producing can be readily estimated, the units of production method will result in good matching of revenues and expenses. Whether it would make sense for this business depends on how good the estimates are. For example, if each lawnmower costs $500, then 40 lawnmowers have been purchased. Is it plausible to assume that each lawnmower can be used to mow 125 (5000 ÷ 40) lawns before it is no longer useful? It does appear that estimated revenues will increase each year until they decline in the fifth year. Therefore, the units of production method would probably make more sense than the straight-line or reducing balance method.

**d i** Net book value:

| | $ |
|---|---|
| Cost | 20 000 |
| Accumulated depreciation | (15 254) |
| | $4 746 |
| Proceeds | 100 |
| Less NBV | (4 746) |
| Loss on disposal | (4 646) |

**ii** The $100 received just reduces the loss on disposal. The lawnmowers were sold because they were no longer useful, therefore they will no longer provide a benefit. Since they will no longer provide a benefit, they should not be included on the statement of financial position as an asset. The fact that there is a loss recorded in the sixth year indicates that the cost of the lawnmowers was not properly matched to the benefit provided by the use of the lawnmowers over their useful life. Since choice of depreciation method involves some estimation as to the appropriate amounts to charge in each period for depreciation expense, it is inevitable that gains and losses on disposal of assets will be recorded. If the units of production method had been used and the estimated number of lawns were actually mowed, there would have been a $100 gain on disposal of the asset. However, cumulative expense for the five years would have been higher. At the end of six years, total expense will be the same under any depreciation method chosen.

## Solution outline for problem 8.3

1 Schedules:

| | $ |
|---|---|
| **Land** | |
| At cost | 320 000 |
| **Building** | |
| At cost | 180 000 |
| Demolition | 1 200 |
| Construction costs | 40 000 |
| Architect's fees | 4 000 |
| Legal fees | 500 |
| | 225 700 |
| Less salvage | 200 |
| | 225 500 |

| | $ |
|---|---|
| **Machinery** | |
| At cost | 200 000 |
| New machinery | 50 000 |
| Sales tax (4%) | 2 000 |
| Freight and installation | 750 |
| Improvement to existing machine | 500 |
| | 253 250 |

2 Shareholders' equity would decline by $400, being repairs to machinery damaged during demolition.

## Solution outline for problem 9.1

Here are some ideas in response to the sentences. You may well think of several other concepts/principles, and probably will make additional points about some of them.

1 The concept/principle related to this is reliability. Some effects on financial statements of this are: accountants are careful that all cash transactions and day-to-day events such as credit sales and purchases are reflected in the financial statements; considerable care is taken to minimise errors and omissions in the accounting system that underlies the financial statements; and auditors ensure that important financial statement data can be traced back to underlying events and evidence.

2 Three concepts/principles related to this are conservatism, reliability and matching. Conservatism results (or should) in financial statements that contain prudent, not overly optimistic estimates of future cash inflows and outflows regarding present assets and liabilities. Reliability has the effect of keeping conservatism in bounds, so that the financial statements are not pessimistic (which would be unfair to present owners and managers). Matching says that estimates affecting revenues should be done on comparable bases to those affecting expenses so that the net profit makes sense, so it also puts some bounds on conservatism.

3 Three concepts/principles related to this are conformance with GAAP, consistency and comparability. Conformance with GAAP ensures that the company's information is prepared in ways the user might expect, to permit meaningful analyses of its performance. The objective of consistency over time results in highlighting inconsistencies so that the user can consider their effects on the information. The goal of comparability refers directly to the idea of 'relative performance' because, if the previous two principles are met, the company can be evaluated by comparison to others like it, or to others the user might consider investing in or lending to.

4 Three concepts/principles related to this are disclosure, decision relevance and understandability. Disclosure has the effect of helping users understand how the accounting numbers were computed, thus helping to make estimates of future effects. Decision relevance is a reminder that the financial statements should be useful both in past-oriented decisions (such as evaluating management's performance or calculating bonuses) and in future-oriented decisions (such as whether to invest in or lend to the company). Understandability requires the preparation of reports that are comprehensible to the recipients.

5 Two concepts/principles related to this are reliability, and conformance with GAAP. The goal of both is partly to minimise the effects of human error, biases and wishes on the information by promoting objective, careful methods of preparing it, and making it possible (in principle) for anyone else who prepares it to come up with, and agree with, the same information.

## Solution outline for problem 9.2

1 No, it is not probable that the future sacrifice of economic benefits will be required.

2 No, it is not probable that the future sacrifice of economic benefits will be required.

3 No, the amount of the liability cannot be measured reliably.

4 While the amount of the liability still cannot be reliably estimated, it appears that it will be at least $1 million, therefore this amount could be taken up at present as a liability/expense.

5 Yes, a liability and an expense of $400 000 should be taken up. It appears that the remainder of the liability cannot be reliably estimated at this stage.

## Solution outline for problem 9.3

1 Conservatism
2 Historical cost (see chapter 1)
3 Accounting period (see chapter 1)
4 Consistency
5 Materiality

## Solution outline for problem 10.1

| | $ |
|---|---|
| Profit from Brassy on cost basis (.4 × $250 000) | 100 000 |
| Profit from Brassy on equity basis (.4 × $600 000) | 240 000 |
| Extra profit if equity basis were used | 140 000 |
| Present profit of China Sports | 800 000 |
| Revised profit | 940 000 |

## Solution outline for problem 10.2

| Date 2002 | | Description | Debits $ | Credits $ |
|---|---|---|---|---|
| Feb | 1 | No entry | | |
| Feb | 28 | DR Cash trust | 14 000 | |
| | | CR Application ($0.20 × 70 000) | | 14 000 |
| Mar | 15 | DR Application | 2 000 | |
| | | (Refund to unsuccessful applicants $0.20 × 10 000) | | |
| | | DR Cash at bank | 12 000 | |
| | | CR Cash trust | | 14 000 |
| Mar | 15 | DR Application | 12 000 | |
| | | CR Share capital | | 12 000 |
| | | DR Allotment | 18 000 | |
| | | CR Share capital ($0.30 × 60 000) | | 18 000 |
| Mar | 31 | DR Cash at bank | 18 000 | |
| | | CR Allotment | | 18 000 |
| May | 1 | DR Call | 15 000 | |
| | | CR Share capital ($0.25 × 60 000) | | 15 000 |
| May | 31 | DR Cash | 14 000 | |
| | | CR Call | | 14 000 |

**Tindale Ltd**
**Capital structure**
**at 31 May 2002**

| | $ |
|---|---|
| Authorised capital | |
| 100 000 shares @ $1.00 | 100 000 |
| Issued capital | |
| 60 000 shares at $1.00 each | 60 000 |
| Less: Uncalled capital | |
| 60 000 shares $0.25 each | (15 000) |
| Called-up capital | |
| 60 000 shares at $0.75 each | 45 000 |
| Less: Calls in arrears | |
| 4 000 shares @ $0.25 each | (1 000) |
| Share capital | 44 000 |

## Solution outline for problem 10.3

1 Estimated expense = $78 500 + $62 000 = $140 500.
Liability = $50 000 + $140 500 – ($84 000 + $78 000) = $28 500.

2

| | | $ | $ |
|---|---|---|---|
| DR | Warranty expense | 140 500 | |
| CR | Warranty liability | | 140 500 |
| DR | Warranty liability | 162 000 | |
| CR | Inventory | | 78 000 |
| CR | Cash (or Wages payable) | | 84 000 |

## Solution outline for problem 11.1

The suggestions below are written at a general level, suited to those with an introductory level of knowledge. Students or instructors who are familiar with companies or industries such as those below may wish to add more specifics.

1 Recognition would be at the point of delivery of the coffee (probably coinciding with receipt of cash).

2 Recognition would be based on either 'percentage completion' (revenue recognition during the production of the houses) or 'completed contract' (recognition once the house is finished and ownership transferred to the buyer).

3 Recognition would be either as gas is delivered (based on meter readings) or based on a convenient 'cycle billing' system, by which customer billings are spread out over the month to remove billing peaks and associated billing costs, based on estimates of usage if necessary, and revenue recognised as customers are billed.

4 Recognition would probably be as each week's magazines are delivered and associated services such as advertising are completed; less allowance for likely percentage of magazines expected to be returned unsold.

5 This probably differs for season tickets and other seats: for the former, recognition as each performance is held (or on a 'run' or monthly basis for convenience, fewer allowances for ticket or performance cancellations); for the latter, as tickets are sold. Note that for an arts organisation not terribly interested in accounting, a simple recognition basis would be 'per season', just accumulating all ticket sales for a year's or season's performances and not troubling to relate this to particular daily performances.

6 For instalment sales, there is usually enough risk of not receiving full payment that revenue is prudently recognised as cash is received (which the 'instalment sales' method of recognising revenue in effect does).

7 If drilling contracts are not very long in duration, recognising revenue when each contract is completed would make sense, as long as receipt of payment is not seriously in doubt. If contracts are longer, some

sort of 'percentage completion' method (see **2** above) may be used, and if receipt of payment is doubtful (for example, if drilling is done on speculation), a cash-receipt-based method would be more appropriate.

**8** Recognition would be at point of delivery of the oil to pipelines or refineries. If a company does its own refining, recognition would be at point of delivery of the refined oil to customers.

**9** When goods are on consignment, the potter does not give up title to them, so would recognise revenue only when the craft shop sold the pottery (probably even later, when the craft shop sends the potter a cash payment at the end of the month or other period).

**10** An appropriate point would be to recognise revenue from TV advertising when the advertising airs. With sports, there are risks of rainouts, technical problems and knockouts in the first round.

**11** Point of delivery of products to customers seems appropriate – no unusual circumstances are indicated (a matching expense recognition of likely customer service and warranty costs may be done at the same time).

**12** Recognition would be at point of delivery of the products to customers.

**13** Recognition would be at the point of the customer's taking possession of the clothing, assuming estimates of returns and doubtful accounts are possible when financial statements are being prepared.

**14** Recognition of revenue as courses are offered (students attend) would be appropriate, but for many universities, teaching terms overlap fiscal year-ends, and tuition revenue may be recognised per teaching semester or academic year without bothering with accrual to a later year-end or deferrals from an earlier year-end.

**15** As donations are actually received in cash (people often pledge to make donations but do not follow through, so recognition on a cash-received basis is prudent). (Nonprofit organisations often use a cash basis of accounting or a strange hybrid of cash and accrual. For example, revenue may be recognised as money is spent, the idea being that revenue is earned when funds are spent for the purposes expected by the donors.)

**16** The kinds of choices would be as in **2** and **7**, probably upon billing at the completion of the contract, because earlier bases are risky as a result of weather problems, plants dying and customer satisfaction. If collection from customers is doubtful, a cash basis might be used, as the gardener probably collects progress payments during the contract to protect the business.

## Solution outline for problem 11.2

1 Revenue recognition points:
- Recognise revenue as cash is received.
- After the outlets have opened, recognise all revenue.
- At the signing of the contract, recognise all revenue.
- Recognise the full revenue after the down payment is received.
- Recognise revenue on some other basis.

2 Ranking, from most conservative to least conservative:
- as cash is received (most conservative)
- after the outlets have opened
- after the down payment is received
- after the signing of the contract (least conservative).

3 Methods of recognising expenses:
- all general and franchise-related costs immediately
- all general expenses, but only 18/28 of the franchise-related costs
- all general expenses, but only 26/28 of the franchise-related costs
- in proportion to the cash received
- some other formula.

4 Matching of expense recognition with revenue recognition:
- 'cash received' revenue with 'proportion of cash received' expenses (for example, ($5000 ÷ $20 000) × ($230 000 ÷ 28) after down payment is received)
- 'after the outlets have opened' with general expenses plus (18 ÷ 28) × $230 000
- 'after the down payment is received' with general expenses plus (26 ÷ 28) × $230 000
- 'after the signing of the contract' with expensing all general and franchise-related costs immediately.

5 After the outlets have opened:

| | $ | $ |
|---|---|---|
| Revenue ($20 000 × 18) | | 360 000 |
| Expenses: | | |
| General | 55 000 | |
| Franchise (18 ÷ 28 × $230 000) | 147 857 | |
| Total expenses | | 202 857 |
| Net profit | | 157 143 |
| As cash is received: | | |
| Revenue (26 × $5 000) | | 130 000 |
| Expenses: | | |
| Bad debts | 24 643 | |
| General | 55 000 | |
| Franchise ([$5 000 ÷ $20 000]) × ([$230 000 ÷ 28]) × 26) | 53 393 | |
| Total expenses | | 133 036 |
| Net loss | | (3 036) |

*Explanation:*
Assuming that the existing $230 000 in franchise-related expenses are evenly distributed to each franchise, the total cost for each franchise to this date is $230 000÷ 28 franchises = $8214.29. Since we are using the cash-received basis for income measurement, revenue is 26 × $5000 = $130 000; franchise expense is ($8214.29 × ($5000 ÷ $20 000) × 26).

The reason that only 26 franchises are included is that two have not paid any money ($0 ÷ $20 000 × $8214.29 = $0 expenses). Bad debt expenses total (4 × $8214.29 × $15 000 ÷ $20 000) = $24643, because four franchisees appear to be incapable of ever paying the remaining $15 000 outstanding.

6 The second revenue recognition policy in question **5** seems to be the best, because The Pie Place and its franchises are new and not really established yet. However, the complexity of its assumptions may be confusing.

7 A typical footnote may read:
The company recognises revenue on a cash basis, and expenses are deferred and recognised according to the percentage that cash received is of the total franchise price remaining to be received. All general expenses are expensed in the period they are incurred. Remaining deferred expenses for any insolvent or closed franchises are written off.

## Solution outline for problem 12.1

1 Cash and cash equivalents are defined as: cash minus bank loan (because the bank loan was a demand loan). The formulae given earlier in the chapter are used to determine these accounts.

Cash received from customers = 42 674 + 0 – 18 723
= 23 951

Cash paid to suppliers = 28 202 + 73 614 – 0 + 1 100 – 45 616
= 57 300

As there are no accrued expenses or prepayments in the statement of financial position, Thomas determined that all expenses (except depreciation and amortisation) were paid in full during the period. Depreciation and amortisation do not affect cash flows. Based on this information, cash flow from operations was determined as follows:

| **Cash flow from operations** | $ |
|---|---|
| Cash received from customers | 23 951 |
| Cash paid to suppliers | (57 300) |
| Cash paid to employees | (25 480) |
| Cash paid for other expenses ($8 726 + $2 461 + $12 000 + $1 629 + $3 444) | (28 260) |
| Cash used in operations | (87 089) |

An analysis of the noncurrent assets shows that the following investments were made: equipment $44 640 (computer $14 900; other equipment and furniture, $29 740); leasehold cost $63 964; software costs $4800. Based on this information, the cash flow from investing activities can be prepared. There is no cash flow from financial activities, as there are no noncurrent liabilities and share capital has not changed. No dividends have been paid, as the change in retained profits (negative $49 378) is equal to the loss for the period. The full statement of cash flows for Mato Pty Ltd is shown below.

**Mato Pty Ltd**
**Cash flow statement**
**for the six months ended 31 August, 2002**

| | $ | $ |
|---|---|---|
| **Cash flows from operating activities** | | |
| Cash received from customers | 23 951 | |
| Cash paid to suppliers | (57 300) | |
| Cash paid to employees | (25 480) | |
| Cash paid for other expenses | (28 260) | (87 089) |
| | $ | $ |
| **Cash flows from investing activities** | | |
| Equipment, computer and furniture acquired | (44 640) | |
| Leasehold improvements made | (63 964) | |
| Software acquired | (4 800) | (113 404) |
| **Cash flows from financing activities** | | 0 |
| Decrease in cash during the six months | | (200 493) |
| Cash on hand, 1 March 2002 | | 130 000 |
| Cash and cash equivalents, 31 August 2002* | | (70 493) |
| * Cash and cash equivalents, August 31, 2002 | | |
| Cash on hand | 4 507 | |
| Demand bank loan | (75 000) | |
| | (70 493) | |

2 The statement of cash flows shows that the dramatic decline in cash has two causes:
- day-to-day operations produced a cash loss of $87 089
- noncurrent asset acquisitions cost $113 404 in cash.

The net result is that a healthy cash balance of $130 000 six months ago was turned into a negative cash balance of $70 493. The company clearly has to get on top of its cash problems quickly.

3 Below is the reconciliation between net loss and cash flow from operations (that is, cash flow from operations using the indirect method).

| | $ | $ |
|---|---|---|
| Net loss for the six months | | (49 378) |
| Add: Back depreciation and amortisation for the period ($3 234 + $6 396 + $480) | | 10 110 |
| | | (39 268) |
| Changes in non-cash working capital accounts: | | |
| Increase in accounts receivable | (18 723) | |
| Increase in inventory | (73 614) | |
| Increase in accounts payable | 44 516 | (47 821) |
| Cash used in operating activities | | (87 089) |

This reconciliation indicates that the reason for the large negative cash flow from operations was a combination of expenses exceeding revenues and the build-up of current assets, especially inventory. The increase in accounts payable helped to finance this, but even after, in essence, borrowing from suppliers, the company still fell far behind in its cash flow.

## Solution outline for problem 12.2

1 Net change in cash and cash equivalents
= \$127 976 – \$238 040 + \$107 000 = –\$3064.
Cash and cash equivalents have gone down \$3064 during the year.

2 a Effects if the event had occurred during the year:
Investing would show an expenditure of \$38 950 and financing would show a cash inflow of \$28 950 from long-term borrowing. The net change in cash and cash equivalents would be \$10 000 lower.

b There would have been a gain on sale of \$880. This gain would have increased the net profit, but would be deducted in the operating section of the cash flow statement to remove the non-cash gain from profit in calculating cash from operations. The proceeds of \$4100 would be included as proceeds in the investing section, reducing the cash expenditure on additional noncurrent assets. The net change in cash and cash equivalent would be \$4100 higher (the cash received).

c Receipts from customers would be \$6000 less, and cash generated from operations would be \$6000 less. The net change in cash and cash equivalents would be \$6000 lower.

d The cash flow statement reports only dividends actually paid. Therefore this \$15 000 would be ignored on the cash flow statement. (It might be included as a deduction from dividends declared in calculating the amount of dividends paid, but this calculation is not usually shown.)

e The demand loan would go into the cash equivalent assets part of cash and cash equivalents, and also into the cash equivalent liabilities part of cash and cash equivalents, so its net effect on cash and cash equivalents would be zero. The amount would not appear anywhere in the body of the cash flow statements, but it would be included in the reconciliation of cash and cash equivalents at the bottom of the cash flow statement (both cash equivalent assets and cash equivalent liabilities would be \$25 000 larger).

3 The decrease in accounts receivable of \$6000 which would be added back to operating profit after tax.

## Solution outline for problem 12.3

**Tut Ltd**
**Statement of cash flows**
**for year ended 30 June 2002**

| | \$ |
|---|---|
| **Cash from operating activities** | |
| Cash received from customers | 522 |
| Cash paid to suppliers and employees (210 + 45 + 132) | (387) |
| Income tax paid | (70) |
| **Net cash flow from operating vehicles** | 65 |
| **Cash from investing activities** | |
| Sale of motor vehicles | 55 |
| Purchase of motor vehicles | (110) |
| Purchase of equipment | (130) |
| **Net cash flow from investing activities** | (185) |
| **Cash from financing activities** | |
| Repayment of borrowings | (20) |
| Final dividend paid | (60) |
| Proceeds from share issue | 170 |
| **Net cash flow from financing activities** | 90 |
| **Net cash outflow** | (30) |
| Cash opening balance | 20 |
| Cash closing balance | (10) |

Reconciliation of net cash provided by operating activities to operating profit after income tax:

| | $000 |
|---|---|
| Operating profit after income tax | 56 |
| Depreciation expense (38 + 50) | 88 |
| Loss on sale of motor vehicles | 25 |
| **Change in assets and liabilities:** | |
| Increase in accounts receivable | (38) |
| Decrease in inventory | 20 |
| Decrease in accounts payable | (60) |
| Decrease in income tax payable | (26) |
| **Net cash provided by operating activities** | 65 |

Workings:

**Accounts receivable**

| | | | |
|---|---|---|---|
| Bal | 105 | Cash* | 522 |
| Sales | 560 | Bal | 143 |
| | 665 | | 665 |

**Inventory**

| | | | |
|---|---|---|---|
| Bal | 220 | COGS | 170 |
| Purchases* | 150 | Bal | 200 |
| | 370 | | 370 |

**Prepaid insurance**

| | | | |
|---|---|---|---|
| Bal | 10 | Insurance exp. | 45 |
| Cash* | 45 | Bal | 10 |
| | 55 | | 55 |

**Equipment**

| | | | |
|---|---|---|---|
| Bal | 450 | Bal | 640 |
| Borrowings | 60 | | |
| Cash* | 130 | | |
| | 640 | | 640 |

**Accum. depreciation – equipment**

| | | | |
|---|---|---|---|
| Bal | 200 | Bal | 150 |
| | | Depn. exp.* | 50 |
| | 200 | | 200 |

**Motor vehicles**

| | | | |
|---|---|---|---|
| Bal | 520 | Disposal | 145 |
| Cash* | 110 | Bal | 485 |
| | 630 | | 630 |

**Accum. depreciation – motor vehicles**

| | | | |
|---|---|---|---|
| Disposal | 65 | Bal | 210 |
| Bal | 183 | Depn. exp.* | 38 |
| | 248 | | 248 |

**Accounts payable**

| | | | |
|---|---|---|---|
| Cash* | 210 | Bal | 265 |
| Bal | 205 | Purchases | 150 |
| | 415 | | 415 |

**Other expenses**

| | | | |
|---|---|---|---|
| Depn. MV | 38 | | |
| Depn. equipment | 50 | | |
| Cash* | 132 | P & L | 220 |
| | 220 | | 220 |

**Borrowings**

| | | | |
|---|---|---|---|
| Cash* | 20 | Bal | 430 |
| Bal | 470 | Equipment | 60 |
| | 490 | | 490 |

**Asset revaluation reserve**

| | | | |
|---|---|---|---|
| Bal | 210 | Land | 80 |
| | | Bal | 130 |
| | 210 | | 210 |

* Balancing figures.

## Solution outline for problem 13.1

| Financial Position end last year | | + Profit impact | | = Financial position end this year | |
|---|---|---|---|---|---|
| | $ | | $ | | $ |
| **Assets** | | **Revenue** | | **Assets** | |
| Receivables up | 8000 | Up | 10 000 | Receivables up | 18 000 |
| **Liabilities** | | **Expenses** | | **Liabilities** | |
| *Other than tax* | | *Other than tax* | | *Other than tax* | |
| Payables up | 3 000 | Exp up | 4 000 | Payables up | 7 000 |
| *Income tax* | | *Income tax* | | *Income tax* | |
| Up | 1 750 | Up | 2 100 | Up | 3 850 |
| **Equity** | | | | **Equity** | |
| *Retained profits* | | *Net profit* | | *Retained profits* | |
| Up | (3 250) | Up | 3 900 | Up | 7 150 |

## Solution outline for problem 13.2

This question can be answered in many ways. You may be cynical and state that accounting is not appropriate for either purpose. Or you may say that external reporting is the most important, or that internal control is. Whatever your position, make sure you can support it with cogent arguments.

One position is to say that financial accounting exists for both purposes, as outlined below.

1 Information for outsiders:
   - It allows comparison by investors because each firm is reporting using the same guidelines (GAAP).
   - An independent auditor reviews the information to ensure that it fairly presents the financial position of the company.
   - The information is for everyone, because supposedly it is to be largely understood by the general users, who take due diligence to analyse the statements.

2 Internal information:
   - It assists in such areas as inventory control, which is important for company control.
   - Incentive plans can be based on the accounting information, which provides control.
   - Since the information is prepared for the owners (shareholders), it may eliminate some management bias and promote clearer evaluation of management performance.

## Solution outline for problem 13.3

Some very sketchy comments, intended to generate ideas:

1 **a** The economic entity that capital markets are presumably interested in is not necessarily the legal entity. For example, a set of consolidated statements is based on the presumed economic entity.

**b** The historical cost basis increases reliability of information, but may reduce relevance to current decisions by market participants.

**c** Reliability aims to increase confidence in objectivity or impartiality of information. But is this term too vague? Is reliability open to too wide an interpretation by preparers of information, and thus too vague to be really useful to markets and other agents?

**d** Although choice is permitted in the presentation of accounting information, there are guidelines that set boundaries. Therefore, markets can have some confidence about the acceptable range of information being presented.

**e** There is potential for management and/or preparers to have undue influence over accountants and auditors. Users rely on the audit report because the auditors are independent. Professional ethics help ensure this independence and the care and expertise required to do a technically competent job of preparing the accounting information.

2 a The financial statements are consolidated. The preparers have used a method of consolidation to create financial statements that represent the commonly controlled entity.
  b Historical cost is the basic measure for most account balances in the large public company's financial statements, including the property, equipment, new debt issued and so on. Since every company uses the original price under historical cost, the statements satisfy one of the main elements of information: objectivity
  c The main piece of evidence relating to reliability is in the audit report. This report gives the external auditor's opinion that the statements are fair
  d The auditor's report also says that the statements have been prepared following GAAP
  e Professional ethics is implied in the presumably expert, unbiased and independent status of the external auditor. That auditor is expected to act professionally and not to follow anyone else's dictates in judging the fairness of the financial statements.

3 These concepts are still relevant to a small, private company. While the larger company's information is of interest to market traders and the private company's is not, they otherwise have many similar users: banks, taxation authorities, managers and perhaps potential owners. Though the use context may differ somewhat, these underlying concepts are still valuable.

## Solution outline for problem 14.1

1 a *Profitability:* ROE has increased from 12 per cent to 13 per cent, while the return on assets has fallen from 9 per cent to 8 per cent. As shown in part **3**, the fall in ROA is a result of the fall in asset turnover.
  b *Asset management:* the average time to collect debtors has stayed constant. However, the days in inventory has increased from 55 days to 72 days, meaning that on average it is taking much longer to sell inventory. These extra days need to be financed by the company. The reasons for the build-up in inventory should be investigated, for example, stocking up for some large orders, as opposed to lack of demand for the product, requires a very different action.
  c *Liquidity:* the current ratio has increased (mainly because of the build-up in inventory; see below) while the quick ratio has dropped below 1 to 0.7, indicating the company may have problems paying its bills in the short term.
  d *Financial structure:* the level of gearing has increased substantially from 1 to 1.4. The ability of the company to pay its interest bill needs to be considered, particularly given the decrease in profitability as indicated by the lower ROA. It would be useful to calculate the interest cover ratio.

2 While ROA has decreased, ROE has increased because of the increase in gearing. Provided the extra funds borrowed earn a return higher than the cost of the debt, shareholders will benefit and the ROE will increase.

3 You can see from the numbers that ROA = profit margin × asset turnover (for example, 0.4 × 20 per cent = 8 per cent for 2002), while the profit margin has increased from 18 per cent to 20 per cent.

4 One likely reason for the fall in asset turnover is the fall in inventory turnover.

5 The current ratio was increased because of the build-up in inventory. It must have been caused by inventory as the quick ratio (which is the same as the current ratio, but it excludes inventory) has dropped.

## Solution outline for problem 14.2

1 Such a concept of performance relates the return to the investment required to earn it, so enabling the relative return to be calculated. This is important, because returns do require investment. People usually don't make investments without expecting a return, and the sizes of each have to be related to each other in order to evaluate the quality of the result. A $1000 return would be great if the investment required was $2000 (a ratio of 50 per cent), but not so great if the investment were $200 000 (only 0.5 per cent).

2 a The interest earned could be compared to the $1200 required to earn it.
  b The consulting earnings could be compared to the $15 000 invested to earn them.
  c This is harder, because the returns are probably non-financial, such as the fun of driving a sports car, and so are not readily comparable to the car's cost. However, this sort of ratio is implicit in many buying decisions, in which we ask ourselves if the benefits we will obtain are worth the cost, and we may well choose a cheaper car if the feeling of wind in our hair isn't all that important relative to what we have to pay for a convertible.

## Solution outline for problem 14.3

1 **a** Total current assets are unaffected (the cash came in and went out in one day).
  **b** Total assets increase by $100 000 000 (the additional equipment).
  **c** Total current liabilities decrease by $50 000 000 (reduced short-term bank loans).
  **d** The current ratio would be improved because the denominator, current liabilities, would decrease without there being any effect on the numerator, current assets.
  **e** No change in shareholders' equity (see **f**, however).
  **f** No direct effect on profit, but there will be increased interest and depreciation expenses in the future. So, unless the additional equipment generates more revenue than that, earnings and shareholders' equity will be reduced in the future.
  **g** No effect on cash and cash equivalents (no net effect on cash, as noted in **a**, and short-term loans are not likely to be part of cash and cash equivalents). (Cash generated by operations, as shown on the cash flow statement, would decrease by $50 000 000, because of the reduction in accounts payable.)
  **h** Cash used for investments would increase by $100 000 000 (the additional equipment).
  **i** Cash provided from financing would increase by $100 000 000 (the borrowing of $150 000 000 less prepayment of $50 000 000).
  **j** The leverage ratio would increase, as the numerator would increase by $100 000 and the denominator would be unchanged.

2 Effect on return on equity could be estimated by estimating the increased profit to be earned from the new equipment and any interest charges on accounts payable that will be saved, and deducting from that the interest costs of the borrowing. All this should be done on an after-tax basis, because return on equity uses net profit as its numerator.

## Solution outline for problem 14.4

1 Return on equity = $6000 ÷ $45 000 = 0.133.

2 The assets financed would earn 13.75 per cent ([6000 + 2000 + 3000] ÷ 80 000), according to the above calculations. The cost of the money borrowed is 8 per cent. Therefore, leverage is positive (5.75 per cent), and the company should go ahead. This will, however, increase the company's risk, because the interest has to be paid and return on assets could decline below that rate.

3 Some possible additional information and ratios (more can be imagined, so this is an outline only):
- terms and security of present debts
- quality of management (especially Mr A.)
- industry and competition prospects
- personal guarantees Mr A. might offer
- interest coverage ratio
- accounts receivable collection and inventory turnover
- profit margin
- income tax information.

## Solution outline for problem 15.1

The major judgements to be made by the accountant are whether sufficient future benefits will be derived and, if so, the period over which to amortise these.

The decision on whether future benefits will be derived will affect whether the development costs are expensed or capitalised. If the accountant decides that sufficient benefits will not be derived, then the entire amount will be expensed in 2001, reducing profit. On the other hand, if it is decided that sufficient benefits will be derived, then the development costs will be capitalised, then amortised. This will mean profit is unaffected in 2001, but will be reduced by the amount of the amortisation expense in subsequent years.

The length of the amortisation period will affect the amount of the amortisation expense each year. A longer period will result in a smaller annual expense, which in turn means a smaller reduction in profit.

## Solution outline for problem 15.2

1 **a** Net profit would go down $46 900 (that is, $67 000 × (1 – .30)).

**b** No immediate cash flow effect, but a cash saving within a year because of lower income tax.

**c** Current tax liability is the only working capital account affected at present. It goes down $20 100 (that is, $67 000 × .30), so working capital is improved by that amount.

2 **a** Net profit would go down $7500 (that is, $25 000 × .30), because of the extra income tax expense recognised.

**b** No effect on current cash flow. Net profit's decline of $7500 is offset by an increased deferred income tax add-back of $7500.

**c** No effect on working capital. No working capital accounts are affected, because the deferred tax in this case is noncurrent.

# Appendix 2

# *Woolworths Limited: 2001 Annual Report*

FINANCIAL REPORT ▸

# Statement of financial performance

| | Note | Consolidated 52 weeks ended 24 June 01 $m | Consolidated 52 weeks ended 25 June 00 $m | Woolworths Limited 52 weeks ended 24 June 01 $m | Woolworths Limited 52 weeks ended 25 June 00 $m |
|---|---|---|---|---|---|
| Revenue from sale of goods | 2a | 20,915.1 | * 20,019.9 | 7,173.1 | 6,874.5 |
| Other operating revenue | 2a | 473.6 | 372.4 | 163.8 | 221.8 |
| Total revenue from operations | | 21,388.7 | 20,392.3 | 7,336.9 | 7,096.3 |
| Cost of sales | | (16,034.6) | (15,353.7) | (5,501.9) | (5,132.2) |
| Gross Profit | | 5,354.1 | 5,038.6 | 1,835.0 | 1,964.1 |
| Other revenue from ordinary activities | 2b | 260.2 | 165.4 | 448.2 | 450.9 |
| Share of loss in associated company accounted for using the equity method | 10b | (1.5) | – | – | – |
| Branch expenses | | (3,648.3) | (3,402.1) | (1,196.0) | (1,225.1) |
| Administration expenses | | (1,257.9) | (1,274.2) | (528.5) | (641.0) |
| Earnings before interest and tax | | 706.6 | 527.7 | 558.7 | 540.0 |
| Interest expense | 3 | (23.8) | (36.7) | (22.7) | (35.2) |
| Interest income | 3 | 10.7 | 8.9 | 10.0 | 8.3 |
| Profit from ordinary activities before income tax expense | | 693.5 | 499.9 | 546.0 | 522.0 |
| Income tax expense | 5 | (217.4) | (178.2) | (52.0) | (27.9) |
| Net profit from ordinary activities after income tax expense | | 476.1 | 321.7 | 494.0 | 494.1 |
| Net profits attributable to outside equity interests | | (0.4) | (0.1) | – | – |
| **Operating net profit attributable to the members of Woolworths Limited** | | **475.7** | **321.6** | **494.0** | **494.1** |
| Decrease (increase) in foreign currency translation reserve | 19 | 1.1 | (0.6) | – | – |
| Decrease in asset revaluation reserve | 19 | – | (15.1) | – | – |
| Total revenue expense and valuation adjustments attributable to members of Woolworths Limited recognised directly in equity | | 1.1 | (15.7) | – | – |
| **Total changes in equity other than those resulting from transactions with owners as owners** | | **476.8** | **305.9** | **494.0** | **494.1** |
| **Earnings per share (EPS)** | | | | | |
| Basic EPS | | 40.16 | 26.27 | – | – |
| Weighted average number of shares used in the calculation of basic EPS (million) | | 1,065.8 | 1,125.0 | – | – |
| Diluted EPS is not materially different | | | | | |

* Sales for the 52 weeks ended 25 June 2000 include wholesale sales tax (WST). Sales adjusted to exclude WST were $18,988.8 million.

# Statement of financial performance

| | Note | Consolidated 52 weeks ended 24 June 01 $m | Consolidated 52 weeks ended 25 June 00 $m | Woolworths Limited 52 weeks ended 24 June 01 $m | Woolworths Limited 52 weeks ended 25 June 00 $m |
|---|---|---|---|---|---|
| **Reconciliation of retained earnings** | | | | | |
| Retained profits at beginning of period | | 368.9 | 562.6 | 74.8 | 97.3 |
| Net profit attributable to the members of Woolworths Limited | | 475.7 | 321.6 | 494.0 | 494.1 |
| Woolworths income notes distribution | | (47.7) | (26.1) | (47.7) | (26.1) |
| Dividends paid or provided | 6 | (284.1) | (243.5) | (284.1) | (243.5) |
| Special dividend of $5.82 (2000: $2.47) per fully paid ordinary share paid to shareholders participating in off market buy-backs | 6 | (232.9) | (247.0) | (232.9) | (247.0) |
| Adjustment due to initial adoption of new accounting standard | | – | 1.3 | – | – |
| **Retained profits at end of period** | | **279.9** | **368.9** | **4.1** | **74.0** |

The statement of financial performance should be read in conjunction with the notes to the financial statements set out on pages 8 to 50.

# Statement of financial position

| | Note | Consolidated As at 24 June 01 $m | Consolidated As at 25 June 00 $m | Woolworths Limited As at 24 June 01 $m | Woolworths Limited As at 25 June 00 $m |
|---|---|---|---|---|---|
| **Current assets** | | | | | |
| Cash | | 256.0 | 350.0 | 196.6 | 298.5 |
| Receivables | 8 | 194.9 | 164.0 | 58.7 | 49.2 |
| Inventories | | 1,731.8 | 1,648.3 | 542.4 | 534.0 |
| Property, plant and equipment | 12 | 126.8 | 98.0 | – | – |
| Current tax asset | | – | – | 1.7 | – |
| Other | 9 | 79.0 | 84.8 | 27.7 | 36.8 |
| Total current assets | | 2,388.5 | 2,345.1 | 827.1 | 918.5 |
| **Non-current assets** | | | | | |
| Receivables | 8 | 44.2 | 47.7 | 1,706.7 | 1,534.5 |
| Investments accounted for using the equity method | 10 | 16.8 | – | – | – |
| Other financial assets | 11 | 1.4 | 1.4 | 96.1 | 71.8 |
| Property, plant and equipment | 12 | 2,130.7 | 2,096.1 | 470.0 | 471.8 |
| Intangibles | 13 | 313.4 | 145.0 | 110.3 | 86.0 |
| Deferred tax assets – timing differences | | 187.7 | 181.0 | 97.9 | 109.1 |
| Other | 9 | 0.5 | 0.5 | 0.5 | 0.5 |
| Total non-current assets | | 2,694.7 | 2,471.7 | 2,481.5 | 2,273.7 |
| **Total assets** | | **5,083.2** | **4,816.8** | **3,308.6** | **3,192.2** |
| **Current liabilities** | | | | | |
| Accounts payable | | 1,666.4 | 1,571.8 | 1,017.0 | 1,007.4 |
| Accruals | | 399.0 | 334.3 | 183.2 | 169.1 |
| Interest bearing liabilities | 14 | 341.7 | 129.9 | 340.2 | 125.2 |
| Current tax liabilities | | 125.0 | 107.2 | – | 11.5 |
| Provisions | 17 | 427.3 | 451.7 | 263.8 | 300.5 |
| Total current liabilities | | 2,959.4 | 2,594.9 | 1,804.2 | 1,613.7 |
| **Non-current liabilities** | | | | | |
| Interest bearing liabilities | 14 | 301.9 | 302.3 | 285.0 | 285.2 |
| Deferred tax liabilities | | 111.7 | 137.8 | 37.1 | 50.9 |
| Provisions | 17 | 184.6 | 150.9 | 70.3 | 41.9 |
| Total non-current liabilities | | 598.2 | 591.0 | 392.4 | 378.0 |
| **Total liabilities** | | **3,557.6** | **3,185.9** | **2,196.6** | **1,991.7** |
| **Net assets** | | **1,525.6** | **1,630.9** | **1,112.0** | **1,200.5** |

## Statement of financial position

| | Note | Consolidated<br>As at<br>24 June 01<br>$m | <br>As at<br>25 June 00<br>$m | Woolworths Limited<br>As at<br>24 June 01<br>$m | <br>As at<br>25 June 00<br>$m |
|---|---|---|---|---|---|
| **Equity** | | | | | |
| Contributed equity | 18 | 476.2 | 494.0 | 476.2 | 494.0 |
| Reserves | 19 | 182.8 | 181.7 | 48.7 | 48.7 |
| Retained profits | | 279.9 | 368.9 | 4.1 | 74.8 |
| Equity attributable to the members of Woolworths Limited | | 938.9 | 1,044.6 | 529.0 | 617.5 |
| Woolworths Income Notes | 21 | 583.0 | 583.0 | 583.0 | 583.0 |
| Outside equity interest in controlled entities: | | | | | |
| Reserves | | 0.9 | 0.9 | – | – |
| Retained profits | | 2.8 | 2.4 | – | – |
| Total outside equity interest | | 3.7 | 3.3 | – | – |
| **Total equity** | **20** | **1,525.6** | **1,630.9** | **1,112.0** | **1,200.5** |

The statement of financial position should be read in conjunction with the notes to the financial statements set out on pages 8 to 50.

# Statement of cash flows

| | Consolidated | | Woolworths Limited | |
|---|---|---|---|---|
| | 52 weeks ended 24 June 01 $m | 52 weeks ended 25 June 00 $m | 52 weeks ended 24 June 01 $m | 52 weeks ended 25 June 00 $m |
| **Cash flows from operating activities** | | | | |
| Receipts from customers | 22,075.7 | 20,031.0 | 7,505.2 | 6,973.7 |
| Receipts from vendors and tenants | 439.9 | 297.1 | 251.5 | 173.3 |
| Payments to suppliers and employees | (21,455.9) | (19,084.9) | (7,493.4) | (6,446.2) |
| Dividends received from related entities | – | – | 348.7 | 376.5 |
| Interest and other borrowing costs paid | (35.7) | (42.5) | (34.6) | (41.0) |
| Interest received | 10.7 | 8.9 | 10.0 | 8.3 |
| Income tax paid | (225.7) | (142.7) | (68.4) | (50.7) |
| Net cash provided by operating activities | 809.0 | 1,066.9 | 519.0 | 993.9 |
| **Cash flows from investing activities** | | | | |
| Proceeds from the sale of property, plant and equipment | 173.1 | 111.0 | 21.2 | 41.4 |
| Proceeds from the sale of businesses | 76.1 | 39.5 | 76.1 | 39.5 |
| Payments for property, plant and equipment | (537.4) | (401.2) | (149.6) | (146.6) |
| Payment for purchase of investments | (18.3) | – | (25.8) | – |
| Advances of employee loans | (30.8) | (19.1) | (30.8) | (19.1) |
| Loans to related entities | – | – | (163.9) | (139.7) |
| Payment for purchase of businesses | (257.0) | (23.2) | (42.6) | (11.8) |
| Proceeds from assignment of employee loans | 45.0 | – | 45.0 | – |
| Net cash used in investing activities | (549.3) | (293.0) | (270.4) | (236.3) |
| **Cash flows from financing activities** | | | | |
| Proceeds from issue of shares | 44.0 | 26.9 | 44.0 | 26.9 |
| Payments for buy-back of shares | (349.4) | (548.4) | (349.4) | (548.4) |
| Proceeds from issue of Woolworths Income Notes | – | 583.0 | – | 583.0 |
| (Repayment of) / proceeds from short term deposits | 0.1 | (0.2) | (0.1) | (0.4) |
| Proceeds from external borrowings | 3,187.0 | 1,685.7 | 3,185.5 | 1,682.1 |
| Repayment of external borrowings | (2,975.6) | (2,205.3) | (2,970.7) | (2,205.0) |
| Dividends paid | (212.1) | (173.5) | (212.1) | (173.5) |
| Woolworths Income Notes distributions | (47.7) | (24.7) | (47.7) | (24.7) |
| Net cash used in financing activities | (353.7) | (656.5) | (350.5) | (660.0) |
| Net increase/(decrease) in cash held | (94.0) | 117.4 | (101.9) | 97.6 |
| Cash at the beginning of the financial period | 350.0 | 232.6 | 298.5 | 200.9 |
| **Cash at the end of the financial period** | **256.0** | **350.0** | **196.6** | **298.5** |

## Non-cash financing and investing activities

| | | | | |
|---|---|---|---|---|
| **Dividend Reinvestment Plan** | | | | |
| In accordance with the Company's Dividend Reinvestment Plan 21% of the dividend paid was reinvested in the shares of the Company. Dividends paid (excluding special buy-back dividend) | 266.8 | 220.8 | 266.8 | 220.8 |
| Issuance of shares under the Plan | (54.7) | (47.3) | (54.7) | (47.3) |
| **Net cash outflow** | **212.1** | **173.5** | **212.1** | **173.5** |

## Statement of cash flows

| | Consolidated | | Woolworths Limited | |
|---|---|---|---|---|
| | 52 weeks ended 24 June 01 $m | 52 weeks ended 25 June 00 $m | 52 weeks ended 24 June 01 $m | 52 weeks ended 25 June 00 $m |
| **Reconciliation of net cash provided by operating activities to operating profit after tax** | | | | |
| Operating profit after income tax | 476.1 | 321.7 | 494.0 | 494.1 |
| Depreciation | 275.0 | 256.6 | 84.3 | 78.9 |
| Amortisation | 34.7 | 32.2 | 13.0 | 13.4 |
| Share of loss of equity accounted associates | 1.5 | – | – | – |
| Provision for diminution in value of other financial assets | – | – | 1.5 | – |
| (Profit)/Loss on sale of businesses | 12.7 | (11.0) | 12.7 | (7.5) |
| (Profit)/Loss on sale of property, plant and equipment | 0.6 | 10.7 | (0.8) | 1.9 |
| Borrowing costs capitalised | (11.9) | (5.8) | (11.9) | (5.8) |
| (Increase)/decrease in deferred tax asset | (0.8) | (5.1) | 11.2 | (22.2) |
| Increase/(decrease) in income tax payable | 18.4 | 28.4 | (13.2) | (5.8) |
| Increase/(decrease) in deferred tax liability | (26.1) | 12.3 | (13.8) | 5.2 |
| (Increase)/decrease in receivables | (39.6) | 14.8 | (19.7) | 99.2 |
| (Increase)/decrease in inventories | (60.0) | (19.0) | (43.0) | (3.9) |
| (Increase)/decrease in sundry debtors and prepayments | 15.5 | (9.0) | 2.2 | (2.6) |
| Increase/(decrease) in payables | 94.6 | 295.0 | 9.6 | 280.3 |
| Increase/(decrease) in sundry payables and provisions | 18.3 | 145.1 | (7.1) | 68.7 |
| **Net cash provided by operating activities** | **809.0** | **1,066.9** | **519.0** | **993.9** |

| | Consolidated | | Woolworths Limited | |
|---|---|---|---|---|
| | 52 weeks ended 24 June 01 $m | 52 weeks ended 25 June 00 $m | 52 weeks ended 24 June 01 $m | 52 weeks ended 25 June 00 $m |
| **Acquisitions of businesses** | | | | |
| Details of the aggregate cash outflow relating to the acquisition of businesses and the aggregate assets and liabilities of those businesses at the date of acquisition were as follows: | | | | |
| **Consideration** | | | | |
| Cash paid | 257.0 | 23.2 | 42.6 | 11.8 |
| **Fair value of net assets acquired** | | | | |
| Property, plant and equipment | 32.4 | 3.5 | 2.5 | 2.0 |
| Prepayments | 17.1 | – | 0.3 | – |
| Other assets | – | (0.1) | – | (0.1) |
| Inventories | 64.6 | 3.7 | 6.5 | 2.2 |
| Liquor licences | 6.6 | 0.6 | 1.9 | – |
| Current income tax asset | 0.6 | – | – | – |
| Deferred tax asset | 6.0 | – | – | – |
| Employee entitlements | (2.5) | – | – | – |
| Other liabilities | (39.7) | | – | – |
| | 85.1 | 7.7 | 11.2 | 4.1 |
| Goodwill on acquisition | 171.9 | 15.5 | 31.4 | 7.7 |
| **Consideration (cash)** | **257.0** | **23.2** | **42.6** | **11.8** |

Details of acquisitions are shown at Note 31.

| | Consolidated | | Woolworths Limited | |
|---|---|---|---|---|
| **Disposal of businesses** | | | | |
| Details of the aggregate cash inflow relating to the sale of businesses and the aggregate assets and liabilities of those businesses at the date of sale were as follows: | | | | |
| **Consideration** | | | | |
| Cash received | 76.1 | 39.5 | 76.1 | 39.5 |
| **Net assets sold** | | | | |
| Plant and equipment | 45.0 | 11.0 | 45.0 | 7.2 |
| Prepayments | 6.7 | 1.5 | 6.7 | 0.9 |
| Inventories | 41.1 | 18.0 | 41.1 | 11.7 |
| Other liabilities | (4.0) | (3.2) | (4.0) | (2.0) |
| Other assets | – | 6.2 | – | 4.0 |
| **Net assets sold** | **88.8** | **33.5** | **88.8** | **21.8** |

# Notes to the financial statements

## 1 Significant accounting policies

The significant accounting policies that have been applied in the preparation of this general purpose financial report are as follows:

### A Basis of preparation

This report has been prepared in accordance with Accounting Standards, Urgent Issues Group Consensus Views, other authoritative pronouncements of the Australian Accounting Standards Board and the Corporations Act 2001.

It has been prepared on the basis of historical cost. The accounting policies adopted are consistent with those of the previous years except as noted below.

The consolidated entity has adopted the presentation and disclosure requirements of Accounting Standards AASB 1018 'Statement of Financial Performance', AASB 1034 'Financial Report Presentation and Disclosures' and AASB 1040 'Statement of Financial Position' for the first time in the preparation of this financial report. In accordance with the requirements of these new/revised standards, comparative amounts have been reclassified in order to comply with the new presentation format. The reclassification of comparative amounts has not resulted in a change in the aggregate amounts of current assets, non-current assets, current liabilities, non-current liabilities or equity, or the net profit of the company or consolidated entity as reported in the prior year financial report.

The financial periods of the Company end on the last Sunday in June of each year. The financial period of the Company ended on 24 June 2001, which comprised 52 weeks and the corresponding financial period to 25 June 2000 comprised 52 weeks.

### B Principles of consolidation

In these financial statements, Woolworths Limited is referred to as 'the Company' and the 'Consolidated' financial statements are those of the consolidated entity, comprising Woolworths Limited and its controlled entities.

All balances and the effects of all transactions between controlled entities that are included in the Consolidated financial statements have been eliminated.

Outside interests in the equity and results of controlled entities are shown as a separate item in the Consolidated financial statements.

Investments in associates are accounted for in the Consolidated financial statements using the equity method. Under this method, the consolidated entity's share of the post acquisition profits or losses of associates is recognised in the consolidated statement of financial performance, and its share of post acquisition movements in reserves is recognised in consolidated reserves. The cumulative post-acquisition movements are adjusted against the cost of the investment. Associates are those entities over which the consolidated entity exercises significant influence, but not control.

### C Revenue recognition

In general, revenue is recognised only when it is probable that the economic benefits comprising the revenue will flow to the entity and that the flow can be reliably measured.

In addition to these general criteria, specific revenue recognition criteria apply as follows:

***Sales revenue***

Sales revenue represents the revenue earned from the provision of products and rendering of services to parties external to the consolidated entity. Sales revenue is only recognised when control of the products has passed to the buyer and for services when a right to be compensated has been attained and the stage of completion of the contract can be reliably measured.

***Interest, rents and dividends***

Interest, rental and dividend revenue is recognised when the consolidated entity has attained control of a right to be compensated for the provision of, or investment of, its assets. With interest and rents, control of the right to be compensated will accrue over time. For dividends, the right to be compensated is usually attained with the approval of the dividend at a meeting of shareholders.

*Proceeds from sale of assets*

The gross proceeds of asset sales are recognised as revenue at the date that an unconditional contract of sale is exchanged with the purchaser.

## D Accounting for acquisitions

Assets and businesses acquired are accounted for using the cost method of accounting, whereby fair values are assigned to all the identifiable underlying assets acquired and the liabilities assumed at the date of acquisition.

Goodwill is brought to account on the basis described in Note 1(O).

## E Income tax

Tax effect accounting is applied using the liability method, whereby the income tax expense for the period is based on the accounting profit after adjustment for permanent differences.

The deferred tax assets and deferred tax liabilities represent the net cumulative effect of items of income and expense that have been brought to account for tax and accounting purposes in different periods.

Deferred tax assets pertaining to timing differences have only been brought to account where the benefits are expected to be realised beyond reasonable doubt.

## F Pre-opening expenses

Pre-opening expenses in connection with new stores are charged to the statement of financial performance in the period in which they are incurred.

## G Stock valuation of finished goods

Short life retail stocks are valued at the lower of average cost or net realisable value.

Long life retail stocks have been valued by the retail inventory method to arrive at cost.

Warehouse stocks are valued at the lower of average cost or net realisable value.

These methods of valuation are considered to achieve a valuation reasonably approximating the lower of cost or net realisable value.

## H Purchase and promotional incentives

Purchase or promotional incentives are taken into income in the period to which the purchase or promotion relates, provided receipt of the incentive is reasonably assured.

## I Recoverable amount of non-current assets

The recoverable amount of a non-current asset is the net amount expected to be recovered through the cash inflows and outflows arising from its continued use and subsequent disposal.

Where the carrying amount of a non-current asset exceeds its recoverable amount, the asset is written down to its recoverable amount. The decrement in the carrying amount is recognised as an expense in the net profit or loss in the reporting period in which the recoverable amount write-down occurs. In determining the recoverable amount, expected future cash flows have not been discounted to their present values.

## J Valuation of non-current assets

Subsequent to initial recognition as assets, all non-current assets are measured at their original cost. This policy was adopted with effect from 28 June 1999, with the directors electing to apply the new accounting standard AASB 1041 'Revaluation of Non-Current Assets' earlier than its operative date. The previous policy was to carry different classes of non-current assets at either cost or valuation. There was also a policy of revaluing freehold land and buildings to fair value at intervals of approximately 3 years.

*Change in accounting policy*

Until 27 June 1999, different classes of non-current assets were carried at either historical cost or valuation. With the exception of freehold land and buildings, which were revalued at approximately 3 yearly intervals, there was no regular policy to ensure that the valuations were current.

Notes to the financial statements ▸ 1 Significant accounting policies (continued)

On applying AASB 1041, with effect from 28 June 1999, the consolidated entity elected to revert to the cost basis for measuring all non-current assets. The directors chose this option because they considered that the cost of complying with the alternative policy permitted by AASB 1041, of revaluing non-current assets with sufficient regularity to ensure that the carrying amount of each item does not materially differ from its fair value at the reporting date, would exceed the benefits that would be gained.

In reverting from a revaluation to a cost basis, the carrying amount as at 27 June 1999 of all classes of non-current assets other than development properties and leasehold improvements, has been deemed to be their cost. For leasehold improvements, adjustments were made to reinstate the amounts of accumulated amortisation that had previously been written back against the asset cost upon revaluation. The adjustments did not result in any change in the carrying value of the leasehold improvements. For development properties, retrospective adjustments were made to measure them at their cost of acquisition less any accumulated depreciation and recoverable amount write-downs, as if they had always been measured using the cost basis.

The retrospective adjustments made at the beginning of the previous year were:

- a reduction in the consolidated carrying value of development properties of $13.8 million
- an increase in consolidated retained profits of $1.3 million, and
- a reduction in the consolidated asset revaluation reserve of $15.1 million.

In the current year the directors elected under section 334(5) of the Corporations Act 2001 to apply the July 2001 revised Accounting Standard AASB 1041 'Revaluation of Non-Current Assets' for the financial year, even though the standard is not required to be applied until annual reporting periods ending on or after 30 September 2001.

## K Current property, plant and equipment

Land and buildings held with the intent of sale within the next twelve months are classified as current assets and are valued at the lower of cost or net realisable value.

## L Depreciation

***(i) Buildings, fixtures, fittings and plant***

Buildings and plant comprising lifts, air conditioning, fire protection systems and other installations are depreciated on a straight-line basis over the estimated useful life of the asset to the consolidated entity. Estimates of remaining useful lives are made on a regular basis for all assets. The expected useful lives are as follows:

| | 2001 | 2000 |
|---|---|---|
| Buildings | 25–40 years | 25–40 years |
| Fixtures, fittings and plant | 3–40 years | 3–40 years |

***(ii) Leasehold improvements***

The cost of leasehold improvements is amortised over the remaining period of the individual leases or the estimated useful life of the improvement to the consolidated entity, whichever is the shorter. Leasehold improvements held at the reporting date are being amortised over a maximum period of 20 years.

***(iii) Plant, equipment and shop fittings***

Plant, equipment and shop fittings (including application software) are depreciated on a straight-line basis over the estimated useful life of the asset to the consolidated entity. Estimates of remaining useful lives are made on a regular basis for all assets.

The expected useful lives are as follows:

| | 2001 | 2000 |
|---|---|---|
| Plant, equipment and fittings | 2.5–40 years | 2.5–40 years |

## M Foreign exchange

***Transactions***

Transactions in foreign currencies within the consolidated entity are converted to local currency at the rate of exchange ruling at the date of the transaction.

Amounts payable to and by the entities within the consolidated entity that are outstanding at period end and are denominated in foreign currencies have been converted to local currency using rates of exchange ruling at the end of the financial period, or where applicable, the contractual exchange rate. The resulting gains or losses are credited or charged to the statement of financial performance.

***Specific commitments***

Exchange gains and losses, and costs, premiums and discounts on transactions intended to hedge the purchase or sale of goods or services are deferred up to the date of, and included in the measurement of the purchase or sale. In the case of hedges of monetary items, exchange gains and losses are brought to account in the period in which the exchange rates change. Gains or costs arising on entry into such hedging transactions are brought to account over the lives of the hedges.

Where a hedging transaction is terminated prior to maturity and the underlying transaction is still expected to occur, any gains or losses occurring prior to termination continue to be deferred and are brought to account in the measurement of the underlying transaction. Where the underlying transaction is no longer expected to occur, any previously deferred gains and losses are taken to statement of financial performance at the date of termination.

Where a hedging transaction is redesignated as a hedge of another transaction, gains and losses arising on the hedge prior to its redesignation are only deferred where the original anticipated transaction is still expected to occur. Where the original transaction is no longer expected to occur, any gains or losses relating to the hedge instrument are included in the statement of financial performance for the period.

***General commitments***

Exchange gains and losses on other hedge transactions are not deferred, but brought to account in the statement of financial performance in the period in which the exchange rates change. Gains or costs arising on entry into these transactions are brought to account at the time of entry and amortised over the lives of the hedges.

***Foreign controlled entities***

All foreign controlled entities are self-sustaining, as each is financially independent of the Company. The accounts of the foreign controlled entities are translated using the current rate method and any exchange differences are taken to the foreign currency translation reserve.

## N Receivables

***Trade and other debtors***

Trade and other debtors are carried at nominal amounts due less any provision for doubtful debts. Provision for doubtful debts is made when collection of the full nominal amount is no longer probable.

***Short term deposits***

Short term deposits are stated at the lower of cost and net realisable value. Interest income is brought to account in the period in which it is earned.

## O Intangibles

***Liquor licences***

Liquor licences are valued at cost, following the change in accounting policy described in Note 1(J). Previously, they were valued at Directors' valuation at 01 June 1998 being the Directors' estimate of the recoverable amount of the licences. On the change in accounting policy, the Directors' valuation has been deemed to be the original cost of the licences in accordance with the transitional provisions contained in Accounting Standard AASB 1041 'Revaluation of Non-Current Assets'.

Liquor licences are amortised over their estimated useful life. The estimate of the useful life of liquor licences has been reassessed. Liquor licences, which were previously considered to have a useful life of 20 years, are now considered to have an indefinite useful life. As a consequence, no amortisation of liquor licences has been charged for the year ended 24 June 2001. Had a change in estimate not taken place, then an amount of $2.4 million would have been charged in the year to 24 June 2001.

***Goodwill***

Goodwill represents the excess of the purchase consideration over the fair value of identifiable net assets acquired at the time of acquisition of some, or all, of the assets or equity of another entity by entities within the consolidated entity.

Goodwill is amortised by the straight-line method over the period during which benefits are expected to be received, a period deemed to be 20 years.

## P Investments

Interests in controlled entities are accounted for in the consolidated accounts as set out in Note 1(B) and at cost in Woolworths Limited's financial statements.

Interests in unlisted shares of associates are carried at the lower of cost and recoverable amount in Woolworths Limited's financial statements.

Interests in partnerships are stated at cost, adjusted by the consolidated entity's share of movements in the net assets of the partnership. The consolidated entity's share of the profit or loss of the partnership is brought to account as it is earned.

Interests in semi-government securities are carried at amortised cost, calculated after accounting for the discount or premium on acquisition. Interest income is taken to account as revenue on an effective yield basis.

## Q Leases

Operating lease payments, where the lessor effectively retains substantially all of the risks and benefits of ownership of the leased items, are charged to the statement of financial performance in the periods in which they are incurred, as this represents the pattern of benefits derived from the leased assets.

The cost of improvements made on or to leasehold properties is accounted for as described in Note 1(L)(ii).

## R Accounts payable and accruals

These amounts represent liabilities for goods and services provided to the consolidated entity which were unpaid at the end of the period. The amounts are unsecured and are usually settled within 45 days of recognition.

## S Interest bearing liabilities

Loans and funds accepted on deposit are carried at their principal amounts, representing the present value of future cash flows associated with servicing of the debt. Interest is recognised as an expense of the period in which it accrues and is recorded as an accrual in the statement of financial position until it is paid. Costs incurred in connection with borrowing are capitalised and amortised over the period of the borrowing.

## T Employee entitlements

***Wages and salaries, annual leave and sick leave***

Liabilities for wages and salaries, annual leave and vested sick leave are recognised, and are measured as the amount unpaid at period end at the current rates of pay in respect of employees' services up to that date.

***Long service leave***

A liability for long service leave is recognised, and is measured as the present value of expected future payments to be made in respect of services provided by employees up to period end. Consideration is given to expected future wage and salary levels, experience of employee departures and periods of service. The expected future cash flows are discounted, using interest rates attaching to Commonwealth Government guaranteed securities which have terms to maturity, matching their estimated timing as closely as possible.

***Employee share schemes***

The cost of the employee share scheme described in Note 25 is not charged as an employee entitlement expense.

*Superannuation*

The Company has a Superannuation Plan that exists to provide defined benefit and/or accumulation type benefits to employees and their dependents on retirement, disability or death.

For funding purposes, actuarial valuations are carried out approximately every 3 years for the Company's liability for the defined benefit and accumulation enhancement portions of the Plan. The Company's commitment in respect of accumulation benefits under the Plan is limited to making the specified contributions in accordance with the Rules of the Plan and/or any statutory obligations. The Company's contributions to the Superannuation Plan are expensed in the statement of financial performance as incurred.

## U Borrowing costs

Borrowing costs include interest, amortisation of discounts or premiums relating to borrowings, amortisation of ancillary costs incurred in connection with the arrangement of borrowings and lease finance charges.

Borrowing costs are recognised as expenses in the period in which they are incurred, except where they are included in the cost of qualifying assets.

Qualifying assets are assets that take more than 12 months to prepare for their intended use or sale.

The capitalisation rate used to determine the amount of borrowing costs to be capitalised is the weighted average interest rate applicable to the consolidated entity's outstanding borrowings during the year, in this case 7.58% (2000: 6.89%).

## V Derivative financial instruments

The consolidated entity enters into forward foreign exchange contracts and interest rate swap agreements. Neither of these types of derivative financial instruments is recognised in the financial statements at inception.

Accounting for forward exchange contracts is in accordance with Note 1(M).

The net amount receivable or payable under interest rate swap agreements is progressively brought to account over the period to settlement.

The amount recognised is adjusted against interest expense during the period.

## W Cash

For purposes of the statement of cash flows, cash includes deposits at call which are readily convertible to cash on hand and are subject to insignificant risk of changes in value, net of outstanding bank overdrafts.

## X Earnings per share

Basic earnings per share is determined by dividing the operating net profit after tax attributable to the members of Woolworths Limited after deducting the Woolworths Income Notes distribution, by the weighted average number of ordinary shares outstanding during the financial period, adjusted for bonus elements in ordinary shares issued during the period.

Diluted earnings per share adjusts the amounts used in the determination of basic earnings per share by taking into account any amounts unpaid on ordinary shares and any reduction in earnings per share that will probably arise from the exercise of options outstanding during the financial period.

## Y Goods and services tax

Revenues, expenses and assets are recognised net of the amount of goods and services tax (GST), except:

(i) where the amount of GST incurred is not recoverable from the taxation authority, it is recognised as part of the acquisition cost of an asset or as part of an item of expense;

or

(ii) for receivables or payables which are recognised inclusive of GST.

The net amount of GST recoverable from, or payable to, the taxation authority is included as part of receivables or payables.

Notes to the financial statements

## 2 Profit from ordinary activities

Profit from ordinary activities before income tax includes the following items of revenue and expense:

| | Consolidated | | Woolworths Limited | |
|---|---|---|---|---|
| | 52 weeks ended 24 June 01 $m | 52 weeks ended 25 June 00 $m | 52 weeks ended 24 June 01 $m | 52 weeks ended 25 June 00 $m |
| **(a) Operating revenue** | | | | |
| Revenue from the sale of goods: | | | | |
| Related parties | – | – | 72.6 | 115.1 |
| Other parties | 20,915.1 | 20,019.9 | 7,100.5 | 6,759.4 |
| Other operating revenue – rebates, discounts received and other | 473.6 | 372.4 | 163.8 | 221.8 |
| Interest: | | | | |
| Related parties | – | – | – | 0.2 |
| Other parties | 10.7 | 8.9 | 10.0 | 8.1 |
| Total operating revenue | 21,399.4 | 20,401.2 | 7,346.9 | 7,104.6 |
| **(b) Other revenue from ordinary activities** | | | | |
| Dividends: | | | | |
| Related parties | – | – | 348.7 | 376.5 |
| Rent: | | | | |
| Related parties | – | – | – | 1.9 |
| Other parties | 11.0 | 9.9 | 2.2 | 2.2 |
| Gross proceeds from disposal of non-current assets | 173.1 | 111.0 | 21.2 | 41.4 |
| Gross proceeds on sale of businesses | 76.1 | 44.5 | 76.1 | 28.9 |
| Total other revenue from ordinary activities | 260.2 | 165.4 | 448.2 | 450.9 |
| **Total revenue** | **21,659.6** | **20,566.6** | **7,795.1** | **7,555.5** |

| | Consolidated | | Woolworths Limited | |
|---|---|---|---|---|
| | 52 weeks ended 24 June 01 $m | 52 weeks ended 25 June 00 $m | 52 weeks ended 24 June 01 $m | 52 weeks ended 25 June 00 $m |
| **(c) Expenses** | | | | |
| Amounts provided for: | | | | |
| Bad and doubtful debts | 2.1 | 4.6 | 1.2 | 0.7 |
| Employee entitlements | 169.9 | 157.2 | 59.1 | 49.7 |
| Self-insured risks | 69.7 | 50.8 | 36.2 | 13.8 |
| Diminution in value of other financial assets | – | – | 1.5 | – |
| Net loss/(profit) on disposal of: | | | | |
| Property, plant, equipment, fixtures and fittings | 0.6 | 10.7 | (0.8) | 1.9 |
| Depreciation of: | | | | |
| Buildings | 12.1 | 9.1 | – | – |
| Plant and equipment, fixtures and fittings | 262.9 | 247.5 | 84.3 | 78.9 |
| Amortisation of: | | | | |
| Leasehold improvements | 25.7 | 24.1 | 7.7 | 8.4 |
| Liquor licences | – | 2.1 | – | 1.3 |
| Goodwill | 9.1 | 6.0 | 5.3 | 3.7 |
| Contributions to defined benefit superannuation plans | 76.3 | 65.3 | 30.9 | 28.1 |
| Operating lease rental expenses: | | | | |
| Leased premises | | | | |
| – minimum lease payments | 496.0 | 434.4 | 189.6 | 151.6 |
| – contingent rentals | 76.9 | 107.3 | 22.5 | 37.3 |
| – sub-leases | 1.3 | 5.0 | 0.5 | 0.1 |
| Leased equipment | | | | |
| – minimum lease payments | 25.8 | – | 13.0 | – |
| Total operating lease rental expenses | 600.0 | 546.7 | 225.6 | 189.0 |
| **(d) Individually significant non-recurring items** | | | | |
| Rationalisation of warehousing and distribution functions | – | (4.3) | – | (4.3) |
| Reversal of provision for write-down in value of assets | 9.3 | 20.7 | 9.3 | 20.7 |
| Gain on disposal of Rockmans business | 2.8 | 11.0 | 2.8 | 7.5 |
| Loss on disposal of Chisholm Manufacturing business | (4.1) | – | (4.1) | – |
| Loss on disposal of Crazy Prices business | (11.4) | | (11.4) | – |
| Restructuring and Project Refresh costs | (1.0) | (68.1) | (1.0) | (68.1) |
| GST implementation costs | – | (53.2) | – | (52.9) |
| Total individually significant non-recurring items | (4.4) | (93.9) | (4.4) | (97.1) |

## Notes to the financial statements

| | Consolidated | | Woolworths Limited | |
|---|---|---|---|---|
| | 52 weeks ended 24 June 01 $m | 52 weeks ended 25 June 00 $m | 52 weeks ended 24 June 01 $m | 52 weeks ended 25 June 00 $m |
| **3 Net finance costs** | | | | |
| Interest income: | | | | |
| Related parties | – | – | – | 0.2 |
| Other parties | 10.7 | 8.9 | 10.0 | 8.1 |
| | 10.7 | 8.9 | 10.0 | 8.3 |
| Interest expense: | | | | |
| Other parties | (35.7) | (42.5) | (34.6) | (41.0) |
| Less: borrowing costs capitalised (Note 1(U)) | 11.9 | 5.8 | 11.9 | 5.8 |
| | (23.8) | (36.7) | (22.7) | (35.2) |
| **Net finance costs** | **(13.1)** | **(27.8)** | **(12.7)** | **(26.9)** |
| **4 Auditors' remuneration** | | | | |
| Audit services: | | | | |
| Deloitte Touche Tohmatsu | 0.577 | – | 0.545 | – |
| BDO | – | 0.781 | – | 0.781 |
| | 0.577 | 0.781 | 0.545 | 0.781 |
| Other services: | | | | |
| Deloitte Touche Tohmatsu | 1.480 | – | 1.480 | – |
| Deloitte Consulting | 0.499 | – | 0.048 | – |
| BDO | – | 0.270 | – | 0.270 |
| | 1.979 | 0.270 | 1.528 | 0.270 |
| **Total auditors' remuneration** | **2.556** | **1.051** | **2.073** | **1.051** |
| **5 Taxation** | | | | |
| Prima facie income tax expense on the current period operating profit before income tax, calculated at 34% (2000 at 36%) | 235.8 | 179.9 | 185.6 | 187.9 |
| Tax effect of permanent differences: | | | | |
| Amortisation of intangibles | 3.1 | 2.9 | 1.8 | 1.8 |
| Depreciation of buildings | 1.7 | 2.4 | – | 0.1 |
| Building allowance deduction | (1.2) | (1.2) | – | – |
| Rebatable dividend income | – | – | (118.5) | (135.5) |
| Tax capital losses not recognised as a deduction | – | 0.4 | – | – |
| Woolworths Income Notes distribution deductible | (16.2) | (9.4) | (16.2) | (9.4) |
| Other permanent differences reducing tax payable | (7.7) | (9.9) | (0.9) | (9.1) |
| Other permanent differences increasing tax payable | 1.9 | 6.2 | 0.2 | 5.0 |
| Income tax expense on current year's operating profit | 217.4 | 171.3 | 52.0 | 40.8 |
| Over provision in prior period | – | (1.5) | – | (14.2) |
| Restatement of deferred tax balances due to change in company income tax rate | – | 8.4 | – | 1.3 |
| **Income tax expense attributable to operating profit** | **217.4** | **178.2** | **52.0** | **27.9** |

| | Consolidated | | Woolworths Limited | |
|---|---|---|---|---|
| | 52 weeks ended 24 June 01 $m | 52 weeks ended 25 June 00 $m | 52 weeks ended 24 June 01 $m | 52 weeks ended 25 June 00 $m |
| Income tax expense attributable to operating profit comprises: | | | | |
| Provision for current income tax liability | 230.6 | 183.8 | 47.0 | 51.9 |
| Provision for deferred tax liability | (19.7) | (9.6) | (8.3) | 7.3 |
| Deferred tax asset | 6.5 | 5.5 | 13.3 | (17.1) |
| Over provision in prior period | – | (1.5) | – | (14.2) |
| | **217.4** | **178.2** | **52.0** | **27.9** |
| Future income tax benefits not brought to account as assets: | | | | |
| Tax losses – capital | 4.5 | – | 4.0 | – |
| | 4.5 | – | 4.0 | – |

The taxation benefits of tax losses not brought to account will only be obtained if:

a) assessable income is derived of a nature and of amount sufficient to enable the benefit from the deductions to be realised;

b) conditions for deductibility imposed by the law are complied with; and

c) no changes in tax legislation adversely affect the realisation of the benefit from the deductions.

On 14 September 1992 the Company entered into a Subvention Agreement under which the tax losses within Industrial Equities Limited (IEL) were used to reduce taxes that the Company and certain of its controlled entities otherwise would have been required to pay to the Australian Tax Office (ATO) in respect of its 1991 and 1992 operating profit. The agreement ensures that the Company and certain of its controlled entities will either make a subvention payment to IEL or to the ATO to the extent that the ATO does not allow IEL losses to be grouped against taxable income of the Company and those controlled entities. These financial statements have been prepared on the assumption that these taxes will be paid to the ATO. This basis is consistent with the prior period.

## 6 Dividends paid or provided

| | | | | |
|---|---|---|---|---|
| Final dividend of 15 cents (2000: 13 cents) per fully paid ordinary share proposed to be paid 5 October 2001 (2000: 5 October 2000) 100% franked at 30% tax rate (2000: 34%) | 155.4 | 137.8 | 155.4 | 137.8 |
| Interim dividend of 12 cents (2000: 10 cents) per fully paid ordinary share paid 27 April 2001 (2000: 28 April 2000) 100% franked at 34% tax rate (2000: 36%) (Class C) | 128.7 | 105.7 | 128.7 | 105.7 |
| Special dividend of $5.82 (2000: $2.47) per fully paid ordinary share paid 22 June 2001 (2000: 7 April 2000) to shareholders participating in the off market share buy-back 100% franked at 34% (2000: 36%) (Class C) | 232.9 | 247.0 | 232.9 | 247.0 |
| **Total dividends paid or provided** | **517.0** | **490.5** | **517.0** | **490.5** |

## Notes to the financial statements ▸ 6 Dividends paid or provided (continued)

| | Consolidated | | Woolworths Limited | |
|---|---|---|---|---|
| | 52 weeks ended 24 June 01 $m | 52 weeks ended 25 June 00 $m | 52 weeks ended 24 June 01 $m | 52 weeks ended 25 June 00 $m |
| Dividends paid in cash or satisfied by the issue of new shares under the Dividend Reinvestment Plan during the years ended 24 June 2001 and 25 June 2000 were as follows: | | | | |
| Paid in cash: | | | | |
| Final and interim dividends | 212.1 | 173.5 | 212.1 | 173.5 |
| Special buy-back dividend | 232.9 | 247.0 | 232.9 | 247.0 |
| Satisfied by the issue of new shares | 54.7 | 47.3 | 54.7 | 47.3 |
| | **499.7** | **467.8** | **499.7** | **467.8** |
| **Franked dividends** | | | | |
| The franked portions of the dividends proposed as at 24 June 2001 will be franked out of existing franking credits or out of franked credits arising from the payment of income tax in the year ending June 2002. | | | | |
| Franking credits available for the subsequent financial year 30% (2000: 34%) franking credits | 402.2 | 417.8 | 83.1 | 143.9 |

The above amounts represent the balances of the franking accounts as at the end of the financial period, adjusted for:

(a) Franking credits that will arise from the payment of income tax payable at the end of the financial period; and

(b) Franking debits that will arise from the payment of dividends proposed at the end of the financial period.

## 7 Segment disclosures

| | Supermarkets | | General merchandise | |
|---|---|---|---|---|
| | 2001 $m | 2000 $m | 2001 $m | 2000 $m |
| **Industry segments** | | | | |
| Sales to customers | 17,519.4 | 16,499.0* | 2,487.8 | 2,444.7* |
| Unallocated revenue | | | | |
| Total revenue excluding interest | 17,519.4 | 16,499.0 | 2,487.8 | 2,444.7 |
| Segment operating profit | 618.6 | 533.0 | 114.2 | 100.3 |
| Unallocated expenses | | | | |
| – Property | | | | |
| – Head office | | | | |
| Net interest | | | | |
| Operating profit before income tax | | | | |
| Segment assets | 2,727.0 | 2,492.1 | 788.5 | 647.4 |
| Unallocated | | | | |
| Total assets | | | | |

| | Wholesale | | Discontinued operations | | Consolidated | |
|---|---|---|---|---|---|---|
| | 2001<br>$m | 2000<br>$m | 2001<br>$m | 2000<br>$m | 2001<br>$m | 2000<br>$m |
| **Industry segments** | | | | | | |
| Sales to customers | 697.8 | 716.5* | 210.1 | 359.7* | 20,915.1 | 20,019.9* |
| Unallocated revenue | | | | | 733.8 | 537.8 |
| Total revenue excluding interest | 697.8 | 716.5 | 210.1 | 359.7 | 21,648.9 | 20,557.7 |
| Segment operating profit/(loss) | 5.0 | 2.9 | (5.3) | 10.8 | 732.5 | 647.0 |
| Unallocated expenses | | | | | | |
| – Property | | | | | 33.1 | 24.8 |
| – Head office | | | | | (59.0) | (144.1) |
| Net interest | | | | | (13.1) | (27.8) |
| Operating profit before income tax | | | | | 693.5 | 499.9 |
| Segment assets | 156.7 | 179.1 | – | 95.8 | 3,672.2 | 3,414.4 |
| Unallocated | | | | | 1,411.0 | 1,402.4 |
| Total assets | | | | | 5,083.2 | 4,816.8 |

* Sales for the 52 weeks ended 25 June 2000 include wholesale sale tax (WST) Sales adjusted to exclude WST were as follows:

| | |
|---|---|
| Supermarkets | 15,723.8 |
| General merchandise | 2,252.1 |
| Wholesale | 675.3 |
| Discontinued operations | 337.6 |
| Total | 18,988.8 |

Inter segment pricing is determined on an arms length basis.

The consolidated entity operates predominantly in Australia. More than 99% of revenue, operating profit before income tax and total assets relate to operations within Australia.

The periods reported are for the 52 weeks ended 24 June 2001 and 25 June 2000, respectively.

Notes to the financial statements

| | Consolidated | | Woolworths Limited | |
|---|---|---|---|---|
| | As at 24 June 01 $m | As at 25 June 00 $m | As at 24 June 01 $m | As at 25 June 00 $m |

## 8 Receivables

| | | | | |
|---|---|---|---|---|
| **Current** | | | | |
| Trade receivables | 91.8 | 85.9 | 9.0 | 11.0 |
| Less: Provision for doubtful debts | (4.1) | (3.4) | (1.3) | (0.4) |
| | 87.7 | 82.5 | 7.7 | 10.6 |
| Other receivables | 103.2 | 75.9 | 46.7 | 32.6 |
| Less: Provision for doubtful debts | (0.8) | (0.8) | (0.4) | (0.6) |
| | 102.4 | 75.1 | 46.3 | 32.0 |
| Short term deposits | 2.2 | 2.3 | 1.9 | 1.9 |
| Staff and other advances | 2.6 | 4.1 | 2.8 | 4.7 |
| | **194.9** | **164.0** | **58.7** | **49.2** |
| **Non-current** | | | | |
| Other debtors | 8.8 | 0.4 | 8.7 | 0.4 |
| Employee loans | 35.4 | 47.3 | 35.4 | 47.3 |
| Loans to controlled entities | – | – | 1,662.6 | 1,486.8 |
| | **44.2** | **47.7** | **1,706.7** | **1,534.5** |

## 9 Other assets

| | | | | |
|---|---|---|---|---|
| **Current** | | | | |
| Prepayments | 78.9 | 84.6 | 27.6 | 36.6 |
| Borrowing costs | 0.6 | 0.5 | 0.6 | 0.5 |
| Less: Amortisation | (0.5) | (0.3) | (0.5) | (0.3) |
| | **79.0** | **84.8** | **27.7** | **36.8** |
| **Non-current** | | | | |
| Borrowing costs | 0.5 | 0.5 | 0.5 | 0.5 |
| | **0.5** | **0.5** | **0.5** | **0.5** |

## 10 Investments accounted for using the equity method

**(a) Details of investment in associates**

| *Name* | *Principal activity* | *% Ownership* | *Investment carrying amount* | |
|---|---|---|---|---|
| GreenGrocer.com.au | On-line retailing | 38.1% | 16.8 | – |
| | | | 16.8 | – |

**(b) Movements in investments in associates**

| | | |
|---|---|---|
| Amount paid on acquisition | 18.3 | – |
| Share of loss from ordinary activities | (1.5) | – |
| Equity accounted amount of investment at end of period | 16.8 | – |

| | Consolidated | | Woolworths Limited | |
|---|---|---|---|---|
| | As at 24 June 01 $m | As at 25 June 00 $m | As at 24 June 01 $m | As at 25 June 00 $m |
| **(c) Commitments** | | | | |
| Share of associates operating lease commitments payable: | | | | |
| Not later than one year | 0.3 | – | | |
| Later than one year, not later than five | 0.4 | – | | |
| Later than five years | – | – | | |
| | 0.7 | – | | |
| Share of associates finance lease commitments payable: | | | | |
| Not later than one year | 0.2 | – | | |
| Later than one year, not later than five | 0.4 | – | | |
| Later than five years | – | – | | |
| | 0.6 | – | | |
| **(d) Summarised financial position of associates** | | | | |
| Aggregate assets and liabilities of associates is as follows: | | | | |
| Current assets | 6.3 | – | | |
| Non current assets | 3.1 | – | | |
| Total assets | 9.4 | – | | |
| Current liabilities | (3.4) | – | | |
| Net assets | 6.0 | – | | |
| Net loss | (3.8) | – | | |
| Woolworths Limited share of accumulated loss | (1.5) | – | | |

## 11 Other financial assets

| | Consolidated | | Woolworths Limited | |
|---|---|---|---|---|
| **Non-current** | | | | |
| Controlled entities: | | | | |
| Unlisted shares at cost | – | – | 78.8 | 71.3 |
| Other corporations: | | | | |
| Associated entity unlisted shares at cost | – | – | 18.3 | – |
| Less: provision for diminution in value of shares | – | – | (1.5) | – |
| | – | – | 16.8 | – |
| Unlisted shares at cost | 0.1 | 0.1 | – | – |
| Interest in partnership | 0.8 | 0.8 | | – |
| Semi-government securities, at cost | 0.5 | 0.5 | 0.5 | 0.5 |
| | **1.4** | **1.4** | **96.1** | **71.8** |

### Semi-government securities

The semi-government securities which were acquired on 21 February 2001 represent NSW Treasury Inscribed Stock. The principal is $500,000 and maturity is 21 August 2001. The current interest rate is 5.33% p.a.

Notes to the financial statements

| | Consolidated | | Woolworths Limited | |
|---|---|---|---|---|
| | As at 24 June 01 $m | As at 25 June 00 $m | As at 24 June 01 $m | As at 25 June 00 $m |

## 12 Property, plant and equipment

| | Consolidated As at 24 June 01 $m | Consolidated As at 25 June 00 $m | Woolworths Limited As at 24 June 01 $m | Woolworths Limited As at 25 June 00 $m |
|---|---|---|---|---|
| **Current** | | | | |
| Development properties: | | | | |
| At cost | 126.8 | 98.0 | – | – |
| | **126.8** | **98.0** | **–** | **–** |
| **Non-current** | | | | |
| Development properties: | | | | |
| At cost | 199.1 | 142.8 | – | – |
| Less: Accumulated depreciation on buildings | (3.8) | (3.1) | – | – |
| | 195.3 | 139.7 | – | |
| Freehold warehouse, retail and other properties: | | | | |
| At cost | 338.1 | 350.7 | – | – |
| Less: Accumulated depreciation on buildings | (18.4) | (11.3) | – | – |
| | 319.7 | 339.4 | – | – |
| Leasehold improvements: | | | | |
| At cost | 342.5 | 309.8 | 133.8 | 125.3 |
| Less: Accumulated amortisation | (130.7) | (108.7) | (47.1) | (40.3) |
| | 211.8 | 201.1 | 86.7 | 85.0 |
| Plant and equipment: | | | | |
| At cost | 3,000.0 | 2,828.7 | 894.7 | 851.5 |
| Less: Accumulated depreciation | (1,596.1) | (1,412.8) | (511.4) | (464.7) |
| | 1,403.9 | 1,415.9 | 383.3 | 386.8 |
| | **2,130.7** | **2,096.1** | **470.0** | **471.8** |
| **Total property, plant and equipment – net book value** | **2,257.5** | **2,194.1** | **470.0** | **471.8** |

## Reconciliations

Reconciliations of the carrying amounts of each class of non-current property, plant and equipment at the beginning and end of the current and previous financial periods are set out below:

| | Development properties | Warehouse, retail and other properties | Leasehold improvements | Plant and equipment |
|---|---|---|---|---|
| **Consolidated – 2001** | | | | |
| Carrying amount at start of period | 139.7 | 339.4 | 201.1 | 1,415.9 |
| Additions | 99.2 | 50.7 | 26.0 | 405.8 |
| Disposals | (38.4) | (23.4) | (7.5) | (148.8) |
| Depreciation/amortisation expense | – | (12.1) | (25.7) | (262.9) |
| Transfers (to)/from current assets | (5.2) | (34.9) | 17.9 | (6.1) |
| **Carrying amount at end of period** | **195.3** | **319.7** | **211.8** | **1,403.9** |
| **Consolidated – 2000** | | | | |
| Carrying amount at start of period | 66.0 | 401.0 | 202.8 | 1,460.5 |
| Additions | 57.0 | 8.9 | 29.1 | 314.2 |
| Disposals | (26.2) | (1.4) | (6.7) | (105.2) |
| Depreciation/amortisation expense | (0.8) | (8.2) | (24.1) | (247.5) |
| Transfers (to)/from current assets | 43.7 | (60.9) | – | (6.1) |
| **Carrying amount at end of period** | **139.7** | **339.4** | **201.1** | **1,415.9** |
| **Woolworths Limited – 2001** | | | | |
| Carrying amount at start of period | – | – | 85.0 | 386.8 |
| Additions | – | – | 8.9 | 143.1 |
| Disposals | – | – | (5.6) | (59.8) |
| Depreciation/amortisation expense | – | – | (7.7) | (84.3) |
| Transfers (to)/from current assets | – | – | 6.1 | (2.5) |
| **Carrying amount at end of period** | **–** | **–** | **86.7** | **383.3** |
| **Woolworths Limited – 2000** | | | | |
| Carrying amount at start of period | – | – | 80.7 | 383.0 |
| Additions | – | – | 14.3 | 124.3 |
| Disposals | – | – | (1.6) | (41.7) |
| Depreciation/amortisation expense | – | – | (8.4) | (78.8) |
| **Carrying amount at end of period** | **–** | **–** | **85.0** | **386.8** |

# Notes to the financial statements

| | Consolidated | | Woolworths Limited | |
|---|---|---|---|---|
| | As at 24 June 01 $m | As at 25 June 00 $m | As at 24 June 01 $m | As at 25 June 00 $m |
| **13 Intangibles** | | | | |
| **Non-current** | | | | |
| Liquor licences: | | | | |
| At cost | 52.5 | 43.8 | 29.2 | 26.3 |
| Accumulated amortisation | (13.1) | (13.1) | (7.8) | (7.8) |
| | 39.4 | 30.7 | 21.4 | 18.5 |
| Goodwill – at cost | 298.4 | 130.1 | 105.9 | 79.1 |
| Accumulated amortisation | (24.4) | (15.8) | (17.0) | (11.6) |
| | 274.0 | 114.3 | 88.9 | 67.5 |
| | **313.4** | **145.0** | **110.3** | **86.0** |

Following the change in the determination of useful life of liquor licences from 20 years to one of indefinite life, no amortisation has been charged in the year to 24 June 2001, as set out in Note 1(O).

## 14 Interest bearing liabilities

| | Consolidated 24 June 01 $m | Consolidated 25 June 00 $m | Woolworths Limited 24 June 01 $m | Woolworths Limited 25 June 00 $m |
|---|---|---|---|---|
| **Current** | | | | |
| ***Unsecured*** | | | | |
| Bank loans | 340.0 | – | 340.0 | – |
| Short term money market loans | – | 125.0 | – | 125.0 |
| Funds accepted on short term deposit | 1.7 | 4.9 | 0.2 | 0.2 |
| | **341.7** | **129.9** | **340.2** | **125.2** |
| **Non-current** | | | | |
| ***Unsecured*** | | | | |
| Other loans | 285.0 | 285.2 | 285.0 | 285.2 |
| | 285.0 | 285.2 | 285.0 | 285.2 |
| ***Secured*** | | | | |
| Bank loans | 16.9 | 17.1 | – | – |
| | **301.9** | **302.3** | **285.0** | **285.2** |

### Bank loans

Unsecured bank loans represent a 3 to 5 year $835 million revolving credit facility, comprising a series of bilateral loan agreements, maturing from financial years 2004 to 2006. Each draw-down under the facility has a term of between one and six months, and may be rolled over on maturity. Interest is payable on roll-over, at a rate calculated as the Bank Bill Swap yield plus a margin. The facility is subject to a negative pledge agreement. The latest maturity date for the loans outstanding at 24 June 2001 is 28 December 2001. The weighted average interest rate on the amounts outstanding was 5.27%.

Secured bank loans represent draw-downs on a multi option facility secured by a mortgage over land and buildings and an equitable charge over the assets of a controlled entity. Interest is payable on this facility at both fixed and variable rates.

### Other loans

Other loans comprise Medium Term Notes of $80 million and $70 million which were issued into the domestic market and mature on 20 August 2007. Interest is payable on these issues, quarterly at the Bank Bill Swap rate plus a margin and semi-annually at a fixed rate on a bond basis, respectively. Senior Notes of $100 million US dollars were issued in the United States capital markets, maturing on 1 September 2007. Under the principal agreement, interest is payable on this debt semi-annually in US dollars, at a fixed rate. The Company has entered into cross currency swaps in respect of these borrowings (refer Note 28) which eliminate all foreign currency exposures.

### Short term money market loans

Short term money market loans represent monies borrowed from financial institutions participating in the money market on an 11am call basis. There were no loans outstanding at 24 June 2001.

### Funds accepted on short term deposit

Funds accepted on short term deposit represent retention monies held on certain construction projects and amounts received from certain retired employees.

## 15 Financing arrangements

| | Consolidated | | Woolworths Limited | |
|---|---|---|---|---|
| | As at 24 June 01 $m | As at 25 June 00 $m | As at 24 June 01 $m | As at 25 June 00 $m |
| Unrestricted access was available at balance date to the following lines of credit: | | | | |
| **Total facilities** | | | | |
| Bank overdrafts | 12.0 | 10.0 | 10.0 | 10.0 |
| Bank loan facilities | 952.5 | 917.5 | 935.0 | 900.0 |
| | 964.5 | 927.5 | 945.0 | 910.0 |
| **Used at balance date** | | | | |
| Bank overdrafts | – | – | – | – |
| Bank loan facilities | 356.9 | 17.1 | 340.0 | – |
| | 356.9 | 17.1 | 340.0 | – |
| **Unused at balance date** | | | | |
| Bank overdrafts | 12.0 | 10.0 | 10.0 | 10.0 |
| Bank loan facilities | 595.6 | 900.4 | 595.0 | 900.0 |
| | **607.6** | **910.4** | **605.0** | **910.0** |

Bank loan facilities may be drawn at any time, subject to the covenants of the lending agreements. All facilities are denominated in Australian dollars. The bank overdraft facilities are unsecured and may be drawn at any time.

## Notes to the financial statements

| | Consolidated | | Woolworths Limited | |
|---|---|---|---|---|
| | As at 24 June 01 $m | As at 25 June 00 $m | As at 24 June 01 $m | As at 25 June 00 $m |

## 16 Foreign currency receivables and payables

The Australian dollar equivalents of unhedged amounts receivable and payable in foreign currencies, calculated at year end exchange rates, are as follows:

| | | | | |
|---|---|---|---|---|
| **Amounts payable** | | | | |
| ***Current*** | | | | |
| United States dollars | 56.3 | 34.1 | 45.4 | 27.3 |
| Hong Kong dollars | 0.5 | 14.8 | 0.5 | 14.7 |
| Japanese yen | – | 0.2 | – | – |
| Other currencies | 0.5 | 1.1 | 0.5 | 1.1 |

## 17 Provisions

| | | | | |
|---|---|---|---|---|
| **Current** | | | | |
| Employee entitlements | 194.7 | 182.5 | 74.9 | 67.5 |
| Self-insured risks | 57.2 | 50.3 | 20.1 | 14.1 |
| Asset write-down | – | 9.3 | – | 9.3 |
| Restructuring and GST costs | 20.0 | 71.8 | 13.4 | 71.8 |
| Dividends | 155.4 | 137.8 | 155.4 | 137.8 |
| | 427.3 | 451.7 | 263.8 | 300.5 |
| **Non-current** | | | | |
| Employee entitlements | 92.8 | 84.8 | 34.2 | 29.6 |
| Self-insured risks | 91.8 | 66.1 | 36.1 | 12.3 |
| | 184.6 | 150.9 | 70.3 | 41.9 |
| **Total provisions** | **611.9** | **602.6** | **334.1** | **342.4** |

## 18 Contributed equity

| | Consolidated | | Woolworths Limited | |
|---|---|---|---|---|
| | As at 24 June 01 $m | As at 25 June 00 $m | As at 24 June 01 $m | As at 25 June 00 $m |
| **Issued and paid-up share capital** | | | | |
| Fully paid ordinary shares: | | | | |
| 1,035,461,356 (2000: 1,059,994,471) | 476.2 | 494.0 | 476.2 | 494.0 |
| Fully paid ordinary shares carry one vote per share. | | | | |
| **Reconciliation of fully paid share capital – ($ millions)** | | | | |
| Balance at beginning of period | 494.0 | 721.4 | 494.0 | 721.4 |
| Issue of shares under employee share plan | 37.4 | 24.9 | 37.4 | 24.9 |
| Issue of shares under employee share issue plan (nil consideration) | – | – | – | – |
| Issue of shares as a result of options exercised under executive share option plan | 6.6 | 1.9 | 6.6 | 1.9 |
| Issue of shares as a result of dividend reinvestment plan | 54.7 | 47.2 | 54.7 | 47.2 |
| Shares bought back | (116.5) | (301.4) | (116.5) | (301.4) |
| **Balance at end of period** | **476.2** | **494.0** | **476.2** | **494.0** |

| **Reconciliation of fully paid share capital – (no of shares)** | **millions** | **millions** | **millions** | **millions** |
|---|---|---|---|---|
| Balance at beginning of period | 1,060.0 | 1,152.8 | 1,060.0 | 1,152.8 |
| Issue of shares under employee share plan | 4.6 | 5.1 | 4.6 | 5.1 |
| Issue of shares under employee share issue plan | 1.5 | 2.7 | 1.5 | 2.7 |
| Issue of shares as a result of options exercised under executive share option plan | 1.8 | 0.6 | 1.8 | 0.6 |
| Issue of shares as a result of dividend reinvestment plan | 7.6 | 9.3 | 7.6 | 9.3 |
| Shares bought back | (40.0) | (110.5) | (40.0) | (110.5) |
| **Balance at end of period** | **1,035.5** | **1,060.0** | **1,035.5** | **1,060.0** |

On 22 June 2001 the company completed an off market buy-back of 40,024,681 shares, representing 4% of ordinary shares on issue on that date. The offer price comprised a return of capital and a fully franked dividend, with the return of capital having a total value of $115.3 million. Costs of $1.2 million relating to the buy-back offer were charged against issued capital.

Notes to the financial statements

| | Consolidated | | Woolworths Limited | |
|---|---|---|---|---|
| | As at 24 June 01 $m | As at 25 June 00 $m | As at 24 June 01 $m | As at 25 June 00 $m |

## 19 Reserves

| | | | | |
|---|---|---|---|---|
| **(a) Reserves** | | | | |
| Capital profits reserve | 63.7 | 63.7 | 2.6 | 2.6 |
| Asset revaluation reserve | 74.4 | 74.4 | 0.6 | 0.6 |
| General reserve | 46.9 | 46.9 | 45.5 | 45.5 |
| Foreign currency translation reserve | (2.2) | (3.3) | – | – |
| | **182.8** | **181.7** | **48.7** | **48.7** |
| **Reconciliation** | | | | |
| **Capital profits reserve** | | | | |
| Balance at beginning of period | 63.7 | 68.6 | 2.6 | 2.6 |
| Transfer from asset revaluation reserve on disposal of non-current assets | – | (4.9) | – | – |
| Balance at end of period | 63.7 | 63.7 | 2.6 | 2.6 |
| **Asset revaluation reserve** | | | | |
| Balance at beginning of period | 74.4 | 84.6 | 0.6 | 0.6 |
| Transfer to capital profits reserve | – | 4.9 | – | – |
| Adjustment resulting from reversion to cost basis on change in accounting policy | – | (15.1) | – | – |
| Balance at end of period | 74.4 | 74.4 | 0.6 | 0.6 |
| **General reserve** | | | | |
| Balance at beginning of period | 46.9 | 46.9 | 45.5 | 45.5 |
| Balance at end of period | 46.9 | 46.9 | 45.5 | 45.5 |
| **Foreign currency translation reserve** | | | | |
| Balance at beginning of period | (3.3) | (2.7) | – | – |
| Net exchange differences on translation of controlled foreign entities | 1.1 | (0.6) | – | – |
| Balance at end of period | (2.2) | (3.3) | – | – |
| **Total reserves** | **182.8** | **181.7** | **48.7** | **48.7** |

| | Consolidated | | Woolworths Limited | |
|---|---|---|---|---|
| | As at 24 June 01 $m | As at 25 June 00 $m | As at 24 June 01 $m | As at 25 June 00 $m |
| **20 Total equity reconciliation** | | | | |
| Total equity at beginning of period | 1,630.9 | 1,484.6 | 1,200.5 | 867.4 |
| Total changes in equity recognised in the statement of financial performance | 476.8 | 305.9 | 494.0 | 494.1 |
| **Transactions with owners as owners:** | | | | |
| – Issue of shares as per note 18 | 98.7 | 74.0 | 98.7 | 74.0 |
| – Shares bought back as per note 18 | (116.5) | (301.4) | (116.5) | (301.4) |
| – Contribution of Woolworths Income Notes (WINS) | – | 583.0 | – | 583.0 |
| – Woolworths Income Notes distribution | (47.7) | (26.1) | (47.7) | (26.1) |
| – Dividends paid or provided | (284.1) | (243.5) | (284.1) | (243.5) |
| – Special dividend | (232.9) | (247.0) | (232.9) | (247.0) |
| Increase in outside equity interest | 0.4 | 0.1 | – | – |
| Adjustment due to initial adoption of accounting standard | – | 1.3 | – | – |
| **Total equity at end of period** | **1,525.6** | **1,630.9** | **1,112.0** | **1,200.5** |
| **21 Woolworths Income Notes** | | | | |
| **Issued and paid-up quasi-equity securities** | | | | |
| Fully paid, on issue: | | | | |
| 6,000,000 securities of $100 face value each | 583.0 | 583.0 | 583.0 | 583.0 |

The Woolworths Income Notes (WINS) are perpetual and have no maturity date, and will not be repaid other than on a winding up of the Company, or at Woolworths option in certain defined circumstances.

The holders of WINS are entitled to a distribution calculated and paid quarterly in arrears, at a margin of 2.00% over the 90 day bank bill swap rate at the beginning of the relevant quarter. The payment of this distribution is contingent upon the Company having sufficient distributable profits in the previous financial period. Dividends may not be paid on Woolworths ordinary shares after non-payment of a distribution until four subsequent quarterly distributions have been made, or the missed distributions have been made up.

## Notes to the financial statements

| | Consolidated | | Woolworths Limited | |
|---|---|---|---|---|
| | As at 24 June 01 $m | As at 25 June 00 $m | As at 24 June 01 $m | As at 25 June 00 $m |
| **22 Contingent liabilities** | | | | |
| The details and estimated maximum amounts of contingent liabilities which may become payable are shown below. No provision has been made in the financial statements in respect of these contingencies. | | | | |
| **Guarantees** | | | | |
| Trading guarantees | 8.4 | 6.8 | 7.9 | 6.7 |
| Workers' compensation self-insurance guarantees | 128.3 | 101.7 | 104.8 | 79.8 |
| Unsecured guarantees in respect of performance covenants in tenancy and other contracts. The total amount of these guarantees is indeterminable but no event has or is anticipated to occur that would result in crystallisation of the liability. | – | – | – | – |
| Under the terms of a Deed of Cross Guarantee, the Company has guaranteed the debts of certain controlled entities, thereby relieving them of the need to prepare financial statements under ASIC Class Order 98/1418. | – | – | – | – |
| **Litigation** | | | | |
| Litigation in progress or threatened against the Company and certain of its controlled entities | 4.5 | 4.5 | 4.5 | 4.5 |
| **Other** | | | | |
| Outstanding letters of credit issued to suppliers | 15.8 | 23.5 | 5.9 | 17.2 |

The remainder of the notes have not been included in the Appendix as they are not relevant to an introductory financial accounting book.

# Independent audit report

**Deloitte Touche Tohmatsu**

To the members of Woolworths Limited

## Scope

We have audited the financial report of Woolworths Limited for the financial year ended 24 June 2001 as set out on pages 1 to 51. The financial report includes the consolidated financial statements of the consolidated entity comprising the company and the entities it controlled at the year's end or from time to time during the financial year. The company's directors are responsible for the financial report. We have conducted an independent audit of the financial report in order to express an opinion on it to the members of the company.

Our audit has been conducted in accordance with Australian Auditing Standards to provide reasonable assurance whether the financial report is free of material misstatement. Our procedures included examination, on a test basis, of evidence supporting the amounts and other disclosures in the financial report, and the evaluation of accounting policies and significant accounting estimates. These procedures have been undertaken to form an opinion whether, in all material respects, the financial report is presented fairly in accordance with Accounting Standards issued in Australia and other mandatory professional reporting requirements and statutory requirements so as to present a view which is consistent with our understanding of the company's and the consolidated entity's financial position, and performance as represented by the results of their operations and their cash flows.

The audit opinion expressed in this report has been formed on the above basis.

## Audit opinion

In our opinion, the financial report of Woolworths Limited is in accordance with:

(a) the Corporations Act 2001, including:

- (i) giving a true and fair view of the Company's and consolidated entity's financial position as at 24 June 2001 and of their performance for the year ended on that date; and
- (ii) complying with Accounting Standards and the Corporations Regulations; and

(b) other mandatory professional reporting requirements.

*Deloitte Touche Tohmatsu* *G. Couttas*

**Deloitte Touche Tohmatsu**
Chartered Accountants

Sydney, 14 September 2001

**G Couttas**
Partner

The liability of Deloitte Touche Tohmatsu is limited by, and to the extent of, the Accountants' Scheme under the Professional Standards Act 1994 (NSW).

# Five year analysis

| | 2001<br>52 weeks | 2000<br>52 weeks | 1999<br>52 weeks | 1998<br>52 weeks | 1997<br>53 weeks |
|---|---|---|---|---|---|
| **Profit and loss** | | | | | |
| **Sales[1] ($m)** | | | | | |
| Food, liquor and groceries | 16,772.3 | 15,251.3 | 14,247.0 | 13,374.5 | 12,583.8 |
| Petrol | 747.1 | 472.5 | 316.4 | - | - |
| Total supermarkets | 17,519.4 | 15,723.8 | 14,563.4 | 13,374.5 | 12,583.8 |
| BIG W | 2,069.8 | 1,913.9 | 1,788.0 | 1,644.5 | 1,516.8 |
| Consumer electronics | 418.0 | 338.2 | 298.6 | 241.9 | 223.1 |
| General merchandise | 2,487.8 | 2,252.1 | 2,086.6 | 1,886.4 | 1,739.9 |
| Wholesale | 697.8 | 675.3 | 520.7 | 388.8 | 151.5 |
| **Total trading operations** | **20,705.0** | **18,651.2** | **17,170.7** | **15,649.7** | **14,475.2** |
| Discontinued operations[2] | 210.1 | 337.6 | 356.6 | 351.4 | 324.5 |
| **Total group** | **20,915.1** | **18,988.8** | **17,527.3** | **16,001.1** | **14,799.7** |
| **EBIT[3] ($m)** | | | | | |
| Food, liquor and groceries | 614.0 | 534.0 | 451.5 | 453.2 | 397.6 |
| Petrol | 4.6 | (1.0) | (2.9) | (3.9) | - |
| Total supermarkets[4] | 618.6 | 533.0 | 448.6 | 449.3 | 397.6 |
| BIG W | 83.4 | 74.3 | 62.2 | 56.2 | 48.0 |
| Consumer electronics | 30.8 | 26.0 | 20.8 | 15.7 | 14.6 |
| General merchandise | 114.2 | 100.3 | 83.0 | 71.9 | 62.6 |
| Wholesale | 5.0 | 2.9 | (2.1) | (9.7) | (4.2) |
| **Total trading operations** | **737.8** | **636.2** | **529.5** | **511.5** | **456.0** |
| Net property income | 33.1 | 24.8 | 33.0 | 22.3 | 15.1 |
| Head office overheads | (59.0) | (50.2) | (40.5) | (33.9) | (45.1) |
| Total unallocated[5] | (25.9) | (25.4) | (7.5) | (11.6) | (30.0) |
| Continuing operations | 711.9 | 610.8 | 522.0 | 499.9 | 426.0 |
| Discontinued operations | (5.3) | 10.8 | 17.4 | 16.3 | 23.0 |
| **Total group** | **706.6** | **621.6** | **539.4** | **516.2** | **449.0** |
| **EBIT to sales (%)** | | | | | |
| Supermarkets | 3.53 | 3.39 | 3.08 | 3.36 | 3.16 |
| General Merchandise | 4.59 | 4.45 | 3.98 | 3.81 | 3.60 |
| Wholesale | 0.72 | 0.43 | (0.40) | (2.49) | (2.77) |
| Total | 3.38 | 3.27 | 3.08 | 3.23 | 3.03 |

| | 2001<br>52 weeks | 2000<br>52 weeks | 1999<br>52 weeks | 1998<br>52 weeks | 1997<br>53 weeks |
|---|---|---|---|---|---|
| **Profit and loss ($m)** | | | | | |
| Sales | 20,915.1 | 18,988.8 | 17,527.3 | 16,001.1 | 14,799.8 |
| Cost of goods sold | 15,561.0 | 13,983.4 | 12,790.3 | 11,710.4 | 10,856.4 |
| Gross profit | 5,354.1 | 5,005.4 | 4,737.0 | 4,290.7 | 3,943.4 |
| Gross profit margin | 25.60% | 26.36% | 27.03% | 26.82% | 26.64% |
| Branch and administration expenses | (3,737.7) | (3,548.3) | (3,400.0) | (3,072.4) | (2,866.4) |
| (excluding rent, depreciation and amortisation) | 17.87% | 18.69% | 19.40% | 19.20% | 19.37% |
| EBITDAR | 1,616.4 | 1,457.1 | 1,337.0 | 1,218.3 | 1,076.9 |
| EBITDAR margin | 7.73% | 7.67% | 7.63% | 7.61% | 7.28% |
| Rent | (600.0) | (546.7) | (527.7) | (479.4) | (442.1) |
| EBITDA | 1,016.4 | 910.4 | 809.3 | 738.9 | 634.8 |
| Depreciation | (300.7) | (282.8) | (265.0) | (219.9) | (184.1) |
| Amortisation of goodwill | (9.1) | (6.0) | (4.9) | (2.8) | (1.7) |
| EBIT | 706.6 | 621.6 | 539.4 | 516.2 | 449.0 |
| Interest | (13.1) | (27.8) | (45.5) | (42.8) | (41.2) |
| WINS distribution | (47.7) | (26.1) | – | – | – |
| Net profit before tax | 645.8 | 567.7 | 493.9 | 473.4 | 407.8 |
| Taxation | (217.4) | (203.6) | (181.3) | (172.7) | (149.5) |
| Normal net profit after tax | 428.4 | 364.1 | 312.6 | 300.7 | 258.3 |
| Adjustment for change in company tax rate | – | (8.4) | – | – | – |
| Abnormal items after tax | – | (60.1) | (55.3) | (21.1) | – |
| Outside equity interests | (0.4) | (0.1) | (0.3) | (0.2) | (0.3) |
| Operating net profit attributable to the members of Woolworths Limited after WINS | 428.0 | 295.5 | 257.0 | 279.4 | 258.0 |
| **Balance sheet ($m)** | | | | | |
| **Funds employed** | | | | | |
| Inventory | 1,731.8 | 1,648.3 | 1,652.6 | 1,562.4 | 1,488.3 |
| Accounts payable | (1,666.4) | (1,571.8) | (1,281.1) | (1,202.7) | (1,101.1) |
| Net investment in inventory | 65.4 | 76.5 | 371.5 | 359.7 | 387.2 |
| Other assets | 320.0 | 443.5 | 424.7 | 342.6 | 301.6 |
| Other creditors | (855.5) | (798.8) | (653.1) | (536.8) | (485.2) |
| Fixed Assets | 2,587.7 | 2,194.1 | 2,216.3 | 1,890.2 | 1,589.3 |
| Total Funds employed[6] | 2,117.6 | 1,915.3 | 2,359.4 | 2,055.7 | 1,792.9 |
| Net tax balances | (49.0) | (64.4) | (28.3) | (52.6) | (85.0) |
| Provision for dividend | (155.4) | (137.8) | (115.2) | (102.6) | (101.1) |
| Net assets employed | 1,913.2 | 1,713.1 | 2,215.9 | 1,900.5 | 1,606.8 |
| Net Debt[7] | (387.6) | (82.2) | (731.3) | (527.9) | (381.1) |
| **Total equity** | **1,526.6** | **1,630.9** | **1,484.6** | **1,372.6** | **1,225.7** |
| Woolworths income notes | (583.0) | (583.0) | – | – | – |
| Outside equity interest | (3.7) | (3.3) | (3.2) | (2.9) | (2.5) |
| **Shareholders funds** | **938.9** | **1,044.6** | **1,481.4** | **1,369.7** | **1,223.2** |

| | 2001 52 weeks | 2000 52 weeks | 1999 52 weeks | 1998 52 weeks | 1997 53 weeks |
|---|---|---|---|---|---|
| **Cash flow ($m)** | | | | | |
| EBITDA | 1,016.4 | 910.4 | 809.3 | 738.9 | 634.8 |
| Movement in net investment in inventory | 34.6 | 276.1 | 4.6 | 28.3 | 52.5 |
| Other operating cash flows | 8.7 | 56.7 | (11.5) | (22.3) | 59.8 |
| Net interest paid | (25.0) | (33.6) | (53.7) | (42.8) | (41.1) |
| Tax paid | (225.7) | (142.7) | (174.7) | (193.1) | (46.2) |
| Operating cash flow | 809.0 | 1,066.9 | 574.0 | 509.0 | 659.8 |
| Gross capital expenditure | (537.4) | (420.8) | (764.9) | (685.0) | (699.4) |
| Proceeds on disposal | 173.1 | 111.0 | 145.7 | 157.7 | 129.2 |
| Other investing cash flows | (185.0) | 16.8 | (32.0) | 3.2 | (19.6) |
| Free cash flow | 259.7 | 773.9 | (77.2) | (15.1) | 70.0 |
| Movement in gross debt | 211.5 | (519.8) | 290.9 | 221.0 | 53.2 |
| Woolworths income notes | - | 583.0 | - | - | - |
| WINS distribution | (47.7) | (24.7) | - | - | - |
| Dividends paid | (212.1) | (173.5) | (154.1) | (153.3) | (96.1) |
| Share buybacks | (349.4) | (548.4) | - | - | - |
| New shares issued | 44.0 | 26.9 | 22.7 | 23.3 | 12.3 |
| Net cash flow | (94.0) | 117.4 | 82.3 | 75.9 | 39.4 |
| **Shareholder value** | | | | | |
| **ROFE[8] (Pre-tax return on funds employed)** | | | | | |
| Before abnormals | 35.04 | 29.08 | 24.43 | 26.83 | 26.33 |
| After abnormals | 35.04 | 24.69 | 20.52 | 25.11 | 26.33 |
| **Du Pont analysis (abnormals excluded)** | | | | | |
| EBIT to sales | 3.38 | 3.27 | 3.08 | 3.23 | 3.03 |
| Debt burden[9] | 91.40 | 91.33 | 91.56 | 91.71 | 90.83 |
| Tax Burden[10] | 66.34 | 64.14 | 63.29 | 63.52 | 63.34 |
| Asset turn[11] | 4.23 | 3.99 | 3.99 | 4.18 | 4.44 |
| Financial leverage[12] | 4.99 | 3.77 | 3.08 | 2.94 | 2.82 |
| Return on investment[13] | 43.19 | 28.92 | 21.88 | 23.15 | 21.88 |
| Earnings per share | | | | | |
| Ordinary share price closing | 10.85 | 6.18 | 5.0 | 5.28 | 4.31 |
| Market capitalisation ($m) | 11,235.2 | 6,550.8 | 5,764.2 | 6,019.2 | 4,842.5 |
| Weighted average shares on issue | 1,065.8 | 1,125.0 | 1,146.2 | 1,132.4 | 1,109.4 |
| Normal basic EPS | 40.16 | 32.36 | 27.25 | 26.54 | 23.26 |
| Total Basic EPS[14] | 40.16 | 26.27 | 22.42 | 24.67 | 23.26 |
| EPS pre goodwill amortisation | 41.01 | 32.89 | 27.67 | 26.78 | 23.41 |
| Interim dividend | 12.0 | 10.0 | 8.0 | 8.0 | 8.0 |
| Final dividend | 15.0 | 13.0 | 10.0 | 9.0 | 8.0 |
| Total dividend | 27.0 | 23.0 | 18.0 | 17.0 | 16.0 |
| Payout ratio (before abnormals) % | 66.37 | 66.88 | 66.28 | 64.34 | 69.53 |
| Payout ratio (after abnormals) % | 66.37 | 82.40 | 80.63 | 69.26 | 69.53 |
| Price/earnings ratio (times) | 27.0 | 23.5 | 22.3 | 21.4 | 18.5 |
| Price/cash flow ratio (times) | 14.28 | 6.50 | 10.00 | 11.70 | 73.00 |

| | 2001<br>52 weeks | 2000<br>52 weeks | 1999<br>52 weeks | 1998<br>52 weeks | 1997<br>53 weeks |
|---|---|---|---|---|---|
| **Growth rates (% increase)** | | | | | |
| Sales | 10.14 | 8.34 | 9.54 | 8.12 | 11.34 |
| Sales per equivalent week | 10.14 | 8.34 | 9.54 | 10.20 | 9.23 |
| Same store sales | 6.31 | 4.74 | 3.99 | 4.20 | 4.30 |
| Sales per square metre | 6.22 | 4.39 | 1.81 | 3.61 | 1.58 |
| EBITDA | 11.63 | 12.49 | 9.53 | 16.40 | 15.38 |
| EBIT | 14.04 | 15.24 | 4.49 | 14.97 | 14.60 |
| NPBT | 13.76 | 14.94 | 4.33 | 16.09 | 13.09 |
| NPAT | 44.84 | 14.98 | (8.02) | 8.29 | 10.45 |
| Normal EPS | 24.12 | 18.75 | 2.68 | 14.10 | 6.60 |
| **Financial strength** | | | | | |
| Interest cover ratio | 11.62 | 11.53 | 11.85 | 12.06 | 10.90 |
| Fixed charges cover | 2.40 | 2.40 | 2.30 | 2.30 | 2.19 |
| Sales to inventory[15] | 12.38 | 11.51 | 10.90 | 10.49 | 10.34 |
| Gross capital expenditure to EBITDA (%) | 52.88 | 46.22 | 94.52 | 92.71 | 110.17 |
| Operating cash flow per share | 0.76 | 0.95 | 0.50 | 0.45 | 0.59 |
| Gearing[16] (%) | 20.26 | 4.80 | 33.01 | 27.80 | 23.72 |
| Current assets to current liabilities (%) | 80.71 | 90.37 | 109.85 | 110.81 | 106.43 |
| Total liabilities to net tangible assets[17] | 71.90 | 64.88 | 67.86 | 65.20 | 64.53 |
| **Productivity** | | | | | |
| **Stores (number)** | | | | | |
| ***Supermarkets*** | | | | | |
| NSW and ACT | 199 | 192 | 178 | 174 | 162 |
| Queensland | 115 | 112 | 111 | 111 | 106 |
| Victoria | 151 | 149 | 145 | 133 | 130 |
| South Australia and Northern Territory | 53 | 51 | 45 | 45 | 43 |
| Western Australia | 57 | 52 | 52 | 50 | 48 |
| Tasmania | 29 | 29 | 28 | 29 | 29 |
| Total Supermarkets | 604 | 585 | 559 | 542 | 518 |
| Freestanding liquor | 130 | 41 | 42 | 38 | 38 |
| Plus Petrol | 166 | 137 | 98 | 49 | 12 |
| ***General merchandise*** | | | | | |
| BIG W | 90 | 87 | 85 | 82 | 78 |
| Dick Smith Electronics | 138 | 123 | 119 | 115 | 113 |
| Powerhouse | 9 | 6 | 4 | 2 | 1 |
| Tandy | 222 | – | – | – | – |
| Crazy Prices | | 135 | 117 | 101 | 86 |
| Rockmans | | | 250 | 257 | 252 |
| **Total** | **1,359** | **1,114** | **1,282** | **1,186** | **1,098** |

**Notes to statistics**

1 Sales for prior periods have been restated to exclude WST.
2 Discontinued operations includes Chisholm Manufacturing and Crazy Prices sold in 2001 and Rockman sold in 2000.
3 EBIT for the periods 1998 to 2000 are as previously reported i.e. excluding individually significant non-recurring items (previously described as abnormal items).
4 Supermarket EBIT for prior periods has been restated to reflect IT costs previously reported as unallocated.
5 Unallocated expense represents corporate costs relating to the Woolworths group as a whole, and profits derived by the group's corporate property division including the disposal of development properties. These amounts are not identifiable against any particular operating segment and accordingly they remain unallocated, as required by Accounting Standard AASB 1005.
6 Funds Employed is net assets excluding net tax balances, provision for dividends and net debt.
7 Net debt is gross debt less cash on hand, cash at bank and cash on short term deposit.
8 Return On Funds Employed (ROFE) is EBIT as a percentage of average funds employed for the year.
9 Debt burden is net operating profit before income tax expressed as a percentage of EBIT before abnormal items.
10 Tax burden is normal profit after income tax expressed as a percentage of normal profit before income tax.
11 Asset turn is Total Sales divided by average Total Assets for the year.
12 Financial leverage is average Total Assets divided by average Shareholders Funds for the year.
13 Return on investment is net profit after income tax, divided by average Shareholders Funds for the year.
14 Total basic earnings per share is net profit after income tax attributable to Members of the Company after WINS distribution, divided into the weighted average number of ordinary shares on issue during the year. The weighted average number of ordinary shares on issue has been calculated in accordance with Accounting Standard AASB 1027. Fully diluted EPS is not significantly different from basic EPS.
15 Sales to inventory is total sales for the period divided by average inventory.
16 Gearing is net repayable debt divided by net repayable debt plus total equity.
17 Total Liabilities excludes deferred income tax liability and provision for dividend and includes outside equity interests.

# Glossary

This glossary provides definitions for many terms in financial accounting. Terms are cross-referenced to other terms where helpful. For additional help in finding things, consult the index at the end of this book.

Some supplementary help in developing this glossary came from: *CICA Handbook*, version in effect 30 June, Canadian Institute of Chartered Accountants, Toronto, 1994; S. Davidson, C. L. Mitchell, C. P. Stickney and R. L. Weil, *Financial Accounting: An Introduction to Concepts, Methods and Uses*, Holt, Rinehart & Winston of Canada, Toronto, 1986; *Funk & Wagnalls Canadian College Dictionary*, Fitzhenry & Whiteside, Markham, Ontario, 1986; and Ross M. Skinner, *Accounting Standards in Evolution*, Holt, Rinehart & Winston of Canada, Toronto, 1987.

## A

**Abnormal items** – items of revenue and expense included in operating profit or loss after tax, which are considered abnormal by reason of their size and effect on operating profit after tax. This classification is only permitted in financial reports prior to 30 June 2001.

**Accelerated depreciation (amortisation)** – a depreciation method, such as reducing balance, that records more depreciation in the earlier years of an asset's life, and less in later years, than does the straight-line method. See **Straight-line depreciation**, **Reducing balance depreciation**.

**Account** – a summary record of an asset, liability, shareholders' equity, revenue or expense, in which the effects of transactions, accruals and adjustments are indicated in dollars (where dollars are the currency of the country). See **General journal**, **General ledger**, **Transaction**.

**Accountant** – a person who performs accounting functions. Professional accountants are those who are granted designations by self-regulating bodies on the basis of special training and successful examination. Examples of designations are Chartered Accountant (CA) and Certified Practising Accountant (CPA).

**Accounting** – 'to account' is to provide a record, such as of funds paid or received for something. Being 'accountable' means to be responsible for, as in to account for one's actions. These two ideas together describe the practice of accounting as the record-keeping and reporting of an enterprise's performance and position in monetary terms. Management is responsible for the decisions made in an enterprise. Accounting provides the reports that summarise the economic results of these decisions for inside use and transmit them to outside interested parties (such as investors, creditors and regulatory agencies). See **Financial accounting**, **Management accounting**.

**Accounting control** – The practice of creating accounting records that provide expected quantities of important assets and liabilities to improve the internal control over those assets. Used by most companies for cash, accounts receivable, sales taxes collected on behalf of governments and employee deductions, and by many companies for investments, inventories, property and equipment and accounts payable. See **Internal control**, **Control account**.

**Accounting entity** – The enterprise for which the accounting is being done. The entity may be a single legal company or other organisation, an economic unit without legal standing (such as a proprietorship) or a group of companies with connected ownership for which consolidated financial statements are prepared.

**Accounting equation** – the double-entry arithmetic by which Asset = Liabilities + Shareholders' equity.

**Accounting policies** – the chosen accounting methods used by a company to recognise economic events on an accrual basis, and to report the financial position and results of operations. For examples, see the notes immediately following the financial statements of any company.

**Accounting policy choice** – a decision between acceptable accounting policies is often needed because more than one acceptable policy exists in many areas.

**Accounting principles** – see **Generally accepted accounting principles (GAAP)**.

**Accounting research** – The practice of studying accounting phenomena to determine their effects on other phenomena such as share prices, and vice-versa.

**Accounting standards** – the mandating of particular accounting methods or policies by an authoritative body. In Australia this is done by the Australian Accounting Standards Board, and in the United States by the Financial Accounting Standards Board. See **Accounting policies**, **Generally accepted accounting principles (GAAP)**.

**Accounts payable** – liabilities representing amounts owed to short-term trade creditors. (An account payable for the debtor is an account receivable for the creditor.)

**Accounts receivable** – amounts owing by debtors (customers), usually arising from sales of goods or services.

**Accrual** – the entering of amounts in the accounts to reflect events or estimates that are economically meaningful but that do not (at present) involve the exchange of cash. An example would be recognising revenue from credit sales before receipt of cash from customers. See **Accrual accounting**, **Deferral**, **Revenue recognition**, **Matching**.

**Accrual accounting** – the method of making an economically meaningful and comprehensive measurement of performance and position by recognising economic events regardless of when cash transactions happen, as opposed to the simpler cash basis of accounting. Under this method, revenues and expenses (and related assets and liabilities) are reflected in the accounts in the period to which they relate.

**Accrual basis** – the use of accrual accounting in preparing financial statements.

**Accrual profit** – the result of subtracting expenses from revenue(s), when both kinds of accounts are calculated by accrual accounting. See **Accrual accounting**, **Net profit**.

**Accrue** – to enter amounts in the accounts to reflect events or estimates that are economically meaningful but do not (at present) involve the exchange of cash. Examples would be recording interest that is building up on a debt before paying it or recording revenue from credit sales before receipt of cash from customers. See **Accrual accounting**, **Revenue recognition**, **Matching**; see also **Deferral**.

**Accrued expense** – an expense recognised in the accounts before paying for it.

**Accumulated depreciation (amortisation)** – a statement of financial position account that accumulates total depreciation (amortisation) expense over a number of years. The account balance is a credit, so is opposite to the debit balance asset cost account. The difference between cost and accumulated depreciation is the 'book value' of the asset. Accumulated depreciation relates to tangible assets and accumulated amortisation relates to intangible assets. See **Book value**, **Contra accounts**, **Fixed assets**, **Amortisation**, **Depreciation**.

**Accumulated foreign currency translation adjustment (foreign currency translation reserve)** – an account arising as a consequence of the method used to convert foreign operations' accounting figures into Australian dollars for the purpose of combining them with the figures for Australian operations. Because statement of financial performance accounts are generally converted at average foreign exchange rates and statement of financial position accounts are generally converted at year-end or historical rates, converted accounts do not quite balance. The difference is put into equity as a separate item, because it does not seem to fit anywhere else, and it is part of the (converted) residual equity of the owners.

**Accumulated funds** – represents the total cumulative amount of surplus/(deficit) that a public sector entity has retained and reinvested in its operations.

**Acid test ratio** – cash, temporary investments, and accounts receivable divided by current liabilities. Also called the quick ratio.

**Adjusted trial balance** – the list of accounts prepared after all the accrual accounting adjustments and corrections have been made, so representing the final account balances used in preparing the financial statements. See **Trial balance**, **Adjusting (journal) entry**.

**Adjusting (journal) entry** – a journal entry to implement accrual accounting by recognising in the accounts economic events not yet adequately accounted for by the routine transactional accounting system. (For example, if there is no transaction to reveal the gradual wear and tear of a fixed asset, an adjusting entry must be made to recognise this depreciation.)

**Adjustment(s)** – see **Adjusting (journal) entry**.

**Ageing of accounts receivable** – the process of classifying accounts receivable by the time that has passed since the account came into existence. This classification is used as an aid to estimating the required provision for doubtful debts for the estimated amount of uncollectable accounts receivable.

**Agency (contract) theory** – is concerned with relationships between people in which one or more of them (the agents, such as managers, auditors, lawyers and doctors) is or are entrusted with acting on behalf of one or more others (the principals, such as owners, creditors, defendants and patients). Agency theory tends to focus on the stewardship role of accounting information (in monitoring and controlling the stewardship of the agent on behalf of the principal). Principals and agents can demand whatever information their specific relationship requires.

**Agent** – a person who is a party to a contract between him- or herself and another, called the principal. The agent's role is to carry out the wishes of the principal, as specified in the contract. Some examples of agents are managers, auditors, lawyers and physicians, who are entrusted with acting on behalf of one or more others (the principals, such as owners, creditors, defendants and patients). Agents have a stewardship responsibility to the principal. See **Contract**, **Stewardship**.

**Aggressive accounting** – seeking out accounting methods and policy choices to meet management objectives for growth, financing, bonuses or other purposes that seem to violate principles such as fairness and conservatism.

**Allocated, allocating** – having spread (spreading) the impact of an event out over time, as in depreciation of an asset's cost over its useful life or recognition of revenue for a long-term contract over several periods. (Allocation is also used, especially in management accounting, [illegible] spreading the impact of an [illegible] activities, such as in allocating the cost of repairs to different departments.)

**Amortisation** – allocation of the cost of an intangible asset to expense over several accounting periods to recognise the 'consumption' of the asset's economic value as it helps to earn revenue over those periods. Amortisation expense for a period thus is deducted from revenue in that period, recognising it as a cost of earning the revenue. See **Depreciation**, **Intangible assets**.

**Analysis, analyse** – the technique, common in accounting, of comparing information derived from different sources or methods in order to understand what has happened, identify errors and answer questions about the effects of possible actions or events. See **Reconciliation**, **'What if' (effects) analysis**. Also used to refer to the detailed study of accounting information, such as by using **Ratios**.

**Annual report** – the document provided annually to the shareholders by the officers of a company. It includes the financial statements, the notes to the financial statements, the auditor's report, supplementary financial information, such as multi-year summaries, and reports from the company's board of directors and management.

**Asset revaluation reserve** – a shareholders' equity account showing the amount by which assets have been revalued.

**Asset valuation** – see **Balance sheet valuation**.

**Asset(s)** – future economic benefits controlled by the entity as a result of past transactions.

**Associated company** – a company, which is not a subsidiary of the investor company, over which the investor has significant influence (generally 20–50 per cent ownership) but not control. See **Equity method**.

**Assurance** – A broader word than 'audit', encompassing auditing and similar procedures to confirm or verify reports or events as fair and proper and assure users of such reports that they may be relied upon. See **Audit**, **Auditor's report**, **Fairness**.

**Audit** – the examination of accounting records and their supporting documentation with the objective of determining the fairness with which the financial statements present the financial position and performance of the company. See **Auditor**, **Auditor's report**.

**Audit committee** – a subcommittee of the board of directors, generally comprising non-executive directors who liaise with the external and internal auditors.

**Auditor** – the person or firm who performs an audit for the purpose of preparing a report on the credibility of the financial statements.

**Auditor's report** – the document accompanying the financial statements that expresses the auditor's opinion on the fairness of the financial statements. The auditor's report explains what the auditor did and states the auditor's opinion.

**Australian Accounting Standards Board (AASB)** – the Australian body that sets financial accounting standards to be followed in the preparation of financial statements.

**Australian Securities and Investments Commission (ASIC)** – the regulatory body that oversees compliance with Australian Corporations Law requirements.

**Authorised capital** – the maximum amount of capital a company is permitted to raise under its memorandum of association.

**Authoritative standards** – written rules and guidelines established by official accounting standard-setters such as the Australian Accounting Standards Board in Australia and the FASB in the United States.

**Available cost** – the total dollar amount represented by the sum of beginning inventory and purchases during the period, thus representing the total dollar cost of inventory available for sale or use during the period.

**Average cost (AVGE)** – an inventory cost flow assumption by which the cost of an individual unit of inventory is the weighted average cost of the beginning inventory and subsequent purchases. See **Weighted average**.

## B

**Bad debts expense** – an expense account that results from the reduction in carrying value of those accounts receivable that have been projected to be uncollectable or doubtful. See **Provision for doubtful debts**.

**Balance (account total)** – the net sum of the amounts added to and subtracted from an account since the account began. In financial accounting's double-entry system, the balance is expressed as a net debit (DR) or net credit (CR). See **Account**, **Double-entry accounting**.

**Balance (in the statement of financial position or the trial balance)** – refers to the double-entry accounting requirement that the sum of the accounts with debit balances and the sum of those with credit balances should be equal. In the statement of financial position, this means that the sum of the assets equals the sum of the liabilities and equity. See **Statement of financial position**, **Accounting equation**, **Trial balance**.

**Balance sheet** – the 'balanced' list of assets, liabilities and owners' equity that constitutes the formal statement of a company's financial position at a specified date, summarising by category the assets, liabilities and shareholders' equity. In Australia, from 30 June 2001, it is referred to as the 'statement of financial position' in published financial statements.

**Balance sheet valuation** – the assignment of numerical values to the balance sheet's assets, liabilities and shareholders' equity accounts.

**Bank overdraft** – a negative bank account balance (withdrawals exceeding deposits), which banks may allow as a *de facto* loan as long as it is temporary. See **Line of credit**.

**Bank reconciliation** – a reconciliation of a bank statement with the figures in a company's cash at bank ledger account.

**Bank statement** – a statement prepared by the bank that provides details of all transactions on a particular account during a period (for example, a month).

**Betterment** – an expenditure to improve an asset's value to the business, commonly extends the asset's functionality and/or useful life; more than just repairs and maintenance, and is added to the value of the asset (capitalised), not expensed.

**Big bath** – a way of manipulating reported income to show even poorer results in a poor year in order to enhance later years' results.

**Board of directors** – the senior level of management, representing and directly responsible to the owners (shareholders). Normally elected annually by the shareholders.

**Bond** – a certificate of debt issued by an enterprise in return for cash, in which a promise is made to repay the debt (usually at a particular date or on a specified schedule) plus interest.

**Bond markets** – capital markets in which debt instruments (bonds and similar items), rather than shares, are traded. See **Capital markets**.

**Bonus issue** – see **Share dividend**.

**Book value** – the amount shown in the accounts for any asset, liability or shareholders' equity item, after deducting any related contra account (for example, the book value of a truck is the recorded cost minus accumulated depreciation). The term is also commonly used to refer to the net amount of total assets less total liabilities (the recorded value of the shareholders' residual interest, which equals total equity: Assets = Liabilities + Equity).

**Book value per share** – total shareholders' equity divided by the number of shares issued.

**Bookkeeping** – the process of recording, classifying and summarising transactions in the books of account.

**Books of original entry** – the journals in which transactions are first recorded.

**Bottom line** – a colloquialism referring to the net profit (the 'bottom line' on the statement of financial performance). See **Net profit**.

## C

**Calls in arrears** – an amount of money due, but not received, on shares that have been allotted.

**Capital** – the owner's contribution to or interest in a business (the equity). Often used specifically to refer to the equity of unincorporated businesses (proprietorships and partnerships). See **Equity**.

**Capital maintenance** – the concept that the owners' equity of a business should be sustained before distributions are paid out of the company to owners.

**Capital market theory** – deals with the behaviour of aggregate markets (such as share markets) and with the role of information in the operation of such markets.

**Capital markets** – markets in which financial instruments, such as shares and bonds, are traded.

**Capitalisation, capitalise** – the recognition of an expenditure that may benefit a future period as an asset rather than as an expense of the period of its occurrence. Expenditures are capitalised if they are likely to lead to future benefits and, thus, meet the criterion to be an asset.

**Capitalised costs** – costs that have been included with an asset on the statement of financial position instead of being deducted as expenses on the statement of financial perfomance.

**Carrying amount** – the amount at which the asset is recorded in the accounting records at a particular date. In application to a depreciable asset, 'carrying amount' means the net amount after deducting accumulated depreciation or amortisation.

**Cash** – currency and coin on hand, balances in bank accounts and other highly liquid assets.

**Cash disbursements** – cash payouts, by cheque, currency or direct deductions from the bank account. See **Cash payments**, **Cash receipts**.

**Cash equivalent assets** – a term used to describe cash plus liquid assets that can be converted into cash almost immediately on demand.

**Cash flow** – the inflows of cash (cash receipts) and outflows of cash (cash disbursements) over a period. Information about cash flow is presented in the **Cash flow statement**.

**Cash flow analysis** – a method of accounting analysis directed at understanding the enterprise's cash inflows, outflows and resulting balances. This analysis lies behind the cash flow statement.

**Cash flow cycle** – the time from payment of goods purchased for manufacture or resale to receipt of cash for final product or sale.

**Cash flow from operations** – cash generated by day-to-day business activities and highlighted as the first section in the statement of cash flows.

**Cash flow statement** – see **Statement of cash flows**.

**Cash flow to total assets** – the ratio of cash from operations divided by total assets.

**Cash payments** – payments by currency, cheque or other bank withdrawal. See **Cash transaction**.

**Cash profit** – cash receipts minus cash disbursements. Roughly equivalent to the cash from operations figure.

**Cash receipts** – cash inflows, by currency, others' cheques or direct bank deposits. See **Cash transaction**, **Cash receipts journal**.

**Cash receipts journal** – the record of customers' cheques and other cash received. See **Books of original entry**.

**Cash received basis** – recognition of revenue only when the cash comes in. See **Revenue recognition**, **Conservatism**.

**Cash transaction** – the simplest kind of economic exchange routinely recorded by financial accounting, and an important starting point for the financial statements.

**Change effects analysis** – analysis of the effects on financial statements of economic or accounting policy changes.

**Chart of accounts** – an organised list of the accounts used in the accounting system. This can be contrasted with the 'trial balance', which displays all the accounts and their debit or credit balances.

**Cheque** – a request by one party that the party's bank pay a specified amount to another party.

**Classification** – choice of where in the financial statements to place an account, such as whether an investment asset should be shown as a current asset or a noncurrent asset.

**Classification policies** – accounting policies covering where within a financial statement an account or description is to appear. See **Accounting policies**.

**Classified financial statements** – financial statements with accounts organised under headings that clarify the accounts' meaning to increase the information value of the statements.

**Close, closing** – the transfer of the temporary accounts (revenues, expenses and dividends declared) to retained earnings at the end of the fiscal period.

**Closing (entries)** – journal entries recorded at year-end to transfer the balances in temporary accounts (revenues, expenses and dividends) to the statement of financial position's account of retained profits, and set those balances to zero in preparation for entering the next year's transactions.

**COGS** – see **Cost of goods sold**.

**COGS expense** – see **Cost of goods sold expense**.

**Commercialisation** – the process by which government entities are exposed to the competitive forces of the market.

**Common shares** – the basic voting ownership interests in a company.

**Common size financial statements** – a technique of analysing financial statements by which statement of financial performance figures are expressed in percentages of revenue, and statement of financial position accounts are expressed in percentages of total assets.

**Company** – a business entity formed under Corporations Law. Ownership of companies is divided into shares owned by shareholders. These shareholders have limited liability in the event of a company's failure.

**Comparability** – information that enables users to identify similarities in and differences between two sets of economic phenomena, such as two different years of a company's financial statements. Comparability between companies and consistency of one company over time are major objectives of financial accounting. See **Fairness**, **Consistency**.

**Completed contract** – a method of revenue recognition for long-term contracts by which the revenue is not reported on the statement of financial perfomance until the contract has been completed. See **Revenue recognition**, **Conservatism**.

**Compound, compounded, compounding** – terms that refer to the frequency by which interest calculated on a loan or other debt is periodically added to the principal, therefore attracting future interest itself. Annual compounding, for example, means that interest built up on a loan starts to bear interest itself on each annual anniversary of the loan. See **Present value**.

**Conservatism** – a prudent reaction to uncertainty to ensure that risks inherent in business situations are adequately considered; also defined as 'the anticipation of possible losses but not possible gains'. In situations where the accountant cannot decide on the superiority of one of two accounting treatments on the basis of accounting principles alone, being conservative means choosing the treatment that has the least favourable impact on the profit of the current period. See **Historical cost** and **Lower of cost or market** for examples of conservatism.

**Consistency** – treatment of like transactions in the same way in consecutive periods so that financial statements will be comparable. The reporting policy implying that procedures, once adopted, should be followed from period to period by a company.

**Consolidated financial statements, consolidation** – a method of preparing financial statements for a group of companies linked by ownership as if they were a single company. Consolidated financial statements recognise that the separate legal entities are components of one economic unit.

**Consolidated goodwill** – a form of **Goodwill** arising only when companies' financial statements are combined in consolidation.

**Constructive** – a constructive obligation is an implied obligation; that is, an obligation that an entity is accustomed to, but is not contractually bound to, such as the payment of Christmas bonuses to staff. See also **Equitable**.

**Contingent liabilities** – liabilities that are contingent on the occurrence of a particular event that has not yet happened. Disclosed in the notes rather than on the statement of financial position.

**Contra accounts** – accounts established to accumulate certain deductions from an asset, liability or owners' equity item. See **Book value**, **Amortisation**, **Depreciation**, **Provision for doubtful debts**.

**Contra asset** – an account that normally has a credit balance but is located in the asset part of the statement of financial position, and deducted from the asset to give a net balance. Examples include accumulated depreciation and provision for doubtful debts.

**Contract** – an oral or written agreement between or among parties, setting out each party's responsibilities and specifying actions agreed to and resulting payments or other settlements. See **Agent**.

**Control account** – a general ledger account for which there is detailed analysis provided in the subsidiary ledger.

**Controlled entity** – see **Subsidiary**.

**Convertible** – a bond or share that can be changed into another kind of security, usually a preferred share that can be converted into a common share.

**Corporate governance** – system by which companies are directed and controlled. Includes policies of board of directors, internal control systems and so on.

**Corporate group** – a group of companies linked by common or mutual ownership. See **Consolidation**.

**Corporatisation** – the process by which public sector entities are organised using ideas consistent with those of large companies; examples are setting up boards of directors for senior managers to report to and making pay structures incentive based. See **Commercialisation**.

**Cost** – the value of an asset when it is acquired by the business. See **Historical cost**.

**Cost basis** – a term usually used to account for a noncurrent intercorporate investment when a company does not have control over another company. The investment is carried at cost, and any receipt of dividends is recorded as revenue for the period. See **Equity method**, **Intercorporate investments**.

**Cost benefit** – the comparison of the benefits of a particular action with its costs, taking action only if the benefits exceed the costs.

**Cost flow assumption** – an assumption made about the order in which units of inventory move into and out of an enterprise, used to compute inventory asset value and cost of goods sold expense in cases where the order of flow is not or cannot be identified. Possible assumptions include FIFO, LIFO and weighted average. See **Cost of goods sold**, **FIFO**, **Weighted average** and **LIFO** for specific examples.

**Cost of capital** – the cost of raising debt or equity funds. For example, the cost of borrowed funds is mostly the interest to be paid to the lender.

**Cost of goods sold (COGS)** – an expense account that reflects the cost of goods that generated the revenue (also called cost of sales). The method of calculating COGS depends on the method of inventory costing. See **Gross profit**, **Cost flow assumption**, **Inventory costing**.

**Credit (CR)** – the right-hand side of double-entry accounting. The term 'credit' can be used as a noun to refer to the right-hand side of a journal entry or account, or as a verb referring to the action of making an entry to the right-hand side of an account. A credit journal entry to the liabilities and equity side of the statement of financial position causes an increase in the account, while a credit to the assets side of the statement of financial position causes a decrease. Credit also refers to the right to buy or borrow on the promise of future payment. See **Double-entry accounting**, **Debit**.

**Credit transaction** – an economic exchange by which at least one party makes a promise to pay cash or other consideration later. This kind of transaction is recognised by most financial accounting systems, especially if it is a routine way of doing business. See **Accounts receivable**, **Accounts payable**.

**Creditor** – one who extends credit – that is, gives someone the right to buy or borrow now in consideration of a promise to pay at a later date.

**Critical event** – the point at which revenue is recognised. The most commonly used example is the point of delivery to a customer, but other points in time may be appropriate, depending on the business.

**Cumulative preference shares** – preference shares that have a priority to a dividend over ordinary shares. This priority is carried forward until all dividend entitlements have been paid before a dividend can be paid to ordinary shareholders.

**Current assets** – cash and other assets, such as temporary investments, inventory, receivables and current prepayments, that are realisable or will be consumed within the normal operating cycle of an enterprise (usually one year). See such current asset categories as **Cash equivalent assets**, **Inventory** and **Accounts receivable**.

**Current liabilities** – debts or estimated claims on the resources of a firm that are expected to be paid within the normal operating cycle of an enterprise (usually one year). See **Cash equivalent liabilities**, **Accounts payable**.

**Current market value** – the estimated sale value of an asset, settlement value of a debt or trading value of an equity share.

**Current ratio** – current assets divided by current liabilities.

**Current value accounting** – a proposed accounting method that uses current or market values to value assets and liabilities and to calculate profit.

**Cut off** – the end of a fiscal period and the procedures used to ensure accuracy in measuring phenomena up to that date.

## D

**Days' sales in receivables** – the ratio of accounts receivable to the daily sales, expressed in number of days' sales represented by accounts receivable. Also called **Collection ratio**, **Days in debtors**.

**DCF** – another phrase for 'present value' analysis of future cash flows. See **Discounted cash flows**, **Present value**.

**Debenture** – a form of **Security** taken by a creditor on a loan or bond, by which the creditor has a general ability to influence or direct management decisions if the debt payments are not made on schedule, not a claim on a specific asset, as a mortgage is.

**Debit (DR)** – the left-hand side of double-entry accounting. The term 'debit' can be used as a noun to refer to the left-hand side of a journal entry or account, or as a verb referring to the action of making an entry on the left-hand side of an account. A debit will increase the amounts on the asset side of the statement of financial position, but decrease the amounts on the liabilities and equity side. See **Double-entry accounting**, **Credit**.

**Debt** – an obligation to make a future payment in return for a benefit already received.

**Debt to assets ratio** – total liabilities divided by total assets.

**Debt to equity ratio, debt–equity ratio, debt/equity ratio** – total liabilities divided by total equity.

**Debtors turnover** – the ratio calculated by dividing credit sales by trade debtors. Also called **Accounts receivable turnover**. See also **Ratios**.

**Decision relevance** – an accounting objective: information should be available to the user at a time and in a form that is useful to the user's decision-making.

**Deferral** – part of accrual accounting, but often used as the opposite to an accrual. A deferral involves keeping a past cash receipt or payment on the statement of financial position – in other words, putting it on the statement of financial performance as revenue or expense at a later time. An example is recognising a deferred revenue liability resulting from a recent cash receipt, such as for a magazine subscription to be delivered later. (By contrast, accruals involve recording a revenue or expense before the cash receipt or payment occurs.)

**Deferred charge** – a noncurrent **Prepaid expense**, by which the costs of issuing bonds, incorporation costs or other expenditures benefiting several future periods are shown as noncurrent assets and usually amortised to expense over several periods, or otherwise charged to expenses in some future period.

**Deferred income tax expense** – an expense account intended to recognise the future tax consequences of profit reported on the current statement of financial performance, but not to be reported on the tax return until a future period. See **Deferred income tax liability**, **Matching**.

**Deferred income tax liability** – a liability (the credit side of deferred income tax expense) that arises when the pretax income shown on the tax return is less than what it would have been had the same accounting principles been used in the tax return as were used in the financial statements. Current reported accounting profit is less than the profit reported on the tax return, so a liability for income tax is implied for later, when the income is reported on the tax return.

**Deferred revenue** – See **Revenue received in advance**, **Unearned revenue**.

**Deficit** – negative retained profits.

**Depletion** – a depreciation method used for physically wasting assets, such as natural resources.

**Depreciation** – allocation of the cost of a noncurrent asset to expense over several accounting periods to recognise the consumption of the asset's economic value as it helps to earn revenue over those periods. The term 'depreciation' is used with respect to tangible assets, while 'amortisation' is used with respect to intangible assets. See **Amortisation**, **Straight-line depreciation**, **Book value**, **Accumulated depreciation**.

**Deprival value** – value to the entity of the future economic benefits that the entity would forego if it were deprived of the asset.

**Direct method of cash flow analysis** – a method of preparing the **Cash flow statement**, especially the cash from operations section, using records of cash receipts and disbursements instead of the adjustments to net income used in the more traditional **Indirect method of cash flow analysis**.

**Direct write-off** – the transfer of the cost of an asset to an expense or **Loss** account by removing the amount entirely from the asset account. Used in cases where there is no prior allowance for the expense or loss, so used when there is no **Contra account** such as **Provision for doubtful debts**.

**Disclosure** – principle of providing sufficient disclosure in accounting reports to enable users to make necessary decisions.

**Discontinued operations** – portions of the business that the enterprise has decided not to keep going and/or to sell to others.

**Discount on bonds** – arises when bonds are issued at a price below their legal face value, such as a $100 bond being issued for $95 cash, indicating a $5 discount.

**Discounted cash flow** – 'present value' analysis of future cash flows by removing their presumed interest components.

**Discretionary expenses** – expenses that depend on management's discretion rather than on the necessities of producing, selling or shipping goods and services. Examples might be donations, political contributions, some maintenance and warranty costs and bonuses not specifically called for in employment contracts.

**Dividend payout ratio** – the ratio of dividends declared to net profit.

**Dividends** – distributions of a portion of net profit to shareholders in the company.

**Double-entry accounting** – the practice of recording two aspects of each transaction or event: the resource effect and the source effect. Though much expanded since its invention several hundred years ago, it is still the basis of bookkeeping and financial accounting.

## E

**Earnings** – a common synonym for net profit. See **Net profit**.

**Earnings before interest and tax (EBIT)** – a measure of profit based on the operating profit before interest and taxes are deducted.

**Earnings per share (EPS)** – the ratio of net profit to the average number of ordinary (voting) shares outstanding, used to allow the owner of the shares to relate the company's earning power to the size of his or her investment.

**E-commerce** –see **Electronic commerce**.

**Economic entity** – the financial accounting definition of an enterprise, used to determine what is to be included in transactions and in the financial statements. Also used to refer to a group of companies considered to be under the same control, so constituting a larger economic group. See **Transaction**, **Consolidation**.

**Effective income tax rate** – the income tax rate the company appears to incur, as deduced from the financial statements. Differs from the statutory or legal rate because of such factors as variations in tax incentives and varying rates across jurisdictions. Can be estimated as the company's income tax expense divided by profit before income tax, both from the statement of financial performance.

**Effects analysis** – see **Change effects analysis**.

**Efficiency (informational efficiency)** – refers to a market's prices quickly and appropriately changing to reflect new information.

**Efficient capital market** – a theoretical description of a capital market whose prices respond quickly and appropriately to information.

**Efficient market hypothesis** – the proposal that capital markets actually are 'efficient', responding quickly, smoothly and appropriately to information. Some seem to be efficient; some do not. See **Efficient capital market**.

**Electronic commerce** – also called e-commerce, it is the conduct of financial transactions, and much of the business transactions behind them, over electronic media such as telecommunication lines or the World Wide Web.

**Electronic funds transfer (EFT)** – the transfer of money between a buyer's bank account and the seller's bank account without the need to write cheques or make deposits. EFT is what happens if a customer uses a bank card to pay for groceries in the supermarket and the amount is automatically deducted from the customer's bank account.

**Employee deductions** – amounts deducted from an employee's gross salary before it is paid to him or her net. These deductions include income tax, superannuation, union fees and health insurance.

**Entity** – see **Economic entity**.

**Entry** – see **Journal entry**.

**Equitable** – normally used in the expression 'equitable obligation', in which sense it refers to a social or moral obligation rather than one required by law.

**Equities** – a term sometimes used to refer to the right-hand side of the statement of financial position (Equities = Liabilities + Owners' equity).

**Equity** – the net assets or residual interest of an owner or shareholder (Assets – Liabilities = Equity). See the components of equity under **Shareholders' equity**, **Retained profits**.

**Equity method** – a method of accounting for intercorporate investments usually used when a company owns between 20 per cent and 50 per cent of another company. The investment is carried at cost, and any profit or loss, multiplied by the percentage ownership of the owned company, is added to or deducted from the investment. Any dividends received are deducted from the investment.

**Exchange** – a transfer of goods, services or money between two parties. In financial accounting, the most significant kind of exchange is external, that is, between the entity and parties it deals with, such as customers, suppliers, owners, employees and creditors. See **Transaction**.

**Expense** – the cost of assets used and/or obligations created in generating revenue. Expenses are defined more formally in SAC 4 as consumptions or losses of future economic benefits in the form of reductions in assets or increases in liabilities of the entity, other than relating to distributions to owners, that result in a decrease in equity during the reporting period. See **Statement of financial performance**, **Revenue**, **Matching**, **Expense recognition**, **Accrual accounting**.

**Expense recognition** – the incorporation of measures of expenses incurred into the measurement of profit by entering into the accounts the amount of expense determined, according to the firm's accounting policies, to be attributable to the current period. See **Matching**, **Revenue recognition**.

**Expensing** – classifying an expenditure or promised expenditure (accrual) as an expense rather than an asset. The opposite of capitalisation.

**External audit** – the audit conducted by an **External auditor**.

**External auditor** – an independent outside auditor appointed to review the financial statements. See **Auditor**.

**Extraordinary items** – means items of revenue and expense that are attributable to transactions or other events of a type that are outside the **Ordinary activities** of the entity and are not of a recurring nature. It is extremely rare for a transaction or other event to give rise to an extraordinary transaction. A transaction or event may be extraordinary for one entity but not extraordinary for another entity, because of the nature of the entities' respective ordinary activities. For example, an earthquake or other natural disaster may give rise to an extraordinary item. Losses sustained as a result of an earthquake or other natural disaster may qualify as an extraordinary expense for entities that do not operate in a region subject to such events.

## F

**Fair value** – the amount for which an asset could be exchanged, or a liability settled, between knowledgeable, willing parties in an arm's length transaction.

**Fairness** – because of all the estimations, judgements and policy choices that go into preparing financial statements, there is no one correct set of figures or disclosures. Instead, there is the idea of fairness, which means playing by the rules and preparing statements honestly, without any intent to deceive or to present any particular view. The opinion paragraph of the auditor's report states that the financial statements 'present fairly . . . in accordance with generally accepted accounting principles'. Attention to fairness in the application of accounting principles requires care and judgement in distinguishing the substance from the form of a transaction and identifying the accepted principles and practices. See **Generally accepted accounting principles**, **Accounting standards**.

**FIFO** – an inventory cost flow assumption by which cost of goods sold is determined from the cost of the beginning inventory and the cost of the oldest purchases; thus the acronym FIFO, which stands for 'first in, first out'. It follows therefore that, under FIFO, ending inventory cost is determined from the cost of the most recent purchases. Since the older inventory is assumed to be sold first, FIFO in a period of inflation usually creates a smaller cost of goods sold and higher profit and ending inventory asset value than LIFO or weighted average. See **Cost flow assumption**.

**Finance lease** – a type of lease that effectively transfers from the lessor to the lessee substantially all the risks and benefits incident to ownership of the leased property.

**Financial accounting** – the reporting in financial statements of the financial position and performance of an enterprise to users external to the enterprise on a regular, periodic basis.

**Financial Accounting Standards Board (FASB)** – the US body responsible for setting the standards that financial reporting must follow.

**Financial assets** – near-cash assets, such as traded shares, bonds, some kinds of loans and accounts receivable, especially as would be held by financial institutions such as banks. Part of the general category of **Financial instruments**.

**Financial instruments** – debts, shares, foreign exchange contracts and other financial obligations and assets, many of which are traded on **Share markets** and other **Capital markets**.

**Financial leverage** – see **Leverage**.

**Financial performance** – the enterprise's ability to generate new resources from day-to-day operations over a period of time, via dealing with customers, employees and suppliers. Measured by the net profit figure in the statement of financial performance, and the cash from operations figure in the cash flow statement, as well as by the details of both statements.

**Financial position** – the enterprise's set of assets, liabilities and owners' equity at a point in time. Measured by the statement of financial position.

**Financial reporting** – use of financial statements and disclosure to report to people outside the enterprise on its financial performance and financial position.

**Financial statement analysis** – use of the financial statements to develop summary measures (ratios) and interpretive comments about an enterprise's financial performance and position. See **Ratios**.

**Financial statements** – the reports for people external to the enterprise (but also of interest to management) referred to in the definition of accounting, which generally comprise a statement of financial position, statement of financial performance, statement of cash flow and the notes to these statements.

**Financing activities** – part of the cash flow statement for those activities that relate to the changing size and composition of the financial structure of the entity.

**First in, first out** – see FIFO.

**Fiscal period** – the period (usually a year, a quarter or a month) over which performance (net profit) is measured and at the end of which position (statement of financial position) is determined.

**Fixed assets** – tangible, noncurrent physical assets that are not expected to be used up in one operating cycle, but are expected to be used in generating revenue for many periods (for example, machines, buildings and land). See **Noncurrent assets**, **Current assets**

**Foreign currency translation** – the conversion of foreign monies into domestic monies at a specific date: either a transaction date, if translating a single transaction, or a financial statement date, if translating a foreign operation for consolidation purposes. See **Accumulated foreign currency translation adjustment**.

**Franchising** – a franchiser sells the right to use the franchiser's name, products or other economic goods to a franchisee.

**Future income tax** – income tax expected to be paid in future years based on business events and income tax calculations done up to the present.

**Future value (FV)** – the amount to which presently held financial assets or liabilities will build up as interest is added to the principal amount invested or borrowed. Often contrasted with **Present value**, which is the future cash flows discounted back to present-day dollars.

## G

**GAAP** – see **Generally accepted accounting principles**.

**GAAS** – see **Generally accepted auditing standards**.

**Gain on sale** – gain that occurs when a company receives a larger amount of proceeds for the sale of an asset than its book value.

**General journal** – an accounting record used mainly to record accrual adjustments (journal entries) not provided for in separate specialised journals.

**General ledger** – a collection of individual accounts that summarises the entire financial accounting system of an enterprise.

**General reserve** – amount of shareholders' funds transferred from retained profits. By transferring to the general reserve account, the company is indicating to shareholders that this amount is not intended to be distributed to shareholders in dividends.

**Generally accepted accounting principles (GAAP)** – principles and methods of accounting that have the general support of standard-setting bodies, general practice, texts and other sources. See **Accounting standards**.

**Generally accepted auditing standards (GAAS)** – the professional standards of care and evidence compilation that auditors are expected to follow when preparing their reports on financial statements. See **Auditor's report**.

**General-purpose financial reports** – financial reports prepared to meet the information needs of a range of users who are unable to command information designed for their individual, specific needs.

**Going concern** – a fundamental assumption in financial accounting that a firm will continue to be financially viable. If a firm is not a going concern, normal accounting principles do not apply. See **Liquidation value**.

**Goods and services tax** – see **GST**.

**Goodwill** – the difference between the price paid for a group of assets and the sum of their apparent fair (market) values. Arises when a bundle of assets or a whole company is acquired and when the difference is positive. ('Badwill', a negative difference, is not recognised.) 'Goodwill on consolidation' often arises when a subsidiary's accounts are consolidated with the parent's.

**Gross margin ratio or gross profit ratio** – equals (revenue – cost of goods sold expense) ÷ revenue.

**Gross profit** – revenue minus cost of goods sold. Also called 'gross margin'.

**GST (goods and services tax)** – the Australian federal sales tax on goods and services (with some exceptions, such as fresh food) that a business collects as a percentage of its own revenue, and remits to the government after deducting any GST the business paid on its own purchases.

## H

**Harmonisation** – the process by which Australian accounting standards become similar to international accounting standards in order to increase comparability of financial statements on a global basis.

**Historical cost** – the dollar value of a transaction on the date it happens, normally maintained in the accounting records from then on because of accounting's reliance on transactions as the basis for recording events. The cost, or historical cost, of an asset is therefore the dollar amount paid for it or promised to be paid as of the date the asset was acquired.

## I

**IASC** – see **International Accounting Standards Committee**.

**Income** – The term used in the USA and Canada and some other countries for the Australian term 'profit'. The (net) income of a business is the residual after deducting expenses from revenues. Also referred to as **Profit** or **Earnings**.

**Income (profit) smoothing** – the manipulation of the announced results for net profit, so that the year-to-year variations in reported profit are reduced.

**Income statement** – a North American term for 'statement of financial performance'. A financial statement that summarises revenues and expenses of a business for a stated period of time and computes the residual net income (revenues minus expenses). Sometimes referred to as 'statement of earnings', 'statement of operations' or 'statement of income.'

**Income tax** – tax assessed on the profit of a business enterprise or the salary or wage of an individual, according to income tax laws.

**Income tax expense** – an estimate of the current and future ('deferred') income tax arising from the profit, as computed on the statement of financial performance and matched to the revenues and expenses shown on the statement.

**Income tax payable** – the liability for the amount of income tax due on the year's profit, calculated according to the income tax law, whether or not it matches the **Income tax expense**.

**Independence** – freedom from financial or other interest that would influence one's decisions. External auditors are expected to be independent of the enterprises they audit, and so can hold no shares or management positions in those enterprises.

**Indirect method of cash flow analysis** – the method of deriving the **Cash flow from operations** section of the Cash flow statement by adjusting net profit for non-cash items.

**Information system** – an organised and systematic way of providing information to decision-makers. Accounting is an information system. See also **Management information system**.

**Input market value** – the market value of an asset calculated as the amount it would cost to replace or reproduce it. See **Replacement cost**.

**Intangible assets** – non-physical noncurrent assets such as copyrights, patents, trademarks, import and export licences, other rights that give a firm an exclusive or preferred position in the marketplace, and goodwill. See **Assets**, **Amortisation**, **Goodwill**.

**Intercorporate investments** – investments by one company in other companies. See **Consolidation**, **Equity method**, **Cost basis**.

**Interest** – the amount charged by a lender for the use of borrowed money.

**Interest coverage ratio** – usually calculated as (profit before interest expense and income tax) ÷ interest expense.

**Intergenerational equity** – concept used in public sector accounting to measure the relative burden to be dispersed over current and future generations of taxpayers.

**Internal auditor** – an auditor who works for the enterprise, and thus verifies information for management's use and to help the enterprise perform better.

**Internal control** – methods of providing physical security and management control over an enterprise's cash, inventories and other assets, and ensuring that management policies are adhered to.

**Internal transactions** – transactions recorded by the entity that do not result from transacting with a third party but are book entries only; for example, depreciation entries and using up supplies.

**International Accounting Standards Committee (IASC)** – a committee, made up of representatives of more than 50 countries, that sets international accounting standards.

**Inventory(ies)** – goods purchased or manufactured by a company for sale, resale or further use in operations, including finished goods, goods in process, raw materials and supplies. See **Current assets**, **Inventory costing**.

**Inventory costing** – comprises various methods of determining the cost of inventory for statement of financial position valuation purposes and of valuing cost of goods sold. The more common methods are FIFO, LIFO and weighted average.

**Inventory turnover** – cost of goods sold expense ÷ average inventory assets.

**Inventory valuation** – the process of determining the amount at which inventory is shown on the statement of financial position, normally the **Lower of cost or market**. See **Inventory costing**.

**Investing activities** – the part of cash flow statement for those activities involving cash that relate to the acquisition and disposal of noncurrent assets.

**Investments** – assets, such as shares or bonds, held for their financial return (for example, interest or dividends), rather than for their use in the enterprise's operations.

**Investors** – people who own investments and who, because of their interest in the value of those shares or bonds, are interested in information about the enterprises issuing such shares and bonds.

## J

**Joint venture** – a business arrangement between companies that is like a corporate partnership.

**Journal entry** – a record of a transaction or accrual adjustment that lists the accounts affected, and in which the total of the debits equals the total of the credits. See **Account**.

**Journals** – chronological or primary records in which accounting transactions of a similar nature are permanently recorded. See **Books of original entry**, **General journal**.

## L

**Last in, first out** – see **LIFO**.

**Lease** – a contract requiring the user of an asset to pay the owner of the asset a predetermined fee for the use of the asset.

**Leasehold improvements** – assets such as fixtures, decorating and alterations installed into rented (leased) premises, which are therefore economic assets for the enterprise, although not strictly owned, because they form part of the leased property. Such improvements are usually depreciated over the period of the lease, as a reasonable estimate of their useful life.

**Ledger** – any book or electronic record that summarises the transactions from the 'books of original entry' in the form of accounts. See **Account**, **General ledger**, **Journals**, **Trial balance**.

**Leverage** – the increased rate of return on owners' equity when assets earn a return larger than the interest rate paid for debt financing of them.

**Leverage ratio** – the ratio of total assets divided by shareholders' equity.

**Leverage return** – the portion of return on equity that is a result of earning more return on borrowed funds than it costs in interest to borrow them.

**Liability** – future sacrifices of economic benefits that the entity is presently obliged to make to other entities as a result of past transactions or other past events (for example, a bank loan, an account payable, a mortgage, an accrued expense or a deferred revenue).

**LIFO** – a cost flow assumption that is the opposite of FIFO. 'Last in, first out' assumes that the units sold are from the most recent purchases, therefore bases the cost of goods sold on the most recent purchases and ending inventory on the oldest purchases. Because of this, in a period of inflation, the LIFO cost of goods sold figure is usually the highest of the inventory costing methods, and the inventory value on the statement of financial position is usually the lowest. See **Cost flow assumption**, **FIFO**, **Weighted average**, **Inventory costing**.

**Line of credit** – advance approval from a bank to borrow money under agreed conditions. A line of credit usually means that the borrower can get the money as needed (for example, when the bank account is overdrawn), without further approval.

**Liquidation value** – the value of a firm's assets if they are all to be sold off when the firm is no longer a going concern. See **Historical cost**, **Fair market value**.

**Liquidity** – the excess of very short-term assets over short-term debts, therefore the measure of a company's ability to pay its immediate obligations in cash as they fall due.

**Listed (shares)** – A listed company (corporation) is one whose shares are available for trading on a **Stock exchange**. See **Public company**.

**Loss, losses** – usually refers to the case of a negative return (proceeds being less than book value) obtained from the disposition of assets (or liabilities) not normally disposed of in the daily course of business, such as from selling land, buildings or other noncurrent assets, or from refinancing debt.

**Loss on sale** – the deficit that occurs when the asset's book value is more than the proceeds received from the sale of the asset.

**Lower of cost or market** – a method of valuing items of inventory where inventory is valued at the lower of original cost or market value (that is, net realisable value).

## M

**Management** – the people (managers) who run the day-to-day operations of an enterprise or other organisation, compared with the shareholders (investors), members and voters who own or legally control the enterprise.

**Management accounting** – accounting information designed to aid management in its operation and control of the firm, and in its general decision-making. Different from financial accounting, which is aimed primarily at users external to the firm.

**Management information system** – the accounting, marketing, production, employee and other record-keeping and reporting systems within the enterprise used by management in its internal decision-making. Often abbreviated as MIS and associated with computer systems. See **Management accounting**, **Electronic commerce**.

**Management of corporate financial disclosure** – steps taken by management to manage the outward flow of information about an enterprise, much as other aspects of the enterprise are managed.

**Manipulation** – the accusation that management, in choosing its accounting and disclosure policies, attempts to make the performance and position measures suit its wishes.

**Market capitalisation** – an estimate of the value of a listed public company made by multiplying the current share price times the number of shares issued and outstanding.

**Market value** – see **Fair market value**.

**Marketable securities** – investments having a ready market for resale and held as a way of earning a return from temporarily unneeded cash.

**Matching** – the concept of recognising expenses in the same accounting period in which the related revenues are recognised. See **Accrual accounting**, **Expense recognition**, **Revenue recognition**.

**Materiality, material** – the magnitude of an omission or misstatement of accounting information that, in the light of surrounding circumstances, makes it probable that a reasonable person relying on the information would have had their judgement changed or influenced by the omission or misstatement. Materiality and decision relevance are both defined in terms of what influences or makes a difference to a decision-maker. A decision not to disclose certain information may be made because it is believed that investors or other users have no need for that kind of information (it is not relevant) or that the amounts involved are too small to make a difference (it is not material).

**Measurement, measuring** – the attachment of dollar figures to assets, liabilities, revenues and expenses in order to produce the figures (values) on the statement of financial position and to enable the computation of profit (revenues minus expenses) and equity (assets minus liabilities). See **Asset valuation**, **Balance sheet valuation**, **Recognition**, **Profit**.

**Merger** – the joining together of two companies such that the owners of both become the owners of the combined company and both companies are approximately equal contributors to the combination.

**Moving average cost** – see **Average cost**.

## N

**Net** – in accounting, net means the residual after one quantity is subtracted from another. Examples are **Net book value**, **Net profit**, **Net-of-tax analysis** and **Net realisable value**.

**Net book value** – the cost of an asset minus any accumulated depreciation, amortisation, provision for doubtful debts and so on.

**Net loss** – negative **Net profit**.

**Net profit** – see **Profit**.

**Net realisable value** – the fair market value that an asset will bring if it is sold through the usual product market minus any completion or disposal costs. See **Fair market value**, **Replacement cost**, **Lower of cost or market**.

**Net-of-tax analysis** – a method of determining the impact of management decisions or accounting changes by which the effects of income tax are included to produce the net after-tax effect of the decision or change.

**Neutrality** – an objective of preparing financial accounting information by which the information should represent phenomena neutrally, without attention to the particular interests of any party or parties. See **Objectivity**, **Independence**.

**Noncontrolling interest** – the portion of a subsidiary company included in consolidated financial statements that is not owned by the controlling (majority) owners of the parent company. See **Minority interest**, **Consolidation**.

**Noncurrent assets** – assets expected to bring benefit for more than one fiscal year.

**Noncurrent liabilities** – liabilities expected to be repaid or otherwise removed more than one year in the future.

**Notes payable** – accounts payable that are supported by signed contracts or other agreements and usually carrying interest. Often used to describe financing obtained from banks and other financial institutions used to provide operating funds or funds for construction before completion of projects, and obtaining of more secured financing, such a mortgage.

**Notes receivable** – accounts receivable supported by signed contracts or other agreements specifying repayment terms, interest rate and other conditions.

**Notes to the financial statements** – notes appended to the statements, providing information about the accounting policies chosen and other supplementary information helpful to interpreting the figures.

**Not-for-profit accounting** – procedures used to account for nonbusiness, nongovernment entities. These procedures increasingly follow **Generally approved accounting principles (GAAP)**.

## O

**Objectivity** – the notion that the information in financial statements must be as free from bias as possible, in order that all user groups can have confidence in it. An accountant attempts to record and report data that are based on objective sources to make the data more acceptable to outside parties. Because completed arm's-length transactions are supported by documents that can be verified by any interested observer, these constitute the preferred basis of measurement. See **Fairness**, **Relevance**, **Reliability**, **Timeliness**, **Verifiability**, **Materiality**.

**Off-balance-sheet financing** – methods of obtaining financing that avoid having to record the sources as liabilities or equity.

**Operating activities** – the part of a cash flow statement that relates to the provision of goods and services.

**Operating lease** – a lease under which the lessor effectively retains substantially all the risks and benefits incidental to ownership of the leased property.

**Operating return** – the return earned by an enterprise before considering the cost of financing, and usually also before considering nonrecurring items.

**Operating statement** – discloses the revenues and expenses of a government entity for a period.

**Opportunity cost** – the return that could have been earned if funds were used in a way other than the way they are being used or are proposed to be used. Called a cost because it is the return given up by not adopting that other way.

**Ordinary activities** – activities, undertaken by an entity as part of its business or to meet its objectives and related activities, in which the entity engages in the furtherance of, incidental to or arising from activities undertaken to meet its objectives.

**Ordinary shares** – the basic voting ownership interests in a company.

**Other assets** – a catch-all category used for current and noncurrent assets that do not fit into other categories, are not material individually but aggregate to a material total.

**Output market value** – the market value of an asset if sold. See **Net realisable value**.

**Outside equity interest (called Minority interest, Noncontrolling interest in other parts of the world)** – shares held by companies outside the consolidated group, which results in an interest in the profit of the consolidated entity; an account in the equities part of the consolidated statement of financial position. The percentage of the subsidiary's equity not owned by the parent company is designated as outside equity interest. An outside equity interest is calculated and deducted from the calculated consolidated net profit. See **Consolidation**.

**Overdraft** – See **Bank overdraft**.

**Overhead cost** – costs of manufacturing inventories or constructing other assets that are incurred indirectly, such as heat, power and supervisors' salaries.

**Owners** – parties who have contributed resources in return for the right to dividends and any residual value (equity) of the enterprise.

**Owner's capital** – the owner's equity of the proprietor of an unincorporated business. See **Capital**, **Equity**.

**Owners' equity** – see **Equity**.

## P

**Par value** – an arbitrary amount placed on each share at incorporation. Although still used in some countries, it is no longer used in Australia.

**Parent** – an entity that controls another entity, and the name of which is usually used in the consolidated financial statements.

**Partnership** – a contractual agreement among individuals to share resources and operations in a jointly run business. This form of business does not have the privilege of limited liability.

**PE ratio** – the price-to-earnings ratio is calculated as the current price of a share in the company divided by its earnings per share. See **Price–earnings ratio**.

**Percentage of completion** – a method of allocating revenue (and associated expenses) over several fiscal periods during which the revenue is earned. Used for long-term construction contracts, franchise revenue and similar multi-period revenues.

**Periodic inventory method** – a method of calculating inventory that uses data on beginning inventory, additions to inventory and an end-of-period count to deduce the cost of goods sold.

**Periodic reporting** – a basic convention of financial accounting that holds that accounting information must be assembled and presented to users at regular intervals (at least yearly, and often quarterly or monthly).

**Perpetual inventory method** – a method of controlling inventory that maintains continuous records on the flow of units of inventory. Thus, there are figures on record for beginning inventory, each unit added to inventory and each unit removed from inventory for sale. From this an ending inventory figure can be determined and checked against the figure from a physical count. This method provides better control than the **Periodic inventory method**, but it is also more costly to maintain the extra records.

**Personal guarantees** – additional **Security** on loans, often taken by banks lending to private companies, in which some or all shareholders sign agreements to contribute personal assets if the company does not repay the loans or pay interest on schedule.

**Petty cash** – a fund set up to make small cash payments.

**Plug** – the double-entry system requires that debits equal credits. If adding up all the debits and the credits does not produce two equal figures, the statements must be adjusted so that a balance occurs. The amount of adjustment needed is often called a 'plug'. This would only be needed if there had been an error somewhere, though sometimes the word plug is used in criticism of accrual, consolidation or other adjustments that produce amounts the critic does not like.

**Posting** – the transfer of journal entries to ledger accounts, thereby making them permanent. The only way to fix a mistake is to use an adjusting or correcting entry and post that.

**Preference shares** – ownership shares having special rights in addition to (or instead of) those going with ordinary shares.

**Premium on bonds** – arises when bonds are issued at a price above their legal face value, such as a $100 bond being issued for $105 cash, indicating a $5 premium.

**Prepaid expense** – an expenditure recorded as a current asset because the benefit will be obtained in the near future (for example, insurance coverage good for the next year).

**Preparers** – managers and accountants who produce financial statements.

**Prepayments (prepaid expenses)** – expenses paid but not yet incurred; an expenditure recorded as a current asset because the benefit will be obtained in the near future (for example, insurance coverage good for the next year).

**Present value** – future cash inflows or outflows reduced to their 'present' amount by removing from them the interest that could have been earned or paid had the money been on hand for investment today.

**Present value analysis** – analysis of future cash flows by removing the presumed interest components of those flows.

**Price–earnings ratio (PE ratio)** – market price of one share of a company divided by earnings per share.

**Price-level-adjusted historical cost** – a rarely used asset valuation method by which the historical cost of each asset is revalued for inflation.

**Principal-agent theory** – see **Agency (contract) theory**.

**Privatisation** – the process by which government-owned entities are sold to a private owner or owners. Large examples of this occurring in Australia include Qantas, the Commonwealth Bank and Telstra.

**Professional ethics** – codes of conduct to guide professionals in applying their professional judgement to their professional activities.

**Professional judgement** – the judgement of professionals about problems in their domain; an example is that of accountants or auditors about financial accounting matters.

**Professionalism** – actions taken according to the levels of competence, ethics and independence expected of professionals.

**Profit** – the excess of revenues over expenses. The (net) profit of a business is the residual after deduction of expenses from revenues. Also referred to as income or earnings. See **Cash profit**, **Gross profit**, **Profit before (income) tax**.

**Profit before (income) tax** – an amount equal to revenue minus all other ordinary expenses except income tax. Some non-taxed or special items, such as extraordinary items, are placed after income tax has been deducted, and are therefore not part of profit before income tax.

**Profit margin** – the percentage of sales revenue that ends up as profit; hence it is the average profit for each dollar of sales.

**Property, plant and equipment** – noncurrent assets that are tangible, and are used in the operating activity of an entity.

**Proprietor approach** – a way of viewing financial statements from the point of view of the proprietor (owner).

**Prospectus** – a formal document, which includes detailed financial information, that is required by law when a company invites the public to subscribe to its securities.

**Provision** – another phrase for a usually noncurrent accrual, such as that for future superannuation costs or warranties. Particularly common when the liability is created to anticipate losses or major expenses involved in discontinuing a business line, refinancing debts or disposing of major assets.

**Provision for doubtful debts** – the estimated amount of accounts receivable that will not be collected (which are 'doubtful'). The provision, which is a contra account to accounts receivable, is used in order to recognise the bad debts expense related to such doubtful accounts, but without removing those accounts from the books, because the firm will still try to collect the amounts owing.

**Provision for employee entitlements** – a liability for future economic benefits to be paid to employees that employees accumulate as a result of the rendering of their services to an employer up to the reporting date, and include, but are not limited to, wages and salaries (including fringe benefits and non-monetary benefits), annual leave, sick leave, long service leave, superannuation and other post-employment benefits.

**Public accounting firm** – the offer of auditing, accounting and related services to the public on a professional basis. Some public accounting firms are very large.

**Public company** – a company whose shares and related securities are sold widely, to members of the public and other investors, and whose securities are likely to be traded on capital markets.

**Purchase order** – a document used when a formal request to buy products or services is made.

## Q

**Qualified opinion** – a report by the external auditors that indicates there is a deficiency in the financial statements.

**Quick ratio** – cash, temporary investments and accounts receivable divided by current liabilities. Also called the acid test ratio. See **Ratios**.

## R

**Ratios, ratio analysis** – numbers produced by dividing one financial statement figure by another figure; for example, the working capital ratio is the total current assets figure divided by the total current liabilities figure. Standard ratios are used to assess aspects of a firm, particularly profitability, solvency and liquidity.

**Realised** – used in this book as a synonym for received, or collected. Revenue is recognised when earned, but that is usually before it is collected, or realised. See **Revenue recognition**, **Recognition**.

**Reclassification (entry)** – a journal entry or repositioning of an account that changes the location of the account within the statement of financial position or within the statement of financial performance, but does not affect profit.

**Recognised** – revenues or expenses (usually) entered into the accounts or given effect in the accounts. See **Recognition**.

**Recognition** – the giving effect in the accounts to revenue believed to be earned, or expenses believed to be incurred, before (or after) the cash is collected or paid. See **Revenue recognition**, **Expense recognition**.

**Reconcile, reconciliation** – the **Analysis** technique of comparing two sets of information that relate to the same account or activity and identifying differences that indicate errors in either or both records. See **Bank reconciliation**.

**Record-keeping** – the bookkeeping and other methods used to create the underlying records on which accounting information is based.

**Reducing balance depreciation** – an accelerated depreciation method by which the annual depreciation expense is calculated as a fixed percentage of the book value of the asset, which declines over time as depreciation is deducted. See **Accelerated depreciation**, **Depreciation**.

**Relevance** – the capacity of information to make a difference in a decision by helping users to form predictions about the outcomes of past, present and future events or to confirm or correct prior expectations. See **Decision relevance**, **Materiality**, **Reliability**, **Timeliness**, **Objectivity**.

**Reliability** – a characteristic of information that is represented faithfully (or faithfully portrays the underlying transactions) and is free from bias and verifiable. See **Relevance**, **Timeliness**, **Materiality**, **Objectivity**.

**Replacement cost** – the price that will have to be paid in order to replace an existing asset with a similar asset. This is likely to be an amount different from fair market value or net realisable value. See also **Lower of cost or market**.

**Resources** – in financial accounting, the recognised assets of the enterprise as shown on the statement of financial position.

**Retail inventory method** – the provision of internal control and deducing of inventory amounts for financial statements by using ratios of cost to selling price; for example, deducing cost of goods sold from sales revenue minus the mark-up on cost. Ending inventory cost can be determined by measuring inventory at retail prices minus mark-up.

**Retained profits (retained earnings)** – profits not yet distributed to owners; the sum of net profits earned over the life of a company, less distributions (dividends declared) to owners.

**Return on assets** – net profit, before deducting interest expense and tax divided by total assets. This measures the operating return before the cost of financing.

**Return on equity (ROE)** – net profit divided by owners' equity. The most frequently used ratio for measuring the business's return to owners.

**Return on funds employed (ROFE)** – the ratio of earnings before interest and tax (EBIT) divided by average funds employed.

**Return on investment (ROI)** – a general term for measures of return related to the investment needed to earn the return. See **Return on assets**, Return on equity.

**Revaluation** – the act of recognising a reassessment of values of noncurrent assets as at a particular date.

**Revaluation decrement** – the amount by which the revalued carrying amount of noncurrent assets as at the revaluation date is less than its previous carrying amount.

**Revaluation increment** – the amount by which the revalued carrying amount of a noncurrent asset as at the revaluation date exceeds its previous carrying amount.

**Revenue** – the amount of benefit received or promised from the sale of goods or services, before any deductions for the cost of providing the goods or services. More formally defined in SAC 4 as 'inflows or other enhancements, or savings in outflows, of future economic benefits in the form of increases in assets or reductions in liabilities of the entity, other than those relating to contributions by owners, that result in an increase in equity during the reporting period'.

**Revenue received in advance** – a liability account used for customer deposits or other cash receipts before the completion of the sale (for example, before delivery).

**Revenue recognition** – the entry into the accounts of the amount of revenue determined, according to the firm's accounting policies, to be attributable to the current period. See **Accrual accounting**, **Accounts receivable**, **Revenue**.

**Risk** – the probable variability in possible future outcomes above and below the expected level of outcomes (for example, returns), but especially below. Risk and return go hand in hand, because a high risk should mean a higher potential return, and vice versa.

## S

**Sales invoice** – a document containing the details of a sale.

**Sales journal** – a record of sales made, used to produce the **Revenue** data in the accounts. See **Books of original entry**.

**Sales return** – the ratio of net income to revenue. See **Ratios**.

**Securities** – shares, bonds and other financial instruments issued by companies and governments, and usually traded on capital markets.

**Securities and Exchange Commission (SEC)** – an agency of the US government that supervises the registration of security issues, prosecutes fraudulent stock manipulations and regulates securities transactions in the United States.

**Segmented information** – financial statement information classified by geographical or economic area of activity in order to provide greater insight into financial performance and position. Segmented information is usually placed at the end of the notes to the financial statements.

**Segregation of duties** – an internal control technique whereby tasks involved in sensitive assets, such as cash, accounts receivable, or inventories, are divided up so that no one both handles the asset and keeps the records of the asset.

**Share buyback** – process by which a company buys its own shares at market value on the stock exchange, then cancels them to reduce the total number of shares on issue. Allowed under certain conditions as specified in the Corporations Law.

**Share capital** – the portion of a company's equity obtained by issuing shares in return for cash or other considerations.

**Share dividend** – a dividend paid by issuing more shares to present shareholders rather than paying them cash.

**Share script** – certificates that show how many of the company's shares are owned by a shareholder.

**Share split** – the reissue of shares in which the number of new shares is some multiple of the previous number. For example, a two-for-one split results in a shareholder owning twice as many shares as before. Because there has been only a change in the number of shares, not in the underlying value of the company, the share price should fall in accordance with the split (therefore the new shares above should have a share price about half the previous price).

**Share (stock) market** – a capital market in which equity shares are traded. Often used as a generic term for capital markets.

**Shareholders** – the holders of a company's share capital, therefore the owners of the company.

**Shareholders' equity** – the sum of shareholders' direct investment (share capital) and indirect investment (retained profits).

**Shares (stock)** – units of share capital, evidenced by certificates and, for public companies, traded on capital markets with other securities.

**Significant influence** – see **Associated company**.

**Significant items** – when a revenue or an expense from ordinary activities is of such a size, nature or incidence that its disclosure is relevant in explaining the financial performance of the entity for the reporting period, its nature and amount must be disclosed separately in the notes in the financial report. The revenues and expenses are not extraordinary items. However, the nature and amount of these items is relevant to users of financial reports in understanding the reported financial performance of the entity and in making decisions. Some of the circumstances that may give rise to the separate disclosure of the nature and amount of revenues and expenses include:

- **a** the write-down of inventories or noncurrent assets and, where applicable, the reversal of such write-downs
- **b** litigation settlements
- **c** reversals of provisions
- **d** restructuring of operations
- **e** changes in accounting policies, other than those changes made to comply with a standard or an urgent issues group consensus view that requires initial adjustments to be recognised as a direct credit to equity or a direct debit to equity.

**Sole trader or sole proprietorship** – a firm that is neither a company nor a partnership, but is under the sole control of one individual. Such a firm is not legally separate from that individual.

**Solvency** – the condition of being able to meet all debts and obligations.

**Source documents** – the evidence required to record a transaction.

**Sources** – the right-hand side of the statement of financial position (liabilities and equity) shows the sources of the enterprise's assets.

**Specific identification** – the accounting for inventories according to the specific cost of the items, which therefore requires some sort of identification of the items, such as by serial number.

**Standard cost** – a method of determining manufactured inventory costs that uses expected normal production costs rather than actual costs.

**Statement of cash flows (cash flow statement)** – a statement that explains the changes in cash equivalent balances during a fiscal period.

**Statement of financial performance** – a financial statement that summarises revenues and expenses of a business for a stated period of time and computes the residual net profit (revenues minus expenses). Sometimes referred to as a profit and loss statement. See components of the statement such as **Revenue**, **Expense**, **Net profit**, **Profit**; see also **Financial performance**.

**Statement of financial position** – the balance sheet as required by Corporations Law.

**Statement of retained profits** – a financial statement or note that summarises the changes in retained profits for the year.

**Stewardship** – the concept that some persons (such as management) are responsible for looking after the assets and interests of other persons (such as shareholders), and that reports should be prepared that will be suitable to allow the 'stewards' to be held accountable for the actions taken on behalf of the other persons.

**Stock** – used to mean shares in the United States, but also sometimes used to mean inventories, as in 'stocktaking' for counting inventories.

**Stock dividend** – the term used for a share dividend in the United States. A **Dividend** paid by issuing more shares to present shareholders rather than paying them cash.

**Stock exchange** – a place where shares and other securities are traded.

**Stock option(s)** – promises, usually made to senior managers, to issue shares to them at specified prices. The prices are usually set to be higher than present prices but lower than expected future prices, to provide an incentive to work to increase those future prices.

**Stockholder** – an alternative term for shareholder, used particularly in the United States.

**Straight-line depreciation (amortisation)** – a method of computing depreciation (amortisation) simply by dividing the difference between the asset's cost and its expected salvage value by the number of years the asset is expected to be used. The depreciation expense is distributed evenly over the periods that comprise the expected useful life of the asset. The most common depreciation method used in Australia.

**Subsidiary** – an entity that is controlled by another entity (the **Parent**). See **Consolidation**.

**Subsidiary ledger** – a set of ledger accounts that collectively provide a detailed analysis of one control account in the general ledger.

**Sum-of-the-year's-digits depreciation** – an accelerated method of computing depreciation that produces a declining annual expense. Used in the United States, but rare in Australia. See **Accelerated depreciation**.

## T

**Temporary differences** – differences between accounting calculations of profit and calculations required for income tax purposes that will eventually net out to zero. These affect income tax expense calculations.

**Temporary investments** – investments made for a short term, often used as a place to put temporarily excess cash to work.

**Time value of money** – money can earn interest, so money received in the future is worth less in 'present value' terms because the lower amount can be invested to grow to the future amount. Money has a time value because interest accrues over time. See **Present value analysis**.

**Timeliness** – timely information is usable because it relates to present decision needs. Information received late may be too late to be usable, since decisions pass it by. See **Relevance**, **Reliability**, **Objectivity**, **Materiality**.

**Total assets turnover** – the ratio of revenue to total assets. See **Ratios**.

**Trade receivables** – **Accounts receivable** that arise in the normal course of business with customers.

**Transaction** – an accounting transaction is the basis of bookkeeping, and is defined by four criteria:

1. *exchange:* there must be an exchange of money, goods or other items that have economic value
2. *externality:* the exchange must be with an outsider; it is not a transaction if it has occurred within the firm
3. *evidence:* there must be an invoice, computer printout or some other source document to show that a transaction has taken place
4. *dollars:* the transaction must be quantifiable in dollars.

**Trial balance** – a list of all the general ledger accounts and their balances. The sum of the accounts with debit balances should equal the sum of those with credit balances.

## U

**Uncalled capital** – amount of issued capital not yet called up by the company.

**Understandability** – one of the concepts underlying the preparation of financial statements is their ability to be understood by users who are willing to exercise diligence in examining the reports and who possess the skills and ability to comprehend accounting practices.

**Unearned revenue** – a liability account used for deposits or other cash receipts before the completion of the sale (for example, before delivery). Also called **Deferred revenue** and **Revenue received in advance**.

**Units-of-production depreciation** – a depreciation method by which the annual depreciation expense varies directly with the year's production volume.

**Unqualified opinion** – An external auditor's report that states the auditor's opinion that the financial statements are fairly presented. This is the kind of auditor's report that most companies receive, because it indicates the auditor found no problems. See **Auditor's report**, **Qualified opinion**.

**Users** – people who use financial statements to assist them in deciding whether to invest in the enterprise, lend it money or take other action involving financial information.

## V

**Valuation** – the determination of the amounts at which assets, liabilities and equity should be shown in the statement of financial position.

**Verifiability** – the ability to trace an accounting entry or figure back to the underlying evidence of its occurrence and validity. See **Source documents**.

## W

**Wages payable** – amounts owing to employees in the form of wages at the end of the period.

**Warrants** – attachments to shares or bonds giving rights to acquire further shares or bonds on specified terms.

**Weighted average** – an inventory cost flow assumption that determines cost of goods sold and ending inventory cost by averaging the cost of all of the inventory available during the period. See **Average**, **LIFO**, **FIFO**, **Inventory costing**.

**'What if' effects analysis** – see **Change effects analysis**.

**Whole-of-government accounts** – in Australia, this refers to the general-purpose financial reports of the Federal Government, the governments of the states of New South Wales, Queensland, South Australia, Tasmania, Victoria and Western Australia, and the governments of the Australian Capital Territory and the Northern Territory.

**Working capital** – the difference between current assets and current liabilities. See **Current assets**, **Current liabilities**.

**Working capital ratio** – current assets divided by current liabilities.

**Write-off** – refers to the elimination of an asset from the statement of financial position. If there is a **Contra account** against the asset already, the write-off is made against the contra, so expense and profit are not affected. If there is no contra account, the write-off (a **Direct write-off**) is made to expense or a loss account, and profit is reduced.

**Written-down value** – for a noncurrent asset, this is the net amount after deducting **Accumulated depreciation (amortisation)**.

## Y

**Yield** – the effective interest rate a financial instrument such as a **Bond** earns, given the amount of money received when it was issued. See **Present value**.

Index